P9-CBC-508

THE
CONSCIOUS
READER

P.O.V.

1st person (I)

3rd limited - narrator doesn't know everything

3rd omniscient - narrator knows everything

THE CONSCIOUS READER

Sixth Edition

CAROLINE SHRODES
Late, The Union Institute

HARRY FINESTONE
California State University, Northridge

MICHAEL SHUGRUE
The College of Staten Island
of the City University of New York

FONTAINE MAURY BELFORD
The Union Institute

ALLYN AND BACON
Boston   London   Toronto   Sydney   Tokyo   Singapore

Editors: D. Anthony English and Eben Ludlow
Editorial Assistants: Ivelisse Elam and Morgan Lance
Marketing Manager: Lisa Kimball
Production Administrator: Rowena Dores
Editorial-Production Service: Tara M. Padykula
Text Designer: Sheree L. Goodman
Cover Administrator: Linda Knowles
Cover Designer: Susan Paradise
Composition Buyer: Linda Cox
Manufacturing Buyer: Louise Richardson

Library of Congress Cataloging-in-Publication Data
The Conscious reader / [edited by] Caroline Shrodes. — 6th
   ed.
      p.   cm.
   Includes index.
   ISBN 0-02-337662-7 (paper)
   1. College readers.   I. Shrodes, Caroline.
PE1122.C586   1995
808'.0427—dc20   94–788
                                                  CIP

This book is printed on
recycled, acid-free paper.

Acknowledgments

   Alda, Alan. "You Have to Know What Your Values Are!" This article appeared in *Redbook*, 1980. Reprinted
by permission.
   Allen, Woody. "My Speech to the Graduates." Originally appeared in *The New York Times*, August 10,
1979. Copyright © 1979 by The New York Times Company. Reprinted by permission.
   Alvarez, A. "Sylvia Plath: A Memoir." From *The Savage God*. Reprinted by permission of George Weiden-
feld & Nicolson Ltd. London.
   Anderson, Sherwood. "Discovery of a Father." From *Sherwood Anderson's Memoirs: A Critical Edition*.
Reprinted by permission of Harold Ober Associates, Incorporated. Copyright © 1939 by *The Reader's Digest*.
Copyright renewed 1966 by Eleanor Copenhaver Anderson.
   Angelou, Maya. "Finishing School" and "Graduation." From *I Know Why the Caged Bird Sings*. Copyright
© 1969 by Maya Angelou. Reprinted by permission of Random House, Inc.
   Atwood, Margaret. "Fiction: Happy Endings." From *Murder in the Dark*. Reprinted by permission of Mar-
garet Atwood. Copyright © 1983 by Coach House Press. "Pornography." First published in *Chatelaine*. Re-
printed by permission of McClelland and Stewart, agents for Margaret Atwood.
   Auden, W. H. "Lay Your Sleeping Head, My Love" and "Unknown Citizen." From *Collected Shorter Poems 1927–1957*. Copyright © 1940 and renewed 1968 by W. H. Auden. Reprinted by permission of Random
House, Inc.
   Baker, Russell. "My Lack of Gumption." From *Growing Up*. Copyright © 1982 by Russell Baker. Reprinted
by permission of Congdon & Weed, Inc.
   Baldwin, James. "The Discovery of What It Means to Be an American." From *Nobody Knows My Name*.

Copyright © 1961 by James Baldwin, copyright renewed 1989. Used by arrangement with the James Baldwin Estate.

Bellow, Saul, and Adrienne Rich. "Three Cheers for Good Marks: Writers on Their Prizes." From the National Book Award Acceptance Speeches. From *The New York Times*, November 16, 1986. Copyright © 1986 by The New York Times Company. Reprinted by permission.

Bettelheim, Bruno. "The Child's Need for Magic." From *The Uses of Enchantment: The Meaning and Importance of Fairy Tales* by Bruno Bettelheim. Copyright © 1975, 1976 by Bruno Bettelheim. Reprinted by permission of Alfred A. Knopf, Inc. "Joey: A 'Mechanical Boy.'" Copyright © 1959 by Scientific American, Inc. All Rights Reserved. Reprinted with permission.

Borges, Jorge Luís. "Borges and Myself." From *The Aleph and Other Stories 1933–1969* by Jorge Luís Borges. English translation copyright © 1968, 1969, 1970 by Emece Editores, S. A. and Norman Thomas di Giovanni; copyright © 1970 by Jorge Luís Borges, Adolfo Bioy Casares and Norman Thomas di Giovanni. Reprinted by permission of the Publisher, Dutton, an imprint of New American Library, a division of Penguin Books USA, Inc. "The Web," trans. Alastair Reid. Copyright © 1986 by the Estate of Jorge Luís Borges and Alastair Reid. All Rights Reserved. Reprinted by permission of the Estate of Jorge Luís Borges. This poem originally appeared in *The New Yorker*, June 2, 1986.

Boyle, T. Coraghessan. "If the River Was Whiskey." From *If the River Was Whiskey*. Copyright © 1989 by T. Coraghessan Boyle. Used by permission of Viking Penguin, a division of Penguin Books USA Inc.

Bradbury, Ray. "Perhaps We Are Going Away." From *The Machineries of Joy*. Reprinted by permission of Don Congdon Associates, Inc. Copyright © 1962, renewed 1990 by Ray Bradbury.

Bradley, David. "Harvest Home." From *Family Portraits* by Carolyn Anthony. Copyright © 1989 by David Bradley. Used by permission of Doubleday, a division of Bantam Doubleday Dell Publishing Group, Inc.

Brodkey, Harold. "Reading, the Most Dangerous Game." Originally appeared in *The New York Times Book Review*, November 24, 1985. Copyright © 1985 by Harold Brodkey. Reprinted by permission of International Creative Management, Inc.

Bronowski, Jacob. "The Reach of the Imagination." Published in *American Scholar*, Spring, 1967. Reprinted by permission of Jacob Bronowski.

Brooks, Gwendolyn. "Life for My Child Is Simple, and Is Good." From *Blacks* by Gwendolyn Brooks. Copyright © 1991 by Gwendolyn Brooks. Reissued by Third World Press, 1991.

Brown, Victoria Bissell. "Abortion Fight Is over Choice." Reprinted from *The Los Angeles Times*, April 1, 1988, by permission of Victoria Bissell Brown.

Buchwald, Art. "Leisure Will Kill You." From *Laid Back in Washington* by Art Buchwald. Copyright © 1981 by Art Buchwald. Reprinted by permission of The Putnam Publishing Group.

Captain X. "Mr. Spock." From *Unfriendly Skies*. Copyright © 1989 by Captain X and Reynolds Dodson. Used by permission of Doubleday, a division of Bantam Doubleday Dell Publishing Group, Inc.

Carver, Raymond. Excerpt from *What We Talk About When We Talk About Love*. Copyright © 1976, 1978, 1980, 1981 by Raymond Carver. Reprinted by permission of Alfred A. Knopf, Inc.

Cheever, John. "Expelled." First appeared in *The New Republic*, October 1, 1930, and again on July 19 and 26, 1982. Copyright © 1930 by John Cheever. Reprinted with the permission of Wylie, Aitken & Stone, Inc.

Cheever, Susan. "Portrait of My Father." From *Home Before Dark*. Copyright © 1984 by Susan Cheever. Reprinted by permission of Houghton Mifflin Co. All Rights Reserved.

Chekhov, Anton. "The Bet." From *The Schoolmistress and Other Stories* by Anton Chekhov. Translated from the Russian by Constance Garnett. Reprinted with permission of Macmillan Publishing Company. Copyright 1921 by Macmillan Publishing Company, renewed 1949 by David Garnett.

Chernin, Kim. "The Flesh and the Devil." From *The Obsession: Reflections on the Tyranny of Slenderness.* Copyright © 1981 by Kim Chernin. Reprinted by permission of HarperCollins Publishers, Inc.

Clark, Walter Van Tilburg. "The Portable Phonograph." From *The Watchful Gods and Other Stories.* Copyright © 1941, 1969 by Walter Van Tilburg Clark. Reprinted by permission of International Famous Agency.

Cofer, Judith Ortiz. "Casa: A Partial Remembrance of a Puerto Rican Childhood." Reprinted from *Prairie Schooner*, by permission of the University of Nebraska Press. Copyright 1989 University of Nebraska Press.

Conroy, Frank. "Think About It." Copyright © 1988 by *Harper's Magazine*, November 1988. All rights reserved. Reprinted by special permission.

Cooke, Patrick. "The Gentle Death." Reprinted by permission from *In Health.* Copyright © 1989.

Copland, Aaron. "How We Listen to Music." From *What to Listen for in Music.* Reprinted by permission of The Aaron Copland Fund for Music.

Cottle, Thomas J. "Goodbye, Kids, Mother's Leaving Home: A Family Separates." From *Atlantic Monthly*, March 1990. Reprinted by permission of Thomas J. Cottle.

Cummings, E. E. "I Like My Body When It Is with Your." From *Complete Poems 1904–1962.* Edited by George J. Firmage. Reprinted by permission of Liveright Publishing Corporation. Copyright © 1923, 1925 and renewed 1951, 1953 by E. E. Cummings. Copyright © 1973, 1976 by the Trustees for the E. E. Cummings Trust. Copyright © 1973, 1976 by George James Firmage. "My Father Moved Through Dooms of Love." From *Complete Poems 1904–1962*, Edited by George J. Firmage. Reprinted by permission of Liveright Publishing Corporation. Copyright © 1923, 1925, 1926, 1931, 1935, 1938, 1939, 1940, 1944, 1945, 1946, 1947, 1948, 1949, 1950, 1951, 1952, 1953, 1954, 1955, 1956, 1957, 1958, 1959, 1960, 1961, 1962 by the Trustees for the E. E. Cummings Trust. Copyright © 1961, 1963, 1968 by Marion Morehouse Cummings.

Didion, Joan. "On Keeping a Notebook." From *Slouching Towards Bethlehem* by Joan Didion. Copyright © 1968 by Joan Didion. Reprinted by permission of Farrar, Straus and Giroux, Inc.

Dillard, Annie. "Sight into Insight." Copyright © 1974 by Annie Dillard. First published in *Harper's Maga-*

Havel, Václav. "Words on Words." From *Open Letters*, trans. A. G. Brain. Copyright © 1991 by Paul Wilson. Reprinted by permission of Alfred A. Knopf, Inc.

Head, Bessie. "The Wind and a Boy." From *The Collector of Treasures and Other Botswana Village Tales*. Copyright © 1977 by the Estate of Bessie Head. Rptd. by permission of Heinemann Publishers, (Oxford) Ltd.

Heilbrun, Carolyn. "Androgyny." From *Toward a Recognition of Androgyny* (New York: Alfred A. Knopf, Publishers, 1973). Reprinted by permission of the author.

Hemingway, Ernest. "Hills Like White Elephants." From *Men Without Women*. Reprinted with permission of Charles Scribner's Sons, an imprint of Macmillan Publishing Company. Copyright 1927 by Charles Scribner's Sons, renewed 1955 by Ernest Hemingway. "Indian Camp." From *In Our Time*. Reprinted with permission of Charles Scribner's Sons, an imprint of Macmillan Publishing Company. Copyright 1925 by Charles Scribner's Sons, renewed 1953 by Ernest Hemingway.

Hoerburger, Rob. "About Men; Gotta Dance!" Originally appeared in *The New York Times Magazine*, July 18, 1993. Copyright © 1993 by The New York Times Company.

Hongo, Garrett. "Kubota." Published in *Ploughshares*, reprinted in *Best American Essays 1991*. Copyright © Garrett Hongo. Reprinted by permission of the author.

Hughes, Langston. "Theme for English B." From *Montage of a Dream Deferred*. Copyright © 1951 by Langston Hughes. Copyright renewed 1979 by George Houston Bass. Reprinted by permission of Harold Ober Associates, Inc.

Hurston, Zora Neale. "How It Feels to Be Colored Me." From *The World Tomorrow* by Zora Neale Hurston. By permission of Lucy A. Hurston.

Huxley, Aldous. "Conditioning the Children." From *Brave New World*. Copyright 1932, 1960 by Aldous Huxley. Reprinted by permission of HarperCollins Publishers, Inc.

Ibsen, Henrik. "An Enemy of the People." From *Six Plays by Henrik Ibsen*. Translated by Eva Le Gallienne. Copyright © 1957 by Eva Le Gallienne. Reprinted by permission of Random House, Inc.

Jacobs, Harriet. "The Women." From *The Black Slave Narratives*, ed. with intro. by John F. Bayliss. Reprinted with permission of Macmillan Publishing Company. Copyright © 1970 by John F. Bayliss.

Jaspers, Karl. "Is Science Evil?" Reprinted from *Commentary*; copyright © 1950 by the American Jewish Committee. Reprinted by permission of the publisher.

Kafka, Franz. "Letter to His Father." From *Dearest Father: Stories and Other Writings*, translated by Ernst Kaiser and Eithene Wilkins, edited by Max Brod. Published by Schocken Books, reprinted by permission of Pantheon Books, a division of Random House, Inc. English translation copyright 1954 by Schocken Books Inc. Renewed 1982 by Schocken Books Inc.

Kaufman, Margo. "Who's Educated? Who Knows?" Originally published in *The New York Times*, November 1, 1992. Copyright 1992 by The New York Times Company. Reprinted by permission.

Keillor, Garrison. "Who Do You Think You Are?" From *We Are Still Married: Stories and Letters* by Garrison Keillor. Copyright © 1982, 1983, 1984, 1985, 1986, 1987, 1988, 1989 by Garrison Keillor. Used by permission of Viking Penguin, a division of Penguin Books USA Inc.

Keller, Helen. "Three Days to See." By permission of the American Foundation for the Blind, Inc.

Kincaid, Jamaica. "A Small Place." From *A Small Place*. Copyright © 1988 by Jamaica Kincaid. Reprinted by permission of Farrar, Straus & Giroux, Inc.

King, Jr., Martin Luther. "Letter from Birmingham Jail." Reprinted by arrangement with The Heirs to the Estate of Martin Luther King, Jr., c/o Joan Daves Agency as agent for the proprietor. Copyright 1963 by the Estate of Martin Luther King, Jr. Copyright renewed 1991 by Coretta Scott King.

Kingston, Maxine Hong. "No Name Woman." From *The Woman Warrior: Memoirs of A Girlhood Among Ghosts* by Maxine Hong Kingston. Copyright © 1975, 1976 by Maxine Hong Kingston. Reprinted by permission of Alfred A. Knopf, Inc.

Kozol, Jonathan. "Distancing the Homeless." From *Rachel and Her Children: Homeless Families in America*. Copyright © 1988 by Jonathan Kozol. Reprinted by permission from Crown Publishers, Inc.

Kroeger, Brooke. "AIDS and the Girl Next Door." Reprinted by permission of the author from September 1989 *Mirabella*, © 1989 Murdock Magazines. All Rights Reserved. Reprinted by permission of author and publisher.

Lawrence, D. H. "Give Her a Pattern." From *Phoenix II: Uncollected Papers of D. H. Lawrence*. Copyright © 1959, 1963, 1968 by The Estate of Frieda Lawrence Ravagli. Reprinted by permission of the publisher, Viking Penguin, a division of Penguin Books USA Inc.

Le Guin, Ursula. "Winged: The Creatures on My Mind." Copyright © 1990 by Ursula Le Guin; first appeared in *Harper's*; reprinted by permission of the author's agent, Virginia Kidd.

Lee, Li-Young. "Persimmons." From *Rose*. Copyright © 1986 by Li-Young Lee. Reprinted by permission of BOA Editions.

Levertov, Denise. "In Mind." From *Poems 1960–1967*. Copyright © 1963 by Denise Levertov. First published in *Poetry*. Reprinted by permission of New Directions Publishing Corporation.

Levine, Mark. "About Face (A Poem called 'Dover Beach')." From *Debt*. Copyright © 1993 by Mark Levine. Reprinted by permission of William Morrow & Company, Inc.

Lifton, Robert Jay. "The Genocidal Mentality." From *Tikkun*, May/June 1990, Vol. 5, No. 3. Reprinted by permission of *Tikkun* magazine, a bimonthly Jewish critique of politics, culture, and society. Subscriptions are available for $25/yr (6 issues) from 5100 Leona St., Oakland, CA 94619.

Machiavelli, Niccolò. "Of Cruelty and Clemency, and Whether It Is Better to Be Loved or Feared." From *The Prince*, trans. Luigi Ricci, rev. by E. R. P. Vincent (1935). By permission of Oxford University Press.

Mairs, Nancy. "On Being a Cripple." From *Plaintext*. Reprinted by permission of The University of Arizona Press. Copyright © 1986.

Reagon, Bernice. "Black Music in Our Hands." Originally published in *Sing Out* Magazine, Winter, 1977. Copyright Bernice Johnson Reagon.

Rich, Adrienne. "The Anger of a Child." From *Of Woman Born: Motherhood as Experience and Institution.* Reprinted by permission of W. W. Norton & Company, Inc. Copyright © 1976 by W. W. Norton & Company, Inc. "Living in Sin" and "Rape" from *The Fact of a Doorframe, Poems Selected and New, 1950–1984.* Reprinted by permission of W. W. Norton & Company, Inc. Copyright © 1981 by Adrienne Rich.

Roethke, Theodore. "Elegy for Jane: My Student, Thrown by a Horse." From *The Collected Poems of Theodore Roethke.* Copyright © 1950 by Theodore Roethke. Reprinted by permission of Doubleday, a division of Bantam, Doubleday Dell Publishing Group, Inc. "My Papa's Waltz." Copyright 1942 by Hearst Magazines, Inc. From *The Collected Poems of Theodore Roethke.* Reprinted by permission of Doubleday, a division of Bantam, Doubleday Dell Publishing Group, Inc. "The Waking." From *The Collected Poems of Theodore Roethke.* Copyright © 1953 by Theodore Roethke. Reprinted by permission of Doubleday, a division of Bantam, Doubleday Dell Publishing Group, Inc. "Some Self-Analysis." From *On the Poet and His Craft: Selected Prose of Theodore Roethke.* Edited by Ralph J. Mills, copyright © 1965 by Beatrice Roethke as Administratrix of the Estate of Theodore Roethke. Reprinted by permission of the University of Washington Press.

Rogers, Natalie. "The Right to Be Me! Confronting Sex Role Expectations." Reprinted from *Emerging Woman.* (Point Reyes Station, CA: Personal Press.)

Rosenblatt, Roger. "Who Killed Privacy?" Originally appeared in *The New York Times Magazine,* January 31, 1993. Copyright © 1993 by The New York Times Company. Reprinted by permission.

Royko, Mike. "The Virtue of Prurience." Originally appeared in *The Chicago Sun-Times,* April 17, 1983. Reprinted by permission of *The Chicago Sun-Times.*

Rubin, Lillian B. "The Approach–Avoidance Dance: Men, Women & Intimacy." From *Intimate Strangers: Men and Women Together.* Copyright © 1983 by Lillian B. Rubin. Reprinted by permission of HarperCollins Publishers, Inc.

Russell, Bertrand. "If We Are to Survive This Dark Time." From *The Basic Writings of Bertrand Russell,* edited by Robert Egner and Lester Denon. Copyright © 1961 by George Allen & Unwin, Ltd. Reprinted by permission of Simon & Schuster, Inc.

Sáenz, Benjamin Alire. "Exiled: The Winds of Sunset Heights." Prologue from *Flowers for the Broken.* Copyright © Benjamin Alire Sáenz. Reprinted by permission of Broken Moon Press.

Santino, Jack. "Rock and Roll as Music; Rock and Roll as Culture." Originally appeared in the July 1990 issue of *The World and I,* a publication of The Washington Times Corporation, copyright © 1990. Reprinted by permission.

Sarton, May. "The Rewards of Living a Solitary Life." Published in *The New York Times,* April 8, 1974. Copyright © 1974 by The New York Times Company. Reprinted by permission.

Sartre, Jean-Paul. "The Passion of the Anti-Semite." From *Anti-Semite and Jew,* trans. George E. Becker. Copyright © 1948 by Schocken Books, a div. of Random House. Copyright renewed © 1976 by Schocken Books, Inc.

Schwartz, Delmore. "In Dreams Begin Responsibilities." From *In Dreams Begin Responsibilities.* Copyright © 1978 by New Directions Publishing Corp. Reprinted by permission of New Directions Publishing Corporation.

Selzer, Richard. "A Question of Mercy." From *Down by Troy.* Copyright © 1992 by Richard Selzer. Reprinted by permission of William Morrow & Company, Inc.

Sexton, Anne. "Her Kind." From *To Bedlam and Part Way Back.* Copyright © 1960 by Anne Sexton, renewed 1988 by Linda G. Sexton. Reprinted by permission of Houghton Mifflin Co. All Rights Reserved.

Silko, Leslie Marmon. "Lullaby." From *Storyteller* by Leslie Marmon Silko. Published by Seaver Books, New York. Copyright © 1981 by Leslie Marmon Silko.

Solzhenitsyn, Aleksandr. "Playing Upon the Strings of Emptiness." A Speech at the National Arts Club. Published in *The New York Times Book Review,* February 7, 1993. Reprinted by permission of the author.

Sophocles. *Antigone.* From *Sophocles, The Oedipus Cycle: An English Version,* by Dudley Fitts and Robert Fitzgerald. Copyright 1939 by Harcourt Brace & Company and renewed 1967 by Dudley Fitts and Robert Fitzgerald. Reprinted by permission of the publisher. All Rights Reserved.

Soto, Gary. "Black Hair." From *Living Up the Street* by Gary Soto. Copyright © 1985 by Gary Soto. Used by permission of Strawberry Hill Press.

Soyinka, Wole. "Telephone Conversation." From *Modern Poetry from Africa.* Copyright © by Wole Soyinka. Reprinted by permission of Brandt & Brandt Literary Agents., Inc.

Steele, Shelby. "On Being Black and Middle Class." Reprinted from *Commentary,* January 1988. Reprinted by permission of the author. All Rights Reserved.

Steffens, Lincoln. "I Go to College." From *The Autobiography of Lincoln Steffens.* Copyright © 1931 by Harcourt Brace & Company and renewed 1959 by Peter Steffens. Reprinted by permission of the publisher.

Steinbeck, John. "The Chrysanthemums." From *The Long Valley.* Copyright 1937, renewed 1965 by John Steinbeck. Used by permission of Viking Penguin, a division of Penguin Books USA Inc.

Swenson, May. "Women." Copyright © 1968 by May Swenson. Reprinted with permission of The Literary Estate of May Swenson.

Tam, Vo Thi. "From Vietnam, 1979." From *American Mosaic: The Immigrant Experience in the Words of Those Who Lived It,* ed. Joan Morrison and Charlotte Fox Zabusky. Copyright © 1980 by Joan Morrison and Charlotte Fox Zabusky. Originally published by Dutton. Reprinted by permission of the University of Pittsburgh Press.

Tavris, Carol. "Uncivil Rights—The Cultural Rules of Anger." From *Anger: The Misunderstood Emotion* by Carol Tavris. Copyright © 1982, 1989 by Carol Tavris. Reprinted by permission of Simon & Schuster, Inc.

Taylor, Elizabeth. "Girl Reading." From *A Dedicated Man*. Copyright © the Elizabeth Taylor Estate. Reprinted by permission of A. M. Heath & Company, Ltd. London.

Terkel, Studs. "Miss U.S.A." From *American Dreams: Lost and Found*. Copyright © 1980 by Studs Terkel. Reprinted by permission of Pantheon Books, a division of Random House, Inc.

Thomas, Dylan. "The Force That Through the Green Fuse Drives the Flower." From *Poems of Dylan Thomas*. Copyright 1939 by New Directions Publishing Corporation. Reprinted by permission of New Directions Publishing Corporation.

Thomas, Lewis. "Humanities and Science." From *Late Night Thoughts on Listening to Mahler's Ninth*. Copyright © 1981 by Lewis Thomas. Used by permission of Viking Penguin, a division of Penguin Books USA, Inc. "Making Science Work." From *Late Night Thoughts on Listening to Mahler's Ninth*. Copyright © 1981 by Lewis Thomas. Used by permission of Viking Penguin, a division of Penguin Books USA, Inc.

Three Rivers, Amoja. "Cultural Etiquette: A Guide for the Well-Intentioned." Published in *Ms.* Magazine, September/October 1991. Copyright © 1990, 1991 by Amoja Three Rivers. Reprinted by permission of the author. Available from Market Wimmin, Auto, WV 24917.

Thurber, James. "The Unicorn in the Garden." From *Fables of Our Time*. Copyright © 1940 by James Thurber, copyright © 1968 by Helen Thurber. Published by Harper & Row.

Tyler, Anne. "Still Just Writing." From *The Writer on Her Work*, edited by Janet Sternburg. Reprinted by permission of W. W. Norton & Company, Inc. Copyright © 1980 by Janet Sternburg.

Walker, Alice. "Beauty: When the Other Dancer Is the Self." From *In Search of Our Mother's Gardens: Womanist Prose*. Copyright © 1983 by Alice Walker, reprinted by permission of Harcourt Brace & Company. "Nineteen Fifty-Five." From *You Can't Keep a Good Woman Down*. Copyright © 1981 by Alice Walker. Reprinted by permission of Harcourt Brace & Company.

Weiner, Jonathan. "The Island Effect: Fire and Rain." From *The Next One Hundred Years*. Copyright © 1990 by Jonathan Weiner. First published in *Lear's* April 1990 issue. Used by permission of Bantam Books, a division of Bantam Doubleday Dell Publishing Group, Inc.

Welty, Eudora. "Finding a Voice." From *One Writer's Beginnings*. Reprinted by permission of Harvard University Press. Copyright © 1983, 1984 by Eudora Welty.

Werner, Peter. "Both Sides Now." From *Stories Parents Seldom Hear: College Students Write About Their Lives and Families*, edited by Harriet Harvey.

White, E. B. "The Second Tree from the Corner." From *The Second Tree from the Corner*. Copyright © 1947 by E. B. White. Copyright renewed. Reprinted by permission of HarperCollins Publishers, Inc..

Wilbur, Richard. "A Finished Man." From *New and Collected Poems*. Originally published in the March 4, 1985 issue of *The New Yorker*.

Wilcove, David S. "What I Saw When I Went to the Forest." From *Wilderness*, Spring 1989, Vol. 51, No. 180. Reprinted by permission.

Willard, Nancy. "Questions My Son Asked Me, Answers I Never Gave Him." From *Household Tales of Moon and Water*. Copyright © 1982 by Nancy Willard. Reprinted by permission of Harcourt Brace & Company.

Williams, William Carlos. "The Use of Force." From *The Farmers' Daughters*. Copyright 1938 by William Carlos Williams. Reprinted by permission of New Directions Publishing Corp.

Wilner, Eleanor. "Emigration." From *Shekhinah*. Reprinted by permission of Eleanor Wilner.

Wilson, Edward O. "Is Humanity Suicidal?" *The New York Times Magazine*, May 30, 1993. Copyright © 1993 by The New York Times Co. Reprinted by permission.

Winn, Marie. "The Plug-in Drug: TV and the American Family." From *The Plug-in Drug*. Copyright © 1977 by Marie Winn Miller. Reprinted by permission of Viking Penguin, a division of Penguin Books, USA Inc.

Woolf, Virginia. "Professions for Women" ("The Angel in the House"). From *The Death of the Moth and Other Essays*. Copyright 1942 by Harcourt Brace & Company and renewed 1971 by Marjorie T. Parsons, reprinted by permission of the publisher.

Wright, Richard. "The Ethics of Living Jim Crow." From *Uncle Tom's Children*. Copyright 1937 by Richard Wright. Reprinted by permission of HarperCollins Publishers, Inc..

Yeats, W. B. "A Prayer for My Daughter." From *The Poems of W. B. Yeats: A New Edition*. Edited by Richard J. Finneran. Reprinted with permission of Macmillan Publishing Company. Copyright 1924 by Macmillan Publishing Company, renewed 1952 by Bertha Georgie Yeats.

Contents

ART AND COMPOSITION

THE SEARCH FOR SELF

Personal Reminiscences

Essays

Fiction

Poetry

PERSONAL RELATIONSHIPS: PARENTS AND CHILDREN

Letters and Personal Reminiscences

Essays

Fiction

Poetry

PERSONAL RELATIONSHIPS: MEN AND WOMEN

Essays

Fiction

Poetry

THE CULTURAL TRADITION: POPULAR CULTURE

Personal Reminiscence

Essays

Fiction

THE CULTURAL TRADITION: ART AND SOCIETY

Personal Reminiscences

Essays

Fiction

Poetry

SCIENCE, THE ENVIRONMENT, AND THE FUTURE

Essays

Fiction

Poetry

Drama

FREEDOM AND HUMAN DIGNITY

Personal Reminiscences

Essays

Fiction

Poetry

Drama

THE EXAMINED LIFE: EDUCATION

Personal Reminiscences

Essays

Fiction

Poetry

THE EXAMINED LIFE: PERSONAL VALUES

Personal Reminiscences

Essays

Fiction

Poetry

Rhetorical Contents

The following arrangement of expository essays will suggest ways in which readers can approach the selections. The classifications are not, of course, rigid, and many selections might fit as easily into one category as another.

Analysis

Argument and Persuasion

Comparison/Contrast

Identification

Illustration

Narration

Preface

> . . . the unexamined life is not worth living.
> —**Plato,** *The Apology*

The academic turmoil of the early 1970s—which may seem remote to-day—provided the background for the first edition of *The Conscious Reader*. The editors, predisposed to support change, wanted to create a reader that would reflect a multidisciplinary approach to the teaching of writing and would recognize cultural diversity. For the former, we included selections to represent a wide range of academic disciplines and interests from psychology to biology and computer science. For the latter, we chose authors who represent the spectrum of American ethnic cultures and the contribution of minorities and women.

We also wanted to stress our belief in the rational mind, in an era in which university faculties were often inclined to measure relevance by spontaneous response. Unhappy with such a superficial concept of relevance, we compiled a book intended to make readers think, to go beyond reading unconsciously. It occurred to one of us (probably to Tony English, our remarkable editor) that we could reinforce our belief by giving the book the name it has since held for twenty years. Today the academic world calls our objective critical reading, but we have never regretted being a little ahead of our time.

Still believing that the development of writing skills depends on the heightening of consciousness, the editors of *The Conscious Reader* invite students to examine and to respond to the basic questions that writers since Plato have posed. The selections included engage our interests by their style and by their focus on issues of universal concern. They reflect the continuity between past and present, serve as a catalyst to self-expression, sharpen our perceptions, and widen our sympathies. Consciousness heightened through reading develops effective writing, and the act of writing fosters self-definition. As we extend awareness by reading, we become increasingly conscious of the reservoir of memories and experiences from which to draw and the variety of forms and techniques that give shape to our writing.

Over two-thirds of the readings in this book are nonfiction prose, primarily exposition or argument. Some of the essays are personal and readily comprehensible and provide models for early writing assignments. Others, more complex, should help students develop the ability to reason abstractly. Although most of the authors included are accomplished literary stylists, others are primarily distinguished for their contributions to popular culture, science, philosophy, or psychology.

We have also included thirty-one stories and thirty-nine poems. The inclusion of imaginative literature in a composition course needs no special justification. It serves a number of important goals: to enhance the pleasure of reading, to educate the emotions as well as the mind, to stimulate original creative efforts, and to provide vicarious experience with which to test the ideas expressed in essays. The dramatic situations, vivid character portrayals, and verbal compression of fiction and poetry also suggest techniques to enliven student writing. We are convinced more than ever that the most stimulating as well as most economical means of helping students to develop conceptual literacy is to expose them to literate essays and imaginative literature, both of which will arrest their interest and challenge their thinking.

This sixth edition of *The Conscious Reader* contains Ibsen's *An Enemy of the People*, which strikes us as a timely reflection on issues facing society in the 1990s. We have also replaced a number of paintings in the section on art and composition. We believe these changes and the increase in the number of selections by women, minority, and Third World writers add to the book's versatility and its capacity to engage the reader deeply.

Each selection has a head note and suggestions for discussion and writing to help students explore multiple levels of understanding. The suggestions invite students to pay careful attention to thought and structure and to compare their experience with the vision of life expressed in the selections. Exploring cultural patterns both similar and alien to one's own should encourage a continuing dialectic in classroom discussion as well as in writing.

The thematic groupings represent a convenient division of the book. The readings begin with the search for self and move to consideration of the self in relation to others—parents, friends, and lovers. The next section focuses on culture, including discussions of both popular culture and art and society. The next section explores many facets of the world of science and technology. The readings continue with a variety of statements about our aspirations and failures to ensure a sense of freedom and human dignity for all. The book concludes with several sections on the examined life. The selections mediate between problems of education and human concerns and then return full cycle to the individual's search for meaning and value.

If there is a dominant theme in these readings, it is that neither understanding of the past nor projections of the future can eliminate conflict from our lives and that opposing forces in the self and society are a part of the human condition. Indeed, it is vital that these forces contend. For it is primarily through conscious recognition and expression of these conflicting forces that we may find our way to a tolerance of ambiguity and to an increased freedom of choice.

Acknowledgments

To Diane Engber, for sharing her knowledge of the women's literature of Africa and the Caribbean; to Karis Towe, for swift and careful research work; to my colleagues at the Union Institute, for their commitment to interdisciplinary and multicultural research; and to the late Caroline Shrodes, for initiating me into the richness of her vision of *The Conscious Reader.*—F. M. B.

To Eve Finestone, who has made the art and composition section possible, and to Anne M. Finestone.   —H. F.

To Robert E. Jackson and to Harry and Mary Miller for their support and encouragement.   —M. S.

For extraordinary assistance and patience, we wish to thank our editors, D. Anthony English and Eben Ludlow. We are grateful, too, for the editorial help offered by Anthony Ven Graitis, Wendy Polhemus-Annibel, and Tara Padykula. We are finally grateful to the reviewers for this sixth edition.

THE
CONSCIOUS
READER

Art and Composition

Discussion of art presents certain problems. It is difficult, sometimes impossible, to discover the thought processes of the visual artist or the "argument" of the painting; moreover, students may be unaware of how much the content of the painting derives from traditions of the form. The contemporary artist George Baselitz argues that painting projects no ideas and does not communicate or express publicly any statements, information, or opinions. A number of contemporary artists even find explication of their work repugnant. Nevertheless, the editors believe that painting can communicate and inspire not only emotions but ideas as well. They further believe that ideas relating to the themes of this text, while accounting for only a part of the total meaning or impact of these paintings, will provoke students to think and to write. Therefore, we offer these paintings in the expectation that students and instructors will find them exciting and will see even more in them for discussion or writing than we have suggested.

Paul Gauguin

Self-Portrait with Halo (1889)

It was the substantial number of Impressionist paintings that French painter Paul Gauguin (1848–1903) had collected when he was a successful Parisian stockbroker that financed his escape from marriage, fatherhood, and bourgeois respectability while in his mid-thirties. Although he had previously exhibited with the Impressionists, it wasn't until this later age that he devoted himself fully to painting.

National Gallery of Art, Washington; Chester Dale Collection.

At the same time as he threw himself into the life of the starving bohemian artist in his garret, he began to develop his own theories of painting. He abandoned the Impressionists' careful scientific study of natural light and the ever-changing fragmentation of color it caused. He sought instead to exercise his own intelligence and to express his own response to a subject by creating new forms and assigning his private meaning to colors. His forms became abstract, stylized, and slightly distorted; he applied colors heavily, without modulation, and outlined them with a thick dark brush. He advised a friend,

A meter of green is greener than a centimeter. . . . How does that tree look to you? Green? All right, then use green, the greenest on your palette. And that shadow, a little bluish? Don't be afraid. Paint it as blue as you can.

In Gauguin's personal vocabulary, a Christ became yellow, the soil red, and a pond white.

His flight from the city led him to the provinces of Provence and Brittany, but eventually, like Europeans for centuries, he followed the call of the exotic, the primitive, the untamed, and the foreign; he sailed for Tahiti and the Marquesas. There Gauguin found the strong bright colors, the simple forms, the decorative patterns of nature and human figures that confirmed the aesthetic he had already established in France. He also found poverty, malnutrition, and syphilis. With the exception of one visit to France, he spent his last twelve years there, creating his great Tahitian masterpieces.

Suggestions for Discussion

1. Why does the painting seem to divide in half? Which half seems to dominate? Examine the forms and lines of Gauguin's face.

2. Describe the multiple symbols. What do they represent? Can you explain the choice of colors? What is the meaning of the halo? Is Gauguin suggesting he should be wearing it? What is suggested by the fact that one apple is red, one green? (Red and green are complementary colors.)

3. What is Gauguin looking at? What is the relationship between the flowers and the snake? What does the direction of his glance tell you about the artist's sense of self?

4. "Art is an abstraction," said Gauguin. How can a self-portrait be an abstraction? What evidence is there that the portrait reflects an introspective person?

5. Compare and contrast this self-portrait with the following one by Frida Kahlo.

Suggestions for Writing

1. Assume you know nothing about Gauguin's life. Write an essay in which you discuss his sense of self, his age, his health, and his values based only on the clues from this self-portrait.

2. How might Gauguin deal with his autobiography in writing rather than in painting? Discuss some differences between the two genres in presenting a self-portrait. What are some of the difficulties and shortcuts of each?

Frida Kahlo

Self-Portrait with a Thorn Necklace
and Hummingbird (1940)

Frida Kahlo (1907–1954) created her autobiography in her scenes of her own life cycle—from conception and birth to marriage, surgeries, miscarriages, and dreams of her death. These basic subjects are informed, however, by a personal vocabulary. For example, in My Grandparents, My Parents and I *she includes herself both as a naked child and as a fetus carefully painted on her mother's white wedding dress; the formal portraits of her parents and grandparents are set against a desert background of the rocky mountains and cacti of Mexico where she was born of mestizo origin.* My Birth *shows most graphically the emergence of the fetus; only the mother's head is covered by a white sheet and over her hangs a* retablo *(a traditional Mexican painting on tin of a miraculous event usually showing figures against an empty background) of the Virgin as Mother of Sorrows pierced with daggers. She painted her own miscarriage on a blood-stained hospital bed surrounded by free-floating objects, such as a fetus, a pelvis, an orchid, and tubes resembling umbilical cords. In short, Kahlo's subject matter was dictated by her own life.*

She was born to a religious Catholic mother of Indian and Spanish parentage and to an agnostic father, a German Jew of Hungarian origin. She vowed as a teenager to bear a child to the famous Mexican painter Diego Rivera, twenty years her senior, before she had even met him. She did indeed marry him at age twenty-two, after she had been left with a limp from polio and had almost died in a horrifying accident that destroyed much of her body and forced her to abandon her medical studies. As a result she suffered many miscarriages, many operations and hospitalizations, and much pain throughout the remainder of her life. She never did have a child.

Kahlo and Rivera shared a commitment to political action (both joined the Communist party along with other leading Mexican artists) as well as a devotion to "Mexicanidad," a rekindling of pride in indigenous Mexican art and culture that had long been eclipsed by imported colonial values. He was a womanizer, and she eventually took male and female lovers. During 1940, the year of this self-portrait, they were divorced and remarried; they later divorced again. They traveled to the United States for Rivera's commissions, but it was not until 1938 that Kahlo gained recognition, selling four paintings and showing in an exhibition of "Masters of Popular Painting: Modern Primitives" at the Museum of Modern Art. At this time she began a friendship with André Breton, a poet and the leader of the French Surrealist movement, who hailed Kahlo as one of them. Although she had seen little of the Surrealists' work, Kahlo shared their interest in dreams, the unconscious, eroticism, pain, and death, and she too floated seemingly unrelated objects in her paintings.

Both in narrative paintings and in a large number of self-portraits, Kahlo presents herself by a rather frank rendering of her face with its slight moustache, almond-shaped eyes, and heavy brows, as well as by her choice of costume, accompanying images, and background. Take into account that she had a large collection of native costumes (particularly from Tehauntupec, an ancient matriarchal society), of pre-Columbian jewelry, and of retablos and folk art; that she honored the Aztec belief in the animal alter ego; that the dead bird and butterflies signify dead warriors; and that she once took the Nahuatl name Xochitl or "flower," which is the sign for artisans.

Suggestions for Discussion

1. How does Kahlo see herself in this portrait? Examine her "costume," her coiffure, her jewels, the pet monkey (who appears in other paintings), and the cat on either side of her. How realistic is each element? Is the background realistic and why has she chosen it? What is the effect of the overall composition? Can you explain her use of color?
2. What does her expression reveal of herself? Is the portrait realistic or symbolic? Do we know this woman from it? What does she want to show in her painting? How successful is it as autobiography? If Kahlo is both subject and object of this work, what is the function of the viewer?

Suggestions for Writing

Write an essay in which you compare Kahlo's self-portrait with that of Gauguin. Organize your essay around one of the following ideas:

1. Compare the two artists' use of color, their sense of design, their expression of the face. Do these elements make one portrait more realistic than the other? Why?
2. Compare the objects in both paintings. What do they mean as symbols? How do we understand their meaning? Are the images universal or personal and private?
3. What does each portrait reveal of its subject? Which one reveals more? For which one could you write a more complete psychological sketch? Which portrait do you find the more successful?

Honoré Daumier

The Uprising (1860)

Honoré Daumier (1808–1879), French painter and caricaturist, was known as the greatest social satirist of his day. Having come with his family to Paris from Marseilles, he began to learn the art of lithography and to contribute to Caricature. *His portrait of King Louis Phillipe as Gargantua led to his imprisonment for six months. After the government suppressed* Caricature, *Daumier contributed to* Charivari *with a series of cartoons that ridiculed the French bourgeois world. The 4,000 lithographs and 1,000 wood engravings, considered merely as cartoons in his lifetime, are now cherished as masterpieces.*

When Henry James, in an article on Daumier in 1890, stated that journalism was the greatest invention of the age, he did so in order to pay tribute to Daumier's lithographs, many of which he had found in a bookstore on the Left Bank in Paris. The French poet Paul Valéry pointed out that Daumier was compared by many to Michelangelo and Rembrandt. Valéry called Daumier the moralist of mankind. The Uprising (1860) is a good example of the power and intensity of his painting.

Suggestions for Discussion

1. Probably inspired by popular demonstrations against the monarchy, Daumier is making a number of statements about people and power in this painting. How does Daumier see the people? Consider colors, shapes, faces, and posture. Notice the buildings and sky. What is their effect on the human subjects?
2. How does Daumier achieve the dominance of the central figure? Consider light, dress, expression. What is the effect of his gesture and the diagonal line formed by it?
3. Comment on the expression on the face of the central figure. Is he a romantic hero? What comment may Daumier be making as he compares the mass and the leader? Why is the leader strongly portrayed, the mass seen as blurred and inchoate?
4. What elements of caricature do you see in the painting?
5. One suggestion about this painting is that the streets can barely contain the mass depicted, and that except for the leader, the mass is totally undifferentiated. Comment.
6. One critic sees this painting as symbolic "of pent-up frustration of the waves of self-rule, of self-reliance, the epic moment in the history of freedom." Comment.

Suggestions for Writing

1. Write an essay characterizing the leader. What qualities do you see in his face and in his stance? Is he totally heroic?
2. For a brief research paper, examine the facts of the anti-monarchical uprising in 1848 France. What in your reading may help account for the painting's scene?

Robert-Victor-Félix Delaunay

Red Eiffel Tower (1911–1912)

Robert-Victor-Félix Delaunay (1885–1941), who showed a precocious ability to paint while still in high school in Paris, was able to devote himself entirely to painting soon after an apprenticeship as a set designer. He was friends first with the post-Impressionists (Gauguin's Pont Aven circle) and

Collection, Solomon R. Guggenheim Museum, New York.
Photo: David Heald.

then he turned to Cubism along with Picasso, Braque, Léger, and the avant-garde poets who were all his friends. The Cubists, reluctant to depend on the evidence of their senses, were more interested in the world of their imagination. Their distinctive characteristic is the study of objects, which they break down into geometric forms and which are seen from several viewpoints and on different planes.

Often using the architecture of cities as subject, Delaunay painted his first of thirty Eiffel Towers in 1910, a fine example for him of benign rather than aggressive technology. With this painting he is on his way toward the more abstract lyrical canvases that celebrate the glory of color and that were so admired by the contemporary German Blue Rider School with which he also exhibited.

Suggestions for Discussion

1. In 1889 the Eiffel Tower was greeted with scorn by Parisians in their beautifully laid-out city of soft-colored stone buildings, grand boulevards, and elegant parks. How does Delaunay speak for this strange fusion of steel and exposed girders? Consider color, form, the emotion aroused in the viewer. What prevents the Tower from appearing cold or mechanical? How does Delaunay create motion? What are his feelings about the future?

2. Choose a contemporary technological construction; for example, a space shuttle, a nuclear power plant, or a multiple-level parking garage. Compare popular reactions to such a construction to reactions to the Tower. How could one describe them in painting or in writing so as to humanize them and to assert humans' control over them?

3. In 1924 the poet Blaise Cendrars said, "No formula of art . . . can pretend to give plastic resolution to the Eiffel Tower. . . . The Tower rose over Paris, slender as a hat-pin. When we retreated from it, it dominated Paris, stark and perpendicular. When we came close, it tilted and leaned over us. Seen from the first platform it corkscrewed around its own axis, and seen from the top it collapsed into itself, doing the splits, its neck pulled in. . . ."

   Discuss this quotation in relation to the painting. Are Delaunay's and Cendrars's attitudes similar? What does the quotation suggest about the difference between the language of the writer and the language of the painter?

Suggestions for Writing

1. Write an imaginative essay in which you convert some construction into something less ominous or more frivolous in order to come to terms with it.

2. Write an essay contrasting this painting with a photograph of the Eiffel Tower. Consider what significant differences in feeling are evoked by the difference in medium.

Pierre-Auguste Renoir

The Luncheon of the Boating Party (1881)

At thirteen, Pierre-Auguste Renoir (1841–1919) actually began earning his living as a painter. He decorated fine porcelains and later fans with flowers, portraits, and copies of eighteenth-century masters. (He had come to Paris from Limoges, home of the great porcelain works.) However, at twenty-one he entered the prestigious Ecole des Beaux-Arts where he made friends with other young painters who were to formulate the new theories of art known as Impressionism. While they all eventually went separate ways, they shared a distaste for the noble subjects of the prevailing tradition and for painting from memory, and they exalted the evidence of the eye rather than the working of the intellect. When many of their group were excluded from the 1863 Salon (the biannual art exhibition), the emperor Napoléon III answered their protests by establishing a subsidiary show that came to be known as the Salon des Refusés. By this time these artists were working outside the established studios and were meeting regularly with avant-garde critics, writers, composers, and photographers (of the new science) to evolve their theories of

e Phillips Collection, Washington, D.C.

art. In 1873 they formed a corporation that held its first exhibition. They went on to hold seven more shows.

In sharp contrast with their own struggle to survive, Monet, Sisley, Pissarro, and Renoir, among others, created scenes of a radiant nature, portraits of beauty and serenity, and scenes of people involved in simple pleasures. Renoir shared their theories of light and its fragmentation of color, of the need to paint spontaneously and immediately out-of-doors, of the use of light brushstrokes to transmit complex colors affected by light and shadow. (One finds dappled cool colors, green, blue, and violet, included in the overall warm pink, rose, peach, and gold that make up the body of a Renoir nude.)

In The Luncheon of the Boating Party Renoir combines his love of the outdoors and his delight in scenes of people at play. It is midday, probably a Sunday, and Renoir and his friends (who have been identified as known models, actresses, artists, titled gentlemen) have rowed down from Paris to an island in the Seine. They are on the upstairs terrace of a popular restaurant.

Suggestions for Discussion

1. What is the general ambience of the scene? Consider the season, the weather, the dress of the diners, their age, their class, their looks. What are they doing? How are they feeling?

2. There are no outlines here, other than those caused by juxtaposition of color. How, then, does Renoir organize his canvas? How can one divide it up? Notice his use of the railing, the awning, the table, the complementary blue of the grasses and orange of the awning. Where else does he use these warm and cool colors?

3. How many groups can you see? Why has the young man standing at the right moved from his seat in the foreground? To make way for a group portrait? What is his function in the composition and that of the man seated with his back to us? What is the purpose of the beautiful still life on the table? (The last course in a French meal is fruit.)

4. Is the euphoria described here real? Complete? Permanent? Do the diners care about tomorrow?

Suggestion for Writing

What do young people do today in their leisure time? How similar or different might such a party be today? Write an essay in which you compare this scene to one in which you have participated.

Jacob Lawrence

Harriet Tubman (1939–1940)
(One of a series of thirty-one)

Harriet Tubman worked as water girl to field hands. She also worked at plowing, carting, and heaving logs.

The parents of Jacob Lawrence (1917–) were part of the African-American migration to the industrial cities of the North following World War I. Born in New Jersey, at age thirteen Lawrence moved to New York City shortly after the flowering of the Harlem Renaissance, when Harlem had become the center for African-American writers, artists, and musicians carving out a cultural identity. Despite the Depression, Harlem was still an exciting place

Hampton University Museum, Hampton, Virginia.

where Lawrence benefited richly from this awakening, from stories and legends told by his family and neighbors, and from his own intensive research at the Schomburg Collection for Research in Black Culture. He received a broad theoretical and practical training in art at WPA (government-financed) art workshops and on a scholarship in art school.

In a 1956 interview Lawrence said,

> *I love to tell a story. The history of the United States fascinates me. Right now, I'm reading in it, looking for any episode that suggests a symbol of struggle. The part the Negro has played in all these events has been greatly overlooked. I intend to bring it out. Of course, where the Negro didn't figure, I leave him out. . . . But fear of "propaganda" doesn't worry me. A great purpose of art is to communicate ideas. Color and design are only means to this end.*

To express his ideas, Lawrence turned to narrative painting following in traditions as varied as those of the modern Mexican muralists, of Goya, Breughel, and African art. Many of his series of paintings constitute biographies of heroic figures: Toussaint l'Ouverture, *the eighteenth-century liberator of Haiti;* Frederick Douglass, *an escaped slave who became a writer and an abolitionist editor;* Harriet Tubman; *and, finally, the white abolitionist John Brown who planned to establish a safe haven for slaves and who led the disastrous raid on Harper's Ferry, Virginia, for which he was hanged. Other series deal with more generalized subjects:* The Migration of the Negro; Hiroshima; Builders, *which celebrates the African-American as worker and craftsperson; and* Eight Sermons of the Creation *from the Book of Genesis. A longtime teacher, Lawrence is presently Professor Emeritus at the University of Washington and an active painter.*

The thirty-one rather small panels of the Harriet Tubman *series tell her story from her childhood as an abused slave and field hand through her frightening escape to the North from where she launched her rescue operation of slaves. Her daring strength became legendary. She advised Frederick Douglass and John Brown, spoke at abolitionist rallies, and was a spy and nurse for the Union army.*

Lawrence provides captions for each painting, but the subject is not always episodic; there is, for example, a lyrical painting of a single cotton plant, a symbol of slavery but a beautiful thing; another of talons covered with eyes and reaching out of the earth to encircle the moon, the searchers who pursued Harriet Tubman as she fled. This painting portrays a woman at work.

Suggestions for Discussion

1. Compare the color tones and the paint strokes used for the woman and for the landscape. Note the lines of the figure and of the landscape. How do they work together? How does the technique express the artist's feelings about Harriet Tubman?

2. Is the painting "propaganda"? How does it differ from a poster with its heavy primary colors? If you did not know this was a heroic historical figure, would you understand the "propaganda"? How?

3. Compare Lawrence's painting with the following one, Degas's *The Ironers.* Compare backgrounds, color tones, subjects' relationship to their background. What seems to be the subjects' attitude toward their work? Compare their "body lan-

guage"; what is the effect of the straight lines, of the curved lines? What is the mood of each painting? How do Lawrence's uncompromising colors and Degas's complex and softer palette affect mood? What is each painter's attitude toward his subject? What is universal in each painting?

Suggestions for Writing

1. Write a portrait of Harriet Tubman to complement Lawrence's visual portrait.

2. What do you think is the purpose of art? Is it what Lawrence calls "propaganda"? Look up the ideas of other artists on the function of art, such as those of the Impressionists. Are the Impressionists to be faulted for being more interested in the theories of art than in the expression of ideas? You might want to read about and consider using abstract art and/or pop art as examples.

Edgar (Hilaire Germain) Degas

The Ironers (c. 1884)

Oil on canvas; 32⅜″ × 29¾″. m.1971.3.P/M.1979.17.p.
Norton Simon Foundation.

Edgar Degas (1834–1917), son of a Parisian banker, did not quite conform to the conservative, upper-middle-class circle he was born to; his father was Neapolitan and his mother was a Creole from New Orleans. After studying the law briefly, he turned to painting, but while he followed the precepts of a classical apprenticeship by copying the masters, he did so by drawing on his own and for an unusually long period of time. Yet like his contemporaries, the Impressionists, he would turn away from traditional subjects, from the heroic, the historic, the elegant, and the ideal to the study of more ordinary people involved in the simple activities of everyday life. Degas met regularly with artists, writers, and photographers at Café Guerbois where the loosely called movement of Impressionism took form, but he did not share their obsession with the outdoors (with the exception of his racetrack scenes) or with natural light and its fleeting effects on color and tone.

His was an urban life; his many preparatory sketches and meticulous drawings were done indoors where his subjects spent their time. While Degas did many portraits of his own class, he was passionately interested in the lives of those who worked: ballet dancers, musicians, entertainers, laundresses, shop girls. And although the finished forms of his subjects are full of grace and beauty, he has caught them at a precise moment when their gestures are casual, even awkward, and always natural. Like the ballet dancers in the wings or at practice, the singer in a club, and the women bathers drying themselves, here the ironers show fatigue and strain, although their bodies are beautifully executed.

Suggestions for Discussion

1. The Japanese wood-block print was greatly admired in Degas's France. The Impressionists collected them and shared their interest in ordinary people at work or at play. Degas regularly used their bird's-eye viewpoint, their asymmetrical arrangements, their cropping of the figure by the picture frame or by another object, their use of negative (seemingly empty) space, their background that seems tilted upward and forward. Look for these characteristics in *The Ironers*.

2. How do straight lines that start outside the canvas lead us into it? Particularly if you start at the left with the edge of the table, see how you are led to different curved lines, which in turn point the way to the one essential vertical, the left arm of the ironer. What is the emotional effect of being led in this way?

3. Degas is painting not merely women, but women at work. What is the purpose of their different poses? How does Degas use objects to define them and their life? How does he handle warm and cool colors; how does he place them; and what is the effect of the blue-white surrounding the ironers? Compare the heavily starched dress shirts with the women's clothing.

Suggestion for Writing

How do the bodies and faces of the ironers compare to Harriet Tubman's in the Lawrence painting? Write an essay comparing the product of their labor. Would Degas agree with Lawrence that color and design are only means to an end? Is Degas making a social comment? You may want to expand the subject of your essay by discussing your preference for the expository or the didactic in painting or writing.

Edward Hopper

Hotel by a Railroad (1952)

Born in a Hudson River port nearby, Edward Hopper (1882–1967) spent most of his adult life in New York City, leaving it three times for Europe, especially Paris, in his twenties and several times for Mexico in later years. Aside from regular vacations on the coast of New England, he lived and worked in the same small apartment in Greenwich Village from 1913 until his death.

He studied at the New York School of Art under the famous teachers William Merritt Chase and Robert Henri, but supported himself as a commercial artist. It was not until his second one-man show at forty-two (at the time of his marriage to a fellow painter) that he could afford to give up his work as a magazine illustrator. He continued to lead a quiet life with his wife in their sparsely furnished apartment (he said he did not like clutter). He eventually won innumerable honors and awards, exhibited widely in prestigious shows,

Hirshhorn Museum and Sculpture Garden, Smithsonian Institution, Gift of Joseph H. Hirshhorn Foundation, 1966.
Photo: Lee Stalsworth.

had his first retrospective show at the Museum of Modern Art in 1933, others at the Whitney Museum of American Art in 1950 and in 1964.

While he did paint landscapes, seascapes, and villages, Hopper seemed to have been fascinated with the city—its restaurants, its theaters, its offices, its apartments glimpsed through open windows, its empty streets. When he left the city as subject, it was often to study the impermanent elements of travel: trains, filling stations, deserted country roads, hotel lobbies, and motel rooms.

In Paris, Hopper had been fascinated not only by the quality of light in the city itself, but also by the glorious effect of light and the interplay of light and shadow found in Impressionist paintings. The Hopper light, however, as he finally developed it, is sharp, even harsh, a pure white often with a yellow pigment, whether it emanates from the strong midday sun, the melancholy tones of evening, or the artificial light of interiors. It does not soften outlines or cause colors to shimmer (as in Renoir's The Luncheon of the Boating Party); rather, it accentuates angles and permits broad areas of solid color to become emphatic.

Suggestions for Discussion

1. What is the role of light in this painting? What is its source? What does it illuminate? Where is the light stronger? What is the emotional effect of this unequal distribution of light?

2. Examine the composition of the painting. Where are the figures and objects placed? What becomes of the softer, curved lines of the armchair and of the woman's bust as one follows the diagonal axis to the right? Why does the movement seem to be toward the right, from the woman to the furniture with its objects to the man? What happens to this movement when we reach the man?

3. The reflection in the mirror would seem to indicate that this is not a small room. Why, then, do we seem to be on top of the figures? Where are we, the viewers, located? Why do we feel we are in the position of a voyeur?

4. What is the relationship between the two people in the room? Are they comfortable with each other? What is the meaning of the woman's dress? What is the object of her and his attention? How does Hopper establish a tension between the interior and the exterior? Why is so much space devoted to the exterior wall, the railroad track, and the building opposite?

Suggestions for Writing

1. In an interview, Hopper said, "Great art is the outward expression of the inner life in the artist, and the inner life will result in his personal vision of the world." Write an essay discussing the relevance of this statement to Hotel by a Railroad. Is there something personal in this painting? Why has Hopper chosen a hotel room as his setting? What adjectives describe the feeling of the scene? Would a voyeur be welcome in the room?

2. Write an essay on the hotel and motel room, the differences between them, their functions, their effect on their lodgers (for example, the traveling salesman, the vacationer, the performer, the diplomat) and vice versa, their attractions and their drawbacks.

The Search for Self

For as long as I could remember, I had been transparent to myself, unselfconscious, learning, doing, most of every day. Now I was in my own way; I myself was a dark object I could not ignore. I couldn't remember how to forget myself. I didn't want to think about myself, to reckon myself in, to deal with myself every livelong minute on top of everything else—but swerve as I might, I couldn't avoid it. I was a boulder blocking my own path. . . .

Must I then lose the world forever, that I had so loved? Was it all, the whole bright and various planet, where I had been so ardent about finding myself alive, only a passion peculiar to children, that I would outgrow even against my will?

—**Annie Dillard,** "So This Was Adolescence"

This crucial day may be the day on which an Algerian taxi-driver tells him how it feels to be an Algerian in Paris. It may be the day on which he passes a café terrace and catches a glimpse of the tense, intelligent and troubled face of Albert Camus. . . .

This is a personal day, a terrible day, the day to which his entire sojourn has been tending. It is the day he realizes that there are no untroubled countries in this fearfully troubled world; that if he has been preparing himself for anything in Europe, he has been preparing himself—for America. In short, the freedom that the American writer finds in Europe brings him, full circle, back to himself, with the responsibility for his development where it always was: in his own hands.

—**James Baldwin,** "The Discovery of What It Means to Be an American"

As I dance, whirling and joyous, happier than I've ever been in my life, another bright-faced dancer joins me. . . . The other dancer has obviously come through all right, as I have done. She is beautiful, whole and free. And she is also me.

—**Alice Walker,** "Beauty: When the Other Dancer Is the Self"

1

I think we are well advised to keep on nodding terms with the people we used to be, whether we find them attractive company or not. Otherwise they turn up unannounced and surprise us, come hammering on the mind's door at 4 A.M. of a bad night and demand to know who deserted them, who betrayed them, who is going to make amends. . . . We forget the loves and the betrayals alike, forget what we whispered and what we screamed, forget who we were.

—**Joan Didion,** "On Keeping a Notebook"

Whether in the pastoral joys of country life or in the labyrinthine city, we Americans are always seeking. We wander, question. But the answer waits in each separate heart—the answer of our own identity and the way by which we can master loneliness and feel that at last we belong.

—**Carson McCullers,** "Loneliness . . . An American Malady"

For writing is discovery. The language that never leaves our head is like colorful yarn, endlessly spun out multicolored threads dropping into a void, momentarily compacted, entangled, fascinating, elusive. . . . Writing that is discovery forces the capturing, the retrieving, the bringing into focus these stray and random thoughts. Sifting through them, we make decisions that are as much about the self as about language.

—**James E. Miller, Jr.,** "Discovering the Self"

Like Biblical stories and myths, fairy tales were the literature which edified everybody—children and adults alike—for nearly all of man's existence. Except that God is central, many Bible stories can be recognized as very similar to fairy tales. In the story of Jonah and the whale, for example, Jonah is trying to run away from his superego's (conscience's) demand that he fight against the wickedness of Nineveh. The ordeal which tests his moral fiber is, as in so many fairy tales, a perilous voyage in which he has to prove himself.

—**Bruno Bettelheim,** "The Child's Need for Magic"

Personal Reminiscences

Annie Dillard

So This Was Adolescence

Annie Dillard (b. 1945), a contributing editor to Harper's, won a Pulitzer Prize in 1975 for Pilgrim at Tinker Creek. More recent books are Living by Fiction, Teaching a Stone to Talk: Expeditions and Encounters, Encounters with Chinese Writers, and The Living. "So This Was Adolescence" is a section of her most recent book, An American Childhood. In this excerpt Dillard experiences adolescence as an identity crisis. She describes her behavior with graphic imagery and questions whether she might "lose the world forever, that I had so loved."

When I was fifteen, I felt it coming; now I was sixteen, and it hit.
My feet had imperceptibly been set on a new path, a fast path into a long tunnel like those many turnpike tunnels near Pittsburgh, turnpike tunnels whose entrances bear on brass plaques a roll call of those men who died blasting them. I wandered witlessly forward and found myself going down, and saw the light dimming; I adjusted to the slant and dimness, traveled further down, adjusted to greater dimness, and so on. There wasn't a whole lot I could do about it, or about anything. I was going to hell on a handcart, that was all, and I knew it and everyone around me knew it, and there it was.

I was growing and thinning, as if pulled. I was getting angry, as if pushed. I morally disapproved most things in North America, and blamed my innocent parents for them. My feelings deepened and lingered. The swift moods of early childhood—each formed by and suited to its occasion—vanished. Now feelings lasted so long they left stains. They arose from nowhere, like winds or waves, and battered at me or engulfed me.
When I was angry, I felt myself coiled and longing to kill someone or bomb something big. Trying to appease myself, during one winter I whipped my bed every afternoon with my uniform belt. I despised the spectacle I made in my own eyes—whipping the bed with a belt, like a creature demented!—and I often began halfheartedly, but I did it daily after school as a desperate discipline, trying to rid myself and the innocent world of my wildness. It was like trying to beat back the ocean.
Sometimes in class I couldn't stop laughing; things were too funny to be borne. It began then, my surprise that no one else saw what was so funny.
I read some few books with such reverence I didn't close them at the finish, but only moved the pile of pages back to the start, without breathing, and began again. I read one such book, an enormous novel, six times that way—closing the binding between sessions, but not between readings.
On the piano in the basement I played the maniacal "Poet and Peasant Overture" so loudly, for so many hours, night after night, I damaged the piano's keys and strings. When I wasn't playing this crashing overture, I played boogie-woogie, or something else, anything else, in octaves—other-

3

wise, it wasn't loud enough. My fingers were so strong I could do push-ups with them. I played one piece with my fists. I banged on a steel-stringed guitar till I bled, and once on a particularly piercing rock-and-roll downbeat I broke straight through one of Father's snare drums.

I loved my boyfriend so tenderly, I thought I must transmogrify into vapor. It would take spectroscopic analysis to locate my molecules in thin air. No possible way of holding him was close enough. Nothing could cure this bad case of gentleness except, perhaps, violence: maybe if he swung me by the legs and split my skull on a tree? Would that ease this insane wish to kiss too much his eyelids' outer corners and his temples, as if I could love up his brain?

I envied people in books who swooned. For two years I felt myself continuously swooning and continuously unable to swoon; the blood drained from my face and eyes and flooded my heart; my hands emptied, my knees unstrung, I bit at the air for something worth breathing—but I failed to fall, and I couldn't find the way to black out. I had to live on the lip of a waterfall, exhausted.

When I was bored I was first hungry, then nauseated, then furious and weak. "Calm yourself," people had been saying to me all my life. Since early childhood I had tried one thing and then another to calm myself, on those few occasions when I truly wanted to. Eating helped; singing helped. Now sometimes I truly wanted to calm myself. I couldn't lower my shoulders; they seemed to wrap around my ears. I couldn't lower my voice although I could see the people around me flinch. I waved my arm in class till the very teachers wanted to kill me.

I was what they called a live wire. I was shooting out sparks that were digging a pit around me, and I was sinking into that pit. Laughing with Ellin at school recess, or driving around after school with Judy in her jeep, exultant, or dancing with my boyfriend to Louis Armstrong across a polished dining-room floor, I got so excited I looked around wildly for aid; I didn't know where I should go or what I should do with myself. People in books split wood.

When rage or boredom reappeared, each seemed never to have left. Each so filled me with so many years' intolerable accumulation it jammed the space behind my eyes, so I couldn't see. There was no room left even on my surface to live. My rib cage was so taut I couldn't breathe. Every cubic centimeter of atmosphere above my shoulders and head was heaped with last straws. Black hatred clogged my very blood. I couldn't peep, I couldn't wiggle or blink; my blood was too mad to flow.

For as long as I could remember, I had been transparent to myself, unself-conscious, learning, doing, most of every day. Now I was in my own way; I myself was a dark object I could not ignore. I couldn't remember how to forget myself. I didn't want to think about myself, to reckon myself in, to deal with myself every livelong minute on top of everything else—but swerve as I might, I couldn't avoid it. I was a boulder blocking my own path. I was a dog barking between my own ears, a barking dog who wouldn't hush.

So this was adolescence. Is this how the people around me had died on their feet—inevitably, helplessly? Perhaps their own selves eclipsed the sun for so many years the world shriveled around them, and when at last their inescapable orbits had passed through these dark egoistic years it was too late, they had adjusted.

Must I then lose the world forever, that I had so loved? Was it all, the whole bright and various planet, where I had been so ardent about finding myself alive, only a _passion_ peculiar to children, that I would outgrow even against my will? ↳ adolescence — complete passion

Suggestions for Discussion

1. What "hit" the author when she was sixteen?

2. How does the metaphor of the tunnel and her movement in it relate to the author's sense of self? How does it relate to her description of what follows?

3. What details of her attitudes and behavior tell you about Annie Dillard's experience of adolescence?

4. What evidence is brought forward that the author was "what they called a live wire"?

5. What does the author mean by being "transparent" to herself? How is that state contrasted with her being in her own way?

6. What images contribute to the reader's understanding of Dillard's sense of crisis?

7. In what sense is Dillard's final questioning a logical conclusion to what has preceded in her narrative?

Suggestions for Writing

1. Recount some of your adolescent experiences and indicate how they related to your sense of self.

2. Draw a portrait of an adolescent you know by examining her/his attitudes and behavior.

3. Compare Dillard's experience of adolescence with that of other writers in this section.

Jack London

What Life Means to Me

Jack London (1876–1916), American novelist and short-story writer, drew upon his extensive travels in such works as The Call of the Wild (1903) and his South Sea tales and developed social themes in such works as The Iron Heel (1907). Although London experienced the loss of many illusions about man's goodness and integrity, he retained his belief in human nobility and excellence.

I was born in the working-class. Early I discovered enthusiasm, ambition, and ideals; and to satisfy these became the problem of my child-life. My environment was crude and rough and raw. I had no outlook, but an uplook rather. My place in society was at the bottom. Here life offered nothing but sordidness and wretchedness, both of the flesh and the spirit; for here flesh and spirit were alike starved and tormented.

Above me towered the colossal edifice of society, and to my mind the only way out was up. Into this edifice I early resolved to climb. Up above, men wore black clothes and boiled shirts, and women dressed in beautiful gowns. Also, there were good things to eat, and there was plenty to eat. This much for the flesh. Then there were the things of the spirit. Up above me, I knew, were unselfishnesses of the spirit, clean and noble thinking, keen intellectual living. I knew all this because I read "Seaside Library" novels, in which, with the exception of the villains and adventuresses, all men and women thought beautiful thoughts, spoke a beautiful tongue, and performed glorious deeds. In short, as I accepted the rising of the sun, I accepted that up above me was all that was fine and noble and gracious, all that gave decency and dignity to life, all that made life worth living and that remunerated one for his travail and misery.

But it is not particularly easy for one to climb up out of the working-class—especially if he is handicapped by the possession of ideals and illusions. I lived on a ranch in California, and I was hard put to find the ladder whereby to climb. I early inquired the rate of interest on invested money, and worried my child's brain into an understanding of the virtues and excellencies of that remarkable invention of man, compound interest. Further, I ascertained the current rates of wages for workers of all ages, and the cost of living. From all this data I concluded that if I began immediately and worked and saved until I was fifty years of age, I could then stop working and enter into participation in a fair portion of the delights and goodnesses that would then be open to me higher up in society. Of course, I resolutely determined not to marry, while I quite forgot to consider at all that great rock of disaster in the working-class world—sickness.

But the life that was in me demanded more than a meagre existence of scraping and scrimping. Also, at ten years of age, I became a newsboy on the streets of a city, and found myself with a changed uplook. All about me were still the same sordidness and wretchedness, and up above me was still the same paradise waiting to be gained; but the ladder whereby to climb was a different one. It was now the ladder of business. Why save my earnings and invest in government bonds, when, by buying two newspapers for five cents, with a turn of the wrist I could sell them for ten cents and double my capital? The business ladder was the ladder for me, and I had a vision of myself becoming a baldheaded and successful merchant prince.

Alas for visions! When I was sixteen I had already earned the title of "prince." But this title was given me by a gang of cut-throats and thieves, by whom I was called "The Prince of the Oyster Pirates." And at that time I had climbed the first rung of the business ladder. I was a capitalist. I owned a boat and a complete oyster-pirating outfit. I had begun to exploit my fellow-creatures. I had a crew of one man. As captain and owner I took two-thirds of the spoils, and gave the crew one-third, though the crew worked just as hard as I did and risked just as much his life and liberty.

This one rung was the height I climbed up the business ladder. One night I went on a raid amongst the Chinese fishermen. Ropes and nets were worth dollars and cents. It was robbery, I grant, but it was precisely the spirit of capitalism. The capitalist takes away the possessions of his fellow-creatures by means of a rebate, or of a betrayal of trust, or by the purchase of senators and supreme-court judges. I was merely crude. That was the only difference. I used a gun.

But my crew that night was one of those inefficients against whom the capitalist is wont to fulminate, because, forsooth, such inefficients increase expenses and reduce dividends. My crew did both. What of his carelessness: he set fire to the big mainsail and totally destroyed it. There weren't any dividends that night, and the Chinese fishermen were richer by the nets and ropes we did not get. I was bankrupt, unable just then to pay sixty-five dollars for a new mainsail. I left my boat at anchor and went off on a bay-pirate boat on a raid up the Sacramento River. While away on this trip, another gang of bay pirates raided my boat. They stole everything, even the anchors; and later on, when I recovered the drifting hulk, I sold it for twenty dollars. I had slipped back the one rung I had climbed, and never again did I attempt the business ladder.

From then on I was mercilessly exploited by other capitalists. I had the muscle, and they made money out of it while I made but a very indifferent living out of it. I was a sailor before the mast, a longshoreman, a roustabout; I worked in canneries, and factories, and laundries; I mowed lawns, and cleaned carpets, and washed windows. And I never got the full product of my toil. I looked at the daughter of the cannery owner, in her carriage, and knew that it was my muscle, in part, that helped drag along that carriage on its rubber tires. I looked at the son of the factory owner, going to college, and knew that it was my muscle that helped, in part, to pay for the wine and good fellowship he enjoyed.

But I did not resent this. It was all in the game. They were the strong. Very well, I was strong. I would carve my way to a place amongst them and make money out of the muscles of other men. I was not afraid of work. I loved hard work. I would pitch in and work harder than ever and eventually become a pillar of society.

And just then, as luck would have it, I found an employer that was of the same mind. I was willing to work, and he was more than willing that I should work. I thought I was learning a trade. In reality, I had displaced two men. I thought he was making an electrician out of me; as a matter of fact, he was making fifty dollars per month out of me. The two men I had displaced had received forty dollars each per month; I was doing the work of both for thirty dollars per month.

This employer worked me nearly to death. A man may love oysters, but too many oysters will disincline him toward that particular diet. And so with me. Too much work sickened me. I did not wish ever to see work again. I fled from work. I became a tramp, begging my way from door to door, wandering over the United States and sweating bloody sweats in slums and prisons.

I had been born in the working-class, and I was now, at the age of eighteen, beneath the point at which I had started. I was down in the cellar of society, down in the subterranean depths of misery about which it is neither nice nor proper to speak. I was in the pit, the abyss, the human cesspool, the shambles and charnel-house of our civilization. This is the part of the edifice of society that society chooses to ignore. Lack of space compels me here to ignore it, and I shall say only that the things I there saw gave me a terrible scare.

I was scared into thinking. I saw the naked simplicities of the complicated civilization in which I lived. Life was a matter of food and shelter. In order to get food and shelter men sold things. The merchant sold shoes, the politician sold his manhood, and the representative of the people, with exceptions, of course, sold his trust; while nearly all sold their honor. Women, too, whether on the street or in the holy bond of wedlock, were prone to sell their flesh. All things were commodities, all people bought and sold. The one commodity that labor had to sell was muscle. The honor of labor had no price in the market-place. Labor had muscle, and muscle alone, to sell.

But there was a difference, a vital difference. Shoes and trust and honor had a way of renewing themselves. They were imperishable stocks. Muscle, on the other hand, did not renew. As the shoe merchant sold shoes, he continued to replenish his stock. But there was no way of replenishing the laborer's stock of muscle. The more he sold of his muscle, the less of it remained to him. It was his one commodity, and each day his stock of it diminished. In the end, if he did not die before, he sold out and put up his shutters. He was a muscle bankrupt, and nothing remained to him but to go down into the cellar of society and perish miserably.

I learned, further, that brain was likewise a commodity. It, too, was different from muscle. A brain seller was only at his prime when he was fifty or sixty years old, and his wares were fetching higher prices than ever. But a laborer was worked out or broken down at forty-five or fifty. I had been in the cellar of society, and I did not like the place as a habitation. The pipes and drains were unsanitary, and the air was bad to breathe. If I could not live on the parlor floor of society, I could, at any rate, have a try at the attic. It was true, the diet there was slim, but the air at least was pure. So I resolved to sell no more muscle, and to become a vender of brains.

Then began a frantic pursuit of knowledge. I returned to California and opened the books. While thus equipping myself to become a brain merchant, it was inevitable that I should delve into sociology. There I found, in a certain class of books, scientifically formulated, the simple sociological concepts I had already worked out for myself. Other and greater minds, before I was born, had worked out all that I had thought and a vast deal more. I discovered that I was a socialist.

The socialists were revolutionists, inasmuch as they struggled to overthrow the society of the present, and out of the material to build the society of the future. I, too, was a socialist and a revolutionist. I joined the groups of working-class and intellectual revolutionists, and for the first time came into intellectual living. Here I found keen-flashing intellects and brilliant wits; for here I met strong and alert-brained, withal horny-handed, members of the working-class; unfrocked preachers too wide in their Christianity for any congregation of Mammon-worshippers; professors broken on the wheel of university subservience to the ruling class and flung out because they were quick with knowledge which they strove to apply to the affairs of mankind.

Here I found, also, warm faith in the human, glowing idealism, sweetnesses of unselfishness, renunciation, and martyrdom—all the splendid, stinging things of the spirit. Here life was clean, noble, and alive. Here life rehabilitated itself, became wonderful and glorious; and I was glad to be alive. I was in touch with great souls who exalted flesh and spirit over dollars and cents, and to whom the thin wail of the starved slum child meant more than all the pomp and circumstance of commerical expansion and world empire. All about me were nobleness of purpose and heroism of effort, and my days and nights were sunshine and starshine, all fire and dew, with before my eyes, ever burning and blazing, the Holy Grail, Christ's own Grail, the warm human, long-suffering and maltreated, but to be rescued and saved at the last.

And I, poor foolish I, deemed all this to be a mere foretaste of the delights of living I should find higher above me in society. I had lost many illusions since the day I read "Seaside Library" novels on the California ranch. I was destined to lose many of the illusions I still retained.

As a brain merchant I was a success. Society opened its portals to me. I entered right in on the parlor floor, and my disillusionment proceeded rapidly. I sat down to dinner with the masters of society, and with the wives and daughters of the masters of society. The women were gowned beautifully, I admit; but to my naïve surprise I discovered that they were of the same clay as all the rest of the women I had known down below in the cellar. "The colonel's lady and Judy O'Grady were sisters under their skins"—and gowns.

It was not this, however, so much as their materialism, that shocked me. It is true, these beautifully gowned, beautiful women prattled sweet little ideals and dear little moralities; but in spite of their prattle the dominant key of the life they lived was materialistic. And they were so sentimentally selfish! They assisted in all kinds of sweet little charities, and informed one of the fact, while all the time the food they ate and the beautiful clothes they wore were bought out of dividends stained with the blood of child labor, and sweated labor, and of prostitution itself. When I mentioned such facts, expecting in my innocence that these sisters of Judy O'Grady would at once strip off their blood-dyed silks and jewels, they became excited and angry, and read me preachments about the lack of thrift, the drink, and the innate depravity that caused all the misery in society's cellar. When I mentioned that I couldn't quite see that it was the lack of thrift, the intemperance, and the depravity of a half-starved child of six that made it work twelve hours every night in a Southern cotton mill, these sisters of Judy O'Grady attacked my private life and called me an "agitator"—as though that, forsooth, settled the argument.

Nor did I fare better with the masters themselves. I had expected to find men who were clean, noble, and alive, whose ideals were clean, noble, and alive. I went about amongst the men who sat in the high places—the preachers, the politicians, the business men, the professors, and the editors. I ate meat with them, drank wine with them, automobiled with them, and studied them. It is true, I found many that were clean and noble; but with rare exceptions, they were not *alive*. I do verily believe I could count the exceptions on the fingers of my two hands. Where they were not alive with rottenness, quick with unclean life, they were merely the unburied dead—clean and noble, like well-preserved mummies, but not alive. In this connection I may especially mention the professors I met, the men who live up to that decadent university ideal, "the passionless pursuit of passionless intelligence."

I met men who invoked the name of the Prince of Peace in their diatribes against war, and who put rifles in the hands of Pinkertons with which to shoot down strikers in their own factories. I met men incoherent with indignation at the brutality of prize-fighting, and who, at the same time, were parties to the adulteration of food that killed each year more babies than even red-handed Herod had killed.

I talked in hotels and clubs and homes and Pullmans and steamer-chairs with captains of industry, and marvelled at how little travelled they were in the realm of intellect. On the other hand, I discovered that their intellect, in the business sense, was abnormally developed. Also, I discovered that their morality, where business was concerned, was nil.

This delicate, aristocratic-featured gentleman, was a dummy director and a tool of corporations that secretly robbed widows and orphans. This gentleman, who collected fine editions and was an especial patron of literature, paid blackmail to a heavy-jowled, black-browed boss of a municipal machine. This editor, who published patent medicine advertisements and did not dare print the truth in his paper about said patent medicines for fear of losing the advertising, called me a scoundrelly demagogue because I told him that his political economy was antiquated and that his biology was contemporaneous with Pliny.

This senator was the tool and the slave, the little puppet of a gross, uneducated machine boss; so was this governor and this supreme-court judge; and all three rode on railroad passes. This man, talking soberly and earnestly about the beauties of idealism and the goodness of God, had just betrayed his comrades in a business deal. This man, a pillar of the church and heavy contributor to foreign missions, worked his shop girls ten hours a day on a starvation wage and thereby directly encouraged prostitution. This man, who endowed chairs in universities, perjured himself in courts of law over a matter of dollars and cents. And this railroad magnate broke his word as a gentleman and a Christian when he granted a secret rebate to one of two captains of industry locked together in a struggle to the death.

It was the same everywhere, crime and betrayal, betrayal and crime—men who were alive, but who were neither clean nor noble, men who were clean and noble but who were not alive. Then there was a great, hopeless mass, neither noble nor alive, but merely clean. It did not sin positively nor deliberately; but it did sin passively and ignorantly by acquiescing in the current immorality and profiting by it. Had it been noble and alive it would not have been ignorant, and it would have refused to share in the profits of betrayal and crime.

I discovered that I did not like to live on the parlor floor of society. Intellectually I was bored. Morally and spiritually I was sickened. I remembered my intellectuals and idealists, my unfrocked preachers, broken professors, and clean-minded, class-conscious workingmen. I remembered my days and nights of sunshine and starshine, where life was all a wild sweet wonder, a spiritual paradise of unselfish adventure and ethical romance. And I saw before me, ever blazing and burning the Holy Grail.

So I went back to the working-class, in which I had been born and where I belonged. I care no longer to climb. The imposing edifice of society above my head holds no delights for me. It is the foundation of the edifice that interests me. There I am content to labor, crowbar in hand, shoulder to shoulder with intellectuals, idealists, and class-conscious workingmen, getting a solid pry now and again and setting the whole edifice rocking. Some day, when we get a few more hands and crowbars to work, we'll topple it over, along with all its rotten life and unburied dead, its monstrous selfishness and sodden materialism. Then we'll cleanse the cellar and build a new habitation for mankind, in which there will be no parlor floor, in which all the rooms will be bright and airy, and where the air that is breathed will be clean, noble, and alive.

Such is my outlook. I look forward to a time when man shall progress upon something worthier and higher than his stomach, when there will be a finer incentive to impel men to action than the incentive of today, which is the incentive of the stomach. I retain my belief in the nobility and excellence of the human. I believe that spiritual sweetness and unselfishness will conquer the gross gluttony of today. And last of all, my faith is in the working-class. As some Frenchman has said, "The stairway of time is ever echoing with the wooden shoe going up, the polished boot descending."

Suggestions for Discussion

1. Discuss the adequacy of London's metaphor of "the colossal edifice of society" in present-day America.

2. Describe the several ways in which London attempted to attain "all that gave decency and dignity to life."

3. Compare eighteen-year-old London's perception of "the naked simplicities of the complicated civilization" in which he lived with that of your classmates.

Suggestions for Writing

1. London has called this piece "What Life Means to Me." Describe in your own words what that is.

2. In a short paper recall an illusion you formerly had and describe the events that destroyed that illusion.

Joan Didion

On Keeping a Notebook

Joan Didion (b. 1934), California-born, began her career when she won *Vogue's* Prix de Paris Award in her senior year of college. She later became an associate editor of *Vogue* and has written columns for *The Saturday Evening Post* and *Life*. Her novels *Run River* (1963); *Play It as It Lays* (1970); *A Book of Common Prayer* (1977); *Democracy* (1984); her collection of essays *Slouching Towards Bethlehem* (1969); and *The White Album* (1975) have established her as an important American writer. She and her husband, writer John Gregory Dunne, have collaborated on several screenplays. In keeping her notebook, as recounted in *Slouching Towards Bethlehem*, the author recounts not facts but feelings, "an indiscriminate and erratic assemblage with meaning only for its maker" and sometimes not for her.

" 'That woman Estelle,' " the note reads, " 'is partly the reason why George Sharp and I are separated today.' *Dirty crepe-de-Chine wrapper, hotel bar, Wilmington RR, 9:45 a.m. August Monday morning.*"

Since the note is in my notebook, it presumably has some meaning to me. I study it for a long while. At first I have only the most general notion of what I was doing on an August Monday morning in the bar of the hotel across from the Pennsylvania Railroad station in Wilmington, Delaware (waiting for a train? missing one? 1960? 1961? why Wilmington?), but I do remember being there. The woman in the dirty crepe-de-Chine wrapper had come down from her room for a beer, and the bartender had heard before the reason why George Sharp and she were separated today. "Sure," he said, and went on mopping the floor. "You told me." At the other end of the bar is a girl. She is talking, pointedly, not to the man beside her but to a cat lying in the triangle of sunlight cast through the open door. She is wearing a plaid silk dress from Peck & Peck, and the hem is coming down.

Here is what it is: the girl has been on the Eastern Shore, and now she is going back to the city, leaving the man beside her, and all she can see ahead are the viscous summer sidewalks and the 3 A.M. long-distance calls that will make her lie awake and then sleep drugged through all the steaming mornings left in August (1960? 1961?). Because she must go directly from the train to lunch in New York, she wishes that she had a safety pin for the hem of the plaid silk dress, and she also wishes that she could forget about the hem and the lunch and stay in the cool bar that smells of disinfectant and malt and make friends with the woman in the crepe-de-Chine wrapper. She is afflicted by a little self-pity, and she wants to compare Estelle's. That is what that was all about.

Why did I write it down? In order to remember, of course, but exactly what was it I wanted to remember? How much of it actually happened? Did any of it? Why do I keep a notebook at all? It is easy to deceive oneself on all those scores. The impulse to write things down is a peculiarly compulsive one, inexplicable to those who do not share it, useful only accidentally, only secondarily, in the way that any compulsion tries to justify itself. I suppose that it begins or does not begin in the cradle. Although I have felt compelled to write things down since I was five years old, I doubt that my daughter ever will, for she is a singularly blessed and accepting child, delighted with life exactly as life presents itself to her, unafraid to go to sleep and unafraid to wake up. Keepers of private notebooks are a different breed altogether, lonely and resistant rearrangers of things, anxious malcontents, children afflicted apparently at birth with some presentiment of loss.

My first notebook was a Big Five tablet, given to me by my mother with the sensible suggestion that I stop whining and learn to amuse myself by writing down my thoughts. She returned the tablet to me a few years ago; the first entry is an account of a woman who believed herself to be freezing to death in the Arctic night, only to find, when day broke, that she had stumbled onto the Sahara Desert, where she would die of the heat before lunch. I have no idea what turn of a five-year-old's mind could have prompted so insistently "ironic" and exotic a story, but it does reveal a certain predilection for the extreme which has dogged me into adult life; perhaps if I were analytically inclined I would find it a truer story than any I might have told about Donald Johnson's birthday party or the day my cousin Brenda put Kitty Litter in the aquarium.

So the point of my keeping a notebook has never been, nor is it now, to have an accurate factual record of what I have been doing or thinking. That would be a different impulse entirely, an instinct for reality which I sometimes envy but do not possess. At no point have I ever been able successfully to keep a diary; my approach to daily life ranges from the grossly negligent to the merely absent, and on those few occasions when I have tried dutifully to record a day's events, boredom has so overcome me that the results are mysterious at best. What is this business about "shopping, typing piece, dinner with E, depressed"? Shopping for what? Typing what piece? Who is E? Was this "E" depressed, or was I depressed? Who cares?

In fact I have abandoned altogether that kind of pointless entry; instead I tell what some would call lies. "That's simply not true," the members of my family frequently tell me when they come up against my memory of a shared event. "The party was *not* for you, the spider was *not* a black widow, *it wasn't that way at all.*" Very likely they are right, for not only have I always had trouble distinguishing between what happened and what merely might have happened, but I remain unconvinced that the distinction, for my purposes, matters. The cracked crab that I recall having for lunch the day my father came home from Detroit in 1945 must certainly be embroidery, worked into the day's pattern to lend verisimilitude; I was ten years old and would not now remember the cracked crab. The day's events did not turn on cracked crab. And yet it is precisely that fictitious crab that makes me see the afternoon all over again, a home movie run all too often, the father bearing gifts, the child weeping, an exercise in family love and guilt. Or that is what it was to me. Similarly, perhaps it never did snow that August in Vermont; perhaps there never were flurries in the night wind, and maybe no one else felt the ground hardening and summer already dead even as we pretended to bask in it, but that was how it felt to me, and it might as well have snowed, could have snowed, did snow.

How it felt to me: that is getting closer to the truth about a notebook. I sometimes delude myself about why I keep a notebook, imagine that some thrifty virtue derives from preserving everything observed. See enough and write it down, I tell myself, and then some morning when the world seems drained of wonder, some day when I am only going through the motions of doing what I am supposed to do, which is write—on that bankrupt morning I will simply open my notebook and there it will all be, a forgotten account with accumulated interest, paid passage back to the world out there: dialogue overheard in hotels and elevators and at the hat-check counter in Pavillon (one middle-aged man shows his hat-check to another and says, "That's my old football number"); impressions of Bettina Aptheker and Benjamin Sonnenberg and Teddy ("Mr. Acapulco") Stauffer; careful *aperçus* about tennis bums and failed fashion models and Greek shipping heiresses, one of whom taught me a significant lesson (a lesson I could have learned from F. Scott Fitzgerald, but perhaps we all must meet the very rich for ourselves) by asking, when I arrived to interview her in her orchid-filled sitting room on the second day of a paralyzing New York blizzard, whether it was snowing outside.

I imagine, in other words, that the notebook is about other people. But of course it is not. I have no real business with what one stranger said to another at the hat-check counter in Pavillon; in fact I suspect that the line "That's my old football number" touched not my own imagination at all, but merely some memory of something once read, probably "The Eighty-Yard

Run." Nor is my concern with a woman in a dirty crepe-de-Chine wrapper in a Wilmington bar. My stake is always, of course, in the unmentioned girl in the plaid silk dress. *Remember what it was to be me:* that is always the point.

It is a difficult point to admit. We are brought up in the ethic that others, any others, all others, are by definition more interesting than ourselves; taught to be diffident, just this side of self-effacing. ("You're the least important person in the room and don't forget it," Jessica Mitford's governess would hiss in her ear on the advent of any social occasion; I copied that into my notebook because it is only recently that I have been able to enter a room without hearing some such phrase in my inner ear.) Only the very young and the very old may recount their dreams at breakfast, dwell upon self, interrupt with memories of beach picnics and favorite Liberty lawn dresses and the rainbow trout in a creek near Colorado Springs. The rest of us are expected, rightly, to affect absorption in other people's favorite dresses, other people's trout.

And so we do. But our notebooks give us away, for however dutifully we record what we see around us, the common denominator of all we see is always, transparently, shamelessly, the implacable "I." We are not talking here about the kind of notebook that is patently for public consumption, a structural conceit for binding together a series of graceful *pensées;* we are talking about something private, about bits of the mind's string too short to use, an indiscriminate and erratic assemblage with meaning only for its maker.

And sometimes even the maker has difficulty with the meaning. There does not seem to be, for example, any point in my knowing for the rest of my life that, during 1964, 720 tons of soot fell on every square mile of New York City, yet there it is in my notebook, labeled "FACT." Nor do I really need to remember that Ambrose Bierce liked to spell Leland Stanford's name "£eland $tanford" or that "smart women almost always wear black in Cuba," a fashion hint without much potential for practical application. And does not the relevance of these notes seem marginal at best?:

> In the basement museum of the Inyo County Courthouse in Independence, California, sign pinned to a mandarin coat: "This MANDARIN COAT was often worn by Mrs. Minnie S. Brooks when giving lectures on her TEAPOT COLLECTION."

> Redhead getting out of car in front of Beverly Wilshire Hotel, chinchilla stole, Vuitton bags with tags reading:
>
> MRS LOU FOX
> HOTEL SAHARA
> VEGAS

Well, perhaps not entirely marginal. As a matter of fact, Mrs. Minnie S. Brooks and her MANDARIN COAT pull me back into my own childhood, for although I never knew Mrs. Brooks and did not visit Inyo County until I was thirty, I grew up in just such a world, in houses cluttered with Indian relics and bits of gold ore and ambergris and the souvenirs my Aunt Mercy Farnsworth brought back from the Orient. It is a long way from that world to Mrs. Lou Fox's world, where we all live now, and is it not just as well to remember that? Might not Mrs. Minnie S. Brooks help me to remember what I am? Might not Mrs. Lou Fox help me to remember what I am not?

But sometimes the point is harder to discern. What exactly did I have in mind when I noted down that it cost the father of someone I know $650 a month to light the place on the Hudson in which he lived before the Crash? What use was I planning to make of this line by Jimmy Hoffa: "I may have my faults, but being wrong ain't one of them"? And although I think it interesting to know where the girls who travel with the Syndicate have their hair done when they find themselves on the West Coast, will I ever make suitable use of it? Might I not be better off just passing it on to John O'Hara? What is a recipe for sauerkraut doing in my notebook? What kind of magpie keeps this notebook? "*He was born the night the Titanic went down.*" That seems a nice enough line, and I even recall who said it, but is it not really a better line in life than it could ever be in fiction?

But of course that is exactly it: not that I should ever use the line, but that I should remember the woman who said it and the afternoon I heard it. We were on her terrace by the sea, and we were finishing the wine left from lunch, trying to get what sun there was, a California winter sun. The woman whose husband was born the night the *Titanic* went down wanted to rent her house, wanted to go back to her children in Paris. I remember wishing that I could afford the house, which cost $1,000 a month. "Someday you will," she said lazily. "Someday it all comes." There in the sun on her terrace it seemed easy to believe in someday, but later I had a low-grade afternoon hangover and ran over a black snake on the way to the supermarket and was flooded with inexplicable fear when I heard the checkout clerk explaining to the man ahead of me why she was finally divorcing her husband. "He left me no choice," she said over and over as she punched the register. "He has a little seven-month-old baby by her, he left me no choice." I would like to believe that my dread then was for the human condition, but of course it was for me, because I wanted a baby and did not then have one and because I wanted to own the house that cost $1,000 a month to rent and because I had a hangover.

It all comes back. Perhaps it is difficult to see the value in having one's self back in that kind of mood, but I do see it; I think we are well advised to keep on nodding terms with the people we used to be, whether we find them attractive company or not. Otherwise they turn up unannounced and surprise us, come hammering on the mind's door at 4 A.M. of a bad night and demand to know who deserted them, who betrayed them, who is going to make amends. We forget all too soon the things we thought we could never forget. We forget the loves and the betrayals alike, forget what we whispered and what we screamed, forget who we were. I have already lost touch with a couple of people I used to be; one of them, a seventeen-year-old, presents little threat, although it would be of some interest to me to know again what it feels like to sit on a river levee drinking vodka-and-orange-juice and listening to Les Paul and Mary Ford and their echoes sing "How High the Moon" on the car radio. (You see I still have the scenes, but I no longer perceive myself among those present, no longer could even improvise the dialogue.) The other one, a twenty-three-year-old, bothers me more. She was always a good deal of trouble, and I suspect she will reappear when I least want to see her, skirts too long, shy to the point of aggravation, always the injured party, full of recriminations and little hurts and stories I do not want to hear again, at once saddening me and angering me with her vulnerability and ignorance, an apparition all the more insistent for being so long banished.

It is a good idea, then, to keep in touch, and I suppose that keeping in touch is what notebooks are all about. And we are all on our own when it comes to keeping those lines open to ourselves: your notebook will never help me, nor mine you. *"So what's new in the whiskey business?"* What could that possibly mean to you? To me it means a blonde in a Pucci bathing suit sitting with a couple of fat men by the pool at the Beverly Hills Hotel. Another man approaches, and they all regard one another in silence for a while. "So what's new in the whiskey business?" one of the fat men finally says by way of welcome, and the blonde stands up, arches one foot and dips it in the pool, looking all the while at the cabaña where Baby Pignatari is talking on the telephone. That is all there is to that, except that several years later I saw the blonde coming out of Saks Fifth Avenue in New York with her California complexion and a voluminous mink coat. In the harsh wind that day she looked old and irrevocably tired to me, and even the skins in the mink coat were not worked the way they were doing them that year, not the way she would have wanted them done, and there is the point of the story. For a while after that I did not like to look in the mirror, and my eyes would skim the newspapers and pick out only the deaths, the cancer victims, the premature coronaries, the suicides, and I stopped riding the Lexington Avenue IRT because I noticed for the first time that all the strangers I had seen for years—the man with the seeing-eye dog, the spinster who read the classified pages every day, the fat girl who always got off with me at Grand Central—looked older than they once had.

It all comes back. Even that recipe for sauerkraut: even that brings it back. I was on Fire Island when I first made that sauerkraut, and it was raining, and we drank a lot of bourbon and ate the sauerkraut and went to bed at ten, and I listened to the rain and the Atlantic and felt safe. I made the sauerkraut again last night and it did not make me feel any safer, but that is, as they say, another story.

Suggestions for Discussion

1. What rhetorical devices does the author use to bring her subject into focus? For example, she compares and contrasts two women in the bar and her daughter and herself.

2. What kinds of details are employed to explain the varied purposes of keeping a notebook?

3. How does the author explain the paradox "I imagine . . . that the notebook is about other people. But of course it is not."

4. Account for the adverbs and adjectives used in the statement "the common denominator of all we see is always, transparently, shamelessly, the implacable 'I.' "

5. How do the citations in the notebook contribute to the central thesis? To the tone? To the author's sense of self? To her writing?

6. Explain: "I have already lost touch with a couple of people I used to be. . . ."

7. T. S. Eliot uses the term *objective correlative* to describe the artist's faculty of achieving emotional impact "by finding a set of objects, a situation, a chain of events, which shall be the formula of that particular emotion such that when the external facts are given, the emotion is immediately evoked." How do the items in the notebook illustrate this theory?

Suggestions for Writing

1. Keep a journal in which you record the events or thoughts of each day. What does it tell you about other people? about yourself?

2. Write an essay on Question 4 or 6 above.

3. Write an essay in which you interweave excerpts from your journal with commentary on them.

Vladimir Nabokov

The Beginning of Consciousness

Vladimir Nabokov (1899–1977) was born in Russia and educated at Trinity College, Cambridge. He was a professor at Cornell University and a regular contributor to popular magazines. Among his works written in English are *The Real Life of Sebastian Knight* (1941); *Pnin* (1957); *Lolita* (1958); *Pale Fire* (1962); two collections of short stories, *Nabokov's Dozen* (1958) and *Nabokov's Quartet* (1966); *King, Queen, Knave* (1968); *Ada* (1969); and an autobiography, *Speak, Memory* (1951). Nabokov describes the awakening of his consciousness as a series of "spaced flashes with intervals between them gradually diminishing until bright blocks of perception are formed, affording memory a slippery hold." His sense of self and his awareness that his parents were his parents came after he had learned numbers and speech.

The cradle rocks above an abyss, and common sense tells us that our existence is but a brief crack of light between two eternities of darkness. Although the two are identical twins, man, as a rule, views the prenatal abyss with more calm than the one he is heading for (at some forty-five hundred heartbeats an hour). I know, however, of a young chronophobiac who experienced something like panic when looking for the first time at homemade movies that had been taken a few weeks before his birth. He saw a world that was practically unchanged—the same house, the same people—and then realized that he did not exist there at all and that nobody mourned his absence. He caught a glimpse of his mother waving from an upstairs window, and that unfamiliar gesture disturbed him, as if it were some mysterious farewell. But what particularly frightened him was the sight of a brand new baby carriage standing there on the porch, with the smug, encroaching air of a coffin; even that was empty, as if, in the reverse course of events, his very bones had disintegrated.

Such fancies are not foreign to young lives. Or, to put it otherwise, first and last things often tend to have an adolescent note—unless, possibly, they are directed by some venerable and rigid religion. Nature expects a full-grown man to accept the two black voids, fore and aft, as stolidly as he accepts the extraordinary visions in between. Imagination, the supreme delight of the immortal and the immature, should be limited. In order to enjoy life, we should not enjoy it too much.

I rebel against this state of affairs. I feel the urge to take my rebellion outside and picket nature. Over and over again, my mind has made colossal efforts to distinguish the faintest of personal glimmers in the impersonal darkness on both sides of my life. That this darkness is caused merely by the walls of time separating me and by bruised fists from the free world of timelessness is a belief I gladly share with the most gaudily painted savage. I have journeyed back in thought—with thought hopelessly tapering off as I went—to remote regions where I groped for some secret outlet only to discover that the prison of time is spherical and without exits. Short of suicide, I have tried everything. I have doffed my identity in order to pass for a conventional spook and steal into realms that existed before I was conceived. I have mentally endured the degrading company of Victorian lady novelists and retired colonels who remembered having, in former lives, been slave messengers on a Roman road or sages under the willows of Lhasa. I have ransacked my oldest dreams for keys and clues—and let me say at once that I reject completely the vulgar, shabby, fundamentally medieval world of Freud, with its crankish quest for sexual symbols (something like searching for Baconian acrostics in Shakespeare's works) and its bitter little embryos spying, from their natural nooks, upon the love life of their parents.

Initially, I was unaware that time, so boundless at first blush, was a prison. In probing my childhood (which is the next best to probing one's eternity) I see the awakening of consciousness as a series of spaced flashes, with the intervals between them gradually diminishing until bright blocks of perception are formed, affording memory a slippery hold. I had learned numbers and speech more or less simultaneously at a very early date, but the inner knowledge that I was I and that my parents were my parents seems to have been established only later, when it was directly associated with my discovering their age in relation to mine. Judging by the strong sunlight that, when I think of that revelation, immediately invades my memory with lobed sun flecks through overlapping patterns of greenery, the occasion may have been my mother's birthday, in late summer, in the country, and I had asked questions and had assessed the answers I received. All this is as it should be according to the theory of recapitulation; the beginning of reflexive consciousness in the brain of our remotest ancestor must surely have coincided with the dawning of the sense of time.

Thus, when the newly disclosed, fresh and trim formula of my own age, four, was confronted with the parental formulas, thirty-three and twenty-seven, something happened to me. I was given a tremendously invigorating shock. As if subjected to a second baptism, on more divine lines than the Greek Catholic ducking undergone fifty months earlier by a howling, half-drowned half-Victor (my mother, through the half-closed door, behind which an old custom bade parents retreat, managed to correct the bungling archpresbyter, Father Konstantin Vetvenitski), I felt myself plunged abruptly into a radiant and mobile medium that was none other than the pure element of time. One shared it—just as excited bathers share shining seawater—with creatures that were not oneself but that were joined to one by time's common flow, an environment quite different from the spatial world, which not only man but apes and butterflies can perceive. At that instant, I became acutely aware that the twenty-seven-year-old being, in soft white and pink, holding my left hand, was my mother, and that the thirty-three-year-old being, in hard white and gold, holding my right hand, was my father. Between them, as they evenly progressed, I strutted, and trotted, and strutted again, from sun fleck to sun fleck, along the middle of a path, which I easily identify today with an alley of ornamental oaklings in the park of our country estate, Vyra, in the former Province of St. Petersburg, Russia. Indeed, from my present ridge or remote, isolated, almost uninhabited time, I see my diminutive self as celebrating, on that August day 1903, the birth of sentient life. If my left-hand-holder and my right-hand-holder had both been present before in my vague infant world, they had been so under the mask of a tender incognito; but now my father's attire, the resplendent uniform of the Horse Guards, with that smooth golden swell of cuirass burning upon his chest and back, came out like the sun, and for several years afterward I remained keenly interested in the age of my parents and kept myself informed about it, like a nervous passenger asking the time in order to check a new watch.

My father, let it be noted, had served his term of military training long before I was born, so I suppose he had that day put on the trappings of his old regiment as a festive joke. To a joke, then, I owe my first gleam of complete consciousness—which again has recapitulatory implications, since the first creatures on earth to become aware of time were also the first creatures to smile.

Suggestions for Discussion

1. How does the author convey the tone of the panic that can be aroused by contemplating the "prenatal abyss"?

2. By specific reference to the text, explain the author's statement that "first and last things often tend to have an adolescent note."

3. Identify all the phrases in this selection that grow out of the image of existence as a "brief crack of light between two eternities of darkness." How literal is this image intended to be? What overtones of experience and myth are there in the image?

4. At the end of the fourth paragraph Nabokov writes, "the beginning of reflexive consciousness in the brain of our remotest ancestor must surely have coincided with the dawning of the sense of time." By what logical process does he arrive at this conclusion? Is the process defensible? Is the conclusion trustworthy?

Suggestions for Writing

1. Recall an incident in your childhood that marked a dramatic change in your concept of yourself or your parents, or your concept of the passage of time.

2. Discuss this paradox in relation to its context: "In order to enjoy life, we should not enjoy it too much."

Peter Werner

Both Sides Now

Peter Werner (pseudonym) as a Yale freshman was one of a small number permitted to enroll in a writing course in the 1970s. He grew up in a large, devout Roman Catholic family in East Meadow, Long Island. After receiving his degree at Yale he studied playwriting in graduate school, and after working in a bank he took a job teaching English in the New York public schools. Werner portrays some of the conflicts and ironies in his experience with "both sides" of the economic structure.

When I was in high school, I don't know how many afternoons I spent upstairs in my bedroom, listening to the neighborhood kids playing roller hockey in the street while I struggled to play the guitar. I was trying to teach myself, and from a huge book of music titled something like *Greatest Hits of the Sixties with Simplified Chords*, I had chosen Joni Mitchell's "Both Sides Now."

The chords were simple, and the song seemed to demand a voice that wasn't too good. As with so many of the folk songs of that era, the lyrics seemed so much more earnest when sung poorly, as if the words demanded to be heard no matter what the quality of the singer's voice. I finally managed to learn the song, and a few more after that, before deciding that as bad as my voice was, it would never sound as earnest as Bob Dylan's, so there was not much point in going on.

And yet to this day I still remember the chords and lyrics to "Both Sides Now," for over the years the song took on an ironic significance as circumstances in my own life changed. What I should have learned from the song was how multifaceted and deeply layered these two sides can be.

When I was living at home, I thought I already had seen both sides. I grew up rather comfortably on suburban Long Island in a family that gradually grew to include eight children. My father supported us all with his job as a space engineer under government contract to NASA.

Then the United States landed a man on the moon, and my father was laid off along with thousands of other space engineers on Long Island. Suddenly we had no money and I saw the "other side." According to government statistics, we were living in poverty, but things weren't much different than before. They were just a bit more strained. For me, the two sides then were simply "richer" and "poorer."

Since coming to Yale I have had a chance to see more of these two sides. Here I learned that in many cases "richer" and "poorer" also define the distinction between "superior" and "inferior." Money, education, and family background all play their part in determining human value. Some people are meant to serve others; others to be served.

As a bursary student, I find myself in a strange position. One minute I'll be on one side, sipping sherry at a reception, while men and women in starched white uniforms offer me hors d'oeuvres from silver platters. The next minute I'll be on the other side, washing dishes in a hot kitchen of one of Yale's dining halls, or wearing a red jacket and serving my fellow class-mates a French dinner. I meet students whose fathers are millionaires, then talk to dining hall workers who try to support a family on seven thousand dollars a year. When I joined the Duke's Men, an informal singing group at Yale, our spring concert tour took us through a series of posh resorts and hotels, a world of servants and masters, another world with two sides.

Here are some glimpses of the two sides:

A Phone Call Home

Tom is one of my three roommates, a blond surfer from a Los Angeles sub-urb. Although our relationship was rather cool early in the year, as the months have progressed we've become close friends. When we're drunk, we call each other by the names of characters taken from a Lawrence novel on our freshman reading list.

I can tell that Tom's family is well off, not by any of Tom's possessions but by his general demeanor and the fact that he's well traveled. I know that Tom thinks my family is comfortable enough, if not abundantly wealthy, and God knows I haven't done anything to make him think otherwise. We're among the last to be able to take advantage of an already slipping fashion dictate that demands that rich and poor alike wear nothing but jeans and cotton T-shirts, and so it's been difficult for me to guess just how much money Tom is used to, and impossible for Tom to realize how poor my own family has become.

We weren't always poor, but we were never wealthy. When my father still had his job as a space engineer, our family often lived in a barn-red colonial home in a suburban neighborhood and had a beige Chrysler Town and Country station wagon parked in the driveway. After my father lost his job, he couldn't find other work as an engineer. He tried his hand at real estate and lost money. There were no savings to draw from, and the family had a desperate struggle hang-ing on to the house and the car. When relatives had no more money to lend us, government assistance became a necessity, and my mother started train-ing as a nurse in order to bring money into the household.

Tonight I find myself chiding Tom for his upper-class prejudices and social naïveté. This always confuses Tom, because he has no way of knowing where I'm coming from and no reason to suspect the personal vindictiveness that creeps into these "consciousness raising" sessions. Tom is trying to convince me that the reason he didn't have any friends among the Chicanos who attended his high school is not because they were poor but because they lived so far away. In fact he does, he insists, have white friends who are really quite poor.

"Listen to this," he says. "I have this friend. There are four kids in his family, and his father makes twenty thousand dollars a year."

I can't quite figure out the moral to this story, although I'm afraid of what's coming. In the best days, my father supported ten people on twenty-three thousand a year.

"Well . . .?" I say, waiting for a conclusion.

Tom says nothing.

"Is that poor? Is twenty thousand dollars a year poor?" I ask, and my voice is angry and condescending.

Tom is annoyed that his humanitarianism in unappreciated. His head cocks back and his eyes go cold.

"Well . . . . my old man makes a hundred grand a year."

Those words, that number, affect me as if I had just been drenched with a bucket of ice water. I want to shout back, "Well, my 'old man' is unemployed and we get six thousand dollars a year from welfare. So how do you like that?" Instead I say nothing.

Tom tries to press his point. He thinks I don't understand.

"Well, how much does your father make?"

"Fuck you," I reply.

Tom shakes his head in disgust and goes into his room to study. He's learned that there's no point in talking to me when I get into one of my moods. And like I've said, he's seen no sign of my family's financial state. When my parents visited on parents' day, the Chrysler was in good condition. My father still had his fine cashmere coat, and my mother's "simple black dress" did not betray its age. So he can't understand my anger.

I think about that number and I realize that there are some who would consider it pocket money, but still it's more than four times what my father ever made, and I resent it. I resent the way Tom takes the money for granted and I resent the way he takes it for granted that my own family is well off. I wish I had the courage to tell him the truth.

How much easier it would be if I were black or Puerto Rican. Then I would be expected to be poor. They could look at me and marvel at how I was advancing. "Look! He goes to Yale!" But to be white and poor. The white rich really don't want to know about it. It upsets them; they think it's disgusting. You're upsetting the order of things. Blacks are poor. Puerto Ricans are poor. They can't help it. They're not smart enough to handle money. But whites aren't handicapped. If they're not rich, it's their own fault. They're not living up to their race. They're a disgrace.

The noise from the stereo is beginning to annoy me. That weirdo David Bowie. It is Tom's record, not mine (which makes it all the more annoying). But the stereo is mine. None of us brought a stereo in September, so the kid who's on welfare had to go home to bring one back. The same thing with the typewriter. The kid whose dad earns a hundred grand a year shows up at Yale without a typewriter. I spend half my summer earnings to buy a decent machine, half that summer slaving in a department store. And Tom just uses it whenever he wants.

Typical, I think. That's why his people are rich and my people aren't.

Bowie keeps whining. It is the same record that was playing when my brother Michael visited in December. Hearing the record, the first thing he said when he came in the door was, "What's going on here? Have you gone gay?"

Michael sat down without taking off his coat, and we tried to catch up with each other on the past few months. After about ten minutes he stood up to remove his coat.

"Boy, it's hot in here."

"Well, you should have taken your coat off."

"I just got sort of used to wearing it around the house. We haven't had any heat this past week."

"What?" I shouted, and broke into laughter. I pictured my family seated around the big oak table in the dining room, eating dinner in their winter coats, my sister Ann trying to avoid dipping her fur cuffs into her food.

"Dad wasn't able to pay the oil bill, so they stopped delivering." Michael was laughing too. He fell back onto the couch and the two of us sat there laughing until tears came to our eyes.

Remembering the laughter, I realize that it would take a great effort to make myself upset about the incident. My family isn't miserable in their predicament; they are able to laugh about it. They're as happy as ever. Then my anger returns when I realize that Tom is happy too.

It's easy not to mind being poor if you think the wealthy are miserable. It's easy to go to see a play or a movie or read a book where the rich are at each other's throats and they're lonely and unhappy and their lives are empty and half of them end up committing suicide. The rich are different and they get their just desserts in the end.

But Tom is really not so different from me. That is one of the reasons we're so close. I can easily see myself in Tom's position through a simple quirk of fate called parentage. I might not have been happier but things would have been much more . . . convenient. Tom is no different, and yet he has so much more. Not only has he money, but he has the ability to enjoy it.

But now it's easy to let the heating incident upset me, and tears of anger burn in my eyes. I remember going home two weeks later for Christmas vacation to discover that, for financial reasons, my family had learned to make do without lunch. My stomach, conditioned to Yale's twenty-one meal plan, was not pleased with this. In the afternoon I would rummage around the kitchen, looking for a quick snack to tide me over until dinner. But there was nothing that could be called "quick." There were no convenience foods that could be taken from a package. They were too expensive. Everything had to be washed or peeled and cooked, and a simple snack would entail a major production. There wasn't even a loaf of bread. My father made fresh rolls before each meal. It was cheaper.

On New Year's Eve, I was particularly hungry. My stomach nagged me all day and I looked forward to supper. But when supper came there was nothing but soup. Soup and the fresh hot rolls I had grown sick of—three to a person. I wanted to cry, but I held back the tears.

I don't now. I pick up my books and go into my room so that no one will see me. I'd like to hate Tom. I'd like so much to hate him but I cannot, and that makes me feel guilty. I am consorting with the enemy.

I try to hate, but the closest I can come to hate is jealousy. I want to have money also. Realizing this, the guilt presses against my lungs like stones. I want to travel. I want to have a swimming pool. I might enjoy a boat. Someday I might be able to have these things, but how could I enjoy them while others were miserable? How do the wealthy do it?

I try to escape to my books. I pick up my Religious Studies assignment. *The Documents of Vatican II.* The words become blurred as I read, the tears swelling in my eyes.

In His goodness and wisdom, God chose to reveal Himself and to make known to us the hidden purpose of His will by which through Christ, the Word made Flesh, man has access to the Father in the Holy Spirit and comes to share in His divine nature. Through His revelation, therefore, the invisible God, out of the abundance of His love, speaks to men as friends and lives among them so that He may invite them and take them into fellowship with Himself.

The book lands in a pile of dust underneath the bed, for in my present state it seems more than likely that Christ was sent forth by Herod. Something had to be done to keep the starving masses from revolting.

My thoughts return to my family at home. My father has taken to going to our church each weekday morning and praying for guidance.

"Just trust in God," he always said. "Don't worry about tomorrow. Everything will work out according to God's will."

I had stopped worrying about tomorrow, but I'd never really trusted in God. And yet things had worked out. For me. But the rest of the family were still at home.

My mother had joined the charismatic movement of our church. She was going to be rebaptized in the Holy Spirit. Born again. But still she was able to say to my father, "Why don't you spend less time in church and more time looking for a job?"

My father laughed and called her a Holy Roller.

My sadness increases, and I want to talk to my parents. I want to call home and hear the voices of my family. They always sound happy. Mary will talk about her school play, *Oklahoma!* And in the background I might hear Paul practicing his French horn. That will cheer me up.

I wait until I've calmed down enough so that my voice will sound normal over the phone. I check my face in the mirror so that my roommates won't see I've been crying.

I go to the phone in the living room and dial my number. It takes a while for the connection to go through. The phone starts ringing, and then there is a click followed by a white fuzzy sound.

A nasal tape-recorded voice speaks.

"The number you have reached, five-five-five, four-eight-nine-five, has been disconnected. Please check the number you are calling to make sure that you have dialed correctly."

I let the receiver fall and the voice starts to repeat itself from the floor. I have dialed correctly. My parents haven't paid the phone bill again. Tears come, and then sobs, and there is nothing I can do to stop them.

In the next room, I can see Tom at his desk, concentrating on his chemistry.

Kevin

Kevin is a full-time dishwasher at Timothy Dwight College. I work with him five days a week. He is twenty-five years old and mentally retarded.

"Peter, are you going home for Thanksgiving?"

"Yes."

"Where do you live?"

"Long Island."

"Are you taking a plane?"

"Kevin, I live on Long Island."

"I know. Are you taking a plane?"

I tell him where Long Island is. I tell him that it's two hours away by car. The next day, Kevin starts again.

"Peter, are you going home for Thanksgiving?"

"Yes."

"Are you taking a plane . . .?"

This goes on every day for two weeks until Thanksgiving arrives.

His affliction is not severe. His speech is normal and he is physically healthy and coordinated, though he is barely five feet tall. He wears the same brown corduroy jeans and tan shoes to work every day, topped by a blue work shirt and a black rubber apron. I remember the pants and shoes when they were new.

"Peter, look what I got for my birthday."

Kevin has a thing about his birthday. He keeps track of it as if it might become lost if he didn't.

"In eight months and ten days I'll be twenty-six years old. Last year the students surprised me on my birthday. They came in and decorated the whole dish machine. The whole place. They didn't do it this year though. Maybe they'll do it again next year. I don't know. Maybe they will. . . .

"In four years I'll be thirty . . . In five years I'll be thirty-one . . . In six years I'll be . . . I'll be . . . How old will I be?"

He's obsessed with rules and instructions. They must not be transgressed. Everything must follow a certain order. There is no room for change.

"Peter, take some trays over there. They need trays. . . . No, not those trays, those are for the coffee cups. Did you hear me? Hey! Where are you going? Bring those back! Those are for the coffee cups!"

Kevin might have the mind of a child, but physically he is a man, and his mind doesn't quite know how to handle this:

"I know about sex. I read those magazines. *Playboy. Playgirl.* I go to the movies. The filthiest movie I every saw, *Superfly.* Oh, boy, you should have seen it. . . .

"If I had a girl in bed you know what I'd do? You know what I'd do? I'd suck her titties. That's what I'd do. . . .

"I got my back pay today. Almost a hundred dollars. Maybe I won't give it to my mother. Maybe I'll get a girlfriend with it. Put on my fancy clothes and get a girlfriend. Go dancing. Maybe she'll let me play sex with her. . . .

"Is that your girlfriend, Peter? Ahhhh. I know you. I bet you're a big lady's man. I bet you've even kissed her. You'll see. I'm gonna kiss a girl some day. . . .

"I'm twenty-five years old and I've never even kissed a girl. Really. Never. I ain't lyin'. Never."

He's proud of his job. He's proud of his salary. Thursday comes and it's payday.

"Whad'ja get, Peter? Lemmee see. I made a hundred and sixty-four dollars this week. Sunday I worked overtime. I'm a good worker. Juan's a good worker too. I make more than he does."

His parents are separated.

"My father's down in Milford. He's married again. I make more than he does."

Thinking about him, I realize now that I've never once seen Kevin do anything to hurt anyone. He's never been selfish, never cruel. His virtues are rather amazing considering the home life that he tells me about.

"My mother takes all my money. She gives me ten dollars a week. I can't do nothin'. If I don't give it to her she'll throw me out of the house. . . .

"My brother's in trouble with the police. He's been stealin' cars and pushin' dope. He got in an accident and the doctor found out they were carryin' drugs in their underwear. The car was stolen. He's sixteen years old. He has to go to a special school now. . . .

"I saw my mother playing sex with one of her boyfriends. I did. I went in her room to get something and there they were, playin' sex. Boy, she was mad. She said, 'Get the hell out of this room!' That was last year."

Due to the recent decision to lay off forty-three dining hall employees, Kevin faces the prospect of losing his job.

"Why does Yale want to do this to me? They have work. I'm a good worker. I never take a break. I'm workin' all day. Who's gonna load the machine if I'm gone? You? You, Peter? You don't know how. You're not fast. You'll be here all night. . . .

"I don't even know how to collect unemployment. I never did it before. I don't want to. They don't mail it to you. You have to go and pick it up. . . .

"They need me here. Who's gonna do all these things? . . . What's gonna happen when I'm gone?"

The Bank Collector

During our spring break, the Duke's Men made a concert tour to Washington and some of the southern states. We spent one night late in our tour at the summer estate of one of the Dukes' girlfriends in Baltimore. Her father is a lung surgeon in Washington.

The estate was on a river leading into Chesapeake Bay. Bolstered by four white pillars, the house stood on a hill about two hundred yards from the private docks, where two sailboats and a motor boat were moored. Inside the house, the floors were covered with Persian rugs and the rooms were filled with antiques.

On one side of the house was a closed-in porch that had a lovely view of the river. It was pleasantly furnished with a green rug and white wicker furniture set against green walls. The large plants that hung from the ceiling thrived in the sun that poured in through the glass windows and doors.

Against one wall was a long shelf holding a collection of antique small mechanical banks. Little metal clowns, acrobats, hunters, and Uncle Sams stood poised, ready to spring into action upon being fed a coin. The amusing figures, painted in bright but now aging colors, created a carnival atmosphere that contrasted with the formality of the rest of the house.

What is it that is so alluring about a carnival? Is it that seductively evil force that always seems to be running through a noisy, crowded, rundown fairground on a hot summer night? Is it the false and deceptive smile of the Kewpie doll?

I looked down at the shelf of antique banks and that same force seemed to be present. The metal figures all wore unchanging smiles that seemed to say they had a secret. They were doing something wrong and getting away with it.

"I see you've found my banks," a voice behind me spoke. I turned to face the doctor.

"Yes. They're very interesting."

"It's not a big collection," he said, sitting down, "but several of them are fine specimens. Quite rare."

I sat down in a chair across from him.

"It's a great hobby," he continued, "but it's expensive. That's why I've only got twenty-three."

I sympathized with him. I bet myself that some of his banks could have cost more than two hundred dollars.

"It used to be you could buy a whole collection for the same amount that just one bank costs today," he said nostalgically. "But now it seems like everybody's got their own collection. The banks are just about all bought up now. You won't find one just sitting around in an antique shop anymore.

"Every now and then someone will put an ad in the classified section of a magazine that he has one for sale, and he'll get offers from all over the country. I had a friend who answered one of them. He recognized that the bank in question was a very rare one, but the guy selling it didn't know it. It turned out there were only two of them left in the whole country. Well, he bought it from this guy for only two thousand dollars.

"The next thing he did was take it to a well-known collector, who was going to give him ten thousand dollars for it. But this guy got a better offer from the Shorelys—you know, the banking Shorelys. Oh, well. Anyway, he sold it to them for twenty-two thousand dollars.

"The collector thought he had it all wrapped up for ten thousand, and it was swept from right under his feet," the doctor chuckled. "Twenty-two thousand dollars. That's a twenty-thousand-dollar profit in just a few days. Not bad."

I was too dumbfounded to say anything. The doctor continued his monologue.

"Here, let me show you one of mine." He went over to the shelf, took down one of the banks, and set it on the table in front of us. The base of the bank was a blue circus pedestal, one of those round structures that trainers train elephants to stand on. In the top of the base was a slot for coins. At the back of the base stood a vertical bar that became a curved fork above the pedestal. A cast-iron acrobat balanced between the sides of the fork on a metal bar which he held on to.

The figure was dressed in a white clown's suit that had been painted on and had now turned creamy with age. He had red buttons and trim, a pair of red pointed slippers, and a red stocking cap. His black face was frozen in a leering grin.

"This one's a prize," the doctor said, giving it a pat. "Look at him. Not a scratch on him. That's all the original paint and there's not a scratch on him. He cost me seven thousand dollars just a few years back. I don't know how much he's worth now. At least twelve. Watch this," he said, reaching into his pocket. He pulled out a nickel and fitted it into the clown's cap. The metal figure bent slowly forward until his head was quite close to the base. The coin fell into the slot in the blue drum, and the figure swung back up again, grinning proudly.

The doctor's face fell. "He's supposed to do a flip, but he needs adjusting. Maybe with something heavier . . ."

He reached into his pocket for a quarter. This time he gave the clown a little push as he fitted the coin into the cap. The clown performed a full flip and he resurfaced with that same evil grin.

"There!" the doctor said proudly. "With something heavier, like a half-dollar, he'll do two flips."

The little metal acrobat swung back and forth on his stand, basking in glory with his huge, gloating grin. I began to understand what evil secret that hunk of metal possessed. He held the power to keep a person fed and alive for several years. That was the power that ran through those atoms of iron. That was the force that gave the metal man life.

The doctor was still speaking.

"You know, if you get your hands on some money these days and you want to invest it, you've got a problem. Look at the stock market. This country's economy is a mess." He smiled at his shelves of banks. "That's what's so great about these things. They're good investments. They're safe. People are taking an interest in these things again. Anything from the early days of America. That's where you should put your money these days, in anything American."

Anything American.

Breakfast at Timothy's

In my job as a dishwasher at Timothy Dwight College I usually worked dinners, but one of the workers had asked me to fill in for him at breakfast one day when he would be away. I needed the money so I agreed, expecting to wash dishes. When I reported to work, though, it turned out that I was expected to work on the serving line.

At all of Yale's dining halls, a hot breakfast is served until nine o'clock. After nine, only continental breakfast is available; students serve themselves cold cereal, toast, or Danish. When nine o'clock rolled around, I still had some scrambled eggs, one piece of French toast, and one piece of regular toast. I decided to finish serving them, rather than bring them back to the kitchen, where they would just be thrown out.

At about ten after nine, a resident fellow of Timothy Dwight showed up for breakfast. He was a tall man, about forty-five years old, with stumpy gray hair and a pair of wire-rimmed glasses. He mumbled something and pointed in the direction of the French toast. I put the toast on a plate and served it to him.

"Okay," he growled, "would you like to give me some eggs? I asked for eggs."

I took another plate and gave him some eggs. He was angry.

"Now would you like to give me some toast to eat with the eggs?" I reached for the last piece of toast and put it on his plate.

"Now," he exploded, "would you like to give me two pieces of toast instead of one piece of toast?"

"That was the last piece," I told him as I put two more pieces of bread in the toaster. Then I remembered that it was after nine o'clock and that I didn't have to be making more toast.

"If you want breakfast," I said, "you should get down here before nine o'clock."

He looked at me, his eyes filled with contempt. He spoke through clenched teeth and the words fell from his lips like bird droppings.

"Tomorrow," he snarled, "you can come and serve me breakfast in my room before nine o'clock."

"Don't count on it," I said. I reached behind me to the toaster and pushed up the slices of bread, half toasted. If he wanted toast, he could make it himself. He stalked out of the kitchen.

When he left, I realized I was shaking. My eyes were burning and it was hard for me to swallow. If I had been alone in my room, I probably would have cried. It hurt to be treated as if I were inferior. I felt a hate for that man stronger than any hate I had ever felt before, and the strength of that hate scared me. I would have liked to see him dead.

In Our Nation's Capital

I sat at a table in the Crystal Room of the Sheraton Carlton Hotel in Washington, D.C. The Duke's Men had been hired to sing at a Saint Patrick's Day luncheon in honor of the Irish ambassador to the United States and of the hotel's manager, who was retiring.

People had gathered an hour earlier to sip cocktails in the Mount Vernon Room, and the Duke's Men hadn't passed up the opportunity either. We were among the first ones there, and we watched the room fill around us with Washington VIPs. The only one that most of us could recognize was J. W. Fulbright. Danny, one of the Duke's Men, whose father is a Washington lawyer, was able to point out important congressmen, aides, consultants, etc. They didn't look like much to me.

More interesting than these stale Washington politicians were the wives they brought with them. Their identities were concealed behind layers of face powder, and most of them were dressed all in green for the occasion. Each of them was responsible for maintaining and advancing the social status of her family, and they were all trying to engage in friendly conversation with women a step ahead of them on the social ladder, in hope that room might be made for them on that step. Their behavior reminded me of the tigers in "Little Black Sambo" who chased each other's tails around a tree in a continuous circle until they turned to butter. Lunch was called, and the women were saved from a similar fate.

I vowed not to sit with any Duke's Men, to force myself to eat and talk with some of these people. I saw it as an educational experience. I sat alone at a table and chased away any of the Duke's Men that tried to join me. Two unassuming men in clerical collars sat down and introduced themselves as monsignors with Irish-sounding names, and that was as far as our conversation went. I began to despair and was unconsoled by the chlorine smell of the hot tuna crepes on my plate. Then a woman who introduced herself as "Grosvenor" sat down and announced that the rest of the seats at the table were reserved for an important congressman, his wife, and an admiral. She greeted the two monsignors, whom she didn't seem very interested in, and started a conversation with me.

She asked me what I was studying, and I told her I was interested in writing. Her eyes lit up, and she told me that she, too, was a writer. She had been an editor for *Business Week*, and a Washington columnist. She was retired, and was now writing a book of amusing anecdotes about "all the famous people" in Washington. I listened intently as she rattled off a story about Prince Charles's visit to Washington.

". . . Well, he was standing on the reception line, and everybody had been carefully screened, you know, and there was a man there and nobody knew who he was or how he got in. . . ."

She was quite tickled by the tale she was telling, and her breath came in short little pants, like that of an overexcited toy poodle.

"Well, finally he reached up to the prince, and he shook his hand and the prince asked, 'And what is your connection?' And do you know what he said?" she gasped. "Do you know what he said? . . . 'Western Union'!"

She repeated "Western Union!" and I realized that I was supposed to laugh. So I laughed politely, trying to figure out the punchline.

The congressman, his wife, and the admiral arrived, and a waiter appeared and filled our wineglasses. Danny later informed me that the congressman was one of the five most powerful men in Washington, along with Ford and Kissinger. His wife was a huge woman with a beaked nose, an elaborate hairdo, and a double chin that danced when she turned her head. She was dressed in pink. The congressman was also fat, and both he and the admiral were bald, roundheaded men whose faces were distorted by thick lenses set in jet-black frames. All of them appeared to be well into their seventies.

Mrs. Grosvenor introduced us, and I remembered to stand up as I shook their hands.

"This young man," Mrs. Grosvenor informed them, "has been most delightful to talk to. He's interested in becoming a writer."

"Awhh," the admiral guffawed, "you'd better tell him to find another field. There's no money in writing. He won't make a cent." He turned to me and looked at me as a father would. "Really, you'd better study something else. Why, you'd be better off in the army!"

"Listen to him," the congressman's wife advised me. "He knows what he's talking about. Why, since the admiral retired, he's simply been raking it in!" The table burst into laughter, and even the two monsignors, who had been totally uninvolved in the conversation, smiled sheepishly.

"He's been . . . He's been . . ." the woman tried to speak through her uncontrollable laughter. "He's been . . . working as a . . . 'consultant'!" And the table was overcome by renewed fits of laughter.

The admiral sat with a huge grin on his face, quite proud of himself.

"You've got to have money, son," he continued, suddenly turning quite somber, "because without money, you're nothing. You don't go anywhere without money."

"He's right, you know." Mrs. Grosvenor frowned. "Money talks."

I waited for more laughter. I waited for them to acknowledge their joke. But there was no laughter, no acknowledgment. These people were serious.

Special People

Mary is a full-time worker at the dining hall where I work part-time as a dishwasher. She's one of those women who can be big and fat but somehow you never notice their size. Although she must be close to sixty, she has a spirited personality that might belong to a sixteen-year-old girl. There is something dry and clean about her; she is the definition of "baby powder fresh." Her hair is dyed dark black; her skin is white with a thin dusting of powder, and her lips bright red with lipstick. She always has a kind word for everyone, and all of the students love her.

One Saturday night, just as we were ready to close the serving line, a busload of Yale alumni appeared with their wives, ready to be served dinner. They were members of the Yale Club of Hartford and had been expected two hours earlier in the evening. But they hadn't arrived, and nobody was ready for them now. General havoc took place in the kitchen as the workers tried to whip up a last-minute meal for the Old Blues and their wives.

I became increasingly annoyed. It especially pained me to see Mary running around excitedly as the Yale Club sat there coolly, waiting to be served. She ran by me in a huff and shouted.

"Quick, Peter! Get some coffee cups! They need coffee cups!"

I walked up to the stack of clean cups with deliberate slowness and started counting them out onto a tray, one by one.

"Hurry up, for Christ's sake," Mary whined. "These people are waiting."

"All right! Don't worry about it. They'll get their goddamn coffee cups," I shouted at her, loud enough for the Yale Club to hear. They looked on in disapproval and Mary walked by them shaking her head.

"Boy, these student workers," she said. "They're so slow!"

I felt terrible.

I had taken my anger out on Mary when she was the one I was angry for. I hated to see her so subservient, and yet it was I who put her down further, and in front of them. So much so that she'd had to defend herself. I couldn't understand how everything had gotten so twisted.

She approached me afterward, when we were cleaning up.

"You know, Peter, you'd better watch it. You were wrong to wise off in front of those people."

"I know, Mary." I tried to apologize. "I'm sorry."

"Those were special people," she said, her face set in earnest, "and you had to go and get wise. They don't like that, you know."

"Oh, Mary," I said, exasperated, "those were not special people."

"Yes they were. The manager made a special trip down here to tell us to make sure that they were well taken care of. You'd better be careful, you know. They might report you. You might lose your job."

She turned to the counter and started shoving cottage cheese into a container.

I almost cried for her. I wanted to take her in my arms and try to convince her that there weren't any "special people," that she was as special as anyone else in the world.

I put my arm on her shoulder.

"Mary, there's no such thing as special people. People are people. That's all."

She stood there, shaking her head and shoveling the cottage cheese.

"Peter, you're wrong. Those were special people and you had to open your big mouth."

"Mary, look at them," I said, pointing toward the dining room. "What's so special about them?"

"Peter. Shush. They'll hear you."

"Mary," I pleaded, "can't you see that you're more special to me than any of those people? That's why I got so mad. I hated seeing you run around for them."

Her eyes suddenly glazed with tears and she hurried to the refrigerator with the cottage cheese.

"Peter, what am I going to do with you?" she called back. "You're gonna give me gray hairs. You're gonna get yourself in trouble too. You don't know your place. Those were special people."

Suggestions for Discussion

1. With what details does Werner describe the ironic significance of the song, "Both Sides Now"? How does he portray the multifaceted and deep-layered character of the two sides?

2. Account for the tone of the section "A Phone Call Home."

3. How can the heating incident both amuse and upset him?

4. How is irony expressed in the juxtaposition of the sketches of Kevin and the bank collector?

5. What does the narrative of "In Our Nation's Capital" tell you about the author's, the admiral's, and Mrs. Grosvenor's values?

6. Compare Mary's and Peter's implicit definition of "special people."

7. What do you infer is Peter's sense of self at the stage of life he portrays in "Both Sides Now"?

Suggestions for Writing

1. Describe one or more of your experiences with "both sides" of the economic structure.

2. On the basis of his descriptions of the people he encountered at Yale and his reactions to them, write a character study of Peter.

Jorge Luís Borges

Borges and Myself
Translated by Norman Thomas di Giovanni

Jorge Luís Borges (1899–1986), Argentine poet, short-story writer, essayist, critic, and university professor, was best known for his esoteric short fiction. He received little recognition in America until the publication in 1968 of English translations of Ficciónes, Labyrinths, and The Aleph and Other Stories. In this short piece the writer speaks of his dual nature, the self who surrenders everything to the creative Borges so that he can weave his tales and poems.

It's to the other man, to Borges, that things happen. I walk along the streets of Buenos Aires, stopping now and then—perhaps out of habit—to look at the arch of an old entranceway or a grillwork gate; of Borges I get news through the mail and glimpse his name among a committee of professors or in a dictionary of biography. I have a taste for hourglasses, maps, eighteenth-century typography, the roots of words, the smell of coffee, and Stevenson's prose; the other man shares these likes, but in a showy way that turns them into stagy mannerisms. It would be an exaggeration to say that we are on bad terms; I live, I let myself live, so that Borges can weave his tales and poems, and those tales and poems are my justification. It is not hard for me to admit that he has managed to write a few worthwhile pages, but these pages cannot save me, perhaps because what is good no longer belongs to anyone—not even the other man—but rather to speech or tradition. In any case, I am fated to become lost once and for all, and only some moment of myself will survive in the other man. Little by little, I have been surrendering everything to him, even though I have evidence of his stubborn habit of falsification and exaggerating. Spinoza held that all things try to keep on being themselves; a stone wants to be a stone and the tiger, a tiger. I shall remain in Borges, not in myself (if it is so that I am someone), but I recognize myself less in his books than in those of others or than in the laborious tuning of a guitar. Years ago, I tried ridding myself of him and I went from myths of the outlying slums of the city to games with time and infinity, but those games are now part of Borges and I will have to turn to other things. And so, my life is a running away, and I lose everything and everything is left to oblivion or to the other man.

Which of us is writing this page I don't know.

Suggestions for Discussion

1. Who is the speaker?
2. What is his relationship to and attitude toward Borges, the writer?
3. With what details are the dual aspects of his personality made clear? Define them.
4. How does he substantiate his belief that he is "fated to become lost once and for all"?
5. On the basis of this brief sketch, what conclusions are you invited to draw about the creative process and about the sources and subject matter of Borges's art?

Suggestions for Writing

1. Read a number of Borges's short stories and analyze the basis of their appeal.
2. The concept of the double appears frequently in literature. Write a sketch of a character in literature (Conrad's "The Secret Sharer," Melville's "Bartleby the Scrivener," Dostoevsky's "The Double," Poe's "William Wilson") who might be described as having a double.
3. Record your daily activities and thoughts for a week, paying no attention to mechanics or organization. Then select one of the journal items for full and logical development.

A. Alvarez

Sylvia Plath: A Memoir

Alfred Alvarez (b. 1929), an English critic, teacher, and writer, has been the poetry editor and critic for *The Observer* since 1956. He is the author and editor of a number of books, most recently *The Day of Atonement* (1991) and *Feeding the Rat* (1989), and is a regular contributor to *The Spectator*. His memoir of Sylvia Plath, which appeared first in *New American Review*, was later included in his book *The Savage God* (1971), a study of suicide. Although Plath was often able to turn her "anger, implacability, and her roused, needle-sharp sense of trouble" into her creativity, even into a kind of celebration, she succumbed to depression and everything, according to Alvarez, who knew her well, finally conspired to destroy her.

They were living in a tiny flat not far from the Regent's Park Zoo. Their windows faced onto a run-down square: peeling houses around a scrappy wilderness of garden. Closer to the Hill, gentility was advancing fast: smart Sunday newspaper house-agents had their boards up, the front doors were all fashionable colors—"Cantaloupe," "Tangerine," "Blueberry," "Thames Green"—and everywhere was a sense of gleaming white interiors, the old houses writ large and rich with new conversions.

Their square, however, had not yet been taken over. It was dirty, cracked, and racketty with children. The rows of houses that led off it were still occupied by the same kind of working-class families they had been built for eighty years before. No one, as yet, had made them chic and quadrupled their price—though that was to come soon enough. The Hughes' flat was one floor up a bedraggled staircase, past a pram in the hall and a bicycle. It was so small that everything seemed sideways on. You inserted yourself into a hallway so narrow and jammed that you could scarcely take off your coat. The kitchen seemed to fit one person at a time, who could span it with arms outstretched. In the living room you sat side by side, longways on, between a wall of books and a wall of pictures. The bedroom off it, with its flowered wallpaper, seemed to have room for nothing except a double bed. But the colors were cheerful, the bits and pieces pretty, and the whole place had a sense of liveliness about it, of things being done. A typewriter stood on a little table by the window, and they took turns at it, each working shifts while the other minded the baby. At night they cleared it away to make room for the child's cot. Later, they borrowed a room from another American poet, W. S. Merwin, where Sylvia worked the morning shift, Ted the afternoon.

This was Ted's time. He was on the edge of a considerable reputation. His first book had been well received and won all sorts of prizes in the States, which usually means that the second book will be an anticlimax. Instead, *Lupercal* effortlessly fulfilled and surpassed all the promises of *The Hawk in the Rain*. A figure had emerged on the drab scene of British poetry, powerful and undeniable. Whatever his natural hesitations and distrust of his own

34

work, he must have had some sense of his own strength and achievement. God alone knew how far he was eventually going, but in one essential way he had already arrived. He was a tall, strong-looking man in a black corduroy jacket, black trousers, black shoes; his dark hair hung untidily forward; he had a long, witty mouth. He was in command.

In those days Sylvia seemed effaced; the poet taking a back seat to the young mother and housewife. She had a long, rather flat body, a longish face, not pretty but alert and full of feeling, with a lively mouth and fine brown eyes. Her brownish hair was scraped severely into a bun. She wore jeans and a neat shirt, briskly American: bright, clean, competent, like a young woman in a cookery advertisement, friendly and yet rather distant.

Her background, of which I knew nothing then, belied her housewifely air: she had been a child prodigy—her first poem was published when she was eight—and then a brilliant student, winning every prize to be had, first at Wellesley High School, then at Smith College: scholarships all the way, straight A's, Phi Beta Kappa, president of this and that college society, and prizes for everything. A New York glossy magazine, *Mademoiselle,* had picked her as an outstanding possibility and wined her, dined her, and photographed her all over Manhattan. Then, almost inevitably, she had won a Fulbright to Cambridge, where she met Ted Hughes. They were married in 1956, on Bloomsday. Behind Sylvia was a self-sacrificing, widowed mother, a schoolteacher who had worked herself into the ground so that her two children might flourish. Sylvia's father—ornithologist, entomologist, ichthyologist, international authority on bumblebees, and professor of biology at Boston University—had died when she was nine. Both parents were of German stock and were German-speaking, academic, and intellectual. When she and Ted went to the States after Cambridge, a glittering university career seemed both natural and assured.

On the surface it was a typical success story: the brilliant examination-passer driving forward so fast and relentlessly that nothing could ever catch up with her. And it can last a lifetime, provided nothing checks the momentum, and the vehicle of all those triumphs doesn't disintegrate into sharp fragments from sheer speed and pressure. But already her progress had twice lurched to a halt. Between her month on *Mademoiselle* and her last year in college she had had the nervous breakdown and suicide attempt which became the theme of her novel, *The Bell Jar.* Then, once reestablished at Smith—"an outstanding teacher," said her colleagues—the academic prizes no longer seemed worth the effort. So in 1958 she had thrown over university life—Ted had never seriously contemplated it—and gone free-lance, trusting her luck and talent as a poet. All this I learned much later. Now Sylvia had simply slowed down; she was subdued, absorbed in her new baby daughter, and friendly only in that rather formal, shallow, transatlantic way that keeps you at your distance.

Ted went downstairs to get the pram ready while she dressed the baby. I stayed behind a minute, zipping up my son's coat. Sylvia turned to me, suddenly without gush:

"I'm so glad you picked *that* poem," she said. "It's one of my favorites but no one else seemed to like it."

For a moment I went completely blank; I didn't know what she was talking about. She noticed and helped me out.

"The one you put in *The Observer* a year ago. About the factory at night."

"For Christ's sake, Sylvia *Plath*." It was my turn to gush. "I'm sorry. It was a lovely poem."

"Lovely" wasn't the right word, but what else do you say to a bright young housewife? I had picked it from a sheaf of poems which had arrived from America, immaculately typed, with self-addressed envelope and international reply coupon efficiently supplied. All of them were stylish and talented but that in itself was not rare in those days. The late fifties was a period of particularly high style in American verse, when every campus worth its name had its own "brilliant" poetic technician in residence. But at least one of these poems had more going for it than rhetorical elegance. It had no title, though later, in *The Colossus*, she called it "Night Shift." It was one of those poems which starts by saying what it is *not* about so strongly that you don't believe the explanations that follow:

> It was not a heart, beating,
> That muted boom, that clangor
> Far off, not blood in the ears
> Drumming up any fever
>
> To impose on the evening.
> The noise came from outside:
> A metal detonating
> Native, evidently, to
>
> These stilled suburbs: nobody
> Startled at it, though the sound
> Shook the ground with its pounding.
> It took root at my coming . . .

It seemed to me more than a piece of good description, to be used and moralized upon as the fashion of that decade dictated. The note was aroused and all the details of the scene seemed continually to be turning inward. It is a poem, I suppose, about fear, and although in the course of it the fear is rationalized and explained (that pounding in the night is caused by machines turning), it ends by reasserting precisely the threatening masculine forces there were to be afraid of. It had its moments of awkwardness—for example, the prissy, pausing flourish in the manner of Wallace Stevens: "Native, evidently, to . . ." But compared with most of the stuff that thudded unsolicited through my letterbox every morning, it was that rare thing: the always unexpected, wholly genuine article.

I was embarrassed not to have known who she was. She seemed embarrassed to have reminded me, and also depressed.

After that I saw Ted occasionally, Sylvia more rarely. He and I would meet for a beer in one of the pubs near Primrose Hill or the Heath, and sometimes we would walk our children together. We almost never talked shop; without mentioning it, we wanted to keep things unprofessional. At some point during the summer Ted and I did a broadcast together. Afterward we collected Sylvia from the flat and went across to their local. The recording had been a success and we stood outside the pub, around the baby's pram, drinking our beers and pleased with ourselves. Sylvia, too, seemed easier, wittier, less

constrained than I had seen her before. For the first time I understood something of the real charm and speed of the girl.

About that time my wife and I moved from our flat near Swiss Cottage to a
house higher up in Hampstead, near the Heath. A couple of days before we
were due to move I broke my leg in a climbing accident, and that put out
everything and everyone, since the house had to be decorated, broken leg or
not. I remember sticking black and white tiles to floor after endless floor, a
filthy dark brown glue coating my fingers and clothes and gumming up my
hair, the great, inert plaster cast dragging behind me like a coffin as I
crawled. There wasn't much time for friends. Ted occasionally dropped in
and I would hobble with him briefly to the pub. But I saw Sylvia not at all.
In the autumn I went to teach for a term in the States.

While I was there *The Observer* sent me her first book of poems to review. It seemed to fit the image I had of her: serious, gifted, withheld, and
still partly under the massive shadow of her husband. There were poems that
had been influenced by him, others which echoed Theodore Roethke or Wallace Stevens; clearly, she was still casting about for her own style. Yet the
technical ability was great, and beneath most of the poems was a sense of
resources and disturbances not yet tapped. "Her poems," I wrote, "rest secure in a mass of experience that is never quite brought out into the daylight. . . . It is this sense of threat, as though she were continually menaced
by something she could see only out of the corners of her eyes, that gives her
work its distinction."

Throughout this time the evidence of the poems and the evidence of the
person were utterly different. There was no trace of the poetry's despair and
unforgiving destructiveness in her social manner. She remained remorse-
lessly bright and energetic: busy with her children and her beekeeping in
Devon, busy flat-hunting in London, busy seeing *The Bell Jar* through the
press, busy typing and sending off her poems to largely unreceptive editors
(just before she died she sent a sheaf of her best poems, most of them now
classics, to one of the national British weeklies; none was accepted). She had
also taken up horse-riding again, teaching herself to ride on a powerful stallion called Ariel, and was elated by this new excitement.

Cross-legged on the red floor, after reading her poems, she would talk
about her riding in her twanging New England voice. And perhaps because I
was also a member of the club, she talked, too, about suicide in much the
same way: about her attempt ten years before which, I suppose, must have
been very much on her mind as she corrected the proofs of her novel, and
about her recent car crash. It had been no accident; she had gone off the road
deliberately, seriously, wanting to die. But she hadn't, and all that was now
in the past. For this reason I am convinced that at this time she was not
contemplating suicide. On the contrary, she was able to write about the act
so freely because it was already behind her. The car crash was a death she
had survived, the death she sardonically felt herself fated to undergo once
every decade:

> I have done it again.
> One year in every ten
> I manage it—

A sort of walking miracle . . .
I am only thirty.
And like the cat I have nine times to die.

This is Number Three . . .

In life, as in the poem, there was neither hysteria in her voice, nor any appeal for sympathy. She talked about suicide in much the same tone as she talked about any other risky, testing activity: urgently, even fiercely, but altogether without self-pity. She seemed to view death as a physical challenge she had, once again, overcome. It was an experience of much the same quality as riding Ariel or mastering a bolting horse—which she had done as a Cambridge undergraduate—or careening down a dangerous snow slope without properly knowing how to ski—an incident, also from life, which is one of the best things in *The Bell Jar*. Suicide, in short, was not a swoon into death, an attempt "to cease upon the midnight with no pain"; it was something to be felt in the nerve-ends and fought against, an initiation rite qualifying her for a *life* of her own.

God knows what wound the death of her father had inflicted on her in her childhood, but over the years this had been transformed into the conviction that to be an adult meant to be a survivor. So, for her, death was a debt to be met once every decade: in order to stay alive as a grown woman, a mother, and a poet, she had to pay—in some partial, magical way—with her life. But because this impossible payment involved also the fantasy of joining or regaining her beloved dead father, it was a passionate act, instinct as much with love as with hatred and despair. Thus in that strange, upsetting poem "The Bee Meeting," the detailed, doubtless accurate description of a gathering of local beekeepers in her Devon village gradually becomes an invocation of some deadly ritual in which she is sacrificial virgin whose coffin, finally, waits in the sacred grove. Why this should happen becomes, perhaps, slightly less mysterious when you remember that her father was an authority on bees; so her beekeeping becomes a way of symbolically allying herself to him, and reclaiming him from the dead.

The tone of all these late poems is hard, factual and, despite the intensity, understated. In some strange way, I suspect she thought of herself as a realist: the deaths and resurrections of "Lady Lazarus," the nightmares of "Daddy," and the rest had all been proved on her pulses. That she brought to them an extraordinary inner wealth of imagery and associations was almost beside the point, however essential it is for the poetry itself. Because she felt she was simply describing the facts as they had happened, she was able to tap in the coolest possible way all her large reserves of skill: those subtle rhymes and half-rhymes, the flexible, echoing rhythms and offhand colloquialism by which she preserved, even in her most anguished probing, complete artistic control. Her internal horrors were as factual and precisely sensed as the barely controllable stallion on which she was learning to ride or the car she had smashed up.

So she spoke of suicide with a wry detachment, and without any mention of the suffering or drama of the act. It was obviously a matter of self-respect that her first attempt had been serious and nearly successful, instead of a mere hysterical gesture. That seemed to entitle her to speak of suicide as a subject, not as an obsession. It was an act she felt she had a right to as a grown woman and a free agent, in the same way as she felt it to be necessary to her development, given her queer conception of the adult as a survivor, an imaginary Jew from the concentration camps of the mind. Because of this there was never any question of motives: you do it because you do it, just as an artist always knows what he knows.

Perhaps this is why she scarcely mentioned her father, however clearly and deeply her fantasies of death were involved with him. The autobiographical heroine of *The Bell Jar* goes to weep at her father's grave immediately before she holes up in a cellar and swallows fifty sleeping pills. In "Daddy," describing the same episode, she hammers home her reasons with repetitions:

> At twenty I tried to die
> And get back, back, back to you.
> I thought even the bones would do.

I suspect that finding herself alone again now, however temporarily and voluntarily, all the anguish she had experienced at her father's death was reactivated: despite herself, she felt abandoned, injured, enraged, and bereaved as purely and defenselessly as she had as a child twenty years before. As a result, the pain that had built up steadily inside her all that time came flooding out. There was no need to discuss motives because the poems did that for her.

These months were an amazingly creative period, comparable, I think, to the "marvellous year" in which Keats produced nearly all the poetry on which his reputation finally rests. Earlier she had written carefully, more or less painfully, with much rewriting and, according to her husband, with constant recourse to *Roget's Thesaurus*. Now, although she abandoned none of her hard-earned skills and discipline, and still rewrote and rewrote, the poems flowed effortlessly, until, at the end, she occasionally produced as many as three a day. She also told me that she was deep into a new novel. *The Bell Jar* was finished, proofread and with her publishers; she spoke of it with some embarrassment as an autobiographical apprentice-work which she had to write in order to free herself from the past. But this new book, she implied, was the genuine article.

Considering the conditions in which she worked, her productivity was phenomenal. She was a full-time mother with a two-year-old daughter, a baby of ten months, and a house to look after. By the time the children were in bed at night she was too tired for anything more strenuous than "music and brandy and water." So she got up very early each morning and worked until the children woke. "These new poems of mine have one thing in common," she wrote in a note for a reading she prepared, but never broadcast, for the BBC, "they were all written at about four in the morning—that still blue, almost eternal hour before the baby's cry, before the glassy music of the milkman, settling his bottles." In those dead hours between night and day, she was able to gather herself into herself in silence and isolation, almost as though she were reclaiming some past innocence and freedom before life got a grip on her. Then she could write. For the rest of the day she was shared among the children, the housework, the shopping, efficient, bustling, harassed, like every other housewife.

Yet lonely she was, touchingly and without much disguise, despite her buoyant manner. Despite, too, the energy of her poems, which are, by any standards, subtly ambiguous performances. In them she faced her private horrors steadily and without looking aside, but the effort and risk involved in doing so acted on her like a stimulant; the worse things got and the more directly she wrote about them, the more fertile her imagination became. Just as disaster, when it finally arrives, is never as bad as it seems in expectation, so she now wrote almost with relief, swiftly as though to forestall further horrors. In a way, this is what she had been waiting for all her life, and now it had come she knew she must use it. "The passion for destruction is also a creative passion," said Michael Bakunin, and for Sylvia also this was true. She turned anger, implacability, and her roused, needle-sharp sense of trouble into a kind of celebration.

I have suggested that her cool tone depends a great deal on her realism, her sense of fact. As the months went by and her poetry became progressively more extreme, this gift of transforming every detail grew steadily until, in the last weeks, each trivial event became the occasion for poetry: a cut finger, a fever, a bruise. Her drab domestic life fused with her imagination richly and without hesitation. Around this time, for example, her husband produced a strange radio play in which the hero, driving to town, runs over a hare, sells the dead animal for five shillings, and with the blood money buys two roses. Sylvia pounced on this, isolating its core, interpreting and adjusting it according to her own needs. The result was the poem "Kindness," which ends:

> The blood jet is poetry,
> There is no stopping it.
> You hand me two children, two roses.

There was, indeed, no stopping it. Her poetry acted as a strange, powerful lens through which her ordinary life was filtered and refigured with extraordinary intensity. Perhaps the elation that comes of writing well and often helped her to preserve that bright American façade she unfailingly presented to the world. In common with her other friends of that period, I chose to believe in this cheerfulness against all the evidence of the poems. Or rather, I believed in it, and I didn't believe. But what could one do? I felt sorry for her but she clearly didn't want that. Her jauntiness forestalled all sympathy, and, if only by her blank refusal to discuss them otherwise, she insisted that her poems were purely poems, autonomous. If attempted suicide is, as some psychiatrists believe, a cry for help, then Sylvia at this time was not suicidal. What she wanted was not help but confirmation: she needed someone to acknowledge that she was coping exceptionally well with her difficult routine life of children, nappies, shopping, and writing. She needed, even more, to know that the poems worked and were good, for although she had gone through a gate Lowell had opened, she was now far along a peculiarly solitary road on which not many would risk following her. So it was important for her to know that her messages were coming back clear and strong. Yet not even her determinedly bright self-reliance could disguise the loneliness that came from her almost palpably, like a heat haze. She asked for neither sympathy nor help but, like a bereaved widow at a wake, she simply wanted company in her mourning. I suppose it provided confirmation that, despite the odds and the internal evidence, she still existed.

It was an unspeakable winter, the worst, they said, in a hundred and fifty years. The snow began just after Christmas and would not let up. By New

Year the whole country had ground to a halt. The trains froze on the tracks, the abandoned trucks froze on the roads. The power stations, overloaded by million upon pathetic million of hopeless electric fires, broke down continually; not that the fires mattered, since the electricians were mostly out on strike. Water pipes froze solid; for a bath you had to scheme and cajole those rare friends with centrally heated houses, who became rarer and less friendly as the weeks dragged on. Doing the dishes became a major operation. The gastric rumble of water in outdated plumbing was sweeter than the sound of mandolins. Weight for weight, plumbers were as expensive as smoked salmon, and harder to find. The gas failed and Sunday joints went raw. The lights failed and candles, of course, were unobtainable. Nerves failed and marriages crumbled. Finally, the heart failed. It seemed the cold would never end. Nag, nag, nag.

In December *The Observer* had published a still uncollected poem by Sylvia called "Event"; in mid-January they published another, "Winter Trees." Sylvia wrote me a note about it, adding that maybe we should take our children to the zoo and she would show me "the nude verdigris of the condor." But she no longer dropped into my studio with poems. Later that month I met the literary editor of one of the big weeklies. He asked me if I had seen Sylvia recently.

"No. Why?"

"I was just wondering. She sent us some poems. Very strange."

"Did you like them?"

"No," he replied. "Too extreme for my taste. I sent them all back. But she sounds in a bad state. I think she needs help."

Her doctor, a sensitive, overworked man, thought the same. He prescribed sedatives and arranged for her to see a psychotherapist. Having been bitten once by American psychiatry, she hesitated for some time before writing for an appointment. But her depression did not lift, and finally the letter was sent. It did no good. Either her letter or that of the therapist arranging a consultation went astray; apparently the postman delivered it to the wrong address. The therapist's reply arrived a day or two after she died. This was one of several links in the chain of accidents, coincidences, and mistakes that ended in her death.

I am convinced by what I know of the facts that this time she did not intend to die. Her suicide attempt ten years before had been, in every sense, deadly serious. She had carefully disguised the theft of the sleeping pills, left a misleading note to cover her tracks, and hidden herself in the darkest, most unused corner of a cellar, rearranging behind her the old firelogs she had disturbed, burying herself away like a skeleton in the nethermost family closet. Then she had swallowed a bottle of fifty sleeping pills. She was found late and by accident, and survived only by a miracle. The flow of life in her was too strong even for the violence she had done it. This, anyway, is her description of the act in *The Bell Jar;* there is no reason to believe it false. So she had learned the hard way the odds against successful suicide; she had learned that despair must be counterpoised by an almost obsessional attention to detail and disguise.

By these lights she seemed, in her last attempt, to be taking care not to succeed. But this time everything conspired to destroy her. An employment agency had found her an *au pair* girl to help with the children and housework while Sylvia got on with her writing. The girl, an Australian, was due to arrive at nine o'clock on the morning of Monday, February 11th. Meanwhile, a recurrent trouble, Sylvia's sinuses were bad; the pipes in her newly converted flat froze solid; there was still no telephone, and no word from the psychotherapist; the weather continued monstrous. Illness, loneliness, depression, and cold, combined with the demands of two small children, were too much for her. So when the weekend came she went off with the babies to stay with friends in another part of London. The plan was, I think, that she would leave early enough on Monday morning to be back in time to welcome the Australian girl. Instead, she decided to go back on the Sunday. The friends were against it but she was insistent, made a great show of her old competence and seemed more cheerful than she had been for some time. So they let her go. About eleven o'clock that night she knocked on the door of the elderly painter who lived below her, asking to borrow some stamps. But she lingered in the doorway, drawing out the conversation until he told her that he got up well before nine in the morning. Then she said goodnight and went back upstairs.

Around six A.M. she went up to the children's room and left a plate of bread and butter and two mugs of milk, in case they should wake hungry before the *au pair* girl arrived. Then she went back down to the kitchen, sealed the door and window as best she could with towels, opened the oven, laid her head in it, and turned on the gas.

The Australian girl arrived punctually at nine A.M. She rang and knocked a long time but could get no answer. So she went off to search for a telephone kiosk in order to phone the agency and make sure she had the right address. Sylvia's name, incidentally, was not on either of the doorbells. Had everything been normal, the neighbor below would have been up by then; even if he had overslept, the girl's knocking should have aroused him. But as it happened, the neighbor was very deaf and slept without his hearing aid. More important, his bedroom was immediately below Sylvia's kitchen. The gas seeped down and knocked him out cold. So he slept on through all the noise. The girl returned and tried again, still without success. Again she went off to telephone the agency and ask what to do; they told her to go back. It was now about eleven o'clock. This time she was lucky: some builders had arrived to work in the frozen-up house, and they let her in. When she knocked on Sylvia's door there was no answer and the smell of gas was overpowering. The builders forced the lock and found Sylvia sprawled in the kitchen. She was still warm. She had left a note saying, "Please call Dr.—" and giving his telephone number. But it was too late.

Had everything worked out as it should—had the gas not drugged the man downstairs, preventing him from opening the front door to the *au pair* girl—there is no doubt she would have been saved. I think she wanted to be; why else leave her doctor's telephone number? This time, unlike the occasion ten years before, there was too much holding her to life. Above all, there were the children: she was too passionate a mother to want to lose them or them to lose her. There were also the extraordinary creative powers she now unequivocally knew she possessed: the poems came daily, unbidden and unstoppable, and she was again working on a novel about which, at last, she had no reservations.

Why, then, did she kill herself? In part, I suppose, it was "a cry for help" which fatally misfired. But it was also a last, desperate attempt to exorcise the death she had summoned up in her poems. I have already suggested that perhaps she had begun to write obsessively about death for two reasons. First, when she and her husband separated, however mutual the arrangement, she went through again the same piercing grief and bereavement she had felt as a child when her father, by his death, seemed to abandon her. Second, I believe she thought her car crash the previous summer had set her free; she had paid her dues, qualified as a survivor, and could now write about it. But, as I have written elsewhere, for the artist himself art is not necessarily therapeutic; he is not automatically relieved of his fantasies by expressing them. Instead, by some perverse logic of creation, the act of formal expression may simply make the dredged-up material more readily available to him. The result of handling it in his work may well be that he finds himself living it out. For the artist, in short, nature often imitates art. Or, to restate the cliché, when an artist holds a mirror up to nature he finds out who and what he is; but the knowledge may change him irredeemably so that he becomes that image.

I think Sylvia, in one way or another, sensed this. In an introductory note she wrote to "Daddy" for the BBC, she said of the poem's narrator, "she has to act out the awful little allegory once over before she is free of it." The allegory in question was, as she saw it, the struggle in her between a fantasy Nazi father and a Jewish mother. But perhaps it was also a fantasy of containing in herself her own dead father, like a woman possessed by a demon (in the poem she actually calls him a vampire). In order for her to be free of him, he has to be released like a genie from a bottle. And this is precisely what the poems did: they bodied forth the death within her. But they also did so in an intensely living and creative way. The more she wrote about death, the stronger and more fertile her imaginative world became. And this gave her everything to live for.

I suspect that in the end she wanted to have done with the theme once and for all. But the only way she could find was "to act out the awful little allegory once over." She had always been a bit of a gambler, used to taking risks. The authority of her poetry was in part due to her brave persistence in following the thread of her inspiration right down to the Minotaur's lair. And this psychic courage had its parallel in her physical arrogance and carelessness. Risks didn't frighten her; on the contrary, she found them stimulating. Freud has written, "Life loses in interest, when the highest stake in the game of living, life itself, may not be risked." Finally, Sylvia took that risk. She gambled for the last time, having worked out that the odds were in her favor, but perhaps, in her depression, not much caring whether she won or lost. Her calculations went wrong and she lost.

It was a mistake, then, and out of it a whole myth has grown. I don't think she would have found it much to her taste, since it is a myth of the poet as a sacrificial victim, offering herself up for the sake of her art, having been dragged by the Muses to that final altar through every kind of distress. In these terms, her suicide becomes the whole point of the story, the act which validates her poems, gives them their interest, and proves her seriousness. So people are drawn to her work in much the same spirit as *Time* featured her at length: not for the poetry but for the gossipy, extra-literary "human interest." Yet just as the suicide adds nothing at all to the poetry, so the myth of Sylvia as a passive victim is a total perversion of the woman she was. It misses altogether her liveliness, her intellectual appetite and harsh wit, her great imaginative resourcefulness and vehemence of feeling, her control. Above all, it misses the courage with which she was able to turn disaster into art. The pity is not that there is a myth of Sylvia Plath but that the myth is not simply that of an enormously gifted poet whose death came recklessly, by mistake, and too soon.

I used to think of her brightness as a façade, as though she were able, in a rather schizoid way, to turn her back on her suffering for the sake of appearances, and pretend it didn't exist. But maybe she was also able to keep her unhappiness in check because she could write about it, because she knew she was salvaging from all those horrors something rather marvelous. The end came when she felt she could stand the subject no longer. She had written it out and was ready for something new.

> The blood-jet is poetry,
> There is no stopping it.

The only method of stopping it she could see, her vision by then blinkered by depression and illness, was that last gamble. So having, as she thought, arranged to be saved, she lay down in front of the gas oven almost hopefully, almost with relief, as though she were saying, "Perhaps this will set me free."

On Friday, February 15th, there was an inquest in the drab, damp coroner's court behind Camden Town: muttered evidence, long silences, the Australian girl in tears. Earlier that morning I had gone with Ted to the undertakers in Mornington Crescent. The coffin was at the far end of a bare, draped room. She lay stiffly, a ludicrous ruff at her neck. Only her face showed. It was gray and slightly transparent, like wax. I had never before seen a dead person and I hardly recognized her; her features seemed too thin and sharp. The room smelled of apples, faint, sweet but somehow unclean, as though the apples were beginning to rot. I was glad to get out into the cold and noise of the dingy streets. It seemed impossible that she was dead.

Even now I find it hard to believe. There was too much life in her long, flat, strongly boned body, and her longish face with its fine brown eyes, shrewd and full of feeling. She was practical and candid, passionate and compassionate. I believe she was a genius. I sometimes catch myself childishly thinking I'll run into her walking on Primrose Hill or the Heath, and we'll pick up the conversation where we left off. But perhaps that is because her poems still speak so distinctly in her accents: quick, sardonic, unpredictable, effortlessly inventive, a bit angry, and always utterly her own.

Suggestions for Discussion

1. What complications do you discern in the author's picture of Sylvia Plath's earlier background, her parents, her domestic life, and her early successes?

2. How does the author relate Sylvia Plath's poetry to her experience, especially in the case of "Daddy"?

3. What details and theories give support to Alvarez's views about the meaning of

suicide for Sylvia Plath, the precipitating events leading to her last attempt, and her lack of intention to succeed in it?

4. Explain the statement in context, "For the artist, in short, nature often imitates art."

5. Study the organization of the memoir. How are earlier events in Plath's life related to the chronologically narrated incidents of the author's association with her? How does the author use his narrative to illuminate the poems he quotes?

6. Toward the end of the memoir, Alvarez objects to readers' being "drawn to her work . . . not for the poetry but for the gossipy, extra-literary 'human interest.' Yet the suicide adds nothing at all to the poetry. . . ." How can this statement be reconciled with his clarification of the poetry noted in Question 5?

Suggestion for Writing

Read the poetry of Sylvia Plath or her early novel *The Bell Jar*. Attempt to account for the enormous impact her writing has on college students.

Maxine Hong Kingston

No Name Woman

Maxine Hong Kingston (b. 1940) was born in Stockton, California, and graduated from the University of California. Her books, *The Woman Warrior* (1976) from which this excerpt has been taken, *China Men* (1980), and *Tripmaster Monkey* (1989), focus on her experiences as a Chinese American. She has won both the National Book Critics Circle and American Book Awards. "No Name Woman" graphically portrays the complex problems of cultural identity and implicitly suggests the author's sense of self.

"You must not tell anyone," my mother said, "what I am about to tell you. In China your father had a sister who killed herself. She jumped into the family well. We say that your father has all brothers because it is as if she had never been born.

"In 1924 just a few days after our village celebrated seventeen hurry-up weddings—to make sure that every young man who went 'out on the road' would responsibly come home—your father and his brothers and your grandfather and his brothers and your aunt's new husband sailed for America, the Gold Mountain. It was your grandfather's last trip. Those lucky enough to get contracts waved good-bye from the decks. They fed and guarded the stowaways and helped them off in Cuba, New York, Bali, Hawaii. 'We'll meet in California next year,' they said. All of them sent money home.

"I remember looking at your aunt one day when she and I were dressing; I had not noticed before that she had such a protruding melon of a stomach.

But I did not think, 'She's pregnant,' until she began to look like other pregnant women, her shirt pulling and the white tops of her black pants showing. She could not have been pregnant, you see, because her husband had been gone for years. No one said anything. We did not discuss it. In early summer she was ready to have the child, long after the time when it could have been possible.

"The village had also been counting. On the night the baby was to be born the villagers raided our house. Some were crying. Like a great saw, teeth strung with lights, files of people walked zigzag across our land, tearing the rice. Their lanterns doubled in the disturbed black water, which drained away through the broken bunds. As the villagers closed in, we could see that some of them, probably men and women we knew well, wore white masks. The people with long hair hung it over their faces. Women with short hair made it stand up on end. Some had tied white bands around their foreheads, arms, and legs.

"At first they threw mud and rocks at the house. Then they threw eggs and began slaughtering our stock. We could hear the animals scream their deaths—the roosters, the pigs, a last great roar from the ox. Familiar wild heads flared in our night windows; the villagers encircled us. Some of the faces stopped to peer at us, their eyes rushing like searchlights. The hands flattened against the panes, framed heads, and left red prints.

"The villagers broke in the front and the back doors at the same time, even though we had not locked the doors against them. Their knives dripped with the blood of our animals. They smeared blood on the doors and walls. One woman swung a chicken, whose throat she had slit, splattering blood in red arcs about her. We stood together in the middle of our house, in the family hall with the pictures and tables of the ancestors around us, and looked straight ahead.

"At that time the house had only two wings. When the men came back, we would build two more to enclose our courtyard and a third one to begin a second courtyard. The villagers rushed through both wings, even your grandparents' rooms, to find your aunt's, which was also mine until the men returned. From this room a new wing for one of the younger families would grow. They ripped up her clothes and shoes and broke her combs, grinding them underfoot. They tore her work from the loom. They scattered the cooking fire and rolled the new weaving in it. We could hear them in the kitchen breaking our bowls and banging the pots. They overturned the great waist-high earthenware jugs; duck eggs, pickled fruits, vegetables burst out and mixed in acrid torrents. The old woman from the next field swept a broom through the air and loosed the spirits-of-the-broom over our heads. 'Pig.' 'Ghost.' 'Pig,' they sobbed and scolded while they ruined our house.

"When they left, they took sugar and oranges to bless themselves. They cut pieces from the dead animals. Some of them took bowls that were not broken and clothes that were not torn. Afterward we swept up the rice and sewed it back up into sacks. But the smells from the spilled preserves lasted. Your aunt gave birth in the pigsty that night. The next morning when I went for the water, I found her and the baby plugging up the family well.

"Don't let your father know that I told you. He denies her. Now that you have started to menstruate, what happened to her could happen to you. Don't humiliate us. You wouldn't like to be forgotten as if you had never been born. The villagers are watchful."

Whenever she had to warn us about life, my mother told stories that ran like this one, a story to grow up on. She tested our strength to establish realities. Those in the emigrant generations who could not reassert brute survival died young and far from home. Those of us in the first American generations have had to figure out how the invisible world the emigrants built around our childhoods fit in solid America.

The emigrants confused the gods by diverting their curses, misleading them with crooked streets and false names. They must try to confuse their offspring as well, who, I suppose, threaten them in similar ways—always trying to get things straight, always trying to name the unspeakable. The Chinese I know hide their names; sojourners take new names when their lives change and guard their real names with silence.

Chinese-Americans, when you try to understand what things in you are Chinese, how do you separate what is peculiar to childhood, to poverty, insanities, one family, your mother who marked your growing with stories, from what is Chinese? What is Chinese tradition and what is the movies?

If I want to learn what clothes my aunt wore, whether flashy or ordinary, I would have to begin, "Remember Father's drowned-in-the-well sister?" I cannot ask that. My mother has told me once and for all the useful parts. She will add nothing unless powered by Necessity, a riverbank that guides her life. She plants vegetable gardens rather than lawns; she carries the odd-shaped tomatoes home from the fields and eats food left for the gods.

Whenever we did frivolous things, we used up energy; we flew high kites. We children came up off the ground over the melting cones our parents brought home from work and the American movie on New Year's Day—*Oh, You Beautiful Doll* with Betty Grable one year, and *She Wore a Yellow Ribbon* with John Wayne another year. After the one carnival ride each, we paid in guilt; our tired father counted his change on the dark walk home.

Adultery is extravagance. Could people who hatch their own chicks and eat the embryos and the heads for delicacies and boil the feet in vinegar for party food, leaving only the gravel, eating even the gizzard lining—could such people engender a prodigal aunt? To be a woman, to have a daughter in starvation time was a waste enough. My aunt could not have been the lone romantic who gave up everything for sex. Women in the old China did not choose. Some man had commanded her to lie with him and be his secret evil. I wonder whether he masked himself when he joined the raid on her family.

Perhaps she encountered him in the fields or on the mountain where the daughters-in-law collected fuel. Or perhaps he first noticed her in the market-place. He was not a stranger because the village housed no strangers. She had to have dealings with him other than sex. Perhaps he worked an adjoining field, or he sold her the cloth for the dress she sewed and wore. His demand must have surprised, then terrified her. She obeyed him; she always did as she was told.

When the family found a young man in the next village to be her husband, she stood tractably beside the best rooster, his proxy, and promised before they met that she would be his forever. She was lucky that he was her age and she would be the first wife, an advantage secure now. The night she first saw him, he had sex with her. Then he left for America. She had almost forgotten what he looked like. When she tried to envision him, she only saw the black and white face in the group photograph the men had had taken before leaving.

The other man was not, after all, much different from her husband. They both gave orders: she followed. "If you tell your family, I'll beat you. I'll kill you. Be here again next week." No one talked sex, ever. And she might have separated the rapes from the rest of living if only she did not have to buy her oil from him or gather wood in the same forest. I want her fear to have lasted just as long as rape lasted so that the fear could have been contained. No drawn-out fear. But women at sex hazarded birth and hence lifetimes. The fear did not stop but permeated everywhere. She told the man, "I think I'm pregnant." He organized the raid against her.

On nights when my mother and father talked about their life back home, sometimes they mentioned an "outcast table" whose business they still seemed to be settling, their voices tight. In a commensal tradition, where food is precious, the powerful older people made wrongdoers eat alone. Instead of letting them start separate new lives like the Japanese, who could become samurais and geishas, the Chinese family, faces averted but eyes glowering sideways, hung on to the offenders and fed them leftovers. My aunt must have lived in the same house as my parents and eaten at an outcast table. My mother spoke about the raid as if she had seen it, when she and my aunt, a daughter-in-law to a different household, should not have been living together at all. Daughters-in-law lived with their husbands' parents, not their own; a synonym for marriage in Chinese is "taking a daughter-in-law." Her husband's parents could have sold her, mortgaged her, stoned her. But they had sent her back to her own mother and father, a mysterious act hinting at disgraces not told me. Perhaps they had thrown her out to deflect the avengers.

She was the only daughter; her four brothers went with her father, husband, and uncles "out on the road" and for some years became western men. When the goods were divided among the family, three of the brothers took land, and the youngest, my father, chose an education. After my grandparents gave their daughter away to her husband's family, they had dispensed all the adventure and all the property. They expected her alone to keep the traditional ways, which her brothers, now among the barbarians, could fumble without detection. The heavy, deep-rooted women were to maintain the past against the flood, safe for returning. But the rare urge west had fixed upon our family, and so my aunt crossed boundaries not delineated in space.

The work of preservation demands that the feelings playing about in one's guts not be turned into action. Just watch their passing like cherry blossoms. But perhaps my aunt, my forerunner, caught in a slow life, let dreams grow and fade and after some months or years went toward what persisted. Fear at the enormities of the forbidden kept her desires delicate, wire and bone. She looked at a man because she liked the way the hair was tucked behind his ears, or she liked the question-mark line of a long torso curving at the shoulder and straight at the hip. For warm eyes or a soft voice or a slow walk— that's all—a few hairs, a line, a brightness, a sound, a pace, she gave up family. She offered us up for a charm that vanished with tiredness, a pigtail that didn't toss when the wind died. Why, the wrong lighting could erase the dearest thing about him.

It could very well have been, however, that my aunt did not take subtle enjoyment of her friend, but, a wild woman, kept rollicking company. Imagining her free with sex doesn't fit, though. I don't know any women like that, or men either. Unless I see her life branching into mine, she gives me no ancestral help.

To sustain her being in love, she often worked at herself in the mirror, guessing at the colors and shapes that would interest him, changing them frequently in order to hit on the right combination. She wanted him to look back.

On a farm near the sea, a woman who tended her appearance reaped a reputation for eccentricity. All the married women blunt-cut their hair in flaps about their ears or pulled it back in tight buns. No nonsense. Neither style blew easily into heart-catching tangles. And at their weddings they displayed themselves in their long hair for the last time. "It brushed the backs of my knees," my mother tells me. "It was braided, and even so, it brushed the backs of my knees."

At the mirror my aunt combed individuality into her bob. A bun could have been contrived to escape into black streamers blowing in the wind or in quiet wisps about her face, but only the older women in our picture album wear buns. She brushed her hair back from her forehead, tucking the flaps behind her ears. She looped a piece of thread, knotted into a circle between her index fingers and thumbs, and ran the double strand across her forehead. When she closed her fingers as if she were making a pair of shadow geese bite, the string twisted together catching the little hairs. Then she pulled the thread away from her skin, ripping the hairs out neatly, her eyes watering from the needles of pain. Opening her fingers, she cleaned the thread, then rolled it along her hairline and the tops of her eyebrows. My mother did the same to me and my sisters and herself. I used to believe that the expression "caught by the short hairs" meant a captive held with a depilatory string. It especially hurt at the temples, but my mother said we were lucky we didn't have to have our feet bound when we were seven. Sisters used to sit on their beds and cry together, she said, as their mothers or their slave removed the bandages for a few minutes each night and let the blood gush back into their veins. I hope that the man my aunt loved appreciated a smooth brow, that he wasn't just a tits-and-ass man.

Once my aunt found a freckle on her chin, at a spot that the almanac said predestined her for unhappiness. She dug it out with a hot needle and washed the wound with peroxide.

More attention to her looks than these pullings of hairs and pickings at spots would have caused gossip among the villagers. They owned work clothes and good clothes, and they wore good clothes for feasting the new seasons. But since a woman combing her hair hexes beginnings, my aunt rarely found an occasion to look her best. Women looked like great sea snails—the corded wood, babies, and laundry they carried were the whorls on their backs. The Chinese did not admire a bent back; goddesses and warriors stood straight. Still there must have been a marvelous freeing of beauty when a worker laid down her burden and stretched and arched.

Such commonplace loveliness, however, was not enough for my aunt. She dreamed of a lover for the fifteen days of New Year's, the time for families to exchange visits, money, and food. She plied her secret comb. And sure enough she cursed the year, the family, the village, and herself.

Even as her hair lured her imminent lover, many other men looked at her. Uncles, cousins, nephews, brothers would have looked, too, had they been home between journeys. Perhaps they had already been restraining their curiosity, and they left, fearful that their glances, like a field of nesting birds, might be startled and caught. Poverty hurt, and that was their first reason for leaving. But another, final reason for leaving the crowded house was the never-said.

She may have been unusually beloved, the precious only daughter, spoiled and mirror gazing because of the affection the family lavished on her. When her husband left, they welcomed the chance to take her back from the in-laws; she could live like the little daughter for just a while longer. There are stories that my grandfather was different from other people, "crazy ever since the little Jap bayoneted him in the head." He used to put his naked penis on the dinner table, laughing. And one day he brought home a baby girl, wrapped up inside his brown western-style greatcoat. He had traded one of his sons, probably my father, the youngest, for her. My grandmother made him trade back. When he finally got a daughter of his own, he doted on her. They must have all loved her, except perhaps my father, the only brother who never went back to China, having once been traded for a girl.

Brothers and sisters, newly men and women, had to efface their sexual color and present plain miens. Disturbing hair and eyes, a smile like no other, threatened the ideal of five generations living under one roof. To focus blurs, people shouted face to face and yelled from room to room. The immigrants I know have loud voices, unmodulated to American tones even after years away from the village where they called their friendships out across the fields. I have not been able to stop my mother's screams in public libraries or over telephones. Walking erect (knees straight, toes pointed forward, not pigeon-toed, which is Chinese-feminine) and speaking in an inaudible voice, I have tried to turn myself American-feminine. Chinese communication was loud, public. Only sick people had to whisper. But at the dinner table, where the family members came nearest one another, no one could talk, not the outcasts nor any eaters. Every word that falls from the mouth is a coin lost. Silently they gave and accepted food with both hands. A preoccupied child who took his bowl with one hand got a sideways glare. A complete moment of total attention is due everyone alike. Children and lovers have no singularity here, but my aunt used a secret voice, a separate attentiveness.

She kept the man's name to herself throughout her labor and dying; she did not accuse him that he be punished with her. To save her inseminator's name she gave silent birth.

He may have been somebody in her own household, but intercourse with a man outside the family would have been no less abhorrent. All the village were kinsmen, and the titles shouted in loud country voices never let kinship be forgotten. Any man within visiting distance would have been neutralized as a lover—"brother," "younger brother," "older brother"—one hundred and fifteen relationship titles. Parents researched birth charts probably not so much to assure good fortune as to circumvent incest in a population that has but one hundred surnames. Everybody has eight million relatives. How useless then sexual mannerisms, how dangerous.

As if it came from an atavism deeper than fear, I used to add "brother" silently to boys' names. It hexed the boys, who would or would not ask me to dance, and made them less scary and as familiar and deserving of benevolence as girls.

But, of course, I hexed myself also—no dates. I should have stood up, both arms waving, and shouted out across libraries, "Hey, you! Love me back." I had no idea, though, how to make attraction selective, how to control its direction and magnitude. If I made myself American-pretty so that the five or six Chinese boys in the class fell in love with me, everyone else—the Caucasian, Negro, and Japanese boys—would too. Sisterliness, dignified and honorable, made much more sense.

Attraction eludes control so stubbornly that whole societies designed to organize relationships among people cannot keep order, not even when they bind people to one another from childhood and raise them together. Among the very poor and the wealthy, brothers married their adopted sisters, like doves. Our family allowed some romance, paying adult brides' prices and providing dowries so that their sons and daughters could marry strangers. Marriage promises to turn strangers into friendly relatives—a nation of siblings.

In the village structure, spirits shimmered among the live creatures, balanced and held in equilibrium by time and land. But one human being flaring up into violence could open up a black hole, a maelstrom that pulled in the sky. The frightened villagers, who depended on one another to maintain the real, went to my aunt to show her a personal, physical representation of the break she had made in the "roundness." Misallying couples snapped off the future, which was to be embodied in true offspring. The villagers punished her for acting as if she could have a private life, secret and apart from them.

If my aunt had betrayed the family at a time of large grain yields and peace, when many boys were born, and wings were being built on many houses, perhaps she might have escaped such severe punishment. But the men—hungry, greedy, tired of planting in dry soil, cuckolded—had had to leave the village in order to send food-money home. There were ghost plagues, bandit plagues, wars with the Japanese, floods. My Chinese brother and sister had died of an unknown sickness. Adultery, perhaps only a mistake during good times, became a crime when the village needed food.

The round moon cakes and round doorways, the round tables of graduated size that fit one roundness inside another, round windows and rice bowls— these talismans had lost their power to warn this family of the law: a family must be whole, faithfully keeping the descent line by having sons to feed the old and the dead, who in turn look after the family. The villagers came to show my aunt and her lover-in-hiding a broken house. The villagers were speeding up the circling of events because she was too shortsighted to see that her infidelity had already harmed the village, that waves of consequences would return unpredictably, sometimes in disguise, as now, to hurt her. This roundness had to be made coin-sized so that she would see its circumference: punish her at the birth of her baby. Awaken her to the inexorable. People who refused fatalism because they could invent small resources insisted on culpability. Deny accidents and wrest fault from the stars.

After the villagers left, their lanterns now scattering in various directions toward home, the family broke their silence and cursed her. "Aiaa, we're going to die. Death is coming. Death is coming. Look what you've done. You've killed us. Ghost! Dead ghost! Ghost! You've never been born." She ran out into the fields, far enough from the house so that she could no longer hear their voices, and pressed herself against the earth, her own land no more. When she felt the birth coming, she thought that she had been hurt. Her body seized together. "They've hurt me too much," she thought. "This is gall, and it will kill me." With forehead and knees against the earth, her body convulsed and then relaxed. She turned on her back, lay on the ground. The black well of sky and stars went out and out and out forever; her body and her complexity seemed to disappear, without home, without a companion, in eternal cold and silence. An agoraphobia rose in her, speeding higher and higher, bigger and bigger; she would not be able to contain it; there would be no end to fear.

Flayed, unprotected against space, she felt pain return, focusing her body. This pain chilled her—a cold, steady kind of surface pain. Inside, spasmodically, the other pain, the pain of the child, heated her. For hours she lay on the ground, alternately body and space. Sometimes a vision of normal comfort obliterated reality: she saw the family in the evening gambling at the dinner table, the young people massaging their elders' backs. She saw them congratulating one another, high joy on the mornings the rice shoots came up. When these pictures burst, the stars drew yet further apart. Black space opened.

She got to her feet to fight better and remembered that old-fashioned women gave birth in their pigsties to fool the jealous, pain-dealing gods, who do not snatch piglets. Before the next spasms could stop her, she ran to the pigsty, each step a rushing out into emptiness. She climbed over the fence and knelt in the dirt. It was good to have a fence enclosing her, a tribal person alone.

Laboring, this woman who had carried her child as a foreign growth that sickened her every day, expelled it at last. She reached down to touch the hot, wet, moving mass, surely smaller than anything human, and could feel that it was human after all—fingers, toes, nails, nose. She pulled it up on to her belly, and it lay curled there, butt in the air, feet precisely tucked one under the other. She opened her loose shirt and buttoned the child inside. After resting, it squirmed and thrashed and she pushed it up to her breast. It turned its head this way and that until it found her nipple. There, it made little snuffling noises. She clenched her teeth at its preciousness, lovely as a young calf, a piglet, a little dog.

She may have gone to the pigsty as a last act of responsibility: she would protect this child as she had protected its father. It would look after her soul, leaving supplies on her grave. But how would this tiny child without family find her grave when there would be no marker for her anywhere, neither in the earth nor the family hall? No one would give her a family hall name. She had taken the child with her into the wastes. At its birth the two of them had felt the same raw pain of separation, a wound that only the family pressing tight could close. A child with no descent line would not soften her life but only trail after her, ghost-like, begging her to give it purpose. At dawn the villagers on their way to the fields would stand around the fence and look.

Full of milk, the little ghost slept. When it awoke, she hardened her breasts against the milk that crying loosens. Toward morning she picked up the baby and walked to the well.

Carrying the baby to the well shows loving. Otherwise abandon it. Turn its face into the mud. Mothers who love their children take them along. It was probably a girl; there is some hope of forgiveness for boys.

"Don't tell anyone you had an aunt. Your father does not want to hear her name. She has never been born." I have believed that sex was unspeakable and words so strong and fathers so frail that "aunt" would do my father mysterious harm. I have thought that my family, having settled among immigrants who had also been their neighbors in the ancestral land, needed to clean their name, and a wrong word would incite the kinspeople even here. But there is more to this silence: they want me to participate in her punishment. And I have.

In the twenty years since I heard this story I have not asked for details nor said my aunt's name; I do not know it. People who can comfort the dead can also chase after them to hurt them further—a reverse ancestor worship. The real punishment was not the raid swiftly inflicted by the villagers, but the family's deliberately forgetting her. Her betrayal so maddened them, they saw to it that she would suffer forever, even after death. Always hungry, always needing, she would have to beg food from other ghosts, snatch and steal it from those whose living descendants give them gifts. She would have to fight the ghosts massed at crossroads for the buns a few thoughtful citizens leave to decoy her away from village and home so that the ancestral spirits could feast unharassed. At peace, they could act like gods, not ghosts, their descent lines providing them with paper suits and dresses, spirit money, paper houses, paper automobiles, chicken, meat, and rice into eternity—essences delivered up in smoke and flames, steam and incense rising from each rice bowl. In an attempt to make the Chinese care for people outside the family, Chairman Mao encourages us now to give our paper replicas to the spirits of outstanding soldiers and workers, no matter whose ancestors they may be. My aunt remains forever hungry. Goods are not distributed evenly among the dead.

My aunt haunts me—her ghost drawn to me because now, after fifty years of neglect, I alone devote pages of paper to her, though not origamied into houses and clothes. I do not think she always means me well. I am telling on her, and she was a spite suicide, drowning herself in the drinking water. The Chinese are always very frightened of the drowned one, whose weeping ghost, wet hair hanging and skin bloated, waits silently by the water to pull down a substitute.

Suggestions for Discussion

1. What is the tone of the author's address to Chinese Americans? In what sense does this paragraph logically follow her mother's story?

2. Why must Chinese emigrants try to confuse their offspring as well as "the gods"?

3. How did the author piece together the reasons for her aunt's adultery?

4. With what details does the reader get a picture of the lives of daughters in old China?

5. What does the phrase "taking a daughter-in-law" as a synonym for marriage tell the reader about men–women relationships in old China?

6. With what details do you learn about differing attitudes toward boys and girls?

7. Compare the conjectured and real behavior of the aunt's lover with hers after her ostracism.

8. How did the economy, plagues, floods, and wars affect attitudes toward adultery?

9. Trace the organization of the aunt's story. Compare the way in which it is narrated in the mother's words and in those of the author. What purpose is served by the author's intervening introspections?

10. How does the author account for the aunt's suicide?

11. How does Kingston convey that the story of her aunt was a story "to grow up on"? Kingston speaks of being haunted by the ghost of her aunt. What do her introspections tell you implicitly of her sense of self?

Suggestions for Writing

1. Narrate a story "to grow up on" that tested your "strength to establish realities."

2. The critic John Leonard called the book, in which this is the first chapter, "a poem turned into a sword." Justify this assessment by analyzing the writer's diction and tone.

Russell Baker

My Lack of Gumption

Russell Baker (b. 1925) has been a journalist throughout his professional career. After graduating from Johns Hopkins University, he worked as a reporter and in 1954 served as a correspondent for the *New York Times* in Washington, D.C., where he was variously assigned to the White House, the State Department, national politics, and the activities of Congress. He subsequently became a columnist for the *New York Times* and won a Pulitzer Prize in 1979. He won a second Pulitzer Prize in 1983 for his autobiography, entitled *Growing Up*, which has been followed by *The Good Times* (1989) and *There's a Country in My Cellar* (1990). Although Baker writes about his boyhood with a light touch and an irreverent humor, there is an overtone of pathos and seriousness in his description of the people and forces that lead to a young boy's development of a sense of self.

I began working in journalism when I was eight years old. It was my mother's idea. She wanted me to "make something" of myself and, after a level-headed appraisal of my strengths, decided I had better start young if I was to have any chance of keeping up with the competition.

The flaw in my character which she had already spotted was lack of "gumption." My idea of a perfect afternoon was lying in front of the radio rereading my favorite Big Little Book, *Dick Tracy Meets Stooge Viller*. My mother despised inactivity. Seeing me having a good time in repose, she was powerless to hide her disgust. "You've got no more gumption than a bump on a log," she said. "Get out in the kitchen and help Doris do those dirty dishes."

My sister Doris, though two years younger than I, had enough gumption for a dozen people. She positively enjoyed washing dishes, making beds, and cleaning the house. When she was only seven she could carry a piece of short-weighted cheese back to the A&P, threaten the manager with legal action, and come back triumphantly with the full quarter-pound we'd paid for and a few ounces extra thrown in for forgiveness. Doris could have made something of herself if she hadn't been a girl. Because of this defect, however, the best she could hope for was a career as a nurse or schoolteacher, the only work that capable females were considered up to in those days.

This must have saddened my mother, this twist of fate that had allocated all the gumption to the daughter and left her with a son who was content with Dick Tracy and Stooge Viller. If disappointed, though, she wasted no energy on self-pity. She would make me make something of myself whether I wanted to or not. "The Lord helps those who help themselves," she said. That was the way her mind worked.

She was realistic about the difficulty. Having sized up the material the Lord had given her to mold, she didn't overestimate what she could do with it. She didn't insist that I grow up to be President of the United States.

Fifty years ago parents still asked boys if they wanted to grow up to be President, and asked it not jokingly but seriously. Many parents who were hardly more than paupers still believed their sons could do it. Abraham Lincoln had done it. We were only sixty-five years from Lincoln. Many a grandfather who walked among us could remember Lincoln's time. Men of grandfatherly age were the worse for asking if you wanted to grow up to be President. A surprising number of little boys said yes and meant it.

I was asked many times myself. No, I would say, I didn't want to grow up to be President. My mother was present during one of these interrogations. An elderly uncle, having posed the usual question and exposed my lack of interest in the Presidency, asked, "Well, what *do* you want to be when you grow up?"

I loved to pick through trash piles and collect empty bottles, tin cans with pretty labels, and discarded magazines. The most desirable job on earth sprang instantly to mind. "I want to be a garbage man," I said.

My uncle smiled, but my mother had seen the first distressing evidence of a bump budding on a log. "Have a little gumption, Russell," she said. Her calling me Russell was a signal of unhappiness. When she approved of me I was always "Buddy."

When I turned eight years old she decided that the job of starting me on the road toward making something of myself could no longer be safely delayed. "Buddy," she said one day, "I want you to come home right after school this afternoon. Somebody's coming and I want you to meet him."

When I burst in that afternoon she was in conference in the parlor with an executive of the Curtis Publishing Company. She introduced me. He bent low from the waist and shook my hand. Was it true as my mother had told him, he asked, that I longed for the opportunity to conquer the world of business?

My mother replied that I was blessed with a rare determination to make something of myself.

"That's right," I whispered.

"But have you got the grit, the character, the never-say-quit spirit it takes to succeed in business?"

My mother said I certainly did.

"That's right," I said.

He eyed me silently for a long pause, as though weighing whether I could be trusted to his confidence, then spoke man-to-man. Before taking a crucial step, he said, he wanted to advise me that working for the Curtis Publishing Company placed enormous responsibility on a young man. It was one of the great companies of America. Perhaps the greatest publishing house in the world. I had heard, no doubt, of the *Saturday Evening Post?*

Heard of it? My mother said that everyone in our house had heard of the *Saturday Post* and that I, in fact, read it with religious devotion.

Then doubtless, he said, we were also familiar with those two monthly pillars of the magazine world, the *Ladies Home Journal* and the *Country Gentlemen.*

Indeed we were familiar with them, said my mother.

Representing the *Saturday Evening Post* was one of the weightiest honors that could be bestowed in the world of business, he said. He was personally proud of being a part of that great corporation.

My mother said he had every right to be.

Again he studied me as though debating whether I was worthy of a knight-hood. Finally: "Are you trustworthy?"

My mother said I was the soul of honesty.

"That's right," I said.

The caller smiled for the first time. He told me I was a lucky young man. He admired my spunk. Too many young men thought life was all play. Those young men would not go far in this world. Only a young man willing to work and save and keep his face washed and his hair neatly combed could hope to come out on top in a world such as ours. Did I truly and sincerely believe that I was such a young man?

"He certainly does," said my mother.

"That's right," I said.

He said he had been so impressed by what he had seen of me that he was going to make me a representative of the Curtis Publishing Company. On the following Tuesday, he said, thirty freshly printed copies of the *Saturday Evening Post* would be delivered at our door. I would place these magazines, still damp with the ink of the presses, in a handsome canvas bag, sling it over my shoulder, and set forth through the streets to bring the best in journalism, fiction, and cartoons to the American public.

He had brought the canvas bag with him. He presented it with reverence fit for a chasuble. He showed me how to drape the sling over my left shoulder and across the chest so that the pouch lay easily accessible to my right hand, allowing the best in journalism, fiction, and cartoons to be swiftly extracted and sold to a citizenry whose happiness and security depended upon us soldiers of the free press.

The following Tuesday I raced home from school, put the canvas bag over my shoulder, dumped the magazines in, and, tilting to the left to balance their weight on my right hip, embarked on the highway of journalism.

We lived in Belleville, New Jersey, a commuter town at the northern fringe of Newark. It was 1932, the bleakest year of the Depression. My father had died two years before, leaving us with a few pieces of Sears, Roebuck furniture and not much else, and my mother had taken Doris and me to live with one of her younger brothers. This was my Uncle Allen. Uncle Allen had made something of himself by 1932. As salesman for a soft-drink bottler in Newark, he had an income of $30 a week; wore pearl-gray spats, detachable collars, and a three-piece suit; was happily married; and took in threadbare relatives.

With my load of magazines I headed toward Belleville Avenue. That's where the people were. There were two filling stations at the intersection with Union Avenue, as well as an A&P, a fruit stand, a bakery, a barber shop, Zuccarelli's drugstore, and a diner shaped like a railroad car. For several hours I made myself highly visible, shifting position now and then from corner to corner, from shop window to shop window, to make sure everyone could see the heavy black lettering on the canvas bag that said the *Saturday Evening Post*. When the angle of the light indicated it was suppertime, I walked back to the house.

"How many did you sell, Buddy?" my mother asked.

"None."

"Where did you go?"

"The corner of Belleville and Union Avenues."

"What did you do?"

"Stood on the corner waiting for somebody to buy a *Saturday Evening Post*."

"You just stood there?"

"Didn't sell a single one."

"For God's sake, Russell!"

Uncle Allen intervened. "I've been thinking about it for some time," he said, "and I've about decided to take the *Post* regularly. Put me down as a regular customer." I handed him a magazine and he paid me a nickel. It was the first nickel I earned.

Afterwards my mother instructed me in salesmanship. I would have to ring doorbells, address adults with charming self-confidence, and break down resistance with a sales talk pointing out that no one, no matter how poor, could afford to be without the *Saturday Evening Post* in the home.

I told my mother I'd changed my mind about wanting to succeed in the magazine business.

"If you think I'm going to raise a good-for-nothing," she replied, "you've got another think coming." She told me to hit the streets with the canvas bag and start ringing doorbells the instant school was out next day. When I objected that I didn't feel any aptitude for salesmanship, she asked how I'd like to lend her my leather belt so she could whack some sense into me. I bowed to superior will and entered journalism with a heavy heart.

My mother and I had fought this battle almost as long as I could remember. It probably started even before memory began, when I was a country child in northern Virginia and my mother, dissatisfied with my father's plain workman's life, determined that I would not grow up like him and his people, with calluses on their hands, overalls on their backs, and fourth-grade educations in their heads. She had fancier ideas of life's possibilities. Introducing me to the *Saturday Evening Post*, she was trying to wean me as early as possible from my father's world where men left with their lunch pails at sunup, worked with their hands until the grime ate into the pores, and died with a few sticks of mail-order furniture as their legacy. In my mother's vision of the better life there were desks and white collars, well-pressed suits, evenings of reading and lively talk, and perhaps—if a man were very, very lucky and hit the jackpot, really made something important of himself—perhaps there might be a fantastic salary of $5,000 a year to support a big house and a Buick with a rumble seat and a vacation in Atlantic City.

And so I set forth with my sack of magazines. I was afraid of the dogs that snarled behind the doors of potential buyers. I was timid about ringing the doorbells of strangers, relieved when no one came to the door, and scared when someone did. Despite my mother's instructions, I could not deliver an engaging sales pitch. When a door opened I simply asked, "Want to buy a *Saturday Evening Post?*" In Belleville few persons did. It was a town of 30,000 people, and most weeks I rang a fair majority of its doorbells. But I rarely sold my thirty copies. Some weeks I canvassed the entire town for six days and still had four or five unsold magazines on Monday evening; then I dreaded the coming of Tuesday morning, when a batch of thirty fresh *Saturday Evening Posts* was due at the front door.

"Better get out there and sell the rest of those magazines tonight," my mother would say.

I usually posted myself then at a busy intersection where a traffic light controlled commuter flow from Newark. When the light turned red I stood on the curb and shouted my sales pitch at the motorists.

"Want to buy a *Saturday Evening Post?*"

One rainy night when car windows were sealed against me I came back soaked and with not a single sale to report. My mother beckoned to Doris.

"Go back down there with Buddy and show him how to sell those magazines," she said.

Brimming with zest, Doris, who was then seven years old, returned with me to the corner. She took a magazine from the bag, and when the light turned red she strode to the nearest car and banged her small fist against the closed window. The driver, probably startled at what he took to be a midget assaulting his car, lowered the window to stare and Doris thrust a *Saturday Evening Post* at him.

"You need this magazine," she piped, "and it only costs a nickel."

Her salesmanship was irresistible. Before the light changed half a dozen times she disposed of the entire batch. I didn't feel humiliated. To the contrary. I was so happy I decided to give her a treat. Leading her to the vegetable store on Belleville Avenue, I bought three apples, which cost a nickel, and gave her one.

"You shouldn't waste money," she said.

"Eat your apple." I bit into mine.

"You shouldn't eat before supper," she said. "It'll spoil your appetite."

Back at the house that evening, she dutifully reported me for wasting a nickel. Instead of a scolding, I was rewarded with a pat on the back for having the good sense to buy fruit instead of candy. My mother reached into her bottomless supply of maxims and told Doris, "An apple a day keeps the doctor away."

By the time I was ten I had learned all my mother's maxims by heart. Asking to stay up past normal bedtime, I knew that a refusal would be explained with, "Early to bed and early to rise, makes a man healthy, wealthy, and wise." If I whimpered about having to get up early in the morning, I could depend on her to say, "The early bird gets the worm."

The one I most despised was, "If at first you don't succeed, try, try again." This was the battle cry with which she constantly sent me back into the hopeless struggle whenever I moaned that I had rung every doorbell in town and knew there wasn't a single potential buyer left in Belleville that week. After listening to my explanation, she handed me the canvas bag and said, "If at first you don't succeed . . ."

Three years in that job, which I would gladly have quit after the first day except for her insistence, produced at least one valuable result. My mother finally concluded that I would never make something of myself by pursuing a life in business and started considering careers that demanded less competitive zeal.

One evening when I was eleven I brought home a short "composition" on my summer vacation which the teacher had graded with an A. Reading it with her own schoolteacher's eye, my mother agreed that it was top-drawer seventh grade prose and complimented me. Nothing more was said about it immediately, but a new idea had taken life in her mind. Halfway through supper she suddenly interrupted the conversation.

"Buddy," she said, "maybe you could be a writer."

I clasped the idea to my heart. I had never met a writer, had shown no previous urge to write, and hadn't a notion how to become a writer, but I loved stories and thought that making up stories must surely be almost as much fun as reading them. Best of all, though, and what really gladdened my heart, was the ease of the writer's life. Writers did not have to trudge through the town peddling from canvas bags, defending themselves against angry dogs, being rejected by surly strangers. Writers did not have to ring doorbells. So far as I could make out, what writers did couldn't even be classified as work.

I was enchanted. Writers didn't have to have any gumption at all. I did not dare tell anybody for fear of being laughed at in the schoolyard, but secretly I decided that what I'd like to be when I grew up was a writer.

Suggestions for Discussion

1. What do the details of Baker's reminiscence suggest to you about the sense of self of an eight- and eleven-year-old boy?

2. What do the mother's responses to the executive of the Curtis Publishing Company tell you about Baker's view of his mother? What does his listing of his mother's maxims convey of his attitude toward his mother? What other devices does Baker use to acquaint the reader with his mother's character?

3. By what means does Baker make his sister, Doris, come to life?

4. Relate the title to the author's sense of self and to his mother's sense of him as a person.

5. With what details does Baker achieve a humorous tone?

Suggestions for Writing

1. Describe your childhood and/or adolescent views of what you might like to do when you were "grown up." You might present the changes that may have occurred in the form of a diary, a monologue, a dialogue, or a narrative in which you reminisce about your early years as Baker does.

2. Baker obviously scoffs at his mother's maxims. Why? Why are these maxims still repeated? What is their value? Their limitation?

Maya Angelou

Finishing School

Maya Angelou (b. 1928) has had careers as a dancer, a writer, a television writer and producer, an actress. She has also served as coordinator of the Martin Luther King Southern Christian Leadership Conference. In 1993 she delivered her poem, "On the Pulse of Morning," at the inauguration of President Clinton. Her books include, among others, I Know Why the Caged Bird Sings (1970), from which this selection is taken, and more recently, I Shall Not Be Moved (1990), Life Doesn't Frighten Me (1993), and Wouldn't Take Nothing for My Journey Now (1993). The irony of the title is immediately apparent to the reader of this graphic portrait of Angelou's racist employer.

Recently a white woman from Texas, who would quickly describe herself as a liberal, asked me about my hometown. When I told her that in Stamps my grandmother had owned the only Negro general merchandise store since the turn of the century, she exclaimed, "Why, you were a debutante." Ridiculous and even ludicrous. But Negro girls in small Southern towns, whether poverty-stricken or just munching along on a few of life's necessities, were given as extensive and irrelevant preparations for adulthood as rich white girls shown in magazines. Admittedly the training was not the same. While white girls learned to waltz and sit gracefully with a tea cup balanced on their knees, we were lagging behind, learning the mid-Victorian values with very little money to indulge them. . . .

We were required to embroider and I had trunkfuls of colorful dishtowels, pillowcases, runners and handkerchiefs to my credit. I mastered the art of crocheting and tatting, and there was a life-time's supply of dainty doilies that would never be used in sacheted dresser drawers. It went without saying that all girls could iron and wash, but the finer touches around the home, like setting a table with real silver, baking roasts, and cooking vegetables without meat, had to be learned elsewhere. Usually at the source of those habits. During my tenth year, a white woman's kitchen became my finishing school.

Mrs. Viola Cullinan was a plump woman who lived in a three-bedroom house somewhere behind the post office. She was singularly unattractive until she smiled, and then the lines around her eyes and mouth which made her look perpetually dirty disappeared, and her face looked like the mask of an impish elf. She usually rested her smile until late afternoon when her women friends dropped in and Miss Glory, the cook, served them cold drinks on the closed-in porch.

The exactness of her house was inhuman. This glass went here and only here. That cup had its place and it was an act of impudent rebellion to place it anywhere else. At twelve-o'clock the table was set. At 12:15 Mrs. Cullinan sat down to dinner (whether her husband had arrived or not). At 12:16 Miss Glory brought out the food.

It took me a week to learn the difference between a salad plate, a bread plate, and a dessert plate.

Mrs. Cullinan kept up the tradition of her wealthy parents. She was from Virginia. Miss Glory, who was a descendant of slaves that had worked for the Cullinans, told me her history. She had married beneath her (according to Miss Glory). Her husband's family hadn't had their money very long and what they had "didn't 'mount to much."

As ugly as she was, I thought privately, she was lucky to get a husband above or beneath her station. But Miss Glory wouldn't let me say a thing against her mistress. She was very patient with me, however, over the housework. She explained the dishware, silverware, and servants' bells. The large round bowl in which soup was served wasn't a soup bowl, it was a tureen. There were goblets, sherbet glasses, ice-cream glasses, wine glasses, green glass coffee cups with matching saucers, and water glasses. I had a glass to drink from, and it sat with Miss Glory's on a separate shelf from the others. Soup spoons, gravy boat, butter knives, salad forks, and carving platter were additions to my vocabulary and in fact almost represented a new language. I was fascinated with the novelty, with the fluttering Mrs. Cullinan and her Alice-in-Wonderland house.

Her husband remains, in my memory, undefined. I lumped him with all the other white men that I had ever seen and tried not to see.

On our way home one evening, Miss Glory told me that Mrs. Cullinan couldn't have children. She said that she was too delicate-boned. It was hard to imagine bones at all under those layers of fat. Miss Glory went on to say that the doctor had taken out all her lady organs. I reasoned that a pig's organs included the lungs, heart and liver, so if Mrs. Cullinan was walking around without those essentials, it explained why she drank alcohol out of unmarked bottles. She was keeping herself embalmed.

When I spoke to Bailey about it, he agreed that I was right, but he also informed me that Mr. Cullinan had two daughters by a colored lady and that I knew them very well. He added that the girls were the spitting image of their father. I was unable to remember what he looked like, although I had just left him a few hours before, but I thought of the Coleman girls. They were very light-skinned and certainly didn't look very much like their mother (no one ever mentioned Mr. Coleman).

My pity for Mrs. Cullinan preceded me the next morning like the Cheshire cat's smile. Those girls, who could have been her daughters, were beautiful. They didn't have to straighten their hair. Even when they were caught in the rain, their braids still hung down straight like tamed snakes. Their mouths were pouty little cupid's bows. Mrs. Cullinan didn't know what she missed. Or maybe she did. Poor Mrs. Cullinan.

For weeks after, I arrived early, left late and tried very hard to make up for her barrenness. If she had had her own children, she wouldn't have had to ask me to run a thousand errands from her back door to the back door of her friends. Poor old Mrs. Cullinan.

Then one evening Miss Glory told me to serve the ladies on the porch. After I set the tray down and turned toward the kitchen, one of the women asked, "What's your name, girl?" It was the speckled-face one. Mrs. Cullinan said, "She doesn't talk much. Her name's Margaret."

"Is she dumb?"

"No. As I understand it, she can talk when she wants to but she's usually quiet as a little mouse. Aren't you, Margaret?"

I smiled at her. Poor thing. No organs and couldn't even pronounce my name correctly.

"She's a sweet little thing, though."

"Well, that may be, but the name's too long. I'd never bother myself. I'd call her Mary if I was you."

I fumed into the kitchen. That horrible woman would never have the chance to call me Mary because if I was starving I'd never work for her. . . .

That evening I decided to write a poem on being white, fat, old and without children. It was going to be a tragic ballad. I would have to watch her carefully to capture the essence of her loneliness and pain.

The very next day, she called me by the wrong name. Miss Glory and I were washing up the lunch dishes when Mrs. Cullinan came to the doorway. "Mary?"

Miss Glory asked, "Who?"

Mrs. Cullinan, sagging a little, knew and I knew. "I want Mary to go down to Mrs. Randall's and take her some soup. She's not been feeling well for a few days."

Miss Glory's face was a wonder to see. "You mean Margaret, ma'am. Her name's Margaret."

"That's too long. She's Mary from now on. Heat that soup from last night and put it in the china tureen and, Mary, I want you to carry it carefully."

Every person I knew had a hellish horror of being "called out of his name." It was a dangerous practice to call a Negro anything that could be loosely construed as insulting because of the centuries of their having been called niggers, jigs, dinges, blackbirds, crows, boots and spooks.

Miss Glory had a fleeting second of feeling sorry for me. Then as she handed me the hot tureen she said, "Don't mind, don't pay that no mind. Sticks and stones may break your bones, but words . . . You know, I been working for her for twenty years."

She held the back door open for me. "Twenty years. I wasn't much older than you. My name used to be Hallelujah. That's what Ma named me, but my mistress give me 'Glory,' and it stuck. I likes it better too."

I was in the little path that ran behind the houses when Miss Glory shouted. "It's shorter too."

For a few seconds it was a tossup over whether I would laugh (imagine being named Hallelujah) or cry (imagine letting some white woman rename you for her convenience). My anger saved me from either outburst. I had to quit the job, but the problem was going to be how to do it. Momma wouldn't allow me to quit for just any reason.

"She's a peach. That woman is a real peach." Mrs. Randall's maid was talking as she took the soup from me, and I wondered what her name used to be and what she answered to now.

For a week I looked into Mrs. Cullinan's face as she called me Mary. She ignored my coming late and leaving early. Miss Glory was a little annoyed because I had begun to leave egg yolk on the dishes and wasn't putting much heart in polishing the silver. I hoped that she would complain to our boss, but she didn't.

Then Bailey solved my dilemma. He had me describe the contents of the cupboard and the particular plates she liked best. Her favorite piece was a casserole shaped like a fish and the green glass coffee cups. I kept his instructions in mind, so on the next day when Miss Glory was hanging out clothes and I had again been told to serve the old biddies on the porch, I dropped the empty serving tray. When I heard Mrs. Cullinan scream, "Mary!" I picked up the casserole and two of the green glass cups in readiness. As she rounded the kitchen door I let them fall on the tiled floor.

I could never absolutely describe to Bailey what happened next, because each time I got to the part where she fell on the floor and screwed up her ugly face to cry, we burst out laughing. She actually wobbled around on the floor and picked up shards of the cups and cried, "Oh, Momma. Oh, dear Gawd. It's Momma's china from Virginia. Oh, Momma, I sorry."

Miss Glory came running in from the yard and the women from the porch crowded around. Miss Glory was almost as broken up as her mistress. "You mean to say she broke our Virginia dishes? What we gone do?"

Mrs. Cullinan cried louder, "That clumsy nigger. Clumsy little black nigger."

Old speckled-face leaned down and asked, "Who did it, Viola? Was it Mary? Who did it?"

Everything was happening so fast I can't remember whether her action preceded her words, but I know that Mrs. Cullinan said, "Her name's Margaret, goddamn it, her name's Margaret." And she threw a wedge of the broken plate at me. It could have been the hysteria which put her aim off, but the flying crockery caught Miss Glory right over her ear and she started screaming.

I left the front door wide open so all the neighbors could hear.

Mrs. Cullinan was right about one thing. My name wasn't Mary.

Suggestions for Discussion

1. With what details does Angelou bring the Cullinan household to life?

2. Angelou's changed views of Mrs. Cullinan are very marked. Characterize the contrasting portraits and suggest the means by which each is made graphic.

3. What is the significance of the name changes? How do they contribute to Angelou's view of Mrs. Cullinan?

4. Angelou uses fresh and surprising language on occasion; how does the phrase (par. 1) "munching along on a few of life's necessities" contribute to her reminiscence? She states that Mrs. Viola Cullinan usually "rested her smile until late afternoon." What does that description tell you about her employer?

5. What does the enumeration of each type of glass and silverware contribute to Angelou's thesis?

6. What is Angelou's central thesis? Relate the title to her experiences. To whom does it appear to be addressed?

7. How would you describe the tone of the piece? Cite examples in which the diction contributes to the tone. Cite examples of irony.

Suggestions for Writing

1. Describe a person or situation in which your initial impressions were reversed or changed. By means of setting, characterization, dialogue, figurative language, and simple narrative account for your shifts in attitude.

2. Write a narrative in which you or a person you know are the victim of discrimination or injustice.

Judith Ortiz Cofer

Casa: A Partial Remembrance of a Puerto Rican Childhood

Judith Ortiz Cofer (b. 1952) is a native of Puerto Rico, although she immigrated to the United States as a small child. Educated in Florida and Georgia, where she still resides, she attended Oxford University as a Scholar of the English Speaking Union, and the prestigious Bread Loaf Writers' Conference. A teacher of both English and Spanish at the university level, she has received a number of awards for her poetry, including grants from the Witter Bynner Foundation and the National Endowment for the Arts. Her publications include, among others, *The Line of the Sun* (1989) and *Silent Dancing* (1990). In this selection she shows the reader how knowledge, of a kind not found in books, is passed from generation to generation through the medium of family storytelling.

At three or four o'clock in the afternoon, the hour of *café con leche*, the women of my family gathered in Mamá's living room to speak of important things and retell familiar stories meant to be overheard by us young girls, their daughters. In Mamá's house (everyone called my grandmother Mamá) was a large parlor built by my grandfather to his wife's exact specifications so that it was always cool, facing away from the sun. The doorway was on the side of the house so no one could walk directly into her living room. First they had to take a little stroll through and around her beautiful garden where prize-winning orchids grew in the trunk of an ancient tree she had hollowed out for that purpose. This room was furnished with several mahogany rocking chairs, acquired at the births of her children, and one intricately carved rocker that had passed down to Mamá at the death of her own mother.

It was on these rockers that my mother, her sisters, and my grandmother sat on these afternoons of my childhood to tell their stories, teaching each other, and my cousin and me, what it was like to be a woman, more specifically, a Puerto Rican woman. They talked about life on the island, and life in *Los Nueva Yores*, their way of referring to the United States from New York City to California: the other place, not home, all the same. They told real-life stories though, as I later learned, always embellishing them with a little or a lot of dramatic detail. And they told *cuentos*, the morality and cautionary tales told by the women in our family for generations: stories that became a part of my subconscious as I grew up in two worlds, the tropical island and the cold city, and that would later surface in my dreams and in my poetry.

One of these tales was about the woman who was left at the altar. Mamá liked to tell that one with histrionic intensity. I remember the rise and fall of her voice, the sighs, and her constantly gesturing hands, like two birds swooping through her words. This particular story usually would come up in a conversation as a result of someone mentioning a forthcoming engagement or wedding. The first time I remember hearing it, I was sitting on the floor at Mamá's feet, pretending to read a comic book. I may have been eleven or twelve years old, at that difficult age when a girl was no longer a child who could be ordered to leave the room if the women wanted freedom to take their talk into forbidden zones, nor really old enough to be considered a part of their conclave. I could only sit quietly, pretending to be in another world, while absorbing it all in a sort of unspoken agreement of my status as silent auditor. On this day, Mamá had taken my long, tangled mane of hair into her ever-busy hands. Without looking down at me and with no interruption of her flow of words, she began braiding my hair, working at it with the quickness and determination that characterized all her actions. My mother was watching us impassively from her rocker across the room. On her lips played a little ironic smile. I would never sit still for *her* ministrations, but even then, I instinctively knew that she did not possess Mamá's matriarchal power to command and keep everyone's attention. This was never more evident than in the spell she cast when telling a story.

"It is not like it used to be when I was a girl," Mamá announced. "Then, a man could leave a girl standing at the church altar with a bouquet of fresh flowers in her hands and disappear off the face of the earth. No way to track him down if he was from another town. He could be a married man, with maybe even two or three families all over the island. There was no way to know. And there were men who did this. Hombres with the devil in their flesh who would come to a pueblo, like this one, take a job at one of the haciendas, never meaning to stay, only to have a good time and to seduce the women."

The whole time she was speaking, Mamá would be weaving my hair into a flat plait that required pulling apart the two sections of hair with little jerks that made my eyes water; but knowing how grandmother detested whining and *boba* (sissy) tears, as she called them, I just sat up as straight and stiff as I did at La Escuela San Jose, where the nuns enforced good posture with a flexible plastic ruler they bounced off of slumped shoulders and heads. As Mamá's story progressed, I noticed how my young Aunt Laura lowered her eyes, refusing to meet Mamá's meaningful gaze. Laura was seventeen, in her last year of high school, and already engaged to a boy from another town who had staked his claim with a tiny diamond ring, then left for Los Nueva Yores to make his fortune. They were planning to get married in a year. Mamá had expressed serious doubts that the wedding would ever take place. In Mamá's eyes, a man set free without a legal contract was a man lost. She believed that marriage was not something men desired, but simply the price they had to pay for the privilege of children and, of course, for what no decent (synonymous with "smart") woman would give away for free.

"María La Loca was only seventeen when *it* happened to her." I listened closely at the mention of this name. María was a town character, a fat middle-aged woman who lived with her old mother on the outskirts of town. She was to be seen around the pueblo delivering the meat pies the two women made for a living. The most peculiar thing about María, in my eyes, was that she walked and moved like a little girl though she had the thick body and wrinkled face of an old woman. She would swing her hips in an exaggerated, clownish way, and sometimes even hop and skip up to someone's house. She spoke to no one. Even if you asked her a question, she would just look at you and smile, showing her yellow teeth. But I had heard that if you got close enough, you could hear her humming a tune without words. The kids yelled out nasty things at her, calling her *La Loca,* and the men who hung out at the bodega playing dominoes sometimes whistled mockingly as she passed by with her funny, outlandish walk. But María seemed impervious to it all, carrying her basket of *pasteles* like a grotesque Little Red Riding Hood through the forest.

María La Loca interested me, as did all the eccentrics and crazies of our pueblo. Their weirdness was a measuring stick I used in my serious quest for a definition of normal. As a Navy brat shuttling between New Jersey and the pueblo, I was constantly made to feel like an oddball by my peers, who made fun of my two-way accent: a Spanish accent when I spoke English, and when I spoke Spanish I was told that I sounded like a *Gringa.* Being the outsider had already turned my brother and me into cultural chameleons. We developed early on the ability to blend into a crowd, to sit and read quietly in a fifth story apartment building for days and days when it was too bitterly cold to play outside, or, set free, to run wild in Mamá's realm, where she took charge of our lives, releasing Mother for a while from the intense fear for our safety that our father's absences instilled in her. In order to keep us from harm when Father was away, Mother kept us under strict surveillance. She even walked us to and from Public School No. 11, which we attended during the months we lived in Paterson, New Jersey, our home base in the states. Mamá freed all three of us like pigeons from a cage. I saw her as my liberator and my model. Her stories were parables from which to glean the *Truth.*

"María La Loca was once a beautiful girl. Everyone thought she would marry the Méndez boy." As everyone knew, Rogelio Méndez was the richest man in town. "But," Mamá continued, knitting my hair with the same intensity she was putting into her story, "this *macho* made a fool out of her and ruined her life." She paused for the effect of her use of the word "macho," which at that time had not yet become a popular epithet for an unliberated man. This word had for us the crude and comical connotation of "male of the species," stud; a *macho* was what you put in a pen to increase your stock.

I peeked over my comic book at my mother. She too was under Mamá's spell, smiling conspiratorially at this little swipe at men. She was safe from Mamá's contempt in this area. Married at an early age, an unspotted lamb, she had been accepted by a good family of strict Spaniards whose name was old and respected, though their fortune had been lost long before my birth. In a rocker Papá had painted sky blue sat Mamá's oldest child, Aunt Nena. Mother of three children, stepmother of two more, she was a quiet woman who liked books but had married an ignorant and abusive widower whose main interest in life was accumulating wealth. He too was in the mainland working on his dream of returning home rich and triumphant to buy the *finca* of his dreams. She was waiting for him to send for her. She would leave her children with Mamá for several years while the two of them slaved away in factories. He would one day be a rich man, and she a sadder woman. Even now her life-light was dimming. She spoke little, an aberration in Mamá's house, and she read avidly, as if storing up spiritual food for the long winters that awaited her in Los Nueva Yores without her family. But even Aunt Nena came alive to Mamá's words, rocking gently, her hands over a thick book in her lap.

Her daughter, my cousin Sara, played jacks by herself on the tile porch outside the room where we sat. She was a year older than I. We shared a bed and all our family's secrets. Collaborators in search of answers, Sara and I discussed everything we heard the women say, trying to fit it all together like a puzzle that, once assembled, would reveal life's mysteries to us. Though she and I still enjoyed taking part in boys' games—chase, volleyball, and even *vaqueros*, the island version of cowboys and Indians involving cap-gun battles and violent shoot-outs under the mango tree in Mamá's back-yard—we loved best the quiet hours in the afternoon when the men were still at work, and the boys had gone to play serious baseball at the park. Then Mamá's house belonged only to us women. The aroma of coffee perking in the kitchen, the mesmerizing creaks and groans of the rockers, and the women telling their lives in *cuentos* are forever woven into the fabric of my imagination, braided like my hair that day I felt my grandmother's hands teaching me about strength, her voice convincing me of the power of story-telling.

That day Mamá told how the beautiful María had fallen prey to a man whose name was never the same in subsequent versions of the story; it was Juan one time, José, Rafael, Diego, another. We understood that neither the name nor any of the *facts* were important, only that a woman had allowed love to defeat her. Mamá put each of us in María's place by describing her wedding dress in loving detail: how she looked like a princess in her lace as she waited at the altar. Then, as Mamá approached the tragic denouement of her story, I was distracted by the sound of my Aunt Laura's violent rocking. She seemed on the verge of tears. She knew the fable was intended for her. That week she was going to have her wedding gown fitted, though no firm date had been set for the marriage. Mamá ignored Laura's obvious discom-fort, digging out a ribbon from the sewing basket she kept by her rocker while describing María's long illness, "a fever that would not break for days." She spoke of a mother's despair: "that woman climbed the church steps on her knees every morning, wore only black as a *promesa* to the Holy Virgin in exchange for her daughter's health." By the time María returned from her honeymoon with death, she was ravished, no longer young or sane. "As you can see, she is almost as old as her mother already," Mamá lamented while tying the ribbon to the ends of my hair, pulling it back with such force that I just knew I would never be able to close my eyes completely again.

"That María's getting crazier every day." Mamá's voice would take a lighter tone now, expressing satisfaction, either for the perfection of my braid, or for a story well told—it was hard to tell. "You know that tune María is always humming?" Carried away by her enthusiasm, I tried to nod, but Mamá still had me pinned between her knees.

"Well, that's the wedding march." Surprising us all, Mamá sang out, "Da, da, dara . . . da, da, dara." Then lifting me off the floor by my skinny shoulders, she would lead me around the room in an impromptu waltz—another session ending with the laughter of women, all of us caught up in the infectious joke of our lives.

Suggestions for Discussion

Relate each of the following quotations to the selection you have just read.

1. "It was on these rockers that my mother, her sisters, and my grandmother sat on these afternoons of my childhood to tell their stories, teaching each other, and my cousin and me, what it was like to be a woman, more specifically, a Puerto Rican woman."

2. "Collaborators in search of answers, Sara and I discussed everything we heard the women say, trying to fit it all together like a puzzle that, once assembled, would reveal life's mysteries to us."

3. "We understood that neither the name nor any of the *facts* were important, only that a woman had allowed love to defeat her."

Suggestions for Writing

1. Children learn much of their culture from eavesdropping on the adult world. Describe a time when you had this experience.

2. Cofer distinguishes between "facts" and "themes." Truth in storytelling has far more to do with one than the other. Write a story in which this is manifest.

Alice Walker

Beauty: When the Other Dancer Is the Self

Alice Walker (b. 1944) has received numerous awards for her fiction: *The Color Purple* (1982), a best-selling novel, was nominated for the Book Critics Circle Award and received the American Book Award, the Candace Award of the National Coalition of 100 Black Women, and a Pulitzer Prize. She has also published two collections of short stories, *You Can't Keep a Good Woman*

Down (1981) and *In Love and Trouble*. Her recent novel is *The Temple of My Familiar* (1989). Her recent book, *In Search of Our Mothers' Gardens: Womanist Prose* (1983), includes this reminiscence of the effect of a traumatic injury to her eye on her self-image.

It is a bright summer day in 1947. My father, a fat, funny man with beautiful eyes and a subversive wit, is trying to decide which of his eight children he will take with him to the county fair. My mother, of course, will not go. She is knocked out from getting most of us ready: I hold my neck stiff against the pressure of her knuckles as she hastily completes the braiding and then be-ribboning of my hair.

My father is the driver for the rich old white lady up the road. Her name is Miss Mey. She owns all the land for miles around, as well as the house in which we live. All I remember about her is that she once offered to pay my mother thirty-five cents for cleaning her house, raking up piles of her magnolia leaves, and washing her family's clothes, and that my mother—she of no money, eight children, and a chronic earache—refused it. But I do not think of this in 1947. I am two and a half years old. I want to go everywhere my daddy goes. I am excited at the prospect of riding in a car. Someone has told me fairs are fun. That there is room in the car for only three of us doesn't faze me at all. Whirling happily in my starchy frock, showing off my biscuit-polished patent-leather shoes and lavender socks, tossing my head in a way that makes my ribbons bounce, I stand, hands on hips, before my father. "Take me, Daddy," I say with assurance; "I'm the prettiest!"

Later, it does not surprise me to find myself in Miss Mey's shiny black car, sharing the back seat with the other lucky ones. Does not surprise me that I thoroughly enjoy the fair. At home that night I tell the unlucky ones all I can remember about the merry-go-round, the man who eats live chickens, and the teddy bears, until they say: that's enough, baby Alice. Shut up now, and go to sleep.

It is Easter Sunday, 1950. I am dressed in a green, flocked, scalloped-hem dress (handmade by my adoring sister, Ruth) that has its own smooth satin petticoat and tiny hot-pink roses tucked into each scallop. My shoes, new T-strap patent leather, again highly biscuit-polished. I am six years old and have learned one of the longest Easter speeches to be heard that day, totally unlike the speech I said when I was two: "Easter lilies / pure and white / blossom in / the morning light." When I rise to give my speech I do so on a great wave of love and pride and expectation. People in the church stop rustling their new crinolines. They seem to hold their breath. I can tell they admire my dress, but it is my spirit, bordering on sassiness (womanishness), they secretly applaud.

"That girl's a little *mess*," they whisper to each other, pleased.

Naturally I say my speech without stammer or pause, unlike those who stutter, stammer, or, worst of all, forget. This is before the word "beautiful" exists in people's vocabulary, but "Oh, isn't she the *cutest* thing!" frequently floats my way. "And got so much sense!" they gratefully add . . . for which thoughtful addition I thank them to this day.

It was great fun being cute. But then, one day, it ended.

I am eight years old and a tomboy. I have a cowboy hat, cowboy boots, checkered shirt and pants, all red. My playmates are my brothers, two and four years older than I. Their colors are black and green, the only difference in the way we are dressed. On Saturday nights we all go to the picture show, even my mother; Westerns are her favorite kind of movie. Back home, "on the ranch," we pretend we are Tom Mix, Hopalong Cassidy, Lash LaRue (we've even named one of our dogs Lash LaRue); we chase each other for hours rustling cattle, being outlaws, delivering damsels from distress. Then my parents decide to buy my brothers guns. These are not "real" guns. They shoot "BBs," copper pellets my brothers say will kill birds. Because I am a girl, I do not get a gun. Instantly I am relegated to the position of Indian. Now there appears a great distance between us. They shoot and shoot at everything with their new guns. I try to keep up with my bow and arrows.

One day while I am standing on top of our makeshift "garage"—pieces of tin nailed across some poles—holding my bow and arrow and looking out toward the fields, I feel an incredible blow in my right eye. I look down just in time to see my brother lower his gun.

Both brothers rush to my side. My eye stings, and I cover it with my hand. "If you tell," they say, "we will get a whipping. You don't want that to happen, do you?" I do not. "Here is a piece of wire," says the older brother, picking it up from the roof; "say you stepped on one end of it and the other flew up and hit you." The pain is beginning to start. "Yes," I say. "Yes, I will say that is what happened." If I do not say this is what happened, I know my brothers will find ways to make me wish I had. But now I will say anything that gets me to my mother.

Confronted by our parents we stick to the lie agreed upon. They place me on a bench on the porch and I close my left eye while they examine the right. There is a tree growing from underneath the porch that climbs past the railing to the roof. It is the last thing my right eye sees. I watch as its trunk, its branches, and then its leaves are blotted out by the rising blood.

I am in shock. First there is intense fever, which my father tries to break using lily leaves bound around my head. Then there are chills: my mother tries to get me to eat soup. Eventually, I do not know how, my parents learn what has happened. A week after the "accident" they take me to see a doctor. "Why did you wait so long to come?" he asks, looking into my eye and shaking his head. "Eyes are sympathetic," he says. "If one is blind, the other will likely become blind too."

This comment of the doctor's terrifies me. But it is really how I look that bothers me most. Where the BB pellet struck there is a glob of whitish scar tissue, a hideous cataract, on my eye. Now when I stare at people—a favorite pastime, up to now—they will stare back. Not at the "cute" little girl, but at her scar. For six years I do not stare at anyone, because I do not raise my head.

Years later, in the throes of a mid-life crisis, I ask my mother and sister whether I changed after the "accident." "No," they say, puzzled. "What do you mean?"

What do I mean?

I am eight, and, for the first time, doing poorly in school, where I have been something of a whiz since I was four. We have just moved to the place where the "accident" occurred. We do not know any of the people around us because this is a different county. The only time I see the friends I knew is when we go back to our old church. The new school is the former state penitentiary. It is a large stone building, cold and drafty, crammed to overflowing with boisterous, ill-disciplined children. On the third floor there is a huge circular imprint of some partition that has been torn out.

"What used to be here?" I ask a sullen girl next to me on our way past it to lunch.

"The electric chair," says she.

At night I have nightmares about the electric chair, and about all the people reputedly "fried" in it. I am afraid of the school, where all the students seem to be budding criminals.

"What's the matter with your eye?" they ask, critically.

When I don't answer (I cannot decide whether it was an "accident" or not), they shove me, insist on a fight.

My brother, the one who created the story about the wire, comes to my rescue. But then brags so much about "protecting" me, I become sick.

After months of torture at the school, my parents decide to send me back to our old community, to my old school. I live with my grandparents and the teacher they board. But there is no room for Phoebe, my cat. By the time my grandparents decide there *is* room, and I ask for my cat, she cannot be found. Miss Yarborough, the boarding teacher, takes me under her wing, and begins to teach me to play the piano. But soon she marries an African—a "prince," she says—and is whisked away to his continent.

At my old school there is at least one teacher who loves me. She is the teacher who "knew me before I was born" and bought my first baby clothes. It is she who makes life bearable. It is her presence that finally helps me turn on the one child at the school who continually calls me "one-eyed bitch." One day I simply grab him by his coat and beat him until I am satisfied. It is my teacher who tells me my mother is ill.

My mother is lying in bed in the middle of the day, something I have never seen. She is in too much pain to speak. She has an abscess in her ear. I stand looking down on her, knowing that if she dies, I cannot live. She is being treated with warm oils and hot bricks held against her cheek. Finally a doctor comes. But I must go back to my grandparents' house. The weeks pass but I am hardly aware of it. All I know is that my mother might die, my father is not so jolly, my brothers still have their guns, and I am the one sent away from home.

"You did not change," they say.

Did I imagine the anguish of never looking up?

I am twelve. When relatives come to visit I hide in my room. My cousin Brenda, just my age, whose father works in the post office and whose mother is a nurse, comes to find me. "Hello," she says. And then she asks, looking at my recent school picture, which I did not want taken, and on which the "glob," as I think of it, is clearly visible, "You still can't see out of that eye?"

"No," I say, and flop back on the bed over my book.

That night, as I do almost every night, I abuse my eye. I rant and rave at it, in front of the mirror. I plead with it to clear up before morning. I tell it I hate and despise it. I do not pray for sight. I pray for beauty.

"You did not change," they say.

I am fourteen and baby-sitting for my brother Bill, who lives in Boston. He is my favorite brother and there is a strong bond between us. Understanding my feelings of shame and ugliness he and his wife take me to a local hospital, where the "glob" is removed by a doctor named O. Henry. There is still a small bluish crater where the scar tissue was, but the ugly white stuff is gone. Almost immediately I become a different person from the girl who does not raise her head. Or so I think. Now that I've raised my head I win the boyfriend of my dreams. Now that I've raised my head I have plenty of friends. Now that I've raised my head classwork comes from my lips as faultlessly as Easter speeches did, and I leave high school as valedictorian, most popular student, and *queen*, hardly believing my luck. Ironically, the girl who was voted most beautiful in our class (and was) was later shot twice through the chest by a male companion, using a "real" gun, while she was pregnant. But that's another story in itself. Or is it?

"You did not change," they say.

It is now thirty years since the "accident." A beautiful journalist comes to visit and to interview me. She is going to write a cover story for her magazine that focuses on my latest book. "Decide how you want to look on the cover," she says. "Glamorous, or whatever."

Never mind "glamorous," it is the "whatever" that I hear. Suddenly all I can think of is whether I will get enough sleep the night before the photography session: if I don't, my eye will be tired and wander, as blind eyes will.

At night in bed with my lover I think up reasons why I should not appear on the cover of a magazine. "My meanest critics will say I've sold out," I say. "My family will now realize I write scandalous books."

"But what's the real reason you don't want to do this?" he asks.

"Because in all probability," I say in a rush, "my eye won't be straight."

"It will be straight enough," he says. Then, "Besides, I thought you'd made your peace with that."

And I suddenly remember that I have.

I remember:

I am talking to my brother Jimmy, asking if he remembers anything unusual about the day I was shot. He does not know I consider that day the last time my father, with his sweet home remedy of cool lily leaves, chose me, and that I suffered and raged inside because of this. "Well," he says, "all I remember is standing by the side of the highway with Daddy, trying to flag down a car. A white man stopped, but when Daddy said he needed somebody to take his little girl to the doctor, he drove off."

I remember:

I am in the desert for the first time. I fall totally in love with it. I am so overwhelmed by its beauty, I confront for the first time, consciously, the meaning of the doctor's words years ago: "Eyes are sympathetic. If one is blind, the other will likely become blind too." I realize I have dashed about the world madly, looking at this, looking at that, storing up images against the fading of the light. *But I might have missed seeing the desert!* The shock of that possibility—and gratitude for over twenty-five years of sight—sends me literally to my knees. Poem after poem comes—which is perhaps how poets pray.

ON SIGHT

I am so thankful I have seen
The Desert
And the creatures in the desert
And the desert Itself.

The desert has its own moon
Which I have seen
With my own eye.

There is no flag on it.

Trees of the desert have arms
All of which are always up
That is because the moon is up
The sun is up
Also the sky
The stars
Clouds
None with flags.

If there *were* flags, I doubt
the trees would point.
Would you?

But mostly, I remember this:

I am twenty-seven, and my baby daughter is almost three. Since her birth
I have worried about her discovery that her mother's eyes are different from
other people's. Will she be embarrassed? I think. What will she say? Every
day she watches a television program called "Big Blue Marble." It begins
with a picture of the earth as it appears from the moon. It is bluish, a little
battered-looking, but full of light, with whitish clouds swirling around it. Every time I see it I weep with love, as if it is a picture of Grandma's house.
One day when I am putting Rebecca down for her nap, she suddenly focuses
on my eye. Something inside me cringes, gets ready to try to protect myself.
All children are cruel about physical differences, I know from experience,
and that they don't always mean to be is another matter. I assume Rebecca
will be the same.

But no-o-o-o. She studies my face intently as we stand, her inside and me
outside her crib. She even holds my face maternally between her dimpled
little hands. Then, looking every bit as serious and lawyerlike as her father,
she says, as if it may just possibly have slipped my attention: "Mommy,
there's a *world* in your eye." (As in, "Don't be alarmed, or do anything
crazy.") And then, gently, but with great interest: "Mommy, where did you
get that world in your eye?"

For the most part, the pain left then. (So what, if my brothers grew up to
buy even more powerful pellet guns for their sons and to carry real guns
themselves. So what, if a young "Morehouse man" once nearly fell off the
steps of Trevor Arnett Library because he thought my eyes were blue.) Crying and laughing I ran to the bathroom, while Rebecca mumbled and sang
herself off to sleep. Yes indeed, I realized, looking into the mirror. There *was*
a world in my eye. And I saw that it was possible to love it: that in fact, for all
it had taught me of shame and anger and inner vision, I *did* love it.

Even to see it drifting out of orbit in boredom, or rolling up out of fatigue, not to mention floating back at attention in excitement (bearing witness, a friend has called it), deeply suitable to my personality, and even characteristic of me.

That night I dream I am dancing to Stevie Wonder's song "Always" (the name of the song is really "As," but I hear it as "Always"). As I dance, whirling and joyous, happier than I've ever been in my life, another bright-faced dancer joins me. We dance and kiss each other and hold each other through the night. The other dancer has obviously come through all right, as I have done. She is beautiful, whole and free. And she is also me.

Suggestions for Discussion

1. How does the author use detail to portray herself at various ages? To portray her mother?

2. What changes in her personality and view of herself take place in the several age periods that Walker describes?

3. The line "you did not change" recurs. What is its relation to the narrative in the several scenes?

4. What is the significance of the repeated reference to raising her head at various stages of the author's development?

5. How does Walker equate prayer with poetry?

6. How does her daughter's comment on her eye affect her attitude?

7. What does the title signify?

Suggestions for Writing

1. Write a series of short vignettes illustrating how you viewed yourself and/or others viewed you at various stages of your development.

2. Describe the ways in which a traumatic episode in your childhood or that of a person close to you has affected your attitudes or behavior.

Garrison Keillor

Who Do You Think You Are?

Garrison Keillor (b. 1942) was the founder and radio host of "A Prairie Home Companion." A frequent contributor to The New Yorker, he has also written Happy to Be Here, Lake Wobegon Days, Leaving Home, and We Are Still Married. The selection that follows reflects his casual, anecdotal, and often flippant style of reminiscence.

It has been a quiet week in Lake Wobegon, my hometown was such a sweet line all those years on the radio, the standard opening of each week's story, a pleasant, modest *useful* sentence, considering how many writers stew over their opening lines (e.g., "Ray opened the refrigerator door and bent down to look for the margarine"), and most stories stop there and wind up in the wastebasket, brilliant stories wasted because the first sentence wasn't as brilliant as what would soon follow, so the writer quit and his masterpiece, his *In Our Time*, his *Great Gatsby*, his *Collected Stories of John Cheever*, never got written because the first sentence opened like a rusty gate, and is it so different for you and me? The marvelous work we could do if only we didn't have to *begin* it but could start in at the middle. The things we could accomplish if only we didn't know what we are doing until later.

It has been a quiet week in Lake Wobegon gets you right in there, into the dim recesses of the Chatterbox Cafe, the air lit up with the smell of hot caramel rolls, where three heavy men in dark-green shirts hunker in the back booth under the Allis Chalmers calendar ("Krebsbach Farm Implement / New & Used Since 1912 / JUniper 5610") and drink black coffee, refilled by Dorothy in her big pink uniform, who doesn't ask if they'd like more (Do bears pee in the woods?), she just pours, as they commiserate on the lousy world situation and console each other with a few beloved old jokes about animals in barrooms. There was this man who trained his dog to go around the corner to Bud's Lounge with a dollar bill under his collar and get a pack of cigarettes and bring them home, until one day the man only had a five, so he put it under the dog's collar and sent him down, waited an hour, and no dog, so he got mad and went to Bud's and there was the pooch sitting up on a stool drinking a vodka gimlet. He said, "You've never done this before!" The dog looked straight ahead and said, "I never had the money before."

One problem with *It has been a quiet week in Lake Wobegon* is that you couldn't go straight from that into talking about dreams of boundless grandeur and the many-rivered generosity of life, but, then, it was that way when I lived there, too. Dreams we did not discuss, they were embarrassing in normal conversation, especially big ones. We sat at supper, Dad at one end, Mother at the other, children in the stanchions along the sides, and talked quietly about the day's events. We might discuss the immediate future such as a history test the day after tomorrow or Bible camp next June, but the distant future, 1964, 1980, was inscrutable, due to the imminence of the Second Coming. And there was to be no grandeur. Once, just to see how it would sound coming out of my mouth, I said I was going to college someday. "College" rhymes with "knowledge." I was ten years old and words were as good as food in my mouth. I chewed my food fast so as to clear the way to be able to say more. "I'm going to go to college," I stated. My sister laughed: Who d'ya think *you* are? She was right, I didn't know.

What I didn't dare mention was my other dream of going into the show business, a faint dream because we were Christian people and wouldn't dream of doing immoral things, though I hoped to find a way around this. I mentioned S.B. to Mrs. Hoglund, the piano teacher, and she told me the story of the famous Swenson Sisters, who hailed from nearby Kimball, a girls' quartet who sang at summer resorts including Moonlite Bay and who, one cold winter day in 1954, won the St. Paul Winter Carnival Outdoor Talent Contest, and the next week boarded the morning Zephyr to Chicago and then the Super Chief to Hollywood. They signed a contract with Fairmont Pictures to make a movie called *Minnesota Moon* but then the producer, Leo Lawrence, took a deep drag on his stogie and growled, "Kids, I love this script, it's beautiful, I loved every bit of it except the cows and the lakes and the farmers—we're going to change them to camels and desert oases and thousands of Bedouins galloping hard over the desolate sands," so the movie became *Moon over Morocco* and the Swenson Sisters became the Casablanca Quartet, dressed in vast black robes, their faces veiled, and their career went down like a concrete block and by 1955 they were back at Gull Lake, singing at Hilmer's Supper Club (Beer & Setups, Fish Fry—All U Can Eat Friday Nites), and their dream was just an old black shell of a burned-down house. What's more, they, who had gone away innocent and filled with shining hope, returned home four hardened women with dark-crimson lipstick who smoked Luckys and drank vodka gimlets and when they laughed, they laughed a deep laugh, like men, laced with pain, and so of course men would have nothing to do with them, and they fell into unnatural forms of love. There ended the story; she would say no more. *They tried to go too far,* and it should be a lesson to the rest of us: not to imagine we *are* somebody but to be content being who we are, Minnesotans.

I'm very proud to be a Minnesotan and have been proud since I was a kid and first traveled to see our beautiful State Capitol building in St. Paul. Our fourth-grade class got up at six o'clock and rode a schoolbus down to meet the governor. We had studied state government for a month, the duties of governor, lieutenant governor, secretary of state, and other state officers, and the legislature and the state commissions and boards, which didn't prepare us for the grandeur and sheer magnificence of the great white temple spread on the crest of a gentle hill, the bank of steps rising to the pillars, the golden horses and golden chariot high above, and the dome, the largest anywhere in the Christian world, so it appeared. We camped in the bus, eating liverwurst sandwiches and drinking green Kool Aid, waiting for our 11:00 A.M. appointment. Mrs. Erickson said that she was trusting us to be on our best behavior indoors, but she didn't have to worry, we were stunned, we shuffled along with the dumb dignity of the barely conscious. Indoors was even more magnificent, such opulence as a child might imagine from fairy tales but never associate with our modest prairie state, long vast echoey marble halls, marble statues, oil paintings, and a room with a gold ceiling and a rug three inches thick, and there was the governor of Minnesota, the leader of our people, physically present in the room with us.

We formed a straight line and gravely filed one by one past Mrs. Erickson, who whispered our name to a grim-faced man, who then whispered it to the governor, who shook our hands and said, "Hello, Stanley, it's good to meet you." This was thrilling, until suddenly, when Mrs. Erickson whispered *Shirley*, Shirley clapped her hand over her mouth and rushed away to the toilet, but her name had gone into the pipeline and when the governor shook Billy's hand he said, "Hello, Shirley, it's good to meet you." He smiled the same warm smile and went right on calling all the rest of the class by the wrong name, including Elaine, who was called Robert. I was called John. He was the governor but he wasn't what you'd call bright.

It was so amazing how many kids (mostly girls) later defended him, saying he was a busy man, had a lot on his mind, had to run the state, etc. We boys said, No, he's dumb. How can you look at a boy and say, Hello, Shirley. The girls said, How do you know Shirley isn't a boy's name, too? Show us where it says Shirley *can't* be a boy's name. How do *you* know? Who do you think *you* are? You're not so smart.

Who do you think you are? You're from Lake Wobegon. You shouldn't think *you're* somebody.

You're no better than the rest of us.

Some of our teachers, however, such as Miss Heinemann, believed that we were good enough and could be improved with proper instruction, and so she set Shakespeare's sonnets in front of us, *Macbeth*, Wordsworth, Chaucer, and expected us to read them and to discuss what was on the page, and if any of us had been so bold as to aspire to a life in literature, she'd have been pleased as punch. The higher the better.

She strolls the aisles between our desks, swishing past in her dull-brown dress, talking about metaphor, the use of language to mean more than what we know it to mean, whereby common things, such as a rose, a birch tree, the dark sky, rain falling, come to mean something else for which there isn't an exact word. She talks about literature as being urgent, impulsively bold, unavoidable, like stopping your car on the highway at night and stepping out and walking alone into dark damp woods because it's unbearable to only know what's in your headlights. Art calls us out of the regulated life into a life that is dangerous, free. I remembered that when I was chosen class poet, to participate in the winter homecoming program and, after the procession of Queen Aileen to the throne and the singing of her favorite song, to stand and recite her favorite poem. Her favorite song was "Vaya Con Dios" but she didn't have a favorite poem, she said, so I said, "That's okay, Aileen, I'll choose a real good one for you." I had in mind a few lines from Whitman's "Song of Myself," beginning:

> I tramp a perpetual journey, (come listen all!)
> My signs are a rain-proof coat, good shoes, and a staff cut from the woods,
> No friend of mine takes his ease in my chair,
> I have no chair, no church, no philosophy,
> I lead no man to a dinner-table, library, exchange,
> But each man and each woman of you I lead upon a knoll,
> My left hand hooking you round the waist,
> My right hand pointing to landscapes of continents and the public road.
>
> Not I, not any one else can travel that road for you,
> You must travel it for yourself.

But first I had to show it to Miss Heinemann for her approval. She was incredulous. "Aileen *Heidenschink* chose this? This is her favorite poem? Aileen?" No, not exactly, Miss H., it's one that I thought might be one that—"I think that on Aileen's big day you might come up with something more appropriate than this. Really. *I have no church, no philosophy?* Aileen is Catholic. Her family will be sitting there. Think."

I *was* thinking, that the Queen's Favorite Poem was a rare occasion when Art had a chance to lift its hoary head and call my classmates toward a higher spiritual life, but Miss Heinemann didn't see it that way; she said, "Don't be mean to Aileen. Find something she'll enjoy, like 'Invictus.' Or else don't do it," which disgusted me, idealist that I was, and also was a huge relief, because the thought of reciting Walt Whitman to a gym full of Lake Wobegon made me sick with fear. So I bowed out as Homecoming Poet on the issue of artistic freedom, keeping my principles intact and taking a big load off my mind at the same time.

Suggestions for Discussion

1. How does Keillor establish the tone of the first paragraph?

2. How do the author's reminiscences relate to the title of the piece?

3. How do some of Keillor's nonstop sentences affect the tone and substance?

4. How does the anecdotal style give the reader a sense of the author's personality?

5. What evidence is there that the author's view of himself and his background is not entirely flippant?

6. What does Keillor's choice of the lines from Whitman's *Song of Myself* tell you about him and his sense of self?

Suggestions for Writing

1. Is the distant future inscrutable for you? If not, describe it.

2. What is your favorite poem? Why is it meaningful to you?

3. Read one of Keillor's books, *Lake Wobegon Days* or *We Are Still Married*, and account for his immense popularity.

Zora Neale Hurston

How It Feels to Be Colored Me

Zora Neale Hurston (1893 or 1903–1960) is now recognized as one of the truly innovative voices in twentieth-century American letters. Born in Florida, she began college while working as a domestic. She was ultimately able to go on to Howard University, a leading center of Black scholarship, and finally to Barnard College where she earned her B.A., and Columbia University where she did graduate work. She was a student of the anthropologist Franz Boas, who urged her to study Southern Black folklore. In the twenties and thirties she was a major figure in the Harlem Renaissance, but she ultimately died unknown, and in poverty. During her career she was a journalist, professor, librarian, folklorist, but, above all, a writer. Five of her books were published during her lifetime, the most prominent being *Mules and Men* (1935), for which she won the Anisfield-Wolf Award, *Their Eyes Were Watching God* (1937), and *Dust Tracks on a Road* (1942). Since 1985, three more collections of her work have been published, the most recent being *Mule Bone: A Comedy of Negro Life* (1991). Here we see Hurston at her most up-beat and affirmative, despite her difficult experiences, refusing the role of victim.

I am colored but I offer nothing in the way of extenuating circumstances except the fact that I am the only Negro in the United States whose grandfather on the mother's side was *not* an Indian chief.

I remember the very day that I became colored. Up to my thirteenth year I lived in the little Negro town of Eatonville, Florida. It is exclusively a colored town. The only white people I knew passed through the town going to or coming from Orlando. The native whites rode dusty horses, the Northern tourists chugged down the sandy village road in automobiles. The town knew the Southerners and never stopped cane chewing when they passed. But the Northerners were something else again. They were peered at cautiously from behind curtains by the timid. The more venturesome would come out on the porch to watch them go past and got just as much pleasure out of the tourists as the tourists got out of the village.

The front porch might seem a daring place for the rest of the town, but it was a gallery seat to me. My favorite place was atop the gate-post. Proscenium box for a born first-nighter. Not only did I enjoy the show, but I didn't mind the actors knowing that I liked it. I usually spoke to them in passing. I'd wave at them and when they returned my salute, I would say something like this: "Howdy-do-well-I-thank-you-where-you-goin'?" Usually the automobile or the horse paused at this, and after a queer exchange of compliments, I would probably "go a piece of the way" with them, as we say in farthest Florida. If one of my family happened to come to the front in time to see me, of course negotiations would be rudely broken off. But even so, it is clear that I was the first "welcome-to-our-state" Floridian, and I hope the Miami Chamber of Commerce will please take notice.

During this period, white people differed from colored to me only in that they rode through town and never lived there. They liked to hear me "speak pieces" and sing and wanted to see me dance the parse-me-la, and gave me generously of their small silver for doing these things, which seemed strange to me for I wanted to do them so much that I needed bribing to stop. Only they didn't know it. The colored people gave no dimes. They deplored any joyful tendencies in me, but I was their Zora nevertheless. I belonged to them, to the nearby hotels, to the county—everybody's Zora.

But changes came in the family when I was thirteen, and I was sent to school in Jacksonville. I left Eatonville, the town of the oleanders, as Zora. When I disembarked from the river-boat at Jacksonville, she was no more. It seemed that I had suffered a sea change. I was not Zora of Orange County any more, I was now a little colored girl. I found it out in certain ways. In my heart as well as in the mirror, I became a fast brown—warranted not to rub nor run.

But I am not tragically colored. There is no great sorrow dammed up in my soul, nor lurking behind my eyes. I do not mind at all. I do not belong to the sobbing school of Negrohood who hold that nature somehow has given them a lowdown dirty deal and whose feelings are all hurt about it. Even in the helter-skelter skirmish that is my life, I have seen that the world is to the strong regardless of a little pigmentation more or less. No, I do not weep at the world—I am too busy sharpening my oyster knife.

Someone is always at my elbow reminding me that I am the granddaughter of slaves. It fails to register depression with me. Slavery is sixty years in the past. The operation was successful and the patient is doing well, thank you. The terrible struggle that made me an American out of a potential slave said "On the line!" The Reconstruction said "Get set!"; and the generation before said "Go!" I am off to a flying start and I must not halt in the stretch to look behind and weep. Slavery is the price I paid for civilization, and the choice was not with me. It is a bully adventure and worth all that I have paid through my ancestors for it. No one on earth ever had a greater chance for glory. The world to be won and nothing to be lost. It is thrilling to think—to know that for any act of mine, I shall get twice as much praise or twice as much blame. It is quite exciting to hold the center of the national stage, with the spectators not knowing whether to laugh or to weep.

The position of my white neighbor is much more difficult. No brown specter pulls up a chair beside me when I sit down to eat. No dark ghost thrusts its leg against mine in bed. The game of keeping what one has is never so exciting as the game of getting.

I do not always feel colored. Even now I often achieve the unconscious Zora of Eatonville before the Hegira. I feel most colored when I am thrown against a sharp white background.

For instance at Barnard. "Beside the waters of the Hudson" I feel my race. Among the thousand white persons, I am a dark rock surged upon, overswept by a creamy sea. I am surged upon and overswept, but through it all, I remain myself. When covered by the waters, I am; and the ebb but reveals me again.

Sometimes it is the other way around. A white person is set down in our midst, but the contrast is just as sharp for me. For instance, when I sit in the drafty basement that is The New World Cabaret with a white person, my color comes. We enter chatting about any little nothing that we have in common and are seated by the jazz waiters. In the abrupt way that jazz orchestras have, this one plunges into a number. It loses no time in circumlocutions, but gets right down to business. It constricts the thorax and splits the heart with its tempo and narcotic harmonies. This orchestra grows rambunctious, rears on its hind legs and attacks the tonal veil with primitive fury, rending it, clawing it until it breaks through to the jungle beyond. I follow those heathen—follow them exultingly. I dance wildly inside myself; I yell within, I whoop; I shake my assegai above my head, I hurl it true to the mark *yeeeeoooww!* I am in the jungle and living in the jungle way. My face is painted red and yellow and my body is painted blue. My pulse is throbbing like a war drum. I want to slaughter something—give pain, give death to what, I do not know. But the piece ends. The men of the orchestra wipe their lips and rest their fingers. I creep back slowly to the veneer we call civilization with the last tone and find the white friend sitting motionless in his seat, smoking calmly.

"Good music they have here," he remarks, drumming the table with his fingertips.

Music! The great blobs of purple and red emotion have not touched him. He has only heard what I felt. He is far away and I see him but dimly across the ocean and the continent that have fallen between us. He is so pale with his whiteness then and I am *so* colored.

*   *   *

At certain times I have no race, I am *me*. When I set my hat at a certain angle and saunter down Seventh Avenue, Harlem City, feeling as snooty as the lions in front of the Forty-Second Street Library, for instance. So far as my feelings are concerned, Peggy Hopkins Joyce on the Boule Mich with her gorgeous raiment, stately carriage, knees knocking together in a most aristocratic manner, has nothing on me. The cosmic Zora emerges. I belong to no race nor time. I am the eternal feminine with its string of beads.

I have no separate feeling about being an American citizen and colored. I am merely a fragment of the Great Soul that surges within the boundaries. My country, right or wrong.

Sometimes, I feel discriminated against, but it does not make me angry. It merely astonishes me. How *can* any deny themselves the pleasure of my company! It's beyond me.

But in the main, I feel like a brown bag of miscellany propped against a wall. Against a wall in company with other bags, white, red and yellow. Pour out the contents, and there is discovered a jumble of small things priceless and worthless. A first-water diamond, an empty spool, bits of broken glass, lengths of string, a key to a door long since crumbled away, a rusty knife-blade, old shoes saved for a road that never was and never will be, a nail bent under the weight of things too heavy for any nail, a dried flower or two, still a little fragrant. In your hand is the brown bag. On the ground before you is the jumble it held—so much like the jumble in the bags, could they be emptied, that all might be dumped in a single heap and the bags refilled without altering the content of any greatly. A bit of colored glass more or less would not matter. Perhaps that is how the Great Stuffer of Bags filled them in the first place—who knows?

Suggestions for Discussion

1. When does Hurston cease to be Zora of Orange County, and become a little colored girl?

2. What does the author mean when she says, "Slavery is the price I paid for civilization"? Do you agree with her?

3. Sometimes Zora feels "cosmic," like "a fragment of the Great Soul," "the eternal feminine . . . " How do these feelings relate to how she understands race?

Suggestions for Writing

1. Hurston describes herself as a "brown bag of miscellany propped against a wall." If someone were to empty the bag that is *you*, what would they find?

2. When did you become aware of how you appeared to the outside world? Did you change because of this? Describe.

John Preston

Medfield, Massachusetts

John Preston (b. 1945), who writes under a variety of pseudonyms, was born in Framingham, Massachusetts, the "hometown" of this selection, and educated at Lake Forest College. An activist in the gay rights movement, he has been a social worker, editor of *Advocate*, and since 1976 a full-time writer. *Franny, the Queen of Provincetown*, was named "Gay Novel of the Year" by the *Frontpage*, and a stage adaptation won the Jane Chambers Gay Playwriting Award, both in 1984. His most recent books include *Hometowns* (1991) and *A Member of the Family* (1992). In the piece that follows the author tries to reconcile the sense of identity his community offers him with the emergence of his identity as a gay man.

Medfield is one of the ancient villages of New England. It was established as a European community in 1649, when pioneers from Dedham moved inland to the location near the headwaters of the Charles River, about twenty-five miles southeast of Boston.

The land on which Medfield was settled had been purchased from Chicatabot, the Sachem of the Neponset nation. He was one of those natives who saw the arrival of the English as, at worst, a neutral event. But it didn't take long for the indigenous people to see that the spread of the Puritan and Pilgrim colonies was threatening their very survival. In 1674, Metacomet, the great leader known to the English as King Philip, organized an alliance of the native nations and led them to battle against the intruders.

The beginning of King Philip's War, as it was called, was fought in the Connecticut Valley. The few communities there were attacked and many of the settlers killed. Within a year Metacomet's warriors were pushing closer to Boston. Medfield was raided on February 19, 1675. Seventeen people were killed and half the buildings were destroyed.

Metacomet was defeated later that winter in a climactic battle in nearby Rhode Island. His campaign was the last serious chance the natives had of sending the English away. Smallpox and other epidemics finished the destruction of the aboriginal nations over the next decades. Medfield's new proprietors, my ancestors, quietly prospered.

When the American Revolution broke out a century later, Medfield was firmly on the side of the rebels. The town meeting communicated regularly with the colonial legislature and the radical Committees of Correspondence, encouraging a strong stance against unfair taxation. When it was apparent that hostilities would break out, the citizens organized a contingent of Minutemen who responded to the call to arms in Concord and Lexington (though they arrived too late to join in the battles).

The Revolution was the last striking event in Medfield's history. Once independence was achieved, Medfield simply became a quintessential Yankee town, the place where I grew up, complete with a phalanx of the white clapboard churches everyone identifies with New England, larded through with extravagant forest parks and with a wealth of substantial wood-frame houses.

When I was born, in 1945, Medfield had fewer than three thousand inhabitants. It was assumed that all of us knew one another. It wasn't just that the population was so small, it was also remarkably stable. Our families had all lived in the same place for so long that it all felt like an extended family. (And there were, in fact, many cousins in town. Not just first cousins, but second and third cousins. We all knew our interlocking heritage at an early age.) The names of all the participants in the colonial and revolutionary events were the same as many of my cousins and classmates and the people in the church my family attended — Harding, Morse, Adams, Lovell, Bullard, Wheelock, and Allen.

We lived our history. When the other kids and I played cowboys and Indians, we did it on the same battlegrounds where our ancestors defeated King Philip. When we studied American history, our teachers taught us the names of the men from Medfield who had fought in the Revolution.

We weren't those for whom this country's history was irrelevant. We weren't left out of the narrative of the white man's ascension. We were, in fact, those for whom American history was written. We were of British ancestry — if not English, then Scots or Irish. We read about people with names that sounded like our own. "Foreign" was, for us, someone of Italian descent. "Alien" was the Roman Catholic church.

As I grew older and came into contact with people from around the state, I discovered a different social criteria. People started to talk about ancestors who'd come from England on the *Mayflower*. I remember going to my mother and asking her if ours had. She looked at me strangely and replied, "Well, whenever any family's lived in a town like ours as long as we have, somebody married somebody who married somebody whose family came over on the *Mayflower*. But, why would you even care?" she asked.

Indeed. Why would anyone look for more than coming from Medfield? There is a story about Yankee insularity that's told in many different forms. A reporter goes up to a lady who's sitting on a bench in a village common and asks her, "If you had the chance to travel to anywhere in the world, where would you go?" The lady looks around her hometown, mystified, and responds, "But why would I go anywhere? I'm already here!" The first times I heard that story, I didn't understand it was a joke. I thought the woman was only speaking the obvious. It's the way we felt about Medfield.

Medfield was a very distinct reality to me. There was even a leftover colonial custom that gave the town a concrete definition. By 1692 the settlements around Boston were growing quickly and their perimeters were hazy because of conflicting land grants and native treaties. The executive power of each town was vested in the Board of Selectmen, three citizens elected by the town meeting to run things between the annual assemblies of the town's voters. The Great and General Court, the romantic name the Commonwealth of Massachusetts still uses for the state legislature, decreed that every five years the selectmen of each town would have to "perambulate the bounds" with the selectmen of its neighbors. The two sets of townspeople had to agree on the markers that separated them.

The requirement for the perambulation stayed on the books until 1973 and even then the rescinding law said, "However, it is enjoyable to keep the old tradition of meeting with the selectmen of adjoining towns for this purpose. It also affords an opportunity to agree to replacement of missing or broken bounds and to discuss subjects of mutual interest." (The Medfield Historical Commission recently reported, "It is also rumored that modern-time selectmen partook of a drink or two at each boundary marker.")

When I was young, I used to walk the bounds of Medfield with the selectmen. The grown-ups' drinking habits weren't important to me, but I was in love with the stones we found with their antiquated signs and the aged oak and maple trees that appeared on the town records as markers between Medfield and Dover, Walpole, Norfolk, and other neighbors.

The living history of the monuments wasn't all I got from these walks. The perambulations gave a firm evidence to just what was my hometown. I was being told that everything on this side of the boundaries was Medfield. Everything on this side of the border was mine.

It's hard to overstate the sense of entitlement that a New England boyhood gave me and my friends. I remember the first time I was taken to Boston. The city seemed large and frightening, at least it did until my mother pointed to the large body of water between Boston and Cambridge and explained that it was the Charles, the same river that separated Medfield from Millis. I realized I couldn't be frightened of someplace that was built on the banks of *my* river.

Even if America wasn't all like Medfield, it certainly acted as though it wanted to be. The new suburban developments that were all the rage in the sixties mimicked the architecture of the buildings that had been standing around our village for centuries. Advertisements for the good life all seemed to take place in our town. Medfield had a wide floodplain to the west, hills to the south, forests to the north. It was the landscape surrounding the "nice people" we saw in magazines and on television. Our lawns were well kept and our trees carefully pruned. A snowstorm was a community event; my mother would make hot chocolate and fresh doughnuts (from scratch) for all the neighborhood children and we'd build snowmen exactly like those pictured on the pages of *The Saturday Evening Post*.

Of course there were blemishes, some of them so well hidden that only those of us inside could see them. There were broken homes and drunken parents. There was economic upheaval as New England's industry migrated to the South after World War II. There were class divisions that were especially apparent to me, since my father's family—he was from Boston's industrial suburbs—was pure working class. We couldn't have been much better off than my aunts and uncles and cousins living in Boston's urban blight, but poverty wasn't as apparent when it was surrounded by beauty like Medfield's. Somerville didn't have Rocky Narrows State Park; Everett didn't have Rocky Woods State Reservation. And, besides, not having a great deal of money had no impact on our status in town. My mother's pedigree made my father's background irrelevant. Her children were of Medfield, and no one ever questioned that.

In fact, we were constantly reminded that our roots were right there on the banks of the Charles. My sisters and brothers and I were continually assaulted by older citizens who would stop us on the street and pinch our cheeks, "Oh, yes, I can see that you must be one of Raymond Blood's family. It's those eyes. Just like his!" My maternal grandfather had died fifteen years before I was born, but townspeople kept on seeing his lineage in my face.

He'd been something of a hero in the town, a World War I veteran who'd prospected for gold in Nevada before he'd returned to take over the family's business, selling feed and grain to the small farmers in the region. To be Raymond Blood's grandson was no small matter. The pinches may have been annoying, but the rest of the message was clear: You are from this place.

Medfield was a town where a boy knew what it meant to belong. It was an environment out of which almost any achievement seemed possible. As we grew older, my friends and I picked and chose from the best colleges, dreamed the most extravagant futures, saw ourselves in any situation we could imagine. Our aspirations were the highest possible and they didn't come out of pressure from striving families or a need to escape a stifling atmosphere. We envisioned ourselves however we chose because we felt it was ours, all of it, the entire American Dream. It was so much ours, we took it so much for granted, that we never even questioned it. It was self-evident.

There must have been many ways I was different from the other kids early on. I'm vaguely aware of being too smart, of not being physical enough, of hating sports. I got grief for all those things in the way any group of peers can deliver it, especially in adolescence. I certainly *felt* different. I certainly *knew* I was different. But the difference didn't define itself right away.

As we became teenagers, things happened that actually eased the sense of deviation. There were forces at work that made us more aware of the things that bound us together and made what might have separated us seem less important. Route 128 had been built in a long arc around Boston's suburbs in the fifties. Originally called a highway to nowhere, it was one of the first freeways whose purpose was to create a flow of traffic around centers of population, not between them. One-twenty-eight quickly got another name: "America's Highway of Technology." New companies with names like Raytheon and Northrop and Digital built enormous high-tech plants along 128. They moved the center of the region's economy out of Boston, toward places like Medfield. The town's population doubled, and then doubled again.

By the time we were in high school, we were faced with new classmates with strange accents and different standards. My friends had earned their extra spending money by trapping beavers and muskrats along the tributaries to the Charles and selling their pelts. These new kids didn't know about traps and they didn't think it was important that their new homes in the spreading developments were ruining the animals' habitat. We were used to having fried clams as a special treat at the local drive-up restaurant; they were only angry that there weren't any fast-food chains. They had strange and exotic—and sexual—dances we hadn't even heard of. We stood in the high school auditorium and wondered how they could act that way in public. When they hiked up on Noon Hill, they didn't know that it had been the place from which King Philip had watched Medfield burn. They thought we were backward and quaint that we even cared about such things.

The local kids closed ranks. I'm sure, as I look back now, that the newcomers must have been puzzled when Mike, the captain of every team sport possible, spent time with me, the class brain. They must have wondered just as much why I would pass afternoons with Philip, who didn't even go to Medfield High School but commuted to Norfolk County Agricultural School, the looked-down-upon "aggie" school in Walpole. And why would my (third) cousin Peter, probably the most handsome youth in town, walk home with me so often?

We defied the new standards; we held to our own. We had all been in the Cub Scouts pack that my mother had founded. We had all sat in the same kindergarten. We had all been a part of Medfield. I was one of the group, and they wouldn't deny me.

When I return to my hometown now, I see that, in most ways, we won. People like Mike and Philip and Peter—and my mother and her friends— simply sat it all out. They waited for the newcomers to leave and then for a new wave of them to come in, the waves of migrating suburbanites who can't tell the difference between Medfield and Northfield, Illinois, or Southfield, Michigan, they've changed addresses so often. My family and friends simply stayed, they had never intended to move. Now, my mother is the town clerk, Mike runs the reunions of our high school class, and last I heard Philip took over his father's job as groundsman for the state hospital.

But I had begun to leave while I was still in high school. I had heard rumors about a different life and a different world. Its gateway, my books and magazines told me, was a bus station in a city. I began to travel to Boston more often, supposedly to visit my urban cousins, but I seldom got as far as Somerville. I would stay, instead, in the Greyhound terminal and wait for one of a series of men to come and initiate me. They were traveling salesmen from Hartford, professors from MIT, students from Northeastern.

Eventually I'd travel further to meet them. I took secret trips to New York when I was supposed to be skiing in New Hampshire. I hitchhiked to Provincetown, the fabulous center of the new world into which I was moving. And, with every move, I left more of Medfield behind.

There was really no way I could see to combine my new life and my old. There was a man in Medfield who was whispered about. He belonged to our church and was the target for endless sympathy because he kept entering and leaving the state hospital. And there were two women down the street, nurses, who were so masculine that it was impossible to ignore their deviance from the other norms of the town. But they offered me nothing. I wasn't like the nurses and I never, ever wanted to be like the man who was so continually institutionalized.

In some ways I moved into my new life with great joy. There was real excitement in it, certainly there was great passion. My explorations took me to places as far away as a New England boy could ever imagine. When it came time to pick my college, I chose one in Illinois, the far horizon of my family's worldview, as far away as they could ever conceive of me going.

I also experienced rage over what was happening to me. I was being taken away from Medfield and everything it stood for. I was the one who should have gotten a law degree and come home to settle into comfortable Charles River Valley politics—perhaps with a seat in the Great and General Court? I should have lived in one of those honestly colonial houses on Pleasant Street. I should have walked through the meadows and the hills as long as I wanted, greeted by people I knew, all of us blanketed in our sense of continuity. History had belonged to us. But I was no longer one of them. I had become too different.

There had become a label for me that was even more powerful than the label of being from Medfield, something I don't think I could have ever envisioned being true.

I remember trying to find some way to come back to Medfield. I remember discovering a hairdresser in a Boston bar who had just opened a shop in town. I wanted desperately to fall in love with him and move back and find some way to be of Medfield again. Another time I did fall in love with a truck driver from Providence, a man of as much overstated masculinity as the nurses down the street. Maybe he and I could create a balance that the town could accept. He drank whiskey with my father, fixed cars with our neighbors, and knew all about the Red Sox. Maybe, between the two of us, we had enough that we could stay in Medfield. It didn't work. And, in those days, no one ever thought it would work in any hometown.

I stopped trying to fit my life into Medfield. I turned my back on it. I belonged to a new world now, one that spun around New York, Chicago, San Francisco, Provincetown. I was danced and bedded away from home, into the arms of someplace no one had ever even told me about.

Suggestions for Discussion

1. Why does Preston spend so much time describing the history of Medfield, Massachusetts?

2. What does the author mean when he says, "There had become a label for me that was even more powerful than the label of being from Medfield, something I don't think I could have ever envisioned being true"?

3. Preston, in the end, turns his back on Medfield. "History had belonged to us. But I was no longer one of them. I had become too different." Would he have different options now? Explain.

Suggestions for Writing

1. Describe a situation where, in order to be true to yourself, you had to give up something that mattered to you very much.

2. Preston's piece is in part about continuity, Medfield and its history, and change, his own discovery that he had to leave. What metaphors might represent the continuity and change in your life?

Essays

James Baldwin

The Discovery of What It Means
to Be an American

James Baldwin (1924–1987) was born in New York of Southern, deeply religious, and poor parents. At fourteen, he became a preacher in the Fireside Pentecostal Church in Harlem. His first novel, *Go Tell It on the Mountain* (1953), reflects his experience as a preacher and, together with *Another Country* (1962), a novel about sex and race, established his reputation as a writer. Since the publication of a lengthy essay, *The Fire Next Time* (1962), he has taken a place as an important spokesman for blacks. He has written significant autobiographical essays and this essay from *Nobody Knows My Name* (1961) examines the ways in which his sojourn in Paris contributed to both his understanding of himself and of America.

"It is a complex fate to be an American," Henry James observed, and the principal discovery an American writer makes in Europe is just how complex this fate is. America's history, her aspirations, her peculiar triumphs, her even more peculiar defeats, and her position in the world—yesterday and today—are all so profoundly and stubbornly unique that the very word "America" remains a new, almost completely undefined and extremely controversial proper noun. No one in the world seems to know exactly what it describes, not even we motley millions who call ourselves Americans.

I left America because I doubted my ability to survive the fury of the color problem here. (Sometimes I still do.) I wanted to prevent myself from becoming *merely* a Negro; or, even, merely a Negro writer. I wanted to find in what way the *specialness* of my experience could be made to connect me with other people instead of dividing me from them. (I was as isolated from Negroes as I was from whites, which is what happens when a Negro begins, at bottom, to believe what white people say about him.)

In my necessity to find the terms on which my experience could be related to that of others, Negroes and whites, writers and non-writers, I proved, to my astonishment, to be as American as any Texas G.I. And I found my experience was shared by every American writer I knew in Paris. Like me, they had been divorced from their origins, and it turned out to make very little difference that the origins of white Americans were European and mine were African—they were no more at home in Europe than I was.

The fact that I was the son of a slave and they were the sons of free men meant less, by the time we confronted each other on European soil, than the fact that we were both searching for our separate identities. When we had found these, we seemed to be saying, why, then, we would no longer need to cling to the shame and bitterness which had divided us so long.

It became terribly clear in Europe, as it never had been here, that we knew more about each other than any European ever could. And it also became clear that, no matter where our fathers had been born, or what they had endured, the fact of Europe had formed us both was part of our identity and part of our inheritance.

I had been in Paris a couple of years before any of this became clear to me. When it did, I, like many a writer before me upon the discovery that his props have all been knocked out from under him, suffered a species of breakdown and was carried off to the mountains of Switzerland. There, in that absolutely alabaster landscape, armed with two Bessie Smith records and a typewriter, I began to try to re-create the life that I had first known as a child and from which I had spent so many years in flight.

It was Bessie Smith, through her tone and her cadence, who helped me to dig back to the way I myself must have spoken when I was a pickaninny, and to remember the things I had heard and seen and felt. I had buried them very deep. I had never listened to Bessie Smith in America (in the same way that, for years, I would not touch watermelon), but in Europe she helped to reconcile me to being a "nigger."

I do not think that I could have made this reconciliation here. Once I was able to accept my role—as distinguished, I must say, from my "place"—in the extraordinary drama which is America, I was released from the illusion that I hated America.

The story of what can happen to an American Negro writer in Europe simply illustrates, in some relief, what can happen to any American writer there. It is not meant, of course, to imply that it happens to them all, for Europe can be very crippling, too; and, anyway, a writer, when he has made his first breakthrough, has simply won a crucial skirmish in a dangerous, unending and unpredictable battle. Still, the breakthrough is important, and the point is that an American writer, in order to achieve it, very often has to leave this country.

The American writer, in Europe, is released, first of all, from the necessity of apologizing for himself. It is not until he *is* released from the habit of flexing his muscles and proving that he is just a "regular guy" that he realizes how crippling this habit has been. It is not necessary for him, there, to pretend to be something he is not, for the artist does not encounter in Europe the same suspicion he encounters here. Whatever the Europeans may actually think of artists, they have killed enough of them off by now to know that they are as real—and as persistent—as rain, snow, taxes or businessmen.

Of course, the reason for Europe's comparative clarity concerning the different functions of men in society is that European society has always been divided into classes in a way that American society never has been. A European writer considers himself to be part of an old and honorable tradition—of intellectual activity, of letters—and his choice of a vocation does not cause him any uneasy wonder as to whether or not it will cost him all his friends. But this tradition does not exist in America.

On the contrary, we have a very deep-seated distrust of real intellectual effort (probably because we suspect that it will destroy, as I hope it does, that myth of America to which we cling so desperately). An American writer fights his way to one of the lowest rungs on the American social ladder by means of pure bull-headedness and an indescribable series of odd jobs. He probably *has* been a "regular fellow" for much of his adult life, and it is not easy for him to step out of that lukewarm bath.

We must, however, consider a rather serious paradox: though American society is more mobile than Europe's, it is easier to cut across social and occupational lines there than it is here. This has something to do, I think, with the problem of status in American life. Where everyone has status, it is also perfectly possible, after all, that no one has. It seems inevitable, in any case, that a man may become uneasy as to just what his status is.

But Europeans have lived with the idea of status for a long time. A man can be as proud of being a good waiter as of being a good actor, and, in neither case, feel threatened. And this means that the actor and the waiter can have a freer and more genuinely friendly relationship in Europe than they are likely to have here. The waiter does not feel, with obscure resentment, that the actor has "made it," and the actor is not tormented by the fear that he may find himself, tomorrow, once again a waiter.

This lack of what may roughly be called social paranoia causes the American writer in Europe to feel—almost certainly for the first time in his life—that he can reach out to everyone, that he is accessible to everyone and open to everything. This is an extraordinary feeling. He feels, so to speak, his own weight, his own value.

It is as though he suddenly came out of a dark tunnel and found himself beneath the open sky. And, in fact, in Paris, I began to see the sky for what seemed to be the first time. It was borne in on me—and it did not make me feel melancholy—that this sky had been there before I was born and would be there when I was dead. And it was up to me, therefore, to make of my brief opportunity the most that could be made.

I was born in New York, but have lived only in pockets of it. In Paris, I lived in all parts of the city—on the Right Bank and the Left, among the bourgeoisie and among *les misérables,* and knew all kinds of people, from pimps and prostitutes in Pigalle to Egyptian bankers in Neuilly. This may sound extremely unprincipled or even obscurely immoral: I found it healthy. I love to talk to people, all kinds of people, and almost everyone, as I hope we still know, loves a man who loves to listen.

This perpetual dealing with people very different from myself caused a shattering in me of preconceptions I scarcely knew I held. The writer is meeting in Europe people who are not American, whose sense of reality is entirely different from his own. They may love or hate or admire or fear or envy this country—they see it, in any case, from another point of view, and this forces the writer to reconsider many things he had always taken for granted. This reassessment, which can be very painful, is also very valuable.

This freedom, like all freedom, has its dangers and its responsibilities. One day it begins to be borne in on the writer, and with great force, that he is living in Europe as an American. If he were living there as a European, he would be living on a different and far less attractive continent.

This crucial day may be the day on which an Algerian taxi-driver tells him how it feels to be an Algerian in Paris. It may be the day on which he passes a café terrace and catches a glimpse of the tense, intelligent and troubled face of Albert Camus. Or it may be the day on which someone asks him to explain Little Rock and he begins to feel that it would be simpler—and, corny as the words may sound, more honorable—to *go* to Little Rock than sit in Europe, on an American passport, trying to explain it.

This is a personal day, a terrible day, the day to which his entire sojourn has been tending. It is the day he realizes that there are no untroubled countries in this fearfully troubled world; that if he has been preparing himself for anything in Europe, he has been preparing himself—for America. In short, the freedom that the American writer finds in Europe brings him, full circle, back to himself, with the responsibility for his development where it always was: in his own hands.

Even the most incorrigible maverick has to be born somewhere. He may leave the group that produced him—he may be forced to—but nothing will efface his origins, the marks of which he carries with him everywhere. I think it is important to know this and even find it a matter for rejoicing, as the strongest people do, regardless of their station. On this acceptance, literally, the life of a writer depends.

The charge has often been made against American writers that they do not describe society, and have no interest in it. Of course, what the American writer is describing is his own situation. But what is *Anna Karenina* describing if not the tragic fate of the isolated individual, at odds with her time and place?

The real difference is that Tolstoy was describing an old and dense society in which everything seemed—to the people in it, though not to Tolstoy—to be fixed forever. And the book is a masterpiece because Tolstoy was able to fathom, and make us see, the hidden laws which really governed this society and made Anna's doom inevitable.

American writers do not have a fixed society to describe. The only society they know is one in which nothing is fixed and in which the individual must fight for his identity. This is a rich confusion, indeed, and it creates for the American writer unprecedented opportunities.

That the tensions of American life, as well as the possibilities, are tremendous is certainly not even a question. But these are dealt with in contemporary literature mainly compulsively; that is, the book is more likely to be a symptom of our tension than an examination of it. The time has come, God knows, for us to examine ourselves, but we can only do this if we are willing to free ourselves of the myth of America and try to find out what is really happening here.

Every society is really governed by hidden laws, by unspoken but profound assumptions on the part of the people, and ours is no exception. It is up to the American writer to find out what these laws and assumptions are. In a society much given to smashing taboos without thereby managing to be liberated from them, it will be no easy matter.

It is no wonder, in the meantime, that the American writer keeps running off to Europe. He needs sustenance for his journey and the best models he can find. Europe has what we do not have yet, a sense of the mysterious and inexorable limits of life, a sense, in a word, of tragedy. And we have what they sorely need: a new sense of life's possibilities.

In this endeavor to wed the vision of the Old World with that of the New, it is the writer, not the statesman, who is our strongest arm. Though we do not wholly believe it yet, the interior life is a real life, and the intangible dreams of people have a tangible effect on the world.

Suggestions for Discussion

1. How does Baldwin's discovery of what it means to be an American relate to his search for identity?

2. How did his Paris sojourn contribute to his sense of self?

3. In what ways did his life in Paris enable him to "find out in what way the *specialness* of my experience could be made to connect me with other people instead of dividing me from them"?

4. How did the Bessie Smith records contribute to Baldwin's search?

5. Compare the attitudes toward writers and toward status of Americans and Europeans.

6. How do the allusions to the Algerian taxi driver, Camus, and the questioner regarding Little Rock relate to Baldwin's understanding of himself and of America?

7. What does the author regard as the responsibility of the writer?

8. What does the author mean when he states that "the interior life is a real life"?

Suggestions for Writing

1. Refer to the text and develop an answer to Question 3.

2. Baldwin believes that America has a "new sense of life's possibilities." What are some of these possibilities?

3. Shelley labeled poets "the potential legislators of the world." Baldwin states that it is the writer, not the statesman, who is our strongest arm in wedding "the vision of the Old World with that of the New." What is your view?

James E. Miller, Jr.

Discovering the Self

James E. Miller, Jr., (b. 1920), American educator and author, has served as a professor of English at the University of Chicago since 1962. The editor of *College English* from 1960 to 1966, he is the author of numerous scholarly works on Fitzgerald, Whitman, and Melville. In this excerpt from his book *Word, Self, Reality* (1972) Miller develops his thesis that by means of language we "proclaim our identities, shape our lives, and leave our impress on the world."

"I speak; therefore I am."

Though this declaration may seem a little strange at first, it can be supported by considerable evidence. The individual establishes his individuality, his distinction as a human being, through language. He *becomes*—through language. Not only does he proclaim his existence, his being, through speech, but also his identity—the special and particular nature that makes him *him*. The declaration may then be rewritten: "I speak; *thus*, I am."

The creation of the self must, by its very nature, be a cooperative affair. The potentiality for language acquisition and language-use appears to be granted as a birthright. But the accident of birth will determine whether the language acquired will be Chinese, Swahili, Spanish, or English. And the same accident will determine the nature of the dialect acquired within the language. These "accidents" assume the presence of people and a culture that together bring the language to the individual.

If, then, the individual creates himself through language, it is only with the help provided by a sympathetic environment; a mother who encourages him to babble, to distinguish sounds and consequences, and then to utter sentences; and a host of other people who act and react linguistically around him. Gradually as the individual develops, he acquires not only language but what might be called a "linguistic personality," a set of language behavior patterns that make up a substantial part of his identity as a person different from other persons.

This *creation of the self*—in the sense of the self's development into a distinctive person with distinctions that are in large part linguistic (or asserted or fulfilled through language)—is a creation of the self in a kind of gross or obvious sense. Few would quarrel with the rough outline sketched above, though some might want to express it in a different set of terms. But there is another, more subtle sense in which we can speak of the creation of the self implied in "I speak; therefore I am." This profounder sense is implied in Alfred North Whitehead's assertion that "it is not going too far to say that the souls of men are the gift from language to mankind." Where a nineteenth-century divine, or a twentieth-century philosopher, might refer to "souls," the modern psychologist might refer to the sense of an enduring self. This sense is generated, sustained, and preserved in language.

One way through which the sense of self is generated appears in the basic human impulse to sort through one's thoughts, or to think through the day's (or a lifetime's) experiences. To follow this impulse throws the individual back on his language resources. The experiences and thoughts that make up one's

---

. . . the mentality of mankind and the language of mankind created each other. If we like to assume the rise of language as a given fact, then it is not going too far to say that the souls of men are the gift from language to mankind.

The account of the sixth day should be written, He gave them speech, and they became souls.

—Alfred North Whitehead, *Modes of Thought,* 1938.

> . . . the fundamental human capacity is the capacity and the need for creative self-expression, for free control of all aspects of one's life and thought. One particularly crucial realization of this capacity is the creative use of language as a free instrument of thought and expression. Now having this view of human nature and human needs, one tries to think about the modes of social organization that would permit the freest and fullest development of the individual, of each individual's potentialities in whatever direction they might take, that would permit him to be fully human in the sense of having the greatest possible scope for his freedom and initiative.
>
> —**Noam Chomsky**, "Linguistics and Politics—Interview," 1969.

life are, in some sense, the essence of the individual, the things that are uniquely his and that make him what he is. In the process of sorting through his thoughts, or of disentangling and examining his tangled experiences, he is in effect defining himself, outlining himself, asserting and proclaiming himself. There can be no more vital activity for the individual: the results and the actions (new thoughts and new experiences) proceeding from it will further define his identity, not only for him but for the world he inhabits. In the old vocabulary, he is in this process revitalizing, reconstituting, refreshing, renewing his soul.

To live an aware life, the individual must begin with an awareness of self. He must conduct a running examination and periodic reexaminations of the self—in language, the medium of furthest reaches, deepest diving, most labyrinthine windings. The sorting through might well begin with the ordinary, everyday experiences of life. A diary or journal enables one to sift through and evaluate experiences, as well as to come to understand them and their significance—or insignificance. Most of us do this sifting and evaluation in moments of reverie or in that state of mental vagabondage just before sleep. There is some (even great) advantage, however, in subjecting ourselves to the discipline of written language, in which the vague and the mushy and the muddled must give way to the specific, the firm, the clearly formulated.

For writing *is* discovery. The language that never leaves our head is like colorful yarn, endlessly spun out multicolored threads dropping into a void,

> It is language . . . that really reveals to man that world which is closer to him than any world of natural objects and touches his weal and woe more directly than physical nature. For it is language that makes his existence in a community possible; and only in society, in relation to a "Thee," can his subjectivity assert itself as a "Me."
>
> —**Ernst Cassirer**, *Language and Myth*, 1946.

I did not exist to write poems, to preach or to paint, neither I nor anyone else. All of that was incidental. Each man had only one genuine vocation—to find the way to himself. He might end up as poet or madman, as prophet or criminal—that was not his affair, ultimately it was of no concern. His task was to discover his own destiny—not an arbitrary one—and live it out wholly and resolutely within himself. Everything else was only a would-be existence, an attempt at evasion, a flight back to the ideas of the masses, conformity and fear of one's own inwardness.

—**Hermann Hesse,** *Demian,* 1925.

momentarily compacted, entangled, fascinating, elusive. We have glimpses that seem brilliant but quickly fade; we catch sight of images that tease us with connections and patterns that too-soon flow on; we hold in momentary view a comprehensive arrangement (insight) that dissolves rapidly and disappears.

Writing that is discovery forces the capturing, the retrieving, the bringing into focus these stray and random thoughts. Sifting through them, we make decisions that are as much about the self as about language. Indeed, writing is largely a process of choosing among alternatives from the images and thoughts of the endless flow, and this choosing is a matter of making up one's mind, and this making up one's mind becomes in effect the making up of one's self. In this way writing that is honest and genuine and serious (though not necessarily without humor or wit) constitutes the discovery of the self. It is not uncommon, before the choices are made, before the words are fixed on paper, to be quite unsure of which way the choices will go. Most people have experienced the phenomenon of their opinions or feelings changing, sometimes markedly, in the process of writing a paper which forces confrontations with language and choices among expressions. All people have experienced the clarification of their views and perspectives as they have worked through the process of placing them on paper. It is not at all unusual to find an individual who is uncertain and unclear about his feelings on a subject or an issue, but who, on discovering his attitude in the process of writing, becomes committed, often dedicated, and sometimes even fanatical: he has come to know himself. When this happens the individual is not being insincere, but is simply experiencing the discoveries of writing—discoveries that are often surprising and frequently exhilarating.

As suggested earlier, in setting forth on this voyage of self-discovery, it is best to begin, not with the problems of the universe, but with what appear to be the trivia of everyday events. Indeed, it might turn out ultimately that the big is somehow indirectly connected with the little. The self-examination which requires simply the writing of an account of one's life for a single day might bring unexpected illumination. Such an account would necessitate reviewing in detail and reliving imaginatively moments of pain and fun, joy and sobriety. A list of the events of that day (or week, month) would require consideration as to what, for an individual, constitutes events. Presumably

YEE-AH! I feel like part of the shadows that make company for me in this warm *amigo* darkness.

I am "My Majesty Piri Thomas," with a high on anything and like a stoned king, I gotta survive my kingdom.

I'm a skinny, dark-face, curly-haired, intense Porty-Ree-can— Unsatisfied, hoping, and always reaching.

—**Piri Thomas,** *Down These Mean Streets,* 1967.

they left some kind of mark—intellectual, emotional, imaginative. What kind of mark, how deep, how long-lasting? There might be public events and private events—events for which there were some, perhaps many, witnesses, and events that had no witnesses at all.

The list of a day's events in an individual's life might be posed against a list of the general public events and happenings—in the community, town, state, country, or world. Where do the two lists intersect, if at all? Did any of the world's events leave any mark on the individual, or did they reach him remotely or impersonally through the mass media, newspapers, radio-TV, and then fade into the distance? A third list might be composed of a close friend's perspective on the personal events on the first list, some of which he will have witnessed (but only externally), and others of which he will be totally unaware. Compilation of these lists, either in fact or imagination, may enable the individual to see the narrative of his life as marking a circle around him, with him—absolutely alone—at the center.

This circle marks the individual's personal turf, material for his intellectual and imaginative use or growth that is his and his alone, impossible to share totally with anyone, no matter how close. One who begins to feel a sense of

Interviewer: Is there anything else you can say to beginning writers?

Simenon: Writing is considered a profession, and I don't think it is a profession. I think that everyone who does not *need* to be a writer, who thinks he can do something else, ought to do something else. Writing is not a profession but a vocation of unhappiness. I don't think an artist can ever be happy.

Interviewer: Why?

Simenon: Because, first, I think that if a man has the urge to be an artist, it is because he needs to find himself. Every writer tries to find himself through his characters, through all his writing.

Interviewer: He is writing for himself?

Simenon: Yes. Certainly.

—**Georges Simenon,** *Writers at Work: The Paris Review Interviews,* 1958.

the preciousness of this material, this segment of life that is his and no one else's, is in fact feeling a sense of the self. If he begins to discover sequence and sense—a kind of unified narrative—in the events of his life for a day, he is making the discovery of self that the process of writing brings about: the unification must come from the individual's unique sensibility and identity.

Henry James had something of all this in mind in some advice he gave to young writers: "Oh, do something from your point of view; an ounce of example is worth a ton of generalities . . . do something with life. Any point of view is interesting that is a direct impression of life. You each have an impression colored by your individual conditions; make that into a picture, a picture framed by your own personal wisdom, your glimpse of the American world. The field is vast for freedom, for study, for observation, for satire, for truth."

Suggestions for Discussion

1. In earlier sections of his book *Word, Self, Reality,* Miller defines language as a form of creation whereby we create both our world and ourselves. With what details does Miller support his belief that it is through language that we create ourselves and our world?

2. What role does environment play in enabling the individual to create himself or herself through language?

3. How does sorting through one's thoughts or thinking through one's experiences relate to self-definition? What role does choice play in this process?

4. How do the quotations from Whitehead, Chomsky, Cassirer, Hesse, Thomas, and Simenon relate to the author's central thesis?

5. Miller maintains the continuity of his thought by careful linking of his paragraphs. Identify the transitional devices that bind each of the paragraphs to the preceding and the following one. Identify the logic that justifies the division of the essay into its constituent paragraphs.

6. Examine the ninth paragraph ("Writing that is discovery . . .") to determine (a) what subject matter is in it, (b) what transitional devices give it internal coherence, (c) what stages of development the discussion undergoes.

7. The eighth paragraph ("For writing *is* discovery") includes an ingenious simile: language is like yarn. Test whether this simile is merely ornamental, useful in conveying the thought, or essential to the thought by rewriting the paragraph in abstract, nonfigurative language and comparing your version with Miller's original.

Suggestions for Writing

1. Keep a journal recording your fleeting impressions, daydreams, night dreams, feelings, and random thoughts as well as your more considered reflections over a period of two weeks. Include your thoughts about your own immediate activities, memories evoked of past events, and reflections on what is going on in the world. Be concerned with getting down on paper as much as possible of what you are feeling and what has gone through your mind and don't concern yourself with the usual mechanics of writing or with the possibly repetitive nature of some of your feelings. At the end of this two-week period, reread your journal and attempt to discover what recurrent patterns of feeling and thought have emerged. Write a

brief analysis of the nature of your own thoughts, what experiences seem to precipitate them, what patterns seem to repeat themselves. What do you make of such
repetitions?

2. Select one of the journal entries that most interests you and elaborate on it in the
form of a short essay or narrative in which you attempt to give shape and unity to
the earlier expression.

3. Make the lists suggested in Miller's essay and write a commentary on your discoveries.

Theodore Roethke

Some Self-Analysis

Theodore Roethke (1908–1963), American poet, taught during the last years
of his life at the University of Washington. The Waking: Poems, 1933–1953
was the winner of the Pulitzer Prize for Poetry in 1953. He received the
Bollingen Award for Poetry in 1958. A collected volume, Words for the Wind,
appeared in 1958, and The Far Field was published posthumously in 1964. In
this statement, written when he was an undergraduate, Roethke recounts
his hopes for the writing course he is taking, assesses his strengths and
limitations as a writer, and expresses his faith in himself.

I expect this course to open my eyes to story material, to unleash my too
dormant imagination, to develop that quality utterly lacking in my nature—a
sense of form. I do not expect to acquire much technique. I expect to be able
to seize upon the significant, reject the trivial. I hope to acquire a greater
love for humanity in all its forms.

I have long wondered just what my strength was as a writer. I am often
filled with tremendous enthusiasm for a subject, yet my writing about it will
seem a sorry attempt. Above all, I possess a driving sincerity,—that prime
virtue of any creative worker. I write only what I believe to be the absolute
truth,—even if I must ruin the theme in so doing. In this respect I feel far
superior to those glib people in my classes who often garner better grades
than I do. They are so often pitiful frauds,—artificial—insincere. They have
a line that works. They do not write from the depths of their hearts. Nothing
of theirs was ever born of pain. Many an incoherent yet sincere piece of
writing has outlived the polished product.

I write only about people and things that I know thoroughly. Perhaps I
have become a mere reporter, not a writer. Yet I feel that this is all my
present abilities permit. I will open my eyes in my youth and store
this raw, living material. Age may bring the fire that molds experience into
artistry.

I have a genuine love of nature. It is not the least bit affected, but an integral and powerful part of my life. I know that Cooper is a fraud—that he doesn't give a true sense of the sublimity of American scenery. I know that Muir and Thoreau and Burroughs speak the truth.

I can sense the moods of nature almost instinctively. Ever since I could walk, I have spent as much time as I could in the open. A perception of nature—no matter how delicate, how subtle, how evanescent,—remains with me forever.

I am influenced too much, perhaps, by natural objects. I seem bound by the very room I'm in. I've associated so long with prosaic people that I've dwarfed myself spiritually. When I get alone under an open sky where man isn't too evident—then I'm tremendously exalted and a thousand vivid ideas and sweet visions flood my consciousness.

I think that I possess story material in abundance. I have had an unusual upbringing. I was let alone, thank God! My mother insisted upon two things,—that I strive for perfection in whatever I did and that I always try to be a gentleman. I played with Italians, with Russians, Poles, and the "sissies" on Michigan Avenue. I was carefully watched, yet allowed to follow my own inclinations. I have seen a good deal of life that would never have been revealed to an older person. Up to the time I came to college then I had seen humanity in diverse forms. Now I'm cramped and unhappy. I don't feel that these idiotic adolescents are worth writing about. In the summer, I turn animal and work for a few weeks in a factory. Then I'm happy.

My literary achievements have been insignificant. At fourteen, I made a speech which was translated into twenty-six languages and used as Red Cross propaganda. When I was younger, it seemed that everything I wrote was eminently successful. I always won a prize when I entered an essay contest. In college, I've been able to get only one "A" in four rhetoric courses. I feel this keenly. If I can't write, what can I do? I wonder.

When I was a freshman, I told Carleton Wells that I knew I could write whether he thought so or not. On my next theme he wrote "You can Write!" How I have cherished that praise!

It is bad form to talk about grades, I know. If I don't get an "A" in this course, it wouldn't be because I haven't tried. I've made a slow start. I'm going to spend Christmas vacation writing. A "B" symbolizes defeat to me. I've been beaten too often.

I do wish that we were allowed to keep our stories until we felt that we had worked them into the best possible form.

I do not have the divine urge to write. There seems to be something surging within,—a profound undercurrent of emotion. Yet there is none of that fertility of creation which distinguishes the real writer.

Nevertheless, I have faith in myself. I'm either going to be a good writer or a poor fool.

Suggestions for Discussion

1. There are a number of paradoxical statements in Roethke's self-analysis, written when he was an undergraduate. Identify and explain.

2. Contrast Roethke's image of himself with what you imagine would be the view of his parents, his instructors, his contemporaries.

Suggestions for Writing

1. Write a statement of your expectations in a course in composition following the format of Roethke's statement. Include an analysis of your strengths and weaknesses, formative influences, sense of present accomplishment, and hopes for the future.

2. In the light of his self-analysis, comment on a selection of Roethke's published poems.

Kim Chernin

The Flesh and the Devil

Kim Chernin (b. 1940), a writer and an editor, was educated at the University of California at Berkeley, and Trinity College, Dublin. Through her ground-breaking work in the area of eating disorders, she has become a powerful voice in the feminist movement. In the 1980s she produced, to significant acclaim, six books: *The Obsession: Reflections on the Tyranny of Slenderness* (1981), *In My Mother's House* (1983), *The Hungry Self* (1985), *The Flame Bearers* (1986), *Reinventing Eve* (1987), and *Sex and Other Sacred Games* (1989). In this selection she relates American women's preoccupation with their bodies not to narcissism, but to self-rejection.

> We know that every woman wants to be thin. Our images of womanhood are almost synonymous with thinness.
> —Susie Orbach

> . . . I must now be able to look at my ideal, this ideal of being thin, of being without a body, and to realize: "it is a fiction."
> —Ellen West

> When the body is hiding the complex, it then becomes our most immediate access to the problem.
> —Marian Woodman

The locker room of the tennis club. Several exercise benches, two old-fashioned hair dryers, a mechanical bicycle, a treadmill, a reducing machine, a mirror, and a scale.

A tall woman enters, removes her towel; she throws it across a bench, faces herself squarely in the mirror, climbs on the scale, looks down.

A silence.

"I knew it," she mutters, turning to me. "I knew it."

And I think, before I answer, just how much I admire her, for this courage beyond my own, this daring to weigh herself daily in this way. And I sympathize. I know what she must be feeling. Not quite candidly, I say: "Up or down?" I am hoping to suggest that there might be people and cultures where gaining weight might not be considered a disaster. Places where women, stepping on scales, might be horrified to notice that they had reduced themselves. A mythical, almost unimaginable land.

"Two pounds," she says, ignoring my hint. "Two pounds." And then she turns, grabs the towel and swings out at her image in the mirror, smashing it violently, the towel spattering water over the glass. "Fat pig," she shouts at her image in the glass. "You fat, fat pig. . . ."

Later, I go to talk with this woman. Her name is Rachel and she becomes, as my work progresses, one of the choral voices that shape its vision.

Two girls come into the exercise room. They are perhaps ten or eleven years old, at that elongated stage when the skeletal structure seems to be winning its war against flesh. And these two are particularly skinny. They sit beneath the hair dryers for a moment, kicking their legs on the faded green upholstery; they run a few steps on the eternal treadmill, they wrap the rubber belt of the reducing machine around themselves and jiggle for a moment before it falls off. And then they go to the scale.

The taller one steps up, glances at herself in the mirror, looks down at the scale. She sighs, shaking her head. I see at once that this girl is imitating someone. The sigh, the headshake are theatrical, beyond her years. And so, too, is the little drama enacting itself in front of me. The other girl leans forward, eager to see for herself the troubling message imprinted upon the scale. But the older girl throws her hand over the secret. It is not to be revealed. And now the younger one, accepting this, steps up to confront the ultimate judgment. "Oh God," she says, this growing girl. "Oh God," with only a shade of imitation in her voice: "Would you believe it? I've gained five pounds."

These girls, too, become a part of my work. They enter, they perform their little scene again and again; it extends beyond them and in it I am finally able to behold something that would have remained hidden—for it does not express itself directly, although we feel its pressure almost every day of our lives. Something, unnamed as yet, struggling against our emergence into femininity. This is my first glimpse of it, out there. And the vision ripens.

I return to the sauna. Two women I have seen regularly at the club are sitting on the bench above me. One of them is very beautiful, the sort of woman Renoir would have admired. The other, who is probably in her late sixties, looks, in the twilight of this sweltering room, very much an adolescent. I have noticed her before, with her tan face, her white hair, her fashionable clothes, her slender hips and jaunty walk. But the effect has not been soothing. A woman of advancing age who looks like a boy.

"I've heard about that illness, anorexia nervosa," the plump one is saying, "and I keep looking around for someone who has it. I want to go sit next to her. I think to myself, maybe I'll catch it. . . ."

"Well," the other woman says to her, "I've felt the same way myself. One of my cousins used to throw food under the table when no one was looking.

Finally, she got so thin they had to take her to the hospital. . . . I always admired her."

What am I to understand from these stories? The woman in the locker room who swings out at her image in the mirror, the little girls who are afraid of the coming of adolescence to their bodies, the woman who admires the slenderness of the anorexic girl. Is it possible to miss the dislike these women feel for their bodies?

And yet, an instant's reflection tells us that this dislike for the body is not a biological fact of our condition as women—we do not come upon it by nature, we are not born to it, it does not arise for us because of anything predetermined in our sex. We know that once we loved the body, delighting in it the way children will, reaching out to touch our toes and count over our fingers, repeating the game endlessly as we come to knowledge of this body in which we will live out our lives. No part of the body exempt from our curiosity, nothing yet forbidden, we know an equal fascination with the feces we eliminate from ourselves, as with the ear we discover one day and the knees that have become bruised and scraped with falling and that warm, moist place between the legs from which feelings of indescribable bliss arise.

From that state to the condition of the woman in the locker room is a journey from innocence to despair, from the infant's naive pleasure in the body, to the woman's anguished confrontation with herself. In this journey we can read our struggle with natural existence—the loss of the body as a source of pleasure. But the most striking thing about this alienation from the body is the fact that we take it for granted. Few of us ask to be redeemed from this struggle against the flesh by overcoming our antagonism toward the body. We do not rush about looking for someone who can tell us how to enjoy the fact that our appetite is large, or how we might delight in the curves and fullness of our own natural shape. We hope instead to be able to reduce the body, to limit the urges and desires it feels, to remove the body from nature. Indeed, the suffering we experience through our obsession with the body arises precisely from the hopeless and impossible nature of this goal.

Cheryl Prewitt, the 1980 winner of the Miss America contest, is a twenty-two-year-old woman, "slender, bright-eyed, and attractive." If there were a single woman alive in America today who might feel comfortable about the size and shape of her body, surely we would expect her to be Ms. Prewitt? And yet, in order to make her body suitable for the swimsuit event of the beauty contest she has just won, Cheryl Prewitt "put herself through a grueling regimen, jogging long distances down back-country roads, pedaling for hours on her stationary bicycle." The bicycle is still kept in the living room of her parents' house so that she can take part in conversation while she works out. This body she has created, after an arduous struggle against nature, in conformity with her culture's ideal standard for a woman, cannot now be left to its own desires. It must be perpetually shaped, monitored, and watched. If you were to visit her at her home in Ackerman, Mississippi, you might well find her riding her stationary bicycle in her parents' living room, "working off the calories from a large slice of homemade coconut cake she has just had for a snack."

And so we imagine a woman who will never be Miss America, a next-door neighbor, a woman down the street, waking in the morning and setting out for her regular routine of exercise. The eagerness with which she jumps up at six o'clock and races for her jogging shoes and embarks upon the cold and arduous toiling up the hill road that runs past her house. And yes, she feels certain that her zeal to take off another pound, tighten another inch of softening flesh, places her in the school of those ancient wise men who formulated that vision of harmony between mind and body. "A healthy mind in a healthy body," she repeats to herself and imagines that it is love of the body which inspires her this early morning. But now she lets her mind wander and encounter her obsession. First it had been those hips, and she could feel them jogging along there with their own rhythm as she jogged. It was they that had needed reducing. Then, when the hips came down it was the thighs, hidden when she was clothed but revealing themselves every time she went to the sauna, and threatening great suffering now that summer drew near. Later, it was the flesh under the arms—this proved singularly resistant to tautness even after the rest of the body had become gaunt. And finally it was the ankles. But then, was there no end to it? What had begun as a vision of harmony between mind and body, a sense of well-being, physical fitness, and glowing health, had become now demonic, driving her always to further exploits, running farther, denying herself more food, losing more weight, always goaded on by the idea that the body's perfection lay just beyond her present achievement. And then, when she began to observe this driven quality in herself, she also began to notice what she had been thinking about her body. For she would write down in her notebook, without being aware of the violence in what she wrote: "I don't care how long it takes. One day I'm going to get my body to obey me. I'm going to make it lean and tight and hard. I'll succeed in this, even if it kills me."

But what a vicious attitude this is, she realizes one day, toward a body she professes to love. Was it love or hatred of the flesh that inspired her now to awaken even before it was light, and to go out on the coldest morning, running with bare arms and bare legs, busily fantasizing what she would make of her body? Love or hatred?

"You know perfectly well we hate our bodies," says Rachel, who calls herself the pig. She grabs the flesh of her stomach between her hands. "Who could love this?"

There is an appealing honesty in this despair, an articulation of what is virtually a universal attitude among women in our culture today. Few women who diet realize that they are confessing to a dislike for the body when they weigh and measure their flesh, subject it to rigorous fasts or strenuous regimens of exercise. And yet, over and over again, as I spoke to women about their bodies, this antagonism became apparent. One woman disliked her thighs, another her stomach, a third the loose flesh under her arms. Many would grab their skin and squeeze it as we talked, with that grimace of distaste language cannot translate into itself. One woman said to me: "Little by little I began to be aware that the pounds I was trying to 'melt away' were my own flesh. Would you believe it? It never occurred to me before. These 'ugly pounds' which filled me with so much hatred were my body."

The sound of this dawning consciousness can be heard now and again among the voices I have recorded in my notebook, heralding what may be a growing awareness of how bitterly the women of this culture are alienated from their bodies. Thus, another woman said to me: "It's true, I never used to like my body." We had been looking at pictures of women from the nine-teenth century; they were large women, with full hips and thighs. "What do you think of them?" I said. "They're like me," she answered, and then began to laugh. "Soft, sensual, and inviting."

The description is accurate; the women in the pictures, and the woman looking at them, share a quality of voluptuousness that is no longer admired by our culture:

> When I look at myself in the mirror I see that there's nothing wrong with me—now! Sometimes I even think I'm beautiful. I don't know why this began to change. It might have been when I started going to the YWCA. It was the first time I saw so many women naked. I realized it was the fuller bodies that were more beautiful. The thin women, who looked so good in clothes, seemed old and worn out. Their bodies were gaunt. But the bodies of the larger women had a certain natural mystery, very different from the false illusion of clothes. And I thought, I'm like them; I'm a big woman like they are and perhaps my body is beautiful. I had always been trying to make my body have the right shape so that I could fit into clothes. But then I started to look at myself in the mirror. Before that I had always looked at parts of myself. The hips were too flabby, the thighs were too fat. Now I began to see myself as a whole. I stopped hearing my mother's voice, asking me if I was going to go on a diet. I just looked at what was really there instead of what should have been there. What was wrong with it? I asked myself. And little by little I stopped disliking my body.

This is the starting point. It is from this new way of looking at an old problem that liberation will come. The very simple idea that an obsession with weight reflects a dislike and uneasiness for the body can have a profound effect upon a woman's life.

> I always thought I was too fat. I never liked my body. I kept trying to lose weight. I just tortured myself. But if I see pictures of myself from a year or two ago I discover now that I looked just fine.
>
> I remember recently going out to buy Häagen Dazs ice cream. I had decided I was going to give myself something I really wanted to eat. I had to walk all the way down to the World Trade Center. But on my way there I began to feel terribly fat. I felt that I was being punished by being fat. I had lost the beautiful self I had made by becoming thinner. I could hear these voices saying to me: "You're fat, you're ugly, who do you think you are, don't you know you'll never be happy?" I had always heard these voices in my mind but now when they would come into consciousness I would tell them to shut up. I saw two men on the street. I was eating the Häagen Dazs ice cream. I thought I heard one of them say "heavy." I thought they were saying: "She's so fat." But I knew that I had to live through these feelings if I was ever to eat what I liked. I just couldn't go on tormenting myself any more about the size of my body.
>
> One day, shortly after this, I walked into my house. I noticed the scales, standing under the sink in the bathroom. Suddenly, I hated them. I was filled with grief for having tortured myself for so many years. They looked like shack-les. I didn't want to have anything more to do with them. I called my boyfriend and offered him the scales. Then, I went into the kitchen. I looked at my shelves. I saw diet books there. I was filled with rage and hatred of them. I hurled them all into a box and got rid of them. Then I looked into the ice box. There was a bottle of Weight Watchers dressing. I hurled it into the garbage and watched it shatter and drip down the plastic bag. Little by little, I started to feel better about myself. At first I didn't eat less, I just worried less about my eating. I allowed myself to eat whatever I wanted. I began to give away the clothes I couldn't fit into. It turned out that they weren't right for me anyway. I

had bought them with the idea of what my body should look like. Now I buy clothes because I like the way they look on me. If something doesn't fit it doesn't fit. I'm not trying to make myself into something I'm not. I weigh more than I once considered my ideal. But I don't seem fat to myself. Now, I can honestly say that I like my body.

Some weeks ago, at a dinner party, a woman who had recently gained weight began to talk about her body.

"I was once very thin," she said, "but I didn't feel comfortable in my body. I fit into all the right clothes. But somehow I just couldn't find myself any longer."

I looked over at her expectantly; she was a voluptuous woman, who had recently given birth to her first child.

"But now," she said as she got to her feet, "now, if I walk or jog or dance, I feel my flesh jiggling along with me." She began to shake her shoulders and move her hips, her eyes wide as she hopped about in front of the coffee table. "You see what I mean?" she shouted over to me. "I love it."

This image of a woman dancing came with me when I sat down to write. I remembered her expression. There was in it something secretive, I thought, something knowing and pleased—the look of a woman who has made peace with her body. Then I recalled the faces of women who had recently lost weight. The haggard look, the lines of strain around the mouth, the neck too lean, the tendons visible, the head too large for the emaciated body. I began to reason:

There must be, I said, for every woman a correct weight, which cannot be discovered with reference to a weight chart or to any statistical norm. For the size of the body is a matter of highly subjective individual preferences and natural endowments. If we should evolve an aesthetic for women that was appropriate to women it would reflect this diversity, would conceive, indeed celebrate and even love, slenderness in a woman intended by nature to be slim, and love the rounded cheeks of another, the plump arms, broad shoulders, narrow hips, full thighs, rounded ass, straight back, narrow shoulders or slender arms, of a woman made that way according to her nature, walking with head high in pride of her body, however it happened to be shaped. And then Miss America, and the woman jogging in the morning, and the woman swinging out at her image in the mirror might say, with Susan Griffin in *Woman and Nature:*

And we are various, and amazing in our variety, and our differences multiply, so that edge after edge of the endlessness of possibility is exposed . . . none of us beautiful when separate but all exquisite as we stand, each moment heeded in this cycle, no detail unlovely. . . .

Suggestions for Discussion

1. Chernin's work led her to the conclusion that America's obsession with thinness has to do with dominating nature, with control. Do you agree? Explain.

2. In their preoccupation with weight women have come to hate their bodies and to derive no sense of pleasure from them, asserts Chernin. With what evidence does she support this statement?

3. Is it possible in our culture to affirm a number of different shapes and sizes of women; to see a variety of body types as beautiful? Or are we always going to have an ideal against which all will be measured?

Suggestions for Writing

1. Eating disorders are a major health crisis in our country. Have you, a friend, or a relation ever suffered from one? What was it like? How did you feel about eating? About yourself? Describe.

2. It has been said that Americans are obsessed with their bodies. Write a story built around at least one example of this obsession.

Carson McCullers

Loneliness . . . An American Malady

Carson McCullers (1917–1967), a Southern writer, was awarded Guggenheim Fellowships in 1942 and in 1946. Her published works include The Heart Is a Lonely Hunter (1940), Reflections in a Golden Eye (1941), The Member of the Wedding (1946), The Ballad of the Sad Café (1951), and Clock Without Hands (1961). This excerpt from The Mortgaged Heart (1971) suggests that the way by which we master loneliness is "to belong to something larger and more powerful than the weak, lonely self."

This city, New York—consider the people in it, the eight million of us. An English friend of mine, when asked why he lived in New York City, said that he liked it here because he could be so alone. While it was my friend's desire to be alone, the aloneness of many Americans who live in cities is an involuntary and fearful thing. It has been said that loneliness is the great American malady. What is the nature of this loneliness? It would seem essentially to be a quest for identity.

To the spectator, the amateur philosopher, no motive among the complex ricochets of our desires and rejections seems stronger or more enduring than the will of the individual to claim his identity and belong. From infancy to death, the human being is obsessed by these dual motives. During our first weeks of life, the question of identity shares urgency with the need for milk. The baby reaches for his toes, then explores the bars of his crib; again and again he compares the difference between his own body and the objects around him, and in the wavering, infant eyes there comes a pristine wonder.

Consciousness of self is the first abstract problem that the human being solves. Indeed, it is this self-consciousness that removes us from lower animals. This primitive grasp of identity develops with constantly shifting emphasis through all our years. Perhaps maturity is simply the history of those mutations that reveal to the individual the relation between himself and the world in which he finds himself.

After the first establishment of identity there comes the imperative need to lose this new-found sense of separateness and to belong to something larger and more powerful than the weak, lonely self. The sense of moral isolation is intolerable to us.

In *The Member of the Wedding* the lonely 12-year-old girl, Frankie Addams, articulates this universal need: "The trouble with me is that for a long time I have just been an *I* person. All people belong to a *We* except me. Not to belong to a *We* makes you too lonesome."

Love is the bridge that leads from the *I* sense to the *We*, and there is a paradox about personal love. Love of another individual opens a new relation between the personality and the world. The lover responds in a new way to nature and may even write poetry. Love is affirmation; it motivates the *yes* responses and the sense of wider communication. Love casts out fear, and in the security of this togetherness we find contentment, courage. We no longer fear the age-old haunting questions: "Who am I?" "Why am I?" "Where am I going?"—and having cast out fear, we can be honest and charitable.

For fear is a primary source of evil. And when the question "Who am I?" recurs and is unanswered, then fear and frustration project a negative attitude. The bewildered soul can answer only: "Since I do not understand 'Who I am,' I only know what I am *not*." The corollary of this emotional incertitude is snobbism, intolerance, and racial hate. The xenophobic individual can only reject and destroy, as the xenophobic nation inevitably makes war.

The loneliness of Americans does not have its source in xenophobia; as a nation we are an outgoing people, reaching always for immediate contacts, further experience. But we tend to seek out things as individuals, alone. The European, secure in his family ties and rigid class loyalties, knows little of the moral loneliness that is native to us Americans. While the European artists tend to form groups or aesthetic schools, the American artist is the eternal maverick—not only from society in the way of all creative minds, but within the orbit of his own art.

Thoreau took to the woods to seek the ultimate meaning of his life. His creed was simplicity and his *modus vivendi* the deliberate stripping of external life to the Spartan necessities in order that his inward life could freely flourish. His objective, as he put it, was to back the world into a corner. And in that way did he discover "What a man thinks of himself, that it is which determines, or rather indicates, his fate."

On the other hand, Thomas Wolfe turned to the city, and in his wanderings around New York he continued his frenetic and lifelong search for the lost brother, the magic door. He too backed the world into a corner, and as he passed among the city's millions, returning their stares, he experienced "That silent meeting [that] is the summary of all the meetings of men's lives."

Whether in the pastoral joys of country life or in the labyrinthine city, we Americans are always seeking. We wander, question. But the answer waits in each separate heart—the answer of our own identity and the way by which we can master loneliness and feel that at last we belong.

Suggestion for Discussion

How does the author establish the connections between loneliness and identity? Between *I* and *We?* Between lack of a sense of identity and fear? Between fear and hatred or destruction? Between Thoreau's search and that of Thomas Wolfe?

Suggestions for Writing

1. Develop or challenge Thoreau's belief, "What a man thinks of himself, that it is which determines, or rather indicates, his fate."

2. Develop an essay in which you argue that country life is or is not more conducive to the development of a sense of self than city life.

Bruno Bettelheim

The Child's Need for Magic

Bruno Bettelheim (1903–1990) was born in Vienna and educated at the University of Vienna. Having survived the Nazi holocaust, he became an American psychoanalyst and educator and was director of the remarkable University of Chicago Sonia Shankman Orthogenic School from 1944 to 1973. He wrote many penetrating works on parents and children and the significance of the holocaust. In this excerpt from *The Uses of Enchantment* (1976), the author believes that fairy tales provide answers to the child's pressing questions about his identity and his world.

Myths and fairy stories both answer the eternal questions: What is the world really like? How am I to live my life in it? How can I truly be myself? The answers given by myths are definite, while the fairy tale is suggestive; its messages may imply solutions, but it never spells them out. Fairy tales leave to the child's fantasizing whether and how to apply to himself what the story reveals about life and human nature.

The fairy tale proceeds in a manner which conforms to the way a child thinks and experiences the world; this is why the fairy tale is so convincing to him. He can gain much better solace from a fairy tale than he can from an effort to comfort him based on adult reasoning and viewpoints. A child trusts what the fairy story tells, because its world view accords with his own.

Whatever our age, only a story conforming to the principles underlying our thought processes carries conviction for us. If this is so for adults, who have learned to accept that there is more than one frame of reference for comprehending the world—although we find it difficult if not impossible truly to think in any but our own—it is exclusively true for the child. His thinking is animistic.

Like all preliterate and many literate people, "the child assumes that his relations to the inanimate world are of one pattern with those to the animate world of people: he fondles as he would his mother the pretty thing that pleased him; he strikes the door that has slammed on him." It should be added that he does the first because he is convinced that this pretty thing loves to be petted as much as he does; and he punishes the door because he is certain that the door slammed deliberately, out of evil intention.

As Piaget has shown, the child's thinking remains animistic until the age of puberty. His parents and teachers tell him that things cannot feel and act; and as much as he may pretend to believe this to please these adults, or not to be ridiculed, deep down the child knows better. Subjected to the rational teachings of others, the child only buries his "true knowledge" deeper in his soul and it remains untouched by rationality; but it can be formed and informed by what fairy tales have to say.

To the eight-year-old (to quote Piaget's examples), the sun is alive because it gives light (and, one may add, it does that because it wants to). To the child's animistic mind, the stone is alive because it can move, as it rolls down a hill. Even a twelve-and-a-half-year-old is convinced that a stream is alive and has a will, because its water is flowing. The sun, the stone, and the water are believed to be inhabited by spirits very much like people, so they feel and act like people.

To the child, there is no clear line separating objects from living things; and whatever has life has life very much like our own. If we do not understand what rocks and trees and animals have to tell us, the reason is that we are not sufficiently attuned to them. To the child trying to understand the world, it seems reasonable to expect answers from those objects which arouse his curiosity. And since the child is self-centered, he expects the animal to talk about the things which are really significant to him, as animals do in fairy tales, and as the child himself talks to his real or toy animals. A child is convinced that the animal understands and feels with him, even though it does not show it openly.

Since animals roam freely and widely in the world, how natural that in fairy tales these animals are able to guide the hero in his search which takes him into distant places. Since all that moves is alive, the child can believe that the wind can talk and carry the hero to where he needs to go, as in "East of the Sun and West of the Moon." In animistic thinking, not only animals feel and think as we do, but even stones are alive; so to be turned into stone simply means that the being has to remain silent and unmoving for a time. By the same reasoning, it is entirely believable when previously silent objects begin to talk, give advice, and join the hero on his wanderings. And since everything is inhabited by a spirit similar to all other spirits (namely, that of the child who has projected his spirit into all these things), because of this inherent sameness it is believable that man can change into animal, or the other way around, as in "Beauty and the Beast" or "The Frog King." Since there is no sharp line drawn between living and dead things, the latter, too, can come to life.

When, like the great philosophers, children are searching for the solutions to the first and last questions—"Who am I? How ought I to deal with life's problems? What must I become?"—they do so on the basis of their animistic thinking. But since the child is so uncertain of what his existence consists, first and foremost comes the question "Who am I?"

As soon as a child begins to move about and explore, he begins to ponder the problem of his identity. When he spies his mirror image, he wonders whether what he sees is really he, or a child just like him standing behind this glassy wall. He tries to find out by exploring whether this other child is really, in all ways, like him. He makes faces, turns this way or that, walks away from the mirror and jumps back in front of it to ascertain whether this other one has moved away or is still there. Though only three years old, the child is already up against the difficult problem of personal identity.

The child asks himself: "Who am I? Where did I come from? How did the world come into being? Who created man and all the animals? What is the purpose of life?" True, he ponders these vital questions not in the abstract, but mainly as they pertain to him. He worries not whether there is justice for individual man, but whether *he* will be treated justly. He wonders who or what projects him into adversity, and what can prevent this from happening to him. Are there benevolent powers in addition to his parents? Are his parents benevolent powers? How should he form himself, and why? Is there hope for him, though he may have done wrong? Why has all this happened to him? What will it mean for his future? Fairy tales provide answers to these pressing questions, many of which the child becomes aware of only as he follows the stories.

From an adult point of view and in terms of modern science, the answers which fairy stories offer are fantastic rather than true. As a matter of fact, these solutions seem so incorrect to many adults—who have become estranged from the ways in which young people experience the world—that they object to exposing children to such "false" information. However, realistic explanations are usually incomprehensible to children, because they lack the abstract understanding required to make sense of them. While giving a scientifically correct answer makes adults think they have clarified things for the child, such explanations leave the young child confused, overpowered, and intellectually defeated. A child can derive security only from the conviction that he understands now what baffled him before—never from being given facts which create *new* uncertainties. Even as the child accepts such an answer, he comes to doubt that he has asked the right question. Since the explanation fails to make sense to him, it must apply to some unknown problem—not the one he asked about.

It is therefore important to remember that only statements which are intelligible in terms of the child's existing knowledge and emotional preoccupations carry conviction for him. To tell a child that the earth floats in space, attracted by gravity into circling around the sun, but that the earth doesn't fall to the sun as the child falls to the ground, seems very confusing to him. The child knows from his experience that everything has to rest on something, or be held up by something. Only an explanation based on that knowledge can make him feel he understands better about the earth in space. More important, to feel secure on earth, the child needs to believe that this world is held firmly in place. Therefore he finds a better explanation in a myth that tells him that the earth rests on a turtle, or is held up by a giant.

If a child accepts as true what his parents tell him—that the earth is a planet held securely on its path by gravity—then the child can only imagine that gravity is a string. Thus the parents' explanation has led to no better understanding or feeling of security. It requires considerable intellectual maturity to believe that there can be stability to one's life when the ground on which one walks (the firmest thing around, on which everything rests) spins with incredible speed on an invisible axis; that in addition it rotates around the sun; and furthermore hurtles through space with the entire solar system. I have never yet encountered a prepubertal youngster who could comprehend all these combined movements, although I have known many who could repeat this information. Such children parrot explanations which according to their own experience of the world are lies, but which they must believe to be true because some adult has said so. The consequence is that children come to distrust their own experience, and therefore themselves and what their minds can do for them.

In the fall of 1973, the comet Kohoutek was in the news. At that time a competent science teacher explained the comet to a small group of highly intelligent second- and third-graders. Each child had carefully cut out a paper circle and had drawn on it the course of the planets around the sun; a paper ellipse, attached by a slit to the paper circle, represented the course of the comet. The children showed me the comet moving along at an angle to the planets. When I asked them, the children told me that they were holding the comet in their hands, showing me the ellipse. When I asked how the comet which they were holding in their hands could also be in the sky, they were all nonplussed.

In their confusion, they turned to their teacher, who carefully explained to them that what they were holding in their hands, and had so diligently created, was only a model of the planets and the comet. The children all agreed that they understood this, and would have repeated it if questioned further. But whereas before they had regarded proudly this circle-cum-ellipse in their hands, they now lost all interest. Some crumpled the paper up, others dropped the model in the wastepaper basket. When the pieces of paper had been the comet to them, they had all planned to take the model home to show their parents, but now it no longer had meaning for them.

In trying to get a child to accept scientifically correct explanations, parents all too frequently discount scientific findings of how a child's mind works. Research on the child's mental processes, especially Piaget's, convincingly demonstrates that the young child is not able to comprehend the two vital abstract concepts of the permanence of quantity, and of reversibility—for instance, that the same quantity of water rises high in a narrow receptacle and remains low in a wide one; and that subtraction reverses the process of addition. Until he can understand abstract concepts such as these, the child can experience the world only subjectively.

Scientific explanations require objective thinking. Both theoretical research and experimental exploration have shown that no child below school age is truly able to grasp these two concepts, without which abstract understanding is impossible. In his early years, until age eight or ten, the child can develop only highly personalized concepts about what he experiences. Therefore it seems natural to him, since the plants which grow on this earth nourish him as his mother did from her breast, to see the earth as a mother or a female god, or at least as her abode.

Even a young child somehow knows that he was created by his parents; so it makes good sense to him that, like himself, all men and where they live were created by a superhuman figure not very different from his parents— some male or female god. Since his parents watch over the child and provide him with his needs in his home, then naturally he also believes that something like them, only much more powerful, intelligent, and reliable—a guardian angel—will do so out in the world.

A child thus experiences the world order in the image of his parents and of what goes on within the family. The ancient Egyptians, as a child does, saw heaven and the sky as a motherly figure (Nut) who protectively bent over the earth, enveloping it and them serenely. Far from preventing man from later developing a more rational explanation of the world, such a view offers security where and when it is most needed—a security which, when the time is ripe, allows for a truly rational world view. Life on a small planet surrounded by limitless space seems awfully lonely and cold to a child—just the opposite of what he knows life ought to be. This is why the ancients needed to feel sheltered and warmed by an enveloping mother figure. To depreciate protective imagery like this as mere childish projections of an immature mind is to rob the young child of one aspect of the prolonged safety and comfort he needs.

True, the notion of a sheltering sky-mother can be limiting to the mind if clung to for too long. Neither infantile projections nor dependence on imaginary protectors—such as a guardian angel who watches out for one when one is asleep, or during Mother's absence—offers true security; but as long as one cannot provide complete security for oneself, imaginings and projections are far preferable to no security. It is such (partly imagined) security which, when experienced for a sufficient length of time, permits the child to develop that feeling of confidence in life which he needs in order to trust himself—a trust necessary for his learning to solve life's problems through his own growing rational abilities. Eventually the child recognizes that what he has taken as literally true—the earth as a mother—is only a symbol.

A child, for example, who has learned from fairy stories to believe that what at first seemed a repulsive, threatening figure can magically change into a most helpful friend is ready to believe that a strange child whom he meets and fears may also be changed from a menace into a desirable companion. Belief in the "truth" of the fairy tale gives him courage not to withdraw because of the way this stranger appears to him at first. Recalling how the hero of many a fairy tale succeeded in life because he dared to befriend a seemingly unpleasant figure, the child believes he may work the same magic.

I have known many examples where, particularly in late adolescence, years of belief in magic are called upon to compensate for the person's having been deprived of it prematurely in childhood, through stark reality having been forced on him. It is as if these young people feel that now is their last chance to make up for a severe deficiency in their life experience; or that without having had a period of belief in magic, they will be unable to meet the rigors of adult life. Many young people who today suddenly seek escape in drug-induced dreams, apprentice themselves to some guru, believe in astrology, engage in practicing "black magic," or who in some other fashion escape from reality into daydreams about magic experiences which are to change their life for the better, were prematurely pressed to view reality in an adult way. Trying to evade reality in such ways has its deeper cause in early formative experiences which prevented the development of the conviction that life can be mastered in realistic ways.

What seems desirable for the individual is to repeat in his life span the process involved historically in the genesis of scientific thought. For a long time in his history man used emotional projections—such as gods—born of his immature hopes and anxieties to explain man, his society, and the universe; these explanations gave him a feeling of security. Then slowly, by his own social, scientific, and technological progress, man freed himself of the constant fear for his very existence. Feeling more secure in the world, and also within himself, man could now begin to question the validity of the images he had used in the past as explanatory tools. From there man's "childish" projections dissolved and more rational explanations took their place. This process, however, is by no means without vagaries. In intervening periods of stress and scarcity, man seeks for comfort again in the "childish" notion that he and his place of abode are the center of the universe.

Translated in terms of human behavior, the more secure a person feels within the world, the less he will need to hold on to "infantile" projections—mythical explanations or fairy-tale solutions to life's eternal problems—and the more he can afford to seek rational explanations. The more secure a man is within himself, the more he can afford to accept an explanation which says his world is of minor significance in the cosmos. Once man feels truly significant in his human environment, he cares little about the importance of his planet within the universe. On the other hand, the more insecure a man is in himself and his place in the immediate world, the more he withdraws into himself because of fear, or else moves outward to conquer for conquest's sake. This is the opposite of exploring out of a security which frees our curiosity.

For these same reasons a child, as long as he is not sure his immediate human environment will protect him, needs to believe that superior powers, such as a guardian angel, watch over him, and that the world and his place within it are of paramount importance. Here is one connection between a family's ability to provide basic security and the child's readiness to engage in rational investigations as he grows up.

As long as parents fully believed that Biblical stories solved the riddle of our existence and its purpose, it was easy to make a child feel secure. The Bible was felt to contain the answers to all pressing questions: the Bible told man all he needed to know to understand the world, how it came into being, and how to behave in it. In the Western world the Bible also provided prototypes for man's imagination. But rich as the Bible is in stories, not even during the most religious of times were these stories sufficient for meeting all the psychic needs of man.

Part of the reason for this is that while the Old and New Testaments and the histories of the saints provided answers to the crucial questions of how to live the good life, they did not offer solutions for the problems posed by the dark sides of our personalities. The Biblical stories suggest essentially only one solution for the asocial aspects of the unconscious: repression of these (unacceptable) strivings. But children, not having their ids in conscious control, need stories which permit at least fantasy satisfaction of these "bad" tendencies, and specific models for their sublimation.

Explicitly and implicitly, the Bible tells of God's demands on man. While we are told that there is greater rejoicing about a sinner who reformed than about the man who never erred, the message is still that we ought to live the good life, and not, for example, take cruel revenge on those whom we hate. As the story of Cain and Abel shows, there is no sympathy in the Bible for the agonies of sibling rivalry—only a warning that acting upon it has devastating consequences.

But what a child needs most, when beset by jealousy of his sibling, is the permission to feel that what he experiences is justified by the situation he is in. To bear up under the pangs of his envy, the child needs to be encouraged to engage in fantasies of getting even someday; then he will be able to manage at the moment, because of the conviction that the future will set things aright. Most of all, the child wants support for his still very tenuous belief that through growing up, working hard, and maturing he will one day be the victorious one. If his present sufferings will be rewarded in the future, he need not act on his jealousy of the moment, the way Cain did.

Like Biblical stories and myths, fairy tales were the literature which edified everybody—children and adults alike—for nearly all of man's existence. Except that God is central, many Bible stories can be recognized as very similar to fairy tales. In the story of Jonah and the whale, for example, Jonah is trying to run away from his superego's (conscience's) demand that he fight against the wickedness of the people of Nineveh. The ordeal which tests his moral fiber is, as in so many fairy tales, a perilous voyage in which he has to prove himself.

Jonah's trip across the sea lands him in the belly of a great fish. There, in great danger, Jonah discovers his higher morality, his higher self, and is wondrously reborn, now ready to meet the rigorous demands of his superego. But the rebirth alone does not achieve true humanity for him: to be a slave neither to the id and the pleasure principle (avoiding arduous tasks by trying to escape from them) nor to the superego (wishing destruction upon the wicked city) means true freedom and higher selfhood. Jonah attains his full humanity only when he is no longer subservient to either institution of his mind, but relinquishes blind obedience to both id and superego and is able to recognize God's wisdom in judging the people of Nineveh not according to the rigid structures of Jonah's superego, but in terms of their human frailty.

Suggestions for Discussion

1. How does Bettelheim distinguish myths from fairy tales? The Bible from fairy tales?

2. Who is Piaget? How has he influenced current thought regarding the way children think and learn?

3. Explain Bettelheim's reference to children as "animistic thinkers." How does this description of them relate to their need for fairy tales?

4. What similarities does the author see between the child and the philosopher? How do they differ?

5. Explain why Bettelheim believes it mistaken to deprive children of fairy tales. How does he relate their need for fairy tales to the difficulties they have in comprehending scientific ideas?

Suggestions for Writing

1. Using one or more fairy tales with which you are familiar, write an essay explaining how magical elements might serve to explain the universe to a child.

2. Write a comparison between a fairy tale and one of the popular children's stories about ordinary life.

Ellen Goodman

The Company Man

Ellen Goodman (b. 1942) was educated at Radcliffe College and pursued a career as a journalist. She was a researcher and reporter for *Newsweek*, a feature writer for the *Boston Globe*, and a syndicated columnist with Washington Post Writers Group. She has been a Nieman fellow at Harvard University and named columnist of the year by the New England Women's Press Association. In 1980 she won a Pulitzer Prize for distinguished commentary. Her books include, among others, *Turning Points* (1979), *At Large* (1981), a collection of newspaper columns, and *Making Sense* (1989). In this essay she portrays a workaholic whose sense of self is totally based upon his identification with his company.

He worked himself to death, finally and precisely, at 3:00 A.M. Sunday morning.

The obituary didn't say that, of course. It said that he died of a coronary thrombosis—I think that was it—but everyone among his friends and acquaintances knew it instantly. He was a perfect Type A, a workaholic, a classic, they said to each other and shook their heads—and thought for five or ten minutes about the way they lived.

This man who worked himself to death finally and precisely at 3:00 A.M. Sunday morning—on his day off—was fifty-one years old and a vice-president. He was, however, one of six vice-presidents, and one of three who might conceivably—if the president died or retired soon enough—have moved to the top spot. Phil knew that.

He worked six days a week, five of them until eight or nine at night, during a time when his own company had begun the four-day week for everyone but the executives. He worked like the Important People. He had no outside "extracurricular interests," unless, of course, you think about a monthly golf game that way. To Phil, it was work. He always ate egg salad sandwiches at his desk. He was, of course, overweight, by 20 or 25 pounds. He thought it was okay, though, because he didn't smoke.

On Saturdays, Phil wore a sports jacket to the office instead of a suit, because it was the weekend.

He had a lot of people working for him, maybe sixty, and most of them liked him most of the time. Three of them will be seriously considered for his job. The obituary didn't mention that.

But it did list his "survivors" quite accurately. He is survived by his wife, Helen, forty-eight years old, a good woman of no particular marketable skills, who worked in an office before marrying and mothering. She had, according to her daughter, given up trying to compete with his work years ago, when the children were small. A company friend said, "I know how much you will miss him." And she answered, "I already have."

"Missing him all these years," she must have given up part of herself which had cared too much for the man. She would be "well taken care of."

His "dearly beloved" eldest of the "dearly beloved" children is a hard-working executive in a manufacturing firm down South. In the day and a half before the funeral, he went around the neighborhood researching his father, asking the neighbors what he was like. They were embarrassed.

His second child is a girl, who is twenty-four and newly married. She lives near her mother and they are close, but whenever she was alone with her father, in a car driving somewhere, they had nothing to say to each other.

The youngest is twenty, a boy, a high-school graduate who has spent the last couple of years, like a lot of his friends, doing enough odd jobs to stay in grass and food. He was the one who tried to grab at his father, and tried to mean enough to him to keep the man at home. He was his father's favorite. Over the last two years, Phil stayed up nights worrying about the boy.

The boy once said, "My father and I only board here."

At the funeral, the sixty-year-old company president told the forty-eight-year-old widow that the fifty-one-year-old deceased had meant much to the company and would be missed and would be hard to replace. The widow didn't look him in the eye. She was afraid he would read her bitterness and, after all, she would need him to straighten out the finances—the stock options and all that.

Phil was overweight and nervous and worked too hard. If he wasn't at the office, he was worried about it. Phil was a Type A, a heart-attack natural. You could have picked him out in a minute from a lineup.

So when he finally worked himself to death, at precisely 3:00 A.M. Sunday morning, no one was really surprised.

By 5:00 P.M. the afternoon of the funeral, the company president had begun, discreetly of course, with care and taste, to make inquiries about his replacement. One of three men. He asked around: "Who's been working the hardest?"

Suggestions for Discussion

1. What does the clause "and thought for five or ten minutes about the way they lived" tell the reader about the author's point of view? About her tone?

2. What is the significance of the statement that the man who died was "one of six vice-presidents, and one of three who might . . . have moved to the top spot"?

3. Why doesn't the author identify the man by name until the end of the third paragraph?

4. Goodman makes statements about Phil, then qualifies them. Cite instances. What is the nature of the qualification? How does this technique add to the characterization? To the tone?

5. What does the brief item on each family member and the company president tell readers about Phil? About themselves?

6. Account for the repetition of Phil's age and the hour of his death.

7. What is the significance of the president's question after the funeral?

8. What is the implicit statement that Goodman makes about workaholics? About large companies?

9. Speculate upon Phil's sense of self.

Suggestions for Writing

1. Make a study of a person you know whose sense of self is based on his or her identification with an institution, a business, a school, or a character in fiction.

2. If you know a workaholic, write a description using incidents and dialogue that illuminate his or her character.

Fiction

Ernest Hemingway

Indian Camp

Ernest Hemingway (1898–1961), novelist and short-story writer, began his career as a reporter and during World War I served with an ambulance unit in France and Italy. After the war he lived in Paris as a correspondent for the Hearst papers. During the Spanish Civil War he went to Spain as a war correspondent. His works include the collections of short stories In Our Time (1925), Men Without Women (1927), The Fifth Column and the First 49 Stories (1938); and the novels The Sun Also Rises (1926), A Farewell to Arms (1929), For Whom the Bell Tolls (1940), and The Old Man and the Sea (1952), which was awarded a Pulitzer Prize. In 1954 he received the Nobel Prize for Literature. This is a story of initiation, from the collection In Our Time, in which the boy is exposed to a violent birth and death.

At the lake shore there was another rowboat drawn up. The two Indians stood waiting.

Nick and his father got in the stern of the boat and the Indians shoved it off and one of them got in to row. Uncle George sat in the stern of the camp rowboat. The young Indian shoved the camp boat off and got in to row Uncle George.

The two boats started off in the dark. Nick heard the oarlocks of the other boat quite a way ahead of them in the mist. The Indians rowed with quick choppy strokes. Nick lay back with his father's arm around him. It was cold on the water. The Indian who was rowing them was working very hard, but the other boat moved further ahead in the mist all the time.

"Where are we going, Dad?" Nick asked.

"Over to the Indian camp. There is an Indian lady very sick."

"Oh," said Nick.

Across the bay they found the other boat beached. Uncle George was smoking a cigar in the dark. The young Indian pulled the boat way up on the beach. Uncle George gave both the Indians cigars.

They walked up from the beach through a meadow that was soaking wet with dew, following the young Indian who carried a lantern. Then they went into the woods and followed a trail that led to the logging road that ran back into the hills. It was much lighter on the logging road as the timber was cut away on both sides. The young Indian stopped and blew out his lantern and they all walked on along the road.

They came around a bend and a dog came out barking. Ahead were the lights of the shanties where the Indian bark-peelers lived. More dogs rushed out at them. The two Indians sent them back to the shanties. In the shanty nearest the road there was a light in the window. An old woman stood in the doorway holding a lamp.

Inside on a wooden bunk lay a young Indian woman. She had been trying to have her baby for two days. All the old women in the camp had been helping her. The men had moved off up the road to sit in the dark and smoke out of range of the noise she made. She screamed just as Nick and the two Indians followed his father and Uncle George into the shanty. She lay in the lower bunk, very big under a quilt. Her head was turned to one side. In the upper bunk was her husband. He had cut his foot very badly with an ax three days before. He was smoking a pipe. The room smelled very bad.

Nick's father ordered some water to be put on the stove, and while it was heating he spoke to Nick.

"This lady is going to have a baby, Nick," he said.

"I know," said Nick.

"You don't know," said his father. "Listen to me. What she is going through is called being in labor. The baby wants to be born and she wants it to be born. All her muscles are trying to get the baby born. That is what is happening when she screams."

"I see," Nick said.

Just then the woman cried out.

"Oh, Daddy, can't you give her something to make her stop screaming?" asked Nick.

"No. I haven't any anaesthetic," his father said. "But her screams are not important. I don't hear them because they are not important."

The husband in the upper bunk rolled over against the wall.

The woman in the kitchen motioned to the doctor that the water was hot. Nick's father went into the kitchen and poured about half of the water out of the big kettle into a basin. Into the water left in the kettle he put several things he unwrapped from a handkerchief.

"Those must boil," he said, and began to scrub his hands in the basin of hot water with a cake of soap he had brought from the camp. Nick watched his father's hands scrubbing each other with the soap. While his father washed his hands very carefully and thoroughly, he talked.

"You see, Nick, babies are supposed to be born head first but sometimes they're not. When they're not they make a lot of trouble for everybody. Maybe I'll have to operate on this lady. We'll know in a little while."

When he was satisfied with his hands he went in and went to work.

"Pull back that quilt, will you, George?" he said. "I'd rather not touch it."

Later when he started to operate Uncle George and three Indian men held the woman still. She bit Uncle George on the arm and Uncle George said, "Damn squaw bitch!" and the young Indian who had rowed Uncle George over laughed at him. Nick held the basin for his father. It all took a long time.

His father picked the baby up and slapped it to make it breathe and handed it to the old woman.

"See, it's a boy, Nick," he said. "How do you like being an interne?"

Nick said, "All right." He was looking away so as not to see what his father was doing.

"There. That gets it," said his father and put something into the basin.

Nick didn't look at it.

"Now," his father said, "there's some stitches to put in. You can watch this or not, Nick, just as you like. I'm going to sew up the incision I made."

Nick did not watch. His curiosity had been gone for a long time.

His father finished and stood up. Uncle George and the three Indian men stood up. Nick put the basin out in the kitchen.

Uncle George looked at his arm. The young Indian smiled reminiscently.

"I'll put some peroxide on that, George," the doctor said.

He bent over the Indian woman. She was quiet now and her eyes were closed. She looked very pale. She did not know what had become of the baby or anything.

"I'll be back in the morning," the doctor said, standing up. "The nurse should be here from St. Ignace by noon and she'll bring everything we need."

He was feeling exalted and talkative as football players are in the dressing room after a game.

"That's one for the medical journal, George," he said. "Doing a Caesarean with a jack-knife and sewing it up with nine-foot, tapered gut leaders."

Uncle George was standing against the wall, looking at his arm.

"Oh, you're a great man, all right," he said.

"Ought to have a look at the proud father. They're usually the worst sufferers in these little affairs," the doctor said. "I must say he took it all pretty quietly."

He pulled back the blanket from the Indian's head. His hand came away wet. He mounted on the edge of the lower bunk with the lamp in one hand and looked in. The Indian lay with his face toward the wall. His throat had been cut from ear to ear. The blood had flowed down into a pool where his body sagged the bunk. His head rested on his left arm. The open razor lay, edge up, in the blankets.

"Take Nick out of the shanty, George," the doctor said.

There was no need of that. Nick, standing in the door of the kitchen, had a good view of the upper bunk when his father, the lamp in one hand, tipped the Indian's head back.

It was just beginning to be daylight when they walked along the logging road back toward the lake.

"I'm terribly sorry I brought you along, Nickie," said his father, all his post-operative exhilaration gone. "It was an awful mess to put you through."

"Do ladies always have such a hard time having babies?" Nick asked.

"No, that was very, very exceptional."

"Why did he kill himself, Daddy?"

"I don't know, Nick. He couldn't stand things, I guess."

"Do many men kill themselves, Daddy?"

"Not very many, Nick."

"Do many women?"

"Hardly ever."

"Don't they ever?"

"Oh, yes. They do sometimes."

"Daddy?"

"Yes."

"Where did Uncle George go?"

"He'll turn up all right."

"Is dying hard, Daddy?"

"No, I think it's pretty easy, Nick. It all depends."

They were seated in the boat, Nick in the stern, his father rowing. The sun was coming up over the hills. A bass jumped, making a circle in the water. Nick trailed his hand in the water. It felt warm in the sharp chill of the morning.

In the early morning on the lake sitting in the stern of the boat with his father rowing, he felt quite sure that he would never die.

Suggestions for Discussion

1. How is the emotional tension of the story built up by the descriptive details of the journey to the Indian camp and the arrival at the shanties?

2. Inside the hut, what images of sight, sound, and smell take you into the heart of the scene?

3. What is the effect of the rather cold, scientific attitude of the doctor-father? Of his laconic explanations to his son interspersed with details of action? Note the verbs he uses.

4. What do Uncle George and the young Indian observers contribute to the reader's rising sense of horror?

5. How are you prepared for the suicide of the husband?

6. Comment on the irony of the concluding conversation and the significance of the experience in Nick's emotional growth and awareness of life and death.

7. Explain the final sentence.

8. By specific reference to the text, support the view that this is primarily a story of Nick's initiation.

Suggestions for Writing

1. Discuss the story as a commentary on the condition of Indians in rural areas or on reservations today.

2. Write about an early experience in which you learned about birth or death, death or violence.

Elizabeth Taylor

Girl Reading

Elizabeth Taylor (1912–1975) was born in England and is distinguished for her short stories. Among her publications are *In a Summer Season* (1961), *The Wedding Group* (1968), and *The Devastating Boys and Other Stories* (1972). She was a frequent contributor to *The New Yorker*. "Girl Reading," from A *Dedicated Man and Other Stories* (1965), is a story of Etta's evolving experience from initial insecurity to a sense of power.

Etta's desire was to belong. Sometimes she felt on the fringe of the family, at other times drawn headily into its very center. At mealtimes—those occasions of argument and hilarity, of thrust and counterstroke, bewildering to her at first—she was especially on her mettle, turning her head alertly from one to another as if watching a fast tennis match. She hoped soon to learn the art of riposte and already used, sometimes unthinkingly, family words and phrases; and had one or two privately treasured memories of even having made them laugh. They delighted in laughing and often did so scoffingly—"at the expense of those less fortunate" as Etta's mother would sententiously have put it.

Etta and Sarah were school friends. It was not the first time that Etta had stayed with the Lippmanns in the holidays. Everyone understood that the hospitality would not be returned, for Etta's mother, who was widowed, went out to work each day. Sarah had seen only the outside of the drab terrace house where her friend lived. She had persuaded her elder brother, David, to take her spying there one evening. They drove fifteen miles to Market Swanford and Sarah, with great curiosity, studied the street names until at last she discovered the house itself. No one was about. The street was quite deserted and the two rows of houses facing one another were blank and silent as if waiting for a hearse to appear. "Do hurry!" Sarah urged her brother. It had been a most dangerous outing and she was thoroughly depressed by it. Curiosity now seemed a trivial sensation compared with the pity she was feeling for her friend's drab life and her shame at having confirmed her own suspicions of it. She was threatened by tears. "Aren't you going in?" her brother asked in great surprise. "Hurry, hurry," she begged him. There had never been any question of her calling at that house.

"She must be very lonely there all through the holidays, poor Etta," she thought, and could imagine hour after hour in the dark house. Bickerings with the daily help she had already heard of and—Etta trying to put on a brave face and make much of nothing—trips to the public library the highlight of the day, it seemed. No wonder that her holiday reading was always so carefully done, thought Sarah, whereas she herself could never snatch a moment for it except at night in bed.

Sarah had a lively conscience about the seriousness of her friend's private world. Having led her more than once into trouble, at school, she had always afterwards felt a disturbing sense of shame; for Etta's work was more important than her own could ever be, too important to be interrupted by escapades. Sacrifices had been made and scholarships must be won. Once—it was a year ago when they were fifteen and had less sense—Sarah had thought up some rough tomfoolery and Etta's blazer had been torn. She was still haunted by her friend's look of consternation. She had remembered too late, as always—the sacrifices that had been made, the widowed mother sitting year after year at her office desk, the holidays that were never taken and the contriving that had to be done.

Her own mother was so warm and worldly. If she had anxieties she kept them to herself, setting the pace of gaiety, up to date and party-loving. She was popular with her friends' husbands who, in their English way, thought of her comfortably as nearly as good company as a man and full of bright ways as well. Etta felt safer with her than with Mr. Lippmann, whose enquiries were often too probing; he touched nerves, his jocularity could be an embarrassment. The boys—Sarah's elder brothers—had their own means of communication which their mother unflaggingly strove to interpret and, on Etta's first visit, she had tried to do so for her, too.

She *was* motherly, although she looked otherwise, the girl decided. Lying in bed at night, in the room she shared with Sarah, Etta would listen to guests driving noisily away or to the Lippmanns returning, full of laughter, from some neighbor's house. Late night door-slamming in the country disturbed only the house's occupants, who all contributed to it. Etta imagined them pottering about downstairs—husband and wife—would hear bottles clinking, laughter, voices raised from room to room, goodnight endearments to cats and dogs and at last Mrs. Lippmann's running footsteps on the stairs and the sound of her jingling bracelets coming nearer. Outside their door she would pause, listening, wondering if they were asleep already. They never were. "Come in!" Sarah would shout, hoisting herself up out of the bed clothes on one elbow, her face turned expectantly towards the door, ready for laughter—for something amusing would surely have happened. Mrs. Lippmann, sitting on one of the beds, never failed them. When they were children, Sarah said, she brought back *petits fours* from parties; now she brought back *faux pas*. She specialised in little stories against herself—Mummy's Humiliations, Sarah named them—tactless things she had said, never-to-be-remedied remarks which sprang fatally from her lips. Mistakes in identity was her particular line, for she never remembered a face, she declared. Having kissed Sarah, she would bend over Etta to do the same. She smelt of scent and gin and cigarette smoke. After this they would go to sleep. The house would be completely quiet for several hours.

Etta's mother had always had doubts about the suitability of this *ménage*. She knew it only at second hand from her daughter, and Etta said very little about her visits and that little was only in reply to obviously resented questions. But she had a way of looking about her with boredom when she returned, as if she had made the transition unwillingly and incompletely. She hurt her mother—who wished only to do everything in the world for her, having no one else to please or protect.

"I should feel differently if we were able to return the hospitality," she told Etta. The Lippmanns' generosity depressed her. She knew that it was despicable to feel jealous, left out, kept in the dark, but she tried to rationalize her feelings before Etta. "I could take a few days off and invite Sarah here," she suggested.

Etta was unable to hide her consternation and her expression deeply wounded her mother. "I shouldn't know what to do with her," she said.

"Couldn't you go for walks? There are the Public Gardens. And take her to the cinema one evening. What do you do at *her* home?"

"Oh, just fool about. Nothing much." Some afternoons they just lay on their beds and ate sweets, keeping all the windows shut and the wireless on loud, and no one ever disturbed them or told them they ought to be out in the fresh air. Then they had to plan parties and make walnut fudge and deflea the dogs. Making fudge was the only one of these things she could imagine them doing in her own home and they could not do it all the time. As for the dreary Public Gardens, she could not herself endure the asphalt paths and the bandstand and the beds of salvias. She could imagine vividly how dejected Sarah would feel.

Early in these summer holidays, the usual letter had come from Mrs. Lipp-mann. Etta, returning from the library, found that the charwoman had gone early and locked her out. She rang the bell, but the sound died away and left an ever more forbidding silence. All the street, where elderly people dozed in stuffy rooms, was quiet. She lifted the flap of the letter-box and called through it. No one stirred or came. She could just glimpse an envelope, lying face up on the doormat, addressed in Mrs. Lippmann's large, loopy, confi-dent handwriting. The house-stuffiness wafted through the letter-box. She imagined the kitchen floor slowly drying, for there was a smell of soapy wa-ter. A tap was steadily dripping.

She leaned against the door, waiting for her mother's return, in a sickness of impatience at the thought of the letter lying there inside. Once or twice, she lifted the flap and had another look at it.

Her mother came home at last, very tired. With an anxious air, she set about cooking supper, which Etta had promised to have ready. The letter was left among her parcels on the kitchen table, and not until they had finished their stewed rhubarb did she send Etta to fetch it. She opened it carefully with the bread knife and deepened the frown on her forehead in preparation for reading it. When she had, she gave Etta a summary of its contents and put forward her objections, her unnerving proposal.

"She wouldn't come," Etta said. "She wouldn't leave her dog."

"But, my dear, she has to leave him when she goes back to school."

"I know. That's the trouble. In the holidays she likes to be with him as much as possible, to make up for it."

Mrs. Salkeld, who had similar wishes about her daughter, looked sad. "It is too one-sided," she gently explained. "You must try to understand how I feel about it."

"They're only too glad to have me. I keep Sarah company when they go out."

They obviously went out a great deal and Mrs. Salkeld suspected that they were frivolous. She did not condemn them for that—they must lead their own lives, but those were in a world which Etta would never be able to afford the time or money to inhabit. "Very well, Musetta," she said, remov-ing the girl further from her by using her full name—used only on formal and usually menacing occasions.

That night she wept a little from tiredness and depression—from disap-pointment, too, at the thought of returning in the evenings to the dark and empty house, just as she usually did, but when she had hoped for company. They were not healing tears she shed and they did nothing but add self-contempt to her other distresses.

A week later, Etta went the short distance by train to stay with the Lipp-manns. Her happiness soon lost its edge of guilt, and once the train had rat-tled over the iron bridge that spanned the broad river, she felt safe in a dif-ferent country. There seemed to be even a different weather, coming from a wider sky, and a riverside glare—for the curves of the railway line brought it close to the even more winding course of the river, whose silver loops could be glimpsed through the trees. There were islands and backwaters and a pale heron standing on a patch of mud.

Sarah was waiting at the little station and Etta stepped down onto the platform as if taking a footing into promised land. Over the station and the gravelly lane outside hung a noonday quiet. On one side were grazing meadows, on the other side the drive gateways of expensive houses. The Gables was indeed gabled and so was its boathouse. It was also turreted and balconied. There was a great deal of woodwork painted glossy white, and a huge-leaved Virginia creeper covered much of the red brick walls—in the front beds were the salvias and lobelias Etta had thought she hated. Towels and swim-suits hung over balcony rails and a pair of tennis shoes had been put out on a window-sill to dry. Even though Mr. Lippmann and his son, David, went to London every day, the house always had—for Etta—a holiday atmosphere.

The hall door stood open and on the big round table were the stacks of new magazines which seemed to her the symbol of extravagance and luxury. At the back of the house, on the terrace overlooking the river, Mrs. Lippmann, wearing tight, lavender pants and a purple shirt, was drinking vodka with a neighbour who had called for a subscription to some charity. Etta was briefly enfolded in scented silk and tinkling bracelets and then released and introduced. Sarah gave her a red, syrupy drink and they sat down on the warm steps among the faded clumps of aubretia and rocked the ice cubes to and fro in their glasses, keeping their eyes narrowed to the sun.

Mrs. Lippmann gossiped, leaning back under a fringed chair-umbrella. She enjoyed exposing the frailties of her friends and family, although she would have been the first to hurry to their aid in trouble. Roger, who was seventeen, had been worse for drink the previous evening, she was saying. Faced with breakfast, his face had been a study of disgust which she now tried to mimic. And David could not eat, either; but from being in love. She raised her eyes to heaven most dramatically, to convey that great patience was demanded of her.

"He eats like a horse," said Sarah. "Etta, let's go upstairs." She took Etta's empty glass and led her back across the lawn, seeming not to care that her mother would without doubt begin to talk about her the moment she had gone.

Rich and vinegary smells of food came from the kitchen as they crossed the hall. (There was a Hungarian cook to whom Mrs. Lippmann spoke in German and a Portuguese "temporary" to whom she spoke in Spanish.) The food was an important part of the holiday to Etta, who had nowhere else eaten *Sauerkraut* or *Apfelstrudel* or cold fried fish, and she went into the dining-room each day with a sense of adventure and anticipation.

On this visit she was also looking forward to the opportunity of making a study of people in love—an opportunity she had not had before. While she unpacked, she questioned Sarah about David's Nora, as she thought of her; but Sarah would only say that she was quite a good sort with dark eyes and an enormous bust, and that as she was coming to dinner that evening, as she nearly always did, Etta would be able to judge for herself.

While they were out on the river all the afternoon—Sarah rowing her in a dinghy along the reedy backwater—Etta's head was full of love in books, even in those holiday set books Sarah never had time for—*Sense and Sensibility* this summer. She felt that she knew what to expect, and her perceptions were sharpened by the change of air and scene, and the disturbing smell of the river, which she snuffed up deeply as if she might be able to store it up in her lungs. "Mother thinks it is polluted," Sarah said when Etta lifted a streaming hand from trailing in the water and brought up some slippery weeds and held them to her nose. They laughed at the idea.

Etta, for dinner, put on the Liberty silk they wore on Sunday evenings at school and Sarah at once brought out her own hated garment from the back of the cupboard where she had pushed it out of sight on the first day of the holidays. When they appeared downstairs, they looked unbelievably dowdy, Mrs. Lippmann thought, turning away for a moment because her eyes had suddenly pricked with tears at the sight of her kind daughter.

Mr. Lippmann and David returned from Lloyd's at half-past six and with them brought Nora—a large, calm girl with an air of brittle indifference towards her fiancé which disappointed but did not deceive Etta, who knew enough to remain undeceived by banter. To interpret from it the private tendernesses it hid was part of the mental exercise she was to be engaged in. After all, David would know better than to have his heart on his sleeve, especially in this *dégagé* family where nothing seemed half so funny as falling in love.

After dinner, Etta telephoned her mother, who had perhaps been waiting for the call, as the receiver was lifted immediately. Etta imagined her standing in the dark and narrow hall with its smell of umbrellas and furniture polish.

"I thought you would like to know I arrived safely."

"What have you been doing?"

"Sarah and I went to the river. We have just finished dinner." Spicy smells still hung about the house. Etta guessed that her mother would have had half a tin of sardines and put the other half by for her breakfast. She felt sad for her and guilty herself. Most of her thoughts about her mother were deformed by guilt.

"What have you been doing?" she asked.

"Oh, the usual," her mother said brightly. "I am just turning the collars and cuffs of your winter blouses. By the way, don't forget to pay Mrs. Lippmann for the telephone call."

"No. I shall have to go now. I just thought . . ."

"Yes, of course, dear. Well, have a lovely time."

"We are going for a swim when our dinner has gone down."

"Be careful of cramp, won't you? But I mustn't fuss from this distance. I know you are in good hands. Give my kind regards to Mrs. Lippmann and Sarah, will you, please. I must get back to your blouses."

"I wish you wouldn't bother. You must be tired."

"I am perfectly happy doing it," Mrs. Salkeld said. But if that were so, it was unnecessary, Etta thought, for her to add, as she did: "And someone has to do it."

She went dully back to the others. Roger was strumming on a guitar, but he blushed and put it away when Etta came into the room.

As the days went quickly by, Etta thought that she was belonging more this time than ever before. Mr. Lippmann, a genial patriarch, often patted her head when passing, in confirmation of her existence, and Mrs. Lippmann let her run errands. Roger almost wistfully sought her company, while Sarah disdainfully discouraged him; for they had their own employments, she implied; her friend—"my best friend," as she introduced Etta to lesser ones or adults—could hardly be expected to want the society of schoolboys. Although he was a year older than themselves, being a boy he was less sophisticated, she explained. She and Etta considered themselves to be rather worldly-wise—Etta having learnt from literature and Sarah from putting two and two together, her favourite pastime. Her parents seemed to her to behave with the innocence of children, unconscious of their motives, so continually betraying themselves to her experienced eye, when knowing more would have made them guarded. She had similarly put two and two together about Roger's behaviour to Etta, but she kept these conclusions to herself—partly from not wanting to make her friend feel self-conscious and partly—for she scorned self-deception—from what she recognised to be jealousy. She and Etta were very well as they were, she thought.

Etta herself was too much absorbed by the idea of love to ever think of being loved. In this house, she had her first chance of seeing it at first hand and she studied David and Nora with such passionate speculation that their loving seemed less their own than hers. At first, she admitted to herself that she was disappointed. Their behaviour fell short of what she required of them; they lacked a romantic attitude to one another and Nora was neither touching nor glorious—neither Viola nor Rosalind. In Etta's mind to be either was satisfactory; to be boisterous and complacent was not. Nora was simply a plump and genial girl with a large bust and a faint moustache. She could not be expected to inspire David with much gallantry and, in spite of all the red roses he brought her from London, he was not above telling her that she was getting fat. Gaily retaliatory, she would threaten him with the bouquet, waving it about his head, her huge engagement ring catching the light, flashing with different colours, her eyes flashing too.

Sometimes, there was what Etta's mother would have called "horseplay," and Etta herself deplored the noise, the dishevelled romping. "We know quite well what it's instead of," said Sarah. "But I sometimes wonder if *they* do. They would surely cut it out if they did."

As intent as a bird-watcher, Etta observed them, but was puzzled that they behaved like birds, making such a display of their courtship, an absurd-looking frolic out of a serious matter. She waited in vain for a sigh or secret glance. At night, in the room she shared with Sarah, she wanted to talk about them more than Sarah, who felt that her own family was the last possible source of glamour or enlightenment. Discussing her bridesmaid's dress was the most she would be drawn into and that subject Etta felt was devoid of romance. She was not much interested in mere weddings and thought them rather banal and public celebrations. "With an overskirt of embroidered net," said Sarah in her decisive voice. "How nice if you could be a bridesmaid, too; but she has all those awful Greenbaum cousins. As ugly as sin, but not to be left out." Etta was inattentive to her. With all her studious nature she had set herself to study love and study it she would. She made the most of what the holiday offered and when the exponents were absent she fell back on the textbooks—*Tess of the D'Urbervilles* and *Wuthering Heights* at that time.

To Roger she seemed to fall constantly into the same pose, as she sat on the river bank, bare feet tucked sideways, one arm cradling a book, the other outstretched to pluck—as if to aid her concentration—at blades of grass. Her face remained pale, for it was always in shadow, bent over her book. Beside her, glistening with oil, Sarah spread out her body to the sun. She was content to lie for hour after hour with no object but to change the colour of her skin and with thoughts crossing her mind as seldom as clouds passed overhead—and in as desultory a way when they did so. Sometimes, she took a book out with her, but nothing happened to it except that it became smothered with oil. Etta, who found sunbathing boring and enervating, read steadily on—her straight, pale hair hanging forward as if to seclude her, to screen her from the curious eyes of passers-by—shaken by passions of the imagination as she was. Voices from boats came clearly across the water, but she did not heed them. People going languidly by in punts shaded their eyes and admired the scarlet geraniums and the greenness of the grass. When motor-cruisers passed, their wash jogged against the mooring stage and swayed into the boathouse, whose lacy fretwork trimmings had just been repainted glossy white.

Sitting there, alone by the boathouse at the end of the grass bank, Roger read, too; but less diligently than Etta. Each time a boat went by, he looked up and watched it out of sight. A swan borne towards him on a wake, sitting neatly on top of its reflection, held his attention. Then his place on the page was lost. Anyhow, the sun fell too blindingly upon it. He would glance again at Etta and briefly, with distaste, at his indolent, spread-eagled sister, who had rolled over on to her stomach to give her shiny back, crisscrossed from the grass, its share of sunlight. So the afternoons passed, and they would never have such long ones in their lives again.

Evenings were more social. The terrace with its fringed umbrellas—symbols of gaiety to Etta—became the gathering place. Etta, listening intently, continued her study of love and as intently Roger studied her and the very emotion which in those others so engrossed her.

"You look still too pale," Mr. Lippmann told her one evening. He put his hands to her face and tilted it to the sun.

"You shan't leave us until there are roses in those cheeks." He implied that only in his garden did sun and air give their full benefit. The thought was there and Etta shared it. "Too much of a bookworm, I'm afraid," he added and took one of her textbooks which she carried everywhere for safety, lest she should be left on her own for a few moments. *Tess of the D'Urbervilles*," read out Mr. Lippmann. "Isn't it deep? Isn't it on the morbid side?" Roger was kicking rhythmically at a table leg in glum embarrassment. "This won't do you any good at all, my dear little girl. This won't put the roses in your cheeks."

"You are doing that," his daughter told him—for Etta was blushing as she always did when Mr. Lippmann spoke to her.

"What's a nice book, Babs?" he asked his wife, as she came out on to the terrace. "Can't you find a nice story for this child?" The house must be full, he was sure, of wonderfully therapeutic novels if only he knew where to lay hands on them. "Roger, you're our bookworm. Look out a nice storybook for your guest. This one won't do her eyes any good." Buying books with small print was a false economy, he thought, and bound to land one in large bills from an eye specialist before long. "A very short-sighted policy," he explained genially when he had given them a little lecture to which no one listened.

His wife was trying to separate some slippery cubes of ice and Sarah sprawled in a cane chair with her eyes shut. She was making the most of the setting sun, as Etta was making the most of romance.

"We like the same books," Roger said to his father. "So she can choose as well as I could."

Etta was just beginning to feel a sense of surprised gratitude, had half turned to look in his direction when the betrothed came through the french windows and claimed her attention.

"In time for a lovely drink," Mrs. Lippmann said to Nora.

"She is too fat already," said David.

Nora swung round and caught his wrists and held them threateningly. "If you say that once more, I'll . . . I'll just . . ." He freed himself and pulled her close. She gasped and panted, but leant heavily against him. "Promise!" she said again.

"Promise what?"

"You won't ever say it again?"

He laughed at her mockingly.

They were less the centre of attention than they thought—Mr. Lippmann was smiling, but rather at the lovely evening and that the day in London was over; Mrs. Lippmann, impeded by the cardigan hanging over her shoulders, was mixing something in a glass jug and Sarah had her eyes closed against the evening sun. Only Etta, in some bewilderment, heeded them. Roger who had his own ideas about love, turned his head scornfully.

Sarah opened her eyes for a moment and stared at Nora, in her mind measuring against her the wedding dress she had been designing. She is too fat for satin, she decided, shutting her eyes again and disregarding the bridal gown for the time being. She returned to thoughts of her own dress, adding a little of what she called "back interest" (though lesser bridesmaids would no doubt obscure it from the congregation—or audience) in the form of long velvet ribbons in turquoise . . . or rose? She drew her brows together and with her eyes still shut said, "All the colours of the rainbow aren't very many, are they?"

"Now, Etta dear, what will you have to drink?" asked Mrs. Lippmann.

Just as she was beginning to ask for some tomato juice, Mr. Lippmann interrupted. He interrupted a great deal, for there were a great many things to be put right, it seemed to him. "Now, Mommy, you should give her a glass of sherry with an egg beaten up in it. Roger, run and fetch a nice egg and a whisk, too . . . all right Babsie dear, I shall do it myself . . . don't worry child," he said, turning to Etta and seeing her look of alarm. "It is no trouble to me. I shall do this for you every evening that you are here. We shall watch the roses growing in your cheeks, shan't we, Mommy?"

He prepared the drink with a great deal of clumsy fuss and sat back to watch her drinking it, smiling to himself, as if the roses were already blossoming. "Good, good!" he murmured, nodding at her as she drained the glass. Every evening, she thought, hoping that he would forget; but horrible though the drink had been, it was also reassuring; their concern for her was reassuring. She preferred it to the cold anxiety of her mother hovering with pills and thermometer.

"Yes," said Mr. Lippmann, "we shall see. We shall see. I think your parents won't know you." He puffed out his cheeks and sketched with a curving gesture the bosom she would soon have. He always forgot that her father was dead. It was quite fixed in his mind that he was simply a fellow who had obviously not made the grade; not everybody could. Roger bit his tongue hard, as if by doing so he could curb his father's. I must remind him again, Sarah and her mother were both thinking.

The last day of the visit had an unexpected hazard as well as its own sadness, for Mrs. Salkeld had written to say that her employer would lend her
his car for the afternoon. When she had made a business call for him in the
neighbourhood she would arrive to fetch Etta at about four o'clock.

"She is really to leave us, Mommy?" asked Mr. Lippmann at breakfast,
folding his newspaper and turning his attention on his family before hurrying
to the station. He examined Etta's face and nodded. "Next time you stay
longer and we make rosy apples of these." He patted her cheeks and ruffled
her hair. "You tell your Mommy and Dadda next time you stay a whole
week."

"She *has* stayed a whole week," said Sarah.

"Then a fortnight, a month."

He kissed his wife, made a gesture as if blessing them all, with his newspaper raised above his head, and went from the room at a trot. "Thank goodness," thought Sarah, "that he won't be here this afternoon to make kind
enquiries about *her* husband."

When she was alone with Etta, she said, "I'm sorry about that mistake he
keeps making."

"I don't mind," Etta said truthfully, "I am only embarrassed because I
know that you are." That's *nothing*, she thought; but the day ahead was a
different matter.

As time passed, Mrs. Lippmann also appeared to be suffering from tension.
She went upstairs and changed her matador pants for a linen skirt. She tidied
up the terrace and told Roger to take his bathing things off his window-sill.
As soon as she had stubbed out a cigarette, she emptied and dusted the ashtray. She was conscious that Sarah was trying to see her with another's eyes.

"Oh, do stop taking photographs," Sarah said tetchily to Roger, who had
been clicking away with his camera all morning. He obeyed her only because
he feared to draw attention to his activities. He had just taken what he hoped
would be a very beautiful study of Etta in a typical pose—sitting on the river
bank with a book in her lap. She had lifted her eyes and was gazing across
the water as if she were pondering whatever she had been reading. In fact,
she had been arrested by thoughts of David and Nora and, although her eyes
followed the print, the scene she saw did not correspond with the lines she
read. She turned her head and looked at the willow trees on the far bank, the
clumps of borage from which moorhens launched themselves. "Perhaps next
time that I see them, they'll be married and it will all be over," she thought.
The evening before, there had been a great deal of high-spirited sparring
about between them. Offence meant and offence taken they assured one another. "If you do that once more . . . I am absolutely serious," cried Nora.
"You are trying not to laugh," David said. "I'm not. I am absolutely serious."
"It will end in tears," Roger had muttered contemptuously. Even good-tem-
pered Mrs. Lippmann had looked down her long nose disapprovingly. And
that was the last, Etta supposed, that she would see of love for a long time.
She was left once again with books. She returned to the one she was reading.

Roger had flung himself on to the grass near by, appearing to trip over a
tussock of grass and collapse. He tried to think of some opening remark
which might lead to a discussion of the book. In the end, he asked abruptly,
"Do you like that?" She sat brooding over it, chewing the side of her finger.
She nodded without looking up and, with a similar automatic gesture, she

waved away a persistent wasp. He leaned forward and clapped his hands together smartly and was relieved to see the wasp drop dead into the grass,
although he would rather it had stung him first. Etta, however, had not noticed this brave deed.

The day passed wretchedly for him; each hour was more filled with the
doom of her departure than the last. He worked hard to conceal his feelings,
in which no one took an interest. He knew that it was all he could do, although no good could come from his succeeding. He took a few more secret
photographs from his bedroom window, and then he sat down and wrote a
short letter to her, explaining his love.

At four o'clock, her mother came. He saw at once that Etta was nervous
and he guessed that she tried to conceal her nervousness behind a much
jauntier manner to her mother than was customary. It would be a bad hour,
Roger decided.

His own mother, in spite of her linen skirt, was gaudy and exotic beside
Mrs. Salkeld, who wore a navy-blue suit which looked as if it had been
sponged and pressed a hundred times—a depressing process unknown to
Mrs. Lippmann. The pink-rimmed spectacles that Mrs. Salkeld wore seemed
to reflect a little colour on to her cheekbones, with the result that she looked
slightly indignant about something or other. However, she smiled a great
deal, and only Etta guessed what an effort it was to her to do so. Mrs. Lippmann gave her a chair where she might have a view of the river and she sat
down, making a point of not looking round the room, and smoothed her
gloves. Her jewellery was real but very small.

"If we have tea in the garden, the wasps get into Anna's rose-petal jam,"
said Mrs. Lippmann. Etta was not at her best, she felt—not helping at all.
She was aligning herself too staunchly with the Lippmanns, so that her
mother seemed a stranger to her, as well. "You see, I am at home here," she
implied, as she jumped up to fetch things or hand things round. She was a
little daring in her familiarity.

Mrs. Salkeld had contrived the visit because she wanted to understand and
hoped to approve of her daughter's friends. Seeing the lawns, the light reflected from the water, later this large, bright room, and the beautiful poppy-
seed cake the Hungarian cook had made for tea, she understood completely
and felt pained. She could see then, with Etta's eyes, their own dark, narrow
house, and she thought of the lonely hours she spent there reading on days of
imprisoning rain. The Lippmanns would even have better weather, she
thought bitterly. The bitterness affected her enjoyment of the poppy-seed
cake. She had, as puritanical people often have, a sweet tooth. She ate the
cake with a casual air, determined not to praise.

"You are so kind to spare Etta to us," said Mrs. Lippmann.

"*You* are kind to invite her," Mrs. Salkeld replied, and then for Etta's
sake, added: "She loves to come to you."

Etta looked self-consciously down at her feet.

"No, I don't smoke," her mother said primly. "Thank you."

Mrs. Lippmann seemed to decide not to, either, but very soon her hand stole
out and took a cigarette—while she was not looking, thought Roger, who was
having some amusement from watching his mother on her best behavior.
Wherever she was, the shagreen cigarette case and the gold lighter were near
by. Ashtrays never were. He got up and fetched one before Etta could do so.

The girls' school was being discussed—one of the few topics the two mothers had in common. Mrs. Lippmann had never taken it seriously. She laughed at the uniform and despised the staff—an attitude she might at least have hidden from her daughter, Mrs. Salkeld felt. The tea-trolley was being wheeled away and her eyes followed the remains of the poppy-seed cake. She had planned a special supper for Etta to return to, but she felt now that it was no use. The things of the mind had left room for an echo. It sounded with every footstep or spoken word in that house where not enough was going on. She began to wonder if there were things of the heart and not the mind that Etta fastened upon so desperately when she was reading. Or was her desire to be in a different place? Lowood was a worse one—she could raise her eyes and look round her own room in relief; Pemberley was better and she would benefit from the change. But how can I help her? she asked herself in anguish. What possible change—and radical it must be—can I ever find the strength to effect? People had thought her wonderful to have made her own life and brought up her child alone. She had kept their heads above water and it had taken all her resources to do so.

Her lips began to refuse the sherry Mrs. Lippmann suggested and then, to her surprise and Etta's astonishment, she said "yes" instead.

It was very early to have suggested it, Mrs. Lippmann thought, but it would seem to put an end to the afternoon. Conversation had been as hard work as she had anticipated and she longed for a dry martini to stop her from yawning, as she was sure it would; but something about Mrs. Salkeld seemed to discourage gin drinking.

"Mother, it isn't half-past five yet," said Sarah.

"Darling, don't be rude to your Mummy. I know perfectly well what the time is." (Who better? she wondered.) "And this isn't a public house, you know."

She had flushed a little and was lighting another cigarette. Her bracelets jangled against the decanter as she handed Mrs. Salkeld her glass of sherry, saying, "Young people are so stuffy," with an air of complicity.

Etta, who had never seen her mother drinking sherry before, watched nervously, as if she might not know how to do it. Mrs. Salkeld—remembering the flavor from Christmas mornings many years ago and—more faintly—from her mother's party trifle—sipped cautiously. In an obscure way she was doing this for Etta's sake. "It may speed her on her way," thought Mrs. Lippmann, playing idly with her charm bracelet, having run out of conversation.

When Mrs. Salkeld rose to go, she looked round the room once more as if to fix it in her memory—the setting where she would imagine her daughter on future occasions.

"And come again soon, there's a darling girl," said Mrs. Lippmann, putting her arm round Etta's shoulder as they walked towards the car. Etta, unused to but not ungrateful for embraces, leaned awkwardly against her. Roger, staring at the gravel, came behind carrying the suitcase.

"I have wasted my return ticket," Etta said.

"Well, that's not the end of the world," her mother said briskly. She thought, but did not say, that perhaps they could claim the amount if they wrote to British Railways and explained.

Mrs. Lippmann's easy affection meant so much less than her own stiff endearments, but she resented it all the same and when she was begged, with enormous warmth, to visit them all again soon her smile was a prim twisting of her lips.

The air was bright with summer sounds, voices across the water and rooks up in the elm trees. Roger stood back listening in a dream to the good-byes and thank-yous. Nor was *this* the end of the world, he told himself. Etta would come again and, better than that, they would also grow older and so be less at the mercy of circumstances. He would be in a position to command his life and turn occasions to his own advantage. Meanwhile, he had done what he could. None the less, he felt such dejection, such an overwhelming conviction that it *was* the end of the world after all, that he could not watch the car go down the drive, and he turned and walked quickly—rudely, off-handedly, his mother thought—back to the house.

Mrs. Salkeld, driving homewards in the lowering sun, knew that Etta had tears in her eyes. "I'm glad you enjoyed yourself," she said. Without waiting for an answer, she added: "They are very charming people." She had always suspected charm and rarely spoke of it, but in this case the adjective seemed called for.

Mr. Lippmann would be coming back from London about now, Etta was thinking. And David will bring Nora. They will all be on the terrace having drinks—dry martinis, not sherry.

She was grateful to her mother about the sherry and understood that it had been an effort towards meeting Mrs. Lippmann's world half-way, and on the way back, she had not murmured one word of criticism—for their world-liness or extravagance or the vulgar opulence of their furnishings. She had even made a kind remark about them.

I might buy her a new dress, Mrs. Salkeld thought—something like the one Sarah was wearing. Though it does seem a criminal waste when she has all her good school clothes to wear out.

They had come onto the main road, and evening traffic streamed by. In the distance the gas holder looked pearl grey and the smoke from factories was pink in the sunset. They were nearly home. Etta, who had blinked her tears back from her eyes, took a sharp breath, almost a sigh.

Their own street with its tall houses was in shadow. "I wish we had a cat," said Etta, as she got out of the car and saw the next door tabby looking through the garden railings. She imagined burying her face in its warm fur, it loving only her. To her surprise, her mother said: "Why not?" Briskly, she went up the steps and turned the key with its familiar grating sound in the lock. The house with its smell—familiar, too—of floor polish and stuffiness, looked secretive. Mrs. Salkeld, hardly noticing this, hurried to the kitchen to put the casserole of chicken in the oven.

Etta carried her suitcase upstairs. On the dressing-table was a jar of mari-golds. She was touched by this—just when she did not want to be touched. She turned her back on them and opened her case. On the top was the book she had left on the terrace. Roger had brought it to her at the last moment. Taking it now, she found a letter inside. Simply "Etta" was written on the envelope.

Roger had felt that he had done all he was capable of and that was to write in the letter those things he could not have brought himself to say, even if he had had an opportunity. No love letter could have been less anticipated and Etta read it twice before she could realise that it was neither a joke nor a mistake. It was the most extraordinary happening of her life, the most incredible.

Her breathing grew slower and deeper as she sat staring before her, pondering her mounting sense of power. It was as if the whole Lippmann family—Nora as well—had proposed to her. To marry Roger—a long, long time ahead though she must wait to do so—would be the best possible way of belonging.

She got up stiffly—for her limbs now seemed too clumsy a part of her body with its fly-away heart and giddy head—she went over to the dressing-table and stared at herself in the glass. "I am I," she thought, but she could not believe it. She stared and stared, but could not take in the tantalising idea.

After a while, she began to unpack. The room was a place of transit, her temporary residence. When she had made it tidy, she went downstairs to thank her mother for the marigolds.

Suggestions for Discussion

1. What does the metaphor of Etta watching a tennis match tell you about Sarah's family?

2. With what details does the reader learn about Sarah and her relationship to Etta? By what means does one learn about Sarah's mother and other members of the family?

3. Why did Etta resent questions from her mother about her visits to the Lippmanns? Why are "Etta's thoughts about her mother deformed by guilt"? How is the guilt conveyed?

4. What do the activities and conversations of Mrs. Lippmann tell you about her attitudes and values?

5. The story is written from the omniscient author point of view, and the focus shifts back and forth from Sarah and Etta to both mothers and to members of Sarah's family. How does the story achieve a singleness of purpose?

6. "Etta's desire was to belong," we are told in the first sentence. With what incidents and commentary is her concern validated? How successful is she in achieving her desire? How is her success communicated?

7. On what are Etta's reflections on love based? How do you account for her disappointment in her observations of David and Nora?

8. Relate the contrasting phrases "things of the mind" and "things of the heart" to Etta's evolving experience.

9. Account for Etta's awareness of a "mounting sense of power." What is the significance of the disbelief that "I am I"?

10. Relate the title to the theme of the story.

Suggestions for Writing

1. Describe a friend, relative, or yourself in a state of being in love.

2. Compare and contrast your family with that of a friend.

3. Develop your own definition and comparison of "things of the mind" and "things of the heart."

4. Drawing upon specific incidents in the story, write a character study of Etta.

Gary Soto

Black Hair

Gary Soto (b. 1952) was born and educated in California, where he is an associate professor in Chicano Studies and English at the University of California at Berkeley. He has published prolifically, both poetry and prose, and has won an impressive series of fellowships and awards. Among these are the Poets' Prize of the Academy of American Poets, the Bess Hopkins Prize for Poetry, a Guggenheim Fellowship, the Levinson Award for Poetry, and the American Book Award from the Before Columbus Foundation. His most recent books are *Pieces of the Heart: New Chicano Fiction* (1993) and *Lesser Evils*. Here we see him as he recounts the grim and almost hopeless life of a young Mexican boy trying to find his way in the world.

There are two kinds of work: One uses the mind and the other uses muscle. As a kid I found out about the latter. I'm thinking of the summer of 1969 when I was a seventeen-year-old runaway who ended up in Glendale, California, to work for Valley Tire Factory. To answer an ad in the newspaper I walked miles in the afternoon sun, my stomach slowly knotting on a doughnut that was breakfast, my teeth like bright candles gone yellow.

I walked in the door sweating and feeling ugly because my hair was still stiff from a swim at the Santa Monica beach the day before. Jules, the accountant and part owner, looked droopily through his bifocals at my application and then at me. He tipped his cigar in the ashtray, asked my age as if he didn't believe I was seventeen, but finally after a moment of silence, said, "Come back tomorrow. Eight-thirty."

I thanked him, left the office, and went around to the chain link fence to watch the workers heave tires into a bin; others carted uneven stacks of tires on hand trucks. Their faces were black from tire dust and when they talked—or cussed—their mouths showed a bright pink.

From there I walked up a commercial street, past a cleaners, a motorcycle shop, and a gas station where I washed my face and hands; before leaving I took a bottle that hung on the side of the Coke machine, filled it with water, and stopped it with a scrap of paper and a rubber band.

The next morning I arrived early at work. The assistant foreman, a potbellied Hungarian, showed me a timecard and how to punch in. He showed me the Coke machine, the locker room with its slimy shower, and also pointed out the places where I shouldn't go: The ovens where the tires were recapped and the customer service area, which had a slashed couch, a coffee table with greasy magazines, and an ashtray. He introduced me to Tully, a fat man with one ear, who worked the buffers that resurfaced the white walls. I was handed an apron and a face mask and shown how to use the buffer: Lift the tire and center, inflate it with a footpedal, press the buffer against the white band until cleaned, and then deflate and blow off the tire with an air hose.

With a paint brush he stirred a can of industrial preserver. "Then slap this blue stuff on." While he was talking a co-worker came up quietly from behind him and goosed him with the air hose. Tully jumped as if he had been struck by a bullet and then turned around cussing and cupping his genitals in his hands as the other worker walked away calling out foul names. When Tully turned to me smiling his gray teeth, I lifted my mouth into a smile because I wanted to get along. He has to be on my side, I thought. He's the one who'll tell the foreman how I'm doing.

I worked carefully that day, setting the tires on the machine as if they were babies, since it was easy to catch a finger in the rim that expanded to inflate the tire. At the day's end we swept up the tire dust and emptied the trash into bins.

At five the workers scattered for their cars and motorcycles while I crossed the street to wash at a burger stand. My hair was stiff with dust and my mouth showed pink against the backdrop of my dirty face. I then ordered a hotdog and walked slowly in the direction of the abandoned house where I had stayed the night before. I lay under the trees and within minutes was asleep. When I woke my shoulders were sore and my eyes burned when I squeezed the lids together.

From the backyard I walked dully through a residential street, and as evening came on, the TV glare in the living rooms and the headlights of passing cars showed against the blue drift of dusk. I saw two children coming up the street with snow cones, their tongues darting at the packed ice. I saw a boy with a peach and wanted to stop him, but felt embarrassed by my hunger. I walked for an hour only to return and discover the house lit brightly. Behind the fence I heard voices and saw a flashlight poking at the garage door. A man on the back steps mumbled something about the refrigerator to the one with the flashlight.

I waited for them to leave, but had the feeling they wouldn't because there was the commotion of furniture being moved. Tired, even more desperate, I started walking again with a great urge to kick things and tear the day from my life. I felt weak and my mind kept drifting because of hunger. I crossed the street to a gas station where I sipped at the water fountain and searched the Coke machine for change. I started walking again, first up a commercial street, then into a residential area where I lay down on some-one's lawn and replayed a scene at home—my Mother crying at the kitchen table, my stepfather yelling with food in his mouth. They're cruel, I thought, and warned myself that I should never forgive them. How could they do this to me.

When I got up from the lawn it was late. I searched out a place to sleep and found an unlocked car that seemed safe. In the backseat, with my shoes off, I fell asleep but woke up startled about four in the morning when the owner, a nurse on her way to work, opened the door. She got in and was about to start the engine when I raised my head up from the backseat to explain my presence. She screamed so loudly when I said "I'm sorry" that I sprinted from the car with my shoes in hand. Her screams faded, then stopped altogether, as I ran down the block where I hid behind a trash bin and waited for a police siren to sound. Nothing. I crossed the street to a church where I slept stiffly on cardboard in the balcony.

I woke up feeling tired and greasy. It was early and a few street lights were still lit, the east growing pink with dawn. I washed myself from a garden hose and returned to the church to break into what looked like a kitchen. Paper cups, plastic spoons, a coffee pot littered on a table. I found a box of Nabisco crackers which I ate until I was full.

At work I spent the morning at the buffer, but was then told to help Iggy, an old Mexican, who was responsible for choosing tires that could be recapped without the risk of exploding at high speeds. Every morning a truck would deliver used tires, and after I unloaded them Iggy would step among the tires to inspect them for punctures and rips on the side walls.

With a yellow chalk he marked circles and Xs to indicate damage and called out "junk." For those tires that could be recapped, he said "goody" and I placed them on my hand truck. When I had a stack of eight I kicked the truck at an angle and balanced them to another work area where Iggy again inspected the tires, scratching Xs and calling out "junk."

Iggy worked only until three in the afternoon, at which time he went to the locker room to wash and shave and to dress in a two-piece suit. When he came out he glowed with a bracelet, watch, rings, and a shiny fountain pen in his breast pocket. His shoes sounded against the asphalt. He was the image of a banker stepping into sunlight with millions on his mind. He said a few low words to workers with whom he was friendly and none to people like me.

I was seventeen, stupid because I couldn't figure out the difference between an F 78 14 and 750 14 at sight. Iggy shook his head when I brought him the wrong tires, especially since I had expressed interest in being his understudy. "Mexican, how can you be so stupid?" he would yell at me, slapping a tire from my hands. But within weeks I learned a lot about tires, from sizes and makes to how they are molded in iron forms to how Valley stole from other companies. Now and then we received a truckload of tires, most of them new or nearly new, and they were taken to our warehouse in the back where the serial numbers were ground off with a sander. On those days the foreman handed out Cokes and joked with us as we worked to get the numbers off.

Most of the workers were Mexican or black, though a few redneck whites worked there. The base pay was a dollar sixty-five, but the average was three dollars. Of the black workers, I knew Sugar Daddy the best. His body carried two hundred and fifty pounds, armfuls of scars, and a long knife that made me jump when he brought it out from his boot without warning. At one time he had been a singer, and had cut a record in 1967 called *Love's Chance*, which broke into the R and B charts. But nothing came of it. No big contract, no club dates, no tours. He made very little from the sales, only enough for an operation to pull a steering wheel from his gut when, drunk and mad at a lady friend, he slammed his Mustang into a row of parked cars.

"Touch it," he smiled at me one afternoon as he raised his shirt, his black belly kinked with hair. Scared, I traced the scar that ran from his chest to the left of his belly button, and I was repelled but hid my disgust.

Among the Mexicans I had few friends because I was different, a *pocho* who spoke bad Spanish. At lunch they sat in tires and laughed over burritos, looking up at me to laugh even harder. I also sat in tires while nursing a Coke and felt dirty and sticky because I was still living on the street and had not had a real bath in over a week. Nevertheless, when the border patrol came to round up the nationals, I ran with them as they scrambled for the fence or hid among the tires behind the warehouse. The foreman, who thought I was an undocumented worker, yelled at me to run, to get away. I did just that. At the time it seemed fun because there was no risk, only a goodhearted feeling of hide-and-seek, and besides it meant an hour away from work on company time. When the police left we came back and some of the nationals made up stories of how they were almost caught—how they out-raced the police. Some of the stories were so convoluted and unconvincing that everyone laughed *mentiras,* especially when one described how he overpowered a policeman, took his gun away, and sold the patrol car. We laughed and he laughed, happy to be there to make up a story.

If work was difficult, so were the nights. I still had not gathered enough money to rent a room, so I spent the nights sleeping in parked cars or in the balcony of a church. After a week I found a newspaper ad for room for rent, phoned, and was given directions. Finished with work, I walked the five miles down Mission Road looking back into the traffic with my thumb out. No rides. After eight hours of handling tires I was frightening, I suppose, to drivers since they seldom looked at me; if they did, it was a quick glance. For the next six weeks I would try to hitchhike, but the only person to stop was a Mexican woman who gave me two dollars to take the bus. I told her it was too much and that no bus ran from Mission Road to where I lived, but she insisted that I keep the money and trotted back to her idling car. It must have hurt her to see me day after day walking in the heat and looking very much the dirty Mexican to the many minds that didn't know what it meant to work at hard labor. That woman knew. Her eyes met mine as she opened the car door, and there was a tenderness that was surprisingly true—one for which you wait for years but when it comes it doesn't help. Nothing changes. You continue on in rags, with the sun still above you.

I rented a room from a middle-aged couple whose lives were a mess. She was a school teacher and he was a fireman. A perfect set up, I thought. But during my stay there they would argue with one another for hours in their bedroom.

When I rang at the front door both Mr. and Mrs. Van Deusen answered and didn't bother to disguise their shock at how awful I looked. But they let me in all the same. Mrs. Van Deusen showed me around the house, from the kitchen and bathroom to the living room with its grand piano. On her fingers she counted out the house rules as she walked me to my room. It was a girl's room with lace curtains, scenic wallpaper of a Victorian couple enjoying a stroll, canopied bed, and stuffed animals in a corner. Leaving, she turned and asked if she could do laundry for me and, feeling shy and hurt, I told her no; perhaps the next day. She left and I undressed to take a bath, exhausted as I sat on the edge of the bed probing my aches and my bruised places. With a towel around my waist I hurried down the hallway to the bathroom where Mrs. Van Deusen had set out an additional towel with a tube of shampoo. I ran the water in the tub and sat on the toilet, lid down, watching the steam curl toward the ceiling. When I lowered myself into the tub I felt my body sting. I soaped a wash cloth and scrubbed my arms until they lightened, even glowed pink, but still I looked unwashed around my neck and face no matter how hard I rubbed. Back in the room I sat in bed reading a magazine, happy and thinking of no better luxury than a girl's sheets, especially after nearly two weeks of sleeping on cardboard at the church.

I was too tired to sleep, so I sat at the window watching the neighbors move about in pajamas, and, curious about the room, looked through the bureau drawers to search out personal things—snapshots, a messy diary, and a high school yearbook. I looked up the Van Deusen's daughter, Barbara, and studied her face as if I recognized her from my own school—a face that said "promise," "college," "nice clothes in the closet." She was a skater and a member of the German Club; her greatest ambition was to sing at the Hollywood Bowl.

After awhile I got into bed and as I drifted toward sleep I thought about her. In my mind I played a love scene again and again and altered it slightly each time. She comes home from college and at first is indifferent to my presence in her home, but finally I overwhelm her with deep pity when I come home hurt from work, with blood on my shirt. Then there was another version: Home from college she is immediately taken with me, in spite of my work-darkened face, and invites me into the family car for a milkshake across town. Later, back at the house, we sit in the living room talking about school until we're so close I'm holding her hand. The truth of the matter was that Barbara did come home for a week, but was bitter toward her parents for taking in boarders (two others besides me). During that time she spoke to me only twice: Once, while searching the refrigerator, she asked if we had any mustard; the other time she asked if I had seen her car keys.

But it was a place to stay. Work had become more and more difficult. I not only worked with Iggy, but also with the assistant foreman who was in charge of unloading trucks. After they backed in I hopped on top to pass the tires down by bouncing them on the tailgate to give them an extra spring so they would be less difficult to handle on the other end. Each truck was weighed down with more than two hundred tires, each averaging twenty pounds, so that by the time the truck was emptied and swept clean I glistened with sweat and my T-shirt stuck to my body. I blew snot threaded with tire dust onto the asphalt, indifferent to the customers who watched from the waiting room.

The days were dull. I did what there was to do from morning until the bell sounded at five; I tugged, pulled, and cussed at tires until I was listless and my mind drifted and caught on small things, from cold sodas to shoes to stupid talk about what we would do with a million dollars. I remember unloading a truck with Hamp, a black man.

"What's better than a sharp lady?" he asked me as I stood sweaty on a pile of junked tires. "Water. With ice," I said.

He laughed with his mouth open wide. With his fingers he pinched the sweat from his chin and flicked at me. "You be too young, boy. A woman can make you a god."

As a kid I had chopped cotton and picked grapes, so I knew work. I knew the fatigue and the boredom and the feeling that there was a good possibility you might have to do such work for years, if not for a lifetime. In fact, as a kid I imagined a dark fate: To marry Mexican poor, work Mexican hours, and in the end die a Mexican death, broke and in despair.

But this job at Valley Tire Company confirmed that there was something worse than field work, and I was doing it. We were all doing it, from foreman to the newcomers like me, and what I felt heaving tires for eight hours a day was felt by everyone—black, Mexican, redneck. We all despised those hours but didn't know what else to do. The workers were unskilled, some undocumented and fearful of deportation, and all struck with an uncertainty at what to do with their lives. Although everyone bitched about work, no one left. Some had worked there for as long as twelve years; some had sons working there. Few quit; no one was ever fired. It amazed me that no one gave up when the border patrol jumped from their vans, baton in hand, because I couldn't imagine any work that could be worse—or any life. What was out there, in the world, that made men run for the fence in fear?

Iggy was the only worker who seemed sure of himself. After five hours of "junking," he brushed himself off, cleaned up in the washroom, and came out gleaming with an elegance that humbled the rest of us. Few would look him straight in the eye or talk to him in our usual stupid way because he was so much better. He carried himself as a man should—with that old world "dignity"—while the rest of us muffed our jobs and talked dully about dull things as we worked. From where he worked in his open shed he would now and then watch us with his hands on his hips. He would shake his head and click his tongue in disgust.

The rest of us lived dismally. I often wondered what the others' homes were like; I couldn't imagine that they were much better than our work place. No one indicated that his outside life was interesting or intriguing. We all looked defeated and contemptible in our filth at the day's end. I imagined the average welcome at home: Rafael, a Mexican national who had worked at Valley for five years, returned to a beaten house of kids who were dressed in mismatched clothes and playing kick-the-can. As for Sugar Daddy, he returned home to a stuffy room where he would read and reread old magazines. He ate potato chips, drank beer, and watched TV. There was no grace in dipping socks into a wash basin where later he would wash his cup and plate.

There was no grace at work. It was all ridicule. The assistant foreman drank Cokes in front of the newcomers as they laced tires in the afternoon sun. Knowing that I had a long walk home, Rudy, the college student, passed me waving and yelling "Hello," as I started down Mission Road on the way home to eat out of cans. Even our plump secretary got into the act by wearing short skirts and flaunting her milky legs. If there was love, it was ugly. I'm thinking of Tully and an older man whose name I can no longer recall fondling one another in the washroom. I had come in cradling a smashed finger to find them pressed together in the shower, their pants undone and partly pulled down. When they saw me they smiled their pink mouths but didn't bother to push away.

How we arrived at such a place is a mystery to me. Why anyone would stay for years is even a deeper concern. You showed up, but from where? What broken life? What ugly past? The foreman showed you the Coke machine, the washroom, and the yard where you'd work. When you picked up a tire, you were amazed at the black it could give off.

Suggestions for Discussion

1. Soto says he cannot imagine any work or any life that could be worse than the one he describes. What makes it so terrible?

2. What does the author mean by "There was no grace at work"? How does this comment relate to how he understands dignity and dullness?

3. As a child Soto imagines a dark fate: "To marry Mexican poor, work Mexican hours, and in the end die a Mexican death, broke and in despair." Why is his experience at the Valley Tire Company even worse?

Suggestions for Writing

1. What is the most disagreeable job you ever had? Why was it so? Describe your workday.

2. In part the protagonist survives by fantasy. How have you used this technique to live through hard times?

David Bradley

Harvest Home

David Bradley (b. 1950) was born in Pennsylvania and educated at the University of Pennsylvania and King's College, London, where he earned an M.A. A writer, he is associate professor of English at Temple University. He has won the PEN/Faulkner Award, and the American Academy of Arts and Letters Award for Literature (1982). His major work is *The Chaneysville Incident* (1981). In the account that follows we see Bradley trying to come to grip with the richness of his family heritage, and all of the ambiguities it brings.

Thanksgiving 1988. In the house my father built my mother and I sit down to dine. A snowy cloth and ivory china give wintry background to browns of turkey and stuffing and gravy, mild yellow of parched corn, mellow orange of candied yams. Amidst those autumnal shades cranberry sauce flares red like flame in fallen leaves, and steam rises like scentless smoke. Head up, eyes open, I chant prefabricated grace (Father, we thank Thee for this our daily bread which we are about to partake of . . .) and long for the extemporaneous artistry of my father, now almost a decade dead. His blessings—couched in archaic diction ("Harvest Home," he called this holiday) and set in meter measured as a tolling bell—were grounded in a childhood in which daily bread was hoped for, not expected; his grace had gravity, unlike this airy ditty I now mutter.

Still, it seems there is even in this doggerel dogma (. . . May it nourish our souls and bodies . . .) an echo of his voice. Hope flutters in me, rises as I come to the end (. . . in Jesus' name and for His sake . . .), then hangs, gliding in the silence, as I pause and listen. My mother sits, head bowed, patient and unsurprised; for nine years I have paused so, just short of "amen." What I wait for she has never asked. And I have never before said.

*   *   *

Once there were more of us. For once we were a mighty clan, complete with house and lineage. As we are dark (and sometimes comely), outsiders might expect us to trace that lineage to Africa, but we have benign contempt for those who pin their pride to ancestries dotted by the Middle Passage or *griot*-given claims to Guinean thrones. For what is Africa (spicy groves, cinnamon trees, or ancient dusky rivers?) to a clan that knows, as we know, the precise when and where of our origin: on March 10, 1836, in Seaford, Delaware. Then and there a justice of the peace named Harry L-something (the paper is browned, the ink faded, and ornate script all but undecipherable) certified that a "Col. man by the name of Peter Bradley" was henceforth a freedman. This Peter was our progenitor.

Outsiders might wonder that we do not fix our origin in 1815, the year of Peter's birth. The reason: the slave laws—what oxymoron that!—decreed that a bondsman had right to neither property nor person. Peter could not own a family, for he did not own himself. But on March 10, Peter's master gave Peter to Peter for Peter's birthday; this not only made him, legally, his own man but entitled him to purchase a (black) woman. He could have owned her, and any children he fathered on her. But he did not. Peter wed a free woman; thus the two sons he sired were free from the moment of their birth. But Peter, by that time, was not. For after being given by his master to himself he gave himself to his Master, and became a minister of the gospel.

Such service became a clan tradition. Both Peter's sons became ministers, licensed by the African Methodist Episcopal Zion Church, the first denomination organized by American blacks who chafed at the unequal opportunity offered by the Methodist Episcopal Church. One son was "M.A."—we do not know his full name, or date of birth. The other was Daniel Francis, born in 1852. Through him our line descends.

Daniel Francis became a minister at the age of nineteen. Although we know nothing of his early assignments, we are sure that they were plentiful, for Zion Methodists followed the dictate of John Wesley that ministers should never stand long in any pulpit, lest they become too powerful. And we know that the Presiding Bishop eventually sent him to Williamsport, Pennsylvania, where he met Cora Alice Brewer. Though in those rigid times, Daniel Francis, at forty-four, would have been called a confirmed bachelor and Cora Alica, at twenty-seven, old enough to be called a spinster, love blossomed into marriage in 1896. The first fruit of the union was a man-child, John, born in 1898. A daughter, Gladys, followed in 1900. More sons, David and Andrew, were born in 1905 and 1906, after the family left Williamsport for Sewickley, Pennsylvania, outside Pittsburgh.

The house came in 1911, when Daniel Francis, who had been reassigned at least five times since Williamsport, was sent to a church called Mt. Pisgah, in the town of Bedford, in the south-central part of Pennsylvania. As Mt. Pisgah had no parsonage, Daniel Francis went ahead of the family to find a place to live. On the train he met a man called Bixler, who offered to sell him an eleven-acre homestead two miles west of Bedford, near the hamlet of Wolfsburg. The price was steep (seven hundred and fifty dollars), the terms usurious (one hundred dollars down, one hundred per year plus annual interest and a widow's dower), but Daniel Francis found both price and terms acceptable, perhaps because there were no other terms at all. And so, in the spring of 1912, our clan took up residence in our first permanent home.

But Daniel Francis did not see the Wolfsburg property as just a home. In early 1915 he announced plans to create what the local weekly, the *Bedford Gazette*, called "an attractive summer resort for those of his race who will gather here from Pittsburgh and Western Pennsylvania." His future plans called for the building of a "large tabernacle for divine services, lectures and entertainments" and in time a normal school for the education of black craftsmen modeled on Tuskegee Institute—Booker T. Washington, Daniel Francis told the *Gazette*, had promised to come to Wolfsburg to speak. Although Booker T. Washington never did appear, a camp meeting was held in August on a sylvan portion of the homestead (christened "Green Brier Grove" in printed advertisements) and the next year a loan from the Bedford County Trust Company liberated the deed from Bixler's clutches and brought Daniel Francis's dream closer to reality. But Zion Methodists, like Wesley, feared empire-building pastors; later that year the bishop kicked Daniel Francis upstairs, appointing him Presiding Elder, the spiritual and financial manager of a group of churches in Pennsylvania and eastern Ohio.

But though the promotion killed a dream, it established our clan's mark of achievement: a successful son is he who follows in his father's footsteps and goes a step further. And though it forced us once again to wander, we never forgot the homestead. Somehow we made mortgage payments. By 1921 the homestead was ours, free and clear. A year later we returned to it. It was not, however, a joyful repatriation. On October 15, 1922, Daniel Francis died of "diabetes mellitus." His first son, John, now at twenty-one our chieftain, paid one hundred dollars for a funeral and secured a permit of removal. We escorted the body of Daniel Francis back to Wolfsburg, he to be buried in Mt. Ross, the local Negro cemetery, we to live.

The homestead did not long save us from wandering. Bedford, which to Daniel Francis seemed prosperous enough to support even black ambitions, soon proved capable of supporting few ambitions at all. White youths who wished to do more than sell hats to each other had to leave, if only to get higher education. Black youths, regardless of ambition, were virtually exiled; Bedford had no place for blacks skilled with pens rather than push brooms, and its small black community offered opportunity for exogamy. Some blacks made do. Bradleys do not make do.

And so we dispersed. Gladys married a man named Caldwell and settled in Cleveland, Ohio. David finished high school, won a scholarship, and went South to college. Andrew, after graduation, attached himself to the local Democratic party—a quixotic alliance, as Bedford blacks were fewer and less powerful than Bedford Democrats—and then went east to Harrisburg, the capital. John, who supported the clan until Andrew's graduation, married and settled in Sewickley, and fathered three daughters. But though we dispersed, the homestead remained—a haven in time of trouble, a gathering place for feasts, a totem signifying that, though we were wanderers, we were not Gypsies.

That is what it signified to outsiders. And so it was that in 1956, our clan's one hundred and twentieth year, the *Gazette*, by then a daily, found our clan of local interest. "The rise of the Bradley family from the enforced degradation of slavery to dignity and high achievement is not unparalleled in the history of the American Negro," wrote reporter Gene Farkas. "But it is certainly one of the more outstanding examples of hard-won Negro accomplishment in the nation and the state. In the annals of Bedford County, the story of the Bradley family is without precedent . . . for it was from these hills and valleys, from the one-room schoolhouse at Wolfsburg and the old Bedford High School . . . that the Bradley boys emerged to eminence and respect."

Cosmopolitans and outsiders would have said that it was Andrew who had risen highest; in 1954, he became State Budget Secretary and the first black to sit in the Pennsylvania Governor's Cabinet. But local interest, and perhaps a sense of our clan's traditions—he even used the phrase "the footsteps of his father"—caused Farkas to give more space to David, who in 1948 had been elected an AME Zion General Officer—a step beyond Daniel Francis's final rank of Presiding Elder. Though his new duties called for travel, he was free to fix his base where he chose; David purchased land adjacent to the homestead and built what Farkas called "a modern stone bungalow," in which he housed both his own family and Cora Alice, who spent her days in the spartan familiarity of the homestead but at night enjoyed the sybaritic comforts of indoor plumbing and central heating.

Farkas did a good job for an outsider. Although he did not specifically mention another of David's contributions to the clan, that he alone of the third generation sired a son to carry on the name, the photographs that accompanied the story did depict the lad, David Jr., then six. And though Farkas did give short shrift to John, not mentioning the names of his wife and children (as he did with David and Andrew) and referring to his occupation with a euphemism (". . . he has worked for a private family for 25 or 30 years"), in this he only reflected the values of outsiders; men who hold advanced degrees and cabinet posts are commonly deemed more noteworthy than those who held rakes in "private" service. Farkas cannot be blamed for this affront to our dignity. How was he to know that the man so slighted was the chief among us? For the tale as Farkas told it was the tale as we told it to him. Sadly, it was the tale as we were telling it to our children. Except at Harvest Home.

Even when I was too young to comprehend a calendar I knew Harvest Home was coming; I could tell by the smell of my grandmother, Cora Alice. Usually she spent her days in the old homestead crocheting, reading the *Gazette,* and listening in on the party line. But the week before Harvest Home she abandoned leisure, stoked up her big Majestic coal stove, and got busy baking: tangy gingerbread, golden pound cakes, and pies of pumpkin, sweet potato, and mince. In the evening she would come back to the house my father built perfumed with molasses and mace, and I would crawl into her lap and lick surreptitiously at the vestiges of brown sugar that clung to her upper arms. The night before the feast she would not return at all. That would be my signal; I would sneak to my window to keep watch on the homestead a hundred yards away. At last I would see a sweep of headlights. I would press my ear against the gelid glass and listen. The sounds of car doors slammed, greetings shouted, would not satisfy me—I would stand, shivering, until I heard an odd and mighty booming. Then I would know the clan was gathered.

The next afternoon would find us in the rear chamber of the homestead, arrayed around a dark Victorian table with saurian legs and dragon feet. To an outsider the order of our seating might have seemed to loosely reflect Fifties customs—most of the children placed at a separate table and all the men at the main table, while the women served. In fact, it reflected our deep reverence for name and blood. The segregated children had the blood—they were of the fifth generation—but had it through their mothers; none had the name. The women who served—including Cora Alice herself, who, although she presided over the gathering, did so from the sideboard—had the name by marriage. The only woman at table not of the blood was my Uncle Andrew's wife, Gussie, who made it clear she waited on no one. She also smoked and drank in public. (My grandmother had declared her mad; she was left alone.) My cousins—the women of our fourth generation—although they'd lost the name through marriage, had the blood and so had seats. Their husbands had seats only as a courtesy to the chief of a related clan—once a husband tried to displace his wife; Cora Alice took away his plate. The men of the third generation had both blood and name, and so had seats of honor. And I too had a seat of honor: a creaky chair, made tall with cushions, set at the table's foot. For I was David, son of David, the only male of the fourth generation, the only hope for the continuation of the name.

I, of course, did not then understand why I alone among the children had a seat at the table. But I was glad I did. For when all closed eyes and bowed heads to listen to my father bless our gathering in fervent baritone extempore, I could raise my head and look down the table, a virtual continent of sustenance—Great Lakes of gravy, Great Plains of yams, tectonic plates of turkey slices thrust upward by the bulk of the bird itself, which rose like Rushmore. But in the place of the visage of Washington or Lincoln this Rushmore was crowned by a huge dark head with massive jowls, pebbly with beard, a broad flat nose, a gently sloping forehead, grizzled brows: the visage of our clan chief, my Uncle John.

Uncle John was titanic. Below his head was a neck thick with muscle and a broad chest, powerful and deep, on which his huge hands prayerfully rested, the fingers like a logjam. When the food was duly blessed the jam burst. For Uncle John did not eat—he fed. His plate—actually a spare meat platter— was filled and refilled with turkey, potatoes, and stuffing all drenched with tureens of gravy, and garnished with enough corn on the cob to fill a field— once I counted a dozen ears lying ravished by his plate, and always I watched his trench work with apprehension, convinced that one day he would explode.

He made all the noise of an explosion. He did not talk—he roared. He roared with jokes—always corny and often in poor taste—and aphorisms— "You can live forever if you don't quit breathin!"—and responses to conversational gambits—once Uncle Andrew twitted him about his shabby clothing. "Rags to riches! I ain't rich yet!" Uncle John roared, off and on for the next twenty years. Mostly, though, he roared with a laugh as big as he was, so concussive it subsumed all ordinary vibrations. Halfway between a boom and a cackle, Uncle John's laugh was like a bushel of corn husks rustling in a hundred-gallon drum. It was not precisely a pleasant sound, but to me it was a Siren song—or perhaps the call of the wild.

When I was small I would leave my place as soon as I could to go and stand beside him. He would be busy devouring dessert—quarters of pie, one each of pumpkin, sweet potato, mince—like Cronus consuming his children, but would catch me up in the crook of his arm and balance me effortlessly on his knee, where I would sit in greatest contentment, remarkably unoffended by his smell—sweat, smoke, and bay rum (which he used for no good reason, since he rarely shaved). When I grew too big for that I would simply stand beside him while he finished eating. Then we would go to kill his car. He didn't call it that, of course. He termed it "blowing out the pipes" and claimed that without it the car—a spavined station wagon—would never climb the mountains between Bedford and Sewickley. But to me, at six or seven, it seemed like bloody murder.

From the back of the wagon he would take a quart jar of kerosene—he called it "coal oil"—and give it to me to hold while he started the engine, raised the hood, and removed the air cleaner. Then he would take the jar and begin to pour the coal oil into the unsuspecting intake manifold. The engine would pause in shock, then sputter, bark, and bellow at the same time, while from the tail pipe issued gouts of greasy black smoke. Meanwhile Uncle John poured more coal oil into the carburetor, his expression like that of a father administering foul-tasting medicine to an ailing child. When the jar was empty he would leap behind the wheel and pump the throttle; the engine would scream and thrash madly on its mounts, while the smoke from the tail pipe would take on bile-green overtones and show tiny flicks of flame. After a while Uncle John—at some clue known to him alone—would stop pumping. The engine would rattle, almost stop. Then the kerosene would clear through the cylinders; the grateful engine would settle into a smooth, fast idle, and Uncle John would smile.

Years later I marveled at all of this, not because the car survived it, but because we did. For it took no mechanical genius to see that we had toyed with tragedy, that that abused engine could easily have exploded, covering us with burning fuel, shredding us with shrapnel, generally blowing us to Kingdom Come. And I marveled that, even had I known that then—which I of course did not—it would have made no difference. Because then—and now—those dangerous pyrotechnics seemed a fitting prerequisite for what followed. For when the smoke showed clean and white I would sit beside Uncle John as he gently blipped the throttle—helping, he said, the pistons settle down—and recounted chronicles of the clan.

Clan history was nothing new—I heard it every day. But what I heard daily were parables, intended to indoctrinate me with the values and courage that had let us rise up from slavery. At Harvest Home, Uncle John told a different story—unpretentious, earthy, human as an unlimed outhouse. Cora Alice told me about Daniel Francis, after the barn was struck by lightning, burning his hands in the steaming ashes as he searched for nails with which to rebuild. Uncle John told me about my grandfather misjudging the dosage when he wormed the mule. David told me about the Christmas Eve when he, knowing his family was too poor for presents, asked for nothing and cried himself to sleep—but woke to find a hand-carved train, three walnuts, and one incredible orange. Uncle John told me about the time my father had the back of his pants gored by a roving bull. My grandmother and father told me of the glory of my people. Uncle John told me that we *were* people. This was vital. For it was something we were forgetting.

On Harvest Home 1957 I was drummed out of my clan. My crime was lying—a peccadillo, outsiders might say, especially as all children tell lies occasionally, some frequently. But I lied almost constantly, even when there was nothing to be gained. My father said I'd rather crawl up Fib Alley than march down Truth Street; this drove him crazy. For he believed a sterling reputation was some shield against the sanctions society—both American and Bedford County—could bring to bear on a Negro male. He was proud that we were held in high repute and feared what would happen to me—to all of us—were our name to lose its luster because of my lying. He announced that he would break me of it.

But he did not realize how good a liar I'd become—so good I took him in. For a while I told him many obvious lies, let him catch and punish me. Then I tapered off. Catching me less often, he assumed I was lying less. But on that morning he discovered . . . well, I don't recall exactly what he discovered; some silken web of half-truths I had been spinning out for weeks. He confronted me, hard evidence in his hands, hot fury in his face.

Corporal punishment was not his way. His cat-o'-ninetails was a Calibanian tongue wetted with Prosperian vocabulary, his lashes sad scenarios starring the local sheriff. That morning he seemed so angry I expected J. Edgar Hoover to make a cameo appearance; I could not imagine what salt he would rub into the wounds—I doubt the usual "thou shalt never amount to anything if thou keepest this up" would suffice. But he was too angry for anything like the usual treatment; he simply looked at me coldly and in a frighteningly quiet voice said, "Bradleys don't lie."

That statement rocked me. For I knew—at least I thought I knew—that it was true. My grandmother did not lie. My father surely did not lie. In the Church he had a reputation for truthfulness—and was in some quarters hated for it. His historical writing was marred by a concern for literal truth; he wouldn't say that two and two were four unless he had a picture of both twos and did the arithmetic three times. And God knows he preached what he saw as truth, and practiced what he preached. So I believed him when he said Bradleys did not lie. But I also knew that I did lie.

On any other day the conclusion of the syllogism—that I was not a Bradley—would have disturbed me. But that day was Harvest Home. I sat in my favored place, accepting accolades and choicest bits of feast food—the heel of the bread, the drumstick of the turkey—that all thought were my due, as sole heir to the name, but I knowing in my heart I had no right to them. I could barely eat.

Later, in the car, I only half listened to Uncle John's chronicle, wondering if I could ever explain to him that I had no right to listen at all. But in the midst of my dilemma I detected a variation from an earlier telling. "Wait," I said. "That's not what you said before."

"No," he said easily. "But don't it work out better that way?"

"Well, yeah," I said—and it did work out better—"but it's not the truth."

"Oh yeah," he said. "The truth. Well, truth is funny. Because you never know it all. So you end up makin' things up to fill in the blanks. Everybody does that. But some folks always makes things up that's make folks sound good, make things sound clean and pretty. Trouble is, the truth usually turns out to be whatever makes the most sense. And if you think you got the whole truth, if it don't make sense, you better make a few things up. And even if you're wrong, it makes a better story." He paused, looked at me. I can't imagine what was on my face—amazement, probably, to hear the head of my clan drumming me back into it as firmly as I'd been drummed out. "Now don't you dare ever tell your daddy I said that," he admonished. And then he sent his laughter rustling and booming around the car.

It is interesting to speculate what would have happened if the *Gazette* had done a follow-up on The Bradley Family Twelve Years Later. By 1968 Andrew had served a second term in the cabinet and served there no longer only because the Democrats had lost the Statehouse—he remained a force in the Party, and had had influence with both the Kennedy and Johnson administrations. He had also followed in at least one of Daniel Francis's footsteps, becoming a trustee of Lincoln University, an institution originally dedicated to the education of blacks. David, meanwhile, retraced his father's footsteps even as he stepped beyond; still a General Officer, he was rumored to be a strong candidate for Bishop, the highest office in the Church, and also preached at Mt. Pisgah, which was now too small to pay its own pastor. David Jr. seemed poised to follow. A senior in high school, he had been admitted to the University of Pennsylvania and awarded several national scholarships. Occasionally he too occupied the pulpit of Mt. Pisgah. Such facts could have led a reporter to believe the Bradley family was still upward bound, might even have caused him or her to see a rising track in tragedy; though Cora Alice had died in 1960, her funeral was resplendent with dignitaries: two ministers and a Presiding Elder of the AME Zion Church, and—the Democrats were then still in power—several state cabinet secretaries and the governor himself. Had such a story been done—it wasn't—the reporter might have written that, after a hundred and thirty-two years of freedom, the Bradleys continued to rise.

To say that, though, the reporter would have had to ignore clippings from the *Gazette* itself—a 1962 story describing the destruction of the Bradley homestead by a fire, photo of the ravished house, its windows like blackened eyes, its clapboard siding stripped away, revealing underlying logs. But to be fair, few reporters would have seen the fire as metaphor. Fewer still would have explored the implications of the fire's aftermath: that for months the house stood unrepaired; that the eventual repairs were minimal; that they were financed by a note cosigned by only David and Andrew; that money to repay the loan was to come from rental of the homestead—to whites. And none, probably, would have understood that the *Gazette*'s account of Cora Alice's funeral reiterated an ancient insult. For although the second paragraph noted the careers of David and Andrew, the clan's chief was not mentioned until the final paragraph, and in passing: "She is survived by another son, John Bradley of Sewickley."

I was only nine when my grandmother died, and so recall little of the pomp and circumstance that surrounded her death. I do recall the lavish spread of ham and turkey and covered dishes brought by neighbors to assuage our grief. I recall that Uncle John ate little. And I recall that at the end of the day I stood beside him on my father's lawn while he looked sadly at the homestead. "I guess that's that," he said, and turned away.

And I do recall my grandmother's final Harvest Home. I remember overhearing my elders in council. The only items on the agenda were her failing health and her refusal to give up her days in the homestead. It was moved and seconded that Uncle Andrew take her to Harrisburg to see a specialist. During discussion the opinion was stated (loudly) that no doctor could cure the fact that my grandmother was ninety years old, but the countermotion ("Let her live the way she wants until she dies") was ruled out of order. The motion carried on a two-to-one vote. Council was adjourned, *sine die.* I remember the meal itself—the mood: heavy, the food: dry, the laughter: absent without leave. And I remember how quiet Uncle John was as he watched my father and Uncle Andrew get my grandmother settled in Uncle Andrew's Chrysler. Mostly I remember how, after my grandmother was driven away, Uncle John went to work with coal oil and a vengeance; I can still hear the sounds he tortured from the engine, the fan belt screaming, the valve lifters chattering like dry bones, the exhaust bellowing like nothing known to man.

Mostly I recall the burning of the house. For if our homestead was once a totem, was it not a totem still? Was not the burning a harbinger of greater doom? For months I would go, sometimes in the dead of night, and circle the hulk of our homestead like a satellite in orbit, pulled down and thrown up simultaneously. In daylight I would peer into the now exposed basement, full of detritus, alive with rats, in darkness sniff the scorched and rotten timber, seeking a message in the rubble and the stench. And when the house was lost to me—repaired and occupied by people my grandmother would have dismissed as poor white trash—I sought a message in the keepsakes of our clan—chipped photographs, browned bills and deeds, yellowed newspaper clippings. When I combined those mementos with my memories I found discrepancies. And when I thought about what made most sense I found a devastating truth: Bradleys did lie.

Most of our lies were common cover-ups of minor moral failures. Others drove to the heart of our history—it seemed doubtful, for example, that Booker T. Washington had ever heard of Daniel Francis. But no lie was as destructive as the one we'd told about my Uncle John.

There are many ways to say it. Then, when clichés were new to me and irony was *terra incognita,* I would have said that Uncle John was our black sheep. Now I say he was the nigger in our woodpile, proof that though Bradley blood flowed in dreamers, power brokers, and preachers, it also flowed in a hewer of wood, a drawer of water, a man content to work in service all his life. This embarrassed us, especially as he was not the least among us; he was the first. And so, while we did not deny him, we denied him his place. We allowed outsiders to see him as a minor footnote to our grand history. And then, made bold by headlines and column inches, tokens Society respects, we had forgotten the rules by which a clan exists and survives. Our junior elders—my father and Uncle Andrew—had rebelled against our rightful leader. This, I decided, was the message of the burned boards and beams of the house of Bradley. Our house had fallen because we had fallen away.

I did not want to fall away. For the years between the burning and my graduation were hard, lonely, desperate years. I needed my people. I needed my clan. I needed my chief. And though I despaired that we had fallen too far from our ways, I hoped that we had not.

I hoped hardest when those years were ending, when to the world outside I seemed poised to take my clan to greater heights. I feared those heights. And so, on the night of my commencement, as my class assembled for its final march, I stood quietly despairing. They chattered about parties and graduation gifts. I wanted only one gift: the presence of my chief. I doubted I would get it. I had sent him an invitation, but Uncle John was almost seventy and Sewickley was more than a hundred mountainous miles away. To make it worse, a violent thunderstorm was raging. Only a fool would make the trip.

But as we marched up to the auditorium door I saw him standing outside the hall, his threadbare coat and tattered sweater soaked with rain, his eyes searching for me in the line of robed seniors. "Who's *that?*" one of my classmates whispered. "My Uncle John," I said. In that moment he saw me. And even in the auditorium they heard, over the pounding of the processional, his booming, rustling laugh.

On Wednesday, September 26, 1979, the *Gazette* recounted the tale of the Bradley clan much as it had in 1956 as part of the page-one obituary of the Reverend David H. Bradley. The burial at Mt. Ross Cemetery would be private, but, later, friends would be received at the Louis Geisel Funeral Home. Memorial services set for the next day, the *Gazette* anticipated, would be appropriately impressive; two AME Zion bishops—mentioned by name—were scheduled to appear. Among the surviving family was listed "John, of Sewickley."

Uncle John was too ill to attend the burial or memorial service, but I prevailed upon the husband of some cousin I did not recall to drive him to the wake, even though his legs were too weak to carry him inside. And so I saw him for the last time when I sat beside him in the car.

He seemed small, shrunken. He joked, but feebly, and when I teased him about the new clothes he was wearing he said, "Rags to riches! Guess I'm gettin' there," but with no force behind it. And he did not even try to laugh. That depressed me, to be honest, more than my father's death, for it told me that my uncle's death would not be long in coming. The death of a father causes grief; the death of a chief causes fear. I was especially fearful. For when he died the chieftainship would descend to me. I was not ready. I was not worthy. And so I sat beside him and cast about for something that would conjure up his laughter.

Inside, I told him, there were two wakes, in adjacent rooms. In our room there was no casket—we'd buried my father that morning. But in the other, in a grand, flower-bedecked coffin lined with crinoline, a rail-thin ancient white lady was laid out. Bedford being a small town, many visitors paid respects in both rooms. Seeing this, the undertaker, to make things more convenient, had opened the doors between the rooms. This caused no problem—until some of my father's ministerial colleagues arrived. Although ignorant of the specific arrangements, they knew just what to do on such sad occasions. Gliding as if on casters, they went to my mother and murmured comfort, then came to give me that two-fisted handshake of condolence before moving on to their next target: the deceased. When they saw no casket they did not panic—they said more comforting words while shaking their heads in sadness, their eyes covertly scanning. Eventually they locked onto the casket in the other room and launched themselves in that direction.

"I should have let them go," I told Uncle John. "But I just couldn't. So I said, 'Gentlemen, please don't go over there. Because if you do you're going to think he suffered a lot more than he did.' " I laughed, hoping that he would laugh too. But his reaction was but a polite chuckle. "Damn," I said. "I should have let them go."

He looked at me and smiled. "Well, don't let it bother you, son. Next time you tell it, you will." And then he did laugh. Not long, but long enough. Not loud, but loud enough.

He died nine months later. I did not attend the funeral. It would have been too quiet. Oh, there would have been sound aplenty—slow hymns, generous lies, even laughter—of a sort. But it would not have been his laughter, a laugh that could shake the earth. And hearing other laughter would have made me know that he and his laugh were gone.

I will never be made to know that, I've decided. I have the right to that decision, for I am clan chief now. I do not have all the wisdom that a chief needs, but I have come to understand some things. I understand that the hypocrisy and hubris that brought our house to ruin were inevitable dangers. For any fool could see that black people in America could not rise on wings of doves. To even think of rising we should have quills of iron, rachises of steel. Of course, we do not have such mighty wings. And so we stiffen our pinfeathers with myths, flap madly, and sometimes gain a certain height.

Suggestions for Discussion

1. Who is the "hero" of the story?

2. What is the significance of the "homestead" to the Bradley family?

3. How is the family misunderstood by those who try to tell its tale? Does the family collaborate in this misunderstanding? Why?

4. Explain the significance of the father's statement, "Bradleys don't lie."

5. Uncle John is both the head of the family and its black sheep. How does the author portray this ambiguity? What are his feelings for his uncle?

Suggestions for Writing

1. Is there a "Harvest Home" equivalent in your family, a time when all generations are gathered together for festivity and celebration? Is it wonderful? Painful? Awkward? Describe it.

2. Who is your favorite relative? Why? What is he or she like? Describe this person in such a way as to enable others to understand why you feel the attachment you do.

Poetry

T. S. Eliot

The Love Song of J. Alfred Prufrock

Thomas Stearns Eliot (1888–1965) was born in St. Louis, was educated at
Harvard University, and studied in Paris and Oxford. He settled in England
in 1914 and became a British subject in 1927. His most influential poem,
The Waste Land, was published in 1922, followed by *The Hollow Men* (1925),
Poems: 1909–1925 (1925), and *Poems: 1909–1935* (1936). His criticism includes *The Use of Poetry and the Use of Criticism* (1933), *Essays Ancient and Modern*
(1936), *Notes Toward the Definition of Culture* (1948), and *To Criticize the Critic*
(1965). His best-known poetic dramas are *Murder in the Cathedral* (1935), *The
Family Reunion* (1939), and *The Cocktail Party* (1950). Prufrock's opposed selves
in this dramatic monologue are separated from each other, the one exploring the idea of human involvement and the other observing it in comfortable isolation.

> *S'io credesse che mia risposta fosse*
> *A persona che mai tornasse al mondo,*
> *Questa fiamma staria senza piu scosse.*
> *Ma perciocche giammai di questo fondo*
> *Non torno vivo alcun, s'i'odo il vero,*
> *Senza tema d'infamia ti rispondo.*

> ["If I believed that my answer would be to one who
> would ever return to the world, this flame would
> shake no more; but since no one ever returns alive
> from this depth, if what I hear is true, I answer you
> without fear of infamy." — Dante's *Inferno*, XXVII, 61–66]

Let us go then, you and I,
When the evening is spread out against the sky
Like a patient etherised upon a table;
Let us go, through certain half-deserted streets,
The muttering retreats
Of restless nights in one-night cheap hotels
And sawdust restaurants with oyster-shells:
Streets that follow like a tedious argument
Of insidious intent
To lead you to an overwhelming question . . .
Oh, do not ask, "What is it?"
Let us go and make our visit.

In the room the women come and go
Talking of Michelangelo.

The yellow fog that rubs its back upon the window-panes,
The yellow smoke that rubs its muzzle on the window-panes

Licked its tongue into the corners of the evening,
Lingered upon the pools that stand in drains,
Let fall upon its back the soot that falls from chimneys,
Slipped by the terrace, made a sudden leap,
And seeing that it was a soft October night,
Curled once about the house, and fell asleep.

   And indeed there will be time
For the yellow smoke that slides along the street,
Rubbing its back upon the window-panes;
There will be time, there will be time
To prepare a face to meet the faces that you meet;
There will be time to murder and create,
And time for all the works and days of hands
That lift and drop a question on your plate;
Time for you and time for me,
And time yet for a hundred indecisions,
And for a hundred visions and revisions,
Before the taking of a toast and tea.

   In the room the women come and go
Talking of Michelangelo.

   And indeed there will be time
To wonder, "Do I dare?" and, "Do I dare?"
Time to turn back and descend the stair,
With a bald spot in the middle of my hair—
[They will say: "How his hair is growing thin!"]
My morning coat, my collar mounting firmly to the chin,
My necktie rich and modest, but asserted by a simple pin—
[They will say: "But how his arms and legs are thin!"]
Do I dare
Disturb the universe?
In a minute there is time
For decisions and revisions which a minute will reverse.

   For I have known them all already, known them all:—
Have known the evenings, mornings, afternoons,
I have measured out my life with coffee spoons;
I know the voices dying with a dying fall
Beneath the music from a farther room.
   So how should I presume?

   And I have known the eyes already, known them all—
The eyes that fix you in a formulated phrase,
And when I am formulated, sprawling on a pin,
When I am pinned and wriggling on the wall,
Then how should I begin
To spit out all the butt-ends of my days and ways?
   And how should I presume?

   And I have known the arms already, known them all—
Arms that are braceleted and white and bare

[But in the lamplight, downed with light brown hair!]
Is it perfume from a dress
That makes me so digress?
Arms that lie along a table, or wrap about a shawl.
    And should I then presume?
    And how should I begin?

Shall I say, I have gone at dusk through narrow streets
And watched the smoke that rises from the pipes
Of lonely men in shirt-sleeves, leaning out of windows? . . .
    I should have been a pair of ragged claws
Scuttling across the floors of silent seas.

And the afternoon, the evening, sleeps so peacefully!
Smoothed by long fingers,
Asleep . . . tired . . . or it malingers,
Stretched on the floor, here beside you and me.
Should I, after tea and cakes and ices,
Have the strength to force the moment to its crisis?
But though I have wept and fasted, wept and prayed,
Though I have seen my head [grown slightly bald] brought in upon a platter,
I am no prophet—and here's no great matter;
I have seen the moment of my greatness flicker,
And I have seen the eternal Footman hold my coat, and snicker,
And in short, I was afraid.

And would it have been worth it, after all,
After the cups, the marmalade, the tea,
Among the porcelain, among some talk of you and me,
Would it have been worth while,
To have bitten off the matter with a smile,
To have squeezed the universe into a ball
To roll it toward some overwhelming question,
To say: "I am Lazarus, come from the dead.
Come back to tell you all, I shall tell you all"—
If one, settling a pillow by her head,
    Should say: "That is not what I meant at all.
    That is not it, at all."

    And would it have been worth it, after all,
Would it have been worth while,
After the sunsets and the dooryards and the sprinkled streets,
After the novels, after the teacups, after the skirts that trail along the floor—
And this, and so much more?—
It is impossible to say just what I mean!
But as if a magic lantern threw the nerves in patterns on a screen:
Would it have been worth while
If one, settling a pillow or throwing off a shawl,
And turning toward the window, should say:
    "That is not it at all,
    That is not what I meant, at all."

No! I am not Prince Hamlet, nor was meant to be;
Am an attendant lord, one that will do
To swell a progress, start a scene or two,
Advise the prince; no doubt, an easy tool,
Deferential, glad to be of use,
Politic, cautious, and meticulous;
Full of high sentence, but a bit obtuse;
At times, indeed, almost ridiculous—
Almost, at times, the Fool.

I grow old . . . I grow old . . .
I shall wear the bottoms of my trousers rolled.

Shall I part my hair behind? Do I dare to eat a peach?
I shall wear white flannel trousers, and walk upon the beach.
I have heard the mermaids singing, each to each.

I do not think that they will sing to me.

I have seen them riding seaward on the waves
Combing the white hair of the waves blown back
When the wind blows the water white and black.

We have lingered in the chambers of the sea
By sea-girls wreathed with seaweed red and brown
Till human voices wake us, and we drown.

Suggestions for Discussion

1. Who are "you and I"?

2. What evidence can you find in the structural development of the poem to support
the view that one self in the dramatic monologue acts out the conflict and the other
assumes the role of observer? Cite lines from the poem in which shifts in mood and
tone occur. How does the poem achieve dramatic unity?

3. Contrast the images of Prufrock's interior world with those of the external world.
How does their recurring juxtaposition illuminate the doubleness of the speaker
and contribute to tone? How is sensory experience used to convey the circularity of
the dialogue with self? Why are the images of the etherized patient, the staircase,
winding streets, cat, and fog especially appropriate dramatic symbols of the speaker's state of mind? Trace the use of sea imagery. How does it function differently in
the metaphor of the crab and the vision of the mermaids? How do both relate to
theme and tone? What do the allusions to John the Baptist, Lazarus, and Hamlet
have in common?

4. Distinguish between the dramatic and the lyric elements. How is the mock heroic
used to satirize both speaker and society? Study the effects of repetition on
rhythm, tone, and meaning. How do the stanzas and the typographical breaks
mark the shifts in tone? Discuss the relationship of tone to syntax, refrain, internal
rhyme, diction, tempo, and melody. Comment on the irony in the title.

5. How does time function in the poem? How does the shift in tense from present to
present perfect and future provide a key to the poem's resolution? What form does
the speaker's recognition take? By what means does the poet evoke sympathy for
Prufrock, who is psychically impotent to establish an intimate human relationship?

To what do you attribute Prufrock's rejection of human encounter? What part does his self-mockery play in our response to him? Does the poem move beyond pathos and self-mockery?

6. In what respect may the poem be viewed as an expression of a search for self?

Suggestions for Writing

1. Write a character study of Prufrock in which you refer directly to the poem.

2. Write a dialogue in which your interior self is counterpointed against your social self or *persona*.

Dylan Thomas

The Force That Through the Green Fuse Drives the Flower

Dylan Thomas (1914–1953) was born in Wales. He was a newspaper reporter for a time and worked for the BBC during World War II. He gained recognition as a lyric poet in his twenties and grew in popularity until his death while on a lecture tour in the United States. His *Collected Poems* appeared in 1953. A collection of his stories, sketches, and essays, *Quite Early One Morning*, was published in 1954; a group of stories and essays, *A Prospect of the Sea*, in 1955; and a verse play, *Under Milk Wood*, in 1954. The poet views natural forces as both destructive and life giving; the poem is an expression of his sense of the energy, both creative and destructive, that runs through all things.

The force that through the green fuse drives the flower
Drives my green age; that blasts the roots of trees
Is my destroyer.
And I am dumb to tell the crooked rose
My youth is bent by the same wintry fever.

The force that drives the water through the rocks
Drives my red blood; that dries the mouthing streams
Turns mine to wax.
And I am dumb to mouth unto my veins
How at the mountain spring the same mouth sucks.

The hand that whirls the water in the pool
Stirs the quicksand; that ropes the blowing wind
Hauls my shroud sail.
And I am dumb to tell the hanging man
How of my clay is made the hangman's lime.

The lips of time leech to the fountain head;
Love drips and gathers, but the fallen blood
Shall calm her sores.
And I am dumb to tell a weather's wind
How time has ticked a heaven round the stars.

And I am dumb to tell the lover's tomb
How at my sheet goes the same crooked worm.

Suggestions for Discussion

1. What images suggest the relationship the poet sees between the world of nature and that of human passions?

2. How does the poet express the sense that the energy that runs through all things is both creator and destroyer? How does the two-line refrain at the end of each stanza relate this theme to the voice of the poet?

3. What images depict contrasting forces of life and death? How does the diction convey the sense of sexual energy?

Eleanor Wilner

Emigration

Eleanor Wilner (b. 1938) was awarded the Juniper Prize for her first book of poetry, maya (1979), and in 1991 received a MacArthur Fellowship. Educated at Goucher College, and the Johns Hopkins University, where she earned her Ph.D., she is a former editor of the American Poetry Review, a contributing editor of Calyx, and a teacher at the Warren Wilson Program for Writers. Her books include Gathering the Wind (1975), a study of the visionary imagination; Sarah's Choice (1989); Otherwise (1993); and Shekhinah (1984), from which the following poem is taken. In it we see two poles of the human psyche as metaphorically exemplified in the lives of the novelist Charlotte Brontë and her friend Mary Taylor.

There are always, in each of us,
these two: the one who stays,
the one who goes away—
Charlotte, who stayed in the rectory
and helped her sisters die in England;
Mary Taylor who went off to Australia
and set up shop with a woman friend.
"Charlotte," Mary said to her, "you are all
like potatoes growing in the dark."

And Charlotte got a plaque in Westminster
Abbey; Mary we get a glimpse of
for a moment, waving her kerchief
on the packet boat, and disappearing.
No pseudonym for her, and nothing
left behind, no trace
but a wide wake closing.

Charlotte stayed, and paid and paid—
the little governess with the ungovernable
heart, that she put on the altar.
She paid the long indemnity of all
who work for what will never wish them well,
who never set a limit to what's owed
and cannot risk foreclosure. So London
gave her fame, though it could never
sit comfortably with her at dinner—
how intensity palls when it is
plain and small and has no fortune.
When she died with her unborn child
the stars turned east
to shine in the gum trees of Australia,
watching over what has sidetracked evolution,
where Mary Taylor lived
to a great old age, Charlotte's letters in a box
beside her bed, to keep her anger hot.

God bless us everyone until we sicken,
until the soul is like a little child
stricken in its corner by the wall; so there is
one who always sits there under lamplight
writing, staying on, and one
who walks the strange hills of Australia,
far too defiant of convention for the novels
drawn daily from the pen's "if only"—
if only Emily had lived,
if only they'd had money, if only
there had been a man who'd loved them truly . . .
when all the time there had been
Mary Taylor, whom no one would remember
except she had a famous friend named Charlotte
with whom she was so loving-angry,
who up and left to be a woman
in that godforsaken outpost past
the reach of fantasy, or fiction.

Suggestions for Discussion

1. When Wilner uses the metaphor ". . . the one who stays, / the one who goes
   away—" to talk about the nature of the human personality, what does she mean?

2. What do Charlotte Brontë, the novelist, and Mary Taylor, her friend, gain and lose
   through their respective decisions to stay at home and to leave?

3. What does the author mean when she describes Charlotte as among those "who work for what will never wish them well"? What is the price her work extracts?

4. Australia is described as a "godforsaken outpost past / the reach of fantasy, or fiction." Why would Mary Taylor want to go there? What does she "win" in doing so?

Suggestions for Writing

1. What is the part of us that stays? What is the part that goes away? Are they different for each of us, or essentially the same?

2. London and Australia are metaphors used to describe these different parts of ourselves. What metaphors would serve this function in the United States today?

Denise Levertov

In Mind

Denise Levertov (b. 1923) was born in England but came to the United States as a young woman. A poet and essayist, her career includes work as an editor, a translator, and a professor, as well as a brief stint in nursing during the Second World War. She holds four honorary degrees, and has won numerous awards for her poetry. These include, most recently, the Bobst and Shelley Prizes. Author of twenty-one volumes of poetry, her current publications include A *Door in the Hive* (1989), *Evening Train* (1992), and *New and Selected Essays* (1992). In the poem that follows she presents portraits of two very different women who inhabit her mind.

There's in my mind a woman
of innocence, unadorned but

fair-featured, and smelling of
apples or grass. She wears

a utopian smock or shift, her hair
is light brown and smooth, and she

is kind and very clean without
ostentation—
        but she has
no imagination.
        And there's a
turbulent moon-ridden girl

or old woman, or both,
dressed in opals and rags, feathers

and torn taffeta,
who knows strange songs—

but she is not kind.

Suggestions for Discussion

1. Each of the women Levertov describes possesses something that the other lacks. Does one woman "make up" for the other?

2. Are the women in Levertov's mind separate women? Or are they both part of the author's secret self, each part of the whole?

3. To which woman figure are you most drawn? Why?

Suggestions for Writing

1. Imagine this poem as a scene in a play. What kind of dialogue would emerge between the two characters?

2. How would you cast the play? Who would role-play each character?

3. Imagine the characters described as men. What would be the masculine equivalents of the two women Levertov describes?

Anne Sexton

Her Kind

Anne Sexton (1928–1974) taught and lectured widely, but was above all a poet. Recipient of three honorary degrees and numerous fellowships, she was also awarded, among others, the Shelley and Pulitzer Prizes. Of her many books the best known are To Bedlam and Part Way Back (1960), from which the following poem is taken; All My Pretty Ones (1962); Live or Die (1966); Transformations (1971); and The Death Notebooks (1974). In "Her Kind" we see another portrayal of the complex and multiple nature of human personality.

I have gone out, a possessed witch,
haunting the black air, braver at night;
dreaming evil, I have done my hitch
over the plain houses, light by light:
lonely thing, twelve-fingered, out of mind.

A woman like that is not a woman, quite.
I have been her kind.

I have found the warm caves in the woods,
filled them with skillets, carvings, shelves,
closets, silks, innumerable goods;
fixed the suppers for the worms and the elves:
whining, rearranging the disaligned.
A woman like that is misunderstood.
I have been her kind.

I have ridden in your car, driver,
waved my nude arms at villages going by,
learning the last bright routes, survivor
where your flames still bite my thigh
and my ribs crack where your wheels wind.
A woman like that is not ashamed to die.
I have been her kind.

Suggestions for Discussion

1. Why does Sexton choose to describe herself as a witch, a housewife, a martyr? How do these characterizations relate to how society has understood and portrayed women?

2. What characterizes each of the three women in the poem? What kinds of metaphors does Sexton use to describe them?

3. Why is the protagonist described as "not a woman, quite," "misunderstood," "not ashamed to die"?

Suggestions for Writing

1. If you were to think of yourself in terms of a number of different characters or *personae*, what would they be? How would they relate to one another?

2. What are some of the stereotypes our culture has used to describe men? Have these had an impact on how men in our culture behave? Explain.

Personal Relationships: Parents and Children

When I was your age I lived with a great dream. The dream grew and I learned how to speak of it and make people listen. Then the dream divided one day when I decided to marry your mother after all, even though I knew she was spoiled and meant no good to me. I was sorry immediately I had married her but, being patient in those days, made the best of it and got to love her in another way. You came along and for a long time we made quite a lot of happiness in our lives. But I was a man divided—she wanted me to work too much for *her* and not enough for my dream. She realized too late that work was dignity, and the only dignity, and tried to atone for it by working herself, but it was too late and she broke and is broken forever.

> —**F. Scott Fitzgerald,** *Dearest Scottie*

Sometimes my mother or father would come up with an image, or a fragment of a story, and we would all weave imaginary plots around it. Sometimes we talked about books or movies or the poetry we recited to each other on Sunday afternoons. Often we talked and speculated about other people, our neighbors and friends. No one ever hesitated to be mean—although the insults were usually also pretty funny. We were so mean to each other, in fact, that guests were often astonished and shocked. They didn't catch the undertone of humor in our quick sarcasms, and there were times when we didn't catch it either. Explosions and tears and sudden departures were not at all uncommon. My brothers called our dinner table "the bear garden."

> —**Susan Cheever,** "Portrait of My Father" from *Home Before Dark*

I will never total it all. I will never come in to say: She was a child seldom smiled at. Her father left me before she was a year old. I had to work her first six years when there was work, or I sent her home and to his relatives. There were years she had care she hated. She was dark and thin and foreign-looking in a world where the prestige went to blondness and curly hair and dimples, she was slow where glibness was prized. She was a child of anxious, not proud, love. We were poor and could not afford for her the soil of easy growth. I was a young mother, I was a distracted mother. There were the other children pushing up, demanding. Her younger sister seemed all that she was not. There were years she did not want me to touch her. She kept too much in herself, her life was such she had to keep too much in herself. My wisdom came too late. She has much to her and probably little will come of it. She is a child of her age, of depression, of war; of fear.

Let her be. So all that is in her will not bloom—but in how many does it? There is still enough left to live by. Only help her to know—help make it so there is cause for her to know—that she is more than this dress on the ironing board, help-less before the iron.

    —**Tillie Olsen,** "I Stand Here Ironing" from *Tell Me a Riddle*

A boy wants something very special from his father. You hear it said that fathers want their sons to be what they feel they cannot themselves be, but I tell you it also works the other way. I know that as a small boy I wanted my father to be a certain thing he was not. I wanted him to be a proud, silent, dignified father. When I was with other boys and he passed along the street, I wanted to feel a glow of pride: "There he is. That is my father."

    —**Sherwood Anderson,** "Discovery of a Father"

My father . . . believed that he (or rather, his wife) could raise children according to his unique moral and intellectual plan, thus proving to the world the values of enlightened, unorthodox child-rearing. I believe that my mother . . . at first genuinely and enthusiastically embraced the experiment, and only later found that in carrying out my father's intense, perfectionist program, she was in conflict with her deep instincts as a mother.

    —**Adrienne Rich,** "The Anger of a Child"

Behind the newspaper Julian was withdrawing into the inner compartment of his mind where he spent most of his time. This was a kind of mental bubble in which he established himself when he could not bear to be a part of what was going on around him. From it he could see out and judge but in it he was safe from any kind of penetration from without. It was the only place where he felt free of the general idiocy of his fellows. His mother had never entered it but from it he could see her with absolute clarity.

. . . She might as well be made to understand what had happened to her. "Don't think that was just an uppity Negro woman," he said. "That was the whole colored race which will no longer take your condescending pennies. That was your black double. She can wear the same hat as you, and to be sure," he added gratuitously (because he thought it was funny), "it looked better on her than it did on you. What all this means," he said, "is that the old world is gone. The old manners are obsolete. . . . You aren't who you think you are."

    —Flannery O'Connor, "Everything That Rises
       Must Converge"

Letters and Personal Reminiscences

Sherwood Anderson

Discovery of a Father

Sherwood Anderson (1876–1941) was an American short-story writer, essayist, and novelist whose writing often reflected his own confusion about man in the modern world of the machine, but whose keen insights into human beings continue to illuminate life for readers of his collection of short stories, *Winesburg, Ohio* (1919), his novels, *Many Marriages* (1922) and *Dark Laughter* (1925), and his semiautobiographical *A Story Teller's Story* (1924). In "Discovery of a Father," from Anderson's *Memoirs* (1939), the boy's negative, even contemptuous, attitude toward his father undergoes a radical change: his earlier wish that his father would be someone else gives way to the secure knowledge that he would never again want another father.

One of the strangest relationships in the world is that between father and son. I know it now from having sons of my own.

A boy wants something very special from his father. You hear it said that fathers want their sons to be what they feel they cannot themselves be, but I tell you it also works the other way. I know that as a small boy I wanted my father to be a certain thing he was not. I wanted him to be a proud, silent, dignified father. When I was with other boys and he passed along the street, I wanted to feel a glow of pride: "There he is. That is my father."

But he wasn't such a one. He couldn't be. It seemed to me then that he was always showing off. Let's say someone in our town had got up a show. They were always doing it. The druggist would be in it, the shoe-store clerk, the horse doctor, and a lot of women and girls. My father would manage to get the chief comedy part. It was, let's say, a Civil War play and he was a comic Irish soldier. He had to do the most absurd things. They thought he was funny, but I didn't.

I thought he was terrible. I didn't see how Mother could stand it. She even laughed with the others. Maybe I would have laughed if it hadn't been my father.

Or there was a parade, the Fourth of July or Decoration Day. He'd be in that, too, right at the front of it, as Grand Marshal or something, on a white horse hired from a livery stable.

He couldn't ride for shucks. He fell off the horse and everyone hooted with laughter, but he didn't care. He even seemed to like it. I remember once when he had done something ridiculous, and right out on Main Street, too. I was with some other boys and they were laughing and shouting at him and he was shouting back and having as good a time as they were. I ran down an alley back of some stores and there in the Presbyterian Church sheds I had a good long cry.

Or I would be in bed at night and Father would come home a little lit up and bring some men with him. He was a man who was never alone. Before he went broke, running a harness shop, there were always a lot of men loafing in the shop. He went broke, of course, because he gave too much credit. He couldn't refuse it and I thought he was a fool. I had got to hating him.

There'd be men I didn't think would want to be fooling around with him. There might even be the superintendent of our schools and a quiet man who ran the hardware store. Once, I remember, there was a white-haired man who was a cashier of the bank. It was a wonder to me they'd want to be seen with such a windbag. That's what I thought he was. I know now what it was that attracted them. It was because life in our town, as in all small towns, was at times pretty dull and he livened it up. He made them laugh. He could tell stories. He'd even get them to singing.

If they didn't come to our house they'd go off, say at night, to where there was a grassy place by a creek. They'd cook food there and drink beer and sit about listening to his stories.

He was always telling stories about himself. He'd say this or that wonderful thing happened to him. It might be something that made him look like a fool. He didn't care.

If an Irishman came to our house, right away father would say he was Irish. He'd tell what county in Ireland he was born in. He'd tell things that happened there when he was a boy. He'd make it seem so real that, if I hadn't known he was born in southern Ohio, I'd have believed him myself.

If it was a Scotchman, the same thing happened. He'd get a burr into his speech. Or he was a German or a Swede. He'd be anything the other man was. I think they all knew he was lying, but they seemed to like him just the same. As a boy that was what I couldn't understand.

And there was Mother. How could she stand it? I wanted to ask but never did. She was not the kind you asked such questions.

I'd be upstairs in my bed, in my room above the porch, and Father would be telling some of his tales. A lot of Father's stories were about the Civil War. To hear him tell it he'd been in about every battle. He'd known Grant, Sherman, Sheridan, and I don't know how many others. He'd been particularly intimate with General Grant so that when Grant went East, to take charge of all the armies, he took Father along.

"I was an orderly at headquarters and Sam Grant said to me, 'Irve,' he said, 'I'm going to take you along with me.'"

It seems he and Grant used to slip off sometimes and have a quiet drink together. That's what my father said. He'd tell about the day Lee surrendered and how, when the great moment came, they couldn't find Grant.

"You know," my father said, "about General Grant's book, his memoirs. You've read of how he said he had a headache and how, when he got word that Lee was ready to call it quits, he was suddenly and miraculously cured.

"Huh," said Father. "He was in the woods with me.

"I was in there with my back against a tree. I was pretty well corned. I had got hold of a bottle of pretty good stuff.

"They were looking for Grant. He had got off his horse and come into the woods. He found me. He was covered with mud.

"I had the bottle in my hand. What'd I care? The war was over. I knew we had them licked."

My father said that he was the one who told Grant about Lee. An orderly riding by had told him, because the orderly knew how thick he was with Grant. Grant was embarrassed.

"But, Irve, look at me. I'm all covered with mud," he said to Father.

And then, my father said, he and Grant decided to have a drink together. They took a couple of shots and then, because he didn't want Grant to show up potted before the immaculate Lee, he smashed the bottle against the tree.

"Sam Grant's dead now and I wouldn't want it to get out on him," my father said.

That's just one of the kind of things he'd tell. Of course, the men knew he was lying, but they seemed to like it just the same.

When we got broke, down and out, do you think he ever brought anything home? Not he. If there wasn't anything to eat in the house, he'd go off visiting around at farm houses. They all wanted him. Sometimes he'd stay away for weeks, Mother working to keep us fed, and then home he'd come bringing, let's say, a ham. He'd got it from some farmer friend. He'd slap it on the table in the kitchen. "You bet I'm going to see that my kids have something to eat," he'd say, and Mother would just stand smiling at him. She'd never say a word about all the weeks and months he'd been away, not leaving us a cent for food. Once I heard her speaking to a woman in our street. Maybe the woman had dared to sympathize with her. "Oh," she said, "it's all right. He isn't ever dull like most of the men in this street. Life is never dull when my man is about."

But often I was filled with bitterness, and sometimes I wished he wasn't my father. I'd even invent another man as my father. To protect my mother I'd make up stories of a secret marriage that for some strange reason never got known. As though some man, say the president of a railroad company or maybe a Congressman, had married my mother, thinking his wife was dead and then it turned out she wasn't.

So they had to hush it up but I got born just the same. I wasn't really the son of my father. Somewhere in the world there was a very dignified, quite wonderful man who was really my father. I even made myself half believe these fancies.

And then there came a certain night. Mother was away from home. Maybe there was church that night. Father came in. He'd been off somewhere for two or three weeks. He found me alone in the house, reading by the kitchen table.

It had been raining and he was very wet. He sat and looked at me for a long time, not saying a word. I was startled, for there was on his face the saddest look I had ever seen. He sat for a time, his clothes dripping. Then he got up.

"Come on with me," he said.

I got up and went with him out of the house. I was filled with wonder but I wasn't afraid. We went along a dirt road that led down into a valley, about a mile out of town, where there was a pond. We walked in silence. The man who was always talking had stopped his talking.

I didn't know what was up and had the queer feeling that I was with a stranger. I didn't know whether my father intended it so. I don't think he did.

The pond was quite large. It was still raining hard and there were flashes of lightning followed by thunder. We were on a grassy bank at the pond's edge when my father spoke, and in the darkness and rain his voice sounded strange.

"Take off your clothes," he said. Still filled with wonder, I began to undress. There was a flash of lightning and I saw that he was already naked.

Naked, we went into the pond. Taking my hand, he pulled me in. It may be that I was too frightened, too full of a feeling of strangeness, to speak. Before that night my father had never seemed to pay any attention to me.

"And what is he up to now?" I kept asking myself. I did not swim very well, but he put my hand on his shoulder and struck out into the darkness.

He was a man with big shoulders, a powerful swimmer. In the darkness I could feel the movements of his muscles. We swam to the far edge of the pond and then back to where we had left our clothes. The rain continued and the wind blew. Sometimes my father swam on his back, and when he did he took my hand in his large powerful one and moved it over so that it rested always on his shoulder. Sometimes there would be a flash of lightning and I could see his face quite clearly.

It was as it was earlier, in the kitchen, a face filled with sadness. There would be the momentary glimpse of his face, and then again the darkness, the wind and the rain. In me there was a feeling I had never known before.

It was a feeling of closeness. It was something strange. It was as though there were only we two in the world. It was as though I had been jerked suddenly out of myself, out of my world of the schoolboy, out of a world in which I was ashamed of my father.

He had become blood of my blood; he the strong swimmer and I the boy clinging to him in the darkness. We swam in silence, and in silence we dressed in our wet clothes and went home.

There was a lamp lighted in the kitchen, and when we came in, the water dripping from us, there was my mother. She smiled at us. I remember that she called us "boys." "What have you boys been up to?" she asked, but my father did not answer. As he had begun the evening's experience with me in silence, so he ended it. He turned and looked at me. Then he went, I thought, with a new and strange dignity, out of the room.

I climbed the stairs to my room, undressed in darkness and got into bed. I couldn't sleep and did not want to sleep. For the first time I knew that I was the son of my father. He was a storyteller as I was to be. It may be that I even laughed a little softly there in the darkness. If I did, I laughed knowing that I would never again be wanting another father.

Suggestions for Discussion

1. How does the author bring the subject into focus?

2. Account for the feelings the narrator had toward his father's public behavior.

3. How do the sentence structure and diction contribute to purpose and tone?

4. How do you explain the father's action in taking the boy swimming? How do you account for the boy's changed view of his father?

Suggestions for Writing

1. Write on one of these topics: a portrait of my father; imaginary parents.

2. Write a narrative in which a seemingly simple event effects a change in attitude.

Franz Kafka

Letter to His Father

Translated by Ernest Kaiser and Eithene Wilkins

Franz Kafka (1883–1924), the German novelist who portrays alienated characters in an absurd world, made little mark during his life but is now considered a major modern writer. Many of his novels have been published posthumously, including *The Trial*, *The Castle*, and *Amerika*. In the letter, also published posthumously, the author in a legalistic manner indicts himself as well as his father in assessing responsibility for his, Kakfa's, insecurity as a person.

Dearest Father:

You asked me recently why I maintain that I am afraid of you. As usual, I was unable to think of any answer to your question, partly for the very reason that I am afraid of you, and partly because an explanation of the grounds for this fear would mean going into far more details than I could even approximately keep in mind while talking. And if I now try to give you an answer in writing, it will still be very incomplete, because even in writing this fear and its consequences hamper me in relation to you and because [anyway] the magnitude of the subject goes far beyond the scope of my memory and power of reasoning. . . .

Compare the two of us: I, to put it in a very much abbreviated form, a Löwy with a certain basis of Kafka, which, however, is not set in motion by the Kafka will to life, business, and conquest, but by a Löwyish spur that urges more secretly, more diffidently, and in another direction, and which often fails to work entirely. You, on the other hand, a true Kafka in strength, health, appetite, loudness of voice, eloquence, self-satisfaction, worldly dominance, endurance, presence of mind, knowledge of human nature, a certain way of doing things on a grand scale, of course with all the defects and weaknesses that go with all these advantages and into which your temperament and sometimes your hot temper drive you. . . .

However it was, we were so different and in our difference so dangerous to each other that, if anyone had tried to calculate in advance how I, the slowly developing child, and you, the full-grown man, would stand to each other, he could have assumed that you would simply trample me underfoot so that nothing was left of me. Well, that didn't happen. Nothing alive can be calculated. But perhaps something worse happened. And in saying this I would all the time beg of you not to forget that I never, and not even for a single moment, believe any guilt to be on your side. The effect you had on me was the effect you could not help having. But you should stop considering it some particular malice on my part that I succumbed to that effect.

I was a timid child. For all that, I am sure I was also obstinate, as children are. I am sure that Mother spoilt me too, but I cannot believe I was particularly difficult to manage; I cannot believe that a kindly word, a quiet taking of me by the hand, a friendly look, could not have got me to do anything that was wanted of me. Now you are after all at bottom a kindly and softhearted person (what follows will not be in contradiction to this, I am speaking only of the impression you made on the child), but not every child has the endurance and fearlessness to go on searching until it comes to the kindliness that lies beneath the surface. You can only treat a child in the way you yourself are constituted, with vigor, noise, and hot temper, and in this case this seemed to you, into the bargain, extremely suitable, because you wanted to bring me up to be a strong brave boy. . . .

There is only one episode in the early years of which I have a direct memory. You may remember it, too. Once in the night I kept on whimpering for water, not, I am certain, because I was thirsty, but probably partly to be annoying, partly to amuse myself. After several vigorous threats had failed to have any effect, you took me out of bed, carried me out onto the *pavlatche* and left me there alone for a while in my nightshirt, outside the shut door. I am not going to say that this was wrong—perhaps at that time there was really no other way of getting peace and quiet that night—but I mention it as typical of your methods of bringing up a child and their effect on me. I dare say I was quite obedient afterwards at that period, but it did me inner harm. What was for me a matter of course, that senseless asking for water, and the extraordinary terror of being carried outside were two things that I, my nature being what it was, could never properly connect with each other. Even years afterwards I suffered from the tormenting fancy that the huge man, my father, the ultimate authority, would come almost for no reason at all and take me out of bed in the night and carry me out onto the *pavlatche*, and that therefore I was such a mere nothing for him.

That then was only a small beginning, but this sense of nothingness that often dominates me (a feeling that is in another respect, admittedly, also a noble and fruitful one) comes largely from your influence. What I would have needed was a little encouragement, a little friendliness, a little keeping open of my road, instead of which you blocked it for me, though of course with the good intention of making me go another road. But I was not fit for that. You encouraged me, for instance, when I saluted and marched smartly, but I was no future soldier, or you encouraged me when I was able to eat heartily or even drink beer with my meals, or when I was able to repeat songs, singing what I had not understood, or prattle to you using your own favorite expressions, imitating you, but nothing of this had anything to do with my future. And it is characteristic that even today you really only encourage me in anything when you yourself are involved in it, when what is at stake is your sense of self-importance.

At that time, and at that time everywhere, I would have needed encouragement. I was, after all, depressed even by your mere physical presence. I remember, for instance, how we often undressed together in the same bathing hut. There was I, skinny, weakly, slight; you strong, tall, broad. Even inside the hut I felt myself a miserable specimen, and what's more, not only in your eyes but in the eyes of the whole world, for you were for me the measure of all things. But then when we went out of the bathing hut before the people, I with you holding my hand, a little skeleton, unsteady, barefoot on the boards, frightened of the water, incapable of copying your swimming strokes, which you, with the best of intentions, but actually to my profound humiliation, always kept on showing me, then I was frantic with desperation and all my bad experiences in all spheres at such moments fitted magnificently together. . . .

In keeping with that, furthermore, was your intellectual domination. You had worked your way up so far alone, by your own energies, and as a result you had unbounded confidence in your opinion. For me as a child that was not yet so dazzling as later for the boy growing up. From your armchair you ruled the world. Your opinion was correct, every other was mad, wild, *meshugge*, not normal. With all this your self-confidence was so great that you had no need to be consistent at all and yet never ceased to be in the right. It did sometimes happen that you had no opinion whatsoever about a matter and as a result all opinions that were at all possible with respect to the matter were necessarily wrong, without exception. You were capable, for instance, of running down the Czechs, and then the Germans, and then the Jews, and what is more, not only selectively but in every respect, and finally nobody was left except yourself. For me you took on the enigmatic quality that all tyrants have whose rights are based on their person and not on reason. At least so it seemed to me.

Now where I was concerned you were in fact astonishingly often in the right, which was a matter of course in talk, for there was hardly ever any talk between us, but also in reality. Yet this too was nothing particularly incomprehensible; in all my thinking I was, after all, under the heavy pressure of your personality, even in that part of it—and particularly in that—which was not in accord with yours. All these thoughts, seemingly independent of you, were from the beginning loaded with the burden of your harsh and dogmatic judgments; it was almost impossible to endure this, and yet to work out one's thoughts with any measure of completeness and permanence. I am not here speaking of any sublime thoughts, but of every little enterprise in childhood. It was only necessary to be happy about something or other, to be filled with the thought of it, to come home and speak of it, and the answer was an ironical sigh, a shaking of the head, a tapping of the table with one finger: "Is that all you're so worked up about?" or "I wish I had your worries!" or "The things some people have time to think about!" or "What can you buy yourself with that?" or "What a song and dance about nothing!" Of course, you couldn't be expected to be enthusiastic about every childish triviality, toiling and moiling as you used to. But that wasn't the point. The point was, rather, that you could not help always and on principle causing the child such disappointments, by virtue of your antagonistic nature, and further that this antagonism was ceaselessly intensified through accumulation of its material, that it finally became a matter of established habit even when for once you were of the same opinion as myself, and that finally these disappointments of the child's were not disappointments in ordinary life but, since what it concerned was your person, which was the measure of all things, struck to the very core. Courage, resolution, confidence, delight in this and that, did not endure to the end when you were against whatever it was or even if your opposition was merely to be assumed; and it was to be assumed in almost everything I did. . . .

You have, I think, a gift for bringing up children: you could, I am sure, have been of use to a human being of your own kind with your methods; such a person would have seen the reasonableness of what you told him, would not have troubled about anything else, and would quietly have done things the way he was told. But for me a child everything you shouted at me was positively a heavenly commandment, I never forgot it, it remained for me the most important means of forming a judgment of the world, above all of forming a judgment of you yourself, and there you failed entirely. Since as a child I was together with you chiefly at meals, your teaching was to a large extent teaching about proper behavior at table. What was brought to the table had to be eaten up, there could be no discussion of the goodness of the food— but you yourself often found the food uneatable, called it "this swill," said "that brute" (the cook) had ruined it. Because in accordance with your strong appetite and your particular habit you ate everything fast, hot and in big mouthfuls, the child had to hurry, there was a somber silence at table, interrupted by admonitions: "Eat first, talk afterwards," or "faster, faster, faster," or "there you are, you see, I finished ages ago." Bones mustn't be cracked with the teeth, but you could. Vinegar must not be sipped noisily, but you could. The main thing was that the bread should be cut straight. But it didn't matter that you did it with a knife dripping with gravy. One had to take care that no scraps fell on the floor. In the end it was under your chair that there were most scraps. At table one wasn't allowed to do anything but eat, but you cleaned and cut your fingernails, sharpened pencils, cleaned your ears with the toothpick. Please, Father, understand me rightly: these would in themselves have been utterly insignificant details, they only became depressing for me because you, the man who was so tremendously the measure of all things for me, yourself did not keep the commandments you imposed on me. Hence the world was for me divided into three parts: into one in which I, the slave, lived under laws that had been invented only for me and which I could, I did not know why, never completely comply with; then into a second world, which was infinitely remote from mine, in which you lived, concerned with government, with the issuing of orders and with annoyance about their not being obeyed; and finally into a third world where everybody else lived happily and free from orders and from having to obey. I was continually in disgrace, either I obeyed your orders, and that was a disgrace, for they applied, after all, only to me, or I was defiant, and that was a disgrace too, for how could I presume to defy you, or I could not obey because, for instance, I had not your strength, your appetite, your skill, in spite of which you expected it of me as a matter of course; this was the greatest disgrace of all. What moved in this way was not the child's reflections, but his feelings. . . .

It was true that Mother was illimitably good to me, but all that was for me in relation to you, that is to say, in no good relation. Mother unconsciously played the part of a beater during a hunt. Even if your method of upbringing might in some unlikely case have set me on my own feet by means of producing defiance, dislike, or even hate in me, Mother canceled that out again by kindness, by talking sensibly (in the maze and chaos of my childhood she was the very pattern of good sense and reasonableness), by pleading for me, and I was again driven back into your orbit, which I might perhaps otherwise have broken out of, to your advantage and to my own. Or it was so that no real reconciliation ever came about, that Mother merely shielded me from you in secret, secretly gave me something, or allowed me to do something, and then where you were concerned I was again the furtive creature, the cheat, the guilty one, who in his worthlessness could only pursue backstairs methods even to get the things he regarded as his right. Of course, I then became used to taking such courses also in quest of things to which, even in my own view, I had no right. This again meant an increase in the sense of guilt.

It is also true that you hardly ever really gave me a whipping. But the shouting, the way your face got red, the hasty undoing of the braces and the laying of them ready over the back of the chair, all that was almost worse for me. It is like when someone is going to be hanged. If he is really hanged, then he's dead and it's all over. But if he has to go through all the preliminaries to being hanged and only when the noose is dangling before his face is told of his reprieve, then he may suffer from it all his life long. Besides, from so many occasions when I had, as you clearly showed you thought, deserved to be beaten, when you were however gracious enough to let me off at the last moment, here again what accumulated was only a huge sense of guilt. On every side I was to blame, I was in debt to you.

You have always reproached me (and what is more either alone or in front of others, you having no feeling for the humiliation of this latter, your children's affairs always being public affairs) for living in peace and quiet, warmth, and abundance, lack for nothing, thanks to your hard work. I think here of remarks that must positively have worn grooves in my brain, like: "When I was only seven I had to push the barrow from village to village." "We all had to sleep in one room." "We were glad when we got potatoes." "For years I had open sores on my legs from not having enough clothes to wear in winter." "I was only a little boy when I was sent away to Pisek to go into business." "I got nothing from home, not even when I was in the army, even then I was sending money home." "But for all that, for all that—Father was always Father to me. Ah, nobody knows what that means these days! What do these children know of things? Nobody's been through that! Is there any child that understands such things today?" Under other conditions such stories might have been very educational, they might have been a way of encouraging one and strengthening one to endure similar torments and deprivations to those one's father had undergone. But that wasn't what you wanted at all; the situation had, after all, become quite different as a result of all your efforts, and there was no opportunity to distinguish oneself in the world as you had done. Such an opportunity would first of all have had to be created by violence and revolution, it would have meant breaking away from home (assuming one had had the resolution and strength to do so and that Mother wouldn't have worked against it, for her part, with other means). But all that was not what you wanted at all, that you termed ingratitude, extravagance, disobedience, treachery, madness. And so, while on the one hand you tempted me to it by means of example, story, and humiliation, on the other hand you forbade it with the utmost severity. . . .

(Up to this point there is in this letter relatively little I have intentionally passed over in silence, but now and later I shall have to be silent on certain matters that it is still too hard for me to confess—to you and to myself. I say this in order that, if the picture as a whole should be somewhat blurred here and there, you should not believe that what is to blame is any lack of evidence; on the contrary, there is evidence that might well make the picture unbearably stark. It is not easy to strike a median position.) Here, it is enough to remind you of early days. I had lost my self-confidence where you were concerned, and in its place had developed a boundless sense of guilt. (In recollection of this boundlessness I once wrote of someone, accurately: "He is afraid the shame will outlive him, even.") I could not suddenly undergo a transformation when I came into the company of other people; on the contrary, with them I came to feel an even deeper sense of guilt, for, as I have already said, in their case I had to make good the wrongs done them by you in the business, wrongs in which I too had my share of responsibility. Besides, you always, of course, had some objection to make, frankly or covertly, to everyone I associated with, and for this too I had to beg his pardon. The mistrust that you tried to instill into me, at business and at home, towards most people (tell me of any single person who was of importance to me in my childhood whom you didn't at least once tear to shreds with your criticism), this mistrust, which oddly enough was no particular burden to you (the fact was that you were strong enough to bear it, and besides, it was in reality perhaps only a token of the autocrat), this mistrust, which for me as a little boy was nowhere confirmed in my own eyes, since I everywhere saw only people excellent beyond all hope of emulation, in me turned into mistrust of myself and into perpetual anxiety in relation to everything else. There, then, I was in general certain of not being able to escape from you.

Suggestions for Discussion

Kafka gave this letter (from which you have only excerpts) to his mother, asking her to give it to his father. Understandably she never did so, but it was found among Kafka's unpublished manuscripts after his death. Although Kafka had asked his friend Max Brod to destroy all unpublished material, Brod did not comply with this request.

1. Study the legalistic manner in which Kafka indicts himself as well as his father. Assuming you were on a jury, evaluate the points for prosecution and defense of both father and son. What would be your final judgment as to responsibility for the boy's insecurity as a person?

2. Study the scenes through which Kafka dramatizes certain moments of special significance in his childhood. In spite of his attempt to be fair, by what means does he enlist sympathy with the child?

3. What seems to be the role of the mother? Why does the boy more closely identify with her and her family than with his father?

Suggestions for Writing

1. Write about a significant moment in your childhood relationship with your parents. What effect may it have had on your self-image?

2. Write on the parents' image versus the child's.

3. Contrast this father with the one portrayed in E. E. Cummings's poem "My Father Moved Through Dooms of Love."

Adrienne Rich

The Anger of a Child

Adrienne Rich (b.1929) has been an activist in the women's movement, and her attitudes are reflected in her poetry, literary criticism, and essays on patriarchy in our culture. Her publications include A Change of World (1951); Snapshots of a Daughter-in-Law (1963); The Will to Change (1971); Your Native Land, Your Life (1986); On Lies, Secrets and Silence: Selected Prose (1979); and Blood, Bread and Poetry (1986). The following excerpt appears in her book Of Woman Born (1976). It reflects her ambivalence toward her parents and "old, smoldering patches of deep-burning anger."

It is hard to write about my mother. Whatever I do write, it is my story I am telling, my version of the past. If she were to tell her own story other landscapes would be revealed. But in my landscape or hers, there would be old, smoldering patches of deep-burning anger. Before her marriage, she had trained seriously for years both as a concert pianist and a composer. Born in a southern town, mothered by a strong, frustrated woman, she had won a scholarship to study with the director at the Peabody Conservatory in Baltimore, and by teaching at girls' schools had earned her way to further study in New York, Paris, and Vienna. From the age of sixteen, she had been a young belle, who could have married at any time, but she also possessed unusual talent, determination, and independence for her time and place. She read—and reads—widely and wrote—as her journals from my childhood and her letters of today reveal—with grace and pungency.

She married my father after a ten years' engagement during which he finished his medical training and began to establish himself in academic medicine. Once married, she gave up the possibility of a concert career, though for some years she went on composing, and she is still a skilled and dedicated pianist. My father, brilliant, ambitious, possessed by his own drive, assumed that she would give her life over to the enhancement of his. She would manage his household with the formality and grace becoming to a medical professor's wife, though on a limited budget; she would "keep up" her music, though there was no question of letting her composing and practice conflict with her duties as a wife and mother. She was supposed to bear him two children, a boy and a girl. She had to keep her household books to the last penny—I still can see the big blue-gray ledgers, inscribed in her clear, strong hand; she marketed by streetcar, and later, when they could afford a car, she drove my father to and from his laboratory or lectures, often awaiting him for hours. She raised two children, and taught us all our lessons, including music. (Neither of us was sent to school until the fourth grade.) I am sure that she was made to feel responsible for all our imperfections.

My father, like the transcendentalist Bronson Alcott, believed that he (or rather, his wife) could raise children according to his unique moral and intellectual plan, thus proving to the world the values of enlightened, unorthodox child-rearing. I believe that my mother, like Abigail Alcott, at first genuinely and enthusiastically embraced the experiment, and only later found that in carrying out my father's intense, perfectionist program, she was in conflict with her deep instincts as a mother. Like Abigail Alcott, too, she must have found that while ideas might be unfolded by her husband, their daily, hourly practice was going to be up to her. ("'Mr. A. aids me in general principles, but nobody can aid me in the detail,' she mourned. . . . Moreover her husband's views kept her constantly wondering if she were doing a good job. 'Am I doing what is right? Am I doing enough? Am I doing too much?'" The appearance of "temper" and "will" in Louisa, the second Alcott daughter, was blamed by her father on her inheritance from her mother.) Under the institution of motherhood, the mother is the first to blame if theory proves unworkable in practice, or if anything whatsoever goes wrong. But even earlier, my mother had failed at one part of the plan: she had not produced a son.

For years, I felt my mother had chosen my father over me, had sacrificed me to his needs and theories. When my first child was born, I was barely in communication with my parents. I had been fighting my father for my right to an emotional life and a selfhood beyond his needs and theories. We were all at a draw. Emerging from the fear, exhaustion, and alienation of my first childbirth, I could not admit even to myself that I wanted my mother, let alone tell her how much I wanted her. When she visited me in the hospital neither of us could uncoil the obscure lashings of feeling that darkened the room, the tangled thread running backward to where she had labored for three days to give birth to me, and I was not a son. Now, twenty-six years later, I lay in a contagious hospital with my allergy, my skin covered with a mysterious rash, my lips and eyelids swollen, my body bruised and sutured, and, in a cot beside my bed, slept the perfect, golden, male child I had brought forth. How could I have interpreted her feelings when I could not begin to decipher my own? My body had spoken all too eloquently, but it was, medically, just my body. I wanted her to mother me again, to hold my baby in her arms as she had once held me; but that baby was also a gauntlet flung down: *my son*. Part of me longed to offer him for her blessing; part of me wanted to hold him up as a badge of victory in our tragic, unnecessary rivalry as women.

But I was only at the beginning. I know now as I could not possibly know then, that among the tangle of feelings between us, in that crucial yet unreal meeting, was her guilt. Soon I would begin to understand the full weight and burden of maternal guilt, that daily, nightly, hourly, *Am I doing what is right? Am I doing enough? Am I doing too much?* The institution of motherhood finds all mothers more or less guilty of having failed their children; and my mother, in particular, had been expected to help create, according to my father's plan, a perfect daughter. This "perfect" daughter, though gratifyingly precocious, had early been given to tics and tantrums, had become permanently lame from arthritis at twenty-two; she had finally resisted her father's Victorian paternalism, his seductive charm and controlling cruelty, had married a divorced graduate student, had begun to write "modern," "obscure," "pessimistic" poetry, lacking the fluent sweetness of Tennyson, had had the final temerity to get pregnant and bring a living baby into the world. She had ceased to be the demure and precocious child or the poetic, seducible adolescent. Something, in my father's view, had gone terribly wrong. I can imagine that whatever else my mother felt (and I know that part of her *was* mutely on my side) she also was made to feel blame. Beneath the "numbness" that she has since told me she experienced at that time, I can imagine the guilt of Everymother, because I have known it myself.

But I did not know it yet. And it is difficult for me to write of my mother now, because I have known it too well. I struggle to describe what it felt like to be her daughter, but I find myself divided, slipping under her skin; a part of me identified too much with her. I know deep reservoirs of anger toward her still exist: the anger of a four-year-old locked in the closet (my father's orders, but my mother carried them out) for childish misbehavior; the anger of a six-year-old kept too long at piano practice (again, at his insistence, but it was she who gave the lessons) till I developed a series of facial tics. (As a mother I know what a child's facial tic is—a lancet of guilt and pain running through one's own body.) And I still feel the anger of a daughter, pregnant, wanting my mother desperately and feeling she had gone over to the enemy.

And I know there must be deep reservoirs of anger in her; every mother has known overwhelming, unacceptable anger at her children. When I think of the conditions under which my mother became a mother, the impossible expectations, my father's distaste for pregnant women, his hatred of all that he could not control, my anger at her dissolves into grief and anger *for* her, and then dissolves back again into anger at her: the ancient, unpurged anger of the child.

My mother lives today as an independent woman, which she was always meant to be. She is a much-loved, much-admired grandmother, an explorer in new realms; she lives in the present and future, not the past. I no longer have fantasies—they are the unhealed child's fantasies, I think—of some infinitely healing conversation with her, in which we could show all our wounds, transcend the pain we have shared as mother and daughter, say everything at last. But in writing these pages, I am admitting, at least, how important her existence is and has been for me.

Suggestions for Discussion

1. What is the tone of Rich's portrait of her father? With what details does it become apparent?

2. With what details does the author convey her anger at her mother?

3. How does the author feel about the relationship of her father and mother?

4. How did Rich recognize her mother's guilt?

5. Account for the author's ambivalence toward her mother.

6. The author concedes that she is writing her "version of the past" and that her mother might tell her story differently. Provide some of the details in the mother's story if told by her.

Suggestions for Writing

1. Write on your views of enlightened child rearing.

2. Recall an episode in your childhood in which you felt anger at your parents.

3. Develop your version of the mother's story.

F. Scott Fitzgerald

Dearest Scottie

F. Scott Fitzgerald (1896–1940) attended Princeton University but did not graduate. He accepted a commission in the army and when stationed at Camp Sheridan he met his future wife, Zelda, about whom he writes in this letter. He wrote copy in an advertising agency in New York while trying to succeed as a novelist. His best-known books are *This Side of Paradise* (1920), which draws upon his experiences at college; *The Beautiful and the Damned* (1922); *Tales of the Jazz Age* (1922); *The Great Gatsby* (1925); and *Tender Is the Night* (1934). The letter that follows reflects not only his disappointment in his daughter and his feeling of bitterness about his marriage but also conveys his sadness that his dream was aborted.

Dearest Scottie:

I don't think I will be writing letters many more years and I wish you would read this letter twice—bitter as it may seem. You will reject it now, but at a later period some of it may come back to you as truth. When I'm talking to you, you think of me as an older person, an "authority," and when I speak of my own youth what I say becomes unreal to you—for the young can't believe in the youth of their fathers. But perhaps this little bit will be understandable if I put it in writing.

When I was your age I lived with a great dream. The dream grew and I learned how to speak of it and make people listen. Then the dream divided one day when I decided to marry your mother after all, even though I knew she was spoiled and meant no good to me. I was sorry immediately I had married her but, being patient in those days, made the best of it and got to love her in another way. You came along and for a long time we made quite a lot of happiness out of our lives. But I was a man divided—she wanted me to work too much for *her* and not enough for my dream. She realized too late that work was dignity, and the only dignity, and tried to atone for it by working herself, but it was too late and she broke and is broken forever.

It was too late also for me to recoup the damage—I had spent most of my resources, spiritual and material, on her, but I struggled on for five years till my health collapsed, and all I cared about was drink and forgetting.

The mistake I made was in marrying her. We belonged to different worlds—she might have been happy with a kind simple man in a southern garden. She didn't have the strength for the big stage—sometimes she pretended, and pretended beautifully, but she didn't have it. She was soft when she should have been hard, and hard when she should have been yielding. She never knew how to use her energy—she's passed that failing on to you.

For a long time I hated *her* mother for giving her nothing in the line of good habit—nothing but "getting by" and conceit. I never wanted to see again in this world women who were brought up as idlers. And one of my chief desires in life was to keep you from being that kind of person, one who brings ruin to themselves and others. When you began to show disturbing signs at about fourteen, I comforted myself with the idea that you were too precocious socially and a strict school would fix things. But sometimes I think that idlers seem to be a special class for whom nothing can be planned, plead as one will with them—their only contribution to the human family is to warm a seat at the common table.

My reforming days are over, and if you are that way I don't want to change you. But I don't want to be upset by idlers inside my family or out. I want my energies and my earnings for people who talk my language.

I have begun to fear that you don't. You don't realize that what I am doing here is the last tired effort of a man who once did something finer and better. There is not enough energy, or call it money, to carry anyone who is dead weight and I am angry and resentful in my soul when I feel that I am doing this. People like ____ ____ and your mother must be carried because their illness makes them useless. But it is a different story that *you* have spent two years doing no useful work at all, improving neither your body nor your mind, but only writing reams and reams of dreary letters to dreary people, with no possible object except obtaining invitations which you could not accept. Those letters go on, even in your sleep, so that I know your whole trip now is one long waiting for the post. It is like an old gossip who cannot still her tongue.

You have reached the age when one is of interest to an adult only insofar as one seems to have a future. The mind of a little child is fascinating, for it looks on old things with new eyes—but at about twelve this changes. The adolescent offers nothing, can do nothing, say nothing that the adult cannot do better. Living with you in Baltimore (and you have told Harold that I alternated between strictness and neglect, by which I suppose you mean the times I was so inconsiderate as to have T.B., or to retire into myself to write, for I had little social life apart from you) represented a rather too domestic duty forced on me by your mother's illness. But I endured your Top Hats and Telephones until the day you snubbed me at dancing school, less willingly after that. . . .

To sum up: What you have done to please me or make me proud is practically negligible since the time you made yourself a good diver at camp (and now you are softer than you have ever been). In your career as a "wild society girl," vintage of 1925, I'm not interested. I don't want any of it—it would bore me, like dining with the Ritz Brothers. When I do not feel you are "going somewhere," your company tends to depress me for the silly waste and triviality involved. On the other hand, when occasionally I see signs of life and intention in you, there is no company in the world I prefer. For there is no doubt that you have something in your belly, some real gusto for life—a real dream of your own—and my idea was to wed it to something solid before it was too late—as it was too late for your mother to learn anything when she got around to it. Once when you spoke French as a child it was enchanting with your odd bits of knowledge—now your conversation is as commonplace as if you'd spent the last two years in the Corn Hollow High School—what you saw in *Life* and read in *Sexy Romances*.

I shall come East in September to meet your boat—but this letter is a declaration that I am no longer interested in your promissory notes but only in what I see. I love you always but I am only interested by people who think and work as I do and it isn't likely that *I* shall change at my age. Whether you will—or want to—remains to be seen.

Daddy

P.S. If you keep the diary, please don't let it be the dry stuff I could buy in a ten-franc guide book. I'm not interested in dates and places, even the Battle of New Orleans, unless you have some unusual reaction to them. Don't try to be witty in the writing, unless it's natural—just true and real.

P.P.S. Will you please read this letter a second time? I wrote it over twice.

Suggestions for Discussion

1. How would you describe the philosophical differences between Fitzgerald and Scottie's mother?

2. What do you infer was Fitzgerald's dream?

3. How valid do you think is Fitzgerald's comparison of the mind of a child with that of an adolescent?

4. Partly by inference the writer provides a picture of Scottie's recent life. What details do you learn of it?

Suggestions for Writing

1. Write the letter that your mother or father might write to you.

2. Imagine you have received a critical letter from your mother or father. How would you answer it?

3. Is it true that the young can't believe in the youth of their fathers (or mothers)?

Susan Cheever

Portrait of My Father

Susan Cheever (b. 1943) was educated at Brown University. She wrote as a professional journalist before she began writing novels. She also taught creative writing at Hofstra University, and has been the recipient of numerous awards and fellowships. Her novels are *Looking for Work* (1980), *A Handsome Man* (1981), *And Women* (1987), and *Elizabeth Cole* (1989). Her recent biography of her father, famous novelist John Cheever, is entitled *Home Before Dark*. By a variety of means—quotations from his journal, statements regarding his philosophy, his contradictions and confusions, his fantasies, and his intimidating qualities—Susan Cheever presents a moving portrait of her father, whom she deeply reveres.

"Susan calls me," my father wrote in his journal in 1952. "It is four or five in the morning. 'I have such awful thoughts, Daddy,' she says. 'I think there is a tiger in the hall and that he will eat me.' She laughs, but she is frightened. It is the hour before light. The dark is troubled for us both. There are no ghosts of men or tigers in the hall, but the dark is hard to bear. There will be great pain and labor before we see this obscurity transformed into sweet morning."

On a cold sunny Monday, about two months before my father died, I checked into New York Hospital and had my own first child, a daughter, Sarah. From the instant I saw her, a tiny red creature bathed in the weird underwater light of the hospital operating room, I loved her with an intensity that life had not prepared me for. As I had grown more pregnant, my father had become sicker. He lost a little every day, and that loss seemed to cast a shadow over all of us. The birth of the baby didn't take away that loss, but it changed everything for me.

My parents drove in to visit me at the hospital the day after she was born. My mother brought a calico mobile, I drank a glass of champagne, and my father's gaunt unbalanced face beamed in at Sarah's plastic bassinet through the transparent wall of the nursery. Her birth seemed to revitalize him. He called the next morning and told me that he felt much better. It was early, but the hospital was already awake. My room was filled with flowers. The cancer was finished, my father had decided. "I've kicked it, Susie," he said. "It's over."

It's a measure of human optimism that we all believed him. For a few weeks it even seemed to be true. He would never be well, of course, but the weakened, wasted father that was left seemed infinitely precious. My first postpregnancy outing was to see him receive the National Medal for Literature at Carnegie Hall. He looked frail, but he spoke with great strength. Afterward my husband and I went backstage. He wasn't there; we found him and the rest of the family ensconced on the banquettes of the Russian Tea Room next door, laughing and eating and ordering more. But early in May, when we took the month-old baby out to visit my parents in Ossining, he looked weaker.

"Make your famous baby noise, John," my mother urged him, and he curled up his lip in a comic high-pitched squeal. Then suddenly he seemed very tired. "Thank you for remembering, dear," he said. That's when I knew he was worse again. As the baby awakened to the world around her that first and last spring, my father waned and faded and grew more absent. The weather stayed warm and sunny. The cherry trees blossomed and shed their pink flowers like a snowfall on the paths in Central Park. The trees turned lush and green. Babies keep odd hours, and often as I watched the sunrise colors well up from the East Side while I fed my daughter, I thought of my father who might be lying awake in his bed in Ossining. In the evening when the baby slept, I called him. By that time, he rarely answered the telephone.

"He won't eat anything," my mother said. Her voice sounded ragged. "Here, Susie, you tell him he has to eat something."

"Hello," my father said in the normal voice that he still managed for telephone hellos and one-word answers.

"Hi, Daddy," I said. "I think you should eat something."

"Yes." His voice had subsided to a grating whisper, and the words were slow and drawn out. Sickness seemed to heighten his sense of social propriety. As his thinking became more chaotic, his manners became more impeccable.

"Shall I call you after dinner?" he said.

"Yes, Daddy." The receiver banged against the telephone as he dropped it.

I remember my father at the head of our family dinner table. First, when there were only three of us, he sat at the end of the plain pine table in the hallway that was the dining room of our apartment on Fifty-ninth Street in New York City.

Later, after we had moved out to Scarborough, he sat at the black modern table next to the window that looked out over the lawns toward Beechwood and the green metal garbage pails behind the estate's big garage. My brother Ben and I sat on opposite sides of the table. At breakfast, before we went to school, Ben would hold a napkin up to his face, slipping food under the bottom edge so that he wouldn't have to look at me. At dinner, nothing like that was allowed. I set the table and my mother cooked and brought the food out in serving dishes and we all sat down and my father said grace.

"Dear Lord, we thank Thee for Thy bounty," he would say while Ben looked longingly at the protection of his napkin. If we children were fighting, as we often were, my father would add a pointed, "And bless this table with peace." And if the dogs were grumbling for scraps under the table, he would also add, "both top and bottom." Then he would say "Amen." My father always said grace. Sometimes he stayed with the short and traditional, sometimes he improvised. Later on, for special occasions, he would base the grace on his favorite quotation, a paraphrase of a line from Jowett's translation of Plato: "Let us consider that the soul of man is immortal, able to endure every sort of good and every sort of evil." Then he would add a paraphrase of the words of the prophet Micah: "So let us live humbly and give thanks unto Our Lord God. Amen."

In the house at Ossining there was a long cherry dining room table with Italian wood and wicker chairs. I always sat on my father's left, with my back to the wall, facing the fireplace with the wing chair in front of it and the long bench next to it that was piled precariously high with galleys of new books and newspapers and magazines: that day's *New York Times*, the local *Ossining Citizen Register*, *The New Yorker*, *The New York Review of Books*, *Newsweek* (when I was working there), *Antaeus*, and sometimes *The Smithsonian* or the *Brown Alumni Monthly*—or anything else that had come in the mail recently enough to have avoided being thrown out. Sometimes at the table my head bumped against the frame of the Piranesi etching that hung on the wall behind me.

I went away to school in 1960, the year my parents bought the house, and Ben went off soon afterward. We three children were rarely there at the same time. When we were, my two brothers sat across from me on the same side of the table. The dogs warmed our feet, sometimes raising themselves for a halfhearted sally after one of the cats. At Christmas vacation, the porch outside would be piled high with snow. In the summer, delicious smells from my mother's flower garden wafted through the open top half of the Dutch door at the end of the room.

The family meal was always served onto our plates by my father from serving platters, and when everyone had said grace and we had all concluded "Amen," my mother would say, "Oh, John, you haven't left yourself anything but the carcass" (if it was a chicken), or "the head" (if it was a fish), or "the tail" (if it was a steak), or "the gristle" (if it was a roast). She was often right. My mother always felt that there wouldn't be enough for her family to eat. Food was so rich and so abundant in our house that even the pets were all overweight. My father, on the other hand, was convinced that somehow he would go hungry—that he would be left out, overlooked, not provided for. He usually managed to make *his* fears seem legitimate, even if it meant heaping our plates to the edges so that there wouldn't be quite enough left for him. "Oh don't worry about me, dear," he would answer my mother. "This is plenty for me." We used to call him Eeyore.

The food, however, was not the main event at our dinner table. Conversation was the main event. Sometimes there was a general discussion of one person's problem: What would I do if Roddy Butler asked me to the dance at the country club? Should Ben major in English at school? Could Fred bring his friend Brad to New Hampshire? Advice, comments, and suggestions came from all quarters. Sometimes it was funny, sometimes it was friendly, sometimes it was harsh or sarcastic. Someone would certainly point out that Roddy had no intention of asking me anywhere, that Ben would be lucky to *pass* English, and that Fred might have trouble keeping his friends if he didn't learn to keep his elbows off the table. There was a lot of joking and very little serious counsel. We learned to make real decisions privately, on our own. My parents' problems were rarely discussed, because that usually ended in tears from my mother or recriminations and sarcasm from my father—and nobody got dessert.

Sometimes my mother or father would come up with an image, or a fragment of a story, and we would all weave imaginary plots around it. Sometimes we talked about books or movies or the poetry we recited to each other on Sunday afternoons. Often we talked and speculated about other people, our neighbors and friends. No one ever hesitated to be mean—although the insults were usually also pretty funny. We were so mean to each other, in fact, that guests were often astonished and shocked. They didn't catch the undertone of humor in our quick sarcasms, and there were times when we didn't catch it either. Explosions and tears and sudden departures were not at all uncommon. My brothers called our dinner table "the bear garden."

"My daughter says that our dinner table is like a shark tank," my father wrote in his journal one day in 1970, between a drunken lunch in honor of his friend Yevtushenko and an evening spent brooding over a bad review of *Bullet Park*. "I go into a spin. I am not a shark, I am a dolphin. Mary is the shark, etc. . . . But what we stumble on is the banality of family situations. Thinking of Susan, she makes the error of daring not to have been invented by me, of laughing at the wrong time and speaking lines I have not written. Does this prove that I am incapable of love or can only love myself? Scotch for breakfast and I do not like these mornings."

By Thanksgiving of 1981, my father was already too sick to eat much. Of course we didn't know how sick. He had had a kidney removed in June, and all summer he had seemed to get better, but in the autumn, as the air cooled and the leaves changed color, he seemed to be weaker again. When Richard Avedon took a picture of him for the cover of *The Dial*, the photograph looked stark and strange. He couldn't ride his bicycle anymore, and so the doctor sent him to a chiropractor. He went twice a week and installed a primitive traction device on Ben's bed upstairs, where he was working then. He wasn't working much, though. *Paradise* had been finished in the spring, and he spent most of his time answering mail and keeping the journal.

My father never quite trusted medicine. On the one hand, he always thought he was fine; at the same time, he always knew he was dying. His perception of physical reality was tenuous at best. Maybe his mother's Christian Science had something to do with it, too. His solution was to stick to small-town doctors and small-town hospitals, where at least he was known and felt comfortable and where it seemed they often told him what he wanted to hear. As a result, when he needed sophisticated diagnosis and expert medical care, he seemed to prefer jolly talk and home remedies. As the pains in his ribs and legs got worse, he was often depressed.

It was the beginning of December by the time he went back into the hospital for some X-rays. The shadows on those heavy plastic sheets showed that cancer had spread from his kidney up to his lungs and down into his legs; and that was why he felt, as he put it, "so lousy." After they saw the X-rays, the doctors told him there was nothing they could do. There was no treatment. The cancer was too far along.

My husband and I were in La Jolla, California, visiting my husband's daughter that week. "It's very bad," my mother said when I called home to see how the X-rays had come out. "It's very bad." Her voice sounded strange. I was sitting on a bed in a hotel room in Southern California. There was a bureau with a few books on it, and my maternity clothes were thrown over a chair. The main street of La Jolla was outside heavily curtained windows.

"They say I'm a dying man," my father said. His voice was still strong, but the laugh in it seemed to fade as I listened. "They say that my bones look moth-eaten." There was an edge of irony to his voice, as if he were talking about someone else. The hotel room had been decorated in Spanish mission style, and the walls and the bedspread were orange. It was the end of the day. Downstairs, people were waiting to meet us for drinks in the Patio Bar. My father told me that my brother Fred would be flying home for the holidays. "Some people will do almost anything to get their children home for Christmas," he said. I leaned back against the headboard, and the ridges of molded wood dug into my spine. A painting of a cowboy hung on the wall. In the distance, I could hear the sound of the sea.

Suggestions for Discussion

1. How does the quotation from her father's journal set the tone for the chapter?

2. What is gained by the juxtaposition of the author's feelings about the birth of her daughter and the declining days of her father? What details sharpen the contrast between the beginning and end of life?

3. In what different contexts are food and the dinner table the subject of discussion? What do these descriptions tell the reader about the writer's father? About the family relationship?

4. What contradictions does the writer see in her father, especially in regard to his attitude toward appearances?

5. Compare the expectations of Fitzgerald and Cheever for their daughters. How does Cheever's response to his daughter's dating reflect his own conflicts?

6. What was the nature of the father–daughter relationship when the latter became a writer?

7. What does the author's description of the setting in the last paragraph contribute to the tone? How does she make the reader know how deeply she cared for her father?

Suggestions for Writing

1. Discuss the banality of family situations.

2. Write a description of someone whose appearance makes a statement about how he or she meets the world. Or write a description of someone whose appearance is very deceptive.

3. Discuss the role that parental expectations play in fostering or inhibiting their children's growth and development.

Garrett Hongo

Kubota

Garrett Hongo (b. 1951) was born in Hawaii, and received his education at Pomona College, and the University of California at Irvine, where he was awarded the M.F.A. He was the founder and artistic director of the Asian Exclusion Act, a theater group, and executive director of the Asian Multi Media Center. A writer, he has been awarded both the Watson and National Endowment for the Arts fellowships, and has won the Hopwood and Lamont Poetry Prizes. In 1989 he was nominated for the Pulitzer Prize in Poetry. His books include Yellow Light (1982), The River of Heaven (1988), and The Open Boat (1993). In the reminiscence that follows he opens up for us the heritage of his grandfather's suffering, and its impact on him, a young nisei boy growing up in post-war America.

On December 8, 1941, the day after the Japanese attack on Pearl Harbor in Hawaii, my grandfather barricaded himself with his family—my grandmother, my teenage mother, her two sisters and two brothers—inside of his home in La'ie, a sugar plantation village on Oahu's North Shore. This was my maternal grandfather, a man most villagers called by his last name, Kubota. It could mean either "Wayside Field" or else "Broken Dreams," depending on which ideograms he used. Kubota ran La'ie's general store, and the previous night, after a long day of bad news on the radio, some locals had come by, pounded on the front door, and made threats. One was said to have brandished a machete. They were angry and shocked, as the whole nation was in the aftermath of the surprise attack. Kubota was one of the few Japanese-Americans in the village and president of the local Japanese language school.

He had become a target for their rage and suspicion. A wise man, he locked all his doors and windows and did not open his store the next day, but stayed closed and waited for news from some official.

He was a *kibei*, a Japanese-American born in Hawaii (a U.S. territory then, so he was thus a citizen) but who was subsequently sent back by his father for formal education in Hiroshima, Japan, their home province. *Kibei* is written with two ideograms in Japanese: one is the word for "return" and the other is the word for "rice." Poetically, it means one who returns from America, known as the Land of Rice in Japanese (by contrast, Chinese immigrants called their new home Mountain of Gold).

Kubota was graduated from a Japanese high school and then came back to Hawaii as a teenager. He spoke English—and a Hawaiian creole version of it at that—with a Japanese accent. But he was well liked and good at numbers, scrupulous and hard working like so many immigrants and children of immigrants. Castle & Cook, a grower's company that ran the sugarcane business along the North Shore, hired him on first as a stock boy and then appointed him to run one of its company stores. He did well, had the trust of management and labor—not an easy accomplishment in any day—married, had children, and had begun to exert himself in community affairs and excel in his own recreations. He put together a Japanese community organization that backed a Japanese language school for children and sponsored teachers from Japan. Kubota boarded many of them, in succession, in his own home. This made dinners a silent affair for his talkative, Hawaiian-bred children, as their stern *sensei*, or teacher, was nearly always at the table and their own abilities in the Japanese language were as delinquent as their attendance. While Kubota and the *sensei* rattled on about things Japanese, speaking Japanese, his children hurried through their suppers and tried to run off early to listen to the radio shows.

After dinner, while the *sensei* graded exams seated in a wicker chair in the spare room and his wife and children gathered around the radio in the front parlor, Kubota sat on the screened porch outside, reading the local Japanese newspapers. He finished reading about the same time as he finished the tea he drank for his digestion—a habit he'd learned in Japan—and then he'd get out his fishing gear and spread it out on the plank floors. The wraps on his rods needed to be redone, gears in his reels needed oil, and, once through with those tasks, he'd painstakingly wind on hundreds of yards of new line. Fishing was his hobby and his passion. He spent weekends camping along the North Shore beaches with his children, setting up umbrella tents, packing a rice pot and hibachi along for meals. And he caught fish. *Ulu'a* mostly, the huge surf-feeding fish known on the mainland as the jack crevalle, but he'd go after almost anything in its season. In Kawela, a plantation-owned bay nearby, he fished for mullet Hawaiian-style with a throw net, stalking the bottom-hugging, gray-backed schools as they gathered at the stream mouths and in the freshwater springs. In an outrigger out beyond the reef, he'd try for *aku*—the skipjack tuna prized for steaks and, sliced raw and mixed with fresh seaweed and cut onions, for *sashimi* salad. In Kahaluu and Ka'awa and on an offshore rock locals called Goat Island, he loved to go torching, stringing lanterns on bamboo poles stuck in the sand to attract *kumu'u*, the red goatfish, as they schooled at night just inside the reef. But in La'ie on Laniloa Point near Kahuku, the northernmost tip of Oahu, he cast twelve- and fourteen-foot surf rods for the huge, varicolored, and fast-running *ulu'a* as they ran for schools of squid and baitfish just beyond the biggest breakers and past the low sand flats wadeable from the shore to nearly a half mile out. At sunset, against the western light, he looked as if he walked on water as he came back, fish and rods slung over his shoulders, stepping along the rock and coral path just inches under the surface of a running tide.

When it was torching season, in December or January, he'd drive out the afternoon before and stay with old friends, the Tanakas or Yoshikawas, shopkeepers like him who ran stores near the fishing grounds. They'd have been preparing for weeks, selecting and cutting their bamboo poles, cleaning the hurricane lanterns, tearing up burlap sacks for the cloths they'd soak with kerosene and tie onto sticks they'd poke into the soft sand of the shallows. Once lit, touched off with a Zippo lighter, these would be the torches they'd use as beacons to attract the schooling fish. In another time, they might have made up a dozen paper lanterns of the kind mostly used for decorating the summer folk dances outdoors on the grounds of the Buddhist church during O-Bon, the Festival for the Dead. But now, wealthy and modern and efficient killers of fish, Tanaka and Kubota used rag torches and Colemans and cast rods with tips made of Tonkin bamboo and butts of American-spun fiberglass. After just one good night, they might bring back a prize bounty of a dozen burlap bags filled with scores of bloody, rigid fish delicious to eat and even better to give away as gifts to friends, family, and special customers.

It was a Monday night, the day after Pearl Harbor, and there was a rattling knock on the front door. Two FBI agents presented themselves, showed identification, and took my grandfather in for questioning in Honolulu. He didn't return home for days. No one knew what had happened or what was wrong. But there was a roundup going on of all those in the Japanese-American community suspected of sympathizing with the enemy and worse. My grandfather was suspected of espionage, of communicating with offshore Japanese submarines launched from the attack fleet days before war began. Torpedo planes and escort fighters, decorated with the insignia of the Rising Sun, had taken an approach route from northwest of Oahu directly across Kahuku Point and on toward Pearl. They had strafed an auxiliary air station near the fishing grounds my grandfather loved and destroyed a small gun battery there, killing three men. Kubota was known to have sponsored and harbored Japanese nationals in his own home. He had a radio. He had wholesale access to firearms. Circumstances and an undertone of racial resentment had combined with wartime hysteria in the aftermath of the tragic naval battle to cast suspicion on the loyalties of my grandfather and all other Japanese-Americans. The FBI reached out and pulled hundreds of them in for questioning in dragnets cast throughout the West Coast and Hawaii.

My grandfather was lucky; he'd somehow been let go after only a few days. Others were not as fortunate. Hundreds, from small communities in Washington, California, Oregon, and Hawaii, were rounded up and, after what appeared to be routine questioning, shipped off under Justice Department orders to holding centers in Leuppe on the Navaho reservation in Arizona, in Fort Missoula in Montana, and on Sand Island in Honolulu Harbor. There were other special camps on Maui in Ha'iku and on Hawaii—the Big Island—in my own home village of Volcano.

Many of these men—it was exclusively the Japanese-American men suspected of ties to Japan who were initially rounded up—did not see their families again for more than four years. Under a suspension of due process that was only after the fact ruled as warranted by military necessity, they were, if only temporarily, "disappeared" in Justice Department prison camps scattered in particularly desolate areas of the United States designated as militarily "safe." These were grim forerunners of the assembly centers and concentration camps for the 120,000 Japanese-American evacuees that were to come later.

I am Kubota's eldest grandchild, and I remember him as a lonely, habitually silent old man who lived with us in our home near Los Angeles for most of my childhood and adolescence. It was the fifties, and my parents had emigrated from Hawaii to the mainland in the hope of a better life away from the old sugar plantation. After some success, they had sent back for my grandparents and taken them in. And it was my grandparents who did the work of the household while my mother and father worked their salaried city jobs. My grandmother cooked and sewed, washed our clothes, and knitted in the front room under the light of a huge lamp with a bright three-way bulb. Kubota raised a flower garden, read up on soils and grasses in gardening books, and planted a zoysia lawn in front and a dichondra one in back. He planted a small patch near the rear block wall with green onions, eggplant, white Japanese radishes, and cucumber. While he hoed and spaded the loamless, clayey earth of Los Angeles, he sang particularly plangent songs in Japanese about plum blossoms and bamboo groves.

Once, in the mid-sixties, after a dinner during which, as always, he had been silent while he worked away at a meal of fish and rice spiced with dabs of Chinese mustard and catsup thinned with soy sauce, Kubota took his own dishes to the kitchen sink and washed them up. He took a clean jelly jar out of the cupboard—the glass was thick and its shape squatty like an old-fashioned. He reached around to the hutch below where he kept his bourbon. He made himself a drink and retired to the living room where I was expected to join him for "talk story," the Hawaiian idiom for chewing the fat.

I was a teenager and, though I was bored listening to stories I'd heard often enough before at holiday dinners, I was dutiful. I took my spot on the couch next to Kubota and heard him out. Usually, he'd tell me about his schooling in Japan where he learned judo along with mathematics and literature. He'd learned the *soroban* there—the abacus, which was the original pocket calculator of the Far East—and that, along with his strong, judo-trained back, got him his first job in Hawaii. This was the moral. "Study *ha-ahd,*" he'd say with pidgin emphasis. "Learn read good. Learn speak da kine *good* English." The message is the familiar one taught to any children of immigrants: succeed through education. And imitation. But this time, Kubota reached down into his past and told me a different story. I was thirteen by then, and I suppose he thought me ready for it. He told me about Pearl Harbor, how the planes flew in wing after wing of formations over his old house in La'ie in Hawaii, and how, the next day, after Roosevelt had made his famous "Day of Infamy" speech about the treachery of the Japanese, the FBI agents had come to his door and taken him in, hauled him off to Honolulu for questioning, and held him without charge for several days. I thought he was lying. I thought he was making up a kind of horror story to shock me and give his moral that much more starch. But it was true. I asked around. I brought it up during history class in junior high school, and my teacher, after silencing me and stepping me off to the back of the room, told me that it was indeed so. I asked my mother and she said it was true. I asked my schoolmates, who laughed and ridiculed me for being so ignorant. We lived in a Japanese-American community, and the parents of most of my classmates were the *nisei* who had been interned as teenagers all through the war. But there was a strange silence around all of this. There was a hush, as if one were invoking the ill powers of the dead when one brought it up. No one cared to speak about the evacuation and relocation for very long. It wasn't in our history books, though we were studying World War II at the time. It wasn't in the family albums of the people I knew and whom I'd visit staying over weekends with friends. And it wasn't anything that the family talked about or allowed me to keep bringing up either. I was given the facts, told sternly and pointedly that "it was war" and that "nothing could be done." "*Shikatta ga nai*" is the phrase in Japanese, a kind of resolute and determinist pronouncement on how to deal with inexplicable tragedy. I was to know it but not to dwell on it. Japanese-Americans were busy trying to forget it ever happened and were having a hard enough time building their new lives after "camp." It was as if we had no history for four years and the relocation was something unspeakable.

But Kubota would not let it go. In session after session, for months it seemed, he pounded away at his story. He wanted to tell me the names of the FBI agents. He went over their questions and his responses again and again. He'd tell me how one would try to act friendly toward him, offering him cigarettes while the other, who hounded him with accusations and threats, left the interrogation room. Good cop, bad cop, I thought to myself, already superficially streetwise from stories black classmates told of the Watts riots and from my having watched too many episodes of *Dragnet* and *The Mod Squad*. But Kubota was not interested in my experiences. I was not made yet, and he was determined that his stories be part of my making. He spoke quietly at first, mildly, but once into his narrative and after his drink was down, his voice would rise and quaver with resentment and he'd make his accusations. He gave his testimony to me and I held it at first cautiously in my conscience like it was an heirloom too delicate to expose to strangers and anyone outside of the world Kubota made with his words. "I give you story now," he once said, "and you learn speak good, eh?" It was my job, as the disciple of his preaching I had then become, Ananda to his Buddha, to reassure him with a promise. "You learn speak good like the Dillingham," he'd say another time, referring to the wealthy scion of the grower family who had once run, unsuccessfully, for one of Hawaii's first senatorial seats. Or he'd then invoke a magical name, the name of one of his heroes, a man he thought particularly exemplary and righteous. "Learn speak dah good Ingrish like *Mistah Inouye*," Kubota shouted. "He *lick* dah Dillingham even in debate. I saw on *terre-bision* myself." He was remembering the debates before the first senatorial election just before Hawaii was admitted to the Union as its fiftieth state. "You *tell* story," Kubota would end. And I had my injunction.

The town we settled in after the move from Hawaii is called Gardena, the independently incorporated city south of Los Angeles and north of San Pedro harbor. At its northern limit, it borders on Watts and Compton, black towns. To the southwest are Torrance and Redondo Beach, white towns. To the rest of L.A., Gardena is primarily famous for having legalized five-card draw poker after the war. On Vermont Boulevard, its eastern border, there is a dingy little Vegas-like strip of card clubs with huge parking lots and flickering neon signs that spell out "The Rainbow" and "The Horseshoe" in timed sequences of varicolored lights. The town is only secondarily famous as the largest community of Japanese-Americans in the United States outside of Honolulu, Hawaii. When I was in high school there, it seemed to me that every *sansei* kid I knew wanted to be a doctor, an engineer, or a pharmacist. Our fathers were gardeners or electricians or nurserymen or ran small businesses catering to other Japanese-Americans. Our mothers worked in civil service for the city or as cashiers for Thrifty Drug. What the kids wanted was a good job, good pay, a fine home, and no troubles. No one wanted to mess with the law—from either side—and no one wanted to mess with language or art. They all talked about getting into the right clubs so that they could go to the right schools. There was a certain kind of sameness, an intensely enforced system of conformity. Style was all. Boys wore moccasin-sewn shoes from Flagg Brothers, black A-1 slacks, and Kensington shirts with high collars. Girls wore their hair up in stiff bouffants solidified in hairspray and knew all the latest dances from the slauson to the funky chicken. We did well in chemistry and in math, no one who was Japanese but me spoke in English class or in history unless called upon, and no one talked about World War II. The day after Robert Kennedy was assassinated, after winning the California Democratic primary, we worked on calculus and elected class coordinators for the prom, featuring the 5th Dimension. We avoided grief. We avoided government. We avoided strong feelings and dangers of any kind. Once punished, we tried to maintain a concerted emotional and social discipline and would not willingly seek to fall out of the narrow margin of protective favor again.

But when I was thirteen, in junior high, I'd not understood why it was so difficult for my classmates, those who were themselves Japanese-American, to talk about the relocation. They had cringed, too, when I tried to bring it up during our discussions of World War II. I was Hawaiian-born. They were mainland-born. Their parents had been in camp, had been the ones to suffer the complicated experience of having to distance themselves from their own history and all things Japanese in order to make their way back and into the American social and economic mainstream. It was out of this sense of shame and a fear of stigma I was only beginning to understand that the *nisei* had silenced themselves. And, for their children, among whom I grew up, they wanted no heritage, no culture, no contact with a defiled history. I recall the silence very well. The Japanese-American children around me were burdened in a way I was not. Their injunction was silence. Mine was to speak.

Away at college, in another protected world in its own way as magical to me as the Hawaii of my childhood, I dreamed about my grandfather. Tired from studying languages, practicing German conjugations or scripting an army's worth of Chinese ideograms on a single sheet of paper, Kubota would come to me as I drifted off into sleep. Or I would walk across the newly mown ball field in back of my dormitory, cutting through a street-side phalanx of ancient eucalyptus trees on my way to visit friends off campus, and I would think of him, his anger, and his sadness.

I don't know myself what makes someone feel that kind of need to have a story they've lived through be deposited somewhere, but I can guess. I think about *The Iliad, The Odyssey, The Peloponnesian Wars* of Thucydides, and a myriad of the works of literature I've studied. A character, almost a *topoi* he occurs so often, is frequently the witness who gives personal testimony about an event the rest of his community cannot even imagine. The sibyl is such a character. And Procne, the maid whose tongue is cut out so that she will not tell that she has been raped by her own brother-in-law, the king of Thebes. There are the dime novels, the epic blockbusters Hollywood makes into miniseries, and then there are the plain, relentless stories of witnesses who have suffered through horrors major and minor that have marked and changed their lives. I myself haven't talked to Holocaust victims. But I've read their survival stories and their stories of witness and been revolted and moved by them. My father-in-law, Al Thiessen, tells me his war stories again and again and I listen. A Mennonite who set aside the strictures of his own church in order to serve, he was a Marine codeman in the Pacific during World War II, in the Signal Corps on Guadalcanal, Morotai, and Bougainville. He was part of the island-hopping maneuver MacArthur had devised to win the war in the Pacific. He saw friends die from bombs which exploded not ten yards away. When he was with the 298th Signal Corps attached to the Thirteenth Air Force, he saw plane after plane come in and crash, just short of the runway, killing their crews, setting the jungle ablaze with oil and gas fires. Emergency wagons would scramble, bouncing over newly bulldozed land men used just the afternoon before for a football game. Every time we go fishing together, whether it's in a McKenzie boat drifting for salmon in Tillamook Bay or taking a lunch break from wading the rifles of a stream in the Cascades, he tells me about what happened to him and the young men in his unit. One was a Jewish boy from Brooklyn. One was a foul-mouthed kid from Kansas. They died. And he *has* to tell me. And I *have* to listen. It's a ritual payment the young owe their elders who have survived. The evacuation and relocation is something like that.

Kubota, my grandfather, had been ill with Alzheimer's disease for some time before he died. At the house he'd built on Kamehameha Highway in Hau'ula, a seacoast village just down the road from La'ie where he had his store, he'd wander out from the garage or greenhouse where he'd set up a workbench, and trudge down to the beach or up toward the line of pines he'd planted while employed by the Work Projects Administration during the thirties. Kubota thought he was going fishing. Or he thought he was back at work for Roosevelt, planting pines as a windbreak or soilbreak on the windward flank of the Ko'olau Mountains, emerald monoliths rising out of sea and cane fields from Waialua to Kaneohe. When I visited, my grandmother would send me down to the beach to fetch him. Or I'd run down Kam Highway a quarter mile or so and find him hiding in the cane field by the roadside, counting stalks, measuring circumferences in the claw of his thumb and forefinger. The look on his face was confused or concentrated, I didn't know which. But I guessed he was going fishing again. I'd grab him and walk him back to his house on the highway. My grandmother would shut him in a room.

Within a few years, Kubota had a stroke and survived it, then he had another one and was completely debilitated. The family decided to put him in a nursing home in Kahuku, just set back from the highway, within a mile or so of Kahuku Point and the Tanaka Store where he had his first job as a stock boy. He lived there three years, and I visited him once with my aunt. He was like a potato that had been worn down by cooking. Everything on him—his eyes, his teeth, his legs and torso—seemed like it had been sloughed away. What he had been was mostly gone now and I was looking at the nub of a man. In a wheelchair, he grasped my hands and tugged on them—violently. His hands were still thick and, I believed, strong enough to lift me out of my own seat into his lap. He murmured something in Japanese—he'd long ago ceased to speak any English. My aunt and I cried a little, and we left him.

I remember walking out on the black asphalt of the parking lot of the nursing home. It was heat-cracked and eroded already, and grass had veined itself into the interstices. There were coconut trees around, a cane field I could see across the street, and the ocean I knew was pitching a surf just beyond it. The green Ko'olaus came up behind us. Somewhere nearby, alongside the beach, there was an abandoned airfield in the middle of the canes. As a child, I'd come upon it playing one day, and my friends and I kept returning to it, day after day, playing war or sprinting games or coming to fly kites. I recognize it even now when I see it on TV—it's used as a site for action scenes in the detective shows Hollywood always sets in the islands: a helicopter chasing the hero racing away in a Ferrari, or gun dealers making a clandestine rendezvous on the abandoned runway. It was the old airfield strafed by Japanese planes the day the major flight attacked Pearl Harbor. It was the airfield the FBI thought my grandfather had targeted in his night fishing and signaling with the long surf poles he'd stuck in the sandy bays near Kahuku Point.

Kubota died a short while after I visited him, but not, I thought, without giving me a final message. I was on the mainland, in California studying for Ph.D. exams, when my grandmother called me with the news. It was a relief. He'd suffered from his debilitation a long time and I was grateful he'd gone. I went home for the funeral and gave the eulogy. My grandmother and I took his ashes home in a small, heavy metal box wrapped in a black *furoshiki*, a large silk scarf. She showed me the name the priest had given to him on his death, scripted with a calligraphy brush on a long, narrow talent of plain wood. Buddhist commoners, at death, are given priestly names, received symbolically into the clergy. The idea is that, in their next life, one of scholarship and leisure, they might meditate and attain the enlightenment the religion is aimed at. *"Shaku Shūchi,"* the ideograms read. It was Kubota's Buddhist name, incorporating characters from his family and given names. It meant "Shining Wisdom of the Law." He died on Pearl Harbor Day, December 7, 1983.

After years, after I'd finally come back to live in Hawaii again, only once did I dream of Kubota, my grandfather. It was the same night I'd heard HR 442, the redress bill for Japanese-Americans, had been signed into law. In my dream that night Kubota was "torching," and he sang a Japanese song, a querulous and wavery folk ballad, as he hung paper lanterns on bamboo poles stuck into the sand in the shallow water of the lagoon behind the reef near Kahuku Point. Then he was at a work table, smoking a hand-rolled cigarette, letting it dangle from his lips Bogart-style as he drew, daintily and skillfully, with a narrow trim brush, ideogram after ideogram on a score of paper lanterns he had hung in a dark shed to dry. He had painted a talismanic mantra onto each lantern, the ideogram for the word "red" in Japanese, a bit of art blended with some superstition, a piece of sympathetic magic appealing to the magenta coloring on the rough skins of the schooling, night-feeding fish he wanted to attract to his baited hooks. He strung them from pole to pole in the dream then, hiking up his khaki worker's pants so his white ankles showed and wading through the shimmering black waters of the sand flats and then the reef. "The moon is leaving, leaving," he sang in Japanese. "Take me deeper in the savage sea." He turned and crouched like an ice racer then, leaning forward so that his unshaven face almost touched the light film of water. I could see the light stubble of beard like a fine, gray ash covering the lower half of his face. I could see his gold-rimmed spectacles. He held a small wooden boat in his cupped hands and placed it lightly on the sea and pushed it away. One of his lanterns was on it and, written in small neat rows like a sutra scroll, it had been decorated with the silvery names of all our dead.

Suggestions for Discussion

1. What do the two renderings of Kubota's name in English, "Wayside Field" and "Broken Dreams," suggest as alternate possibilities for interpretations of his life? What of his death name, "Shining Wisdom of the Law"?

2. Why does no one among Hongo's family and friends want to talk about the evacuation and relocation of the *nisei* (Japanese-Americans) during the Second World War? Why will Kubota not stop talking about it?

3. How are the stories we are told part of our "making"?

Suggestions for Writing

1. Hongo says of his generation, "We avoided grief. . . . We avoided strong feelings and dangers of any kind." Does this describe you? Your friends? Explain.

2. ". . . he *has* to tell me. And I *have* to listen. It's a ritual payment the young owe their elders who have survived." Relate this comment to your own experience with someone from a previous generation.

Essays

Bruno Bettelheim

Joey: A "Mechanical Boy"

Bruno Bettelheim (1903–1990) was born in Vienna and educated at the University of Vienna. Having survived the Nazi holocaust, he became an American psychoanalyst and educator and was director of the remarkable University of Chicago Sonia Shankman Orthogenic School from 1944 to 1973. He has written many penetrating works on parents and children and the significance of the holocaust. Bettelheim clarifies the concept of emotional development in a machine age by drawing upon the experiences of a single individual, Joey. The illustration is developed by taking an extreme and atypical example of a boy who "froze himself" in the image of the machine.

Joey, when we began our work with him, was a mechanical boy. He functioned as if by remote control, run by machines of his own powerfully creative fantasy. Not only did he himself believe that he was a machine but, more remarkably, he created this impression in others. Even while he performed actions that are intrinsically human, they never appeared to be other than machine-started and executed. On the other hand, when the machine was not working he had to concentrate on recollecting his presence, for he seemed not to exist. A human body that functions as if it were a machine and a machine that duplicates human functions are equally fascinating and frightening. Perhaps they are so uncanny because they remind us that the human body can operate without a human spirit, that body can exist without soul. And Joey was a child who had been robbed of his humanity.

Not every child who possesses a fantasy world is possessed by it. Normal children may retreat into realms of imaginary glory or magic powers, but they are easily recalled from these excursions. Disturbed children are not always able to make the return trip; they remain withdrawn, prisoners of the inner world of delusion and fantasy. In many ways Joey presented a classic example of this state of infantile autism. In any age, when the individual has escaped into a delusional world, he has usually fashioned it from bits and pieces of the world at hand. Joey, in his time and world, chose the machine and froze himself in its image. His story has a general relevance to the understanding of emotional development in a machine age.

Joey's delusion is not uncommon among schizophrenic children today. He wanted to be rid of his unbearable humanity, to become completely automatic. He so nearly succeeded in attaining this goal that he could almost convince others, as well as himself, of his mechanical character. The descriptions of autistic children in the literature take for their point of departure and comparison the normal or abnormal human being. To do justice to Joey I would have to compare him simultaneously to a most inept infant and a highly complex piece of machinery. Often we had to force ourselves by a conscious act of will to realize that Joey was a child. Again and again his acting-out of his delusions froze our own ability to respond as human beings.

During Joey's first weeks with us we would watch absorbedly as this at once fragile-looking and imperious nine-year-old went about his mechanical existence. Entering the dining room, for example, he would string an imaginary wire from his "energy source"—an imaginary electric outlet—to the table. There he "insulted" himself with paper napkins and finally plugged himself in. Only then could Joey eat, for he firmly believed that the "current" ran his ingestive apparatus. So skillful was the pantomime that one had to look twice to be sure there was neither wire nor outlet nor plug. Children and members of our staff spontaneously avoided stepping on the "wires" for fear of interrupting what seemed the source of his very life.

For long periods of time, when his "machinery" was idle, he would sit so quietly that he would disappear from the focus of the most conscientious observation. Yet in the next moment he might be "working" and the center of our captivated attention. Many times a day he would turn himself on and shift noisily through a sequence of higher and higher gears until he "exploded," screaming "crash, crash!" and hurling items from his ever present apparatus—radio tubes, light bulbs, even motors or, lacking these, any handy breakable object. (Joey had an astonishing knack for snatching bulbs and tubes unobserved.) As soon as the object thrown had shattered, he would cease his screaming and wild jumping and retire to mute, motionless nonexistence.

Our maids, inured to difficult children, were exceptionally attentive to Joey; they were apparently moved by his extreme infantile fragility, so strangely coupled with megalomaniacal superiority. Occasionally some of the apparatus he fixed to his bed to "live him" during his sleep would fall down in disarray. This machinery he contrived from masking tape, cardboard, wire and other paraphernalia. Usually the maids would pick up such things and leave them on a table for the children to find, or disregard them entirely. But Joey's machine they carefully restored: "Joey must have the carburetor so he can breathe." Similarly they were on the alert to pick up and preserve the motors that ran him during the day and the exhaust pipes through which he exhaled.

How had Joey become a human machine? From intensive interviews with his parents we learned that the process had begun even before birth. Schizophrenia often results from parental rejection, sometimes combined ambivalently with love. Joey, on the other hand, had been completely ignored.

"I never knew I was pregnant," his mother said, meaning that she had already excluded Joey from her consciousness. His birth, she said, "did not make any difference." Joey's father, a rootless draftee in the wartime civilian army, was equally unready for parenthood. So, of course, are many young couples. Fortunately most such parents lose their indifference upon the baby's birth. But not Joey's parents. "I did not want to see or nurse him," his mother declared. "I had no feeling of actual dislike—I simply didn't want to take care of him." For the first three months of his life Joey "cried most of the time." A colicky baby, he was kept on a rigid four-hour feeding schedule, was not touched unless necessary and was never cuddled or played with. The mother, preoccupied with herself, usually left Joey alone in the crib or playpen during the day. The father discharged his frustrations by punishing Joey when the child cried at night.

Soon the father left for overseas duty, and the mother took Joey, now a year and a half old, to live with her at her parents' home. On his arrival the grandparents noticed that ominous changes had occurred in the child. Strong and healthy at birth, he had become frail and irritable; a responsive baby, he had become remote and inaccessible. When he began to master speech, he talked only to himself. At an early date he became preoccupied with machinery, including an old electric fan which he could take apart and put together again with surprising deftness.

Joey's mother impressed us with a fey quality that expressed her insecurity, her detachment from the world and her low physical vitality. We were struck especially by her total indifference as she talked about Joey. This seemed much more remarkable than the actual mistakes she made in handling him. Certainly he was left to cry for hours when hungry, because she fed him on a rigid schedule; he was toilet-trained with great rigidity so that he would give no trouble. These things happen to many children. But Joey's existence never registered with his mother. In her recollections he was fused at one moment with one event or person; at another, with something or somebody else. When she told us about his birth and infancy, it was as if she were talking about some vague acquaintance, and soon her thoughts would wander off to another person or to herself.

When Joey was not yet four, his nursery school suggested that he enter a special school for disturbed children. At the new school his autism was immediately recognized. During his three years there he experienced a slow improvement. Unfortunately a subsequent two years in a parochial school destroyed this progress. He began to develop compulsive defenses, which he called his "preventions." He could not drink, for example, except through elaborate piping systems built of straws. Liquids had to be "pumped" into him, in his fantasy, or he could not suck. Eventually his behavior became so upsetting that he could not be kept in the parochial school. At home things did not improve. Three months before entering the Orthogenic School he made a serious attempt at suicide.

To us Joey's pathological behavior seemed the external expression of an overwhelming effort to remain almost nonexistent as a person. For weeks Joey's only reply when addressed was "Bam." Unless he thus neutralized whatever we said, there would be an explosion, for Joey plainly wished to close off every form of contact not mediated by machinery. Even when he was bathed he rocked back and forth with mute, engine-like regularity, flooding the bathroom. If he stopped rocking, he did this like a machine too; suddenly he went completely rigid. Only once, after months of being lifted from his bath and carried to bed, did a small expression of puzzled pleasure appear on his face as he said very softly: "They even carry you to bed here."

For a long time after he began to talk he would never refer to anyone by name, but only as "that person" or "the little person" or "the big person." He was unable to designate by its true name anything to which he attached feelings. Nor could he name his anxieties except through neologisms or word contaminations. For a long time he spoke about "master paintings" and "a master painting room" (*i.e.*, masturbating and masturbating room). One of his machines, the "criticizer," prevented him from "saying words which have un-pleasant feelings." Yet he gave personal names to the tubes and motors in his collection of machinery. Moreover, these dead things had feelings; the tubes bled when hurt and sometimes got sick. He consistently maintained this reversal between animate and inanimate objects.

In Joey's machine world everything, on pain of instant destruction, obeyed inhibitory laws much more stringent than those of physics. When we came to know him better, it was plain that in his momemts of silent withdrawal, with his machine switched off, Joey was absorbed in pondering the compulsive laws of his private universe. His preoccupation with machinery made it difficult to establish even practical contacts with him. If he wanted to do something with a counselor, such as play with a toy that had caught his vague attention, he could not do so: "I'd like this very much, but first I have to turn off the machine." But by the time he had fulfilled all the requirements of his preventions, he had lost interest. When a toy was offered to him, he could not touch it because his motors and his tubes did not leave him a hand free. Even certain colors were dangerous and had to be strictly avoided in toys and clothing, because "some colors turn off the current, and I can't touch them because I can't live without the current."

Joey was convinced that machines were better than people. Once when he bumped into one of the pipes on our jungle gym he kicked it so violently that his teacher had to restrain him to keep him from injuring himself. When she explained that the pipe was much harder than his foot, Joey replied: "That proves it. Machines are better than the body. They don't break; they're much harder and stronger." If he lost or forgot something, it merely proved that his brain ought to be thrown away and replaced by machinery. If he spilled something his arm should be broken and twisted off because it did not work properly. When his head or arm failed to work as it should, he tried to punish it by hitting it. Even Joey's feelings were mechanical. Much later in his therapy, when he had formed a timid attachment to another child and had been rebuffed, Joey cried: "He broke my feelings."

Gradually we began to understand what had seemed to be contradictory in Joey's behavior—why he held on to the motors and tubes, then suddenly destroyed them in a fury, then set out immediately and urgently to equip himself with new and larger tubes. Joey had created these machines to run his body and mind because it was too painful to be human. But again and again he became dissatisfied with their failure to meet his need and rebellious at the way they frustrated his will. In a recurrent frenzy he "exploded" his light bulbs and tubes, and for a moment became a human being—for one crowning instant he came alive. But as soon as he had asserted his dominance through the self-created explosion, he felt his life ebbing away. To keep on existing he had immediately to restore his machines and replenish the electricity that supplied his life energy.

What deep-seated fears and needs underlay Joey's delusional system? We were long in finding out, for Joey's preventions effectively concealed the secret of his autistic behavior. In the meantime we dealt with his peripheral problems one by one.

During his first year with us Joey's most trying problem was toilet behavior. This surprised us, for Joey's personality was not "anal" in the Freudian sense; his original personality damage had antedated the period of his toilet-training. Rigid and early toilet-training, however, had certainly contributed to his anxieties. It was our effort to help Joey with this problem that led to his first recognition of us as human beings.

Going to the toilet, like everything else in Joey's life, was surrounded by elaborate preventions. We had to accompany him; he had to take off all his clothes; he could only squat, not sit, on the toilet seat; he had to touch the wall with one hand, in which he also clutched frantically the vacuum tubes that powered his elimination. He was terrified lest his whole body be sucked down.

To counteract this fear we gave him a metal wastebasket in lieu of a toilet. Eventually, when eliminating into the wastebasket, he no longer needed to take off all his clothes, nor to hold on to the wall. He still needed the tubes and motors which, he believed, moved his bowels for him. But here again the all-important machinery was itself a source of new terrors. In Joey's world the gadgets had to move their bowels, too. He was terribly concerned that they should, but since they were so much more powerful than men, he was also terrified that if his tubes moved their bowels, their feces would fill all of space and leave him no room to live. He was thus always caught in some fearful contradiction.

Our readiness to accept his toilet habits, which obviously entailed some hardship for his counselors, gave Joey the confidence to express his obsessions in drawings. Drawing these fantasies was the first step toward letting us in, however distantly, to what concerned him most deeply. It was the first step in a year-long process of externalizing his anal preoccupations. As a result he began seeing feces everywhere; the whole world became to him a mire of excrement. At the same time he began to eliminate freely wherever he happened to be. But with this release from his infantile imprisonment in compulsive rules, the toilet and the whole process of elimination became less dangerous. Thus far it had been beyond Joey's comprehension that anybody could possibly move his bowels without mechanical aid. Now Joey took a further step forward; defecation became the first physiological process he could perform without the help of vacuum tubes. It must not be thought that he was proud of this ability. Taking pride in his achievement presupposes that one accomplished it of one's own free will. He still did not feel himself an autonomous person who could do things on his own. To Joey defecation still seemed enslaved to some incomprehensible but utterly binding cosmic law, perhaps the law his parents had imposed on him when he was being toilet-trained.

It was not simply that his parents had subjected him to rigid, early training. Many children are so trained. But in most cases the parents have a deep emotional investment in the child's performance. The child's response in turn makes training an occasion for interaction between them and for the building of genuine relationships. Joey's parents had no emotional investment in him. His obedience gave them no satisfaction and won him no affection or approval. As a toilet-trained child he saved his mother labor, just as household machines saved her labor. As a machine he was not loved for his performance, nor could he love himself.

So it had been with all other aspects of Joey's existence with his parents. Their reactions to his eating or noneating, sleeping or wakening, urinating or defecating, being dressed or undressed, washed or bathed did not flow from any unitary interest in him, deeply embedded in their personalities. By treating him mechanically his parents made him a machine. The various functions of life—even the parts of his body—bore no integrating relationship to one another or to any sense of self that was acknowledged and confirmed by others. Though he had acquired mastery over some functions, such as toilet-training and speech, he had acquired them separately and kept them isolated from each other. Toilet-training had thus not gained him a pleasant feeling of body mastery; speech had not led to communication of thought or feeling. On the contrary, each achievement only steered him away from self-mastery and integration. Toilet-training had enslaved him. Speech left him talking in neologisms that obstructed his and our ability to relate to each other. In Joey's development the normal process of growth had been made to run backward. Whatever he had learned put him not at the end of his infantile development toward integration but, on the contrary, farther behind than he was at its very beginning. Had we understood this sooner, his first years with us would have been less baffling.

It is unlikely that Joey's calamity could befall a child in any time and culture but our own. He suffered no physical deprivation; he starved for human contact. Just to be taken care of is not enough for relating. It is a necessary but not a sufficient condition. At the extreme where utter scarcity reigns, the forming of relationships is certainly hampered. But our society of mechanized plenty often makes for equal difficulties in a child's learning to relate. Where parents can provide the simple creature-comforts for their children only at the cost of significant effort, it is likely that they will feel pleasure in being able to provide for them; it is this, the parents' pleasure, that gives children a sense of personal worth and sets the process of relation in motion. But if comfort is so readily available that the parents feel no particular pleasure in winning it for their children, then the children cannot develop the feeling of being worthwhile around the satisfaction of their basic needs. Of course parents and children can and do develop relationships around other situations. But matters are then no longer so simple and direct. The child must be on the receiving end of care and concern given with pleasure and without the exaction of return if he is to feel loved and worthy of respect and consideration. This feeling gives him the ability to trust; he can entrust his well-being to persons to whom he is so important. Out of such trust the child learns to form close and stable relationships.

For Joey relationship with his parents was empty of pleasure in comfort-giving as in all other situations. His was an extreme instance of a plight that sends many schizophrenic children to our clinics and hospitals. Many months passed before he could relate to us; his despair that anybody could like him made contact impossible.

When Joey could finally trust us enough to let himself become more infantile, he began to play at being a papoose. There was a corresponding change in his fantasies. He drew endless pictures of himself as an electrical papoose. Totally enclosed, suspended in empty space, he is run by unknown, unseen powers through wireless electricity.

As we eventually came to understand, the heart of Joey's delusional system was the artificial, mechanical womb he had created and into which he had locked himself. In his papoose fantasies lay the wish to be entirely reborn in a womb. His new experiences in the school suggested that life, after all, might be worth living. Now he was searching for a way to be reborn in a better way. Since machines were better than men, what was more natural than to try rebirth through them? This was the deeper meaning of his electrical papoose.

As Joey made progress, his pictures of himself became more dominant in his drawings. Though still machine-operated, he has grown in self-importance. Another great step forward is represented in a picture in which he has acquired hands that do something, and he has had the courage to make a picture of the machine that runs him. Later still the papoose became a person, rather than a robot encased in glass.

Eventually Joey began to create an imaginary family at the school: the "Carr" family. Why the Carr family? In the car he was enclosed as he had been in his papoose, but at least the car was not stationary; it could move. More important, in a car one was not only driven but also could drive. The Carr family was Joey's way of exploring the possibility of leaving the school, of living with a good family in a safe, protecting car.

Joey at last broke through his prison. In this brief account it has not been possible to trace the painfully slow process of his first true relations with other human beings. Suffice it to say that he ceased to be a mechanical boy and became a human child. This newborn child was, however, nearly 12 years old. To recover the lost time is a tremendous task. That work has occupied Joey and us ever since. Sometimes he sets to it with a will; at other times the difficulty of real life makes him regret that he ever came out of his shell. But he has never wanted to return to his mechanical life.

One last detail and this fragment of Joey's story has been told. When Joey was 12, he made a float for our Memorial Day parade. It carried the slogan: "Feelings are more important than anything under the sun." Feelings, Joey had learned, are what make for humanity; their absence, for a mechanical existence. With this knowledge Joey entered the human condition.

Suggestions for Discussion

1. What is meant by "mechanical boy"? How does the author account for Joey's behavior? How does the author develop his analogy?

2. What cause–effect relationships are discussed and how are they illustrated and supported?

3. How does the author illustrate his statement that "in Joey's development the normal process of growth had been made to run backward"?

4. How does the analogy of labor-saving devices contribute to your understanding of Joey's problem? How does the succeeding paragraph further illuminate the analogy?

5. What is the relationship of Joey's Memorial Day slogan to the concluding sentence? To the author's central purpose?

6. With what concrete illustrations does the author make clear each of the following dualities: human–mechanical; fragile–imperious; internalize–externalize; explosions–preventions?

7. How does the diction, appropriate to the vocabulary of a machine, contribute to

the tone? Provide emphasis? Refer both to the author's descriptions and to Joey's own choice of words.

8. What is Bettelheim's attitude toward Joey? Toward his mother? How do you know?

9. From what point of view does Bettelheim narrate the story of Joey? Is he speaking solely as a psychiatrist? Is he also passing judgment upon society? Discuss.

Suggestions for Writing

1. Formulate your own definition of childhood schizophrenia by referring to specific details in the text.

2. Describe a sensitive or rebellious child or adolescent by providing concrete illustrations of his behavior and by showing your subject interacting with family, friends, or teachers.

3. Clarify a general concept by drawing upon the experiences of a single individual. Beginning with an observation about the family, the university, an occupation, a leisure activity, attempt to illustrate your concept by narrating the experiences of a single individual.

4. Explore how such current studies as Laura Schreibman's *Autism* (1988) and Michael Powers's *Children with Autism* (1989) challenge Bettelheim's theories.

Victoria Bissell Brown

Abortion Fight Is over Choice

Victoria Bissell Brown teaches American Women's History at San Diego State University. Her portrait of a mother and her adolescent daughter and their reconciliation focuses on their respective views of choice.

The local broadcaster announced that after the commercial he would be interviewing a leader in the anti-abortion movement. "Turn it off," I snapped at my daughter, "I can't bear to listen to that."

She gave me the kind of look children in the 1960s gave parents who refused to watch anti-war demonstrations on TV news. That look asked how could I have such a closed mind? How could I be so Establishment? And how could I be so curt, so final, so decisive about what my 13-year-old daughter says she regards as possibly the killing of babies?

Standing there in my kitchen, biscuit dough on my hands, I felt the full force of the abortion backlash. At that moment, my daughter saw me not as a soft-hearted liberal—a political persona I've grown comfortable with—but as a cold-hearted killer, one who sacrifices the unborn in the name of some abstract right to privacy. It was not the fact that she disagreed with me that was so disturbing. She's a teen-ager, she disagrees with me every day. What was so disturbing was the success of the anti-abortion movement at depicting people like me as heartless, amoral abstractionists who care more about rights than about life.

It seems to me that this is where I came in some 20 years ago. Only back then the opponents of abortion laws were the ones who were the heartless killers. Back then, we charged them with caring more about abstract principles than real life. Back then, we were the ones who showed the gruesome pictures—of women butchered on dirty kitchen tables, of women dead from unnecessary infections, of fetuses punctured by coat hangers, of women poisoned from drinking lye.

The movement for abortion rights did not begin and was not fueled by a passion for the right to privacy. That is the principle that convinced the Supreme Court, but the heart of this movement is nothing so anemic as a legalistic principle. The heart of this movement is a deep concern for the lives, the health and the well-being of American women.

That is the point I tried to make to my daughter. As the biscuits cooked and the interview came on the television, we sat and discussed the matter as only a mother and adolescent daughter can. Which is to say that we were alternately snarly and sensitive; there were bursts of honesty as well as of anger; there were questions and accusations; there were tears and occasional smiles. We were momentarily locked in a primal tug of wills over the most primal of issues.

We began, of course, with the fundamentals. "How do you know you're not killing a person?" she asked. Because I know that a 10-week-old fetus cannot survive outside a woman's womb, I know that it has no cognitive abilities. I know that it has no capacity for love or work, I know that it has no relationships or responsibilities. And I weigh that knowledge against the certitude that a pregnant woman is, most definitely, a person with relationships and responsibilities that only she can calculate.

I know that the research on women considering abortions shows that they aren't consumed with the question of privacy rights; they're consumed with the question of responsibilities—to their other children, to their parents, to their employers or teachers, to their husbands or lovers, to themselves, to that embryo. Few women make this decision casually; no women make it because they want to assert their right to privacy. Women decide to abort pregnancies because the ties that bind them in every other corner of their lives take priority over the very tenuous tie that binds them to that very tenuous bit of life in their wombs.

My daughter paid attention to these remarks, but seemed unmoved.

The television interview intruded. "What advice do you give to single women?" asked the interviewer. "We advise chastity," responded the pretty, powdered, softly bow-tied lady on the screen. I looked sideways at my daughter.

"What do you think of that?" I asked her. "Well," she sniffed, "I don't think people should be irresponsible about sex." That answer should have warmed the cockles of my maternal heart, but it didn't. It sounded cold-hearted, abstract—a principle unrelated to real life uttered by one who has yet to experience her first kiss.

My innocent child holds the conviction that women are—or should be—sufficiently in control of their lives so that they could always prevent pregnancy, either through contraception or by simply saying "no." It seems that she is, after all, the daughter of a feminist. This child of the women's movement expects women to be in charge of their lives. After all, her mother had only one child and no abortions—why can't everyone else be similarly well regulated? So great is women's progress (on TV and among the privileged white elite of my daughter's experience) that she simply cannot imagine women as victims of either the law or contraceptive failure or male sexual demands.

In abstract principle, she's right of course. In the best of all possible worlds, women would have the personal socialization and the economic independence that would allow them to say "no," and they would have medical and legal protections against unwanted pregnancies. But we don't live in abstract principle, and this isn't the best of all possible worlds, and despite what the softly bow-tied lady on TV said, making abortion illegal will not decrease premarital—or "irresponsible"—sex. It will only bring back all those couples who "had" to get married and all those women who were maimed or killed by underworld abortionists and all those mothers who abandoned all personal goals and resigned themselves to the vagaries of reproductive chance.

My daughter's eyes glazed over a bit, the way they do when I started sounding like a history professor. This story doesn't end with her throwing her arms around me and swearing her allegiance to my politics. It ends with my husband serving some almost-burned biscuits and my daughter and me making amends at a funny matinee.

She's not going to acquiesce to me on this. She wants the autonomy to make her own choice about abortion. And in that, she is true to the proud tradition of the abortion rights movement.

Suggestions for Discussion

1. What do the rhetorical questions contribute to the mother's sense of her daughter's view of her?

2. What was the nature of the abortion backlash the mother feels in relation to her thirteen-year-old daughter's attitudes?

3. What really disturbed the mother in relation to her teenage daughter?

4. What is the nature of the principle that guided the Supreme Court in its *Roe v. Wade* decision?

5. What were the "fundamentals" discussed by mother and daughter?

6. What issues outweigh the question of privacy rights in the research on women considering abortions?

7. In what respect does the mother view the child as naive?

8. How does the mother reconcile her daughter's attitude with her own?

Suggestions for Writing

1. Analyze the character of the mother, the daughter, and the relationship between them.

2. Discuss the significance of "choice" in any aspect of your life or in that of one of your friends or parents.

Thomas J. Cottle

Goodbye, Kids, Mother's Leaving Home

Thomas J. Cottle (b. 1937) is a psychologist and educator. This article is adapted from his book, *Children's Secrets*, published in 1990. Other books are *Reward and Betrayal* and *Hidden Survivors*. In this selection, Willie's parents' separation and their imposition of secrecy leave him vulnerable, miserable, and unsure of his sanity.

Most families, for obvious reasons, would like to give the impression to the outside world, if not to their own members, that their home lives are ideal. Children, in the main, "appreciate" this myth, since the rumblings of parental wars and the threat of separation are hardly stabilizing influences on a child's personality. Parents and children alike "appreciate" the knowledge that arguments need not automatically end in separation or, for that matter, death, as children often imagine. The real and fantasized stability of the family helps all its members to believe in its ultimate strength and to have faith in the idea that families can wage war yet end up as allies.

Much of this is self-evident. It is also evident that families, adults and children alike have begun to quake under the strain of ubiquitous divorces, although divorce rates lead to a series of myths of their own. That a growing percentage of marriages end in divorce has caused many couples to look upon their own marriages as far more frail, precarious, and strained than they ever recognized. Like microbes carrying vicious illness, the threat of divorce is in the air, and a not insignificant number of families now huddle together waiting for the disease to reach them. Equally important, as the nature of family life generally becomes more publicly discussed, the sacredness of marriage, and more particularly the marriage bond, is eroded, and marriage, in many people's eyes, becomes just another one of life's everyday institutions.

I am not suggesting that divorce is an innocuous event for the people involved. Quite the contrary. For these people, family stability may well remain a sacred concept and a hope. Despite the prevalence of divorce, it can cause great pain in the people who institute it, not to mention in the people innocently victimized by it. As a notion, a practice, a reality, divorce is no longer something that people must keep secret. Yet, ironically, the very "speakableness" of divorce may be one of the matters that causes many people a special hurt: namely, one finds a tendency in our culture to substitute "speakability" for the successful resolution of human problems. All one has to do is speak about divorce, death, abortion, and one's tensions or misgivings, fears or doubts, are automatically dissipated. Letting a ghost out of a closet hardly guarantees the demise of the ghost. Secret closets may house other ghosts. In fact, secrecy itself generates ghosts.

My work with young people from divorced families is not easily summarized. Some children come out of a divorce psychologically wounded, and as the metaphor would suggest, the wound seems to heal over time. Other chil-

205

dren do not emerge so fortunate; their scars are visible. In some instances I have found children flourishing after their parents' divorce, suggesting that life for them prior to the divorce had been unbearably stressful. Whether or not these children will someday reveal scars cannot yet be known, but for the moment, divorce, they claim, brought life-saving relief.

While divorce may be perceived by some children as abandonment, my own impression is that automatically equating divorce with abandonment is not necessarily helpful. Many divorced parents work hard not to show signs of abandonment, even though some of the children of these parents may speak about abandonment before they speak about family dissolution. In other words, a sense of abandonment may be heard in a child's early accounts of his or her parents' divorce, but eventually the new environment established for the child may help to dispel this sense. However, in the case of Willie Fryer, nothing about the "new" environment in which he found himself by dint of his parents' impending separation could possibly have counteracted the hurt *not* of divorce but of outright human abandonment. And the fact that he was meant to keep these experiences and his feelings about them secret only exacerbated his despair.

Willie Fryer, seventeen years old, came from a well-to-do family, had long blond curls, a shaggy appearance, soft blue eyes, and broad hands. Willie Fryer's father was a professor of law, his mother a journalist. Both were talented, hardworking people. They loved their three children, but they wanted successful careers too. Their children (Willie was the second born) grew up with the knowledge that adults lead two lives, their work life and their family life, and there was no sense in children screaming for their parents between the hours of eight and six, Monday through Friday. They just wouldn't be there. Nor did the children think of the summer as a time when families vacationed together. The family typically stayed home; the children were sent to day camp. Everybody left the house at eight in the morning and returned at six in the evening. Still, it was a close family, even if its five members grew up leading separate lives.

Indeed, that was another thing the Fryers taught their children: Dependence is a dangerous stance. After the child reaches a certain age, there is no reason for him or her to be dependent on anyone, especially parents. People must learn to be self-sufficient, self-possessed. That way, the shock of life's vicissitudes, as Martin Fryer repeatedly reminded his son, will be reduced. Love people, he would tell his children, but never need them to the point of dependency. Shirley Fryer preached the same lesson, particularly to her daughters. Needing and loving are two foods, she would say. Too many people, and especially girls, confuse them. Don't let one substitute for the other. To Willie, she would add, "There is no man who can be happy, ultimately happy, when he's married to a woman who *needs* him rather than *loves* him. If she loves him she'll enrich his life. If she only needs him and pretends to love him to satisfy her need, she'll bring him down. She may be loyal, but if you want loyalty, marry a German shepherd!"

Willie Fryer was told many things by his parents, but his mother's remark about distinguishing between love and need remained the most prominent. The message made sense to him, although it carried a bit of fright as well, not that he could define this feeling. The idea that people who needed him would drag him down could not have been more dramatic. He could see it with his school friends. As a young teenager, he had close friends. But there was also a group who pretended to be his friends. In their way they expressed a need to be his friend, but his mother was correct. They were driven by a fascination for him, not by a concern for him. They were the people to look out for.

If further proof of his mother's statement was necessary, Sylvie Jenner provided it. Willie began dating her when they were in the eighth grade, and at seventeen Sylvie needed Willie, but it was love that held them together. Never did he feel brought down by her needs. He once asked her, "Do you love me 'cause you need me, or need me 'cause you love me?" Sylvie looked confused. "If I know what you're talking about," she answered, "I think I don't love you *or* need you. Or is that a song?" Willie remembers thinking the idea was right, but that it was just too soon to tell. When he told his mother of the exchange with Sylvie, Shirley Fryer laughed. Willie could see she approved of what he had tried to do. She agreed that it was too soon to tell. He would use the same words when he told me of his mother's decision to leave the family.

Willie Fryer did indeed have broad hands. When we went for beer at the Silver Parrot one afternoon, his hand was practically wrapped around the entire tall glass. I often remarked to myself on the contrast of that broad hand ready to crush the glass and the delicate manner with which Willie sipped his beer. He seemed somewhat self-conscious about sitting in a college hangout when he was a high school senior. Or perhaps the self-consciousness grew out of our conversation. The hand of a man, I would think, the drinking style of a boy.

In Willie's case, it was not important how we met, or what he felt the nature of our friendship to be. As he himself told Sylvie, the point was that if he didn't speak to someone soon, he was going to explode. He needed what he called an outsider. So we met on and off for several months, talking mostly about books, politics, and, as it was the autumn of his senior year, college applications and the things he might want to study in university. The subject of his mother's leaving, something I knew nothing about, arose with Willie saying: "I've got a little problem I thought you might be able to help me out with. I don't know exactly what you can do about it, but maybe you know somebody." This last phrase, so common among young people holding tightly to precious secrets, always sounds so poignant. "Maybe you know somebody." Somebody to do what? I always want to say. Listen? Fix it? Kiss the hurt? Or, in Willie Fryer's case, Love you but not need you? The noise in the Silver Parrot was so great I could barely hear Willie's words.

"About a year and a half ago my mom came to me with this little problem. Well, problem isn't the right word . . . listen, you got to stop me if you've heard this one before. I mean, I'm sure a lot of kids have stories like this one, so don't let me cry into your beer, okay? What I was saying, it wasn't really a problem, it was just a message. She had grown a little tired—that's the way she said it—of being a mother and a wife and a journalist. She couldn't do everything at once and be happy. So she had to give something up. It wasn't going to be journalism since that meant a lot to her, and we were all pretty much grown up so we didn't need a mother, like children need a mother, and besides, you know my mother and needing. So she had decided she was going to leave my father, and us. I tell you, when she said it, I felt like I was living in the middle of that expression, pulling the plug out. I mean, it was like somebody pulling the floor out, not the rug. I mean the floor, so you fall down, down, down, like into endless space.

"But here's the interesting thing: I must not have had any expression on my face. Just a look, like, go on, Mother, keep talking, I'm still listening. I couldn't even get the feeling I was feeling. It was just boom, except for one thing. She said it in a way that sort of made it impossible for me to say anything, or feel anything. Like, I had to keep anything I was thinking from her. So she said a little bit more, like how her leaving everybody didn't mean she didn't love us and that it was her work that was making her do it. She talked about how in the old days, when people weren't meant to live as long as they do now, it was all right for a man and a woman to get married for life, but in modern times it's probably too long to stay together forever. It's nice to say it in a marriage vow and all that, but death, if you're lucky, doesn't come for a long, long time, so you could probably have a couple of families and still not be that old. She's talking on and on and I'm feeling like someone's choking the air out of my lungs but I'm not to let on I'm being choked. I didn't want to bother her. She'd obviously prepared her little speech, and I wasn't about to let it all come to nothing because this nice big fifteen-year-old kid—this was two years ago—was breaking down on the floor sobbing. And this was no big male thing on my part. I would have gladly cried if I thought I could have with her standing there. But if *she* could be calm, *I* could be calm. So I kept giving her the look, 'Keep going, Ma, I'm still listening.'

"Now comes the end of the speech: Don't tell Dad. The girls have known for a couple of weeks. They were told not to tell anybody, not even me, and now the three of us know but the old man doesn't. I mean the four of us know. Great game! And when does he find out? She's not sure. In time. She knows she has to make a break, but she's just not sure when, and she doesn't want to worry him because he's in the middle of a big project at work. So we get to keep a little secret. I'll tell you how I felt then, especially when she said, 'You want to tell me anything?' and all I could say was, 'Not really. Maybe I'll think of something.' I felt like all the clocks in the world stopped and time went back to the beginning. All of us had to start all over again. It was like I was a new me. After all, no more mother; that makes me different from what I was when she came into my room. She went out the door and all the clocks stopped. I remember that night my younger sister looked at me and she didn't have anything written on her face. I couldn't tell what she was thinking. Then all of a sudden she has this big grin and she says, 'Merry Christmas, Lone Ranger.' I said, 'Merry Christmas, Tonto.' It was April then.

"So now the Fryers are leading a wonderful life. There's a little time bomb in the house, ticking away under my father's nose, maybe I should say in his bed, but he doesn't know it. At least he lets us *think* he doesn't know it. But he couldn't have known it and pretended like that. But none of us, not even my mother, knew when the time bomb was going off. Every night in bed, I'd say to myself, well, it wasn't today, maybe it won't happen. Then, as the time goes on, you begin to forget about it. Like, all secrets are fantastic, upsetting, whatever, in the beginning, but then the excitement wears off. Still, that feeling of, well, starting life all over again, and this time without a mother, I mean being born all over again without a mother, that didn't leave me. I was starting a second time, really a third time, and it was going to be a fourth time before it was over.

"When my mother gave me that speech, years before, about loving and needing, I think that's when I started to live life all over again. She was warning me, even if she wasn't aware of it. But knowing her, she probably was. I didn't know what was coming off, but I was being told, Stop the old clocks and start the new ones, pal, your old lady's going away one of these days. In a sense, that was like the first secret she was telling me. Be prepared: there's a time bomb being manufactured. Then the time bomb becomes real, which was when she told me she was leaving. The next time the clock stops and starts all over again is six months after she made her little speech. Now both my parents come to me one night. My sister Patty is with me this time. They're both so straight-faced they look like they're going to ask me for the toothpaste. My father by now knows everything. The bomb went off and nothing. No one heard a noise. If it hit him, no one could have guessed by the way he was looking at us. So what can I think? They made their plans and they're neither delighted nor upset, and we're waiting around for the next step. Do they sell the house? Do we go with *her*? Do we go with *him*? Do they quit their jobs? No, that much I knew. Jobs come first after children reach six years old. So the clocks are going off again and I'm sitting on my bed feeling like a goddamn refugee. Just tell me when to pack and which country I'm supposed to walk to. And can I take my security blanket? This is all happening on Thanksgiving vacation. They waited until Thanksgiving vacation in case we got a little upset so we could take it easy a couple of days and not miss school. Thoughtful. Thoughtful people.

"Here's a funny thing. For a minute there, while the two of them like a couple of football coaches were giving us their half-time speech, how we're going to have to play a little better the second half—the second half of our life is more like it—I was actually feeling relieved. She waited so damn long she had me believing she wouldn't go through with it. I might have been better had she just said she was going and gone. But now I didn't have to keep the secret anymore. At least it was out in the open and we could talk about it. And don't think they didn't try to get us to talk about it. Probably because all the books said when you knife your kids in the back be sure they get a chance to talk about it with you; it makes them feel better. Except that Patty and I looked at each other and didn't have a thing to say. I don't think we talked about it for weeks. Fact, I don't *ever* remember talking about it. Patty said, 'Where do we go?' My mother said, 'You'll stay here with your father. I'll see you regularly.' But get this, she tacked on the trailer, 'Willie, you must have some questions. You're never this quiet.' Oh yeah, man, I got a question. Do you think you could take your foot off my chest long enough so I could take a breath of air?

"It was really terrific. If anybody had made a movie of us they could have sold it to television for one of these afternoon specials which are supposed to help children learn about *real* family problems, except we didn't have any problems because our family was breaking up amicably. That's my father's word. My mother called it *peaceably*, in case Patty or me didn't know the word amicably. Anyway, I felt relieved because no more secrets. I couldn't have said anything if they tortured me. But the more she kept saying 'Willie, you must have something to say,' the more I could have killed her. She has a great way of not letting anybody express any emotion and she thinks they're purposely holding back. But she strangles us. That, maybe, is the biggest secret I was asked to keep in my entire life: my emotions. I *had* to keep them secret because she didn't have a way to deal with them, or the time. In fact, that may be why I keep saying that thing about time stopping and starting all over again. There never was time for our feelings. Our feelings were the big secret, *our* big time bombs, which weren't allowed to go off because Mommy and Daddy's work schedules would have been messed up. Can you imagine the three of us, the most wordy children in America, not saying a thing about what was going on? I mean, that has to go beyond a pledge of secrecy. She never said we couldn't talk to one another about it. Although she did, in her way. She kept us from raising anything with her, or with each other, or with anybody, that would keep her from getting where she wanted to go. This time she wanted to get out of the house. Can you see Patty and me exchanging Christmas greetings in the middle of the *spring*? 'Merry Christmas, Lone Ranger?' What the hell were we doing?"

"You want to hear the kicker? They take one secret off the agenda for us, now they got another one. This time it's my father who's breaking the big news. He's just been told by my mother a couple of days before how she had decided to walk out. So what's on my father's mind? We shouldn't breathe a word of this to anyone. It was the right word for him to use too, because I couldn't breathe anymore at all. For his business and reputation, and her business and reputation, divorce wouldn't look good. My mother pointed out that when men leave women it doesn't look so bad as when women leave men. Either way, though, it ends up looking like there's something wrong with the woman. Either she's not good enough to keep her husband, or she's unstable and leaves him. So, there we were, pledged to secrecy all over again. And there was the clock stopping and starting again. I was beginning to feel like a car bumping along a dirt road without any gas.

"As you can see, I'm not doing all that well with my parents, but I've got to be among the world's top secret-keepers. I didn't tell Sylvie for a long, long time. When she'd come over she wouldn't ask where my mother was because she knew my parents worked. She didn't see anything different because the three little Fryers were such good secret-keepers, or is the word good liars! I didn't tell a soul; I led my life like a good little boy, and let myself choke on the whole scene. The secrets were still going strong in the Fryer home. If the split bothered anybody at 18 Willow Road, nobody could have told. But that's not really amazing. The amazing thing is that my parents kept up the secret, thanks to the sealed lips of their beloved children, one of whom's birthday was forgotten this year, and last year, too. They arranged to go to certain important social events together, the whole works, just to let people think they were together. People still wrote to her at home, thinking she lived at home. Great, huh? No one at their jobs knew, and the people they work with are the biggest gossips I've ever met. The fact is, the greatest family project the Fryers ever undertook was the keeping of that secret. My father must have known better than anyone how good we were at it, because we kept the one before it from him pretty darn well.

"That's my story. I still feel strangled to death, like I can't get air, and like every time I turn around I hear clocks stopping and starting and stopping and starting. I guess I feel too that I can't be young anymore, which isn't all that bad, not that I have any idea anymore who I am. Who I really am, I mean. No, that's a lie. I do know who I am, up to a point. I just can't put it into words; but I can sort of feel who I am. It's my parents I don't know. Talk about people you live with, or used to live with, or are *supposed* to live with, being strangers. Jesus, I don't know who they are, who they were, *what* they are. The big secret is the charade. The all-night, all-day drama playing over at Willow Road. The people are real, the events are real, only the emotions are fictitious to protect the innocent, as if anybody could be innocent after what's been going on.

"I think my parents are asking us to keep a far more important and dangerous secret than they think. Sometimes I think my mother's worse than my father, then I think he's worse. Both of them, in my eyes, are really sick people. They both need a team of psychiatrists working on them. But they don't see it, and nobody who is friends with them thinks there's anything wrong. Not telling anybody they're separated is a little matter next to the fact that their whole life is a lie. A lie when they were together, and when they're apart. That's what I can't tell anybody. Not even Sylvie. I have to be loyal to them. They think I'm loyal by not talking about their separation. They probably think I'm afraid to jeopardize their jobs because I may not have enough money for college, but that's a lot of crap! I couldn't care less about that. It's *them* I think about; not money for clothes and cars and college. And both my sisters are the same.

"I'm being loyal, acting the way I am, but the act is taking it out of me. It's changing me, which is all right, but it's making me think there are things I once thought I could do that I don't think I can do anymore. It's cutting into my confidence. You can't grow up worrying about your parents or putting them out of your mind. It's normal for kids to grow up and find out that, well, your dad and mom aren't as great as you thought when you were small. Sure. But I have another problem. I have to grow up and put them behind me, or try to convince them that one of us is crazy, and I know it isn't me because *I'm* not going around asking people to keep secrets about *my* life. Believe me, I have a much healthier relationship with Sylvie than they ever had, and certainly better than that crazy business they have going between them now. Nobody goes through life with the strength they *could* have when their parents run around like that. This secret business is absolutely foolish, crazy. I say it's both. I also say I'm going to crack.

"You want the last straw? The secret-makers have just come up with their latest dandy. For the last six months they *have* been telling some people they're separated, although we're still not supposed to talk about it. But here's the latest: My mother is going to write a book about it. It, that means about us, the little counterspies of Willow Road. So now she really doesn't want me to talk about any of these things until I tell her how I've lived through the last few years. You want to see a grown man or almost grown man cry? I'd love to. But they've taken the tears out of me. I'd love to have a good old-fashioned cry, or laugh, or anything over this. But all that secret-keeping business, all that holding things in, I don't have a damn thing to let out. Maybe that's what I've been trying to say. The secrets took it all out of me. I told nothing in exchange for giving up every feeling I've had. Wow. I feel I've been talking a whole day. Tell me, after hearing this, you think I'm crazy? Or maybe I should ask, you think I *need* my parents, or *love* my parents?"

Suggestions for Discussion

1. With what details do you learn of Willie's family background? What do you learn of his mother's and father's values?

2. What distinction does Mrs. Fryer make between *needing* and *loving?* How does Willie react to her remark? Why does he later feel it was prophetic?

3. How would you describe Willie's response to his mother's news about leaving her husband?

4. What are the several occasions when "the clocks stop" for Willie?

5. What images does Willie use to describe his feelings when both his parents let him know his mother is leaving?

6. What is the irony in his parents' description of the break up?

7. How does the admonition to keep the matter secret affect Willie?

8. How does the situation affect Willie's sense of self?

9. Why does Willie sum up his story to the counselor by asking whether he loves or needs his parents?

Suggestions for Writing

1. In a narrative or an exposition suggest or explain your sense of the difference between needing and loving.

2. Draw upon the details and imagery in the text to describe Willie's attitudes and feelings. What seemed to him to be the cruelest acts of his parents?

3. Discuss a situation in which divorce seems to be the preferred solution to marital incompatibility.

Fiction

T. Coraghessan Boyle

If the River Was Whiskey

T. Coraghessian Boyle (b. 1948) has both an M.F.A. and a Ph.D. from Iowa University, and presently is a writer, musician, and professor at the University of California at Los Angeles. Winner of the St. Lawrence and Aga Khan prizes, he is the author of nine books of fiction and autobiography. These include, among others, *If the River Was Whiskey* (1989), *East Is East* (1990), *T. Coraghessian Boyle* (1991), and *Road to Wellville* (1993). The story included here explores the disintegrating relationship between a father and his family.

The water was a heartbeat, a pulse, it stole the heat from his body and pumped it to his brain. Beneath the surface, magnified through the shimmering lens of his face mask, were silver shoals of fish, forests of weed, a silence broken only by the distant throbbing hum of an outboard. Above, there was the sun, the white flash of a faraway sailboat, the weatherbeaten dock with its weatherbeaten rowboat, his mother in her deck chair, and the vast depthless green of the world beyond.

He surfaced like a dolphin, spewing water from the vent of his snorkel, and sliced back to the dock. The lake came with him, two bony arms and the wedge of a foot, the great heaving splash of himself flat out on the dock like something thrown up in a storm. And then, without pausing even to snatch up a towel, he had the spinning rod in hand and the silver lure was sizzling out over the water, breaking the surface just above the shadowy arena he'd fixed in his mind. His mother looked up at the splash. "Tiller," she called, "come get a towel."

His shoulders quaked. He huddled and stamped his feet, but he never took his eyes off the tip of the rod. Twitching it suggestively, he reeled with the jerky, hesitant motion that would drive lunker fish to a frenzy. Or so he'd read, anyway.

"Tilden, do you hear me?"

"I saw a Northern," he said. "A big one. Two feet maybe." The lure was in. A flick of his wrist sent it back. Still reeling, he ducked his head to wipe his nose on his wet shoulder. He could feel the sun on his back now and he envisioned the skirted lure in the water, sinuous, sensual, irresistible, and he waited for the line to quicken with the strike.

The porch smelled of pine—old pine, dried up and dead—and it depressed him. In fact, everything depressed him—especially this vacation. Vacation. It was a joke. Vacation from what?

He poured himself a drink—vodka and soda, tall, from the plastic half-gallon jug. It wasn't noon yet, the breakfast dishes were in the sink, and Tiller and Caroline were down at the lake. He couldn't see them through the screen of trees, but he heard the murmur of their voices against the soughing of the branches and the sadness of the birds. He sat heavily in the creaking wicker chair and looked out on nothing. He didn't feel too hot. In fact, he felt as if he'd been cored and dried, as if somebody had taken a pipe cleaner and run it through his veins. His head ached too, but the vodka would take care of that. When he finished it, he'd have another, and then maybe a grilled swiss on rye. Then he'd start to feel good again.

His father was talking to the man and his mother was talking to the woman. They'd met at the bar about twenty drinks ago and his father was into his could-have-been, should-have-been, way-back-when mode, and the man, bald on top and with a ratty beard and long greasy hair like his father's, was trying to steer the conversation back to building supplies. The woman had whole galaxies of freckles on her chest, and she leaned forward in her sundress and told his mother scandalous stories about people she'd never heard of. Tiller had drunk all the Coke and eaten all the beer nuts he could hold. He watched the Pabst Blue Ribbon sign flash on and off above the bar and he watched the woman's freckles move in and out of the gap between her breasts. Outside it was dark and a cool clean scent came in off the lake.

"Uh huh, yeah," his father was saying, "the To the Bone Band. I played rhythm and switched off vocals with Dillie Richards. . . ."

The man had never heard of Dillie Richards.

"Black dude, used to play with Taj Mahal?"

The man had never heard of Taj Mahal.

"Anyway," his father said, "we used to do all this really outrageous stuff by people like Muddy, Howlin' Wolf, Luther Allison—"

"She didn't," his mother said.

The woman threw down her drink and nodded and the front of her dress went crazy. Tiller watched her and felt the skin go tight across his shoulders and the back of his neck, where he'd been burned the first day. He wasn't wearing any underwear, just shorts. He looked away. "Three abortions, two kids," the woman said. "And she never knew who the father of the second one was."

"Drywall isn't worth a damn," the man said. "But what're you going to do?"

"Paneling?" his father offered.

The man cut the air with the flat of his hand. He looked angry. "Don't talk to me about paneling," he said.

Mornings, when his parents were asleep and the lake was still, he would take the rowboat to the reedy cove on the far side of the lake where the big pike lurked. He didn't actually know if they lurked there, but if they lurked anywhere, this would be the place. It looked fishy, mysterious, sunken logs looming up dark from the shadows beneath the boat, mist rising like steam, as if the bottom were boiling with ravenous, cold-eyed, killer pike that could slice through monofilament with a snap of their jaws and bolt ducklings in a gulp. Besides, Joe Matochik, the old man who lived in the cabin next door and could charm frogs by stroking their bellies, had told him that this was where he'd find them.

It was cold at dawn and he'd wear a thick homeknit sweater over his T-shirt and shorts, sometimes pulling the stretched-out hem of it down like a skirt to warm his thighs. He'd take an apple with him or a slice of brown bread and peanut butter. And of course the orange lifejacket his mother insisted on.

When he left the dock he was always wearing the lifejacket—for form's sake and for the extra warmth it gave him against the raw morning air. But when he got there, when he stood in the swaying basin of the boat to cast his Hula Popper or Abu Relfex, it got in the way and he took it off. Later, when the sun ran through him and he didn't need the sweater, he balled it up on the seat beside him, and sometimes, if it was good and hot, he shrugged out of his T-shirt and shorts too. No one could see him in the cove, and it made his breath come quick to be naked like that under the morning sun.

"I heard you," he shouted, and he could feel the veins stand out in his neck, the rage come up in him like something killed and dead and brought back to life. "What kind of thing is that to tell a kid, huh? About his own father?"

She wasn't answering. She'd backed up in a corner of the kitchen and she wasn't answering. And what could she say, the bitch? He'd heard her. Dozing on the trundle bed under the stairs, wanting a drink but too weak to get up and make one, he'd heard voices from the kitchen, her voice and Tiller's. "Get used to it," she said, "he's a drunk, your father's a drunk," and then he was up off the bed as if something had exploded inside of him and he had her by the shoulders—always the shoulders and never the face, that much she'd taught him—and Tiller was gone, out the door and gone. Now, her voice low in her throat, a sick and guilty little smile on her lips, she whispered, "It's true."

"Who are you to talk?—you're shit-faced yourself." She shrank away from him, that sick smile on her lips, her shoulders hunched. He wanted to smash things, kick in the damn stove, make her hurt.

"At least I have a job," she said.

"I'll get another one, don't you worry."

"And what about Tiller? We've been here two weeks and you haven't done one damn thing with him, nothing, zero. You haven't even been down to the lake. Two hundred feet and you haven't even been down there once." She came up out of the corner now, feinting like a boxer, vicious, her sharp little fists balled up to drum on him. She spoke in a snarl. "What kind of father are you?"

He brushed past her, slammed open the cabinet, and grabbed the first bottle he found. It was whiskey, cheap whiskey, Four Roses, the shit she drank. He poured out half a water glass full and drank it down to spite her. "I hate the beach, boats, water, trees. I hate you."

She had her purse and she was halfway out the screen door. She hung there a second, looking as if she'd bitten into something rotten. "The feeling's mutual," she said, and the door banged shut behind her.

There were too many complications, too many things to get between him and the moment, and he tried not to think about them. He tried not to think about his father—or his mother either—in the same way that he tried not to think about the pictures of the bald-headed stick people in Africa or meat in its plastic wrapper and how it got there. But when he did think about his father he thought about the river-was-whiskey day.

It was a Tuesday or Wednesday, middle of the week, and when he came home from school the curtains were drawn and his father's car was in the driveway. At the door, he could hear him, the *chunk-chunk* of the chords and the rasping nasal whine that seemed as if it belonged to someone else. His father was sitting in the dark, hair in his face, bent low over the guitar. There was an open bottle of liquor on the coffee table and a clutter of beer bottles. The room stank of smoke.

It was strange, because his father hardly ever played his guitar anymore—he mainly just talked about it. In the past tense. And it was strange too—and bad—because his father wasn't at work. Tiller dropped his bookbag on the telephone stand. "Hi, Dad," he said.

His father didn't answer. Just bent over the guitar and played the same song, over and over, as if it were the only song he knew. Tiller sat on the sofa and listened. There was a verse—one verse—and his father repeated it three or four times before he broke off and slurred the words into a sort of chant or hum, and then he went back to the words again. After the fourth repetition, Tiller heard it:

> If the river was whiskey,
> And I was a divin' duck,
> I'd swim to the bottom,
> Drink myself back up.

For half an hour his father played that song, played it till anything else would have sounded strange. He reached for the bottle when he finally stopped, and that was when he noticed Tiller. He looked surprised. Looked as if he'd just woke up. "Hey, ladykiller Tiller," he said, and took a drink from the mouth of the bottle.

Tiller blushed. There'd been a Sadie Hawkins dance at school and Janet Rumery had picked him for her partner. Ever since, his father had called him ladykiller, and though he wasn't exactly sure what it meant, it made him blush anyway, just from the tone of it. Secretly, it pleased him. "I really liked the song, Dad," he said.

"Yeah?" His father lifted his eyebrows and made a face. "Well, come home to Mama, doggie-o. Here," he said, and he held out an open beer. "You ever have one of these, ladykiller Tiller?" He was grinning. The sleeve of his shirt was torn and his elbow was raw and there was a hard little clot of blood over his shirt pocket. "With your sixth-grade buddies out behind the handball court, maybe? No?"

Tiller shook his head.

"You want one? Go ahead, take a hit."

Tiller took the bottle and sipped tentatively. The taste wasn't much. He looked up at his father. "What does it mean?" he said. "The song, I mean—the one you were singing. About the whiskey and all."

His father gave him a long slow grin and took a drink from the big bottle of clear liquor. "I don't know," he said finally, grinning wider to show his tobacco-stained teeth. "I guess he just liked whiskey, that's all." He picked up a cigarette, made as if to light it, and then put it down again. "Hey," he said, "you want to sing it with me?"

All right, she'd hounded him and she'd threatened him and she was going to leave him, he could see that clear as day. But he was going to show her. And the kid too. He wasn't drinking. Not today. Not a drop.

He stood on the dock with his hands in his pockets while Tiller scrambled around with the fishing poles and oars and the rest of it. Birds were screeching in the trees and there was a smell of diesel fuel on the air. The sun cut into his head like a knife. He was sick already.

"I'm giving you the big pole, Dad, and you can row if you want."

He eased himself into the boat and it fell away beneath him like the mouth of a bottomless pit.

"I made us egg salad, Dad, your favorite. And I brought some birch beer."

He was rowing. The lake was churning underneath him, the wind was up and reeking of things washed up on the shore, and the damn oars kept slipping out of the oarlocks, and he was rowing. At the last minute he'd wanted to go back for a quick drink, but he didn't, and now he was rowing.

"We're going to catch a pike," Tiller said, hunched like a spider in the stern.

There was spray off the water. He was rowing. He felt sick. Sick and depressed.

"We're going to catch a pike, I can feel it. I know we are," Tiller said, "I know it. I just know it."

It was too much for him all at once—the sun, the breeze that was so sweet he could taste it, the novelty of his father rowing, pale arms and a dead cigarette clenched between his teeth, the boat rocking, and the birds whispering—and he closed his eyes a minute, just to keep from going dizzy with the joy of it. They were in deep water already. Tiller was trolling with a plastic worm and spinner, just in case, but he didn't have much faith in catching anything out here. He was taking his father to the cove with the submerged logs and beds of weed—that's where they'd connect, that's where they'd catch pike.

"Jesus," his father said when Tiller spelled him at the oars. Hands shaking, he crouched in the stern and tried to light a cigarette. His face was gray and the hair beat crazily around his face. He went through half a book of matches and then threw the cigarette in the water. "Where are you taking us, anyway," he said, "—the Indian Ocean?"

"The pike place," Tiller told him. "You'll like it, you'll see."

The sun was dropping behind the hills when they got there, and the water went from blue to gray. There was no wind in the cove. Tiller let the boat glide out across the still surface while his father finally got a cigarette lit, and then he dropped anchor. He was excited. Swallows dove at the surface, bullfrogs burped from the reeds. It was the perfect time to fish, the hour when the big lunker pike would cruise among the sunken logs, hunting.

"All right," his father said, "I'm going to catch the biggest damn fish in the lake," and he jerked back his arm and let fly with the heaviest sinker in the tackle box dangling from the end of the rod. The line hissed through the guys and there was a thunderous splash that probably terrified every pike within half a mile. Tiller looked over his shoulder as he reeled in his silver spoon. His father winked at him, but he looked grim.

It was getting dark, his father was out of cigarettes, and Tiller had cast the spoon so many times his arm was sore, when suddenly the big rod began to buck. "Dad! Dad!" Tiller shouted, and his father lurched up as if he'd been stabbed. He'd been dozing, the rod propped against the gunwale, and Tiller had been studying the long suffering-lines in his father's face, the grooves in his forehead, and the puffy discolored flesh beneath his eyes. With his beard and long hair and with the crumpled suffering look on his face, he was the picture of the crucified Christ Tiller had contemplated a hundred times at church. But now the rod was bucking and his father had hold of it and he was playing a fish, a big fish, the tip of the rod dipping all the way down to the surface.

"It's a pike, Dad, it's a pike!"

His father strained at the pole. His only response was a grunt, but Tiller saw something in his eyes he hardly recognized anymore, a connection, a charge, as if the fish were sending a current up the line, through the pole, and into his hands and body and brain. For a full three minutes he played the fish, his slack biceps gone rigid, the cigarette clamped in his mouth, while Tiller hovered over him with the landing net. There was a surge, a splash, and the thing was in the net, and Tiller had it over the side and into the boat. "It's a pike," his father said, "goddamnit, look at the thing, look at the size of it."

It wasn't a pike. Tiller had watched Joe Matochik catch one off the dock one night. Joe's pike had been dangerous, full of teeth, a long, lean, tapering strip of muscle and pounding life. This was no pike. It was a carp. A fat, pouty, stinking, ugly mud carp. Trash fish. They shot them with arrows and threw them up on the shore to rot. Tiller looked at his father and felt like crying.

"It's a pike," his father said, and already the thing in his eyes was gone, already it was over, "it's a pike. Isn't it?"

It was late—past two, anyway—and he was drunk. Or no, he was beyond drunk. He'd been drinking since morning, one tall vodka and soda after another, and he didn't feel a thing. He sat on the porch in the dark and he couldn't see the lake, couldn't hear it, couldn't even smell it. Caroline and Tiller were asleep. The house was dead silent.

Caroline was leaving him, which meant that Tiller was leaving him. He knew it. He could see it in her eyes and he heard it in her voice. She was soft once, his soft-eyed lover, and now she was hard, unyielding, now she was his worst enemy. They'd had the couple from the roadhouse in for drinks and burgers earlier that night and he'd leaned over the table to tell the guy something—Ed, his name was—joking really, nothing serious, just making conversation. "Vodka and soda," he said, "that's my drink. I used to drink vodka and grapefruit juice, but it tore the lining out of my stomach." And then Caroline, who wasn't even listening, stepped in and said, "Yeah, and that"—pointing to the glass—"tore the lining out of your brain." He looked up at her. She wasn't smiling.

All right. That was how it was. What did he care? He hadn't wanted to come up here anyway—it was her father's idea. Take the cabin for a month, the old man had said, pushing, pushing in that way he had, and get yourself turned around. Well, he wasn't turning around, and they could all go to hell.

After a while the chill got to him and he pushed himself up from the chair and went to bed. Caroline said something in her sleep and pulled away from him as he lifted the covers and slid in. He was awake for a minute or two, feeling depressed, so depressed he wished somebody would come in and shoot him, and then he was asleep.

In his dream, he was out in the boat with Tiller. The wind was blowing, his hands were shaking, he couldn't light a cigarette. Tiller was watching him. He pulled at the oars and nothing happened. Then all of a sudden they were going down, the boat sucked out from under them, the water icy and black, beating in on them as if it were alive. Tiller called out to him. He saw his son's face, saw him going down, and there was nothing he could do.

Suggestions for Discussion

1. When Tiller describes his father as into his "could-have-been, should-have-been, way-back-when mode," what does he mean? What does this tell us about his father?

2. What is the significance of the river-was-whiskey day in Tiller's relationship with his father?

3. Boyle contrasts the world of nature and the world of human relationships. At several significant points they converge. Why does Tiller want to cry when his father catches a "trash" fish? Why does his father dream Tiller is drowning and he cannot save him?

Suggestions for Writing

1. Describe a moment when you had to face a hard truth about someone you loved.

2. Sometimes things that happen in an instant can change your whole life. Describe one.

===============

William Carlos Williams

The Use of Force

William Carlos Williams (1883–1963) practiced medicine in Rutherford, New Jersey, the factory town in which he was born. *Selected Poems* appeared in 1949, *Collected Later Poetry* (1950), and *Collected Poems* (1951). His long epic poem, *Paterson*, won the National Book Award for Poetry in 1950. *Desert Music* appeared in 1954, *Journey to Love* in 1955. He has also written novels, *White Mule* (1937) and *In the Money* (1940); short stories, *Life Along the Passaic* (1938), *Selected Essays* (1954); and an *Autobiography* (1951). He received the Bollingen Award for poetry in 1953. The simple and direct language in this short story heightens the intensity of the feelings of the doctor, parents, and child.

They were new patients to me, all I had was the name, Olson.
Please come down as soon as you can, my daughter is very sick.
When I arrived I was met by the mother, a big startled looking woman, very clean and apologetic who merely said, Is this the doctor? and let me in. In the back, she added. You must excuse us, doctor, we have her in the kitchen where it is warm. It is very damp here sometimes.

The child was fully dressed and sitting on her father's lap near the kitchen table. He tried to get up, but I motioned for him not to bother, took off my overcoat and started to look things over. I could see that they were all very nervous, eyeing me up and down distrustfully. As often, in such cases, they weren't telling me more than they had to, it was up to me to tell them; that's why they were spending three dollars on me.

The child was fairly eating me up with her cold, steady eyes, and no expression to her face whatever. She did not move and seemed, inwardly, quiet; an unusually attractive little thing, and as strong as a heifer in appearance. But her face was flushed, she was breathing rapidly, and I realized that she had a high fever. She had magnificent blonde hair, in profusion. One of those picture children often reproduced in advertising leaflets and the photogravure sections of the Sunday papers.

She's had a fever for three days, began the father and we don't know what it comes from. My wife has given her things, you know, like people do, but it don't do no good. And there's been a lot of sickness around. So we tho't you'd better look her over and tell us what is the matter.

As doctors often do I took a trial shot at it as a point of departure. Has she had a sore throat?

Both parents answered me together, No . . . No, she says her throat don't hurt her.

Does your throat hurt you? added the mother to the child. But the little girl's expression didn't change nor did she move her eyes from my face.

Have you looked?

I tried to, said the mother, but I couldn't see.

As it happens we had been having a number of cases of diphtheria in the school to which this child went during that month and we were all, quite apparently, thinking of that, though no one had as yet spoken of the thing.

Well, I said, suppose we take a look at the throat first. I smiled in my best professional manner and asking for the child's first name I said, come on, Mathilda, open your mouth and let's take a look at your throat.

Nothing doing.

Aw, come on, I coaxed, just open your mouth wide and let me take a look. Look, I said opening both hands wide, I haven't anything in my hands. Just open up and let me see.

Such a nice man, put in the mother. Look how kind he is to you. Come on, do what he tells you to. He won't hurt you.

At that I ground my teeth in disgust. If only they wouldn't use the word "hurt" I might be able to get somewhere. But I did not allow myself to be hurried or disturbed but speaking quietly and slowly I approached the child again.

As I moved my chair a little nearer suddenly with one catlike movement both her hands clawed instinctively for my eyes and she almost reached them too. In fact she knocked my glasses flying and they fell, though unbroken, several feet away from me on the kitchen floor.

Both the mother and father almost turned themselves inside out in embarrassment and apology. You bad girl, said the mother, taking her and shaking her by one arm. Look what you've done. The nice man . . .

For heaven's sake, I broke in. Don't call me a nice man to her. I'm here to look at her throat on the chance that she might have diphtheria and possibly die of it. But that's nothing to her. Look here, I said to the child, we're going to look at your throat. You're old enough to understand what I'm saying. Will you open it now by yourself or shall we have to open it for you?

Not a move. Even her expression hadn't changed. Her breaths however were coming faster and faster. Then the battle began. I had to do it. I had to have a throat culture for her own protection. But first I told the parents that it was entirely up to them. I explained the danger but said that I would not insist on a throat examination so long as they would take the responsibility.

If you don't do what the doctor says you'll have to go to the hospital, the mother admonished her severely.

Oh yeah? I had to smile to myself. After all, I had already fallen in love with the savage brat, the parents were contemptible to me. In the ensuing struggle they grew more and more abject, crushed, exhausted while she surely rose to magnificent heights of insane fury of effort bred of her terror of me.

The father tried his best, and he was a big man but the fact that she was his daughter, his shame at her behavior, and his dread of hurting her made him release her just at the critical times when I had almost achieved success, till I wanted to kill him. But his dread also that she might have diphtheria made him tell me to go on, go on though he himself was almost fainting, while the mother moved back and forth behind us raising and lowering her hands in an agony of apprehension.

Put her in front of you on your lap, I ordered, and hold both her wrists.

But as soon as he did the child let out a scream. Don't, you're hurting me. Let go of my hands. Let them go I tell you. Then she shrieked terrifyingly, hysterically. Stop it! Stop it! You're killing me!

Do you think she can stand it, doctor! said the mother.

You get out, said the husband to his wife. Do you want her to die of diphtheria?

Come on now, hold her, I said.

Then I grasped the child's head with my left hand and tried to get the wooden tongue depressor between her teeth. She fought, with clenched teeth, desperately! But now I also had grown furious—at a child. I tried to hold myself down but I couldn't. I know how to expose a throat for inspection. And I did my best. When finally I got the wooden spatula behind the last teeth and just the point of it into the mouth cavity, she opened up for an instant but before I could see anything she came down again and gripped the wooden blade between her molars; she reduced it to splinters before I could get it out again.

Aren't you ashamed, the mother yelled at her. Aren't you ashamed to act like that in front of the doctor?

Get me a smooth-handled spoon of some sort, I told the mother. We're going through with this. The child's mouth was already bleeding. Her tongue was cut and she was screaming in wild hysterical shrieks. Perhaps I should have desisted and come back in an hour or more. No doubt it would have been better. But I have seen at least two children lying dead in bed of neglect in such cases, and feeling that I must get a diagnosis now or never I went at it again. But the worst of it was that I too had got beyond reason. I could have torn the child apart in my own fury and enjoyed it. It was a pleasure to attack her. My face was burning with it.

The damned little brat must be protected against her own idiocy, one says to one's self at such times. Others must be protected against her. It is a social necessity. And all these things are true. But a blind fury, a feeling of adult shame, bred of a longing for muscular release are the operatives. One goes on to the end.

In the final unreasoning assault I overpowered the child's neck and jaws. I forced the heavy silver spoon back of her teeth and down her throat till she gagged. And there it was—both tonsils covered with membrane. She had fought valiantly to keep me from knowing her secret. She had been hiding that sore throat for three days at least and lying to her parents in order to escape just such an outcome as this.

Now truly she was furious. She had been on the defensive before but now she attacked. Tried to get off her father's lap and fly at me while tears of defeat blinded her eyes.

Suggestions for Discussion

1. How do you explain the child's resistance to the doctor?

2. Account for the doctor's statement: "I had already fallen in love with the savage brat; the parents were contemptible to me."

3. How are the doctor's feelings reflected during the struggle? How does he rationalize them?

4. Attempt to recreate the child's relationship with each of her parents.

5. Comment on the use of force. What alternatives did the doctor have?

Suggestion for Writing

Create a scene in which there is interaction between the child and her parents.

Flannery O'Connor

Everything That Rises Must Converge

Flannery O'Connor (1925–1965), born in Georgia, was educated in Georgia schools and the University of Iowa. She received the O. Henry Award in 1957 and a Ford Foundation grant in 1959. Her books include the novels *Wise Blood* (1952) and *The Violent Bear It Away* (1960). Her collection of short stories, *Everything That Rises Must Converge*, was published posthumously in 1965. The tension between mother and son is aggravated by the racial conflict and leads to a tragic resolution in which the internal conflict merges with the climax of the racial incident.

Her doctor had told Julian's mother that she must lose twenty pounds on account of her blood pressure, so on Wednesday nights Julian had to take her downtown on the bus for a reducing class at the Y. The reducing class was designed for working girls over fifty, who weighed from 165 to 200 pounds. His mother was one of the slimmer ones, but she said ladies did not tell their age or weight. She would not ride the buses by herself at night since they had been integrated, and because the reducing class was one of her few pleasures, necessary for her health, and *free*, she said Julian could at least put himself out to take her, considering all she did for him. Julian did not like to consider all she did for him, but every Wednesday night he braced himself and took her.

She was almost ready to go, standing before the hall mirror, putting on her hat, while he, his hands behind him, appeared pinned to the door frame, waiting like Saint Sebastian for the arrows to begin piercing him. The hat was new and had cost her seven dollars and a half. She kept saying, "Maybe I shouldn't have paid that for it. No, I shouldn't have. I'll take it off and return it tomorrow. I shouldn't have bought it."

Julian raised his eyes to heaven. "Yes, you should have bought it," he said. "Put it on and let's go." It was a hideous hat. A purple velvet flap came down on one side of it and stood up on the other; the rest of it was green and looked like a cushion with the stuffing out. He decided it was less comical than jaunty and pathetic. Everything that gave her pleasure was small and depressed him.

She lifted the hat one more time and set it down slowly on top of her head. Two wings of gray hair protruded on either side of her florid face, but her eyes, sky-blue, were as innocent and untouched by experience as they must have been when she was ten. Were it not that she was a widow who had struggled fiercely to feed and clothe and put him through school and who was supporting him still, "until he got on his feet," she might have been a little girl that he had to take to town.

"It's all right, it's all right," he said. "Let's go." He opened the door himself and started down the walk to get her going. The sky was a dying violet and the houses stood out darkly against it, bulbous liver-colored monstrosities of a uniform ugliness though no two were alike. Since this had been a fashionable neighborhood forty years ago, his mother persisted in thinking they did well to have an apartment in it. Each house had a narrow collar of dirt around it in which sat, usually, a grubby child. Julian walked with his hands in his pockets, his head down and thrust forward and his eyes glazed with the determination to make himself completely numb during the time he would be sacrificed to her pleasure.

The door closed and he turned to find the dumpy figure, surmounted by the atrocious hat, coming toward him. "Well," she said, "you only live once and paying a little more for it, I at least won't meet myself coming and going."

"Some day I'll start making money," Julian said gloomily—he knew he never would—"and you can have one of those jokes whenever you take the fit." But first they would move. He visualized a place where the nearest neighbors would be three miles away on either side.

"I think you're doing fine," she said, drawing on her gloves. "You've only been out of school a year. Rome wasn't built in a day."

She was one of the few members of the Y reducing class who arrived in hat and gloves and who had a son who had been to college. "It takes time," she said, "and the world is in such a mess. This hat looked better on me than any of the others, though when she brought it out I said, 'Take that thing back. I wouldn't have it on my head,' and she said, 'Now wait till you see it on,' and when she put it on me, I said, 'We-ull,' and she said, 'If you ask me, that hat does something for you and you do something for the hat, and besides,' she said 'with that hat, you won't meet yourself coming and going.'"

Julian thought he could have stood his lot better if she had been selfish, if she had been an old hag who drank and screamed at him. He walked along, saturated in depression, as if in the midst of his martyrdom he had lost his faith. Catching sight of his long, hopeless, irritated face, she stopped suddenly with a grief-stricken look, and pulled back on his arm. "Wait on me," she said. "I'm going back to the house and take this thing off and tomorrow I'm going to return it. I was out of my head. I can pay the gas bill with that seven-fifty."

He caught her arm in a vicious grip. "You are not going to take it back," he said. "I like it."

"Well," she said, "I don't think I ought . . ."

"Shut up and enjoy it," he muttered, more depressed than ever.

"With the world in the mess it's in," she said, "it's a wonder we can enjoy anything. I tell you, the bottom rail is on the top."

Julian sighed.

"Of course," she said, "if you know who you are, you can go anywhere." She said this every time he took her to the reducing class. "Most of them in it are not our kind of people," she said, "but I can be gracious to anybody. I know who I am."

"They don't give a damn for your graciousness," Julian said savagely. "Knowing who you are is good for one generation only. You haven't the foggiest idea where you stand now or who you are."

She stopped and allowed her eyes to flash at him. "I most certainly do know who I am," she said, "and if you don't know who you are, I'm ashamed of you."

"Oh hell," Julian said.

"Your great-grandfather was a former governor of this state," she said. "Your grandfather was a prosperous landowner. Your grandmother was a God-high."

"Will you look around you," he said tensely, "and see where you are now?" and he swept his arm jerkily out to indicate the neighborhood, which the growing darkness at least made less dingy.

"You remain what you are," she said. "Your great-grandfather had a plantation and two hundred slaves."

"There are no more slaves," he said irritably.

"They were better off when they were," she said. He groaned to see that she was off on that topic. She rolled onto it every few days like a train on an open track. He knew every stop, every junction, every swamp along the way, and knew the exact point at which her conclusion would roll majestically into the station: "It's ridiculous. It's simply not realistic. They should rise, yes, but on their own side of the fence."

"Let's skip it," Julian said.

"The ones I feel sorry for," she said, "are the ones that are half white. They're tragic."

"Will you skip it?"

"Suppose we were half white. We would certainly have mixed feelings."

"I have mixed feelings now," he groaned.

"Well let's talk about something pleasant," she said. "I remember going to Grandpa's when I was a little girl. Then the house had double stairways that went up to what was really the second floor—all the cooking was done on the first. I used to like to stay down in the kitchen on account of the way the walls smelled. I would sit with my nose pressed against the plaster and take deep breaths. Actually the place belonged to the Godhighs but your grandfather Chestny paid the mortgage and saved it for them. They were in reduced circumstances," she said, "but reduced or not, they never forgot who they were."

"Doubtless that decayed mansion reminded them," Julian muttered. He never spoke of it without contempt or thought of it without longing. He had seen it once when he was a child before it had been sold. The double stairways had rotted and been torn down. Negroes were living in it. But it remained in his mind as his mother had known it. It appeared in his dreams regularly. He would stand on the wide porch, listening to the rustle of oak leaves, then wander through the high-ceilinged hall into the parlor that opened onto it and gaze at the worn rugs and faded draperies. It occurred to him that it was he, not she, who could have appreciated it. He preferred its threadbare elegance to anything he could name and it was because of it that all the neighborhoods they had lived in had been a torment to him—whereas she had hardly known the difference. She called her insensitivity "being adjustable."

"And I remember the old darky who was my nurse, Caroline. There was no better person in the world. I've always had a great respect for my colored friends," she said. "I'd do anything in the world for them and they'd . . ."

"Will you for God's sake get off that subject?" Julian said. When he got on a bus by himself, he made it a point to sit down beside a Negro, in reparation as it were for his mother's sins.

"You're mighty touchy tonight," she said. "Do you feel all right?"

"Yes I feel all right," he said. "Now lay off."

She pursed her lips. "Well, you certainly are in a vile humor," she observed. "I just won't speak to you at all."

They had reached the bus stop. There was no bus in sight and Julian, his hands still jammed in his pockets and his head thrust forward, scowled down the empty street. The frustration of having to wait on the bus as well as ride on it began to creep up his neck like a hot hand. The presence of his mother was borne in upon him as she gave a pained sigh. He looked at her bleakly. She was holding herself very erect under the preposterous hat, wearing it like a banner of her imaginary dignity. There was in him an evil urge to break her spirit. He suddenly unloosened his tie and pulled it off and put it in his pocket.

She stiffened. "Why must you look like *that* when you take me to town?" she said. "Why must you deliberately embarrass me?"

"If you'll never learn where you are," he said, "you can at least learn where I am."

"You look like a—thug," she said.

"Then I must be one," he murmured.

"I'll just go home," she said. "I will not bother you. If you can't do a little thing like that for me . . ."

Rolling his eyes upward, he put his tie back on. "Restored to my class," he muttered. He thrust his face toward her and hissed, "True culture is in the mind, the *mind*," he said, and tapped his head, "the mind."

"It's in the heart," she said, "and in how you do things and how you do things is because of who you *are*."

"Nobody in the damn bus cares who you are."

"I care who I am," she said icily.

The lighted bus appeared on top of the next hill and as it approached, they moved out into the street to meet it. He put his hand under her elbow and hoisted her up on the creaking step. She entered with a little smile, as if she were going into a drawing room where everyone had been waiting for her. While he put in the tokens, she sat down on one of the broad front seats for three which faced the aisle. A thin woman with protruding teeth and long yellow hair was sitting on the end of it. His mother moved up beside her and left room for Julian beside herself. He sat down and looked at the floor across the aisle where a pair of thin feet in red and white canvas sandals were planted.

His mother immediately began a general conversation meant to attract anyone who felt like talking. "Can it get any hotter?" she said and removed from her purse a folding fan, black with a Japanese scene on it, which she began to flutter before her.

"I reckon it might could," the woman with the protruding teeth said, "but I know for a fact my apartment couldn't get no hotter."

"It must get the afternoon sun," his mother said. She sat forward and looked up and down the bus. It was half filled. Everybody was white. "I see we have the bus to ourselves," she said. Julian cringed.

"For a change," said the woman across the aisle, the owner of the red and white canvas sandals. "I come on one the other day and they were thick as fleas—up front and all through."

"The world is in a mess everywhere," his mother said. "I don't know how we've let it get in this fix."

"What gets my goat is all those boys from good families stealing automobile tires," the woman with the protruding teeth said. "I told my boy, I said you may not be rich but you been raised right and if I ever catch you in any such mess, they can send you on to the reformatory. Be exactly where you belong."

"Training tells," his mother said. "Is your boy in high school?"

"Ninth grade," the woman said.

"My son just finished college last year. He wants to write but he's selling typewriters until he gets started," his mother said.

The woman leaned forward and peered at Julian. He threw her such a malevolent look that she subsided against the seat. On the floor across the aisle there was an abandoned newspaper. He got up and got it and opened it out in front of him. His mother discreetly continued the conversation in a lower tone but the woman across the aisle said in a loud voice, "Well that's nice. Selling typewriters is close to writing. He can go right from one to the other."

"I tell him," his mother said, "that Rome wasn't built in a day."

Behind the newspaper Julian was withdrawing into the inner compartment of his mind where he spent most of his time. This was a kind of mental bubble in which he established himself when he could not bear to be a part of what was going on around him. From it he could see out and judge but in it he was safe from any kind of penetration from without. It was the only place where he felt free of the general idiocy of his fellows. His mother had never entered it but from it he could see her with absolute clarity.

The old lady was clever enough and he thought that if she had started from any of the right premises, more might have been expected of her. She lived according to the laws of her own fantasy world, outside of which he had never seen her set foot. The law of it was to sacrifice herself for him after she had first created the necessity to do so by making a mess of things. If he had permitted her sacrifices, it was only because her lack of foresight had made them necessary. All of her life had been a struggle to act like a Chestny without the Chestny goods, and to give him everything she thought a Chestny ought to have; but since, said she, it was fun to struggle, why complain? And when you had won, as she had won, what fun to look back on the hard times! He could not forgive her that she had enjoyed the struggle and that she thought *she* had won.

What she meant when she said she had won was that she had brought him up successfully and had sent him to college and that he had turned out so well—good looking (her teeth had gone unfilled so that his could be straightened), intelligent (he realized he was too intelligent to be a success), and with a future ahead of him (there was of course no future ahead of him). She excused his gloominess on the grounds that he was still growing up and his radical ideas on his lack of practical experience. She said he didn't yet know a thing about "life," that he hadn't even entered the real world—when already he was as disenchanted with it as a man of fifty.

The further irony of all this was that in spite of her, he had turned out so well. In spite of going to only a third-rate college, he had, on his own initiative, come out with a first-rate education; in spite of growing up dominated by a small mind, he had ended up with a large one; in spite of all her foolish views, he was free of prejudice and unafraid to face facts. Most miraculous of all, instead of being blinded by love for her as she was for him, he had cut himself emotionally free of her and could see her with complete objectivity. He was not dominated by his mother.

The bus stopped with a sudden jerk and shook him from his meditation. A woman from the back lurched forward with little steps and barely escaped falling in his newspaper as she righted herself. She got off and a large Negro got on. Julian kept his paper lowered to watch. It gave him a certain satisfaction to see injustice in daily operation. It confirmed his view that with a few exceptions there was no one worth knowing within a radius of three hundred miles. The Negro was well dressed and carried a briefcase. He looked around and then sat down on the other end of the seat where the woman with the red and white canvas sandals was sitting. He immediately unfolded a newspaper and obscured himself behind it. Julian's mother's elbow at once prodded insistently into his rib. "Now you see why I won't ride on these buses by myself," she whispered.

The woman with the red and white canvas sandals had risen at the same time the Negro sat down and had gone further back in the bus and taken the seat of the woman who had got off. His mother leaned forward and cast her an approving look.

Julian rose, crossed the aisle, and sat down in the place of the woman with the canvas sandals. From this position, he looked serenely across at his mother. Her face had turned an angry red. He stared at her, making his eyes the eyes of a stranger. He felt his tension suddenly lift as if he had openly declared war on her.

He would have liked to get in conversation with the Negro and to talk with him about art or politics or any subject that would be above the comprehension of those around them, but the man remained entrenched behind his paper. He was either ignoring the change of seating or had never noticed it. There was no way for Julian to convey his sympathy.

His mother kept her eyes fixed reproachfully on his face. The woman with the protruding teeth was looking at him avidly as if he were a type of monster new to her.

"Do you have a light?" he asked the Negro.

Without looking away from his paper, the man reached in his pocket and handed him a packet of matches.

"Thanks," Julian said. For a moment he held the matches foolishly. A NO SMOKING sign looked down upon him from over the door. This alone would not have deterred him; he had no cigarettes. He had quit smoking some months before because he could not afford it. "Sorry," he muttered and handed back the matches. The Negro lowered the paper and gave him an annoyed look. He took the matches and raised the paper again.

His mother continued to gaze at him but she did not take advantage of his momentary discomfort. Her eyes retained their battered look. Her face seemed to be unnaturally red, as if her blood pressure had risen. Julian allowed no glimmer of sympathy to show on his face. Having got the advantage, he wanted desperately to keep it and carry it through. He would have liked to teach her a lesson that would last her a while, but there seemed no way to continue the point. The Negro refused to come out from behind his paper.

Julian folded his arms and looked stolidly before him, facing her but as if he did not see her, as if he had ceased to recognize her existence. He visualized a scene in which, the bus having reached their stop, he would remain in his seat and when she said, "Aren't you going to get off?" he would look at her as at a stranger who had rashly addressed him. The corner they got off on was usually deserted, but it was well lighted and it would not hurt her to walk by herself the four blocks to the Y. He decided to wait until the time came and then decide whether or not he would let her get off by herself. He would have to be at the Y at ten to bring her back, but he could leave her wondering if he was going to show up. There was no reason for her to think she could always depend on him.

He retired again into the high-ceilinged room sparsely settled with large pieces of antique furniture. His soul expanded momentarily but then he became aware of his mother across from him and the vision shriveled. He studied her coldly. Her feet in little pumps dangled like a child's and did not quite reach the floor. She was training on him an exaggerated look of reproach. He felt completely detached from her. At that moment he could with pleasure have slapped her as he would have slapped a particularly obnoxious child in his charge.

He began to imagine various unlikely ways by which he could teach her a lesson. He might make friends with some distinguished Negro professor or lawyer and bring him home to spend the evening. He would be entirely justified but her blood pressure would rise to 300. He could not push her to the extent of making her have a stroke, and moreover, he had never been successful at making any Negro friends. He had tried to strike up an acquaintance on the bus with some of the better types, with ones that looked like professors or ministers or lawyers. One morning he had sat down next to a distinguished-looking dark brown man who had answered his questions with a sonorous solemnity but who had turned out to be an undertaker. Another day he had sat down beside a cigar-smoking Negro with a diamond ring on his finger, but after a few stilted pleasantries, the Negro had rung the buzzer and risen, slipping two lottery tickets into Julian's hand as he climbed over him to leave.

He imagined his mother lying desperately ill and his being able to secure only a Negro doctor for her. He toyed with that idea for a few minutes and then dropped it for a momentary vision of himself participating as a sympathizer in a sit-in demonstration. This was possible but he did not linger with it. Instead, he approached the ultimate horror. He brought home a beautiful suspiciously Negroid woman. Prepare yourself, he said. There is nothing you can do about it. This is the woman I've chosen. She's intelligent, dignified, even good, and she's suffered and she hasn't thought it *fun*. Now persecute us, go ahead and persecute us. Drive her out of here, but remember, you're driving me too. His eyes were narrowed and through the indignation he had generated, he saw his mother across the aisle, purple-faced, shrunken to the dwarf-like proportions of her moral nature, sitting like a mummy beneath the ridiculous banner of her hat.

He was tilted out of his fantasy again as the bus stopped. The door opened with a sucking hiss and out of the dark a large, gaily dressed, sullenlooking colored woman got on with a little boy. The child, who might have been four, had on a short plaid suit and a Tyrolean hat with a blue feather in it. Julian hoped that he would sit down beside him and that the woman would push in beside his mother. He could think of no better arrangement.

As she waited for her tokens, the woman was surveying the seating possibilities—he hoped with the idea of sitting where she was least wanted. There was something familiar-looking about her but Julian could not place what it was. She was a giant of a woman. Her face was set not only to meet opposition but to seek it out. The downward tilt of her large lower lip was like a warning sign: DON'T TAMPER WITH ME. Her bulging figure was encased in a green crepe dress and her feet overflowed in red shoes. She had on a hideous hat. A purple velvet flap came down on one side of it and stood up on the other; the rest of it was green and looked like a cushion with the stuffing out. She carried a mammoth red pocketbook that bulged throughout as if it were stuffed with rocks.

To Julian's disappointment, the little boy climbed up on the empty seat beside his mother. His mother lumped all children, black and white, into the common category, "cute," and she thought little Negroes were on the whole cuter than little white children. She smiled at the little boy as he climbed on the seat.

Meanwhile the woman was bearing down upon the empty seat beside Julian. To his annoyance, she squeezed herself into it. He saw his mother's face change as the woman settled herself next to him and he realized with satisfaction that this was more objectionable to her than it was to him. Her face seemed almost gray and there was a look of dull recognition in her eyes, as if suddenly she had sickened at some awful confrontation. Julian saw that it was because she and the woman had, in a sense, swapped sons. Though his mother would not realize the symbolic significance of this, she would feel it. His amusement showed plainly on his face.

The woman next to him muttered something unintelligible to herself. He was conscious of a kind of bristling next to him, a muted growling like that of an angry cat. He could not see anything but the red pocketbook upright on the bulging green thighs. He visualized the woman as she had stood waiting for her tokens—the ponderous figure, rising from the red shoes upward over the solid hips, the mammoth bosom, the haughty face, to the green and purple hat.

His eyes widened.

The vision of the two hats, identical, broke upon him with the radiance of a brilliant sunrise. His face was suddenly lit with joy. He could not believe that Fate had thrust upon his mother such a lesson. He gave a loud chuckle so that she would look at him and see that he saw. She turned her eyes on him slowly. The blue in them seemed to have turned a bruised purple. For a moment he had an uncomfortable sense of her innocence, but it lasted only a second before principle rescued him. Justice entitled him to laugh. His grin hardened until it said to her as plainly as if he were saying aloud: Your punishment exactly fits your pettiness. This should teach you a permanent lesson.

Her eyes shifted to the woman. She seemed unable to bear looking at him and to find the woman preferable. He became conscious again of the bristling presence at his side. The woman was rumbling like a volcano about to become active. His mother's mouth began to twitch slightly at one corner. With a sinking heart, he saw incipient signs of recovery on her face and realized that this was going to strike her suddenly as funny and was going to be no lesson at all. She kept her eyes on the woman and an amused smile came over her face as if the woman were a monkey that had stolen her hat. The little Negro was looking up at her with large fascinated eyes. He had been trying to attract her attention for some time.

"Carver!" the woman said suddenly. "Come heah!"

When he saw that the spotlight was on him at last, Carver drew his feet up and turned himself toward Julian's mother and giggled.

"Carver!" the woman said. "You heah me? Come heah!"

Carver slid down from the seat but remained squatting with his back against the base of it, his head turned slyly around toward Julian's mother, who was smiling at him. The woman reached a hand across the aisle and snatched him to her. He righted himself and hung backwards on her knees, grinning at Julian's mother. "Isn't he cute?" Julian's mother said to the woman with the protruding teeth.

"I reckon he is," the woman said without conviction.

The Negress yanked him upright but he eased out of her grip and shot across the aisle and scrambled, giggling wildly, onto the seat beside his love.

"I think he likes me," Julian's mother said, and smiled at the woman. It was the smile she used when she was being particularly gracious to an inferior. Julian saw everything lost. The lesson had rolled off her like rain on a roof.

The woman stood up and yanked the little boy off the seat as if she were snatching him from contagion. Julian could feel the rage in her at having no weapon like his mother's smile. She gave the child a sharp slap across his leg. He howled once and then thrust his head into her stomach and kicked his feet against her shins. "Be-have," she said vehemently.

The bus stopped and the Negro who had been reading the newspaper got off. The woman moved over and set the little boy down with a thump between herself and Julian. She held him firmly by the knee. In a moment he put his hands in front of his face and peeped at Julian's mother through his fingers.

"I see yoooooooo!" she said and put her hand in front of her face and peeped at him.

The woman slapped his hand down. "Quit yo' foolishness," she said, "before I knock the living Jesus out of you!"

Julian was thankful that the next stop was theirs. He reached up and pulled the cord. The woman reached up and pulled it at the same time. Oh my God, he thought. He had the terrible intuition that when they got off the bus together, his mother would open her purse and give the little boy a nickel. The gesture would be as natural to her as breathing. The bus stopped and the woman got up and lunged to the front, dragging the child, who wished to stay on, after her. Julian and his mother got up and followed. As they neared the door, Julian tried to relieve her of her pocketbook.

"No," she murmured, "I want to give the little boy a nickel."

"No!" Julian hissed. "No!"

She smiled down at the child and opened her bag. The bus door opened and the woman picked him up by the arm and descended with him, hanging at her hip. Once in the street she set him down and shook him.

Julian's mother had to close her purse while she got down the bus step but as soon as her feet were on the ground, she opened it again and began to rummage inside. "I can't find but a penny," she whispered, "but it looks like a new one."

"Don't do it!" Julian said fiercely between his teeth. There was a streetlight on the corner and she hurried to get under it so that she could better see into her pocketbook. The woman was heading off rapidly down the street with the child still hanging backward on her hand.

"Oh little boy!" Julian's mother called and took a few quick steps and caught up with them just beyond the lamppost. "Here's a bright new penny for you," and she held out the coin, which shone bronze in the dim light.

The huge woman turned and for a moment stood, her shoulders lifted and her face frozen with frustrated rage, and stared at Julian's mother. Then all at once she seemed to explode like a piece of machinery that had been given one ounce of pressure too much. Julian saw the black fist swing out with the red pocketbook. He shut his eyes and cringed as he heard the woman shout, "He don't take nobody's pennies!" When he opened his eyes, the woman was disappearing down the street with the little boy staring wide-eyed over her shoulder. Julian's mother was sitting on the sidewalk.

"I told you not to do that," Julian said angrily. "I told you not to do that!"

He stood over her for a minute, gritting his teeth. Her legs were stretched out in front of her and her hat was on her lap. He squatted down and looked her in the face. It was totally expressionless. "You got exactly what you deserved," he said. "Now get up."

He picked up her pocketbook and put what had fallen out back in it. He picked the hat up off her lap. The penny caught his eye on the sidewalk and he picked that up and let it drop before her eyes into the purse. Then he stood up and leaned over and held his hands out to pull her up. She remained immobile. He sighed. Rising above them on either side were black apartment buildings, marked with irregular rectangles of light. At the end of the block a man came out of a door and walked off in the opposite direction. "All right," he said, "suppose somebody happens by and wants to know why you're sitting on the sidewalk?"

She took the hand and, breathing hard, pulled heavily up on it and then stood for a moment, swaying slightly as if the spots of light in the darkness were circling around her. Her eyes, shadowed and confused, finally settled on his face. He did not try to conceal his irritation. "I hope this teaches you a lesson," he said. She leaned forward and her eyes raked his face. She seemed trying to determine his identity. Then, as if she found nothing familiar about him, she started off with a headlong movement in the wrong direction.

"Aren't you going on to the Y?" he asked.

"Home," she muttered.

"Well, are we walking?"

For answer she kept going. Julian followed along, his hands behind him. He saw no reason to let the lesson she had had go without backing it up with an explanation of its meaning. She might as well be made to understand what had happened to her. "Don't think that was just an uppity Negro woman," he said. "That was the whole colored race which will no longer take your condescending pennies. That was your black double. She can wear the same hat as you, and to be sure," he added gratuitously (because he thought it was funny), "it looked better on her than it did on you. What all this means," he said, "is that the old world is gone. The old manners are obsolete and your graciousness is not worth a damn." He thought bitterly of the house that had been lost for him. "You aren't who you think you are," he said.

She continued to plow ahead, paying no attention to him. Her hair had come undone on one side. She dropped her pocketbook and took no notice. He stooped and picked it up and handed it to her but she did not take it.

"You needn't act as if the world had come to an end," he said, "because it hasn't. From now on you've got to live in a new world and face a few realities for a change. Buck up," he said, "it won't kill you."

She was breathing fast.

"Let's wait on the bus," he said.

"Home," she said thickly.

"I hate to see you behave like this," he said. "Just like a child. I should be able to expect more of you." He decided to stop where he was and make her stop and wait for a bus. "I'm not going any farther," he said, stopping. "We're going on the bus."

She continued to go on as if she had not heard him. He took a few steps and caught her arm and stopped her. He looked into her face and caught his breath. He was looking into a face he had never seen before. "Tell Grandpa to come get me," she said.

He stared, stricken.

"Tell Caroline to come get me," she said.

Stunned, he let her go and she lurched forward again, walking as if one leg were shorter than the other. A tide of darkness seemed to be sweeping her from him. "Mother!" he cried. "Darling, sweetheart, wait!" Crumpling, she fell to the pavement. He dashed forward and fell at her side, crying, "Mamma, Mamma!" He turned her over. Her face was fiercely distorted. One eye, large and staring, moved slightly to the left as if it had become unmoored. The other remained fixed on him, raked his face again, found nothing and closed.

"Wait here, wait here!" he cried and jumped up and began to run for help toward a cluster of lights he saw in the distance ahead of him. "Help, help!" he shouted, but his voice was thin, scarcely a thread of sound. The lights drifted farther away the faster he ran and his feet moved numbly as if they carried him nowhere. The tide of darkness seemed to sweep him back to her, postponing from moment to moment his entry into the world of guilt and sorrow.

Suggestions for Discussion

1. Trace the steps in the rising action of the story, noting shifts between internal and external action. Study the transitions from one narrative mode to another. How are they effected? What point of view is adopted? What is gained or lost by this device?

2. Characterize the son, distinguishing between his apparent self-image and the individual as you see him.

3. What is the central conflict? What details of setting define the conflict? How is it extended into a larger social area? Comment on the way in which each scene heightens the tension and prepares for the climax.

4. How is your impression of the mother's character created? What is your reaction to the Negro woman's striking of the mother, the son's behavior, and the resulting amnesia? Do you assume that the mother will die? Has the author prepared you for acceptance of the climax, or does it seem contrived? If so, why?

5. What is the central symbol of identity and status in the story? What symbolic elements are used in the description of scene?

6. Find examples of irony and relate them to the controlling purpose of the story.

7. Relate the title to the central theme(s) of the story.

Suggestions for Writing

1. Select one of the above questions for development.

2. The relationship between experience and insight is a central theme of the story. Support this statement by specific references.

3. Compare your view of personal identity with that of your mother and/or father.

William Maxwell

What He Was Like

William Maxwell, Jr. (b. 1908) has degrees from both the University of Illinois and Harvard University. After a brief stint as an English professor, he spent his entire professional career as a member of the editorial staff of The New Yorker. A writer as well as an editor, he has been the recipient of the American Writer's Award and a grant from the National Institute of Arts and Letters. Among other books, he has written Over by the River, and Other Stories (1977) and So Long, See You Tomorrow (1980).

He kept a diary, for his own pleasure. Because the days passed by so rapidly, and he found it interesting to go back and see how he had occupied his time, and with whom. He was aware that his remarks were sometimes far from kind, but the person they were about was never going to read them, so what difference did it make? The current diary was usually on his desk, the previous ones on a shelf in his clothes closet, where they were beginning to take up room.

His wife's uncle, in the bar of the Yale Club, said, "I am at the age of funerals." Now, thirty-five years later, it was his turn. In his address book the names of his three oldest friends had lines drawn through them. "Jack is dead," he wrote in his diary. "I didn't think that would happen. I thought he was immortal. . . . Louise is dead. In her sleep. . . . Richard has been dead for over a year and I still do not believe it. So impoverishing."

He himself got older. His wife got older. They advanced deeper into their seventies without any sense of large changes but only of one day's following another, and of the days being full, and pleasant, and worth recording. So he went on doing it. They all got put down in his diary, along with his feelings about old age, his fear of dying, his declining sexual powers, his envy of the children that he saw running down the street. To be able to run like that! He had to restrain himself from saying to young men in their thirties and forties, "You do appreciate, don't you, what you have?" In his diary he wrote, "If I had my life to live over again—but one doesn't. One goes forward instead, dragging a cart piled high with lost opportunities."

Though his wife had never felt the slightest desire to read his diary, she knew when he stopped leaving it around as carelessly as he did his opened mail. Moving the papers on his desk in order to dust it, she saw where he had hidden the current volume, was tempted to open it and see what it was he didn't want her to know, and then thought better of it and replaced the papers, exactly as they were before.

"To be able to do in your mind," he wrote, "what it is probably not a good idea to do in actuality is a convenience not always sufficiently appreciated." Though in his daily life he was as cheerful as a cricket, the diaries were more and more given over to dark thoughts, anger, resentment, indecencies, regrets, remorse. And now and then the simple joy in being alive. "If I stopped recognizing that I want things that it is not appropriate for me to want," he wrote, "wouldn't this inevitably lead to my not wanting anything at all—which as people get older is a risk that must be avoided at all costs?" He wrote, "Human beings are not like a clock that is wound up at birth and runs until the mainspring is fully unwound. They live because they want to. And when they stop wanting to, the first thing they know they are in a doctor's office being shown an X-ray that puts a different face on everything."

After he died, when the funeral had been got through, and after the number of telephone calls had diminished to a point where it was possible to attend to other things, his wife and daughter together disposed of the clothes in his closet. His daughter folded and put in a suit box an old, worn corduroy coat that she remembered the feel of when her father had rocked her as a child. His wife kept a blue-green sweater that she was used to seeing him in. As for the rest, he was a common size, and so his shirts and suits were easily disposed of to people who were in straitened circumstances and grateful for a warm overcoat, a dark suit, a pair of pigskin gloves. His shoes were something else again, and his wife dropped them into the Goodwill box, hoping that somebody would turn up who wore size-9A shoes, though it didn't seem very likely. Then the two women were faced with the locked filing cabinet in his study, which contained business papers that they turned over to the executor, and most of the twenty-seven volumes of his diary.

"Those I don't know what to do with, exactly," his wife said. "They're private and he didn't mean anybody to read them."

"Did he say so?" his daughter asked.

"No."

"Then how do you know he didn't want anybody to read them?"

"I just know."

"You're not curious?"

"I was married to your father for forty-six years and I know what he was like."

Which could only mean, the younger woman decided, that her mother had, at some time or other, looked into them. But she loved her father, and felt a very real desire to know what he was like as a person and not just as a father. So she put one of the diaries aside and took it home with her.

When her husband got home from his office that night, her eyes were red from weeping. First he made her tell him what the trouble was, and then he went out to the kitchen and made a drink for each of them, and then he sat down beside her on the sofa. Holding his free hand, she began to tell him about the shock of reading the diary.

"He wasn't the person I thought he was. He had all sorts of secret desires. A lot of it is very dirty. And some of it is more unkind than I would have believed possible. And just not like him—except that it *was* him. It makes me feel I can never trust anybody ever again."

"Not even me?" her husband said soberly.

"Least of all, you."

They sat in silence for a while. And then he said, "I was more comfortable with him than I was with my own father. And I think, though I could be mistaken, that he liked me."

"Of course he liked you. He often said so."

"So far as his life is concerned, if you were looking for a model to—"

"I don't see how you can say that."

"I do, actually. In his place, though, I think I would have left instructions that the diaries were to be disposed of unread. . . . We could burn it. Burn all twenty-seven volumes."

"No."

"Then let's put it back," he said, reaching for the diary. "Put it back in the locked file where your mother found it."

"And leave it there forever?"

"For a good long while. He may have been looking past our shoulders. It would be like him. If we have a son who doesn't seem to be very much like you or me, or like anybody in your family or mine, we can give him the key to the file—"

"If I had a son, the *last* thing in the world I'd want would be for him to read this filth!"

"—and tell him he can read them if he wants to. And if he doesn't want to, he can decide what should be done with them. It might be a help to him to know that there was somebody two generations back who wasn't in every respect what he seemed to be."

"Who was, in fact—"

"Since he didn't know your father, he won't be shocked and upset. You stay right where you are while I make us another of these."

But she didn't. She didn't want to be separated from him, even for the length of time it would take him to go out to the kitchen and come back with a Margarita suspended from the fingers of each hand, lest in that brief interval he turn into a stranger.

Suggestions for Discussion

1. What does the father mean when he writes, "To be able to do in your mind what it is probably not a good idea to do in actuality is a convenience not always sufficiently appreciated"?

2. How well can we truly know another person?

3. What does it mean when the father stops leaving the diary lying around? When he does not destroy it before his death?

4. How much of your own most private self—that is, what you might reveal in a diary—do you actually share with another person?

Suggestions for Writing

1. Write about an incident in which someone is revealed to be very different from the way you had assumed that person to be.

2. Maxwell says, "One goes forward . . . dragging a cart piled high with lost opportunities." Write about some of the "lost opportunities" one might find in your cart.

Delmore Schwartz

In Dreams Begin Responsibilities

Delmore Schwartz (1913–1966), American poet and critic, was a teacher of English at Harvard University from 1940 to 1947. He is best known for In Dreams Begin Responsibilities (1938), which consists of a story, poems, and verse-drama, and for a collection of poems, Summer Knowledge: New and Selected Poems, 1938–1958 (1959). He was an editor of Partisan Review and poetry editor of The New Republic. The six sections of the narrative "In Dreams Begin Responsibilities" follow a logical time sequence determined by the movie framework of the son's dream. This convention permits the narrator-son to imagine events in the premarital lives of his parents and enter into their emotional states in scenes filtered through his own perceptions and feelings.

I

I think it is the year 1909. I feel as if I were in a moving-picture theater, the long arm of light crossing the darkness and spinning, my eyes fixed upon the screen. It is a silent picture, as if an old Biograph one, in which the actors are dressed in ridiculously old-fashioned clothes, and one flash succeeds another with sudden jumps, and the actors, too, seem to jump about, walking too fast. The shots are full of rays and dots, as if it had been raining when the picture was photographed. The light is bad.

It is Sunday afternoon, June 12th, 1909, and my father is walking down the quiet streets of Brooklyn on his way to visit my mother. His clothes are newly pressed, and his tie is too tight in his high collar. He jingles the coins in his pocket, thinking of the witty things he will say. I feel as if I had by now relaxed entirely in the soft darkness of the theater; the organist peals out the obvious approximate emotions on which the audience rocks unknowingly. I am anonymous. I have forgotten myself: it is always so when one goes to a movie, it is, as they say, a drug.

My father walks from street to street of trees, lawns and houses, once in a while coming to an avenue on which a street-car skates and gnaws, progressing slowly. The motorman, who has a handle-bar mustache, helps a young lady wearing a hat like a feathered bowl onto the car. He leisurely makes change and rings his bell as the passengers mount the car. It is obviously Sunday, for everyone is wearing Sunday clothes and the street-car's noises emphasize the quiet of the holiday (Brooklyn is said to be the city of churches). The shops are closed and their shades drawn but for an occasional stationery store or drugstore with great green balls in the window.

My father has chosen to take this long walk because he likes to walk and think. He thinks about himself in the future and so arrives at the place he is to visit in a mild state of exaltation. He pays no attention to the houses he is passing, in which the Sunday dinner is being eaten, nor to the many trees which line each street, now coming to their full green and the time when they will enclose the whole street in leafy shadow. An occasional carriage passes, the horses' hooves falling like stones in the quiet afternoon, and once in a while an automobile, looking like an enormous upholstered sofa, puffs and passes.

My father thinks of my mother, of how lady-like she is, and of the pride which will be his when he introduces her to his family. They are not yet engaged and he is not yet sure that he loves my mother, so that, once in a while, he becomes panicky about the bond already established. But then he reassures himself by thinking of the big men he admires who are married: William Randolph Hearst and William Howard Taft, who has just become the President of the United States.

My father arrives at my mother's house. He has come too early and so is suddenly embarrassed. My aunt, my mother's younger sister, answers the loud bell with her napkin in her hand, for the family is still at dinner. As my father enters, my grandfather rises from the table and shakes hands with him. My mother has run upstairs to tidy herself. My grandmother asks my father if he has had his dinner and tells him that my mother will be down soon. My grandfather opens the conversation by remarking about the mild June weather. My father sits uncomfortably near the table, holding his hat in his hand. My grandmother tells my aunt to take my father's hat. My uncle, twelve years old, runs into the house, his hair tousled. He shouts a greeting to my father, who has often given him nickels, and then runs upstairs, as my grandmother shouts after him. It is evident that the respect in which my father is held in this house is tempered by a good deal of mirth. He is impressive, but also very awkward.

II

Finally my mother comes downstairs and my father, being at the moment engaged in conversation with my grandfather, is made uneasy by her entrance, for he does not know whether to greet my mother or to continue the conversation. He gets up from his chair clumsily and says "Hello" gruffly. My grandfather watches this, examining their congruence, such as it is, with a critical eye, and meanwhile rubbing his bearded cheek roughly, as he always does when he reasons. He is worried; he is afraid that my father will not make a good husband for his oldest daughter. At this point something happens to the film, just as my father says something funny to my mother: I am awakened to myself and my unhappiness just as my interest has become most intense. The audience begins to clap impatiently. Then the trouble is attended to, but the film has been returned to a portion just shown, and once more I see my grandfather rubbing his bearded cheek, pondering my father's character. It is difficult to get back into the picture once more and forget myself, but as my mother giggles at my father's words, the darkness drowns me.

My father and mother depart from the house, my father shaking hands with my grandfather once more, out of some unknown uneasiness. I stir uneasily also, slouched in the hard chair of the theater. Where is the older uncle, my mother's older brother? He is studying in his bedroom upstairs, studying for his final examinations at the College of the City of New York, having been dead of double pneumonia for the last twenty-one years. My mother and father walk down the same quiet streets once more. My mother is holding my father's arm and telling him of the novel she has been reading and my father utters judgments of the characters as the plot is made clear to him. This is a habit which he very much enjoys, for he feels the utmost superiority and confidence when he is approving or condemning the behavior of other people. At times he feels moved to utter a brief "Ugh" whenever the story becomes what he would call sugary. This tribute is the assertion of his manliness. My mother feels satisfied by the interest she has awakened; and she is showing my father how intelligent she is and how interesting.

They reach the avenue, and the street-car leisurely arrives. They are going to Coney Island this afternoon, although my mother really considers such pleasures inferior. She has made up her mind to indulge only in a walk on the boardwalk and a pleasant dinner, avoiding the riotous amusements as being beneath the dignity of so dignified a couple.

My father tells my mother how much money he has made in the week just past, exaggerating an amount which need not have been exaggerated. But my father has always felt that actualities somehow fall short, no matter how fine they are. Suddenly I begin to weep. The determined old lady who sits next to me in the theater is annoyed and looks at me with an angry face, and being intimidated, I stop. I drag out my handkerchief and dry my face, licking the drop which has fallen near my lips. Meanwhile I have missed something, for here are my father and mother alighting from the street-car at the last stop, Coney Island.

III

They walk toward the boardwalk and my mother commands my father to inhale the pungent air from the sea. They both breathe in deeply, both of them laughing as they do so. They have in common a great interest in health, although my father is strong and husky, and my mother is frail. They are both full of theories about what is good to eat and not good to eat, and sometimes have heated discussions about it, the whole matter ending in my father's announcement, made with a scornful bluster, that you have to die sooner or later anyway. On the boardwalk's flagpole, the American flag is pulsing in an intermittent wind from the sea.

My father and mother go to the rail of the boardwalk and look down on the beach where a good many bathers are casually walking about. A few are in the surf. A peanut whistle pierces the air with its pleasant and active whine, and my father goes to buy peanuts. My mother remains at the rail and stares at the ocean. The ocean seems merry to her; it pointedly sparkles and again and again the pony waves are released. She notices the children digging in the wet sand, and the bathing costumes of the girls who are her own age. My father returns with the peanuts. Overhead the sun's lightning strikes and strikes, but neither of them are at all aware of it. The boardwalk is full of people dressed in their Sunday clothes and casually strolling. The tide does not reach as far as the boardwalk, and the strollers would feel no danger if it did. My father and mother lean on the rail of the boardwalk and absently stare at the ocean. The ocean is becoming rough; the waves come in slowly, tugging strength from far back. The moment before they somersault, the moment when they arch their backs so beautifully, showing white veins in the green and black, that moment is intolerable. They finally crack, dashing fiercely upon the sand, actually driving, full force downward, against it, bouncing upward and forward, and at last petering out into a small stream of bubbles which slides up the beach and then is recalled. The sun overhead does not disturb my father and my mother. They gaze idly at the ocean, scarcely interested in its harshness. But I stare at the terrible sun which breaks up sight, and the fatal merciless passionate ocean. I forget my parents. I stare fascinated, and finally, shocked by their indifference, I burst out weeping once more. The old lady next to me pats my shoulder and says: "There, there, young man, all of this is only a movie, only a movie," but I look up once more at the terrifying sun and the terrifying ocean, and being unable to control my tears I get up and go to the men's room, stumbling over the feet of the other people seated in my row.

IV

When I return, feeling as if I had just awakened in the morning sick for lack of sleep, several hours have apparently passed and my parents are riding on the merry-go-round. My father is on a black horse, my mother on a white one, and they seem to be making an eternal circuit for the single purpose of snatching the nickel rings which are attached to an arm of one of the posts. A hand organ is playing; it is inseparable from the ceaseless circling of the merry-go-round.

For a moment it seems that they will never stop, and I feel as if I were looking down from the fiftieth story of a building. But at length they do get off; even the hand organ has ceased for a moment. There is a sudden and sweet stillness, as if the achievement of so much motion. My mother has acquired only two rings, my father, however, ten of them, although it was my mother who really wanted them.

They walk on along the boardwalk as the afternoon descends by imperceptible degrees into the incredible violet of dusk. Everything fades into a relaxed glow, even the ceaseless murmuring from the beach. They look for a place to have dinner. My father suggests the best restaurant on the boardwalk and my mother demurs, according to her principles of economy and housewifeliness.

However they do go to the best place, asking for a table near the window so that they can look out upon the boardwalk and the mobile ocean. My father feels omnipotent as he places a quarter in the waiter's hand in asking for a table. The place is crowded and here too there is music, this time from a kind of string trio. My father orders with a fine confidence.

As their dinner goes on, my father tells of his plans for the future and my mother shows with expressive face how interested she is, and how impressed. My father becomes exultant, lifted up by the waltz that is being played and his own future begins to intoxicate him. My father tells my mother that he is going to expand his business, for there is a great deal of money to be made. He wants to settle down. After all, he is twenty-nine, he has lived by himself since his thirteenth year, he is making more and more money, and he is envious of his friends when he visits them in the security of their homes, surrounded, it seems, by the calm domestic pleasures, and by delightful children, and then as the waltz reaches the moment when the dancers all swing madly, then, then with awful daring, then he asks my mother to marry him, although awkwardly enough and puzzled as to how he had arrived at the question, and she, to make the whole business worse, begins to cry, and my father looks nervously about, not knowing at all what to do now, and my mother says: "It's all I've wanted from the first moment I saw you," sobbing, and he finds all of this very difficult, scarcely to his taste, scarcely as he thought it would be, on his long walks over Brooklyn Bridge in the revery of a fine cigar, and it was then, at that point, that I stood up in the theater and shouted: "Don't do it! It's not too late to change your minds, both of you. Nothing good will come of it, only remorse, hatred, scandal, and two children whose characters are monstrous." The whole audience turned to look at me, annoyed, the usher came hurrying down the aisle flashing his searchlight, and the old lady next to me tugged me down into my seat, saying: "Be quiet. You'll be put out, and you paid thirty-five cents to come in." And so I shut my eyes because I could not bear to see what was happening. I sat there quietly.

<hr>

V

But after a while I begin to take brief glimpses and at length I watch again with thirsty interest, like a child who tries to maintain his sulk when he is offered the bribe of candy. My parents are now having their picture taken in a photographer's booth along the boardwalk. The place is shadowed in the mauve light which is apparently necessary. The camera is set to the side on its tripod and looks like a Martian man. The photographer is instructing my parents in how to pose. My father has his arm over my mother's shoulder, and both of them smile emphatically. The photographer brings my mother a bouquet of flowers to hold in her hand, but she holds it at the wrong angle. Then the photographer covers himself with the black cloth which drapes the camera and all that one sees of him is one protruding arm and his hand with which he holds tightly to the rubber ball which he squeezes when the picture is taken. But he is not satisfied with their appearance. He feels that somehow there is something wrong in their pose. Again and again he comes out from his hiding place with new directions. Each suggestion merely makes matters worse. My father is becoming impatient. They try a seated pose. The photographer explains that he has his pride, he wants to make beautiful pictures, he is not merely interested in all of this for the money. My father says: "Hurry up, will you? We haven't got all night." But the photographer only scurries about apologetically, issuing new directions. The photographer charms me, and I approve of him with all my heart, for I know exactly how he feels, and as he criticizes each revised pose according to some obscure idea of rightness, I become quite hopeful. But then my father says angrily: "Come on, you've had enough time, we're not going to wait any longer." And the photographer, sighing unhappily, goes back into the black covering, and holds out his hand, saying: "One, two, three, Now!", and the picture is taken, with my father's smile turned to a grimace and my mother's bright and false. It takes a few minutes for the picture to be developed and as my parents sit in the curious light they become depressed.

VI

They have passed a fortune-teller's booth and my mother wishes to go in, but my father does not. They begin to argue about it. My mother becomes stubborn, my father once more impatient. What my father would like to do now is walk off and leave my mother there, but he knows that that would never do. My mother refuses to budge. She is near tears, but she feels an uncontrollable desire to hear what the palm-reader will say. My father consents angrily and they both go into the booth which is, in a way, like the photographer's, since it is draped in black cloth and its light is colored and shadowed. The place is too warm, and my father keeps saying that this is all nonsense, pointing to the crystal ball on the table. The fortune-teller, a short, fat woman garbed in robes supposedly exotic, comes into the room and greets them, speaking with an accent, but suddenly my father feels that the whole thing is intolerable; he tugs at my mother's arm but my mother refuses to budge. And then, in terrible anger, my father lets go of my mother's arm and strides out, leaving my mother stunned. She makes a movement as if to go after him, but the fortune-teller holds her and begs her not to do so, and I in my seat in the darkness am shocked and horrified. I feel as if I were walking a tight-rope one hundred feet over a circus audience and suddenly the rope is showing signs of breaking, and I get up from my seat and begin to shout once more the first words I can think of to communicate my terrible fear, and once more the usher comes hurrying down the aisle flashing his searchlight, and the old lady pleads with me, and the shocked audience has turned to stare at me, and I keep shouting: "What are they doing? Don't they know what they are doing? Why doesn't my mother go after my father and beg him not to be angry? If she does not do that, what will she do? Doesn't my father know what he is doing?" But the usher has seized my arm, and is dragging me away, and as he does so, he says: "What are *you* doing? Don't you know you can't do things like this, you can't do whatever you want to do, even if other people aren't about? You will be sorry if you do not do what you should do. You can't carry on like this, it is not right, you will find that out soon enough, everything you do matters too much," and as he said that, dragging me through the lobby of the theater, into the cold light, I woke up into the bleak winter morning of my twenty-first birthday, the window-sill shining with its lip of snow, and the morning already begun.

Suggestions for Discussion

1. Trace the development of the narrative in the six sections that follow the time sequence of the movie framework of the son's dream. How does the use of the son as narrator provide a double vision?

2. Relate the title to the action and theme of the story.

3. Describe the son's emotional state. How does it relate to the events of each episode?

4. Analyze the relationship of the parents to each other and that of the son to the parents.

5. Is there a resolution to the conflict? What do you assume will be the son's future?

6. Relate the following images to the theme of the story: the movie audience, the usher, the old lady, the Coney Island scene, the turbulent ocean, the photographer, the fortune teller.

Suggestion for Writing

Draw a portrait of your parents by means of an imaginary dialogue or a narrative.

Tillie Olsen

I Stand Here Ironing

Tillie Olsen (b. 1913) was born in Omaha, Nebraska, but has lived most of her adult life in the San Francisco Bay Area. She worked for a time in manual and clerical jobs but in later years received a number of literary awards: a Stanford University Creative Writing Fellowship, a Ford Foundation grant in literature, and a Radcliffe Institute for Independent Study Fellowship. She is best known for her collection of stories, *Tell Me a Riddle* (1956), from which this story was selected, and *Silences* (1979). The tension of the story lies in the writer's conception of the distance between what might have been and what is.

I stand here ironing, and what you asked me moves tormented back and forth with the iron.

"I wish you would manage the time to come in and talk with me about your daughter. I'm sure you can help me understand her. She's a youngster who needs help and whom I'm deeply interested in helping."

"Who needs help." . . . . Even if I came, what good would it do? You think because I am her mother I have a key, or that in some way you could use me as a key? She has lived for nineteen years. There is all that life that has happened outside of me, beyond me.

And when is there time to remember, to sift, to weigh, to estimate, to total? I will start and there will be an interruption and I will have to gather it all together again. Or I will become engulfed with all I did or did not do, with what should have been and what cannot be helped.

She was a beautiful baby. The first and only one of our five that was beautiful at birth. You do not guess how new and uneasy her tenancy in her now-loveliness. You did not know her all those years she was thought homely, or see her poring over her baby pictures, making me tell her over and over how beautiful she had been—and would be, I would tell her—and was now, to the seeing eye. But the seeing eyes were few or nonexistent. Including mine.

I nursed her. They feel that's important nowadays. I nursed all the children, but with her, with all the fierce rigidity of first motherhood, I did like the books then said. Though her cries battered me to trembling and my breasts ached with swollenness, I waited till the clock decreed.

Why do I put that first? I do not even know if it matters, or if it explains anything.

She was a beautiful baby. She blew shining bubbles of sound. She loved motion, loved light, loved color and music and textures. She would lie on the floor in her blue overalls patting the surface so hard in ecstasy her hands and feet would blur. She was a miracle to me, but when she was eight months old I had to leave her daytimes with the woman downstairs to whom she was no miracle at all, for I worked or looked for work and for Emily's father, who "could no longer endure" (he wrote in his good-bye note) "sharing want with us."

I was nineteen. It was the pre-relief, pre-WPA world of the depression. I would start running as soon as I got off the streetcar, running up the stairs, the place smelling sour, and awake or asleep to startle awake, when she saw me she would break into a clogged weeping that could not be comforted, a weeping I can hear yet.

After a while I found a job hashing at night so I could be with her days, and it was better. But it came to where I had to bring her to this family and leave her.

It took a long time to raise the money for her fare back. Then she got chicken pox and I had to wait longer. When she finally came, I hardly knew her, walking quick and nervous like her father, looking like her father, thin, and dressed in a shoddy red that yellowed her skin and glared at the pockmarks. All the baby loveliness gone.

She was two. Old enough for nursery school they said, and I did not know then what I know now—the fatigue of the long day, and the lacerations of group life in the kinds of nurseries that are only parking places for children.

Except that it would have made no difference if I had known. It was the only place there was. It was the only way we could be together, the only way I could hold a job.

And even without knowing, I knew. I knew the teacher that was evil because all these years it has curdled into my memory, the little boy hunched in the corner, her rasp, "why aren't you outside, because Alvin hits you? that's no reason, go out, scaredy." I knew Emily hated it even if she did not clutch and implore "don't go Mommy" like the other children, mornings.

She always had a reason why we should stay home. Momma, you look sick. Momma, I feel sick. Momma, the teachers aren't there today, they're sick. Momma, we can't go, there was a fire there last night. Momma, it's a holiday today, no school, they told me.

But never a direct protest, never rebellion. I think of our others in their three-, four-year-oldness—the explosions, the tempers, the denunciations, the demands—and I feel suddenly ill. I put the iron down. What in me demanded that goodness in her? And what was the cost, the cost to her of such goodness?

The old man living in the back once said in his gentle way: "You should smile at Emily more when you look at her." What *was* in my face when I looked at her? I loved her. There were all the acts of love.

It was only with the others I remembered what he said, and it was the face of joy, and not of care or tightness or worry I turned to them—too late for Emily. She does not smile easily, let alone almost always as her brothers and sisters do. Her face is closed and sombre, but when she wants, how fluid. You must have seen it in her pantomimes, you spoke of her rare gift for comedy on the stage that rouses a laughter out of the audience so dear they applaud and applaud and do not want to let her go.

Where does it come from, that comedy? There was none of it in her when she came back to me that second time, after I had had to send her away again. She had a new daddy now to learn to love, and I think perhaps it was a better time.

Except when we left her alone nights, telling ourselves she was old enough.

"Can't you go some other time, Mommy, like tomorrow?" she would ask. "Will it be just a little while you'll be gone? Do you promise?"

The time we came back, the front door open, the clock on the floor in the hall. She rigid awake. "It wasn't just a little while. I didn't cry. Three times I called you, just three times, and then I ran downstairs to open the door so you could come faster. The clock talked loud. I threw it away, it scared me what it talked."

She said the clock talked loud again that night I went to the hospital to have Susan. She was delirious with the fever that comes before red measles, but she was fully conscious all the week I was gone and the week after we were home when she could not come near the new baby or me.

She did not get well. She stayed skeleton thin, not wanting to eat, and night after night she had nightmares. She would call for me, and I would rouse from exhaustion to sleepily call back: "You're all right, darling, go to sleep, it's just a dream," and if she still called, in a sterner voice, "now go to sleep, Emily, there's nothing to hurt you." Twice, only twice, when I had to get up for Susan anyhow, I went in to sit with her.

Now when it is too late (as if she would let me hold and comfort her like I do the others) I get up and go to her at once at her moan or restless stirring. "Are you awake, Emily? Can I get you something?" And the answer is always the same: "No, I'm all right, go back to sleep, Mother."

They persuaded me at the clinic to send her away to a convalescent home in the country where "she can have the kind of food and care you can't manage for her, and you'll be free to concentrate on the new baby." They still send children to that place. I see pictures on the society page of sleek young women planning affairs to raise money for it, or dancing at the affairs, or decorating Easter eggs or filling Christmas stockings for the children.

They never have a picture of the children so I do not know if the girls still wear those gigantic red bows and the ravaged looks on the every other Sunday when parents can come to visit "unless otherwise notified"—as we were notified the first six weeks.

Oh it is a handsome place, green lawns and tall trees and fluted flower beds. High up on the balconies of each cottage the children stand, the girls in their red bows and white dresses, the boys in white suits and giant red ties. The parents stand below shrieking up to be heard and the children shriek down to be heard, and between them the invisible wall "Not To Be Contaminated by Parental Germs or Physical Affection."

There was a tiny girl who always stood hand in hand with Emily. Her parents never came. One visit she was gone. "They moved her to Rose Cottage," Emily shouted in explanation. "They don't like you to love anybody here."

She wrote once a week, the labored writing of a seven-year-old. "I am fine. How is the baby. If I write my leter nicly I will have a star. Love" There never was a star. We wrote every other day, letters she could never hold or keep but only hear read—once. "We simply do not have room for children to keep any personal possessions," they patiently explained when we pieced one Sunday's shrieking together to plead how much it would mean to Emily, who loved so to keep things, to be allowed to keep her letters and cards.

Each visit she looked frailer. "She isn't eating," they told us.

(They had runny eggs for breakfast or mush with lumps, Emily said later, I'd hold it in my mouth and not swallow. Nothing ever tasted good, just when they had chicken.)

It took us eight months to get her released home, and only the fact that she gained back so little of her seven lost pounds convinced the social worker.

I used to try to hold and love her after she came back, but her body would stay stiff, and after a while she'd push away. She ate little. Food sickened her, and I think much of life too. Oh she had physical lightness and brightness, twinkling by on skates, bouncing like a ball up and down up and down over the jump rope, skimming over the hill; but these were momentary.

She fretted about her appearance, thin and dark and foreign-looking at a time when every little girl was supposed to look or thought she should look a chubby blonde replica of Shirley Temple. The doorbell sometimes rang for her, but no one seemed to come and play in the house or be a best friend. Maybe because we moved so much.

There was a boy she loved painfully through two school semesters. Months later she told me how she had taken pennies from my purse to buy him candy. "Licorice was his favorite and I brought him some every day, but he still liked Jennifer better'n me. Why, Mommy?" The kind of question for which there is no answer.

School was a worry to her. She was not glib or quick in a world where glibness and quickness were easily confused with ability to learn. To her overworked and exasperated teachers she was an overconscientious "slow learner" who kept trying to catch up and was absent entirely too often.

I let her be absent, though sometimes the illness was imaginary. How different from my now-strictness about attendance with the others. I wasn't working. We had a new baby, I was home anyhow. Sometimes, after Susan grew old enough, I would keep her home from school, too, to have them all together.

Mostly Emily had asthma, and her breathing, harsh and labored, would fill the house with a curiously tranquil sound. I would bring the two old dresser mirrors and her boxes of collections to her bed. She would select beads and single earrings, bottle tops and shells, dried flowers and pebbles, old post-cards and scraps, all sorts of oddments; then she and Susan would play King-dom, setting up landscapes and furniture, peopling them with action.

Those were the only times of peaceful companionship between her and Susan. I have edged away from it, that poisonous feeling between them, that terrible balancing of hurts and needs I had to do between the two, and did so badly, those earlier years.

Oh there are conflicts between the others too, each one human, needing, demanding, hurting, taking—but only between Emily and Susan, no, Emily toward Susan that corroding resentment. It seems so obvious on the surface, yet it is not obvious. Susan, the second child, Susan, golden- and curly-haired and chubby, quick and articulate and assured, everything in appear-ance and manner Emily was not; Susan, not able to resist Emily's precious things, losing or sometimes clumsily breaking them; Susan telling jokes and riddles to company for applause while Emily sat silent (to say to me later: that was *my* riddle, Mother, I told it to Susan); Susan, who for all the five years' difference in age was just a year behind Emily in developing physically.

I am glad for that slow physical development that widened the difference between her and her contemporaries, though she suffered over it. She was too vulnerable for that terrible world of youthful competition, of preening and parading, of constant measuring of yourself against every other, of envy, "If I had that copper hair," "If I had that skin. . . ." She tormented herself enough about not looking like the others, there was enough of the unsure-ness, the having to be conscious of words before you speak, the constant caring—what are they thinking of me? without having it all magnified by the merciless physical drives.

Ronnie is calling. He is wet and I change him. It is rare there is such a cry now. That time of motherhood is almost behind me when the ear is not one's own but must always be racked and listening for the child cry, the child call. We sit for a while and I hold him, looking out over the city spread in charcoal with its soft aisles of light. "*Shoogily*," he breathes and curls closer. I carry him back to bed, asleep. *Shoogily*. A funny word, a family word, inherited from Emily, invented by her to say: *comfort*.

In this and other ways she leaves her seal, I say aloud. And startle at my saying it. What do I mean? What did I start to gather together, to try and make coherent? I was at the terrible, growing years. War years. I do not remember them well. I was working, there were four smaller ones now, there was not time for her. She had to help be a mother, and housekeeper, and shopper. She had to set her seal. Mornings of crisis and near hysteria trying to get lunches packed, hair combed, coats and shoes found, everyone to school or Child Care on time, the baby ready for transportation. And al-ways the paper scribbled on by a smaller one, the book looked at by Susan then mislaid, the homework not done. Running out to that huge school where she was one, she was lost, she was a drop; suffering over the unpreparedness, stammering and unsure of her classes.

There was so little time left at night after the kids were bedded down. She would struggle over books, always eating (it was in those years she developed her enormous appetite that is legendary in our family) and I would be ironing, or preparing food for the next day, or writing V-mail to Bill, or tending the baby. Sometimes, to make me laugh, or out of her despair, she would imitate happenings or types at school.

I think I said once: "Why don't you do something like this in the school amateur show?" One morning she phoned me at work, hardly understandable through the weeping: "Mother, I did it. I won, I won; they gave me first prize; they clapped and clapped and wouldn't let me go."

Now suddenly she was Somebody, and as imprisoned in her difference as she had been in anonymity.

She began to be asked to perform at other high schools, even in colleges, then at city and statewide affairs. The first one we went to, I only recognized her that first moment when thin, shy, she almost drowned herself into the curtains. Then: Was this Emily? The control, the command, the convulsing and deadly clowning, the spell, then the roaring, stamping audience, unwilling to let this rare and precious laughter out of their lives.

Afterwards: You ought to do something about her with a gift like that—but without money or knowing how, what does one do? We have left it all to her, and the gift has as often eddied inside, clogged and clotted, as been used and growing.

She is coming. She runs up the stairs two at a time with her light graceful step, and I know she is happy tonight. Whatever it was that occasioned your call did not happen today.

"Aren't you ever going to finish the ironing, Mother? Whistler painted his mother in a rocker. I'd have to paint mine standing over an ironing board." This is one of her communicative nights and she tells me everything and nothing as she fixes herself a plate of food out of the icebox.

She is so lovely. Why did you want me to come in at all? Why were you concerned? She will find her way.

She starts up the stairs to bed. "Don't get me up with the rest in the morning." "But I thought you were having midterms." "Oh, those," she comes back in, kisses me, and says quite lightly, "in a couple of years when we'll all be atom-dead they won't matter a bit."

She has said it before. She *believes* it. But because I have been dredging the past, and all that compounds a human being is so heavy and meaningful in me, I cannot endure it tonight.

I will never total it all. I will never come in to say: She was a child seldom smiled at. Her father left me before she was a year old. I had to work her first six years when there was work, or I sent her home and to his relatives. There were years she had care she hated. She was dark and thin and foreign-looking in a world where the prestige went to blondeness and curly hair and dimples, she was slow where glibness was prized. She was a child of anxious, not proud, love. We were poor and could not afford for her the soil of easy growth. I was a young mother, I was a distracted mother. There were the other children pushing up, demanding. Her younger sister seemed all that she was not. There were years she did not want me to touch her. She kept too much in herself, her life was such she had to keep too much in herself. My wisdom came too late. She has much to her and probably little will come of it. She is a child of her age, of depression, of war, of fear.

Let her be. So all that is in her will not bloom—but in how many does it? There is still enough left to live by. Only help her to know—help make it so there is cause for her to know—that she is more than this dress on the ironing board, helpless before the iron.

Suggestions for Discussion

1. In this story in which the mother speaks of her daughter, who is the listener? What evidence is there that she is speaking to herself as well as to the unnamed listener? How does this technique affect the emotional impact of the story?

2. What is the symbolic and real significance of the title and the opening and concluding allusions to ironing?

3. As you review the chronology of events in the lives of the mother and Emily, how would you characterize the changes in their attitudes, feelings, and behavior?

4. In what respects might it be said that the author portrays two lives that move beyond the personal and reflect a universal phenomenon?

5. What attitude toward life is expressed in the final paragraph?

Suggestions for Writing

1. After stating in your own words the attitude toward life expressed in the last paragraph, discuss your view of it by making reference to your own experience or your observation of others (real or fictional).

2. Rewrite the story of Emily chronologically. What is lost of the author's artistry?

3. Write a monologue in which Emily is the speaker.

Louise Erdrich

A Wedge of Shade

Louise Erdrich (b. 1954) is a leading voice among Native American writers. Born in Minnesota, of Chippewa extraction, she received her B.A. from Dartmouth and her M.A. from Johns Hopkins University. She has won the Nelson Algren Award and the National Book Critics Circle Award for Fiction, and she was first on the New York Times Bestseller List with her novels The Beet Queen (1986) and Tracks (1988). Her most recent books include Baptism of Desire (1989), The Crown of Columbus (1991), and The Bingo Palace (1994). This short story deals with the intensity of family bonds and the difficulty of loosening them to claim one's own life.

Every place that I could name you, in the whole world around us, has better things about it than Argus, North Dakota. I just happened to grow up there for eighteen years, and the soil got to be part of me, the air has something in it that I breathed. Argus water doesn't taste as good as water in the cities. Still, the first thing I do, walking back into my mother's house, is stand at the kitchen sink and toss down glass after glass.

"Are you filled up?" My mother stands behind me. "Sit down if you are."

She's tall and board-square, French-Chippewa, with long arms and big knuckles. Her face is rawboned, fierce, and almost masculine in its edges and planes. Several months ago, a beauty operator convinced her that she should feminize her look with curls. Now the permanent, grown out in grizzled streaks, bristles like the coat of a terrier. I don't look like her. Not just the hair, since hers is salt-and-pepper and mine is a reddish brown, but my build. I'm short, boxy, more like my Aunt Mary. Like her, I can't seem to shake this town. I keep coming back here.

"There's jobs at the beet plant," my mother says.

This rumor, probably false, since the plant is in a slump, drops into the dim, close air of the kitchen. We have the shades drawn because it's a hot June, over a hundred degrees, and we're trying to stay cool. Outside, the water has been sucked from everything. The veins in the leaves are hollow, the ditch grass is crackling. The sky has absorbed every drop. It's a thin whitish-blue veil stretched from end to end over us, a flat gauze tarp. From the depot, I've walked here beneath it, dragging my suitcase.

We're sweating as if we're in an oven, a big messy one. For a week, it's been too hot to clean much or even move, and the crops are stunted, failing. The farmer next to us just sold his field for a subdivision, but the construction workers aren't doing much. They're wearing wet rags on their heads, sitting near the house sites in the brilliance of noon. The studs of wood stand upright over them, but uselessly—nothing casts shadows. The sun has dried them up, too.

"The beet plant," my mother says again.

"Maybe so," I say, and then, because I've got something bigger on my mind, "Maybe I'll go out there and apply."

"Oh?" She is intrigued now.

"God, this is terrible!" I take the glass of water in my hand and tip some onto my head. I don't feel cooler, though; I just feel the steam rising off me.

"The fan broke down," she states. "Both of them are kaput now. The motors or something. If Mary would get the damn tax refund, we'd run out to Pamida, buy a couple more, set up a breeze. Then we'd be cool out here."

"Your garden must be dead," I say, lifting the edge of the pull shade.

"It's sick, but I watered. And I won't mulch; that draws the damn slugs."

"Nothing could live out there, no bug." My eyes smart from even looking at the yard, which is a clear sheet of sun, almost incandescent.

"You'd be surprised."

I wish I could blurt it out, just tell her. Even now, the words swell in my mouth, the one sentence, but I'm scared, and with good reason. There is this about my mother: it is awful to see her angry. Her lips press together and she stiffens herself within, growing wooden, silent. Her features become fixed and remote, she will not speak. It takes a long time, and until she does you are held in suspense. Nothing that she ever says, in the end, is as bad as that feeling of dread. So I wait, half believing that she'll figure out my secret for herself, or drag it out of me, not that she ever tries. If I'm silent, she hardly notices. She's not like Aunt Mary, who forces me to say more than I know is on my mind.

My mother sighs. "It's too hot to bake. It's too hot to cook. But it's too hot to eat anyway."

She's talking to herself, which makes me reckless. Perhaps she is so preoccupied by the heat that I can slip my announcement past her. I should just say it, but I lose nerve, make an introduction that alerts her. "I have something to tell you."

I've cast my lot; there's no going back unless I think quickly. My thoughts hum.

But she waits, forgetting the heat for a moment.

"Ice," I say. "We have to have ice." I speak intensely, leaning toward her, almost glaring, but she is not fooled.

"Don't make me laugh," she says. "There's not a cube in town. The refrigerators can't keep cold enough." She eyes me the way a hunter eyes an animal about to pop from its den and run.

"O.K." I break down. "I really do have something." I stand, turn my back. In this lightless warmth I'm dizzy, almost sick. Now I've gotten to her and she's frightened to hear, breathless.

"Tell me," she urges. "Go on, get it over with."

And so I say it. "I got married." There is a surge of relief, a wind blowing through the room, but then it's gone. The curtain flaps and we're caught again, stunned in an even denser heat. It's now my turn to wait, and I whirl around and sit right across from her. Now is the time to tell her his name, a Chippewa name that she'll know from the papers, since he's notorious. Now is the time to get it over with. But I can't bear the picture she makes, the shock that parts her lips, the stunned shade of hurt in her eyes. I have to convince her, somehow, that it's all right.

"You hate weddings! Just think, just picture it. Me, white net. On a day like this. You, stuffed in your summer wool, and Aunt Mary, God knows . . . and the tux, the rental, the groom . . ."

Her head had lowered as my words fell on her, but now her forehead tips up and her eyes come into view, already hardening. My tongue flies back into my mouth.

She mimics, making it a question, "The groom . . ."

I'm caught, my lips half open, a stuttering noise in my throat. How to begin? I have rehearsed this, but my lines melt away, my opening, my casual introductions. I can think of nothing that would convince her of how much more he is than the captions beneath the photos. There is no picture adequate, no representation that captures him. So I just put my hand across the table and I touch her hand. "Mother," I say, as if we're in a staged drama, "he'll arrive here shortly."

There is something forming in her, some reaction. I am afraid to let it take complete shape. "Let's go out and wait on the steps, Mom. Then you'll see him."

"I do not understand," she says in a frighteningly neutral voice. This is what I mean. Everything is suddenly forced, unnatural—we're reading lines.

"He'll approach from a distance." I can't help speaking like a bad actor. "I told him to give me an hour. He'll wait, then he'll come walking down the road."

We rise and unstick our blouses from our stomachs, our skirts from the backs of our legs. Then we walk out front in single file, me behind, and settle ourselves on the middle step. A scrubby box-elder tree on one side casts a light shade, and the dusty lilacs seem to catch a little breeze on the other. It's not so bad out here, still hot, but not so dim, contained. It is worse past the trees. The heat shimmers in a band, rising off the fields, out of the spars and bones of houses that will wreck our view. The horizon and the edge of town show through the gaps in the framing now, and as we sit we watch the workers move, slowly, almost in a practiced recital, back and forth. Their head-cloths hang to their shoulders, their hard hats are dabs of yellow, their white T-shirts blend into the fierce air and sky. They don't seem to be doing anything, although we hear faint thuds from their hammers. Otherwise, except for the whistles of a few birds, there is silence. Certainly we don't speak.

It is a longer wait than I anticipated, maybe because he wants to give me time. At last the shadows creep out, hard, hot, charred, and the heat begins to lengthen and settle. We are going into the worst of the afternoon when a dot at the end of the road begins to form.

Mom and I are both watching. We have not moved our eyes around much, and we blink and squint to try and focus. The dot doesn't change, not for a long while. And then it suddenly springs clear in relief—a silhouette, lost for a moment in the shimmer, reappearing. In that shining expanse he is a little wedge of moving shade. He continues, growing imperceptibly, until there are variations in the outline, and it can be seen that he is large. As he passes the construction workers, they turn and stop, all alike in their hats, stock-still.

Growing larger yet, as if he has absorbed their stares, he nears us. Now we can see the details. He is dark, the first thing. His arms are thick, his chest is huge, and the features of his face are wide and open. He carries nothing in his hands. He wears a black T-shirt, the opposite of the construction workers, and soft jogging shoes. His jeans are held under his stomach by a belt with a star beaded on the buckle. His hair is long, in a tail. I am the wrong woman for him. I am paler, shorter, un-magnificent. But I stand up. Mom joins me, and I answer proudly when she asks, "His name?"

"His name is Gerry—" Even now I can't force his last name through my lips. But Mom is distracted by the sight of him anyway.

We descend one step, and stop again. It is here we will receive him. Our hands are folded at our waists. We're balanced, composed. He continues to stroll toward us, his white smile widening, his eyes filling with the sight of me as mine are filling with him. At the end of the road behind him, another dot has appeared. It is fast-moving and the sun flares off it twice: a vehicle. Now there are two figures—one approaching in a spume of dust from the rear, and Gerry, unmindful, not slackening or quickening his pace, continuing on. It is like a choreography design. They move at parallel speeds in front of our eyes. Then, at the same moment, at the end of our yard, they conclude the performance; both of them halt.

Gerry stands, looking toward us, his thumbs in his belt. He nods respectfully to Mom, looks calmly at me, and half smiles. He raises his brows, and we're suspended. Officer Lovchik emerges from the police car, stooped and tired. He walks up behind Gerry and I hear the snap of handcuffs, then I jump. I'm stopped by Gerry's gaze, though, as he backs away from me, still smiling tenderly. I am paralyzed halfway down the walk. He kisses the air while Lovchik cautiously prods at him, fitting his prize into the car. And then the doors slam, the engine roars, and they back out and turn around. As they move away there is no siren. I think I've heard Lovchik mention questioning. I'm sure it is lots of fuss for nothing, a mistake, but it cannot be denied—this is terrible timing.

I shake my shoulders, smooth my skirt, and turn to my mother with a look of outrage. "How do you like that?" I try.

She's got her purse in one hand, her car keys out.

"Let's go," she says.

"O.K.," I answer. "Fine. Where?"

"Aunt Mary's."

"I'd rather go and bail him out, Mom."

"Bail," she says. "*Bail?*"

She gives me such a look of cold and furious surprise that I sink immediately into the front seat, lean back against the vinyl. I almost welcome the sting of the heated plastic on my back, thighs, shoulders.

Aunt Mary lives at the rear of the butcher shop she runs. As we walk toward the "House of Meats," her dogs are rugs in the dirt, flattened by the heat of the day. Not one of them barks at us to warn her. We step over them and get no more reaction than a whine, the slow beat of a tail. Inside, we get no answers either, although we call Aunt Mary up and down the hall. We enter the kitchen and sit at the table, which holds a half-ruined watermelon. By the sink, in a tin box, are cigarettes. My mother takes one and carefully puts a match to it, frowning. "I know what," she says. "Go check the lockers."

There are two—a big freezer full of labelled meats and rental space, and another, smaller one that is just a side cooler. I notice, walking past the meat display counter, that the red beacon beside the outside switch of the cooler is glowing. That tells you when the light is on inside.

I pull the long metal handle toward me and the thick door swishes open. I step into the cool, spicy air. Aunt Mary is there, too proud to ever register a hint of surprise. She simply nods and looks away as though I've just been out for a minute, although we've not seen one another in six months or more. She is relaxing on a big can of pepper labelled "Zanzibar," reading a scientific-magazine article. I sit down on a barrel of alum. With no warning, I drop my bomb; "I'm married." It doesn't matter how I tell it to Aunt Mary, because she won't be, refuses to be, surprised.

"What's he do?" she simply asks, putting aside the sheaf of paper. I thought the first thing she'd do was scold me for fooling my mother. But it's odd, for two women who have lived through boring times and disasters, how rarely one comes to the other's defense, and how often they are each willing to take advantage of the other's absence. But I'm benefiting here. It seems that Aunt Mary is truly interested in Gerry. So I'm honest.

"He's something like a political activist. I mean he's been in jail and all. But not for any crime, you see; it's just because of his convictions."

She gives me a long, shrewd stare. Her skin is too tough to wrinkle, but she doesn't look young. All around us hang loops of sausages, every kind you can imagine, every color, from the purple-black of blutwurst to the pale-whitish links that my mother likes best. Blocks of butter and headcheese, a can of raw milk, wrapped parcels, and cured bacons are stuffed onto the shelves around us. My heart has gone still and cool inside me, and I can't stop talking.

"He's the kind of guy it's hard to describe. Very different. People call him a free spirit, but that doesn't say it either, because he's very disciplined in some ways. He learned to be neat in jail." I pause. She says nothing, so I go on. "I know it's sudden, but who likes weddings? I hate them —all that mess with the bridesmaids' gowns, getting material to match. I don't have girl-friends. I mean, how embarrassing, right? Who would sing 'O Perfect Love'? Carry the ring?"

She isn't really listening.

"What's he do?" she asks again.

Maybe she won't let go of it until I discover the right answer, like a game with nouns and synonyms.

"He—well, he agitates," I tell her.

"Is that some kind of factory work?"

"Not exactly, no, it's not a nine-to-five job or anything . . . "

She lets the magazine fall, now, cocks her head to one side, and stares at me without blinking her cold yellow eyes. She has the look of a hawk, of a person who can see into the future but won't tell you about it. She's lost business for staring at customers, but she doesn't care.

"Are you telling me that he doesn't . . . " Here she shakes her head twice, slowly, from one side to the other, without removing me from her stare. "That he doesn't have regular work?"

"Oh, what's the matter, anyway?" I say roughly. "I'll work. This is the nineteen-seventies."

She jumps to her feet, stands over me—a stocky woman with terse fea-tures and short, thin points of gray hair. Her earrings tremble and flash— small fiery opals. Her brown plastic glasses hang crooked on a cord around her neck. I have never seen her become quite so instantly furious, so dis-turbed. "We're going to fix that," she says.

The cooler immediately feels smaller, the sausages knock at my shoulder, and the harsh light makes me blink. I am as stubborn as Aunt Mary, how-ever, and she knows that I can go head to head with her. "We're married and that's final." I manage to stamp my foot.

Aunt Mary throws an arm back, blows air through her cheeks, and waves away my statement vigorously. "You're a little girl. How old is *he?*"

I frown at my lap, trace the threads in my blue cotton skirt, and tell her that age is irrelevant.

"Big word," she says sarcastically. "Let me ask you this. He's old enough to get a job?"

"Of course he is; what do you think? O.K., he's older than me. He's in his thirties."

"Aha, I knew it."

"Geez! So what? I mean, haven't you ever been in love, hasn't someone ever gotten you *right here?*" I smash my fist on my chest.

We lock eyes, but she doesn't waste a second in feeling hurt. "Sure, sure I've been in love. You think I haven't? I know what it feels like, you smart-ass. You'd be surprised. But he was no lazy son of a bitch. Now, listen . . ." She stops, draws breath, and I let her. "Here's what I mean by 'fix.' I'll teach the sausage-making trade to him—to you, too—and the grocery business. I've about had it anyway, and so's your mother. We'll do the same as my aunt and uncle—leave the shop to you and move to Arizona. I like this place." She looks up at the burning safety bulb, down at me again. Her face drags in the light. "But what the hell. I always wanted to travel."

I'm stunned, a little flattened out, maybe ashamed of myself. "You hate going anywhere," I say, which is true.

The door swings open and Mom comes in with us. She finds a milk can and balances herself on it, sighing at the delicious feeling of the air, absorbing from the silence the fact that we have talked. She hasn't anything to add, I guess, and as the coolness hits, her eyes fall shut. Aunt Mary's too. I can't help it, either, and my eyelids drop, although my brain is conscious and alert. From the darkness, I can see us in the brilliance. The light rains down on us. We sit the way we have been sitting, on our cans of milk and pepper, upright and still. Our hands are curled loosely in our laps. Our faces are blank as the gods'. We could be statues in a tomb sunk into the side of a mountain. We could be dreaming the world up in our brains.

It is later, and the weather has no mercy. We are drained of everything but simple thoughts. It's too hot for feelings. Driving home, we see how field after field of beets has gone into shock, and even some of the soybeans. The plants splay, limp, burned into the ground. Only the sunflowers continue to struggle upright, bristling but small.

What drew me in the first place to Gerry was the unexpected. I went to hear him talk just after I enrolled at the university, and then I demonstrated when they came and got him off the stage. He always went so willingly, accommodating everyone. I began to visit him. I sold lunar calendars and posters to raise his bail and eventually free him. One thing led to another, and one night we found ourselves alone in a Howard Johnson's coffee shop downstairs from where they put him up when his speech was finished. There were much more beautiful women after him; he could have had his pick of Swedes or Yankton Sioux girls, who are the best-looking of all. But I was different, he says. He liked my slant on life. And then there was no going back once it started, no turning, as though it was meant. We had no choice.

I have this intuition as we near the house, in the fateful quality of light, as in the turn of the day the heat continues to press and the blackness, into which the warmth usually lifts, lowers steadily: We must come to the end of something; there must be a close to this day.

As we turn into the yard we see that Gerry is sitting on the porch stairs. Now it is our turn to be received. I throw the car door open and stumble out before the motor even cuts. I run to him and hold him, as my mother, pursuing the order of events, parks carefully. Then she walks over, too, holding her purse by the strap. She stands before him and says no word but simply looks into his face, staring as if he's cardboard, a man behind glass who cannot see her. I think she's rude, but then I realize that he is staring back, that they are the same height. Their eyes are level.

He puts his hand out. "My name is Gerry."

"Gerry what?"

"Nanapush."

She nods, shifts her weight. "You're from that line, the old strain, the ones . . ." She does not finish.

"And my father," Gerry says, "was Old Man Pillager."

"Kashpaws," she says, "are my branch, of course. We're probably related through my mother's brother." They do not move. They are like two opponents from the same divided country, staring across the border. They do not shift or blink, and I see that they are more alike than I am like either one of them—so tall, solid, dark-haired. They could be mother and son.

"Well, I guess you should come in," she offers. "You are a distant relative, after all." She looks at me. "Distant enough."

Whole swarms of mosquitoes are whining down, discovering us now, so there is no question of staying where we are. And so we walk into the house, much hotter than outside, with the gathered heat. Instantly the sweat springs from our skin and I can think of nothing else but cooling off. I try to force the windows higher in their sashes, but there's no breeze anyway; nothing stirs, no air.

"Are you sure," I gasp, "about those fans?"

"Oh, they're broke, all right," my mother says, distressed. I rarely hear this in her voice. She switches on the lights, which makes the room seem hotter, and we lower ourselves into the easy chairs. Our words echo, as though the walls have baked and dried hollow.

"Show me those fans," says Gerry.

My mother points toward the kitchen. "They're sitting on the table. I've already tinkered with them. See what you can do."

And so he does. After a while she hoists herself and walks out back to him. Their voices close together now, absorbed, and their tools clank frantically, as if they are fighting a duel. But it is a race with the bell of darkness and their waning energy. I think of ice. I get ice on the brain.

"Be right back," I call out, taking the car keys from my mother's purse. "Do you need anything?"

There is no answer from the kitchen but a furious sputter of metal, the clatter of nuts and bolts spilling to the floor.

I drive out to the Superpumper, a big new gas-station complex on the edge of town, where my mother most likely has never been. She doesn't know about convenience stores, has no credit cards for groceries or gas, pays only with small bills and change. She never has used an ice machine. It would grate on her that a bag of frozen water costs eighty cents, but it doesn't bother me. I take the plastic-foam cooler and I fill it for a couple of dollars. I buy two six-packs of Shasta soda and I plunge them in among the uniform cubes of ice. I drink two myself on the way home, and I manage to lift the whole heavy cooler out of the trunk, carry it to the door.

The fans are whirring, beating the air. I hear them going in the living room the minute I come in. The only light shines from the kitchen. Gerry and my mother have thrown the pillows from the couch onto the living-room floor, and they are sitting in the rippling currents of air. I bring the cooler in and put it near us. I have chosen all dark flavors—black cherry, grape, red berry, cola—so as we drink the darkness swirls inside us with the night air, sweet and sharp, driven by small motors.

I drag more pillows down from the other rooms upstairs. There is no question of attempting the bedrooms, the stifling beds. And so, in the dark, I hold hands with Gerry as he settles down between my mother and me. He is huge as a hill between the two of us, solid in the beating wind.

Suggestions for Discussion

1. What does the metaphor "a wedge of shade" have to do with the relationships between the characters in the story?

2. Erdrich uses light and dark, hot and cold, movement and stillness as ways of making us both respond to and understand what is happening in the story. How does she do this? What feelings are evoked? What do we come to know through these metaphors?

3. What reconciles Mom to Gerry?

Suggestions for Writing

1. Metaphors engage us in what is going on without ever becoming explicit about it. Write about a metaphor that expresses something you want to say about a relationship important to you.

2. Write a brief story about what happens in a family when a stranger enters it to stay.

Poetry

E. E. Cummings

My Father Moved Through Dooms of Love

Edward Estlin Cummings (1894–1963) was an American whose novel *The Enormous Room* (1922) and whose books of poetry *&* and *XLI Poems* (1925) established his reputation as an avant-garde writer interested in experimenting with stylistic techniques. Awarded several important prizes for poetry, he also was Charles Eliot Norton Lecturer at Harvard University in 1952 and published *i: six nonlectures* (1953). The theme of wholeness and reconciliation of opposites in the father's character is implictly expressed in this poem in which images of death, hate, and decay are counterpointed against images that celebrate life and growth.

> my father moved through dooms of love
> through sames of am through haves of give,
> singing each morning out of each night
> my father moved through depths of height
>
> this motionless forgetful where
> turned at his glance to shining here;
> that if (so timid air is firm)
> under his eyes would stir and squirm
>
> newly as from unburied which
> floats the first who, his april touch
> drove sleeping selves to swarm their fates
> woke dreamers to their ghostly roots
>
> and should some why completely weep
> my father's fingers brought her sleep:
> vainly no smallest voice might cry
> for he could feel the mountains grow.
>
> Lifting the valleys of the sea
> my father moved through griefs of joy;
> praising a forehead called the moon
> singing desire into begin
>
> joy was his song and joy so pure
> a heart of star by him could steer
> and pure so now and now so yes
> the wrists of twilight would rejoice
>
> keen as midsummer's keen beyond
> conceiving mind of sun will stand,
> so strictly (over utmost him
> so hugely) stood my father's dream

his flesh was flesh his blood was blood:
no hungry man but wished him food;
no cripple wouldn't creep one mile
uphill to only see him smile.

Scorning the pomp of must and shall
my father moved through dooms of feel;
his anger was as right as rain
his pity was as green as grain

septembering arms of year extend
less humbly wealth to foe and friend
than he to foolish and to wise
offered immeasurable is

proudly and (by octobering flame
beckoned) as earth will downward climb,
so naked for immortal work
his shoulders marched against the dark

his sorrow was as true as bread:
no liar looked him in the head;
if every friend became his foe
he'd laugh and build a world with snow.

My father moved through theys of we,
singing each new leaf out of each tree
(and every child was sure that spring
danced when she heard my father sing)

then let men kill which cannot share,
let blood and flesh be mud and mire,
scheming imagine, passion willed,
freedom a drug that's bought and sold

giving to steal and cruel kind,
a heart to fear, to doubt a mind,
to differ a disease of same,
conform the pinnacle of am

though dull were all we taste as bright,
bitter all utterly things sweet,
maggoty minus and dumb death
all we inherit, all bequeath

and nothing quite so least as truth
—i say though hate were why men breathe—
because my father lived his soul
love is the whole and more than all

Suggestions for Discussion

1. Study the verbal juxtapositions that seem antithetical: "dooms of love"; "depths of height"; "griefs of joy." How is the theme of wholeness and reconciliation of opposites in the character of the father implicitly expressed?

2. Cite passages in which the natural imagery of life, love, birth, and rebirth is counterpointed against images of death, hate, and decay.

3. Contrast this father with Kafka's in "Letter to His Father."

Sylvia Plath

Daddy

Sylvia Plath (1932–1963) began her career while still a college student by
serving as guest editor of *Mademoiselle*. She studied in both the United
States and England, taught at Smith College, and then settled in England,
where she lived until her suicide. Her poetry is collected in *The Colossus*
(1960), *Ariel* (1965), *Crossing the Water* (1971), and *Winter Trees* (1972), and she
contributed to such magazines as *Seventeen*, *Atlantic*, and *The Nation*. *The Bell
Jar*, her only novel, was written about her late-adolescent attempt at suicide
and was published posthumously in 1963 under the pseudonym Victoria
Lucas. In "Daddy," the poet as child recalls the past and reinvokes her brutal image of her father.

> You do not do, you do not do
> Any more, black shoe
> In which I have lived like a foot
> For thirty years, poor and white,
> Barely daring to breath or Achoo.
>
> Daddy, I have had to kill you.
> You died before I had time—
> Marble-heavy, a bag full of God,
> Ghastly statue with one grey toe
> Big as a Frisco seal
>
> And a head in the freakish Atlantic
> Where it pours bean green over blue
> In the waters off beautiful Nauset.
> I used to pray to recover you.
> Ach, du.
>
> In the German tongue, in the Polish town
> Scraped flat by the roller
> Of wars, wars, wars.
> But the name of the town is common.
> My Polack friend

Says there are a dozen or two.
So I never could tell where you
Put your foot, your root,
I never could talk to you.
The tongue stuck in my jaw.

It stuck in a barb wire snare.
Ich, ich, ich, ich
I could hardly speak.
I thought every German was you.
And the language obscene

An engine, an engine
Chuffing me off like a Jew.
A Jew to Dachau, Auschwitz, Belsen.
I began to talk like a Jew.
I think I may well be a Jew.

The snows of the Tyrol, the clear beer of Vienna
Are not very pure or true.
With my gypsy ancestress and my weird luck
And my Taroc pack and my Taroc pack
I may be a bit of a Jew.

I have always been scared of *you*,
With your Luftwaffe, your gobbledygoo.
And your neat moustache
And your Aryan eye, bright blue.
Panzer-man, panzer-man, O You—

Not God but a swastika
So black no sky could squeak through.
Every woman adores a Fascist,
The boot in the face, the brute
Brute heart of a brute like you.

You stand at the blackboard, daddy,
In the picture I have of you,
A cleft in your chin instead of your foot
But no less a devil for that, no not
Any less the black man who

Bit my pretty red heart in two.
I was ten when they buried you.
At twenty I tried to die
And get back, back, back to you.
I thought even the bones would do.

But they pulled me out of the sack,
And they stuck me together with glue.
And then I knew what to do.
I made a model of you,
A man in black with a Meinkampf look

And a love of the rack and the screw.
And I said I do, I do.
So daddy, I'm finally through.
The black telephone's off at the root,
The voice just can't worm through.

If I've killed one man, I've killed two—
The vampire who said he was you
And drank my blood for a year,
Seven years, if you want to know.
Daddy, you can lie back now.

There's a stake in your fat black heart
And the villagers never liked you.
They are dancing and stamping on you.
They always *knew* it was you.
Daddy, daddy, you bastard, I'm through.

Suggestions for Discussion

1. Discuss the theme and mood of the poem. Comment on the relative maturity or insight the narrator has achieved through the distance of time.

2. What may Sylvia Plath's father have had in common with Kafka's father?

3. To what extent does your reading of A. Alvarez's "Sylvia Plath: A Memoir" illuminate your reading of the poem?

Theodore Roethke

My Papa's Waltz

Theodore Roethke (1908–1963), American poet, taught during the last years of his life at the University of Washington. *The Waking: Poems, 1933–1953* was the winner of the Pulitzer Prize for Poetry in 1953. He received the Bollingen Award for Poetry in 1958. A collected volume, *Words for the Wind*, appeared in 1958, and *The Far Field* was published posthumously in 1964. The poet remembers his antic father and his own difficult childhood.

The whiskey on your breath
Could make a small boy dizzy;
But I hung on like death:
Such waltzing was not easy.

We romped until the pans
Slid from the kitchen shelf;
My mother's countenance
Could not unfrown itself.

The hand that held my wrist
Was battered on one knuckle;
At every step I missed
My right ear scraped a buckle.

You beat time on my head
With a palm caked hard by dirt,
Then waltzed me off to bed
Still clinging to your shirt.

Suggestion for Discussion

Compare the relationship of father and son in this poem with that in Anderson's "Discovery of a Father." Contrast the two mothers.

William Butler Yeats

A Prayer for My Daughter

William Butler Yeats (1865–1939), the leading poet of the Irish literary revival and a playwright, was born near Dublin and educated in London and Dublin. He wrote plays for the Irish National Theatre Society (later called the Abbey Theatre). For a number of years he served as a senator of the Irish Free State. His volumes of poetry range from *The Wanderings of Oisin* (1889) to *The Last Poems* (1939). *The Collected Poems of W. B. Yeats* appeared in 1933, 1950, and 1956; *The Collected Plays of W. B. Yeats* were published in 1934 and 1952. From his view of a chaotic, threatening world, the poet prays for the harmony and order he considers requisite to the growth of his daughter.

Once more the storm is howling, and half hid
Under this cradle-hood and coverlid
My child sleeps on. There is no obstacle
But Gregory's wood and one bare hill
Whereby the haystack- and roof-levelling wind,
Bred on the Atlantic, can be stayed;
And for an hour I have walked and prayed
Because of the great gloom that is in my mind.

I have walked and prayed for this young child an hour
And heard the sea-wind scream upon the tower,
And under the arches of the bridge, and scream
In the elms above the flooded stream;
Imagining in excited reverie
That the future years had come,
Dancing to a frenzied drum,
Out of the murderous innocence of the sea.

May she be granted beauty and yet not
Beauty to make a stranger's eye distraught,
Or hers before a looking-glass, for such,
Being made beautiful overmuch,
Consider beauty a sufficient end,
Lose natural kindness and maybe
The heart-revealing intimacy
That chooses right, and never find a friend.

Helen, being chosen, found life flat and dull
And later had much trouble from a fool,
While that great Queen, that rose out of the spray,
Being fatherless, could have her way
Yet chose a bandy-leggèd smith for man.
It's certain that fine women eat
A crazy salad with their meat
Whereby the Horn of Plenty is undone.

In courtesy I'd have her chiefly learned;
Hearts are not had as a gift but hearts are earned
By those that are not entirely beautiful;
Yet many, that have played the fool
For beauty's very self, has charm made wise,
And many a poor man that has roved,
Loved and thought himself beloved,
From a glad kindness cannot take his eyes.

May she become a flourishing hidden tree
That all her thoughts may like the linnet be,
And have no business but dispensing round
Their magnanimities of sound.
Nor but in merriment began a chase,
Nor but in merriment a quarrel.
O may she live like some green laurel
Rooted in one dear perpetual place.

My mind, because the minds that I have loved,
The sort of beauty that I have approved,
Prosper but little, has dried up of late,
Yet knows that to be choked with hate
May well be of all evil chances chief.
If there's no hatred in a mind
Assault and battery of the wind
Can never tear the linnet from the leaf.

An intellectual hatred is the worst,
So let her think opinions are accursed.
Have I not seen the loveliest woman born
Out of the mouth of Plenty's horn,
Because of her opinionated mind
Barter that horn and every good
By quiet natures understood
For an old bellows full of angry wind?

Considering that, all hatred driven hence,
The soul recovers radical innocence
And learns at last that it is self-delighting,
Self-appeasing, self-affrighting,
And that its own sweet will is Heaven's will;
She can, though every face should scowl
And every windy quarter howl
Or every bellows burst, be happy still.

And may her bridegroom bring her to a house
Where all's accustomed, ceremonious;
For arrogance and hatred are the wares
Peddled in the thoroughfares.
How but in custom and in ceremony
Are innocence and beauty born?
Ceremony's a name for the rich horn,
And custom for the spreading laurel tree.

Suggestions for Discussion

1. Is he imposing on her a conservative ideal of womanhood?

2. What words or images suggest that he might quarrel with the ideas of feminists today?

3. Discuss: "How but in custom and in ceremony / Are innocence and beauty born?"

4. What seems to be the poet's concept of happiness for a woman?

Gwendolyn Brooks

Life for My Child Is Simple, and Is Good

Gwendolyn Brooks (b. 1917) is an American poet who grew up in Chicago's slums. Her works, which focus on contemporary Black life in the United States, include A Street in Bronzeville (1949); Annie Allen (1949), which won a Pulitzer Prize; The Bean Eaters (1960); and, most recently, The Near Johannesburg Boy and Other Poems (1987). She also has written a novel and a book for children. In this brief poem the writer sets forth her hopes for her son's joy and growth.

Life for my child is simple, and is good.
He knows his wish. Yes, but that is not all.
Because I know mine too.
And we both want joy of undeep and unabiding things,
Like kicking over a chair or throwing blocks out of a window
Or tipping over an icebox pan
Or snatching down curtains or fingering an electric outlet
Or a journey or a friend or an illegal kiss.
No. There is more to it than that.
It is that he has never been afraid.
Rather, he reaches out and lo the chair falls with a beautiful crash,
And the blocks fall, down on the people's heads,
And the water comes slooshing sloopily out across the floor.
And so forth.
Not that success, for him, is sure, infallible.
But never has he been afraid to reach.
His lesions are legion.
But reaching is his rule.

Suggestions for Discussion

1. Compare Brooks's hopes for her child with those of Yeats for his daughter.

2. What do the joys of "unabiding things" have in common?

3. What oppositions are posed in the poem, and how are they resolved?

Nancy Willard

Questions My Son Asked Me,
Answers I Never Gave Him

Nancy Willard (b. 1936) received her Ph.D. from the University of Michigan. She has won the Hopwood Award, a Woodrow Wilson Fellowship, and an O. Henry Award for the best short story in 1970. Her publications include In His Country: Poems (1966), Skin of Grace (1967), The Carpenter of the Sun: Poems (1974), Water Waker (1990), and The Sorcerer's Apprentice (1994). In this poem Willard responds to her child's questions concerning the nature of his universe with tenderness and whimsy.

1. Do gorillas have birthdays?
   Yes. Like the rainbow they happen,
   like the air they are not observed.

2. Do butterflies make a noise?
The wire in the butterfly's tongue
hums gold.
Some men hear butterflies
even in winter.

3. Are they part of our family?
They forgot us, who forgot how to fly.

4. Who tied my navel? Did God tie it?
God made the thread: O man, live forever!
Man made the knot: enough is enough.

5. If I drop my tooth in the telephone
will it go through the wires and bite someone's ear?
I have seen earlobes pierced by a tooth of steel.
It loves what lasts.
It does not love flesh.
It leaves a ring of gold in the wound.

6. If I stand on my head
will the sleep in my eye roll up into my head?
Does the dream know its own father?
Can bread go back to the field of its birth?

7. Can I eat a star?
Yes, with the mouth of time
that enjoys everything.

8. Could we xerox the moon?
This is the first commandment:
I am the moon, thy moon.
Thou shalt have no other moons before thee.

9. Who invented water?
The hands of the air, that wanted to wash each other.

10. What happens at the end of numbers?
I see three men running toward a field.
At the edge of the tall grass, they turn into light.

11. Do the years ever run out?
God said, I will break time's heart.
Time ran down like an old phonograph.
It lay flat as a carpet.
At rest on its threads I am learning to fly.

Suggestions for Discussion

1. Since each question is answered, why does the author suggest in her title that she did not answer it?

2. What do the son's questions tell you about him? Note the range of his questions.

3. What do the writer's answers tell you about her? How would you characterize the answers?

4. How does figurative language affect the tone? Describe the tone of the answers. In Question 3 Willard says we "forgot how to fly." What does she mean? The figure of flying is repeated in the last stanza. What is its significance? How does it relate to the question?

5. On the basis of the questions and answers, how would you describe the relationship of mother and son?

Suggestion for Writing

Write your own answer(s) to a hypothetical question you are either asking yourself or someone is asking you.

Personal Relationships: Men and Women

The men of our culture have stripped themselves of the fineries of the earth so that they might work more freely to plunder the universe for treasures to deck my lady in. New raw materials, new processes, new machines are all brought into her service. My lady must therefore be the chief spender as well as the chief symbol of spending ability and monetary success. While her mate toils in his factory, she totters about the smartest streets and plushiest hotels with his fortune upon her back and bosom, fingers, and wrists, continuing that essential expenditure in his house which is her frame and her setting, enjoying that silken idleness which is the necessary condition of maintaining her mate's prestige and her qualification to demonstrate it.

> **—Germaine Greer,** "The Stereotype"

Modern woman isn't really a fool. But modern man is. That seems to me the only plain way of putting it. The modern man is a fool, and the modern young man is a prize fool. He makes a greater mess of his women than men have ever made. Because he absolutely doesn't know *what* he wants her to be. We shall see the changes in the woman-pattern follow one another fast and furious now, because the young men hysterically don't know what they want. Two years hence women may be in crinolines—there was a pattern for you!—or a bead flap, like naked negresses in mid-Africa—or they may be wearing brass armor, or the uniform of the Horse Guards. They may be anything. Because the young men are off their heads, and don't know what they want.

> **D. H. Lawrence,** "Give Her a Pattern"

That the test did reveal something other than the superficiality of its makers I realized only many years later. What it revealed was that there is a large class of men and women both, to which I belong, who are essentially androgynous. That doesn't mean we're gay, or low in the appropriate hormones, or uncomfortable performing the jobs traditionally assigned our sexes. (A few years after that summer, I was leading troops in combat and, unfashionable as it now is to admit this, having a very good time. War is exciting. What a pity the 20th century went and spoiled it with high-tech weapons.)

    —Noel Perrin, "The Androgynous Man"

Strange how things change. The image of manhood against which I am measured has changed so much that now, almost twenty years later, I am told I am not sensitive *enough*. When tensions build in our relationship, Shelley will admonish me for being out of touch with my feelings. . . .

    How can I explain it to her? How can any man explain it to any woman? Women are not raised to abort all tears. They are not measured by their toughness. They are not expected to bang against each other on hockey rinks and football fields and basketball courts. They do not go out into the woods to play soldiers. They do not settle disagreements by punching each other. For them, tears are a badge of femininity. For us, they are a masculine demerit.

    —Mark Gerzon, "Manhood: The Elusive Goal"

Her mind only vaguely grasped what he was saying. Her physical being was for the moment predominant. She was not thinking of his words, only drinking in the tones of his voice. She wanted to reach out her hand in the darkness and touch him with the sensitive tips of her fingers upon the face or the lips. She wanted to draw close to him and whisper against his cheek—she did not care what—as she might have done if she had not been a respectable woman.

    —Kate Chopin, "A Respectable Woman"

Essays

Mary Wollstonecraft

A Vindication of the Rights of Woman

Mary Wollstonecraft (1759–1797), whose husband was the radical William Godwin and whose daughter became Mrs. Percy Bysshe Shelley, was a schoolteacher, a governess, and a member of a publishing firm. Her *Vindication of the Rights of Woman* (1792) was an extraordinary defense of the rights of eighteenth-century women. This eighteenth-century diatribe against those who would keep women enslaved was written with the wish to persuade women to acquire strength of mind and body.

My own sex, I hope, will excuse me, if I treat them like rational creatures, instead of flattering their *fascinating* graces, and viewing them as if they were in a state of perpetual childhood, unable to stand alone. I earnestly wish to point out in what true dignity and human happiness consists—I wish to persuade women to endeavor to acquire strength, both of mind and body, and to convince them that the soft phrases, susceptibility of heart, delicacy of sentiment, and refinement of taste, are almost synonymous with epithets of weakness, and that those beings who are only the objects of pity and that kind of love, which has been termed its sister, will soon become objects of contempt.

Dismissing, then, those pretty feminine phrases, which the men condescendingly use to soften our slavish dependence, and despising that weak elegancy of mind, exquisite sensibility, and sweet docility of manners, supposed to be the sexual characteristics of the weaker vessel, I wish to show that elegance is inferior to virtue, that the first object of laudable ambition is to obtain a character as a human being, regardless of the distinction of sex; and that secondary views should be brought to this simple touchstone.

This is a rough sketch of my plan; and should I express my conviction with the energetic emotions that I feel whenever I think of the subject, the dictates of experience and reflection will be felt by some of my readers. Animated by this important object, I shall disdain to cull my phrases or polish my style; I aim at being useful, and sincerity will render me unaffected; for, wishing rather to persuade by the force of my arguments, than dazzle by the elegance of my language, I shall not waste my time in rounding periods, or in fabricating the turgid bombast of artificial feelings, which, coming from the head, never reach the heart. I shall be employed about things, not words! and, anxious to render my sex more respectable members of society, I shall try to avoid that flowery diction which has slided from essays into novels, and from novels into familiar letters and conversation.

These pretty superlatives, dropping glibly from the tongue, vitiate the taste, and create a kind of sickly delicacy that runs away from simple unadorned truth; and a deluge of false sentiments and overstretched feelings,

271

stifling the natural emotions of the heart, render the domestic pleasures insipid, that ought to sweeten the exercise of those severe duties, which educate a rational and immortal being for a nobler field of action.

The education of women has, of late, been more attended to than formerly; yet they are still reckoned a frivolous sex, and ridiculed or pitied by the writers who endeavor by satire or instruction to improve them. It is acknowledged that they spend many of the first years of their lives in acquiring a smattering of accomplishments; meanwhile strength of body and mind are sacrificed to libertine notions of beauty, to the desire of establishing themselves—the only way women can rise in the world—by marriage. And this desire making mere animals of them, when they marry they act as such children may be expected to act—they dress; they paint, and nickname God's creatures. Surely these weak beings are only fit for a seraglio!—Can they be expected to govern a family with judgment, or take care of the poor babes whom they bring into the world?

If then it can be fairly deduced from the present conduct of the sex, from the prevalent fondness for pleasure which takes place of ambition, and those nobler passions that open and enlarge the soul; that the instruction which women have hitherto received has only tended, with the constitution of civil society, to render them insignificant objects of desire—mere propagators of fools!—if it can be proved that in aiming to accomplish them, without cultivating their understandings, they are taken out of their sphere of duties, and made ridiculous and useless when the short-lived bloom of beauty is over,* I presume that *rational* men will excuse me for endeavoring to persuade them to become more masculine and respectable.

Indeed the word masculine is only a bugbear: there is little reason to fear that women will acquire too much courage or fortitude; for their apparent inferiority with respect to bodily strength, must render them, in some degree, dependent on men in the various relations of life; but why should it be increased by prejudices that give a sex to virtue, and confound simple truths with sensual reveries?

Women are, in fact, so much degraded by mistaken notions of female excellence, that I do not mean to add a paradox when I assert, that this artificial weakness produces a propensity to tyrannize, and gives birth to cunning, the natural opponent of strength, which leads them to play off those contemptible infantine airs that undermine esteem even whilst they excite desire. Let men become more chaste and modest, and if women do not grow wiser in the same ratio, it will be clear that they have weaker understandings. It seems scarcely necessary to say, that I now speak of the sex in general. Many individuals have more sense than their male relatives; and, as nothing preponderates where there is a constant struggle for an equilibrium, without it has naturally more gravity, some women govern their husbands without degrading themselves, because intellect will always govern.

*A lively writer, I cannot recollect his name, asks what business women turned of forty have to do in the world?

Suggestions for Discussion

1. Why does the author urge women to reject their conventional image of weakness?

2. How does she relate diction and style to the cause of women's rights? The author acknowledges that her feelings are "energetic." How are you made aware of the strength of her conviction? Why is *fascinating* italicized?

3. How does her own use of language affect her purpose and tone?

4. With what details does she convey her view of marriage? How would you characterize her attitude toward members of her own sex?

5. What evidence is there in this brief excerpt that the author is detached from her subject? Deeply involved?

6. According to Wollstonecraft, how does the education of women both reflect and foster the concept of their frivolity and weakness? What does she see as its effect on the family?

7. What causal relationship is established in the last paragraph?

8. How does the concept of self function in the author's argument?

9. What rhetorical devices are used to persuade the reader?

Suggestions for Writing

1. Imagine a dialogue between Mary Wollstonecraft and D. H. Lawrence, whose essay follows. Focus on points of agreement and disagreement.

2. ". . . the first object of laudable ambition is to obtain a character as a human being, regardless of the distinction of sex." Discuss this statement in the light of your reading on the search for self.

3. Defend or refute the comment that the word *masculine*, as applied to women, is "only a bugbear."

D. H. Lawrence

Give Her a Pattern

D. H. Lawrence (1885–1930) was a schoolteacher before he turned to writing and became one of the great English novelists of the twentieth century. His best-known novels, which focus on relationships between men and women, include *Sons and Lovers* (1913), *Women in Love* (1920), and *Lady Chatterley's Lover* (1928). He also wrote short stories, essays, poetry, and literary criticism. In "Give Her a Pattern," Lawrence castigates men for not accepting women as real human beings of the feminine sex.

The real trouble about women is that they must always go on trying to adapt themselves to men's theories of women, as they always have done. When a woman is thoroughly herself, she is being what her type of man wants her to be. When a woman is hysterical it's because she doesn't quite know what to be, which pattern to follow, which man's picture of woman to live up to.

For, of course, just as there are many men in the world, there are many masculine theories of what women should be. But men run to type, and it is the type, not the individual, that produces the theory, or "ideal" of woman. Those very grasping gentry, the Romans, produced a theory or ideal of the matron, which fitted in very nicely with the Roman property lust. "Caesar's wife should be above suspicion."—So Caesar's wife kindly proceeded to be above it, no matter how far below it the Caesar fell. Later gentlemen like Nero produced the "fast" theory of woman, and later ladies were fast enough for everybody. Dante arrived with a chaste and untouched Beatrice, and chaste and untouched Beatrices began to march self-importantly through the centuries. The Renaissances discovered the learned woman, and learned women buzzed mildly into verse and prose. Dickens invented the child-wife, so child-wives have swarmed ever since. He also fished out his version of the chaste Beatrice, a chaste but marriageable Agnes. George Eliot imitated this pattern, and it became confirmed. The noble woman, the pure spouse, the devoted mother took the field, and was simply worked to death. Our own poor mothers were this sort. So we younger men, having been a bit frightened of our noble mothers, tended to revert to the child-wife. We weren't very inventive. Only the child-wife must be a boyish little thing—that was the new touch we added. Because young men are definitely frightened of the real female. She's too risky a quantity. She is too untidy, like David's Dora. No, let her be a boyish little thing, it's safer. So a boyish little thing she is.

There are, of course, other types. Capable men produce the capable woman ideal. Doctors produce the capable nurse. Business men produce the capable secretary. And so you get all sorts. You can produce the masculine sense of honor (whatever that highly mysterious quantity may be) in women, if you want to.

There is, also, the eternal secret ideal of men—the prostitute. Lots of women live up to this idea: just because men want them to.

And so, poor woman, destiny makes away with her. It isn't that she hasn't got a mind—she has. She's got everything that man has. The only difference is that she asks for a pattern. Give me a pattern to follow! That will always be woman's cry. Unless of course she has already chosen her pattern quite young, then she will declare she is herself absolutely, and no man's idea of women has any influence over her.

Now the real tragedy is not that women ask and must ask for a pattern of womanhood. The tragedy is not, even, that men give them such abominable patterns, child-wives, little-boy-baby-face girls, perfect secretaries, noble spouses, self-sacrificing mothers, pure women who bring forth children in virgin coldness, prostitutes who just make themselves low, to please the men; all the atrocious patterns of womanhood that men have supplied to woman; patterns all perverted from any real natural fullness of a human being. Man is willing to accept woman as an equal, as man in skirts, as an angel, a devil, a baby-face, a machine, an instrument, a bosom, a womb, a pair of legs, a servant, an encyclopaedia, an ideal, or an obscenity; the one thing he won't accept her as, is a human being, a real human being of the feminine sex.

And, of course, women love living up to strange patterns, weird patterns—the more uncanny the better. What could be more uncanny than the present pattern of the Eton-boy girl with flower-like artificial complexion? It is just weird. And for its very weirdness women like living up to it. What can be more gruesome than the little-boy-baby-face pattern? Yet the girls take it on with avidity.

But even that isn't the real root of the tragedy. The absurdity, and often, as in the Dante–Beatrice business, the inhuman nastiness of the pattern—for Beatrice had to go on being chaste and untouched all her life, according to Dante's pattern, while Dante had a cozy wife and kids at home—even that isn't the worst of it. The worst of it is, as soon as a woman has really lived up to the man's pattern, the man dislikes her for it. There is intense secret dislike for the Eton-young-man girl, among the boys, now that she is actually produced. Of course, she's very nice to show in public, absolutely the thing. But the very young men who have brought about her production detest her in private and in their private hearts are appalled by her.

When it comes to marrying, the pattern goes all to pieces. The boy marries the Eton-boy girl, and instantly he hates the *type*. Instantly his mind begins to play hysterically with all the other types, noble Agneses, chaste Beatrices, clinging Doras, and lurid *filles de joie*. He is in a wild welter of confusion. Whatever pattern the poor woman tries to live up to, he'll want another. And that's the condition of modern marriage.

Modern woman isn't really a fool. But modern man is. That seems to me the only plain way of putting it. The modern man is a fool, and the modern young man a prize fool. He makes a greater mess of his women than men have ever made. Because he absolutely doesn't know *what* he wants her to be. We shall see the changes in the woman-pattern follow one another fast and furious now, because the young men hysterically don't know what they want. Two years hence women may be in crinolines—there was a pattern for you!—or a bead flap, like naked negresses in mid-Africa—or they may be wearing brass armor, or the uniform of the Horse Guards. They may be anything. Because the young men are off their heads, and don't know what they want.

The women aren't fools, but they *must* live up to some pattern or other. They *know* the men are fools. They don't really respect the pattern. Yet a pattern they must have, or they can't exist.

Women are not fools. They have their own logic, even if it's not the masculine sort. Women have the logic of emotion, men have the logic of reason. The two are complementary and mostly in opposition. But the woman's logic of emotion is no less real and inexorable than the man's logic of reason. It only works differently.

And the woman never really loses it. She may spend years living up to a masculine pattern. But in the end, the strange and terrible logic of emotion will work out the smashing of that pattern, if it has not been emotionally satisfactory. This is the partial explanation of the astonishing changes in women. For years they go on being chaste Beatrices or child-wives. Then on a sudden—bash! The chaste Beatrice becomes something quite different, the child-wife becomes a roaring lioness! The pattern didn't suffice, emotionally.

Whereas men are fools. They are based on a logic of reason, or are supposed to be. And then they go and behave, especially with regard to women,
in a more-than-feminine unreasonableness. They spend years training up the
little-boy-baby-face type, till they've got her perfect. Then the moment they
marry her, they want something else. Oh, beware, young women, of the
young men who adore you! The moment they've got you they'll want something utterly different. The moment they marry the little-boy-baby-face, instantly they begin to pine for the noble Agnes, pure and majestic, or the
infinite mother with deep bosom of consolation, or the perfect business
woman, or the lurid prostitute on black silk sheets; or, most idiotic of all, a
combination of all the lot of them at once. And that is the logic of reason!
When it comes to women, modern men are idiots. They don't know what
they want, and so they never want, permanently, what they get. They want a
cream cake that is at the same time ham and eggs and at the same time
porridge. They are fools. If only women weren't bound by fate to play up to
them!

For the fact of life is that women *must* play up to man's pattern. And she
only gives her best to a man when he gives her a satisfactory pattern to play
up to. But today, with a stock of ready-made, worn-out idiotic patterns to live
up to, what can women give to men but the trashy side of their emotions?
What could a woman possibly give to a man who wanted her to be a boy-
baby-face? What could she possibly give him but the dribblings of an idiot?—
And, because women aren't fools, and aren't fooled even for very long at a
time, she gives him some nasty cruel digs with her claws, and makes him cry
for mother dear!—abruptly changing his pattern.

Bah! men are fools. If they want anything from women, let them give
women a decent, satisfying idea of womanhood—not these trick patterns of
washed-out idiots.

Suggestions for Discussion

1. Consider the title "Give Her a Pattern" in the light of Lawrence's attitude toward
women. As he sketches some of the patterns imposed on women by men through
the ages, whom does he regard as villain? Is there any evidence that he regards
both men and women as victims of their culture?

2. What details provide the basis for the statement that the one thing man "won't
accept her as, is a human being, a real human being of the feminine sex"?

3. Observe the repetition of the charge that modern men are fools. What does
Lawrence mean by the statement that women are bound by fate to play up to
men? How does he suggest that women are not as great "fools" as men?

4. What is the basis for his fatalistic attitude toward the possibility of real change in
relationships between men and women?

5. What relationship does he make between art and nature?

6. How does he lead up to a definition of woman's tragedy?

7. How are comparison and contrast employed to develop his thesis?

8. How do structure, diction, exclamatory sentences, and metaphor contribute to
tone and purpose?

9. What rhetorical devices are used to persuade the reader?

Suggestions for Writing

1. Write on modern female stereotypes and the mass media.
2. ". . . women love living up to strange patterns." What are some of these patterns today?
3. "When it comes to marrying, the pattern goes all to pieces." Can you illustrate?
4. Discuss and illustrate the "terrible logic of emotion" from your own experience.

Virginia Woolf

The Angel in the House

Virginia Woolf (1882–1941) was an English novelist and critic known for her experimentation with the form of the novel. Her works include *The Voyage Out* (1915), *Night and Day* (1919), *Jacob's Room* (1922), *Mrs. Dalloway* (1925), *To the Lighthouse* (1927), *Orlando: A Biography* (1928), *The Waves* (1931), *The Years* (1937), *Between the Acts* (1941), and several collections of essays. With her husband, Leonard Woolf, she founded the Hogarth Press. Although Woolf was able to overcome certain obstacles to honest writing, she states that women still have "many ghosts to fight, many prejudices to overcome."

When your secretary invited me to come here, she told me that your Society is concerned with the employment of women and she suggested that I might tell you something about my own professional experiences. It is true I am a woman; it is true I am employed; but what professional experiences have I had? It is difficult to say. My profession is literature; and in that profession there are fewer experiences for women than in any other, with the exception of the stage—fewer, I mean, that are peculiar to women. For the road was cut many years ago—by Fanny Burney, by Aphra Behn, by Harriet Martineau, by Jane Austen, by George Eliot—many famous women, and many more unknown and forgotten, have been before me, making the path smooth, and regulating my steps. Thus, when I came to write, there were very few material obstacles in my way. Writing was a reputable and harmless occupation. The family peace was not broken by the scratching of a pen. No demand was made upon the family purse. For ten and sixpence one can buy paper enough to write all the plays of Shakespeare—if one has a mind that way. Pianos and models, Paris, Vienna, and Berlin, masters and mistresses, are not needed by a writer. The cheapness of writing paper is, of course, the reason why women have succeeded as writers before they have succeeded in the other professions.

But to tell you my story—it is a simple one. You have only got to figure to yourselves a girl in a bedroom with a pen in her hand. She had only to move that pen from left to right—from ten o'clock to one. Then it occurred to her to do what is simple and cheap enough after all—to slip a few of those pages into an envelope, fix a penny stamp in the corner, and drop the envelope into the red box at the corner. It was thus that I became a journalist; and my effort was rewarded on the first day of the following month—a very glorious day it was for me—by a letter from an editor containing a cheque for one pound ten shillings and sixpence. But to show you how little I deserve to be called a professional woman, how little I know of the struggles and difficulties of such lives, I have to admit that instead of spending that sum upon bread and butter, rent, shoes and stockings, or butcher's bills, I went out and bought a cat—a beautiful cat, a Persian cat, which very soon involved me in bitter disputes with my neighbours.

What could be easier than to write articles and to buy Persian cats with the profits? But wait a moment. Articles have to be about something. Mine, I seem to remember, was about a novel by a famous man. And while I was writing this review, I discovered that if I were going to review books I should need to do battle with a certain phantom. And the phantom was a woman, and when I came to know her better I called her after the heroine of a famous poem. The Angel in the House. It was she who used to come between me and my paper when I was writing reviews. It was she who bothered me and wasted my time and so tormented me that at last I killed her. You who come of a younger and happier generation may not have heard of her—you may not know what I mean by the Angel in the House. I will describe her as shortly as I can. She was intensely sympathetic. She was immensely charming. She was utterly unselfish. She excelled in the difficult arts of family life. She sacrificed herself daily. If there was chicken, she took the leg; if there was a draught she sat in it—in short she was so constituted that she never had a mind or a wish of her own, but preferred to sympathize always with the minds and wishes of others. Above all—I need not say it—she was pure. Her purity was supposed to be her chief beauty—her blushes, her great grace. In those days—the last of Queen Victoria—every house had its Angel. And when I came to write I encountered her with the very first words. The shadow of her wings fell on my page; I heard the rustling of her skirts in the room. Directly, that is to say, I took my pen in hand to review that novel by a famous man, she slipped behind me and whispered: "My dear, you are a young woman. You are writing about a book that has been written by a man. Be sympathetic; be tender; flatter; deceive; use all the arts and wiles of our sex. Never let anybody guess that you have a mind of your own. Above all, be pure." And she made as if to guide my pen. I now record the one act for which I take some credit to myself, though the credit rightly belongs to some excellent ancestors of mine who left me a certain sum of money—shall we say five hundred pounds a year?—so that it was not necessary for me to depend solely on charm for my living. I turned upon her and caught her by the throat. I did my best to kill her. My excuse, if I were to be had up in a court of law, would be that I acted in self-defense. Had I not killed her she would have killed me. She would have plucked the heart out of my writing. For, as I found, directly I put pen to paper, you cannot review even a novel without having a mind of your own, without expressing what you think to be the truth about human relations, morality, sex. And all these questions, according to the Angel in the House, cannot be dealt with freely and openly by women; they must charm, they must conciliate, they must—to put it bluntly—tell lies if they are to succeed. Thus, whenever I felt the shadow of her wing or the radiance of her halo upon my page, I took up the inkpot and flung it at her. She died hard. Her fictitious nature was of great assistance to her. It is far harder to kill a phantom than a reality. She was always creeping back when I thought I had despatched her. Though I flatter myself that I killed her in the end, the struggle was severe; it took much time that had better have been spent upon learning Greek grammar; or in roaming the world in search of adventures. But it was a real experience; it was an experience that was bound to befall all women writers at that time. Killing the Angel in the House was part of the occupation of a woman writer.

But to continue my story. The Angel was dead; what then remained? You may say that what remained was a simple and common object—a young woman in a bedroom with an inkpot. In other words, now that she had rid herself of falsehood, that young woman had only to be herself. Ah, but what is "herself"? I mean, what is a woman? I assure you, I do not know. I do not believe that you know. I do not believe that anybody can know until she has expressed herself in all the arts and professions open to human skill. That indeed is one of the reasons why I have come here—out of respect for you, who are in process of showing us by your experiments what a woman is, who are in process of providing us, by your failures and successes, with that extremely important piece of information.

But to continue the story of my professional experiences. I made one pound ten and six by my first review; and I bought a Persian cat with the proceeds. Then I grew ambitious. A Persian cat is all very well, I said; but a Persian cat is not enough. I must have a motor car. And it was thus that I became a novelist—for it is a very strange thing that people will give you a motor car if you will tell them a story. It is a still stranger thing that there is nothing so delightful in the world as telling stories. It is far pleasanter than writing reviews of famous novels. And yet, if I am to obey your secretary and tell you my professional experiences as a novelist, I must tell you about a very strange experience that befell me as a novelist. And to understand it you must try first to imagine a novelist's state of mind. I hope I am not giving away professional secrets if I say that a novelist's chief desire is to be as unconscious as possible. He has to induce in himself a state of perpetual lethargy. He wants life to proceed with the utmost quiet and regularity. He wants to see the same faces, to read the same books, to do the same things day after day, month after month, while he is writing, so that nothing may break the illusion in which he is living—so that nothing may disturb or disquiet the mysterious nosings about, feelings round, darts, dashes and sudden discoveries of that very shy and illusive spirit, the imagination. I suspect that this state is the same both for men and women. Be that as it may, I want you to imagine me writing a novel in a state of trance. I want you to figure to yourselves a girl sitting with a pen in her hand, which for minutes, and indeed for hours, she never dips into the inkpot. The image that comes to my mind when I think of this girl is the image of a fisherman lying sunk in dreams on the verge of a deep lake with a rod held out over the water. She was letting her imagination sweep unchecked round every rock and cranny of the world that lies submerged in the depths of our unconscious being. Now came the experience, the experience that I believe to be far commoner with women writers than with men. The line raced through the girl's fingers. Her imagination had rushed away. It had sought the pools, the depths, the dark places where the largest fish slumber. And then there was a smash. There was an explosion. There was foam and confusion. The imagination had dashed itself against something hard. The girl was roused from her dream. She was indeed in a state of the most acute and difficult distress. To speak without figure she had thought of something, something about the body, about the passions which it was unfitting for her as a woman to say. Men, her reason told her, would be shocked. The consciousness of what men will say of a woman who speaks the truth about her passions had roused her from her artist's state of unconsciousness. She could write no more. The trance was over. Her imagination could work no longer. This I believe to be a very common experience with women writers—they are impeded by the extreme conventionality of the other sex. For though men sensibly allow themselves great freedom in these respects, I doubt that they realize or can control the extreme severity with which they condemn such freedom in women.

These then were two very genuine experiences of my own. These were two of the adventures of my professional life. The first—killing the Angel in the House—I think I solved. She died. But the second, telling the truth about my own experiences as a body, I do not think I solved. I doubt that any woman has solved it yet. The obstacles against her are still immensely powerful—and yet they are very difficult to define. Outwardly, what is simpler than to write books? Outwardly, what obstacles are there for a woman rather than for a man? Inwardly, I think, the case is very different; she has still many ghosts to fight, many prejudices to overcome. Indeed it will be a long time still, I think, before a woman can sit down to write a book without finding a phantom to be slain, a rock to be dashed against. And if this is so in literature, the freest of all professions for women, how is it in the new professions which you are now for the first time entering?

Those are the questions that I should like, had I time, to ask you. And indeed, if I have laid stress upon these professional experiences of mine, it is because I believe that they are, though in different forms, yours also. Even when the path is nominally open—when there is nothing to prevent a woman from being a doctor, a lawyer, a civil servant—there are many phantoms and obstacles, as I believe, looming in her way. To discuss and define them is I think of great value and importance; for thus only can the labor be shared, the difficulties be solved. But besides this, it is necessary also to discuss the ends and the aims for which we are fighting, for which we are doing battle with these formidable obstacles. Those aims cannot be taken for granted; they must be perpetually questioned and examined. The whole position, as I see it—here in this hall surrounded by women practising for the first time in history I know not how many different professions—is one of extraordinary interest and importance. You have won rooms of your own in the house hitherto exclusively owned by men. You are able, though not without great labor and effort, to pay the rent. You are earning your five hundred pounds a year. But this freedom is only a beginning; the room is your own, but it is still bare. It has to be furnished; it has to be decorated; it has to be shared. How are you going to furnish it, how are you going to decorate it? With whom are you going to share it, and upon what terms? These, I think, are questions of the utmost importance and interest. For the first time in history you are able to ask them; for the first time you are able to decide for yourselves what the answers should be. Willingly would I stay and discuss those questions and answers—but not tonight. My time is up; and I must cease.

Suggestions for Discussion

1. What are the characteristics of this phantom, the Angel in the House? Do they persist today?

2. Why does the author say she had to kill the Angel?

3. What remaining obstacles to truth did she find? In what ways may women still encounter these obstacles?

4. What are the implications in the concluding paragraph concerning relationships with men?

5. "Ah, but what is 'herself'? I mean, what is a woman?" Discuss these rhetorical questions in relation to purpose and tone.

6. What points of agreement or disagreement might Woolf have with Lawrence?

7. What rhetorical devices are employed to persuade the reader?

Suggestions for Writing

1. Describe an Angel in the House you know.

2. Does this phantom of the Angel still haunt contemporary drama, movies, fiction, advertising?

3. Apply one or more of Woolf's generalizations to a woman poet or writer of fiction.

Cynthia Ozick

We Are the Crazy Lady

Cynthia Ozick (b. 1928) is an American novelist who has written fiction, essays, poetry, and translations in various magazines and reviews. Winner of a number of awards, she is the author of, among others, *Trust* (1966); *The Pagan Rabbi and Other Stories* (1971); *Bloodshed and Three Novellas* (1976); *Levitation: Five Fictions* (1981); and *The Cannibal Galaxy* (1983). A series of episodes in the 1950s and 1960s in which the writer experiences sexual discrimination are ironically narrated.

I. The Crazy Lady Double

A long, long time ago, in another century—1951, in fact—when you, dear younger readers, were most likely still in your nuclear-family playpen (where, if female, you cuddled a rag-baby to your potential titties, or, if male, let down virile drool over your plastic bulldozer), Lionel Trilling told me never, never to use a parenthesis in the very first sentence. This was in a graduate English seminar at Columbia University. To get into this seminar, you had to submit to a grilling wherein you renounced all former allegiance to the then-current literary religion, New Criticism, which considered that only the text existed, not the world. I passed the interview by lying, cunningly, and against my real convictions. I said that probably the world *did* exist—and walked triumphantly into the seminar room.

There were four big tables arranged in a square, with everyone's feet sticking out into the open middle of the square. You could tell who was nervous, and how much, by watching the pairs of feet twist around each other. Professor Trilling presided awesomely from the high bar of the square. His head was a majestic granite-gray, like a centurion in command; he *looked* famous. His clean shoes twitched only slightly, and only when he was angry.

It turned out he was angry at me a lot of the time. He was angry because he thought me a disrupter, a rioter, a provocateur, and a fool; also crazy. And this was twenty years ago, before these things were *de rigueur* in the universities. Everything was very quiet in those days. There were only the Cold War and Korea and Joe McCarthy and the Old Old Nixon, and the only revolutionaries around were in Henry James's *The Princess Casamassima.*

Habit governed the seminar. Where you sat the first day was where you settled forever. So, to avoid the stigmatization of the ghetto, I was careful not to sit next to the other woman in the class: the Crazy Lady.

At first the Crazy Lady appeared to be remarkably intelligent. She was older than the rest of us, somewhere in her thirties (which was why we thought of her as a Lady), with wild tan hair, a noticeably breathing bosom, eccentric gold-rimmed old-pensioner glasses, and a tooth-crowded wild mouth that seemed to get wilder the more she talked. She talked like a motorcycle, fast and urgent. Everything she said was almost brilliant, only not actually on point, and frenetic with hostility. She was tough and negative. She volunteered a lot and she stood up and wobbled with rage, pulling at her hair and mouth. She fought Trilling point for point, piecemeal and wholesale, mixing up queerly-angled literary insights with all sorts of private and public fury. After the first meetings, he was fed up with her. The rest of us accepted that she probably wasn't all there, but in a room where everyone was on the make for recognition—you talked to save your life, and the only way to save your life was to be the smartest one that day—she was a nuisance, a distraction, a pain in the ass. The class became a bunch of Good Germans, determinedly indifferent onlookers to a vindictive match between Trilling and the Crazy Lady, until finally he subdued her by shutting his eyes, and, when that didn't always work, by cutting her dead and lecturing right across the sound of her strong, strange voice.

All this was before R. D. Laing had invented the superiority of madness, of course, and, cowards all, no one liked the thought of being tarred with the Crazy Lady's brush. Ignored by the boss, in the middle of everything she would suddenly begin to mutter to herself. She mentioned certain institutions she'd been in, and said we all belonged there. The people who sat on either side of her shifted chairs. If the Great Man ostracized the Crazy Lady, we had to do it too. But one day the Crazy Lady came in late and sat down in the seat next to mine, and stayed there the rest of the semester.

Then an odd thing happened. There, right next to me, was the noisy Crazy Lady, tall, with that sticking-out sighing chest of hers, orangey curls dripping over her nose, snuffling furiously for attention. And there was I, a brownish runt, a dozen years younger and flatter and shyer than the Crazy Lady, in no way her twin, physically or psychologically. In those days I was bone-skinny, small, sallow and myopic, and so scared I could trigger diarrhea at one glance from the Great Man. All this stress on looks is important. The Crazy Lady and I had our separate bodies, our separate brains. We handed in our separate papers.

But the Great Man never turned toward me, never at all, and if ambition broke feverishly through shyness so that I dared to push an idea audibly out of me, he shut his eyes when I put up my hand. This went on for a long time. I never got to speak, and I began to have the depressing feeling that Lionel Trilling hated me. It was no small thing to be hated by the man who had written "Wordsworth and the Rabbis" and *Matthew Arnold*, after all. What in hell was going on? I was in trouble, because, like everyone else in that demented contest, I wanted to excel. Then, one slow afternoon, wearily, the Great Man let his eyes fall on me. He called me by name, but it was not my name—it was the Crazy Lady's. The next week the papers came back—and there, right at the top of mine, in the Great Man's own handwriting, was a rebuke to the Crazy Lady for starting an essay with a parenthesis in the first sentence, a habit he took to be a continuing sign of that unruly and unfocused mentality so often exhibited in class. And then a Singular Revelation crept coldly through me. Because the Crazy Lady and I sat side by side, because we were a connected blur of Woman, Lionel Trilling, master of ultimate distinctions, couldn't tell us apart. The Crazy Lady and I! He couldn't tell us apart! It didn't matter that the Crazy Lady was crazy! *He couldn't tell us apart!*

Moral 1: All cats are gray at night,
          all darkies look alike.

Moral 2: Even among intellectual humanists, every woman has a *Doppelgänger*—every other woman.

II. The Lecture, 1

I was invited by a women's group to be guest speaker at a Book-Author Luncheon. The women themselves had not really chosen me: the speaker had been selected by a male leader and imposed on them. The plan was that I would autograph copies of my book, eat a good meal and then lecture. The woman in charge of the programming phoned to ask me what my topic would be. This was a matter of some concern, since they had never had a woman author before, and no one knew how the idea would be received. I offered as my subject "The Contemporary Poem."

When the day came, everything went as scheduled—the autographing, the food, the welcoming addresses. Then it was time to go to the lectern. I aimed at the microphone and began to speak of poetry. A peculiar rustling sound flew up from the audience. All the women were lifting their programs to the light, like hundreds of wings. Confused murmurs ran along the walls. I began to feel very uncomfortable. Then I too took up the program. It read, "Topic: The Contemporary Home."

Moral: Even our ears practice the caste system.

III. The Lecture, 2

I was in another country, the only woman at a philosophical seminar lasting three days. On the third day, I was to read a paper. I had accepted the invitation with a certain foreknowledge. I knew, for instance, that I could not dare to be the equal of any other speaker. To be an equal would be to be less. I understood that mine had to be the most original and powerful paper of all. I had no choice; I had to toil beyond my most extreme possibilities. This was not ambition, but only fear of disgrace.

For the first two days, I was invisible. When I spoke, people tapped impatiently, waiting for the interruption to be over with. No one took either my presence or my words seriously. At meals, I sat with my colleagues' wives.

The third day arrived, and I read my paper. It was successful beyond my remotest imaginings. I was interviewed, and my remarks appeared in newspapers in a language I could not understand. The Foreign Minister invited me to his home. I hobnobbed with famous poets.

Now my colleagues noticed me. But they did not notice me as a colleague. They teased and kissed me. I had become their mascot.

Moral: There is no route out of caste which does not instantly lead back into it.

IV. Propaganda

For many years, I had noticed that no book of poetry by a woman was ever reviewed without reference to the poet's sex. The curious thing was that, in the two decades of my scrutiny, there were *no* exceptions whatever. It did not matter whether the reviewer was a man or woman: in every case the question of the "feminine sensibility" of the poet was at the center of the reviewer's response. The maleness of male poets, on the other hand, hardly ever seemed to matter.

Determined to ridicule this convention, I wrote a tract, a piece of purely tendentious mockery, in the form of a short story. I called it "Virility."

The plot was, briefly, as follows: A very bad poet, lustful for fame, is despised for his pitiful lucubrations and remains unpublished. But luckily, he comes into possession of a cache of letters written by his elderly spinster aunt, who lives an obscure and secluded working-class life in a remote corner of England. The letters contain a large number of remarkable poems; the aunt, it turns out, is a genius. The bad poet publishes his find under his own name, and instantly attains world-wide adulation. Under the title *Virility*, the poems become immediate classics. They are translated into dozens of languages and are praised and revered for their unmistakably masculine qualities: their strength, passion, wisdom, energy, boldness, brutality, worldliness, robustness, authenticity, sensuality, compassion. A big, handsome sweating man, the poet swaggers from country to country, courted everywhere, pursued by admirers, yet respected by the most demanding critics.

Meanwhile, the old aunt dies. The supply of genius runs out. Bravely and contritely the poor poet confesses his ruse, and, in a burst of honesty, publishes the last batch under the real poet's name. The book is entitled *Flowers from Liverpool*. But the poems are at once found negligible and dismissed: "Thin feminine art," say the reviews, "a lovely girlish voice." Also: "Choked with female inwardness," and "The fine womanly intuition of a competent poetess." The poems are utterly forgotten.

I included this fable in a collection of short stories. In every review, the salvo went unnoticed. Not one reviewer recognized that the story was a sly tract. Not one reviewer saw the smirk or the point. There was one delicious comment, though. "I have some reservations," a man in Washington, D.C., wrote, "about the credibility of some of her male characters when they are chosen as narrators."

Moral: In saying what is obvious, never choose cunning. Yelling works better.

V. Hormones

During a certain period of my life, I was reading all the time, and fairly obsessively. Sometimes, though, sunk in a book of criticism or philosophy, I would be brought up short. Consider: here is a paragraph that excites the intellect. Inwardly, one assents passionately to its premises; the writer's idea is an exact diagram of one's own deepest psychology or conviction; one feels oneself seized as for a portrait. Then the disclaimer: "It is, however, otherwise with the female sex. . . ." A rebuke from the World of Thinking. *I didn't mean you, lady.* In the instant one is in possession of one's humanity most intensely, it is ripped away.

These moments I discounted. What is wrong—intrinsically, psychologically, culturally, morally—can be dismissed.

But to dismiss in this manner is to falsify one's most genuine actuality. A Jew reading of the aesthetic glories of European civilization without taking notice of his victimization during, say, the era of the building of the great cathedrals, is self-forgetful in the most dangerous way. So would be a black who read of King Cotton with an economist's objectivity.

I am not offering any strict analogy between the situation of women and the history of Jews or colonialized blacks, as many politically radical women do (though the analogy with blacks is much the more frequent one). It seems to me to be abusive of language in the extreme when some women speak, in the generation after Auschwitz, in the very hour of the Bengali horror, of the "oppression" of women. Language makes culture, and we make a rotten culture when we abuse words. We raise up rotten heroines. I use "rotten" with particular attention to its precise meanings: foul, putrid, tainted, stinking. I am thinking now especially of a radical women's publication, *Off Our Backs*, which not long ago presented Leila Khaled, terrorist and foiled murderer, as a model for the political conduct of women.

But if I would not support the extreme analogy (and am never surprised when black women, who have a more historical comprehension of actual, not figurative, oppression, refuse to support the analogy), it is anyhow curious to see what happens to the general culture when any enforced class in any historical or social condition is compelled to doubt its own self-understanding, when identity is extremely defined, when individual humanity is called into question as being different from "standard" humanity. What happens is that the general culture, along with the object of its debasement, is also debased. If you laugh at women, you play Beethoven in vain. If you laugh at women, your laboratory will lie.

We can read in Charlotte Perkins Gilman's 1912 essay, "Are Women Human Beings?", an account of an opinion current sixty years ago. Women, said one scientist, are not only "not the human race—they are not even half the human race, but a sub-species set apart for purposes of reproduction merely."

Though we are accustomed to the idea of "progress" in science, if not in civilization generally, the fact is that more information has led to something very like regression.

I talked with an intelligent physician, the Commissioner of Health of a middle-sized city in Connecticut, a man who sees medicine not discretely but as part of the social complex. He treated me to a long list of all the objective differences between men and women, including particularly an account of current endocrinal studies relating to female hormones. Aren't all of these facts? he asked. How can you distrust facts? Very good, I said, I'm willing to take your medically-educated word for it. I'm not afraid of facts, I welcome facts—*but a congeries of facts is not equivalent to an idea*. This is the essential fallacy of the so-called "scientific" mind. People who mistake facts for ideas are incomplete thinkers; they are gossips.

You tell me, I said, that my sense of my own humanity as being "standard" humanity—which is, after all, a subjective idea—is refuted by hormonal research. My psychology, you tell me, which in your view is the source of my ideas, is the result of my physiology. It is not I who express myself, it is my hormones which express me. A part is equal to the whole, you say. Worse yet, the whole is simply the issue of the part: my "I" is a flash of chemicals. You are willing to define all my humanity by hormonal investigation under a microscope. This you call "objective irrefutable fact," as if tissue-culture were equivalent to culture. But each scientist can assemble his own (subjective) constellation of "objective irrefutable fact," just as each social thinker can assemble his own (subjective) selection of traits that define "humanity." Who can prove what is "standard" humanity, and which sex, class, or race is to be exempted from whole participation in it? On what basis do you regard female hormones as causing a modification from normative humanity? And what better right do you have to define normative humanity by what males have traditionally apperceived than by what females have traditionally apperceived—assuming (as I, lacking presumptuousness, do not) that their apperceptions have not been the same? Only Tiresias—that mythological character who was both man and woman consecutively—is in a position to make the comparison and present the proof. And then not even Tiresias, because to be a hermaphrodite is to be a monster, and not human.

"Why are you so emotional about all this?" said the Commissioner of Health. "You see how it is? Those are your female hormones working on you right now."

Moral: Defamation is only applied research.

VI. Ambition

After thirteen years, I at last finished a novel. The first seven years were spent in a kind of apprenticeship—the book that came out of that time was abandoned without much regret. A second one was finished in six weeks and buried. It took six years to write the third novel, and this one was finally published.

How I lived through those years is impossible to recount in a short space. I was a recluse, a priest of Art. I read seas of books. I believed in the idea of masterpieces. I was scornful of the world of journalism, jobs, everydayness. I did not live like any woman I knew. I lived like some men I had read about—Flaubert, or Proust, or James—the subjects of those literary biographies I endlessly drank in. I did not think of them as men, but as writers. I read the diaries of Virginia Woolf, and biographies of George Eliot, but I did not think of them as women. I thought of them as writers. I thought of myself as a writer.

It goes without saying that all this time my relatives regarded me as abnormal. I accepted this. It seemed to me, from what I had read, that most writers were abnormal. Yet on the surface, I could easily have passed for normal. The husband goes to work, the wife stays home—that is what is normal. Well, I was married. My husband went to his job every day. His job paid the rent and bought the groceries. I stayed home, reading and writing, and felt myself to be an economic parasite. To cover guilt, I joked that I had been given a grant from a very private, very poor, foundation—my husband.

But my relatives never thought of me as a parasite. The very thing I was doubtful about—my economic dependence—they considered my due as a woman. They saw me not as a failed writer without an income, but as a childless housewife, a failed woman. They did not think me abnormal because I was a writer, but because I was not properly living my life as a woman. In one respect we were in agreement utterly—my life was failing terribly, terribly. For me it was because, already deep into my thirties, I had not yet published a book. For them, it was because I had not yet borne a child.

I was a pariah, not only because I was a deviant, but because I was not recognized as the kind of deviant I meant to be. A failed woman is not the same as a failed writer. Even as a pariah I was the wrong kind of pariah.

Still, relations are only relations. What I aspired to, what I was in thrall to, was Art, was Literature, not familial contentment. I knew how to distinguish the trivial from the sublime. In Literature and in Art, I saw, my notions were not pariah notions. There, I inhabited the mainstream. So I went on reading and writing. I went on believing in Art, and my intention was to write a masterpiece. Not a saucer of well-polished craft (the sort of thing "women writers" are always accused of being accomplished at), but something huge, contemplative, Tolstoyan. My ambition was a craw.

I called the book *Trust*. I began it in the summer of 1957 and finished it in November of 1963, on the day President John Kennedy was assassinated. In manuscript, it was 801 pages divided into four parts: "America," "Europe," "Birth," and "Death." The title was meant to be ironic. In reality, it was about distrust. It seemed to me I had touched on distrust in every order or form of civilization. It seemed to me I had left nothing out. It was (though I did not know this then) a very hating book. What it hated above all was the whole—the whole—of Western Civilization. It told how America had withered into another Europe. It dreamed dark and murderous pagan dreams, and hated what it dreamed.

In style, the book was what has come to be called "mandarin": a difficult, aristocratic, unrelenting virtuoso prose. It was, in short, unreadable. I think I knew this. I was sardonic enough to say, echoing Joyce about *Finnegans Wake*, "I expect you to spend your life at this." In any case, I had spent a decade-and-a-half of my own life at it. Though I did not imagine the world would fall asunder at its appearance, I thought—at the very least—the ambition, the all-swallowingness, the wild insatiability of the writer would be plain to everyone who read it. I had, after all, taken History for my subject: not merely History as an aggregate of events, but History as a judgment on events. No one could say my theme was flighty. Of all the novelists I read (and in those days I read them all, broiling in the envy of the unpublished, which is like no envy on earth), who else had dared so vastly?

During that period, Françoise Sagan's first novel was published. I held the thin little thing and laughed. Women's pulp!

My own novel, I believed, contained everything—the whole world.

But there was one element I had consciously left out. Though on principle I did not like to characterize it or think about it much, the truth is I was thinking about it all the time. It was only a fiction-technicality, but I was considerably afraid of it. It was the question of the narrator's "sensibility." The narrator, as it happened, was a young woman; I had chosen her to be the eye—and the "I"—of the novel because all the other characters in some way focused on her. She was the one most useful to my scheme. Nevertheless, I wanted her not to live. Everything I was reading in reviews of other people's books made me fearful: I would have to be very cautious; I would have to drain my narrator of emotive value of any kind, because I was afraid to be pegged as having written a "woman's" novel. Nothing was more certain to lead to that than a point-of-view seemingly lodged in a woman, and no one takes a woman's novel seriously. I was in terror, above all, of sentiment and feelings, those telltale taints. I kept the fury and the passion for other, safer, characters.

So what I left out of my narrator entirely, sweepingly, with exquisite consciousness of what exactly I *was* leaving out, was any shred of "sensibility." I
stripped her of everything, even a name. I crafted and carpentered her. She
was for me a bloodless device, fulcrum or pivot, a recording voice, a language-
machine. She confronted moment or event, took it in, gave it out. And what
to me was all the more wonderful about this nameless fiction-machine I had
invented was that the machine itself, though never alive, was a character in
the story, without ever influencing the story. My machine-narrator was there
for efficiency only, for flexibility, for craftiness, for subtlety, but never, never,
as a "woman." I wiped the "woman" out of her. And I did it out of fear, out
of vicarious vindictive critical imagination, out of the terror of my ambition,
out of, maybe, paranoia. I meant my novel to be taken for what it really was.
I meant to make it impossible for it to be mistaken for something else.

Publication. Review in *The New York Times* Sunday Book Review.

Review is accompanied by a picture of a naked woman seen from the back.
Her bottom is covered by some sort of drapery.

Title of review: "Daughter's Reprieve."

Excerpts from review: "These events, interesting in themselves, exist to
reveal the sensibility of the narrator." "She longs to play some easy feminine
role." "She has been unable to define herself as a woman." "The main body
of the novel, then, is a revelation of the narrator's inner, turbulent, psychic
drama."

O rabid rotten Western Civilization, where are you? O judging History, O
foul Trust and fouler Distrust, where?

O Soap Opera, where did you come from?

(Meanwhile the review in *Time* was calling me a "housewife.")

Pause.

All right, let us take up the rebuttals.

Q. Maybe you *did* write a soap opera without knowing it. Maybe you only
thought you were writing about Western Civilization when you were really
only rewriting Stella Dallas.

A. A writer may be unsure of everything—trust the tale not the teller is a
good rule—but not of his obsessions; of these he is certain. If I were rewriting
Stella Dallas, I would turn her into the Second Crusade and demobilize her.

Q. Maybe you're like the blind Jew who wants to be a pilot, and when
they won't give him the job he says they're anti-Semitic. Look, the book was
lousy, you deserved a lousy review.

A. You mistake me, I never said it was a bad review. It was in fact an
extremely favorable review, full of gratifying adjectives.

Q. Then what's eating you?

A. I don't know. Maybe the question of language. By language I mean
literacy. See the next section, please.

Q. No Moral for *this* section?

A. Of course. If you look for it, there will always be a decent solution for
female ambition. For instance, it is still not too late to enroll in a good secre-
tarial school.

Q. Bitter, bitter! You mean your novel failed?

A. Perished, is dead and buried. I sometimes see it exhumed on the shelf
in the public library. It's always there. No one ever borrows it.

Q. Dummy! You should've written a soap opera. Women are good at that.

A. Thank you. You almost remind me of a Second Moral: In conceptual life, junk prevails. Even if you do not produce junk, it will be taken for junk.

Q. What does that have to do with women?

A. The products of women are frequently taken for junk.

Q. And if a woman *does* produce junk . . . ?

A. Glory—they will treat her almost like a man who produces junk. They will say her name on television. Do please go on to the next section. Thank you.

VII. Conclusion, and a Peek

Actually I had two more stories to tell you. One was about Mr. Machismo, a very angry, well-groomed, *clean man* (what a pity he isn't a woman—ah, deprived of vaginal spray) who defines as irresponsible all those who do not obey him, especially his mother and sister. A highly morbid and titillating Gothic tale. The other story was about Mr. Littletable, the Petty Politician, at the Bankers' Feast—how he gathered up the wives in a pretty garland, threw them a topic to chatter over. A Bronx neighborhood where you can buy good lox, I think it was. Having set them all up so nicely, he went off to lick the nearest Vice-President-of-Morgan-Guaranty.

But these are long stories, Ladies and Gentlemen. No room up there for another Woman's Novel.

Suggestions for Discussion

1. How does the author establish tone? What are its components? Cite examples.

2. Find examples of effective metaphoric language and show how they contribute to purpose and tone.

3. What is the causal relationship between the experiences and the "morals"? State each "moral" in your own words. How does the phrasing of the "morals" contribute to tone?

4. How does the author develop the paradox that more information leads to repression?

5. Cite examples of irony.

6. What generalization does each incident illustrate?

Suggestions for Writing

1. Out of your own experience and observation develop the thesis underlying one of the author's "morals."

2. Write a sketch or narrative recounting an experience in which your sexual identity made a difference in the outcome.

3. Develop or refute the following statements of the author: "If you laugh at women, you play Beethoven in vain. If you laugh at women, your laboratory will lie."

Germaine Greer

The Stereotype

Germaine Greer (b. 1939) is an Australian-born writer and educator, best known as a standard bearer of the women's liberation movement and as the author of the best-selling *The Female Eunuch* (1971), from which this selection is taken, and of *Sex and Destiny: The Politics of Human Fertility* (1984). The stereotype—the Eternal Feminine—sought by women as well as by men, reduces a woman to a cipher and castrates her.

In that mysterious dimension where the body meets the soul the stereotype is born and has her being. She is more body than soul, more soul than mind. To her belongs all that is beautiful, even the very word beauty itself. All that exists, exists to beautify her. The sun shines only to burnish her skin and gild her hair; the wind blows only to whip up the color in her cheeks; the sea strives to bathe her; flowers die gladly so that her skin may luxuriate in their essence. She is the crown of creation, the masterpiece. The depths of the sea are ransacked for pearl and coral to deck her; the bowels of the earth are laid open that she might wear gold, sapphires, diamonds, and rubies. Baby seals are battered with staves, unborn lambs ripped from their mothers' wombs, millions of moles, muskrats, squirrels, minks, ermines, foxes, beavers, chinchillas, ocelots, lynxes, and other small and lovely creatures die untimely deaths that she might have furs. Egrets, ostriches, and peacocks, butterflies and beetles yield her their plumage. Men risk their lives hunting leopards for her coats, and crocodiles for her handbags and shoes. Millions of silkworms offer her their yellow labors; even the seamstresses roll seams and whip lace by hand, so that she might be clad in the best that money can buy. The men of our civilization have stripped themselves of the fineries of the earth so that they might work more freely to plunder the universe for treasures to deck my lady in. New raw materials, new processes, new machines are all brought into her service. My lady must therefore be the chief spender as well as the chief symbol of spending ability and monetary success. While her mate toils in his factory, she totters about the smartest streets and plushiest hotels with his fortune upon her back and bosom, fingers, and wrists, continuing that essential expenditure in his house which is her frame and her setting, enjoying that silken idleness which is the necessary condition of

> Taught from infancy that beauty is woman's scepter, the mind shapes itself to the body, and roaming round its gilt cage, only seeks to adorn its prison.
>
> —**Mary Wollstonecraft,** A *Vindication of the Rights of Woman,* 1792.

maintaining her mate's prestige and her qualification to demonstrate it. Once upon a time only the aristocratic lady could lay claim to the title of crown of creation: only her hands were white enough, her feet tiny enough, her waist narrow enough, her hair long and golden enough; but every well-to-do burgher's wife set herself up to ape my lady and to follow fashion, until my lady was forced to set herself out like a gilded doll overlaid with monstrous rubies and pearls like pigeon's eggs. Nowadays the Queen of England still considers it part of her royal female role to sport as much of the family jewelry as she can manage at any one time on all public occasions, although the male monarchs have escaped such showcase duty, which develops exclusively upon their wives.

At the same time as woman was becoming the showcase for wealth and caste, while men were slipping into relative anonymity and "handsome is as handsome does," she was emerging as the central emblem of western art. For the Greeks the male and female body had beauty of a human, not necessarily a sexual, kind; indeed they may have marginally favored the young male form as the most powerful and perfectly proportioned. Likewise the Romans showed no bias towards the depiction of femininity in their predominantly monumental art. In the Renaissance the female form began to predominate, not only as the mother in the predominant emblem of *madonna con bambino*, but as an aesthetic study in herself. At first naked female forms took their chances in crowd scenes or diptychs of Adam and Eve, but gradually Venus claims ascendancy, Mary Magdalene ceases to be wizened and emaciated, and becomes nubile and ecstatic, portraits of anonymous young women, chosen only for their prettiness, begin to appear, are gradually disrobed, and renamed Flora or Primavera. Painters begin to paint their own wives and mistresses and royal consorts as voluptuous beauties, divesting them of their clothes if desirable, but not of their jewelry. Susanna keeps her bracelets on in the bath, and Hélène Fourment keeps ahold of her fur as well!

What happened to women in painting happened to her in poetry as well. Her beauty was celebrated in terms of the riches which clustered around her: her hair was gold wires, her brow ivory, her lips ruby, her teeth gates of pearl, her breasts alabaster veined with lapis lazuli, her eyes as black as jet. The fragility of her loveliness was emphasized by the inevitable comparisons with the rose, and she was urged to employ her beauty in love-making before it withered on the stem. She was for consumption; other sorts of imagery spoke of her in terms of cherries and cream, lips as sweet as honey and skin white as milk, breasts like cream uncurdled, hard as apples. Some celebrations yearned over her finery as well, her lawn more transparent than morning mist, her lace as delicate as gossamer, the baubles that she toyed with and the favors that she gave. Even now we find the thriller hero describing his classy dames' elegant suits, cheeky hats, well-chosen accessories and footwear; the imagery no longer dwells on jewels and flowers but the consumer emphasis is the same. The mousy secretary blossoms into the feminine stereotype when she reddens her lips, lets down her hair, and puts on something frilly.

Nowadays women are not expected, unless they are Paola di Liegi or Jackie Onassis, and then only on gala occasions, to appear with a king's ransom deployed upon their bodies, but they are required to look expensive, fashionable, well-groomed, and not to be seen in the same dress twice. If the duty of the few may have become less onerous, it has also become the duty of the many. The stereotype marshals an army of servants. She is supplied with cosmetics, underwear, foundation garments, stockings, wigs, postiches, and hairdressing as well as her outer garments, her jewels, and furs. The effect is to be built up layer by layer, and it is expensive. Splendor has given way to fit, line, and cut. The spirit of competition must be kept up, as more and more women struggle toward the top drawer, so that the fashion industry can rely upon an expanding market. Poorer women fake it, ape it, pick up on the fashions a season too late, use crude effects, mistaking the line, the sheen, the gloss of the high-class article for a garish simulacrum. The business is so complex that it must be handled by an expert. The paragons of the stereotype must be dressed, coifed, and painted by the experts and the style-setters, although they may be encouraged to give heart to the housewives studying their lives in pulp magazines by claiming a lifelong fidelity to their own hair and soap and water. The boast is more usually discouraging than otherwise, unfortunately.

As long as she is young and personable, every woman may cherish the dream that she may leap up the social ladder and dim the sheen of luxury by sheer natural loveliness; the few examples of such a feat are kept before the eye of the public. Fired with hope, optimism, and ambition, young women study the latest forms of the stereotype, set out in *Vogue, Nova, Queen,* and other glossies, where the mannequins stare from among the advertisements for fabulous real estate, furs, and jewels. Nowadays the uniformity of the year's fashions is severely affected by the emergence of the pert female designers who direct their appeal to the working girl, emphasizing variety, comfort, and simple, striking effects. There is no longer a single face of the year: even Twiggy has had to withdraw into marketing and rationed personal appearances, while the Shrimp works mostly in New York. Nevertheless the stereotype is still supreme. She has simply allowed herself a little more variation.

The stereotype is the Eternal Feminine. She is the Sexual Object sought by all men, and by all women. She is of neither sex, for she has herself no sex at all. Her value is solely attested by the demand she excites in others. All she must contribute is her existence. She need achieve nothing, for she is the reward of achievement. She need never give positive evidence of her moral character because virtue is assumed from her loveliness, and her passivity. If any man who has no right to her be found with her she will not be punished, for she is morally neuter. The matter is solely one of male rivalry. Innocently she may drive men to madness and war. The more trouble she can cause, the more her stocks go up, for possession of her means more the more demand she excites. Nobody wants a girl whose beauty is imperceptible to all but him; and so men welcome the stereotype because it directs their taste into the most commonly recognized areas of value, although they may protest because some aspects of it do not tally with their fetishes. There is scope in the stereotype's variety for most fetishes. The leg man may follow miniskirts, the tit man can encourage see-through blouses and plunging necklines, although the man who likes fat women may feel constrained to enjoy them in secret. There are stringent limits to the variations on the stereotype, for nothing must interfere with her function as sex object. She may wear leather, as long as she cannot actually handle a motorbike: she may wear rubber, but it ought

> The myth of the strong black woman is the other side of the coin of the myth of the beautiful dumb blonde. The white man turned the white woman into a weak-minded, weak-bodied, delicate freak, a sex pot, and placed her on a pedestal; he turned the black woman into a strong self-reliant Amazon and deposited her in his kitchen. . . . The white man turned himself into the Omnipotent Administrator and established himself in the Front Office.
>
> **—Eldridge Cleaver,** "The Allegory of the Black Eunuchs," *Soul on Ice,* 1968.

not to indicate that she is an expert diver or waterskier. If she wears athletic clothes the purpose is to underline her unathleticism. She may sit astride a horse, looking soft and curvy, but she must not crouch over its neck with her rump in the air.

Because she is the emblem of spending ability and the chief spender, she is also the most effective seller of this world's goods. Every survey ever held has shown that the image of an attractive woman is the most effective advertising gimmick. She may sit astride the mudguard of a new car, or step into it ablaze with jewels; she may lie at a man's feet stroking his new socks; she may hold the petrol pump in a challenging pose, or dance through woodland glades in slow motion in all the glory of a new shampoo; whatever she does her image sells. The gynolatry of our civilization is written large upon its face, upon hoardings, cinema screens, television, newspapers, magazines, tins, packets, cartons, bottles, all consecrated to the reigning deity, the female fetish. Her dominion must not be thought to entail the rule of women, for she is not a woman. Her glossy lips and mat complexion, her unfocused eyes and flawless fingers, her extraordinary hair all floating and shining, curling, and gleaming, reveal the inhuman triumph of cosmetics, lighting, focusing, and printing, cropping and composition. She sleeps unruffled, her lips red and juicy and closed, her eyes as crisp and black as if new painted, and her false lashes immaculately curled. Even when she washes her face with a new and creamier toilet soap her expression is as tranquil and vacant and her paint as flawless as ever. If ever she should appear tousled and troubled, her features are miraculously smoothed to their proper veneer by a new washing powder or a bouillon cube. For she is a doll: weeping, pouting, or smiling, running or reclining, she is a doll. She is an idol, formed of the concatenation of lines and masses, signifying the lineaments of satisfied impotence.

Her essential quality is castratedness. She absolutely must be young, her body hairless, her flesh buoyant, and *she must not have a sexual organ.* No musculature must distort the smoothness of the lines of her body, although she may be painfully slender or warmly cuddly. Her expression must betray no hint of humor, curiosity, or intelligence, although it may signify hauteur to an extent that is actually absurd, or smoldering lust, very feebly signified by drooping eyes and a sullen mouth (for the stereotype's lust equals irrational submission), or, most commonly, vivacity and idiot happiness. Seeing that

> She was created to be the toy of man, his rattle, and it must
> jingle in his ears whenever, dismissing reason, he chooses to
> be amused.
>
> —**Mary Wollstonecraft,** A *Vindication of the Rights of
> Woman,* 1792.

the world despoils itself for this creature's benefit, she must be happy; the entire structure would topple if she were not. So the image of woman appears plastered on every surface imaginable, smiling interminably. An apple pie evokes a glance of tender beatitude, a washing machine causes hilarity, a cheap box of chocolates brings forth meltingly joyous gratitude, a Coke is the cause of a rictus of unutterable brilliance, even a new stick-on bandage is saluted by a smirk of satisfaction. A real woman licks her lips and opens her mouth and flashes her teeth when photographers appear: *she* must arrive at the premiere of her husband's film in a paroxysm of delight, or his success might be murmured about. The occupational hazard of being a Playboy Bunny is the aching facial muscles brought on by the obligatory smiles.

So what is the beef? Maybe I couldn't make it. Maybe I don't have a pretty smile, good teeth, nice tits, long legs, a cheeky ass, a sexy voice. Maybe I don't know how to handle men and increase my market value, so that the rewards due to the feminine will accrue to me. Then again, maybe I'm sick of the masquerade. I'm sick of pretending eternal youth. I'm sick of belying my own intelligence, my own will, my own sex. I'm sick of peering at the world through false eyelashes, so everything I see is mixed with a shadow of bought hairs; I'm sick of weighting my head with a dead mane, unable to move my neck freely, terrified of rain, of wind, of dancing too vigorously in case I sweat into my lacquered curls. I'm sick of the Powder Room. I'm sick of pretending that some fatuous male's self-important pronouncements are the objects of my undivided attention, I'm sick of going to films and plays when someone else wants to, and sick of having no opinions of my own about either. I'm sick of being a transvestite. I refuse to be a female impersonator. I am a woman, not a castrate.

April Ashley was born male. All the information supplied by genes, chromosomes, internal and external sexual organs added up to the same thing.

> Discretion is the better part of Valerie
> though all of her is nice
> lips as warm as strawberries
> eyes as cold as ice
> the very best of everything
> only will suffice
> not for her potatoes
> and puddings made of rice
>
> —**Roger McGough,** Discretion.

> To what end is the laying out of the embroidered Hair, em-
> bared Breasts; vermilion Cheeks, alluring looks, Fashion
> gates, and artful Countenances, effeminate intangling and in-
> snaring Gestures, their Curls and Purls of proclaiming Petu-
> lancies, boulstered and laid out with such example and au-
> thority in these our days, as with Allowance and beseeming
> Conveniency?
>
> Doth the world wax barren through decrease of Genera-
> tions, and become, like the Earth, less fruitful heretofore?
> Doth the Blood lose his Heat or do the Sunbeams become
> waterish and less fervent, than formerly they have been, that
> men should be thus inflamed and persuaded on to lust?
>
> —**Alex. Niccholes,** A *Discourse of Marriage and Wiving,*
> 1615.

April was a man. But he longed to be a woman. He longed for the stereotype, not to embrace, but to be. He wanted soft fabrics, jewels, furs,
makeup, the love and protection of men. So he was impotent. He couldn't
fancy women at all, although he did not particularly welcome homosexual
addresses. He did not think of himself as a pervert, or even as a transvestite,
but as a woman cruelly transmogrified into manhood. He tried to die, became a female impersonator, but eventually found a doctor in Casablanca
who came up with a more acceptable alternative. He was to be castrated, and
his penis used as the lining of a surgically constructed cleft, which would be a
vagina. He would be infertile, but that has never affected the attribution of
femininity. April returned to England, resplendent. Massive hormone treatment had eradicated his beard, and formed tiny breasts: he had grown his
hair and bought feminine clothes during the time he had worked as an impersonator. He became a model, and began to illustrate the feminine stereotype
as he was perfectly qualified to do, for he was elegant, voluptuous, beautifully
groomed, and in love with his own image. On an ill-fated day he married the
heir to a peerage, the Hon. Arthur Corbett, acting out the highest achievement of the feminine dream, and went to live with him in a villa in Marbella.
The marriage was never consummated. April's incompetence as a woman is
what we must expect from a castrate, but it is not so very different after all
from the impotence of feminine women, who submit to sex without desire,
with only the infantile pleasure of cuddling and affection, which is their favorite reward. As long as the feminine stereotype remains the definition of the
female sex, April Ashley is a woman, regardless of the legal decision ensuing
from her divorce. She is as much a casualty of the polarity of the sexes as we
all are. Disgraced, unsexed April Ashley is our sister and our symbol.

Suggestions for Discussion

1. How does the author develop the concept that "beauty is woman's scepter"? How
   does the long series of examples in the first paragraph contribute to purpose and
   tone?

2. What does the author mean by the stereotype? How does she develop and support her extended definition?

3. In what context does the author invoke the first person? How does its intrusion affect purpose and tone?

4. What purpose is served by the introduction of April Ashley? Do the last two sentences constitute an appropriate summation of what has gone before? Explain.

Suggestion for Writing

Drawing on your own experience and observation, write an essay on stereotypes.

Natalie Rogers

The Right to Be Me!
Confronting Sex Role Expectations

Natalie Rogers initiated with her father, Carl Rogers, residential workshops in the "Person-Centered Approach." She is a client-centered psychotherapist and works with both individuals and groups. She has developed training programs for women counselors and has led professional women's groups in many foreign countries. This chapter, from her book, Emerging Woman, suggests how the conditioning forces of family and society led to her "collusion" in a marriage that deprived her of a sense of worth.

I have spent some time trying to discover how I came to be the woman I am. How much of what I am was set by cultural role expectations? What, in my childhood, adolescence, and adult life was prescribed for me? How much freedom do I have to *choose* my role? What is it I want? In order to understand the role expectations placed on me, I have looked for those people and incidents which have influenced my attitudes toward myself.

Metaphors of Childhood

As I look back on my girlhood, I see myself in a sailboat. It is a small, tubby boat my father had built in our garage. Mother made the sails—their division of labor. We were proud of the stability of the "Snark" even though it was not the sleek racing boat that others sailed on the lake.

"Come on Nat, want to join me for a sail?" My brother takes the initiative. "See if you can put up the jib, I'll rig the mainsail. You can hold the tiller while I shove off. . . . Okay, good girl, get to the jib and pull the sheets in. The jib will pull us around. . . . There we go, swell—we can relax now. When I get us away from this tricky shore wind I'll let you take the tiller."

As the wind fills the mainsail and I pull tight the jib to keep it from luffing, I feel proud. I hope I'm doing it right. As we heel in the wind I let it out a little; and, looking to the captain, I ask, "Is this okay?"

"Well, you could let it out a little further," comes the knowledgeable reply. I tidy the boat, coiling the ropes, looping the end through the coil, and hanging it neatly on the cleat. As we gain full speed, the wind strokes my face and excitement wells inside me. I look at my brother with question in my eyes, "Now?"

"Okay, you can take the tiller, but take it easy, the gusts come up suddenly."

As we switch places the boat levels off, I pull in the mainsail, hold the tiller tight, and heel us until the deck is cutting the lake.

"You've got it too tight! We'll go faster if you let it out," comes the advice.

I know this is true, but I enjoy the risky feeling of balancing on the edge. I slice the water, bracing my feet against the cockpit, leaning hard against the rope. A storm cloud appears. My brother announces that he is taking us in. I relinquish my seat feeling secure in his presence.

The memory of sailing in the boat with my father and brother is a simple, joyful recollection. Being the crew for one or two men skippers while Mom was on the shore making lunch became a significant metaphor in my development as a female. I was proud to be a good crew: I knew how to keep the boat shipshape to the requirements of the captains. As crew, I was pleasing the men in my life, getting their praise for doing what was expected of me. It was exciting to be a part of their action. I didn't have to take command of the boat—I liked that feeling of being protected from the full responsibility, yet being part of the excitement. I used to think, "Too bad for you, Mom, you're not out here with the adventure of making the boat heel, or of racing toward home before the squall comes up." I must have felt proud to be included with the men and somewhat disdainful of the woman left on shore, yet glad that she was there with the warm soup when we got back.

It doesn't take an analyst to see that I was being well trained for my role as a woman. I wanted to please the men I loved, to take part in their more exciting world, to take the tiller only on occasion (to take responsibility for the direction of others only occasionally), and with their approval and guidance. Mother's life was necessary and appreciated—but not as exciting. There was, and still is, an element in me that says, "I'll be more adventurous than you." Though I was appreciated, loved, and included, the expectation seemed to be that I would not be capable of being captain of a ship. I would ask for a turn at the tiller with full knowledge that I could only be second best. They (the men) had the *real* understanding of how things worked.

As a girl, I was being subtly trained to believe:

Men take the major responsibility for leadership and direction in life. They are to have control.

Women are to be helpers toward the destination that men choose. A good helper is pleasing, serving, accommodating.

Men have the real knowledge and understanding; women ask them for the truth.

Women get their "goodies" (self-esteem) by being praised and adored for being all of the above!

These were all an unspoken part of my growing up, and I never thought to question this role. It is only recently, in the process of writing these pages and leading women's groups, that I have come to realize what such training did to limit the scope of my personal horizons.

I am now aware that the seeds of some of my present anger started germinating in childhood, as my parents and brother acted out the roles society demanded of them.

Looking at a favorite snapshot of me and my older brother, I see us standing on the back porch—he with his arm protectively around my shoulders. The expression on my face says I am enjoying cuddling under his wing. What a comforting role, this! And to this day, when a man puts his arm around me with the "I'll take care of you" stance, I yield to that longing. But I *now* know I can allow myself to be temporarily protected as long as it is not my role in *life*.

As a model for being a wife and mother, my mother set very high standards. She was nurturing and supportive, always there to do things for us, feed us, and take care of us. She cooked, cleaned, did the laundry, took care of our needs for love, discipline, schooling, and play. My father worked long hours in a clinic for disturbed children and wrote at night. She was taking care to see that he had the time to do his important work and would not need to be bothered with the mundane things in life. Although she had interests of her own, the message from mother was that "Children and husband come first, my own needs come last." We prospered under this in many ways, but at what cost to her? This model played some havoc with me. When it came to my own marriage, I took on that same model without questioning whether it was right for me.

The words "career woman" were pejorative in our home. They meant being cold, unfeminine, unmotherly, competitive, and aggressive. It was a wife's role to be emotionally supportive, to do everything possible to promote her husband's ideas and profession. Of course, in those days, I never consciously thought about what my parents were to each other or what impressions it left on me. I saw them peacefully discussing issues. I saw them caring and touching each other. I observed the division of labor and the feeling of who was dealing with the "world" and who was taking care of "home." Later I acted on what I had learned without being aware of it.

Marriage: Collusion of Two Members for the Benefit of One

The night before my wedding, like the picture of the sailboat, is a clear memory.

I can't sleep, naturally. I'm too excited. It's hard to believe tomorrow is the day I've dreamed of for so long. Marriage, to the one I will always love—my heart feels large, warm, and tender.

Amazing I have no doubts or fears. Some brides do, I know. I just want to give and be loved and share our lives. I wonder, wonder what our life will be like now that we are sealing it forever? Sounds delicious. I'm so happy I could burst!

I remember the choices I *thought* I had when I graduated from college. "If I don't find a man to marry I'll go on to graduate school to become a psychologist." It seemed like a very lonely possible second choice. It never occurred to me I could do both. Nor did anyone expect me to do both.

In retrospect, what I did to myself and how my husband colluded with me in the state of matrimony is incredible. I wrote to him, before marriage, that I thought he was better at most things than I, and that I looked forward to "living my life for him." When I read this "love" letter twenty years later, I set a match to it instantly. As I did so, I realized that I had been asking him to be the graduate student, the psychologist, the political activist, the thinker, and doer, when that is what I wanted for myself. I *married* one instead of *becoming* one.

The fact that I was at least as good as my husband-to-be in all areas—in human relations, in intellectual ability, in the "how to fix it" department, in life experience of being independent and responsible for myself—was somehow forgotten as I entered into a commitment to be a wife. To this day, I don't know whether my feelings of self-worth were really that low or whether I was responding to the powerful pressures of what a good wife is supposed to be. Apparently, being second best was one of my definitions of love.

I had applied to graduate school at Harvard (where he had already been accepted). I was told I wouldn't be accepted unless I was a full-time student. In this same letter to my fiancé, I wrote, "It will take at least half-time to take care of you." This was said without malice or resentment. It was what I expected of myself. The concept that we might share equally in educational opportunities and in taking care of each other never occurred to either of us. Instead, I edited, typed, helped organize his papers, occasionally went with him to classes to take his notes, or to the library to assist him in research. He was proud of all that I did, giving me praise—apparently I enjoyed and needed this approval. It kept me doing the second-class work throughout our marriage. I don't ever remember wondering why I wasn't going to classes and writing papers for myself. No one else asked why either.

Why should a man question what this role does to a woman? His ego and his work benefit greatly from this system. I was quite content with my role. I seemed to go to any length to get praise and approval. It was making a gourmet casserole, or the most original hors d'oeuvre, or running an efficient and tasteful house—that kept me going. Not that there is anything inherently wrong with any of those achievements. But what was happening to my *brain?* Except for the times that I was helping him think through the data for his books, or the decisions he had to make, or how to teach his class, I was not developing my own ability to think. I was hiding behind his ideas. He was using my thoughts in his work (without giving me credit).

I seldom said, "This is my opinion," or "Those are the dilemmas in the world as I view them." My identity as a thinking person, capable of sifting information, analyzing, and coming to conclusions, was given over to him. I believe I was acting out what was expected of me by my family, my husband, and society, without questioning any of it.

And yet, what a contrast to the person I had started to become before my marriage. In college I was quite a strong, independent-thinking young woman. At a woman's college I was turned on by new ideas, by testing my own intelligence. Delving into philosophy, religion, and literature, I questioned my own beliefs, or lack of them, searching for my place in the universe. (In a coed high school I had known well the need to act less intelligent than I was in order to be attractive to the boys.) Now I thrived on the personal attention of the professors—women and men—who wanted to hear about my philosophical struggles. I was valued for my ability to think and enjoyed the intellectual sparring with adults; and, since there were no men in the classes, I did not hold myself back intellectually. When I married, apparently I took off my thinking cap.

One part of the marriage myth that did not disappoint me was motherhood. I truly enjoyed being a mother and put a lot of my creative energy and intelligence into being with my children. I treasured being with my daughters while they were young. I experienced them as important persons from the day they responded to my love with a smile—and that was the day they were born! (No doctor will ever convince me those smiles were due to "gas bubbles.")

Playing with my children was fun. For hours I'd sit on the floor building blocks, crayoning, watching, encouraging, and chatting while they discovered how to hammer down the peg or build a tower. Their discoveries were exciting to me.

When I pushed Janet in the stroller to the park, I was happy to be alone with her. Some mothers sat together on a bench more interested in each other than their kids—which puzzled me.

When the girls were older, I created Sunday art-time where materials and possible projects with paint, collage, and clay were available to all of us at the kitchen table. As a family we enjoyed our playtimes together.

However, I resented having to be the sole disciplinarian of the family, and this was the one issue in our marriage that I assertively fought about. As bedtime approached, father and daughters would be happily engaged in story telling. Fine! Except that usually there was no ending to it unless I put my foot down. It was like having a fourth child—since I had to convince him to close the books or end the tale, as well. My request for shared responsibility for the disciplining was not heard. In the various parent groups I have run, this is one of the biggest complaints on the part of mothers: not being able to get fathers to share in the necessary task of setting appropriate limits for the children and consistently following them through. My husband preferred the role of playmate to the kids when they were young, rather than accept his share of the disciplining. I felt like the ogre.

If I were to relive my married life, I would still choose to spend most of my time, for those twelve to fifteen years, being a mother. It is one of the most enjoyable careers I can imagine. But I would also have a different attitude about my rights to time off and sharing of household responsibilities. I would not feel guilty when I took time for myself to read, write, study, or be with others.

By a subtle process which many women will recognize, I began to lose my identity in the marriage. His friends and colleagues became my friends. His career became my motivation. I protected and promoted his time and space to work. The telephone rang constantly—for him. Our system was that I would answer it, screen the call as to its immediate importance, and interrupt his writing or thinking only if absolutely necessary. I was a competent receptionist—but who protected any time for me?

Those were the days I would be introduced as Mrs. ———. The first question asked me was, "What does your husband do?" And I'd be discussing his involvements for hours. It occurred to me one week when he was out of town that I didn't really know who I was when he was gone. My identity was defined by his presence. Who was I and what did I believe in when he was away?

> He was torn about leaving me to go on this speaking tour. Having him gone for a week is a totally new experience. Is it possible that except for my three trips to the hospital to give birth, we have not been apart one night in eight years? I think it is true. I have such mixed feelings—I'm glad to have a few evenings to myself after the kids are in bed, and yet I don't feel I am all here. Part of me walked out the door and got in that taxi.
>
> Having S. here alone for supper was a nice experience. She didn't seem to think anything was strange, but as we sat eating leftover pot roast (the kids had eaten) and talking about life—her thoughts and mine—I realized I didn't *have* many thoughts of my own. Or do I? I'm just not used to saying them. I'm not sure my opinions or knowledge have validity any more. I feel I depend on my husband's interpretation or answers for everything (outside of the house and children). S. seemed interested in my opinions—she certainly has hers!
>
> This gives me some new insights. I need to do something about me. If I don't talk about him and his work, or my kids and their life, what *do* I talk about? More importantly, what do I think about if I'm not thinking of them?

Once I recognized how symbiotic we were, it became important to me to re-establish my own areas of interest. I decided to go back to school in the field of psychology. The encouragement of Abe Maslow helped me gain courage to become a student. (I already felt I was too old and stale to compete at age thirty.) I had also gained support from my father over the years to publish my psychological writing ("Play Therapy at Home," 1957: *Merrill-Palmer Quarterly*, Winter).* Today, as I counsel women, I often hear their sense of isolation and lack of self-worth as they toy with the idea of further education. I know how important supportive individuals can be at that time.

I had adopted the notion that a man's work is always more important than a woman's. Therefore, when I started graduate school, I took one course a semester, feeling somewhat guilty as I rushed off to school while my husband babysat. He made me feel this was something he was "giving'" me, for which I should be grateful. It didn't occur to me (or to him) that I was entitled to further education. Neither of us imagined that my work was important as work, or that my ideas might contribute just as much to the world as his.

The ultimate in thinking "His work is more important than mine" was captured in a rather humorous event. I was nine months' pregnant and close to delivery. My husband, on leaving for work, reminded me what a very important day this was in his career. "Don't have the baby today," he said. A fetus doesn't seem to have the same accommodating personality as a wife, so I did have the baby that day. When I called to let him know his important day was going to be interrupted by me and our child, I apologized rather than acknowledged that my work of the day was *more* important than his.

---

*Also published in Clark Moustakas' book, *Psychotherapy with Children, The Living Relationship*. It appears in the chapter, "Parents as Therapists."

When I look at our photo album I see pictures of a loving honeymoon in Europe with our tiny English car, hikes and picnics with the kids, birthday celebrations and travels. There is warmth in our faces, radiance and laughter in the children. Together. As many hours of as many days as possible, together. We shared our lives focusing on the world and the children. Bedtime stories, Saturday walks, family art projects on Sundays. Together we built a nest, a house out of which each of us could fly, only to return to its safety and warmth.

My wings seem to be broken or is it a cage I am in? Each time I go out for a test flight and come back, I awake the next day, my wings hurting. Am I so afraid to fly? Or is the male bird in this nest putting holes in my wings when I'm not aware of it? He says, "Go, I am proud to see you fly!" Yet the nest feels cold when I return. I ache.

Is he aware that every time I test out an idea or opinion at the dinner table he either puts it down, pushes it aside, or talks on endlessly until I am lost in the fog? I lose my sense of self.

Or does he realize that when I come home after class or writing my thesis that there is hostility in the air? Or pouting?

. . . and a year later:

What is wrong with me? Every day I drive to pick up Janet at the end of the MTA line as she comes home from high school. And every day I get on the highway and miss the exit! It seems dangerous that I can't keep my mind on the road. Then I turn around to go back to the exit and discover I've passed it again! Where was my mind? Why do I think of death all the time? Why? When I love my kids, I have a nice home, I have a husband who loves me (we never argue), I have security. Why am I in this awful funk?

Who Am I?

To the outside world the image of our marriage was of two handsome people doing exciting things. Inside, I was lonely and unhappy, and blamed it totally on myself. I would look at the trees silhouetted against the orange sky of the setting sun and say to myself, "I know that is an exquisite scene and in years past I would *feel* it. Now I am dead inside."

Women, I find, tend to blame the failure of marriage on themselves. As the carriers of the emotional condition of a relationship, they feel they are to blame if something goes wrong.

It is apparent to me now that I was unaware of my needs and feelings and had little ability to express my resentments or demand rights for myself.

Today, I can also see that part of my depression was caused by society's role expectation—my feelings of inadequacy were built into the system. This system we have created produces second-class citizenship for women and causes much pain.

My emotional pain found vent in constant fantasies of flight, of packing my bags and leaving without saying good-bye to anyone since I couldn't understand—to say nothing of trying to explain to the children I loved—why I felt I had to go. My other fantasy was the peace of total oblivion or nonexistence.

This eventually worked its way into many specific fantasies of death, with all the attached guilt feelings for even thinking of leaving the people who loved me.

It was a bright sunny New England Sunday, but I could *feel* nothing. My husband and children were home. Life seemed normal, whatever that meant. There were no fights or hassles. Inside I was so empty and numb. I remember telling my husband and children that I was going to take the car for the day—to be alone. (An unusual event for me.) Without knowing where I was going or why, I started driving. I remember stopping as I went on a country road, not to *do* anything, just to turn around. Back to what? Away from what? I was confused, groggy, didn't know. I saw a Turnpike sign and followed it. Started West with no destination, no inkling if I would return. Tears rolled down my face as I was driving. It was as though the dam broke loose—I could barely see—yet there was no pain. My foot got heavy on the accelerator, I pushed it to ninety. "My God, why doesn't a cop stop me?" I thought. Part of me was hoping that someone would see me speeding and report me. Another part of me wanted to hit the railing on the next curve. Three hours went by without stopping—the tears kept flowing. As my foot got tired from pressing the accelerator, I exited on to a country road. I came to a halt in front of a pond with a marshy bottom and cat-tails. I sat for how long? An hour or two wondering if I could drive me and the car into the pond to an end. Wondering what was wrong with me, feeling blank.

As I began to experience my mortality, my choice—to end my life or to live—I finally felt the pain. I sobbed and sobbed. This time with feeling. Feeling of potential loss of my children and their potential loss of me. Love and guilt. Who would help me understand me? Who would care? Who would see beyond the reserved, collected, smooth exterior? Who would see beyond the pretty face and graceful body? My loneliness was profound. I felt alienated from myself, from the ones I loved, and the world. I felt completely vulnerable. If anyone ever knew what I had just been through, would they forgive me? Would I forgive myself? As I sat in the car staring at the muck of the pond which mirrored my internal state, I looked at my own death, and took the first step back to myself.

Finding some paper to scribble on, I wrote a note to a psychiatrist colleague: "Would you help me? I think I'm destroying our marriage." (Notice where I put the blame.)

When I returned home, I found my husband and daughters having a quiet, creative Sunday with art materials—something I had always initiated for the family. It was eerie to see them carry on with my project, as though I were already dead—as though at some level they knew what had happened to me that day. I said to myself, "Yes, they could go on without me. My husband would take on those duties and characteristics which are mine, and life would continue in my absence." It was sobering. Rather than have them ask me questions about my day, I went to a movie. By morning, life had returned to normal; or so we pretended.

That timid note to the psychiatrist was a muted scream. If I had told the truth, I would have said, "I feel like I am being swallowed up alive—there is nothing left of me and I would just as soon disappear into the mist as to be devoured by this relationship."

It was a big step for me to say, "I'm hurting—I need help." I knew people needed me, but I didn't know that I needed people. With help, I began to work my way out of the bottom of the well by finding my own strengths and voicing some of my needs. What I needed was room to change, and support in my experiments and learnings. I needed to be myself instead of all those things *expected of me*. Eventually, I went to a five-day workshop without my husband or children. My mother encouraged me in taking this step. She thought it would be an enriching experience for me, and offered to take care of my children and husband in my absence. It was the first time I had been on my own since my marriage thirteen years earlier. I was amazed when people responded to me as a warm, intelligent, caring human being with my own identity. People were relating to *me*—not as wife, not as mother, but just plain me. It was like coming out from under the deep shade of a tree where others could only vaguely see me, into the bright sunlight, where I stood in full view. Both the warmth and the exposure seemed risky and exhilarating.

I think the process by which a woman loses her identity in marriage is well expressed in an article by a *man*, Joel Roache, in *Ms.* magazine. He took care of the home while his wife had a turn at her career. He describes very clearly his initial joy in doing the job well. However as time went on, the demands of the job left no time for himself, and his transformation from a self-assured individual to an angry, unsympathetic second-class citizen was complete. He says, "I was getting my sense of fulfillment, of self-esteem, through *her*, while she was getting it through her work. I was a full-fledged house-husband."

Marriage in Crisis

During the next few years, our marriage was in "an identity crisis" as Margaret Mead defines it: "For years the wife, always alert and attentive to the immediate needs of her family for food and comfort, clothes and transportation, play and rest, seldom has a thought of herself alone. Then one day she begins to look more carefully at . . . what it means to become a person with goals of one's own, as distinguished from a total commitment to homemaking. But such a crisis is not—or need not become—a catastrophe. It is also a signal that the partners are ready, if they can but find their way, for a new stage of living together. They are ready, if each is willing for the other to grow as a person, to broaden and deepen what they have to share."

We tried, during this period, to understand what each other's needs were. We had long talks and went to our first marriage counselor. Unfortunately, she listened to my verbal husband delve into his childhood years while I sat in mute pain as the scenario of our relationship was re-enacted in her presence, without her recognizing my silent agony. Today, when I counsel couples, I am acutely aware of "equal time for each" and of the poignant non-verbal messages being sent. There I was, in the counselor's office, listening, as usual, while the talk went on.

I made efforts to establish my new feelings of selfhood within the marriage relationship. I was certainly gaining a sense of myself outside of the relationship. But the ways my husband maintained control and created dependence were numerous. As I started to earn a couple of thousand dollars a year, I was excited by my new sense of self-worth; and I "asked" my husband if I might put the money in an account of my own to spend on special gifts from me to our family, such as family vacations. He said "No." In this instance, I am not sure whether my husband was blind to my need to feel good about my small earning power, or whether he wanted to maintain control of the family purse. Now I wonder, why did I *give away my power* by "asking"? I could have told him what I planned to do with the money. By training and role expectation, women frequently hand the power to men without realizing it.

At one point, I said I wanted to buy my own car—that is, to shop, evaluate, bargain, and make a decision. Distasteful though it was, I took it for a challenge. Somehow, at the last minute, my spouse went out and made the final choice, negotiated the final deal, and proudly brought the car home to me. This took away my sense of power and exemplified his inability to understand my need to relearn the self-sufficiency I had when I was twenty.

We tried getting help with another family therapist. This time I made various attempts at getting myself heard. When I interrupted, I was told "You are not polite, you're intrusive, you are not listening!" When I shouted that I had to speak, I was told, "You are angry."

It was fortunate for me these sessions were tape-recorded. I could document for myself that he used three quarters of each hour. Instead of feeling crazy, I felt validated.

My feelings of being trapped and cornered led me to rage and tears. While thus being gagged, I was simultaneously told that I was beautiful, talented, sensual, and that he loved and wanted me. By putting me on such a pedestal, he was keeping me in my place (another familiar place for many women).

I finally realized what should have been apparent years before: my husband liked the marriage relationship when I was living my life through and for him. He couldn't hear what a real toll this situation had taken on me. I was told I was selfish for wanting more for myself. How many women have heard they are selfish when they don't give of themselves 100% of the time? I was being driven crazy by a double message: his *words* were "develop your own interests, your own selfhood." Yet his *actions* and nonverbal communications were punishing me for being interested in my own life and effective at what I was doing.

Wanting more for myself was extremely threatening to my husband and our marriage system, which in turn made him more controlling and intimidating. The end of our marriage occurred when I found my anger at his trying to keep me in the one-down position. It was incredible to discover, within myself and within him, that what was once a deep and sensitive love and caring could turn to such distrust, contempt, and hate. I had never experienced rage before. I was shocked—since I am a mild-tempered, trusting person—to find I can be provoked to distrust and violent anger. A lot of my hostile feelings toward this particular man were provoked by the ways he dealt with me. Some of my angry feelings were aimed at society for creating such an unequal world.

My anger gave me the energy—a life-saving force, I'd say—to pull out of the relationship. Our divorce, in my opinion, was a product of our inability or unwillingness to work ourselves out of an unequal situation. The person who has a "good deal" in any system is going to be reluctant to change. I chose the only road to psychic survival.

Some marriages make it through the identity crises. Some do not. In my present counseling practice, I am keenly sensitive to women and men who are growing to new selfhood, and how this shakes up established patterns in a relationship.

Suggestions for Discussion

1. How does the sailing episode relate to the author's feeling that she was being well trained for her role as a woman?

2. What message did Rogers receive regarding the proper role of wife and mother?

3. What was the nature of the author's collusion with her husband? How did it affect her sense of self?

4. How do the diary entries reinforce the author's point of view?

5. Discuss some of the ironies in Rogers's description of her life with her husband.

6. What insights did the author gain from the therapy and the workshop?

7. What events precipitated the "identity crisis" in Rogers's marriage and ultimately led to her divorce?

Suggestions for Writing

1. Select one of the questions the author asks herself and reflect on it with references to your experience.

2. Discuss your attitude toward the italicized statements that Rogers was being subtly trained to believe.

3. Discuss double messages that you have received from your family or from society at large.

Carolyn Heilbrun

Androgyny

Carolyn Heilbrun (b. 1926) was professor of English literature at Columbia University. She has written *Toward a Recognition of Androgyny* (1973), from which the following selection is taken; *Writing a Woman's Life* (1988); and *Hamlet's Mother and Other Women* (1990), as well as a number of articles and reviews; a history of the Garnetts (a literary family); and a study of Christopher Isherwood. Under the name Amanda Cross, she has written a number of mystery novels. Androgyny defines a condition in which there are no assigned roles for men and women, but rather a full range of experience is open to both sexes.

"When a subject is highly controversial," Virginia Woolf observed to an audience forty-five years ago, "and any question about sex is that, one cannot hope to tell the truth. One can only show how one came to hold whatever opinion one does hold." My opinion is easily enough expressed: I believe that our future salvation lies in a movement away from sexual polarization and the prison of gender toward a world in which individual roles and the modes of personal behavior can be freely chosen. The ideal toward which I believe we should move is best described by the term "androgyny." This ancient Greek word—from *andro* (male) and *gyn* (female)—defines a condition under which the characteristics of the sexes, and the human impulses expressed by men and women, are not rigidly assigned. Androgyny seeks to liberate the individual from the confines of the appropriate.

There will always be those to whom a clear demarcation between proper behavior for one sex and the other will seem fundamental, as though it had been laid down at the creation. Probably both the traditionalist and the revolutionary are to some extent deluded in this, as in other matters. Thinking about profound social change, conservatives always expect disaster, while revolutionaries confidently anticipate utopia. Both are wrong. But in the end, I am convinced, the future lies with those who believe salvation likelier to spring from the imagination of possibility than from the delineation of the historical.

Yet recognition, not revolution, is the object of this essay. My method is to use the vast world of myth and literature as a universe in which to seek out the sometimes obscure signs of androgyny. My hope is that the occasional interpretation I bring to the literature of the past will suggest new ways of responding to the circumstances of our own lives and the literature of our own times. Once the name of androgyny has been spoken and some of its past appearances identified, the reader to whom the idea is not viscerally unbearable will begin to see this largely undefined phenomenon in many places. The idea of androgyny, at first startling, rapidly becomes less so. If this essay succeeds in its purpose, the reader returning to it later will be struck by the familiarity and simplicity of its central idea. . . .

Androgyny suggests a spirit of reconciliation between the sexes; it suggests, further, a full range of experience open to individuals who may, as women, be aggressive, as men, tender; it suggests a spectrum upon which human beings choose their places without regard to propriety or custom. The unbounded and hence fundamentally indefinable nature of androgyny is best evoked by borrowing a description of Dionysus from the critic Thomas Rosenmeyer's discussion of the *Bacchae* of Euripides: "Dionysus, who is Euripides' embodiment of universal vitality, is described variously by chorus, herdsman, commoners, and princes. The descriptions do not tally, for the god cannot be defined. He can perhaps be totaled but the sum is never definitive; further inspection adds new features to the old. If a definition is at all possible it is a definition by negation or cancelation. For one thing, Dionysus appears to be neither woman nor man; or, better, he presents himself as woman-in-man, or man-in-woman, the unlimited personality. . . . In the person of the god strength mingles with softness, majestic terror with coquettish glances. To follow him or to comprehend him we must ourselves give up our precariously controlled, socially desirable sexual limitations." A better description of the difficulties of defining androgyny could not be hoped for, although we have perhaps reached the stage where the social desirability of sexual limitations is in question. Such, at least, is my hope.

Unfortunately, it is easier to know what we fear from androgyny than what we may hope from it. The question of who will go through doorways first, or who will care for young children, is immediate and practical; the rewards to men from sharing their professional haunts with highly trained women are at best unclear. Change which threatens our established institutions and habits threatens our individual security, regardless of whether those institutions serve us individually well or ill. When Simone de Beauvoir remarked that men have found in women more complicity than the oppressor usually finds in the oppressed, she expressed an understanding of this fear of lost security, palpable to women as to men.

Androgyny appears to threaten men and women even more profoundly in their sexual than in their social roles. There has been a fear, not only of homosexuality or the appearance of homosexuality, but of impotence and frigidity as the consequence of less rigid patterns of sexual behavior. That we already have more than enough impotence and frigidity is apparently blamed more comfortably on the changing of roles than on strict adherence to them. If the man does not pursue, assuming aggressive attitudes, if the woman does not limit her response to consent or refusal, assuming passive attitudes, may we not lose altogether our skill at sexual performance? Women, terrified of "unmanning" men or making themselves less "feminine" and compliant, have failed to explore with men the possibilities inherent in heterosexual love freed from ritualized attitudes. Yet the complicity of women and the insistence of men on maintaining the old sexual order is daily less to be relied on. More and more women, many men, are coming to realize that the delight inherent in male-female relationships, whether in conversation or passion, is capable only of enhancement as the androgynous ideal is approached.

Those youths so often seen almost anywhere in the world today—their long hair and costumes making uneasy, in both senses of the word, the immediate identification of gender—suggest a new homage to androgyny. Indeed, the androgynous ideal is gaining acceptance faster than I had dared hope when I began this book. Then the danger I felt in suggesting so startling an idea was palpable. In the first introduction that I wrote my remarks were hedged about with protestations, defenses, caveats, for I much feared that I would be misunderstood. But ideas move rapidly when their time comes. Today one may speak of androgyny without assuming a defensive tone. One danger perhaps remains: that androgyny, an ideal, might be confused with hermaphroditism, an anomalous physical condition.

Homosexuality and bisexuality have seemed to occur very often in those societies and among those artists who have produced androgynous works. Readers of my own generation may find themselves at first uncomfortable, as I did, in the recognition of widespread homosexuality. Yet I have come to realize that today's youth are less threatened than were we by this subject and, in all likelihood, future generations will be still less concerned.

I made, in this connection, an interesting discovery when I returned in the *Symposium* to Plato's actual story of the circular beings who existed before the split of humans into male and female halves. As Aristophanes, the character in the *Symposium* who presents this myth of sexuality tells the tale; there were originally three wholes: all male, all female, male and female;

each person seeking his other, original half might be in search with equal likelihood for someone of the same or of the other sex. I did one of those instant surveys among my friends and acquaintances which are the delight of the pedagogical profession, to discover that I was not alone in having blocked out the homosexual wholes of Plato's parable. Perhaps we all need to be reminded of the necessity of remaining open to new, or newly recovered, ways of being.

In a certain sense this book* is a tribute to the persistence of Victorianism. Most of us nowadays regard the Victorian age as part of the very remote past. Its major ideas, no longer thought to be the imprisoning conventions of our youth, are now consigned to the museum of antique beliefs, where we study them with a certain condescension and amusement. How quaint and implausible they were; how remote their power now seems. Or so we believe. Yet in the matter of sexual polarization and the rejection of androgyny we still accept the convictions of Victorianism; we view everything, from our study of animal habits to our reading of literature, through the paternalistic eyes of the Victorian era.

Masculine domination of life accompanied by extreme sexual polarization was not, of course, unique to the nineteenth century. Patriarchy reached its apotheosis in the years of Victoria's reign, but it is a habit thousands of years old, its roots deep in the Judaeo-Christian tradition. Whether or not patriarchy arose as a reaction to matriarchy is not readily established, and has not easily been accepted at any time by those considered the proper authorities. The opinions of J. J. Bachofen, for example, the chief expounder in the nineteenth century of the belief in an early matriarchy, are not now in academic fashion. For any purposes, however, the verification of theories of prehistoric matriarchy, even were that possible, is not important. Nor is it particularly important to decide whether the male principle at one time ruled the world well. Indeed, one might sensibly argue that the patriarchy, whether or not it supplanted a matriarchy, was necessary to human development and has brought many blessings. Yet I believe that it has also brought many curses to our almost dying earth. What is important now is that we free ourselves from the prison of gender and, before it is too late, deliver the world from the almost exclusive control of the masculine impulse.

If we are still, in our definition of sexual roles, the heirs of the Victorian age, we must also recognize that our definitions of the terms "masculine" and "feminine" are themselves little more than unexamined, received ideas. According to the conventional view, "masculine" equals forceful, competent, competitive, controlling, vigorous, unsentimental, and occasionally violent; "feminine" equals tender, genteel, intuitive rather than rational, passive, unaggressive, readily given to submission. The "masculine" individual is popularly seen as a maker, the "feminine" as a nourisher. Qualities which the Victorians considered admirable in men they thought perverted in women, an attitude which Freud did much to sanctify. The confident assurance that directing traffic or driving trucks somehow disqualifies women for their "feminine" roles, that the care of young children or the working of crewels disqualifies men for their masculine roles, is indicative of the rigidity with which human beings have been divided, not by talent, inclination, or attribute, but

*This essay is an introduction to a book of critical pieces on Victorian writers.

by gender. Recently, for example, *The New York Times* related the story of a young girl who, for lack of enough good boy players, had been drafted onto a Little League baseball team. The ensuing ruckus might have been justified had someone been caught practicing medicine without training or license, though the response where this does happen is less hysterical. The girl was thrown off the team together with the manager who had been unpolitical enough to let her play. There followed long discussions about the weakness and physical vulnerability of girls, the wisdom of their partaking in sports, and so forth. But the obvious points were nowhere mentioned: she had qualified for the team by being able to play better than any available boy, and whatever physical disabilities her sex may be thought to have endowed her with, so wide is the extent of individual variation that she was clearly better able to cope with the rigors of competitive contact sports than many boys. What she had outraged were preconceived ideas of the "feminine" role and the "masculine" rights to certain activities. If in fact a graph showing the frequency distribution of athletic ability in girls is superimposed upon one for boys, the upper end of the graph, signifying highest ability, will perhaps be all male, the lower end perhaps all female, but a wide intermediate range will comprise both sexes. This pattern (or its reverse, with females at the upper end) recurs for almost every human attribute that is thought to be associated with sex, apart from primary sex characteristics.

Yet so wedded are we to the conventional definitions of "masculine" and "feminine" that it is impossible to write about androgyny without using these terms in their accepted, received sense. I have done so throughout this essay, and have placed the terms in quotation marks to make my usage clear. What is more, the term "masculine" is often used pejoratively in what follows. My reason for so using it must be carefully explained.

Because "masculine" traits are now and have for so many years been the dominant ones, we have ample evidence of the danger the free play of such traits brings in its wake. By developing in men the ideal "masculine" characteristics of competitiveness, aggressiveness, and defensiveness, and by placing in power those men who most embody these traits, we have, I believe, gravely endangered our own survival. Unless we can effectively check the power of manly men and the women who willingly support them, we will experience new Vietnams, My Lais, Kent States. Even the animal world is now threatened by the aggression of man, the hunter. So long as we continue to believe the "feminine" qualities of gentleness, lovingness, and the counting of cost in human rather than national or property terms are out of place among rulers, we can look forward to continued self-brutalization and perhaps even to self-destruction.

In appearing to exalt feminine traits, I mean to suggest that these, since they have been so drastically undervalued, must now gain respect, so that a sort of balance is achieved among those in power, and within individuals. Obviously, not all women embody "feminine" characteristics: the parent who said that the National Guard at Kent State should have shot all the students was a mother. Such women are described by Simone de Beauvoir as "the poetesses of the bourgeoisie since they represent the most conservative element in this threatened class. . . . they orchestrate the grand mystification intended to persuade women to 'stay womanly.' " But for the most part, and especially for literary artists, the "feminine" impulses are most frequently embodied in women. The cry within literary works for more balanced human experience, from *The Trojan Women* to *Saint Joan*, has largely been the cry of women.

If the argument on behalf of androgyny sounds, more often than not, like a feminist or "women's lib" cry, that is because of the power men now hold, and because of the political weakness of women. If "feminine" resounds throughout this essay with the echoes of lost virtue, while "masculine" thuds with the accusation of misused power, this is a reflection on our current values, not on the intrinsic virtues of either "masculine" or "feminine" impulses. Humanity requires both.

So typical a Victorian as Leslie Stephen may, in his opinions on androgyny, be seen as equally typical of our own day. Creator of the *Dictionary of National Biography* and father, in a certain sense, of the Bloomsbury group, Leslie Stephen found the condition of androgyny to be evil. He used the words "masculine" and "manly" to indicate the highest praise; for purposes of denigration, "effeminate" and "morbid" were synonymous. His biographer Noel Annan summed up Stephen's views on the sexes in the statement that "men must be manly and women womanly; and the slightest androgynous taint must be condemned."

Yet the androgynous ideal, as Norman O. Brown has shown, persists in all the dreams of mysticism even through the nineteenth century:

> In the West, cabalistic mysticism has interpreted Genesis 1:27—"God created man in his own image . . . male and female created he them"—as implying the androgynous nature of God and of human perfection before the Fall. From cabalism this notion passed into the Christian mysticism of Boehme, where it is fused with the Pauline mysticism of Galatians 3:28—"There can be no male and female; for ye are all one man in Christ Jesus." In neglecting Boehme, or this side of Boehme, later Protestantism only keeps its head in the sand; for, as Berdyaev writes; "The great anthropological myth which alone can be the basis of an anthropological metaphysic is the myth about the androgyne. . . . According to his Idea, to God's conception of him, man is a complete, masculinely feminine being, solar and telluric, logoic and cosmic at the same time. . . . Original sin is connected in the first instance with division into two sexes and the Fall of the androgyne, i.e., of man as a complete being."

In the East, Taoist mysticism, as Needham shows, seeks to recover the androgynous self: one of the famous texts of the Tao Te Ching says:

> He who knows the male, yet cleaves to what is female,
> Becomes like a ravine, receiving all things under heaven.
> [Thence] the eternal virtue never leaks away.
> This is returning to the state of infancy.

And since poetry, as well as psychoanalysis, is the modern heir of the mystical tradition, the hermaphroditic ideal is central, for example, in the message of Rilke. In *Letters to a Young Poet* he writes: "And perhaps the sexes are more related than we think, and the great renewal of the world will perhaps consist in this, that man and maid, freed from all false feeling and aversion, will seek each other not as opposites, but as brother and sister, as neighbors, and will come together as *human beings*." But deeper than the problem of the relation between the sexes is the problem of the reunification of the sexes in the self. In Rilke as artist, according to his friend Lou Andreas

Salome, "both sexes unite into an entity." And Rilke, in his call to God to perfect him as an artist, calls on God to make him a hermaphrodite.

What poets understood, psychologists discovered. Donald W. MacKinnon, director of the Institute of Personality Assessment and Research at the University of California in Berkeley, wrote in 1962: "[Openness to experience] may be observed, for example, in the realm of sexual identifications and interests, where creative males give more expression to the feminine side of their nature than do less creative men. On a number of tests of masculinity–femininity, creative men score relatively high on femininity, and this despite the fact that, as a group, they do not present an effeminate appearance or give evidence of increased homosexual interests or experiences. Their elevated scores on femininity indicate rather an openness to their feelings and emotions, a sensitive intellect and understanding self-awareness and wide ranging interests including many which in the American culture are thought of as more feminine, and these traits are observed and confirmed by other techniques of assessment. If one were to use the language of the Swiss psychiatrist C. G. Jung, it might be said that creative persons are not so completely identified with their masculine *persona* roles as to blind themselves to or deny expression to the more feminine traits of the *anima*."

Joseph Campbell in *The Masks of God*, his comprehensive and incisive account of world mythology, tells us that the patriarchal, anti-androgynous view is distinguished "by its setting apart of all pairs of opposites—male and female, life and death, true and false, good and evil." Though Campbell identifies the androgynous ideal as the "archaic view," which predated the patriarchal, we must not therefore suppose that his ideal is to be encountered only "in the dark backward and abysm of time. . . ."

Suggestions for Discussion

1. To what extent is androgyny, as defined by Heilbrun, a liberating mode of personal behavior? To what extent do you feel that human impulses expressed by men and women are rigidly assigned?

2. How valid is the concern that androgyny is a threat to the sexual roles of men and women?

3. How valid is the author's view that the androgynous ideal is rapidly gaining acceptance? If true, to what do you attribute such a shift in attitude?

4. Defend or challenge the author's statement that we ought to free ourselves from the "prison of gender" and, before it is too late, deliver the world from the almost exclusive control of the masculine impulse.

5. In what sense do the author's views transcend the personal and embrace political and societal concerns?

Suggestions for Writing

1. Discuss your sense of the possibilities inherent in heterosexual love freed from ritualized attitudes.

2. Write on any of the above questions for discussion.

3. Discuss the author's statement: "deeper than the problem of the relation between the sexes is the problem of the reunification of the sexes in the self."

4. Write on one of the following topics: the prison of gender; sexual polarization; a spirit of reconciliation between the sexes; the unlimited personality; the imprisoning conventions of youth; the patriarchy as a bringer of blessings or of curses.

Noel Perrin

The Androgynous Man

Noel Perrin (b. 1927), a professor of English and, since 1991, a professor of environmental studies at Dartmouth College, is a frequent contributor to *The New Yorker* and other periodicals. He also practices farming in Vermont. Among his published works are A *Passport Secretly Green* (1961), *First Person Rural: Essays of a Sometime Farmer* (1980), *Third Person Rural: More Essays of a Sometime Farmer* (1981), *Last Person Rural* (1991), and *Solo: Life with an Electric Car* (1992). The writer cites a number of examples to support his view that the androgynous man has a range of choices denied the macho man.

The summer I was 16, I took a train from New York to Steamboat Springs, Colo., where I was going to be assistant horse wrangler at a camp. The trip took three days, and since I was much too shy to talk to strangers, I had quite a lot of time for reading. I read all of "Gone With the Wind." I read all the interesting articles in a couple of magazines I had, and then I went back and read all the dull stuff. I also took all the quizzes, a thing of which magazines were even fuller then than now.

The one that held my undivided attention was called "How Masculine/Feminine Are You?" It consisted of a large number of inkblots. The reader was supposed to decide which of four objects each blot most resembled. The choices might be a cloud, a steam engine, a caterpillar and a sofa.

When I finished the test, I was shocked to find that I was barely masculine at all. On a scale of 1 to 10, I was about 1.2. Me, the horse wrangler? (And not just wrangler, either. That summer, I had to skin a couple of horses that died—the camp owner wanted the hides.)

The results of that test were so terrifying to me that for the first time in my life I did a piece of original analysis. Having unlimited time on the train, I looked at the "masculine" answers over and over, trying to find what it was that distinguished real men from people like me—and eventually I discovered two very simple patterns. It was "masculine" to think the blots looked like man-made objects, and "feminine" to think they looked like natural objects. It was masculine to think they looked like things capable of causing harm, and feminine to think of innocent things.

Even at 16, I had the sense to see that the compilers of the test were using rather limited criteria—maleness and femaleness are both more complicated than *that*—and I breathed a huge sigh of relief. I wasn't necessarily a wimp, after all.

That the test did reveal something other than the superficiality of its makers I realized only many years later. What it revealed was that there is a large class of men and women both, to which I belong, who are essentially androgynous. That doesn't mean we're gay, or low in the appropriate hormones, or uncomfortable performing the jobs traditionally assigned our sexes. (A few years after that summer, I was leading troops in combat and, unfashionable as it now is to admit this, having a very good time. War is exciting. What a pity the 20th century went and spoiled it with high-tech weapons.)

What it does mean to be spiritually androgynous is a kind of freedom. Men who are all-male, or he-man, or 100 percent red-blooded Americans, have a little biological set that causes them to be attracted to physical power, and probably also to dominance. Maybe even to watching football. I don't say this to criticize them. Completely masculine men are quite often wonderful people: good husbands, good (though sometimes overwhelming) fathers, good members of society. Furthermore, they are often so unself-consciously at ease in the world that other men seek to imitate them. They just aren't as free as us androgynes. They pretty nearly have to be what they are; we have a range of choices open.

The sad part is that many of us never discover that. Men who are not 100 percent red-blooded Americans—say, those who are only 75 percent red-blooded—often fail to notice their freedom. They are too busy trying to copy the he-men ever to realize that men, like women, come in a wide variety of acceptable types. Why this frantic imitation? My answer is mere speculation, but not casual. I have speculated on this for a long time.

Partly they're just envious of the he-man's unconscious ease. Mostly they're terrified of finding that there may be something wrong with them deep down, some weakness at the heart. To avoid discovering that, they spend their lives acting out the role that the he-man naturally lives. Sad.

One thing that men owe to the women's movement is that this kind of failure is less common than it used to be. In releasing themselves from the single ideal of the dependent woman, women have more or less incidentally released a lot of men from the single ideal of the dominant male. The one mistake the feminists have made, I think, is in supposing that *all* men need this release, or that the world would be a better place if all men achieved it. It wouldn't. It would just be duller.

So far I have been pretty vague about just what the freedom of the androgynous man is. Obviously it varies with the case. In the case I know best, my own, I can be quite specific. It has freed me most as a parent. I am, among other things, a fairly good natural mother. I like the nurturing role. It makes me feel good to see a child eat—and it turns me to mush to see a 4-year-old holding a glass with both small hands, in order to drink. I even enjoyed sewing patches on the knees of my daughter Amy's Dr. Dentons when she was at the crawling stage. All that pleasure I would have lost if I had made myself stick to the notion of the paternal role that I started with.

Or take a smaller and rather ridiculous example. I feel free to kiss cats. Until recently it never occurred to me that I would want to, though my daughters have been doing it all their lives. But my elder daughter is now 22, and in London. Of course, I get to look after her cat while she is gone. He's a big, handsome farm cat named Petrushka, very unsentimental, though used from kittenhood to being kissed on the top of the head by Elizabeth. I've gotten very fond of him (he's the adventurous kind of cat who likes to climb hills with you), and one night I simply felt like kissing him on the top of the head, and did. Why did no one tell me sooner how silky cat fur is?

Then there's my relation to cars. I am completely unembarrassed by my inability to diagnose even minor problems in whatever object I happen to be driving, and don't have to make some insider's remark to mechanics to try to establish that I, too, am a "Man With His Machine."

The same ease extends to household maintenance. I do it, of course. Service people are expensive. But for the last decade my house has functioned better than it used to because I've had the aid of a volume called "Home Repairs Any Woman Can Do," which is pitched just right for people at my technical level. As a youth, I'd as soon have touched such a book as I would have become a transvestite. Even though common sense says there is really nothing sexual whatsoever about fixing sinks.

Or take public emotion. All my life I have easily been moved by certain kinds of voices. The actress Siobhan McKenna's, to take a notable case. Give her an emotional scene in a play, and within 10 words my eyes are full of tears. In boyhood, my great dread was that someone might notice. I struggled manfully, you might say, to suppress this weakness. Now, of course, I don't see it as a weakness at all, but as a kind of fulfillment. I even suspect that the true he-men feel the same way, or one kind of them does, at least, and it's only the poor imitators who have to struggle to repress themselves.

Let me come back to the inkblots, with their assumption that masculine equates with machinery and science, and feminine with art and nature. I have no idea whether the right pronoun for God is He, She or It. But this I'm pretty sure of. If God could somehow be induced to take that test, God would not come out macho, and not feminismo, either, but right in the middle. Fellow androgynes, it's a nice thought.

Suggestions for Discussion

1. In what ways does the magazine test reflect society's stereotypes of masculine and feminine?

2. What is Perrin's definition of androgyny and why does he believe it to be liberating?

3. What is the writer's view of the strengths and limitations of the completely masculine man? Why are what he calls the "75 percent red-blooded" Americans sad to contemplate?

4. What elements of androgyny discussed by Carolyn Heilbrun does Perrin leave out?

Suggestions for Writing

1. Support or challenge the assumption that "masculine equates with machinery and science, and feminine with art and nature."

2. Drawing upon your own life or your observation of a friend, describe what might be called androgynous experiences.

Betty Friedan

The Quiet Movement of American Men

Betty Friedan (b. 1921) has been active as a feminist, recorder of the movement, and lecturer at universities and professional associations throughout the world. Her first major book, *The Feminist Mystique* (1963), was critical of women's roles in post–World War II America. Later she brought feminist concerns up to date in *The Second Stage* (1981), from which this selection was taken, and published *The Fountain of Age* (1993). Friedan believes that the women's movement has had a profound effect on men, and she recounts a number of problems, shifts in values, and possible solutions.

It is nothing like the women's movement, and probably never will be. Each man seems to be struggling with it quietly—at twenty-five or thirty-five, or before it is too late, at forty-five or fifty. It is a change not yet fully visible, not clearly identified or understood by the experts and rarely spoken about by men themselves. Nobody is marching. Most men are turned off by the "men's lib" groups, which try to copy women's. With men there is no explosion of anger, no enemy to rage against, no list of grievances or demands for benefits and opportunities clearly valuable and previously denied, as with women. And yet I believe that American men are at the edge of a momentous change in their very identity as men, going beyond the change catalyzed by the women's movement.

It is a deceptively quiet movement, a shifting in direction, a saying "no" to old patterns, a searching for new values, a struggling with basic questions that each man seems to be dealing with alone. He may be going through the same outward motions that have always defined men's lives—making it, or struggling to make it, in the corporate rat race, the office, the plant, college, the ball park; making it with women; getting married; having children. Or he may be deciding not to get married, or thinking in a new way about having children, or no longer really trying to make it in traditional terms. He is not issuing a public statement. He is just grappling with private questions: success, promotion, senior partner, vice-president, $65,000 a year—is that what he really wants out of life? Will he ever get it? What will it be worth? What kind of a man is he anyhow, asking questions like this? Other men are satisfied with their lives, aren't they? But what does he want out of life for himself? How does he fulfill himself as a man?

Asking these questions about himself, he doesn't feel so angry at women. He feels awkward, isolated, confused. Yet he senses that something is happening with men, something large and historic, and he wants to be part of it. He carries the baby in his backpack, shops at the supermarket on Saturday, bakes his own bread with a certain showing-off quality.

It's happened to some men because of the economy: layoffs from jobs that looked secure, as in the auto industry; company takeovers, budget cuts; a dead end suddenly in a career that he had put his all into for years. Or, after

317

sweating it through to the Ph.D., no jobs in his field. Or making it to the top at forty or forty-five—and then having to figure out what to do next—fight off the younger men coming up, or join another company?

Some men just know they don't want to be like their fathers, or like those senior partners, who have heart attacks at fifty—but they don't know what other way there is to be.

It started for many men almost unwillingly, as a response to the women's movement. Women changing their own lives forced men or made it possible for men to change theirs. Some men seem to be making these moves quite independently of women. But they sense, we sense, it's related somehow. The rhetoric of sexual politics that characterized the first stage of the women's movement seemed to demand a hostile stance from the men. But that rhetoric and the response it elicited obscured the real reasons that these changes were threatening to some men, and also obscured the fact that many men supported, and felt a surprising relief about, the women's movement.

At first glance, all it looked like was endless arguments about his doing his share of the housework, the cooking, the cleaning, the dishes, taking out the garbage, scrubbing out the toilet bowl and mopping the kitchen floor without leaving streaks; or about his responsibility for taking care of the children, changing diapers, getting them to bed, into snowsuits, to the park, to the pediatrician. These disputes arose because it was no longer *automatic* that her job was to take care of the house and the kids and all the other details of life, and that his job was to support everyone. Now she was working to support them, too.

But that wasn't the entire issue. Even if she didn't have a job outside the home, she suddenly had to be treated as a person too, as he was. She had a right to her own life and interests. He could help with the kids and the house at night, or on weekends. (The arguments over the housework were worse when she didn't have a job.)

He felt wronged, injured. He had been working so hard to support her and the kids and now he was her "oppressor," a "male chauvinist pig," if he didn't scrub all the pots and pans to boot. "You make dinner," she said. "I'm going to my design class." He felt scared when she walked out like that. If she didn't need him for her identity, her status, her sense of importance, if she was going to get all that for herself, if she could support herself and have a life independent of him, wouldn't she stop loving him? Why would she stay with him? Wouldn't she just leave? So he was supposed to be the big male oppressor, right? How could he admit the big secret—that maybe he needed her more than she needed him? That he felt like a baby when he became afraid she would leave? That he suddenly didn't know what he felt, what he was *supposed* to feel—as a man?

I believe much of the hostility men express toward women comes from their very dependence on our love, from those needy feelings that men aren't supposed to have—just as the excesses of our attacks on our male "oppressors" stemmed from our dependence on men. That old, excessive dependence (which was supposed to be natural in women) made us feel we had to be more independent than any man in order to be able to move at all. Our explosion of rage and our attacks on men, however justified, often masked our own timidity and fear of risking ourselves in a complex, competitive world, in ways never required of us before.

And the more a man pretended to a dominant, cool, masculine superiority he didn't really feel—the more he was forced to carry the burden alone of supporting the whole family against the rough odds of that grim outside economic world—the more threatened and the more hostile he felt.

Sam, an aerospace engineer in Seattle, told me that the period when his wife "tried to be just a housewife" was the worst time in his marriage.

"It was not only her staying home and losing confidence in herself, and the resentment and hostility against me after she joined the consciousness-raising group. It was her loss of confidence in me. If you decide you're going to stay home and be taken care of and you have to depend for everything on this guy, you get afraid—*Can he do it?* It all depended on me, and I was in a constant panic, but I'd say, 'Don't worry.'

"Susie was tired of her job anyhow. It wasn't such a great job—neither is mine if you want to know—but she had an excuse, wanting to stay home with her kids. The pressure was on me, hanging by my fingernails, barely paying the bills each month. But it was crazy. Here I was, not knowing where the next check was coming from after the government contract ran out, suddenly supporting a wife and kids all by myself.

"It's better now that she's working and bringing some money in. But I don't just *help* with the kids now. She has to be at work before I do, so I give them breakfast and get them off to school. The nights she works late, I make dinner, help with the homework, and get everyone to bed. But I don't feel so panicky now—and she isn't attacking me any more."

Phil, a doctor in his thirties who started out to be a surgeon but who now has a small-town family practice in New Jersey, talks to me as he makes pickles, with his kids running around underfoot in the country kitchen that is next to his office.

"I was going to be a surgeon, supercool, in my gleaming white uniform," he says, "the man my mother wanted me to be but I knew I wasn't. So I married a nurse and she stayed home to raise our children, and she was supposed to fulfill herself through my career. It didn't work for either of us. I went through tortures before every operation. I couldn't sleep.

"Then Ellen started turning against me. I always said the children needed her at home, full-time mothering. Maybe because *I* was so scared inside. Maybe she didn't have the nerve to try to do her own thing professionally. All she seemed to want was revenge on me, as if she were locked into some kind of sexual battle against me, playing around, looking elsewhere for true love.

"She got into a women's consciousness-raising group, and I even joined a men's one. At home, I'd grovel, the male chauvinist pig repenting, not letting on how hurt, angry, offended I felt. The worst was when our little girl tried to be as tough as Mummy and went *yuk* at every word I said.

"When Ellen finally got up the nerve to do her own thing—she's a nurse-midwife now—it was a relief. The other stuff stopped. She could come back to being my wife. I'm coming out of this, redefining myself, no longer in terms of success or failure as a doctor (though I still am a doctor) and not as superior or inferior to her. It was a blow to my ego, but what a relief, to take off my surgical mask! I'm discovering my own value in the family.

"Now that I'm not so hurt and angry and afraid that she'll leave me, I can see that it's a hell of a fight for a woman to be seen as a person. I think she's been hiding from herself the fear of accomplishing anything on her own so she made me the villain. Well, I'm happy now to take on the kids while she practices her profession, though every time she goes out of town, I practically wet my pants. I tell my own patients now, the mothers, don't make the kids that dependent on you. That's what my mother did to me. I was so afraid of those messy, needy feelings I couldn't get away from, even as a surgeon. You know, it's as hard for me to feel like a person as it is for her. We couldn't either of us get that from each other."

The change is harder to discern among men because men have a harder time talking about their feelings than women do. They certainly don't talk about their feelings to other men. It's part of the masculine mystique—the definition of man by his "score," competing against other men—that he constantly keep his guard up. And after all, since men have the power and position in society that women are making all the fuss about, why should men want to change unless women make them do so? When men began talking to me about their own new questions (and some refused—which never happened with women—and some just couldn't seem to talk about their feelings, only about abstractions like the economy or the state of the nation), it reminded me of "the problem that has no name" as I heard it from the women I was interviewing for *The Feminine Mystique* twenty years ago, when, each one feeling she was alone, American women were poised unconsciously on the brink of the women's movement.

"Maybe men feel more need to pretend," says a Detroit sales engineer, temporarily laid off, struggling to take "equal responsibility" for the kids and the house, now that his wife has gone to work in a department store. "When I used to see a man on the street with his children on a weekday, I assumed he was unemployed, a loser. Now, it's so common—daddies with their children, at ease. Now, even if a man is unemployed, like I am right now, well, that job is not what makes me a man. I'm not just a breadwinner. I'm a person, I have feelings myself."

With all the attention on the women's movement these past fifteen years, it hasn't been noticed that many of the old bases for men's identity have become shaky. If being a man is defined, for example, as being dominant, superior, as *not-being-a-woman,* that definition becomes an illusion hard to maintain when most of the important work of society no longer requires brute muscular force. The Vietnam war probably was the beginning of the end of the hunter-caveman, gun-toting he-man mystique.

The signs that machismo was dying in the U.S. appeared about the same time as the women's movement emerged in the sixties. The long-haired young men, and their elders imitating them or clubbing them down from repressed envy, began saying they didn't have to be tight-lipped, crewcut or poker-faced like John Wayne to be a man. They didn't have to be all-powerful, superior to everyone in the world, and to napalm all the children in Vietnam and Cambodia and the green leaves off the trees, to prove they were men. They could be sensitive, tender, compassionate, they didn't have to have big muscles, when there were no bears to kill, they could admit they were afraid and they could even cry—and they were still men, their own men.

Books were written such as *The Greening of America,* and hippies played their guitars, chanting "Make love, not war." And the young men said they were not going to live their whole lives for the dollar like their fathers, about the same time as the young women said they were not going to spend their lives as housewife "service stations" like their mothers. How the adventurous good life could be lived on other terms wasn't quite clear. It didn't have to be, while the counterculture was sustained by the allowances from Daddy.

But all that supposedly stopped a while ago, with the end of the Vietnam war, inflation, recession, the job crunch and the energy crisis. Or did it? At the dawn of the eighties, the signs of a quiet, complex, continuing movement among men emerged not just as counterculture, but as shifting currents in the mainstream, converging on the women's movement for the second stage. The men I have been interviewing around the country these past months are not hippies playing games on those allowances from Daddy. They are members of the college classes in which everyone wanted to be a lawyer, a doctor, an MBA. They are the men who fought in Vietnam, or went to graduate school to stay out of the war, or they are assembly-line workers whose line has stopped.

Vietnam was somehow the watershed. If men stop defining themselves by going to war or getting power from jobs woman can't have, what is left? What does it mean to be a man, except not-being-a-woman—being physically superior, able to beat all the other men up? The fact is, when a man admits those "messy, needy feelings" that men as well as women have—and which that brutal, brittle machismo is supposed to hide, but only makes worse—he can't *play* the same kind of man any more.

Tony, who lives now on the Outer Banks of North Carolina, was a pilot in Vietnam when it started for him.

"I was a captain, coming up for major. I had all the medals, could have gone on for twenty years in the Air Force. Sitting up there over Nam, the commander, under heavy fire, the guys screaming into the mikes, the bombers and fighters moving in, me giving the orders, I was caught up in it, crazy-wild, excited. And then I woke up one day and found myself clicking my empty gun at civilians. I knew I had to get out. The next mission, sitting up there, it felt for real, and for the first time, I was frightened. It's so heavy, the medals, the games, and then suddenly realizing that you are dropping napalm on real people."

He "could fly any piece of machinery," so he took a job with an airline. "All I wanted was security," he says. "After one year I was furloughed because the company was having financial difficulties. There was no security. So I came back to this town where I grew up and took a job as a schoolteacher, working with seventh and eighth graders who were reading at the second-grade level. It was the 'reading lab,' the pits, the bottom, and a woman's job. It's the hardest job I've ever done, teaching those kids, and it gets the least respect. Flying a 323,000-pound Lockheed Starlifter can't compare." As a pilot, Tony made $34,000 a year; as a teacher, he makes $12,000.

"But maybe now," he says, "with the ladies moving in and picking up some of the financial slack—my wife works for a florist, and as a waitress, nights—a guy can say 'I'm not going to get much of anywhere, with the money anyhow—how much of it is really going to rub off on me? Why don't

I do something really worthwhile from a human point of view?" Now with the ladies out earning, it frees a man from being strapped down to just one job for his whole life. After school, I take out my boat, which I built myself, and if I make some extra money fishing, fine. But there are more important things in life than the dollar bill."

In *Breaktime*, a controversial study of men "living without work in a nine-to-five world," Bernard Lefkowitz reports a 71 percent increase in the number of working-aged men who have left the labor force since 1968 and who are not looking for work. According to Lefkowitz, the "stop-and-go pattern of work" is becoming the predominant pattern, rather than the lifetime jobs and careers men used to pursue both for economic security and for their masculine identity. "In the depression of the 30s," says Lefkowitz, "men were anxious because they were not working. In the 70s, men became anxious because their work was not paying off in the over-all economic security they had expected."

"I thought seriously of killing myself," says a St. Louis man who was forced to resign at the age of fifty when the company he headed was taken over by a large conglomerate. "I saved up the arsenic pills I take for my heart condition. How could I live without that company to run, my office, my staff, six hundred employees, the wheeling and dealing? But then I realized how much of it I'd really hated: the constant worry, getting in at 6 A.M. to read the reports of six vice-presidents, fighting the union to keep wages down, and being hated, knuckling under to people I despised to get accounts. The only good thing was knowing I'd made it to president of a company when my father never got past store clerk. Now I want to work for myself, to live, enjoy the sunsets, and raise begonias. But my kids are gone now, and my wife started her career late, and all she wants is to get ahead in the agency."

It is not only, or even mainly, "losers" making such shifts in values and life style, if not actual jobs. In a *Playboy* survey in 1979, the men from the most oppressed backgrounds were the only group whose main concern was "getting ahead," making more money. The majority of the men polled, age eighteen to forty-nine, valued "personal growth," "self-fulfillment," "love," and "family life" more than making more money and "getting ahead."

But the hold of the old success drive, the competitiveness that always defined men before, hasn't disappeared overnight. It makes for uneasiness, even for men wanting to live by new values.

A young man in Chicago refuses an extra assignment, which would mean working nights and traveling on weekends, on top of his regular job. It doesn't matter that it will probably lead to a big promotion. "We're having another child," he tells his boss, "and I'm committed to sharing the responsibilities at home because my wife's going to law school at night. It hasn't and won't interfere with my job—you were more than satisfied with my last report. But I'm not taking on anything extra. My family is more important to me."

"That man isn't going to get far," his puzzled boss tells a colleague. "Too bad. He was the pick of the litter."

The colleague asks, "What if they all start acting like that? Where are we going to find the men to run the economy, for God's sake, if they all start putting their families first?"

There's a danger today for men and women who may try to get out of their own binds by reversing roles. Exchanging one obsolete model of a half-life for another, they may copy the worst aspects of the old feminine or masculine mystique instead of building from their own enduring, evolving strengths, and liberating their buried feelings or untried potential in the new experiences now open to them until, sharing parenting and work, they create new role models of wholeness.

I've observed men, suppressing their own disenchantment with sterile corporate jobs or bureaucratic professions, watch bemused as some women jump in, eagerly taking courses in "assertiveness training." I've also seen men shaken, threatened and secretly envious when some women, whose identities, after all, do not depend solely on those jobs, move from strengths that must be rooted in their own female experience and *resist* these same dehumanizing corporate practices men have acquiesced in, too long and to no real advantage.

On the other hand, a woman may become uneasy when a man is so intent on dropping out of the rat race that he clearly yearns for a superwoman to support him as she used to yearn for that strong man to take care of her whole life. "My husband wants me to have another child, and he will quit his job altogether and stay home and take care of the kids," a woman in Vermont told me. "Why should that work for him when it didn't work for me? Maybe I don't want him to take over the family that much. I'd resent it, just working to support him."

Beaten, desperate or self-denigrating "inadequate" men, playing into woman's pent-up hunger for power in the world or simply into her own harassed desperation, toy with fantasies that such reversals would be good. "What I need is a wife," she may joke, trying to be superwoman and doing it all herself, not really able yet to give up or share equally her old power in the home and family. But that half-life which made her insecure can also shake his sense of self.

It didn't really work when Phil, in the first flush of liberation from his surgical mask, reversed roles with Ellen. He stayed home full time after they moved to the country, "mothering" their children, cooking and cleaning, even meekly doing all the dishes "including the pots and pans my daughters were supposed to share," while Ellen went off to work. Is there something suspicious about such an excessively repentant male chauvinist pig? "Let her have the bigtime medical career," he urged, with no trace of outward bitterness, as his wife took on acupuncture on top of her new midwife training. "She shouldn't be a nurse any more and take orders from men. She's a natural healer; she's the one who should have gone to medical school. I'll grow our own vegetables and heal myself."

But, in the first place, she didn't make nearly as much money as a nurse as he could as a doctor. And when she came home, the house was never clean enough, the meat loaf wasn't seasoned right, he'd forgotten to put the potatoes in, and she would rush around, tired as she was, doing it all over, making him feel just as guilty as she had in the old days.

"Then I began to feel like a martyr," he says. "Nobody appreciated how hard I worked, taking care of the house and kids all day. Anyhow, she missed that security, the money and all the rest of it, of my being a doctor. Working as much as I want to, with my family practice, and bringing money in again, I don't have to feel guilty if the house isn't all that clean on my shift. And now that they're treating her like a professional at the hospital, she doesn't notice the dust on the window sills so much."

Most men sense they are really dependent on women for security and love and intimacy, just as most women learn, after the old resentment-making imbalances are out of the way, that they are dependent on men for these same qualities. Most husbands will put up with quite a lot to weather their wives' periods of transition as they change their attitudes and redefine their roles (though maybe not quite as much as most wives have always had to put up with from their husbands!).

In a recent lecture on "The Male Sex Role: An Insider's View," sociologist William J. Goode stated that he did not think there was or would be a real masculine backlash to women's demand for equality, though men for a time may both exaggerate and deny the threat to them. Nor did he think that, whatever problems or discomforts might be involved for either sex, women would ever give up the new sense of self-respect and the freedom they now enjoy. "Males will stubbornly resist, but reluctantly adjust: because women will continue to want more equality and will be unhappy if they do not get it; because men on the average will prefer that their women be happy; because neither will find an adequate substitute for the other sex; because neither will be able to find an alternative social system."

Men may feel unjustly threatened by the women's movement because they know they personally didn't create the system or conspire to dominate women. Consciously they aren't even aware of how pervasively the social structure, attitudes and laws give them advantages. Men therefore "assume that their greater accomplishments are actually due to their inborn superiority, so they are more aware of their burdens and responsibilities than their unearned advantages," says Goode. In other words, men notice only the difficulties in their lives. They take the comforts as their due. And because they take their superiority for granted, "men view even small losses of differences, of advantages or opportunities as large threats."

But the change that disturbs men most, Goode says, "is a loss of centrality, a decline in the extent to which they are the center of attention. Boys and grown men have always taken for granted that what they were doing was more important than what the other sex was doing. Women's attention was focused on them." Far more troubling to men than women's demand for equal opportunity and pay is the simple fact that "the center of attention shifts more to women now."

The threat is also somewhat exaggerated because the women now holding the desirable jobs only men had held before are so visible, so different, that the mass media plays them up. Even so, their numbers are still too small to constitute any real threat to men's dominance.

Yet men are right in sensing inexorable forces that are undermining their previous claim to natural superiority. But these threatening forces are not created by women. As Goode reports, "The conditions we now live in are different from those of any prior civilization, and they give less support to men's claim of superiority than any other historical era." More and more, the work is done by specialists and machines. And there is new awareness that in today's complex society the top posts in government and business are not best filled by the stereotypical male but by people, male or female, sensitive to others' needs, adept at obtaining cooperation—in short, with the intuitions and social skills and nurturing qualities once considered feminine.

So *men* envy *women* the women's movement. They envy women the zest and energy with which we approach jobs that hold no novelty or challenge for *them*. These jobs also seem like exciting new challenges to women because we are not saddled with that burdensome mandate to be superior and dominant. We do not yet have the need to suppress feelings of weakness and vulnerability that men have been locked into for so long. As a young man put it to me, after several years of wandering, dropping out of school and trying to find himself, "Every guy I know is in trouble. They can't seem to get it together. They don't know what they want. Only the women seem to be getting it together now."

Whatever a woman does today, she is somehow ahead of where she used to be, of where her mother or older sisters were.

The practical problems remain, emerging more clearly now from the fog of reaction and backlash. As men seek for themselves the liberation that began with the women's movement, both men and women have to confront the conflict between their human needs—for love, for family, for meaning in work and purpose in life—and the demands of the workplace as it is structured today.

A family therapist from Philadelphia, watching his three-year-old learn to throw a ball, talked of the conflict between his own profession and his personal family needs. "I was working at one of the big family-training centers in the country," he said. "There was constant theoretical discussion about getting the father back into the family. But the way our own jobs were set up, you had to work fifty to sixty hours a week. To really get anywhere you had to put in seventy hours, work nights, weekends. You didn't have time for your own family. You were supposed to make the job Number One in your life, and I wouldn't do that. My life is Number One, and my family—my job is only to be a good therapist. To play the office politics and be one of the big guns you had to devote your whole life to it. I started my own practice where I keep my own hours. Most of the other family therapists at the center are now divorced."

Recent managerial studies have shown that the long working hours and the frequent corporate transfers that kept many men from stong daily involvements with their families or with any other fulfilling commitments for interests besides their jobs were not all that necessary for the work of the company. But the long hours and the transfers do serve to keep a man dependent for his very identity, as well as his livelihood, on the corporation—a "company man."

This process is pinpointed in a depth study of executives in a major Connecticut company by Diana Rothbard Margolis published in 1980, *The Managers—Corporate Life in America*. "Security is not all that binds," this study explains. "Beyond the large paychecks, the benefit plans . . . the corporation controls a trump—the manager's identity. Paradoxically, managers must depend on the corporation for their definition of self precisely because they are moved around so frequently in their jobs. . . . With interests narrowed by the demands of their [corporate] initiation, a manager's thirst for money, status and security grows until other needs are eclipsed. . . . For corporation managers, needs usually fulfilled by human relationships become increasingly difficult to satisfy because almost all relationships outside their nuclear family are distant and fleeting. So like half-starved people who in the absence of proteins will fatten themselves on starches, managers and their families hunger for goods money cannot buy, but reach for those it can."

Is it necessary for a man to leave the corporate mainstream to find himself—and his new identity in the family? Might he not be able to turn that corner for himself by acting, along with women, to change those dehumanizing corporate conditions? With productivity declining and absenteeism increasing, corporations will have to come to terms with men's insistence on human terms and meaning in work—which could conceivably strengthen the system, as women's equality is giving new strength to the family.

It seems strange to suggest that there is a new American frontier, a new adventure for men, in this new struggle for wholeness, for openness to feeling, for living and sharing life on equal terms with women, taking equal responsibility for children—the human liberation that began with the women's movement. Unlike the American hero of the past, the new frontier liberates men from the isolating silence of that lonely cowboy. "I'm not just my work now, not just a breadwinner, I can do something just for myself," says Avery. "But to tell you the truth, my fantasies now tend to be in terms of the family. I'd like to take the kids and Judy on the same trip backpacking to Canada I took at nineteen. It's not my fantasy to go off to the South Seas alone like Gauguin."

Men aren't really going to be able to escape, or want to escape, the work world, any more than most women can or want to escape the family. The men in *Breaktime* had to or wanted to go back to work after their unemployment insurance or savings ran out—but on terms now which left them more room to be human, enabled them to use their own abilities and control their own lives more (if not in the job itself, then by reducing the job's importance and putting their main energies into other pursuits). The new statistics showing how frequently men are changing jobs indicate that somehow, even in this turbulent economy, men are taking more control of their own lives instead of being passive robots of the corporation. And new statistics showing for the first time a decline in the number of hours American women spend on housework suggest that when women no longer need all that power and status from the perfectly clean house because they're getting a little more power in the world—they don't let their houses run them.

Instead of being defined by their jobs or careers, more and more young men—and survivors of the midlife crisis—are holding down one or more part-time jobs, like women (taxi driver, teaching one course, waiter, bartender, apartment-house "super" or country caretaker in return for free rent), while "their own thing" may be the cello, ecology, dance, or studying Greek mythology—not for pay at all. Says my young friend David, "I seem to know fewer and fewer men who answer 'What do you do?' in terms of their job. It's 'What is your *shtik?*'"

In the second stage of this struggle that is changing everyone's life, men's and women's needs converge. There are conscious choices now, for men as well as women—to set up their lives in such a way as to achieve a more equitable balance between success in work and gratification in personal life. And here is the missing link, the power that was lacking when women tried to solve these problems by taking it all on themselves as superwomen, the power women did not and will not have, to change the structure of jobs by and for themselves alone. But if young men now need and want self-fulfillment beyond their jobs and the life-grounding women have always had in the family—as much as women now need and want some voice and active power in the world—there will be a new, and sufficient, *combined* force for the second stage.

So this is the other half of Stage Two of the struggle that began with women's movement for equality—men's liberation. Men, it seems, are now seeking new life patterns as much as women are. They envy women's freedom to express their feelings and their private questions and the support they got from each other in those years of the women's movement.

After talking to these men, I wonder about women who struggle so hard to succeed in traditional male roles. A West Point officer, like a number of executives I've met who are dealing with women colleagues as equals for the first time, seemed to have a strange awe, fear, envy almost, of women's power, a sense that women know some secret men don't. (Or maybe, now that women are there, in the man's world, the men are afraid women will discover how hollow men's power can be.)

This is tricky, because there's been so much hypocrisy about the power of women. But the West Point man says, "It always defined women as against men—that we went to war. 'Winners never quit,' 'Quitters never win,' etc. The worst insult was to be called the four- and five-letter words for women's sex. Now the women are in the locker room, too. They have a powerful advantage because they weren't brought up with the black-and-white view of the world: 'If he knocks you down, you're a pussy.' 'He has the courage, so you have to knock him down.' Women aren't stuck with the notion that that kind of courage is necessary, or even possible. They just cast about for ways to do what has to be done, push through the phoniness, the lies, to the concrete reality of it. They know it's not black and white, it's gray. It makes men feel guilty for having believed the lie in the first place, and then for having given up so easily. Men are jealous and afraid of women, maybe envious of their power. It may sound corny, but there is power in women's ability to create life, closeness to life, that men don't have, always chasing power, in the company, in the army.

"Speaking for myself, I need reassurance from women. And now there's all this rhetoric that all the things men bragged about are no good. So men are left with gaping holes in their identity, their equation of life. And now that women feel unfettered ambition is absolutely necesary to get ahead in their own careers, they can't turn around and help men. Men don't like to admit their fear of women, and women don't like to be feared, but the hidden secret is coming out now, and it's freaking people. It's scary to have power over people and be able to control them, the way women do with feelings.

"It seems to me, beginning with the Vietnam war, more and more men are reaching a turning point where if they don't turn the corner and get beyond these black-and-white games, they start to die. Women will make a mistake if they reach that turning point and start to imitate men. Will the women move in and take our place? Men can't be role models for women, not even in the army. We badly need some new role models ourselves."

Suggestions for Discussion

1. What supporting evidence does Friedan provide that American men "are at the edge of a momentous change in their very identity as men"?

2. What questions does the author believe that men are asking?

3. How do dependency and need affect men's attitudes toward women and women's feelings about men?

4. What are some of the signs that "machismo was dying" and what brought about the change?

5. What are the dangers in role reversals?

6. What is sociologist Goode's view of men's response to the women's movement?

7. What is Friedan's suggested solution for the identity problem facing men in the corporate mainstream?

8. How does the author define the second stage of the struggle?

9. How does the West Point man view men's problems?

Suggestions for Writing

1. Compare Friedan's views with those of Noel Perrin in *The Androgynous Man*. Whose analysis seems more valid to you? Draw upon your observation and experience.

2. Read Friedan's book, *The Second Stage*, and try to account for the displeasure expressed by some feminists in its point of view.

3. Discuss any one of the questions above by bringing to bear your observation and experience.

4. Develop a character study of a man (or woman) who is trying to reconcile her or his career goals with a sense of self-fulfillment.

Brooke Kroeger

AIDS and the Girl Next Door

Brooke Kroeger, a New York City writer, is the author of "Nellie Bly: Daredevil, Reporter, Feminist" (1994). Only by a fluke did "the girl next door" learn that she was HIV-positive and that the source of her infection could not be identified.

There was just no point in joining an AIDS support group for women. What, besides impending death, did she have in common with convicts and heroin addicts? She'd graduated from college and become a professional, a twenty-eight-year-old comer in her field, earning forty thousand dollars a year, the daughter of a respected upper-middle-class family. A gay men's group might have made a better demographic fit. For the time being, no appropriate group exists. Most of the heterosexual men and women with the background to be helpful to her are walking around with the AIDS virus and don't even know it.

But then, neither would she, if not for a series of coincidences that bore the mark of Providence. This is why she has agreed to be interviewed. She thinks there is a message she had better get across. In deference to her family, she asks that her name and any identifying details be excluded from the story.

What makes her story worth telling is that she is utterly ordinary, the girl next door. It was only by a fluke that a doctor would think to suggest that someone with her socioeconomic profile and no symptoms should be tested for AIDS—and that the test would come back HIV-positive.

The story began with a case of fatigue and a stubborn rash in the folds of her groin that would not go away. She would have ignored them both if the raw skin hadn't been so aggravating in the summer heat of 1988. And even though she had good reason to be tired—fourteen-hour, adrenalin-charged workdays would wear anyone out—it felt too much like the mononucleosis of her adolescence. Time for a physical.

The physician examined her carefully. The fatigue was easily explained away. She was working too hard. As for the rash, nylon stockings and relentless humidity made it a common summertime affliction. Still, the rash struck him as meaner than most. He ordered a full blood workup for the new patient.

"So," he said, "it's the 1980s. Tell me about your sex life."

She quickly determined where this conversation might lead, but found the doctor easy to talk to and had no problem answering his questions. She had lost her virginity at twenty, the oldest among her friends, and married the first man she slept with, but divorced him two years later. Depression dulled her very Roman Catholic sensibilities and she "got wild" for about two years. Though she had been celibate for the nine months before the examination, there had been fifteen partners before that. For the most part, they were friends who became lovers or lovers who became friends. There were two one-night stands, but the men were not strangers. Nothing kinky. No violence. No one the least bit exotic. No anal intercourse except for one distasteful, twenty-second attempt while she was married that did not result in penetration or ejaculation. And no condoms; they didn't seem necessary. She knew all these men of the Brooks-Brothers-Suit Brigade. There is, to this day, no reason to think that any of her partners were bisexual or users of intravenous drugs or frequenters of prostitutes. None of them is known to be sick.

The doctor asked her if she would like him to order an AIDS test. He had no particular reason to suggest it, but was mindful of the times. The test would involve nothing more than another entry on the printout of results for which her blood had already been drawn.

She needed only a moment to decide. It *was* the 1980s. Responsible people check their cholesterol and submit to the AIDS test.

"Sure," she said. "Do it."

Over the coming weeks, the test would be repeated twice to confirm its devastating result. From a source that remains unknown, she had contracted the HIV infection. Her most recent tests show that the virus is active. Nevertheless, she feels terrific. She has gained a not-necessarily desired twenty-five pounds since she was diagnosed. She swims everyday, goes horseback riding, foxhunts, plays squash. Her doctor says he thinks the virulence of her rash may have been an indication of a taxed immune system, but this is hindsight. If it weren't for having casually agreed to being tested, she would have walked around for who knows how long oblivious to her infectiousness. There is no published estimate of how many others may be in her situation.

"I could be acting as wild as I was after my divorce or even wilder," she says. "I could be married and giving this to my baby."

The case of Alison Gertz, a twenty-three-year-old New Yorker raised on Park Avenue, is similar to this woman's in that their backgrounds make them atypical of the most common AIDS sufferers in this country, and a cause for concern to the general heterosexual population. What distinguishes the two cases is that Alison Gertz was able to identify the source of her infection: a bartender whom she says she slept with once. He since has died of AIDS.

By the end of May 1989, the Centers for Disease Control (CDC) reported a total of 97,193 cases of AIDS in the United States since 1981, and of that number 56,468 deaths. Heterosexual cases accounted for only 4 percent of that total, or 4,305 cases. To qualify as a heterosexual case, the individual must report specific heterosexual contact with someone who is considered to be at high risk for AIDS—a bisexual, an I.V.-drug user, a hemophiliac, someone who received a blood transfusion before screening began, or someone of African or Caribbean origin (in those countries, AIDS occurs predominantly in heterosexuals).

The woman interviewed for this story is not yet a statistic. There is no national register of people who carry the HIV virus but have not yet developed AIDS. Fewer than thirty states require reporting of those who test HIV-positive and she does not live in one of them. Because the source of her infection is not known, when she does develop AIDS her case will have to be classified as "No Identifiable Risk (NIR)."

Nonetheless, it is presumed that she was infected through sexual contact. Fully 75 percent of AIDS sufferers who have been listed as NIR ultimately are moved to other categories after follow-up studies reveal that they or one of their partners actually belonged to a high-risk group. The source of infection for the other 25 percent remains a mystery.

Jeanette Stehr-Green, M.D., a section chief in AIDS surveillance, CDC, explains why there has been no move at the national level to keep count of those who are HIV-positive but not yet suffering from AIDS. "Many of those who would be HIV-positive are not motivated to get tested," she says, "so there is no way we could count all of them. Many don't know they are at risk. Many are denying their risk. Many may realize their risk but don't feel that getting tested will change anything anyway."

The CDC estimates that the total number of people in the United States who are HIV-positive—from all causes—is somewhere between 1 million and 1.5 million. Working backwards from that figure, Jody Robinson, M.D., a Washington, D.C., physician with a background in immunology, epidemiology, and international medicine, estimates the number of infected heterosexuals to be as high as 400,000 (regardless of how they got the virus). If Dr. Robinson is anywhere near correct—and no one at the CDC is willing to say—then the potential threat to the general heterosexual population could be greater than usually presumed. These infected persons can be assumed to have relations from time to time with people who would have no other risk of infection.

"I think this is a reasonable estimate," says Elizabeth M. Whelan, Ph.D., president of the American Council on Science and Health. "The I.V.-drug-using community is the potential bridge to the general spread of AIDS."

When the woman interviewed for this story asked her doctor if she needed to furnish him with a list of the names and addresses of all her sexual partners, he said, "No, only if you want."

"Only if you want?" she shot back. "ONLY IF YOU WANT? What the f—— is that when someone is out there spreading death?" She thought surely it would be required by law.

The federal government does require any state accepting certain types of federal funds for its AIDS programs to set up partner-notification services. However, it has been left to each state to interpret this requirement. "By definition, the process is voluntary," says Cathy Raevsky, deputy section chief of the Sexually Transmitted Diseases/AIDS Section of the Colorado Health Department's AIDS program, considered to have one of the most aggressive notification systems in the country.

Together, the woman and her doctor drafted a letter, sent without signature, to all the men she had slept with. She located all but one of them. The letter explained that she had contracted the HIV virus and urged that they be tested.

"All of them know how to find me," she says. "You would think that there would have been a letter from at least one of them, even an anonymous one, saying he was HIV-positive and I should be tested. But I've heard nothing and it's been almost a year."

Dr. Robinson has brandished the threat of AIDS to the general, heterosexual population in a series of op-ed page pieces for *The Wall Street Journal*, *The Washington Post*, the *Chicago Tribune*, the *St. Louis Post-Dispatch* and *The Atlanta Constitution*. His premise is that people should not be lulled into a false sense of security because of their conventional lifestyles or the relatively small number of recorded cases of heterosexual AIDS in this country.

As he explains it, the most efficient means of transmitting the AIDS virus are anal intercourse and inoculation into the vascular system. "This has skewed the sense of this disease in the eyes of the public because of the preponderance of cases who have gotten the disease through these extraordinarily efficient means."

If the median incubation rate for the virus is ten years, and the first cases in this country were only recognized eight years ago in 1981, then it makes sense that the first two waves of infection were among people in those communities in which infection could occur most efficiently—homosexuals, hemophiliacs, heroin addicts. Those who have been infected by somewhat less efficient means—vaginal intercourse—would likely take longer to surface.

For Dr. Robinson the experience with AIDS in Africa serves as a case in point. There, the ratio of infection among heterosexual men and women is 1:1. Here, the ratio is 4:1 men to women. In Africa, he believes, the disease has been spreading longer, even though homosexuality and I.V.-drug use are rare. It is also a place with a high degree of untreated venereal diseases, untreated skin sores, and uncircumcised males—all of which enhance the spread of AIDS infection. In short, if the Africa example is adjusted to the prevailing conditions in this country, it may well mean that the worst is yet to come.

At CDC, however, the view is less alarming for those not already considered to be at risk. Nevertheless, there is cause for concern.

"We are not seeing an explosive increase in heterosexual AIDS," says Mary Chamberland, M.D., a medical epidemiologist with CDC's AIDS program. "But that is not to minimize the problem. In big urban centers, among African-Americans and Hispanics and drug users and prostitutes, it is a big problem. But for most people, heterosexual AIDS is not something that poses a very significant risk.

"But the risk is not zero," she says, "and the woman you have just described is a very good example. It points out the need for education. Everybody does need to take prudent precautions."

Our girl next door has stopped spending time worrying about who her "donor" was. What's important is maintaining a good outlook; eating a high-protein diet; monitoring her T-cell count for signs of a turn in her condition; and deepening her spiritual life, a journey that began long before she discovered her condition. She still spends time with her good friends and they are many. She is someone people like to be with. She has a great sense of humor. She's someone with good values who likes to party.

She is at peace with her situation. It is difficult to imagine the emotional upheavals she has weathered in the past ten months—the shock of discovery, the anxiety attacks, the depression, the suicide attempt. "You don't know me," she says. "But you can't imagine how uncharacteristic my behavior was."

When the test result first came back, she says her reaction was primordial. "My hands and feet went ice cold. I thought I would lose control of my bowels. I stood up and started pacing like an animal in a cage, looking out the window. I kept focusing on the shame. There is so much shame attached to this illness."

Her sister, brother-in-law, and their two children arrived at her apartment, by chance, to spend the weekend.

"I was in complete shock," she says. "When my sister asked what happened at the doctor's office, I told her I was anemic and had to take it easy. I love to eat. We ordered a pizza and I couldn't eat it. Nobody would believe there could be a pizza on the table and I wouldn't eat it. My heart was racing out of my chest. I know now I was having an anxiety attack. The doctor had given me a prescription for Valium. I had never taken it before, not even for a back injury. But I filled it immediately. I needed to get my pulse rate below one hundred. I lost nine pounds getting through that weekend. I thought I was wasting away."

Her sister left; Monday morning she called work and told her boss she had pneumonia. She bought a first-class air ticket on the first possible flight to see her brother.

"It was like a bad Bette Davis movie. It was eight-thirty in the morning and I was slugging Bloody Marys one after the other. And smoking cigarettes. The stewardess didn't know what to make of me. I didn't know how sick I was. I was only dealing with death. Only death."

Her brother calmed her down, got her thinking straight, and put her in touch with a lawyer so she could understand her legal situation. Subsequently her parents and sister were told. The whole family has been a mainstay of support.

But the journey she started toward deepening her religious life stopped cold when her first test result came back. She was severely depressed. She went through a phase of seeing the world as one big germ—compulsively washing her hands, being afraid to touch doorknobs, avoiding hospitals and sick people, fearing any sneeze in her presence.

The worst bout of depression came at Thanksgiving. She attended her tenth high-school reunion and finished the evening with drinking and reminiscing and a 5:30 A.M. breakfast at the home of one of her oldest and dearest friends. She made her confession. The poignance was palpable. The friend and her husband then went upstairs to bed and she remained at the kitchen table with her bottle of Xanax, prescribed by a psychiatrist she had been seeing who had been no help at all. She doesn't recall how many pills she took, but before she passed out, she called her sister, who rushed her to their mother's house and then to a hospital where she spent a week recuperating.

"Until you've done this, you can't imagine the humor," she says. "They treat you like a psychiatric patient because you've tried to kill yourself and they make you have nurses around the clock to make sure you don't try to do it again. I convinced them that I was fine and would not harm myself in order to get them to release me. But I was still clinically depressed, certainly still in danger. That tells you how much faith I have in psychiatrists anymore."

She stayed with her parents for several days, lying in bed, crying, refusing to eat. Her mother would cry with her and that would make her feel worse.

Her mother left an Advent calendar by her bedside. For each day in the countdown to Christmas, there was a verse. She can't remember which one, or what about the experience of reading it every day made the difference, but "something clicked," she says. "I hadn't prayed for three months, but this was perfect, as if it had been written for me. It was loving, forgiving, hopeful."

"And that's when I started getting better," she goes on. "That was my cure. You know, my family has all been praying for a miracle, for a cure, and after this I said, 'This is my cure.' A cure is not only physical, you know. I started feeling and caring and thinking about life again."

She tries not to moralize, knowing how pointless that would be. But she wishes those wild years had never happened, that she had possessed the wisdom at the time to realize how fruitless all the empty activity was. She wishes she had insisted on condoms and spermicides.

"The truth is, I could no more have pulled a condom out of my purse—I couldn't have even raised the question. There is so much pressure from men—so much competition for so few men—women will continue to say yes to men and be too bashful to be cautious. But there is just no dignity in finding out you have AIDS because you were too dignified to ask a man to wear a condom."

As for now, she has taken medical leave from work. It will probably be permanent. She doesn't feel sick in the least and she is not currently undergoing any treatment. A protocol was tried but proved too toxic for her system. Instead of experimenting with other drugs, her doctors think it is best to wait until she may really need them. In the meantime, she concentrates on simplifying her life. She contemplates entering a religious community and hopes to volunteer for an AIDS hotline ("I'm sure I could handle the suicide calls," she jokes). She spends a lot of time with her family.

"I'm not withering away," she says. "Just because it doesn't look like I'm running frantic and busily producing doesn't mean I'm not running frantic and busily producing."

Getting involved with someone, she says, is not in the cards.

"My forever will be a lot shorter than his forever," she says. "And that's not fair."

Neither is AIDS. But that kind of thinking is not part of whom she has become.

Suggestions for Discussion

1. What makes the woman's story worth telling? Why is she called "the girl next door"?

2. What is the significance of the phrase "Brooks-Brothers-Suit Brigade"?

3. Why was the woman astounded when her doctor said "only if you want" when she asked if she needed to furnish him with a list of the names and addresses of all her sexual partners?

4. Trace the varied responses to the condition of "the girl next door."

5. How does she account for her carelessness in her relationships with men?

6. What is her outlook on the future?

Suggestions for Writing

1. What kind of educational program might protect young women from becoming HIV-positive?

2. Describe "a girl next door" among your friends and acquaintances and suggest the ways in which she relates to others.

3. Describe a situation in which "friends became lovers" or in which "lovers became friends."

Mark Gerzon

Manhood
The Elusive Goal

Mark Gerzon is the author of The Whole World Is Watching: A Young Man Looks at Youth's Dissent (1969); A Childhood for Every Child: The Politics of Parenthood (1973); A Choice of Heroes (1982), from which this chapter was selected; and

Coming Into Our Own (1992). Manhood is an elusive goal because our culture does not provide an appropriate rite of passage for young men who are "caught between the competing ideals of chauvinism and liberation."

> There is no steady unretracing progress in this life
> . . . Once gone through, we trace the round again;
> and are infants, boys, and men, and Ifs eternally.
> —Melville, *Moby-Dick*

It was not coincidence that when love entered my life, so did violence. I fell in love for the first time with a high school classmate, Diana. She was a cheerleader, the most feminine of all roles. Even now, almost twenty years later, I think of her when I see cheerleaders practicing. In one cheer, they would shout each letter of each member of the starting line-up's name as they ran onto the basketball court, heralding them as if they were heroes. They had mastered the art of feminine support: they remained on the sidelines while acclaiming the men who played the game.

In this, Diana was wholehearted. In winter, her face would glow when the ball swished through the hoop; she would look crestfallen when it fell short. In autumn, chanting "Hit 'em again, hit 'em again, harder, harder," her body pulsed to the rhythm of her words. Even if she was not the most beautiful cheerleader, she was certainly the most magnetic. She made us feel like men.

Before she and I started dating, she went with a fellow two years my senior, a leading figure in one of the male clubs known for its toughness. Since he and Diana had broken up (or so she said), I felt no qualms when our study dates became romantic. Soon she and I were together almost constantly. When she invited me to a party sponsored by her club, I accepted. After all, she was "mine."

Midway through the evening, however, her former beau arrived with several of his hefty club brothers behind him. "They want you," a friend warned me, then quickly disappeared. My strategy, which was to pretend that I had not noticed their arrival, became impractical when three of them had me cornered. And I had no club brothers to back me up.

"Let's go outside," said Diana's old beau.

"What for?" I was still playing dumb.

The purpose of our outing was to settle with our fists who Diana belonged to. He obviously felt that he had staked his claim first and that I was trespassing on his territory. I believed that she had the right to choose for herself to whom she wanted to belong. Neither of us, perhaps not even Diana herself, considered it odd that at the age of sixteen she should belong to anyone.

As it turned out, the other boy friend and I didn't fight, at least not that night. "Why'd you let him talk you out of it?" one of his buddies asked him. He was outraged at being deprived of what was to be the high point of his evening.

A few weeks later, after a basketball game, my adversary and I passed each other under the bleachers. Without warning, he punched me hard in my right eye. My fist was raised to return the blow when several arms pressed me back against the wall.

"Whatsa matter?" he shouted at me contemptuously. "Are you gonna cry?"

The impatient crowd pushed us in opposite directions. Stunned, I felt my eye to check if it was bleeding. Only then did I feel the tell-tale moistness. Although no tears trickled down my cheeks, they were still evidence against my manliness. First, I had weaseled out of a fight. Next, I let him hit me without ever returning the blow. But the most damaging evidence of all were my barely averted tears. To be hit and to cry was the ultimate violation of the code of masculine conduct.

That happened half a lifetime ago. I no longer see my unwillingness to fight as an indictment of my character. Had I been as old and as tough as my adversary, perhaps I would have handled our conflict differently. Perhaps I would have fought. Perhaps I even might have won. Instead, aware of my relative weakness and inexperience, I chose not to. I wanted to protect my eyes, my mouth, my groin. I thought I might need them in the future. But the deeper reason had nothing to do with self-protection but with love. I could not understand what the winner of a fight would gain. Would Diana accept the verdict of our brawl? Like a Kewpie doll at the fairgrounds, would she let herself be claimed by whichever contestant came out on top? If her love could be won by violence, I was not sure I wanted it. I wanted her to love me for who I was, not for how I fought.

My problem, my friends told me then, was that I was too sensitive.

Strange how things change. The image of manhood against which I am measured has changed so much that now, almost twenty years later, I am told I am not sensitive *enough*. When tensions build in our relationship, Shelley will admonish me for being out of touch with my feelings. "You are always so defensive, always trying to protect yourself," she will say. "Why can't you be more open to your feelings?"

How can I explain it to her? How can any man explain it to any woman? Women are not raised to abort all tears. They are not measured by their toughness. They are not expected to bang against each other on hockey rinks and football fields and basketball courts. They do not go out into the woods to play soldiers. They do not settle disagreements by punching each other. For them, tears are a badge of femininity. For us, they are a masculine demerit.

Nothing has made me see this more clearly than talking with Richard Ryan, a former alcoholic. Sitting in the sun one afternoon by a lake near his home, Richard reminded me of a masculine rite of passage I had almost forgotten.

"After I gave this rap about alcoholism at the high school, this kid came up to me and said, 'Can I talk with you privately, Mr. Ryan?' Usually that means that either the kid's parents are alcoholic or he is. But not this kid. He said to me, 'Mr. Ryan, I've never been drunk, never smoked a joint. What's wrong with me?'

"So I said to him, 'Nothing's wrong with you, man. You're doin' fine.'

" 'But why do I feel I have to lie to my friends about it?' he asked. 'If they knew I didn't drink or smoke they'd make fun of me.' "

Richard Ryan rolled over onto his stomach as he finished the story. Either the sun or his emotions made him hide his face.

"I always felt like I had to lie as a kid," Ryan told me. "I liked to bake cookies. I liked to watch my kid brothers and sisters. I liked to write poetry. But my dad made me feel that was wrong somehow. So I started to pretend I *didn't* want to do it."

I had heard the lament so often now that I pushed him for specifics. "But what did your dad do? Did he walk in and say, 'Get out of the kitchen' or 'That's women's work'?"

"No, no. Nothing like that. It was more subtle." He thought for a moment. "For example, when my mother's mother died, I wanted to be her pallbearer. Grandma had been very special to me. I felt like she'd carried me all my life. When she died, I wanted to carry her once. So I asked my dad if I could be a pallbearer. He said, 'Only if you promise not to cry. Pallbearers can't cry!' I knew if I lied and said I wouldn't, he'd let me. But I felt like that'd be betraying her. How could I go to her funeral and not cry? Since I wouldn't promise, my dad refused to let me do it."

Now in his mid-thirties, Ryan runs a project called Creative Drug Education. He visits high schools and talks about alcohol and drug abuse. But he doesn't preach. He tells his own story:

"When I used to go out and get bombed, guys would say, 'He drinks like a man' or 'He holds it like a man.' Being drunk, I really felt like I was something great. The other guys and I, we were like a pack, and drinking was our bond. We'd get together and, because we drank, we'd say stuff and hug each other and do all sorts of things we'd never let ourselves do if we were sober."

Only after reaching the age of thirty did Richard realize he was an alcoholic. "I've only recently felt I can be who I am," he continues. "All those years I felt I had to blot out a whole side of myself. I used alcohol to make myself feel good about myself. After I quit drinking, I thought I was free. But then I realized I was addicted to smoking. And I mean *addicted*. My withdrawal from nicotine was almost as bad as from booze—the shakes, sweating, couldn't sleep. I found it hard to be around people without a cigarette in my hand. It was the whole Marlboro man thing—it made me look cool, made me feel like a man. When a friend told me I should stop, I told him, 'Anybody can quit smoking. It takes a real man to face cancer.' I said it as a joke, but I meant it. That's how sick I was."

Richard no longer looks sick. He is big and muscular. We swam out to the middle of the lake and back and, when we dried off, he wasn't even out of breath. He is respected by the people with whom he works. Teachers tell me he is more effective with young people who use drugs than anyone they've ever met.

As we walked back to the car, I saw a sadness in him, a wound that had not yet healed.

"What you thinking about?" I asked, not knowing a better way to probe.

He laughed. "Oh, I was just thinking about Grandma's funeral. You know what? Every one of those pallbearers cried."

In Western societies, there are clearly no longer any rites of passage. The very existence of terms such as teenager (the German word is *Halbwüchsiger*, half-grown) shows that the absence of this social institution results in an in-between stage. All too often adult society avoids this whole question by regarding those in their teens in terms of the high school health book definition. Adolescence, it says, is the period when the person is no longer a child, but not yet an adult. This is defining the concept of adolescence by avoiding it altogether. This is why we have a youth culture. It is where adolescents go (and sometimes stay) before they become grownups.

Despite the absence of any established initiation rite, young men need one. By default, other institutions take the place of these missing rites. Some commentators on growing up in America point to sports or fraternities, for example, to demonstrate that our culture does have various kinds of initiation rites. But they are wrong.

Sports, for instance, can hardly serve as the means for gaining manhood. Sports are games. Except for the professionals who make their living from them, these games have little connection with real life. Moreover, only a small minority of males in American high schools and colleges can participate in athletics. As dozens of articles document, sports play a key role in enabling boys and young men to test their physical prowess, but they do not alone make a boy a man.

Fraternities, too, are a painfully inadequate means for gaining manhood. Except for token community service projects once a year, most fraternities are disconnected from society. How can they provide a socially recognized initiation rite when they involve only members of the younger generation? Frat members do not go off into seclusion with the adults of the "tribe." They go off into seclusion with themselves. They are initiated into youth culture, perhaps, but not into the world of adults.

The young man facing adulthood cannot reach across this great divide. He has only rites of impasse. There is no ritual—not sexual, economic, military, or generational—that can confirm his masculinity. Maturity eludes him. Our culture is famous for its male adolescent pain. From James Dean in *Rebel Without a Cause* and Dustin Hoffman in *The Graduate* to the more recent box office hits *Breaking Away, My Bodyguard,* and *Ordinary People,* young men try to prove they are grown men. But to no avail. None of the surrogate initiation rites—car duels, college diplomas, after-work drinking rituals, first paychecks, sports trophies—answers their deepest needs. None has proven to be what William James called the "moral equivalent of war."

The only rituals that confirm manhood now are imitations of war. The military academies, for example, like boot camp itself, involve many of the ingredients of primitive rites of passage. Young men are secluded with older men. They must endure tests of psychological or physical endurance.

Pat Conroy's novel *The Lords of Discipline,* which depicts life in a southern military academy, and Lucian K. Truscott IV's *Dress Gray,* which portrays West Point, showed how boys are turned into men—the kind of men the military needs. But, as we have recognized, the Soldier is no longer the hero. The Vietnam war was "billed on the marquee as a John Wayne shoot-'em-up test of manhood," wrote Mark Baker in *Nam,* but it ended up "a warped version of *Peter Pan* . . . a brutal Never Never Land where little boys didn't have to grow up. They just grew old before their time." Similarly, the heroes of Conroy's and Truscott's tales are not the brave soldier but the dissenter. Nevertheless, because military service is the only rite of passage available, men are drawn to it like moths to light. We need to prove our manhood and will take whatever paths our culture offers.

With the option of going to war foreclosed, young men seek to prove themselves by performing other manly deeds. The most obvious surrogates for war often involve violence too. It is not directed at the enemy, but at each other and ourselves.

Each week, the news media overflow with accounts of young men between the ages of fifteen and twenty-five who have committed acts of violence. Too old to be boys, too young to have proven themselves men, they are finding their own rites of passage. Here are three, culled from the newspapers:

A Boy Scout leader smashes his new car on a country road at 100 miles per hour: he is "showing off" to the four scouts who were riding with him. Now they are all dead.

A 16-year-old who lives in a comfortable suburb throws a large rock from a freeway overpass through the windshield of a car. The victim, a 31-year-old housewife, suffers a concussion but survives. "You do it for the thrill," the boy says. "It's a boring town," says one of his classmates.

A teenage boy is so upset that his girl friend has jilted him that he threatens to kill himself. Talking to her on the phone, he says he will drive over to her house and smash his car into the tree in her front yard if she will not go out with him. She refuses. So he does it, killing himself.

Many movies are made as surrogate rites of passage for young men. They are designed for the guy who, in actor Clint Eastwood's words, "sits alone in the theater. He's young and he's scared. He doesn't know what he's going to do with his life. He wishes he could be self-sufficient, like the man he sees up there on the screen, somebody who can look out for himself, solve his own problems." The heroes of these films are men who are tough and hard, quick to use violence, wary of women. Whether cowboys, cops, or superheroes, they dominate everything—women, nature, and other men. Young men cannot outmaneuver the Nazis as Indiana Jones did in *Raiders of the Lost Ark*, or battle Darth Vader, or outsmart Dr. No with James Bond's derring-do. To feel like heroes they turn to the other sex. They ask young women for more than companionship, or sex, or marriage. They ask women to give them what their culture could not—their manhood.

Half the nation's teenagers have had sex before they graduate from high school. The easiest way to prove oneself a man today is to make it with a girl. First we make out or put the make on her. Then we make it. We are not, like our "primitive" forebears, joining together with a woman as adults. We are coming together in order to become adults, if not in society's eyes, then in our own.

"You in her pants yet?" one of the high school jocks asks his classmate in *Ordinary People*, the Academy Award–winning movie directed by Robert Redford. We prove our manhood on the football field or the basketball court by scoring points against other men. We prove our manhood in sex by scoring with women.

The young man, armed with lines like "Don't you love me?" is always ready for action. He wants to forge ahead, explore new territory. After all, he has nothing to lose. He has no hymen, no uterus. He is free to play the role of bold adventurer, coaxing the reluctant girl to let him sow his wild oats in her still virgin land. "I love you, but I don't feel ready," she may say. She may be afraid that her refusal may jeopardize her relationship with her young explorer, but she is even more afraid to get pregnant. She may feel less mature than her sex-hungry companion. But the emotional reality may be precisely the opposite. Certain of her femininity and of her pregnability, she dares to wait until the time is right. Insecure about his masculinity and obsessed with proving it—to himself and his buddies, if not to her—he needs to score in order to feel that he has made the team.

Sonny Burns, the sexually insecure hero of Dan Wakefield's *Going All the Way*, finds himself engaged in an amorous overture on a double date. But he admits to himself, and to a generation of readers, that he is doing so not because he finds his date exciting. On the contrary, she bores him. He does so because he wants to impress his buddy in the front seat. He must prove he is a man, and a man takes whatever "pussy" he can get. Pretending to be passionate, he thinks about the high school rating system, according to which boys reported their sexual scores: "The next day, when the guys asked you what you got the night before, you could say you got finger action inside the pants. That wasn't as good as really fucking but it rated right along with dry-humping and was much better than just the necking stuff like frenching and getting covered-tit or bare-tit. It was really pretty much of a failure if you parked with a girl and got only covered-tit."

Even if he wins, the victory is private. There are no fans in the bleachers as he crosses home plate and scores. He has not proved himself a man to adult males, as did young men in traditional rites of passage. His sexual conquest is a rite of passage only in his own mind. If adult society were to pass judgment on these back-seat gymnastics, it would probably be negative. The responsible adult would ask him if he was ready for marriage. Could he support her if he had to? And of course the answers are no. He has become an adult sexually, not socially. He has proved his virility in the dark of night. By the light of day, the proof has vanished.

As Margaret Mead pointed out in *Male and Female*, our culture leaves adolescents in a quandary. We give them extraordinary freedom but tell them not to use it. "We permit and encourage situations in which young people can indulge in any sort of sex behavior that they elect," wrote Mead a generation ago. "We actually place our young people in a virtually intolerable situation, giving them the entire setting for behaviour for which we then punish them when it occurs." It is a cultural arrangement for which some young women pay an awful price.

Whether veiled in fiction or revealed in autobiography, women recall the ritual of modern courtship with caustic humor at best, more often with bitterness. So objectified do they feel that they develop a detached attitude toward their bodies. Reports the cheerleader heroine in Lisa Alther's *Kinflicks:* "Joe Bob would dutifully knead my breasts through my uniform jacket and padded bra, as though he were a housewife poking plums to determine their ripeness." Later, she would observe him sucking "at my nipples while I tried to decide what to do with my hands to indicate my continuing involvement in the project."

But Alther's good-natured response is not typical. Other sagas of car-seat courtships and apartment affairs leave their heroines harboring a deep distaste for men. Some declare themselves feminists or lesbians. Some become depressed. Others, as in Judith Rossner's *Looking for Mr. Goodbar*, are killed by their lovers. And a few, after great turmoil, find a man who will treat them gently, with genuine care.

The movie theater, that public living room for a nation of young lovers, reflects this yearning too. For those who have grown weary of the macho hero whose physical prowess is enough, Hollywood has provided a counter-type. For those who are not infatuated with the Soldier, there are now movies about the anti-soldier. "In what may be an emerging genre in the movies," wrote Paul Starr in his review of *Coming Home, An Unmarried Woman*, and *Alice Doesn't Live Here Anymore*, "there appears a character who expresses in his personality and in his relations with the heroine a new idea of masculinity. He might be described as the emotionally competent hero . . . He is the man to whom women turn as they try to change their own lives: someone who is strong and affectionate, capable of intimacy . . . masculine without being dominating." The new hero, though perhaps not rugged and tough in the familiar mold, can be intimate. He can feel. "The new softer image of masculinity seems to represent what is distinctive and significant in recent films, and I expect we will see more of the post-feminist hero because the old, strong, silent type no longer seems adequate as lover—or as person."

Who, then, is to be the young man's hero? The gentle, post-feminist figure extolled by the new genre of films and by the roughly five thousand men's consciousness-raising groups across America? Or the self-sufficient, hard-hitting tough that Eastwood tries to embody and that the military breeds? Faced with such polarized and politicized choices, how does a boy become a man? By being hard or by being soft?

From the sensible to the absurd, we have answers. We have so many shifting, contradictory criteria for manhood that they confuse rather than inspire.

American boys coming of age encounter sexual chaos. A chorus of liberation advocates, now with bass as well as soprano voices, encourages them to free themselves from the oppressive male role, to become softer, and to consider themselves women's equals. But another vociferous group beckons them in another direction. For every pro-feminist man, there is his counterpart, who denounces those "fuzzy-headed housemales, purporting to represent 'men's liberation,' but sponsored by NOW." One Minnesota men's rights leader argued, for example, that men who support women's liberation are "eunuchs," motivated by an "urge to slip into a pair of panties." According to him and his followers: "Men's liberation means establishing the right of males to be men, not to liberate them from being men."

The hard-liners and soft-liners both have their respective magazines, organizations, and conferences. Repulsed by the cacophony, most young men try to ignore it. But the questions gnaw at them anyway. Although the pro- and anti-feminist activists irritate them, young men cannot deny their own uncertainty. They are caught between the competing ideals of chauvinism and liberation. The old archetypes do not work; the new ones remain vague and incomplete. If we are not to be John Wayne, then who?

Into the vacuum created by the demise of the old archetypes rush myriad images. Each hopes to inspire a following. Masculinity becomes the target for everyone from toothpaste advertisers to Hollywood superstars. These salesmen of self-help all have their diagnoses for the young man struggling to find his own identity. Some take the pose of proud aging lions, defending the traditional masculine role as Western civilization enters a precipitous, psychosexual decline. In *Sexual Suicide*, George Gilder warned of the imminent feminization of man and masculinization of woman and called on men to reassert their superiority.

Others do not oppose liberation but rather seem to exploit it. Cynically catering to masculine insecurity, they describe the world of white-collar commuters as a stark and brutal asphalt jungle in which men must constantly flex their aggressive personalities in order to survive. According to Michael Korda, author of *Power!* and *Success!*, life is nothing more than a series of encounters in which one dominates or is dominated, intimidates or is intimidated, achieves power over or is oneself overpowered. "Your gain is inevitably someone else's loss," philosophizes this latter-day Nietzsche, "your failure someone else's victory."

There are also the advocates of liberation who seek to free us from the manacles of machismo. Although they are constructive in intent, they too increase the confusion. In their attempt to free us from one-sidedness, they double our load. They now want us to be "assertive *and* yielding, independent *and* dependent, job *and* people oriented, strong *and* gentle, in short, both masculine *and* feminine." The prescriptions are not wrong, just overwhelming. Their lists of do's and don'ts, like Gail Sheehy's *Passages*, seem too neat, too tidy. They write of "masculinity in crisis" with such certainty. They encourage us to cry with such stoicism. They advise us to "be personal, be intimate with men" with such authority. It is all too much.

Whichever model young men choose, they know the traditional expectation of their culture. At least until the seventies, Americans of all ages and of all educational and income levels were in wide agreement about what traits are masculine. According to one study, based on more than a thousand interviews, men are expected to be very aggressive, not at all emotional, very dominant, not excitable, very competitive, rough, and unaware of others' feelings. And women are expected to be more or less the opposite.

If this is what maleness is, then a young man must find ways to demonstrate those traits. Without a rite of passage, he can only prove what he is *not*. Not a faggot, a pussy, a queer. Not a pushover, a loser, or a lightweight. Not a dimwit or a dunce. Not a jerk or a nobody. Not a prick or a pansy. Not, above all, anything that is feminine. Indeed, without clear rites of passage, the only way to be a man is essentially negative: to not be a woman.

If we are to be masculine, then they must be feminine. We convince ourselves that women are yielding, that they are more interested in our careers than in their own, that they are interested in sex whenever we are, that they are fulfilled by raising children. That, we assume, is who they are. Should one of them act differently, then something is wrong, not with our assumptions, but with her.

Having entered physical manhood, we are nevertheless emotionally unsure of ourselves. The more unsure we are, the more we stress that we are not "feminine" and the more we are threatened when women act "masculine." We try to rid ourselves of any soft, effeminate qualities. We gravitate toward all-male cliques in the form of sports teams, social clubs, or professional groups. When we are with a woman, it is virtually always in a sexually charged atmosphere. To be merely friends is nearly impossible because it suggests that we have something in common. We are trying, after all, to prove precisely the opposite, which is why so many marriages fail.

Suggestions for Discussion

1. How did the author's adolescent confrontation with the cheerleader affect him? How does he view it from his adult perspective?

2. With what details from the text can you explain the circumstances that led Gerzon's friends to call him too sensitive when he was an adolescent and almost twenty years later to regard him as not sensitive enough?

3. How does the author's talk with a former alcoholic confirm his feeling that societal forces make it difficult if not impossible for men always to be in touch with their feelings and not defensive about them?

4. What reasons does Gerzon offer for an appropriate rite of passage or initiation rite for young men? Why does he regard sports and fraternities as inadequate in helping a boy achieve manhood?

5. How do recent fiction and films support the author's statement that none of the surrogate initiation rites have provided what William James called the "moral equivalent of war"?

6. What does Gerzon mean when he says that many movies are made as "surrogate rites of passage for young men"?

7. What are some of the differences in attitude expressed by male and female novelists?

8. With what details does the author describe what appears to be an emerging genre in the movies?

9. The author believes that young men are "caught between the competing ideals of chauvinism and liberation." Restate this point of view in your own words and provide examples in defending or challenging it.

10. To what does the author attribute the failure of many marriages?

Suggestions for Writing

1. What do you see as the primary difficulties for boys in achieving manhood?

2. What do you see as the primary difficulties that girls experience in achieving adulthood?

3. Discuss Question 9 above.

Lillian B. Rubin

The Approach–Avoidance Dance

Lillian B. Rubin (b. 1924) is a writer and therapist in the San Francisco Bay Area. She has written a number of books about gender issues, including *Intimate Strangers: Men and Women Together* (1983), from which this selection is taken. Rubin describes the basic differences in the conditioning of men and women as they affect commitment and intimacy in their relationships.

> For one human being to love another, that is perhaps the most difficult of all our tasks, the ultimate, the last test and proof, the work for which all other work is but preparation.
> —**Rainer Maria Rilke**

Intimacy. We hunger for it, but we also fear it. We come close to a loved one, then we back off. A teacher I had once described this as the "go away a little closer" message. I call it the approach–avoidance dance.

The conventional wisdom says that women want intimacy, men resist it. And I have plenty of material that would *seem* to support that view. Whether in my research interviews, in my clinical hours, or in the ordinary course of my life, I hear the same story told repeatedly. "He doesn't talk to me," says a woman. "I don't know what she wants me to talk about," says a man. "I want to know what he's feeling," she tells me. "I'm not feeling anything," he insists. "Who can feel nothing?" she cries. "I can," he shouts. As the heat rises, so does the wall between them. Defensive and angry, they retreat—stalemated by their inability to understand each other.

Women complain to each other all the time about not being able to talk to their men about the things that matter most to them—about what they themselves are thinking and feeling, about what goes on in the hearts and minds of the men they're relating to. And men, less able to expose themselves and their conflicts—those within themselves or those with the women in their lives—either turn silent or take cover by holding women up to derision. It's one of the norms of male camaraderie to poke fun at women, to complain laughingly about the mystery of their minds, wonderingly about their ways. Even Freud did it when, in exasperation, he asked mockingly, "What do women want? Dear God, what do they want?"

But it's not a joke—not for the women, not for the men who like to pretend it is.

> The whole goddamn business of what you're calling intimacy bugs the hell out of me. I never know what you women mean when you talk about it. Karen complains that I don't talk to her, but it's not talk she wants, it's some other damn thing, only I don't know what the hell it is. Feelings, she keeps asking for. So what am I supposed to do if I don't have any to give her or to talk about just because she decides it's time to talk about feelings? Tell me, will you; maybe we can get some peace around here.

The expression of such conflicts would seem to validate the common understandings that suggest that women want and need intimacy more than men do—that the issue belongs to women alone; that, if left to themselves, men would not suffer it. But things are not always what they seem. And I wonder: "If men would renounce intimacy, what is their stake in relationships with women?"

Some would say that men need women to tend to their daily needs—to prepare their meals, clean their houses, wash their clothes, rear their children—so that they can be free to attend to life's larger problems. And, given the traditional structure of roles in the family, it has certainly worked that way most of the time. But, if that were all men seek, why is it that, even when they're not relating to women, so much of their lives is spent in search of a relationship with another, so much agony experienced when it's not available?

These are difficult issues to talk about—even to think about—because the subject of intimacy isn't just complicated, it's slippery as well. Ask yourself: What is intimacy? What words come to mind, what thoughts?

It's an idea that excites our imagination, a word that seems larger than life to most of us. It lures us, beckoning us with a power we're unable to resist. And, just because it's so seductive, it frightens us as well—seeming sometimes to be some mysterious force from outside ourselves that, if we let it, could sweep us away.

But what is it we fear?

Asked what intimacy is, most of us—men and women—struggle to say something sensible, something that we can connect with the real experience of our lives. "Intimacy is knowing there's someone who cares about the children as much as you do." "Intimacy is a history of shared experience." "It's sitting there having a cup of coffee together and watching the eleven o'clock news." "It's knowing you care about the same things." "It's knowing she'll always understand." "It's him sitting in the hospital for hours at a time when I was sick." "It's knowing he cares when I'm hurting." "It's standing by me when I was out of work." "It's seeing each other at our worst." "It's sitting across the breakfast table." "It's talking when you're in the bathroom." "It's knowing we'll begin and end each day together."

These seem the obvious things—the things we expect when we commit our lives to one another in a marriage, when we decide to have children together. And they're not to be dismissed as inconsequential. They make up the daily experience of our lives together, setting the tone for a relationship in important and powerful ways. It's sharing such commonplace, everyday events that determines the temper and the texture of life, that keeps us living together even when other aspects of the relationship seem less than perfect. Knowing someone is there, is constant, and can be counted on in just the ways these thoughts express provides the background of emotional security and stability we look for when we enter a marriage. Certainly a marriage and the people in it will be tested and judged quite differently in an unusual situation or in a crisis. But how often does life present us with circumstances and events that are so out of the range of ordinary experience?

These ways in which a relationship feels intimate on a daily basis are only one part of what we mean by intimacy, however—the part that's most obvious, the part that doesn't awaken our fears. At a lecture where I spoke of these issues recently, one man commented also, "Intimacy is putting aside the masks we wear in the rest of our lives." A murmur of assent ran through the audience of a hundred or so. Intuitively we say "yes." Yet this is the very issue that also complicates our intimate relationships.

On the one hand, it's reassuring to be able to put away the public persona—to believe we can be loved for who we *really* are, that we can show our shadow side without fear, that our vulnerabilities will not be counted against us. "The most important thing is to feel I'm accepted just the way I am," people will say.

But there's another side. For, when we show ourselves thus without the masks, we also become anxious and fearful. "Is it possible that someone could love the *real* me?" we're likely to ask. Not the most promising question for the further development of intimacy, since it suggests that, whatever else another might do or feel, it's we who have trouble loving ourselves. Unfortunately, such misgivings are not usually experienced consciously. We're aware only that our discomfort has risen, that we feel a need to get away. For the person who has seen the "real me" is also the one who reflects back to us an image that's usually not wholly to our liking. We get angry at that, first at ourselves for not living up to our own expectations, then at the other, who becomes for us the mirror of our self-doubts—a displacement of hostility that serves intimacy poorly.

There's yet another level—one that's further below the surface of consciousness, therefore, one that's much more difficult for us to grasp, let alone to talk about. I'm referring to the differences in the ways in which women and men deal with their inner emotional lives—differences that create barriers between us that can be high indeed. It's here that we see how those early childhood experiences of separation and individuation—the psychological tasks that were required of us in order to separate from mother, to distinguish ourselves as autonomous persons, to internalize a firm sense of gender identity—take their toll on our intimate relationships.

Stop a woman in mid-sentence with the question, "What are you feeling right now?" and you might have to wait a bit while she reruns the mental tape to capture the moment just passed. But, more than likely, she'll be able to do it successfully. More than likely, she'll think for a while and come up with an answer.

The same is not true of a man. For him, a similar question usually will bring a sense of wonderment that one would even ask it, followed quickly by an uncomprehending and puzzled response. "What do you mean?" he'll ask. "I was just talking," he'll say.

I've seen it most clearly in the clinical setting where the task is to get to the feeling level—or, as one of my male patients said when he came into therapy, to "hook up the head and the gut." Repeatedly when therapy begins, I find myself having to teach a man how to monitor his internal states—how to attend to his thoughts and feelings, how to bring them into consciousness. In the early stages of our work, it's a common experience to say to a man, "How does that feel?," and to see a blank look come over his face. Over and over, I find myself listening as a man speaks with calm reason about a situation which I know must be fraught with pain. "How do you feel about that?" I'll ask. "I've just been telling you," he's likely to reply. "No," I'll say, "you've told me what happened, not how you *feel* about it." Frustrated, he might well respond, "You sound just like my wife."

It would be easy to write off such dialogues as the problems of men in therapy, of those who happen to be having some particular emotional difficulties. But it's not so, as any woman who has lived with a man will attest. Time and again women complain: "I can't get him to verbalize his feelings." "He talks, but it's always intellectualizing." "He's so closed off from what he's feeling, I don't know how he lives that way." "If there's one thing that will eventually ruin this marriage, it's the fact that he can't talk about what's going on inside him." "I have to work like hell to get anything out of him that resembles a feeling that's something besides anger. That I get plenty of—me and the kids, we all get his anger. Anything else is damn hard to come by with him." One woman talked eloquently about her husband's anguish over his inability to get problems in his work life resolved. When I asked how she knew about his pain, she answered:

> I pull for it, I pull hard, and sometimes I can get something from him. But it'll be late at night in the dark—you know, when we're in bed and I can't look at him while he's talking and he doesn't have to look at me. Otherwise, he's just defensive and puts on what I call his bear act, where he makes his warning, go-away faces, and he can't be reached or penetrated at all.

To a woman, the world men live in seems a lonely one—a world in which their fears of exposing their sadness and pain, their anxiety about allowing their vulnerability to show, even to a woman they love, is so deeply rooted inside them that, most often, they can only allow it to happen "late at night in the dark."

Yet, if we listen to what men say, we will hear their insistence that they *do* speak of what's inside them, *do* share their thoughts and feelings with the women they love. "I tell her, but she's never satisfied," they complain. "No matter how much I say, it's never enough," they grumble.

From both sides, the complaints have merit. The problem lies not in what men don't say, however, but in what's not there—in what, quite simply, happens so far out of consciousness that it's not within their reach. For men have integrated all too well the lessons of their childhood—the experiences that taught them to repress and deny their inner thoughts, wishes, needs, and fears; indeed, not even to notice them. It's real, therefore, that the kind of inner thoughts and feelings that are readily accessible to a woman generally are unavailable to a man. When he says, "I don't know what I'm feeling," he isn't necessarily being intransigent and withholding. More than likely, he speaks the truth.

Partly that's a result of the ways in which boys are trained to camouflage their feelings under cover of an exterior of calm, strength, and rationality. Fears are not manly. Fantasies are not rational. Emotions, above all, are not for the strong, the sane, the adult. Women suffer them, not men—women, who are more like children with what seems like their never-ending preoccupation with their emotional life. But the training takes so well because of their early childhood experience when, as very young boys, they had to shift their identification from mother to father and sever themselves from their earliest emotional connection. Put the two together and it does seem like suffering to men to have to experience that emotional side of themselves, to have to give it voice.

This is the single most dispiriting dilemma of relations between women and men. He complains, "She's so emotional, there's no point in talking to her." She protests, "It's him you can't talk to, he's always so darned rational." He says, "Even when I tell her nothing's the matter, she won't quit." She says, "How can I believe him when I can see with my own eyes that something's wrong?" He says, "Okay, so something's wrong! What good will it do to tell her?" She cries, "What are we married for? What do you need me for, just to wash your socks?"

These differences in the psychology of women and men are born of a complex interaction between society and the individual. At the broadest social level is the rending of thought and feeling that is such a fundamental part of

Western thought. Thought, defined as the ultimate good, has been assigned to men; feeling, considered at best a problem, has fallen to women.

So firmly fixed have these ideas been that, until recently, few thought to question them. For they were built into the structure of psychological thought as if they spoke to an eternal, natural, and scientific truth. Thus, even such a great and innovative thinker as Carl Jung wrote, "The woman is increasingly aware that love alone can give her her full stature, just as the man begins to discern that spirit alone can endow his life with its highest meaning. Fundamentally, therefore, both seek a psychic relation one to the other, because love needs the spirit, and the spirit love, for their fulfillment."*

For a woman, "love"; for a man, "spirit"—each expected to complete the other by bringing to the relationship the missing half. In German, the word that is translated here as spirit is *Geist*. But *The New Cassell's German Dictionary* shows that another primary meaning of *Geist* is "mind, intellect, intelligence, wit, imagination, sense of reason." And, given the context of these words, it seems reasonable that *Geist* for Jung referred to a man's highest essence—his mind. There's no ambiguity about a woman's calling, however. It's love.

Intuitively, women try to heal the split that these definitions of male and female have foisted upon us.

> I can't stand that he's so damned unemotional and expects me to be the same. He lives in his head all the time, and he acts like anything that's emotional isn't worth dealing with.

Cognitively, even women often share the belief that the rational side, which seems to come so naturally to men, is the more mature, the more desirable.

> I know I'm too emotional, and it causes problems between us. He can't stand it when I get emotional like that. It turns him right off.

Her husband agrees that she's "too emotional" and complains:

> Sometimes she's like a child who's out to test her parents. I have to be careful when she's like that not to let her rile me up because otherwise all hell would break loose. You just can't reason with her when she gets like that.

It's the rational-man–hysterical-woman script, played out again and again by two people whose emotional repertoire is so limited that they have few real options. As the interaction between them continues, she reaches for the strongest tools she has, the mode she's most comfortable and familiar with: She becomes progressively more emotional and expressive. He falls back on his best weapons: He becomes more rational, more determinedly reasonable. She cries for him to attend to her feelings, whatever they may be. He tells her coolly, with a kind of clenched-teeth reasonableness, that it's silly for her to feel that way, that she's just being emotional. And of course she is. But that dismissive word "just" is the last straw. She gets so upset that she does, in fact, seem hysterical. He gets so bewildered by the whole interaction that his only recourse is to build the wall of reason even higher. All of which makes things measurably worse for both of them.

*Carl Gustav Jung, *Contributions to Analytical Psychology* (New York: Harcourt, Brace & Co., 1928), p. 185.

The more I try to be cool and calm her the worse it gets. I swear, I can't figure her out. I'll keep trying to tell her not to get so excited, but there's nothing I can do. Anything I say just makes it worse. So then I try to keep quiet, but . . . wow, the explosion is like crazy, just nuts.

And by then it *is* a wild exchange that any outsider would agree was "just nuts." But it's not just her response that's off, it's his as well—their conflict resting in the fact that we equate the emotional with the nonrational.

This notion, shared by both women and men, is a product of the fact that they were born and reared in this culture. But there's also a difference between them in their capacity to apprehend the *logic* of emotions—a difference born in their early childhood experiences in the family, when boys had to repress so much of their emotional side and girls could permit theirs to flower.

. . . It should be understood: Commitment itself is not a problem for a man; he's good at that. He can spend a lifetime living in the same family, working at the same job—even one he hates. And he's not without an inner emotional life. But when a relationship requires the sustained verbal expression of that inner life and the full range of feelings that accompany it, then it becomes burdensome for him. He can act out anger and frustration inside the family, it's true. But ask him to express his sadness, his fear, his dependency—all those feelings that would expose his vulnerability to himself or to another—and he's likely to close down as if under some compulsion to protect himself.

All requests for such intimacy are difficult for a man, but they become especially complex and troublesome in relations with women. It's another of those paradoxes. For, to the degree that it's possible for him to be emotionally open with anyone, it is with a woman—a tribute to the power of the childhood experience with mother. Yet it's that same early experience and his need to repress it that raises his ambivalence and generates his resistance.

He moves close, wanting to share some part of himself with her, trying to do so, perhaps even yearning to experience again the bliss of the infant's connection with a woman. She responds, woman style—wanting to touch him just a little more deeply, to know what he's thinking, feeling, fearing, wanting. And the fear closes in—the fear of finding himself again in the grip of a powerful woman, of allowing her admittance only to be betrayed and abandoned once again, of being overwhelmed by denied desires.

So he withdraws.

It's not in consciousness that all this goes on. He knows, of course, that he's distinctly uncomfortable when pressed by a woman for more intimacy in the relationship, but he doesn't know why. And, every so often, his behavior doesn't please him any more than it pleases her. But he can't seem to help it.

Suggestions for Discussion

1. What is the basic conflict raised in the first paragraphs? Why is it as applicable to men as to women?

2. Why do people wear masks and how does wearing them affect one's feelings about oneself and about "the other"?

3. What are the differences with which women and men deal with their emotional lives? What accounts for these differences?

4. How is Jung's view of men–women relationships illustrated in the paragraphs that follow? In the light of Friedan's essay, is the distinction Jung makes necessarily valid today?

5. What is the source of our equating the emotional with the non-rational?

6. What is the major cause of male withdrawal?

Suggestions for Writing

1. What is your definition of intimacy? What is the nature of the relationship that fosters it? What factors diminish it?

2. Describe the masks that you or someone close to you wear. How do the masks affect intimacy?

3. From your observation and experience, how valid is Rubin's thesis?

Margaret Atwood

Fiction: Happy Endings

Margaret Atwood (b. 1939) has lived both in the United States and Europe, but her home is in Toronto. She is best known as the author of the novels *The Edible Woman* (1976); *Surfacing* (1981); *Life Before Man* (1980); *Bodily Harm* (1982); the powerful political thriller, *The Handmaid's Tale* (1986); *Cat's Eye* (1989); and *The Robber Bride* (1993). She also has written short stories, television plays, children's books, criticism, and poetry. She did graduate work at Harvard on a Woodrow Wilson Fellowship and has taught at a number of Canadian and American universities. In this understated critique of happy endings, the author comments bitterly upon the relationships of men and women and the vicissitudes of life.

John and Mary meet. What happens next? If you want a happy ending, try A.

A

John and Mary fall in love and get married. They both have worthwhile and remunerative jobs which they find stimulating and challenging. They buy a charming house. Real estate values go up. Eventually, when they can afford live-in help, they have two children, to whom they are devoted. The children turn out well. John and Mary have a stimulating and challenging sex life and worthwhile friends. They go on fun vacations together. They retire. They both have hobbies which they find stimulating and challenging. Eventually they die. This is the end of the story.

B

Mary falls in love with John but John doesn't fall in love with Mary. He merely uses her body for selfish pleasure and ego gratification of a tepid kind. He comes to her apartment twice a week and she cooks him dinner, you'll notice that he doesn't even consider her worth the price of a dinner out, and after he's eaten the dinner he fucks her and after that he falls asleep, while she does the dishes so he won't think she's untidy, having all those dirty dishes lying around, and puts on fresh lipstick so she'll look good when he wakes up, but when he wakes up he doesn't even notice, he puts on his socks and his shorts and his pants and his shirt and his tie and his shoes, the reverse order from the one in which he took them off. He doesn't take off Mary's clothes, she takes them off herself, she acts as if she's dying for it every time, not because she likes sex exactly, she doesn't but she wants John to think she does because if they do it often enough surely he'll get used to her, he'll come to depend on her and they will get married, but John goes out the door with hardly so much as a good-night and three days later he turns up at six o'clock and they do the whole thing over again.

Mary gets run down. Crying is bad for your face, everyone knows that and so does Mary but she can't stop. People at work notice. Her friends tell her John is a rat, a pig, a dog, he isn't good enough for her, but she can't believe it. Inside John, she thinks, is another John, who is much nicer. This other John will emerge like a butterfly from a cocoon, a Jack from a box, a pit from a prune, if the first John is only squeezed enough.

One evening John complains about the food. He has never complained about the food before. Mary is hurt.

Her friends tell her they've seen him in a restaurant with another woman, whose name is Madge. It's not even Madge that finally gets to Mary: it's the restaurant. John has never taken Mary to a restaurant. Mary collects all the sleeping pills and aspirins she can find, and takes them and half a bottle of sherry. You can see what kind of a woman she is by the fact that it's not even whiskey. She leaves a note for John. She hopes he'll discover her and get her to the hospital in time and repent and then they can get married, but this fails to happen and she dies.

John marries Madge and everything continues as in A.

C

John, who is an older man, falls in love with Mary, and Mary, who is only twenty-two, feels sorry for him because he's worried about his hair falling out. She sleeps with him even though she's not in love with him. She met him at work. She's in love with someone called James, who is twenty-two also and not yet ready to settle down.

John on the contrary settled down long ago: this is what is bothering him. John has a steady respectable job and is getting ahead in his field, but Mary isn't impressed by him, she's impressed by James, who has a motorcycle, being free. Freedom isn't the same for girls, so in the meantime Mary spends Thursday evenings with John. Thursdays are the only days John can get away.

John is married to a woman called Madge and they have two children, a charming house which they bought just before the real estate values went up, and hobbies which they find stimulating and challenging, when they have the time. John tells Mary how important she is to him, but of course he can't leave his wife because a commitment is a commitment. He goes on about this more than is necessary and Mary finds it boring, but older men can keep it up longer so on the whole she has a fairly good time.

One day James breezes in on his motorcycle with some top-grade California hybrid and James and Mary get higher than you'd believe possible and and they climb into bed. Everything becomes very underwater, but along comes John, who has a key to Mary's apartment. He finds them stoned and entwined. He's hardly in any position to be jealous, considering Madge, but nevertheless he's overcome with despair. Finally he's middle-aged, in two years he'll be bald as an egg and he can't stand it. He purchases a handgun, saying he needs it for target practice—this is the thin part of the plot, but it can be dealt with later—and shoots the two of them and himself.

Madge, after a suitable period of mourning, marries an understanding man called Fred and everything continues as in A, but under different names.

D

Fred and Madge have no problems. They get along exceptionally well and are good at working out any little difficulties that may arise. But their charming house is by the seashore and one day a giant tidal wave approaches. Real estate values go down. The rest of the story is about what caused the tidal wave and how they escape from it. They do, though thousands drown. Some of the story is about how the thousands drown, but Fred and Madge are virtuous and lucky. Finally on high ground they clasp each other, wet and dripping and grateful, and continue as in A.

E

Yes, but Fred has a bad heart. The rest of the story is about how kind and understanding they both are until Fred dies. Then Madge devotes herself to charity work until the end of A. If you like, it can be "Madge," "cancer," "guilty and confused," and "birdwatching."

F

If you think this is all too bourgeois, make John a revolutionary and Mary a counterespionage agent and see how far that gets you. You'll still end up with A, though in between you may get a lustful brawling saga of passionate involvement, a chronicle of our times, sort of.

You'll have to face it, the endings are the same however you slice it. Don't be deluded by any other endings, they're all fake, either deliberately fake, with malicious intent to deceive, or just motivated by excessive optimism if not by downright sentimentality.

The only authentic ending is the one provided here:

John and Mary die. John and Mary die. John and Mary die.

So much for endings. Beginnings are always more fun. True connoisseurs, however, are known to favor the stretch in between, since it's the hardest to do anything with.

That's about all that can be said for plots, which anyway are just one thing after another, a what and a what and a what.

Now try How and Why.

Suggestions for Discussion

1. In the spare language of A there are simple undeveloped declarative sentences. What is the effect on substance and tone?

2. What is the author saying about men–women relationships in B and C? What is the significance of the ending in B and C in which everything continues as in A?

3. What does Atwood mean when she says that plots are "just one thing after another, a what and a what and a what"?

4. In her last sentence the author says "Now try How and Why." What is she saying about plots, about fiction, and about relationships?

Suggestions for Writing

1. In her discussion of Mary and John the author poses a number of problems in men–women relationships. Discuss them drawing on illustrations from your observation or experience.

2. Discuss what you believe to be the major areas of disagreement in marriage.

3. Review a book in which you find an illogical happy ending.

Fiction

Nathaniel Hawthorne

The Birthmark

Nathaniel Hawthorne (1804–1864) was born of New England Puritan stock in Salem, Massachusetts. His first publication, *Twice-Told Tales* (1837), was followed by the novels *The Scarlet Letter* (1850), *The House of the Seven Gables* (1851), and *The Marble Faun* (1860). Other short fiction includes a second series of *Twice-Told Tales* (1842), *Mosses from an Old Manse* (1846), and *The Snow Image and Other Twice-Told Tales* (1851). In "The Birthmark," Aylmer's love for Georgiana deteriorates into self-love and an obsessive sense of his own omnipotence; his faith in science is reduced to an unconscious belief in the possibility of magical exorcism. The opposed forces in his personality become completely separated, and when they cease to contend there is no possibility of a reconciliation between them.

In the latter part of the last century there lived a man of science, an eminent proficient in every branch of natural philosophy, who not long before our story opens had made experience of a spiritual affinity more attractive than any chemical one. He had left his laboratory to the care of an assistant, cleared his fine countenance from the furnace smoke, washed the stain of acids from his fingers, and persuaded a beautiful woman to become his wife. In those days, when the comparatively recent discovery of electricity and other kindred mysteries of Nature seemed to open paths into the region of miracle, it was not unusual for the love of science to rival the love of woman in its depth and absorbing energy. The higher intellect, the imagination, the spirit, and even the heart might all find their congenial aliment in pursuits which, as some of their ardent votaries believed, would ascend from one step of powerful intelligence to another, until the philosopher should lay his hand on the secret of creative force and perhaps make new worlds for himself. We know not whether Aylmer possessed this degree of faith in man's ultimate control over Nature. He had devoted himself, however, too unreservedly to scientific studies ever to be weaned from them by any second passion. His love for his young wife might prove the stronger of the two; but it could only be by intertwining itself with his love of science and uniting the strength of the latter to his own.

Such a union accordingly took place, and was attended with truly remarkable consequences and a deeply impressive moral. One day, very soon after their marriage, Aylmer sat gazing at his wife with a trouble in his countenance that grew stronger until he spoke.

"Georgiana," said he, "has it never occurred to you that the mark upon your cheek might be removed?"

"No, indeed," said she, smiling; but, perceiving the seriousness of his manner, she blushed deeply. "To tell you the truth, it has been so often called a charm that I was simple enough to imagine it might be so."

"Ah, upon another face perhaps it might," replied her husband; "but never on yours. No, dearest Georgiana, you came so nearly perfect from the hand of Nature that this slightest possible defect, which we hesitate whether to term a defect or a beauty, shocks me, as being the visible mark of earthly imperfection."

"Shocks you, my husband!" cried Georgiana, deeply hurt; at first reddening with momentary anger, but then bursting into tears. "Then why did you take me from my mother's side? You cannot love what shocks you!"

To explain this conversation, it must be mentioned that in the centre of Georgiana's left cheek there was a singular mark, deeply interwoven, as it were, with the texture and substance of her face. In the usual state of her complexion—a healthy though delicate bloom—the mark wore a tint of deeper crimson, which imperfectly defined its shape amid the surrounding rosiness. When she blushed it gradually became more indistinct, and finally vanished amid the triumphant rush of blood that bathed the whole cheek with its brilliant glow. But if any shifting motion caused her to turn pale there was the mark again, a crimson stain upon the snow, in what Aylmer sometimes deemed an almost fearful distinctness. Its shape bore not a little similarity to the human hand, though of the smallest pygmy size. Georgiana's lovers were wont to say that some fairy at her birth hour had laid her tiny hand upon the infant's cheek, and left this impress there in token of the magic endowments that were to give her such sway over all hearts. Many a desperate swain would have risked life for the privilege of pressing his lips to the mysterious hand. It must not be concealed, however, that the impression wrought by this fairy sign manual varied exceedingly according to the difference of temperament in the beholders. Some fastidious persons—but they were exclusively of her own sex—affirmed that the bloody hand, as they chose to call it, quite destroyed the effect of Georgiana's beauty and rendered her countenance even hideous. But it would be as reasonable to say that one of those small blue stains which sometimes occur in the purest statuary marble would convert the Eve of Powers to a monster. Masculine observers, if the birthmark did not heighten their admiration, contented themselves with wishing it away, that the world might possess one living specimen of ideal loveliness without the semblance of a flaw. After his marriage,—for he thought little or nothing of the matter before,—Aylmer discovered that this was the case with himself.

Had she been less beautiful,—if Envy's self could have found aught else to sneer at,—he might have felt his affection heightened by the prettiness of this mimic hand, now vaguely portrayed, now lost, now stealing forth again and glimmering to and fro with every pulse of emotion that throbbed within her heart; but, seeing her otherwise so perfect, he found this one defect grow more and more intolerable with every moment of their united lives. It was the fatal flaw of humanity which Nature, in one shape or another, stamps ineffaceably on all her productions, either to imply that they are temporary and finite, or that their perfection must be wrought by toil and pain. The crimson hand expressed the ineludible grip in which mortality clutches the highest and purest of earthly mould, degrading them into kindred with the lowest, and even with the very brutes, like whom their visible frames return to dust. In this manner, selecting it as the symbol of his wife's liability to sin, sorrow, decay, and death, Aylmer's sombre imagination was not long in rendering the birthmark a frightful object, causing him more trouble and horror than ever Georgiana's beauty, whether of soul or sense, had given him delight.

At all the seasons which should have been their happiest he invariably, and without intending it, nay, in spite of a purpose to the contrary, reverted to this one disastrous topic. Trifling as it at first appeared, it so connected itself with innumerable trains of thought and modes of feeling that it became the central point of all. With the morning twilight Aylmer opened his eyes upon his wife's face and recognized the symbol of imperfection; and when they sat together at the evening hearth his eyes wandered stealthily to her cheek, and beheld, flickering with the blaze of the wood fire, the spectral hand that wrote mortality where he would fain have worshipped. Georgiana soon learned to shudder at his gaze. It needed but a glance with the peculiar expression that his face often wore to change the roses of her cheek into a deathlike paleness, amid which the crimson hand was brought strongly out, like a bas relief of ruby on the whitest marble.

Late one night, when the lights were growing dim so as hardly to betray the stain on the poor wife's cheek, she herself, for the first time, voluntarily took up the subject.

"Do you remember, my dear Aylmer," said she, with a feeble attempt at a smile, "have you any recollection, of a dream last night about this odious hand?"

"None! none whatever!" replied Aylmer, starting; but then he added, in a dry, cold tone, affected for the sake of concealing the real depth of his emotion, "I might well dream of it; for, before I fell asleep, it had taken a pretty firm hold of my fancy."

"And you did dream of it?" continued Georgiana hastily; for she dreaded lest a gush of tears should interrupt what she had to say. "A terrible dream! I wonder that you can forget it. Is it possible to forget this one expression?—'It is in her heart now; we must have it out!' Reflect, my husband; for by all means I would have you recall that dream."

The mind is in a sad state when Sleep, the all-involving, cannot confine her spectres within the dim region of her sway, but suffers them to break forth, affrighting this actual life with secrets that perchance belong to a deeper one. Aylmer now remembered his dream. He had fancied himself with his servant Aminadab, attempting an operation for the removal of the birthmark; but the deeper went the knife, the deeper sank the hand, until at length its tiny grasp appeared to have caught hold of Georgiana's heart; whence, however, her husband was inexorably resolved to cut or wrench it away.

When the dream had shaped itself perfectly in his memory Aylmer sat in his wife's presence with a guilty feeling. Truth often finds its way to the mind close muffled in robes of sleep, and then speaks with uncompromising directness of matters in regard to which we practise an unconscious self-deception during our waking moments. Until now he had not been aware of the tyrannizing influence acquired by one idea over his mind, and of the lengths which he might find in his heart to go for the sake of giving himself peace.

"Aylmer," resumed Georgiana, solemnly, "I know not what may be the cost to both of us to rid me of this fatal birthmark. Perhaps its removal may cause cureless deformity; or it may be the stain goes as deep as life itself. Again: do we know that there is a possibility, on any terms, of unclasping the firm grip of this little hand which was laid upon me before I came into the world?"

"Dearest Georgiana, I have spent much thought upon the subject," hastily interrupted Aylmer. "I am convinced of the perfect practicability of its removal."

"If there be the remotest possibility of it," continued Georgiana, "let the attempt be made, at whatever risk. Danger is nothing to me; for life, while this hateful mark makes me the object of your horror and disgust—life is a burden which I would fling down with joy. Either remove this dreadful hand, or take my wretched life! You have deep science. All the world bears witness of it. You have achieved great wonders. Cannot you remove this little, little mark, which I cover with the tips of two small fingers? Is this beyond your power, for the sake of your own peace, and to save your poor wife from madness?"

"Noblest, dearest, tenderest wife," cried Aylmer, rapturously, "doubt not my power. I have already given this matter the deepest thought—thought which might almost have enlightened me to create a being less perfect than yourself. Georgiana, you have led me deeper than ever into the heart of science. I feel myself fully competent to render this dear cheek as faultless as its fellow; and then, most beloved, what will be my triumph when I shall have corrected what Nature left imperfect in her fairest work! Even Pygmalion, when his sculptured woman assumed life, felt not greater ecstasy than mine will be."

"It is resolved, then," said Georgiana, faintly smiling. "And, Aylmer, spare me not, though you should find the birthmark take refuge in my heart at last."

Her husband tenderly kissed her cheek—her right cheek—not that which bore the impress of the crimson hand.

The next day Aylmer apprised his wife of a plan that he had formed whereby he might have opportunity for the intense thought and constant watchfulness which the proposed operation would require; while Georgiana, likewise, would enjoy the perfect repose essential to its success. They were to seclude themselves in the extensive apartments occupied by Aylmer as a laboratory, and where, during his toilsome youth, he had made discoveries in the elemental powers of Nature that had roused the admiration of all the learned societies in Europe. Seated calmly in this laboratory, the pale philosopher had investigated the secrets of the highest cloud region and of the profoundest mines; he had satisfied himself of the causes that kindled and kept alive the fires of the volcano; and had explained the mystery of fountains, and how it is that they gush forth; some so bright and pure, and others with such rich medicinal virtues, from the dark bosom of the earth. Here, too, at an earlier period, he had studied the wonders of the human frame, and attempted to fathom the very process by which Nature assimilates all her precious influences from earth and air, and from the spiritual world, to create and foster man, her masterpiece. The latter pursuit, however, Aylmer had long laid aside in unwilling recognition of the truth—against which all seekers sooner or later stumble—that our great creative Mother, while she amuses us with apparently working in the broadest sunshine, is yet severely careful to keep her own secrets, and, in spite of her pretended openness, shows us nothing but results. She permits us, indeed, to mar, but seldom to mend, and, like a jealous patentee, on no account to make. Now, however,

Aylmer resumed these half-forgotten investigations; not, of course, with such hopes or wishes as first suggested them; but because they involved much physiological truth and lay in the path of his proposed scheme for the treatment of Georgiana.

As he led her over the threshold of the laboratory, Georgiana was cold and tremulous. Aylmer looked cheerfully into her face, with intent to reassure her, but was so startled with the intense glow of the birthmark upon the whiteness of her cheek that he could not restrain a strong convulsive shudder. His wife fainted.

"Aminadab! Aminadab!" shouted Aylmer, stamping violently on the floor.

Forthwith there issued from an inner apartment a man of low stature, but bulky frame, with shaggy hair hanging about his visage, which was grimed with the vapors of the furnace. This personage had been Aylmer's underworker during his whole scientific career, and was admirably fitted for that office by his great mechanical readiness, and the skill with which, while incapable of comprehending a single principle, he executed all the details of his master's experiments. With his vast strength, his shaggy hair, his smoky aspect, and the indescribable earthiness that incrusted him, he seemed to represent man's physical nature; while Aylmer's slender figure, and pale, intellectual face, were no less apt a type of the spiritual element.

"Throw open the door of the boudoir, Aminadab," said Aylmer, "and burn a pastil."

"Yes, master," answered Aminadab, looking intently at the lifeless form of Georgiana; and then he muttered to himself, "If she were my wife, I'd never part with that birthmark."

When Georgiana recovered consciousness she found herself breathing an atmosphere of penetrating fragrance, the gentle potency of which had recalled her from her deathlike faintness. The scene around her looked like enchantment. Aylmer had converted those smoky, dingy, sombre rooms, where he had spent his brightest years in recondite pursuits, into a series of beautiful apartments not unfit to be the secluded abode of a lovely woman. The walls were hung with gorgeous curtains, which imparted the combination of grandeur and grace that no other species of adornment can achieve; and, as they fell from the ceiling to the floor, their rich and ponderous folds, concealing all angles and straight lines, appeared to shut in the scene from infinite space. For aught Georgiana knew, it might be a pavilion among the clouds. And Aylmer, excluding the sunshine, which would have interfered with his chemical processes, had supplied its place with perfumed lamps, emitting flames of various hue, but all uniting in a soft, impurpled radiance. He now knelt by his wife's side, watching her earnestly, but without alarm; for he was confident in his science, and felt that he could draw a magic circle round her within which no evil might intrude.

"Where am I? Ah, I remember," said Georgiana, faintly; and she placed her hand over her cheek to hide the terrible mark from her husband's eyes.

"Fear not, dearest!" exclaimed he. "Do not shrink from me! Believe me, Georgiana, I even rejoice in this single imperfection, since it will be such a rapture to remove it."

"O, spare me!" sadly replied his wife. "Pray do not look at it again. I never can forget that convulsive shudder."

In order to soothe Georgiana, and, as it were, to release her mind from the burden of actual things, Aylmer now put in practice some of the light and playful secrets which science had taught him among its profounder lore. Airy figures, absolutely bodiless ideas, and forms of unsubstantial beauty came and danced before her, imprinting their momentary footsteps on beams of light. Though she had some indistinct idea of the method of these optical phenomena, still the illusion was almost perfect enough to warrant the belief that her husband possessed sway over the spiritual world. Then again, when she felt a wish to look forth from her seclusion, immediately, as if her thoughts were answered, the procession of external existence flitted across a screen. The scenery and the figures of actual life were perfectly represented, but with that bewitching yet indescribable difference which always makes a picture, an image, or a shadow so much more attractive than the original. When wearied of this, Aylmer bade her cast her eyes upon a vessel containing a quantity of earth. She did so, with little interest at first; but was soon startled to perceive the germ of a plant shooting upward from the soil. Then came the slender stalk; the leaves gradually unfolded themselves; and amid them was a perfect and lovely flower.

"It is magical!" cried Georgiana. "I dare not touch it."

"Nay, pluck it," answered Aylmer,—"pluck it, and inhale its brief perfume while you may. The flower will wither in a few moments and leave nothing save its brown seed vessels; but thence may be perpetuated a race as ephemeral as itself."

But Georgiana had no sooner touched the flower than the whole plant suffered a blight, its leaves turning coal-black as if by the agency of fire.

"There was too powerful a stimulus," said Aylmer, thoughtfully.

To make up for this abortive experiment, he proposed to take her portrait by a scientific process of his own invention. It was to be effected by rays of light striking upon a polished plate of metal. Georgiana assented; but, on looking at the result, was affrighted to find the features of the portrait blurred and indefinable; while the minute figure of a hand appeared where the cheek should have been. Aylmer snatched the metallic plate and threw it into a jar of corrosive acid.

Soon, however, he forgot these mortifying failures. In the intervals of study and chemical experiment he came to her flushed and exhausted, but seemed invigorated by her presence, and spoke in glowing language of the resources of his art. He gave a history of the long dynasty of the alchemists, who spent so many ages in quest of the universal solvent by which the golden principle might be elicited from all things vile and base. Aylmer appeared to believe that, by the plainest scientific logic, it was altogether within the limits of possibility to discover this long-sought medium; "but," he added, "a philosopher who should go deep enough to acquire the power would attain too lofty a wisdom to stoop to the exercise of it." Not less singular were his opinions in regard to the elixir vitae. He more than intimated that it was at his option to concoct a liquid that should prolong life for years, perhaps interminably; but that it would produce a discord in Nature which all the world, and chiefly the quaffer of the immortal nostrum, would find cause to curse.

"Aylmer, are you in earnest?" asked Georgiana, looking at him with amazement and fear. "It is terrible to possess such power, or even to dream of possessing it."

"O, do not tremble, my love," said her husband. "I would not wrong either you or myself by working such inharmonious effects upon our lives; but I would have you consider how trifling, in comparison, is the skill requisite to remove this little hand."

At the mention of the birthmark, Georgiana, as usual, shrank as if a red-hot iron had touched her cheek.

Again Aylmer applied himself to his labors. She could hear his voice in the distant furnace room giving directions to Aminadab, whose harsh, uncouth, misshapen tones were audible in response, more like the grunt or growl of a brute than human speech. After hours of absence, Aylmer reappeared and proposed that she should now examine his cabinet of chemical products and natural treasures of the earth. Among the former he showed her a small vial, in which, he remarked, was contained a gentle yet most powerful fragrance, capable of impregnating all the breezes that blow across a kingdom. They were of inestimable value, the contents of that little vial; and, as he said so, he threw some of the perfume into the air and filled the room with piercing and invigorating delight.

"And what is this?" asked Georgiana, pointing to a small crystal globe containing a gold-colored liquid. "It is so beautiful to the eye that I could imagine it the elixir of life."

"In one sense it is," replied Aylmer; "or rather, the elixir of immortality. It is the most precious poison that ever was concocted in this world. By its aid I could apportion the lifetime of any mortal at whom you might point your finger. The strength of the dose would determine whether he were to linger out years, or drop dead in the midst of a breath. No king on his guarded throne could keep his life if I, in my private station, should deem that the welfare of millions justified me in depriving him of it."

"Why do you keep such a terrific drug?" inquired Georgiana in horror.

"Do not mistrust me, dearest," said her husband, smiling; "its virtuous potency is yet greater than its harmful one. But see! here is a powerful cosmetic. With a few drops of this in a vase of water, freckles may be washed away as easily as the hands are cleansed. A stronger infusion would take the blood out of the cheek, and leave the rosiest beauty a pale ghost."

"Is it with this lotion that you intend to bathe my cheek?" asked Georgiana, anxiously.

"O, no," hastily replied her husband; "this is merely superficial. Your case demands a remedy that shall go deeper."

In his interviews with Georgiana, Aylmer generally made minute inquiries as to her sensations, and whether the confinement of the rooms and the temperature of the atmosphere agreed with her. These questions had such a particular drift that Georgiana began to conjecture that she was already subjected to certain physical influences, either breathed in with the fragrant air or taken with her food. She fancied likewise, but it might be altogether fancy, that there was a stirring up of her system—a strange, indefinite sensation creeping through her veins, and tingling, half painfully, half pleasurably, at her heart. Still, whenever she dared to look into the mirror, there she beheld herself pale as a white rose and with the crimson birthmark stamped upon her cheek. Not even Aylmer now hated it so much as she.

To dispel the tedium of the hours which her husband found it necessary to devote to the processes of combination and analysis, Georgiana turned over the volumes of his scientific library. In many dark old tomes she met with chapters full of romance and poetry. They were the works of the philosophers of the middle ages, such as Albertus Magnus, Cornelius Agrippa, Paracelsus, and the famous friar who created the prophetic Brazen Head. All these antique naturalists stood in advance of their centuries, yet were imbued with some of their credulity, and therefore were believed, and perhaps imagined themselves to have acquired from the investigation of Nature a power above Nature, and from physics a sway over the spiritual world. Hardly less curious and imaginative were the early volumes of the Transactions of the Royal Society, in which the members, knowing little of the limits of natural possibility, were continually recording wonders or proposing methods whereby wonders might be wrought.

But to Georgiana, the most engrossing volume was a large folio from her husband's own hand, in which he had recorded every experiment of his scientific career, its original aim, the methods adopted for its development, and its final success or failure, with the circumstances to which either event was attributable. The book, in truth, was both the history and emblem of his ardent, ambitious, imaginative, yet practical and laborious life. He handled physical details as if there were nothing beyond them; yet spiritualized them all and redeemed himself from materialism by his strong and eager aspiration towards the infinite. In his grasp the veriest clod of earth assumed a soul. Georgiana, as she read, reverenced Aylmer and loved him more profoundly than ever, but with a less entire dependence on his judgment than heretofore. Much as he had accomplished, she could not but observe that his most splendid successes were almost invariably failures, if compared with the ideal at which he aimed. His brightest diamonds were the merest pebbles, and felt to be so by himself, in comparison with the inestimable gems which lay hidden beyond his reach. The volume, rich with achievements that had won renown for its author, was yet as melancholy a record as ever mortal hand had penned. It was the sad confession and continual exemplification of the shortcomings of the composite man, the spirit burdened with clay and working in matter, and of the despair that assails the higher nature at finding itself so miserably thwarted by the earthly part. Perhaps every man of genius, in whatever sphere, might recognize the image of his own experience in Aylmer's journal.

So deeply did these reflections affect Georgiana that she laid her face upon the open volume and burst into tears. In this situation she was found by her husband.

"It is dangerous to read in a sorcerer's books," said he with a smile, though his countenance was uneasy and displeased. "Georgiana, there are pages in that volume which I can scarcely glance over and keep my senses. Take heed lest it prove detrimental to you."

"It has made me worship you more than ever," said she.

"Ah, wait for this one success," rejoined he, "then worship me if you will. I shall deem myself hardly unworthy of it. But come, I have sought you for the luxury of your voice. Sing to me, dearest."

So she poured out the liquid music of her voice to quench the thirst of his spirit. He then took his leave with a boyish exuberance of gayety, assuring her that her seclusion would endure but a little longer, and that the result was already certain. Scarcely had he departed when Georgiana felt irresistibly impelled to follow him. She had forgotten to inform Aylmer of a symptom which for two or three hours past had begun to excite her attention. It was a sensation in the fatal birthmark, not painful, but which induced a restlessness throughout her system. Hastening after her husband, she intruded for the first time into the laboratory.

The first thing that struck her eye was the furnace, that hot and feverish worker, with the intense glow of its fire, which by the quantities of soot clustered above it seemed to have been burning for ages. There was a distilling apparatus in full operation. Around the room were retorts, tubes, cylinders, crucibles, and other apparatus of chemical research. An electrical machine stood ready for immediate use. The atmosphere felt oppressively close, and was tainted with gaseous odors which had been tormented forth by the process of science. The severe and homely simplicity of the apartment, with its naked walls and brick pavement, looked strange, accustomed as Georgiana had become to the fantastic elegance of her boudoir. But what chiefly, indeed almost solely, drew her attention, was the aspect of Aylmer himself.

He was pale as death, anxious and absorbed, and hung over the furnace as if it depended upon his utmost watchfulness whether the liquid which it was distilling should be the draught of immortal happiness or misery. How different from the sanguine and joyous mien that he had assumed for Georgiana's encouragement!

"Carefully now, Aminadab; carefully, thou human machine; carefully, thou man of clay," muttered Aylmer, more to himself than his assistant. "Now, if there be a thought too much or too little, it is all over."

"Ho! ho!" mumbled Aminadab. "Look, master! look!"

Aylmer raised his eyes hastily, and at first reddened, then grew paler than ever, on beholding Georgiana. He rushed towards her and seized her arm with a grip that left the print of his fingers upon it.

"Why do you come hither? Have you no trust in your husband?" cried he, impetuously. "Would you throw the blight of that fatal birthmark over my labors? It is not well done. Go, prying woman! go!"

"Nay, Aylmer," said Georgiana with the firmness of which she possessed no stinted endowment, "it is not you that have a right to complain. You mistrust your wife; you have concealed the anxiety with which you watch the development of this experiment. Think not so unworthily of me, my husband. Tell me all the risk we run, and fear not that I shall shrink; for my share in it is far less than your own."

"No, no, Georgiana!" said Aylmer, impatiently; "it must not be."

"I submit," replied she, calmly. "And, Aylmer, I shall quaff whatever draught you bring me; but it will be on the same principle that would induce me to take a dose of poison if offered by your hand."

"My noble wife," said Aylmer, deeply moved, "I knew not the height and depth of your nature until now. Nothing shall be concealed. Know, then, that this crimson hand, superficial as it seems, has clutched its grasp into your being with a strength of which I had no previous conception. I have already administered agents powerful enough to do aught except to change your entire physical system. Only one thing remains to be tried. If that fail us we are ruined."

"Why did you hesitate to tell me this?" asked she.

"Because, Georgiana," said Aylmer, in a low voice, "there is danger."

"Danger? There is but one danger—that this horrible stigma shall be left upon my cheek!" cried Georgiana. "Remove it, remove it, whatever be the cost, or we shall both go mad!"

"Heaven knows your words are too true," said Aylmer, sadly. "And now, dearest, return to your boudoir. In a little while all will be tested."

He conducted her back and took leave of her with a solemn tenderness which spoke far more than his words how much was now at stake. After his departure Georgiana became rapt in musings. She considered the character of Aylmer and did it completer justice than at any previous moment. Her heart exulted, while it trembled, at his honorable love—so pure and lofty that it would accept nothing less than perfection nor miserably make itself contented with an earthlier nature than he had dreamed of. She felt how much more precious was such a sentiment than that meaner kind which would have borne with the imperfection for her sake, and have been guilty of treason to holy love by degrading its perfect idea to the level of the actual; and with her whole spirit she prayed that, for a single moment, she might satisfy his highest and deepest conception. Longer than one moment she well knew it could not be; for his spirit was ever on the march, ever ascending, and each instant required something that was beyond the scope of the instant before.

The sound of her husband's footsteps aroused her. He bore a crystal goblet containing a liquor colorless as water, but bright enough to be the draught of immortality. Aylmer was pale; but it seemed rather the consequence of a highly-wrought state of mind and tension of spirit than of fear or doubt.

"The concoction of the draught has been perfect," said he, in answer to Georgiana's look. "Unless all my science have deceived me, it cannot fail."

"Save on your account, my dearest Aylmer," observed his wife, "I might wish to put off this birthmark of mortality by relinquishing mortality itself in preference to any other mode. Life is but a sad possession to those who have attained precisely the degree of moral advancement at which I stand. Were I weaker and blinder, it might be happiness. Were I stronger, it might be endured hopefully. But, being what I find myself, methinks I am of all mortals the most fit to die."

"You are fit for heaven without tasting death!" replied her husband. "But why do we speak of dying? The draught cannot fail. Behold its effect upon this plant."

On the window seat there stood a geranium diseased with yellow blotches which had overspread all its leaves. Aylmer poured a small quantity of the liquid upon the soil in which it grew. In a little time, when the roots of the plant had taken up the moisture, the unsightly blotches began to be extinguished in a living verdure.

"There needed no proof," said Georgiana, quietly. "Give me the goblet. I joyfully stake all upon your word."

"Drink, then, thou lofty creature!" exclaimed Aylmer, with fervid admiration. "There is no taint of imperfection on thy spirit. Thy sensible frame, too, shall soon be all perfect."

She quaffed the liquid and returned the goblet to his hand.

"It is grateful," said she, with a placid smile. "Methinks it is like water from a heavenly fountain; for it contains I know not what of unobtrusive fragrance and deliciousness. It allays a feverish thirst that had parched me for many days. Now, dearest, let me sleep. My earthly senses are closing over my spirit like the leaves around the heart of a rose at sunset."

She spoke the last words with a gentle reluctance, as if it required almost more energy than she could command to pronounce the faint and lingering syllables. Scarcely had they loitered through her lips ere she was lost in slumber. Aylmer sat by her side, watching her aspect with the emotions proper to a man the whole value of whose existence was involved in the process now to be tested. Mingled with this mood, however, was the philosophic investigation characteristic of the man of science. Not the minutest symptom escaped him. A heightened flush of the cheek, a slight irregularity of breath, a quiver of the eyelid, a hardly perceptible tremor through the frame,—such were the details which, as the moments passed, he wrote down in his folio volume. Intense thought had set its stamp upon every previous page of that volume; but the thoughts of years were all concentrated upon the last.

While thus employed, he failed not to gaze often at the fatal hand, and not without a shudder. Yet once, by a strange and unaccountable impulse, he pressed it with his lips. His spirit recoiled, however, in the very act; and Georgiana, out of the midst of her deep sleep, moved uneasily and murmured as if in remonstrance. Again Aylmer resumed his watch. Nor was it without avail. The crimson hand, which at first had been strongly visible upon the marble paleness of Georgiana's cheek, now grew more faintly outlined. She remained not less pale than ever; but the birthmark, with every breath that came and went lost somewhat of its former distinctness. Its presence had been awful; its departure was more awful still. Watch the stain of the rainbow fading out of the sky, and you will know how that mysterious symbol passed away.

"By Heaven! it is well nigh gone!" said Aylmer to himself, in almost irrepressible ecstasy. "I can scarcely trace it now. Success! success! And now it is like the faintest rose color. The lightest flush of blood across her cheek would overcome it. But she is so pale!"

He drew aside the window curtain and suffered the light of natural day to fall into the room and rest upon her cheek. At the same time he heard a gross, hoarse chuckle, which he had long known as his servant Aminadab's expression of delight.

"Ah, clod! ah, earthly mass!" cried Aylmer, laughing in a sort of frenzy, "you have served me well! Matter and spirit—earth and heaven—have both done their part in this! Laugh, thing of the senses! You have earned the right to laugh."

These exclamations broke Georgiana's sleep. She slowly unclosed her eyes and gazed into the mirror which her husband had arranged for that purpose. A faint smile flitted over her lips when she recognized how barely perceptible was now that crimson hand which had once blazed forth with such disastrous brilliancy as to scare away all their happiness. But then her eyes sought Aylmer's face with a trouble and anxiety that he could by no means account for.

"My poor Aylmer!" murmured she.

"Poor? Nay, richest, happiest, most favored!" exclaimed he. "My peerless bride, it is successful! You are perfect!"

"My poor Aylmer," she repeated, with a more than human tenderness, "you have aimed loftily; you have done nobly. Do not repent that, with so high and pure a feeling, you have rejected the best the earth could offer. Aylmer, dearest Aylmer, I am dying!"

Alas! it was too true! The fatal hand had grappled with the mystery of life, and was the bond by which an angelic spirit kept itself in union with a mortal frame. As the last crimson tint of the birthmark—that sole token of human imperfection—faded from her cheek, the parting breath of the now perfect woman passed into the atmosphere, and her soul, lingering a moment near her husband, took its heavenward flight. Then a hoarse, chuckling laugh was heard again! Thus ever does the gross fatality of earth exult in its invariable triumph over the immortal essence which, in this dim sphere of half development, demands the completeness of a higher state. Yet, had Aylmer reached a profounder wisdom, he need not thus have flung away the happiness which would have woven his mortal life of the selfsame texture with the celestial. The momentary circumstance was too strong for him; he failed to look beyond the shadowy scope of time, and, living once for all in eternity, to find the perfect future in the present.

Suggestions for Discussion

1. What do you regard as the forces motivating Aylmer's attitude and behavior?

2. Discuss the multiple ways in which the dream advances the story's development. Justify or challenge the statement that Aylmer's dream marks the climax of the story.

3. Examine the language and imagery with special reference to the birthmark and the varied responses to it. How does the juxtaposition of religious and sexual imagery contribute to characterization, meaning, and tone? What is the function of the animistic detail? How does the contrasting imagery describing Georgiana's chambers and Aylmer's laboratory advance the action?

4. By what means are the polarities between the earthly and the spiritual developed? How are they reflected in the descriptions of Aylmer and Aminadab? What support can you find for the idea that Aminadab is presented as Aylmer's double, representing the submerged aspect of Aylmer's personality (note the significance of Aminadab spelled backward)? How would you define the opposing forces in Aylmer? At what point do they cease to contend? In responding to this question, identify the rising action, climax, falling action, and resolution.

5. What has been gained and lost by the use of the omniscient author point of view? How necessary are the author's interpolations to the reader's understanding of the story's latent meaning? Note especially the author's comments upon the dream; the expository first paragraph; the passage beginning, "It was the fatal flaw of humanity," and the later one on "the shortcomings of the composite man." (Cf. *Hamlet*, I, iv, 11. 23–38.)

6. Trace the changes that take place in Georgiana's consciousness in the course of the action. If her last words to Aylmer reflect a tragic recognition of what Aylmer has rejected, to what does she remain blind? Discuss the irony in her becoming the instrument of her own fate.

7. Find the examples of the skillful use of foreshadowing. How is suspense maintained? While the reader experiences a mounting sense of impending doom, does he completely surrender his disbelief in the possibility that a miracle might be wrought?

Suggestions for Writing

1. Define the relationship of Aylmer and Georgiana. To what extent is the story dated? Under what circumstances could the action of the story take place today?

2. Discuss "The Birthmark" as a story of moral flaw or of psychological determination. Bring to bear what evidence you can for either point of view by specific allusion to the imagery, setting, and characterizations.

Kate Chopin

A Respectable Woman

Kate Chopin (1851–1904) was an early feminist who did not begin to write until her late thirties. Her first novel, At Fault (1890), was followed by two volumes of short stories, Bayou Folk (1894) and A Night in Acadie (1897), and her masterpiece, The Awakening (1899). The "respectable woman" undergoes a metamorphosis after her earlier indifference to her husband's friend.

Mrs. Baroda was a little provoked to learn that her husband expected his friend, Gouvernail, up to spend a week or two on the plantation.

They had entertained a good deal during the winter; much of the time had also been passed in New Orleans in various forms of mild dissipation. She was looking forward to a period of unbroken rest, now, and undisturbed tête-à-tête with her husband, when he informed her that Gouvernail was coming up to stay a week or two.

This was a man she had heard much of but never seen. He had been her husband's college friend; was now a journalist, and in no sense a society man or "a man about town," which were, perhaps, some of the reasons she had never met him. But she had unconsciously formed an image of him in her mind. She pictured him tall, slim, cynical; with eye-glasses, and his hands in his pockets; and she did not like him. Gouvernail was slim enough, but he wasn't very tall nor very cynical; neither did he wear eye-glasses nor carry his hands in his pockets. And she rather liked him when he first presented himself.

But why she liked him she could not explain satisfactorily to herself when she partly attempted to do so. She could discover in him none of those brilliant and promising traits which Gaston, her husband, had often assured her that he possessed. On the contrary, he sat rather mute and receptive before her chatty eagerness to make him feel at home and in face of Gaston's frank and wordy hospitality. His manner was as courteous toward her as the most exacting woman could require; but he made no direct appeal to her approval or even esteem.

Once settled at the plantation he seemed to like to sit upon the wide portico in the shade of one of the big Corinthian pillars, smoking his cigar lazily and listening attentively to Gaston's experience as a sugar planter.

"This is what I call living," he would utter with deep satisfaction, as the air that swept across the sugar field caressed him with its warm and scented velvety touch. It pleased him also to get on familiar terms with the big dogs that came about him, rubbing themselves sociably against his legs. He did not care to fish, and displayed no eagerness to go out and kill grosbecs when Gaston proposed doing so.

Gouvernail's personality puzzled Mrs. Baroda, but she liked him. Indeed, he was a lovable, inoffensive fellow. After a few days, when she could understand him no better than at first, she gave over being puzzled and remained piqued. In this mood she left her husband and her guest, for the most part, alone together. Then finding that Gouvernail took no manner of exception to her action, she imposed her society upon him, accompanying him in his idle

366

strolls to the mill and walks along the batture. She persistently sought to penetrate the reserve in which he had unconsciously enveloped himself.

"When is he going—your friend?" she one day asked her husband. "For my part, he tires me frightfully."

"Not for a week yet, dear. I can't understand; he gives you no trouble."

"No. I should like him better if he did; if he were more like others, and I had to plan somewhat for his comfort and enjoyment."

Gaston took his wife's pretty face between his hands and looked tenderly and laughingly into her troubled eyes. They were making a bit of toilet sociably together in Mrs. Baroda's dressing-room.

"You are full of surprises, ma belle," he said to her. "Even I can never count upon how you are going to act under given conditions." He kissed her and turned to fasten his cravat before the mirror.

"Here you are," he went on, "taking poor Gouvernail seriously and making a commotion over him, the last thing he would desire or expect."

"Commotion!" she hotly resented. "Nonsense! How can you say such a thing? Commotion, indeed! But, you know, you said he was clever."

"So he is. But the poor fellow is run down by overwork now. That's why I asked him here to take a rest."

"You used to say he was a man of ideas," she retorted, unconciliated. "I expected him to be interesting, at least. I'm going to the city in the morning to have my spring gowns fitted. Let me know when Mr. Gouvernail is gone; I shall be at my Aunt Octavie's."

That night she went and sat alone upon a bench that stood beneath a live oak tree at the edge of the gravel walk.

She had never known her thoughts or her intentions to be so confused. She could gather nothing from them but the feeling of a distinct necessity to quit her home in the morning. *quit her home → quit her husb*

Mrs. Baroda heard footsteps crunching the gravel; but could discern in the darkness only the approaching red point of a lighted cigar. She knew it was Gouvernail, for her husband did not smoke. She hoped to remain unnoticed, but her white gown revealed her to him. *innocence → invoked by her husband* He threw away his cigar and seated himself upon the bench beside her; without a suspicion that she might object to his presence.

"Your husband told me to bring this to you, Mrs. Baroda," he said, handing her a filmy, white scarf with which she sometimes enveloped her head and shoulders. She accepted the scarf from him with a murmur of thanks, and let it lie in her lap.

He made some commonplace observation upon the baneful effect of the night air at that season. Then as his gaze reached out into the darkness, he murmured, half to himself:

"'Night of south winds—night of the large few stars!
Still nodding night—'"

She made no reply to this apostrophe to the night, which indeed, was not addressed to her.

Gouvernail was in no sense a diffident man, for he was not a self-conscious one. His periods of reserve were not constitutional, but the result of moods. Sitting there beside Mrs. Baroda, his silence melted for the time.

He talked freely and intimately in a low, hesitating drawl that was not unpleasant to hear. He talked of the old college days when he and

Gaston had been a good deal to each other; of the days of keen and blind ambitions and large intentions. Now there was left with him, at least, a philosophic acquiescence to the existing order—only a desire to be permitted to exist, with now and then a little whiff of genuine life, such as he was breathing now.

Her mind only vaguely grasped what he was saying. Her physical being was for the moment predominant. She was not thinking of his words, only drinking in the tones of his voice. She wanted to reach out her hand in the darkness and touch him with the sensitive tips of her fingers upon the face or the lips. She wanted to draw close to him and whisper against his cheek—she did not care what—as she might have done if she had not been a respectable woman. → who had never respe

The stronger the impulse grew to bring herself near him, the further, in fact, did she draw away from him. As soon as she could do so without an appearance of too great rudeness, she rose and left him there alone.

Before she reached the house, Gouvernail had lighted a fresh cigar and ended his apostrophe to the night.

Mrs. Baroda was greatly tempted that night to tell her husband—who was also her friend—of this folly that had seized her. But she did not yield to the temptation. Beside being a respectable woman she was a very sensible one; and she knew there are some battles in life which a human being must fight alone.

When Gaston arose in the morning, his wife had already departed. She had taken an early train to the city. She did not return till Gouvernail was gone from under her roof.

There was some talk of having him back during the summer that followed. That is, Gaston greatly desired it; but this desire yielded to his wife's strenuous opposition.

However, before the year ended, she proposed, wholly from herself, to have Gouvernail visit them again. Her husband was surprised and delighted with the suggestion coming from her.

"I am glad, chère amie, to know that you have finally overcome your dislike for him; truly he did not deserve it."

"Oh," she told him, laughingly, after pressing a long, tender kiss upon his lips, "I have overcome everything! you will see. This time I shall be very nice to him."

Suggestions for Discussion

1. How do you learn that Mrs. Baroda is ambivalent about Gouvernail?

2. Why do you think Mrs. Baroda left for the city? What precipitated the move?

3. What details suggest to you that this story was written in an earlier era?

4. What is the significance of the title? Relate it to the theme of the story. Is it used ironically?

5. What are you led to surmise is the relationship of Mrs. Baroda to her husband?

6. What do you think will happen on Gouvernail's next visit? How are you prepared for it?

Suggestion for Writing

Write an essay on Question 4 or 6 above.

James Thurber

The Unicorn in the Garden

James Thurber (1894–1961), American humorist and artist, began contributing in 1927 to The New Yorker, in which most of his work first appeared. His
humorous essays and short stories are collected in such books as The Owl in
the Attic (1931), My Life and Hard Times (1933), The Thurber Carnival (1945), The
Beast in Me (1948), and Lanterns and Lances (1961). He also wrote the short
story "The Secret Life of Walter Mitty," several fantasies for children, and
with Elliot Nugent, a comedy called The Male Animal (1940). "The Unicorn in
the Garden," a fable of hostile feelings between husband and wife, ends
with a surprise twist.

Once upon a sunny morning a man who sat in a breakfast nook looked up
from his scrambled eggs to see a white unicorn with a gold horn quietly cropping the roses in the garden. The man went up to the bedroom where his
wife was still asleep and woke her. "There's a unicorn in the garden," he
said. "Eating roses." She opened one unfriendly eye and looked at him. "The
unicorn is a mythical beast," she said, and turned her back to him. The man
walked slowly downstairs and out into the garden. The unicorn was still
there; he was now browsing among the tulips. "Here, unicorn," said the
man, and he pulled up a lily and gave it to him. The unicorn ate it gravely.
With a high heart, because there was a unicorn in his garden, the man went
upstairs and roused his wife again. "The unicorn," he said, "ate a lily." His
wife sat up in bed and looked at him, coldly. "You are a booby," she said,
"and I am going to have you put in the booby-hatch." The man, who had
never liked the words "booby" and "booby-hatch," and who liked them even
less on a shining morning when there was a unicorn in the garden, thought
for a moment. "We'll see about that," he said. He walked over to the door.
"He has a golden horn in the middle of his forehead," he told her. Then he
went back to the garden to watch the unicorn; but the unicorn had gone
away. The man sat down among the roses and went to sleep.

As soon as the husband had gone out of the house, the wife got up and dressed
as fast as she could. She was very excited and there was a gloat in
her eye. She telephoned the police and she telephoned a psychiatrist; she told
them to hurry to her house and bring a strait-jacket. When the police and the
psychiatrist arrived they sat down in chairs and looked at her, with great interest. "My husband," she said, "saw a unicorn this morning." The police looked
at the psychiatrist and the psychiatrist looked at the police. "He told me it ate
a lily," she said. The psychiatrist looked at the police and the police looked
at the psychiatrist. "He told me it had a golden horn in the middle of its forehead," she said. At a solemn signal from the psychiatrist, the police leaped from
their chairs and seized the wife. They had a hard time subduing her, for she put
up a terrific struggle, but they finally subdued her. Just as they got her into the
strait-jacket, the husband came back into the house.

"Did you tell your wife you saw a unicorn?" asked the police. "Of course not," said the husband. "The unicorn is a mythical beast." "That's all I wanted to know," said the psychiatrist. "Take her away. I'm sorry, sir, but your wife is as crazy as a jay bird." So they took her away, cursing and screaming, and shut her up in an institution. The husband lived happily ever after.

Moral: Don't count your boobies until they are hatched.

Suggestions for Discussion

1. From what details do you become aware of the hostile feelings between husband and wife?

2. What is Thurber's attitude toward his characters, including the psychiatrist? Refer to the diction, the role of the unicorn, the setting, the details of the action, the twist at the end, the moral, and the drawing.

3. What other "moral" might be appropriate to append to this fable?

4. What evidence can you find that the author is (or is not) detached from his subject?

Suggestions for Writing

1. Write an imaginary description of the events leading up to the situation at the beginning of the fable.

2. Read "The Secret Life of Walter Mitty" and compare situation, tone, and resolution with those of the fable of the unicorn.

3. Write a fable depicting a domestic relationship.

John Steinbeck

The Chrysanthemums

John Steinbeck (1902–1968) wrote novels, short stories, travel sketches, and essays. Born in Salinas, California, he studied at Stanford University. Before he achieved success as a writer, he worked as ranch hand, laborer, and newspaperman. Among his novels are *Tortilla Flat* (1935), *Of Mice and Men* (1937), *The Grapes of Wrath* (1939), which was awarded a Pulitzer Prize, and *East of Eden* (1952). In 1962 he was awarded the Nobel Prize for Literature. Although Elisa's encounter with the tinker in "The Chrysanthemums" leads to her awareness of herself as a woman and of formerly submerged feelings, nothing in her external world has been significantly altered. Her isolation, vitality, and creative energy leave her unfulfilled as a woman.

The high grey-flannel fog of winter closed off the Salinas Valley from the sky and from all the rest of the world. On every side it sat like a lid on the mountains and made of the great valley a closed pot. On the broad, level land floor the gang plows bit deep and left the black earth shining like metal where the shares had cut. On the foothill ranches across the Salinas River, the yellow stubble fields seemed to be bathed in pale cold sunshine, but there was no sunshine in the valley now in December. The thick willow scrub along the river flamed with sharp and positive yellow leaves.

It was a time of quiet and of waiting. The air was cold and tender. A light wind blew up from the southwest so that the farmers were mildly hopeful of a good rain before long; but fog and rain do not go together.

Across the river, on Henry Allen's foothill ranch there was little work to be done, for the hay was cut and stored and the orchards were plowed up to receive the rain deeply when it should come. The cattle on the higher slopes were becoming shaggy and rough-coated.

Elisa Allen, working in her flower garden, looked down across the yard and saw Henry, her husband, talking to two men in business suits. The three of them stood by the tractor shed, each man with one foot on the side of the little Fordson. They smoked cigarettes and studied the machine as they talked.

Elisa watched them for a moment and then went back to her work. She was thirty-five. Her face was lean and strong and her eyes were as clear as water. Her figure looked blocked and heavy in her gardening costume, a man's black hat pulled low down over her eyes, clodhopper shoes, a figured print dress almost completely covered by a big corduroy apron with four big pockets to hold the snips, the trowel and scratcher, the seeds and the knife she worked with. She wore heavy leather gloves to protect her hands while she worked.

She was cutting down the old year's chrysanthemum stalks with a pair of short and powerful scissors. She looked down toward the men by the tractor shed now and then. Her face was eager and mature and handsome; even her work with the scissors was over-eager, over-powerful. The chrysanthemum stems seemed too small and easy for her energy.

She brushed a cloud of hair out of her eyes with the back of her glove, and left a smudge of earth on the cheek in doing it. Behind her stood the neat white farm house with red geraniums close-banked around it as high as the windows. It was a hard-swept looking little house, with hard-polished windows, and a clean mud-mat on the front steps.

Elisa cast another glance toward the tractor shed. The strangers were getting into their Ford coupe. She took off a glove and put her strong fingers down into the forest of new green chrysanthemum sprouts that were growing around the old roots. She spread the leaves and looked down among the close-growing stems. No aphids were there, no sowbugs or snails or cutworms. Her terrier fingers destroyed such pests before they could get started.

Elisa started at the sound of her husband's voice. He had come near quietly, and he leaned over the wire fence that protected her flower garden from cattle and dogs and chickens.

"At it again," he said. "You've got a strong new crop coming."

Elisa straightened her back and pulled on the gardening glove again. "Yes. They'll be strong this coming year." In her tone and on her face there was a little smugness.

"You've got a gift with things," Henry observed. "Some of those yellow chrysanthemums you had this year were ten inches across. I wish you'd work out in the orchard and raise some apples that big."

Her eyes sharpened. "Maybe I could do it, too. I've a gift with things, all right. My mother had it. She could stick anything in the ground and make it grow. She said it was having planters' hands that knew how to do it."

"Well, it sure works with flowers," he said.

"Henry, who were those men you were talking to?"

"Why, sure, that's what I came to tell you. They were from the Western Meat Company. I sold those thirty head of three-year-old steers. Got nearly my own price, too."

"Good," she said. "Good for you."

"And I thought," he continued, "I thought how it's Saturday afternoon, and we might go into Salinas for dinner at a restaurant, and then to a picture show—to celebrate, you see."

"Good," she repeated. "Oh, yes. That will be good."

Henry put on his joking tone. "There's fights tonight. How'd you like to go to the fights?"

"Oh, no," she said breathlessly. "No, I wouldn't like fights."

"Just fooling, Elisa. We'll go to a movie. Let's see. It's two now. I'm going to take Scotty and bring down those steers from the hill. It'll take us maybe two hours. We'll go in town about five and have dinner at the Cominos Hotel. Like that?"

"Of course I'll like it. It's good to eat away from home."

"All right, then. I'll go get up a couple of horses."

She said, "I'll have plenty of time to transplant some of these sets, I guess."

She heard her husband calling Scotty down by the barn. And a little later she saw the two men ride up the pale yellow hillside in search of the steers.

There was a little square sandy bed kept for rooting the chrysanthemums. With her trowel she turned the soil over and over, and smoothed it and patted it firm. Then she dug ten parallel trenches to receive the sets. Back at the chrysanthemum bed she pulled out the little crisp shoots, trimmed off the leaves of each one with her scissors and laid it on a small orderly pile.

A squeak of wheels and plod of hoofs came from the road. Elisa looked up. The country road ran along the dense bank of willows and cottonwoods that bordered the river, and up this road came a curious vehicle, curiously drawn. It was an old spring-wagon, with a round canvas top on it like the cover of a prairie schooner. It was drawn by an old bay horse and a little grey-and-white burro. A big stubble-bearded man sat between the cover flaps and drove the crawling team. Underneath the wagon, between the hind wheels, a lean and rangy mongrel dog walked sedately. Words were painted on the canvas in clumsy, crooked letters. "Pots, pans, knives, sisors, lawn mores. Fixed." Two rows of articles and the triumphantly definitive "Fixed" below. The black paint had run down in little sharp points beneath each letter.

Elisa, squatting on the ground, watched to see the crazy, loose-jointed wagon pass by. But it didn't pass. It turned into the farm road in front of her house, crooked old wheels skirling and squeaking. The rangy dog darted from between the wheels and ran ahead. Instantly the two ranch shepherds flew out at him. Then all three stopped, and with stiff and quivering tails, with taut straight legs, with ambassadorial dignity, they slowly circled, sniffing daintily. The caravan pulled up to Elisa's wire fence and stopped. Now the newcomer dog, feeling out-numbered, lowered his tail and retired under the wagon with raised hackles and bared teeth.

The man on the wagon seat called out. "That's a bad dog in a fight when he gets started."

Elisa laughed. "I see he is. How soon does he generally get started?"

The man caught up her laughter and echoed it heartily. "Sometimes not for weeks and weeks," he said. He climbed stiffly down, over the wheel. The horse and the donkey drooped like unwatered flowers.

Elisa saw that he was a very big man. Although his hair and beard were greying, he did not look old. His worn black suit was wrinkled and spotted with grease. The laughter had disappeared from his face and eyes the moment his laughing voice ceased. His eyes were dark, and they were full of the brooding that gets in the eyes of teamsters and of sailors. The calloused hands he rested on the wire fence were cracked, and every crack was a black line. He took off his battered hat.

"I'm off my general road, ma'am," he said. "Does this dirt road cut over across the river to the Los Angeles highway?"

Elisa stood up and shoved the thick scissors in her apron pocket. "Well, yes, it does, but it winds around and then fords the river. I don't think your team could pull through the sand."

He replied with some asperity, "It might surprise you what them beasts can pull through."

"When they get started?" she asked.

He smiled for a second. "Yes. When they get started."

"Well," said Elisa, "I think you'll save time if you go back to the Salinas road and pick up the highway there."

He drew a big finger down the chicken wire and made it sing. "I ain't in any hurry, ma'am. I go from Seattle to San Diego and back every year. Takes all my time. About six months each way. I aim to follow nice weather."

Elisa took off her gloves and stuffed them in the apron pocket with the scissors. She touched the under edge of her man's hat, searching for fugitive hairs. "That sounds like a nice kind of a way to live," she said.

He leaned confidentially over the fence. "Maybe you noticed the writing on my wagon. I mend pots and sharpen knives and scissors. You got any of them things to do?"

"Oh, no," she said quickly. "Nothing like that." Her eyes hardened with resistance.

"Scissors is the worst thing," he explained. "Most people just ruin scissors trying to sharpen 'em but I know how. I got a special tool. It's a little bobbit kind of thing, and patented. But it sure does the trick."

"No. My scissors are all sharp."

"All right, then. Take a pot," he continued earnestly, "a bent pot, or a pot with a hole. I can make it like new so you don't have to buy no new ones. That's a saving for you."

"No," she said shortly. "I tell you I have nothing like that for you to do."

His face fell to an exaggerated sadness. His voice took on a whining undertone. "I ain't had a thing to do today. Maybe I won't have no supper tonight. You see I'm off my regular road. I know folks on the highway clear from Seattle to San Diego. They save their things for me to sharpen up because they know I do it so good and save them money."

"I'm sorry," Elisa said irritably. "I haven't anything for you to do."

His eyes left her face and fell to searching the ground. They roamed about until they came to the chrysanthemum bed where she had been working. "What's them plants, ma'am?"

The irritation and resistance melted from Elisa's face. "Oh, those are chrysanthemums, giant whites and yellows. I raise them every year, bigger than anybody around here."

"Kind of a long-stemmed flower? Looks like a quick puff of colored smoke?" he asked.

"That's it. What a nice way to describe them."

"They smell kind of nasty till you get used to them," he said.

"It's a good bitter smell," she retorted, "not nasty at all."

He changed his tone quickly. "I like the smell myself."

"I had ten-inch blooms this year," she said.

The man leaned farther over the fence. "Look. I know a lady down the road a piece, has got the nicest garden you ever seen. Got nearly every kind of flower but no chrysanthemums. Last time I was mending a copper-bottom washtub for her (that's a hard job but I do it good), she said to me, 'If you ever run acrost some nice chrysanthemums I wish you'd try to get me a few seeds.' That's what she told me."

Elisa's eyes grew alert and eager. "She couldn't have known much about chrysanthemums. You can raise them from seed, but it's much easier to root the little sprouts you see there."

"Oh," he said. "I s'pose I can't take none to her, then."

"Why yes you can," Elisa cried. "I can put some in damp sand, and you can carry them right along with you. They'll take root in the pot if you keep them damp. And then she can transplant them."

"She'd sure like to have some, ma'am. You say they're nice ones?"

"Beautiful," she said. "Oh, beautiful." Her eyes shone. She tore off the battered hat and shook out her dark pretty hair. "I'll put them in a flower pot, and you can take them right with you. Come into the yard."

While the man came through the picket gate Elisa ran excitedly along the geranium-bordered path to the back of the house. And she returned carrying a big red flower pot. The gloves were forgotten now. She kneeled on the ground by the starting bed and dug up the sandy soil with her fingers and scooped it into the bright new flower pot. Then she picked up the little pile of shoots she had prepared. With her strong fingers she pressed them into the sand and tamped around them with her knuckles. The man stood over her. "I'll tell you what to do," she said. "You remember so you can tell the lady."

"Yes, I'll try to remember."

"Well, look. These will take root in about a month. Then she must set them out, about a foot apart in good rich earth like this, see?" She lifted a handful of dark soil for him to look at. "They'll grow fast and tall. Now remember this. In July tell her to cut them down, about eight inches from the ground."

"Before they bloom?" he asked.

"Yes, before they bloom." Her face was tight with eagerness. "They'll come right up again. About the last of September the buds will start."

She stopped and seemed perplexed. "It's the budding that takes the most care," she said hesitantly. "I don't know how to tell you." She looked deep into his eyes, searchingly. Her mouth opened a little, and she seemed to be listening. "I'll try to tell you," she said. "Did you ever hear of planting hands?"

"Can't say I have, ma'am."

"Well, I can only tell you what it feels like. It's when you're picking off the buds you don't want. Everything goes right down into your fingertips. You watch your fingers work. They do it themselves. You can feel how it is. They pick and pick the buds. They never make a mistake. They're with the plant. Do you see? Your fingers and the plant. You can feel that, right up your arm. They know. They never make a mistake. You can feel it. When you're like that you can't do anything wrong. Do you see that? Can you understand that?"

She was kneeling on the ground looking up at him. Her breast swelled passionately.

The man's eyes narrowed. He looked away, self-consciously. "Maybe I know," he said. "Sometimes in the night in the wagon there—"

Elisa's voice grew husky. She broke in on him. "I've never lived as you do, but I know what you mean. When the night is dark—why, the stars are sharp-pointed, and there's quiet. Why, you rise up and up! Every pointed star gets driven into your body. It's like that. Hot and sharp and—lovely."

Kneeling there, her hand went out toward his legs in the greasy black trousers. Her hesitant fingers almost touched the cloth. Then her hand dropped to the ground. She crouched low like a fawning dog.

He said, "It's nice, just like you say. Only when you don't have no dinner, it ain't."

She stood up then, very straight, and her face was ashamed. She held the flower pot out to him and placed it gently in his arms. "Here. Put it in your wagon, on the seat, where you can watch it. Maybe I can find something for you to do."

At the back of the house she dug in the can pile and found two old and battered aluminum saucepans. She carried them back and gave them to him. "Here, maybe you can fix these."

His manner changed. He became professional. "Good as new I can fix them." At the back of his wagon he set a little anvil, and out of an oily tool box dug a small machine hammer. Elisa came through the gate to watch him while he pounded out the dents in the kettles. His mouth grew sure and knowing. At a difficult part of the work he sucked his under-lip.

"You sleep right in the wagon?" Elisa asked.

"Right in the wagon, ma'am. Rain or shine I'm dry as a cow in there."

"It must be nice," she said. "It must be very nice. I wish women could do such things."

"It ain't the right kind of a life for a woman."

Her upper lip raised a little, showing her teeth. "How do you know? How can you tell?" she said.

"I don't know ma'am," he protested. "Of course I don't know. Now here's your kettles, done. You don't have to buy no new ones."

"How much?"

"Oh, fifty cents'll do. I keep my prices down and my work good. That's why I have all them satisfied customers up and down the highway."

Elisa brought him a fifty-cent piece from the house and dropped it in his hand. "You might be surprised to have a rival some time. I can sharpen scissors, too. And I can beat the dents out of little pots. I could show you what a woman might do."

He put his hammer back in the oily box and shoved the little anvil out of sight. "It would be a lonely life for a woman, ma'am, and a scarey life, too, with animals creeping under the wagon all night." He climbed over the singletree, steadying himself with a hand on the burro's white rump. He settled himself in the seat, picked up the lines. "Thank you kindly, ma'am," he said. "I'll do like you told me; I'll go back and catch the Salinas road."

"Mind," she called, "if you're long in getting there, keep the sand damp."

"Sand, ma'am? . . . Sand? Oh, sure. You mean round the chrysanthemums. Sure I will." He clucked his tongue. The beasts leaned luxuriously into their collars. The mongrel dog took his place between the back wheels. The wagon turned and crawled out the entrance road and back the way it had come, along the river.

Elisa stood in front of her wire fence watching the slow progress of the caravan. Her shoulders were straight, her head thrown back, her eyes half-closed, so that the scene came vaguely into them. Her lips moved silently, forming the words "Good-bye—good-bye." Then she whispered. "That's a bright direction. There's a glowing there." The sound of her whisper startled her. She shook herself free and looked about to see whether anyone had been listening. Only the dogs had heard. They lifted their heads toward her from their sleeping in the dust, and then stretched out their chins and settled asleep again. Elisa turned and ran hurriedly into the house.

In the kitchen she reached behind the stove and felt the water tank. It was full of hot water from the noonday cooking. In the bathroom she tore off her soiled clothes and flung them into the corner. And then she scrubbed herself with a little block of pumice, legs and thighs, loins and chest and arms, until her skin was scratched and red. When she had dried herself she stood in front of a mirror in her bedroom and looked at her body. She tightened her stomach and threw out her chest. She turned and looked over her shoulder at her back.

After a while she began to dress, slowly. She put on her newest under-clothing and her nicest stockings and the dress which was the symbol of her prettiness. She worked carefully on her hair, pencilled her eyebrows and rouged her lips.

Before she was finished she heard the little thunder of hoofs and the shouts of Henry and his helper as they drove the red steers into the corral. She heard the gate bang shut and set herself for Henry's arrival.

His step sounded on the porch. He entered the house calling "Elisa, where are you?"

"In my room, dressing. I'm not ready. There's hot water for your bath. Hurry up. It's getting late."

When she heard him splashing in the tub, Elisa laid his dark suit on the bed, and shirt and socks and tie beside it. She stood his polished shoes on the floor beside the bed. Then she went to the porch and sat primly and stiffly down. She looked toward the river road where the willow-line was still yellow with frosted leaves so that under the high grey fog they seemed a thin band of sunshine. This was the only color in the grey afternoon. She sat unmoving for a long time. Her eyes blinked rarely.

Henry came banging out of the door, shoving his tie inside his vest as he came. Elisa stiffened and her face grew tight. Henry stopped short and looked at her. "Why—why, Elisa. You look so nice!"

"Nice? You think I look nice? What do you mean by 'nice'?"

Henry blundered on. "I don't know. I mean you look different, strong and happy."

"I am strong? Yes, strong. What do you mean 'strong'?"

He looked bewildered. "You're playing some kind of a game," he said helplessly. "It's a kind of a play. You look strong enough to break a calf over your knee, happy enough to eat it like a watermelon."

For a second she lost her rigidity. "Henry! Don't talk like that. You didn't know what you said." She grew complete again. "I'm strong," she boasted. "I never knew before how strong."

Henry looked down toward the tractor shed, and when he brought his eyes back to her, they were his own again. "I'll get out the car. You can put on your coat while I'm starting."

Elisa went into the house. She heard him drive to the gate and idle down his motor, and then she took a long time to put on her hat. She pulled it here and pressed it there. When Henry turned the motor off she slipped into her coat and went out.

The little roadster bounced along on the dirt road by the river, raising the birds and driving the rabbits into the brush. Two cranes flapped heavily over the willow-line and dropped into the river-bed.

Far ahead on the road Elisa saw a dark speck. She knew.

She tried not to look as they passed it, but her eyes would not obey. She whispered to herself sadly. "He might have thrown them off the road. That wouldn't have been much trouble, not very much. But he kept the pot," she explained. "He had to keep the pot. That's why he couldn't get them off the road."

The roadster turned a bend and she saw the caravan ahead. She swung full around toward her husband so she could not see the little covered wagon and the mismatched team as the car passed them.

In a moment they had left behind them the man who had not known or needed to know what she said, the bargainer. She did not look back.

To Henry, she said loudly, to be heard above the motor, "It will be good, to-night, a good dinner."

"Now you're changed again," Henry complained. He took one hand from the wheel and patted her knee. "I ought to take you in to dinner oftener. It would be good for both of us. We get so heavy out on the ranch."

"Henry," she asked, "could we have wine at dinner?"

"Sure. Say! That will be fine."

She was silent for a while; then she said, "Henry, at those prize fights do the men hurt each other very much?"

"Sometimes a little, not often. Why?"

"Well, I've read how they break noses, and blood runs down their chests. I've read how the fighting gloves get heavy and soggy with blood."

He looked round at her. "What's the matter, Elisa? I didn't know you read things like that." He brought the car to a stop, then turned to the right over the Salinas River bridge.

"Do any women ever go to the fights?" she asked.

"Oh, sure, some. What's the matter, Elisa? Do you want to go? I don't think you'd like it, but I'll take you if you really want to go."

She relaxed limply in the seat. "Oh, no. I don't want to go. I'm sure I don't." Her face was turned away from him. "It will be enough if we can have wine. It will be plenty." She turned up her coat collar so he could not see that she was crying weakly—like an old woman.

Suggestions for Discussion

1. What descriptive details prepare you for Elisa's emotional isolation?

2. The action, rising in emotional intensity to its climax, is developed in four scenes. Describe Elisa's feelings in each scene and attempt to account for them.

3. Discuss the possible symbolic functions of the scissors, the chrysanthemum shoots, the wine, and the fights. How are they related to the complication and resolution of the action?

4. How is the tinker's deception foreshadowed?

5. By what means are we made aware of the change in Elisa's image of herself? How adequately does the story account for Elisa's frustration? Explain the fluctuations in her appearance and mood. By what means are we made aware that her relationship with Henry is not satisfying?

Suggestions for Writing

1. Relate the story to the essay by Germaine Greer, "The Stereotype."
2. Write a character study of Elisa.
3. Portray in narrative form a marital relationship in which there is a failure in communication.

Ernest Hemingway

Hills Like White Elephants

Ernest Hemingway (1898–1961), novelist and short-story writer, began his career as a reporter and during World War I served with an ambulance unit in France and Italy. After the war he lived in Paris as a correspondent for the Hearst papers. During the Spanish Civil War he went to Spain as a war correspondent. His works include the collections of short stories In Our Time (1925), Men Without Women (1927), The Fifth Column and the First 49 Stories (1938); and the novels The Sun Also Rises (1926), A Farewell to Arms (1929), For Whom the Bell Tolls (1940), and The Old Man and the Sea (1952), which was awarded a Pulitzer Prize. In 1954 he received the Nobel Prize for Literature. In dialogue that is elliptical and ironic Hemingway dramatizes the plight of the two lovers, their different views of the immediate problem and of their future.

The hills across the valley of the Ebro were long and white. On this side there was no shade and no trees and the station was between two lines of rails in the sun. Close against the side of the station there was the warm shadow of the building and a curtain, made of strings of bamboo beads, hung across the open door into the bar, to keep out flies. The American and the girl with him sat at a table in the shade, outside the building. It was very hot and the express from Barcelona would come in forty minutes. It stopped at this junction for two minutes and went on to Madrid.

"What should we drink?" the girl asked. She had taken off her hat and put it on the table.

"It's pretty hot," the man said.

"Let's drink beer."

"Dos cervezas," the man said into the curtain.

"Big ones?" a woman asked from the doorway.

"Yes. Two big ones."

The woman brought two glasses of beer and two felt pads. She put the felt pads and the beer glasses on the table and looked at the man and the girl.

The girl was looking off at the line of hills. They were white in the sun and the country was brown and dry.

"They look like white elephants," she said.

"I've never seen one," the man drank his beer.

"No, you wouldn't have."

"I might have," the man said. "Just because you say I wouldn't have doesn't prove anything."

The girl looked at the bead curtain. "They've painted something on it," she said. "What does it say?"

"Anis del Toro. It's a drink."

"Could we try it?"

The man called "Listen" through the curtain. The woman came out from the bar.

"Four reales."

"We want two Anis del Toro."

"With water?"

"Do you want it with water?"

"I don't know," the girl said. "Is it good with water?"

"It's all right."

"You want them with water?" asked the woman.

"Yes, with water."

"It tastes like licorice," the girl said and put the glass down.

"That's the way with everything."

"Yes," said the girl. "Everything tastes of licorice. Especially all the things you've waited so long for, like absinthe."

"Oh, cut it out."

"You started it," the girl said. "I was being amused. I was having a fine time."

"Well, let's try and have a fine time."

"All right. I was trying. I said the mountains looked like white elephants. Wasn't that bright?"

"That was bright."

"I wanted to try this new drink. That's all we do, isn't it—look at things and try new drinks?"

"I guess so."

The girl looked across the hills.

"They're lovely hills," she said. "They don't really look like white elephants. I just meant the coloring of their skin through the trees."

"Should we have another drink?"

"All right."

The warm wind blew the bead curtain against the table.

"The beer's nice and cool," the man said.

"It's lovely," the girl said.

"It's really an awfully simple operation, Jig," the man said. "It's not really an operation at all."

The girl looked at the ground the table legs rested on.

"I know you wouldn't mind it, Jig. It's really not anything. It's just to let the air in."

The girl did not say anything.

"I'll go with you and I'll stay with you all the time. They just let the air in and then it's all perfectly natural."

"Then what will we do afterward?"

"We'll be fine afterward. Just like we were before."

"What makes you think so?"

"That's the only thing that bothers us. It's the only thing that's made us unhappy."

The girl looked at the bead curtain, put her hand out and took hold of two of the strings of beads.

"And you think then we'll be all right and be happy."

"I know we will. You don't have to be afraid. I've known lots of people that have done it."

"So have I," said the girl. "And afterward they were all happy."

"Well," the man said, "if you don't want to you don't have to. I wouldn't have you do it if you didn't want to. But I know it's perfectly simple."

"And you really want to?"

"I think it's the best thing to do. But I don't want you to do it if you don't really want to."

"And if I do it you'll be happy and things will be like they were and you'll love me?"

"I love you now. You know I love you."

"I know. But if I do it, then it will be nice again if I say things are like white elephants, and you'll like it?"

"I'll love it. I love it now but I just can't think about it. You know how I get when I worry."

"If I do it you won't ever worry?"

"I won't worry about that because it's perfectly simple."

"Then I'll do it. Because I don't care about me."

"What do you mean?"

"I don't care about me."

"Well, I care about you."

"Oh, yes. But I don't care about me. And I'll do it and then everything will be fine."

The girl stood up and walked to the end of the station. Across, on the other side, were fields of grain and trees along the banks of the Ebro. Far away, beyond the river, were mountains. The shadow of a cloud moved across the field of grain and she saw the river through the trees.

"And we could have all this," she said. "And we could have everything and every day we make it more impossible."

"What did you say?"

"I said we could have everything."

"We can have everything."

"No, we can't."

"We can have the whole world."

"No, we can't."

"We can go everywhere."

"No, we can't. It isn't ours any more."

"It's ours."

"No, it isn't. And once they take it away, you never get it back."

"But they haven't taken it away."

"We'll wait and see."

"Come on back in the shade," he said. "You mustn't feel that way."

"I don't feel any way," the girl said. "I just know things."

"I don't want you to do anything that you don't want to do—"

"Nor that isn't good for me," she said. "I know. Could we have another beer?"

"All right. But you've got to realize—"

"I realize," the girl said. "Can't we maybe stop talking?"

They sat down at the table and the girl looked across at the hills on the dry side of the valley and the man looked at her and at the table.

"You've got to realize," he said, "that I don't want you to do it if you don't want to. I'm perfectly willing to go through with it if it means anything to you."

"Doesn't it mean anything to you? We could get along."

"Of course it does. But I don't want anybody but you. I don't want any one else. And I know it's perfectly simple."

"Yes, you know it's perfectly simple."

"It's all right for you to say that, but I do know it."

"Would you do something for me now?"

"I'd do anything for you."

"Would you please please please please please please please stop talking?"

He did not say anything but looked at the bags against the wall of the station. There were labels on them from all the hotels where they had spent nights.

"But I don't want you to," he said, "I don't care anything about it."

"I'll scream," the girl said.

The woman came out through the curtains with two glasses of beer and put them down on the damp felt pads. "The train comes in five minutes," she said.

"What did she say?" asked the girl.

"That the train is coming in five minutes."

The girl smiled brightly at the woman, to thank her.

"I'd better take the bags over to the other side of the station," the man said. She smiled at him.

"All right. Then come back and we'll finish the beer."

He picked up the two heavy bags and carried them around the station to the other tracks. He looked up the tracks but could not see the train. Coming back, he walked through the barroom, where people waiting for the train were drinking. He drank an Anis at the bar and looked at the people. They were all waiting reasonably for the train. He went out through the bead curtain. She was sitting at the table and smiled at him.

"Do you feel better?" he asked.

"I feel fine," she said. "There's nothing wrong with me. I feel fine."

Suggestions for Discussion

1. What is the relationship of the title to the theme of the story? How does "white elephant" relate to the girl's dilemma?

2. Why are the early lines of dialogue evasive of the couple's real concerns?

3. What is Jig's real fear?

4. What is the nature of the man's arguments? What is the irony in his lines?

5. What is the nature of the girl's attitude toward their relationship? What statement does she make that clarifies her feelings about it?

6. What accounts for Jig's pessimism about the future?

7. How would you characterize the man, Jig, and their relationship?

8. At one point Jig begs the man to stop talking and threatens to scream. What precipitates her exhortation that he stop?

9. What is the irony in Jig's last statement?

Suggestions for Writing

1. With respect to the text describe Jig's sense of self and the kind of relationship she seeks with her lover.

2. Cite the evidence that Hemingway is not sympathetic to the man.

3. Continue the dialogue several months later.

Carson McCullers

The Sojourner

Carson McCullers (1917–1967), a Southern writer, was awarded Guggenheim fellowships in 1942 and in 1946. Her published works include *The Heart Is a Lonely Hunter* (1940), *Reflections in a Golden Eye* (1941), *The Member of the Wedding* (1946), *The Ballad of the Sad Café* (1951), and *Clock Without Hands* (1961). After a rootless man relives and revisits his past, the experience enables him to acknowledge the waste of his years, the brevity of life, and his need to reorder his relationships with those close to him.

The twilight border between sleep and waking was a Roman one this morning: splashing fountains and arched, narrow streets, the golden lavish city of blossoms and age-soft stone. Sometimes in this semiconsciousness he sojourned again in Paris, or German war rubble, or a Swiss skiing and a snow hotel. Sometimes, also, in a fallow Georgia field at hunting dawn. Rome it was this morning in the yearless region of dreams.

John Ferris awoke in a room in a New York hotel. He had the feeling that something unpleasant was awaiting him—what it was, he did not know. The feeling, submerged by matinal necessities, lingered even after he had dressed and gone downstairs. It was a cloudless autumn day and the pale sunlight sliced between the pastel skyscrapers. Ferris went into the next-door drugstore and sat at the end booth next to the window glass that overlooked the sidewalk. He ordered an American breakfast with scrambled eggs and sausage.

Ferris had come from Paris to his father's funeral which had taken place the week before in his home town in Georgia. The shock of death had made him aware of youth already passed. His hair was receding and the veins in his now naked temples were pulsing and prominent and his body was spare except for an incipient belly bulge. Ferris had loved his father and the bond between them had once been extraordinarily close—but the years had somehow unraveled this filial devotion; the death, expected for a long time, had left him with an unforeseen dismay. He had stayed as long as possible to be near his mother and brothers at home. His plane for Paris was to leave the next morning.

Ferris pulled out his address book to verify a number. He turned the pages with growing attentiveness. Names and addresses from New York, the capitals of Europe, a few faint ones from his home state in the South. Faded, printed names, sprawled drunken ones. Betty Wills: a random love, married now. Charlie Williams: wounded in the Hürtgen Forest, unheard of since. Grand old Williams—did he live or die? Don Walker: a B.T.O. in television, getting rich. Henry Green: hit the skids after the war, in a sanitarium now, they say. Cozie Hall: he had heard that she was dead. Heedless, laughing Cozie—it was strange to think that she too, silly girl, could die. As Ferris closed the address book, he suffered a sense of hazard, transience, almost of fear.

It was then that his body jerked suddenly. He was staring out of the window when there, on the sidewalk, passing by, was his ex-wife. Elizabeth passed quite close to him, walking slowly. He could not understand the wild quiver of his heart, nor the following sense of recklessness and grace that lingered after she was gone.

Quickly Ferris paid his check and rushed out to the sidewalk. Elizabeth stood on the corner waiting to cross Fifth Avenue. He hurried toward her meaning to speak, but the lights changed and she crossed the street before he reached her. Ferris followed. On the other side he could easily have overtaken her, but he found himself lagging unaccountably. Her fair hair was plainly rolled, and as he watched her Ferris recalled that once his father had remarked that Elizabeth had a "beautiful carriage." She turned at the next corner and Ferris followed, although by now his intention to overtake her had disappeared. Ferris questioned the bodily disturbance that the sight of Elizabeth aroused in him, the dampness of his hands, the hard heartstrokes.

It was eight years since Ferris had last seen his ex-wife. He knew that long ago she had married again. And there were children. During recent years he had seldom thought of her. But at first, after the divorce, the loss had almost destroyed him. Then after the anodyne of time, he had loved again, and then again. Jeannine, she was now. Certainly his love for his ex-wife was long since past. So why the unhinged body, the shaken mind? He knew only that his clouded heart was oddly dissonant with the sunny, candid autumn day. Ferris wheeled suddenly and, walking with long strides, almost running, hurried back to the hotel.

Ferris poured himself a drink, although it was not yet eleven o'clock. He sprawled out in an armchair like a man exhausted, nursing his glass of bourbon and water. He had a full day ahead of him as he was leaving by plane the next morning for Paris. He checked over his obligations: take luggage to Air France, lunch with his boss, buy shoes and an overcoat. And something— wasn't there something else? Ferris finished his drink and opened the telephone directory.

His decision to call his ex-wife was impulsive. The number was under Bailey, the husband's name, and he called before he had much time for self-debate. He and Elizabeth had exchanged cards at Christmastime, and Ferris had sent a carving set when he received the announcement of her wedding. There was no reason *not* to call. But as he waited, listening to the ring at the other end, misgiving fretted him.

Elizabeth answered; her familiar voice was a fresh shock to him. Twice he had to repeat his name, but when he was identified, she sounded glad. He explained he was only in town for that day. They had a theater engagement, she said—but she wondered if he would come by for an early dinner. Ferris said he would be delighted.

As he went from one engagement to another, he was still bothered at odd moments by the feeling that something necessary was forgotten. Ferris bathed and changed in the late afternoon, often thinking about Jeannine: he would be with her the following night. "Jeannine," he would say, "I happened to run into my ex-wife when I was in New York. Had dinner with her. And her husband, of course. It was strange seeing her after all these years."

Elizabeth lived in the East Fifties, and as Ferris taxied uptown he glimpsed at intersections the lingering sunset, but by the time he reached his destination it was already autumn dark. The place was a building with a marquee and a doorman, and the apartment was on the seventh floor.

"Come in, Mr. Ferris."

Braced for Elizabeth or even the unimagined husband, Ferris was astonished by the freckled red-haired child; he had known of the children, but his mind had failed somehow to acknowledge them. Surprise made him step back awkwardly.

"This is our apartment," the child said politely. "Aren't you Mr. Ferris? I'm Billy. Come in."

In the living room beyond the hall, the husband provided another surprise; he too had not been acknowledged emotionally. Bailey was a lumbering red-haired man with a deliberate manner. He rose and extended a welcoming hand.

"I'm Bill Bailey. Glad to see you. Elizabeth will be in, in a minute. She's finishing dressing."

The last words struck a gliding series of vibrations, memories of the other years. Fair Elizabeth, rosy and naked before her bath. Half-dressed before the mirror of her dressing table, brushing her fine, chestnut hair. Sweet, casual intimacy, the soft-fleshed loveliness indisputably possessed. Ferris shrank from the unbidden memories and compelled himself to meet Bill Bailey's gaze.

"Billy, will you please bring that tray of drinks from the kitchen table?"

The child obeyed promptly, and when he was gone Ferris remarked conversationally, "Fine boy you have there."

"We think so."

Flat silence until the child returned with a tray of glasses and a cocktail shaker of Martinis. With the priming drinks they pumped up conversation:

Russia, they spoke of, and the New York rain-making, and the apartment situation in Manhattan and Paris.

"Mr. Ferris is flying all the way across the ocean tomorrow," Bailey said to the little boy who was perched on the arm of his chair, quiet and well behaved. "I bet you would like to be a stowaway in his suitcase."

Billy pushed back his limp bangs. "I want to fly in an airplane and be a newspaperman like Mr. Ferris." He added with sudden assurance, "That's what I would like to do when I am big."

Bailey said, "I thought you wanted to be a doctor."

"I do!" said Billy. "I would like to be both. I want to be a atom-bomb scientist too."

Elizabeth came in carrying in her arms a baby girl.

"Oh, John!" she said. She settled the baby in the father's lap. "It's grand to see you. I'm awfully glad you could come."

The little girl sat demurely on Bailey's knees. She wore a pale pink crepe de Chine frock, smocked around the yoke with rose, and a matching silk hair ribbon tying back her pale soft curls. Her skin was summer tanned and her brown eyes flecked with gold and laughing. When she reached up and fingered her father's horn-rimmed glasses, he took them off and let her look through them a moment. "How's my old Candy?"

Elizabeth was very beautiful, more beautiful perhaps than he had ever realized. Her straight clean hair was shining. Her face was softer, glowing and serene. It was a madonna loveliness, dependent on the family ambiance.

"You've hardly changed at all," Elizabeth said, "but it has been a long time."

"Eight years." His hand touched his thinning hair self-consciously while further amenities were exchanged.

Ferris felt himself suddenly a spectator—an interloper among these Baileys. Why had he come? He suffered. His own life seemed so solitary, a fragile column supporting nothing amidst the wreckage of the years. He felt he could not bear much longer to stay in the family room.

He glanced at his watch. "You're going to the theater?"

"It's a shame," Elizabeth said, "but we've had this engagement for more than a month. But surely, John, you'll be staying home one of these days before long. You're not going to be an expatriate, are you?"

"Expatriate," Ferris repeated. "I don't much like the word."

"What's a better word?" she asked.

He thought for a moment. "Sojourner might do."

Ferris glanced again at his watch, and again Elizabeth apologized. "If only we had known ahead of time—"

"I just had this day in town. I came home unexpectedly. You see, Papa died last week."

"Papa Ferris is dead?"

"Yes, at Johns Hopkins. He had been sick there nearly a year. The funeral was down home in Georgia."

"Oh, I'm so sorry, John. Papa Ferris was always one of my favorite people."

The little boy moved from behind the chair so that he could look into his mother's face. He asked, "Who is dead?"

Ferris was oblivious to apprehension; he was thinking of his father's death. He saw again the outstretched body on the quilted silk within the coffin. The corpse flesh was bizarrely rouged and the familiar hands lay massive and joined above a spread of funeral roses. The memory closed and Ferris awakened to Elizabeth's calm voice.

"Mr. Ferris's father, Billy. A really grand person. Somebody you didn't know."

"But why did you call him *Papa* Ferris?"

Bailey and Elizabeth exchanged a trapped look. It was Bailey who answered the questioning child. "A long time ago," he said, "your mother and Mr. Ferris were once married. Before you were born—a long time ago."

"Mr. Ferris?"

The little boy stared at Ferris, amazed and unbelieving. And Ferris's eyes, as he returned the gaze, were somehow unbelieving too. Was it indeed true that at one time he had called this stranger, Elizabeth, Little Butterduck during nights of love, that they had lived together, shared perhaps a thousand days and nights and—finally—endured in the misery of sudden solitude the fiber by fiber (jealousy, alcohol and money quarrels) destruction of the fabric of married love?

Bailey said to the children, "It's somebody's suppertime. Come on now."

"But Daddy! Mama and Mr. Ferris—I—"

Billy's everlasting eyes—perplexed and with a glimmer of hostility—reminded Ferris of the gaze of another child. It was the young son of Jeannine—a boy of seven with a shadowed little face and knobby knees whom Ferris avoided and usually forgot.

"Quick march!" Bailey gently turned Billy toward the door. "Say good night now, son."

"Good night, Mr. Ferris." He added resentfully, "I thought I was staying up for the cake."

"You can come in afterward for the cake," Elizabeth said. "Run along now with Daddy for your supper."

Ferris and Elizabeth were alone. The weight of the situation descended on those first moments of silence. Ferris asked permission to pour himself another drink and Elizabeth set the cocktail shaker on the table at his side. He looked at the grand piano and noticed the music on the rack.

"Do you still play as beautifully as you used to?"

"I still enjoy it."

"Please play, Elizabeth."

Elizabeth rose immediately. Her readiness to perform when asked had always been one of her amiabilities; she never hung back, apologized. Now as she approached the piano there was the added readiness of relief.

She began with a Bach prelude and fugue. The prelude was as gaily iridescent as a prism in a morning room. The first voice of the fugue, an announcement pure and solitary, was repeated intermingling with a second voice, and again repeated within an elaborated frame, the multiple music, horizontal and serene, flowed with unhurried majesty. The principal melody was woven with two other voices, embellished with countless ingenuities—now dominant, again submerged, it had the sublimity of a single thing that does not fear surrender to the whole. Toward the end, the density of the material gathered for the last enriched insistence on the dominant first motif and with a chorded final statement the fugue ended. Ferris rested his head on the chair back and closed his eyes. In the following silence a clear, high voice came from the room down the hall.

"Daddy, how *could* Mama and Mr. Ferris—" A door was closed.

The piano began again—what was this music? Unplaced, familiar, the limpid melody had lain a long while dormant in his heart. Now it spoke to him of another time, another place—it was the music Elizabeth used to play. The delicate air summoned a wilderness of memory. Ferris was lost in the riot of past longings, conflicts, ambivalent desires. Strange that the music, catalyst for this tumultuous anarchy, was so serene and clear. The singing melody was broken off by the appearance of the maid.

"Miz Bailey, dinner is out on the table now."

Even after Ferris was seated at the table between his host and hostess, the unfinished music still overcast his mood. He was a little drunk.

"*L'improvisation de la vie humaine,*" he said. "There's nothing that makes you so aware of the improvisation of human existence as a song unfinished. Or an old address book."

"Address book?" repeated Bailey. Then he stopped, noncommittal and polite.

"You're still the same old boy, Johnny," Elizabeth said with a trace of the old tenderness.

It was a Southern dinner that evening, and the dishes were his old favorites. They had fried chicken and corn pudding and rich, glazed candied sweet potatoes. During the meal Elizabeth kept alive a conversation when the silences were overlong. And it came about that Ferris was led to speak of Jeannine.

"I first knew Jeannine last autumn—about this time of the year—in Italy. She's a singer and she had an engagement in Rome. I expect we will be married soon."

The words seemed so true, inevitable, that Ferris did not at first acknowledge to himself the lie. He and Jeannine had never in that year spoken of marriage. And indeed, she was still married—to a White Russian moneychanger in Paris from whom she had been separated for five years. But it was too late to correct the lie. Already Elizabeth was saying: "This really makes me glad to know. Congratulations, Johnny."

He tried to make amends with truth. "The Roman autumn is so beautiful. Balmy and blossoming." He added, "Jeannine has a little boy of six. A curious trilingual little fellow. We go to the Tuileries sometimes."

A lie again. He had taken the boy once to the gardens. The sallow foreign child in shorts that bared his spindly legs had sailed his boat in the concrete pond and ridden the pony. The child had wanted to go in to the puppet show. But there was not time, for Ferris had an engagement at the Scribe Hotel. He had promised they would go to the guignol another afternoon. Only once had he taken Valentin to the Tuileries.

There was a stir. The maid brought in a white-frosted cake with pink candles. The children entered in their night clothes. Ferris still did not understand.

"Happy birthday, John," Elizabeth said. "Blow out the candles."

Ferris recognized his birthday date. The candles blew out lingeringly and there was the smell of burning wax. Ferris was thirty-eight years old. The veins in his temples darkened and pulsed visibly.

"It's time you started for the theater."

Ferris thanked Elizabeth for the birthday dinner and said the appropriate good-byes. The whole family saw him to the door.

A high, thin moon shone above the jagged, dark skyscrapers. The streets were windy, cold. Ferris hurried to Third Avenue and hailed a cab. He gazed at the nocturnal city with the deliberate attentiveness of departure and perhaps farewell. He was alone. He longed for flight-time and the coming journey.

The next day he looked down on the city from the air, burnished in sunlight, toylike, precise. Then America was left behind and there was only the Atlantic and the distant European shore. The ocean was milky pale and placid beneath the clouds. Ferris dozed most of the day. Toward dark he was thinking of Elizabeth and the visit of the previous evening. He thought of Elizabeth among her family with longing, gentle envy and inexplicable regret. He sought the melody, the unfinished air, that had so moved him. The cadence, some unrelated tones, were all that remained; the melody itself evaded him. He had found instead the first voice of the fugue that Elizabeth had played—it came to him, inverted mockingly and in a minor key. Suspended above the ocean the anxieties of transience and solitude no longer troubled him and he thought of his father's death with equanimity. During the dinner hour the plane reached the shore of France.

At midnight Ferris was in a taxi crossing Paris. It was a clouded night and mist wreathed the lights of the Place de la Concorde. The midnight bistros gleamed on the wet pavements. As always after a transocean flight the change of continents was too sudden. New York at morning, this midnight Paris. Ferris glimpsed the disorder of his life: the succession of cities, of transitory loves; and time, the sinister glissando of the years, time always.

"Vite! Vite!" he called in terror. "Dépêchez-vous."

Valentin opened the door to him. The little boy wore pajamas and an outgrown red robe. His grey eyes were shadowed and, as Ferris passed into the flat, they flickered momentarily.

"J'attends Maman."

Jeannine was singing in a night club. She would not be home before another hour. Valentin returned to a drawing, squatting with his crayons over the paper on the floor. Ferris looked down at the drawing—it was a banjo player with notes and wavy lines inside a comicstrip balloon.

"We will go again to the Tuileries."

The child looked up and Ferris drew him closer to his knees. The melody, the unfinished music that Elizabeth had played came to him suddenly. Unsought, the load of memory jettisoned—this time bringing only recognition and sudden joy.

"Monsieur Jean," the child said, "did you see him?"

Confused, Ferris thought only of another child—the freckled, family-loved boy. "See who, Valentin?"

"Your dead papa in Georgia." The child added, "Was he okay?"

Ferris spoke with rapid urgency: "We will go often to the Tuileries. Ride the pony and we will go into the guignol. We will see the puppet show and never be in a hurry any more."

"Monsieur Jean," Valentin said. "The guignol is now closed."

Again, the terror, the acknowledgment of wasted years and death. Valentin, responsive and confident, still nestled in his arms. His cheek touched the soft cheek and felt the brush of the delicate eyelashes. With inner desperation he pressed the child close—as though an emotion as protean as his love could dominate the pulse of time.

Suggestions for Discussion

1. In *The Mortgaged Heart* McCullers suggests that the way by which we master loneliness is "to belong to something larger and more powerful than the weak, lonely self." How is this belief developed in her short story?

2. What do the descriptions in the opening four paragraphs tell you about Ferris? In particular, try to account for his emotional response to the names in his address book.

3. From the moment Ferris catches a glimpse of Elizabeth on the sidewalk outside the restaurant to his flight to Paris and his taxi ride across the city, the reader gains an understanding of Elizabeth and of their relationship. What details clarify your knowledge of Elizabeth? Of Ferris?

4. What is Ferris's response to his evening at the Baileys? How does the playing of the fugue and the second piece he couldn't identify affect Ferris?

5. Why does Ferris lie to Elizabeth about his relationship with Jeannine and Valentin?

6. How are you prepared for Ferris's new relationship with Valentin?

7. What is the meaning of the last sentence? Relate it to what has gone before in Ferris's life.

Suggestions for Writing

1. Discuss the McCullers quotation in Question 1.

2. Write a narrative growing out of your observation or experience about the effects of divorce on the former mates and/or the children.

Leslie Marmon Silko

Lullaby

Leslie Marmon Silko (b. 1948) received her B.A. from the University of New Mexico, and has taught both there and at the University of Arizona. She grew up on the Laguna Pueblo Reservation, where she presently lives. In addition to having won the Pushcart and Chicago Review Poetry Prizes, she has been awarded fellowships from the National Endowment for the Arts and, in 1983, from the MacArthur Foundation. Among her recent books are *Storyteller* (1981), *The Delicacy and Strength of Lace* (1986), and *Almanac of the Dead* (1991).

The sun had gone down but the snow in the wind gave off its own light. It came in thick tufts like new wool—washed before the weaver spins it. Ayah reached out for it like her own babies had, and she smiled when she remembered how she had laughed at them. She was an old woman now, and her life had become memories. She sat down with her back against the wide cottonwood tree, feeling the rough bark on her back bones; she faced east and listened to the wind and snow sing a high-pitched Yeibechei song. Out of the wind she felt warmer, and she could watch the wide, fluffy snow fill in her tracks, steadily, until the direction she had come from was gone. By the light of the snow she could see the dark outline of the big arroyo a few feet away. She was sitting on the edge of Cebolleta Creek, where in the springtime the thin cows would graze on grass already chewed flat to the ground. In the wide, deep creek bed where only a trickle of water flowed in the summer, the skinny cows would wander, looking for new grass along winding paths splashed with manure.

Ayah pulled the old Army blanket over her head like a shawl. Jimmie's blanket—the one he had sent to her. That was a long time ago and the green wool was faded, and it was unraveling on the edges. She did not want to think about Jimmie. So she thought about the weaving and the way her mother had done it. On the tall wooden loom set into the sand under a tamarack tree for shade. She could see it clearly. She had been only a little girl when her grandma gave her the wooden combs to pull the twigs and burrs from the raw, freshly washed wool. And while she combed the wool, her grandma sat beside her spinning a silvery strand of yarn around the smooth cedar spindle. Her mother worked at the loom with yarns dyed bright yellow and red and gold. She watched them dye the yarn in boiling black pots full of beeweed petals, juniper berries, and sage. The blankets her mother made were soft and woven so tight that rain rolled off them like birds' feathers. Ayah remembered sleeping warmly on cold windy nights, wrapped in her mother's blankets on the hogan's sandy floor.

The snow drifted now, with the northwest wind hurling it in gusts. It drifted up around her black overshoes—old ones with little metal buckles. She smiled at the snow which was trying to cover her little by little. She could remember when they had no black rubber overshoes; only the high buckskin leggings that they wrapped over their elkhide moccasins. If the snow was dry or frozen, a person could walk all day and not get wet; and in the evenings the beams of the ceiling would hang with lengths of pale buckskin leggings drying out slowly.

She felt peaceful remembering. She didn't feel cold any more. Jimmie's blanket seemed warmer than it had ever been. And she could remember the morning he was born. She could remember whispering to her mother, who was sleeping on the other side of the hogan, to tell her it was time now. She did not want to wake the others. The second time she called to her, her mother stood up and pulled on her shoes; she knew. They walked to the old stone hogan together, Ayah walking a step behind her mother. She waited alone learning the rhythms of the pains while her mother went to call the old woman to help them. The morning was already warm even before dawn and Ayah smelled the bee flowers blooming and the young willow growing at the springs. She could remember that so clearly, but his birth merged into the births of the other children and to her it became all the same birth. They named him for the summer morning and in English they called him Jimmie.

It wasn't like Jimmie died. He just never came back, and one day a dark blue sedan with white writing on its doors pulled up in front of the boxcar shack where the rancher let the Indians live. A man in a khaki uniform trimmed in gold gave them a yellow piece of paper and told them that Jimmie was dead. He said the Army would try to get the body back and then it would be shipped to them; but it wasn't likely because the helicopter had burned after it crashed. All of this was told to Chato because he could understand English. She stood inside the doorway holding the baby while Chato listened. Chato spoke English like a white man and he spoke Spanish too. He was taller than the white man and he stood straighter too. Chato didn't explain why; he just told the military man they could keep the body if they found it. The white man looked bewildered; he nodded his head and left. Then Chato looked at her and shook his head, and then he told her, "Jimmie isn't coming home anymore," and when he spoke, he used the words to speak of the dead. She didn't cry then, but she hurt inside with anger. And she mourned him as the years passed, when a horse fell with Chato and broke his leg, and the white rancher told them he wouldn't pay Chato until he could work again. She mourned Jimmie because he would have worked for his father then; he would have saddled the big bay horse and ridden the fence lines each day, with wire cutters and heavy gloves, fixing the breaks in the barbed wire and putting the stray cattle back inside again.

She mourned him after the white doctors came to take Danny and Ella away. She was at the shack alone that day they came. It was back in the days before they hired Navajo women to go with them as interpreters. She recognized one of the doctors. She had seen him at the children's clinic at Cañoncito about a month ago. They were wearing khaki uniforms and they waved papers at her and a black ball-point pen, trying to make her understand their English words. She was frightened by the way they looked at the children, like the lizard watches the fly. Danny was swinging on the tire swing on the elm tree behind the rancher's house, and Ella was toddling around the front door, dragging the broomstick horse Chato made for her. Ayah could see they wanted her to sign the papers, and Chato had taught her to sign her name. It was something she was proud of. She only wanted them to go, and to take their eyes away from her children.

She took the pen from the man without looking at his face and she signed the papers in three different places he pointed to. She stared at the ground by their feet and waited for them to leave. But they stood there and began to point and gesture at the children. Danny stopped swinging. Ayah could see his fear. She moved suddenly and grabbed Ella into her arms; the child squirmed, trying to get back to her toys. Ayah ran with the baby toward Danny; she screamed for him to run and then she grabbed him around his chest and carried him too. She ran south into the foothills of juniper trees and black lava rock. Behind her she heard the doctors running, but they had been taken by surprise, and as the hills became steeper and the cholla cactus were thicker, they stopped. When she reached the top of the hill, she stopped to listen in case they were circling around her. But in a few minutes she heard a car engine start and they drove away. The children had been too surprised to cry while she ran with them. Danny was shaking and Ella's little fingers were gripping Ayah's blouse.

She stayed up in the hills for the rest of the day, sitting on a black lava boulder in the sunshine where she could see for miles all around her. The sky was light blue and cloudless, and it was warm for late April. The sun warmth relaxed her and took the fear and anger away. She lay back on the rock and watched the sky. It seemed to her that she could walk into the sky, stepping through clouds endlessly. Danny played with little pebbles and stones, pretending they were birds' eggs and then little rabbits. Ella sat at her feet and dropped fistfuls of dirt into the breeze, watching the dust and particles of sand intently. Ayah watched a hawk soar high above them, dark wings gliding; hunting or only watching, she did not know. The hawk was patient and he circled all afternoon before he disappeared around the high volcanic peak the Mexicans called Guadalupe.

Late in the afternoon, Ayah looked down at the gray boxcar shack with the paint all peeled from the wood: the stove pipe on the roof was rusted and crooked. The fire she had built that morning in the oil drum stove had burned out. Ella was asleep in her lap now and Danny sat close to her, complaining that he was hungry; he asked when they would go to the house. "We will stay up here until your father comes," she told him, "because those white men were chasing us." The boy remembered then and he nodded at her silently.

If Jimmie had been there he could have read those papers and explained to her what they said. Ayah would have known then, never to sign them. The doctors came back the next day and they brought a BIA policeman with them. They told Chato they had her signature and that was all they needed. Except for the kids. She listened to Chato sullenly; she hated him when he told her it was the old woman who died in the winter, spitting blood; it was her old grandma who had given the children this disease. "They don't spit blood," she said coldly. "The whites lie." She held Ella and Danny close to her, ready to run to the hills again. "I want a medicine man first," she said to Chato, not looking at him. He shook his head. "It's too late now. The policeman is with them. You signed the paper." His voice was gentle.

It was worse than if they had died: to lose the children and to know that somewhere, in a place called Colorado, in a place full of sick and dying strangers, her children were without her. There had been babies that died soon after they were born, and one that died before he could walk. She had carried them herself, up to the boulders and great pieces of the cliff that long ago crashed down from Long Mesa; she laid them in the crevices of sandstone and buried them in fine brown sand with round quartz pebbles that washed down the hills in the rain. She had endured it because they had been with her. But she could not bear this pain. She did not sleep for a long time after they took her children. She stayed on the hill where they had fled the first time, and she slept rolled up in the blanket Jimmie had sent her. She carried the pain in her belly and it was fed by everything she saw: the blue sky of their last day together and the dust and pebbles they played with; the swing in the elm tree and broomstick horse choked life from her. The pain filled her stomach and there was no room for food or for her lungs to fill with air. The air and the food would have been theirs.

She hated Chato, not because he let the policeman and doctors put the screaming children in the government car, but because he had taught her to sign her name. Because it was like the old ones always told her about learning their language or any of their ways: It endangers you. She slept alone on the hill until the middle of November when the first snows came. Then she made a bed for herself where the children had slept. She did not lie down beside Chato again until many years later, when he was sick and shivering and only her body could keep him warm. The illness came after the white rancher told Chato he was too old to work for him anymore, and Chato and his old woman should be out of the shack by the next afternoon because the rancher had hired new people to work there. That had satisfied her. To see how the white man repaid Chato's years of loyalty and work. All of Chato's fine-sounding English talk didn't change things.

It snowed steadily and the luminous light from the snow gradually diminished into the darkness. Somewhere in Ceboletta a dog barked and other village dogs joined with it. Ayah looked in the direction she had come, from the bar where Chato was buying the wine. Sometimes he told her to go on ahead and wait; and then he never came. And when she finally went back looking for him, she would find him passed out at the bottom of the wooden steps to Azzie's Bar. All the wine would be gone and most of the money too, from the pale blue check that came to them once a month in a government envelope. It was then that she would look at his face and his hands, scarred by ropes and the barbed wire of all those years, and she would think, this man is a stranger; for forty years she had smiled at him and cooked his food, but he remained a stranger. She stood up again, with the snow almost to her knees, and she walked back to find Chato.

It was hard to walk in the deep snow and she felt the air burn in her lungs. She stopped a short distance from the bar to rest and readjust the blanket. But this time he wasn't waiting for her at the bottom step with his old Stetson hat pulled down and his shoulders hunched up in his long wool overcoat.

She was careful not to slip on the wooden steps. When she pushed the door open, warm air and cigarette smoke hit her face. She looked around slowly and deliberately, in every corner, in every dark place that the old man might find to sleep. The bar owner didn't like Indians in there, especially Navajos, but he let Chato come in because he could talk Spanish like he was one of them. The men at the bar stared at her, and the bartender saw that she left the door open wide. Snowflakes were flying inside like moths and melting into a puddle on the oiled wood floor. He motioned to her to close the door, but she did not see him. She held herself straight and walked across the room slowly, searching the room with every step. The snow in her hair melted and she could feel it on her forehead. At the far corner of the room, she saw red flames at the mica window of the old stove door; she looked behind the stove just to make sure. The bar got quiet except for the Spanish polka music playing on the jukebox. She stood by the stove and shook the snow from her blanket and held it near the stove to dry. The wet wool smell reminded her of newborn goats in early March, brought inside to warm near the fire. She felt calm.

In past years they would have told her to get out. But her hair was white now and her face was wrinkled. They looked at her like she was a spider crawling slowly across the room. They were afraid; she could feel the fear. She looked at their faces steadily. They reminded her of the first time the white people brought her children back to her that winter. Danny had been shy and hid behind the thin white woman who brought them. And the baby had not known her until Ayah took her into her arms, and then Ella had nuzzled close to her as she had when she was nursing. The blonde woman was nervous and kept looking at a dainty gold watch on her wrist. She sat on the bench near the small window and watched the dark snow clouds gather around the mountains; she was worrying about the unpaved road. She was frightened by what she saw inside too: the strips of venison drying on a rope across the ceiling and the children jabbering excitedly in a language she did not know. So they stayed for only a few hours. Ayah watched the government car disappear down the road and she knew they were already being weaned from these lava hills and from this sky. The last time they came was in early June, and Ella stared at her the way the men in the bar were now staring. Ayah did not try to pick her up; she smiled at her instead and spoke cheerfully to Danny. When he tried to answer her, he could not seem to remember and he spoke English words with the Navajo. But he gave her a scrap of paper that he had found somewhere and carried in his pocket; it was folded in half, and he shyly looked up at her and said it was a bird. She asked Chato if they were home for good this time. He spoke to the white woman and she shook her head. "How much longer?" he asked, and she said she didn't know; but Chato saw how she stared at the boxcar shack. Ayah turned away then. She did not say good-bye.

She felt satisfied that the men in the bar feared her. Maybe it was her face and the way she held her mouth with teeth clenched tight, like there was nothing anyone could do to her now. She walked north down the road, searching for the old man. She did this because she had the blanket, and there would be no place for him except with her and the blanket in the old adobe barn near the arroyo. They always slept there when they came to Cebolleta. If the money and the wine were gone, she would be relieved because then they could go home again; back to the old hogan with a dirt roof and rock walls where she herself had been born. And the next day the old man could go back to the few sheep they still had, to follow along behind them, guiding them, into dry sandy arroyos where sparse grass grew. She knew he did not like walking behind old ewes when for so many years he rode big quarter horses and worked with cattle. But she wasn't sorry for him; he should have known all along what would happen.

There had not been enough rain for their garden in five years; and that was when Chato finally hitched a ride into the town and brought back brown boxes of rice and sugar and big tin cans of welfare peaches. After that, at the first of the month they went to Ceboletta to ask the postmaster for the check; and then Chato would go to the bar and cash it. They did this as they planted the garden every May, not because anything would survive the summer dust, but because it was time to do this. The journey passed the days that smelled silent and dry like the caves above the canyon with yellow painted buffaloes on their walls.

He was walking along the pavement when she found him. He did not stop or turn around when he heard her behind him. She walked beside him and she noticed how slowly he moved now. He smelled strong of woodsmoke and urine. Lately he had been forgetting. Sometimes he called her by his sister's name and she had been gone for a long time. Once she had found him wandering on the road to the white man's ranch, and she asked him why he was going that way; he laughed at her and said, "You know they can't run that ranch without me," and he walked on determined, limping on the leg that had been crushed many years before. Now he looked at her curiously, as if for the first time, but he kept shuffling along, moving slowly along the side of the highway. His gray hair had grown long and spread out on the shoulders of the long overcoat. He wore the old felt hat pulled down over his ears. His boots were worn out at the toes and he had stuffed pieces of an old red shirt in the holes. The rags made his feet look like little animals up to their ears in snow. She laughed at his feet; the snow muffled the sound of her laugh. He stopped and looked at her again. The wind had quit blowing and the snow was falling straight down; the southeast sky was beginning to clear and Ayah could see a star.

"Let's rest awhile," she said to him. They walked away from the road and up the slope to the giant boulders that had tumbled down from the red sandrock mesa throughout the centuries of rainstorms and earth tremors. In a place where the boulders shut out the wind, they sat down with their backs against the rock. She offered half of the blanket to him and they sat wrapped together.

The storm passed swiftly. The clouds moved east. They were massive and full, crowding together across the sky. She watched them with the feeling of horses—steely blue-gray horses startled across the sky. The powerful haunches pushed into the distances and the tail hairs streamed white mist behind them. The sky cleared. Ayah saw that there was nothing between her and the stars. The light was crystalline. There was no shimmer, no distortion through earth haze. She breathed the clarity of the night sky; she smelled the purity of the half moon and the stars. He was lying on his side with his knees pulled up near his belly for warmth. His eyes were closed now, and in the light from the stars and the moon, he looked young again.

She could see it descend out of the night sky: an icy stillness from the edge of the thin moon. She recognized the freezing. It came gradually, sinking snowflake by snowflake until the crust was heavy and deep. It had the strength of the stars in Orion, and its journey was endless. Ayah knew that with the wine he would sleep. He would not feel it. She tucked the blanket around him, remembering how it was when Ella had been with her; and she felt the rush so big inside her heart for the babies. And she sang the only song she knew to sing for babies. She could not remember if she had ever sung it to her children, but she knew that her grandmother had sung it and her mother had sung it:

> The earth is your mother,
>   she holds you.
> The sky is your father,
>   he protects you.
> Sleep,
> sleep.
> Rainbow is your sister,
>   she loves you.
> The winds are your brothers,

they sing to you.
Sleep,
sleep.
We are together always
We are together always
There never was a time
when this
was not so.

Suggestions for Discussion

1. Silko's story is in part about the different ways we have to say good-bye to the people we love and to parts of our life. What has Ayah lost? And how?

2. Why does the author call the story "Lullaby"? To whom is the lullaby sung and for what reason? What do the words of the lullaby tell us about the worldview of the Navajo?

3. How does Ayah's connection with her own past parallel her connection with the natural world?

Suggestions for Writing

1. Think of a lullaby or nursery rhyme that has special meaning for you. Use it as the focal point of a story about yourself.

2. Write a lullaby or a sleep/comfort song that describes what you find peaceful and reassuring.

3. Outline the plot of a western movie from the perspective of Ayah.

Raymond Carver

What We Talk About When
We Talk About Love

Raymond Carver (1939–1988) was born in Clatskaine, Oregon, and lived in the Pacific Northwest until his death. He received a number of honors including a Guggenheim Fellowship, National Endowment for the Arts grants, and the Mildred and Harold Strauss Living Award. Four collections of his short stories have been published: *Will You Please Be Quiet, Please* (1976), nominated for the National Book Award; *What We Talk About When We Talk About Love* (1981); *Cathedral* (1984), nominated for the National Book Critics Circle Award; and *The Stories of Raymond Carver* (1985). Although two couples are seated around the kitchen table drinking gin, the primary focus is on Mel and to a lesser degree his second wife, Terri. In Mel's reminiscences about his personal and professional life and in his behavior, he expresses differing and perhaps contradictory views of love.

Purpose P.O.V. Setting place time situation Characters Plot Theme

My friend Mel McGinnis was talking. Mel McGinnis is a cardiologist, and sometimes that gives him the right.

The four of us were sitting around his kitchen table drinking gin. Sunlight filled the kitchen from the big window behind the sink. There were Mel and me and his second wife, Teresa—Terri, we called her—and my wife, Laura. We lived in Albuquerque then. But we were all from somewhere else.

There was an ice bucket on the table. The gin and the tonic water kept going around, and we somehow got on the subject of love. Mel thought real love was nothing less than spiritual love. He said he'd spent five years in a seminary before quitting to go to medical school. He said he still looked back on those years in the seminary as the most important years in his life.

Terri said the man she lived with before she lived with Mel loved her so much he tried to kill her. Then Terri said, "He beat me up one night. He dragged me around the living room by my ankles. He kept saying, 'I love you, I love you, you bitch.' He went on dragging me around the living room. My head kept knocking on things." Terri looked around the table. "What do you do with love like that?"

She was a bone-thin woman with a pretty face, dark eyes, and brown hair that hung down her back. She liked necklaces made of turquoise, and long pendant earrings.

"My God, don't be silly. That's not love, and you know it," Mel said. "I don't know what you'd call it, but I sure know you wouldn't call it love."

"Say what you want to, but I know it was," Terri said. "It may sound crazy to you, but it's true just the same. People are different, Mel. Sure, sometimes he may have acted crazy. Okay. But he loved me. In his own way maybe, but he loved me. There was love there, Mel. Don't say there wasn't."

Mel let out his breath. He held his glass and turned to Laura and me. "The man threatened to kill me," Mel said. He finished his drink and reached for the gin bottle. "Terri's a romantic. Terri's of the kick-me-so-I'll-know-you-love-me school. Terri, hon, don't look that way." Mel reached across the table and touched Terri's cheek with his fingers. He grinned at her.

"Now he wants to make up," Terri said.

"Make up what?" Mel said. "What is there to make up? I know what I know. That's all."

"How'd we get started on this subject, anyway?" Terri said. She raised her glass and drank from it. "Mel always has love on his mind," she said. "Don't you, honey?" She smiled, and I thought that was the last of it.

"I just wouldn't call Ed's behavior love. That's all I'm saying, honey," Mel said. "What about you guys?" Mel said to Laura and me. "Does that sound like love to you?"

"I'm the wrong person to ask," I said. "I didn't even know the man. I've only heard his name mentioned in passing. I wouldn't know. You'd have to know the particulars. But I think what you're saying is that love is an absolute."

Mel said, "The kind of love I'm talking about is. The kind of love I'm talking about, you don't try to kill people."

Laura said, "I don't know anything about Ed, or anything about the situation. But who can judge anyone else's situation?"

. I touched the back of Laura's hand. She gave me a quick smile. I picked up Laura's hand. It was warm, the nails polished, perfectly manicured. I encircled the broad wrist with my fingers, and I held her.

"When I left, he drank rat poison," Terri said. She clasped her arms with her hands. "They took him to the hospital in Santa Fe. That's where we lived then, about ten miles out. They saved his life. But his gums went crazy from it. I mean they pulled away from his teeth. After that, his teeth stood out like fangs. My God," Terri said. She waited a minute, then let go of her arms and picked up her glass.

"What people won't do!" Laura said.

"He's out of the action now," Mel said. "He's dead."

Mel handed me the saucer of limes. I took a section, squeezed it over my drink, and stirred the ice cubes with my finger.

"It gets worse," Terri said. "He shot himself in the mouth. But he bungled that too. Poor Ed," she said. Terri shook her head.

"Poor Ed nothing," Mel said. "He was dangerous."

Mel was forty-five years old. He was tall and rangy with curly soft hair. His face and arms were brown from the tennis he played. When he was sober, his gestures, all his movements, were precise, very careful.

"He did love me though, Mel. Grant me that," Terri said. "That's all I'm asking. He didn't love me the way you love me. I'm not saying that. But he loved me. You can grant me that, can't you?"

"What do you mean, he bungled it?" I said.

Laura leaned forward with her glass. She put her elbows on the table and held her glass in both hands. She glanced from Mel to Terri and waited with a look of bewilderment on her open face, as if amazed that such things happened to people you were friendly with.

"How'd he bungle it when he killed himself?" I said.

"I'll tell you what happened," Mel said. "He took this twenty-two pistol he'd bought to threaten Terri and me with. Oh, I'm serious, the man was always threatening. You should have seen the way we lived in those days. Like fugitives. I even bought a gun myself. Can you believe it? A guy like me? But I did. I bought one for self-defense and carried it in the glove compartment. Sometimes I'd have to leave the apartment in the middle of the night. To go to the hospital, you know? Terri and I weren't married then, and my first wife had the house and kids, the dog, everything, and Terri and I were living in this apartment here. Sometimes, as I say, I'd get a call in the middle of the night and have to go in to the hospital at two or three in the morning. It'd be dark out there in the parking lot, and I'd break into a sweat before I could even get to my car. I never knew if he was going to come up out of the shrubbery or from behind a car and start shooting. I mean, the man was crazy. He was capable of wiring a bomb, anything. He used to call my service at all hours and say he needed to talk to the doctor, and when I'd return the call, he'd say, 'Son of a bitch, your days are numbered.' Little things like that. It was scary, I'm telling you."

"I still feel sorry for him," Terri said.

"It sounds like a nightmare," Laura said. "But what exactly happened after he shot himself?"

Laura is a legal secretary. We'd met in a professional capacity. Before we knew it, it was a courtship. She's thirty-five, three years younger than I am.

In addition to being in love, we like each other and enjoy one another's company. She's easy to be with.

"What happened?" Laura said.

Mel said, "He shot himself in the mouth in his room. Someone heard the shot and told the manager. They came in with a passkey, saw what had happened, and called an ambulance. I happened to be there when they brought him in, alive but past recall. The man lived for three days. His head swelled up to twice the size of a normal head. I'd never seen anything like it, and I hope I never do again. Terri wanted to go in and sit with him when she found out about it. We had a fight over it. I didn't think she should see him like that. I didn't think she should see him, and I still don't."

"Who won the fight?" Laura said.

"I was in the room with him when he died," Terri said. "He never came up out of it. But I sat with him. He didn't have anyone else."

"He was dangerous," Mel said. "If you call that love, you can have it."

"It was love," Terri said. "Sure, it's abnormal in most people's eyes. But he was willing to die for it. He did die for it."

"I sure as hell wouldn't call it love," Mel said. "I mean, no one knows what he did it for. I've seen a lot of suicides, and I couldn't say anyone ever knew what they did it for."

Mel put his hands behind his neck and tilted his chair back. "I'm not interested in that kind of love," he said. "If that's love, you can have it."

Terri said, "We were afraid. Mel even made a will out and wrote to his brother in California who used to be a Green Beret. Mel told him who to look for if something happened to him."

Terri drank from her glass. She said, "But Mel's right—we lived like fugitives. We were afraid. Mel was, weren't you, honey? I even called the police at one point, but they were no help. They said they couldn't do anything until Ed actually did something. Isn't that a laugh?" Terri said.

She poured the last of the gin into her glass and waggled the bottle. Mel got up from the table and went to the cupboard. He took down another bottle.

"Well, Nick and I know what love is," Laura said. "For us, I mean," Laura said. She bumped my knee with her knee. "You're supposed to say something now," Laura said, and turned her smile on me.

For an answer, I took Laura's hand and raised it to my lips. I made a big production out of kissing her hand. Everyone was amused.

"We're lucky," I said.

"You guys," Terri said. "Stop that now. You're making me sick. You're still on the honeymoon, for God's sake. You're still gaga, for crying out loud. Just wait. How long have you been together now? How long has it been? A year? Longer than a year?"

"Going on a year and a half," Laura said, flushed and smiling.

"Oh, now," Terri said. "Wait awhile."

She held her drink and gazed at Laura.

"I'm only kidding," Terri said.

Mel opened the gin and went around the table with the bottle.

"Here, you guys," he said. "Let's have a toast. I want to propose a toast. A toast to love. To true love," Mel said.

We touched glasses.

"To love," we said.

Outside in the backyard, one of the dogs began to bark. The leaves of the aspen that leaned past the window ticked against the glass. The afternoon sun was like a presence in this room, the spacious light of ease and generosity. We could have been anywhere, somewhere enchanted. We raised our glasses again and grinned at each other like children who had agreed on something forbidden.

"I'll tell you what real love is," Mel said. "I mean, I'll give you a good example. And then you can draw your own conclusions." He poured more gin into his glass. He added an ice cube and a sliver of lime. We waited and sipped our drinks. Laura and I touched knees again. I put a hand on her warm thigh and left it there.

"What do any of us really know about love?" Mel said. "It seems to me we're just beginners at love. We say we love each other and we do, I don't doubt it. I love Terri and Terri loves me, and you guys love each other too. You know the kind of love I'm talking about now. Physical love, that impulse that drives you to someone special, as well as love of the other person's being, his or her essence, as it were. Carnal love and, well, call it sentimental love, the day-to-day caring about the other person. But sometimes I have a hard time accounting for the fact that I must have loved my first wife too. But I did, I know I did. So I suppose I am like Terri in that regard. Terri and Ed." He thought about it and then he went on. "There was a time when I thought I loved my first wife more than life itself. But now I hate her guts. I do. How do you explain that? What happened to that love? What happened to it, is what I'd like to know. I wish someone could tell me. Then there's Ed. Okay, we're back to Ed. He loves Terri so much he tries to kill her and he winds up killing himself." Mel stopped talking and swallowed from his glass. "You guys have been together eighteen months and you love each other. It shows all over you. You glow with it. But you both loved other people before you met each other. You've both been married before, just like us. And you probably loved other people before that too, even. Terri and I have been together five years, been married for four. And the terrible thing, the terrible thing is, but the good thing too, the saving grace, you might say, is that if something happened to one of us— excuse me for saying this—but if something happened to one of us tomorrow, I think the other one, the other person, would grieve for a while, you know, but then the surviving party would go out and love again, have someone else soon enough. All this, all of this love we're talking about, it would just be a memory. Maybe not even a memory. Am I wrong? Am I way off base? Because I want you to set me straight if you think I'm wrong. I want to know. I mean, I don't know anything, and I'm the first one to admit it."

"Mel, for God's sake," Terri said. She reached out and took hold of his wrist. "Are you getting drunk? Honey? Are you drunk?"

"Honey, I'm just talking," Mel said. "All right? I don't have to be drunk to say what I think. I mean, we're all just talking, right?" Mel said. He fixed his eyes on her.

"Sweetie, I'm not criticizing," Terri said.

She picked up her glass.

"I'm not on call today," Mel said. "Let me remind you of that. I am not on call," he said.

"Mel, we love you," Laura said.

Mel looked at Laura. He looked at her as if he could not place her, as if she was not the woman she was.

"Love you too, Laura," Mel said. "And you, Nick, love you too. You know something?" Mel said. "You guys are our pals," Mel said.

He picked up his glass.

Mel said, "I was going to tell you about something. I mean, I was going to prove a point. You see, this happened a few months ago, but it's still going on right now, and it ought to make us feel ashamed when we talk like we know what we're talking about when we talk about love."

"Come on now," Terri said. "Don't talk like you're drunk if you're not drunk."

"Just shut up for once in your life," Mel said very quietly. "Will you do me a favor and do that for a minute? So as I was saying, there's this old couple who had this car wreck out on the interstate. A kid hit them and they were all torn to shit and nobody was giving them much chance to pull through."

Terri looked at us and then back at Mel. She seemed anxious, or maybe that's too strong a word.

Mel was handing the bottle around the table.

"I was on call that night," Mel said. "It was May or maybe it was June. Terri and I had just sat down to dinner when the hospital called. There'd been this thing out on the interstate. Drunk kid, teenager, plowed his dad's pickup into this camper with this old couple in it. They were up in their mid-seventies, that couple. The kid—eighteen, nineteen, something—he was DOA. Taken the steering wheel through his sternum. The old couple, they were alive, you understand. I mean, just barely. But they had every-thing. Multiple fractures, internal injuries, hemorrhaging, contusions, lacera-tions, the works, and they each of them had themselves concussions. They were in a bad way, believe me. And, of course, their age was two strikes against them. I'd say she was worse off than he was. Ruptured spleen along with everything else. Both kneecaps broken. But they'd been wearing their seatbelts and, God knows, that's what saved them for the time being."

"Folks, this is an advertisement for the National Safety Council," Terri said. "This is your spokesman, Dr. Melvin R. McGinnis, talking." Terri laughed. "Mel," she said, "sometimes you're just too much. But I love you, hon," she said.

"Honey, I love you," Mel said.

He leaned across the table. Terri met him halfway. They kissed.

"Terri's right," Mel said as he settled himself again. "Get those seatbelts on. But seriously, they were in some shape, those oldsters. By the time I got down there, the kid was dead, as I said. He was off in a corner, laid out on a gurney. I took one look at the old couple and told the ER nurse to get me a neurologist and an orthopedic man and a couple of surgeons down there right away."

He drank from his glass. "I'll try to keep this short," he said. "So we took the two of them up to the OR and worked like fuck on them most of the night. They had these incredible reserves, those two. You see that once in a while. So we did everything that could be done, and toward morning we're giving them a fifty–fifty chance, maybe less than that for her. So here they are, still alive the next morning. So, okay, we move them into the ICU, which is where they both kept plugging away at it for two weeks, hitting it better and better on all the scopes. So we transfer them out to their own room."

Mel stopped talking. "Here," he said, "let's drink this cheapo gin the hell up. Then we're going to dinner, right? Terri and I know a new place. That's where we'll go, to this new place we know about. But we're not going until we finish up this cut-rate, lousy gin."

Terri said, "We haven't actually eaten there yet. But it looks good. From the outside, you know."

"I like food," Mel said. "If I had it to do all over again, I'd be a chef, you know? Right, Terri?" Mel said.

He laughed. He fingered the ice in his glass.

"Terri knows," he said. "Terri can tell you. But let me say this. If I could come back again in a different life, a different time and all, you know what? I'd like to come back as a knight. You were pretty safe wearing all that armor. It was all right being a knight until gunpowder and muskets and pistols came along."

"Mel would like to ride a horse and carry a lance," Terri said.

"Carry a woman's scarf with you everywhere," Laura said.

"Or just a woman," Mel said.

"Shame on you," Laura said.

Terri said, "Suppose you came back as a serf. The serfs didn't have it so good in those days," Terri said.

"The serfs never had it good," Mel said. "But I guess even the knights were vessels to someone. Isn't that the way it worked? But then everyone is always a vessel to someone. Isn't that right? Terri? But what I liked about knights, besides their ladies, was that they had that suit of armor, you know, and they couldn't get hurt very easy. No cars in those days, you know? No drunk teenagers to tear into your ass."

"Vassals," Terri said.

"What?" Mel said.

"Vassals," Terri said. "They were called vassals, not vessels."

"Vassals, vessels," Mel said, "what the fuck's the difference? You knew what I meant anyway. All right," Mel said. "So I'm not educated. I learned my stuff. I'm a heart surgeon, sure, but I'm just a mechanic. I go in and I fuck around and I fix things. Shit," Mel said.

"Modesty doesn't become you," Terri said.

"He's just a humble sawbones," I said. "But sometimes they suffocated in all that armor, Mel. They'd even have heart attacks if it got too hot and they were too tired and worn out. I read somewhere that they'd fall off their horses and not be able to get up because they were too tired to stand with all that armor on them. They got trampled by their own horses sometimes."

"That's terrible," Mel said. "That's a terrible thing, Nicky. I guess they'd just lay there and wait until somebody came along and made a shish kebab out of them."

"Some other vessel," Terri said.

"That's right," Mel said. "Some vassal would come along and spear the bastard in the name of love. Or whatever the fuck it was they fought over in those days."

"Same things we fight over these days," Terri said.

Laura said, "Nothing's changed."

The color was still high in Laura's cheeks. Her eyes were bright. She brought her glass to her lips.

Mel poured himself another drink. He looked at the label closely as if studying a long row of numbers. Then he slowly put the bottle down on the table and slowly reached for the tonic water.

"What about the old couple?" Laura said. "You didn't finish that story you started."

Laura was having a hard time lighting her cigarette. Her matches kept going out.

The sunshine inside the room was different now, changing, getting thinner. But the leaves outside the window were still shimmering, and I stared at the pattern they made on the panes and on the Formica counter. They weren't the same patterns, of course.

"What about the old couple?" I said.

"Older but wiser," Terri said.

Mel stared at her.

Terri said, "Go on with your story, hon. I was only kidding. Then what happened?"

"Terri, sometimes," Mel said.

"Please, Mel," Terri said. "Don't always be so serious, sweetie. Can't you take a joke?"

"Where's the joke?" Mel said.

He held his glass and gazed steadily at his wife.

"What happened?" Laura said.

Mel fastened his eyes on Laura. He said, "Laura, if I didn't have Terri and if I didn't love her so much, and if Nick wasn't my best friend, I'd fall in love with you. I'd carry you off, honey," he said.

"Tell your story," Terri said. "Then we'll go to that new place, okay?"

"Okay," Mel said. "Where was I?" he said. He stared at the table and then he began again.

"I dropped in to see each of them every day, sometimes twice a day if I was up doing other calls anyway. Casts and bandages, head to foot, the both of them. You know, you've seen it in the movies. That's just the way they looked, just like in the movies. Little eye-holes and nose-holes and mouth-holes. And she had to have her legs slung up on top of it. Well, the husband was very depressed for the longest while. Even after he found out that his wife was going to pull through, he was still very depressed. Not about the accident, though. I mean, the accident was one thing, but it wasn't everything. I'd get up to his mouth-hole, you know, and he'd say no, it wasn't the accident exactly but it was because he couldn't see her through his eye-holes. He said that was what was making him feel so bad. Can you imagine? I'm telling you, the man's heart was breaking because he couldn't turn his goddamn head and *see* his goddamn wife."

Mel looked around the table and shook his head at what he was going to say.

"I mean, it was killing the old fart just because he couldn't *look* at the fucking woman."

We all looked at Mel.

"Do you see what I'm saying?" he said.

Maybe we were a little drunk by then. I know it was hard keeping things in focus. The light was draining out of the room, going back through the window where it had come from. Yet nobody made a move to get up from the table to turn on the overhead light.

"Listen," Mel said. "Let's finish this fucking gin. There's about enough left here for one shooter all around. Then let's go eat. Let's go to the new place."

"He's depressed," Terri said. "Mel, why don't you take a pill?"

Mel shook his head. "I've taken everything there is."

"We all need a pill now and then," I said.

"Some people are born needing them," Terri said.

She was using her finger to rub at something on the table. Then she stopped rubbing.

"I think I want to call my kids," Mel said. "Is that all right with everybody? I'll call my kids," he said.

Terri said, "What if Marjorie answers the phone? You guys, you've heard us on the subject of Marjorie? Honey, you know you don't want to talk to Marjorie. It'll make you feel even worse."

"I don't want to talk to Marjorie," Mel said. "But I want to talk to my kids."

"There isn't a day goes by that Mel doesn't say he wishes she'd get married again. Or else die," Terri said. "For one thing," Terri said, "she's bankrupting us. Mel says it's just to spite him that she won't get married again. She has a boyfriend who lives with her and the kids, so Mel is supporting the boyfriend too."

"She's allergic to bees," Mel said. "If I'm not praying she'll get married again, I'm praying she'll get herself stung to death by a swarm of fucking bees."

"Shame on you," Laura said.

"Bzzzzzzz," Mel said, turning his fingers into bees and buzzing them at Terri's throat. Then he let his hands drop all the way to his sides.

"She's vicious," Mel said. "Sometimes I think I'll go up there dressed like a beekeeper. You know, that hat that's like a helmet with the plate that comes down over your face, the big gloves, and the padded coat? I'll knock on the door and let loose a hive of bees in the house. But first I'd make sure the kids were out, of course."

He crossed one leg over the other. It seemed to take him a lot of time to do it. Then he put both feet on the floor and leaned forward, elbows on the table, his chin cupped in his hands.

"Maybe I won't call the kids, after all. Maybe it isn't such a hot idea. Maybe we'll just go eat. How does that sound?"

"Sounds fine to me," I said. "Eat or not eat. Or keep drinking. I could head right on out into the sunset."

"What does that mean, honey?" Laura said.

"It just means what I said," I said. "It means I could just keep going. That's all it means."

"I could eat something myself," Laura said. "I don't think I've ever been so hungry in my life. Is there something to nibble on?"

"I'll put out some cheese and crackers," Terri said.

But Terri just sat there. She did not get up to get anything.

Mel turned his glass over. He spilled it out on the table.

"Gin's gone," Mel said.

Terri said, "Now what?"

I could hear my heart beating. I could hear everyone's heart. I could hear the human noise we sat there making, not one of us moving, not even when the room went dark.

Suggestions for Discussion

1. In what respects does the setting for the discussion between the two couples affect the dialogue?

2. Characterize each of the participants by referring to their behavior, their expressions of love, and their attitudes toward love. For example, how do Terri and Mel differ in their views of love?

3. What to Mel is both the "terrible thing" and the "saving grace" about love?

4. What is the significance of Mel's story about the elderly couple whom he treated in the hospital? Why does he use vulgar language in describing their relationship? Mel has earlier described love as carnal and sentimental. How adequate are those adjectives in describing the love of the elderly couple?

5. Why is Mel's story of the elderly couple troubling to Nick and Laura? How do you know?

6. Note the changes in Mel's statements about love. To what extent are his differing statements of attitude affected by his drinking? By his earlier years in the seminary? By his profession as a cardiologist?

7. Are there discrepancies between Mel's views and his behavior? Why do you think he is a pill taker?

Suggestions for Writing

1. You have read a number of writers on the meaning of love. Drawing upon these readings, and your experience and observation, develop in either narrative or expository form your feelings and thoughts about love.

2. Interview a number of your contemporaries. What appears to be their sense of the meaning of love? To what extent is their behavior consonant with their attitude?

Katherine Anne Porter

Rope

Katherine Anne Porter (1890–1980), American short-story writer, novelist, and critic, was born in Texas and educated in convent schools in Texas and New Orleans. She was a visiting lecturer at numerous colleges and universities and lived and traveled in Mexico, Germany, and France. Her books include *Flowering Judas* (1930); *Noon-Wine* (1937); *Pale Horse, Pale Rider* (1939); critical essays, *The Days Before* (1952); and a novel, *Ship of Fools* (1962). In "Rope," the frustration of husband and wife, expressed in displaced anger, is followed by an expression of the more enduring ties of a shared life.

On the third day after they moved to the country he came walking back from the village carrying a basket of groceries and a twenty-four-yard coil of rope. She came out to meet him, wiping her hands on her green smock. Her hair was tumbled, her nose was scarlet with sunburn; he told her that already she looked like a born country woman. His gray flannel shirt stuck to him, his heavy shoes were dusty. She assured him he looked like a rural character in a play.

Had he brought the coffee? She had been waiting all day long for coffee. They had forgot it when they ordered at the store the first day.

Gosh, no, he hadn't. Lord, now he'd have to go back. Yes, he would if it killed him. He thought, though, he had everything else. She reminded him it was only because he didn't drink coffee himself. If he did he would remember it quick enough. Suppose they ran out of cigarettes? Then she saw the rope. What was that for? Well, he thought it might do to hang clothes on, or something. Naturally, she asked him if he thought they were going to run a laundry. They already had a fifty-foot line hanging right before his eyes. Why, hadn't he noticed it, really? It was a blot on the landscape to her.

He thought there were a lot of things a rope might come in handy for. She wanted to know what, for instance. He thought a few seconds, but nothing occurred. They could wait and see, couldn't they? You need all sorts of strange odds and ends around a place in the country. She said, yes, that was so; but she thought just at that time when every penny counted, it seemed funny to buy more rope. That was all. She hadn't meant anything else. She hadn't just seen, not at first, why he felt it was necessary.

Well, thunder, he had bought it because he wanted to, and that was all there was to it. She thought that was reason enough, and couldn't understand why he hadn't said so, at first. Undoubtedly it would be useful, twenty-four yards of rope, there were hundreds of things, she couldn't think of any at the moment, but it would come in. Of course. As he had said, things always did in the country.

But she was a little disappointed about the coffee, and oh, look, look, look at the eggs! Oh, my, they're all running! What had he put on top of them? Hadn't he known eggs mustn't be squeezed? Squeezed, who had squeezed them, he wanted to know. What a silly thing to say. He had simply brought them along in the basket with the other things. If they got broke it was the grocer's fault. He should know better than to put heavy things on top of eggs.

She believed it was the rope. That was the heaviest thing in the pack, she saw him plainly when he came in from the road, the rope was a big package on top of everything. He desired the whole wide world to witness that this was not a fact. He had carried the rope in one hand and the basket in the other, and what was the use of her having eyes if that was the best they could do for her?

Well, anyhow, she could see one thing plain: no eggs for breakfast. They'd have to scramble them now, for supper. It was too damned bad. She had planned to have steak for supper. No ice, meat wouldn't keep. He wanted to know why she couldn't finish breaking the eggs in a bowl and set them in a cool place.

Cool place! if he could find one for her, she'd be glad to set them there. Well, then, it seemed to him they might very well cook the meat at the same time they cooked the eggs and then warm up the meat for tomorrow. The idea simply choked her. Warmed-over meat, when they might as well have had it fresh. Second best and scraps and makeshifts, even to the meat! He rubbed her shoulder a little. It doesn't really matter so much, does it, darling? Sometimes when they were playful, he would rub her shoulder and she would arch and purr. This time she hissed and almost clawed. He was getting ready to say that they could surely manage somehow when she turned on him and said, if he told her they could manage somehow she would certainly slap his face.

He swallowed the words red hot, his face burned. He picked up the rope and started to put it on the top shelf. She would not have it on the top shelf, the jars and tins belonged there; positively she would not have the top shelf cluttered up with a lot of rope. She had borne all the clutter she meant to bear in the flat in town, there was space here at least and she meant to keep things in order.

Well, in that case, he wanted to know what the hammer and nails were doing up there? And why had she put them there when she knew very well he needed that hammer and those nails upstairs to fix the window sashes? She simply slowed down everything and made double work on the place with her insane habit of changing things around and hiding them.

She was sure she begged his pardon, and if she had had any reason to believe he was going to fix the sashes this summer she would have left the hammer and nails right where he put them; in the middle of the bedroom floor where they could step on them in the dark. And now if he didn't clear the whole mess out of there she would throw them down the well.

Oh, all right, all right—could he put them in the closet? Naturally not, there were brooms and mops and dustpans in the closet, and why couldn't he find a place for his rope outside her kitchen? Had he stopped to consider there were seven God-forsaken rooms in the house, and only one kitchen?

He wanted to know what of it? And did she realize she was making a complete fool of herself? And what did she take him for, a three-year-old idiot? The whole trouble with her was she needed something weaker than she was to heckle and tyrannize over. He wished to God now they had a couple of children she could take it out on. Maybe he'd get some rest.

Her face changed at this, she reminded him he had forgot the coffee and had bought a worthless piece of rope. And when she thought of all the things they actually needed to make the place even decently fit to live in, well, she could cry, that was all. She looked so forlorn, so lost and despairing he couldn't believe it was only a piece of rope that was causing all the racket. What *was* the matter, for God's sake?

Oh, would he please hush and go away, and *stay* away, if he could, for five minutes? By all means, yes, he would. He'd stay away indefinitely if she wished. Lord, yes, there was nothing he'd like better than to clear out and never come back. She couldn't for the life of her see what was holding him, then. It was a swell time. Here she was, stuck, miles from a railroad, with a half-empty house on her hands, and not a penny in her pocket, and everything on earth to do; it seemed the God-sent moment for him to get out from under. She was surprised he hadn't stayed in town as it was until she had come out and done the work and got things straightened out. It was his usual trick.

It appeared to him that this was going a little far. Just a touch out of bounds, if she didn't mind his saying so. Why the hell had he stayed in town the summer before? To do a half-dozen extra jobs to get the money he had sent her. That was it. She knew perfectly well they couldn't have done it otherwise. She had agreed with him at the time. And that was the only time so help him he had ever left her to do anything by herself.

Oh, he could tell that to his great-grandmother. She had her notion of what had kept him in town. Considerably more than a notion, if he wanted to know. So, she was going to bring all that up again, was she? Well, she could just think what she pleased. He was tired of explaining. It may have looked funny but he had simply got hooked in, and what could he do? It was impossible to believe that she was going to take it seriously. Yes, yes, she knew how it was with a man: if he was left by himself a minute, some woman was certain to kidnap him. And naturally he couldn't hurt her feelings by refusing!

Well, what was she raving about? Did she forget she had told him those two weeks alone in the country were the happiest she had known for four years? And how long had they been married when she said that? All right, shut up! If she thought that hadn't stuck in his craw.

She hadn't meant she was happy because she was away from him. She meant she was happy getting the devilish house nice and ready for him. That was what she had meant, and now look! Bringing up something she had said a year ago simply to justify himself for forgetting her coffee and breaking the eggs and buying a wretched piece of rope they couldn't afford. She really thought it was time to drop the subject, and now she wanted only two things in the world. She wanted him to get that rope from underfoot, and go back to the village and get her coffee, and if he could remember it, he might bring a metal mitt for the skillets, and two more curtain rods, and if there were any rubber gloves in the village, her hands were simply raw, and a bottle of milk of magnesia from the drugstore.

He looked out at the dark blue afternoon sweltering on the slopes, and mopped his forehead and sighed heavily and said, if only she could wait a minute for *anything*, he was going back. He had said so, hadn't he, the very instant they found he had overlooked it?

Oh, yes, well . . . run along. She was going to wash windows. The country was so beautiful! She doubted they'd have a moment to enjoy it. He meant to go, but he could not until he had said that if she wasn't such a hopeless melancholiac she might see that this was only for a few days. Couldn't she remember anything pleasant about the other summers? Hadn't they ever had any fun? She hadn't time to talk about it, and now would he please not leave that rope lying around for her to trip on? He picked it up, somehow it had toppled off the table, and walked out with it under his arm.

Was he going this minute? He certainly was. She thought so. Sometimes it seemed to her he had second sight about the precisely perfect moment to leave her ditched. She had meant to put the mattresses out to sun, if they put them out this minute they would get at least three hours, he must have heard her say that morning she meant to put them out. So of course he would walk off and leave her to it. She supposed he thought the exercise would do her good.

Well, he was merely going to get her coffee. A four-mile walk for two pounds of coffee was ridiculous, but he was perfectly willing to do it. The habit was making a wreck of her, but if she wanted to wreck herself there was nothing he could do about it. If he thought it was coffee that was making a wreck of her, she congratulated him: he must have a damned easy conscience.

Conscience or no conscience, he didn't see why the mattresses couldn't very well wait until tomorrow. And anyhow, for God's sake, were they living in the house, or were they going to let the house ride them to death? She paled at this, her face grew livid about the mouth, she looked quite dangerous, and reminded him that housekeeping was no more her work than it was his: she had other work to do as well, and when did he think she was going to find time to do it at this rate?

Was she going to start on that again? She knew as well as he did that his work brought in the regular money, hers was only occasional, if they depended on what *she* made—and she might as well get straight on this question once for all!

That was positively not the point. The question was, when both of them were working on their own time, was there going to be a division of the housework, or wasn't there? She merely wanted to know, she had to make her plans. Why, he thought that was all arranged. It was understood that he was to help. Hadn't he always, in summers?

Hadn't he, though? Oh, just hadn't he? And when, and where, and doing what? Lord, what an uproarious joke!

It was such a very uproarious joke that her face turned slightly purple, and she screamed with laughter. She laughed so hard she had to sit down, and finally a rush of tears spurted from her eyes and poured down into the lifted corners of her mouth. He dashed towards her and dragged her up to her feet and tried to pour water on her head. The dipper hung by a string on a nail and he broke it loose. Then he tried to pump water with one hand while she struggled in the other. So he gave it up and shook her instead.

She wrenched away, crying for him to take his rope and go to hell, she had simply given him up: and ran. He heard her high-heeled bedroom slippers clattering and stumbling on the stairs.

He went out around the house into the lane; he suddenly realized he had a blister on his heel and his shirt felt as if it were on fire. Things broke so suddenly you didn't know where you were. She could work herself into a fury about simply nothing. She was terrible, damn it: not an ounce of reason. You might as well talk to a sieve as that woman when she got going. Damned if he'd spend his life humoring her! Well, what to do now? He would take back the rope and exchange it for something else. Things accumulated, things were mountainous, you couldn't move them or sort them out or get rid of them. They just lay around and rotted. He'd take it back. Hell, why should he? He wanted it. What was it anyhow? A piece of rope. Imagine anybody caring more about a piece of rope than about a man's feelings. What earthly right had she to say a word about it? He remembered all the useless, meaningless things she bought for herself: Why? because I wanted it; that's why! He stopped and selected a large stone by the road. He would put the rope behind it. He would put it in the tool-box when he got back. He'd heard enough about it to last him a life-time.

When he came back she was leaning against the post box beside the road waiting. It was pretty late, the smell of broiled steak floated nose high in the cooling air. Her face was young and smooth and fresh looking. Her unmanageable funny black hair was all on end. She waved to him from a distance, and he speeded up. She called out that supper was ready and waiting, was he starved?

You bet he was starved. Here was the coffee. He waved it at her. She looked at his other hand. What was that he had there?

Well, it was the rope again. He stopped short. He had meant to exchange it but forgot. She wanted to know why he should exchange it, if it was something he really wanted. Wasn't the air sweet now, and wasn't it fine to be here?

She walked beside him with one hand hooked into his leather belt. She pulled and jostled him a little as he walked, and leaned against him. He put his arm clear around her and patted her stomach. They exchanged wary smiles. Coffee, coffee for the Ootsum-Wootsums! He felt as if he were bringing her a beautiful present.

He was a love, she firmly believed, and if she had had her coffee in the morning, she wouldn't have behaved so funny . . . There was a whippoorwill still coming back, imagine, clear out of season, sitting in the crab-apple tree calling all by himself. Maybe his girl stood him up. Maybe she did. She hoped to hear him once more, she loved whippoorwills . . . He knew how she was, didn't he?

Sure, he knew how she was.

Suggestions for Discussion

1. Think of the multiple uses of rope and determine the ways in which the title serves as a metaphor for the quarrel and the bond between husband and wife. What does the phrase "enough rope" connote? How might it relate to the story?

2. What is the purpose of the indirect approach to the narrative through a third-person narrator? Is it more or less effective than if told from the point of view of husband or wife? Account for the frequent questions and their effect.

3. With what details are the character of husband and wife revealed?

4. What are the ostensible and real causes of the quarrel? Is the mechanism of displacement at work? Explain.

5. How do you learn of the husband and wife's economic situation?

6. How serious was the husband's threat to go away? How did the wife respond?

7. Account for the shift in tone on the husband's return. What other changes in tone do you find?

8. What does the introduction of the whippoorwill add to the resolution of the story?

9. Why was the wife particularly incensed at the time the husband asked if they were "going to let the house ride them to death"?

10. What effect is achieved by referring to the characters as husband and wife rather than as Dan and Mary or other proper names?

11. In what sense is this a story of affirmation?

Suggestions for Writing

1. Retell the story from the wife's or the husband's point of view.

2. Discuss the mechanism of displacement in human relationships. Account for it and illustrate it.

3. Argue for or against the idea that the title "Rope" is symbolic of the relationship. If you were to retitle the story, what title would you give it and why?

Poetry

William Shakespeare

When in Disgrace with Fortune and Men's Eyes (Sonnet 29)

Let Me Not to the Marriage of True Minds (Sonnet 116)

William Shakespeare (1564–1616) is generally acknowledged to be the greatest playwright in the English language. He was born in Stratford-upon-Avon, England. By 1592 he had become an actor and playwright in London, and in 1599 he helped establish the famous Globe Theatre. In addition to the sonnets, his works include historical plays, comedies such as A *Midsummer Night's Dream*, and tragedies such as *Macbeth, Hamlet, King Lear,* and *Othello.* The self-doubt in Sonnet 29 is resolved with the poet's thoughts of his love. In Sonnet 116 the poet attests to the inviolability and permanence of love.

Sonnet 29

When, in disgrace with fortune and men's eyes,
I all alone beweep my outcast state,
And trouble deaf heaven with my bootless cries,
And look upon myself and curse my fate;
Wishing me like to one more rich in hope,
Featured like him, like him with friends possessed,
Desiring this man's art, and that man's scope,
With what I most enjoy contented least;
Yet in these thoughts myself almost despising,
Haply I think on thee, and then my state,
Like to the lark at break of day arising
From sullen earth, sings hymns at heaven's gate;
For thy sweet love remembered such wealth brings
That then I scorn to change my state with kings.

Sonnet 116

Let me not to the marriage of true minds
Admit impediments. Love is not love
Which alters when it alteration finds,
Or bends with the remover to remove:
Oh, no! it is an ever-fixed mark,
That looks on tempests and is never shaken;

It is the star to every wandering bark,
Whose worth's unknown, although his height be taken.
Love's not Time's fool, though rosy lips and cheeks
Within his bending sickle's compass come;
Love alters not with his brief hours and weeks,
But bears it out even to the edge of doom.
If this be error and upon me proved,
I never writ, nor no man ever loved.

Suggestions for Discussion

1. How does the imagery in each of the sonnets contribute to its unity?

2. How does dramatic understatement at the end of the second of the two sonnets reinforce the theme?

William Blake

The Clod and the Pebble
The Garden of Love

William Blake (1757–1827), poet and artist, illustrated his poems with his own engravings. His works include *Songs of Innocence* (1789), *Songs of Experience* (1794), *The Marriage of Heaven and Hell* (1790), *The Gates of Paradise* (1793), and *Visions of the Daughters of Albion* (1793). The poems that follow suggest some of the contradictions inherent in concepts of love.

The Clod and the Pebble

"Love seeketh not Itself to please,
    Nor for itself hath any care,
But for another gives its ease,
    And builds a Heaven in Hell's despair."

So sung the Clod of Clay,
    Trodden with the cattle's feet,
But a Pebble in the brook
    Warbled out these metres meet:

"Love seeketh only Self to please,
    To bind another to its delight,
Joys in another's loss of ease,
    And builds a Hell in Heaven's Despite."

The Garden of Love

I went to the Garden of Love,
And I saw what I never had seen:
A Chapel was built in the midst,
Where I used to play on the green.

And the gates of this Chapel were shut,
And "Thou shalt not" writ over the door:
So I turned to the Garden of Love
That so many sweet flowers bore;

And I saw it was filled with graves,
And tomb-stones where flowers should be;
And Priests in black gowns were walking their rounds,
And binding with briars my joys and desires.

Suggestion for Discussion

Both of Blake's poems suggest some of the contradictions inherent in concepts of "love." What are they and what seems to be the poet's conclusion?

W. H. Auden

Lay Your Sleeping Head, My Love

Wystan Hugh Auden (1907–1973), English poet educated at Oxford University, was early recognized as a leader of the poets of his generation. His poetry collections include *The Orators* (1932), *The Double Man* (1941), *The Shield of Achilles* (1955), *Homage to Clio* (1960), *About the House* (1965), and *The Age of Anxiety* (1947), which won a Pulitzer Prize in 1948. His autobiography, *Certain World: A Commonplace Book*, was published in 1970. Auden also experimented with drama, and his criticism was collected in *The Dyer's Hand* in 1963. In 1967 he was made a fellow of Christ College, Oxford. The writer speaks of the threats to love in this poem that weaves back and forth between the present and future, the concrete and abstract.

Lay your sleeping head, my love,
Human on my faithless arm;
Time and fevers burn away
Individual beauty from
Thoughtful children, and the grave
Proves the child ephemeral:

But in my arms till break of day
Let the living creature lie,
Mortal, guilty, but to me
The entirely beautiful.

Soul and body have no bounds:
To lovers as they lie upon
Her tolerant enchanted slope
In their ordinary swoon,
Grave the vision Venus sends
Of supernatural sympathy,
Universal love and hope;
While an abstract insight wakes
Among the glaciers and the rocks
The hermit's sensual ecstasy.
Eye and knocking heart may bless,

Certainty, fidelity
On the stroke of midnight pass
Like vibrations of a bell,
And fashionable madmen raise
Their pedantic boring cry:
Every farthing of the cost,
All the dreaded cards foretell,
Shall be paid, but from this night
Not a whisper, not a thought,
Not a kiss nor look be lost.

Beauty, midnight, vision dies:
Let the winds of dawn that blow
Softly round your dreaming head
Such a day of sweetness show
Eye and knocking heart may bless,
Find the mortal world enough;
Noons of dryness see you fed
By the involuntary powers,
Nights of insult let you pass
Watched by every human love.

Suggestions for Discussion

1. What images are employed by the speaker to suggest the hazards of love?

2. Account for the movement from present to future and from particular to general.

Edna St. Vincent Millay

Love Is Not All

Edna St. Vincent Millay (1892–1950), American poet, wrote "Renascence," her first major poem, while she was still in college. Her early works such as *A Few Figs from Thistles* (1920) exhibited a cynical flippancy that deepened into bitter disillusionment in later works such as *The Harp-Weaver and Other Poems* (1923), a Pulitzer Prize selection, and *The Buck in the Snow* (1928). In this sonnet the poet exalts the power of love.

> Love is not all; it is not meat nor drink
> Nor slumber nor a roof against the rain,
> Nor yet a floating spar to men that sink
> And rise and sink and rise and sink again;
> Love can not fill the thickened lung with breath,
> Nor clean the blood, nor set the fractured bone;
> Yet many a man is making friends with death
> Even as I speak, for lack of love alone.
> It well may be that in a difficult hour,
> Pinned down by pain and moaning for release,
> Or nagged by want past resolution's power,
> I might be driven to sell your love for peace,
> To trade the memory of this night for food.
> It well may be. I do not think I would.

E. E. Cummings

I Like My Body When It Is with Your

E. E. Cummings (1894–1962) was an American whose book *The Enormous Room* (1922) and whose poetry *&* and *XLI Poems* (1925) established his reputation as an avant-garde writer interested in experimenting with stylistic techniques. Awarded several important prizes for poetry, he was also Charles Eliot Norton Lecturer at Harvard University in 1952 and wrote *i: six nonlectures* (1953). The repetitions and typography as well as the sensory detail contribute to Cummings's expression of joy in physical love.

i like my body when it is with your
body. It is so quite new a thing.
Muscles better and nerves more.
i like your body. i like what it does,
i like its hows. i like to feel the spine
of your body and its bones, and the trembling
-firm-smooth ness and which i will
again and again and again
kiss, i like kissing this and that of you,
i like, slowly stroking the, shocking fuzz
of your electric fur, and what-is-it comes
over parting flesh . . . . And eyes big love-crumbs,

and possibly i like the thrill

of under me you so quite new

Suggestions for Discussion

1. Account for the appeal of the poem.

2. How do the repetitions and the typography contribute to the poem's effectiveness?
   What distinguishes this poem from prose?

Adrienne Rich

Living in Sin
Rape

Adrienne Rich (b. 1929), contemporary American poet, is the author of, among others, A Change of World (1951), The Diamond Cutters (1955), Snapshots of a Daughter-in-Law (1963), Necessities of Life (1966), Of Woman Born (1976), Of Your Native Land, Your Life (1986), An Atlas of the Difficult World (1991), and What Is Found There (1993). She has contributed to such magazines as Poetry, The Nation, and The New York Review of Books. Her awards include a Guggenheim grant, the National Book Award (1976), the Ruth Lilly Poetry Prize (1986), and a MacArthur foundation grant. The graphic physical images in "Living in Sin" suggest that the lovers are emerging from an illusory world into a world of reality. "Rape," published in Diving Into the Wreck (1973), reflects the poet's anger in her ironic attribution of the crime and the portrait of the cop who is pleased by the hysteria of the speaker's voice.

Living in Sin

She had thought the studio would keep itself;
no dust upon the furniture of love.

Half heresy, to wish the taps less vocal,
the panes relieved of grime. A plate of pears,
a piano with a Persian shawl, a cat
stalking the picturesque amusing mouse
had risen at his urging.
Not that at five each separate stair would writhe
under the milkman's tramp; that morning light
so coldly would delineate the scraps
of last night's cheese and three sepulchral bottles;
that on the kitchen shelf among the saucers
a pair of beetle-eyes would fix her own—
envoy from some black village in the mouldings . . .
Meanwhile he, with a yawn,
sounded a dozen notes upon the keyboard,
declared it out of tune, shrugged at the mirror,
rubbed at his beard, went out for cigarettes;
while she, jeered by the minor demons,
pulled back the sheets and made the bed and found
a towel to dust the table-top,
and let the coffee-pot boil over on the stove.
By evening she was back in love again,
though not so wholly but throughout the night
she woke sometimes to feel the daylight coming
like a relentless milkman up the stairs.

Suggestions for Discussion

1. What physical images in the studio scene imply that the lovers are emerging from an illusory world into a world of reality?

2. Comment on the irony of the title. Do you perceive an end or a beginning to the relationship? Consider the clues in the final lines.

Rape

There is a cop who is both prowler and father:
he comes from your block, grew up with your brothers,
had certain ideals.
You hardly know him in his boots and silver badge,
on horseback, one hand touching his gun.

You hardly know him but you have to get to know him:
he has access to machinery that could kill you.
He and his stallion clop like warlords among the trash,
his ideals stand in the air, a frozen cloud
from between his unsmiling lips.

And so, when the time comes, you have to turn to him,
the maniac's sperm still greasing your thighs,
your mind whirling like crazy. You have to confess
to him, you are guilty of the crime
of having been forced.

And you see his blue eyes, the blue eyes of all the family
whom you used to know, grow narrow and glisten,
his hand types out the details
and he wants them all
but the hysteria in your voice pleases him best.

You hardly know him but now he thinks he knows you:
he has taken down your worst moment
on a machine and filed it in a file.
He knows, or thinks he knows, how much you imagined;
he knows, or thinks he knows, what you secretly wanted.

He has access to machinery that could get you put away;
and if, in the sickening light of the precinct,
and if, in the sickening light of the precinct,
your details sound like a portrait of your confessor,
will you swallow, will you deny them, will you lie your way home?

Suggestions for Discussion

1. How do the lines "you are guilty of the crime of having been forced" convey the author's point of view? How do you know she is being ironic?

2. With what details do you learn of the cop's pleasure in the narrator's report? How does the narrator view the cop?

3. What does the last series of questions signify?

Suggestion for Writing

Discuss the changing attitudes of society and the law toward the victims of rape.

May Swenson

Women Should Be Pedestals

May Swenson (1919–1989) is an American poet best known for *Another Animal* (1954), *A Cage of Spines* (1958), *To Mix with Time* (1963), *Poems to Solve* (1966), and *Half Sun Half Sleep* (1967). She has won numerous prizes and grants, including Guggenheim, Ford Foundation, and Rockefeller Foundation fellowships, the National Institute of Arts and Letters Award, and the

Shelley Award. The poet's anger is reflected in the pedestal and rocking horse metaphors.

Women
should be
pedestals
moving
pedestals
moving
to the
motions
of men

Or they
should be
little horses
those wooden
sweet
oldfashioned
painted
rocking
horses

the gladdest things in the toyroom

The
pegs
of their
ears
so familiar
and dear
to the trusting
fists
To be chafed

feelingly
and then
unfeelingly
To be
joyfully
ridden
rockingly
ridden until
the restored

egos dismount and the legs stride away

Immobile
sweetlipped
sturdy
and smiling
women
should always
be waiting

willing
to be set
into motion
Women
should be
pedestals
to men

Suggestions for Discussion

1. How does the central metaphor define the author's point of view? How does it contribute to tone?

2. How does the second extended metaphor contribute to purpose and tone?

3. How do alliteration and repetition function in the poem?

4. Comment on the function of the verbs and adjectives in creating mood and tone.

Suggestion for Writing

Using the same title, write an ironic sketch or poem.

The Cultural Tradition: Popular Culture

I wince when I'm called a former beauty queen or Miss U.S.A.

   —**Studs Terkel,** "Miss U.S.A."

"How can I go to work," I yelled, "when I've got so much leisure time on my hands?"

   —**Art Buchwald,** "Leisure Will Kill You"

And so the American family muddles on, dimly aware that something is amiss but distracted from an understanding of its plight by an endless stream of television images.

   —**Marie Winn,** "The Plug-in Drug: TV and the American Family"

In short, television works on the same imaginative and intellectual level as psychoactive drugs.

   —**Pete Hamill,** "Crack and the Box"

The trouble is, people nowadays simply assume that they have the right to know about everyone—and indeed, in the course of events, that they *will* know about everyone, and everyone will know about them.

   —**Roger Rosenblatt,** "Who Killed Privacy?"

We live in a rock and roll culture.

   —**Jack Santino,** "Rock and Roll as Music; Rock and Roll as Culture"

I believe that Black musicians/artists have a responsibility to be conscious of their world and to let their consciousness be heard in their songs.

   —**Bernice Reagon,** "Black Music in Our Hands"

Dinomania dramatizes a conflict between institutions with disparate purposes—museums and theme parks.

> —**Stephen Jay Gould,** "Dinomania"

By the end of my football career, I had learned that physical injury—giving it and taking it—is the real currency of the sport.

> —**John McMurtry,** "Kill 'Em! Crush 'Em! Eat 'Em Raw!"

. . . dance has in fact become a kind of physical and psychic redemption.

> —**Rob Hoerburger,** "Gotta Dance"

They was crying and crying and didn't even know what they was crying for. One day this is going to be a pitiful country, I thought.

> —**Alice Walker,** "Nineteen Fifty-Five"

Personal Reminiscence

Studs Terkel

Miss U.S.A.

Studs Terkel (b. 1912), long associated with radio station WFMT in Chicago, won the Pulitzer Prize for General Non-Fiction in 1985. He gained fame as an oral historian with the publication of Division Street (1966), Hard Times (1970), Working (1974), and American Dreams: Lost and Found (1980), from which the following selection is taken. More recent books include The Good War (1985), an oral history of World War II; The Great Divide: Second Thoughts on the American Dream (1991); and How Blacks and Whites Think and Feel About the American Obsession (1992). In "Miss U.S.A.," Terkel interviews Emma Knight, a perceptive and outspoken former beauty queen.

Emma Knight, Miss U.S.A., 1973. She is twenty-nine.

I wince when I'm called a former beauty queen or Miss U.S.A. I keep thinking they're talking about someone else. There are certain images that come to mind when people talk about beauty queens. It's mostly what's known as t and a, tits and ass. No talent. For many girls who enter the contest, it's part of the American Dream. It was never mine.

You used to sit around the TV and watch Miss America and it was exciting, we thought, glamorous. Fun, we thought. But by the time I was eight or nine, I didn't feel comfortable. Soon I'm hitting my adolescence, like fourteen, but I'm not doing any dating and I'm feeling awkward and ugly. I'm much taller than most of the people in my class. I don't feel I can compete the way I see girls competing for guys. I was very much of a loner. I felt intimidated by the amount of competition females were supposed to go through with each other. I didn't like being told by *Seventeen* magazine: Subvert your interests if you have a crush on a guy, get interested in what he's interested in. If you play cards, be sure not to beat him. I was very bad at these social games.

After I went to the University of Colorado for three and a half years, I had it. This was 1968 through '71. I came home for the summer. An agent met me and wanted me to audition for commercials, modeling, acting jobs. Okay. I started auditioning and winning some.

I did things actors do when they're starting out. You pass out literature at conventions, you do print ads, you pound the pavements, you send out your resumés. I had come to a model agency one cold day, and an agent came out and said: "I want you to enter a beauty contest." I said: "No, uh-uh, never, never, never. I'll lose, how humiliating." She said: "I want some girls to represent the agency, might do you good." So I filled out the application blank: hobbies, measurements, blah, blah, blah. I got a letter: "Congratulations. You have been accepted as an entrant into the Miss Illinois-Universe contest." Now what do I do? I'm stuck.

You have to have a sponsor. Or you're gonna have to pay several hundred dollars. So I called up the lady who was running it. Terribly sorry, I can't do this. I don't have the money. She calls back a couple of days later: "We found you a sponsor, it's a lumber company."

It was in Decatur. There were sixty-some contestants from all over the place. I went as a lumberjack: blue jeans, hiking boots, a flannel shirt, a pair of suspenders, and carrying an axe. You come out first in your costume and you introduce yourself and say your astrological sign or whatever it is they want you to say. You're wearing a banner that has the sponsor's name on it. Then you come out and do your pirouettes in your one-piece bathing suit, and the judges look at you a lot. Then you come out in your evening gown and pirouette around for a while. That's the first night.

The second night, they're gonna pick fifteen people. In between, you had judges' interviews. For three minutes, they ask you anything they want. Can you answer questions? How do you handle yourself? Your poise, personality, blah, blah, blah. They're called personality judges.

I thought: This will soon be over, get on a plane tomorrow, and no one will be the wiser. Except that my name got called as one of the fifteen. You have to go through the whole thing all over again.

I'm thinking: I don't have a prayer. I'd come to feel a certain kind of distance, except that they called my name. I was the winner, Miss Illinois. All I could do was laugh. I'm twenty-two, standing up there in a borrowed evening gown, thinking: What am I doing here: This is like Tom Sawyer becomes an altar boy.

I was considered old for a beauty queen, which is a little horrifying when you're twenty-two. That's very much part of the beauty queen syndrome: the young, untouched, unthinking human being.

I had to go to this room and sign the Miss Illinois-Universe contract right away. Miss Universe, Incorporated, is the full name of the company. It's owned by Kayser-Roth, Incorporated, which was bought out by Gulf & Western. Big business.

I'm sitting there with my glass of champagne and I'm reading over this contract. They said: "Oh, you don't have to read it." And I said: "I never sign anything that I don't read." They're all waiting to take pictures, and I'm sitting there reading this long document. So I signed it and the phone rang and the guy was from a Chicago paper and said: "Tell me, is it Miss or Ms.?" I said: "It's Ms." He said: "You're kidding." I said: "No, I'm not." He wrote an article the next day saying something like it finally happened: a beauty queen, a feminist. I thought I was a feminist before I was a beauty queen, why should I stop now?

Then I got into the publicity and training and interviews. It was a throwback to another time where crossed ankles and white gloves and teacups were present. I was taught how to walk around with a book on my head, how to sit daintily, how to pose in a bathing suit, and how to frizz my hair. They wanted curly hair, which I hate.

One day the trainer asked me to shake hands. I shook hands. She said: "That's wrong. When you shake hands with a man, you always shake hands ring up." I said: "Like the pope? Where my hand is up, like he's gonna kiss it?" Right. I thought: Holy mackerel! It was a very long February and March and April and May.

I won the Miss U.S.A. pageant. I started to laugh. They tell me I'm the only beauty queen in history that didn't cry when she won. It was on network television. I said to myself: "You're kidding." Bob Barker, the host, said: "No, I'm not kidding." I didn't know what else to say at that moment. In the press releases, they call it the great American Dream. There she is, Miss America, your ideal. Well, not my ideal, kid.

The minute you're crowned, you become their property and subject to whatever they tell you. They wake you up at seven o'clock next morning and make you put on a negligee and serve you breakfast in bed, so that all the New York papers can come in and take your picture sitting in bed, while you're absolutely bleary-eyed from the night before. They put on the Kayser-Roth negligee, hand you the tray, you take three bites. The photographers leave, you whip off the negligee, they take the breakfast away, and that's it. I never did get any breakfast that day. (Laughs).

You immediately start making personal appearances. The Jaycees or the chamber of commerce says: "I want to book Miss U.S.A. for our Christmas Day parade." They pay, whatever it is, seven hundred fifty dollars a day, first-class air fare, round trip, expenses, so forth. If the United Fund calls and wants me to give a five-minute pitch on queens at a luncheon, they still have to pay a fee. Doesn't matter that it's a charity. It's one hundred percent to Miss Universe, Incorporated. You get your salary. That's your prize money for the year. I got fifteen thousand dollars, which is all taxed in New York. Maybe out of a check of three thousand dollars, I'd get fifteen hundred dollars.

From the day I won Miss U.S.A. to the day I left for Universe, almost two months, I got a day and a half off. I made about two hundred fifty appearances that year. Maybe three hundred. Parades, shopping centers, and things. Snip ribbons. What else do you do at a shopping center? Model clothes. The nice thing I got to do was public speaking. They said: "You want a ghost writer?" I said: "Hell, no, I know how to talk." I wrote my own speeches. They don't trust girls to go out and talk because most of them can't.

One of the big execs from General Motors asked me to do a speech in Washington, D.C., on the consumer and the energy crisis. It was the fiftieth anniversary of the National Management Association. The White House, for some reason, sent me some stuff on it. I read it over, it was nonsense. So I stood up and said: "The reason we have an energy crisis is because we are, industrially and personally, pigs. We have a short-term view of the resources available to us; and unless we wake up to what we're doing to our air and our water, we'll have a dearth, not just a crisis." Oh, they weren't real pleased. (Laughs.)

What I resent most is that a lot of people didn't expect me to live this version of the American Dream for myself. I was supposed to live it their way.

When it came out in a newspaper interview that I said Nixon should resign, that he was a crook, oh dear, the fur flew. They got very upset until I got an invitation to the White House. They wanted to shut me up. The Miss Universe corporation had been trying to establish some sort of liaison with the White House for several years. I make anti-Nixon speeches and get this invitation.

I figured they're either gonna take me down to the basement and beat me up with a rubber hose or they're gonna offer me a cabinet post. They had a list of fifteen or so people I was supposed to meet. I've never seen such a bunch of people with raw nerve endings. I was dying to bring a tape recorder but thought if you mention the word "Sony" in the Nixon White House, you're in trouble. They'd have cardiac arrest. But I'm gonna bring along a pad and paper. They were patronizing. And when one of 'em got me in his office and talked about all the journalists and television people being liberals, I brought up blacklisting, *Red Channels,* and the TV industry. He changed the subject.

Miss Universe took place in Athens, Greece. The junta was still in power. I saw a heck of a lot of jeeps and troops and machine guns. The Americans were supposed to keep a low profile. I had never been a great fan of the Greek junta, but I knew darn well I was gonna have to keep my mouth shut. I was still representing the United States, for better or for worse. Miss Philippines won. I ran second.

At the end of the year, you're run absolutely ragged. That final evening, they usually have several queens from past years come back. Before they crown the new Miss U.S.A., the current one is supposed to take what they call the farewell walk. They call over the PA: Time for the old queen's walk. I'm now twenty-three and I'm an old queen. And they have this idiot farewell speech playing over the airwaves as the old queen takes the walk. And you're sitting on the throne for about thirty seconds, then you come down and they announce the name of the new one and you put the crown on her head. And then you're old.

As the new one is crowned, the reporters and photographers rush on the stage. I've seen photographers shove the girl who has just given her reign up thirty seconds before, shove her physically. I was gone by that time. I had jumped off the stage in my evening gown. It is very difficult for girls who are terrified of this ending. All of a sudden (snaps fingers), you're out. Nobody gives a damn about the old one.

Miss U.S.A. and remnants thereof is the crown stored in the attic in my parents' home. I don't even know where the banners are. It wasn't me the fans of Miss U.S.A. thought was pretty. What they think is pretty is the banner and crown. If I could put the banner and crown on that lamp, I swear to God ten men would come in and ask it for a date. I'll think about committing an axe murder if I'm not called anything but a former beauty queen. I can't stand it any more.

Several times during my year as what's-her-face I had seen the movie *The Sting.* There's a gesture the characters use which means the con is on: they rub their nose. In my last fleeting moments as Miss U.S.A., as they were playing that silly farewell speech and I walked down the aisle and stood by the throne, I looked right into the camera and rubbed my finger across my nose. The next day, the pageant people spent all their time telling people that I hadn't done it. I spent the time telling them that, of course, I had. I simply meant: the con is on. (Laughs.)

Miss U.S.A. is in the same graveyard that Emma Knight the twelve-year-old is. Where the sixteen-year-old is. All the past selves. There comes a time when you have to bury those selves because you've grown into another one. You don't keep exhuming the corpses.

If I could sit down with every young girl in America for the next fifty years, I could tell them what I liked about the pageant. I could tell them what I hated. It wouldn't make any difference. There're always gonna be girls who want to enter the beauty pageant. That's the fantasy: the American Dream.

Suggestions for Discussion

1. What sequence of events led Emma Knight to win the title of Miss U.S.A.?

2. Describe her life as Miss U.S.A.

3. What evidence does she show of her interest in politics? In women's rights?

4. For what reasons does she signal "the con is on" at the end of her reign?

Suggestions for Writing

1. Explain why Emma Knight believes there will always be "girls who want to enter the beauty pageant." Do you agree?

2. Describe a contest in which you were a participant. Use details that the casual observer would not know.

Essays

Art Buchwald

Leisure Will Kill You

Art Buchwald (b. 1925), the nationally syndicated columnist, won the Pulitzer Prize in 1982 for his humorous, critical writings. Among his more than two dozen books are The Buchwald Stops Here (1978), You Can Fool All of the People All of the Time (1986, While Reagan Slept (1987), Lighten Up, George (1991), and Laid Back in Washington (1981), from which the following droll selection is taken. A memoir, Leaving Home, was published in 1993.

This country is producing so much leisure equipment for the home that nobody has any leisure time anymore to enjoy it. A few months ago I bought a television tape recorder to make copies of programs when I was out of the house.

Last week I recorded the Nebraska–Oklahoma football game. When I came home in the evening, I decided to play it back. But my son wanted to play "Baseball" on the TV screen with his Atari Computer. We finished four innings when my wife came in the room and asked me if I would like to listen to the Vienna Opera on our hi-fi stereo set. I told her I was waiting to finish the baseball match so I could watch the football game I had recorded.

She said if I watched the football game for three hours, I would miss *Love Boat*. I told her I would record *Love Boat* and we could watch it later in the evening. She protested that *Casablanca* was showing on Channel 5 at 11:30 and she wanted to see it again.

"Don't worry," I assured her, "we can watch *Love Boat* late Saturday and *Casablanca* on Sunday morning when we get up."

"But if we watch *Casablanca* tomorrow morning when can we see the instant Polaroid movies you took of Ben yesterday afternoon?"

"We'll see them after we play backgammon on the new table."

"If we do that," my daughter said, "we won't be able to see the Washington Redskins–New York Giants football game."

"I'll record the Redskins-Giants football game and we'll watch it while *60 Minutes* is on the air. We can see *60 Minutes* at 11 o'clock."

"But," my son said, "you promised to play the pinball machine with me at 11."

"Okay, we'll play pinball at 11 and watch *60 Minutes* at midnight."

My wife said, "Why don't we listen to the Vienna Opera while we're eating and then we can save an hour to play computer golf?"

"That's good thinking," I said. "The only problem is I've rented a TV tape for *Cleopatra* and that runs for three hours."

"You could show it on Monday night," she suggested.

"I can't do that. I have to return the tape Monday afternoon or be charged for it another week. I have an idea. I won't go to work Monday morning and we'll watch it then."

"I was hoping to use our Jacuzzi Monday morning," my wife said.

"Okay, then I'll tape *Cleopatra* and you can see it Monday afternoon."

430

"I'm using the set Monday afternoon," my son said, "to play digital hockey on the TV screen."

"You can't do that," I said. "I have to watch the *Today* show in the afternoon if I'm going to watch *Cleopatra* in the morning."

"Why can't you watch the *Today* show at dinnertime?" my wife asked.

"Because the Wolfingtons are coming over to hear me play 'Tea for Two' on the electric organ."

"I thought we might play computer bridge at dinner," my wife said.

"We'll play it after my encore," I assured her.

"Then when will we see *Monday Night Football?*" my son wanted to know.

"Tuesday," I said.

"Does that mean you're not going to work on Tuesday?" my wife asked.

"How can I go to work," I yelled, "when I've got so much leisure time on my hands?"

Suggestions for Discussion

1. Explain Buchwald's observation that our "country is producing so much leisure equipment for the home that nobody has any leisure time anymore to enjoy it." Do you agree? State your reasons.

2. Discuss whether or not the conflicts that Buchwald sets up in this short essay are realistic, believable, and resolvable.

3. Suggest solutions to the conflicts Buchwald identifies.

4. Discuss Buchwald's use of exaggeration and accumulated detail to give humor to his essay.

Suggestions for Writing

1. Identify and discuss dangers to the individual and to the family posed by excessive amounts of leisure.

2. Depict a busy scene in your own home.

Marie Winn

The Plug-in Drug: TV and the American Family

Marie Winn is the author of *The Playground Book, The Sick Book, The Baby Reader,* and other books for parents and children. Long interested in the impact of media on American family life, she has written *Children Without Childhood* (1984), *Unplugging the Plug-in Drug* (1987), and *The Plug-in Drug* (1977), from which the following analysis of television on family life is taken.

A quarter of a century after the introduction of television into American society, a period that has seen the medium become so deeply ingrained in American life that in at least one state the television set has attained the rank of a legal necessity, safe from repossession in case of debt along with clothes, cooking utensils, and the like, television viewing has become an inevitable and ordinary part of daily life. Only in the early years of television did writers and commentators have sufficient perspective to separate the activity of watching television from the actual content it offers the viewer. In those early days writers frequently discussed the effects of television on family life. However, a curious myopia afflicted those early observers: almost without exception they regarded television as a favorable, beneficial, indeed, wondrous influence upon the family.

"Television is going to be a real asset in every home where there are children," predicts a writer in 1949.

"Television will take over your way of living and change your children's habits, but this change can be a wonderful improvement," claims another commentator.

"No survey's needed, of course, to establish that television has brought the family together in one room," writes *The New York Times* television critic in 1949.

Each of the early articles about television is invariably accompanied by a photograph or illustration showing a family cozily sitting together before the television set, Sis on Mom's lap, Buddy perched on the arm of Dad's chair, Dad with his arm around Mom's shoulder. Who could have guessed that twenty or so years later Mom would be watching a drama in the kitchen, the kids would be looking at cartoons in their room, while Dad would be taking in the ball game in the living room?

Of course television sets were enormously expensive in those early days. The idea that by 1975 more than 60 percent of American families would own two or more sets was preposterous. The splintering of the multiple-set family was something the early writers could not foresee. Nor did anyone imagine the number of hours children would eventually devote to television, the common use of television by parents as a child pacifier, the changes television would effect upon child-rearing methods, the increasing domination of family schedules by children's viewing requirements—in short, the *power* of the new medium to dominate family life.

After the first years, as children's consumption of the new medium increased, together with parental concern about the possible effects of so much television viewing, a steady refrain helped to soothe and reassure anxious parents. "Television always enters a pattern of influences that already exist: the home, the peer group, the school, the church, and culture generally," write the authors of an early and influential study of television's effects on children. In other words, if the child's home life is all right, parents need not worry about the effects of all that television watching.

But television does not merely influence the child; it deeply influences that "pattern of influences" that is meant to ameliorate its effects. Home and family life has changed in important ways since the advent of television. The peer group has become television-oriented, and much of the time children spend together is occupied by television viewing. Culture generally has been transformed by television. Therefore it is improper to assign to television the subsidiary role its many apologists (too often members of the television industry) insist it plays. Television is not merely one of a number of important influences upon today's child. Through the changes it has made in family life, television emerges as *the* important influence in children's lives today.

Television's contribution to family life has been an equivocal one. For while it has, indeed, kept the members of the family from dispersing, it has not served to bring them *together*. By its domination of the time families spend together, it destroys the special quality that distinguishes one family from another, a quality that depends to a great extent on what a family *does*, what special rituals, games, recurrent jokes, familiar songs, and shared activities it accumulates.

"Like the sorcerer of old," writes Urie Bronfenbrenner, "the television set casts its magic spell, freezing speech and action, turning the living into silent statues so long as the enchantment lasts. The primary danger of the television screen lies not so much in the behavior it produces—although there is danger there—as in the behavior it prevents: the talks, the games, the family festivities and arguments through which much of the child's learning takes place and through which his character is formed. Turning on the television set can turn off the process that transforms children into people."

Yet parents have accepted a television-dominated family life so completely that they cannot see how the medium is involved in whatever problems they might be having. A first-grade teacher reports:

"I have one child in the group who's an only child. I wanted to find out more about her family life because this little girl was quite isolated from the group, didn't make friends, so I talked to her mother. Well, they don't have time to do anything in the evening, the mother said. The parents come home after picking up the child at the baby-sitter's. Then the mother fixes dinner while the child watches TV. Then they have dinner and the child goes to bed. I said to this mother, 'Well, couldn't she help you fix dinner? That would be a nice time for the two of you to talk,' and the mother said, 'Oh, but I'd hate to have her miss "Zoom." It's such a good program!' "

Even when families make efforts to control television, too often its very presence counterbalances the positive features of family life. A writer and mother of two boys aged 3 and 7 described her family's television schedule in an article in *The New York Times:*

> We were in the midst of a full-scale War. Every day was a new battle and every program was a major skirmish. We agreed it was a bad scene all around and were ready to enter diplomatic negotiations. . . . In principle we have agreed on 2½ hours of TV a day, "Sesame Street," "Electric Company" (with dinner gobbled up in between) and two half-hour shows between 7 and 8:30 which enables the grown-ups to eat in peace and prevents the two boys from destroying one another. Their pre-bedtime choice is dreadful, because, as Josh recently admitted, "There's nothing much on I really like." So . . . it's "What's My Line" or "To Tell the Truth." . . . Clearly there is a need for first-rate children's shows at this time. . . .

Consider the "family life" described here: Presumably the father comes home from work during the "Sesame Street"–"Electric Company" stint. The children are either watching television, gobbling their dinner, or both. While the parents eat their dinner in peaceful privacy, the children watch another hour of television. Then there is only a half-hour left before bedtime, just enough time for baths, getting pajamas on, brushing teeth, and so on. The children's evening is regimented with an almost military precision. They watch their favorite programs, and when there is "nothing much on I really like," they watch whatever else is on—because *watching* is the important thing. Their mother does not see anything amiss with watching programs just for the sake of watching; she only wishes there were some first-rate children's shows on at those times.

Without conjuring up memories of the Victorian era with family games and long, leisurely meals, and large families, the question arises: isn't there a better family life available than this dismal, mechanized arrangement of children watching television for however long is allowed them, evening after evening?

Of course, families today still do *special* things together at times: go camping in the summer, go to the zoo on a nice Sunday, take various trips and expeditions. But their *ordinary* daily life together is diminished—that sitting around at the dinner table, that spontaneous taking up of an activity, those little games invented by children on the spur of the moment when there is nothing else to do, the scribbling, the chatting, and even the quarreling, all the things that form the fabric of a family, that define a childhood. Instead, the children have their regular schedule of television programs and bedtime, and the parents have their peaceful dinner together.

The author of the article in the *Times* notes that "keeping a family sane means mediating between the needs of both children and adults." But surely the needs of adults are being better met than the needs of the children, who are effectively shunted away and rendered untroublesome, while their parents enjoy a life as undemanding as that of any childless couple. In reality, it is those very demands that young children make upon a family that lead to growth, and it is the way parents accede to those demands that builds the relationships upon which the future of the family depends. If the family does not accumulate its backlog of shared experiences, shared *everyday* experiences that occur and recur and change and develop, then it is not likely to survive as anything other than a caretaking institution.

Family Rituals

Ritual is defined by sociologists as "that part of family life that the family likes about itself, is proud of, and wants formally to continue." Another text notes that "the development of a ritual by a family is an index of the common interest of its members in the family as a group."

What has happened to family rituals, those regular, dependable, recurrent happenings that gave members of a family a feeling of *belonging* to a home rather than living in it merely for the sake of convenience, those experiences that act as the adhesive of family unity far more than any material advantages?

Mealtime rituals, going-to-bed rituals, illness rituals, holiday rituals, how many of these have survived the inroads of the television set?

A young woman who grew up near Chicago reminisces about her childhood and gives an idea of the effects of television upon family rituals:

"As a child I had millions of relatives around—my parents both come from relatively large families. My father had nine brothers and sisters. And so every holiday there was this great swoop-down of aunts, uncles, and millions of cousins. I just remember how wonderful it used to be. These thousands of cousins would come and everyone would play and ultimately, after dinner, all the women would be in the front of the house, drinking coffee and talking, all the men would be in the back of the house, drinking and smoking, and all the kids would be all over the place, playing hide and seek. Christmas time was particularly nice because everyone always brought all their toys and games. Our house had a couple of rooms with go-through closets, so there were always kids running in a great circle route. I remember it was just wonderful.

"And then all of a sudden one year I remember becoming suddenly aware of how different everything had become. The kids were no longer playing Monopoly or Clue or the other games we used to play together. It was because we had a television set which had been turned on for a football game. All of that socializing that had gone on previously had ended. Now everyone was sitting in front of the television set, on a holiday, at a family party! I remember being stunned by how awful that was. Somehow the television had become more attractive."

As families have come to spend more and more of their time together engaged in the single activity of television watching, those rituals and pastimes that once gave family life its special quality have become more and more uncommon. Not since prehistoric times when cave families hunted, gathered, ate, and slept, with little time remaining to accumulate a culture of any significance, have families been reduced to such a sameness.

Real People

It is not only the activities that a family might engage in together that are diminished by the powerful presence of television in the home. The relationships of the family members to each other are also affected, in both obvious and subtle ways. The hours that the young child spends in a one-way relationship with television people, an involvement that allows for no communication or interaction, surely affect his relationships with real-life people.

Studies show the importance of eye-to-eye contact, for instance, in real-life relationships, and indicate that the nature of a person's eye-contact patterns, whether he looks another squarely in the eye or looks to the side or shifts his gaze from side to side, may play a significant role in his success or failure in human relationships. But no eye contact is possible in the child-television relationship, although in certain children's programs people purport to speak directly to the child and the camera fosters this illusion by focusing directly upon the person being filmed. (Mr. Rogers is an example, telling the child "I like you, you're special," etc.) How might such a distortion of real-life relationships affect a child's development of trust, of openness, of an ability to relate well to other *real* people?

Bruno Bettelheim writes:

Children who have been taught, or conditioned, to listen passively most of the day to the warm verbal communications coming from the TV screen, to the deep emotional appeal of the so-called TV personality, are often unable to respond to real persons because they arouse so much less feeling than the skilled actor. Worse, they lose the ability to learn from reality because life experiences are much more complicated than the ones they see on the screen. . . .

A teacher makes a similar observation about her personal viewing experiences:
"I have trouble mobilizing myself and dealing with real people after watching a few hours of television. It's just hard to make that transition from watching television to a real relationship. I suppose it's because there was no effort necessary while I was watching, and dealing with real people always requires a bit of effort. Imagine, then, how much harder it might be to do the same thing for a small child, particularly one who watches a lot of television every day."

But more obviously damaging to family relationships is the elimination of opportunities to talk, and perhaps more important, to argue, to air grievances, between parents and children and brothers and sisters. Families frequently use television to avoid confronting their problems, problems that will not go away if they are ignored but will only fester and become less easily resolvable as time goes on.

A mother reports:
"I find myself, with three children, wanting to turn on the TV set when they're fighting. I really have to struggle not to do it because I feel that's telling them this is the solution to the quarrel—but it's so tempting that I often do it."

A family therapist discusses the use of television as an avoidance mechanism:
"In a family I know the father comes home from work and turns on the television set. The children come and watch with him and the wife serves them their meal in front of the set. He then goes and takes a shower, or works on the car or something. She then goes and has her own dinner in front of the television set. It's a symptom of a deeper-rooted problem, sure. But it would help them all to get rid of the set. It would be far easier to work on what the symptom really means without the television. The television simply encourages a double avoidance of each other. They'd find out more quickly what was going on if they weren't able to hide behind the TV. Things wouldn't necessarily be better, of course, but they wouldn't be anesthetized."

The decreased opportunities for simple conversation between parents and children in the television-centered home may help explain an observation made by an emergency room nurse at a Boston hospital. She reports that parents just seem to sit there these days when they come in with a sick or seriously injured child, although talking to the child would distract and comfort him. "They don't seem to know *how* to talk to their own children at any length," the nurse observes. Similarly, a television critic writes in *The New York Times:* "I had just a day ago taken my son to the emergency ward of a hospital for stitches above his left eye, and the occasion seemed no more real to me than Maalot or 54th Street, south-central Los Angeles. There was distance and numbness and an inability to turn off the total institution. I didn't behave at all; I just watched. . . ."

A number of research studies substantiate the assumption that television interferes with family activities and the formation of family relationships. One survey shows that 78 percent of the respondents indicated no conversation taking place during viewing except at specified times such as commercials. The study notes: "The television atmosphere in most households is one of quiet absorption on the part of family members who are present. The nature of the family social life during a program could be described as 'parallel' rather than interactive, and the set does seem to dominate family life when it is on." Thirty-six percent of the respondents in another study indicated that television viewing was the only family activity participated in during the week.

In a summary of research findings on television's effect on family interactions James Gabardino states: "The early findings suggest that television had a disruptive effect upon interaction and thus presumably human development. . . . It is not unreasonable to ask: 'Is the fact that the average American family during the 1950's came to include two parents, two children, and a television set somehow related to the psychosocial characteristics of the young adults of the 1970's?'"

Undermining the Family

In its effect on family relationships, in its facilitation of parental withdrawal from an active role in the socialization of their children, and in its replacement of family rituals and special events, television has played an important role in the disintegration of the American family. But of course it has not been the only contributing factor, perhaps not even the most important one. The steadily rising divorce rate, the increase in the number of working mothers, the decline of the extended family, the breakdown of neighborhoods and communities, the growing isolation of the nuclear family—all have seriously affected the family.

As Urie Bronfenbrenner suggests, the sources of family breakdown do not come from the family itself, but from the circumstances in which the family finds itself and the way of life imposed upon it by those circumstances. "When those circumstances and the way of life they generate undermine relationships of trust and emotional security between family members, when they make it difficult for parents to care for, educate and enjoy their children, when there is no support or recognition from the outside world for one's role as a parent and when time spent with one's family means frustration of career, personal fulfillment, and peace of mind, then the development of the child is adversely affected," he writes.

But while the roots of alienation go deep into the fabric of American social history, television's presence in the home fertilizes them, encourages their wild and unchecked growth. Perhaps it is true that America's commitment to the television experience masks a spiritual vacuum, an empty and barren way of life, a desert of materialism. But it is television's dominant role in the family that anesthetizes the family into accepting its unhappy state and prevents it from struggling to better its condition, to improve its relationships, and to regain some of the richness it once possessed.

Others have noted the role of mass media in perpetuating an unsatisfactory *status quo*. Leisure-time activity, writes Irving Howe, "must provide relief from work monotony without making the return to work too unbearable; it must provide amusement without insight and pleasure without disturbance—as distinct from art which gives pleasure through disturbance. Mass culture is thus oriented towards a central aspect of industrial society: the depersonalization of the individual." Similarly, Jacques Ellul rejects the idea that television is a legitimate means of educating the citizen: "Education . . . takes place only incidentally. The clouding of his consciousness is paramount. . . ."

And so the American family muddles on, dimly aware that something is amiss but distracted from an understanding of its plight by an endless stream of television images. As family ties grow weaker and vaguer, as children's lives become more separate from their parents', as parents' educational role in their children's lives is taken over by television and schools, family life becomes increasingly more unsatisfying for both parents and children. All that seems to be left is Love, an abstraction that family members *know* is necessary but find great difficulty giving each other because the traditional opportunities for expresssing love within the family have been reduced or destroyed.

For contemporary parents, love toward each other has increasingly come to mean successful sexual relations, as witnessed by the proliferation of sex manuals and sex therapists. The opportunities for manifesting other forms of love through mutual support, understanding, nurturing, even, to use an unpopular word, *serving* each other, are less and less available as mothers and fathers seek their independent destinies outside the family.

As for love of children, this love is increasingly expressed through supplying material comforts, amusements, and educational opportunities. Parents show their love for their children by sending them to good schools and camps, by providing them with good food and good doctors, by buying them toys, books, games, and a television set of their very own. Parents will even go further and express their love by attending PTA meetings to improve their children's schools, or by joining groups that are acting to improve the quality of their children's television programs.

But this is love at a remove, and is rarely understood by children. The more direct forms of parental love require time and patience, steady, dependable, ungrudgingly given time actually spent *with* a child, reading to him, comforting him, playing, joking, and working with him. But even if a parent were eager and willing to demonstrate that sort of direct love to his children today, the opportunities are diminished. What with school and Little League and piano lessons and, of course, the inevitable television programs, a day seems to offer just enough time for a good-night kiss.

Suggestions for Discussion

1. Why did early critics regard television as a "favorable, beneficial, indeed, wondrous influence upon the family"?

2. Explain why television has not served to bring members of the family together.

3. Cite examples of the loss of social interaction in families described by Winn.

4. Explain Winn's belief that "television has played an important role in the disintegration of the American family." Do you agree?

Suggestions for Writing

1. Describe and comment on television viewing in your own home.

2. Compare and contrast Winn's depiction of family interaction with Art Buchwald's.

=====

Pete Hamill

Crack and the Box

Pete Hamill, the distinguished New York journalist long associated with the New York *Post*, is the author of seven novels, including *Loving Women* (1990). In the essay that follows, Hamill argues that "television works on the same imaginative and intellectual level as psychoactive drugs." In 1994 he published *A Drinking Life: A Memoir*.

One sad rainy morning last winter, I talked to a woman who was addicted to crack cocaine. She was twenty-two, stiletto-thin, with eyes as old as tombs. She was living in two rooms in a welfare hotel with her children, who were two, three, and five years of age. Her story was the usual tangle of human woe: early pregnancy, dropping out of school, vanished men, smack and then crack, tricks with johns in parked cars to pay for the dope. I asked her why she did drugs. She shrugged in an empty way and couldn't really answer beyond "makes me feel good." While we talked and she told her tale of squalor, the children ignored us. They were watching television.

Walking back to my office in the rain, I brooded about the woman, her zombielike children, and my own callous indifference. I'd heard so many versions of the same story that I almost never wrote them anymore; the sons of similar women, glimpsed a dozen years ago, are now in Dannemora or Soledad or Joliet; in a hundred cities, their daughters are moving into the same loveless rooms. As I walked, a series of homeless men approached me for change, most of them junkies. Others sat in doorways, staring at nothing. They were additional casualties of our time of plague, demoralized reminders that although this country holds only 2 percent of the world's population, it consumes 65 percent of the world's supply of hard drugs.

Why, for God's sake? Why do so many millions of Americans of all ages, races, and classes choose to spend all or part of their lives stupefied? I've talked to hundreds of addicts over the years; some were my friends. But none could give sensible answers. They stutter about the pain of the world, about despair or boredom, the urgent need for magic or pleasure in a society empty of both. But then they just shrug. Americans have the money to buy drugs;

the supply is plentiful. But almost nobody in power asks, *Why?* Least of all, George Bush and his drug warriors.

William Bennett talks vaguely about the heritage of sixties permissiveness, the collapse of Traditional Values, and all that. But he and Bush offer the traditional American excuse: It Is Somebody Else's Fault. This posture set the stage for the self-righteous invasion of Panama, the bloodiest drug arrest in world history. Bush even accused Manuel Noriega of "poisoning our children." But he never asked *why* so many Americans demand the poison.

And then, on that rainy morning in New York, I saw another one of those ragged men staring out at the rain from a doorway. I suddenly remembered the inert postures of the children in that welfare hotel, and I thought: *television.*

Ah, no, I muttered to myself: too simple. Something as complicated as drug addiction can't be blamed on television. Come on. . . . but I remembered all those desperate places I'd visited as a reporter, where there were no books and a TV set was always playing and the older kids had gone off somewhere to shoot smack, except for the kid who was at the mortuary in a coffin. I also remembered when I was a boy in the forties and early fifties, and drugs were a minor sideshow, a kind of dark little rumor. And there was one major difference between that time and this: television.

We had unemployment then; illiteracy, poor living conditions, racism, governmental stupidity, a gap between rich and poor. We didn't have the all-consuming presence of television in our lives. Now two generations of Americans have grown up with television from their earliest moments of consciousness. Those same American generations are afflicted by the pox of drug addiction.

Only thirty-five years ago, drug addiction was not a major problem in this country. There were drug addicts. We had some at the end of the nineteenth century, hooked on the cocaine in patent medicines. During the placid fifties, Commissioner Harry Anslinger pumped up the budget of the old Bureau of Narcotics with fantasies of reefer madness. Heroin was sold and used in most major American cities, while the bebop generation of jazz musicians got jammed up with horse.

But until the early sixties, narcotics were still marginal to American life; they weren't the $120-billion market they make up today. If anything, those years have an eerie innocence. In 1955 there were 31,700,000 TV sets in use in the country (the number is now past 184 million). But the majority of the audience had grown up without the dazzling new medium. They embraced it, were diverted by it, perhaps even loved it, but they weren't *formed* by it. That year, the New York police made a mere 1,234 felony drug arrests; in 1988 it was 43,901. They confiscated ninety-seven *ounces* of cocaine for the entire year; last year it was hundreds of pounds. During each year of the fifties in New York, there were only about a hundred narcotics-related deaths. But by the end of the sixties, when the first generation of children *formed* by television had come to maturity (and thus to the marketplace), the number of such deaths had risen to 1,200. The same phenomenon was true in every major American city.

In the last Nielsen survey of American viewers, the average family was watching television seven hours a day. This has never happened before in history. No people has ever been entertained for seven hours a *day.* The

Elizabethans didn't go to the theater seven hours a day. The pre-TV generation did not go to the movies seven hours a day. Common sense tells us that this all-pervasive diet of instant imagery, sustained now for forty years, must have changed us in profound ways.

Television, like drugs, dominates the lives of its addicts. And though some lonely Americans leave their sets on without watching them, using them as electronic companions, television usually absorbs its viewers the way drugs absorb their users. Viewers can't work or play while watching television; they can't read; they can't be out on the streets, falling in love with the wrong people, learning how to quarrel and compromise with other human beings. In short they are asocial. So are drug addicts.

One Michigan State University study in the early eighties offered a group of four- and five-year-olds the choice of giving up television or giving up their fathers. Fully one third said they would give up Daddy. Given a similar choice (between cocaine or heroin and father, mother, brother, sister, wife, husband, children, job), almost every stone junkie would do the same.

There are other disturbing similarities. Television itself is a consciousness-altering instrument. With the touch of a button, it takes you out of the "real" world in which you reside and can place you at a basketball game, the back alleys of Miami, the streets of Bucharest, or the cartoony living rooms of Sitcom Land. Each move from channel to channel alters mood, usually with music or a laugh track. On any given evening, you can laugh, be frightened, feel tension, thump with excitement. You can even tune in *MacNeil/Lehrer* and feel sober.

But none of these abrupt shifts in mood is *earned*. They are attained as easily as popping a pill. Getting news from television, for example, is simply not the same experience as reading it in a newspaper. Reading is *active*. The reader must decode little symbols called words, then create images or ideas and make them connect; at its most basic level, reading is an act of the imagination. But the television viewer doesn't go through that process. The words are spoken to him by Dan Rather or Tom Brokaw or Peter Jennings. There isn't much decoding to do when watching television, no time to think or ponder before the next set of images and spoken words appears to displace the present one. The reader, being active, works at his or her own pace; the viewer, being passive, proceeds at a pace determined by the show. Except at the highest levels, television never demands that its audience take part in an act of imagination. Reading always does.

In short, television works on the same imaginative and intellectual level as psychoactive drugs. If prolonged television viewing makes the young passive (dozens of studies indicate that it does), then moving to drugs has a certain coherence. Drugs provide an unearned high (in contrast to the earned rush that comes from a feat accomplished, a human breakthrough earned by sweat or thought or love).

And because the television addict and the drug addict are alienated from the hard and scary world, they also feel they make no difference in its complicated events. For the junkie, the world is reduced to him and the needle, pipe, or vial; the self is absolutely isolated, with no desire for choice. The television addict lives the same way. Many Americans who fail to vote in presidential elections must believe they have no more control over such a choice than they do over the casting of *L.A. Law*.

The drug plague also coincides with the unspoken assumption of most television shows: Life should be *easy*. The most complicated events are summarized on TV news in a minute or less. Cops confront murder, chase the criminals, and bring them to justice (usually violently) within an hour. In commercials, you drink the right beer and you get the girl. *Easy!* So why should real life be a grind? Why should any American have to spend years mastering a skill or a craft, or work eight hours a day at an unpleasant job, or endure the compromises and crises of a marriage? Nobody *works* on television (except cops, doctors, and lawyers). Love stories on television are about falling in love or breaking up; the long, steady growth of a marriage—its essential *dailiness*—is seldom explored, except as comedy. Life on television is almost always simple: good guys and bad, nice girls and whores, smart guys and dumb. And if life in the real world isn't that simple, well, hey, man, have some dope, man, be happy, feel good.

The doper always whines about how he *feels*; drugs are used to enhance his feelings or obliterate them, and in this the doper is very American. No other people on earth spend so much time talking about their feelings; hundreds of thousands go to shrinks, they buy self-help books by the millions, they pour out intimate confessions to virtual strangers in bars or discos. Our political campaigns are about emotional issues now, stated in the simplicities of adolescence. Even alleged statesmen can start a sentence, "I feel that the Sandinistas should . . ." when they once might have said, "I *think*. . . ." I'm convinced that this exaltation of cheap emotions over logic and reason is one by-product of hundreds of thousands of hours of television.

Most Americans under the age of fifty have now spent their lives absorbing television; that is, they've had the structures of drama pounded into them. Drama is always about conflict. So news shows, politics, and advertising are now all shaped by those structures. Nobody will pay attention to anything as complicated as the part played by Third World debt in the expanding production of cocaine; it's much easier to focus on Manuel Noriega, a character right out of *Miami Vice*, and believe that even in real life there's a Mister Big.

What is to be done? Television is certainly not going away, but its addictive qualities can be controlled. It's a lot easier to "just say no" to television than to heroin or crack. As a beginning, parents must take immediate control of the sets, teaching children to watch specific television *programs*, not "television," to get out of the house and play with other kids. Elementary and high schools must begin teaching television as a subject, the way literature is taught, showing children how shows are made, how to distinguish between the true and the false, how to recognize cheap emotional manipulation. All Americans should spend more time reading. And thinking.

For years, the defenders of television have argued that the networks are only giving the people what they want. That might be true. But so is the Medellín cartel.

Suggestions for Discussion

1. Explain Hamill's observation that we live in a "time of plague."

2. Discuss the ties he sees between television and drug addiction. Do you agree or disagree with his conclusions? Why?

3. Comment on Hamill's assertion that "television works on the same imaginative and intellectual level as psychoactive drugs."

4. What recommendations does he make? Do you find them sound? Explain.

Suggestions for Writing

1. Explore the power of television viewing on your life and/or on the lives of others you know. You might keep a log for a week or more to ascertain what and when you watch.

2. Write a response to Hamill's controversial assertions.

Roger Rosenblatt

Who Killed Privacy?

Roger Rosenblatt, essayist, television commentator, and playwright, is the author of Children of War *(1992),* Life Itself: Abortion in the American Mind *(1992), and* The Man in the Water *(1993). In the following essay he argues that "people nowadays simply assume that they have the right to know about everyone."*

I don't know about you, but my life has not been significantly improved by watching any of the three versions of the Amy Fisher story (one version fewer than the story of Jesus), or by learning of the doings of "Dallas" in the palace, or by seeing Fergie topless or Woody humorless, or even—hard as this may be to swallow—by photographs surreptitiously taken of Chelsea Clinton's cat, Socks. I could, if need be, spend the rest of my days without learning one more fact about Socks or any of those other subjects. (I guess the royals aren't subjects.) I am out of things, of course. This is the age where everything is known, everything told.

"If I had to choose my place of birth," Rousseau exclaimed in a fit of nonsense, "I would have chosen a state in which everyone knew everyone else, so that neither the obscure tactics of vice nor the modesty of virtue could have escaped public scrutiny and judgment." Jean-Jacques, say bonjour to Ron Galella.

I really ought not to sound too above it all, because I do not in the least understand this general lust for publicity, this death, this murder and suicide of private life. Socks's father had it right. "The boom mike," the President complained with a forced smile, "has done what 12 years of the Reagan-Bush Supreme Court couldn't do to abolish the right to privacy." Here is precisely what puzzles me: Privacy in our time has not only been invaded; it's been eagerly surrendered. Do people no longer see themselves as private beings? What do *you* think, Socks?

It's difficult to tell the manifestations of this phase or phenomenon or whatever it is from the causes. Technology, for instance, offers both. Bill Clinton's reference to the boom mike is quaint compared with the new spying and surveillance devices that have made a multimillion-dollar industry of what used to be the obscure tactics of vice. A recent science magazine bears an advertisement for a book called "How to Eavesdrop on Your Neighbor," a twist on the Welcome Wagon. An Atlanta mail-order house offered Listenaider, which amplifies nearby sounds and is designed to look like a Walkman. With Mail Inspector one may spray envelopes to read their contents. With a Tracman vehicle tracking system, anybody may follow anybody else's car.

Also available is a voice changer that alters one's telephone voice; this is useful, its makers say, for a man who wishes to pretend he has a secretary. A monitor phone permits one to spy on another room of one's own house; a scanner, to listen in on the police and fire departments. With several devices on the premises, a wife could listen in on her husband disguising his voice as his secretary's, and contact the police.

Since there are as many debugging devices produced as those that bug, one may envision a small, idiotic universe in which everyone spies or thwarts spies in an area the size of an embassy bedroom; but in fact this world of perpetual mutual observation is wide. Businesses spend loads of time and money looking in on competing businesses. Trinet America and its parent company, American Business Information Inc. of Omaha, recently brought out a computer program called "Lists-on-Disk" which, for a license that costs $750 a year, issues factual information on 9.2 million private and public businesses—type, location, number of employees, ownership, revenues and so forth.

When companies are not poking around about one another, they always have us. The Lotus Development Corporation offered and then withdrew something called "Marketplace: Households," a CD-ROM containing essential information on 120 million citizens, things like marital status, income, buying habits—information readily compiled from one of the large credit bureaus, Equifax Inc. Though "Marketplace: Households" was removed from the market, *The New York Times* wrote that "such programs will not go away" because they offer gold mines for small businesses. In any case, what used to be deemed private information on practically everyone has been available for the taking for years, thanks to financial organizations like TRW, which, in spite of frequent citations for harmful inaccuracies, continues to offer data on credit cards, personal loans and tax liens on more than 170 million Americans, including, almost certainly, you.

As business goes, so goes the United States Government. In 1990 Congress proposed legislation that would allow Federal agencies wider latitude than ever in sharing confidential financial information obtained from banks. Under the Right to Financial Privacy Act of 1978, such information cannot be exchanged unless a customer is notified first. Under the new legislation, no prior notification would be necessary; the law would permit agencies to share information on deposits, mortgages and other loans. This bill must have looked especially interesting in the light of Congress's check-kiting scandal of

1991, during which several Congressmen protested reporters' inquiries on the grounds that their privacy was being violated.

The fact is, most people are no longer shocked by the devices or the impulses of public exposure, and in many contexts are happy to contribute to the exposure themselves. See the television shows of Oprah, Donahue and Geraldo, which were once the refuges for nymphomaniacal nuns with eating disorders and now provide lecterns for Presidential candidates. Video telephones are newly for sale, which will be successful only if everyone wants to be seen as well as heard, since a gizmo at one end requires another at another. The entire presumption of private life has been turned on its head. Liz Smith observed astutely, and with equal amusement and irritation, that her province of gossip is regularly raided by front-page news.

The age of grievance, too, is both a cause and effect of this atmosphere. For the past 30 years or so, people have tended to see themselves, and have tended to be seen, as members of interest groups (racial, national, sexual) and not as individuals, making every life both political and potentially publishable; the leap between a private complaint and a public cause is semiautomatic. Multiculturalism insists that everybody is a class of being, as do other bad current ideas. The practice of "outing" homosexuals implies contradictorily that homosexuals have a right to private choice but not to private lives.

My own guess is that television has had more to do with hastening the death of privacy than anything else—not television shows per se, but camcorders, those home TV cameras owned by seemingly everyone. There used to be a sweet kind of shyness displayed by ordinary people whenever they appeared on television. I remember how passers-by used to look at themselves on television monitors in the NBC window at Rockefeller Center—how, tickled with the sight of themselves, they would point, giggle and blush. No more. With the advent of camcorders, everybody is on television, is a TV "personality," taking exposure in stride.

It is astonishing, and heartbreaking, to watch parents of children who were caught in a fire or a crossfire appearing before local TV news cameras mere moments after a tragedy. They are ready for their appearance, even if they have never been on television before, because they know how it is done, how one is to pose, look and speak.

If ordinary citizens do not feel uncomfortable about airing their lives in this way, it should hardly be surprising that celebrities, who live to be noticed, are eager to disclose the details of their brutalized childhoods and bestial "relationships." La Toya Jackson, Patti Davis, Roseanne tell more than anyone wants to know about life with father and mother. What the principals won't reveal the media will. Magic Johnson goes public about his HIV. But the earth would have continued to spin without anyone knowing that Arthur Ashe had AIDS; that was the press's doing. Ashe was endangering no one. The fact that he is a public figure does not deprive him of the right to personal anguish. It was moving, if anachronistic, to hear Anthony Perkins's family announce that the circumstances leading to the actor's death by AIDS were nobody's business.

I wonder, incidentally, if AIDS itself does not, in some atmospheric way, contribute to the sense that people are no longer safe as private entities—if the terrible omnipresence of the pandemic doesn't reinforce the idea that everyone in the world is helplessly exposed.

With AIDS or any serious communicable disease the question of what is or is not private gets complicated, as several school boards and distraught families have learned. But the non-right to privacy has been extended to genetic diseases as well. The March of Dimes Birth Defect Foundation conducted a survey asking if someone other than the patient—an insurance company, an employer—has the right to know if that patient has a genetic defect. Fifty-seven percent of the respondents said yes.

Things also get more problematic when it comes to revelations about political candidates, especially the Presidential variety, where the issue becomes one of "What do we have here?" No one deeply cared if Bill Clinton or George Bush had a G(J)ennifer, because it seemed clear to most voters that the ability of both men to govern was not impaired by their alleged scandals. Yet Gary Hart's boaty fling seemed to indicate a person out of control, so a distinction was drawn.

To give exposure its due, if there were not this tendency to shout private news, sexual harassment would still be a dirty little secret. And it is at least arguable that the men's movement, sans grunts and howls, has encouraged a useful unlocking of spirits. Without the climate of revelation there might have been no Pentagon papers or Watergate, either—though there is a difference between privacy and secrecy. The camcorder has valuable applications, too, as the nation discovered through Rodney King.

The trouble is, people nowadays simply assume that they have the right to know about everyone—and indeed, in the course of events, that they *will* know about everyone, and everyone will know about them. This suggests the possibility of two interesting aftereffects:

People will behave better as a result of the continual prospect of public exposure. People will abjure the interior life, and live only in the open.

To the first proposition, I bravely offer the observation: Who knows? In the 45,000 or so years the species has been around, people have improved incrementally by learning to get along a little better in masses, so perhaps the exposed life is a first evolutionary step toward more companionable communities. Perhaps.

But if the penalty for achieving community involves the forfeiture of thinking of ourselves as private beings, we're in a fix. Robert Warshow once asked: "How shall we regain the use of our experience in the world of mass culture?" He was considering the natural opposition of culture and democracy. It is possible that the publicizing of private lives is an extension of the old democratizing impulse to make everybody equal—by exposing them equally. Yet the idea that it is somehow more egalitarian, thus more American, to dry every life on the line undermines individualism, that other basic notion of the Republic.

Privacy is more difficult to cultivate than publicity because it involves being alone with oneself. John V. Kelleher, professor emeritus of Irish studies at Harvard, used to quote an Old Irish maxim: "Strife is better than loneliness." And privacy requires both. Maybe that's what's at the bottom of this intense desire to know and tell all—a fear of keeping one's own company, of Emersonian self-reliance, which is dreaded in direct proportion to an increase of state power or the power of other institutions over one's life. The more I open myself to the State of New York or to the Ajax Corporation the less I think of myself in control of my destiny, the less I seek that control, the less I am.

Private thoughts are more complicated and confused than public announcements, thus usually more true. Praising Elizabeth Bishop's "power of reticence," Octavio Paz complained that "20th-century poetry has become garrulous. We are drowning not in a sea but in a swamp of words. We have forgotten that poetry is not in what words say but in what is said between them, that which appears fleetingly in pauses and silences. In the poetry workshops of universities there should be a required course for young poets: learning to be silent." Ralph Ellison made a variation on the same point in "Invisible Man," where the narrator admires Louis Armstrong for playing the blues in the breaks between the notes—private space felt by him alone. Earl (the Pearl) Monroe played basketball like that. When the defenders were down, the Pearl was up; he played the game in his own imagined air.

I know it sounds paradoxical, but the killing of privacy is, in some fundamental way, a supremely antisocial act. Everybody goes public, and who cares? Who sympathizes? On the other hand, the person who nurtures and preserves a private existence encourages the respect and imitation of others. Under the best circumstances a general decorum ensues; people feel more comfortable with one another for the walls they erect and defend. Civilizations are made of such interacting privacies, since civilizations tend to rely more on communion than communication.

Out of our private gropings and self-inspections grow our imaginative values—private language, imagery, memory. In the caves of the mind one bats about to discover a light entirely of one's own which, though it should turn out to be dim, is still worth a life.

Suggestions for Discussion

1. Discuss Rosenblatt's criticism of the "general lust for publicity, this death, this murder and suicide of private life." Comment on the language of his critique.

2. Explain the "age of grievance" to which he refers.

3. Give examples to show that "most people are no longer shocked by the devices or the impulses of public exposure, and in many contexts are happy to contribute to the exposure themselves."

Suggestions for Writing

1. Give three or four examples of startling revelations about people that you have observed on television. Would you feel comfortable revealing such personal information about yourself? Discuss.

2. Discuss Rosenblatt's assertion that for the past thirty years or so, "people have tended to see themselves, and have tended to be seen, as members of interest groups (racial, national, sexual) and not as individuals." What examples can you offer to support or refute his observation?

Jack Santino

Rock and Roll as Music;
Rock and Roll as Culture

Jack Santino won four Emmy Awards for his 1982 film, *Miles of Smiles, Years of Struggle: The Untold Story of the Black Pullman Porter*. His book, *Miles of Smiles, Years of Struggle: Stories of Black Pullman Porters*, was published in 1989. A professor in the Department of Popular Culture at Bowling Green State University in Ohio, he teaches popular music from a sociocultural as well as aesthetic perspective. In the following essay, he traces the pervasive influence of rock music over the past forty years.

Here we are, in the 1990s, and rock and roll music, in some form or other, is still the dominant popular musical form in the USA, and maybe the world. Who would have thought, almost forty years ago, when Big Joe Turner, Fats Domino, and Bo Diddley began having hit records that crossed over to the white charts, that rock and roll music would become the business and cultural force that it is today? Who would have thought, when Bill Haley's "Rock Around the Clock," or Hank Ballard and the Midnighters' "Work With Me Annie" were attacked for their supposed ill effects on youth, that a similar debate would be raging almost forty years later about songs and music that evolved and developed out of their efforts?

Rock and roll was seen as a menace to society by many in the fifties. Much of the reaction to the early crossover and cover hits was overtly racist. When a song intended for one market, such as blacks, becomes popular with another market, such as whites, it is called a crossover hit. When a song that has been recorded by one artist, for example, Little Richard, is recorded by another—for instance, Pat Boone—the re-recording is called a cover record. There were crossovers and covers of country and western material, but most of the early rock and roll crossovers did in fact go from the "race" or rhythm and blues charts to the pop charts. This meant an influx of black music on popular radio. Likewise, the cover records tended to be by whites of black artists' work. During the wave of rock and roll bashing and record smashing that began almost simultaneously with the music's sudden popularity, the very fact that much of the music was derived from black tradition was frequently raised as an issue. That the music had a beat, and that this syncopation was African American in origin, was pointed to as self-evident proof that the music was both inferior and corrupting.

On the other hand, rock and roll was also considered by many to be simply a fad, the latest in a long line of trivialities embraced by whimsical youth. This attitude continued well into the 1960s. The Beatles, for instance, were dismissed for years before it dawned on people that they were (1) not a fad, (2) important, and (3) good. It took a long time before adults figured out what the kids knew all along—rock and roll is here to stay.

448

The Origins of Rock and Roll

I remember seeing Elvis Presley on the *Ed Sullivan Show* in 1956. Although I was young, I knew who he was because my two older sisters had told me all about him. They were very interested in seeing him, and so was I. Watching him on television, I was fascinated by the performance and my sisters loved him, but my parents decided he was "on dope." "Look at his eyes!" my mother said, as if offering proof. Recently I was discussing Elvis with a colleague who also remembered seeing him on television for the first time. His story was identical to mine, right down to his mother's exclamation: "He must be on dope. Look at his eyes!" Actually, despite Presley's later addiction to drugs, at that time he was not "on" anything. But he managed to divide parents from children with his looks, his singing, and his stage movements. At that moment in 1956, a generation gap was created.

A similar thing happened in 1964, when the Beatles performed on the *Ed Sullivan Show*. Kids loved them and parents hated them—both their music and their appearance. In 1982, however, when Michael Jackson achieved a similar kind of superfame, also after national exposure on television, many parents took their children to see him on the Jacksons' Victory Tour. They viewed Jackson as the functional equivalent of the Elvis or the Beatles they remembered and cherished in ther own youth and wanted to give their children the opportunity to see this generation's rock hero live. In fact, this is one of the reasons Michael Jackson declined in popularity rather quickly— too many parents liked him. Along with overexposure and his well-publicized idiosyncracies, Jackson was immediately cast into a "good boy" role, as Elvis and the Beatles had been before him, thus clearing the way for such "bad boy" artists as Jerry Lee Lewis, the Rolling Stones, and Prince.

Rock and Roll's Evolving Audience

We live in a rock and roll culture. Since the 1950s, generations have grown up with the music—and to some extent it has grown up with them— while new artists and new styles continue to emerge. A generation gap still exists, however, although somewhat narrowed. Young people today may enjoy musicians who were popular before they were born, such as Chuck Berry, but how many parents today who grew up with fifties and sixties rock music enjoy Prince, or Bon Jovi, or the Dead Milkmen? "Rock and roll" means different things to people, depending on, among other things, how old they are, and although a great many adults consider themselves rock fans, they have difficulty in understanding, much less appreciating, the music that their kids enjoy.

I teach popular music, from a sociocultural as well as an aesthetic perspective, in the nation's only academic Department of Popular Culture, at Bowling Green State University in Bowling Green, Ohio. I believe that the best teaching involves learning on the part of both the students and the instructor, and this is certainly true in my case. Through my teaching I am continually exposed to the various tastes and perceptions of the current generation of college students. From them, I find out not merely who is currently popular, who they like and dislike and why, but also how they view the artists of the past in the light of their own experiences. For instance, during the sixties, the Monkees were viewed as a "plastic" band, consisting of nonmusician actors hired by a corporate entrepreneur (Don Kirshner) to play the roles of imitation Beatles, singing songs written for them by professional songwriters. Although they sold a lot of records, the counterculture hated them. Today, the issues of authenticity and sincerity I alluded to above simply are not relevant to the audience that hears, buys, and enjoys listening to the Monkees' records. Most of my students see no difference whatsoever between the Beatles and the Monkees, while many consumers in the sixties viewed the two bands as polar opposites. Moreover, this example points to another fact: The audience for popular music is diversified. The so-called counterculture may have despised the Monkees, but somebody liked them. They had the best selling album of 1966, along with several No. 1 singles.

If we accept the fact that there is such diversity in the tastes of the consumers of rock and roll music, we must then realize that the term is frequently used in a general way to encompass a great number of musical styles, both black and white. This is how I am using it. With this in mind, I would say that despite the fact that their view of the rock/pop music is different from mine, my students and I share a rock and roll culture.

Rock music (I am using the terms rock and roll and rock interchangeably, although not everyone does[1]) is one of the distinctive features of postwar life, along with television, the Cold War, space travel, and the atomic bomb. For instance, I can expect that everyone in my classroom will be familiar with most of the more popular songs of Elvis Presley, Chuck Berry, or Buddy Holly. They hear them on the radio and on television, they are used in commercials, they are covered by later artists—in short, it is difficult to be alive in America and not know these songs. The same thing is true for popular sixties music, especially the Beatles, the Beach Boys, and Detroit's Motown artists such as the Supremes, the Four Tops, and the Temptations.

However, if I play songs that were popular a year or two preceding the first nationally popular rock hits, or if I drop back to the forties and play something from the Big Band era, these college-age young people are totally unfamiliar with the material, no matter how popular it was in its day. Neither do they know much about other genres, such as blues or country. This is not to say, however, that within the apparently limited category of "rock" that there is not a wide variety of musical styles available to them. Often, these styles give rise to specific subcultures which have their own dress code and concomitant values, such as the punks.

Interweaving and Evolving Styles

This has always been the case. In his important and influential work *The Sound of the City*, Charlie Gillett says that when the music we call rock and roll achieved national popularity in the mid-fifties, it actually included five distinct regional styles: Memphis rockabilly (Elvis, Carl Perkins, Jerry Lee Lewis), Chicago rhythm and blues (Bo Diddley, Chuck Berry), New Orleans

[1]Ed Ward, Geoffrey Stokes, and Ken Tucker, eds., *Rock of Ages: The Rolling Stone History of Rock and Roll* (Englewood Cliffs, N.J.: Prentice-Hall, Inc., 1986), 249.

piano boogie (Fats Domino, Little Richard), the group harmony singing known as doo-wop, centered in New York but found in other urban areas as well (the Platters, the Moonglows, the Penguins), and Northern band rock and roll (Bill Haley and the Comets, from Chester, Pennsylvania). While one may question the specific number of styles Gillett identifies or argue for the inclusion of other styles as well, the principle is a sound one. Different styles of music, derived from blues, country, and gospel—often tied to a geographical region and sometimes to ethnicity as well—all became identified as rock and roll largely because they shared an emphasis on a beat that was appealing to a generation of young people.[2]

Since then, we have seen styles come and go, some to return again, others to wield an influence on later music. If rock is, generally speaking, a synthesis of rhythm and blues (i.e., black) music and country and western (i.e., white) music, and I believe it is, the music that resulted was the beginning, not the end, of a dynamic process. For instance, an interest in American blues inspired young, white British musicians to form bands such as the Rolling Stones and Cream. Their music led in turn to the development of heavy metal music in the 1970s through such blues-based British bands as Led Zeppelin. And heavy metal itself has changed greatly and spun new subgenres in the past twenty years: speed metal, glam metal, bubblegum metal, and so forth. England's Beatles, who were heavily influenced by Americans such as Buddy Holly and the Everly Brothers, went on to influence virtually every rock act in the world, including the early art-rockers, who also contributed to the rise of heavy metal. New styles are created out of the syntheses of the old, but these new styles became the raw materials for further developments.

There are and have been so many styles of rock or rock-derived music in the past thirty years that I could not exhaustively list them all in the space of this article, let alone describe, define, or discuss each of them. A partial list would include surf music, girl-group, Merseybeat, California country rock, psychedelic, punk, new wave, doo-wop, Motown, soul, funk, rap, disco, industrial, and synth-pop. Each has its audience, though neither the audiences nor the musical styles are mutually exclusive. For many adolescents, music becomes a basis of personal and group identity. The music is something they can relate to and feel is their own; they signal their taste by their dress, their hair styles, perhaps even the words they use. They associate with others who share their tastes and, implicitly, their values. Many such subcultures have formed around musical styles over the years. Rockabilly musicians in Memphis were "cats." In the sixties rock had unprecedented influence, giving rise to the hippie life-style. Rock in Britain became associated with Teddy Boys, mods, rockers, and, later, punks. Often, these rock subcultures are shocking and threatening to the rest of us, because the symbols that are used to identify one as a member are loaded with antisocial or rebellious meaning: motorcycle jackets, shoulder-length hair on men, spiked bracelets, and razor blades.

However, we should be aware that the members of these subgroups—the people wearing such things—have redefined these symbols in their own terms and are usually not the threats they appear to be. Wearing forbidden items, breaking the rules for acceptable public appearance, helps define the group in many ways. Of course, it helps individuals identify each other as

[2]Charlie Gillett, *The Sound of the City* (New York: Pantheon Books, 1970), 23–35.

having reasonably similar tastes, but it also defines an in-group/out-group di-chotomy, an "us against them" outlook. The choice of sacrilegious and taboo paraphernalia, such as crucifixes or swastikas, brings forth the wrath of out-siders and helps the kids perpetuate in their own mind their sense that they are both prejudged and misunderstood by adults.

Rock and Roll as Big Business

Rock and roll is a way of life; certainly it is music, but it is also big busi-ness. Selling records, compact discs, tapes, and concert appearances is at the center of a multi-billion-dollar international industry. The success of a popu-lar musician depends as much on monetary backing, good publicity, and sharp business agents as it does on talent. Creating an image is an all-impor-tant part of the process. The leather-jacketed Beatles, for instance, were cleaned up and put into suits by their manager, Brian Epstein, to help them achieve commercial success. Ironically, their being marketed as cheeky but cute and cuddly British boys led to the self-conscious image-mongering of the Rolling Stones as unkempt ruffians.

Today, the music video has become a major marketing tool which has in-tensified the importance of visual image, often at the expense of the musi-cianship. Legend has it that Fabian was discovered sitting on the front step of his Philadelphia row house. His dark good looks appealed to the "talent scouts," but when the sixteen-year-old Fabian Forte explained that he could not sing, he was assured that this was not a problem. More recently, certain bands such as Duran Duran are said to be the contemporary versions of es-sentially the same process. They are routinely described as having been cre-ated by and for videos.

Such assessment may not be fair. Most popular musicians are groomed for a mass audience; not all make it. Artists who create music aimed at the wid-est possible market are not necessarily poor musicians. I have noticed that my students feel that artists have "sold out" when they achieve great popular-ity, for example, artists such as Bruce Springsteen and such former college favorites as Genesis and U2. The question really has to do with the extent to which an artist is willing to change in order to achieve this popularity, and whether the artist considers this change morally or aesthetically compromis-ing. Forgotten in such judgments is the fact that rock music is indeed an industry whose first concern is making money, and that most if not all popu-lar recording artists hope to appeal to a broad audience and, yes, make a lot of money. Sociologist Simon Frith sees this as a central contradiction in rock and roll music: It is and always has been an outlaw form, rebellious, rene-gade, at odds with authority. On the other hand, it is very much a part of the Establishment it apparently rejects: It is a commerical endeavor that gener-ates fortunes for large corporations. Thus, Frith feels that the image of rock as an outlaw form is illusory, designed to add to its mystique and help sell more units.[3] Nevertheless, rock's most enduring artists are unquestionably talented musicians.

[3]Simon Frith, *Sound Effects: Youth, Leisure, and the Politics of Rock 'n' Roll* (New York: Pantheon Books, 1981).

The Cultural Impact of Rock and Roll

Beyond all of this, however, is the question of rock as a social force. As a genre that breaks social rules, rock remains true to itself and appealing to its mostly younger audience specifically by stirring up controversy and angering adults. The kids' aesthetics are the reverse of the adults': the more tasteless and shocking the better. As a product of big business, however, rock is scrutinized for songs and lyrics that might tarnish the corporations' image or offend consumers, or rather, consumers' parents. Despite such well-publicized philanthropic and humanitarian efforts such as the Live-Aid concert or the song "We Are the World," both of which raised money for famine-plagued Ethiopia, rock music is seen as a threat to the young, and to society in general. Satanic imagery, references to violence, rape, drugs, and sex, along with provocatively explicit music videos, frighten the very parents who grew up with rock in the fifties and sixties. The current situation is different, they say, more extreme, more vile, and I have no doubt that it is. However, my students have taught me that the situation is more complex than it seems.

Often songs are judged out of the context of the entire album in which the kids will usually hear them. The Rolling Stones' "Under Cover of the Night" has been cited for its violence; my students answer that if you listen to the entire 1983 album *Undercover,* although the song showcases violence, the entire album is actually antiviolent. Likewise, some songs that are about suicide are not necessarily promoting it but rather attempting to demonstrate the futility of it. Nevertheless, many people feel that these songs (and others with less redeeming social qualities) contribute to the proliferation of society's evils. Companies have responded by initiating a labeling system that cautions consumers about potentially offensive material contained in the recordings. Opponents maintain this is censorship and a curtailment of free speech. From practical experience I can say that the labels in actuality do little to prevent the sale of these recordings to minors, but proponents of the system feel it is a necessary step, and that the free speech issue is outweighed by social urgency.

What is the effect of music—or any other popular medium, such as television or movies—on its audience? No one really knows. It has not been systematically measured and it may be immeasurable. One thing we do know: It depends on the person listening. There are a great many other factors involved as well, such as which specific music are we talking about, under what conditions is it being listened to, and in what situation? A youngster may be more vulnerable to suggestion at certain times, such as after the death of a parent, for instance, than at others. Lawsuits have been brought against singers such as Ozzy Osbourne by parents who feel that his work influenced—in fact, caused—their child to commit suicide. Under such circumstances, parents are distraught and feel understandably passionate about the issue. I am not a fan of Ozzy Osbourne's, and I believe that artists do have a responsibility to consider the effects of their work on their young audience, but it is hard to believe that a child could be driven to such an extreme act by a single piece of music unless there were many other problems already involved. I am not a psychologist, but it occurs to me that a teenager who spends a great deal of time listening to death-oriented music may in fact be asking for help. A fascination with this kind of material may be symptomatic of a deeper problem, one that parents should address before things get to the point of irrevocable tragedy.

It is too easy to blame rock stars for the existence of troubled teenagers. Millions of young people listen to the same records without killing themselves or committing crimes against others. I think we have to consider the personality of the listener as the primary rather than the secondary factor. People seek out music that reinforces their own attitudes and moods; they bring themselves to the music. Charles Manson heard the Beatles' "Helter Skelter" as a call for mass murder, but the rest of us did not.

Furthermore, we need to look closely at the great variety of material that is routinely lumped together in discussions of rock lyrics. There are many different genres, styles, and songs involved, and they may not all be of the same order. Is a song about masturbation to be treated the same as a song that urges its audience to kill? How much of the negative reaction to some of this material has to do with personal morality or individual political points of view? People have defended the use of Satanic imagery to me as simply an artistic use of mythological symbolism, and they frequently point to Milton's *Paradise Lost* as the epitome of an artistic use of the story of Satan. Indeed, Milton portrays Satan sympathetically. Are we to deny Milton the use of the Bible for poetic purposes? Should we take Milton off the library shelves? Many of the people who want to curtail such symbolism believe in the literal, biblical truth of Satan, and see any reference to him as evil. However, not everyone in the United States shares this belief. Are we then dealing with constitutional issues of religious freedom?

It seems obvious that people have a right to write and sing what they want. But parents also have a right and a duty to monitor their children's entertainments. To the extent that rock remains a music of the young, we find a clash of two principles: the artists' right to free expression versus the parents' right to raise their children as they see fit. However, it is important to remind ourselves that rock stars are no longer exclusively in their teens and twenties. A forty-year-old Bruce Springsteen might well write about sex, as poets have always done. It would be unrealistic to expect him not to. In the past, rock performers were themselves young, and this is still true to a large extent, but as the decades have passed, both the audience and the musicians have aged. Last year (1989) saw tours by the Who, the Jefferson Airplane, the Kinks, the Rolling Stones, Bob Dylan, Ringo Starr, and Paul McCartney, all veterans of the sixties. Certainly there are younger musicians playing today, but the point is that these adult musicians cannot be expected to write or sing about teenage concerns.

Furthermore, such things as suicide, drugs, sex, and violence *are* teenage concerns. While artists have a responsibility not to glamorize them, that does not mean these themes should not be explored. Rock songs often work as fantasy explorations of situations that a young person has confronted or at least can imagine confronting. A teenager imagines him- or herself into the song, explores it, but does not necessarily live it. Adolescence is a time of identity formation, when peer-group pressure is very powerful, and when one explores any number of alternative identities: Today, I am a vegetarian, deeply concerned about world ecology; tomorrow I wear leather and chains. Rock music is a part of this testing out of identities, of ideas. It is a fictive form, and it may in fact *help* young people gain a sense of their identity.

Moreover, rock does not exist in a vacuum. It is not the only popular entertainment that has grown more violent and more sexually explicit in recent years. Compare the slasher films of today with the horror films of the sixties or fifties. Even a superheroic movie such as *Robocop*, whose audience would obviously contain a great many children, came very close to receiving an X-rating for violence. Language restrictions have loosened in film and television, and popular television shows are certainly much more explicit than ever before. Comic books are undergoing a similar controversy, due again to their traditional appeal to youngsters. Today's comics are often labeled "Intended For Mature Audiences," and feature the same range of subjects and themes as described above for rock. Creators say that comics are a medium like any other, and that they are free to produce what they want, for readers of all age groups, while others feel that comics are and will always be for kids, and therefore should not contain certain materials under any circumstances. My point is that, in the midst of all this opening up across all the popular media, why should anyone expect that rock music would not reflect the same changes? Is it any more exploitative when rock deals with these themes than television shows such as, say, *Dynasty*, or *Geraldo?* Songs may in fact be written about gang rape, and I find these reprehensible, but I find the slasher films reprehensible also. Rock music is a part of society. It should not be singled out as the single effective agent of change within society.

Redeeming Qualities

Rock also has its positive side, seldom addressed in this debate. Beyond such altruistic efforts as the above-mentioned Live-Aid concert, or Quake-Aid, held to raise money for earthquake victims in Northern California, or benefits to save the whales, or George Harrison's Concert for Bangladesh (way back in 1971), rock can be inspirational on a personal level. Most rock songs do *not* contain off-color lyrics or deal with extremely antisocial behavior. What of all the songs that celebrate fidelity, or that reject drug-taking as a way of life? The truth is, it is far more convincing for kids to hear Rolling Stone Keith Richards talk of the dangers of heroin than to hear Nancy Reagan pronounce "Just say no."

Ultimately, rock and roll is as much a creation of its audience as it is of the artists or the businessmen. Songs that deal with taboo subjects, such as Prince's "Darling Nikki" (masturbation), do not necessarily corrupt their listeners. Prince's fans are quite aware of his tendency to write explicitly about sex. He also writes frequently about God, leading some to see him as a kind of contemporary mystic, using sexual imagery to describe spiritual yearning. As I said, these issues are much more complex than the simpleminded arguments being raised on both sides suggest, and until we deal with them in all their complexity, we will continue to get nowhere. We need to hear out the young people who listen to Prince, or Madonna, or heavy metal, or rap. How do *they* perceive the music? What does it mean to them? They can tell us more about it than we can tell them. Which kids are attracted to which styles, and which musicians? While some rock and roll is nihilistic, much of it is romantic and often melodramatic. This is what has always appealed to me about it, and I think today's youth feel the same. How often do they hear something positive, something altruistic, in rock and roll? Two decades ago, Crosby, Stills, and Nash exhorted parents to "teach your children well," and also, for children, to "teach your parents well." The advice is still good. Let us learn from each other.

Suggestions for Discussion

1. Explain Santino's statement that we "live in a rock and roll culture."
2. Why do some people find certain rock subcultures "shocking and threatening"?
3. What significance does the music video have in contemporary rock music?
4. How do rock lyrics exemplify the "clash of two principles: the artists' right to free expression versus the parents' right to raise their children as they see fit"?
5. Discuss the positive side of rock.

Suggestions for Writing

1. Analyze the lyrics of a favorite rock song.
2. Discuss a rock group that has stirred controversy.
3. Write about the positive contributions made by one or more rock performers or groups.

Bernice Reagon

Black Music in Our Hands

Bernice Reagon, the editor of Black American Culture and Scholarship (1985), grew up in Albany, Georgia, and attended Albany State College and Spelman College before earning her doctorate in Black history and music from Howard University in 1975. Having served as a director of the Washington, D.C., Black Repertory Company and as consultant in Black music to the Smithsonian Institution, she asserts the importance of "Black music that functions in relation to the people and community who provide the nurturing compost that makes its creation and continuation possible."

In the early 1960s, I was in college at Albany State. My major interests were music and biology. In music I was a contralto soloist with the choir, studying Italian arias and German lieder. The black music I sang was of three types:

(1) Spirituals sung by the college choir. These were arranged by such people as Nathaniel Dett and William Dawson and had major injections of European musical harmony and composition. (2) Rhythm 'n' Blues, music done by

and for Blacks in social settings. This included the music of bands at proms, juke boxes, and football game songs. (3) Church music; gospel was a major part of Black church music by the time I was in college. I was a soloist with the gospel choir.

Prior to the gospel choir, introduced in my church when I was twelve, was many years' experience with unaccompanied music—Black choral singing, hymns, lined out by strong song leaders with full, powerful, richly ornate congregational responses. These hymns were offset by upbeat, clapping call-and-response songs.

I saw people in church sing and pray until they shouted. I knew *that* music as a part of a cultural expression that was powerful enough to take people from their conscious selves to a place where the physical and intellectual being worked in harmony with the spirit. I enjoyed and needed that experience. The music of the church was an integral part of the cultural world into which I was born.

Outside of church, I saw music as good, powerful sounds you made or listened to. Rhythm and blues—you danced to; music of the college choir—you clapped after the number was finished.

The Civil Rights Movement changed my view of music. It was after my first march. I began to sing a song and in the course of singing changed the song so that it made sense for that particular moment. Although I was not consciously aware of it, this was one of my earliest experiences with how my music was supposed to *function*. This music was to be integrative of and consistent with everything I was doing at that time; it was to be tied to activities that went beyond artistic affairs such as concerts, dances, and church meetings.

The next level of awareness came while in jail. I had grown up in a rural area outside the city limits, riding a bus to public school or driving to college. My life had been a pretty consistent, balanced blend of church, school, and proper upbringing. I was aware of a Black educated class that taught me in high school and college, of taxi cabs I never rode in, and of people who used buses I never boarded. I went to school with their children.

In jail with me were all these people. All ages. In my section were women from about thirteen to eighty years old. Ministers' wives and teachers and teachers' wives who had only nodded at me or clapped at a concert or spoken to my mother. A few people from my classes. A large number of people who rode segregated city buses. One or two women who had been drinking along the two-block stretch of Little Harlem as the march went by. Very quickly, clashes arose: around age, who would have authority, what was proper behavior?

The Albany Movement was already a singing movement, and we took the songs to jail. There the songs I had sung because they made me feel good or because they said what I thought about a specific issue did something. I would start a song and everybody would join in. After the song, the differences among us would not be as great. Somehow, making a song required an expression of that which was common to us all. The songs did not feel like the same songs I had sung in college. This music was like an instrument, like holding a tool in your hand.

I found that although I was younger than many of the women in my section of the jail, I was asked to take on leadership roles. First as a song leader and then in most other matters concerning the group, especially in discussions, or when speaking with prison officials.

I fell in love with that kind of music. I saw that to define music as something you listen to, something that pleases you, is very different from defining it as an instrument with which you can drive a point. In both instances, you can have the same song. But using it as an instrument makes it a different kind of music.

The next level of awareness occurred during the first mass meeting after my release from jail. I was asked to lead the song that I had changed after the first march. When I opened my mouth and began to sing, there was a force and power within myself I had never heard before. Somehow this music—music I could use as an instrument to do things with, music that was mine to shape and change so that it made the statement I needed to make—released a kind of power and required a level of concentrated energy I did not know I had. I liked the feeling.

For several years, I worked with the Movement eventually doing Civil Rights songs with the Freedom Singers. The Freedom Singers used the songs, interspersed with narrative, to convey the story of the Civil Rights Movement's struggles. The songs were more powerful than spoken conversation. They became a major way of making people who were not on the scene feel the intensity of what was happening in the south. Hopefully, they would move the people to take a stand, to organize support groups or participate in various projects.

The Georgia Sea Island Singers, whom I first heard at the Newport Festival, were a major link. Bessie Jones, coming from within twenty miles of Albany, Georgia, had a repertoire and song-leading style I recognized from the churches I had grown up in. She, along with John Davis, would talk about songs that Black people had sung as slaves and what those songs meant in terms of their struggle to be free. The songs did not sound like the spirituals I had sung in college choirs; they sounded like the songs I had grown up with in church. There I had been told the songs had to do with worship of Jesus Christ.

The next few years I spent focusing on three components: (1) The music I had found in the Civil Rights Movement. (2) Songs of the Georgia Sea Island Singers and other traditional groups, and the ways in which those songs were linked to the struggles of Black peoples at earlier times. (3) Songs of the church that now sounded like those traditional songs and came close to having, for many people, the same kind of freeing power.

There was another experience that helped to shape my present-day use of music. After getting out of jail, the mother of the church my father pastored was at the mass meeting. She prayed, a prayer I had heard hundreds of times. I had focused on its sound, tune, rhythm, chant, whether the moans came at the proper pace and intensity. That morning I heard every word that she said. She did not have to change one word of prayer she had been praying for much of her Christian life for me to know she was addressing the issues we were facing at that moment. More than her personal prayer, it felt like an analysis of the Albany, Georgia, Black community.

My collection, study, and creation of Black music has been, to a large extent, about freeing the sounds and the words and the messages from casings in which they have been put, about hearing clearly what the music has to say about Black people and their struggle.

When I first began to search, I looked for what was then being called folk music, rather than for other Black forms, such as jazz, rhythm and blues, or gospel. It slowly dawned on me that during the Movement we had used all those forms. When we were relaxing in the office, we made up songs using popular rhythm and blues tunes; songs based in rhythm and blues also came out of jails, especially from the sit-in movement and the march to Selma, Alabama. "Oh Wallace, You Never Can Jail Us All" is an example from Selma. "You Better Leave Segregation Alone" came out of the Nashville Freedom Rides and was based on a bit by Little Willie John, "You Better Leave My Kitten Alone." Gospel choirs became the major musical vehicle in the urban center of Birmingham, with the choir led by Carlton Reese. There was also a gospel choir in the Chicago work, as well as an instrumental ensemble led by Ben Branch.

Jazz had not been a strong part of my musical life. I began to hear it as I traveled north. Thelonious Monk and Charlie Mingus played on the first SNCC benefit at Carnegie Hall. I heard of and then heard Coltrane. Then I began to pick up the pieces that had been laid by Charlie Parker and Coleman Hawkins and whole lifetimes of music. This music had no words. But, it had power, intensity, and movement under various degrees of pressure; it had vocal texture and color. I could feel that the music knew how it felt to be Black and Angry, Black and Down, Black and Loved, Black and Fighting.

I now believe that Black music exists in every place where Black people run, every corner where they live, every level on which they struggle. We have been here a long while, in many situations. It takes all that we have created to sing our song. I believe that Black musicians/artists have a responsibility to be conscious of their world and to let their consciousness be heard in their songs.

And we need it all—blues, gospel, ballads, children's games, dance, rhythms, jazz, lovesongs, topical songs—doing what it has always done. We need Black music that functions in relation to the people and community who provide the nurturing compost that makes its creation and continuation possible.

Suggestions for Discussion

1. Analyze the careful structure of Reagon's essay.

2. Discuss the levels of awareness about music that the author describes. What examples does she use to illustrate each?

3. Discuss her assertion that music is "tied to activities that" go "beyond artistic affairs." Are her examples convincing? Explain.

Suggestions for Writing

1. Describe the special significance of certain music to your life.

2. Compare and contrast Bernice Reagon's essay with Aaron Copland's "How We Listen to Music."

Stephen Jay Gould

Dinomania

Stephen Jay Gould (b. 1941) teaches paleontology at Harvard University. His many books include *The Panda's Thumb* (1982), *Time's Arrow* (1987), *Wonderful Life* (1989), and *Bully for Brontosaurus* (1992). In this essay he brings his special knowledge about dinosaurs to an engaging, stimulating review of the *Jurassic Park* craze.

1

Macbeth's soliloquy on his intended murder of King Duncan provides our canonical quotation for the vital theme that deeds spawn unintended consequences in distant futures. "If it were done when 'tis done," Macbeth muses, "then 'twere well it were done quickly." The act must be swift but, even more importantly, the sequelae must be contained, as Macbeth hopes to

> trammel up the consequence, and catch
> With his surcease success; that but this blow
> Might be the be-all and the end-all here.

Yet Macbeth fears that big events must unleash all the genies of unknowable futures—for "bloody instructions, which, being taught, return to plague th' inventor."

I doubt that Henry Fairfield Osborn considered these lines, or imagined any popular future for his new discoveries, when he published a conventionally dull, descriptive paper in 1924 on three genera of dinosaurs recently found in Mongolia on the famous Gobi Desert expedition. In this paper, entitled "Three New Theropoda, *Protoceratops* Zone, Central Mongolia,"[1] Osborn named, and described for the first time, the "skull and jaws, one front claw and adjoining phalanges" of a small, but apparently lithe and skillful carnivore. He called his new creature *Velociraptor mongoliensis* to honor these inferred skills, for *Velociraptor* means "quick seizer." *Velociraptor*, Osborn wrote, "seems to have been an alert, swift-moving carnivorous dinosaur." He then describes the teeth as "perfectly adapted to the sudden seizure of . . . swift-moving prey. . . . The long rostrum and wide gape of the jaws indicate that the prey was not only living but of considerable size."

Osborn was America's greatest vertebrate paleontologist, but he was also the politically conservative, socially prominent, imperious president of the American Museum of Natural History in New York. He would, I think, have

[1] *American Museum Novitates*, No. 144 (November 7, 1924).

been quite surprised, and not at all amused, to learn that, nearly seventy years later, his creature would win a new, and vastly extended, status as the primary dinosaur hero (or villain, depending on your modes of rooting) in *Jurassic Park,* the biggest blockbuster film of all time.

Public fascination has always followed these prehistoric beasts. Just ten years after Richard Owen coined the word dinosaur in 1840, sculptor Waterhouse Hawkins was hard at work on a series of full-scale models to display in the Crystal Palace during the Great Exhibition of 1851. (The Palace burned down in 1936, but Hawkins's dinosaurs, recently spruced up with a coat of paint, can still be seen in Sydenham, south of London.)

But the popular acclaim of dinosaurs has been fitful and episodic. We saw them in *King Kong* (thanks to Willis O'Brien and his brilliant technique of stop-motion filming using models, later magnified). We filled our cars under the sign of the jolly green giant *Brontosaurus,* the logo of Sinclair Oil (who also provided a fine exhibit at the 1939 World's Fair in New York). But dinosaurs never became a big or truly pervasive cultural icon, and some decades largely ignored them. I was a "dinosaur nut" as a kid growing up in New York during the late Forties and early Fifties. Hardly anyone knew or cared about them, and I was viewed as a nerd and misfit on that ultimate field of vocational decision—the school playground at recess. I was called "fossil face"; the only other like-minded kid in the school became "dino" (I am pleased to report that he also became a professional natural historian). The names weren't funny, and they hurt.

During the last twenty years, however, dinosaurs have vaulted to a steady level of culturally pervasive popularity—from gentle Barney, who teaches proper values to young children on a PBS television series, to ferocious monsters who can promote films from G to R ratings. This dinosaurian flooding of popular consciousness guarantees that no paleontologist can ever face a journalist and avoid what seems to be the most pressing question of the Nineties: Why are children so fascinated with dinosaurs?

The question may be commonplace, but it remains poorly formulated by conflating two quite separate issues. The first—call it the Jungian or archetypal theme—seeks the universal reason that stirs the soul of childhood (invariably fatuous and speculative, hence my dislike of the question). To this inquiry, I know no better response than the epitome proposed by a psychologist colleague: "big, fierce, and extinct"—in other words, alluringly scary, but basically safe.

Most inquirers stop here, supposing the question resolved when they feel satisfied about archetypal fascination. But this theme cannot touch the heart of current dinomania, culminating in the extraordinary response to *Jurassic Park,* for an obvious, but oddly disregarded, reason: dinosaurs were just as big, as fierce, and as extinct forty years ago, but only a few nerdy kids, and even fewer professional paleontologists, gave a damn about them. We must therefore pose the second question: Why now and not before?

We might propose two solutions to this less general, but more resolvable, question—one that I wish were true (but almost cannot be), and one that I deeply regret (but must surely be correct). As a practicing paleontologist, I would love to believe that current dinomania arose as a direct product of our research, and of all the fascinating new ideas that our profession has generated about dinosaurs. The slow, lumbering, stupid, robotic, virtually behaviorless behemoths of my childhood have been replaced by lithe, agile, potentially warm-blooded, adequately smart, and behaviorally complex creatures. The giant sauropods were mired in ponds during my youth, for many paleontologists regarded them as too heavy to hold up their own bodies on land. Now they stride across the plains, necks and tails outstretched. In some reconstructions, they even rear up on their hind legs to reach high vegetation, or to scare off predators (they are so depicted in the first *Brachiosaurus* scene of *Jurassic Park*, and in the full-scale fiberglass model of *Barosaurus* in the rotunda of the American Museum of Natural History—though most of my colleagues consider such a posture ridiculously unlikely).

When I was a child, ornithopods laid their eggs and then walked away forever. Today, these same creatures are the very models of maternal, caring, politically correct dinosaurs. They watch over their nests, care for their young, form cooperative herds, and bear such lovely peaceful names as *Maiasauria*, the earth mother lizard (in contrast with such earlier monikers as *Pachycephalosaurus*, the thick bonehead). Even their extinction now appears in a much more interesting light. They succumbed to vaguely speculative types of "climatic change" in my youth; now we have firm evidence for extraterrestrial impact as the trigger for their final removal.

But how can this greening of dinosaurs be the major reason for present faddishness—for if we credit the Jungian theme at all, then the substrate for fascination has always been present, even in the bad old days of dumb and lumbering dinosaurs (who were still big, fierce, and extinct). What promotes this substrate to overt and pervasive dinomania? To such questions about momentary or periodic fads, one quintessentially American source usually supplies a solution—recognition and exploitation of commercial possibilities.

When I was growing up on the streets of New York City, yo-yo crazes would sweep through kiddie culture every year or two, usually lasting for a month or so. These crazes were not provoked by any technological improvement in the design of yo-yos (just as more competent dinosaurs do not engender dinomania). Similarly, a Jungian substrate rooted in control over contained circular motion will not explain why every kid needed a yo-yo in July 1951, but not in June 1950 (just as dinosaurs are always available, but only sometimes exploited).

The answer, in short, must lie in commercialization. Every few years, someone figured out how to make yo-yos sell. At some point about twenty years ago, some set of forces discovered how to turn the Jungian substrate into profits from a plethora of products. You just need a little push to kick the positive feedback machine of human herding and copying behavior into its upward spiral (especially powerful in kids with disposable income).

I'd love to know the source of the initial push (a good theme for cultural historians). Should we look to the great expansion of museum gift shops from holes-in-the-wall run by volunteers to glitzy operations crucial to the financial health of their increasingly commercialized parent institutions? Or did some particular product, or character, grip enough youthful imaginations at some point? Should we be looking for an evil genius, or just for an initial chaotic fluctuation, then amplified by cultural loops of positive feedback?

2

Contemporary culture presents no more powerful symbol, or palpable product, of pervasive, coordinated commercialization than the annual release of "blockbuster" films for the summer viewing season. The movies themselves are sufficiently awesome, but when you consider the accompanying publicity machines, and the flood of commercial tie-ins from lunch pails to coffee mugs to T-shirts, the effort looks more like a military blitzkrieg than an offer of entertainment. Therefore every American who is not mired in some Paleozoic pit surely knows that dinomania has reached its apogee with the release of Steven Spielberg's film version of Michael Crichton's novel *Jurassic Park*. As a paleontologist, I could not possibly feel more ambivalent about the result—marveling and cursing, laughing and moaning. One can hardly pay greater tribute to the importance of an event than to proclaim the impossibility of neutrality before it.

John Hammond (an entrepreneur with more than a touch of evil in the book, but kindly and merely overenthusiastic in the film) has built the ultimate theme park (for greedy profits in the book, for mixed but largely honorable motives in the film) by remaking living dinosaurs out of DNA extracted from dinosaur blood preserved within mosquitoes and other biting insects entombed in fossil Mesozoic amber. Crichton deserves high praise for developing the most clever and realistic of all scenarios for such an impossible event, for such plausibility is the essence of science fiction at its best. (The idea, as Crichton acknowledged, had been kicking around paleontological labs for quite some time.)

Until a few months ago, the record for oldest extracted DNA belonged to a twenty-million-year-old magnolia leaf from Idaho.[2] A group of my colleagues managed to recover nearly the entire sequence—1,320 of 1,431 base pairs—of a chloroplast gene prominently involved in photosynthesis. (Most DNA lies in chromosomes of the nucleus, but mitochondria—energy factories—and chloroplasts—sites of photosynthesis in plants—also contain small DNA programs.)

But amber has also been yielding results during the past year. In the September 25, 1991, issue of *Science* a group of colleagues reported the successful extraction of several DNA fragments (fewer than two hundred base pairs each) from a 25–30-million-year-old termite encased in amber.[3] Then, in a publishing event tied to the opening of *Jurassic Park*, the June 10, 1993, issue of the leading British journal *Nature*—same week as the film's premiere—reported results of another group of colleagues on the extraction of two slightly larger fragments (315 and 226 base pairs) from a fossil weevil.[4]

[2] S. J. Gould, "Magnolias from Moscow," *Natural History*, September 1992; P. S. Soltis, D. E. Soltis, and C. J. Smiley, "An rbcL sequence from a Miocene *Taxodium*," *Proceedings of the National Academy of Sciences*, January 1992, pp.449–451.

[3] R. De Salle, J. Gatesy, W. Wheeler, and D. Grimaldi, "DNA sequences from a fossil termite in Oligo-Miocene amber and their phylogenetic implications," *Science*, Volume 257 (September 25, 1992), pp. 1933–1936.

[4] R. J. Cano, H. N. Poinar, N. J. Pieniazek, A. Acra, and G. O. Poinar, "Amplification and sequencing of DNA from a 120–135 million year old weevil," *Nature*, Volume 363 (June 10, 1993), pp. 536–538.

The amber enclosing this insect is 120–135 million years old—not quite as ancient as Jurassic, but from the next geological period, called Cretaceous, when dinosaurs were also dominant creatures of the land (most of the *Jurassic Park* dinosaurs are Cretaceous in any case).[5]

The nearly complete blurring of pop and professional domains represents one of the most interesting by-products—a basically positive one in my view—of the *Jurassic Park* phenomenon. When a staid and distinguished British journal uses the premiere of an American film to set the sequencing of its own articles, then we have reached an ultimate integration. Museum shops sell the most revolting dinosaur kitsch. Movies employ the best paleontologists as advisers to heighten the realism of their creatures. Orwell's pigs have become human surrogates walking on two legs—and "already it was impossible to say which was which" (nor do I know anymore who was the pig, and who the person, at the outset—that is, if either category be appropriate).

If all this welcome scientific activity gives people the idea that dinosaurs might actually be re-created by Crichton's narrative, I hasten (with regret) to pour frigid water upon this greatest reverie of any aficionado of past life. Aristotle wisely taught us that one swallow doesn't make a summer—nor, his modern acolytes might add, does one gene (or just a fragment thereof) make an organism. Only the most prominent, easily extracted, or multiply copied bits of fossil DNA have sequenced—and we have no reason to believe that anything approaching the complete genetic program of an organism has been preserved in such ancient rocks. (The magnolia study, for example, found no nuclear DNA at all, while the recovered chloroplast gene occurs in numerous copies per cell, with a correspondingly better chance of preservation. More than 90 percent of the attempts yielded no DNA at all. The amber DNA is nuclear, but represents fragments of coding for the so-called 16S and 18S ribosomal RNA genes—among the most commonly and easily recovered segments of the genetic program.)

DNA is not a geological stable compound. We may recover fragments, or even a whole gene, here and there, but no wizardry can make an organism from just a few percent of its codes. *Jurassic Park* honorably acknowledged this limitation by having their genetic engineers use modern frog DNA to fill in the missing spaces in their dinosaur programs. But in so doing, they commit their worst scientific blunder—the only one that merits censure as a deep philosophical error, rather than a studied superficial mistake consciously permitted to bolster the drama of science fiction.

An amalgamated code of, say, 50 percent dinosaur DNA and 50 percent

[5]Pardon some trivial professional carping, but only two of the dinosaurs featured in the film version of *Jurassic Park* actually lived during the Jurassic period—the giant sauropod *Brachiosaurus*, and the small *Dilophosaurus*. All the others come from the subsequent Cretaceous period—a perfectly acceptable mixing given the film's premise that amber of any appropriate age might be scanned for dinosaur blood. Still, the majority might rule in matters of naming, though I suppose that Cretaceous Park just doesn't have the same ring. When I met Michael Crichton (long before the film's completion), I had to ask him the small-minded professional's question: "Why did you place a Cretaceous dinosaur on the cover of *Jurassic Park*?" (for the book's dust jacket—and now the film's logo—features a Cretaceous *Tyrannosaurus rex*). I was delighted with his genuine response: "Oh, my God, I never thought of that. We were just fooling around with different cover designs, and this one looked best." Fair enough; he took the issue seriously, and I would ask no more.

frog DNA would never foster the embryological development of a functioning organism. This form of reductionism is simply silly. An animal is an integrated entity, not the summation of its genes, one by one. Fifty percent of your genetic code doesn't make a perfectly good half of you; it makes no functioning organism at all. Genetic engineers might get by with a missing dab or two, but large holes cannot be plugged with DNA from a different zoological class (frogs are amphibians, dinosaurs are reptiles, and their lines diverged in the Carboniferous Period, more than 100 million years before the origin of dinosaurs). The embryological decoding of a DNA program into an organism represents nature's most complex orchestration. You need all the proper instruments and conductors of an evolutionarily unique symphony. You cannot throw in half a rock band playing its own tunes by its own rules and hope for harmony.

When a scientist soberly states that something cannot be done, the public has every right to express doubts based on numerous historical precedents for results proclaimed impossible, but later both achieved and far surpassed. But the implausibility of reconstructing dinosaurs by the amber scenario resides in a different category of stronger argument.

Most proclamations of impossibility only illustrate a scientist's lack of imagination about future discovery—impossible to see the moon's backside because you can't fly there, impossible to see an atom because light microscopy cannot resolve such dimensions. The object was always there: atoms and the moon's far side. We only lacked a technology that was possible in principle to attain, but unimagined in practice.

But when we say that a particular historical item—like a dinosaur species—can't be recovered, we are invoking a different and truly ineluctable brand of impossibility. If all information about a historical event has been lost, then it just isn't there anymore and the event cannot be reconstructed. We are not lacking a technology to see something that actually exists; rather, we have lost all information about the thing itself, and no technology can recover an item from the void. Suppose I want to know the name of every soldier who fought in the Battle of Marathon. The records, I suspect, simply don't exist—never, nowhere, and nohow. No future technology, no matter how sophisticated, can recover events with crucially missing information. So it is, I fear, with dinosaur DNA. We may make gene machines more powerful by orders of magnitude than anything we can now even conceive. But if full programs of dinosaur DNA exist nowhere—and we can find only the scrap of a gene here and there—then we have permanently lost these particular items of history.

3

I liked the book version of *Jurassic Park*. In addition to using the best possible scenario for making dinosaurs, Crichton based the book's plot upon an interesting invocation of currently fashionable chaos theory. To allay the fears of his creditors, John Hammond brings a set of experts to Jurassic Park, hoping to win their endorsement. His blue ribbon panel includes two paleontologists and a preachy iconoclast of a mathematician named Ian Malcolm—the novel's intellectual and philosophical center. Malcolm urges—often, color-fully, and at length—a single devastating critique based on his knowledge of chaos and fractals: the park's safety system must collapse because it is too precariously complex in its coordination of so many, and so intricate, fail-safe devices. Moreover, the park must fail both unpredictably and spectacularly—and does it ever! Malcolm explains,

> It's chaos theory. But I notice nobody is willing to listen to the consequences of the mathematics. Because they imply very large consequences for human life. Much larger than Heisenberg's principle or Gödel's theorem, which everybody rattles on about. . . . But chaos theory concerns everyday life. . . . I gave all this information to Hammond long before he broke ground on this place. You're going to engineer a bunch of prehistoric animals and set them on an island? Fine. A lovely dream. Charming. But it won't go as planned. It is inherently unpredictable.
>
> We have soothed ourselves into imagining sudden change as something that happens outside the normal order of things. An accident, like a car crash. Or beyond our control, like a fatal illness. We do not conceive a sudden, radical, irrational change as built into the very fabric of existence. Yet it is. And chaos theory teaches us. . . .

Moreover, Malcolm uses this argument —not the usual and romantic pap about "man treading where God never intended" (to invoke the old language as well as the old cliché)—to urge our self-restraint before such scientific power:

> And now chaos theory proves that unpredictability is built into our daily lives. It is as mundane as the rainstorm we cannot predict. And so the grand vision of science, hundreds of years old—the dream of total control—had died, in our century.

This reliance on chaos as a central theme did, however, throw the book's entire story line into a theoretically fatal inconsistency—one that, to my surprise, no reviewer seemed to catch at the time. The book's second half is, basically, a grand old, rip-roaring chase novel, with survivors managing (and with nary a scratch to boot) to prevail through a long sequence of independent and excruciatingly dangerous encounters with dinosaurs. By the same argument that complex sequences cannot proceed as planned—that is, in this case, toward the novelistic necessity of at least some characters surviving—not a human soul in the park should have stood a chance of proceeding harmless through such a sequence. Malcolm even says so: "Do you have any idea how unlikely it is that you, or any of us, will get off this island alive?" But I'm willing to accept the literary convention for bending nature's laws in this case.

I expected to like the film even more. The boy dinosaur nut still dwells within me, and I have seen them all, from *King Kong* to *One Million Years B.C.*, to *Godzilla*. The combination of a better story line, with such vast improvement in monster-making technology, and all done by the most masterly hands in the world, seemed to guarantee success at a spectacular new level of achievement. I did not feel that I wasted my two hours or my seven bucks (plus another two for the indigestible "raptor bites" candy tie-in), but I was deeply disappointed by much about the movie.

The dinosaurs themselves certainly delivered. As a practicing paleontologist, I confess to wry amusement at the roman-à-cleffery embedded in the reconstructions. I could recognize nearly every provocative or *outré* idea of my colleagues, every social tie-in now exploited by dinosaurs in their commanding role as cultural icons. The herbivores are so sweet and idyllic. The giant brachiosaurs low to each other like cattle in the peaceable kingdom. They rear up on their hind legs to find the juiciest leaves. The smaller species care for and help each other—down to such subtle details as experienced elders keeping young *Gallimimus* in the safer center of the fleeing herd.

Even the carnivores are postmodernists of another type. The big old fearsome standard, *Tyrannosaurus rex*, presides over Jurassic Park in all her glory (and in her currently fashionable posture, with head down, tail up, and vertebral column nearly parallel to the ground). But the mantle of carnivorous heroism has clearly passed to the much smaller *Velociraptor*, Henry Fairfield Osborn's Mongolian jewel. Downsizing and diversity are in; constrained hugeness has become a tragic flaw. *Velociraptor* is everything that modern corporate life values in a tough competitor—mean, lean, lithe, and intelligent. They hunt in packs, using a fine military technique of feinting by one beast in front, followed by attack from the side by a co-conspirator. In the film's best moment of wry parody of its own inventions, the wonderfully stereotyped stiff-upper-lip-British-hunter Muldoon gets the center beast in his gun's sight, only to realize too late that the side-hunting companion is a few inches from his head. He looks at the side beast, says "Clever girl" in a tone of true admiration (all of Jurassic Park's dinosaurs are engineered to be female in another ultimately failed attempt to control their reproduction), and then gets gobbled to death.

Even so, Spielberg didn't choose to challenge pop culture's canonical dinosaurs in all details of accuracy and professional speculation; blockbusters must, to some extent, play upon familiarity. Ironically, he found the true size of *Velociraptor*—some six feet in length—too small for the scary effects desired, and enlarged them to nearly ten feet, thus moving partway back toward the old stereotype, otherwise so effectively challenged. He experimented, in early plans and models, with bright colors favored by some of my colleagues on the argument that bird-like behavior (and closeness to bird ancestry) might imply avian styles of coloration for the smaller dinosaurs (the original *Velociraptor* models were tiger striped). But he eventually opted for conventional reptilian dullness ("Your same old, ordinary, dinosaur shit-green," lamented one of my graduate students).

But let me not carp. The dinosaur scenes are spectacular. Intellectuals too often either pay no attention to such technical wizardry or, even worse, actually disdain special effects with such dismissive epithets as "merely mechanical." I find such small-minded parochialism outrageous. Nothing can be more complex than a living organism, with all the fractal geometry of its form and behavior (compared with the almost childishly simple lines of our buildings, and of almost anything else in the realm of human construction).[6] The use of technology to render accurate and believable animals therefore becomes one of the greatest all-time challenges to human ingenuity.

---

[6]My colleague Rhonda Shearer pointed out to me that *Jurassic Park* can be interpreted in the context of socially changing views about geometry. On the contrast between complex nature and Euclidian geometry, see Rhonda Roland Shearer, "Chaos theory and fractal geometry: their potential impact on the future of art," *Leonardo*, Volume 25 (1992), pp. 143–152.

The field has a long and honorable history of continually improving techniques—and who would dare deny this story a place in the annals of human intellectual achievement. An old debate among historians of science asks whether most key technological inventions arise from practical need (more often in war than in any other activity), or from opportunities to fool around during periods of maximal freedom from practical pressures. My friend Cyril Smith, the wisest scientist-humanist I ever knew, strongly advocated the centrality of "play domains" as the major field for innovations with immense practical utility down the road. (He argued that block-and-tackle was invented, or at least substantially improved, in order to lift animals from underground storage pits to the game floor of the Roman Colosseum.) Yes, *Jurassic Park* is "just" a movie—but for this very reason, it had freedom (and money) to develop techniques of reconstruction, particularly computer generation or CG, to new heights of astonishing realism. And yes, it matters—for immediately aesthetic reasons, and for all manner of practical possibilities in the future.

Spielberg originally felt that computer generation had not yet progressed far enough, and that he would have to do all his dinosaur scenes with the fascinating array of modeling techniques long used, but constantly improving, in Hollywood—stop-motion with small models, people dressed in dinosaur suits, puppetry of various sorts, robotics with hydraulic apparatus moved by people sitting at consoles. (All this is described clearly, if uncritically, in *The Making of Jurassic Park*, the formula-book by Don Shay and Jody Duncan— just one of the innumerable commercial tie-ins generated by all blockbusters, but a worthy effort in this case.)

But computer generation improved spectacularly during the two-year gestation of *Jurassic Park*, and dinosaurs are entirely machine-constructed in some of the most spectacular scenes—meaning, of course, that performers interacted with empty space during the actual shooting. (Cartoons have been computer-generated for many years, but remember the entirely different problem that Spielberg faced. Roger Rabbit was supposed to be a "toon"; the computer-generated dinosaurs of *Jurassic Park* must be indistinguishable from real beasts.) I learned, after watching the film, that my two favorite dinosaur scenes—the fleeing herd of *Gallimimus*, and the final attack of *Tyrannosaurus* upon the last two *Velociraptors*—were entirely computer-generated.

The effect does not always work. The very first dinosaur scene—when paleontologist Grant hops out of his vehicle to encounter a computer-generated *Brachiosaurus*—is the film's worst flop. Grant is clearly not in the same space as the dinosaur, and I could only think of Victor Mature, similarly out of synch with his beasts, in *One Million Years B.C.*

The dinosaurs are wonderful, but they aren't on the set enough of the time (yes, I know how much more they cost than human actors). Unfortunately, the plot line for the human actors reduces to pap and romantic drivel of the worst kind, the very antithesis of the book's grappling with serious themes. It is so ironic, but I fear that mammon and the perception (false I hope) of the need to dumb-down for mass audiences have brought us to this impasse of utter inconsistency. How cruel, how perverse, that we invest the most awesome expertise (and millions of bucks) in the dinosaurs, sparing no knowledge or expense to render every detail, every possible nuance, in the most accurate and realistic way. I have nothing but praise for the thought and care, the months and years that went into each dinosaur model, the pushing of computer generation to a new world of utility, the concern for rendering every detail with consummate care, even the tiny bits that few will see and the little sounds that fewer will hear. I think of medieval sculptors who lavished all their skills upon invisible statues on the parapets, for God's view is best (internal satisfaction based on personal excellence in modern translation). How perverse that we permit a movie to do all this so superbly well, and then throw away the story because we think that the public will reject, or fail to comprehend, any complexity beyond a Neanderthal "duh" or a brontosaurian bellow. I just don't believe it.

We feel this loss most in the reconstruction of the mathematician Ian Malcolm as the antithesis of his character in the book. He still presents himself as a devotee of chaos theory ("a chaotician"), but he no longer uses its argument (as previously documented in this article) to formulate his criticism of the park. Instead, he is given the oldest diatribe, the most hackneyed and predictable staple of every Hollywood monster film since *Frankenstein:* man (again I prefer the old gender-biased term for such an archaic line) must not disturb the proper and given course of nature; man must not tinker in God's realm. What dullness and disappointment (and Malcolm, in the film, is a frightful and tendentious bore, obviously so recognized by Spielberg, for he effectively puts Malcolm out of action with a broken leg about halfway through).

Not only have we heard this silly argument a hundred times before (can Spielberg really believe that his public could comprehend no other reason for criticizing a dinosaur park?), but its formulation by Malcolm utterly negates his proclaimed persona as a theoretician of chaos. In the film's irony of ironies, Malcolm's argument becomes the precise antithesis of chaos and also relies on whopping inconsistency to boot. Consider these two flubs that make the story line completely incoherent:

1. As Malcolm rails against genetic reconstruction of lost organisms, Hammond asks him if he would really hesitate to bring the California condor back to life (from preserved DNA) should the last actual bird die. Malcolm answers that he would not object, and would view such an act as benevolent, because the condor's death would have been an accident based on human malfeasance, not an expression of nature's proper course. But we must not bring back dinosaurs because they disappeared along a natural and intended route: "Dinosaurs," he says, "had their shot, and nature selected them for extinction." But such an implied scenario of groups emerging, flourishing, and dying, one after the other in an intended and predictable course, is the antithesis of chaos theory and its crucial emphasis on the great accumulating effect of apparently insignificant perturbations, and on the basic unpredictability of long historical sequences. How can a chaotician talk about nature's proper course at all?

2. If "nature selected them for extinction," and if later mammals therefore represent such an improvement, why can the dinosaurs of Jurassic Park beat any mammal in the place, including the most arrogant primate of them all. You can't have it both ways. If you take dinosaur revisionism seriously, and portray them as smart and capable creatures able to hold their own with

mammals, then you can't argue against reviving them by claiming that their extinction was both predictable and appointed as life ratcheted onward to greater complexity.

Since Malcolm actually preaches the opposite of chaos theory, but presents himself as a chaotician and must therefore talk about it, the film's material on chaos is reduced to an irrelevant caricature in the most embarrassing of all scenes—Malcolm's half-hearted courting of the female paleontologist (before he learns of her partnership with the male paleontologist), by grasping her hand, dripping water on the top and using chaos theory to explain why we can't tell which side the drop will run down! How are the mighty fallen.

4

In the film, John Hammond flies his helicopter to a site in Montana, under excavation by Ellie Sattler and Alan Grant, the two paleontologists chosen to "sign off" on his park and satisfy his investors. They say at first that they cannot come, for they are hard at work on the crucial phase of collecting a fossil *Velociraptor*. Hammond promises to support their research for three years if they will spend one weekend at his site. Grant and Sattler suddenly realize that they would rather be no place else on earth; the *Velociraptor* can wait (little do they know. . . .).

This scene epitomizes the ambivalence that I feel about the *Jurassic Park* phenomenon, and about dinomania in general. Natural history is, and has always been, a beggar's game. Our work as natural historians has never been funded by or for itself. We have always depended upon patrons, and upon other people's perceptions of the utility of our data. We sucked up to princes who wanted to stock their baroque *Wunderkammern* with the most exotic specimens. We sailed on colonial vessels for nations that viewed the cataloguing of faunas and floras as one aspect of control (we helped Bligh bring breadfruit from Tahiti to feed slaves in the West Indies). Many, but not all, of these partnerships have been honorable from our point of view, but we have never had the upper hand. Quite the contrary, our hand has always been out.

Few positions are more precarious than that of the little guy in associations based on such unequal sizes and distributions of might. The power brokers need our expertise, but we are so little in comparison, so quickly bedazzled, and often silenced, by promises (three years as a lifetime's dream for the paleontologists and an insignificant tax write-off for Hammond), so easily swallowed up—if we do not insist on maintaining our island of intact values and concerns in the midst of such a different, and giant, operation. How shall we sing the Lord's song in a strange land?

I do not blame the prince, the captain, or his modern counterparts: the government grantor, the commercial licenser, or the blockbuster filmmaker. These folks know what they want, and they are usually upfront about their needs and bargains. It is our job to stay whole, not be swallowed in compromise, not to execute a pact of silence, or endorsement, for proffered payoff. The issue is more structural than ethical: we are small, though our ideas may be powerful. If we merge, we are lost.

Mass commercial culture is engulfing, vastly bigger than we can ever be. Mass culture forces compromises, even for the likes of Steven Spielberg. He is given the resources to prepare and film his magnificent special effects; but I cannot believe that he feels comfortable about ballyhooing all the ridiculous kitsch now for sale under the coordinated marketing program of movie tie-ins (from fries in a dinosaur's mouth at McDonald's—sold to kids too young for the movie's scary scenes—to a rush on amber rings at fancy jewelry stores); and I cannot imagine that either he or Michael Crichton is truly satisfied with their gutless and incoherent script as an enjoined substitute for an interesting book. Imagine, then, what compromises the same commercial world forces upon the tiny principality of paleontological research?

As a symbol of our dilemma, consider the plight of natural history museums in the light of commercial dinomania. In the past decade, nearly every major or minor natural history museum has succumbed (not always unwisely) to two great commercial temptations: to sell many scientifically worthless, and often frivolous, or even degrading, dinosaur products in their gift shops; and to mount, at high and separate admissions charges, special exhibits of colorful robotic dinosaurs that move and growl but (so far as I have ever been able to judge) teach nothing of scientific value about these animals. Such exhibits could be wonderful educational aids, if properly labeled and integrated with more traditional material; but I have never seen these robots presented for much more than their colors and sound effects (the two aspects of dinosaurs that must, for obvious reasons, remain most in the realm of speculation).

If you ask my colleagues in museum administration why they have permitted such incursions into their precious and limited spaces, they will reply that these robotic displays bring large crowds into the museum, mostly of people who otherwise would never come. These folks can then be led or cajoled into viewing the regular exhibits, and the museum's primary mission of science education receives a giant boost.

I cannot fault the logic of this argument, but I fear that my colleagues are expressing a wish or a hope, not an actual result, and not even an outcome actively pursued by most museums. If the glitzy displays were dispersed among teaching exhibits, if they were used as a springboard for educational programs (sometimes they are), then a proper balance of mammon and learning might be reached. But, too often, the glitz occupies a separate wing (where the higher admission charges can be monitored), and the real result gets measured in increased body counts and profits.

One major museum geared all its fancy fund-raising apparatus for years to the endowment of a new wing—and then filled it with a huge gift shop, a fancy restaurant, and an Omnimax theater, thus relegating the regular exhibits to neglect and disrepair. Another museum intended the dinosaur robots as a come-on to guide visitors to the permanent exhibits. But they found that the robots wouldn't fit into the regular museum. Did they cancel the show? Not at all. They moved it to another building on the extreme opposite end of campus—and even fewer people visited the regular museum as a result.

I may epitomize my argument in the following way: institutions have central purposes that define their integrity and being. Dinomania dramatizes a conflict between institutions with disparate purposes—museums and theme parks. Museums exist to display authentic objects of nature and culture—yes, they must teach; and yes, they may certainly include all manner of computer graphics and other virtual displays to aid in this worthy effort; but they must remain wed to authenticity. Theme parks are gala places of entertainment, committed to using the best displays and devices from the increasingly sophisticated arsenals of virtual reality to titillate, to scare, to thrill, even to teach.

I happen to love theme parks, so I do not speak from a rarefied academic post in a dusty museum office. But theme parks are, in many ways, the antithesis of museums. If each institution respects the other's essence and place, this opposition poses no problem. But theme parks belong to the realm of commerce, museums to the world of education—and the first is so much bigger than the second. Commerce will swallow museums if educators try to copy the norms of business for immediate financial reward.

Speaking about the economics of major sporting events, Mr. Steinbrenner once opined that "it's all about getting the fannies into the seats." If we have no other aim than to stuff more bodies in, and to extract more dollars per fanny, then we might as well convert our museums to theme parks and fill the gift shops with coffee mugs. But then we will be truly lost—necessarily smaller and not as oomphy as Disneyland or Jurassic Park, but endowed with no defining integrity of our own.

Our task is hopeless if museums, in following their essences and respecting authenticity, condemn themselves to marginality, insolvency, and empty corridors. But, fortunately, this need not and should not be our fate. We have an absolutely wonderful product to flog—real objects of nature. We may never get as many fannies as *Jurassic Park*, but we can and do attract multitudes for the right reasons. Luckily, and I do not pretend to understand why, authenticity stirs the human soul (and attracts fannies aplenty). The appeal is cerebral and entirely conceptual, not at all visual.

Casts and replicas are now sufficiently like the originals that no one but the most seasoned expert can possibly tell the difference. But a cast of the Rosetta stone is plaster (however intriguing and informative), while the object itself, on display in the British Museum, is magic. A fiberglass *Tyrannosaurus* merits a good look; the real bones send shivers down my spine as I think of the animal that bore them some 70 million years ago. Even the wily John Hammond knew this principle and awarded museums their garland of ultimate respect. He wanted to build the greatest theme park in the history of the world—but he could do so only by abandoning the virtual reality of most models, and stocking his own park with real, living dinosaurs, reconstructed from authentic dinosaur DNA. (The conscious ironies and recursions embedded in *Jurassic Park*'s own reality are clear enough—for the best dinosaurs are computer-generated within a movie based on a novel.)

For paleontologists, *Jurassic Park* is both our greatest opportunity and our most oppressive incubus—a spur for unparalleled general interest in our subject, and the source of a commercial flood that may truly extinguish dinosaurs by turning them from sources of awe into clichés and commodities. Will we have strength to stand up in this deluge? Preliminary signs are not encouraging.

New York's Museum of Natural History—where Osborn once presided; where he first described *Velociraptor;* where his bust still proclaims, "For him the dry bones came to life and giant forms of ages past rejoined the pageant of the living" —has just mounted a special exhibit (June 11–September 12, 1993) called "The Dinosaurs of Jurassic Park," commanding an additional entrance fee of $5.00 for adults and $2.50 for children. In its advertisement (*New York Times,* June 13), the museum proclaims: "This one-of-a-kind exhibition features spectacular life-size dinosaurs, realistic special effects, and props from the movie, alongside actual dinosaur fossils from the Museum." Do they not see that they have inverted the proper order—and that we will ultimately lose if authentic fossils are not primary, and cultural artifacts derivative?

But we do have one powerful advantage, if we cleave to our purpose as purveyors of authenticity. Commercial dinosaurs may dominate the moment, but must be ephemeral, for they have no support beyond their immediate profitability. Macbeth, in his soliloquy, recognized a special problem facing his plans, for he could formulate no justification beyond personal advantage:

> I have no spur
> To prick the sides of my intent,
> but only
> Vaulting ambition, which o'er-
> leaps itself.

This too shall pass, and nothing of human manufacture can possibly challenge the staying power of real dinosaur bones—sixty-five million years (at least) in the making.

Suggestions for Discussion

1. What reasons does Gould offer for children's fascination with dinosaurs? Does he find one explanation more convincing than others?

2. Explain what he means by the "nearly complete blurring of pop and professional domains." Offer examples from your own experience.

3. Evaluate his critique of Michael Crichton's novel and of the film *Jurassic Park.*

4. Discuss the purpose and effectiveness of Gould's use of quotations from Shakespeare.

5. What does he offer as the "right" reasons for an interest in "real objects of nature"?

Suggestions for Writing

1. Write your own review of *Jurassic Park* or of a similar film or novel. Use Gould's arguments in your analysis.

2. Discuss in some detail a scientific activity from your experience.

John McMurtry

Kill 'Em! Crush 'Em! Eat 'Em Raw!

John McMurtry (b. 1939) is a professor of philosophy at the University of Guelph in Canada. A former college linebacker and a player for the Calgary Stampeders in the Canadian Football League, McMurtry examines in this essay the widespread violence in football.

A few months ago my neck got a hard crick in it. I couldn't turn my head; to look left or right I'd have to turn my whole body. But I'd had cricks in my neck since I started playing grade-school football and hockey, so I just ignored it. Then I began to notice that when I reached for any sort of large book (which I do pretty often as a philosophy teacher at the University of Guelph) I had trouble lifting it with one hand. I was losing the strength in my left arm, and I had such a steady pain in my back I often had to stretch out on the floor of the room I was in to relieve the pressure.

A few weeks later I mentioned to my brother, an orthopedic surgeon, that I'd lost the power in my arm since my neck began to hurt. Twenty-four hours later I was in a Toronto hospital not sure whether I might end up with a wasted upper limb. Apparently the steady pounding I had received playing college and professional football in the late fifties and early sixties had driven my head into my backbone so that the discs had crumpled together at the neck—"acute herniation"—and had cut the nerves to my left arm like a pinched telephone wire (without nerve stimulation, of course, the muscles atrophy, leaving the arm crippled). So I spent my Christmas holidays in the hospital in heavy traction and much of the next three months with my neck in a brace. Today most of the pain has gone, and I've recovered most of the strength in my arm. But from time to time I still have to don the brace, and surgery remains a possibility.

Not much of this will surprise anyone who knows football. It is a sport in which body wreckage is one of the leading conventions. A few days after I went into hospital for that crick in my neck, another brother, an outstanding football player in college, was undergoing spinal surgery in the same hospital two floors above me. In his case it was a lower, more massive herniation, which every now and again buckled him so that he was unable to lift himself off his back for days at a time. By the time he entered the hospital for surgery he had already spent several months in bed. The operation was successful, but, as in all such cases, it will take him a year to recover fully.

These aren't isolated experiences. Just about anybody who has ever played football for any length of time, in high school, college or one of the professional leagues, has suffered for it later physically.

Indeed, it is arguable that body shattering is the very *point* of football, as killing and maiming are of war. (In the United States, for example, the game results in 15 to 20 deaths a year and about 50,000 major operations on knees alone.) To grasp some of the more conspicuous similarities between football and war, it is instructive to listen to the imperatives most frequently issued to the players by their coaches, teammates and fans. "Hurt 'em!" "Level 'em!" "Kill 'em!" "Take 'em apart!" Or watch for the plays that are most enthusiastically applauded by the fans. Where someone is "smeared," "knocked silly," "creamed," "nailed," "broken in two," or even "crucified." (One of my coaches when I played corner linebacker with the Calgary Stampeders in 1961 elaborated, often very inventively, on this language of destruction: admonishing us to "unjoin" the opponent, "make 'im remember you" and "stomp 'im like a bug.") Just as in hockey, where a fight will bring fans to their feet more often than a skillful play, so in football the mouth waters most of all for the really crippling block or tackle. For the kill. Thus the good teams are "hungry," the best players are "mean," and "casualties" are as much a part of the game as they are of a war.

The family resemblance between football and war is, indeed, striking. Their languages are similar: "field general," "long bomb," "blitz," "take a shot," "front line," "pursuit," "good hit," "the draft" and so on. Their principles and practices are alike: mass hysteria, the art of intimidation, absolute command and total obedience, territorial aggression, censorship, inflated insignia and propaganda, blackboard maneuvers and strategies, drills, uniforms, formations, marching bands and training camps. And the virtues they celebrate are almost identical: hyper-aggressiveness, coolness under fire and suicidal bravery. All this has been implicitly recognized by such jock-loving Americans as media stars General Patton and President Nixon, who have talked about war as a football game. Patton wanted to make his Second World War tank men look like football players. And Nixon, as we know, was fond of comparing attacks on Vietnam to football plays and drawing coachly diagrams on a blackboard for TV war fans.

One difference between war and football, though, is that there is little or no protest against football. Perhaps the most extraordinary thing about the game is that the systematic infliction of injuries excites in people not concern, as would be the case if they were sustained at, say, a rock festival, but a collective rejoicing and euphoria. Players and fans alike revel in the spectacle of a combatant felled into semi-consciousness, "blindsided," "clotheslined" or "decapitated." I can remember, in fact, being chided by a coach in pro ball for not "getting my hat" injuriously into a player who was already lying helpless on the ground. (On another occasion, after the Stampeders had traded the celebrated Joe Kapp to BC, we were playing the Lions in Vancouver and Kapp was forced on one play to run with the ball. He was coming "down the chute," his bad knee wobbling uncertainly, so I simply dropped on him like a blanket. After I returned to the bench I was reproved for not exploiting the opportunity to unhinge his bad knee.)

After every game, of course, the papers are full of reports on the day's injuries, a sort of post-battle "body count," and the respective teams go to work with doctors and trainers, tape, whirlpool baths, cortisone and morphine to patch and deaden the wounds before the next game. Then the whole drama is reenacted—injured athletes held together by adhesive, braces and drugs—and the days following it are filled with even more feverish activity to put on the show yet again at the end of the next week. (I remember being so taped up in college that I earned the nickname "mummy.") The team that survives this merry-go-round spectacle of skilled masochism with the fewest incapacitating injuries usually wins. It is a sort of victory by ordeal: "We hurt them more than they hurt us."

My own initiation into this brutal circus was typical. I loved the game from the moment I could run with a ball. Played shoeless on a green open field with no one keeping score and in a spirit of reckless abandon and laughter, it's a very different sport. Almost no one gets hurt and it's rugged, open and exciting (it still is for me). But then, like everything else, it starts to be regulated and institutionalized by adult authorities. And the fun is over.

So it was as I began the long march through organized football. Now there was a coach and elders to make it clear by their behavior that beating other people was the only thing to celebrate and that trying to shake someone up every play was the only thing to be really proud of. Now there were severe rule enforcers, audiences, formally recorded victors and losers, and heavy equipment to permit crippling bodily moves and collisions (according to one American survey, more than 80 percent of all football injuries occur to fully equipped players). And now there was the official "given" that the only way to keep playing was to wear suffocating armor, to play to defeat, to follow orders silently and to renounce spontaneity for joyless drill. The game had been, in short, ruined. But because I loved to play and play skillfully, I stayed. And progressively and inexorably, as I moved through high school, college and pro leagues, my body was dismantled. Piece by piece.

I started off with torn ligaments in my knee at 13. Then, as the organization and the competition increased, the injuries came faster and harder. Broken nose (three times), broken jaw (fractured in the first half and dismissed as a "bad wisdom tooth," so I played with it for the rest of the game), ripped knee ligaments again. Torn ligaments in one ankle and a fracture in the other (which I remember feeling relieved about because it meant I could honorably stop drill-blocking a 270-pound defensive end). Repeated rib fractures and cartilage tears (usually carried, again, through the remainder of the game). More dislocations of the left shoulder than I can remember (the last one I played with because, as the Calgary Stampeder doctor said, it "couldn't be damaged any more"). Occasional broken or dislocated fingers and toes. Chronically hurt lower back (I still can't lift with it or change a tire without worrying about folding). Separated right shoulder (as with many other injuries, like badly bruised hips and legs, needled with morphine for the games). And so on. The last pro game I played—against the Winnipeg Blue Bombers in the Western finals in 1961—I had a recently dislocated left shoulder, a more recently wrenched right shoulder and a chronic pain center in one leg. I was so tied up with soreness I couldn't drive my car to the airport. But it never occurred to me or anyone else that I miss a play as a corner linebacker.

By the end of my football career, I had learned that physical injury—giving it and taking it—is the real currency of the sport. And that in the final analysis the "winner" is the man who can hit to kill even if only half his limbs are working. In brief, a warrior game with a warrior ethos into which (like almost everyone else I played with) my original boyish enthusiasm had been relentlessly taunted and conditioned.

In thinking back on how all this happened, though, I can pick out no villains. As with the social system as a whole, the game has a life of its own. Everyone grows up inside it, accepts it and fulfills its dictates as obediently as helots. Far from ever questioning the principles of the activity, people simply concentrate on executing these principles more aggressively than anybody around them. The result is a group of people who, as the leagues become of a higher and higher class, are progressively insensitive to the possibility that things could be otherwise. Thus, in football, anyone who might question the wisdom or enjoyment of putting on heavy equipment on a hot day and running full speed at someone else with the intention of knocking him senseless would be regarded simply as not really a devoted athlete and probably "chicken." The choice is made straightforward. Either you, too, do your very utmost to efficiently smash and be smashed, or you admit incompetence or cowardice and quit. Since neither of these admissions is very pleasant, people generally keep any doubts they have to themselves and carry on.

Of course, it would be a mistake to suppose that there is more blind acceptance of brutal practices in organized football than elsewhere. On the contrary, a recent Harvard study has approvingly argued that football's characteristics of "impersonal acceptance of inflicted injury," an overriding "organization goal," the "ability to turn oneself on and off" and being, above all, "out to win" are of "inestimable value" to big corporations. Clearly, our sort of football is no sicker than the rest of our society. Even its organized destruction of physical well-being is not anomalous. A very large part of our wealth, work and time is, after all, spent in systematically destroying and harming human life. Manufacturing, selling and using weapons that tear opponents to pieces. Making ever bigger and faster predator-named cars with which to kill and injure one another by the million every year. And devoting our very lives to outgunning one another for power in an ever more destructive rat race. Yet all these practices are accepted without question by most people, even zealously defended and honored. Competitive, organized injuring is integral to our way of life, and football is simply one of the more intelligible mirrors of the whole process: a sort of colorful morality play showing us how exciting and rewarding it is to Smash Thy Neighbor.

Now it is fashionable to rationalize our collaboration in all this by arguing that, well, man *likes* to fight and injure his fellows and such games as football should be encouraged to discharge this original-sin urge into less harmful channels than, say, war. Public-show football, this line goes, plays the same sort of cathartic role as Aristotle said stage tragedy does: without real blood (or not much), it releases players and audience from unhealthy feelings stored up inside them.

As an ex-player in the seasonal coast-to-coast drama, I see little to recommend such a view. What organized football did to me was make me *suppress* my natural urges and re-express them in an alienating, vicious form. Spontaneous desires for free bodily exuberance and fraternization with competitors were shamed and forced under ("If it ain't hurtin' it ain't helpin'") and in their place were demanded armored mechanical moves and cool hatred of all opposition. Endless authoritarian drill and dressing-room harangues (ever wonder why competing teams can't prepare for a game in the same dressing room?) were the kinds of mechanisms employed to reconstruct joyful energies into mean and alien shapes. I am quite certain that everyone else around me was being similarly forced into this heavily equipped military precision and angry antagonism, because there was always a mutinous attitude about full-dress practices, and everybody (the pros included) had to concentrate incredibly hard for days to whip themselves into just one hour's hostility a week against another club. The players never speak of these things. course, because everyone is so anxious to appear tough.

The claim that men like seriously to battle one another to some sort of finish is a myth. It only endures because it wears one of the oldest and most propagandized of masks—the romantic combatant. I sometimes wonder whether the violence all around us doesn't depend for its survival on the existence and preservation of this tough-guy disguise.

As for the effect of organized football on the spectator, the fan is not released from supposed feelings of violent aggression by watching his athletic heroes perform it so much as encouraged in the view that people-smashing is an admirable mode of self-expression. The most savage attackers, after all, are, by general agreement, the most efficient and worthy players of all (the biggest applause I ever received as a football player occurred when I ran over people or slammed them so hard they couldn't get up). Such circumstances can hardly be said to lessen the spectators' martial tendencies. Indeed it seems likely that the whole show just further develops and titillates the North American addiction for violent self-assertion. . . . Perhaps, as well, it helps explain why the greater the zeal of U.S. political leaders as football fans (Johnson, Nixon, Agnew), the more enthusiastic the commitment to hard-line politics. At any rate there seems to be a strong correlation between people who relish tough football and people who relish intimidating and beating the hell out of commies, hippies, protest marchers and other opposition groups.

Watching well-advertised strong men knock other people round, make them hurt, is in the end like other tastes. It does not weaken with feeding and variation in form. It grows.

I got out of football in 1962. I had asked to be traded after Calgary had offered me a $25-a-week-plus-commissions off-season job as a clothing-store salesman. ("Dear Mr. Finks:" I wrote. [Jim Fink was then the Stampers' general manager.] "Somehow I do not think the dialectical subtleties of Hegel, Marx and Plato would be suitably oriented amidst the environmental stimuli of jockey shorts and herringbone suits. I hope you make a profitable sale or trade of my contract to the East.") So the Stampeders traded me to Montreal. In a preseason intersquad game with the Alouettes I ripped the cartilages in my ribs on the hardest block I'd ever thrown. I had trouble breathing and I had to shuffle-walk with my torso on a tilt. The doctor in the local hospital said three weeks rest, the coach said scrimmage in two days. Three days later I was back home reading philosophy.

Suggestions for Discussion

1. Explain why McMurtry gave up professional football.

2. What conclusions does he draw about the language used to describe football? Do you think the language is merely colorful or contributes to a climate of violence? Give specific examples from his essay or from your own experience.

3. Discuss the author's conclusion that football is "a sort of colorful morality play showing us how exciting and rewarding it is to Smash Thy Neighbor."

Suggestions for Writing

1. Describe the positive and negative effects of your own participation in football or another sport.

2. Write about whether or not you would encourage your own children to participate in a contact sport.

Rob Hoerburger

Gotta Dance!

Rob Hoerburger, an editor of the New York Times Magazine, writes about dancing, "something that most of my life I had feared would bring me ridicule."

I walked into the confessional a repentant sinner and walked out a dancer. The priest who heard my sins half-jokingly suggested that for my penance I join the church's production of *West Side Story*, which he was directing. I was 27 at the time and hadn't performed on a stage since fourth grade, but I figured at the very least I could help out with the lights.

Instead, I ended up with the featured role of Riff, the leader of the Jets, mostly because of a lucky break (as in the ankle of the actor originally cast), and the usual dearth of male bodies in community-theater productions. After months of rehearsal, I was comfortable enough with the dialogue and the singing, but the dancing—and *West Side Story* is *mostly* dancing—petrified me. Right up to opening night, I was never sure which foot I would land on.

My anxiety was born of some taboo I had long ago internalized about dancing not being masculine. The typical after-school and after-supper pastimes for boys in my suburban neighborhood were baseball and football. Forget that dancing can actually develop the timing and coordination needed to play second base, or that dancers have physiques that gym rats only dream about. Any parent signing his or her son up for dance class instead of (or even in addition to) Little League was practically subject to child-abuse charges—because invariably that boy would be subject to the cruel taunts of his peers.

This unspoken prohibition was especially painful because secretly I loved to dance. Sports were O.K., but there were many nights when I would forgo the pickup game of baseball on the street, throw on some Motown and whirl around my room for a few hours. But always behind closed doors. Now here I was about to make a public spectacle of myself, and in *West Side Story* no less.

Most of the other men in the cast expressed similar anxiety, but we got a reprieve in that the choreography de-emphasized the more balletic turns in favor of macho posturing and finger-snapping and the climbing of fences. When the steps did get a little more complicated, I took the choreographer's advice to "show a lot of attitude" and chalked the rest up to the power of prayer. And I vowed to get better.

But childhood taboos die hard. It took me a year and a half to summon the courage to enroll in a dance class in Manhattan. As I signed my name for a year's worth of lessons, a lifetime of aversion—my own and my friends'—to dancing in public flashed through my head. I thought of linebackers in high school who took and gave poundings on the football field but sweated through the box step at the prom. And I knew firefighters and fleet-footed detectives who had been in shootouts who cowered at the sight of a wood floor with strobe light above it. Even after John Travolta gyrated through *Saturday Night Fever*, tough guys still didn't dance.

I had been assured that there would be other men in the class, but when I arrived for the first one I was surrounded by leggy women in tights and tutus. The only other man was the instructor, Jeff, a former Broadway dancer who had been in *A Chorus Line* early in its run. He wore makeup and several earrings. Would I have felt more comfortable if he looked like Cal Ripken? Probably, but then I didn't have time to dwell on it, because I was immediately barraged with not only new steps but a new language ("plié," "relevé," "jazz third") and lessons in attire. ("This is not aerobics," Jeff would say, casting gentle aspersions at my jock wear—sneakers and sweats, which I clung to as the last bastions of my maleness.)

I tried to hide in the back lines, but in dance studios even the support beams have mirrors. I heard my name a lot in those first weeks: "Keep your shoulders down." "Other hand." "Watch your head." Yet every time I was tempted to quit, I also heard Jeff's words of encouragement: "If you get only 25 percent of the routine, I'll be happy" or "Just showing up is the victory."

Eventually the routines seemed less tyrannical, and I started to relax. I even compromised on my attire—retaining my Nike T-shirt but trading the sweats and sneakers for black satin jazz pants and jazz shoes. ("Now those," Jeff said, "have style.") And the benefits of the class were instantaneous—walking to my train after each session, I felt a kind of honorable exhaustion, having coaxed into consciousness muscles I hadn't even known existed. It was the same sense of physical satisfaction that I'd felt hitting a bases-clearing double or finishing a half-marathon.

My lessons were interrupted when the next show came along: *Man of La Mancha*, which required me to age 30 years but hardly afforded me an opportunity to show off my new steps. When the show finished its run, I returned to the studio, only to find Jeff out sick and the class being taught by a drill-sergeant substitute. She demanded that each dancer cross the floor individually while she exhorted, "Kick that leg higher—and now *sell* it." Under Jeff's kid-gloves tutelage, I had imagined myself as Fred Astaire, but now, under this magnifying glass, I turned back into Fred Flintstone—stumbling, clumsy, self-conscious, as if all the inhibitions I had been whittling away suddenly gathered themselves back into an intractable whole. On my third or fourth solo flight across the floor I kept going into the locker room, up the stairs and out the door.

Jeff's absence turned out to be permanent—his illness was forcing him to retire—and the studio closed soon after that, a victim of the economy's own failing health. Then I got word of a cast call for a local production of *South Pacific*, a show whose feats are primarily vocal, at least for the men. Reluctantly, I auditioned and made the male chorus. It looked as if my dancing days would be indefinitely deferred.

The men did have one big number—*There Is Nothin' Like a Dame*—which basically involved animated marching. Posture and expression were key, and, because Jeff had emphasized these in class, I had no trouble picking up the routine. The choreographer even singled me out to demonstrate a couple of steps, and the other men—most of whom had never danced on stage before and were wearing the same long faces I did during *West Side Story*—were saying things like "Obviously you've done this before." Now I was being celebrated for something that most of my life I had feared would bring me ridicule.

After much fine-tuning and many weeks of rehearsal, the other men came around, and by the time the show opened there was a buzz about *There Is Nothin' Like a Dame*. The women in the show had three times as many dance numbers and their steps were much fancier. But the novelty appeal of "men who can move" ran high, and when we successfully executed a kickline at the end of the song we brought down the house.

At moments like that, and the many since I've had dancing in public and private, I remember that trip to the confession booth, and realize that dance has in fact become a kind of physical and psychic redemption. But it isn't penance anymore.

Suggestions for Discussion

1. Discuss Hoerburger's anxiety "about dancing not being masculine," an anxiety shared by most of the other men in the cast of an amateur production of *West Side Story*. How does he overcome his anxiety?

2. In what ways has dancing become "a kind of physical and psychic redemption" for the author?

Suggestions for Writing

1. Discuss your psychological responses to certain sports or other kinds of physical activity. Were you afraid you might be injured? Anxious to succeed? Worried about competing successfully? Concerned about your image? How did you overcome your negative responses and reinforce positive ones?

2. Research and write brief biographical sketches of five major modern dancers.

Fiction

Alice Walker

Nineteen Fifty-Five

Alice Walker (b. 1944) has won the Pulitzer Prize and the American Book Award for her fiction. Her books include *Meridian* (1976), *The Color Purple* (1982), and *You Can't Keep a Good Woman Down* (1981), from which the following story is taken.

1955

The car is a brandnew red Thunderbird convertible, and it's passed the house more than once. It slows down real slow now, and stops at the curb. An older gentleman dressed like a Baptist deacon gets out on the side near the house, and a young fellow who looks about sixteen gets out on the driver's side. They are white, and I wonder what in the world they are doing in this neighborhood.

Well, I say to J. T., put your shirt on, anyway, and let me clean these glasses offa the table.

We had been watching the ballgame on TV. I wasn't actually watching, I was sort of daydreaming, with my foots up in J. T.'s lap.

I seen 'em coming on up the walk, brisk, like they coming to sell something, and then they rung the bell, and J. T. declined to put on a shirt but instead disappeared into the bedroom where the other television is. I turned down the one in the living room; I figured I'd be rid of these two double quick and J. T. could come back out again.

Are you Gracie Mae Still? asked the old guy, when I opened the door and put my hand on the lock inside the screen.

And I don't need to buy a thing, said I.

What makes you think we're sellin'? he asks, in that hearty Southern way that makes my eyeballs ache.

Well, one way or another and they're inside the house and the first thing the young fellow does is raise the TV a couple of decibels. He's about five feet nine, sort of womanish looking, with real dark white skin and a red pouting mouth. His hair is black and curly and he looks like a Loosianna creole.

About one of your songs, says the deacon. He is maybe sixty, with white hair and beard, white silk shirt, black linen suit, black tie, and black shoes. His cold gray eyes look like they're sweating.

One of my songs?

Traynor here just *loves* your songs. Don't you, Traynor? He nudges Traynor with his elbow. Traynor blinks, says something I can't catch in a pitch I don't register.

482

The boy learned to sing and dance livin' round you people out in the country. Practically cut his teeth on you.

Traynor looks up at me and bites his thumbnail.

I laugh.

Well, one way or another they leave with my agreement that they can record one of my songs. The deacon writes me a check for five hundred dollars, the boy grunts his awareness of the transaction, and I am laughing all over myself by the time I rejoin J. T.

Just as I am snuggling down beside him though I hear the front door bell going off again.

Forgit his hat? asks J. T.

I hope not, I say.

The deacon stands there leaning on the door frame and once again I'm thinking of those sweaty-looking eyeballs of his. I wonder if sweat makes your eyeballs pink because his are sure pink. Pink and gray and it strikes me that nobody I'd care to know is behind them.

I forgot one little thing, he says pleasantly. I forgot to tell you Traynor and I would like to buy up all of those records you made of the song. I tell you we sure do love it.

Well, love it or not, I'm not so stupid as to let them do that without making 'em pay. So I says, Well, that's gonna cost you. Because, really, that song never did sell all that good, so I was glad they was going to buy it up. But on the other hand, them two listening to my song by themselves, and nobody else getting to hear me sing it, give me a pause.

Well, one way or another the deacon showed me where I would come out ahead on any deal he had proposed so far. Didn't I give you five hundred dollars? he asked. What white man—and don't even mention colored—would give you more? We buy up all your records of that particular song: first, you git royalties. Let me ask you, how much you sell that song for in the first place? Fifty dollars? A hundred, I say. And no royalties from it yet, right? Right. Well, when we buy up all of them records you gonna git royalties. And that's gonna make all them race record shops sit up and take notice of Gracie Mae Still. And they gonna push all them other records of yourn they got. And you no doubt will become one of the big name colored recording artists. And then we can offer you another five hundred dollars for letting us do all this for you. And by God you'll be sittin' pretty! You can go out and buy you the kind of outfit a star should have. Plenty sequins and yards of red satin.

I had done unlocked the screen when I saw I could get some more money out of him. Now I held it wide open while he squeezed through the opening between me and the door. He whipped out another piece of paper and I signed it.

He sort of trotted out to the car and slid in beside Traynor, whose head was back against the seat. They swung around in a u-turn in front of the house and then they was gone.

J. T. was putting his shirt on when I got back to the bedroom. Yankees beat the Orioles 10–6, he said. I believe I'll drive out to Paschal's pond and go fishing. Wanta go?

While I was putting on my pants J. T. was holding the two checks.

I'm real proud of a woman that can make cash money without leavin' home, he said. And I said *Umph*. Because we met on the road with me singing in first one little low-life jook after another, making ten dollars a night for myself if I was lucky, and sometimes bringin' home nothing but my life. And J. T. just loved them times. The way I was fast and flashy and always on the go from one town to another. He loved the way my singin' made the dirt farmers cry like babies and the womens shout Honey, hush! But that's mens. They loves any style to which you can get 'em accustomed.

1956

My little grandbaby called me one night on the phone: Little Mama, Little Mama, there's a white man on the television singing one of your songs! Turn on channel 5.

Lord, if it wasn't Traynor. Still looking half asleep from the neck up, but kind of awake in a nasty way from the waist down. He wasn't doing too bad with my song either, but it wasn't just the song the people in the audience was screeching and screaming over, it was that nasty little jerk he was doing from the waist down.

Well, Lord have mercy, I said, listening to him. If I'da closed my eyes, it could have been me. He had followed every turning of my voice, side streets, avenues, red lights, train crossings and all. It give me a chill.

Everywhere I went I heard Traynor singing my song, and all the little white girls just eating it up. I never had so many ponytails switched across my line of vision in my life. They was so *proud*. He was a *genius*.

Well, all that year I was trying to lose weight anyway and that and high blood pressure and sugar kept me pretty well occupied. Traynor had made a smash from a song of mine, I still had seven hundred dollars of the original one thousand dollars in the bank, and I felt if I could just bring my weight down, life would be sweet.

1957

I lost ten pounds in 1956. That's what I give myself for Christmas. And J. T. and me and the children and their friends and grandkids of all description had just finished dinner—over which I had put on nine and a half of my lost ten—when who should appear at the front door but Traynor. Little Mama, Little Mama! It's that white man who sings
. The children didn't call it my song anymore. Nobody did. It was funny how that happened. Traynor and the deacon had bought up all my records, true, but on his record he had put "written by Gracie Mae Still." But that was just another name on the label, like "produced by Apex Records."

On the TV he was inclined to dress like the deacon told him. But now he looked presentable.

Merry Christmas, said he.

And same to you, Son.

I don't know why I called him Son. Well, one way or another they're all our sons. The only requirement is that they be younger than us. But then again, Traynor seemed to be aging by the minute.

You looks tired, I said. Come on in and have a glass of Christmas cheer.

J. T. ain't never in his life been able to act decent to a white man he wasn't working for, but he poured Traynor a glass of bourbon and water, then he took all the children and grandkids and friends and whatnot out to the den. After while I heard Traynor's voice singing the song, coming from the stereo console. It was just the kind of Christmas present my kids would consider cute.

I looked at Traynor, complicit. But he looked like it was the last thing in the world he wanted to hear. His head was pitched forward over his lap, his hands holding his glass and his elbows on his knees.

I done sung that song seem like a million times this year, he said. I sung it on the Grand Ole Opry, I sung it on the Ed Sullivan show. I sung it on Mike Douglas, I sung it at the Cotton Bowl, the Orange Bowl. I sung it at Festivals. I sung it at Fairs. I sung it overseas in Rome, Italy, and once in a submarine *underseas*. I've sung it and sung it, and I'm making forty thousand dollars a day offa it, and you know what, I don't have the faintest notion what that song means.

Whatchumean, what do it mean? It mean what it says. All I could think was: These suckers is making forty thousand a *day* offa my song and now they gonna come back and try to swindle me out of the original thousand.

It's just a song, I said. Cagey. When you fool around with a lot of no count mens you sing a bunch of 'em. I shrugged.

Oh, he said. Well. He started brightening up. I just come by to tell you I think you are a great singer.

He didn't blush, saying that. Just said it straight out.

And I brought you a little Christmas present too. Now you take this little box and you hold it until I drive off. Then you take it outside under that first streetlight back up the street aways in front of that greenhouse. Then you open the box and see . . . Well, just *see*.

What had come over this boy, I wondered, holding the box. I looked out the window in time to see another white man come up and get in the car with him and then two more cars full of white mens start out behind him. They was all in long black cars that looked like a funeral procession.

Little Mama, Little Mama, what it is? One of my grandkids come running up and started pulling at the box. It was wrapped in gay Christmas paper—the thick, rich kind that's hard to picture folks making just to throw away.

J. T. and the rest of the crowd followed me out of the house, up the street to the streetlight and in front of the greenhouse. Nothing was there but somebody's gold-grilled white Cadillac. Brandnew and most distracting. We got to looking at it so till I almost forgot the little box in my hand. While the others were busy making 'miration I carefully took off the paper and ribbon and folded them up and put them in my pants pocket. What should I see but a pair of genuine solid gold caddy keys.

Dangling the keys in front of everybody's nose, I unlocked the caddy, motioned for J. T. to git in on the other side, and us didn't come back home for two days.

1960

Well, the boy was sure nuff famous by now. He was still a mite shy of twenty but already they was calling him the Emperor of Rock and Roll.

Then what should happen but the draft.

Well, says J. T. There goes all the Emperor of Rock and Roll business.

But even in the army the womens was on him like white on rice. We watched it on the News.

Dear Gracie Mae [he wrote from Germany],

How you? Fine I hope as this leaves me doing real well. Before I come in the army I was gaining a lot of weight and gitting jittery from making all them dumb movies. But now I exercise and eat right and get plenty of rest. I'm more awake than I been in ten years.

I wonder if you are writing any more songs?

Sincerely,
Traynor

I wrote him back:

Dear Son,

We is all fine in the Lord's good grace and hope this finds you the same. J. T. and me be out all times of the day and night in that car you give me—which you know you didn't have to do. Oh, and I do appreciate the mink and the new self-cleaning oven. But if you send anymore stuff to eat from Germany I'm going to have to open up a store in the neighborhood just to get rid of it. Really, we have more than enough of everything. The Lord is good to us and we don't know Want.

Glad to here you is well and gitting your right rest. There ain't nothing like exercising to help that along. J. T. and me work some part of every day that we don't go fishing in the garden.

Well, so long Soldier.

Sincerely,
Gracie Mae

He wrote:

Dear Gracie Mae,

I hope you and J. T. like that automatic power tiller I had one of the stores back home send you. I went through a mountain of catalogs looking for it—I wanted something that even a woman could use.

I've been thinking about writing some songs of my own but every time I finish one it don't seem to be about nothing I've actually lived myself. My agent keeps sending me other people's songs but they just sound mooney. I can hardly git through 'em without gagging.

Everybody still loves that song of yours. They ask me all the time what do I think it means, really. I mean, they want to know just what I want to know. Where out of your life did it come from?

Sincerely,
Traynor

1968

I didn't see the boy for seven years. No. Eight. Because just about everybody was dead when I saw him again. Malcolm X, King, the president and his brother, and even J. T. J. T. died of a head cold. It just settled in his head like a block of ice, he said, and nothing we did moved it until one day he just leaned out the bed and died.

His good friend Horace helped me put him away, and then about a year later Horace and me started going together. We was sitting out on the front porch swing one summer night, dusk-dark, and I saw this great procession of lights winding to a stop.

Holy Toledo! said Horace. (He's got a real sexy voice like Ray Charles.)

Look *at* it. He meant the long line of flashy cars and the white men in white summer suits jumping out on the drivers' sides and standing at attention. With wings they could pass for angels, with hoods they could be the Klan.

Traynor comes waddling up the walk.

And suddenly I know what it is he could pass for. An Arab like the ones you see in storybooks. Plump and soft and with never a care about weight. Because with so much money, who cares? Traynor is almost dressed like someone from a storybook too. He has on, I swear, about ten necklaces. Two sets of bracelets on his arms, at least one ring on every finger, and some kind of shining buckles on his shoes, so that when he walks you get a quite a few twinkling lights.

Gracie Mae, he says, coming up to give me a hug. J. T.

I explain that J. T. passed. That this is Horace.

Horace, he says, puzzled but polite, sort of rocking back on his heels, Horace.

That's it for Horace. He goes in the house and don't come back.

Looks like you and me is gained a few, I say.

He laughs. The first time I ever heard him laugh. It don't sound much like a laugh and I can't swear that it's better than no laugh a'tall.

He's gitting fat for sure, but he's still slim compared to me. I'll never see three hundred pounds again and I've just about said (excuse me) fuck it. I got to thinking about it one day an' I thought: aside from the fact that they say it's unhealthy, my fat ain't never been no trouble. Mens always have loved me. My kids ain't never complained. Plus they's fat. And fat like I is I looks distinguished. You see me coming and know somebody's *there.*

Gracie Mae, he says, I've come with a personal invitation to you to my house tomorrow for dinner. He laughed. What did it sound like? I couldn't place it. See them men out there? he asked me. I'm sick and tired of eating with them. They don't never have nothing to talk about. That's why I eat so much. But if you come to dinner tomorrow we can talk about the old days. You can tell me about that farm I bought you.

I sold it, I said.

You did?

Yeah, I said, I did. Just cause I said I liked to exercise by working in a garden didn't mean I wanted five hundred acres! Anyhow, I'm a city girl now. Raised in the country it's true. Dirt poor—the whole bit—but that's all behind me now.

Oh well, he said, I didn't mean to offend you.

We sat a few minutes listening to the crickets.

Then he said: You wrote that song while you was still on the farm, didn't you, or was it right after you left?

You had somebody spying on me? I asked.

You and Bessie Smith got into a fight over it once, he said.

You *is* been spying on me!

But I don't know what the fight was about, he said. Just like I don't know what happened to your second husband. Your first one died in the Texas electric chair. Did you know that? Your third one beat you up, stole your touring costumes and your car and retired with a chorine to Tuskegee. He laughed. He's still there.

I had been mad, but suddenly I calmed down. Traynor was talking very dreamily. It was dark but seems like I could tell his eyes weren't right. It was like some*thing* was sitting there talking to me but not necessarily with a person behind it.

You gave up on marrying and seem happier for it. He laughed again. I married but it never went like it was supposed to. I never could squeeze any of my own life either into it or out of it. It was like singing somebody else's record. I copied the way it was sposed to be *exactly* but I never had a clue what marriage meant.

I bought her a diamond ring big as your fist. I bought her clothes. I built her a mansion. But right away she didn't want the boys to stay there. Said they smoked up the bottom floor. Hell, there were *five* floors.

No need to grieve, I said. No need to. Plenty more where she come from.

He perked up. That's part of what that song means, ain't it? No need to grieve. Whatever it is, there's plenty more down the line.

I never really believed that way back when I wrote that song, I said. It was all bluffing then. The trick is to live long enough to put your young bluffs to use. Now if I was to sing that song today I'd tear it up. 'Cause I done lived long enough to know it's *true*. Them words could hold me up.

I ain't lived that long, he said.

Look like you on your way, I said. I don't know why, but the boy seemed to need some encouraging. And I don't know, seem like one way or another you talk to rich white folks and you end up reassuring *them*. But what the hell, by now I feel something for the boy. I wouldn't be in his bed all alone in the middle of the night for nothing. Couldn't be nothing worse than being famous the world over for something you don't even understand. That's what I tried to tell Bessie. She wanted that same song. Overheard me practicing it one day, said, with her hands on her hips: Gracie Mae, I'ma sing your song tonight. I *likes* it.

Your lips be too swole to sing, I said. She was mean and she was strong, but I trounced her.

Ain't you famous enough with your own stuff? I said. Leave mine alone. Later on, she thanked me. By then she was Miss Bessie Smith to the World, and I was still Miss Gracie Mae Nobody from Notasulga.

The next day all these limousines arrived to pick me up. Five cars and twelve bodyguards. Horace picked that morning to start painting the kitchen.

Don't paint the kitchen, fool, I said. The only reason that dumb boy of ours is going to show me his mansion is because he intends to present us with a new house.

What you gonna do with it? he asked me, standing there in his shirtsleeves stirring the paint.

Sell it. Give it to the children. Live in it on weekends. It don't matter what I do. He sure don't care.

Horace just stood there shaking his head. Mama you sure looks *good*, he says. Wake me up when you git back.

Fool, I say, and pat my wig in front of the mirror.

The boy's house is something else. First you come to this mountain, and then you commence to drive and drive up this road that's lined with magnolias. Do magnolias grow on mountains? I was wondering. And you come to lakes and you come to ponds and you come to deer and you come up on some sheep. And I figure these two is sposed to represent England and Wales. Or something out of Europe. And you just keep on coming to stuff. And it's all pretty. Only the man driving my car don't look at nothing but the road. Fool. And then *finally*, after all this time, you begin to go up the driveway. And there's more magnolias—only they're not in such good shape. It's sort of cool up this high and I don't think they're gonna make it. And then I see this building that looks like if it had a name it would be The Tara Hotel. Columns and steps and outdoor chandeliers and rocking chairs. Rocking chairs? Well, and there's the boy on the steps dressed in a dark green satin jacket like you see folks wearing on TV late at night, and he looks sort of like a fat Dracula with all that house rising behind him, and standing beside him there's this little white vision of loveliness that he introduces as his wife.

He's nervous when he introduces us and he says to her: This is Gracie Mae Still, I want you to know me. I mean . . . and she gives him a look that would fry meat.

Won't you come in, Gracie Mae, she says, and that's the last I see of her.

He fishes around for something to say or do and decides to escort me to the kitchen. We go through the entry and the parlor and the breakfast room and the dining room and the servants' passage and finally get there. The first thing I notice is that, altogether, there are five stoves. He looks about to introduce me to one.

Wait a minute, I say. Kitchens don't do nothing for me. Let's go sit on the front porch.

Well, we hike back and we sit in the rocking chairs rocking until dinner.

Gracie Mae, he says down the table, taking a piece of fried chicken from the woman standing over him, I got a little surprise for you.

It's a house, ain't it? I ask, spearing a chitlin.

You're getting *spoiled*, he says. And the way he says *spoiled* sounds funny. He slurs it. It sounds like his tongue is too thick for his mouth. Just that quick he's finished the chicken and is now eating chitlins *and* a pork chop. *Me* spoiled, I'm thinking.

I already got a house. Horace is right this minute painting the kitchen. I bought that house. My kids feel comfortable in that house.

But this one I bought you is just like mine. Only a little smaller.

I still don't need no house. And anyway who would clean it?

He looks surprised.

Really, I think, some peoples advance *so* slowly.

I hadn't thought of that. But what the hell, I'll get you somebody to live in.

I don't want other folks living 'round me. Makes me nervous.

You *don't?* It *do?*

What I want to wake up and see folks I don't even know for?

He just sits there downtable staring at me. Some of that feeling is in the song, ain't it? Not the words, the *feeling*. What I want to wake up and see folks I don't even know for? But I see twenty folks a day I don't even know, including my wife.

This food wouldn't be bad to wake up to though, I said. The boy had found the genius of corn bread.

He looked at me real hard. He laughed. Short. They want what you got but they don't want you. They want what I got only it ain't mine. That's what makes 'em so hungry for me when I sing. They getting the flavor of something but they ain't getting the thing itself. They like a pack of hound dogs trying to gobble up a scent.

You talking 'bout your fans?

Right. Right. He says.

Don't worry 'bout your fans, I say. They don't know their asses from a hole in the ground. I doubt there's a honest one in the bunch.

That's the point. Dammit, that's the point! He hits the table with his fist. It's so solid it don't even quiver. You need a honest audience! You can't have folks that's just gonna lie right back to you.

Yeah, I say, it was small compared to yours, but I had one. It would have been worth my life to try to sing 'em somebody else's stuff that I didn't know nothing about.

He must have pressed a buzzer under the table. One of his flunkies zombies up.

Git Johnny Carson, he says.

On the phone? asks the zombie.

On the phone, says Traynor, what you think I mean, git him offa the front porch? Move your ass.

So two weeks later we's on the Johnny Carson show.

Traynor is all corseted down nice and looks a little bit fat but mostly good. And all the women that grew up on him and my song squeal and squeal. Traynor says: The lady who wrote my first hit record is here with us tonight, and she's agreed to sing it for all of us, just like she sung it forty-five years ago. Ladies and Gentlemen, the great Gracie Mae Still!

Well, I had tried to lose a couple of pounds my own self, but failing that I had me a very big dress made. So I sort of rolls over next to Traynor, who is dwarfted by me, so that when he puts his arm around back of me to try to hug me it looks funny to the audience and they laugh.

I can see this pisses him off. But I smile out there at 'em. Imagine squealing for twenty years and not knowing why you're squealing? No more sense of endings and beginnings than hogs.

It don't matter, Son, I say. Don't fret none over me.

I commence to sing. And I sound—wonderful. Being able to sing good ain't all about having a good singing voice a'tall. A good singing voice helps. But when you come up in the Hard Shell Baptist church like I did you understand early that the fellow that sings is the singer. Them that waits for programs and arrangements and letters from home is just good voices occupying body space.

So there I am singing my own song, my own way. And I give it all I got and enjoy every minute of it. When I finish Traynor is standing up clapping and clapping and beaming at first me and then the audience like I'm his mama for true. The audience claps politely for about two seconds.

Traynor looks disgusted.

He comes over and tries to hug me again. The audience laughs.

Johnny Carson looks at us like we both weird.

Traynor is mad as hell. He's supposed to sing something called a love ballad. But instead he takes the mike, turns to me and says: Now see if my imitation still holds up. He goes into the same song, *our song*, I think, looking out at his flaky audience. And he sings it just the way he always did. My voice, my tone, my inflection, everything. But he forgets a couple of lines. Even before he's finished the matronly squeals begin.

He sits down next to me looking whipped.

It don't matter, Son, I say, patting his hand. You don't even know those people. Try to make the people you know happy.

Is that in the song? he asks.

Maybe, I say.

1977

For a few years I hear from him, then nothing. But trying to lose weight takes all the attention I got to spare. I finally faced up to the fact that my fat is the hurt I don't admit, not even to myself, and that I been trying to bury it from the day I was born. But also when you git real old, to tell the truth, it ain't as pleasant. It gits lumpy and slack. Yuck. So one day I said to Horace, I'ma git this shit offa me.

And he fell in with the program like he always try to do and Lord such a procession of salads and cottage cheese and fruit juice!

One night I dreamed Traynor had split up with his fifteenth wife. He said: *You meet 'em for no reason. You date 'em for no reason. You marry 'em for no reason. I do it all but I swear it's just like somebody else doing it. I feel like I can't remember Life.*

The boy's in trouble, I said to Horace.

You've always said that, he said.

I have?

Yeah. You always said he looked asleep. You can't sleep through life if you wants to live it.

You not such a fool after all, I said, pushing myself up with my cane and hobbling over to where he was. Let me sit down on your lap, I said, while this salad I ate takes effect.

In the morning we heard Traynor was dead. Some said fat, some said heart, some said alcohol, some said drugs. One of the children called from Detroit. Them dumb fans of his is on a crying rampage, she said. You just ought to turn on the t.v.

But I didn't want to see 'em. They was crying and crying and didn't even know what they was crying for. One day this is going to be a pitiful country, I thought.

Suggestions for Discussion

1. What parallels with the career of Elvis Presley does Walker suggest?

2. Describe the relationship between Traynor and Gracie Mae Still.

3. Characterize Gracie Mae.

4. Why does Traynor shower Gracie Mae with gifts?

5. How does Gracie Mae respond to Traynor's death?

Suggestions for Writing

1. Discuss loneliness as a theme in "Nineteen Fifty-Five."

2. Discuss Walker's use of dialect to add color and develop characterization.

The Cultural Tradition:
Art and Society

The whole New Critical period I went through, and the scholarly period that followed it, betrayed me, I think, into an excessive concern with significance.

> **—John Gardner,** "Learning from Disney and Dickens"

I think I was born with the impression that what happened in books was much more reasonable, and interesting, and *real*, in some ways, than what happened in life.

> **—Anne Tyler,** "Still Just Writing"

The memory is a living thing—it too is in transit. But during its moment, all that is remembered joins, and lives—the old and the young, the past and the present, the living and the dead.

> **—Eudora Welty,** "Finding a Voice"

In this sense fiction became the agency of my efforts to answer the questions, Who am I, what am I, how did I come to be? What shall I make of the life around me, what celebrate, what reject, how confront the snarl of good and evil which is inevitable?

> **—Ralph Ellison,** "On Becoming a Writer"

Works of art, in my opinion, are the only objects in the material universe to possess internal order, and that is why, though I don't believe that only art matters, I do believe in Art for Art's sake.

> **—E. M. Forster,** "Art for Art's Sake"

Yet standards there are, timeless as the universe itself. And when you have committed yourself to them, you have acquired a passport to that elusive but immutable realm of truth.

—Marya Mannes, "How Do You Know It's Good?"

I, too, dislike it; there are things that are important beyond all this fiddle. Reading it, however, with a perfect contempt for it, one discovers in it after all, a place for the genuine.

—Marianne Moore, "Poetry"

Is there a clear line between erotica and violent pornography, or are they on an escalating continuum? Is this a "men versus women" issue, with all men secretly siding with the pro-porners and all women secretly siding against?

—Margaret Atwood, "Pornography"

Where are the Hittites?

Why does no one find it remarkable that in most world cities today there are Jews but not one single Hittite, even though the Hittites had a great flourishing civilization while the Jews nearby were a weak and obscure people? . . .

Where are the Hittites? Show me one Hittite in New York City.

—Walker Percy, "The Delta Factor"

Personal Reminiscences

John Gardner

Learning from Disney and Dickens

John Champlin Gardner, Jr. (1933–1982), was a medieval and classical scholar, a professor of English literature, head of the Creative Writing Program at the State University of New York at Binghamton, and author of novels, short stories, critical works, translations from Old and Middle English, and even opera librettos. In *On Moral Fiction* (1978), he calls upon the artist to act as a moral agent, saying, "I agree with Tolstoy. . . . The highest purpose of art is to make people good by choice." This essay from *The New York Times*, which he titled "Cartoons," is part of a book of essays by various writers, *In Praise of What Persists*, edited by Stephen Berg. Gardner wrote this memoir of his development as a writer shortly before his death in a motorcycle accident.

Trying to figure out the chief influences on my work as a writer turns out to be mainly a problem of deciding what not to include. I grew up in a family where literary influence was everywhere, including under the bridge on our dirt road, where I kept my comic books. My father is a memorizer of poetry and scripture, a magnificent performer in the old reciter tradition. (I once did a reading in Rochester, N.Y., near Batavia, where I grew up. After I'd finished several people remarked that I was a wonderful reader—"though not quite up to your father, of course.") He did readings of everything from Edgar Guest to Shakespeare and The Book of Job at the monthly Grange meetings, in schools, churches, hospitals. While he milked the cows, my mother (who'd once been his high school English teacher) would read Shakespeare's plays aloud to him from her three-legged stool behind the gutter, and he would take, yelling from the cow's flank, whatever part he'd decided on that night—Macbeth, King Lear, Hamlet, and so on.

My mother was a well-known performer too, except that she mainly sang. She had one of those honeysweet Welsh soprano voices and sang everything from anthems to the spirituals she'd learned from an old black woman who took care of her during her childhood in Missouri. Often my mother performed in blackface, with a red bandana, a practice that may sound distasteful unless you understand that she wasn't kidding; she was authentic, flatting, quarter-toning, belting it out: She was amazing. They frequently worked together, my mother and father, and were known all over western New York. Sometimes they were in plays—my mother often directed—and wherever they went, riding around in the beat-up farm truck or just sitting in the kitchen, they sang, always in harmony, like crazy people.

The house was full of books, very few of them books that would now be thought fashionable aside from the Shakespeare and Dickens. My parents read aloud a lot—the narrative poems of Scott, miles of Longfellow, spooky stories by Edgar Allan Poe, the poems of Tennyson and Browning, also rather

495

goofy religious writers (I loved them; what did I know?) like Lloyd C. Douglas and some woman whose name escapes me now, who wrote Jesus-filled love stories with titles like "A Patch of Blue." My grandmother, who was bedridden through much of my childhood, was especially fond of this religious lady, and one of my more pleasant chores was to read her these tender little novels. The climax was always the moment the boy shyly touched the girl's hand. I've never found anything more sexually arousing than that Jesus-filled, long-delayed touch. I mean it was smut, it nearly made me a pervert, and not a court in the land could nail her.

My favorite authors, at least when I was between the ages of 8 and 18, were in what might be described as the nonrealistic tradition: God, Dickens, and Disney. One of my less pleasant chores when I was young was to read the Bible from one end to the other. Reading the Bible straight through is at least 70 percent discipline, like learning Latin. But the good parts are, of course, simply amazing. God is an extremely uneven writer, but when He's good, nobody can touch him. I learned to find the good parts easily (some very sexy stuff here too), and both the poetry and the storytelling had a powerful effect on what I think good fiction ought to be!

Dickens I ran into when I was in my early teens, when I began to find the Hardy boys tiresome and unconvincing. I never liked realism much, but the irrealism of two boys having long conversations while riding on motorcycles (I was big on motorcycles myself) was more than I could put up with. Running across Dickens was like finding a secret door. I read book after book, and when I'd finished the last one I remember feeling a kind of horror, as if suddently the color had gone out of the world; then luckily I discovered that when you went back to one of the ones you had read first, you couldn't remember half of it, you could read it again and find it even better, so life wasn't quite as disappointing as for a moment I'd thought.

For me at that time Disney and Dickens were practically indistinguishable. Both created wonderful cartoon images, told stories as direct as fairy tales, knew the value of broad comedy spiced up with a little weeping. I have since learned that Dickens is occasionally profound, as Disney never deigns to be; but that was never why I valued Dickens or have, now, a bust of him in my study to keep me honest. Unconsciously—without ever hearing the term, in fact—I learned about symbolism from Dickens and Disney, with the result that I would never learn to appreciate, as I suppose one should, those realistic writers who give you life data without resonance, things merely as they are. Dickens's symbolism may never be very deep—the disguised witches and fairy princesses, Uriah Heep and his mother flapping around like buzzards, or all the self-conscious folderol of "A Tale of Two Cities"—but in my experience, anyway, it spoils you forever for books that never go oo-boom.

There were other important influences during this period of my life, probably the most important of which was opera. The Eastman School of Music presented operas fairly often (and of course played host to traveling opera companies, including the Met). From Dickens and Disney (not to mention God) it took no adjustment to become opera-addicted. The plots of most operas (not all, heaven knows) are gloriously simple-minded or, to put it more favorably, elemental; the stage is nothing if not a grand cartoon (Wagner's mountainscapes and gnomes, Mozart's crazies, Humperdinck's angels, the weirdness and clowning that show up everywhere from "La Bohème" to "The Tales of Hoffmann"). I was by this time playing French horn, and of course I'd always been around singing. So I got hooked at once—hence my special fondness now for writing librettos.

By the time I reached college my taste was, I'm afraid, hopelessly set. Predictably I was ravished by Melville—all those splendid cartoon images, for instance Ahab and the Chinese coolies he's kept hidden until the first time he needs to lower away after whale—and of course by Milton, who must be considered one of the all-time great cartoonists, as when Satan

> Puts on swift wings, and toward the Gates of Hell
> Explores his solitary flight; sometimes
> He scours the right hand coast, sometimes the left,
> Now shaves with level wing the Deep, then soars
> Up the fiery concave touring high.

(It's true, Milton's a little boring now and then, and Milton teachers often don't properly value the cartoonist in him and want to know things about "Paradise Lost" that only some kind of crazy could get seriously interested in; but never mind.) I'm afraid the embarrassing truth is that the whole literary tradition opened out, for me, from Disney and his kind. I got caught up in the mighty cartoons of Homer and Dante (much later Virgil and Apollonius), the less realistic 18th- and 19th-century novelists (Fielding, Smollett, Collins, and the rest), the glorious mad Russians (Tolstoy, Dostoyevsky, Bely), and those kinds of poets who fill one's head with strange, intense visions, like Blake, Coleridge, and Keats.

For me the whole world of literature was at this time one of grand cartoons. I thought of myself mainly as a chemistry major and took courses in English just for fun. I guess I thought literature was unserious, like going to the movies or playing in a dance band, even an orchestra. It did not seem to me that one ought to spend one's life on mere pleasure, like a butterfly or cricket. Beethoven, Shakespeare, Richard Strauss, Conan Doyle might be a delight, but to fritter away one's life in the arts seemed, well, not quite honest. Then I came across the New Criticism.

At the first college I went to (for two years) I'd read nearly all of the Modern Library, partly for fun, partly because I felt ignorant around my fellow students, people who could talk with seeming wisdom about Camus and Proust, Nietzsche and Plato—I soon discovered they hadn't really read what they claimed to have read, they'd just come from the right part of town—but I'd never in any serious sense "studied" literature. (I took a couple of courses where one was examined on what Carlyle and Cardinal Newman said, without much emphasis on why or to whom.) But when I moved to Washington University in St. Louis I got a whole new vision of what literature was for— that is, the vision of the New Criticism. Like the fanatic I've always been, I fell to analyzing fiction, digging out symbols and structural subtleties, learning about "levels" and so on.

I don't say this was a foolish activity—in fact I think the New Critics were basically right: It's much more interesting and rewarding to talk about how literature "works" than to read biographies of the writer, which is mainly what the New Criticism replaced. Working with the famous books by Cleanth Brooks and Robert Penn Warren, I began to love things in fiction and poetry that I'd never before noticed, things like meaning and design, and, like all my generation, I made the great discovery that literature is worthwhile, not a thing to be scorned by serious puritans but a thing to be embraced and turned cunningly to advantage. I learned that literature is Good for you, and that writers who are not deeply philosophical should be scorned. I began to read realists—two of whom, Jane Austen and James Joyce, I actually liked— and I began to write "serious" fiction; that is, instead of writing pleasant jingles or stories I desperately hoped would be published in *The Saturday Evening Post* or maybe *Manhunt*, I began shyly eyeing *The Kenyon Review*. With a sigh of relief (though I'd enjoyed them, in a way) I quit math and science and signed up, instead, for courses in philosophy and sociology and psychology, which I knew would make me a better person and perhaps a famous writer so brilliant and difficult that to get through my books you would need a teacher.

This period lasted longer than I care to admit. On the basis of my earnestness and a more or less astonishing misreading of Nietzsche (I was convinced that he was saying that only fiction can be truly philosophical) I won a Woodrow Wilson Fellowship to the University of Iowa, where I meant to study in the famous Writers' Workshop but soon ended up taking medieval language and literature, the literature God had been nudging me toward all along: "Beowulf," "The Divine Comedy," the Gawain poet, and Chaucer. The scales fell from my eyes. My New Critical compulsion to figure out exactly how everything works, how every nuance plays against every other, had suddenly an immense field to plow. I continued to read and think about other literature—I went through a Thomas Mann phase, a Henry James phase, and so on—but I found myself spending more and more time trying to figure out medieval works.

It seems to me that when I began working on medieval literature, in the late 50's and early 60's, scholars knew very little about even the greatest works in that literature. No one had really figured out the structure of the works of the Gawain poet, not to mention "Beowulf" or the poetry of Chaucer. People were still arguing about whether or not "Beowulf" is a Christian poem; people were still trying to shuffle around "The Canterbury Tales." The usual New Critical method, which is to stare and stare at the work until it becomes clear, was useless on this material, because again and again you found yourself staring at something that felt like a symbol or an allusion, or felt that maybe it ought to be some kind of joke but you couldn't see the humor. To figure out the poem you had to figure out the world it came from—read the books the poets knew, try to understand esthetic principles abandoned and forgotten centuries ago. One had no choice but to become a sort of scholar.

Literary detective work is always fun, for a certain kind of mind at least, but the work I did on medieval literature, then on later classical literature, was for me the most exciting detective work I've ever done or heard of. The thing was, not only did you solve interesting puzzles, but when you got them solved you found you'd restored something magnificent, a work of art—in the case of "Beowulf" or "The Canterbury Tales"—supremely beautiful and noble. One unearthed tricks of the craft that nobody'd known or used for a long, long time—tricks one could turn on one's own work, making it different from anybody else's and yet not crazy, not merely novel.

I think every writer wants to sound like him- or herself; that's the main reason one sees so many experimental novels. And of course the risk in the pursuit of newness is that, in refusing to do what the so-called tradition does, one ends up doing exactly the same thing everybody else trying to get outside the tradition does. For better or worse (I'm no longer much concerned about whether it's better or worse), I joined up with an alternative tradition, one with which I felt almost eerily comfortable. My church-filled childhood delighted in discovering a Christianity distant enough—in fact, for all practical purposes, *dead* enough—to satisfy nostalgia without stirring embarrassment and annoyance, as modern Christianity does. For instance, when one reads about "ensoulment" in a medieval book—that is, when one reads arguments on precisely when the soul enters the fetus, and the argument comes from someone of the 13th century—one can read with interest; but when one hears a living Christian hotly debating ensoulment, hoping to be able to support abortion without feelings of guilt, one shrinks away, tries to get lost in the crowd.

I found in medieval culture and art, in other words, exactly what I needed as an instrument for looking at my own time and place. I of course never became for a moment a medieval Christian believer, but medieval ideas and attitudes gave me a means of triangulating, a place to stand. And, needless to say, medieval literature had built into it everything I'd liked best from the beginning, back in the days of God, Dickens, and Disney, of grotesques (cartoon people and places), noble feeling, humor (God was perhaps a little short on humor), and real storytelling.

I said earlier that I'm no longer much concerned about whether the work I've done and am doing is for better or worse. That is not quite as true as I might wish. Egoistic ambition is the kind of weed that grows out of dragon's blood: The more you chop it away the more it flourishes. But it's true that at a certain point in one's career one begins to face up to one's limitations, and the way to stay sane at such a moment is to soften one's standards a little— find good reasons for approving lumpy but well-intentioned work, one's own and everybody else's.

To put all this another way, when I think back now over the influences which have helped to shape the way I write, I notice with a touch of dismay that they were as much bad influences as good ones. I won't criticize God (anyway, He's almost certainly been misquoted), but clearly the influence of Dickens and Disney was not all to the good. Both of them incline one toward stylized gestures. Instead of looking very closely at the world and writing it down, the way James Joyce does, brilliantly getting down, say, the way an old man moves his tongue over his gums, or the way a beautiful woman idly plays with her bracelets, a writer like me, seduced by cartoon vision, tends to go again and again for the same gestural gimmicks, a consistent pattern of caricature (compare the way doors in Dostoyevsky are forever flying open or slamming).

I look over my fiction of 20 years and see it as one long frenzy of tics—
endlessly repeated words like *merely* and *grotesque,* a disproportionate number of people with wooden fingers and a dreary penchant for frowning
thoughtfully or darting their eyes around like maniacs. I seem incapable of
writing a story in which people do not babble philosophically, not really because they're saying things I want to get said but because earnest babbling is
one of the ways I habitually give vitality to my short-legged, overweight,
twitching cartoon creations. And needless to say, from artists like Dickens
and Disney I get my morbid habit of trying to make the reader fall into tender weeping.

The whole New Critical period I went through, and the scholarly period
that followed it, betrayed me, I think, into an excessive concern with significance. It's probably the case that novels and stories are more interesting if, in
some sense or another, they mean something. But it has begun to dawn on
me that—in fiction, as in all the arts—a little meaning goes a long way. I
think what chiefly made me notice this is the work of my creative writing
students. Until about five years ago, I never taught creative writing, only
medieval literature and now and then a little Greek. When I began to look
hard and often at student writing, I soon discovered that one of the main
mistakes in their writing is that students think (probably because they've
taken too many English literature courses) that fiction is supposed to tell us
things—instruct us, improve us, show us.

In a sense of course they're right, but only in a subtle and mysterious
sense. When one has analyzed every symbolically neat detail in a story like
"Death in Venice" or "Disorder and Early Sorrow"—when one has accounted for every verbal repetition, every pattern and relationship, and set
down in alphabetical order every thought to be lifted or wrenched from the
story—one discovers that, when you come right down to it, Mann has told us
nothing we didn't know already. More by my writing students' early bad examples (they later get better) than by all the good literary examples I ever
read, I've come to see that fiction simply dramatizes. It gives importance to
ideas, it seems to me, pretty much in the way the string on which a handful
of pearls have been strung gives a kind of importance to the pearls. When I
read my earliest, most ingeniously constructed fictions ("The Resurrection"
and "Grendel") I find I can no longer figure the damn things out—would
that I'd kept all my charts! Insofar as such books are interesting, for me at
least, they're interesting because I like the characters and hope, as I reread,
that life (the rest of the book) won't treat them too badly.

I don't mean, of course, that I intend never again to use symbols or to
design my stories so that the reader has the kind of experience William James
described with such delight: "There goes the same thing I saw before again."
What I do mean is that when I was 3 or 4, or 12 or 13, I understood fiction
more profoundly than I understood it through most of my writing years. I
understood that a story, like a painting, or like a symphony, is one of the most
wonderful, one of the most useless, things in the world. The magnificence of a
work of art lies precisely in the fact that nobody made the artist make it, he just
did, and—except when one's in school—nobody makes the receiver read it, or
look at it, or listen to it; he just does. The influence of my writing students has
been to lead me to understand (or imagine I understand) that art's value is not
that it expresses life's meaning (though presumably it does, as do butterflies
and crickets) but that it is, simply, splendidly, *there.*

I think of the performances my mother and father would sometimes do at, for instance, the monthly meetings of the Grange. The way the night would go is this: First everybody would crowd into one immense room with trestle-tables and white-paper tablecloths, the tables all loaded down with food, all the redfaced farmers and their plump wives and children finding folding chairs near friends, and somebody would tap a water glass with the side of his spoon and would say a quick, self-conscious prayer, and then everybody would eat.

It was a wonderfully pleasant social time, lots of jokes and stories and abundant country food; but it wasn't a time they chose solely for its pleasantness: If you wanted to get farmers to come from all over the county late at night, after chores, you had to feed them. Then they'd all go into another room and have their business meeting—how much or how little they should organize, how to keep the feed-mills, the truckers, and the United States Congress in line. Nobody much cared for the business meeting, though sometimes somebody would "get off a good one," as they used to say.

Then, when the work was done my mother and father would stand there in the middle of the big, bright room and say poems or sing. How strange it seemed to me that all these serious, hard-working people should sit there grinning for an hour or more, listening, for instance, to my father telling them an endless, pointless story of a ghost in armor, or a ship rescued by pigeons, or somebody called Dangerous Dan McGrew. It was absurd. I wasn't just imagining it. The whole thing was deeply, weirdly absurd. Clearly if one is to devote a lifetime to doing something as crazy as that, one had better do it well—not necessarily because there is any great virtue in doing it well but only because, if one does it badly, people may wake up and notice that what one's doing is crazy.

Suggestions for Discussion

1. John Gardner, like Anne Tyler, describes his family and their influence on him. How are the two families different and similar?

2. Why did Gardner learn so much from Dickens and Disney? To what kind of writers does he contrast them? Explain his statement that when he was young, God, Dickens, and Disney were his favorite authors.

3. Explain how Gardner became interested first in literature as a serious occupation and then in the study of medieval literature. Why did medieval literature become so important to him? How did literary study influence his own writing?

4. How similar in tone is the memoir to the one by Anne Tyler?

5. What does Gardner mean by "cartoons" in literature?

6. Why does Gardner both begin and end the essay with an account of his parents?

Suggestions for Writing

1. In an essay, compare and contrast the memoirs by Gardner and Tyler. Discuss the structure and tone of each.

2. Write an essay explaining why Gardner lists Disney in the same breath as God and Dickens. How are Disney's cartoons related to art?

Anne Tyler

Still Just Writing

Anne Tyler (b. 1941) won creative writing awards while majoring in Russian at Duke, where she received her degree at 19. She went on to graduate study in Russian, worked as a librarian, and wrote her first novel at 22. She has written numerous short stories situated in the contemporary South and several novels, including *Searching for Caleb* (1975), *Earthly Possessions* (1977), *Dinner at the Homesick Restaurant* (1982), *The Accidental Tourist* (1985), *Breathing Lessons* (1988), for which she won the Pulitzer Prize in 1989, and *Saint Maybe* (1991). This essay, published in 1980 in *The Writer on Her Work*, explains with understated wit how she has managed at the same time to be a successful writer, wife, and mother of two daughters.

While I was painting the downstairs hall I thought of a novel to write. Really I just thought of a character; he more or less wandered into my mind, wearing a beard and a broad-brimmed leather hat. I figured that if I sat down and organized this character on paper, a novel would grow up around him. But it was March and the children's spring vacation began the next day, so I waited.

After spring vacation the children went back to school, but the dog got worms. It was a little complicated at the vet's and I lost a day. By then it was Thursday; Friday is the only day I can buy the groceries, pick up new cedar chips for the gerbils, scrub the bathrooms. I waited till Monday. Still, that left me four good weeks in April to block out the novel.

By May I was ready to start actually writing, but I had to do it in patches. There was the follow-up treatment at the vet, and then a half-day spent trailing the dog with a specimen tin so the lab could be sure the treatment had really worked. There were visits from the washing machine repairman and the Davey tree man, not to mention briefer interruptions by the meter reader, five Jehovah's Witnesses, and two Mormons. People telephoned wanting to sell me permanent light bulbs and waterproof basements. An Iranian cousin of my husband's had a baby; the cousin's uncle died; then the cousin's mother decided to go home to Iran and needed to know where to buy a black American coat before she left. There *are* no black American coats; don't Americans wear mourning? I told her no, but I checked around at all the department stores anyway because she didn't speak English. Then I wrote chapters one and two. I had planned to work till 3:30 every day, but it was a month of early quittings: once for the children's dental appointment, once for the cat's rabies shot, once for our older daughter's orthopedist, and twice for her gymnastic meets. Sitting on the bleachers in the school gymnasium, I told myself I could always use this in a novel someplace, but I couldn't really picture writing a novel about 20 little girls in leotards trying to walk the length of a wooden beam without falling off. By the time I'd written chapter three, it was Memorial Day and the children were home again.

Characters on Hold

I knew I shouldn't expect anything from June. School was finished then and camp hadn't yet begun. I put the novel away. I closed down my mind and planted some herbs and played cribbage with the children. Then on the 25th, we drove one child to a sleepaway camp in Virginia and entered the other in a day camp, and I was ready to start work again. First I had to take my car in for repairs and the mechanics lost it, but I didn't get diverted. I sat in the garage on a folding chair while they hunted my car all one afternoon, and I hummed a calming tune and tried to remember what I'd planned to do next in my novel. Or even what the novel was about, for that matter. My character wandered in again in his beard and his broad-brimmed hat. He looked a little pale and knuckly, like someone scrabbling at a cliff edge so as not to fall away entirely.

I had high hopes for July, but it began with a four-day weekend, and on Monday night we had a long-distance call from our daughter's camp in Virginia. She was seriously ill in a Charlottesville hospital. We left our youngest with friends and drove three hours in a torrent of rain. We found our daughter frightened and crying, and another child (the only other child I knew in all of Virginia) equally frightened and crying down in the emergency room with possible appendicitis, so I spent that night alternating between a chair in the pediatraic wing and a chair in the emergency room. By morning, it had begun to seem that our daughter's illness was typhoid fever. We loaded her into the car and took her back to Baltimore, where her doctor put her on drugs and prescribed a long bed-rest. She lay in bed six days, looking wretched and calling for fluids and cold cloths. On the seventh day she got up her same old healthy self, and the illness was declared to be not typhoid fever after all but a simple virus, and we shipped her back to Virginia on the evening train. The next day I was free to start writing again but sat, instead, on the couch in my study, staring blankly at the wall.

Part-Time Creativity

I could draw some conclusions here about the effect that being a woman/wife/mother has upon my writing, except that I am married to a writer who is also a man/husband/father. He published his first novel while he was a medical student in Iran; then he came to America to finish his training. His writing fell by the wayside, for a long while. You can't be on call in the emergency room for 20 hours and write a novel during the other four. Now he's a child psychiatrist, fulltime, and he writes his novels in the odd moments here and there—when he's not preparing a lecture, when he's not on the phone with a patient, when he's not attending classes at the psychoanalytic institute. He writes in Persian, still, in those black-and-white speckled composition books. Sometimes one of the children will interrupt him in English and he will answer in Persian, and they'll say, "What?" and he'll look up blankly, and it seems a sheet has to fall from in front of his eyes before he remembers where he is and switches to English. Often, I wonder what he would be doing now if he didn't have a family to support. He cares deeply about his writing and he's very good at it, but every morning at 5:30 he gets up and puts on a suit and tie and drives in the dark to the hospital. Both of us, in different ways, seem to be hewing our creative time in small, hard chips from our living time.

Drained and Drawn

Occasionally, I take a day off. I go to a friend's house for lunch, or weed the garden, or rearrange the linen closet. I notice that at the end of one of these days, when my husband asks me what I've been doing, I tend to exaggerate any hardships I may have encountered. ("A pickup nearly sideswiped me on Greenspring Avenue. I stood in line an hour just trying to buy the children some flip-flops.") It seems sinful to have lounged around so. Also, it seems sinful that I have more choice than my husband as to whether or not to undertake any given piece of work. I can refuse to do an article if it doesn't appeal to me, refuse to change a short story, refuse to hurry a book any faster than it wants to go—all luxuries. My husband, on the other hand, is forced to rise and go off to that hospital every blessed weekday of his life. *His* luxury is that no one expects him to drop all else for two weeks when a child has chicken pox. The only person who has no luxuries at all, it seems to me, is the woman writer who is the sole support of her children. I often think about how she must manage. I think that if I were in that position, I'd have to find a job involving manual labor. I have spent so long erecting partitions around the part of me that writes—learning how to close the door on it when ordinary life intervenes, how to close the door on ordinary life when it's time to start writing again—that I'm not sure I could fit the two parts of me back together now.

Before we had children I worked in a library. It was a boring job, but I tend to like doing boring things. I would sit on a stool alphabetizing Russian catalogue cards and listening to the other librarians talking around me. It made me think of my adolescence, which was spent listening to the tobacco stringers while I handled tobacco. At night I'd go home from the library and write. I never wrote what the librarians said, exactly, but having those voices in my ears all day helped me summon up my own characters' voices. Then our first baby came along—an insomniac. I quit work and stayed home all day with her and walked her all night. Even if I had found the time to write, I wouldn't have had the insides. I felt drained; too much care and feeling were being drawn out of me. And the only voices I heard now were by appointment—people who came to dinner, or invited us to dinner, and who therefore felt they had to make deliberate conversation. That's one thing writers never have, and I still miss it: the easy-going, on-again-off-again, gossipy murmurs of people working alongside each other all day.

Free and Useful

I enjoyed tending infants (though I've much preferred the later ages), but it was hard to be solely, continually in their company and not to be able to write. And I couldn't think of any alternative. I know it must be possible to have a child raised beautifully by a housekeeper, but every such child I've run into has seemed dulled and doesn't use words well. So I figured I'd better stick it out. As it happened, it wasn't that long—five years, from the time our first daughter was born till our second started nursery school and left me with my mornings free. But while I was going through it I thought it would be a lot longer. I couldn't imagine any end to it. I felt that everything I wanted to write was somehow coagulating in my veins and making me fidgety and slow. Then after a while I didn't have anything to write anyhow, but I still had the fidgets. I felt useless, no matter how many diapers I washed or strollers I pushed. The only way I could explain my life to myself was to imagine that I was living in a very small commune. I had spent my childhood in a commune, or what would nowadays be called a commune, and I was used to the idea of division of labor. What we had here, I told myself, was a perfectly sensible arrangement: One member was the liaison with the outside world, bringing in money; another was the caretaker, reading the Little Bear books to the children and repairing the electrical switches. This second member might have less physical freedom, but she had much more freedom to arrange her own work schedule. I must have sat down a dozen times a week and very carefully, consciously thought it all through. Often, I was merely trying to convince myself that I really did pull my own weight.

Strung Up

This Iranian cousin who just had the baby: She sits home now and cries a lot. She was working on her master's degree and is used to being out in the world more. "Never mind," I tell her, "you'll soon be out again. This stage doesn't last long."

"How long?" she asks.

"Oh . . . three years, if you just have the one."

"Three years!"

I can see she's appalled. Her baby is beautiful, very dark and Persian; and what's more, he sleeps—something I've rarely seen a baby do. What I'm trying to say to her (but of course, she'll agree without really hearing me) is that he's worth it. It seems to me that since I've had children, I've grown richer and deeper. They may have slowed down my writing for a while, but when I did write, I had more of a self to speak from. After all, who else in the world do you *have* to love, no matter what? Who else can you absolutely not give up on? My life seems more intricate. Also more dangerous.

After the children started school, I put up the partitions in my mind. I would rush around in the morning braiding their hair, packing their lunches; then the second they were gone I would grow quiet and climb the stairs to my study. Sometimes a child would come home early and I would feel a little tug between the two parts of me; I'd be absent-minded and short-tempered. Then gradually I learned to make the transition more easily. It feels like a sort of string that I tell myself to loosen. When the children come home, I drop the string and close the study door and that's the end of it. It doesn't always work perfectly, of course. There are times when it doesn't work at all:

If a child is sick, for instance, I can't possibly drop the children's end of the string, and I've learned not to try. It's easier just to stop writing for a while. Or if they're home but otherwise occupied, I no longer attempt to sneak off to my study to finish that one last page; I know that instantly, as if by magic, assorted little people will be pounding on my door requiring Band-Aids, tetanus shots, and a complete summation of the facts of life.

Last spring, I bought a midget tape recorder to make notes on. I'd noticed that my best ideas came while I was running the vacuum cleaner, but I was always losing them. I thought this little recorder would help. I carried it around in my shirt pocket. But I was ignoring the partitions, is what it was; I was letting one half of my life intrude upon the other. A child would be talking about her day at school and suddenly I'd whip out the tape recorder and tell it, "Get Morgan out of that cocktail party; he's not the type to drink." "Huh?" the child would say. Both halves began to seem ludicrous, unsynchronized. I took the recorder back to Radio Shack.

Faith and Adaptation

A few years ago, my parents went to the Gaza Strip to work for the American Friends Service Committee. It was a lifelong dream of my father's to do something with the AFSC as soon as all his children were grown, and he'd been actively preparing for it for years. But almost as soon as they got there, my mother fell ill with a mysterious fever that neither the Arab nor the Israeli hospitals could diagnose. My parents had to come home for her treatment, and since they'd sublet their house in North Carolina, they had to live with us. For four months, they stayed here—but only on a week-to-week basis, not knowing when they were going back, or whether they were going back at all, or how serious my mother's illness was. It was hard for her, of course, but it should have been especially hard in another way for my father, who had simply to hang in suspended animation for four months while my mother was whisked in and out of hospitals. However, I believe he was as pleased with life as he always is. He whistled Mozart and puttered around insulating our windows. He went on long walks collecting firewood. He strolled over to the meetinghouse and gave a talk on the plight of the Arab refugees. "Now that we seem to have a little time," he told my mother, "why not visit the boys?" and during one of her outpatient periods he took her on a gigantic cross-country trip to see all my brothers and any other relatives they happened upon. Then my mother decided she ought to go to a faith healer. (She wouldn't usually do such a thing, but she was desperate.) "Oh. Okay," my father said, and he took her to a faith healer, whistling all the way. And when the faith healer didn't work, my mother said, "I think this is psychosomatic. Let's go back to Gaza." My father said, "Okay," and reserved two seats on the next plane over. The children and I went to see them the following summer: My mother's fever was utterly gone, and my father drove us down the Strip, weaving a little Renault among the tents and camels, cheerfully whistling Mozart.

I hold this entire, rambling set of events in my head at all times, and remind myself of it almost daily. It seems to me that the way my father lives (infinitely adapting, and looking around him with a smile to say, "Oh! So *this* is where I am!") is also the way to slip gracefully through a choppy life of writing novels, plastering the dining room ceiling, and presiding at slumber parties. I have learned, bit by bit, to accept a school snow-closing as an unexpected holiday, an excuse to play 17 rounds of Parcheesi instead of typing up a short story. When there's a midweek visitation of uncles from Iran (hordes of great, bald, yellow men calling for their glasses of tea, sleeping on guest beds, couches, two armchairs pushed together, and discarded crib mattresses), I have decided that I might as well listen to what they have to say, and work on my novel tomorrow instead. I smile at the uncles out of a kind of clear, swept space inside me. What this takes, of course, is a sense of limitless time, but I'm getting that. My life is beginning to seem unusually long. And there's a danger to it: I could wind up as passive as a piece of wood on a wave. But I try to walk a middle line.

Wait for Heaven

I was standing in the schoolyard waiting for a child when another mother came up to me. "Have you found work yet?" she asked. "Or are you still just writing?"

Now, how am I supposed to answer that?

I could take offense, come to think of it. Maybe the reason I didn't is that I halfway share her attitude. They're *paying* me for this? For just writing down untruthful stories? I'd better look around for more permanent employment. For I do consider writing to be a finite job. I expect that any day now, I will have said all I have to say; I'll have used up all my characters, and then I'll be free to get on with my real life. When I make a note of new ideas on index cards, I imagine I'm clearing out my head, and that soon it will be empty and spacious. I file the cards in a little blue box, and I can picture myself using the final card one day—ah! through at last!—and throwing the blue box away. I'm like a dentist who continually fights tooth decay, working toward the time when he's conquered it altogether and done himself out of a job. But my head keeps loading up again; the little blue box stays crowded and messy. Even when I feel I have no ideas at all, and can't possibly start the next chapter, I have a sense of something still bottled in me, trying to get out.

People have always seemed funny and strange to me, and touching in unexpected ways. I can't shake off a sort of mist of irony that hangs over whatever I see. Probably that's what I'm trying to put across when I write; I may believe that I'm the one person who holds this view of things. And I'm always hurt when a reader says that I choose only bizarre or eccentric people to write about. It's not a matter of choice; it just seems to me that even the most ordinary person, in real life, will turn out to have something unusual at his center. I like to think that I might meet up with one of my past characters at the very next street corner. The odd thing is, sometimes I have. And if I were remotely religious, I'd believe that a little gathering of my characters would be waiting for me in heaven when I died. "*Then* what happened?" I'd ask them. "How have things worked out, since the last time I saw you?"

Eudora's Legacy

I think I was born with the impression that what happened in books was much more reasonable, and interesting, and *real,* in some ways, than what happened in life. I hated childhood, and spent it sitting behind a book waiting for adulthood to arrive. When I ran out of books I made up my own. At night, when I couldn't sleep, I made up stories in the dark. Most of my plots involved girls going west in covered wagons. I was truly furious that I'd been born too late to go west in a covered wagon.

I know a poet who says that in order to be a writer, you have to have had rheumatic fever in your childhood. I've never had rheumatic fever, but I believe that any kind of setting-apart situation will do as well. In my case, it was emerging from that commune—really an experimental Quaker community in the wilderness—and trying to fit into the outside world. I was eleven. I had never used a telephone and could strike a match on the soles of my bare feet. All the children in my new school looked very peculiar to me, and I certainly must have looked peculiar to them. I am still surprised, to this day, to find myself where I am. My life is so streamlined and full of modern conveniences. How did I get here? I have given up hope, by now, of ever losing my sense of distance; in fact, I seem to have come to cherish it. Neither I nor any of my brothers can stand being out among a crowd of people for any length of time at all.

I spent my adolescence planning to be an artist, not a writer. After all, books had to be about major events, and none had ever happened to me. All I knew were tobacco workers, stringing the leaves I handed them and talking up a storm. Then I found a book of Eudora Welty's short stories in the high school library. She was writing about Edna Earle, who was so slow-witted she could sit all day just pondering how the tail of the *C* got through the loop of the *L* on the Coca-Cola sign. Why, I knew Edna Earle. You mean you could *write* about such people? I have always meant to send Eudora Welty a thank-you note, but I imagine she would find it a little strange.

The Write of Passage

I wanted to go to Swarthmore College, but my parents suggested Duke instead, where I had a full scholarship, because my three brothers were coming along right behind me and it was more important for boys to get a good education than for girls. That was the first and last time that my being female was ever a serious issue. I still don't think it was just, but I can't say it ruined my life. After all, Duke had Reynolds Price, who turned out to be the only person I ever knew who could actually teach writing. It all worked out, in the end.

I believe that for many writers, the hardest time is that dead spot after college (where they're wonder-children, made much of) and before their first published work. Luckily, I didn't notice that part; I was so vague about what I wanted to do that I could hardly chafe at not yet doing it. I went to graduate school in Russian studies; I scrubbed decks on a boat in Maine; I got a job ordering books from the Soviet Union. Writing was something that crept in around the edges. For a while I lived in New York, where I became addicted to riding any kind of train or subway, and while I rode I often felt I was nothing but an enormous eye, taking things in and turning them over and sorting them out. But who would I tell them to, once I'd sorted them? I have never had more than three or four close friends, at any period of my life; and anyway, I don't talk well. I am the kind of person who wakes up at four in the morning and suddenly thinks of what she should have said yesterday at lunch. For me, writing something down was the only road out.

Rewarding Routines and Rituals

You would think, since I waited so long and so hopefully for adulthood, that it would prove to be a disappointment. Actually, I figure it was worth the wait. I like everything about it but the paperwork—the income tax and protesting the Sears bill and renewing the Triple-A membership. I always did count on having a husband and children, and here they are. I'm surprised to find myself a writer but have fitted it in fairly well, I think. The only real trouble that writing has ever brought me is an occasional sense of being invaded by the outside world. Why do people imagine that writers, having chosen the most private of professions, should be any good at performing in public, or should have the slightest desire to tell their secrets to interviewers from ladies' magazines? I feel I am only holding myself together by being extremely firm and decisive about what I will do and what I will not do. I will write my books and raise the children. Anything else just fritters me away. I know this makes me seem narrow, but in fact, I *am* narrow. I like routine and rituals and I hate leaving home; I have a sense of digging my heels in. I refuse to drive on freeways. I dread our annual vacation. Yet I'm continually prepared for travel: It is physically impossible for me to buy any necessity without buying a travel-sized version as well. I have a little toilet kit, with soap and a nightgown, forever packed and ready to go. How do you explain that?

As the outside world grows less dependable, I keep buttressing my inside world, where people go on meaning well and surprising other people with little touches of grace. There are days when I sink into my novel like a pool and emerge feeling blank and bemused and used up. Then I drift over to the schoolyard, and there's this mother wondering if I'm doing anything halfway useful yet. Am I working? Have I found a job? No, I tell her.

I'm still just writing.

Suggestions for Discussion

1. This essay is about a writer who is a woman, wife, and mother. Would a male writer have written a much different essay?

2. In what ways does the author keep her life compartmentalized? What advantages are there for her in doing so?

3. Anne Tyler writes about her difficulties objectively and without self-pity. What impact does this style of writing have?

4. Is this a formal or an informal essay? Explain your answer.

5. Explain the relevance of two incidents to the theme of the essay: her daughter's illness while at camp and her mother's illness which began on the Gaza Strip.

6. Why does Tyler say she is not a good talker? In what way is the writer's job different from most others?

Suggestions for Writing

1. This essay explains a professional writer's methods of coping with the details of life from a woman's point of view. Write an essay showing how your gender shapes the way you meet your daily duties and imposes restraints on you.

2. Tyler presents her family as both loving and cohesive. Write an essay in which you explain how the love in this family is expressed. Is it supportive of the parents' lives?

Eudora Welty

Finding a Voice

Eudora Welty (b. 1909), the preeminent Southern novelist and short-story writer, has published *Delta Wedding* (1946); *Losing Battles* (1970); *The Optimist's Daughter* (1972), for which she won the Pulitzer Prize; *Collected Stories* (1980); and *Eudora Welty's Photographs* (1989). She was awarded the Presidential Medal of Freedom in 1980 and the National Medal of Arts in 1987. In the following excerpt from her reminiscence, *One Writer's Beginnings* (1985), she explores the source of one of the characters she has created.

What discoveries I've made in the course of writing stories all begin with the particular, never the general. They are mostly hindsight: arrows that I now find I myself have left behind me, which have shown me some right, or wrong, way I have come. What one story may have pointed out to me is of no avail in the writing of another. But "avail" is not what I want; freedom ahead is what each story promises—beginning anew. And all the while, as further hindsight has told me, certain patterns in my work repeat themselves without my realizing. There would be no way to know this, for during the writing of any single story, there is no other existing. Each writer must find out for himself, I imagine, on what strange basis he lives with his own stories.

I had been writing a number of stories, more or less one after the other, before it belatedly dawned on me that some of the characters in one story were, and had been all the time, the same characters who had appeared already in another story. Only I'd written about them originally under different names, at different periods in their lives, in situations not yet interlocking but ready for it. They touched on every side. These stories were all related (and the fact was buried in their inceptions) by the strongest ties—identities, kinships, relationships, or affinities already known or remembered or foreshadowed. From story to story, connections between the characters' lives, through their motives or actions, sometimes their dreams, already existed: there to be found. Now the whole assembly—some of it still in the future—fell, by stages, into place in one location already evoked, which I saw now was a focusing point for all the stories. What had drawn the characters together there was one strong strand in them all: they lived in one way or another in a dream or in romantic aspiration, or under an illusion of what their lives were coming to, about the meaning of their (now) related lives.

The stories were connected most provocatively of all to me, perhaps, through the entry into my story-telling mind of another sort of tie—a shadowing of Greek mythological figures, gods and heroes that wander in various guises, at various times, in and out, emblems of the characters' heady dreams.

Writing these stories, which eventually appeared joined together in the book called *The Golden Apples*, was an experience in a writer's own discovery of affinities. In writing, as in life, the connections of all sorts of relationships and kinds lie in wait of discovery, and give out their signals to the Geiger counter of the charged imagination, once it is drawn into the right field.

The characters who go to make up my stories and novels are not portraits. Characters I invent along with the story that carries them. Attached to them are what I've borrowed, perhaps unconsciously, bit by bit, of persons I have seen or noticed or remembered in the flesh—a cast of countenance here, a manner of walking there, that jump to the visualizing mind when a story is underway. (Elizabeth Bowen said, "Physical detail cannot be invented." It can only be chosen.) I don't write by invasion into the life of a real person: my own sense of privacy is too strong for that; and I also know instinctively that living people to whom you are close—those known to you in ways too deep, too overflowing, ever to be plumbed outside love—do not yield to, could never fit into, the demands of a story. On the other hand, what I do make my stories out of is the *whole* fund of my feelings, my responses to the real experiences of my own life, to the relationships that formed and changed it, that I have given most of myself to, and so learned my way toward a dramatic counterpart. Characters take on life sometimes by luck, but I suspect it is when you can write most entirely out of yourself, inside the skin, heart, mind, and soul of a person who is not yourself, that a character becomes in his own right another human being on the page.

It was not my intention—it never was—to invent a character who should speak for me, the author, in person. A character is in a story to fill a role there, and the character's life along with its expression of life is defined by that surrounding—indeed is created by his own story. Yet, it seems to me now, years after I wrote *The Golden Apples*, that I did bring forth a character with whom I came to feel oddly in touch. This is Miss Eckhart, a woman who has come from away to give piano lessons to the young of Morgana. She is formidable and eccentric in the eyes of everyone, is scarcely accepted in the town. But she persisted with me, as she persisted in spite of herself with the other characters in the stories.

Where did the character of Miss Eckhart come from? There was my own real-life piano teacher, "eligible" to the extent that she swatted my hands at the keyboard with a fly-swatter if I made a mistake; and when she wrote "Practice" on my page of sheet music she made her "P" as Miss Eckhart did—a cat's face with a long tail. She did indeed hold a recital of her pupils every June that was a fair model for Miss Eckhart's, and of many another as well, I suppose. But the character of Miss Eckhart was miles away from that of the teacher I knew as a child, or from that of anybody I did know. Nor was she like other teacher-characters I was responsible for: my stories and novels suddenly appear to me to be full of teachers, with Miss Eckhart different from them all.

What the story "June Recital" most acutely shows the reader lies in her inner life. I haven't the slightest idea what my real teacher's life was like inside. But I knew what Miss Eckhart's was, for it protruded itself well enough into the story.

As I looked longer and longer for the origins of this passionate and strange character, at last I realized that Miss Eckhart came from me. There wasn't any resemblance in her outward identity: I am not musical, not a teacher, nor foreign in birth; not humorless or ridiculed or missing out in love; nor have I yet let the world around me slip from my recognition. But none of that counts. What counts is only what lies at the solitary core. She derived from what I already knew for myself, even felt I had always known. What I have put into her is my passion for my own life work, my own art. Exposing yourself to risk is a truth Miss Eckhart and I had in common. What animates and possesses me is what drives Miss Eckhart, the love of her art and the love of giving it, the desire to give it until there is no more left. Even in the small and literal way, what I had done in assembling and connecting all the stories in *The Golden Apples*, and bringing them off as one, was not too unlike the June recital itself.

Not in Miss Eckhart as she stands solidly and almost opaquely in the surround of her story, but in the making of her character out of my most inward and most deeply feeling self, I would say I have found my voice in my fiction.

Of course any writer is in part all of his characters. How otherwise would they be known to him, occur to him, become what they are? I was also part Cassie in that same story, the girl who hung back, and indeed part of most of the main characters in the connected stories into whose minds I go. Except for Virgie, the heroine. She is right outside me. She is powerfully like Miss Eckhart, her co-equal in stubborn and passionate feeling, while more expressive of it—but fully apart from me. And as Miss Eckhart's powers shrink and fade away, the young Virgie grows up more rampant, and struggles into some sort of life independent from all the rest.

If somewhere in its course your work seems to you to have come into a life of its own, and you can stand back from it and leave it be, you are looking then at your subject—so I feel. This is how I came to regard the character of Virgie in *The Golden Apples*. She comes into her own in the last of the stories, "The Wanderers." Passionate, recalcitrant, stubbornly undefeated by failure or hurt or disgrace or bereavement, all the while heedlessly wasting of her gifts, she knows to the last that there is a world that remains out there, a world living and mysterious, and that she is of it.

Inasmuch as Miss Eckhart might have been said to come from me, the author, Virgie, at her moments, might have always been my subject.

Through learning at my later date things I hadn't known, or had escaped or possibly feared realizing, about my parents—and myself—I glimpse our whole family life as if it were freed of that clock time which spaces us apart so inhibitingly, divides young and old, keeps our living through the same experiences at separate distances.

It is our inward journey that leads us through time—forward or back, seldom in a straight line, most often spiraling. Each of us is moving, changing, with respect to others. As we discover, we remember; remembering, we discover; and most intensely do we experience this when our separate journeys converge. Our living experience at those meeting points is one of the charged dramatic fields of fiction.

I'm prepared now to use the wonderful word *confluence*, which of itself exists as a reality and a symbol in one. It is the only kind of symbol that for me as a writer has any weight, testifying to the pattern, one of the chief patterns, of human experience.

Here I am leading to the last scenes in my novel, *The Optimist's Daughter:*

She had slept in the chair, like a passenger who had come on an emergency journey in a train. But she had rested deeply.

She had dreamed that she *was* a passenger, and riding with Phil. They had ridden together over a long bridge.

Awake, she recognized it: it was a dream of something that had really happened. When she and Phil were coming down from Chicago to Mount Salus to be married in the Presbyterian Church, they came on the train. Laurel, when she travelled back and forth between Mount Salus and Chicago, had always taken the sleeper. She and Phil followed the route on the day train, and she saw it for the first time.

When they were climbing the long approach to a bridge after leaving Cairo, rising slowly higher until they rode above the tops of bare trees, she looked down and saw the pale light widening and the river bottoms opening out, and then the water appearing, reflecting the low, early sun. There were two rivers. Here was where they came together. This was the confluence of the waters, the Ohio and the Mississippi.

They were looking down from a great elevation and all they saw was at the point of coming together, the bare trees marching in from the horizon, the rivers moving into one, and as he touched her arm she looked up with him and saw the long, ragged, pencil-faint line of birds within the crystal of the zenith, flying in a V of their own, following the same course down. All they could see was sky, water, birds, light, and confluence. It was the whole morning world.

And they themselves were a part of the confluence. Their own joint act of faith had brought them here at the very moment and matched its occurrence, and proceeded as it proceeded. Direction itself was made beautiful, momentous. They were riding as one with it, right up front. It's our turn! she'd thought exultantly. And we're going to live forever.

Left bodiless and graveless of a death made of water and fire in a year long gone, Phil could still tell her of her life. For her life, any life, she had to believe, was nothing but the continuity of its love.

She believed it just as she believed that the confluence of the waters was still happening at Cairo. It would be there the same as it ever was when she went flying over it today on her way back—out of sight, for her, this time, thousands of feet below, but with nothing in between except thin air.

Of course the greatest confluence of all is that which makes up the human memory—the individual human memory. My own is the treasure most dearly regarded by me, in my life and in my work as a writer. Here time, also, is subject to confluence. The memory is a living thing—it too is in transit. But during its moment, all that is remembered joins, and lives—the old and the young, the past and the present, the living and the dead.

As you have seen, I am a writer who came of a sheltered life. A sheltered life can be a daring life as well. For all serious daring starts from within.

Suggestions for Discussion

1. Discuss her observation that the "characters who go to make up my stories and novels are not portraits. Characters I invent along with the story that carries them."

2. Why did she "come in touch" with the character of Miss Eckhart?

3. Explain her use of the word *confluence*.

Suggestions for Writing

1. Document her observation that "each of us is moving, changing, with respect to others."

2. Use your memory to recreate a scene or character of significance.

Ralph Ellison

On Becoming a Writer

Ralph Ellison (1914–1994), the distinguished American writer, was born in Oklahoma City. In the 1930s he was a student at the Tuskegee Institute, which granted him an honorary Ph.D. in Human Letters in 1963. He held honorary degrees from other American universities and has been a visiting professor of writing in many of them. He was Emeritus Professor of English at New York University. He is best known for The Invisible Man (1952). His other works include Going to the Territory (1986) and Shadow and Act (1964), a collection of essays from which is taken the following reminiscence of becoming aware of what it means to be an "American Negro."

In the beginning writing was far from a serious matter; it was a reflex of reading, an extension of a source of pleasure, escape, and instruction. In fact, I had become curious about writing by way of seeking to understand the aesthetic nature of literary power, the devices through which literature could command my mind and emotions. It was not, then, the *process* of writing which initially claimed my attention, but the finished creations, the artifacts, poems, plays, novels. The act of learning writing technique was, therefore, an amusing investigation of what seemed at best a secondary talent, an exploration, like dabbling in sculpture, of one's potentialities as a "Renaissance

Man." This, surely, would seem a most unlikely and even comic concept to introduce here; and yet, it is precisely because I come from where I do (the Oklahoma of the years between World War I and the Great Depression) that I must introduce it, and with a straight face.

Anything and everything was to be found in the chaos of Oklahoma; thus the concept of the Renaissance Man has lurked long within the shadow of my past, and I shared it with at least a half dozen of my Negro friends. How we actually acquired it I have never learned, and since there is no true sociology of the dispersion of ideas within the American democracy, I doubt if I ever shall. Perhaps we breathed it in with the air of the Negro community of Oklahoma City, the capital of that state whose Negroes were often charged by exasperated white Texans with not knowing their "place." Perhaps we took it defiantly from one of them. Or perhaps I myself picked it up from some transplanted New Englander whose shoes I had shined on a Saturday afternoon. After all, the most meaningful tips do not always come in the form of money, nor are they intentionally extended. Most likely, however, my friends and I acquired the idea from some book or some idealistic Negro teacher, some dreamer seeking to function responsibly in an environment which at its most normal took on some of the mixed character of nightmare and of dream.

One thing is certain, ours was a chaotic community, still characterized by frontier attitudes and by that strange mixture of the naive and sophisticated, the benign and malignant, which makes the American past so puzzling and its present so confusing; that mixture which often affords the minds of the young who grow up in the far provinces such wide and unstructured latitude, and which encourages the individual's imagination—up to the moment "reality" closes in upon him—to range widely and, sometimes, even to soar.

We hear the effects of this in the Southwestern jazz of the 30's, that joint creation of artistically free and exuberantly creative adventurers, of artists who had stumbled upon the freedom lying within the restrictions of their musical tradition as within the limitations of their social background, and who in their own unconscious way have set an example for any Americans, Negro or white, who would find themselves in the arts. They accepted themselves and the complexity of life as they knew it, they loved their art and through it they celebrated American experience definitively in sound. Whatever others thought or felt, this was their own powerful statement, and only non-musical assaults upon their artistic integrity—mainly economically inspired changes of fashion—were able to compromise their vision.

Much of so-called Kansas City jazz was actually brought to perfection in Oklahoma by Oklahomans. It is an important circumstance for me as a writer to remember, because while these musicians and their fellows were busy creating out of tradition, imagination, and the sounds and emotions around them, a freer, more complex, and driving form of jazz, my friends and I were exploring an idea of human versatility and possibility which went against the barbs or over the palings of almost every fence which those who controlled social and political power had erected to restrict our roles in the life of the country. Looking back, one might say that the jazzmen, some of whom we idolized, were in their own way better examples for youth to follow than were most judges and ministers, legislators and governors (we were stuck with the notorious Alfalfa Bill Murray). For as we viewed these pillars of society from the confines of our segregated community we almost always saw crooks, clowns, or hypocrites. Even the best were revealed by their attitudes toward us as lacking the respectable qualities to which they pretended and for which they were accepted outside by others, while despite the outlaw nature of their art, the jazzmen were less torn and damaged by the moral compromises and insincerities which have so sickened the life of our country.

Be that as it may, our youthful sense of life, like that of many Negro children (though no one bothers to note it—especially the specialists and "friends of the Negro" who view our Negro-American life as essentially non-human) was very much like that of Huckleberry Finn, who is universally so praised and enjoyed for the clarity and courage of his moral vision. Like Huck, we observed, we judged, we imitated and evaded as we could the dullness, corruption, and blindness of "civilization." We were undoubtedly comic because, as the saying goes, we weren't supposed to know what it was all about. But to ourselves we were "boys," members of a wild, free, outlaw tribe which transcended the category of race. Rather we were Americans born into the forty-sixth state, and thus, into the context of Negro-American post-Civil War history, "frontiersmen." And isn't one of the implicit functions of the American frontier to encourage the individual to a kind of dreamy wakefulness, a state in which he makes—in all ignorance of the accepted limitations of the possible—rash efforts, quixotic gestures, hopeful testings of the complexity of the known and the given?

Spurring us on in our controlled and benign madness was the voracious reading of which most of us were guilty and the vicarious identification and empathetic adventuring which it encouraged. This was due, in part, perhaps to the fact that some of us were fatherless—my own father had died when I was three—but most likely it was because boys are natural romantics. We were seeking examples, patterns to live by, out of a freedom which for all its being ignored by the sociologists and subtle thinkers, was implicit in the Negro situation. Father and mother substitutes also have a role to play in aiding the child to help create himself. Thus we fabricated our own heroes and ideals catch-as-catch-can; and with an outrageous and irreverent sense of freedom. Yes, and in complete disregard of ideas of respectability or the surreal incongruity of some of our projections. Gamblers and scholars, jazz musicians and scientists, Negro cowboys and soldiers from the Spanish-American and First World Wars, movie stars and stunt men, figures from the Italian Renaissance and literature, both classical and popular, were combined with the special virtues of some local bootlegger, the eloquence of some Negro preacher, the strength and grace of some local athlete, the ruthlessness of some businessman-physician, the elegance in dress and manners of some head-waiter or hotel doorman.

Looking back through the shadows upon this absurd activity, I realize now that we were projecting archetypes, recreating folk figures, legendary heroes, monsters even, most of which violated all ideas of social hierarchy and order and all accepted conceptions of the hero handed down by cultural, religious, and racist tradition. But we, remember, were under the intense spell of the early movies, the silents as well as the talkies; and in our community, life was not so tightly structured as it would have been in the traditional South—or even in deceptively "free" Harlem. And our imaginations processed reality and dream, natural man and traditional hero, literature and folklore, like maniacal editors turned loose in some frantic film-cutting room. Remember, too, that being boys, yet in the play-stage of our development, we were dream-serious in our efforts. But serious nevertheless, for *culturally* play is a prepa-ration, and we felt that somehow the human ideal lay in the vague and con-stantly shifting figures—sometimes comic but always versatile, picaresque, and self-effacingly heroic—which evolved from our wildly improvisatory pro-jections: figures neither white nor black, Christian nor Jewish, but represen-tative of certain desirable essences, of skills and powers, physical, aesthetic, and moral.

The proper response to these figures was, we felt, to develop ourselves for the performance of many and diverse roles, and the fact that certain definite limitations had been imposed upon our freedom did not lessen our sense of obligation. Not only were we to prepare but we were to perform—not with mere competence but with an almost reckless verve; with, may we say (with-out evoking the quaint and questionable notion of *négritude*) Negro-American style? Behind each artist there stands a traditional sense of style, a sense of the felt tension indicative of expressive completeness; a mode of humanizing reality and of evoking a feeling of being at home in the world. It is something which the artist shares with the group, and part of our boyish activity ex-pressed a yearning to make any and everything of quality *Negro-American;* to appropriate it, possess it, recreate it in our own group and individual images.

And we recognized and were proud of our group's own style wherever we discerned it, in jazzmen and prize-fighters, ballplayers, and tap dancers; in gesture, inflection, intonation, timbre, and phrasing. Indeed, in all those nu-ances of expression and attitude which reveal a culture. We did not fully understand the cost of that style, but we recognized within it an affirmation of life beyond all question of our difficulties as Negroes.

Contrary to the notion currently projected by certain specialists in the "Negro problem" which characterizes the Negro American as self-hating and defensive, we did not so regard ourselves. We felt, among ourselves at least, that we were supposed to be whoever we would and could be and do any-thing and everything which other boys did, and do it better. Not defensively, because we were ordered to do so; nor because it was held in the society at large that we were naturally, as Negroes, limited—but because we de-manded it of ourselves. Because to measure up to our own standards was the only way of affirming our notion of manhood.

Hence it was no more incongruous, as seen from our own particular per-spective in this land of incongruities, for young Negro Oklahomans to project themselves as Renaissance men than for white Mississippians to see them-selves as ancient Greeks or noblemen out of Sir Walter Scott. Surely our fantasies have caused far less damage to the nation's sense of reality, if for no other reason than that ours were expressive of a more democratic ideal. Re-member, too, as William Faulkner made us so vividly aware, that the slaves often took the essence of the aristocratic ideal (as they took Christianity) with far more seriousness than their masters, and that we, thanks to the tight tele-scoping of American history, were but two generations from that previous condition. Renaissance men, indeed!

I managed, by keeping quiet about it, to cling to our boyish ideal during three years in Alabama, and I brought it with me to New York, where it not only gave silent support to my explorations of what was then an unknown territory, but served to mock and caution me when I became interested in the Communist ideal. And when it was suggested that I try my hand at writing it was still with me.

The act of writing requires a constant plunging back into the shadow of the past where time hovers ghostlike. When I began writing in earnest I was forced, thus, to relate myself consciously and imaginatively to my mixed background as American, as Negro-American, and as a Negro from what in its own belated way was a pioneer background. More important, and inseparable from this particular effort, was the necessity of determining my true relationship to that body of American literature to which I was most attracted and through which, aided by what I could learn from the literatures of Europe, I would find my own voice and to which I was challenged, by way of achieving myself, to make some small contribution, and to whose composite picture of reality I was obligated to offer some necessary modifications.

This was no matter of sudden insight but of slow and blundering discovery, of a struggle to stare down the deadly and hypnotic temptation to interpret the world and all its devices in terms of race. To avoid this was very important to me, and in light of my background far from simple. Indeed, it was quite complex, involving as it did, a ceaseless questioning of all those formulas which historians, politicians, sociologists, and an older generation of Negro leaders and writers—those of the so-called "Negro Renaissance"—had evolved to describe my group's identity, its predicament, its fate, and its relation to the larger society and the culture which we share.

Here the question of reality and personal identity merge. Yes, and the question of the nature of the reality which underlies American fiction and thus the human truth which gives fiction viability. In this quest, for such it soon became, I learned that nothing could go unchallenged; especially that feverish industry dedicated to telling Negroes who and what they are, and which can usually be counted upon to deprive both humanity and culture of their complexity. I had undergone, not too many months before taking the path which led to writing, the humiliation of being taught in a class in sociology at a Negro college (from Park and Burgess, the leading textbook in the field) that Negroes represented the "lady of the races." This contention the Negro instructor passed blandly along to us without even bothering to wash his hands, much less his teeth. Well, I had no intention of being bound by any such humiliating definition of my relationship to American literature. Not even to those works which depicted Negroes negatively. Negro-Americans have a highly developed ability to abstract desirable qualities from those around them, even from their enemies, and my sense of reality could reject bias while appreciating the truth revealed by achieved art. The pleasure which I derived from reading had long been a necessity, and in the *act* of reading, that marvelous collaboration between the writer's artful vision and the reader's sense of life, I had become acquainted with other possible selves; freer, more courageous and ingenuous and, during the course of the narrative at least, even wise.

At the time I was under the influence of Ernest Hemingway, and his description, in *Death in the Afternoon*, of his thinking when he first went to Spain became very important as translated in my own naïve fashion. He was trying to write, he tells us, and I found the greatest difficulty aside from knowing truly what you really felt, rather than what you were supposed to feel, and had been taught to feel, was to put down what really happened in action; what the actual things were which produced the emotion that you experienced. . . .

His statement of moral and aesthetic purpose which followed focused my own search to relate myself to American life through literature. For I found the greatest difficulty for a Negro writer was the problem of revealing what he truly felt, rather than serving up what Negroes were supposed to feel, and were encouraged to feel. And linked to this was the difficulty, based upon our long habit of deception and evasion, of depicting what really happened within our areas of American life, and putting down with honesty and without bowing to ideological expediencies the attitudes and values which give Negro-American life its sense of wholeness and which render it bearable and human and, when measured by our own terms, desirable.

I was forced to this awareness through my struggles with the craft of fiction; yes, and by my attraction (soon rejected) to Marxist political theory, which was my response to the inferior status which society sought to impose upon me (I did not then, now, or ever *consider* myself inferior).

I did not know my true relationship to America—what citizen of the U. S. really does?—but I did know and accept how I felt inside. And I also knew, thanks to the old Renaissance Man, what I expected of myself in the matter of personal discipline and creative quality. Since by the grace of the past and the examples of manhood picked willy-nilly from the continuing-present of my background, I rejected all negative definitions imposed upon me by others, there was nothing to do but search for those relationships which were fundamental.

In this sense fiction became the agency of my efforts to answer the questions, Who am I, what am I, how did I come to be? What shall I make of the life around me, what celebrate, what reject, how confront the snarl of good and evil which is inevitable? What does American society *mean* when regarded out of my *own* eyes, when informed by my *own* sense of the past and viewed by my *own* complex sense of the present? How, in other words, should I think of myself and my pluralistic sense of the world, how express my vision of the human predicament, without reducing it to a point which would render it sterile before that necessary and tragic—though enhancing—reduction which must occur before the fictive vision can come alive? It is quite possible that much potential fiction by Negro-Americans fails precisely at this point: through the writers' refusal (often through provincialism or lack of courage or through opportunism) to achieve a vision of life and a resourcefulness of craft commensurate with the complexity of their actual situation. Too often they fear to leave the uneasy sanctuary of race to take their chances in the world of art.

Suggestions for Discussion

1. Discuss the significance to Ellison of his Oklahoma experience.

2. What distinction does Ellison make between "the process of writing" and "the finished creations, the artifacts, poems, plays, novels"?

3. Describe his use of literature to relate himself to American life.

Suggestions for Writing

1. Discuss a piece of fiction that has helped you "answer the questions, who am I, what am I, how did I come to be?"

2. Relate the importance of where you "come from" to your understanding of yourself.

Essays

Aaron Copland

How We Listen to Music

Aaron Copland (1900–1990) studied music in the United States and France.
His French teacher, Nadia Boulanger, was the first to conduct his Symphony for Organ and Orchestra in 1925. Much of Copland's work reflects
the influence of American jazz and folk music: for example, in *John Henry*
(1940) and in his well-known ballets *Billy the Kid* (1938), *Rodeo* (1942), and
Appalachian Spring (1944). His major symphonic works are *El Salon Mexico*
(1936) and *The Third Symphony*; he also has written music for films. Copland
has remained a major influence in contemporary music and was awarded
the National Medal for Arts in 1986. He has also written about music for
the general public. This essay from *What to Listen for in Music* (1939, 1957)
provides a defense for the difficulty of contemporary music and explains
the obligations of the intelligent listener.

We all listen to music according to our separate capacities. But, for the
sake of analysis, the whole listening process may become clearer if we break
it up into its component parts, so to speak. In a certain sense we all listen to
music on three separate planes. For lack of a better terminology, one might
name these: (1) the sensuous plane, (2) the expressive plane, (3) the sheerly
musical plane. The only advantage to be gained from mechanically splitting
up the listening process into these hypothetical planes is the clearer view to
be had of the way in which we listen.

The simplest way of listening to music is to listen for the sheer pleasure of
the musical sound itself. That is the sensuous plane. It is the plane on which
we hear music without thinking, without considering it in any way. One turns
on the radio while doing something else and absent-mindedly bathes in the
sound. A kind of brainless but attractive state of mind is engendered by the
mere sound appeal of the music.

You may be sitting in a room reading this book. Imagine one note struck
on the piano. Immediately that one note is enough to change the atmosphere
of the room—providing that the sound element in music is a powerful and
mysterious agent, which it would be foolish to deride or belittle.

The surprising thing is that many people who consider themselves qualified music lovers abuse that plane in listening. They go to concerts in order
to lose themselves. They use music as a consolation or an escape. They enter
an ideal world where one doesn't have to think of the realities of everyday
life. Of course they aren't thinking about the music either. Music allows them
to leave it, and they go off to a place to dream, dreaming because of and
apropos of the music yet never quite listening to it.

Yes, the sound appeal of music is a potent and primitive force, but you
must not allow it to usurp a disproportionate share of your interest. The sensuous plane is an important one in music, a very important one, but it does
not constitute the whole story.

521

There is no need to digress further on the sensuous plane. Its appeal to every normal human being is self-evident. There is, however, such a thing as becoming more sensitive to the different kinds of sound stuff as used by various composers. For all composers do not use that sound stuff in the same way. Don't get the idea that the value of music is commensurate with its sensuous appeal or that the loveliest sounding music is made by the greatest composer. If that were so, Ravel would be a greater creator than Beethoven. The point is that the sound element varies with each composer, that his usage of sound forms an integral part of his style and must be taken into account when listening. The reader can see, therefore, that a more conscious approach is valuable even on this primary plane of music listening.

The second plane on which music exists is what I have called the expressive one. Here, immediately, we tread on controversial ground. Composers have a way of shying away from any discussion of music's expressive side. Did not Stravinsky himself proclaim that his music was an "object," a "thing," with a life of its own, and with no other meaning than its own purely musical existence? This intransigent attitude of Stravinsky's may be due to the fact that so many people have tried to read different meanings into so many pieces. Heaven knows it is difficult enough to say precisely what it is that a piece of music means, to say it definitely, to say it finally so that everyone is satisfied with your explanation. But that should not lead one to the other extreme of denying to music the right to be "expressive."

My own belief is that all music has an expressive power, some more and some less, but that all music has a certain meaning behind the notes and that the meaning behind the notes constitutes, after all, what the piece is saying, what the piece is about. The whole problem can be stated quite simply by asking, "Is there a meaning to music?" My answer to that would be, "Yes." And "Can you state in so many words what the meaning is?" My answer to that would be, "No." Therein lies the difficulty.

Simple-minded souls will never be satisfied with the answer to the second of these questions. They always want music to have a meaning, and the more concrete it is the better they like it. The more the music reminds them of a train, a storm, a funeral, or any other familiar conception the more expressive it appears to be to them. This popular idea of music's meaning—stimulated and abetted by the usual run of musical commentator—should be discouraged wherever and whenever it is met. One timid lady once confessed to me that she suspected something seriously lacking in her appreciation of music because of her inability to connect it with anything definite. That is getting the whole thing backward, of course.

Still, the question remains, How close should the intelligent music lover wish to come to pinning a definite meaning to any particular work? No closer than a general concept, I should say. Music expresses, at different moments, serenity or exuberance, regrets or triumph, fury or delight. It expresses each of these moods, and many others, in a numberless variety of subtle shadings and differences. It may even express a state of meaning for which there exists no adequate word in any language. In that case, musicians often like to say that it has only a purely musical meaning. They sometimes go further and say that *all* music has only a purely musical meaning. What they really mean is that no appropriate word can be found to express the music's meaning and that, even if it could, they do not feel the need of finding it.

But whatever the professional musician may hold, most musical novices still search for specific words with which to pin down their musical reactions. That is why they always find Tschaikovsky easier to "understand" than Beethoven. In the first place, it is easier to pin a meaning-word on a Tschaikovsky piece than on a Beethoven one. Much easier. Moreover, with the Russian composer, every time you come back to a piece of his it almost always says the same thing to you, whereas with Beethoven it is often quite difficult to put your finger right on what he is saying. And any musician will tell you that that is why Beethoven is the greater composer. Because music which always says the same thing to you will necessarily soon become dull music, but music whose meaning is slightly different with each hearing has a greater chance of remaining alive.

Listen, if you can, to the forty-eight fugue themes of Bach's *Well Tempered Clavichord*. Listen to each theme, one after another. You will soon realize that each theme mirrors a different world of feeling. You will also soon realize that the more beautiful a theme seems to you the harder it is to find any word that will describe it to your complete satisfaction. Yes, you will certainly know whether it is a gay theme or a sad one. You will be able, in other words, in your own mind, to draw a frame of emotional feeling around your theme. Now study the sad one a little closer. Try to pin down the exact quality of its sadness. Is it pessimistically sad or resignedly sad; is it fatefully sad or smilingly sad?

Let us suppose that you are fortunate and can describe to your own satisfaction in so many words the exact meaning of your chosen theme. There is still no guarantee that anyone else will be satisfied. Nor need they be. The important thing is that each one feel for himself the specific expressive quality of a theme or, similarly, an entire piece of music. And if it is a great work of art, don't expect it to mean exactly the same thing to you each time you return to it.

Themes or pieces need not express only one emotion, of course. Take such a theme as the first main one of the *Ninth Symphony*, for example. It is clearly made up of different elements. It does not say only one thing. Yet anyone hearing it immediately gets a feeling of strength, a feeling of power. It isn't a power that comes simply because the theme is played loudly. It is a power inherent in the theme itself. The extraordinary strength and vigor of the theme results in the listener's receiving an impression that a forceful statement has been made. But one should never try to boil it down to "the fateful hammer of life," etc. That is where the trouble begins. The musician, in his exasperation, says it means nothing but the notes themselves, whereas the nonprofessional is only too anxious to hang on to any explanation that gives him the illusion of getting closer to the music's meaning.

Now, perhaps, the reader will know better what I mean when I say that music does have an expressive meaning but that we cannot say in so many words what that meaning is.

The third plane on which music exists is the sheerly musical plane. Besides the pleasurable sound of music and the expressive feeling that it gives off, music does exist in terms of the notes themselves and of their manipulation. Most listeners are not sufficiently conscious of this third plane. . . .

Professional musicians, on the other hand, are, if anything, too conscious of the mere notes themselves. They often fall into the error of becoming so engrossed with their arpeggios and staccatos that they forget the deeper aspects of the music they are performing. But from the layman's standpoint, it is not so much a matter of getting over bad habits on the sheerly musical plane as of increasing one's awareness of what is going on, in so far as the notes are concerned.

When the man in the street listens to the "notes themselves" with any degree of concentration, he is most likely to make some mention of the melody. Either he hears a pretty melody or he does not, and he generally lets it go at that. Rhythm is likely to gain his attention next, particularly if it seems exciting. But harmony and tone color are generally taken for granted, if they are thought of consciously at all. As for music's having a definite form of some kind, that idea seems never to have occurred to him.

It is very important for all of us to become more alive to music on its sheerly musical plane. After all, an actual musical material is being used. The intelligent listener must be prepared to increase his awareness of the musical material and what happens to it. He must hear the melodies, the rhythms, the harmonies, the tone colors in a more conscious fashion. But above all he must, in order to follow the line of the composer's thought, know something of the principles of musical form. Listening to all of these elements is listening on the sheerly musical plane.

Let me repeat that I have split up mechanically the three separate planes on which we listen merely for the sake of greater clarity. Actually, we never listen on one or the other of these planes. What we do is to correlate them— listening in all three ways at the same time. It takes no mental effort, for we do it instinctively.

Perhaps an analogy with what happens to us when we visit the theater will make this instinctive correlation clearer. In the theater, you are aware of the actors and actresses, costumes and sets, sounds and movements. All these give one the sense that the theater is a pleasant place to be in. They constitute the sensuous plane in our theatrical reactions.

The expressive plane in the theater would be derived from the feeling that you get from what is happening on the stage. You are moved to pity, excitement, or gayety. It is this general feeling, generated aside from the particular words being spoken, a certain emotional something which exists on the stage, that is analogous to the expressive quality in music.

The plot and plot development is equivalent to our sheerly musical plane. The playwright creates and develops a character in just the same way that a composer creates and develops a theme. According to the degree of your awareness of the way in which the artist in either field handles his material you will become a more intelligent listener.

It is easy enough to see that the theatergoer never is conscious of any of these elements separately. He is aware of them all at the same time. The same is true of music listening. We simultaneously and without thinking listen on all three planes.

In a sense, the ideal listener is both inside and outside the music at the same moment, judging it and enjoying it, wishing it would go one way and watching it go another—almost like the composer at the moment he composes it; because in order to write his music, the composer must also be inside and outside his music, carried away by it and yet coldly critical of it. A subjective and objective attitude is implied in both creating and listening to music.

What the reader should strive for, then, is a more *active* kind of listening. Whether you listen to Mozart or Duke Ellington, you can deepen your understanding of music only by being a more conscious and aware listener — not someone who is just listening, but someone who is listening *for* something.

Suggestions for Discussion

1. According to Copland, on what different levels do we listen to music?

2. Why does Copland believe that listening to music as an escape is an inadequate response to it?

3. Does Copland believe that a musical composition can have meaning? Does he believe it possible to state that meaning easily?

4. How, according to Copland, is the meaning of a musical composition related to its expressive power? What boundaries does Copland place on the expressive power of music? Explain his use of Bach in this regard.

5. What for Copland are significant differences between Tschaikovsky and Beethoven? Why does he consider Beethoven the greater composer?

6. What are the elements of the third plane of music? How do professional musicians and listeners of music differ about this third plane? What criticism does Copland make of musicians? What obligation does the intelligent listener have to this plane?

7. Explain Copland's analogy between the elements in music and in drama. What important differences exist for the audience in its response to both forms of art?

8. Contrast E. M. Forster's position with Copland's in the matter of meaning in the arts. Can you account for their different points of view?

Suggestions for Writing

1. Listen to a composition by Bach and to one by Duke Ellington and, insofar as you can, discuss the music on all three levels.

2. Summarize the arguments of Copland and Mannes about the problems of responding to art. Which of these essays do you find most helpful for your own response? Explain your position in detail.

Mike Royko

The Virtue of Prurience

Mike Royko (b. 1932) is a Chicagoan through and through: he was born there and worked on Chicago newspapers most of his life. He was for many years a columnist for the Chicago *Sun-Times* and now writes for the Chicago *Tribune*. He has won the Pulitzer Prize for his commentary, was named Best Newspaper Columnist in America in 1985, 1987, 1988, 1989, and 1990, and has written a number of books. This essay on censorship provides a good example of how to treat a serious subject with wit.

My first right-wing endeavor—helping get a book banned—has failed miserably. I now can appreciate how frustrating life in our permissive society must be for such grim-lipped groups as the Moral Majority.

Normally, I don't favor censorship and have never before tried to get anything banned. But several months ago, I joined in a crusade that was being led by Bill and Barbara Younis of Hannibal, N.Y.

Bill and Barbara are parents of an 18-year-old high school senior, and they became alarmed when they discovered that their daughter was being required to read a book they considered vulgar.

They went to the school superintendent and demanded that the book be removed from the reading list. He refused.

So they asked friends and neighbors to sign petitions supporting them, and they demanded that the school board ban the book.

That's when I found out about it. A reporter from that part of New York called to ask me what I thought of the censorship efforts.

I responded by dropping the phone, shouting, "Hot damn, yowee!" and dancing gleefully around my office.

I reacted that way because it is a book that I wrote about 12 years ago. It is called "Boss" and is about Mayor Richard J. Daley, power, and Chicago politics.

Before long, there were news stories about the censorship efforts of the Younises, and my phone started ringing with calls from other writers.

One of them said:

"You slick devil, how did you ever pull that off?"

I'm just lucky, I guess.

"Well, I don't get it. My last book was so torrid and lurid that I blushed while writing it. And there hasn't even been a hint from anybody about banning it."

You're just unlucky, I guess.

Another writer called and said: "This is so unfair. In my last book, George did it with Lucy, Lucy did it with Wally, Wally did it with Evelyn, Evelyn did it with George, George did it with Wally, Lucy did it with Sally, and then they all did it together."

Sounds exhausting.

"What I don't understand, is why you, but not me. I mean, I could really use a break like that."

Maybe I just live right.

What they were talking about was the tremendous commercial value of being banned. By anyone, anywhere, just as long as you are banned. It works this way:

If you can get a book banned in, say, Minneapolis, and there is a great furor about it, the book will suddenly become a best-seller next door in St. Paul. Sure, you won't sell any books in Minneapolis. But for every book you don't sell in Minneapolis, you'll sell 10 in St. Paul.

That's all part of the forbidden-fruit syndrome. Tell people they can't have or do something, and they immediately want to do it.

With this in mind, I called my publisher and said: "Get those presses rolling. We're going to sell a ton."

He said: "Not yet. You haven't been banned yet. And just being threatened with censorship isn't enough. You've got to be tossed off the shelves."

So I got on the phone and called Mr. and Mrs. Younis.

"Your book is vulgar," they said. "It is filled with swear words."

I know. That's the way Chicago politicians talk, so I quoted them. But you're right. It's vulgar. Shocking.

"You agree?"

Hell . . . I mean, heck, yes. And I'm behind you 100 percent.

"You are?"

Of course I am. I think what you're doing is terrific. And if I were there, I'd sign your petition.

"You would?"

Darn right. I don't want 18-year-olds reading words like (bleep) and (censored) and (deleted). Who ever heard of 18-year-olds being exposed to such language?

"Would you send us a letter expressing your support?"

Of course. I'll do more than that. I'll write a column urging that my book be banned.

And I did.

Since then, I've been thumbing through travel folders, real-estate brochures for tropical hideaways, yachting magazines, and girlie magazines, anticipating life as a rich and censored author.

Nothing ever works out.

The school board set up a three-member committee to review the book and the Younises' complaint.

Then a hearing was held. Mr. and Mrs. Younis, bless them, came to the hearing and said things like: "It's got the kind of language you see painted on bridges. Books like this encourage young ladies to become prostitutes."

That's dynamite stuff. Would you want your daughter to read a book that would encourage her to enter the employ of a brothel? I should hope not.

Despite this, the committee ruled that the book would remain on the reading list.

Mr. and Mrs. Younis have now removed three of their four children from the school system and say they will send them to private schools.

A noble effort, but it doesn't do me much good. As the school superintendent said:

"We made our decision, and it was a good one. There is nothing wrong with that book."

Doggone busybody.

Suggestions for Discussion

1. What is the tone of Royko's essay? How does he achieve the right tone? Is it appropriate to the subject of the essay? Explain its title.

2. Why are fellow authors jealous of Royko? What examples of their works does he use? How are those works different from his? Should the book about George and Lucy and the others be banned? Explain.

3. What is "the forbidden-fruit syndrome"?

4. What serious issue does Royko suggest in his description of the Younis couple?

5. Why is censorship a danger to human freedom? Are there instances in which censorship might safely be imposed?

Suggestions for Writing

1. Royko says, "Tell people they can't have or do something, and they immediately want to do it." Write an essay illustrating this comment. Explain why you think Royko's observation about people may be accurate.

2. Write an essay in which you discuss a play, movie, poem, painting, or novel that you think should be banned. Explain your reasons. If you don't believe in banning anything, explain why, giving your reasons carefully.

E. M. Forster

Art for Art's Sake

Edward Morgan Forster (1879–1970) was a British novelist educated at King's College, Cambridge. He lived for a time in Italy, was a member of the Bloomsbury Group of writers and artists in London, and spent the major part of his life in Cambridge. His works include *Where Angels Fear to Tread* (1905), *A Room with a View* (1908), and *A Passage to India* (1924). In this essay from *Two Cheers for Democracy* (1951), Forster explains the importance of art as a source of comfort and order in a troubled society.

I believe in art for art's sake. It is an unfashionable belief, and some of my statements must be of the nature of an apology. Sixty years ago I should have faced you with more confidence. A writer or a speaker who chose "Art for Art's Sake" for his theme sixty years ago could be sure of being in the swim, and could feel so confident of success that he sometimes dressed himself in aesthetic costumes suitable to the occasion—in an embroidered dressing-gown, perhaps, or a blue velvet suit with a Lord Fauntleroy collar; or a toga, or a kimono, and carried a poppy or a lily or a long peacock's feather in his mediaeval hand. Times have changed. Not thus can I present either myself or my theme to-day. My aim rather is to ask you quietly to reconsider for a few minutes a phrase which has been much misused and much abused, but which has, I believe, great importance for us—has, indeed, eternal importance.

Now we can easily dismiss those peacock's feathers and other affectations—they are but trifles—but I want also to dismiss a more dangerous heresy, namely the silly idea that only art matters, an idea which has somehow got mixed up with the idea of art for art's sake, and has helped to discredit it. Many things besides art, matter. It is merely one of the things that matter, and high though the claims are that I make for it, I want to keep them in proportion. No one can spend his or her life entirely in the creation or the appreciation of masterpieces. Man lives, and ought to live, in a complex world, full of conflicting claims, and if we simplified them down into the aesthetic he would be sterilised. Art for art's sake does not mean that only art matters and I would also like to rule out such phrases as, "The Life of Art," "Living for Art," and "Art's High Mission." They confuse and mislead.

What does the phrase mean? Instead of generalising, let us take a specific instance—Shakespeare's *Macbeth*, for example, and pronounce the words, "*Macbeth* for *Macbeth's* sake." What does that mean? Well, the play has several aspects—it is educational, it teaches us something about legendary Scotland, something about Jacobean England, and a good deal about human nature and its perils. We can study its origins, and study and enjoy its dramatic technique and the music of its diction. All that is true. But *Macbeth* is furthermore a world of its own, created by Shakespeare and existing in virtue of its own poetry. It is in this aspect *Macbeth* for *Macbeth's* sake, and that is what I intend by the phrase "art for art's sake." A work of art—whatever else it may be—is a self-contained entity, with a life of its own imposed on it by its creator. It has internal order. It may have external form. That is how we recognise it.

Take for another example that picture of Seurat's which I saw two years ago in Chicago—"*La Grande Jatte*." Here again there is much to study and to enjoy: the pointillism, the charming face of the seated girl, the nineteenth-century Parisian Sunday sunlight, the sense of motion in immobility. But here again there is something more; "*La Grande Jatte*" forms a world of its own, created by Seurat and existing by virtue of its own poetry: "*La Grande Jatte*" pour "*La Grande Jatte*": *l'art pour l'art*. Like *Macbeth* it has internal order and internal life.

It is to the conception of order that I would now turn. This is important to my argument, and I want to make a digression, and glance at order in daily life, before I come to order in art.

In the world of daily life, the world which we perforce inhabit, there is much talk about order, particularly from statesmen and politicians. They tend, however, to confuse order with orders, just as they confuse creation with regulations. Order, I suggest, is something evolved from within, not something imposed from without; it is an internal stability, a vital harmony, and in the social and political category, it has never existed except for the convenience of historians. Viewed realistically, the past is really a series of *dis*orders, succeeding one another by discoverable laws, no doubt, and certainly marked by an increasing growth of human interference, but disorders all the same. So that, speaking as a writer, what I hope for today is a disorder which will be more favourable to artists than is the present one, and which will provide them with fuller inspirations and better material conditions. It will not last—nothing lasts—but there have been some advantageous disorders in the past—for instance, in ancient Athens, in Renaissance Italy, eighteenth-century France, periods in China and Persia—and we may do something to accelerate the next one. But let us not again fix our hearts where true joys are not to be found. We were promised a new order after the first world war through the League of Nations. It did not come, nor have I faith in present promises, by whomsoever endorsed. The implacable offensive of Science forbids. We cannot reach social and political stability for the reason that we continue to make scientific discoveries and to apply them, and thus to destroy the arrangements which were based on more elementary discoveries. If Science would discover rather than apply—if, in other words, men were more interested in knowledge than in power—mankind would be in a far safer position, the stability statesmen talk about would be a possibility, there could be a new order based on vital harmony, and the earthly millennium might approach. But Science shows no signs of doing this: she gave us the internal combustion engine, and before we had digested and assimilated it with terrible pains into our social system, she harnessed the atom, and destroyed any new order that seemed to be evolving. How can man get into harmony with his surroundings when he is constantly altering them? The future of our race is, in this direction, more unpleasant than we care to admit, and it has sometimes seemed to me that its best chance lies through apathy, uninventiveness, and inertia. Universal exhaustion might promote that Change of Heart which is at present so briskly recommended from a thousand pulpits. Universal exhaustion would certainly be a new experience. The human race has never undergone it, and is still too perky to admit that it may be coming and might result in a sprouting of new growth through the decay.

I must not pursue these speculations any further—they lead me too far from my terms of reference and maybe from yours. But I do want to emphasize that order in daily life and in history, order in the social and political category, is unattainable under our present psychology.

Where is it attainable? Not in the astronomical category, where it was for many years enthroned. The heavens and the earth have become terribly alike since Einstein. No longer can we find a reassuring contrast to chaos in the night sky and look up with George Meredith to the stars, the army of unalterable law, or listen for the music of the spheres. Order is not there. In the entire universe there seem to be only two possibilities for it. The first of them—which again lies outside my terms of reference—is the divine order, the mystic harmony, which according to all religions is available for those who can contemplate it. We much admit its possibility, on the evidence of the adepts, and we must believe them when they say that it is attained, if attainable, by prayer. "O thou who changest not, abide with me," said one of its poets. "*Ordina questo amor, o tu che m'ami,*" said another: "Set love in order thou who lovest me." The existence of a divine order, though it cannot be tested, has never been disproved.

The second possibility for order lies in the aesthetic category, which is my subject here: the order which an artist can create in his own work, and to that we must now return. A work of art, we are all agreed, is a unique product. But why? It is unique not because it is clever or noble or beautiful or enlightened or original or sincere or idealistic or useful or educational—it may embody any of those qualities—but because it is the only material object in the universe which may possess internal harmony. All the others have been pressed into shape from outside, and when their mold is removed they collapse. The work of art stands up by itself, and nothing else does. It achieves something which has often been promised by society, but always delusively. Ancient Athens made a mess—but the *Antigone* stands up. Renaissance Rome made a mess—but the ceiling of the Sistine got painted. James I made a mess—but there was *Macbeth*. Louis XIV—but there was *Phedre*. Art for art's sake? I should just think so, and more so than ever at the present time.

It is the one orderly product which our muddling race has produced. It is the cry of a thousand sentinels, the echo from a thousand labyrinths; it is the lighthouse which cannot be hidden: *c'est le meilleur témoignage que nous puissions donner de notre dignité.* Antigone for Antigone's sake, *Macbeth* for *Macbeth*'s, "*La Grande Jatte*" pour "*La Grande Jatte.*"

If this line of argument is correct, it follows that the artist will tend to be an outsider in the society to which he has been born, and that the nineteenth century conception of him as a Bohemian was not inaccurate. The conception erred in three particulars: it postulated an economic system where art could be a full-time job, it introduced the fallacy that only art matters, and it over-stressed idiosyncracy and waywardness—the peacock-feather aspect—rather than order. But it is a truer conception than the one which prevails in official circles on my side of the Atlantic—I don't know about yours: the conception which treats the artist as if he were a particularly bright government advertiser and encourages him to be friendly and matey with his fellow citizens, and not to give himself airs.

Estimable is mateyness, and the man who achieves it gives many a pleasant little drink to himself and to others. But it has no traceable connection with the creative impulse, and probably acts as an inhibition on it. The artist who is seduced by mateyness may stop himself from doing the one thing which he, and he alone, can do—the making of something out of words or sounds or paint or clay or marble or steel or film which has internal harmony and presents order to a permanently disarranged planet. This seems worth doing, even at the risk of being called uppish by journalists. I have in mind an article which was published some years ago in the London *Times*, an article called "The Eclipse of the Highbrow," in which the "Average Man" was exalted, and all contemporary literature was censured if it did not toe the line, the precise position of the line being naturally known to the writer of the article. Sir Kenneth Clark, who was at that time director of our National Gallery, commented on this pernicious doctrine in a letter which cannot be too often quoted. "The poet and the artist," wrote Clark, "are important precisely because they are not average men; because in sensibility, intelligence, and power of invention they far exceed the average." These memorable words, and particularly the words "power of invention," are the Bohemian's passport. Furnished with it, he slinks about society, saluted now by a brickbat and now by a penny, and accepting either of them with equanimity. He does not consider too anxiously what his relations with society may be, for he is aware of something more important than that—namely the invitation to invent, to create order, and he believes he will be better placed for doing this if he attempts detachment. So round and round he slouches, with his hat pulled over his eyes, and maybe with a louse in his beard, and—if he really wants one—a peacock's feather in his hand.

If our present society should disintegrate—and who dare prophesy that it won't?—this old-fashioned and démodé figure will become clearer: the Bohemian, the outsider, the parasite, the rat—one of those figures which have at present no function either in a warring or a peaceful world. It may not be dignified to be a rat, but many of the ships are sinking, which is not dignified either—the officials did not build them properly. Myself, I would sooner be a swimming rat than a sinking ship—at all events I can look around me for a little longer—and I remember how one of us, a rat with particularly bright eyes called Shelley, squeaked out, "Poets are the unacknowledged legislators of the world," before he vanished into the waters of the Mediterranean.

What laws did Shelley propose to pass? None. The legislation of the artist is never formulated at the time, though it is sometimes discerned by future generations. He legislates through creating. And he creates through his sensitiveness and power to impose form. Without form the sensitiveness vanishes. And form is as important today, when the human race is trying to ride the whirlwind, as it ever was in those fixed agitating days of the past, when the earth seemed solid and the stars fixed, and the discoveries of science were made slowly, slowly. Form is not tradition. It alters from generation to generation. Artists always seek a new technique, and will continue to do so as long as their work excites them. But form of some kind is imperative. It is the surface crust of the internal harmony, it is the outward evidence of order.

My remarks about society may have seemed too pessimistic, but I believe that society can only represent a fragment of the human spirit, and that another fragment can only get expressed through art. And I wanted to take this opportunity, this vantage ground, to assert not only the existence of art, but its pertinacity. Looking back into the past, it seems to me that that is all there has ever been: vantage grounds for discussion and creation, little vantage grounds in the changing chaos, where bubbles have been blown and webs spun, and the desire to create order has found temporary gratification, and the sentinels have managed to utter their challenges, and the huntsmen, though lost individually, have heard each other's calls through the impenetrable wood, and the lighthouses have never ceased sweeping the thankless seas. In this pertinacity there seems to me, as I grow older, something more and more profound, something which does in fact concern people who do not care about art at all.

In conclusion, let me summarise the various categories that have laid claim to the possession of Order.

(1) The social and political category. Claim disallowed on the evidence of history and of our own experience. If man altered psychologically, order here might be attainable: not otherwise.

(2) The astronomical category. Claim allowed up to the present century, but now disallowed on the evidence of the physicists.

(3) The religious category. Claim allowed on the evidence of the mystics.

(4) The aesthetic category. Claim allowed on the evidence of various works of art, and on the evidence of our own creative impulses, however weak these may be or however imperfectly they may function. Works of art, in my opinion, are the only objects in the material universe to possess internal order, and that is why, though I don't believe that only art matters, I do believe in Art for Art's Sake.

Suggestions for Discussion

1. Why does Forster make clear that the belief in art for art's sake does not mean a belief that only art matters?

2. Where does art stand, for Forster, in the list of things that matter?

3. Explain Forster's phrase, "*Macbeth* for *Macbeth*'s sake." How does he use it to explain his main argument?

4. Explain Forster's comparison of the order of art with order in life. How does this comparison function in his argument?

5. What does Forster mean by claiming that a work of art is a unique product?

6. Examine Forster's categories that have laid claim to the possession of order. Why does he reject all but the religious and aesthetic categories?

Suggestions for Writing

1. Write a paper explaining Forster's defense of art.

2. Obviously, many people feel differently from Forster about the autonomy of art. In Marxist countries, for example, art is often considered to be a servant of the state. Write a paper in which you argue for or against Forster's position.

Marya Mannes

How Do You Know It's Good?

Marya Mannes (1904–1990), although she has written fiction and poetry, has made her reputation as a tirelessly questioning essayist and journalist. Her essays have appeared in a variety of magazines from *Vogue*, on the one hand, to *The New Republic*, on the other. Her essays on euthanasia were collected in *Last Rights* (1974), and she wrote about television in *Who Owns the Air?* (1960). Her other essay collections include *More in Anger* (1958), *The New York I Know* (1961), and *But Will It Sell?* (1964), in which this essay appears. "How Do You Know It's Good?" challenges educated citizens to assert their independence of fads and trends in the arts and to question critics who popularize fads. She believes that all observers have an obligation to make intelligent judgments about art.

Suppose there were no critics to tell us how to react to a picture, a play, or a new composition of music. Suppose we wandered innocent as the dawn into an art exhibition of unsigned paintings. By what standards, by what values would we decide whether they were good or bad, talented or untalented, successes or failures? How can we ever know that what we think is right?

For the last fifteen or twenty years the fashion in criticism or appreciation of the arts has been to deny the existence of any valid criteria and to make the words "good" or "bad" irrelevant, immaterial, and inapplicable. There is no such thing, we are told, as a set of standards, first acquired through experience and knowledge and later imposed on the subject under discussion. This has been a popular approach, for it relieves the critic of the responsibility of judgment and the public of the necessity of knowledge. It pleases those resentful of disciplines, it flatters the empty-minded by calling them open-minded, it comforts the confused. Under the banner of democracy and the kind of equality which our forefathers did *not* mean, it says, in effect, "Who are you to tell us what *is* good or bad?" This is the same cry used so long and so effectively by the producers of mass media who insist that it is the public, not they, who decides what it wants to hear and see, and that for a critic to say that *this* program is bad and *this* program is good is purely a reflection of personal taste. Nobody recently has expressed this philosophy more succinctly than Dr. Frank Stanton, the highly intelligent president of CBS television. At a hearing before the Federal Communications Commission, this phrase escaped him under questioning: "One man's mediocrity is another man's good program."

There is no better way of saying "No values are absolute." There is another important aspect to this philosophy of *laissez faire:* It is the fear, in all observers of all forms of art, of guessing wrong. This fear is well come by, for who has not heard of the contemporary outcries against artists who later were called great? Every age has its arbiters who do not grow with their times, who cannot tell evolution from revolution or the difference between frivolous faddism, amateurish experimentation, and profound and necessary change. Who wants to be caught *flagrante delicto* with an error of judgment as serious as this? It is far safer, and certainly easier, to look at a picture or a play or a poem and to say "This is hard to understand, but it may be good," or simply to welcome it as a new form. The word "new"—in our country especially—has magical connotations. What is new must be good; what is old is probably bad. And if a critic can describe the new in language that nobody can understand, he's safer still. If he has mastered the art of saying nothing with exquisite complexity, nobody can quote him later as saying anything.

But all these, I maintain, are forms of abdication from the responsibility of judgment. In creating, the artist commits himself; in appreciating, you have a commitment of your own. For after all, it is the audience which makes the arts. A climate of appreciation is essential to its flowering, and the higher the expectations of the public, the better the performance of the artist. Conversely, only a public ill-served by its critics could have accepted as art and as literature so much in these last years that has been neither. If anything goes, everything goes; and at the bottom of the junkpile lie the discarded standards too.

But what are these standards? How do you get them? How do you know they're the right ones? How can you make a clear pattern out of so many intangibles, including that greatest one, the very private I?

Well for one thing, it's fairly obvious that the more you read and see and hear, the more equipped you'll be to practice that art of association which is at the basis of all understanding and judgment. The more you live and the more you look, the more aware you are of a consistent pattern—as universal as the stars, as the tides, as breathing, as night and day—underlying everything. I would call this pattern and this rhythm an order. Not order—*an* order. Within it exists an incredible diversity of forms. Without it lies chaos—the wild cells of destruction—sickness. It is in the end up to you to distinguish between the diversity that is health and the chaos that is sickness, and you can't do this without a process of association that can link a bar of Mozart with the corner of a Vermeer painting, or a Stravinsky score with a

Picasso abstraction; or that can relate an aggressive act with a Franz Kline painting and a fit of coughing with a John Cage composition.

There is no accident in the fact that certain expressions of art live for all time and that others die with the moment, and although you may not always define the reasons, you can ask the questions. What does an artist say that is timeless; how does he say it? How much is fashion, how much is merely reflection? Why is Sir Walter Scott so hard to read now, and Jane Austen not? Why is baroque right for one age and too effulgent for another?

Can a standard of craftsmanship apply to art of all ages, or does each have its own, and different, definitions? You may have been aware, inadvertently, that craftsmanship has become a dirty word these years because, again, it implies standards—something done well or done badly. The result of this convenient avoidance is a plentitude of actors who can't project their voices, singers who can't phrase their songs, poets who can't communicate emotion, and writers who have no vocabulary—not to speak of painters who can't draw. The dogma now is that craftsmanship gets in the way of expression. You can do better if you don't know *how* you do it, let alone *what* you're doing.

I think it is time you helped reverse this trend by trying to rediscover craft: the command of the chosen instrument, whether it is a brush, a word, or a voice. When you begin to detect the difference between freedom and sloppiness, between serious experimentation and egotherapy, between skill and slickness, between strength and violence, you are on your way to separating the sheep from the goats, a form of segregation denied us for quite a while. All you need to restore it is a small bundle of standards and a Geiger counter that detects fraud, and we might begin our tour of the arts in an area where both are urgently needed: contemporary painting.

I don't know what's worse: to have to look at acres of bad art to find the little good, or to read what the critics say about it all. In no other field of expression has so much double-talk flourished, so much confusion prevailed, and so much nonsense been circulated: further evidence of the close interdependence between the arts and the critical climate they inhabit. It will be my pleasure to share with you some of this double-talk so typical of our times.

Item one: preface for a catalogue of an abstract painter:

"Time-bound meditation experiencing a life; sincere with plastic piety at the threshold of hallowed arcana; a striving for pure ideation giving shape to inner drive; formalized patterns where neural balances reach a fiction." End of quote. Know what this artist paints like now?

Item two: a review in the *Art News:*

". . . a weird and disparate assortment of material, but the monstrosity which bloomed into his most recent cancer of aggregations is present in some form everywhere. . . ." Then, later, "A gluttony of things and processes terminated by a glorious constipation."

Item three, same magazine, review of an artist who welds automobile fragments into abstract shapes:

Each fragment . . . is made an extreme of human exasperation, torn at and fought all the way, has its rightness of form as if by accident. *Any technique that requires order or discipline would just be the human ego.* No, these must be egoless, uncontrolled, undesigned and different enough to give you a bang—fifty miles an hour around a telephone pole. . . .

"Any technique that requires order of discipline would just be the human ego." What does he mean—"just be"? What are they really talking about? Is this journalism? Is it criticism? Or is it that other convenient abdication from standards of performance and judgment practiced by so many artists and critics that they, like certain writers who deal only in sickness and depravity, "reflect the chaos about them"? Again, whose chaos? Whose depravity?

I had always thought that the prime function of art was to create order *out* of chaos—again, not the order of neatness or rigidity or convention or artifice, but the order of clarity by which one will and one vision could draw the essential truth out of apparent confusion. I still do. It is not enough to use parts of a car to convey the brutality of the machine. This is as slavishly representative, and just as easy, as arranging dried flowers under glass to convey nature.

Speaking of which, i.e., the use of real materials (burlap, old gloves, bottletops) in lieu of pigment, this is what one critic had to say about an exhibition of Assemblage at the Museum of Modern Art last year:

Spotted throughout the show are indisputable works of art, accounting for a quarter or even a half of the total display. But the remainder are works of non-art, anti-art, and art substitutes that are the aesthetic counterparts of the social deficiencies that land people in the clink on charges of vagrancy. These aesthetic bankrupts . . . have no legitimate ideological roof over their heads and not the price of a square intellectual meal, much less a spiritual sandwich, in their pockets.

I quote these words of John Canady of *The New York Times* as an example of the kind of criticism which puts responsibility to an intelligent public above popularity with an intellectual coterie. Canaday has the courage to say what he thinks and the capacity to say it clearly: two qualities notably absent from his profession.

Next to art, I would say that appreciation and evaluation in the field of music is the most difficult. For it is rarely possible to judge a new composition at one hearing only. What seems confusing or fragmented at first might well become clear and organic a third time. Or it might not. The only salvation here for the listener is, again, an instinct born of experience and association which allows him to separate intent from accident, design from experimentation, and pretense from conviction. Much of contemporary music is, like its sister art, merely a reflection of the composer's own fragmentation: an absorption in self and symbols at the expense of communication with others. The artist, in short, says to the public: If you don't understand this, it's because you're dumb. I maintain that you are not. You may have to go part way or even halfway to meet the artist, but if you must go the whole way, it's his fault, not yours. Hold fast to that. And remember it too when you read new poetry, that estranged sister of music.

A multitude of causes, unknown to former times, are now acting with a combined force to blunt the discriminating powers of the mind, and, unfitting it for all voluntary exertion, to reduce it to a state of almost savage torpor. The most effective of these causes are the great national events which are daily taking place and the increasing accumulation of men in cities, where the uniformity of their occupations produces a craving for extraordinary incident, which the rapid communication of intelligence hourly gratifies. To this tendency of life and manners, the literature and theatrical exhibitions of the country have conformed themselves.

This startlingly applicable comment was written in the year 1800 by William Wordsworth in the preface to his "Lyrical Ballads"; and it has been cited by Edwin Muir in his recently published book "The Estate of Poetry." Muir states that poetry's effective range and influence have diminished alarmingly in the modern world. He believes in the inherent and indestructible qualities of the human mind and the great and permanent objects that act upon it, and suggests that the audience will increase when "poetry loses what obscurity is left in it by attempting greater themes, for great themes have to be stated clearly." If you keep that firmly in mind and resist, in Muir's words, "the vast dissemination of secondary objects that isolate us from the natural world," you have gone a long way toward equipping yourself for the examination of any work of art.

When you come to theatre, in this extremely hasty tour of the arts, you can approach it on two different levels. You can bring to it anticipation and innocence, giving yourself up, as it were, to the life on the stage and reacting to it emotionally, if the play is good, or listlessly, if the play is boring; a part of the audience organism that expresses its favor by silence or laughter and its disfavor by coughing and rustling. Or you can bring to it certain critical faculties that may heighten, rather than diminish, your enjoyment.

You can ask yourselves whether the actors are truly in their parts or merely projecting themselves; whether the scenery helps or hurts the mood; whether the playwright is honest with himself, his characters, and you. Somewhere along the line you can learn to distinguish between the true creative act and the false arbitrary gesture; between fresh observation and stale cliché; between the avant-garde play that is pretentious drivel and the avant-garde play that finds new ways to say old truths.

Purpose and craftsmanship—end and means—these are the keys to your judgment in all the arts. What is this painter trying to say when he slashes a broad band of black across a white canvas and lets the edges dribble down? Is it a statement of violence? Is it a self-portrait? If it is *one* of these, has he made you believe it? Or is this a gesture of the ego or a form of therapy? If it shocks you, what does it shock you into?

And what of this tight little painting of bright flowers in a vase? Is the painter saying anything new about flowers? Is it different from a million other canvases of flowers? Has it any life, any meaning, beyond its statement? Is there any pleasure in its forms or texture? The question is not whether a thing is abstract or representational, whether it is "modern" or conventional. The question, inexorably, is whether it is good. And this is a decision which only you, on the basis of instinct, experience, and association, can make for yourself. It takes independence and courage. It involves, moreover, the risk of wrong decision and the humility, after the passage of time, of recognizing it as such. As we grow and change and learn, our attitudes can change too, and what we once thought obscure or "difficult" can later emerge as coherent and illuminating. Entrenched prejudices, obdurate opinions are as sterile as no opinions at all.

Yet standards there are, timeless as the universe itself. And when you have committed yourself to them, you have acquired a passport to that elusive but immutable realm of truth. Keep it with you in the forests of bewilderment. And never be afraid to speak up.

Suggestions for Discussion

1. What is the problem posed in the first paragraph of this essay? How is this problem significant for the rest of the discussion?

2. How does Mannes relate Dr. Frank Stanton's remarks about television in the second paragraph to the issue of "good" and "bad" in high culture as well as popular culture?

3. What, according to Mannes, is a major cause of the philosophy of laissez faire in art criticism? What does she see as the dangers in the statement, "No values are absolute"? To what extent does she believe that values may be absolute?

4. How does Mannes believe we can achieve standards for judging art?

5. Why does Mannes object so strongly to the attack on craftsmanship in art? What is the argument in favor of ignoring craftsmanship? How do you respond to the conflict she describes?

6. Mannes gives some examples of what she calls double-talk in art criticism. Examine these examples. Can you make clear sense from them? How does Mannes attack these examples?

7. What is Mannes's definition of order in art? Is her definition one with which you agree?

8. Why does Mannes approve of her quotation from a review by John Canaday?

9. How do the author's criteria for judging painting and sculpture apply to music and theatre?

10. What is the tone of the essay? How is it achieved? What role does the pronoun *you* play in establishing the tone?

Suggestions for Writing

1. Examine a modern painting and explain why you think it is good. Remember Mannes's advice about what you must avoid in writing about art.

2. Collect some criticism of an art exhibition or gallery show in your area and go see the paintings or sculpture. Write an essay in which you evaluate the criticism based on your own experience of the work. You may want to write a comparable essay about a music performance or a play or a film.

3. Compare and contrast Mannes's arguments with those of E. M. Forster.

Ira Glasser

Artistic Freedom: A Gathering Storm

Ira S. Glasser (b. 1938) was born in Brooklyn and studied mathematics at Queens College (New York City) and at Ohio State University. He was associate editor and then editor of *Current Magazine* from 1962 to 1967 and briefly lectured in mathematics at Sarah Lawrence College. He was the New York director of the American Civil Liberties Union until becoming its executive director in 1978. Since 1974 he has also served as director of the Asian American Legal Defense and Education Fund. The New York Association of Black School Supervisors gave him their Martin Luther King, Jr. Award in 1971. He contributes articles to various professional journals as well as a column for *Civil Liberties*, the publication of the ACLU. This essay, the subject of one of his columns, demonstrates why Glasser and the ACLU regard the rising tendency to censorship in the late eighties and early nineties as a serious threat to First Amendment rights.

The roots of current efforts to curb freedom of artistic expression reach back to the early 1980s, when religious fundamentalists and other authoritarians attempted to censor books, films and television. Libraries, museums, schools, theaters, television stations, bookstores and video shops all came under sustained pressure to restrict the display or availability of images and words felt to offend various self-appointed monitors of morality and taste.

This censorship movement found powerful allies in government. Attorney General Edwin Meese enthusiastically joined the crusade, heading up a Presidential commission convened to establish a behavioral link between vaguely defined "pornography" and sex crimes (a link that has eluded social scientists for decades), and to establish a rationale for prosecuting the purveyors of "offensive" artworks.

Today, we are reaping the harvest of those earlier efforts: a climate in which artistic expression—from rock music lyrics to unconventional imagery in photography, to political symbolism in paintings and sculpture, to unique cinematic visions of reality—is under sustained assault. Today, artistic freedom is threatened across the country by escalating (if more refined) pressure from private groups, new censorship laws, and politically-inspired funding cuts.

For example, in 1985 Tipper Gore's Parents' Music Resource Center (PMRC) pressured record companies to label song lyrics that allegedly encourage sex, suicide, drugs, alcohol and belief in "the occult." The Recording Industry Association of America, feeling the heat from the PMRC, agreed to support "warning" labels. Today, retail outlets around the country are using such labels to decide what records to sell, and to whom. Hastings, the nation's eighth largest book and music store chain, places "18 for Purchase" stickers on 74 rock albums and refuses to sell them to underage consumers.

The other large chains are similarly restricting record sales, according to what criteria no one knows. One chain recently decided not to stock labeled records at all. Obviously, these actions on the part of the large chains, which dominate record sales nationwide, are bound to engender self-censorship tendencies in composers and recording artists—who need the chains to gain access to their market.

Predictably, these retail labeling practices, combined with the recording industry's drift toward self-censorship, are now prompting politicians to begin introducing laws that *require* labeling.

In December 1989, the Pennsylvania legislature passed a bill banning the sale to minors of "sexually explicit" albums, unless the album covers bear a day-glo label that reads: "WARNING: May contain explicit lyrics descriptive of or advocating one or more of the following: suicide, incest, bestiality, sadomasochism, sexual activity in a violent context, murder, morbid violence, illegal use of drugs or alcohol. PARENTAL ADVISORY." Retailers caught selling such material without a label are subject to a $300 fine and 90 days in jail. The state representative who introduced the bill was quoted recently as saying that his intent is not to censor song lyrics, but to label them "just as we do for corn flakes and pesticides and many other things."

Similar legislation has been introduced in Missouri, Virginia, Arizona, Iowa, New Mexico, Illinois, Oklahoma, Delaware, Kansas and Florida. The Missouri bill adds nudity and adultery to the danger zone; Florida includes books and magazines and would prohibit the sale of labeled materials to minors. Maryland would also label racist and anti-Semitic content in music lyrics (presumably, local prosecutors would identify the guilty lyrics). The state representative who introduced the Missouri bill has sent a copy of it to his counterparts in 35 states, encouraging them to duplicate his effort. One wonders, if it is acceptable to label records, whether labels on books are next.

In some states, prosecutors are not waiting for these new censorship proposals to become law. For example, the ACLU represented an Alabama retailer whose record store was raided in June 1988; 25 rap music tapes were confiscated and he was arrested, under the state's obscenity law. The day before the raid, the store owner had sold a rap cassette containing lyrics that were "offensive" to an undercover police officer. This was the first case in which recorded music was the basis for an obscenity prosecution.

The store owner was convicted in municipal court and fined $500. He then requested a jury trial, as was his right under Alabama law. At the trial, held this February, the ACLU presented a music critic and linguist as expert witnesses to argue that such obscenity convictions would have a widespread chilling effect on artists. On February 22, the jury overturned the conviction. We regard it as a hopeful sign that the people of Alabama would chafe so readily at the threat of prosecutors deciding what music they can and cannot hear.

The visual arts are also under assault. Only a few weeks into 1990, the city of New Haven, Connecticut ordered the dismantling of an exhibition of Vietnam War photographs on the grounds that they were "too explicit." In November 1989, in Washington, D.C. a black artist's outdoor portrait of Jesse Jackson as blond, blue-eyed and white-skinned, was attacked with sledgehammers by a group of offended black men. A painting that depicts the late

Chicago Mayor Harold Washington in women's underwear, when exhibited last year at the Art Institute of Chicago, provoked offended city aldermen to call out the police to literally arrest the painting and remove it from the premises. The ACLU is suing the city for damages and injunctive relief on behalf of the artist, to whom the painting was later returned in a damaged condition.

Another controversy at the Art Institute of Chicago last summer, surrounding the display of a sculpture by "Dread" Scott Tyler that invited viewers to trod upon an American flag spread out on the floor, ultimately led to the enactment of new city, state and federal bans on flag desecration! Senator Robert Dole (R-KA) said at the time, "I don't know much about art, but I know desecration when I see it."

The flag issue did not go away. On June 21, 1989, the U.S. Supreme Court handed down its anxiously awaited decision in the flag burning case, *Texas v. Johnson*. The Texas statute that banned flag-burning as part of a political protest, said the Court, was unconstitutional under the First Amendment. Ironically, the decision ignited a firestorm that raged so out of control as to underscore the total insignificance of the conflagration Gregory Johnson had visited upon the 1984 Republican convention in Dallas.

Let's amend the Constitution, said President Bush one week after the decision. And so commenced a campaign to attach to the First Amendment an exception that would allow enactment of a law prohibiting "desecration" of the American flag. With great haste and nearly without dissent, Congress passed "sense of the Congress" resolutions condemning the Supreme Court decision.

Mercifully, the proposed consitutional amendment did not pass. But a new federal law prohibiting "desecration" of the flag did. That law has now been declared unconstitutional by two federal courts, and appeals are on the way to the U.S. Supreme Court. If the Supreme Court upholds the lower court decisions, that could recharge efforts to amend the Constitution. And while proponents of flag desecration laws are primarily interested in restricting political expression, if such laws are allowed to stand there will be no way to limit their sweep through the arts.

Censorship of visual images has also been enabled by federal funding restrictions. Last summer, Senator Jesse Helms, outraged by two exhibits underwritten by the National Endowment for the Arts (NEA), one of them featuring homoerotic photographs by Robert Mapplethorpe, introduced a federal law that would have broadly restricted NEA funding of "offensive" art. The mere introduction of the Helms bill had an immediate censorious effect: The Corcoran Gallery in Washington cancelled its plans to mount the Mapplethorpe exhibit that had been the object of Helms' wrath. Congress rejected the initial Helms bill but enacted legislation that prohibits funding of "obscene" art, seems to define all homoerotic art as *per se* obscene, and establishes a regime of surveillance over artistic expression.

To even *read* the restrictions and guidelines that the new law imposes on the NEA is to be chilled! The law establishes a federal commission to review the NEA's grant-making process; requires the NEA to give Congress 30 days notice of its intention to award futher grants to the institutions responsible for the Mapplethorpe exhibit, so that Congress may review the plan; and puts

Congress on record as disavowing the previous NEA grants to those institutions, as well as the NEA fellowship awarded to painter Andres Serrano, who created a work thought to defame the Christian religion.

The very first application of the guidelines realized their potential for being wielded as a political weapon. Prior to enactment of the law, a small New York City gallery called Artists' Space had obtained a $10,000 NEA grant to help mount a show dealing with AIDS. After the new legislation took effect, the gallery director reported to the NEA that the show's catalogue and some of its imagery might be controversial. Incoming NEA chair John Frohnmeyer responded by threatening to withdraw the grant entirely, on the grounds that an essay in the catalogue criticized public officials—including Senator Helms. Said Frohnmeyer: "Political discourse ought to be in the political arena and not in a show sponsored by the Endowment."

One of the most disturbing things about current efforts to corral expression in the arts and in popular culture is that such efforts are increasingly broad-based.

For example: In the early 1980s, some feminists and legal scholars began to argue that pornography is a type of civil rights violation and gained passage of local ordinances broadly outlawing images that "denigrate" women. The ACLU challenged these laws and helped strike them down in court.

Interestingly, these laws are founded on the same reasoning that the Meese Commission on Pornography used to advocate the shutting down of bookstores and video shops, and prosecution of their owners for trafficking in "obscene" materials.

Similar efforts to categorize speech that "denigrates" as a civil rights violation are now occurring on numerous college and university campuses. As deeply troubling as the resurgence of racial tensions among students is, it is also troubling that the regulations and policies being devised by universities to respond to these tensions echo the standards of Jesse Helms. The original Helms law would have prohibited grants of NEA funds for artistic expression that "denigrates, debases or reviles a person, group or class of citizens on the basis of race, creed, sex, handicap or national origin," or that "denigrates any religion or non-religion."

Thus, it turns out that overbroad campus regulations intended to protect minorities and women from racial and sexual harassment are lending a veil of legitimacy to the efforts of people like Jesse Helms, whose targets are unconventional art. Similarly, restrictions on rock lyrics are now not only rationalized on the grounds that the music presumably encourages drug use, promiscuity and violence, but also because its content is presumably racist, sexist, anti-Semitic and/or homophobic. Wrote Tipper Gore, on the op-ed page of the *Washington Post* January 8, 1990: "Words like 'bitch' and 'nigger' are dangerous. Racial and sexual epithets, whether screamed across a street or camouflaged by the rhythms of a song, turn people into objects less than human . . . [w]e must raise our voices in protest and put pressure on those who not only reflect this hatred but also package, polish, promote, and market it."

Another, and inevitable, twist of fate is the fact that campus rules prohibiting racist speech are being turned against minority students themselves and their kinfolk in the arts. Recently, a student group at Columbia University tried to invoke campus rules against racist speech to bar an appearance on campus by a controversial member of the black rap group, Public Enemy, who had made some allegedly anti-Semitic remarks last summer.

Permitting restraints on expression in one area only fuels efforts to restrain it in another. Censorship is as indivisible as the First Amendment itself. That is why the ACLU challenges *all* censorship—whether it is an attempt to prohibit "unpatriotic" uses of the flag, racist speech on campuses, sexually explicit rock lyrics, the banning of films or NEA funding for certain artistic expression.

Suggestions for Discussion

1. What is the major point that Glasser makes in this essay? Explain his assertion that "censorship is as indivisible as the First Amendment itself."

2. Discuss the various areas of art that, according to Glasser, have been intimidated by the threat of censorship. What common thread does he see running through the movement to censor art?

3. Even in this short discussion, Glasser enables us to see how complex and ambiguous the issues of censorship become. Discuss these ambiguities and complexities in several of the examples cited.

Suggestions for Writing

1. The Mapplethorpe and Serrano works are the ones most frequently cited in the controversy over funding by the National Endowment for the Arts. Write an essay in which you explain why. (You will need to do some library research if you are not familiar with the works.) Make some personal commentary on these controversies.

2. Why does the American Civil Liberties Union oppose censorship in any form? Do you agree with their position? Use Glasser's remarks as a basis for your conclusions.

3. Why does one find opposing political movements (for example, the feminist movement and religious fundamentalism) sometimes in agreement over censorship? How would they answer Glasser's comments? Write an essay explaining this issue and make a personal comment on it.

Margaret Atwood

Pornography

Margaret Atwood (b. 1939) was born in Ottawa, Canada, and was educated at the University of Toronto and Radcliffe College. She is a novelist, best known for *The Handmaid's Tale* (1986), as well as a poet, critic, and professor. Her other novels include *The Edible Woman* (1969) and *Life Before Man* (1979); her collections of poetry include *Double Persephone* (1961) and *The Circle Game*

(1966). She has also written a controversial study of Canadian literature, *Survival* (1972), compiled *The New Oxford Book of Canadian Verse in English* (1983), and written another novel, *Cat's Eye* (1989). Her *Selected Poems* (originally published in 1976) has appeared in several editions, the latest in 1992. In this essay she attempts to state clearly why pornography is intolerable and why a discussion of banning it has created much confusion.

When I was in Finland a few years ago for an international writers' conference, I had occasion to say a few paragraphs in public on the subject of pornography. The context was a discussion of political repression, and I was suggesting the possibility of a link between the two. The immediate result was that a male journalist took several large bites out of me. Prudery and pornography are two halves of the same coin, said he, and I was clearly a prude. What could you expect from an Anglo-Canadian? Afterward, a couple of pleasant Scandinavian men asked me what I had been so worked up about. All "pornography" means, they said, is graphic depictions of whores, and what was the harm in that?

Not until then did it strike me that the male journalist and I had two entirely different things in mind. By "pornography," he meant naked bodies and sex. I, on the other hand, had recently been doing the research for my novel *Bodily Harm*, and was still in a state of shock from some of the material I had seen, including the Ontario Board of Film Censors' "outtakes." By "pornography," I meant women getting their nipples snipped off with garden shears, having meat hooks stuck into their vaginas, being disemboweled; little girls being raped; men (yes, there are some men) being smashed to a pulp and forcibly sodomized. The cutting edge of pornography, as far as I could see, was no longer simple old copulation, hanging from the chandelier or otherwise: it was death, messy, explicit and highly sadistic. I explained this to the nice Scandinavian men. "Oh, but that's just the United States," they said. "Everyone knows they're sick." In their country, they said, violent "pornography" of that kind was not permitted on television or in movies; indeed, excessive violence of any kind was not permitted. They had drawn a clear line between erotica, which earlier studies had shown did not incite men to more aggressive and brutal behavior toward women, and violence, which later studies indicated did.

Some time after that I was in Saskatchewan, where, because of the scenes in *Bodily Harm*, I found myself on an open-line radio show answering questions about "pornography." Almost no one who phoned in was in favor of it, but again they weren't talking about the same stuff I was, because they hadn't seen it. Some of them were all set to stamp out bathing suits and negligees, and, if possible, any depictions of the female body whatsoever. God, it was implied, did not approve of female bodies, and sex of any kind, including that practised by bumblebees, should be shoved back into the dark, where it belonged. I had more than a suspicion that *Lady Chatterley's Lover*, Margaret Laurence's *The Diviners*, and indeed most books by most serious modern authors would have ended up as confetti if left in the hands of these callers.

For me, these two experiences illustrate the two poles of the emotionally heated debate that is now thundering around this issue. They also underline the desirability and even the necessity of defining the terms. "Pornography" is now one of those catchalls, like "Marxism" and "feminism," that have become so broad they can mean almost anything, ranging from certain verses in the Bible, ads for skin lotion and sex texts for children to the contents of Penthouse, Naughty '90s postcards and films with titles containing the word *Nazi* that show vicious scenes of torture and killing. It's easy to say that sensible people can tell the difference. Unfortunately, opinions on what constitutes a sensible person vary.

But even sensible people tend to lose their cool when they start talking about this subject. They soon stop talking and start yelling, and the name-calling begins. Those in favor of censorship (which may include groups not noticeably in agreement on other issues, such as some feminists and religious fundamentalists) accuse the others of exploiting women through the use of degrading images, contributing to the corruption of children, and adding to the general climate of violence and threat in which both women and children live in this society; or, though they may not give much of a hoot about actual women and children, they invoke moral standards and God's supposed aversion to "filth," "smut" and deviated *perversion,* which may mean ankles.

The camp in favor of total "freedom of expression" often comes out howling as loud as the Romans would have if told they could no longer have innocent fun watching the lions eat up Christians. It too may include segments of the population who are not natural bedfellows: those who proclaim their God-given right to freedom, including the freedom to tote guns, drive when drunk, drool over chicken porn and get off on videotapes of women being raped and beaten, may be waving the same anticensorship banner as responsible liberals who fear the return of Mrs. Grundy, or gay groups for whom sexual emancipation involves the concept of "sexual theatre." *Whatever turns you on* is a handy motto, as is *A man's home is his castle* (and if it includes a dungeon with beautiful maidens strung up in chains and bleeding from every pore, that's his business).

Meanwhile, theoreticians theorize and speculators speculate. Is today's pornography yet another indication of the hatred of the body, the deep mind-body split, which is supposed to pervade Western Christian society? Is it a backlash against the women's movement by men who are threatened by uppity female behavior in real life, so like to fantasize about women done up like outsize parcels, being turned into hamburger, kneeling at their feet in slavelike adoration or sucking off guns? Is it a sign of collective impotence, of a generation of men who can't relate to real women at all but have to make do with bits of celluloid and paper? Is the current flood just a result of smart marketing and aggressive promotion by the money men in what has now become a multibillion-dollar industry? If they were selling movies about men getting their testicles stuck full of knitting needles by women with swastikas on their sleeves, would they do as well, or is this penchant somehow peculiarly male? If so, why? Is pornography a power trip rather than a sex one? Some say that those ropes, chains, muzzles and other restraining devices are an argument for the immense power female sexuality still wields in the male imagination: you don't put these things on dogs unless you're afraid of them. Others, more literary, wonder about the shift from the 19th-century Magic Women or Femme Fatale image to the lollipop-licker, airhead or turkey-carcass treatment of women in porn today. The proporners don't care much about theory: they merely demand product. The anti-porners don't care about it in the final analysis either: there's dirt on the street, and they want it cleaned up, now.

It seems to me that this conversation, with its *You're-a-prude/You're-a-pervert* dialectic, will never get anywhere as long as we continue to think of this material as just "entertainment." Possibly we're deluded by the packaging, the format: magazine, book, movie, theatrical presentation. We're used to thinking of these things as part of the "entertainment industry," and we're used to thinking of ourselves as free adult people who ought to be able to see any kind of "entertainment" we want to. That was what the First Choice pay-TV debate was all about. After all, it's only entertainment, right? Entertainment means fun, and only a killjoy would be antifun. What's the harm?

This is obviously the central question: *What's the harm?* If there isn't any real harm to any real people, then the antiporners can tsk-tsk and/or throw up as much as they like, but they can't rightfully expect more legal controls or sanctions. However, the no-harm position is far from being proven.

(For instance, there's a clear-cut case for banning—as the federal government has proposed—movies, photos and videos that depict children engaging in sex with adults: real children are used to make the movies, and hardly anybody thinks this is ethical. The possibilities for coercion are too great.)

To shift the viewpoint, I'd like to suggest three other models for looking at "pornography"—and here I mean the violent kind.

Those who find the idea of regulating pornographic materials repugnant because they think it's Fascist or Communist or otherwise not in accordance with the principles of an open democratic society should consider that Canada has made it illegal to disseminate material that may lead to hatred toward any group because of race or religion. I suggest that if pornography of the violent kind depicted these acts being done predominantly to Chinese, to blacks, to Catholics, it would be off the market immediately, under the present laws. Why is hate literature illegal? Because whoever made the law thought that such material might incite real people to do real awful things to other real people. The human brain is to a certain extent a computer: garbage in, garbage out. We only hear about the extreme cases (like that of American multimurderer Ted Bundy) in which pornography has contributed to the death and/or mutilation of women and/or men. Although pornography is not the only factor involved in the creation of such deviance, it certainly has upped the ante by suggesting both a variety of techniques and the social acceptability of such actions. Nobody knows yet what effect this stuff is having on the less psychotic.

Studies have shown that a large part of the market for all kinds of porn, soft and hard, is drawn from the 16-to-21-year-old population of young men. Boys used to learn about sex on the street, or (in Italy, according to Fellini movies) from friendly whores, or, in more genteel surroundings, from girls, their parents, or, once upon a time, in school, more or less. Now porn has been added, and sex education in the schools is rapidly being phased out. The buck has been passed, and boys are being taught that all women secretly like to be raped and that real men get high on scooping out women's digestive tracts.

Boys learn their concept of masculinity from other men: is this what most men want them to be learning? If word gets around that rapists are "normal" and even admirable men, will boys feel that in order to be normal, admirable and masculine they will have to be rapists? Human beings are enormously flexible, and how they turn out depends a lot on how they're educated, by the society in which they're immersed as well as by their teachers. In a society that advertises and glorifies rape or even implicitly condones it, more women get raped. It becomes socially acceptable. And at a time when men and the traditional male role have taken a lot of flak and men are confused and casting around for an acceptable way of being male (and, in some cases, not getting much comfort from women on that score), this must be at times a pleasing thought.

It would be naïve to think of violent pornography as just harmless entertainment. It's also an educational tool and a powerful propaganda device. What happens when boy educated on porn meets girl brought up on Harlequin romances? The clash of expectations can be heard around the block. She wants him to get down on his knees with a ring, he wants her to get down on all fours with a ring in her nose. Can this marriage be saved?

Pornography has certain things in common with such addictive substances as alcohol and drugs: for some, though by no means for all, it induces chemical changes in the body, which the user finds exciting and pleasurable. It also appears to attract a "hard core" of habitual users and a penumbra of those who use it occasionally but aren't dependent on it in any way. There are also significant numbers of men who aren't much interested in it, not because they're undersexed but because real life is satisfying their needs, which may not require as many appliances as those of users.

For the "hard core," pornography may function as alcohol does for the alcoholic: tolerance develops, and a little is no longer enough. This may account for the short viewing time and fast turnover in porn theatres. Mary Brown, chairwoman of the Ontario Board of Film Censors, estimates that for every one mainstream movie requesting entrance to Ontario, there is one porno flick. Not only the quantity consumed but the quality of explicitness must escalate, which may account for the growing violence: once the big deal was breasts, then it was genitals, then copulation, then that was no longer enough and the hard users had to have more. The ultimate kick is death, and after that, as the Marquis de Sade so boringly demonstrated, multiple death.

The existence of alcoholism has not led us to ban social drinking. On the other hand, we do have laws about drinking and driving, excessive drunkenness and other abuses of alcohol that may result in injury or death to others.

This leads us back to the key question: what's the harm? Nobody knows, but this society should find out fast, before the saturation point is reached. The Scandinavian studies that showed a connection between depictions of sexual violence and increased impulse toward it on the part of male viewers would be a starting point, but many more questions remain to be raised as well as answered. What, for instance, is the crucial difference between men who are users and men who are not? Does using affect a man's relationship with actual women, and, if so, adversely? Is there a clear line between erotica and violent pornography, or are they on an escalating continuum? Is this a "men versus women" issue, with all men secretly siding with the proporners and all women secretly siding against? (I think not; there *are* lots of men who don't think that running their true love through the Cuisinart is the best way they can think of to spend a Saturday night, and they're just as nauseated by films of someone else doing it as women are.) Is pornography merely an expression of the sexual confusion of this age or an active contributor to it?

Nobody wants to go back to the age of official repression, when even piano legs were referred to as "limbs" and had to wear pantaloons to be decent. Neither do we want to end up in George Orwell's *1984*, in which pornography is turned out by the State to keep the proles in a state of torpor, sex itself is considered dirty and the approved practise is only for reproduction. But Rome under the emperors isn't such a good model either.

If all men and women respected each other, if sex were considered joyful and life-enhancing instead of a wallow in germ-filled glop, if everyone were in love all the time, if, in other words, many people's lives were more satisfactory for them than they appear to be now, pornography might just go away on its own. But since this is obviously not happening, we as a society are going to have to make some informed and responsible decisions about how to deal with it.

Suggestions for Discussion

1. Identify the following in the essay: D. H. Lawrence's *Lady Chatterley's Lover*, Margaret Laurence's *The Diviners*, Mrs. Grundy, the Marquis de Sade.

2. Summarize Atwood's major argument against pornography. What action does she believe society should take against it?

3. How do the Scandinavian countries deal with pornography? How do they define it?

4. Is Atwood too pessimistic about the ability of people who watch or read pornography to resist translating it into action by themselves?

Suggestions for Writing

1. Write a paper in which you express your agreement or disagreement with Atwood's definition of pornography.

2. Does Atwood's position result in censorship? Are you opposed to censorship? Write a paper in which you discuss censorship and pornography as defined by Atwood.

3. Is pornography an issue for women or is it important to both sexes? Write a paper in which you explain your opinion.

Noel Perrin

Science Fiction: Imaginary Worlds and Real-Life Questions

Noel Perrin (b. 1927), a professor of English and, since 1991, a professor of environmental studies at Dartmouth College, is a frequent contributor to *The New Yorker* and other periodicals. He also practices farming in Vermont. Among his published works are A *Passport Secretly Green* (1961), *First Person*

Rural: Essays of a Sometime Farmer (1980), *Third Person Rural: More Essays of a Sometime Farmer* (1981), *Last Person Rural* (1991), and *Solo: Life with an Electric Car* (1992). This personal account of his role in making science fiction respectable at Dartmouth also claims that it is an art form demanding serious consideration.

Fourteen years ago I began to teach a course in science fiction at Dartmouth College. Spaceships figured in the reading, along with faster-than-light travel, telepathic robots and in one story some bright orange aliens who rather resembled tennis balls on legs.

Not all my colleagues in the English department were embarrassed by the new course, just most. Say, 25 out of 30. In general, they knew just enough about science fiction—without, perhaps, having read any except those two special cases, "Brave New World" and "Nineteen Eighty-Four"—to know that it was a formula genre, like the murder mystery, and not worthy of attention in the classroom. But they were powerless to stop the new course, or at least it would have taken a concerted effort. I was chairman of the department at the time, and my last year in office I spent such credit as I had left on getting the science fiction course approved.

Why did I want a science fiction course? It is not self-evident that Dartmouth students need to hear about tennis-ball-shaped aliens. Was I maybe pandering to popular taste, as chairmen often do when they want to build enrollment? (If so, it worked. About 160 students signed up that first year, and still more would have if we hadn't quickly closed the course.)

If I was pandering, it certainly wasn't conscious. I wanted the course for what seemed to me the very highest of reasons. I thought that the most important questions of the 20th century got more attention in works of science fiction than anywhere else. Fairly often they even got answers.

Some of these questions are quite specific. What might it feel like to live in the age after a nuclear war? Just how possible will it be, perhaps in the not so distant future, to turn all work over to robots? Since we can splice genes, what kind of creatures will we make of ourselves? Others are as broad as questions can get. What is the good life for human beings? What are our duties, if any, to other life-forms? If we can, should be abolish death? (That's a genuine issue. Some scientists think a form of immortality is no more than a century away.)

Philosophers once used to ask some of the same questions. A few of them still do. But to most philosophers the broad questions seem naïve, the product of an outdated metaphysics, and the narrow ones demand a range of technical knowledge most philosophers don't have.

More recently, novelists pondered many of the more metaphysical issues—until both they and critics realized that literature is self-referential and not much of a guide to the real world. Mainstream fiction now mostly flows in more private directions.

But science fiction, immensely sophisticated about technology, has stayed naïve about metaphysics—naïve in the sense that most science fiction writers continue to suppose that questions of value can be meaningfully discussed. (I suppose that, too. If I didn't, I would probably resign my job.) In fact, science fiction has become the chief refuge for metaphysics. It is where you go in literature if you want to hear people openly and seriously talking about meaning, and especially meaning in a world increasingly made and controlled by ourselves.

That is the main reason I wanted a science fiction course, but it is not the only one. There is also the question of literary merit. I support as much as any of my colleagues the notion that a genre needs to have attained a high level of distinction before it deserves to be taught in a course. I also think science fiction has attained that level. But it is not amazing that most professors of English failed to perceive that in 1975.

To begin with, though science fiction was well out of its infancy in 1975— was in fact about a hundred years old—it still seemed new. For example, with rare exceptions, it attained the dignity of being published in hard cover only in the 1960's. More serious science fiction was (and is) hard to distinguish from a couple of seedy cousins. If you were to pose the three for a group picture, you would put science fiction in the middle, clean-faced and intelligent. On one side, wearing stage armor, would be the sword-and-sorcery novel. On the other, holding a couple of laser pistols and wearing a gaudy helmet, space opera. Both these genres *are* formulaic, derivative, unworthy of being taught. And both are so interactive with science fiction that they can sometimes inhabit the same book. But science fiction is a much more serious genre, which, instead of trafficking in pure fantasy, attempts to be scientifically and logically responsible to the real universe.

Frank Herbert's "Dune," for example, is part sword-and-sorcery—though in his case I prefer the politer name of heroic fantasy. There are witches in the book, prophecies, much hand-to-hand combat. But the book is also full of spaceships, personal atomic weapons and advanced ecology, and is partly science fiction.

Or take Larry Niven and Jerry Pournelle's book "The Mote in God's Eye," once described by Robert A. Heinlein, one of the eminences of the field, as possibly the finest science fiction novel he'd ever read. The half of the book devoted to the alien creatures called Moties is indeed major science fiction. But the other half! That takes place aboard a starship of the Imperial Space Navy (I can see my colleagues grinning at the very name), and it reeks of space opera.

I doubt if any of my colleagues had read or even heard of "The Mote in God's Eye" in 1975. But they had certainly picked up on its vibes, as one would have said back then. They knew about space opera, and they erroneously thought that no science fiction existed without it.

In fact, enough science fiction of high literary quality, pure and unmixed with either space opera or fantasy, already existed to fill two or three courses. Easy to assert, hard to prove. What I shall do is name a few of the ones I actually used. The one that gave me the most private amusement was a novella written back in 1909. The author, an Englishman, had been reading H. G. Wells and had been so put off by what he saw as Wells's mindless faith in technology that he wrote his own work of science fiction as a riposte. Thus it came about that in the spring of 1975 one member of the department was teaching E. M. Forster's "Passage to India" in the 20th-century British novel course while I was simultaneously teaching "The Machine Stops" by the same E. M. Forster in the new science fiction course. It fitted in nicely. Just as Forster had written in response to Wells, so Arthur C. Clarke much later was moved to answer Forster in "The City and the Stars"; and that brooding novel—it deals with earthly immortality—was also in the course.

But there are not a lot of Huxleys, Orwells and Forsters who once or twice in their lives come trailing clouds of respectability into science fiction. Most of the good work (and virtually all of the bad) is by people who start out in science fiction, and who, along with all their books, were invisible to my colleagues in 1975. Such were three of the other works I taught.

The star of the course was undoubtedly Walter Miller's extraordinary novel, "A Canticle for Leibowitz." It's the best and wisest of all novels about the world after a nuclear war, and also the most exhilarating to read. You didn't know a novel about a radioactive world *could* be exhilarating? You haven't read "Canticle" then.

Then I had Samuel R. Delany's story "We, in Some Strange Power's Employ, Move on a Rigorous Line." It's about employees of the one great power company that serves the whole planet, maybe 60 years from now, when the remotest Tibetan village is guaranteed access to electricity. It's also about what constitutes the good life, and about destiny, and about ambition. It operates on more levels that William Empson could have counted, including one on which the story plays off Spenser's "Faerie Queene," though so unobtrusively that no Dartmouth student has yet noticed. Mr. Delany is the first major black science fiction writer to emerge, not that I knew that in 1975. I just knew that he had written a classic story.

And I also taught Ursula K. Le Guin's "Left Hand of Darkness," a novel that goes so far beyond either feminism or male chauvinism as to leave people attached to either gender gasping in the dust. One way I know the book's power is that it has consistently stimulated good papers from students—some of the best papers I have ever got in any course.

A book focused on sex and gender is, of course, bound to be deeply interesting to 20-year-olds. I mean, even more interesting than to the rest of us. But "Left Hand" does more than speculate on what human beings would be like if all of us belonged to both sexes and were likely to be active in a male phase one month and female the next. It tells a heroic story. It develops rounded characters, most of them two-sexed inhabitants of the planet Gethen, but one a male visitor from Earth. (His nickname among Gethenians is "the pervert.") It brings a whole imagined world into plenary existence. There is nothing of formula here. There is high literature.

Three student generations have passed since those books were picked. (Not that I mean to claim pioneer status for the course. The first regular science fiction course seems to have been given at Colgate University in 1962.) If much good literature was available back then, vastly more is now. The late 20th century has been the golden age of science fiction.

In this country, writer after fine writer has emerged. I think of Michael Bishop, whose novella "Death and Designation Among the Asadi" gives so powerful a sense of what it would really be like to encounter—and not to understand—an alien intelligence that one understands even Columbus differently after reading it. I think of Alice Sheldon, the woman who wrote as James Tiptree, Jr. Her depiction of life aboard a United Nations starship in the novella "A Momentary Taste of Being" is to the Niven-Pournelle account of the Imperial Space Navy as a real horse is to a child's drawing. I think of

Judith Moffett, who just two or three years ago turned from a successful career as a poet to a still more successful one as a writer of science fiction. Her first novel, "Pennterra," the only work of Quaker science fiction I know, already establishes her as a presence in the field. It's as interesting ecologically as literarily.

Meanwhile, translation of major work from other parts of the world has proceeded rapidly. The most impressive examples have come from the Soviet Union and its satellites. Science fiction has its Borges in the person of Stanislaw Lem of Poland. I'm thinking especially of "The Cyberiad," his mock-epic about cybers—that is, cybernetic beings, or robots. Mr. Lem's elaborate fantasies are less *outré* than the reader first supposes. In the real world, computer science students at the Massachusetts Institute of Technology are already wondering—as he has in this fiction—whether it will constitute murder when someone first unplugs a self-aware robot.

Among the Eastern Europeans, I particularly admire Arkady and Boris Strugatsky, Russian brothers whose jointly written novels dominate Soviet science fiction and are among the best in the world. If American publishers had the decency to keep them in print, I would always have had one in the course—most often, probably, "Roadside Picnic," despite the bad translation in which it comes to us. The concept of the book is wonderful—that at some point a few years hence a group of aliens pauses briefly on Earth without our ever noticing and carelessly leaves a little debris behind when they go, like sandwich bags and soda cans after a picnic. We, like, ants, find it. And it is as mysterious to us as a soda can to an ant, which doesn't even know what Nutrasweet *is*, let alone its risks.

In 1989 I don't suppose that more than half the department is embarrassed by the existence of the course. Maybe less. But not many of my colleagues see it as important, either. I no longer teach the course. (I burn out on any course after a few years—13 with science fiction is my record for longevity.) The department's response has been to "bracket" the course. It will stay in the catalogue, but for now at least it will not be taught.

I admit that some of my colleagues' literary misgivings have been justified. Not about the books, but about me. I have found the metaphysics too tempting. Once a colleague came across a copy of my final exam. There was a perfectly decent question or two about narrational mode and so on, but there was also a question that asked simply, "If it were in your power to air-condition this planet, would you?"

Of course I can see why a literary theorist might shudder at such an exam. And I would be perfectly happy to have the department hire a replacement who would deal with science fiction in more rigorous and analytical ways. Such is the power of the genre that the metaphysics would come through anyway.

Suggestions for Discussion

1. What is Perrin's basic argument for including a course in science fiction in the English department curriculum? Does he make a good case? How?

2. What distinction does Perrin make between science fiction on one hand and the sword-and-sorcery novel and space opera on the other? With what works of space opera are you familiar?

3. Discuss Perrin's reasons for describing works by Miller, Delany, Le Guin, and others as profound works of fiction. Have you read any of the works he mentions? Does his description of them make you want to read them? Why?

4. What is the tone of this essay? How does Perrin establish it? Why does he disparage his final examination question that he quotes?

5. Discuss Perrin's statement that if he did not believe questions of value can be meaningfully discussed, he would give up teaching.

Suggestions for Writing

1. Write a paper in which you explain whether you think a work of science fiction has significance as literature. Notice how Perrin presents his evaluations and attempt to follow his example in your own essay.

2. Write an essay in which you discuss the proposition that what Perrin calls sword-and-sorcery works and space opera are not serious works of literature. Use as many examples, including film, as you think necessary to persuade your reader.

E. L. Doctorow

Ultimate Discourse

E. L. Doctorow (b. 1931), born in New York City, graduated with honors in philosophy from Kenyon College and has received two honorary doctorate degrees. He has worked as an editor in publishing and as a member of the English faculty at Sarah Lawrence College, Yale University, University of California, Irvine, and since 1982 has been a professor at New York University. He has received numerous honors, including the National Book Critics Circle Award for *Ragtime* (1975). He has served as director of the Authors Guild and is a member of the American Academy and the Institute for Arts and Letters. Among his works are *The Book of Daniel* (1971), *Drinks Before Dinner* (1979), *Loon Lake* (1980), and *Billy Bathgate* (1988). In 1990 he won the National Book Critics Circle Award and the PEN/Faulkner Award and was elected to the American Academy and Institute of Arts and Letters. In this brief essay he explains why fiction occupies a significant place in our lives.

When I was a boy everyone in my family was a good storyteller, my mother and father, my brother, my aunts and uncles and grandparents; all of them were people to whom interesting things seemed to happen. The events they spoke of were of a daily, ordinary sort, but when narrated or acted out they took on great importance and excitement as I listened.

Of course, when you bring love to the person you are listening to, the story has to be interesting, and in one sense the task of a professional writer who publishes books is to overcome the terrible loss of not being someone the reader knows and loves.

But apart from that, the people whose stories I heard as a child must have had a very firm view of themselves in the world. They must have been strong enough as presences in their own minds to trust that people would listen to them when they spoke.

I know now that everyone in the world tells stories. Relatively few people are given to mathematics or physics, but narrative seems to be within everyone's grasp, perhaps because it comes of the nature of language itself.

The moment you have nouns and verbs and prepositions, the moment you have subjects and objects, you have stories.

For the longest time there would have been nothing but stories, and no sharper distinction between what was real and what was made up than between what was spoken and what was sung. Religious arousal and scientific discourse, simple urgent communication and poetry, all burned together in the intense perception of a metaphor—that, for instance, the sun was a god's chariot driven across the heavens.

Stories were as important to survival as a spear or a hoe. They were the memory of the knowledge of the dead. They gave counsel. They connected the visible to the invisible. They distributed the suffering so that it could be borne.

In our era, even as we separate the functions of language, knowing when we speak scientifically we are not speaking poetically, and when we speak theologically we are not speaking the way we do to each other in our houses, and even as our surveys demand statistics, and our courts demand evidence, and our hypotheses demand proof—our minds are still structured for storytelling.

What we call fiction is the ancient way of knowing, the total discourse that antedates all the special vocabularies of modern intelligence.

The professional writer of fiction is a conservative who cherishes the ultimate structures of the human mind. He cultivates within himself the universal disposition to think in terms of conflict and its resolution, and in terms of character undergoing events, and of the outcome of events being not at all sure, and therefore suspenseful—the whole thing done, moreover, from a confidence of narrative that is grounded in our brains as surely as the innate talent to construe the world grammatically.

The fiction writer, looking around him, understands the homage a modern up-to-date world of nonfiction specialists pays to his craft—even as it isolates him and tells him he is a liar. Newsweeklies present the events of the world as installments in a serial melodrama. Weather reports on television are constructed with exact attention to conflict (high-pressure areas clashing with lows), suspense (the climax of tomorrow's prediction coming after the commercial), and the consistency of voice (the personality of the weathercaster). The marketing and advertising of product-facts is unquestionably a fictional enterprise. As is every government's representations of its activities. And modern psychology, with its concepts of *sublimation, repression, identity crisis, complex,* and so on, proposes the interchangeable parts for the stories of all of us; in this sense it is the industrialization of storytelling.

But nothing is as good at fiction as fiction. It is the most ancient way of knowing but also the most modern, managing when it's done right to burn all the functions of language back together into powerful fused revelation. Because it is total discourse it is ultimate discourse. It excludes nothing. It will express from the depth and range of its sources truths that no sermon or experiment or news report can begin to apprehend. It will tell you without shame what people do with their bodies and think with their minds. It will deal evenhandedly with their microbes or their intuitions. It will know their nightmares and blinding moments of moral crisis. You will experience love, if it so chooses, or starvation or drowning or dropping through space or holding a hot pistol in your hand with the police pounding on the door. This is the way it is, it will say, this is what it feels like.

Fiction is democratic, it reasserts the authority of the single mind to make and remake the world. By its independence from all institutions, from the family to the government, and with no responsibility to defend their hypocrisy or murderousness, it is a valuable resource and instrument of survival.

Fiction gives counsel. It connects the present with the past, and the visible with the invisible. It distributes the suffering. It says we must compose ourselves in our stories in order to exist. It says if we don't do it, someone else will do it for us.

Suggestions for Discussion

1. Doctorow suggests that storytelling is basic to everyone, a universal activity. How does he distinguish between the stories people tell to their loved ones and those authors write for publication?

2. What does Doctorow say is the origin of the urge to tell stories? Explain his assertion that storytelling fuses the elements of religion, science, and poetry.

3. Although the fused elements became separate in modern times, how does fiction remain fundamental to all activity? How, for example, is it used by representatives of government and business and by professional psychologists?

4. Doctorow says that "nothing is as good at fiction as fiction." Explain his reasons for this assertion.

Suggestions for Writing

1. Doctorow not only calls fiction the "ultimate discourse," but he says that it is also democratic. Write an essay in which you explain both of these assertions. Do you agree? Why?

2. Doctorow states that fiction "says we must compose ourselves in our stories in order to exist. It says if we don't do it, someone else will do it for us." Explain what he means by these remarks, particularly by the last sentence.

Saul Bellow
Adrienne Rich

From the National Book Award
Acceptance Speeches

Each year since 1950, the American Book Awards have been presented for the best book of the year in two categories, fiction and nonfiction. Excerpts follow from the acceptance speeches of Saul Bellow (b. 1915), who won the award in 1965 for his novel *Herzog,* and Adrienne Rich (b. 1929), who won in 1974 for *Diving Into the Wreck: Poems, 1971–72.*

Saul Bellow

The fact that there are so many weak, poor and boring stories and novels written and published in America has been ascribed by our rebels to the horrible squareness of our institutions, the idiocy of power, the debasement of sexual instincts and the failure of writers to be alienated enough. The poems and novels of these same rebellious spirits, and their theoretical statements, are grimy and gritty and very boring too, besides being nonsensical, and it is evident now that polymorphous sexuality and vehement declarations of alienation are not going to produce great works of art either.

There is nothing left for us novelists to do but think. For unless we think, unless we make a clearer estimate of our condition, we will continue to write kid stuff, to fail in our function, we will lack serious interests and become truly irrelevant.

Here the critics must share the blame. They too have failed to describe the situation. Literature has for several generations been its own source, its own province, has lived upon its own traditions, and accepted a romantic separation or estrangement from the common world. This estrangement, though it produced some masterpieces, has by now enfeebled literature. The separatism of writers is accompanied by the more or less conscious acceptance of a theory of modern civilization. This theory says in effect that modern mass society is frightful, brutal, hostile to whatever is pure in the human spirit, a wasteland and a horror. To its ugliness, its bureaucratic regiments, its thefts, its lies, its wars and its unparalleled cruelties, the artist can never be reconciled. This is one of the traditions on which literature has lived uncritically. But it is the task of artists and critics in every generation to look with their own eyes. Perhaps they will see even worse evils, but they will at least be seeing for themselves. They will not, they cannot permit themselves, generation after generation, to hold views they have not examined for themselves.

By such willful blindness we lose the right to call ourselves artists; we have accepted what we ourselves condemn—narrow specialization, professional-

556

ism and snobbery and the formation of a caste. And unfortunately the postures of this caste, postures of liberation and independence and creativity, are attractive to poor souls dreaming everywhere of a fuller, freer life. The writer is admired, the writer is envied. But what has he to say for himself? Why, he says, just as writers have said for more than a century, [is it] that he is cut off from the life of his own society, despised by its overlords who are cynical and have nothing but contempt for the artist, without a true public, estranged. He dreams of ages when the poet or the painter expressed a perfect unit of time and place, had real acceptance, and enjoyed a vital harmony with his surroundings—he dreams of a golden age. In fact, without the golden age, there is no wasteland.

Well, this is no age of gold. It is only what it is. Can we do no more than complain about it? We writers have better choices. We can either shut up because the times are too bad, or continue because we have an instinct to make books, a talent to enjoy, which even these disfigured times cannot obliterate. Isolated professionalism is death. Without the common world the novelist is nothing but a curiosity and will find himself in a glass case along some dull museum corridor of the future.

We live in a technological age which seems insurmountably hostile to the artist. He must fight for his life, for his freedom, along with everyone else— for justice and equality, threatened by mechanization and bureaucracy. This is not to advise the novelist to rush immediately into the political sphere. But in the first stage he must begin to exert his intelligence, long unused. If he is to reject politics, he must understand what he is rejecting. He must begin to think, and to think not merely of his own narrower interests and needs.

Adrienne Rich

[This] statement . . . was prepared by three of the women nominated for the National Book Award for poetry, with the agreement that it would be read by whichever of us, if any, was chosen.

We, Audre Lord, Adrienne Rich and Alice Walker, together accept this award in the name of all the women whose voices have gone and still go unheard in a patriarchal world, and in the name of those who, like us, have been tolerated as token women in this culture, often at great cost and in great pain. We believe that we can enrich ourselves more in supporting and giving to each other than by competing against each other; and that poetry—if it *is* poetry—exists in a realm beyond ranking and comparison. We symbolically join together here in refusing the terms of patriarchal competition and declaring that we will share this prize among us, to be used as best we can for women. . . . We dedicate this occasion to the struggle for self-determination of all women, of every color, identification or derived class: the poet, the housewife, the lesbian, the mathematician, the mother, the dishwasher, the pregnant teen-ager, the teacher, the grandmother, the prostitute, the philosopher, the waitress, the women who will understand what we are doing here and those who will not understand yet; the silent women whose voices have been denied us, the articulate women who have given us strength.

Suggestions for Discussion

1. What advice does Bellow offer writers?

2. To what use did Rich put her opportunity to speak?

3. What common problems do both writers identify in modern society?

4. Explain what you perceive to be the principal difference between the speeches.

Suggestions for Writing

1. Write a brief address in which you identify an important issue for serious discussion.

2. Write a commentary on either of the excerpts.

===

Walker Percy

The Delta Factor

Walker Percy (1916–1990) was one of the most distinguished southern writers in this country. Born in Birmingham, Alabama, he was educated at the University of North Carolina and received an M.D. from Columbia University. The success of his first novel, *The Moviegoer* (1961), confirmed him in his belief that he should be a writer rather than a medical doctor. His other works include *The Last Gentleman* (1966) and its sequel, *Second Coming* (1980). Both novels portray a southerner who returns home in search of moral values. *Love in the Ruins* (1971) treats satirically a scientist whose main preoccupation is to change the mechanistic culture of the country. "The Delta Factor" is from *The Message in the Bottle* (1975), a collection of essays on language and its impact on how we live.

How I Discovered the Delta Factor Sitting at My Desk One Summer Day in Louisiana in the 1950s Thinking About an Event in the Life of Helen Keller on Another Summer Day in Alabama in 1887

In the beginning was Alpha and the end is Omega, but somewhere between occurred Delta, which was nothing less than the arrival of man himself and his breakthrough into the daylight of language and consciousness and knowing, of happiness and sadness, of being with and being alone, of being right and being wrong, of being himself and being not himself, and of being at home and being a stranger.

1

Why does man feel so sad in the twentieth century?

Why does man feel so bad in the very age when, more than in any other age, he has succeeded in satisfying his needs and making over the world for his own use?

Why has man entered on an orgy of war, murder, torture, and self-destruction unparalleled in history and in the very century when he had hoped to see the dawn of universal peace and brotherhood?

Why do people often feel bad in good environments and good in bad environments?

Why do people often feel so bad in good environments that they prefer bad environments?

Why does a man often feel better in a bad environment?

Why is a man apt to feel bad in a good environment, say suburban Short Hills, New Jersey, on an ordinary Wednesday afternoon? Why is the same man apt to feel good in a very bad environment, say an old hotel on Key Largo during a hurricane?

Why have more people been killed in the twentieth century than in all other centuries put together?

Why is war man's greatest pleasure?

Why is man the only creature that wages war against its own species?

What would man do if war were outlawed?

Why is it that the only time I ever saw my uncle happy during his entire life was the afternoon of December 7, 1941, when the Japanese bombed Pearl Harbor?

Why did he shortly thereafter become miserable when he learned that he was too old to go to Europe to shoot at Germans and stand a good chance of being shot by Germans?

Why is it that the only time he was happy before was in the Argonne Forest in 1918 when he was shooting at Germans and stood a good chance of being shot by Germans?

Why was he sad from 1918 to 1941 even though he lived in as good an environment as man can devise, indeed had the best of all possible worlds in literature, music, and art?

Why is it that a man riding a good commuter train from Larchmont to New York, whose needs and drives are satisfied, who has a good home, loving wife and family, good job, who enjoys unprecedented "cultural and recreational facilities," often feels bad without knowing why?

Why is it that if such a man suffers a heart attack and, taken off the train at New Rochelle, regains consciousness and finds himself in a strange place, he then comes to himself for the first time in years, perhaps in his life, and begins to gaze at his own hand with a sense of wonder and delight?

What is the difference between such a man, a commuter who feels bad without knowing why, and another commuter who feels bad without knowing why but who begins to read a book about a man who feels bad without knowing why?

Why does it make a man feel better to read a book about a man like himself feeling bad?

Why was it that Jean-Paul Sartre, sitting in a French café and writing *Nausea*, which is about the absurdity of human existence and the nausea of life in the twentieth century—why was he the happiest man in France at the time?

Why was it that when Franz Kafka would read aloud to his friends stories about the sadness and alienation of life in the twentieth century everyone would laugh until tears came?

Why is it harder to study a dogfish on a dissecting board in a zoological laboratory in college where one has proper instruments and a proper light than it would be if one were marooned on an island and, having come upon a dogfish on the beach and having no better instrument than a pocketknife or bobby pin, one began to explore the dogfish?

Why is it all but impossible to read Shakespeare in school now but will not be fifty years from now when the Western world has fallen into ruins and a survivor sitting among the vines of the Forty-second Street library spies a moldering book and opens it to *The Tempest*?

Why is it difficult to see a painting in a museum but not if someone should take you by the hand and say, "I have something to show you in my house," and lead you through a passageway and upstairs into the attic and there show the painting to you?

Why are Americans intrigued by the idea of floating down the Mississippi River on a raft but not down the Hudson?

Why do more people commit suicide in San Francisco, the most beautiful city in America, than in any other city?

Why is the metaphor *Flesh is grass*, which is not only wrong (flesh is not grass) but inappropriate (flesh is not even like grass), better and truer than the sentence *Flesh is mortal*, which is quite accurate and logical?

What would you do if a stranger came up to you on a New York street and, before disappearing into the crowd, gave you a note which read: "I know your predicament; it is such and such. Be at the southeast corner of Lindell Boulevard and Kingshighway in St. Louis at 9 a.m., April 16—I have news of the greatest importance"?

Where are the Hittites?

Why does no one find it remarkable that in most world cities today there are Jews but not one single Hittite, even though the Hittites had a great flourishing civilization while the Jews nearby were a weak and obscure people?

When one meets a Jew in New York or New Orleans or Paris or Melbourne, it is remarkable that no one considers the event remarkable. What are they doing here? But it is even more remarkable to wonder, if there are Jews here, why are there not Hittites here?

Where are the Hittites? Show me one Hittite in New York City.

Given two men living in Short Hills, New Jersey, each having satisfied his needs, working at rewarding jobs, participating in meaningful relationships with other people, etc., etc.: one feels good, the other feels bad; one feels at home, the other feels homeless. Which one is sick? Which is better off?

Why do people driving around on beautiful Sunday afternoons like to see bloody automobile wrecks?

Why did the young French couple driving through the countryside with their baby, having heard the news of a crash nearby of an airliner killing three hundred people and littering the forest with bits of flesh, speed frantically toward the scene, stop the car, and, carrying the baby, rush toward the dead, running through thickets to avoid police barricades? Did they have relatives on the plane?

Why did French and German veterans of Verdun, a catastrophic battle in which one million men were killed, keep returning to Verdun for years after the war, sit quietly in a café at Lemmes on the Sacred Way, speaking softly of those terrible times, and even camp out for a week in the shell hole or trench where they spent the worst days of their lives?

Why is the good life which men have achieved in the twentieth century so bad that only news of world catastrophes, assassinations, plane crashes, mass murders, can divert one from the sadness of ordinary mornings?

Why do young people look so sad, the very young who, seeing how sad their elders are, have sought a new life of joy and freedom with each other and in the green fields and forests, but who instead of finding joy look even sadder than their elders?

2

What does a man do when he finds himself living after an age has ended and he can no longer understand himself because the theories of man of the former age no longer work and the theories of the new age are not yet known, for not even the name of the new age is known, and so everything is upside down, people feeling bad when they should feel good, good when they should feel bad?

What a man does is start afresh as if he were newly come into a new world, which in fact it is; start with what he knows for sure, look at the birds and beasts, and like a visitor from Mars newly landed on earth notice what is different about man.

If beasts can be understood as organisms living in environments which are good or bad and to which the beast responds accordingly as it has evolved to respond, how is man to be understood if he feels bad in the best environment?

Where does one start with a theory of man if the theory of man as an organism in an environment doesn't work and all the attributes of man which were accepted in the old modern age are now called into question: his soul, mind, freedom, will, Godlikeness?

There is only one place to start: the place where man's singularity is there for all to see and cannot be called into question, even in a new age in which everything else is in dispute.

That singularity is language.

Why is it that men speak and animals don't?

What does it entail to be a speaking creature, that is, a creature who names things and utters sentences about things which other similar creatures understand and misunderstand?

Why is it that every normal man on earth speaks, that is, can utter an unlimited number of sentences in a complex language, and that not one single beast has ever uttered a word?

Why are there not some "higher" animals which have acquired a primitive language?

Why are there not some "lower" men who speak a crude, primitive language?

Why is there no such thing as a primitive language?

Why is there such a gap between nonspeaking animals and speaking man, when there is no other such gap in nature?

How can a child learn to speak a language in three years without anyone taking trouble about it, that is, utter and understand an unlimited number of sentences, while a great deal of time and trouble is required to teach a chimpanzee a few hand signals?

Why is it that scientists, who know a great deal about the world, know less about language than about the back side of the moon, even though language is the one observable behavior which most clearly sets man apart from the beasts and the one activity in which all men, scientists included, engage more than in any other?

Why is it that scientists know a good deal about what it is to be an organism in an environment but very little about what it is to be a creature who names things and utters and understands sentences about things?

Why is it that scientists have a theory about everything under the sun but do not have a theory of man?

Is it possible that a theory of man is nothing more nor less than a theory of the speaking creature?

Is it possible that the questions about man's peculiar upside-down and perverse behavior, which he doesn't understand, have something to do with his strange gift of speech, which he also doesn't understand?

Is it possible that man's peculiar predicament, his unhappiness in the twentieth century, his upside-down behavior, disliking things which according to his theory he ought to like, liking things which according to his theory he ought not to like, has come to pass because the old modern age has ended and man has not the beginning of an understanding of himself in the new age because the old theories don't work any more, because they showed man as monster, as centaur organism-plus-soul, as one not different from beasts yet somehow nevertheless possessing "freedom" and "dignity" and "individuality" and "mind" and such—and that such theories, monstrous as they are, worked for a while in the old modern age because there was still enough left of belief in Judeo-Christianity to make such talk of "sacredness of the individual" sound good even while such individuals were being slaughtered by the millions, and because science was still young and exuberant and no one noticed or cared about the contradiction in scientists' understanding other men as organisms-beasts and putting them into the world of things to understand and so putting themselves above the world and other men?

But time ran out and the old modern world ended and the old monster theory no longer works. Man knows he is something more than an organism in an environment, because for one thing he acts like anything but an organism in an environment. Yet he no longer has the means of understanding the traditional Judeo-Christian teaching that the "something more" is a soul somehow locked in the organism like a ghost in a machine. What is he then? He has not the faintest idea. Entered as he is into a new age, he is like a child who sees everything in his new world, names everything, knows everything except himself.

When man doesn't know whether he is an organism or a soul or both, and if both how he can be both, it is good to start with what he does know.

This book is about two things, man's strange behavior and man's strange gift of language, and about how understanding the latter might help in understanding the former.

I have made the assumption that the proper study of man is man and that there does not presently exist a theory of man. Accordingly, the book is an attempt to sketch the beginnings of a theory of man for a new age, the sort of crude guess a visitor from Mars might make if he landed on earth and spent a year observing man and the beasts.

It is the meager fruit of twenty years' off-and-on thinking about the subject, of coming at it from one direction, followed by failure and depression and giving up, followed by making up novels to raise my spirits, followed by a new try from a different direction or from an old direction but at a different level, followed by failure, followed by making up another novel, and so on.

As it stands, it is nothing more than a few trails blazed through a dark wood, most dead-ended. I should consider it worthwhile even if it established no more than that there is such a wood—for not even that much is known now—and that it is very dark indeed. . . .

I make no apologies for being an amateur in such matters, since the one thing that has been clear to me from the beginning is that language is too important to be left to linguisticians. Indeed everything is too important to be left to the specialist of that thing, and the layman is already too deprived by the surrendering of such sovereignty.

If justification is needed, I plead the justification of the visitor from Mars: it is necessary in this case to be to a degree an outsider in order to see these particular woods for the trees.

One must be a Martian or a survivor poking among the ruins to see how extremely odd the people were who lived there.

Suggestions for Discussion

1. The first half of this selection is devoted to a series of provocative questions. How can you summarize the tone of those questions? The meaning? The purpose?

2. What role does Percy believe language plays in explaining our role in the universe?

3. Explain the following question: "Why do people driving around on beautiful Sunday afternoons like to see bloody automobile wrecks?"

4. Explain the question in the last paragraph at the end of part 1.

5. Explain Percy's reasons for focusing on language in his effort to answer the questions in part 1.

6. Discuss the two paragraphs in part 2 beginning with, "Is it possible that man's peculiar predicament . . . has come to pass because the old modern age has ended . . . ?" and closing with the statement ". . . he is like a child who sees everything in his new world, names everything, knows everything except himself."

Suggestions for Writing

1. At the end of part 2, Percy explains why he has embarked on a study of language and its relation to human behavior. Write an essay in which you attempt to summarize his position on the major issues facing human beings at this time. Consider whether Percy was a religious man.

2. Choose two or three questions from either part of the essay and write answers. Your discussion should attempt to be complete.

Aleksandr Solzhenitsyn

Playing Upon the Strings of Emptiness

Aleksandr Solzhenitsyn (b. 1918), a Russian writer, was born in Kislovodsk, grew up in Rostov, and studied mathematics at the university there. During World War II he rose to the rank of captain in the Soviet artillery and was decorated for bravery. While still serving on the German front in 1945, he was arrested for criticizing Stalin and sentenced to eight years in prison where he became familiar with other political prisoners. His novel *One Day in the Life of Ivan Denisovich* (1962) was published through the intervention of Nikita Khrushchev. Its publication made the author famous. As his subsequent novels, *The First Circle* (1964) and *Cancer Ward* (1966), were regarded as too critical of the Soviet Union, he was censored and expelled from the Union of Soviet Writers. He was awarded the Nobel Prize for Literature in 1970, but, wishing to remain in the Soviet Union, he refused it. Since he also refused to remain silent about Soviet repression, he was arrested and forcibly deported in 1974. Soon after, he accepted his Nobel Prize. He is perhaps best known for *The Gulag Archipelago* (1973), which records the prison operations of Soviet totalitarianism from 1918 to 1956. After many years of exile in the United States, Solzhenitsyn returned to Russia after the overturn of the government of the Soviet Union. In 1993 he received the medal of honor of the National Arts Club. His wife received the award on his behalf and read his acceptance speech, printed here, translated by his sons, Ignat and Stephan. The reader, aware of the author's experience with repression in the Soviet Union, should not be surprised by the conservatism of his position in this speech.

There is a long-accepted truth about art that "style is the man" ("*le style est l'homme*"). This means that every work of a skilled musician, artist or writer is shaped by an absolutely unique combination of personality traits, creative abilities and individual, as well as national, experience. And since such a combination can never be repeated, art (but I shall here speak primarily of literature) possesses infinite variety across the ages and among different peoples. The divine plan is such that there is no limit to the appearance of ever new and dazzling creative talents, none of whom, however, negate in any way the works of their outstanding predecessors, even though they may be 500 or 2,000 years removed. The unending quest for what is new and fresh is never closed to us, but this does not deprive our grateful memory of all that came before.

No new work of art comes into existence (whether consciously or unconsciously) without an organic link to what was created earlier. But it is equally true that a healthy conservatism must be flexible both in terms of creation and perception, remaining equally sensitive to the old and to the new, to venerable and worthy traditions, and to the freedom to explore, without which no future can ever be born. At the same time the artist must not forget that creative *freedom* can be dangerous, for the fewer artistic limitations he imposes on his own work, the less chance he has for artistic success. The loss of a responsible organizing force weakens or even ruins the structure, the meaning and the ultimate value of a work of art.

Every age and every form of creative endeavor owes much to those outstanding artists whose untiring labors brought forth new meanings and new rhythms. But in the 20th century the necessary equilibrium between tradition and the search for the new has been repeatedly upset by a falsely understood "avant-gardism"—a raucous, impatient "avant-gardism" at any cost. Dating from before World War I, this movement undertook to destroy all commonly accepted art—its forms, language, features and properties—in its drive to build a kind of "superart," which would then supposedly spawn the New Life itself. It was suggested that literature should start anew "on a blank sheet of paper." (Indeed, some never went much beyond this stage.) Destruction, thus, became the apotheosis of this belligerent avant-gardism. It aimed to tear down the entire centuries-long cultural tradition, to break and disrupt the natural flow of artistic development by a sudden leap forward. This goal was to be achieved through an empty pursuit of novel forms as an end in itself, all the while lowering the standards of craftsmanship for oneself to the point of slovenliness and artistic crudity, at times combined with a meaning so obscured as to shade into unintelligibility.

This aggressive impulse might be interpreted as a mere product of personal ambition, were it not for the fact that in Russia (and I apologize to those gathered here for speaking mostly of Russia, but in our time it is impossible to bypass the harsh and extensive experience of my country), in Russia this impulse and its manifestations preceded and foretold the most *physically* destructive revolution of the 20th century. Before erupting on the streets of Petrograd, this cataclysmic revolution erupted on the pages of the artistic and literary journals of the capital's bohemian circles. It is there that we first heard scathing imprecations against the entire Russian and European way of life, the calls to sweep away all religions or ethical codes, to tear down, overthrow, and trample all existing traditional culture, along with the self-extolment of the desperate innovators themselves, innovators who never did succeed in producing anything of worth. Some of these appeals literally called for the destruction of the Racines, the Murillos and the Raphaels, "so that bullets would bounce off museum walls." As for the classics of Russian literature, they were to be "thrown overboard from the ship of modernity." Cultural history would have to begin anew. The cry was "Forward, forward!" — its authors already called themselves "futurists," as though they had now stepped over and beyond the present, and were bestowing upon us what was undoubtedly the genuine art of the Future.

But no sooner did the revolution explode in the streets, than those "futurists" who only recently, in their manifesto entitled "A Slap in the Face of Public Taste," had preached an "insurmountable hatred toward the existing language" — these same "futurists" changed their name to the "Left Front," now directly joining the revolution at its leftmost flank. It thus became clear that the earlier outbursts of this "avant-gardism" were no mere literary froth, but had very real embodiment in life. Beyond their intent to overturn the entire culture, they aimed to uproot life itself. And when the Communists gained unlimited power (their own battle cry called for tearing the existing world "down to its foundations," so as to build a new Unknown Beautiful World in its stead, with equally unlimited brutality) they not only opened wide the gates of publicity and popularity to this horde of so-called "avant-gardists," but even gave some of them, as to faithful allies, power to administrate over culture.

Granted, neither the ragings of this pseudo-"avant-garde" nor its power over culture lasted long; there followed a general coma of all culture. We in the U.S.S.R. began to trudge, downcast, through a 70-year-long ice age, under whose heavy glacial cover one could barely discern the secret heartbeat of a handful of great poets and writers. These were almost entirely unknown to their own country, not to mention the rest of the world, until much later. With the ossification of the totalitarian Soviet regime, its inflated pseudoculture ossified as well, turning into the loathsome ceremonial forms of so-called "socialist realism." Some individuals have been eager to devote numerous critical analyses to the essence and significance of this phenomenon. I would not have written a single one, for it is outside the bounds of art altogether: the *object* of study, the style of "socialist realism," never existed. One does not need to be an expert to see that it consisted of nothing more than servility, a style defined by "What would you care for?" or "Write whatever the Party commands." What scholarly discussion can possibly take place here?

And now, having lived through these 70 lethal years inside Communism's iron shell, we are crawling out, though barely alive. A new age has clearly begun, both for Russia and for the whole world. Russia lies utterly ravaged and poisoned; its people are in a state of unprecedented humiliation, and are on the brink of perishing physically, perhaps even biologically. Given the current conditions of national life, and the sudden exposure and ulceration of the wounds amassed over the years, it is only natural that literature should experience a pause. The voices that bring forth the nation's literature need time before they can begin to sound once again.

However, some writers have emerged who appreciate the removal of censorship and the new, unlimited artistic freedom mostly in one sense: for allowing uninhibited "self-expression." The point is to *express* one's own perception of one's surroundings, often with no sensitivity toward today's ills and scars, and with a visible emptiness of heart; to express the personality of an author, whether it is significant or not; to express it with no sense of responsibility toward the morals of the public, and especially of the young; and at times thickly lacing the language with obscenities which for hundreds of years were considered unthinkable to put in print, but now seem to be almost in vogue.

The confusion of minds after 70 years of total oppression is more than understandable. The artistic perception of the younger generations finds itself in shock, humiliation, resentment, amnesia. Unable to find in themselves the strength fully to withstand and refute Soviet dogma in the past, many young writers have now given in to the more accessible path of pessimistic relativism. Yes, they say, Communist doctrines were a great lie; but then again, absolute truths do not exist anyhow, and trying to find them is pointless. Nor is it worth the trouble to strive for some kind of higher meaning.

And in one sweeping gesture of vexation, classical Russian literature— which never disdained reality and sought the truth—is dismissed as next to worthless. Denigrating the past is deemed to be the key to progress. And so it has once again become fashionable in Russia to ridicule, debunk, and toss overboard the great Russian literature, steeped as it is in love and compassion toward all human beings, and especially toward those who suffer. And in order to facilitate this operation of discarding, it is announced that the lifeless and servile "socialist realism" had in fact been an organic continuation of full-blooded Russian literature.

Thus we witness, through history's various thresholds, a recurrence of one and the same perilous anti-cultural phenomenon, with its rejection of and contempt for all foregoing tradition, and with its mandatory hostility toward whatever is universally accepted. Before, it burst in upon us with the fanfares and gaudy flags of "futurism"; today the term "post-modernism" is applied. (Whatever the meaning intended for this term, its lexical makeup involves an incongruity: the seeming claim that a person can think and experience *after* the period in which he is destined to live.)

For a post-modernist, the world does not possess values that have reality. He even has an expression for this: "the world as text," as something secondary, as the text of an author's work, wherein the primary object of interest is the author himself in his relationship to the work, his own introspection. Culture, in this view, ought to be directed inward at itself (which is why these works are so full of reminiscences, to the point of tastelessness); it alone is valuable and real. For this reason the concept of play acquires a heightened importance—not the Mozartian playfulness of a Universe overflowing with joy, but a forced playing upon the strings of emptiness, where an author need have no responsibility to anyone. A denial of any and all ideals is considered courageous. And in this voluntary self-delusion, "post-modernism" sees itself as the crowning achievement of all previous culture, the final link in its chain. (A rash hope, for already there is talk of the birth of "conceptualism," a term that has yet to be convincingly defined in terms of its relationship to *art*, though no doubt this too will duly be attempted. And then there is already *post-avant-gardism;* and it would be no surprise if we were to witness the appearance of a "post-post-modernism," or of a "post-futurism.") We could have sympathy for this constant searching, but only as we have sympathy for the suffering of a sick man. The search is doomed by its theoretical premises to forever remaining a secondary or ternary exercise, devoid of life or of a future.

But let us shift our attention to the more complex flow of this process. Even though the 20th century has seen the more bitter and disheartening lot fall to the peoples under Communist domination, our whole world is living through a century of spiritual illness, which could not but give rise to a similar ubiquitous illness in art. Although for other reasons, a similar "post-modernist" sense of confusion about the world has also arisen in the West.

Alas, at a time of an unprecedented rise in the material benefits of civilization and ever-improving standards of living, the West, too, has been undergoing an erosion and obscuring of high moral and ethical ideals. The spiritual axis of life has grown dim, and to some lost artists the world has now appeared in seeming senselessness, as an absurd conglomeration of debris.

Yes, world culture today is of course in crisis, a crisis of great severity. The newest directions in art seek to outpace this crisis on the wooden horse of clever stratagems—on the assumption that if one invents deft, resourceful new methods, it will be as though the crisis never was. Vain hopes. Nothing worthy can be built on a neglect of higher meanings and on a relativistic view of concepts and culture as a whole. Indeed, something greater than a phenomenon confined to art can be discerned shimmering here beneath the surface—shimmering not with light but with an ominous crimson glow.

Looking intently, we can see that behind these ubiquitous and seemingly innocent experiments of rejecting "antiquated" tradition there lies a deep-seated hostility toward any spirituality. This relentless cult of novelty, with its assertion that art need not be good or pure, just so long as it is new, newer, and newer still, conceals an unyielding and long-sustained attempt to undermine, ridicule and uproot all moral precepts. There is no God, there is no truth, the universe is chaotic, all is relative, "the world as text," a text any post-modernist is willing to compose. How clamorous it all is, but also—how helpless.

For several decades now, world literature, music, painting and sculpture have exhibited a stubborn tendency to grow not higher but to the side, not toward the highest achievements of craftsmanship and of the human spirit but toward their disintegration into a frantic and insidious "novelty." To decorate public spaces we put up sculptures that estheticize pure ugliness—but we no longer register surprise. And if visitors from outer space were to pick up our music over the airwaves, how could they ever guess that earthlings once had a Bach, a Beethoven and a Schubert, now abandoned as out of date and obsolete?

If we, the creators of art, will obediently submit to this downward slide, if we cease to hold dear the great cultural tradition of the foregoing centuries together with the spiritual foundations from which it grew—we will be contributing to a highly dangerous fall of the human spirit on earth, to a degeneration of mankind into some kind of lower state, closer to the animal world.

And yet, it is hard to believe that we will allow this to occur. Even in Russia, so terribly ill right now, we wait and hope that after the coma and a period of silence, we shall feel the breath of a reawakening Russian literature, and that we shall witness the arrival of fresh new forces—of our younger brothers.

Suggestions for Discussion

1. Explain the writer's point that God provides the opportunity for many skilled, original, and diverse artists. How does he relate this occurrence to the tradition of literature? What does he mean by "healthy conservatism"?

2. What distinguishes twentieth-century literature from the tradition of the past?

3. What is Solzhenitsyn's reaction to "avant-gardism"? Why does he believe that this art movement differs from any other art movement in previous times? Why does he regard the "avant-garde" as destructive?

4. What is the tone of this speech? Is it suited to the subject? Does Solzhenitsyn distinguish between the literature of the West and that of Russia? According to the author, what role did communism play in the development of twentieth-century literature?

5. Discuss the author's use of the term "post-modernism." How does he trace the rise of post-modernism to the loss of spirituality in the West?

Suggestions for Writing

1. Write a paper in which you attempt to summarize and evaluate the author's conservative hostility to twentieth-century literature.

2. T. S. Eliot's essay "Tradition and the Individual Talent" makes several points similar to the one made in this speech. Write a paper in which you compare and contrast the arguments of both authors. (You will find the other essay in the *Collected Essays* of T. S. Eliot.)

Fiction

Willa Cather

The Sculptor's Funeral

Willa Cather (1873–1947) was born in Virginia and grew up in Nebraska. On leaving the University of Nebraska, where as an undergraduate she had written for a Lincoln newspaper, she worked in Pittsburgh as a reporter and then as a teacher, and wrote her first collection of stories, *The Troll Garden* (1905). Her works include *My Antonia* (1918), *A Lost Lady* (1923), *The Professor's House* (1925), *Death Comes for the Archbishop* (1927), and *Sapphira and the Slave Girl* (1940), which dealt with her native Virginia. She celebrated the frontier spirit, whether of art or of action. However, in this story, she shows how small-town intolerance and demands for conformity are inimical to artistic impulses and creativity.

A group of the townspeople stood on the station siding of a little Kansas town, awaiting the coming of the night train, which was already twenty minutes overdue. The snow had fallen thick over everything; in the pale starlight the line of bluffs across the wide, white meadows south of the town made soft, smoke-coloured curves against the clear sky. The men on the siding stood first on one foot and then on the other, their hands thrust deep into their trousers pockets, their overcoats open, their shoulders screwed up with the cold; and they glanced from time to time toward the southeast, where the railroad track wound along the river shore. They conversed in low tones and moved about restlessly, seeming uncertain as to what was expected of them. There was but one of the company who looked as though he knew exactly why he was there; and he kept conspicuously apart; walking to the far end of the platform, returning to the station door, then pacing up the track again, his chin sunk in the high collar of his overcoat, his burly shoulders drooping forward, his gait heavy and dogged. Presently he was approached by a tall, spare, grizzled man clad in a faded Grand Army suit, who shuffled out from the group and advanced with a certain deference, craning his neck forward until his back made the angle of a jackknife three-quarters open.

"I reckon she's a-goin' to be pretty late agin tonight, Jim," he remarked in a squeaky falsetto. "S'pose it's the snow?"

"I don't know," responded the other man with a shade of annoyance, speaking from out an astonishing cataract of red beard that grew fiercely and thickly in all directions.

The spare man shifted the quill toothpick he was chewing to the other side of his mouth. "It ain't likely that anybody from the East will come with the corpse, I s'pose," he went on reflectively.

"I don't know," responded the other, more curtly than before.

"It's too bad he didn't belong to some lodge or other. I like an order funeral myself. They seem more appropriate for people of some repytation," the spare man continued, with an ingratiating concession in his shrill voice, as he carefully placed his toothpick in his vest pocket. He always carried the flag at the G.A.R. funerals in the town.

The heavy man turned on his heel, without replying, and walked up the siding. The spare man shuffled back to the uneasy group. "Jim's ez full ez a tick, ez ushel," he commented commiseratingly.

Just then a distant whistle sounded, and there was a shuffling of feet on the platform. A number of lanky boys of all ages appeared as suddenly and slimily as eels wakened by the crack of thunder; some came from the waiting-room, where they had been warming themselves by the red stove, or half asleep on the slat benches; others uncoiled themselves from baggage trucks or slid out of express wagons. Two clambered down from the driver's seat of a hearse that stood backed up against the siding. They straightened their stooping shoulders and lifted their heads, and a flash of momentary animation kindled their dull eyes at that cold, vibrant scream, the worldwide call for men. It stirred them like the note of a trumpet; just as it had often stirred the man who was coming home to-night, in his boyhood.

The night express shot, red as a rocket, from out the eastward marsh lands and wound along the river shore under the long lines of shivering poplars that sentineled the meadows, the escaping steam hanging in grey masses against the pale sky and blotting out the Milky Way. In a moment the red glare from the headlight streamed up the snow-covered track before the siding and glittered on the wet, black rails. The burly man with the dishevelled red beard walked swiftly up the platform toward the approaching train, uncovering his head as he went. The group of men behind him hesitated, glanced questioningly at one another, and awkwardly followed his example. The train stopped, and the crowd shuffled up to the express car just as the door was thrown open, the spare man in the G.A.R. suit thrusting his head forward with curiosity. The express messenger appeared in the doorway, accompanied by a young man in a long ulster and traveling cap.

"Are Mr. Merrick's friends here?" inquired the young man.

The group of the platform swayed and shuffled uneasily. Philip Phelps, the banker, responded with dignity: "We have come to take charge of the body. Mr. Merrick's father is very feeble and can't be about."

"Send the agent out here," growled the express messenger, "and tell the operator to lend a hand."

The coffin was got out of its rough box and down on the snowy platform. The townspeople drew back enough to make room for it and then formed a close semicircle about it, looking curiously at the palm leaf which lay across the black cover. No one said anything. The baggage man stood by his truck, waiting to get at the trunks. The engine panted heavily, and the fireman dodged in and out among the wheels with his yellow torch and long oilcan, snapping the spindle boxes. The young Bostonian, one of the dead sculptor's pupils who had come with the body, looked about him helplessly. He turned to the banker, the only one of that black, uneasy, stoop-shouldered group who seemed enough of an individual to be addressed.

"None of Mr. Merrick's brothers are here?" he asked uncertainly.

The man with the red beard for the first time stepped up and joined the group. "No, they have not come yet: the family is scattered. The body will be taken directly to the house." He stooped and took hold of one of the handles of the coffin.

"Take the long hill road up, Thompson, it will be easier on the horses," called the liveryman as the undertaker snapped the door of the hearse and prepared to mount to the driver's seat.

Laird, the red-bearded lawyer, turned again to the stranger: "We didn't know whether there would be any one with him or not," he explained. "It's a long walk, so you'd better go up in the hack." He pointed to a single battered conveyance, but the young man replied stiffly: "Thank you, but I think I will go up with the hearse. If you don't object," turning to the undertaker, "I'll ride with you."

They clambered up over the wheels and drove off in the starlight up the long, white hill toward the town. The lamps in the still village were shining from under the low, snow-burdened roofs; and beyond, on every side, the plains reached out into emptiness, peaceful and wide as the soft sky itself, and wrapped in a tangible, white silence.

When the hearse backed up to a wooden sidewalk before a naked, weather-beaten frame house, the same composite, ill-defined group that had stood upon the station siding was huddled about the gate. The front yard was an icy swamp, and a couple of warped planks, extending from the sidewalk to the door, made a sort of rickety footbridge. The gate hung on one hinge, and was opened wide with difficulty. Steavens, the young stranger, noticed that something black was tied to the knob of the front door.

The grating sound made by the casket, as it was drawn from the hearse, was answered by a scream from the house; the front door was wrenched open, and a tall, corpulent woman rushed out bareheaded into the snow and flung herself upon the coffin, shrieking: "My boy, my boy! And this is how you've come home to me!"

As Steavens turned away and closed his eyes with a shudder of unutterable repulsion, another woman, also tall, but flat and angular, dressed entirely in black, darted out of the house and caught Mrs. Merrick by the shoulders, crying sharply: "Come, come, mother; you mustn't go on like this!" Her tone changed to one of obsequious solemnity as she turned to the banker: "The parlour is ready, Mr. Phelps."

The bearers carried the coffin along the narrow boards, while the undertaker ran ahead with the coffin rests. They bore it into a large, unheated room that smelled of dampness and disuse and furniture polish, and set it down under a hanging lamp ornamented with jingling glass prisms and before a "Rogers group" of John Alden and Priscilla, wreathed with smilax. Henry Steavens stared about him with the sickening conviction that there had been some horrible mistake, and that he had somehow arrived at the wrong destination. He looked painfully about over the clover-green Brussels, the fat plush upholstery; among the hand-painted china plaques and panels, and vases, for some mark of identification, for something that might once conceivably have belonged to Harvey Merrick. It was not until he recognized his friend in the crayon portrait of a little boy in kilts and curls hanging above the piano, that he felt willing to let any of these people approach the coffin.

"Take the lid off, Mr. Thompson; let me see my boy's face," wailed the elderly woman between her sobs. This time Steavens looked fearfully, almost beseechingly into her face, red and swollen under its masses of strong, black, shiny hair. He flushed, dropped his eyes, and then, almost incredulously, looked again. There was a kind of power about her face—a kind of brutal handsomeness, even, but it was scarred and furrowed by violence, and so coloured and coarsened by fiercer passions that grief seemed never to have laid a gentle finger there. The long nose was distended and knobbed at the end, and there were deep lines on either side of it; her heavy, black brows almost met across her forehead, her teeth were large and square, and set far apart—teeth that could tear. She filled the room; the men were obliterated, seemed tossed about like twigs in an angry water, and even Steavens felt himself being drawn into the whirlpool.

The daughter—the tall, raw-boned woman in crêpe, with a mourning comb in her hair which curiously lengthened her long face—sat stiffly upon the sofa, her hands, conspicuous for their large knuckles, folded in her lap, her mouth and eyes drawn down, solemnly awaiting the opening of the coffin. Near the door stood a mulatto woman, evidently a servant in the house, with a timid bearing and an emaciated face pitifully sad and gentle. She was weeping silently, the corner of her calico apron lifted to her eyes, occasionally suppressing a long, quivering sob. Steavens walked over and stood beside her.

Feeble steps were heard on the stairs, and an old man, tall and frail, odorous of pipe smoke, with shaggy, unkempt grey hair and a dingy beard, tobacco stained about the mouth, entered uncertainly. He went slowly up to the coffin and stood rolling a blue cotton handkerchief between his hands, seeming so pained and embarrassed by his wife's orgy of grief that he had no consciousness of anything else.

"There, there, Annie, dear, don't take on so," he quavered timidly, putting out a shaking hand and awkwardly patting her elbow. She turned with a cry, and sank upon his shoulder with such violence that he tottered a little. He did not even glance toward the coffin, but continued to look at her with a dull, frightened, appealing expression, as a spaniel looks at the whip. His sunken cheeks slowly reddened and burned with miserable shame. When his wife rushed from the room, her daughter strode after her with set lips. The servant stole up to the coffin, bent over it for a moment, and then slipped away to the kitchen, leaving Steavens, the lawyer, and the father to themselves. The old man stood trembling and looking down at his dead son's face. The sculptor's splendid head seemed even more noble in its rigid stillness than in life. The dark hair had crept down upon the wide forehead; the face seemed strangely long, but in it there was not that beautiful and chaste repose which we expect to find in the faces of the dead. The brows were so drawn that there were two deep lines above the beaked nose, and the chin was thrust forward defiantly. It was as though the strain of life had been so sharp and bitter that death could not at once wholly relax the tension and smooth the countenance into perfect peace—as though he were still guarding something precious and holy, which might even yet be wrested from him.

The old man's lips were working under his stained beard. He turned to the lawyer with timid deference: "Phelps and the rest are comin' back to set up with Harve, ain't they?" he asked. "Thank 'ee, Jim, thank 'ee." He brushed the hair back gently from his son's forehead. "He was a good boy, Jim; always a good boy. He was ez gentle ez a child and the kindest of 'em all—only we didn't none of us ever onderstand him." The tears trickled slowly down his beard and dropped upon the sculptor's coat.

"Martin, Martin. Oh, Martin! come here," his wife wailed from the top of the stairs. The old man started timorously: "Yes, Annie, I'm coming." He turned away, hesitated, stood for a moment in miserable indecision; then reached back and patted the dead man's hair softly, and stumbled from the room.

"Poor old man, I didn't think he had any tears left. Seems as if his eyes would have gone dry long ago. At his age nothing cuts very deep," remarked the lawyer.

Something in his tone made Steavens glance up. While the mother had been in the room, the young man had scarcely seen any one else; but now, from the moment he first glanced into Jim Laird's florid face and bloodshot eyes, he knew that he had found what he had been heartsick at not finding before—the feeling, the understanding that must exist in some one, even here.

The man was red as his beard, with features swollen and blurred by dissipation, and a hot, blazing blue eye. His face was strained—that of a man who is controlling himself with difficulty—and he kept plucking at his beard with a sort of fierce resentment. Steavens, sitting by the window, watched him turn down the glaring lamp, still its jangling pendants with an angry gesture, and then stand with his hands locked behind him, staring down into the master's face. He could not help wondering what link there could have been between the porcelain vessel and so sooty a lump of potter's clay.

From the kitchen an uproar was sounding; when the dining-room door opened, the import of it was clear. The mother was abusing the maid for having forgotten to make the dressing for the chicken salad which had been prepared for the watchers. Steavens had never heard anything in the least like it; it was injured, emotional, dramatic abuse, unique and masterly in its excruciating cruelty, as violent and unrestrained as had been her grief of twenty minutes before. With a shudder of disgust the lawyer went into the dining room and closed the door into the kitchen.

"Poor Roxy's getting it now," he remarked when he came back. "The Merricks took her out of the poorhouse years ago; and if her loyalty would let her, I guess the poor old thing could tell tales that would curdle your blood. She's the mulatto woman who was standing in here a while ago, with her apron to her eyes. The old woman is a fury; there never was anybody like her for demonstrative piety and ingenious cruelty. She made Harvey's life a hell for him when he lived at home; he was so sick ashamed of it. I never could see how he kept himself so sweet."

"He was wonderful," said Steavens slowly, "wonderful; but until tonight I have never known how wonderful."

"That is the true and eternal wonder of it, anyway; that it can come even from such a dung heap as this," the lawyer cried, with a sweeping gesture which seemed to indicate much more than the four walls within which they stood.

"I think I'll see whether I can get a little air. The room is so close I am beginning to feel rather faint," murmured Steavens, struggling with one of the windows. The sash was stuck, however, and would not yield, so he sat down dejectedly and began pulling at his collar. The lawyer came over, loosened the sash with one blow of his red fist and sent the window up a few inches. Steavens thanked him, but the nausea which had been gradually climbing into his throat for the last half hour left him with but one desire—a desperate feeling that he must get away from this place with what was left of Harvey Merrick. Oh, he comprehended well enough now the quiet bitterness of the smile that he had seen so often on his master's lips!

He remembered that once, when Merrick returned from a visit home, he brought with him a singularly feeling and suggestive bas-relief of a thin, faded old woman, sitting and sewing something pinned to her knee; while a full-lipped, full-blooded little urchin, his trousers held up by a single gallus, stood beside her, impatiently twitching her gown to call her attention to a butterfly he had caught. Steavens, impressed by the tender and delicate modelling of the thin, tired face, had asked him if it were his mother. He remembered the dull flush that had burned up in the sculptor's face.

The lawyer was sitting in a rocking-chair beside the coffin, his head thrown back and his eyes closed. Steavens looked at him earnestly, puzzled at the line of the chin, and wondering why a man should conceal a feature of such distinction under that disfiguring shock of beard. Suddenly, as though he felt the young sculptor's keen glance, he opened his eyes.

"Was he always a good deal of an oyster?" he asked abruptly. "He was terribly shy as a boy."

"Yes, he was an oyster, since you put it so," rejoined Steavens. "Although he could be very fond of people, he always gave one the impression of being detached. He disliked violent emotion; he was reflective, and rather distrustful of himself—except, of course, as regarded his work. He was surefooted enough there. He distrusted men pretty thoroughly and women even more, yet somehow without believing ill of them. He was determined, indeed, to believe the best, but he seemed afraid to investigate."

"A burnt dog dreads the fire," said the lawyer grimly, and closed his eyes.

Steavens went on and on, reconstructing that whole miserable boyhood. All this raw, biting ugliness had been the portion of the man whose tastes were refined beyond the limits of the reasonable—whose mind was an exhaustless gallery of beautiful impressions, and so sensitive that the mere shadow of a poplar leaf flickering against a sunny wall would be etched and held there forever. Surely, if ever a man had the magic word in his fingertips, it was Merrick. Whatever he touched, he revealed its holiest secret; liberated it from enchantment and restored to it its pristine loveliness, like the Arabian prince who fought the enchantress spell for spell. Upon whatever he had come in contact with, he had left a beautiful record of the experience—a sort of ethereal signature; a scent, a sound, a colour that was his own.

Steavens understood now the real tragedy of his master's life; neither love nor wine, as many had conjectured; but a blow which had fallen earlier and cut deeper than these could have done—a shame not his, and yet so unescapably his, to hide in his heart from his very boyhood. And without—the frontier warfare; the yearning of a boy, cast ashore upon a desert of newness and ugliness and sordidness, for all that is chastened and old, and noble with traditions.

At eleven o'clock the tall, flat woman in black crêpe entered and announced that the watchers were arriving, and asked them "to step into the dining-room." As Steavens rose, the lawyer said dryly: "You go on—it'll be a good experience for you, doubtless; as for me, I'm not equal to that crowd tonight; I've had twenty years of them."

As Steavens closed the door after him he glanced back at the lawyer, sitting by the coffin in the dim light, with his chin resting on his hand.

The same misty group that had stood before the door of the express car shuffled into the dining room. In the light of the kerosene lamp they separated and became individuals. The minister, a pale, feeble-looking man with white hair and blond chin-whiskers, took his seat beside a small side table and placed his Bible upon it. The Grand Army man sat down behind the stove and tilted his chair back comfortably against the wall, fishing his quill toothpick from his waistcoat pocket. The two bankers, Phelps and Elder, sat off in a corner behind the dinner table, where they could finish their discussion of the new usury law and its effect on chattel security loans. The real estate agent, an old man with a smiling, hypocritical face, soon joined them. The coal and lumber dealer and the cattle shipper sat on opposite sides of the hard coal-burner, their feet on the nickelwork. Steavens took a book from his pocket and began to read. The talk around him ranged through various topics of local interest while the house was quieting down. When it was clear that the members of the family were in bed, the Grand Army man hitched his shoulders and, untangling his long legs, caught his heels on the rounds of his chair.

"S'pose there'll be a will, Phelps?" he queried in his weak falsetto.

The banker laughed disagreeably, and began trimming his nails with a pearl-handled pocketknife.

"There'll scarcely be any need for one, will there?" he queried in his turn.

The restless Grand Army man shifted his position again, getting his knees still nearer his chin. "Why, the ole man says Harve's done right well lately," he chirped.

The other banker spoke up. "I reckon he means by that Harve ain't asked him to mortgage any more farms lately, so as he could go on with his education."

"Seems like my mind don't reach back to a time when Harve wasn't bein' edycated," tittered the Grand Army man.

There was a general chuckle. The minister took out his handkerchief and blew his nose sonorously. Banker Phelps closed his knife with a snap. "It's too bad the old man's sons didn't turn out better," he remarked with reflective authority. "They never hung together. He spent money enough on Harve to stock a dozen cattle farms and he might as well have poured it into Sand Creek. If Harve had stayed at home and helped nurse what little they had, and gone into stock on the old man's bottom farm, they might all have been well fixed. But the old man had to trust everything to tenants and was cheated right and left."

"Harve never could have handled stock none," interposed the cattleman. "He hadn't it in him to be sharp. Do you remember when he bought Sander's mules for eight-year olds, when everybody in town knew that Sander's father-in-law give 'em to his wife for a wedding present eighteen years before, an' they was full-grown mules then."

Every one chuckled, and the Grand Army man rubbed his knees with a spasm of childish delight.

"Harve never was much account for anything practical, and he shore was never fond of work," began the coal and lumber dealer. "I mind the last time he was home; the day he left, when the old man was out to the barn helpin' his hand hitch up to take Harve to the train, and Cal Moots was patchin' up the fence, Harve, he come out on the step and sings out, in his ladylike voice: 'Cal Moots, Cal Moots! please come cord my trunk.'"

"That's Harve for you," approved the Grand Army man gleefully. "I kin hear him howlin' yet when he was a big feller in long pants and his mother used to whale him with a rawhide in the barn for lettin' the cows get foundered in the cornfield when he was drivin' 'em home from pasture. He killed a cow of mine that-a-way onct—a pure Jersey and the best milker I had, an' the ole man had to put up for her. Harve, he was watchin' the sun set acrost the marshes when the anamile got away; he argued that sunset was oncommon fine."

"Where the old man made his mistake was in sending the boy East to school," said Phelps, stroking his goatee and speaking in a deliberate, judicial tone. "There was where he got his head full of trapesing to Paris and all such folly. What Harve needed, of all people, was a course in some first-class Kansas City business college."

The letters were swimming before Steavens's eyes. Was it possible that these men did not understand, that the palm of the coffin meant nothing to them? The very name of their town would have remained forever buried in the postal guide had it not been now and again mentioned in the world in connection with Harvey Merrick's. He remembered what his master had said to him on the day of his death, after the congestion of both lungs had shut off any probability of recovery, and the sculptor had asked his pupil to send his body home. "It's not a pleasant place to be lying while the world is moving and doing and bettering," he had said with a feeble smile, "but it rather seems as though we ought to go back to the place we came from in the end. The townspeople will come in for a look at me; and after they have had their say I shan't have much to fear from the judgment of God. The wings of the Victory, in there"—with a weak gesture toward his studio—"will not shelter me."

The cattleman took up the comment. "Forty's young for a Merrick to cash in; they usually hang on pretty well. Probably he helped it along with whisky."

"His mother's people were not long-lived, and Harvey never had a robust constitution," said the minister mildly. He would have liked to say more. He had been the boy's Sunday-school teacher, and had been fond of him; but he felt that he was not in a position to speak. His own sons had turned out badly, and it was not a year since one of them had made his last trip home in the express car, shot in a gambling house in the Black Hills.

"Nevertheless, there is no disputin' that Harvey frequently looked upon the wine when it was red, also variegated, and it shore made an oncommon fool of him," moralized the cattleman.

Just then the door leading into the parlor rattled loudly and everyone started involuntarily, looking relieved when only Jim Laird came out. His red face was convulsed with anger, and the Grand Army man ducked his head when he saw the spark in his blue, bloodshot eye. They were all afraid of Jim; he was a drunkard, but he could twist the law to suit his client's needs as no other man in all western Kansas could do; and there were many who tried. The lawyer closed the door gently behind him, leaned back against it and folded his arms, cocking his head a little to one side. When he assumed this attitude in the courtroom, ears were always pricked up, as it usually foretold a flood of withering sarcasm.

"I've been with you gentlemen before," he began in a dry, even tone, "when you've sat by the coffins of boys born and raised in this town; and, if I remember rightly, you were never any too well satisfied when you checked them up. What's the matter, anyhow? Why is it that reputable young men are as scarce as millionaires in Sand City? It might almost seem to a stranger that there was some way something the matter with your progressive town. Why did Ruben Sayer, the brightest young lawyer you ever turned out, after he had come home from the university as straight as a die, take to drinking and forge a check and shoot himself? Why did Bill Merrit's son die of the shakes in a saloon in Omaha? Why was Mr. Thomas's son, here, shot in a gambling-house? Why did young Adams burn his mill to beat the insurance companies and go to the pen?"

The lawyer paused and unfolded his arms, laying one clenched fist quietly on the table. "I'll tell you why. Because you drummed nothing but money and knavery into their ears from the time they wore knickerbockers; because you carped away at them as you've been carping here tonight, holding our friends Phelps and Elder up to them for their models, as our grandfathers held up George Washington and John Adams. But the boys, worse luck, were young and raw at the business you put them to; and how could they match coppers with such artists as Phelps and Elder? You wanted them to be successful rascals; they were only unsuccessful ones—that's all the difference. There was only one boy ever raised in this borderland between ruffianism and civilization, who didn't come to grief, and you hated Harvey Merrick more for winning out than you hated all the other boys who got under the wheels. Lord, Lord, how you did hate him! Phelps, here, is fond of saying that he could buy and sell us all out any time he's a mind to; but he knew Harve wouldn't have given a tinker's damn for his bank and all his cattle farms put together; and a lack of appreciation, that way, goes hard with Phelps.

"Old Nimrod, here, thinks Harve drank too much; and this from such as Nimrod and me!

"Brother Elder says Harve was too free with the old man's money—fell short in filial consideration, maybe. Well, we can all remember the very tone in which brother Elder swore his own father was a liar, in the county court; and we all know that the old man came out of that partnership with his son as bare as a sheared lamb. But maybe I'm getting personal, and I'd better be driving ahead at what I want to say."

The lawyer paused a moment, squared his heavy shoulders, and went on: "Harvey Merrick and I went to school together, back East. We were dead in earnest, and we wanted you all to be proud of us some day. We meant to be great men. Even I, and I haven't lost my sense of humour, gentlemen, I meant to be a great man. I came back here to practise, and I found you didn't in the least want me to be a great man. You wanted me to be a shrewd lawyer—oh, yes! Our veteran here wanted me to get him an increase of pension, because he had dyspepsia; Phelps wanted a new country survey that would put the widow Wilson's little bottom farm inside his south line; Elder wanted to lend money at 5 percent a month, and get it collected; old Stark here wanted to wheedle old women up in Vermont into investing their annuities in real-estate mortgages that are not worth the paper they are written on. Oh, you needed me hard enough, and you'll go on needing me; and that's why I'm not afraid to plug the truth home to you this once.

"Well, I came back here and became the damned shyster you wanted me to be. You pretend to have some sort of respect for me; and yet you'll stand up and throw mud at Harvey Merrick, whose soul you couldn't dirty and whose hands you couldn't tie. Oh, you're a discriminating lot of Christians! There have been times when the sight of Harvey's name in some Eastern paper has made me hang my head like a whipped dog; and, again, times when I liked to think of him off there in the world, away from all this hogwallow, doing his great work and climbing the big, clean up-grade he'd set for himself.

"And we? Now that we've fought and lied and sweated and stolen, and hated as only the disappointed strugglers in a bitter, dead little Western town know how to do, what have we got to show for it? Harvey Merrick wouldn't have given one sunset over your marshes for all you've got put together, and you know it. It's not for me to say why, in the inscrutable wisdom of God, a genius should ever have been called from his place of hatred and bitter waters; but I want this Boston man to know that the drivel he's been hearing here tonight is the only tribute any truly great man could ever have from such a lot of sick, side-tracked, burnt-dog, land-poor sharks as the here-present financiers of Sand City—upon which town may God have mercy!"

The lawyer thrust out his hand to Steavens as he passed him, caught up his overcoat in the hall, and had left the house before the Grand Army man had had time to lift his ducked head and crane his long neck about at his fellows.

Next day Jim Laird was drunk and unable to attend the funeral services. Steavens called twice at his office, but was compelled to start East without seeing him. He had a presentiment that he would hear from him again, and left his address on the lawyer's table; but if Laird found it, he never acknowledged it. The thing in him that Harvey Merrick had loved must have gone underground with Harvey Merrick's coffin; for it never spoke again, and Jim got the cold he died of driving across the Colorado mountains to defend one of Phelps's sons who had got into trouble out there by cutting government timber.

Suggestions for Discussion

1. Discuss the details Cather uses to characterize the small Kansas town to which the dead sculptor's body is brought for burial. Why is Steavens repelled by the furnishings in the house of Merrick's mother?

2. The sculptor's mother is overcome by grief. Steavens is repelled by her outburst of emotion. Why? Explain how Cather arranges details so that we will agree with Steavens.

3. How does Cather contrast Mrs. Merrick with her daughter? What function do both characters have in the story?

4. Why does Cather portray Jim Laird as a heavy drinker? What is his function in the story?

5. What was the real tragedy of the dead sculptor's life? How had it affected his work?

6. What is the theme of Cather's story? Why does she use the long speech by Laird to express it?

Suggestion for Writing

Cather's view of the artist as somehow alienated from his society is illustrated in this story. Write a paper dealing with the issue, using examples of well-known artists. You might make this a research project by investigating the life of Beethoven, Mozart, Baudelaire, or Poe. What about the relation of the artists to society in other cultures; for example, China, India, or Bali?

Poetry

Marianne Moore

Poetry

Marianne Moore (1877–1972) was born in Missouri, graduated from Bryn Mawr College, taught at an Indian school, worked in the New York Public Library, edited *The Dial* between 1925 and 1929, and was a distinguished resident of Brooklyn Heights. Her first collection of poems was published in 1921, her *Collected Poems* in 1951. Among her works are *Predilection* (1955), a volume of critical essays, a poetic translation of La Fontaine's *Fables* (1954), and the volume of poetry *Tell Me, Tell Me* (1967). In the following poem, as she appears to put poetry in its place and dismisses high-flown theories about art, she affirms the power of the genuine article and the real significance of poetry.

I, too, dislike it: there are things that are important beyond all this fiddle,
Reading it, however, with a perfect contempt for it, one discovers in
it after all, a place for the genuine.
    Hands that can grasp, eyes
    that can dilate, hair that can rise
       if it must, these things are important not because a

high-sounding interpretation can be put upon them but because they are
useful. When they become so derivative as to become unintelligible,
the same thing may be said for all of us, that we
    do not admire what
    we cannot understand: the bat
       holding on upside down or in quest of something to

eat, elephants pushing, a wild horse taking a roll, a tireless wolf under
a tree, the immovable critic twitching his skin like a horse that feels a flea,
the base-
    ball fan, the statistician—
    nor is it valid
       to discriminate against "business documents and

school-books"; all these phenomena are important. One must make a
    distinction
however: when dragged into prominence by half poets, the result is not
    poetry,
nor till the poets among us can be
    "literalists of
    the imagination"—above
       insolence and triviality and can present

for inspection, "imaginary gardens with real toads in them," shall we have
　it. In the meantime, if you demand on the one hand,
　　the raw material of poetry in
　　　all its rawness and
　　　that which is on the other hand
　　　　genuine, you are interested in poetry.

Suggestions for Discussion

1. Why does the poet, on one hand, refer to poetry as "all this fiddle" and, on the
　 other, find in it "a place for the genuine"?

2. What does the poet list as the important parts of poetry? Why does she dismiss the
　 unintelligible in poetry?

3. Moore wants poets to become " 'literalists of the imagination.' " Relate this phrase to
　 her belief that the poets must create " 'imaginary gardens with real toads in them.' "

Suggestions for Writing

1. Write a paper in which you compare the view of poetry in this poem with the view
　 that poetry is a romantic outburst of pure emotion. What arguments would you use
　 in defense of either position?

2. Rewrite the poem in prose sentences in a paragraph. Write a comment on what
　 you have done with the poem. How have you changed it? Does your change effect
　 a change in defining the piece as a poem?

===============

Rita Dove

Beauty and the Beast

Rita Dove (b. 1952), born in Akron, Ohio, and educated at Miami University
in Oxford, Ohio, was appointed the first black poet laureate of the United
States in 1993. She is a Commonwealth Professor of English at the University of Virginia. Her books of poetry include *The Yellow House on the Corner*
(1980); *Museum* (1983); *Thomas and Beulah* (1987), for which she won the Pulitzer Prize; *Grace Notes* (1989); and *Selected Poems* (1993). She has also written
a play, a collection of short stories, *Fifth Sunday* (1985), and a novel, *Through
the Ivory Gate* (1992). "Beauty and the Beast" illustrates how the artist transforms an ever-popular fairy tale into a statement on the human condition.

　　　Darling, the plates have been cleared away,
　　　the servants are in their quarters.
　　　What lies will we lie down with tonight?
　　　The rabbit pounding in your heart, my

child legs, pale from a life of petticoats?
My father would not have had it otherwise
when he trudged the road home with our souvenirs.
You are so handsome it eats my heart away . . .

Beast, when you lay stupid with grief
at my feet, I was too young to see anything
die. Outside, the roses are folding
lip upon red lip. I miss my sisters—

they are standing before their clouded mirrors.
Gray animals are circling under the windows.
Sisters, don't you see what will snatch you up—
the expected, the handsome, the one who needs us?

Suggestions for Discussion

1. Who is the speaker in this poem? Try to put together the characteristics of the speaker from suggestions in the poem to describe the nature of the person speaking.

2. Why does the speaker refer to the Beast as lying "stupid with grief / at my feet"? The speaker asks several other questions in the poem. How are they related to each other?

Suggestion for Writing

Write an essay in which you compare and contrast the events of the fairy tale with the remarks of the speaker in the poem. Summarize clearly the significance of the speaker's statements and questions to the Beast and to her sisters.

Li-Young Lee

Persimmons

Li-Young Lee (b. 1957) was born in Jakarta, Indonesia, of Chinese parents. His father, a political prisoner for one year, fled Indonesia with his family in 1959. They arrived in the United States in 1964, after living in Hong Kong, Macao, and Japan. Li-Young Lee studied at the University of Pittsburgh, the University of Arizona, and SUNY at Brockport. He and his family live in Chicago where he works as an artist. His poems in *Rose*, of which this is one, deal lyrically with the relations between parents and children, men and women, and the creation of art through painting or poetry.

In sixth grade Mrs. Walker
slapped the back of my head
and made me stand in the corner
for not knowing the difference
between *persimmon* and *precision.*
How to choose

persimmons. This is precision.
Ripe ones are soft and brown-spotted.
Sniff the bottoms. The sweet one
will be fragrant. How to eat:
put the knife away, lay down newspaper.
Peel the skin tenderly, not to tear the meat.
Chew the skin, suck it,
and swallow. Now, eat
the meat of the fruit,
so sweet,
all of it, to the heart.

Donna undresses, her stomach is white.
In the yard, dewy and shivering
with crickets, we lie naked,
face-up, face-down.
I teach her Chinese.
Crickets: *chin chin.* Dew: I've forgotten.
Naked: I've forgotten.
Ni, wo: you and me.
I part her legs,
remember to tell her
she is beautiful as the moon.

Other words
that got me into trouble were
fight and *fright, wren* and *yarn.*
Fight was what I did when I was frightened,
fright was what I felt when I was fighting.
Wrens are small, plain birds,
yarn is what one knits with.
Wrens are soft as yarn.
My mother made birds out of yarn.
I loved to watch her tie the stuff;
a bird, a rabbit, a wee man.

Mrs. Walker brought a persimmon to class
and cut it up
so everyone could taste
a *Chinese apple.* Knowing
it wasn't ripe or sweet, I didn't eat
but watched the other faces.

My mother said every persimmon has a sun
inside, something golden, glowing,
warm as my face.

Once, in the cellar, I found two wrapped in newspaper,
forgotten and not yet ripe.
I took them and set both on my bedroom windowsill,
where each morning a cardinal
sang, *The sun, the sun.*

Finally understanding
he was going blind,
my father sat up all one night
waiting for a song, a ghost.
I gave him the persimmons,
swelled, heavy as sadness,
and sweet as love.

This year, in the muddy lighting
of my parents' cellar, I rummage, looking
for something I lost.
My father sits on the tired, wooden stairs,
black cane between his knees,
hand over hand, gripping the handle.
He's so happy that I've come home.
I ask how his eyes are, a stupid question.
All gone, he answers.

Under some blankets, I find a box.
Inside the box I find three scrolls.
I sit beside him and untie
three paintings by my father:
Hibiscus leaf and a white flower.
Two cats preening.
Two persimmons, so full they want to drop from the cloth.

He raises both hands to touch the cloth,
asks, *Which is this?*

This is persimmons, Father.

Oh, the feel of the wolftail on the silk,
the strength, the tense
precision in the wrist.
I painted them hundreds of times
eyes closed. These I painted blind.
Some things never leave a person:
scent of the hair of one you love,
the texture of persimmons,
in your palm, the ripe weight.

Suggestions for Discussion

1. Discuss the way Lee uses the difficulties he had with English words *(persimmon/ precision, fight/fright, wren/yarn)* to create the ideas for this poem.

2. In what ways does the poem reveal the relations between members of the narrator's family? Between the two young lovers? What special bond exists between the narrator in the poem and his father?

3. What statements does the father make about the nature of art in the final stanza of the poem? In the seven-line stanza before the end of the poem?

4. Why has the poet chosen the persimmon as the title for this poem?

Suggestions for Writing

1. Write a paper explaining the structure of the poem. What are its parts? How does the poet help the reader discover them?

2. Write two paragraphs summarizing the poet's ideas on the art of poetry. How does this poem differ from the following one, "Why I Am Not a Painter," in its comment on poetry?

Frank O'Hara

Why I Am Not a Painter

Frank O'Hara (1926–1966) did not have a wide audience during his lifetime, but since his death his reputation has grown, and numerous articles and several biographies have appeared. After his education at Harvard (B.A.) and the University of Michigan (M.A.), where he won the Hopwood Award for poetry, he moved to New York City where he worked for the Museum of Modern Art. He became an intimate of the painters who formed what has been called the New York School, and many of his poems express the concerns of his abstract expressionist friends. "Why I Am Not a Painter" comically reflects O'Hara's beliefs about the difference between the two media.

I am not a painter, I am a poet.
Why? I think I would rather be
a painter, but I am not. Well,

for instance, Mike Goldberg
is starting a painting. I drop in.
"Sit down and have a drink" he

says. I drink; we drink. I look
up. "You have SARDINES in it."
"Yes, it needed something there."
"Oh." I go and the days go by
and I drop in again. The painting
is going on, and I go, and the days
go by. I drop in. The painting is
finished. "Where's SARDINES?"
All that's left is just
letters, "It was too much," Mike says.

But me? One day I am thinking of
a color: orange. I write a line
about orange. Pretty soon it is a
whole page of words, not lines.
Then another page. There should be
so much more, not of orange, of
words, of how terrible orange is
and life. Days go by. It is even in
prose, I am a real poet. My poem
is finished and I haven't mentioned
orange yet. It's twelve poems, I call
it ORANGES. And one day in a gallery
I see Mike's painting, called SARDINES.

Suggestions for Discussion

1. Explain the speaker's conversation with Mike Goldberg about his new painting. Why does he paint over the word *sardines?*

2. How does the speaker begin to write a poem? How different is this approach from that of his friend the painter?

3. Why does Goldberg name his painting *Sardines?* Why does the poet name his poem "Oranges"?

4. Explain the title of the poem. How is the poem somewhat comic?

Suggestions for Writing

1. A number of O'Hara's poems deal, as this one does, with the art of poetry. Read O'Hara's *Selected Poems* (1974) for examples, and write a paper relating "Why I Am Not a Painter" to several other poems on this topic.

2. O'Hara is known as a humorous poet. How does the poem in the text show this quality? From his *Selected Poems* choose several other poems that also are humorous; for example, "A True Account of Talking to the Sun at Fire Island" and "Ave Maria." Write a paper about humor in O'Hara's poetry.

Science, the Environment, and the Future

Science . . . is neither human nor inhuman. So far as the well-being of humanity is concerned, science needs guidance from other sources. Science in itself is not enough — or should not be.
> **— Karl Jaspers,** "Is Science Evil?"

The universe is vast and men are but tiny specks on an insignificant planet. But the more we realize our minuteness and our impotence in the face of cosmic forces, the more astonishing becomes what human beings have achieved.
> **— Bertrand Russell,** "If We Are to Survive This Dark Time"

The power that man has over nature and himself, and that a dog lacks, lies in his command of imaginary experience. He alone has the symbols which fix the past and play with the future.
> **— Jacob Bronowski,** "The Reach of the Imagination"

At the moment we are an ignorant species, flummoxed by the puzzles of who we are, where we came from, and what we are for. It is a gamble to bet on science for moving ahead, but it is, in my view, the only game in town.
> **— Lewis Thomas,** "Making Science Work"

So the creationists distort. An attack on some parts of Darwin's views is equated with a rejection of evolution.
> **— Niles Eldredge,** "Creationism Isn't Science"

A generation of research has revealed that when natural landscapes are chopped into little pieces, ecological processes go
awry and species go extinct.

> — **David S. Wilcove,** "What I Saw When I Went to the
> Forest"

And beyond the rich, rolling, ancient panorama of rising, interlocking ridges I saw — spread vividly out before my mind's unhappy eye — our modern panorama of Los Angeles and the
Love Canal, Beirut and Chernobyl, Ethiopia and the East
Bronx.

> — **Colin Fletcher,** "A Bend in the Road"

Darwin's dice have rolled badly for Earth. It was a misfortune
for the living world in particular, many scientists believe, that
a carnivorous primate and not some more benign form of animal made the breakthrough.

> — **Edward O. Wilson,** "Is Humanity Suicidal?"

Essays

Francis Bacon

Idols of the Mind

Sir Francis Bacon (1561–1626) was a lawyer, essayist, philosopher, and statesman. Among his best-known works are *The Advancement of Learning* (1605), *The New Organum* (1620), and *The New Atlantis* (1627). He is considered the originator of modern scientific induction because of his insistence on observation and experimentation as a means to knowledge. In "Idols of the Mind," from *The New Organum*, Bacon illustrates those habits of thought that inhibit human understanding and the spirit of scientific inquiry.

XXIII

There is a great difference between the Idols of the human mind and the Ideals of the divine. That is to say, between certain empty dogmas, and the true signatures and marks set upon the works of creation as they are found in nature.

XXXVIII

The idols and false notions which are now in possession of the human understanding, and have taken deep root therein, not only so beset men's minds that truth can hardly find entrance, but even after entrance obtained, they will again in the very instauration of the sciences meet and trouble us, unless men being forewarned of the danger fortify themselves as far as may be against their assaults.

XXXIX

There are four classes of Idols which beset men's minds. To these for distinction's sake I have assigned names,—calling the first class *Idols of the Tribe;* the second, *Idols of the Cave;* the third, *Idols of the Market Place;* the fourth, *Idols of the Theater.*

XL

The formation of ideas and axioms by true induction is no doubt the proper remedy to be applied for the keeping off and clearing away of idols. To point them out, however, is of great use; for the doctrine of Idols is to the Interpretation of Nature what the doctrine of the refutation of Sophisms is to common Logic.

XLI

The Idols of the Tribe have their foundation in human nature itself, and in the tribe or race of men. For it is a false assertion that the sense of man is the measure of things. On the contrary, all perceptions as well of the sense as of the mind are according to the measure of the individual and not according to the measure of the universe. And the human understanding is like a false mirror, which, receiving rays irregularly, distorts and discolors the nature of things by mingling its own nature with it.

XLII

The Idols of the Cave are the idols of the individual man. For everyone (besides the errors common to human nature in general) has a cave or den of his own, which refracts and discolours the light of nature; owing either to his own proper and peculiar nature; or to his education and conversation with others; or to the reading of books, and the authority of those whom he esteems and admires; or to the differences of impressions, accordingly as they take place in a mind preoccupied and predisposed or in a mind indifferent and settled; or the like. So that the spirit of man (according as it is meted out to different individuals) is in fact a thing variable and full of perturbation, and governed as it were by chance. Whence it was well observed by Heraclitus that men look for sciences in their own lesser worlds, and not in the greater or common world.

XLIII

There are also Idols formed by the intercourse and association of men with each other, which I call Idols of the Market Place, on account of the commerce and consort of men there. For it is by discourse that men associate; and words are imposed according to the apprehension of the vulgar. And therefore the ill and unfit choice of words wonderfully obstructs the understanding. Nor do the definitions or explanations wherewith in some things learned men are wont to guard and defend themselves, by any means set the matter right. But words plainly force and overrule the understanding, and throw all into confusion, and lead men away into numberless empty controversies and idle fancies.

XLIV

Lastly, there are Idols which have immigrated into men's minds from the various dogmas of philosophies, and also from wrong laws of demonstration. These I call Idols of the Theater; because in my judgment all the received systems are but so many stage-plays, representing worlds of their own creation after an unreal and scenic fashion. Nor is it only of the systems now in vogue, or only of the ancient sects and philosophies, that I speak; for many more plays of the same kind may yet be composed and in like artificial manner set forth; seeing that errors the most widely different have nevertheless causes for the most part alike. Neither again do I mean this only of entire systems, but also of many principles and axioms in science, which by tradition, credulity, and negligence have come to be received.

But of these several kinds of Idols I must speak more largely and exactly, that the understanding may be duly cautioned.

XLV

The human understanding is of its own nature prone to suppose the existence of more order and regularity in the world than it finds. And though there be many things in nature which are singular and unmatched, yet it devises for them parallels and conjugates and relatives which do not exist. Hence the fiction that all celestial bodies move in perfect circles; spirals and dragons being (except in name) utterly rejected. Hence too the element of Fire with its orb is brought in, to make up the square with the other three which the sense perceives. Hence also the ratio of density of the so-called elements is arbitrarily fixed at ten to one. And so on of other dreams. And these fancies affect not dogmas only, but simple notions also.

XLVI

The human understanding when it has once adopted an opinion (either as being the received opinion or as being agreeable to itself) draws all things else to support and agree with it. And though there be a greater number and weight of instances to be found on the other side, yet these it either neglects and despises, or else by some distinction sets aside and rejects; in order that by this great and pernicious predetermination the authority of its former conclusions may remain inviolate. And therefore it was a good answer that was made by one who when they showed him hanging in a temple a picture of those who had paid their vows as having escaped shipwreck, and would have him say whether he did not now acknowledge the power of the gods,— "Aye," asked he again, "but where are they painted that were drowned after their vows?" And such is the way of all superstition, whether in astrology, dreams, omens, divine judgments, or the like; wherein men, having a delight in such vanities, mark the events where they are fulfilled, but where they fail, though this happen much oftener, neglect and pass them by. But with far more subtlety does this mischief insinuate itself into philosophy and the sciences; in which the first conclusion colors and brings into conformity with itself all that come after, though far sounder and better. Besides, independently of that delight and vanity which I have described, it is the peculiar and perpetual error of the human intellect to be more moved and excited by affirmatives than by negatives; whereas it ought properly to hold itself indifferently disposed towards both alike. Indeed in the establishment of any true axiom, the negative instance is the more forcible of the two.

XLVII

The human understanding is moved by those things most which strike and enter the mind simultaneously and suddenly, and so fill the imagination; and then it feigns and supposes all other things to be somehow, though it cannot see how, similar to those few things by which it is surrounded. But for that going to and fro to remote and heterogeneous instances, by which axioms are tried as in the fire, the intellect is altogether slow and unfit, unless it be forced thereto by severe laws and overruling authority.

XLVIII

The human understanding is unquiet; it cannot stop or rest, and still presses onward, but in vain. Therefore it is that we cannot conceive of any end or limit to the world; but always as of necessity it occurs to us that there is something beyond. Neither again can it be conceived how eternity has flowed down to the present day; for that distinction which is commonly received of infinity in time past and in time to come can by no means hold; for it would thence follow that one infinity is greater than another, and that infinity is wasting away and tending to become finite. The like subtlety arises touching the infinite divisibility of lines, from the same inability of thought to stop. But this inability interferes more mischievously in the discovery of causes: for although the most general principles in nature ought to be held merely positive, as they are discovered, and cannot with truth be referred to a cause; nevertheless the human understanding being unable to rest still seeks something prior in the order of nature. And then it is that in struggling toward that which is further off it falls back upon that which is more nigh at hand; namely, on final causes: which have relation clearly to the nature of man rather than to the nature of the universe; and from this source have strangely defiled philosophy. But he is no less an unskilled and shallow philosopher who seeks causes of that which is most general, than he who in things subordinate and subaltern omits to do so.

XLIX

The human understanding is no dry light, but receives an infusion from the will and affections; whence proceed sciences which may be called "sciences as one would." For what a man had rather were true he more readily believes. Therefore he rejects difficult things from impatience of research; sober things, because they narrow hope; the deeper things of nature, from superstition; the light of experience, from arrogance and pride, lest his mind should seem to be occupied with things mean and transitory; things not commonly believed, out of deference to the opinion of the vulgar. Numberless in short are the ways, and sometimes imperceptible, in which the affections color and infect the understanding.

L

But by far the greatest hindrance and aberration of the human understanding proceeds from the dullness, incompetency, and deceptions of the senses; in that things which strike the sense outweigh things which do not immediately strike it, though they be more important. Hence it is that speculation commonly ceases where sight ceases; insomuch that of things invisible there is little or no observation. Hence all the working of the spirits enclosed in tangible bodies lies hid and unobserved by men. So also all the more subtle changes of form in the parts of coarser substances (which they commonly call alteration, though it is in truth local motion through exceedingly small spaces) is in like manner unobserved. And yet unless these two things just mentioned be searched out and brought to light, nothing great can be achieved in nature, as far as the production of works is concerned. So again the essential nature of our common air, and of all bodies less dense than air (which are very many), is almost unknown. For the sense by itself is a thing infirm and erring; neither can instruments for enlarging or sharpening the senses do much; but all the truer kind of interpretation of nature is effected by instances and experiments fit and apposite; wherein the sense decides touching the experiment only, and the experiment touching the point in nature and the thing itself.

LI

The human understanding is of its own nature prone to abstractions and gives a substance and reality to things which are fleeting. But to resolve nature into abstractions is less to our purpose than to dissect her into parts; as did the school of Democritus, which went further into nature than the rest. Matter rather than forms should be the object of our attention, its configurations and changes of configuration, and simple action, and law of action or motion; for forms are figments of the human mind, unless you will call those laws of action forms.

LII

Such then are the idols which I call *Idols of the Tribe;* and which take their rise either from the homogeneity of the substance of the human spirit, or from its preoccupation, or from its narrowness, or from its restless motion, or from an infusion of the affections, or from the incompetency of the senses, or from the mode of impression.

LIII

The *Idols of the Cave* take their rise in the peculiar constitution, mental or bodily, of each individual; and also in education, habit, and accident. Of this kind there is a great number and variety; but I will instance those the pointing out of which contains the most important caution, and which have most effect in disturbing the clearness of the understanding.

LIV

Men become attached to certain particular sciences and speculations, either because they fancy themselves the authors and inventors thereof, or because they have bestowed the greatest pains upon them and become most habituated to them. But men of this kind, if they betake themselves to philosophy and contemplations of a general character, distort and color them in obedience to their former fancies; a thing especially to be noticed in Aristotle, who made his natural philosophy a mere bond-servant to his logic, thereby rendering it contentious and well nigh useless. The race of chemists again out of a few experiments of the furnace have built up a fantastic philosophy, framed with reference to a few things; and Gilbert also, after he had employed himself most laboriously in the study and observation of the lodestone, proceeded at once to construct an entire system in accordance with his favourite subject.

LVI

There are found some minds given to an extreme admiration of antiquity, others to an extreme love and appetite for novelty; but few so duly tempered that they can hold the mean, neither carping at what has been well laid down by the ancients, nor despising what is well introduced by the moderns. This however turns to the great injury of the sciences and philosophy; since these affectations of antiquity and novelty are the humors of partisans rather than judgments; and truth is to be sought for not in the felicity of any age, which is an unstable thing, but in the light of nature and experience, which is eternal. These factions therefore must be abjured, and care must be taken that the intellect be not hurried by them into assent.

LVIII

Let such then be our provision and contemplative prudence for keeping off and dislodging the *Idols of the Cave*, which grow for the most part either out of the predominance of a favourite subject, or out of an excessive tendency to compare or to distinguish, or out of partiality for particular ages, or out of the largeness or minuteness of the objects contemplated. And generally let every student of nature take this as a rule—that whatever his mind seizes and dwells upon with peculiar satisfaction is to be held in suspicion, and that so much the more care is to be taken in dealing with such questions to keep the understanding even and clear.

LIX

But the *Idols of the Market Place* are the most troublesome of all: idols which have crept into the understanding through the alliances of words and names. For men believe that their reason governs words; but it is also true that words react on the understanding; and this it is that had rendered philosophy and the sciences sophistical and inactive. Now words, being commonly framed and applied according to the capacity of the vulgar, follow those lines of division which are most obvious to the vulgar understanding. And whenever an understanding of greater acuteness or a more diligent observation would alter those lines to suit the true divisions of nature, words stand in the way and resist the change. Whence it comes to pass that the high and formal discussions of learned men end oftentimes in disputes about words and names; with which (according to the use and wisdom of the mathematicians) it would be more prudent to begin, and so by means of definitions reduce them to order. Yet even definitions cannot cure this evil in dealing with natural and material things; since the definitions themselves consist of words, and those words beget others: so that it is necessary to recur to individual instances, and those in due series and order; as I shall say presently when I come to the method and scheme for the formation of notions and axioms.

LX

The idols imposed by words on the understanding are of two kinds. They are either names of things which do not exist (for as there are things left unnamed through lack of observation, so likewise are there names which result from fantastic suppositions and to which nothing in reality corresponds), or they are names of things which exist, but yet confused and ill-defined, and hastily and irregularly derived from realities. Of the former kind are Fortune, the Prime Mover, Planetary Orbits, Element of Fire, and like fictions which owe their origin to false and idle theories. And this class of idols is more easily expelled, because to get rid of them it is only necessary that all theories should be steadily rejected and dismissed as obsolete.

But the other class, which springs out of a faulty and unskillful abstraction, is intricate and deeply rooted. Let us take for example such a word as *humid;* and see how far the several things which the word is used to signify agree with each other; and we shall find the word *humid* to be nothing else than a mark loosely and confusedly applied to denote a variety of actions which will not bear to be reduced to any constant meaning. For it both signifies that which easily spreads itself round any other body; and that which in itself is indeterminate and cannot solidify; and that which readily yields in every direction; and that which easily divides and scatters itself; and that which easily unites and collects itself; and that which readily flows and is put in motion;

and that which readily clings to another body and wets it; and that which is easily reduced to a liquid, or being solid easily melts. Accordingly when you come to apply the word—if you take it in one sense, flame is humid; if in another, air is not humid; if in another, fine dust is humid; if in another, glass is humid. So that it is easy to see that the notion is taken by abstraction only from water and common and ordinary liquids, without any due verification.

There are however in words certain degrees of distortion and error. One of the least faulty kinds is that of names of substances, especially of lowest species and well-deduced (for the notion of *chalk* and of *mud* is good, of *earth* bad); a more faulty kind is that of actions, as *to generate, to corrupt, to alter;* the most faulty is of qualities (except such as are the immediate objects of the sense) as *heavy, light, rare, dense,* and the like. Yet in all these cases some notions are of necessity a little better than others, in proportion to the greater variety of subjects that fall within the range of the human sense.

LXI

But the *Idols of the Theater* are not innate, nor do they steal into the understanding secretly, but are plainly impressed and received into the mind from the play-books of philosophical systems and the perverted rules of demonstration. To attempt refutations in this case would be merely inconsistent with what I have already said: for since we agree neither upon principles nor upon demonstrations there is no place for argument. And this is so far well, inasmuch as it leaves the honor of the ancients untouched. For they are no wise disparaged—the question between them and me being only as to the way. For as the saying is, the lame man who keeps the right road outstrips the runner who takes a wrong one. Nay it is obvious that when a man runs the wrong way, the more active and swift he is the further he will go astray.

But the course I propose for the discovery of sciences is such as leaves but little to the acuteness and strength of wits, but places all wits and understandings nearly on a level. For as in the drawing of a straight line or a perfect circle, much depends on the steadiness and practice of the hand, if it be done by aim of hand only, but if with the aid of rule or compass, little or nothing; so is it exactly with my plan. But though particular confutations would be of no avail, yet touching the sects and general divisions of such systems I must say something; something also touching the external signs which show that they are unsound; and finally something touching the causes of such great infelicity and of such lasting and general agreement in error; that so the access to truth may be made less difficult, and the human understanding may the more willingly submit to its purgation and dismiss its idols.

LXII

Idols of the Theater, or of Systems, are many, and there can be and perhaps will be yet many more. For were it not that now for many ages men's minds have been busied with religion and theology; and were it not that civil governments, especially monarchies, have been averse to such novelties, even in matters speculative; so that men labor therein to the peril and harming of their fortunes—not only unrewarded, but exposed also to contempt and envy; doubtless there would have arisen many other philosophical sects like to those which in great variety flourished once among the Greeks. For as on the phenomena of the heavens many hypotheses may be constructed, so likewise (and more also) many various dogmas may be set up and established on the phenomena of philosophy. And in the plays of this philosophical theater you may observe the same thing which is found in the theater of the poets, that stories invented for the stage are more compact and elegant, and more as one would wish them to be, than true stories out of history.

LXVII

A caution must also be given to the understanding against the intemperance which systems of philosophy manifest in giving or withholding assent; because intemperance of this kind seems to establish Idols and in some sort to perpetuate them, leaving no way open to reach and dislodge them.

This excess is of two kinds: the first being manifest in those who are ready in deciding, and render sciences dogmatic and magisterial: the other in those who deny that we can know anything, and so introduce a wandering kind of inquiry that leads to nothing: of which kinds the former subdues, the latter weakens the understanding. For the philosophy of Aristotle, after having by hostile confutations destroyed all the rest (as the Ottomans serve their brothers), has laid down the law on all points; which done, he proceeds himself to raise new questions of his own suggestion, and dispose of them likewise; so that nothing may remain that is not certain and decided: a practice which holds and is in use among his successors.

LXVIII

So much concerning the several classes of Idols, and their equipage: all of which must be renounced and put away with a fixed and solemn determination, and the understanding thoroughly freed and cleansed; the entrance into the kingdom of man, founded on the sciences, being not much other than the entrance into the kingdom of heaven, whereinto none may enter except as a little child.

Suggestions for Discussion

1. Bacon names the four idols he is going to discuss. They can be represented diagramatically as follows:

of Tribe	of Cave	of Market Place	of Theater

Relate each aphorism to one of the idols Bacon has named. How does each aphorism apply to or illustrate an idol?

2. In discussing the idols of the market place Bacon deals with nonexistent and ill-defined things. Why does he separate the two? He rapidly disposes of the first category with a number of short examples. The second he divides into three degrees of distortion. What are the degrees? Why does Bacon deal with ill-defined things more precisely than with nonexistent things?

3. For almost every division or subdivision Bacon provides an example or illustration. List at least one example for each. Which are the most important examples? Which divisions have no examples? Why?

4. The language of the aphorisms often has an archaic flavor. Examples: *instauration, whence.* What elements other than archaic words contribute to this flavor? What examples are no longer meaningful to a modern reader?

5. Bacon frequently uses vivid imagery. The concept of "idols of the mind" is imagistic. Discuss some of the images and show how they function to support his arguments in the aphorisms.

Suggestions for Writing

1. Select one of the idols and define it in your own words. Using contemporary illustrations, write an essay (approximately 500 words) to apply the idol to your own world.

2. You may wish to write a paper on some idols of the American mind. Follow Bacon's idols as a guide and try to classify your categories as Bacon does.

Bertrand Russell

If We Are to Survive This Dark Time

Bertrand Arthur William Russell (1872–1970), third Earl Russell, studied at Trinity College, Cambridge, where he later was lecturer and fellow. He lost his post because of his opposition to World War I. With Alfred North Whitehead he wrote *Principia Mathematica* (1910–1913), a major contribution to symbolic logic that helped determine much of the course of modern philosophy. Among his many other works are *The Analysis of Mind* (1921), *Human Knowledge, Its Scope and Limits* (1948), and *The Impact of Science on Society* (1952). He was also an educator and a spokesman for many causes, popular and unpopular, all his life. He won the Nobel Prize for Literature in 1950. This essay (1961) clearly distinguishes between democratic and totalitarian concepts of man and society and projects hope for the future.

There is only too much reason to fear that Western civilization, if not the whole world, is likely in the near future to go through a period of immense sorrow and suffering and pain—a period during which, if we are not careful to remember them, the things that we are attempting to preserve may be forgotten in bitterness and poverty and disorder. Courage, hope, and unshakable conviction will be necessary if we are to emerge from the dark time spiritually undamaged. It is worthwhile, before the actual danger is upon us, to collect our thoughts, to marshal our hopes, and to plant in our hearts a firm belief in our ideals.

It is not the first time that such disasters have threatened the Western world. The fall of Rome was another such time, and in that time, as now, varying moods of despair, escape, and robust faith were exemplified in the writings of leading men. What emerged and became the kernel of the new civilization was the Christian Church. Many pagans were noble in their thoughts and admirable in their aspirations, but they lacked dynamic force.

Plotinus, the founder of neo-Platonism, was the most remarkable of the pagans of that time. In his youth he hoped to play some part in world affairs and accompanied the emperor in a campaign against Persia, but the Roman soldiers murdered the emperor and decided to go home. Plotinus found his way home as best he could, and decided to have done with practical affairs.

He then retired into meditation and wrote books full of beauty, extolling the eternal world and the inactive contemplation of it. Such philosophy, however admirable in itself, offered no cure for the ills from which the empire was suffering.

I think Plotinus was right in urging contemplation of eternal things, but he was wrong in thinking of this as enough to constitute a good life. Contemplation, if it is to be wholesome and valuable, must be married to practice; it must inspire action and ennoble the aims of practical statesmanship. While it remains secluded in the cloister it is only a means of escape.

Boethius, who represents the very last blossoming of Roman civilization, was a figure of more use to our age. After a lifetime spent in public administration and in trying to civilize a Gothic king, he fell into disfavour and was condemned to death. In prison he composed his great book, *The Consolations of Philosophy*, in which, with a combination of majestic calm and sweet reasonableness, he sets forth, as imperturbably as though he were still a powerful minister, the joys of contemplation, the delight in the beauty of the world and the hopes for mankind, which, even in that situation, did not desert him. Throughout the Dark Ages his book was studied and it transmitted to happier times the last purified legacy of the ancient world.

The sages of our times have a similar duty to perform. It is their duty to posterity to crystallize the achievements, the hopes, and the ideals which have made our time great—to study them with monumental simplicity, so they may shine like a beacon light through the coming darkness.

Two very different conceptions of human life are struggling for mastery of the world. In the West we see man's greatness in the individual life. A great society for us is one which is composed of individuals who, as far as is humanly possible, are happy, free, and creative. We do not think that individuals should be alike. We conceive society as like an orchestra, in which the different performers have different parts to play and different instruments upon which to perform, and in which cooperation results from a conscious common purpose. We believe that each individual should have his proper pride. He should have his personal conscience and his personal aims, which he should be free to develop except where they can be shown to cause injury to others. We attach importance to the diminution of suffering and poverty, to the increase of knowledge, and the production of beauty and art. The State for us is a convenience, not an object of worship.

The Russian government has a different conception of the ends of life. The individual is thought of no importance: he is expendable. What is important is the State, which is regarded as something almost divine and having a welfare of its own not consisting in the welfare of citizens. This view, which Marx took over from Hegel, is fundamentally opposed to the Christian ethic, which in the West is accepted by free-thinkers as much as by Christians. In the Soviet world human dignity counts for nothing.

It is thought right and proper that men should be groveling slaves, bowing down before the semidivine beings who embody the greatness of the State. When a man betrays his dearest friend and causes him, as a penalty for a moment's peevish indiscretion, to vanish into the mysterious horror of a Siberian labor camp; when a schoolchild, as a result of indoctrination by his teacher, causes his parents to be condemned to death; when a man of exceptional courage, after struggling against evils, is tried, convicted, and abjectly confesses that he has sinned in opposing the Moloch power of the authorities, neither the betrayal nor the confession brings any sense of shame to the perpetrator, for has he not been engaged in the service of his divinity?

It is this conception that we have to fight, a conception which, to my mind and to that of most men who appreciate what the Western world stands for, would, if it prevailed, take everything out of life that gives it value, leaving nothing but a regimented collection of grovelling animals. I cannot imagine a greater or more profound cause for which to fight. But if we are to win a victory—not only on the battlefield but in the hearts of men and in the institutions that they support—we must be clear in our own minds as to what it is that we value, and we must, like Boethius, fortify our courage against the threat of adversity.

While Russia underestimates the individual, there are those in the West who unduly magnify the separateness of separate persons. No man's ego should be enclosed in granite walls; its boundaries should be translucent. The first step in wisdom, as well as in morality, is to open the windows of the ego as wide as possible. Most people find little difficulty in including their children within the compass of their desires. In slightly lesser degree they include their friends, and in time of danger their country. Very many men feel that what hurts their country hurts them. In 1940 I knew Frenchmen living prosperously in America who suffered from the fall of France almost as they would have suffered from the loss of a leg. But it is not enough to enlarge our sympathies to embrace our own country. If the world is ever to have peace it will be necessary to learn to embrace the whole human race in the same kind of sympathy which we now feel toward our compatriots. And if we are to retain calm and sanity in difficult times, it is a great help if the furniture of our minds contains past and future ages.

Few things are more purifying to our conception of values than to contemplate the gradual rise of man from his obscure and difficult beginnings to his present eminence. Man, when he first emerged, was a rare and hunted species, not so fleet as the deer, not so nimble as the monkey, unable to defend himself against wild beasts, without the protection of warm fur against rain and cold, living precariously upon the food that he could gather, without weapons, without domestic animals, without agriculture.

The one advantage that he possessed—intelligence—gave him security. He learned the use of fire, of bows and arrows, of language, of domestic animals and, at last, of agriculture. He learned to co-operate in communities, to build great palaces and pyramids, to explore the world in all directions and, at last, to cope with disease and poverty. He studied the stars, he invented geometry, and he learned to substitute machines for muscles in necessary labour. Some of the most important of these advances are very recent and are as yet confined to Western nations.

In the former days most children died in infancy, mortality in adult life was very high, and in every country the great majority of the population endured abject poverty. Now certain nations have succeeded in preserving the lives of the overwhelming majority of infants, in lowering enormously the adult death rate, and in nearly eliminating abject poverty. Other nations, where disease and abject poverty are still the rule, could achieve the same level of well-being by adopting the same methods. There is, therefore, a new hope for mankind.

The hope cannot be realized unless the causes of present evils are understood. But it is the hope that needs to be emphasized. Modern man is master of his fate. What he suffers he suffers because he is stupid or wicked, not because it is nature's decree. Happiness is his if he will adopt the means that lie ready to his hands.

We of the Western world, faced with Communism's hostile criticism, have been too modest and too defensive in our attitude. Throughout the long ages since life began the mechanism of evolution has involved cruel suffering, endless struggle for bare subsistence, and in the end, in most cases, death by starvation. This is the law in the animal kingdom, and it remained, until the present century, the law among human beings also. Now, at last, certain nations have discovered how to prevent abject poverty, how to prevent the pain and sorrow and waste of useless births condemned to premature death, and how to substitute intelligence and care for the blind ruthlessness of nature.

The nations that have made this discovery are trustees for the future of mankind. They must have the courage of their new way of life and not allow themselves to be bemused or bewildered by the slogans of the semicivilized. We have a right to hopes that are rational, that can be itemized and set forth in statistics. If we allow ourselves to be robbed of these hopes for the sake of irrational dreams, we shall be traitors to the human race.

If bad times lie ahead of us, we should remember while they last the slow march of man, chequered in the past by devastations and retrogressions, but always resuming the movement toward progress. Spinoza, who was one of the wisest of men and who lived consistently in accordance with his own wisdom, advised men to view passing events "under the aspect of eternity." Those who can learn to do this will find a painful present much more bearable than it would otherwise be. They can see it as a passing moment—a discord to be resolved, a tunnel to be traversed. The small child who has hurt himself weeps as if the world contained nothing but sorrow, because his mind is confined to the present. A man who has learned wisdom from Spinoza can see even a lifetime of suffering as a passing moment in the life of humanity. And the human race itself, from its obscure beginning to its unknown end, is only a minute episode in the life of the universe.

What may be happening elsewhere we do not know, but it is improbable that the universe contains nothing better than ourselves. With increase of wisdom our thoughts acquire a wider scope both in space and in time. The child lives in the minute, the boy in the day, the instinctive man in the year. The man imbued with history lives in the epoch. Spinoza would have us live not in the minute, the day, the year or the epoch but in eternity. Those who learn to do this will find that it takes away the frantic quality of misfortune and prevents the trend towards madness that comes with overwhelming disaster. He spent the last day of his life telling cheerful anecdotes to his host. He had written: "The wise man thinks less about death than about anything else," and he carried out this precept when it came to his own death.

I do not mean that the wise man will be destitute of emotion—on the contrary, he will feel friendship, benevolence, and compassion in a higher degree than the man who has not emancipated himself from personal anxieties. His ego will not be a wall between him and the rest of mankind. He will feel, like Buddha, that he cannot be completely happy while anybody is miserable. He will feel pain—a wider and more diffused pain than that of the egoist—but he will not find the pain unendurable. He will not be driven by it to invent comfortable fairy-tales which assure him that the sufferings of others are illusory. He will not lose poise and self-control. Like Milton's Satan, he will say:

> The mind is its own place, and in itself
> Can make a Heav'n of Hell, a Hell of Heav'n.

Above all, he will remember that each generation is trustee to future generations of the mental and moral treasure that man has accumulated through the ages. It is easy to forget the glory of man. When King Lear is going mad he meets Edgar, who pretends to be mad and wears only a blanket. King Lear moralizes: "Unaccommodated, man is no more but such a poor, bare, forked animal as thou art."

This is half of the truth. The other half is uttered by Hamlet:

"What a piece of work is a man! how noble in reason; how infinite in faculty! In form and moving how express and admirable; in action how like an angel! in apprehension how like a god!"

Soviet man, crawling on his knees to betray his friends and family to slow butchery, is hardly worthy of Hamlet's words, but it is possible to be worthy of them. It is possible for every one of us. Every one of us can enlarge his mind, release his imagination, and spread wide his affection and benevolence. And it is those who do this whom ultimately mankind reveres. The East reveres Buddha, the West reveres Christ. Both taught love as the secret of wisdom. The earthly life of Christ was contemporary with that of the Emperor Tiberius, who spent his life in cruelty and disgusting debauchery. Tiberius had pomp and power; in his day millions trembled at his nod. But he is forgotten by historians.

Those who live nobly, even if in their day they live obscurely, need not fear that they will have lived in vain. Something radiates from their lives, some light that shows the way to their friends, their neighbours—perhaps to long future ages. I find many men nowadays oppressed with a sense of impotence, with the feeling that in the vastness of modern societies there is nothing of importance that the individual can do. This is a mistake. The individual, if he is filled with love of mankind, with breadth of vision, with courage and with endurance, can do a great deal.

As geological time goes, it is but a moment since the human race began and only the twinkling of an eye since the arts of civilization were first invented. In spite of some alarmists, it is hardly likely that our species will completely exterminate itself. And so long as man continues to exist, we may be pretty sure that, whatever he may suffer for a time, and whatever brightness may be eclipsed, he will emerge sooner or later, perhaps strengthened and reinvigorated by a period of mental sleep. The universe is vast and men are but tiny specks on an insignificant planet. But the more we realize our minuteness and our impotence in the face of cosmic forces, the more astonishing becomes what human beings have achieved.

It is to the possible achievements of man that our ultimate loyalty is due, and in that thought the brief troubles of our unquiet epoch become endurable. Much wisdom remains to be learned, and if it is only to be learned through adversity, we must endeavour to endure adversity with what fortitude we can command. But if we can acquire wisdom soon enough, adversity may not be necessary and the future of man may be happier than any part of his past.

Suggestions for Discussion

1. How does the first paragraph summarize the concerns that Russell treats in the rest of the essay?

2. What is the function of Russell's references to Plotinus and Boethius?

3. Russell distinguishes between totalitarian and democratic governments in their attitude toward individual freedom. Explain his argument.

4. What is the tone of this essay? Why does Russell hold out promise of hope in "this dark time"?

Suggestion for Writing

Write an essay in which you define Russell's "dark time." Your essay should attempt to evaluate his optimism in face of the difficulties that he considers to lie ahead.

Karl Jaspers

Is Science Evil?

Karl Jaspers (1883–1969) was a German philosopher who deeply influenced the modern existentialist movement in philosophy and literature. His works include *Reason and Anti-Reason in Our Time* (1952), *Tragedy Is Not Enough* (1952), and *The Future of Man* (1961). In "Is Science Evil?" published in *Commentary* in 1950, Jaspers answers the accusation that modern science is responsible for the perverted experiments of Nazi doctors. Pointing out that crimes

against humanity appeared long before science appeared, Jaspers defines
the limits of science, but asserts its commitment to reason and truth.

No one questions the immense significance of modern science. Through
industrial technology it has transformed our existence, and its insights have
transformed our consciousness, all this to an extent hitherto unheard of. The
human condition throughout the millennia appears relatively stable in comparison with the impetuous movement that has now caught up mankind as a
result of science and technology, and is driving it no one knows where. Science has destroyed the substance of many old beliefs and has made others
questionable. Its powerful authority has brought more and more men to the
point where they wish to know and not believe, where they expect to be
helped by science and only by science. The present faith is that scientific
understanding can solve all problems and do away with all difficulties.

Such excessive expectations result inevitably in equally excessive disillusionment. Science has still given no answer to man's doubts and despair. Instead, it has created weapons able to destroy in a few moments that which
science itself helped build up slowly over the years. Accordingly, there are
today two conflicting viewpoints: first, the superstition of science, which
holds scientific results to be as absolute as religious myths used to be, so that
even religious movements are now dressed in the garments of pseudoscience.
Second, the hatred of science, which sees it as a diabolical evil of mysterious
origin that has befallen mankind.

These two attitudes—both nonscientific—are so closely linked that they
are usually found together, either in alternation or in an amazing compound.

A very recent example of this situation can be found in the attack
against science provoked by the trial in Nuremberg of those doctors who,
under Nazi orders, performed deadly experiments on human beings. One
of the most esteemed medical men among German university professors
has accepted the verdict on these crimes as a verdict on science itself, as a
stick with which to beat "purely scientific and biological" medicine, and even
the modern science of man in general: "this invisible spirit sitting on the
prisoner's bench in Nuremberg, this spirit that regards men merely as objects, is not present in Nuremberg alone—it pervades the entire world."
And he adds, if this generalization may be viewed as an extenuation of the
crime of the accused doctors, that is only a further indictment of purely scientific medicine.

Anyone convinced that true scientific knowledge is possible only of things
that *can* be regarded as objects, and that knowledge of the subject is possible
only when the subject attains a form of objectivity; anyone who sees science
as the one great landmark on the road to truth, and sees the real achievements of modern physicians as derived exclusively from biological and scientific medicine—such a person will see in the above statements an attack on
what he feels to be fundamental to human existence. And he may perhaps
have a word to say in rebuttal.

In the special case of the crimes against humanity committed by Nazi doctors and now laid at the door of modern science, there is a simple enough
argument. Science was not needed at all, but only a certain bent of mind for
the perpetration of such outrages. Such crimes were already possible millen-

nia ago. In the Buddhist Pali canon, there is the report of an Indian prince who had experiments performed on criminals in order to determine whether they had an immortal soul that survived their corpses: "You shall—it was ordered—put the living man in a tub, close the lid, cover it with a damp hide, lay on a thick layer of clay, put it in the oven, and make a fire. This was done. When we knew the man was dead, the tub was drawn forth, uncovered, the lid removed, and we looked carefully inside to see if we could perceive the escaping soul. But we saw no escaping soul." Similarly, criminals were slowly skinned alive to see if their souls could be observed leaving their bodies. Thus there were experiments on human beings before modern science.

Better than such a defense, however, would be a consideration of what modern science really genuinely is, and what its limits are.

Science, both ancient and modern, has, in the first place, three indispensable characteristics:

First, it is *methodical* knowledge. I know something scientifically only when I also know the method by which I have this knowledge, and am thus able to ground it and mark its limits.

Second, it is *compellingly certain*. Even the uncertain—i.e., the probable or improbable—I know scientifically only insofar as I know it clearly and compellingly as such, and know the degree of its uncertainty.

Third, it is *universally valid*. I know scientifically only what is identically valid for every inquirer. Thus scientific knowledge spreads over the world and remains the same. Unanimity is a sign of universal validity. When unanimity is not attained, when there is a conflict of schools, sects, and trends of fashion, then universal validity becomes problematic.

This notion of science as methodical knowledge, compellingly certain, and universally valid, was long ago possessed by the Greeks. Modern science has not only purified this notion; it has also transformed it: a transformation that can be described by saying that modern science is *indifferent to nothing*. Everything—the smallest and meanest, the furthest and strangest—that is in any way and at any time *actual*, is relevant to modern science, simply because it *is*. Modern science wants to be thoroughly universal, allowing nothing to escape it. Nothing shall be hidden, nothing shall be silent, nothing shall be a secret.

In contrast to the science of classical antiquity, modern science is *basically unfinished*. Whereas ancient science had the appearance of something completed, to which the notion of progress was not essential, modern science progresses into the infinite. Modern science has realized that a finished and total world-view is scientifically impossible. Only when scientific criticism is crippled by making particulars absolute can a closed view of the world pretend to scientific validity—and then it is a false validity. Those great new unified systems of knowledge—such as modern physics—that have grown up in the scientific era, deal only with single aspects of reality. And reality as a whole has been fragmented as never before; whence the openness of the modern world in contrast to the closed Greek cosmos.

However, while a total and finished world-view is no longer possible to modern science, the idea of a unity of the sciences has now come to replace it. Instead of the cosmos of the world, we have the cosmos of the sciences.

Out of dissatisfaction with all the separate bits of knowledge is born the desire to unite all knowledge. The ancient sciences remained dispersed and without mutual relations. There was lacking to them the notion of a concrete totality of science. The modern sciences, however, seek to relate themselves to each other in every possible way.

At the same time the modern sciences have increased their claims. They put a low value on the possibilities of speculative thinking, they hold thought to be valid only as part of definite and concrete knowledge, only when it has stood the test of verification and thereby become infinitely modified. Only superficially do the modern and the ancient atomic theories seem to fit into the same theoretical mold. Ancient atomic theory was applied as a plausible interpretation of common experience; it was a statement complete in itself of what might possibly be the case. Modern atomic theory has developed through experiment, verification, refutation: that is, through an incessant transformation of itself in which theory is used not as an end in itself but as a tool of inquiry. Modern science, in its questioning, pushes to extremes. For example: the rational critique of appearance (as against reality) was begun in antiquity, as in the concept of perspective and its application to astronomy, but it still had some connection with immediate human experiences; today, however, this same critique, as in modern physics for instance, ventures to the very extremes of paradox, attaining a knowledge of the real that shatters any and every view of the world as a closed and complete whole.

So it is that in our day a scientific attitude has become possible that addresses itself inquisitively to everything it comes across, that is able to know what it knows in a clear and positive way, that can distinguish between the known and the unknown, and that has acquired an incredible mass of knowledge. How helpless was the Greek doctor or the Greek engineer! The ethos of modern science is the desire for reliable knowledge based on dispassionate investigation and criticism. When we enter its domain we feel as though we were breathing pure air, and seeing the dissolution of all vague talk, plausible opinions, haughty omniscience, blind faith.

But the greatness and the limitations of science are inseparable. It is a characteristic of the greatness of modern science that it comprehends its own limits:

(1) Scientific, objective knowledge is not a knowledge of Being. This means that scientific knowledge is particular, not general, that it is directed toward specific objects, and not toward Being itself. Through knowledge itself, science arrives at the most positive recognition of what it does *not* know.

(2) Scientific knowledge or understanding cannot supply us with the aims of life. It cannot lead us. By virtue of its very clarity it directs us elsewhere for the sources of our life, our decisions, our love.

(3) Human freedom is not an object of science, but is the field of philosophy. Within the purview of science there is no such thing as liberty.

These are clear limits, and the person who is scientifically minded will not expect from science what it cannot give. Yet science has become, nevertheless, the indispensable element of all striving for truth, it has become the premise of philosophy and the basis in general for whatever clarity and candor are today possible. To the extent that it succeeds in penetrating all obscurities and unveiling all secrets, science directs to the most profound, the most genuine secret.

The unique phenomenon of modern science, so fundamentally different from anything in the past, including the science of the Greeks, owes its character to the many sources that were its origin; and these had to meet together in Western history in order to produce it.

One of these sources was Biblical religion. The rise of modern science is scarcely conceivable without its impetus. Three of the motives that have spurred research and inquiry seem to have come from it:

(1) The ethos of Biblical religion demanded truthfulness at all costs. As a result, truthfulness became a supreme value and at the same time was pushed to the point where it became a serious problem. The truthfulness demanded by God forbade making the search for knowledge a game or amusement, an aristocratic leisure activity. It was a serious affair, a calling in which everything was at stake.

(2) The world is the creation of God. The Greeks knew the cosmos as that which was complete and ordered, rational and regular, eternally subsisting. All else was nothing, merely material, not knowable and not worth knowing. But if the world is the creation of God, then everything that exists is worth knowing, just because it is God's creation; there is nothing that ought not to be known and comprehended. To know is to reflect upon God's thought. And God as creator is—in Luther's words—present even in the bowels of a louse.

The Greeks remained imprisoned in their closed world-view, in the beauty of their rational cosmos, in the logical transparency of the rational whole. Not only Aristotle and Democritus, but Thomas Aquinas and Descartes, too, obey this Greek urge, so paralyzing to the spirit of science, toward a closed universe. Entirely different is the new impulse to unveil the totality of creation. Out of this there arises the pursuit through knowledge of that reality which is not in accord with previously established laws. In the Logos itself [the Word, Reason] there is born the drive toward repeated self-destruction—not as self-immolation, but in order to arise again and ever again in a process that is to be continued infinitely. This science springs from a Logos that does not remain closed within itself, but is open to an anti-Logos which it permeates by the very act of subordinating itself to it. The continuous, unceasing reciprocal action of theory and experiment is the simple and great example and symbol of the universal process that is the dialectic between Logos and anti-Logos.

This new urge for knowledge sees the world no longer as simply beautiful. This knowledge ignores the beautiful and the ugly, the good and the wicked. It is true that in the end, *omne ens est bonum* [all Being is good], that is, as a creation of God. This goodness, however, is no longer the transparent and self-sufficient beauty of the Greeks. It is present only in the love of all existent things as created by God, and it is present therefore in our confidence in the significance of inquiry. The knowledge of the createdness of all worldly things replaces indifference in the face of the flux of reality with limitless questioning, an insatiable spirit of inquiry.

But the world that is known and knowable is, as created Being, Being of the second rank. For the world is unfathomable, it has its ground in another, a Creator, it is not self-contained and it is not containable by knowledge. The Being of the world cannot be comprehended as definitive, absolute reality but points always to another.

The idea of creation makes worthy of love whatever is, for it is God's creation; and it makes possible, by this, an intimacy with reality never before attained. But at the same time it gives evidence of the incalculable distance from that Being which is not merely created Being but Being itself, God.

(3) The reality of this world is full of cruelty and horror for men. "That's the way things are," is what man must truthfully say. If, however, God is the world's creator, then he is responsible for his creation. The question of justifying God's way becomes with Job a struggle with the divine for the knowledge of reality. It is a struggle against God, for God. God's existence is undisputed and just because of this the struggle arises. It would cease if faith were extinguished.

This God, with his unconditional demand for truthfulness, refuses to be grasped through illusions. In the Bible, he condemns the theologians who wish to console and comfort Job with dogmas and sophisms. This God insists upon science, whose content always seems to bring forth an indictment of him. Thus we have the adventure of knowledge, the furtherance of unrestricted knowledge—and at the same time, a timidity, an awe in the face of it. There was an inner tension to be observed in many scientists of the past century, as if they heard: God's will is unconfined inquiry, inquiry is in the service of God—and at the same time: it is an encroachment on God's domain, all shall not be revealed.

This struggle goes hand in hand with the struggle of the man of science against all that he holds most dear, his ideals, his beliefs; they must be proven, newly verified, or else transformed. Since God could not be believed in if he were not able to withstand all the questions arising from the facts of reality, and since the seeking of God involves the painful sacrifice of all illusions, so true inquiry is the struggle against all personal desires and expectations.

This struggle finds its final test in the struggle of the scientist with his own theses. It is the determining characteristic of the modern scientist that he seeks out the strongest points in the criticism of his opponents and exposes himself to them. What in appearance is self-destructiveness becomes, in this case, productive. And it is evidence of a degradation of science when discussion is shunned or condemned, when men imprison themselves and their ideas in a milieu of like-minded savants and become fanatically aggressive to all outside it.

That modern science, like all things, contains its own share of corruption, that men of science only too often fail to live up to its standards, that science can be used for violent and criminal ends, that man will steal, plunder, abuse, and kill to gain knowledge—all this is no argument against science.

To be sure, science as such sets up no barriers. As science, it is neither human nor inhuman. So far as the well-being of humanity is concerned, science needs guidance from other sources. Science in itself is not enough—or should not be. Even medicine is only a scientific means, serving an eternal ideal, the aid of the sick and the protection of the healthy.

When the spirit of a faithless age can become the cause of atrocities all over the world, then it can also influence the conduct of the scientist and the behavior of the physician, especially in those areas of activity where science itself is confused and unguided. It is not the spirit of science but the spirit of its vessels that is depraved. Count Keyserling's dictum—"The roots of truth-seeking lie in primitive aggression"—is as little valid for science as it is for any genuine truth seeking. The spirit of science is in no way primarily aggressive, but becomes so only when truth is prohibited; for men rebel against the glossing over of truth or its suppression.

In our present situation the task is to attain to that true science which knows what it knows at the same time that it knows what it cannot know. This science shows us the ways to the truth that are the indispensable precondition of every other truth. We know what Mephistopheles knew when he thought he had outwitted Faust:

> *Verachte nur Vernunft und Wissenschaft*
> *Des Menschen allerhöchste Kraft*
> *So habe ich Dich schon unbedingt.*

> (Do but scorn Reason and Science
> Man's supreme strength
> Then I'll have you for sure.)

Suggestions for Discussion

1. What is the function of the first two paragraphs of the essay? How is the third paragraph linked to the first two?

2. How does Jaspers use the Nuremberg trial to develop his ideas? Discuss Jaspers's statement that there were experiments on human beings before science.

3. What role do the three characteristics of science play in Jaspers's defense of science?

4. Explain Jaspers's statement that "modern science is *basically unfinished.*" Is this statement part of his defense of science? How does it also serve as a definition of the limits of scientific knowledge? What are the limits?

5. How does Jaspers relate the limits of science to the area of what is unknowable scientifically? What is Jaspers's attitude toward this area?

Suggestions for Writing

1. Although Jaspers's essay is complex, is it difficult to read? If you think not, explain how the language and the organization of the essay contribute to its clarity.

2. Why does Jaspers close his essay with a quotation from Goethe's *Faust?* Write a paper in which you relate the quotation to the essay.

Jacob Bronowski

The Reach of the Imagination

Jacob Bronowski (1908–1974) was a Polish-born American scientist who has played a significant role in the scientific and cultural life of America. He has been particularly active in attempting to explain scientific concepts to humanists. He wrote *The Common Sense of Science* (1951), *Science and Human*

Values (1959), and William Blake, *A Man with a Mask* (1965). His *Ascent of Man* (1974), a series of television essays that combined art, philosophy, and science, was a major effort to bridge the gap between the worlds of science and humanism. "The Reach of the Imagination" argues that imagination is common to literature and science and inspires creativity in both.

For three thousand years, poets have been enchanted and moved and perplexed by the power of their own imagination. In a short and summary essay I can hope at most to lift one small corner of that mystery; and yet it is a critical corner. I shall ask, What goes on in the mind when we imagine? You will hear from me that one answer to this question is fairly specific: which is to say, that we can describe the working of the imagination. And when we describe it as I shall do, it becomes plain that imagination is a specifically *human* gift. To imagine is the characteristic act, not of the poet's mind, or the painter's, or the scientist's, but of the mind of man.

My stress here on the word *human* implies that there is a clear difference in this between the actions of men and those of other animals. Let me then start with a classical experiment with animals and children which Walter Hunter thought out in Chicago about 1910. That was the time when scientists were agog with the success of Ivan Pavlov in forming and changing the reflex actions of dogs, which Pavlov had first announced in 1903. Pavlov had been given a Nobel Prize the next year, in 1904; although in fairness I should say that the award did not cite his work on the conditioned reflex, but on the digestive gland.

Hunter duly trained some dogs and other animals on Pavlov's lines. They were taught that when a light came on over one of three tunnels out of their cage, that tunnel would be open; they could escape down it, and were rewarded with food if they did. But once he had fixed that conditioned reflex, Hunter added to it a deeper idea: he gave the mechanical experiment a new dimension, literally—the dimension of time. Now he no longer let the dog go to the lighted tunnel at once; instead, he put out the light, and then kept the dog waiting a little while before he let him go. In this way Hunter timed how long an animal can remember where he has last seen the signal light to his escape route.

The results were and are staggering. A dog or a rat forgets which one of three tunnels has been lit up within a matter of seconds—in Hunter's experiment, ten seconds at most. If you want such an animal to do much better than this, you must make the task much simpler: you must face him with only two tunnels to choose from. Even so, the best that Hunter could do was to have a dog remember for five minutes which one of two tunnels had been lit up.

I am not quoting these times as if they were exact and universal: they surely are not. Hunter's experiment, more than fifty years old now, had many faults of detail. For example, there were too few animals, they were oddly picked, and they did not all behave consistently. It may be unfair to test a dog for what he *saw*, when he commonly follows his nose rather than his eyes. It may be unfair to test any animal in the unnatural setting of a laboratory cage. And there are higher animals, such as chimpanzees and other primates, which certainly have longer memories than the animals that Hunter tried.

Yet when all these provisos have been made (and met, by more modern experiments) the facts are still startling and characteristic. An animal cannot recall a signal from the past for even a short fraction of the time that a man can—for even a short fraction of the time that a child can. Hunter made comparable tests with six-year-old children, and found, of course, that they were incomparably better than the best of his animals. There is a striking and basic difference between a man's ability to imagine something that he saw or experienced, and an animal's failure.

Animals make up for this by other and extraordinary gifts. The salmon and the carrier pigeon can find their way home as we cannot: they have, as it were, a practical memory that man cannot match. But their actions always depend on some form of habit: on instinct or on learning, which reproduce by rote a train of known responses. They do not depend, as human memory does, on calling to mind the recollection of absent things.

Where is it that the animal falls short? We get a clue to the answer, I think, when Hunter tells us how the animals in his experiment tried to fix their recollection. They most often pointed themselves at the light before it went out, as some gun dogs point rigidly at the game they scent—and get the name *pointer* from the posture. The animal makes ready to act by building the signal into its action. There is a primitive imagery in its stance, it seems to me; it is as if the animal were trying to fix the light on its mind by fixing it in its body. And indeed, how else can a dog mark and (as it were) name one of the three tunnels, when he has no such words as *left* and *right*, and no such numbers as *one, two, three?* The directed gesture of attention and readiness is perhaps the only symbolic device that the dog commands to hold on to the past, and thereby to guide himself into the future.

I used the verb *to imagine* a moment ago, and now I have some ground for giving it a meaning. *To imagine* means to make images and to move them about inside one's head in new arrangements. When you and I recall the past, we imagine it in this direct and homely sense. The tool that puts the human mind ahead of the animal is imagery. For us, memory does not demand the preoccupation that it demands in animals, and it lasts immensely longer, because we fix it in images or other substitute symbols. With the same symbolic vocabulary we spell out the future—not one but many futures, which we weigh one against another.

I am using the word *image* in a wide meaning, which does not restrict it to the mind's eye as a visual organ. An image in my usage is what Charles Peirce called a *sign*, without regard for its sensory quality. Peirce distinguished between different forms of signs, but there is no reason to make his distinction here, for the imagination works equally with them all, and that is why I call them all images.

Indeed, the most important images for human beings are simply words, which are abstract symbols. Animals do not have words, in our sense: there is no specific center for language in the brain of any animal, as there is in the human being. In this respect at least we know that the human imagination depends on a configuration in the brain that has only evolved in the last one or two million years. In the same period, evolution has greatly enlarged the front lobes in the human brain, which govern the sense of the past and the future; and it is a fair guess that they are probably the seat of our other images. (Part of the evidence for this guess is that damage to the front lobes in primates reduces them to the state of Hunter's animals.) If the guess turns out to be right, we shall know why man has come to look like a highbrow or an egghead: because otherwise there would not be room in his head for his imagination.

The images play out for us events which are not present to our senses, and thereby guard the past and create the future—a future that does not yet exist, and may never come to exist in that form. By contrast, the lack of symbolic ideas, or their rudimentary poverty, cuts off an animal from the past and the future alike, and imprisons him in the present. Of all the distinctions between man and animal, the characteristic gift which makes us human is the power to work with symbolic images: the gift of imagination.

This is really a remarkable finding. When Philip Sidney in 1580 defended poets (and all unconventional thinkers) from the Puritan charge that they were liars, he said that a maker must imagine things that are not. Halfway between Sidney and us, William Blake said, "What is now proved was once only imagined." About the same time, in 1796, Samuel Taylor Coleridge for the first time distinguished between the passive fancy and the active imagination, "the living Power and prime Agent of all human Perception." Now we see that they were right, and precisely right: the human gift is the gift of imagination—and that is not just a literary phrase.

Nor is it just a literary gift; it is, I repeat, characteristically human. Almost everything that we do that is worth doing is done in the first place in the mind's eye. The richness of human life is that we have many lives; we live the events that do not happen (and some that cannot) as vividly as those that do; and if thereby we die a thousand deaths, that is the price we pay for living a thousand lives. (A cat, of course, has only nine.) Literature is alive to us because we live its images, but so is any play of the mind—so is chess: the lines of play that we foresee and try in our heads and dismiss are as much a part of the game as the moves that we make. John Keats said that the unheard melodies are sweeter, and all chess players sadly recall that the combinations that they planned and which never came to be played were the best.

I make this point to remind you, insistently, that imagination is the manipulation of images in one's head; and that the rational manipulation belongs to that, as well as the literary and artistic manipulation. When a child begins to play games with things that stand for other things, with chairs or chessmen, he enters the gateway to reason and imagination together. For the human reason discovers new relations between things not by deduction, but by that unpredictable blend of speculation and insight that scientists call induction, which—like other forms of imagination—cannot be formalized. We see it at work when Walter Hunter inquires into a child's memory, as much as when Blake and Coleridge do. Only a restless and original mind would have asked Hunter's questions and could have conceived his experiments, in a science that was dominated by Pavlov's reflex arcs and was heading toward the behaviorism of John Watson.

Let me find a spectacular example for you from history. What is the most famous experiment that you had described to you as a child? I will hazard that it is the experiment that Galileo is said to have made in Sidney's age, in Pisa about 1590, by dropping two unequal balls from the Leaning Tower. There, we say, is a man in the modern mold, a man after our own hearts: he insisted on questioning the authority of Aristotle and St. Thomas Aquinas, and seeing with his own eyes whether (as they said) the heavy ball would reach the ground before the light one. Seeing is believing.

Yet seeing is also imagining. Galileo did challenge the authority of Aristotle, and he did look at his mechanics. But the eye that Galileo used was the mind's eye. He did not drop balls from the Leaning Tower of Pisa—and if he had, he would have got a very doubtful answer. Instead, Galileo made an imaginary experiment in his head, which I will describe as he did years later in the book he wrote after the Holy Office silenced him: *Discorsi . . . intorno a due nuove scienze,* which was smuggled out to be printed in the Netherlands in 1638.

Suppose, said Galileo, that you drop two unequal balls from the tower at the same time. And suppose that Aristotle is right—suppose that the heavy ball falls faster, so that it steadily gains on the light ball, and hits the ground first. Very well. Now imagine the same experiment done again, with only one difference: this time the two unequal balls are joined by a string between them. The heavy ball will again move ahead, but now the light ball holds it back and acts as a drag or brake. So the light ball will be speeded up and the heavy ball will be slowed down; they must reach the ground together because they are tied together, but they cannot reach the ground as quickly as the heavy ball alone. Yet the string between them has turned the two balls into a single mass which is heavier than either ball—and surely (according to Aristotle) this mass should therefore move faster than either ball? Galileo's imaginary experiment has uncovered a contradiction; he says trenchantly, "You see how, from your assumption that a heavier body falls more rapidly than a lighter one, I infer that a (still) heavier body falls more slowly." There is only one way out of the contradiction: the heavy ball and the light ball must fall at the same rate, so that they go on falling at the same rate when they are tied together.

This argument is not conclusive, for nature might be more subtle (when the two balls are joined) than Galileo has allowed. And yet it is something more important: it is suggestive, it is stimulating, it opens a new view—in a word, it is imaginative. It cannot be settled without an actual experiment, because nothing that we imagine can become knowledge until we have translated it into, and backed it by, real experience. The test of imagination is experience. But then, that is as true of literature and the arts as it is of science. In science, the imaginary experiment is tested by confronting it with physical experience; and in literature, the imaginative conception is tested by confronting it with human experience. The superficial speculation in science is dismissed because it is found to falsify nature; and the shallow work of art is discarded because it is found to be untrue to our own nature. So when Ella Wheeler Wilcox died in 1919, more people were reading her verses than Shakespeare's; yet in a few years her work was dead. It had been buried by its poverty of emotion and its trivialness of thought: which is to say that it had been proved to be as false to the nature of man as, say, Jean Baptiste Lamarck and Trofim Lysenko were false to the nature of inheritance. The strength of the imagination, its enriching power and excitement, lies in its interplay with reality—physical and emotional.

I doubt if there is much to choose here between science and the arts: the imagination is not much more free, and not much less free, in one than in the other. All great scientists have used their imagination freely, and let it ride them to outrageous conclusions without crying "Halt!" Albert Einstein fiddled with imaginary experiments from boyhood, and was wonderfully ignorant of the facts that they were supposed to bear on. When he wrote the first of his beautiful papers on the random movement of atoms, he did not know that the Brownian motion which it predicted could be seen in any laboratory. He was sixteen when he invented the paradox that he resolved ten years later, in 1905, in the theory of relativity, and it bulked much larger in his mind than the experiment of Albert Michelson and Edward Morley which had upset every other physicist since 1881. All his life Einstein loved to make up teasing puzzles like Galileo's, about falling lifts and the detection of gravity; and they carry the nub of the problems of general relativity on which he was working.

Indeed, it could not be otherwise. The power that man has over nature and himself, and that a dog lacks, lies in his command of imaginary experience. He alone has the symbols which fix the past and play with the future, possible and impossible. In the Renaissance, the symbolism of memory was thought to be mystical, and devices that were invented as mnemonics (by Giordano Bruno, for example, and by Robert Fludd) were interpreted as magic signs. The symbol is the tool which gives man his power, and it is the same tool whether the symbols are images or words, mathematical signs or mesons. And the symbols have a reach and a roundness that goes beyond their literal and practical meaning. They are the rich concepts under which the mind gathers many particulars into one name, and many instances into one general induction. When a man says *left* and *right*, he is outdistancing the dog not only in looking for a light; he is setting in train all the shifts of meaning, the overtones and the ambiguities, between *gauche* and *adroit* and *dexterous*, between *sinister* and the sense of right. When a man counts *one*, *two*, *three*, he is not only doing mathematics; he is on the path to the mysticism of numbers in Pythagoras and Vitruvius and Kepler, to the Trinity and the signs of the Zodiac.

I have described imagination as the ability to make images and to move them about inside one's head in new arrangements. This is the faculty that is specifically human, and it is the common root from which science and literature both spring and grow and flourish together. For they do flourish (and languish) together; the great ages of science are the great ages of all the arts, because in them powerful minds have taken fire from one another breathless and higgledy-piggledy, without asking too nicely whether they ought to tie their imagination to falling balls or a haunted island. Galileo and Shakespeare, who were born in the same year, grew into greatness in the same age; when Galileo was looking through his telescope at the moon, Shakespeare was writing *The Tempest* and all Europe was in ferment, from Johannes Kepler to Peter Paul Rubens, and from the first table of logarithms by John Napier to the Authorized Version of the Bible.

Let me end with a last and spirited example of the common inspiration of literature and science, because it is as much alive today as it was three hundred years ago. What I have in mind is man's ageless fantasy, to fly to the moon. I do not display this to you as a high scientific enterprise; on the contrary, I think we have more important discoveries to make here on earth than wait for us, beckoning, at the horned surface of the moon. Yet I cannot belittle the fascination which that ice-blue journey has had for the imagination of men, long before it drew us to our television screens to watch the tumbling astronauts. Plutarch and Lucian, Ariosto and Ben Jonson wrote about it, before the days of Jules Verne and H. G. Wells and science fiction. The seventeenth century was heady with new dreams and fables about voyages to the moon. Kepler wrote one full of deep scientific ideas, which (alas) simply got his mother accused of witchcraft. In England, Francis Godwin wrote a wild and splendid work, *The Man in the Moone*, and the astronomer John Wilkins wrote a wild and learned one, *The Discovery of a New World*. They did not draw a line between science and fancy; for example, they all tried to guess just where in the journey the earth's gravity would stop. Only Kepler understood that gravity has no boundary, and put a law to it—which happened to be the wrong law.

All this was a few years before Isaac Newton was born, and it was all in his head that day in 1666 when he sat in his mother's garden, a young man of twenty-three, and thought about the reach of gravity. This was how he came to conceive his brilliant image, that the moon is like a ball which has been thrown so hard that it falls exactly as fast as the horizon, all the way round the earth. The image will do for any satellite, and Newton modestly calculated how long therefore an astronaut would take to fall round the earth once. He made it ninety minutes, and we have all seen now that he was right; but Newton had no way to check that. Instead he went on to calculate how long in that case the distant moon would take to round the earth, if indeed it behaves like a thrown ball that falls in the earth's gravity, and if gravity obeyed a law of inverse squares. He found that the answer would be twenty-eight days.

In that telling figure, the imagination that day chimed with nature, and made a harmony. We shall hear an echo of that harmony on the day when we land on the moon, because it will be not a technical but an imaginative triumph, that reaches back to the beginning of modern science and literature both. All great acts of imagination are like this, in the arts and in science, and convince us because they fill out reality with a deeper sense of rightness. We start with the simplest vocabulary of images, with *left* and *right* and *one, two, three*, and before we know how it happened the words and the numbers have conspired to make a match with nature: we catch in them the pattern of mind and matter as one.

Suggestions for Discussion

1. Although Bronowski proposes to discuss the imagination of man, he begins his essay by describing an experiment conducted on animals. How does Bronowski use the experiment to explore or define man's imagination?

2. Bronowski uses the metaphor of "reaching" in the essay. What objects does the imagination reach for? What is the function of the metaphor in the argument?

3. Explain how Bronowski uses Galileo and Newton in his argument.

Suggestion for Writing

Write a paper in which you compare Bronowski the scientist with Whitman the poet, based entirely on this essay and the poem by Whitman "When I Heard the Learn'd Astronomer." Might Whitman have been surprised at the poetic nature of Bronowski the scientist?

Alan B. Durning

Asking How Much Is Enough

Alan B. Durning graduated with honors from Oberlin College and Conservatory from which he holds degrees in philosophy and music. He is a senior researcher at the Worldwatch Institute in Washington, D.C., investigating global problems. Among the papers he has either written or co-authored are "Action at the Grassroots: Fighting Poverty and Environmental Issues" (1988), "Poverty and the Environment: Reversing the Downward Spiral" (1989), and "Apartheid's Environmental Toll" (1990). He also contributes to various periodicals on these issues. This selection appeared in the *San Francisco Chronicle* (March 13, 1991) and is an excerpt from the Worldwatch Institute's 1991 "State-of-the-World Report."

Early in the age of affluence that followed World War II, an American retailing analyst named Victor Lebow proclaimed, "Our enormously productive economy . . . demands that we make consumption our way of life, that we convert the buying and use of goods into rituals, that we seek our spiritual satisfaction, our ego satisfaction, in consumption. . . . We need things consumed, burned up, worn out, replaced and discarded at an ever increasing rate."

Americans have responded to Lebow's call, and much of the world has followed.

Consumption has become a central pillar of life in industrial lands and is even embedded in social values. Opinion surveys in the world's two largest economies—Japan and the United States—show consumerist definitions of success becoming ever more prevalent.

In Taiwan, a billboard demands "Why Aren't You a Millionaire Yet?" The Japanese speak of the "new three sacred treasures": color television, air conditioning and the automobile.

The affluent life-style born in the United States is emulated by those who can afford it around the world. And many can: the average person today is 4.5 times richer than were his or her great-grandparents at the turn of the century.

Needless to say, that new global wealth is not evenly spread among the earth's people. One billion live in unprecedented luxury; 1 billion live in destitution. Even American children have more pocket money—$230 a year—than the half-billion poorest people alive.

Overconsumption by the world's fortunate is an environmental problem unmatched in severity by anything but perhaps population growth. Their surging exploitation of resources threatens to exhaust or unalterably disfigure forests, soils, water, air and climate.

Ironically, high consumption may be a mixed blessing in human terms, too. The time-honored values of integrity of character, good work, friend-

618

ship, family and community have often been sacrificed in the rush to riches.

Thus, many in the industrial lands have a sense that their world of plenty is somehow hollow—that, hoodwinked by a consumerist culture, they have been fruitlessly attempting to satisfy what are essentially social, psychological and spiritual needs with material things.

Of course, the opposite of overconsumption—poverty—is no solution to either environmental or human problems. It is infinitely worse for people and bad for the natural world too. Dispossessed peasants slash-and-burn their way into the rain forests of Latin America, and hungry nomads turn their herds out onto fragile African rangeland, reducing it to desert.

If environmental destruction results when people have either too little or too much, we are left to wonder how much is enough. What level of consumption can the earth support? When does having more cease to add appreciably to human satisfaction?

Answering these questions definitively is impossible, but for each of us in the world's consuming class, asking is essential nonetheless. Unless we see that more is not always better, our efforts to forestall ecological decline will be overwhelmed by our appetites.

In simplified terms, an economy's total burden on the ecological systems that undergird it is a function of three factors: the size of the population, average consumption and the broad set of technologies—everything from mundane clothesline to the most sophisticated satellite communications system—the economy uses to provide goods and services.

Changing agricultural patterns, transportation systems, urban design, energy uses and the like could radically reduce the total environmental damage caused by the consuming societies, while allowing those at the bottom of the economic ladder to rise without producing such egregious effects.

Japan, for example, uses a third as much energy as the Soviet Union to produce a dollar's worth of goods and services, and Norwegians use half as much paper and cardboard apiece as their neighbors in Sweden, though they are equals in literacy and richer in monetary terms.

Some guidance on what the earth can sustain emerges from an examination of current consumption patterns around the world.

For three of the most ecologically important types of consumption—transportation, diet and use of raw materials—the world's people are distributed unevenly over a vast range. Those at the bottom clearly fall below the "too little" line, while those at the top, in what could be called the cars-meat-and-disposables class, clearly consume too much.

About 1 billion people do most of their traveling, aside from the occasional donkey or bus ride, on foot, many of them never going more than 500 miles from their birthplaces. Unable to get to jobs easily, attend school or bring their complaints before government offices, they are severely hindered by the lack of transportation options.

The massive middle class of the world, numbering some 3 billion, travels by bus and bicycle. Mile for mile, bikes are cheaper than any other vehicles, costing less than $100 new in most of the Third World and requiring no fuel.

The world's automobile class is relatively small: only 8 percent of humans, about 400 million people, own cars. Their cars are directly responsible for an estimated 13 percent of carbon dioxide emissions from fossil fuels world-wide, along with air pollution, acid rain and a quarter-million traffic fatalities a year.

Car owners bear indirect responsibility for the far-reaching impacts of their chosen vehicle. The automobile makes itself indispensable: cities sprawl, public transit atrophies, shopping centers multiply, workplaces scatter. As suburbs spread, families start to need a car for each driver.

One-fifth of American households own three or more vehicles, more than half own at least two, and 65 percent of new American houses are built with two-car garages.

Today, working Americans spend nine hours a week behind the wheel. To make these homes-away-from-home more comfortable, 90 percent of new cars have air conditioning, doubling their contributions to climate change and adding emissions of ozone-depleting chlorofluorocarbons.

Some in the auto class are also members of a more select group: the global jet set. Although an estimated 1 billion people travel by air each year, the overwhelming majority of trips are taken by a small group. The 4 million Americans who account for 41 percent of domestic trips, for example, cover five times as many miles a year as average Americans.

Furthermore, because each mile traveled by air uses more energy than one traveled by car, jetsetters consume six-and-a-half times as much energy for transportation as other car-class members.

The global food consumption ladder has three rungs. At the bottom, the world's 630 million poorest people are unable to provide themselves with a healthy diet, according to the latest World Bank estimates.

On the next rung, the 3.4 billion grain eaters of the world's middle class get enough calories and plenty of plant-based protein, giving them the healthiest basic diet of the world's people. They typically receive less than 20 percent of their calories from fat, a level low enough to protect them from the consequences of excessive dietary fat.

The top of the ladder is populated by the meat eaters, those who obtain close to 40 percent of their calories from fat. These 1.25 billion people eat three times as much fats per person as the remaining 4 billion, mostly be-cause they eat so much red meat. The meat class pays the price of its diet in high death rates from the so-called diseases of affluence—heart disease, stroke and certain types of cancer.

The earth also pays for the high-fat diet. Indirectly, the meat-eating quar-ter of humanity consumes nearly 40 percent of the world's grain—grain that fattens the livestock they eat. Meat production is behind a substantial share of the environmental strains induced by the present global agricultural sys-tem, from soil erosion to overpumping of underground water.

In the extreme case of American beef, producing 2 pounds of steak re-quires 10 pounds of grain and the energy equivalent of 2 gallons of gasoline, not to mention the associated soil erosion, water consumption, pesticide and fertilizer runoff, groundwater depletion and emissions of the greenhouse gas methane.

Beyond the effects of livestock production, the affluent diet rings up an ecological bill through its heavy dependence on long-distance transport. North Europeans eat lettuce trucked from Greece and decorate their tables with flowers flown in from Kenya. Japanese eat turkey from the United States and ostrich from Australia.

One-fourth of the grapes eaten in the United States are grown 5,500 miles away, in Chile, and the typical mouthful of American food travels 1,000 miles from farm field to dinner plate.

Processing and packaging add further resource costs to the way the affluent eat. Extensively packaged foods are energy gluttons, but even seemingly simple foods need a surprising amount of energy to prepare: ounce for ounce, getting canned corn to the consumer takes 10 times the energy of providing fresh corn in season. Frozen corn, if left in the freezer for much time, takes even more energy.

To be sure, canned and frozen vegetables make a healthy diet easy even in the dead of winter; more of a concern are the new generation of microwave-ready instant meals. Loaded with disposable pans and multilayer packaging, their resource inputs are orders of magnitude larger than preparing the same dishes at home from scratch.

In raw material consumption, the same pattern emerges.

In the throwaway economy, packaging becomes an end in itself, disposables proliferate, and durability suffers. Four percent of consumer expenditures on goods in the United States goes for packaging—$225 a year.

Likewise, the Japanese use 30 million "disposable" single-roll cameras each year, and the British dump 12.5 billion diapers. Americans toss away 180 million razors annually, enough paper and plastic plates and cups to feed the world a picnic six times a year, and enough aluminum cans to make 6,000 DC-10 airplanes.

Where disposability and planned obsolescence fail to accelerate the trip from cash register to junk heap, fashion sometimes succeeds. Most clothing goes out of style long before it is worn out; lately, the realm of fashion has even colonized sports footwear. Kevin Ventrudo, chief financial officer of California-based L.A. Gear, which saw sales multiply 50 times in four years, told the Washington Post, "If you talk about shoe performance, you only need one or two pairs. If you're talking fashion, you're talking endless pairs of shoes."

In transportation, diet and use of raw materials, as consumption rises on the economic scale, so does waste—both of resources and of health. Bicycles and public transit are cheaper, more efficient and healthier transport options than cars. A diet founded on the basics of grains and water is gentle to the earth and the body.

And a lifestyle that makes full use of raw materials for durable goods without succumbing to the throwaway mentality is ecologically sound while still affording many of the comforts of modernity.

Suggestions for Discussion

1. How are luxury and poverty both bad for the state of the world's environment, according to Durning?

2. Discuss the opening quotation that increased consumption has become the most significant goal in America and other industrialized countries. Relate this to the Taiwan billboard and the Japanese version of the "new three sacred treasures."

3. Why is more consumption not always the better goal for consumers? What factors determine what is better?

4. Discuss Durning's comments on both the inequities and consequences of excessive use of fuel, consumption of food, and the "throwaway" economy.

Suggestions for Writing

1. Durning makes certain assumptions about eating and what foods are best for people. Write a short research paper in which you either confirm or contradict his statements. In order to write this paper, you will have to study the consequences of eating certain foods.

2. Write a paper in which you discuss "throwaway" consumption. Give explicit examples with which you are familiar. Do you agree with Durning's assertions? Would you be willing personally to give up throwaway consumption?

Grant Fjermedal

Artificial Intelligence

Grant Fjermedal has written Magic Bullets: A Revolution in Cancer Treatment (1984) and The Tomorrow Makers: A Brave New World of Living Brain Machines (1986). This essay, published in Omni, an excerpt from The Tomorrow Makers, presents in dramatic fashion the choice that people one day may be able to make between dying or continuing to live forever by transferring one's capacity for thinking from one's brain to a machine.

I'm sure that Hans Moravec is at least as sane as I am, but he certainly brought to mind the classic mad scientist as we sat in his fifth-floor office at Carnegie-Mellon University on a dark and stormy night. It was nearly midnight, and he mixed for each of us a bowl of chocolate milk and Cheerios, with slices of banana piled on top.

Then, with banana-slicing knife in hand, Moravec, the senior research scientist at Carnegie-Mellon's Mobile Robot Laboratory, outlined for me how he could create a robotic immortality for Everyman, a deathless universe in which life would go on forever. By creating computer copies of our minds and transferring, or downloading, this program into robotic bodies, Moravec explained, humans could survive for centuries.

"You are in an operating room. A robot brain surgeon is in attendance. . . . Your skull but not your brain is anesthetized. You are fully conscious. The surgeon opens your braincase and peers inside." This is how

Moravec described the process in a paper he wrote called "Robots That Rove." The robotic surgeon's "attention is directed at a small clump of about one hundred neurons somewhere near the surface. Using high-resolution 3-D nuclear-magnetic-resonance holography, phased-array radio encephalography, and ultrasonic radar, the surgeon determines the three-dimensional structure and chemical makeup of that neural clump. It writes a program that models the behavior of the clump and starts it running on a small portion of the computer sitting next to you."

That computer sitting next to you in the operating room would in effect be your new brain. As each area of your brain was analyzed and simulated, the accuracy of the simulation would be tested as you pressed a button to shift between the area of the brain just copied and the simulation. When you couldn't tell the difference between the original and the copy, the surgeon would transfer the simulation of your brain into the new, computerized one and repeat the process on the next area of your biological brain.

"Though you have not lost consciousness or even your train of thought, your mind—some would say soul—has been removed from the brain and transferred to a machine," Moravec said, "In a final step your old body is disconnected. The computer is installed in a shiny new one, in the style, color, and material of your choice."

As we sat around Moravec's office I asked what would become of the original human body after the downloading. "You just don't bother waking it up again if the copying went successfully," he said. "It's so messy. Humans have got so many problems that you might just want to leave it retired. You don't take your junker car out if you've got a new one."

Moravec's idea is the ultimate in life insurance: Once one copy of the brain's contents has been made, it will be easy to make multiple backup copies, and these could be stashed in hiding places around the world, allowing you to embark on any sort of adventure without having to worry about aging or death. As decades pass into centuries you could travel the globe and then the solar system and beyond—always keeping an eye out for the latest in robotic bodies into which you could transfer your computer mind.

If living forever weren't enough, you could live forever several times over by activating some of your backup copies and sending different versions of yourself out to see the world. "You could have parallel experiences and merge the memories later," Moravec explained.

In the weeks and months that followed my stay at Carnegie-Mellon, I was intrigued by how many researchers seemed to believe downloading would come to pass. The only point of disagreement was when—certainly a big consideration to those of us still knocking around in mortal bodies. Although some of the researchers I spoke with at Carnegie-Mellon, MIT, and Stanford and in Japan thought that downloading was still generations away, there were others who believed achieving robotic immortality was imminent and seemed driven by private passions never to die.

The significance of the door Moravec is trying to open is not lost on others. Olin Shivers, a Carnegie-Mellon graduate student who works closely with Moravec as well as with Allen Newell, one of the founding fathers of artificial intelligence, told me, "Moravec wants to design a creature, and my professor Newell wants to design a creature. We are all, in a sense, trying to play God."

At MIT I was surprised to find Moravec's concept of downloading given consideration by Marvin Minsky, Donner Professor of Science and another father of artificial intelligence. Minsky is trying to learn how the billions of brain cells work together to allow a person to think and remember. If he succeeds, it will be a big step toward figuring out how to join perhaps billions of computer circuits together to allow a computer to receive the entire contents of the human mind.

"If a person is like a machine, once you get a wiring diagram of how he works, you can make copies," Minsky told me.

Although Minsky doesn't think he'll live long enough to download (he's fifty-seven now), he would consider it. "I think it would be a great thing to do," he said. "I've spent a long time learning things, and I'd hate to see it all go away."

Minsky also said he would have no qualms about waving good-bye to his human body and taking up residence within a robot. "Why not avoid getting sick and things like that?" he asked. "It's hard to see anything against it. I think people will get fed up with bodies after a while. Then you'll have another population problem: You'll have all the people of the past, as well as the new ones."

Another believer is Danny Hillis, one of Minsky's Ph.D. students and the founding scientist of Thinking Machines, a Cambridge-based company that is trying to create the kind of computer that might someday receive the contents of a brain. During my research several computer scientists would point to Hillis's connection machine as an example of a new order of computer architecture, one that's comparable to the human brain. (Hillis's connection machine doesn't have one large central processing unit as other computers do but a network of 64,000 small units—roughly analogous in concept, if not in size, to the brain's network of 40 billion neuronal processing units.)

"I've added up the things I want to do in my life, and it's about fifteen hundred years' worth of stuff," Hillis, now twenty-eight, told me one day as we stood out on the sixth-floor sun deck of the Thinking Machines building. "I enjoy having a body as much as anyone else does, but if it's a choice between downloading into a computer—even one that's stuck in a room someplace—and still being able to think versus just dying, I would certainly take that opportunity to think."

Gerald J. Sussman, a thirty-six-year-old MIT professor and a computer hacker of historic proportions, expressed similar sentiments. "Everyone would like to be immortal. I don't think the time is quite right, but it's close. I'm afraid, unfortunately, that I'm in the last generation to die."

"Do you really think that we're that close?" I asked.

"Yes," he answered, which reminded me of something Moravec had written not too long ago: "We are on a threshold of a change in the universe comparable to the transition from nonlife to life."

Suggestions for Discussion

1. Summarize the major thesis of this brief essay. Is it one that you take seriously? Explain your response.

2. What method does Fjermedal use to develop his essay? What is its tone? Is there an element of ambiguity in the tone?

3. Define the term *downloading.*

4. Explain the significance of the quotation in the last paragraph.

5. How close does this essay come to what we think of as science fiction?

Suggestions for Writing

1. Write an essay in which you describe a world inhabited by surrogate brains. What would be the advantages, disadvantages of such a world? Is it one that you would want to inhabit? Explain your response to this question.

2. Using this essay and others in this text, write a paper examining the directions of research in the fields of computer science.

Edward O. Wilson

Is Humanity Suicidal?

Edward O. Wilson (b. 1929) was born in Birmingham, Alabama, and educated at the University of Alabama and Harvard. The Frank B. Baird, Jr. Professor of Science at Harvard, he has taught at many universities in the United States and abroad and holds a number of honorary degrees. Having won many prizes for his research, he also was awarded the Pulitzer Prize for General Non-Fiction in 1979, demonstrating that he belongs to that limited number of distinguished scientists who also write extremely well. He is a member of the National Academy of Science, a Fellow of the American Academy of Arts and Science, and an honorary member of the Royal Society of London. In "Is Humanity Suicidal?" Wilson states what human beings must do to avoid the eventual disappearance of the species *Homo sapiens* on earth.

Imagine that on an icy moon of Jupiter—say, Ganymede—the space station of an alien civilization is concealed. For millions of years its scientists have closely watched the earth. Because their law prevents settlement on a living planet, they have tracked the surface by means of satellites equipped with sophisticated sensors, mapping the spread of large assemblages of organisms, from forests, grasslands and tundras to coral reefs and the vast planktonic meadows of the sea. They have recorded millennial cycles in the climate, interrupted by the advance and retreat of glaciers and scattershot volcanic eruptions.

The watchers have been waiting for what might be called the Moment. When it comes, occupying only a few centuries and thus a mere tick in geological time, the forests shrink back to less than half their original cover. Atmospheric carbon dioxide rises to the highest level in 100,000 years. The ozone layer of the stratosphere thins, and holes open at the poles. Plumes of nitrous oxide and other toxins rise from fires in South America and Africa, settle in the upper troposphere and drift eastward across the oceans. At night the land surface brightens with millions of pinpoints of light, which coalesce into blazing swaths across Europe, Japan and eastern North America. A semicircle of fire spreads from gas flares around the Persian Gulf.

It was all but inevitable, the watchers might tell us if we met them, that from the great diversity of large animals, one species or another would eventually gain intelligent control of Earth. That role has fallen to *Homo sapiens*, a primate risen in Africa from a lineage that split away from the chimpanzee line five to eight million years ago. Unlike any creature that lived before, we have become a geophysical force, swiftly changing the atmosphere and climate as well as the composition of the world's fauna and flora. Now in the midst of a population explosion, the human species has doubled to 5.5 billion during the past 50 years. It is scheduled to double again in the next 50 years. No other single species in evolutionary history has even remotely approached the sheer mass in protoplasm generated by humanity.

Darwin's dice have rolled badly for Earth. It was a misfortune for the living world in particular, many scientists believe, that a carnivorous primate and not some more benign form of animal made the breakthrough. Our species retains hereditary traits that add greatly to our destructive impact. We are tribal and aggressively territorial, intent on private space beyond minimal requirements and oriented by selfish sexual and reproductive drives. Cooperation beyond the family and tribal levels comes hard.

Worse, our liking for meat causes us to use the sun's energy at low efficiency. It is a general rule of ecology that (very roughly) only about 10 percent of the sun's energy captured by photosynthesis to produce plant tissue is converted into energy in the tissue of herbivores, the animals that eat the plants. Of that amount, 10 percent reaches the tissue of the carnivores feeding on the herbivores. Similarly, only 10 percent is transferred to carnivores that eat carnivores. And so on for another step or two. In a wetlands chain that runs from marsh grass to grasshopper to warbler to hawk, the energy captured during green production shrinks a thousandfold.

In other words, it takes a great deal of grass to support a hawk. Human beings, like hawks, are top carnivores, at the end of the food chain whenever they eat meat, two or more links removed from the plants; if chicken, for example, two links, and if tuna, four links. Even with most societies confined today to a mostly vegetarian diet, humanity is gobbling up a large part of the rest of the living world. We appropriate between 20 and 40 percent of the sun's energy that would otherwise be fixed into the tissue of natural vegetation, principally by our consumption of crops and timber, construction of buildings and roadways and the creation of wastelands. In the relentless search for more food, we have reduced animal life in lakes, rivers and now, increasingly, the open ocean. And everywhere we pollute the air and water, lower water tables and extinguish species.

The human species is, in a word, an environmental abnormality. It is possible that intelligence in the wrong kind of species was foreordained to be a fatal combination for the biosphere. Perhaps a law of evolution is that intelligence usually extinguishes itself.

This admittedly dour scenario is based on what can be termed the juggernaut theory of human nature, which holds that people are programmed by their genetic heritage to be so selfish that a sense of global responsibility will come too late. Individuals place themselves first, family second, tribe third and the rest of the world a distant fourth. Their genes also predispose them to plan ahead for one or two generations at most. They fret over the petty problems and conflicts of their daily lives and respond swiftly and often ferociously to slight challenges to their status and tribal security. But oddly, as psychologists have discovered, people also tend to underestimate both the likelihood and impact of such natural disasters as major earthquakes and great storms.

The reason for this myopic fog, evolutionary biologists contend, is that it was actually advantageous during all but the last few millennia of the two million years of existence of the genus *Homo*. The brain evolved into its present form during this long stretch of evolutionary time, during which people existed in small, preliterate hunter-gatherer bands. Life was precarious and short. A premium was placed on close attention to the near future and early reproduction, and little else. Disasters of a magnitude that occur only once every few centuries were forgotten or transmuted into myth. So today the mind still works comfortably backward and forward for only a few years, spanning a period not exceeding one or two generations. Those in past ages whose genes inclined them to short-term thinking lived longer and had more children than those who did not. Prophets never enjoyed a Darwinian edge.

The rules have recently changed, however. Global crises are rising within the life span of the generation now coming of age, a foreshortening that may explain why young people express more concern about the environment than do their elders. The time scale has contracted because of the exponential growth in both the human population and technologies impacting the environment. Exponential growth is basically the same as the increase of wealth by compound interest. The larger the population, the faster the growth; the faster the growth, the sooner the population becomes still larger. In Nigeria, to cite one of our more fecund nations, the population is expected to double from its 1988 level to 216 million by the year 2010. If the same rate of growth were to continue to 2110, its population would exceed that of the entire present population of the world.

With people everywhere seeking a better quality of life, the search for resources is expanding even faster than the population. The demand is being met by an increase in scientific knowledge, which doubles every 10 to 15 years. It is accelerated further by a parallel rise in environment-devouring technology. Because Earth is finite in many resources that determine the quality of life—including arable soil, nutrients, fresh water and space for natural ecosystems—doubling of consumption at constant time intervals can bring disaster with shocking suddenness. Even when a nonrenewable resource has been only half used, it is still only one interval away from the end. Ecologists like to make this point with the French riddle of the lily pond. At first there is only one lily pad in the pond, but the next day it doubles, and thereafter each of its descendants doubles. The pond completely fills with lily pads in 30 days. When is the pond exactly half full? Answer: on the 29th day.

Yet, mathematical exercises aside, who can safely measure the human capacity to overcome the perceived limits of Earth? The question of central interest is this: Are we racing to the brink of an abyss, or are we just gathering speed for a takeoff to a wonderful future? The crystal ball is clouded; the human condition baffles all the more because it is both unprecedented and bizarre, almost beyond understanding.

In the midst of uncertainty, opinions on the human prospect have tended to fall loosely into two schools. The first, exemptionalism, holds that since humankind is transcendent in intelligence and spirit, so must our species have been released from the iron laws of ecology that bind all other species. No matter how serious the problem, civilized human beings, by ingenuity, force of will and—who knows—divine dispensation, will find a solution.

Population growth? Good for the economy, claim some of the exemptionalists, and in any case a basic human right, so let it run. Land shortages? Try fusion energy to power the desalting of sea water, then reclaim the world's deserts. (The process might be assisted by towing icebergs to coastal pipelines.) Species going extinct? Not to worry. That is nature's way. Think of humankind as only the latest in a long line of exterminating agents in geological time. In any case, because our species has pulled free of old-style, mindless Nature, we have begun a different order of life. Evolution should now be allowed to proceed along this new trajectory. Finally, resources? The planet has more than enough resources to last indefinitely, if human genius is allowed to address each new problem in turn, without alarmist and unreasonable restrictions imposed on economic development. So hold the course, and touch the brakes lightly.

The opposing idea of reality is environmentalism, which sees humanity as a biological species tightly dependent on the natural world. As formidable as our intellect may be and as fierce our spirit, the argument goes, those qualities are not enough to free us from the constraints of the natural environment in which our human ancestors evolved. We cannot draw confidence from successful solutions to the smaller problems of the past. Many of Earth's vital resources are about to be exhausted, its atmospheric chemistry is deteriorating and human populations have already grown dangerously large. Natural ecosystems, the wellsprings of a healthful environment, are being irreversibly degraded.

At the heart of the environmentalist world view is the conviction that human physical and spiritual health depends on sustaining the planet in a relatively unaltered state. Earth is our home in the full, genetic sense, where humanity and its ancestors existed for all the millions of years of their evolution. Natural ecosystems—forests, coral reefs, marine blue waters—maintain the world exactly as we would wish it to be maintained. When we debase the global environment and extinguish the variety of life, we are dismantling a support system that is too complex to understand, let alone replace, in the foreseeable future. Space scientists theorize the existence of a virtually unlimited array of other planetary environments, almost all of which are uncongenial to human life. Our own Mother Earth, lately called Gaia, is a specialized conglomerate of organisms and the physical environment they create on a day-to-day basis, which can be destabilized and turned lethal by careless activity. We run the risk, conclude the environmentalists, of beaching ourselves upon alien shores like a great confused pod of pilot whales.

If I have not done so enough already by tone of voice, I will now place myself solidly in the environmentalist school, but not so radical as to wish a turning back of the clock, not given to driving spikes into Douglas firs to prevent logging and distinctly uneasy with such hybrid movements as ecofeminism, which holds that Mother Earth is a nurturing home for all life and should be revered and loved as in premodern (paleolithic and archaic) societies and that ecosystematic abuse is rooted in androcentric—that is to say, male-dominated—concepts, values and institutions.

Still, however soaked in androcentric culture, I am radical enough to take seriously the question heard with increasing frequency: Is humanity suicidal? Is the drive to environmental conquest and self-propagation embedded so deeply in our genes as to be unstoppable?

My short answer—opinion if you wish—is that humanity is not suicidal, at least not in the sense just stated. We are smart enough and have time enough to avoid an environmental catastrophe of civilization-threatening dimensions. But the technical problems are sufficiently formidable to require a redirection of much of science and technology, and the ethical issues are so basic as to force a reconsideration of our self-image as a species.

There are reasons for optimism, reasons to believe that we have entered what might someday be generously called the Century of the Environment. The United Nations Conference on Environment and Development, held in Rio de Janeiro in June 1992, attracted more than 120 heads of government, the largest number ever assembled, and helped move environmental issues closer to the political center stage; on November 18, 1992, more than 1,500 senior scientists from 69 countries issued a "Warning to Humanity," stating that overpopulation and environmental deterioration put the very future of life at risk. The greening of religion has become a global trend, with theologians and religious leaders addressing environmental problems as a moral issue. In May 1992, leaders of most of the major American denominations met with scientists as guests of members of the United States Senate to formulate a "Joint Appeal by Religion and Science for the Environment." Conservation of biodiversity is increasingly seen by both national governments and major landowners as important to their country's future. Indonesia, home to a large part of the native Asian plant and animal species, has begun to shift to land-management practices that conserve and sustainably develop the remaining rain forests. Costa Rica has created a National Institute of Biodiversity. A pan-African institute for biodiversity research and management has been founded, with headquarters in Zimbabwe.

Finally, there are favorable demographic signs. The rate of population increase is declining on all continents, although it is still well above zero almost everywhere and remains especially high in sub-Saharan Africa. Despite entrenched traditions and religious beliefs, the desire to use contraceptives in family planning is spreading. Demographers estimate that if the demand were fully met, this action alone would reduce the eventual stabilized population by more than two billion.

In summary, the will is there. Yet the awful truth remains that a large part of humanity will suffer no matter what is done. The number of people living in absolute poverty has risen during the past 20 years to nearly one billion and is expected to increase another 100 million by the end of the decade. Whatever progress has been made in the developing countries, and that includes an overall improvement in the average standard of living, is threatened by a continuance of rapid population growth and the deterioration of forests and arable soil.

Our hopes must be chastened further still, and this is in my opinion the central issue, by a key and seldom-recognized distinction between the nonliving and living environments. Science and the political process can be adapted to manage the nonliving, physical environment. The human hand is now upon the physical homeostat. The ozone layer can be mostly restored to the upper atmosphere by elimination of CFCs, with these substances peaking at six times the present level and then subsiding during the next half century. Also, with procedures that will prove far more difficult and initially expensive, carbon dioxide and other greenhouse gases can be pulled back to concentrations that slow global warming.

The human hand, however, is not upon the biological homeostat. There is no way in sight to micromanage the natural ecosystems and the millions of species they contain. That feat might be accomplished by generations to come, but then it will be too late for the ecosystems—and perhaps for us. Despite the seemingly bottomless nature of creation, humankind has been chipping away at its diversity, and Earth is destined to become an impoverished planet within a century if present trends continue. Mass extinctions are being reported with increasing frequency in every part of the world. They include half the freshwater fishes of peninsular Malaysia, 10 birds native to Cebu in the Philippines, half the 41 tree snails of Oahu, 44 of the 68 shallow-water mussels of the Tennessee River shoals, as many as 90 plant species growing on the Centinela Ridge in Ecuador, and in the United States as a whole, about 200 plant species, with another 680 species and races now classified as in danger of extinction. The main cause is the destruction of natural habitats, especially tropical forests. Close behind, especially on the Hawaiian archipelago and other islands, is the introduction of rats, pigs, beard grass, lantana and other exotic organisms that outbreed and extirpate native species.

The few thousand biologists worldwide who specialize in diversity are aware that they can witness and report no more than a very small percentage of the extinctions actually occurring. The reason is that they have facilities to keep track of only a tiny fraction of the millions of species and a sliver of the planet's surface on a yearly basis. They have devised a rule of thumb to characterize the situation: that whenever careful studies are made of habitats before and after disturbance, extinctions almost always come to light. The corollary: the great majority of extinctions are never observed. Vast numbers of species are apparently vanishing before they can be discovered and named.

There is a way, nonetheless, to estimate the rate of loss indirectly. Independent studies around the world and in fresh and marine waters have revealed a robust connection between the size of a habitat and the amount of biodiversity it contains. Even a small loss in area reduces the number of species. The relation is such that when the area of the habitat is cut to a tenth of its original cover, the number of species eventually drops by roughly one-half. Tropical rain forests, thought to harbor a majority of Earth's species (the reason conservationists get so exercised about rain forests), are being reduced by nearly that magnitude. At the present time they occupy about the same area as that of the 48 conterminous United States, representing a little less than half their original, prehistoric cover; and they are shrinking each year by about 2 percent, an amount equal to the state of Florida. If the typical value (that is, 90 percent area loss causes 50 percent eventual extinction) is applied, the projected loss of species due to rain forest destruction worldwide is half a percent across the board for all kinds of plants, animals and microorganisms.

When area reduction and all the other extinction agents are considered together, it is reasonable to project a reduction by 20 percent or more of the rain forest species by the year 2020, climbing to 50 percent or more by mid-century, if nothing is done to change current practice. Comparable erosion is likely in other environments now under assault, including many coral reefs and Mediterranean-type heathlands of Western Australia, South Africa and California.

The ongoing loss will not be replaced by evolution in any period of time that has meaning for humanity. Extinction is now proceeding thousands of times faster than the production of new species. The average life span of a species and its descendants in past geological eras varied according to group (like mollusks or echinoderms or flowering plants) from about 1 to 10 million years. During the past 500 million years, there have been five great extinction spasms comparable to the one now being inaugurated by human expansion. The latest, evidently caused by the strike of an asteroid, ended the Age of Reptiles 66 million years ago. In each case it took more than 10 million years for evolution to completely replenish the biodiversity lost. And that was in an otherwise undisturbed natural environment. Humanity is now destroying most of the habitats where evolution can occur.

The surviving biosphere remains the great unknown of Earth in many respects. On the practical side, it is hard even to imagine what other species have to offer in the way of new pharmaceuticals, crops, fibers, petroleum substitutes and other products. We have only a poor grasp of the ecosystem services by which other organisms cleanse the water, turn soil into a fertile living cover and manufacture the very air we breathe. We sense but do not fully understand what the highly diverse natural world means to our esthetic pleasure and mental well-being.

Scientists are unprepared to manage a declining biosphere. To illustrate, consider the following mission they might be given. The last remnant of a rain forest is about to be cut over. Environmentalists are stymied. The contracts have been signed, and local landowners and politicians are intransigent. In a final desperate move, a team of biologists is scrambled in an attempt to preserve the biodiversity by extraordinary means. Their assignment is the following: collect samples of all the species of organisms quickly, before the cutting starts; maintain the species in zoos, gardens and laboratory cultures or else deep-freeze samples of the tissues in liquid nitrogen, and finally, establish the procedure by which the entire community can be reassembled on empty ground at a later date, when social and economic conditions have improved.

The biologists cannot accomplish this task, not if thousands of them came with a billion-dollar budget. They cannot even imagine how to do it. In the forest patch live legions of species: perhaps 300 birds, 500 butterflies, 200 ants, 50,000 beetles, 1,000 trees, 5,000 fungi, tens of thousands of bacteria and so on down a long roster of major groups. Each species occupies a precise niche, demanding a certain place, an exact microclimate, particular nutrients and temperature and humidity cycles with specified timing to trigger phases of the life cycle. Many, perhaps most, of the species are locked in symbioses with other species; they cannot survive and reproduce unless arrayed with their partners in the correct idiosyncratic configurations.

Even if the biologists pulled off the taxonomic equivalent of the Manhattan Project, sorting and preserving cultures of all the species, they could not then put the community back together again. It would be like unscrambling an egg with a pair of spoons. The biology of the micro-organisms needed to reanimate the soil would be mostly unknown. The pollinators of most of the flowers and the correct timing of their appearance could only be guessed. The "assembly rules," the sequence in which species must be allowed to colonize in order to coexist indefinitely, would remain in the realm of theory.

In its neglect of the rest of life, exemptionalism fails definitively. To move ahead as though scientific and entrepreneurial genius will solve each crisis that arises implies that the declining biosphere can be similarly manipulated. But the world is too complicated to be turned into a garden. There is no biological homeostat that can be worked by humanity; to believe otherwise is to risk reducing a large part of Earth to a wasteland.

The environmentalist vision, prudential and less exuberant than exemptionalism, is closer to reality. It sees humanity entering a bottleneck unique in history, constricted by population and economic pressures. In order to pass through to the other side, within perhaps 50 to 100 years, more science and entrepreneurship will have to be devoted to stabilizing the global environment. That can be accomplished, according to expert consensus, only by halting population growth and devising a wiser use of resources than has been accomplished to date. And wise use for the living world in particular means preserving the surviving ecosystems, micromanaging them only enough to save the biodiversity they contain, until such time as they can be understood and employed in the fullest sense for human benefit.

Suggestions for Discussion

1. Wilson's essay begins by imagining that at the space station of an alien civilization the environmental history of our planet has been secretly tracked. What advantage does he gain in using this introductory device?

2. Explain Wilson's statement in the fourth paragraph: "Darwin's dice have rolled badly for Earth." What does he mean when he states later in the essay, "It is possible that intelligence in the wrong kind of species was foreordained to be a fatal combination for the biosphere"?

3. Who are the "exemptionalists"? What do they believe about humans' ability to control the environment? How does Wilson interpret their beliefs?

4. What is the "environmentalist world view"? To which school of belief does Wilson belong? Why?

5. According to the author, what can humankind do to save itself from extinction?

Suggestions for Writing

1. Write a paper explaining the difficulties we face in trying to protect the rain forests. Why is it necessary for us to attempt to do so?

2. Is Wilson optimistic about the future of human beings on earth? Write a paper carefully explaining his position. Do you agree? Explain your own position on the issue.

Niles Eldredge

Creationism Isn't Science

Niles Eldredge (b. 1925), born in Brooklyn, New York, and educated as an undergraduate and graduate at Columbia University, is the curator of the Department of Invertebrates at the American Museum of Natural History in New York. The author of a number of books, including *Time Frame* (1985), *Life Pulse* (1987), and *Miner's Canary* (1991), he is a scientist deeply concerned about Darwinism and other theories of evolution that derive from Charles Darwin's *On the Origin of Species* (1859). Following the publication of Darwin's book, a violent argument ensued between science and religion that appeared to come to a close after the Scopes Trial in 1925. In recent years, however, with the rise of fundamentalist religion in the United States, an argument has flowered that creationism has as much validity as a theory as Darwin's theory of evolution. Eldredge attempts to show in this essay why the two theories are not equal and how the zeal of creationists is undermining the teaching of science in the schools.

Despite this country's apparent modernism, the creationist movement once again is growing. The news media proclaimed a juryless trial in California as "Scopes II" and those who cling to the myth of progress wonder how the country could revert to the primitive state it was in when Darrow and Bryan battled it out in the hot summer of 1925 in Dayton, Tennessee. But the sad truth is that we have not progressed. Creationism never completely disappeared as a political, religious, and educational issue. Scopes was convicted of violating the Tennessee statute forbidding the teaching of the evolutionary origins of mankind (although in fact he was ill and never really did teach the evolution segment of the curriculum). The result was a drastic cutback in serious discussion of evolution in many high school texts until it became respectable again in the 1960s.

Although technological advances since 1925 have been prodigious, and although science news magazines are springing up like toadstools, the American public appears to be as badly informed about the real nature of science as it ever was. Such undiluted ignorance, coupled with the strong anti-intellectual tradition in the US, provides a congenial climate for creationism to leap once more to the fore, along with school prayer, sex education, Proposition 13, and the other favorite issues of the populist, conservative movement. Much of the success of recent creationist efforts lies in a prior failure to educate our children about science—how it is done, by whom, and how its results are to be interpreted.

Today's creationists usually cry for "equal time" rather than for actually substituting the Genesis version of the origin of things for the explanations preferred by modern science. (The recent trial in California is an anachronism in this respect because the plaintiff simply affirmed that his rights of religious freedom were abrogated by teaching him that man "descended from

633

apes"). At the heart of the creationists' contemporary political argument is an appeal to the time-honored American sense of fair play. "Look," they say, "evolution is only a theory. Scientists cannot agree on all details either of the exact course of evolutionary history, or how evolution actually takes place." True enough. Creationists then declare that many scientists have grave doubts that evolution actually has occurred—a charge echoed by Ronald Reagan during the campaign, and definitely false. They argue that since evolution is only a theory, why not, in the spirit of fair play, give equal time to equally plausible explanations of the origin of the cosmos, of life on earth, and of mankind? Why not indeed?

The creationist argument equates a biological, evolutionary system with a non-scientific system of explaining life's exuberant diversity. Both systems are presented as authoritarian, and here lies the real tragedy of American science education: the public is depressingly willing to see merit in the "fair play, equal time" argument precisely because it views science almost wholly in this authoritarian vein. The public is bombarded with a constant stream of oracular pronouncements of new discoveries, new truths, and medical and technological innovations, but the American education system gives most people no effective choice but to ignore, accept on faith, or reject out of hand each new scientific finding. Scientists themselves promote an Olympian status for their profession; it's small wonder that the public has a tough time deciding which set of authoritarian pronouncements to heed. So why not present them all and let each person choose his or her own set of beliefs?

Of course, there has to be some willingness to accept the expertise of specialists. Although most of us "believe" the earth is spherical, how many of us can design and perform an experiment to show that it must be so? But to stress the authoritarianism of science is to miss its essence. Science is the enterprise of comparing alternative ideas about what the cosmos is, how it works, and how it came to be. Some ideas are better than others, and the criterion for judging which are better is simply the relative power of different ideas to fit our observations. The goal is greater understanding of the natural universe. The method consists of constantly challenging received ideas, modifying them, or, best of all, replacing them with better ones.

So science is ideas, and the ideas are acknowledged to be merely approximations to the truth. Nothing could be further from authoritarianism—dogmatic assertions of what is true. Scientists deal with ideas that appear to be the best (the closest to the truth) given what they think they know about the universe at any given moment. If scientists frequently act as if their ideas *are* the truth, they are simply showing their humanity. But the human quest for a rational coming-to-grips with the cosmos recognizes imperfection in observation and thought, and incorporates the frailty into its method. Creationists disdain this quest, preferring the wholly authoritarian, allegedly "revealed" truth of divine creation as an understanding of our beginnings. At the same time they present disagreement among scientists as an expression of scientific failure in the realm of evolutionary biology.

To the charge that "evolution is *only* a theory," we say "all science is theory." Theories are ideas, or complex sets of ideas, which explain some aspect of the natural world. Competing theories sometimes coexist until one drives the other out, or until both are discarded in favor of yet another theory. But it is true that one major theory usually holds sway at any one time. All biologists, including biochemists, molecular geneticists, physiologists, behaviorists, and anatomists, see a pattern of similarity interlocking the spectrum of millions of species, from bacteria to timber wolves. Darwin finally convinced the world that this pattern of similarity is neatly explained by "descent with modification." If we imagine a genealogical system where an ancestor produces one or more descendants, we get a pattern of progressive similarity. The whole array of ancestors and descendants will share some feature inherited from the first ancestor; as each novelty appears, it is shared only with later descendants. All forms of life have the nucleic acid RNA. One major branch of life, the vertebrates, all share backbones. All mammals have three inner ear bones, hair, and mammary glands. All dogs share features not found in other carnivores, such as cats. In other words, dogs share similarities among themselves in addition to having general mammalian features, plus general vertebrate features, as well as anatomical and biochemical similarities shared with the rest of life.

How do we test the basic notion that life has evolved? The notion of evolution, like any scientific idea, should generate predictions about the natural world, which we can discover to be true or false. The grand prediction of evolution is that there should be one basic scheme of similarities interlocking all of life. This is what we have consistently found for over 100 years, as thousands of biologists daily compared different organisms. Medical experimentation depends upon the interrelatedness of life. We test drugs on rhesus monkeys and study the effects of caffeine on rats because we cannot experiment on ourselves. The physiological systems of monkeys are more similar to our own than to rats. Medical scientists know this and rely on this prediction to interpret the significance of their results in terms of human medicine. Very simply, were life not all interrelated, none of this would be possible. There would be chaos, not order, in the natural world. There is no competing, rational biological explanation for this order in nature, and there hasn't been for a long while.

Creationists, of course, have an alternative explanation for this order permeating life's diversity. It is simply the way the supernatural creator chose to pattern life. But any possible pattern could be there, including chaos—an absence of any similarity among the "kinds" of organisms on earth—and creationism would hold that it is just what the creator made. There is nothing about this view of life that smacks of prediction. It tells us nothing about what to expect if we begin to study organisms in detail. In short, there is nothing in this notion that allows us to go to nature to test it, to verify or reject it.

And there is the key difference. Creationism (and it comes in many guises, most of which do not stem from the Judeo-Christian tradition) is a belief system involving the supernatural. Testing an idea with our own experiences in the natural universe is simply out of bounds. The mystical revelation behind creationism is the opposite of science, which seeks rational understanding of the cosmos. Science thrives on alternative explanations, which must be equally subject to observational and experimental testing. No form of creationism even remotely qualifies for inclusion in a science curriculum.

Creationists have introduced equal-time bills in over 10 state legislatures, and recently met with success when Governor White of Arkansas signed such a bill into law on March 19 (reportedly without reading it). Creationists also have lobbied extensively at local school boards. The impact has been enormous. Just as the latest creationist bill is defeated in committee, and some of their more able spokesmen look silly on national TV, one hears of a local school district in the Philadelphia environs where some of the teachers have adopted the "equal time" or "dual model" approach to discussing "origins" in the biology curriculum on their own initiative. Each creationist "defeat" amounts to a Pyrrhic victory for their opponents. Increasingly, teachers are left to their own discretion, and whether out of personal conviction, a desire to be "fair," or fear of parental reprisal, they are teaching creationism along with evolution in their biology classes. It is simply the path of least resistance.

Acceptance of equal time for two alternative authoritarian explanations is a startling blow to the fabric of science education. The fundamental notion a student should get from high school science is that people can confront the universe and learn about it directly. Just one major inroad against this basic aspect of science threatens all of science education. Chemistry, physics, and geology—all of which spurn biblical revelation in favor of direct experience, as all science must—are jeopardized every bit as much as biology. That some creationists have explicitly attacked areas of geology, chemistry, and physics (in arguments over the age of the earth, for example) underscores the more general threat they pose to all science. We must remove science education from its role as authoritarian truthgiver. This view distorts the real nature of science and gives creationists their most potent argument.

The creationists' equal-time appeal maintains that evolution itself amounts to a religious belief (allied with a secular humanism) and should not be included in a science curriculum. But if it is included, goes the argument, it must appear along with other religious notions. Both are authoritarian belief systems, and neither is science, according to this creationist ploy.

The more common creationist approach these days avoids such sophistry and maintains that both creationism and evolution belong in the realm of science. But apart from some attempts to document the remains of Noah's Ark on the flanks of Mt. Ararat, creationists have been singularly unsuccessful in posing testable theories about the origin, diversity, and distribution of plants and animals. No such contributions have appeared to date either in creationism's voluminous literature or, more to the point, in the professional biological literature. "Science creationism" consists almost exclusively of a multipronged attack on evolutionary biology and historical geology. No evidence, for example, is presented in favor of the notion that the earth is only 20,000 years old, but many arguments attempt to poke holes in geochemists' and astronomers' reckoning of old Mother Earth's age at about 4.6 billion years. Analysis of the age of formation of rocks is based ultimately on the theories of radioactive decay in nuclear physics. (A body of rock is dated, often by several different means, in several different laboratories. The results consistently agree. And rocks shown to be roughly the same age on independent criteria (usually involving fossils) invariably check out to be roughly the same age when dated radiometrically. The system, although not without its flaws, works.) The supposed vast age of any particular rock can be shown to be false, but not by quoting Scripture.

All of the prodigious works of "scientific creationism" are of this nature. All can be refuted. However, before school boards or parent groups, creationists are fond of "debating" scientists by bombarding the typically ill-prepared biologist or geologist with a plethora of allegations, ranging from the second law of thermodynamics (said to falsify evolution outright) to the supposed absence of fossils intermediate between "major kinds." No scientist is equally at home in all realms of physics, chemistry, geology, and biology in this day of advanced specialization. Not all the proper retorts spring readily to mind. Retorts there are, but the game is usually lost anyway, as rebuttals strike an audience as simply another set of authoritarian statements they must take on faith.

Although creationists persist in depicting both science and creationism as two comparable, monolithic belief systems, perhaps the most insidious attack exploits free inquiry in science. Because we disagree on specifics, some of my colleagues and I are said now to have serious doubts that evolution has occurred. Distressing as this may be, the argument actually highlights the core issue raised by creationism. The creationists are acknowledging that science is no monolithic authoritarian belief system. But even though they recognize that there are competing ideas within contemporary biology, the creationists see scientific debate as a sign of weakness. Of course, it really is a sign of vitality.

Evolutionary theory since the 1940s (until comparatively recently) has focused on a single coherent view of the evolutionary process. Biologists of all disciplines agree to a remarkable degree on the outlines of this theory, the so-called "modern synthesis." In a nutshell, this was a vindication of Darwin's original position: that evolution is predominantly an affair of gradual progressive change. As environmental conditions changed, natural selection (a culling process similar to the "artificial" selection practiced by animal breeders) favored those variants best suited to the new conditions. Thus evolutionary change is fundamentally adaptive. The modern synthesis integrated the newly arisen science of genetics with the Darwinian view and held that the entire diversity of life could be explained in these simple terms.

Some biologists have attacked natural selection itself, but much of the current uproar in evolutionary biology is less radical in implication. Some critics see a greater role for random processes. Others, like me, see little evidence of gradual, progressive change in the fossil record. We maintain that the usual explanation—the inadequacy of the fossil record—is itself inadequate to explain the non-change, the maintenance of status quo which lasts in some cases for 10 million years or more in our fossil bones and shells. In this view, change (presumably by natural selection causing adaptive modifications) takes place in bursts of a few thousand years, followed usually by immensely longer periods of business as usual.

Arguments become heated. Charges of "straw man," "no evidence," and so on are flung about—which shows that scientists, like everyone, get their egos wrapped up in their work. They believe passionately in their own ideas, even if they are supposed to be calm, cool, dispassionate, and able to evaluate all possibilities evenly. (It is usually in the collective process of argument that the better ideas win out in science; seldom has anyone single-handedly evinced the open-mindedness necessary to drop a pet idea.) But nowhere in this *sturm und drang* has any of the participants come close to denying that evolution has occurred.

So the creationists distort. An attack on some parts of Darwin's views is equated with a rejection of evolution. They conveniently ignore that Darwin merely proposed one of many sets of ideas on *how* evolution works. The only real defense against such tactics lies in a true appreciation of the scientific enterprise—the trial-and-error comparison of ideas and how they seem to fit the material universe. If the public were more aware that scientists are expected to disagree, that what a scientist writes today is not the last word, but a progress report on some very intensive thinking and investigation, creationists would be far less successful in injecting an authoritarian system of belief into curricula supposedly devoted to free, open rational inquiry into the nature of natural things.

Suggestions for Discussion

1. Eldredge refers to the Scopes II trial in California. What was the first Scopes trial in Tennessee about? What issues about evolution were raised in 1925 by the trial, and how are they relevant today?

2. What does Eldredge have to say about the relationship between the populist–conservative movement and creationism? How do you define *creationism?*

3. Explain Eldredge's response to the claim that since Darwinian evolution is only a theory, equal time in the schools should be given to the proponents of creationism.

4. For Eldredge, what are the dangers of accepting the authoritarianism of science? What does he believe the real function of the scientific enterprise to be? How do creationists, according to Eldredge, misunderstand the meaning of the constant debates raging in the scientific community?

5. What causes one major scientific theory to predominate for a given period of time? Summarize Eldredge's explanation of why Darwin's theory has held the support of scientists for such a long period.

6. Why does Eldredge believe that creationism does not lend itself to testing? What is the significance of testing theories?

7. For Eldredge, what is the most significant danger of the struggle by creationists for equal time in the schools? How do creationists take advantage, according to Eldredge, of scientific authoritarianism? Why does Eldredge believe that debates among scientists are a sign of vitality?

8. Summarize Eldredge's description of recent debates among evolutionists and his claim that these debates are distorted by creationists.

Suggestions for Writing

1. Write a paper in which you explain how one may believe in God without accepting the position of the creationists. Document your argument with examples.

2. Do you believe that creationists should be allowed equal time with biologists in the schools? If you do, explain your position.

3. Write a paper in which you summarize Eldredge's position and contrast it with arguments by a creationist. State why you agree with one side of the argument or the other.

Lewis Thomas

Making Science Work

Lewis Thomas (1913–1993), born in Flushing, New York, was an M.D. from Harvard whose career centered on the Sloan-Kettering Cancer Center in New York of which he was President Emeritus. He was also a member of several medical faculties in New York. He wrote articles for medical journals as well as popular essays that presented science to the lay public. He received numerous honorary degrees and awards, including the National Book Award for Arts and Letters (1975) for *The Lives of a Cell: Notes of a Body Watcher* (1974). His other works include *The Medusa and the Snail* (1979), *Late Night Thoughts on Listening to Mahler's Ninth Symphony* (1983), *Et Cetera, Et Cetera* (1990), and *The Fragile Species* (1992). The following essay focuses on the remarkable advances science has made in this country and suggests how society can maintain the momentum of scientific thought.

For about three centuries we have been doing science, trying science out, using science for the construction of what we call modern civilization. Every dispensable item of contemporary technology, from canal locks to dial telephones to penicillin to the Mars Lander, was pieced together from the analysis of data provided by one or another series of scientific experiments—also the technologies we fear the most for the threat they pose to civilization: radioactivity from the stored, stacked bombs or from leaking, flawed power plants, acid rain, pesticides, leached soil, depleted ozone, and increased carbon dioxide in the outer atmosphere.

Three hundred years seems a long time for testing a new approach to human interliving, long enough to settle back for critical appraisal of the scientific method, maybe even long enough to vote on whether to go on with it or not. There is an argument. Voices have been raised in protest since the beginning, rising in pitch and violence in the nineteenth century during the early stages of the industrial revolution, summoning urgent crowds into the streets any day these days on the issue of nuclear energy. Give it back, say some of the voices, it doesn't really work, we've tried it and it doesn't work, go back three hundred years and start again on something else less chancy for the race of man.

The scientists disagree, of course, partly out of occupational bias, but also from a different way of viewing the course and progress of science in the past fifty years. As they see it, science is just at its beginning. The principal discoveries in this century, taking all in all, are the glimpses of the depth of our ignorance about nature. Things that used to seem clear and rational, matters of absolute certainty—Newtonian mechanics, for example—have slipped through our fingers, and we are left with a new set of gigantic puzzles, cosmic uncertainties, ambiguities; some of the laws of physics are amended every few years, some are canceled outright, some undergo revised versions of legislative intent as if they were acts of Congress.

In biology, it is one stupefaction after another. Just thirty years ago we called it a biological revolution when the fantastic geometry of the DNA molecule was exposed to public view and the linear language of genetics was decoded. For a while things seemed simple and clear; the cell was a neat little machine, a mechanical device ready for taking to pieces and reassembling, like a tiny watch. But just in the last few years it has become almost imponderably complex, filled with strange parts whose functions are beyond today's imagining. DNA is itself no longer a straightforward set of instructions on a tape. There are long strips of what seem nonsense in between the genes, edited out for the assembly of proteins but essential nonetheless for the process of assembly; some genes are called jumping genes, moving from one segment of DNA to another, rearranging the messages, achieving instantly a degree of variability that we once thought would require eons of evolution. The cell membrane is no longer a simple skin for the cell; it is a fluid mosaic, a sea of essential mobile signals, an organ in itself. Cells communicate with one another, exchange messages like bees in a hive, regulate one another. Genes are switched on, switched off, by molecules from the outside whose nature is a mystery; somewhere inside are switches which, when thrown one way or the other, can transform any normal cell into a cancer cell, and sometimes back again.

It is not just that there is more to do, there is everything to do. Biological science, with medicine bobbing somewhere in its wake, is under way, but only just under way. What lies ahead, or what *can* lie ahead if the efforts in basic research are continued, is much more than the conquest of human disease or the amplification of agricultural technology or the cultivation of nutrients in the sea. As we learn more about the fundamental processes of living things in general we will learn more about ourselves, including perhaps the ways in which our brains, unmatched by any other neural structures on the planet, achieve the earth's awareness of itself. It may be too much to say that we will become wise through such endeavors, but we can at least come into possession of a level of information upon which a new kind of wisdom might be based. At the moment we are an ignorant species, flummoxed by the puzzles of who we are, where we came from, and what we are for. It is a gamble to bet on science for moving ahead, but it is, in my view, the only game in town.

The near views in our instruments of the dead soil of Mars, the bizarre rings of Saturn, and the strange surfaces of Saturn, Jupiter, Venus, and the rest, literally unearthly, are only brief glances at what is ahead for mankind in the exploration of our own solar system. In theory, there is no reason why human beings cannot make the same journeys in person, or out beyond into the galaxy.

We will solve our energy problems by the use of science, and in no other way. The sun is there, to be sure, ready for tapping, but we cannot sit back in the lounges of political lobbies and make guesses and wishes; it will take years, probably many years, of research. Meanwhile, there are other possibilities needing deeper exploration. Nuclear fission power, for all its present disadvantages, including where on earth to put the waste, can be made safer and more reliable by better research, while hydrogen fusion, inexhaustibly fueled from the oceans and much safer than fission, lies somewhere ahead. We may learn to produce vast amounts of hydrogen itself, alcohol or methane, when we have learned more about the changeable genes of single-celled microorganisms. If we are to continue to burn coal in large amounts, we will need research models for predicting how much more carbon dioxide we can inject into the planet's atmosphere before we run into the danger of melting the ice shelves of western Antarctica and flooding all our coasts. We will need science to protect us against ourselves.

It has become the fashion to express fear of computers—the machines will do our thinking, quicker and better than human thought, construct and replicate themselves, take over and eventually replace us—that sort of thing. I confess to apprehensions of my own, but I have a hunch that those are on my mind because I do not know enough about computers. Nor, perhaps, does anyone yet, not even the computer scientists themselves. For my comfort, I know for sure only one thing about the computer networks now being meshed together like interconnected ganglia around the earth: what they contain on their microchips are bits of information put there by human minds; perhaps they will do something like thinking on their own, but it will still be a cousin of human thought once removed and, because of newness, potentially of immense usefulness.

The relatively new term "earth science" is itself an encouragement. It is nice to know that our own dear planet has become an object of as much obsessive interest to large bodies of professional researchers as a living cell, and almost as approachable for discovering the details of how it works. Satellites scrutinize it all day and night, recording the patterns of its clouds, the temperatures at all parts of its surface, the distribution and condition of its forests, crops, waterways, cities, and barren places. Seismologists and geologists have already surprised themselves over and over again, probing the movement of crustal plates afloat on something or other, maybe methane, deep below the surface, meditating the evidences now coming in for the reality and continuing of continental drift, and calculating with increasing precision the data that describe the mechanisms involved in earthquakes. Their instruments are becoming as neat and informative as medicine's CAT scanners; the earth has deep secrets still, but they are there for penetrating.

The astronomers have long since become physicists, the physicists are astronomers; both are, as well, what we used to call chemists, examining the levels of ammonia or formaldehyde in clouds drifting billions of light-years away, measuring the concentrations of methane in the nearby atmosphere of Pluto, running into paradoxes. Contemporary physics lives off paradox. Niels Bohr said that a great truth is one for which the opposite is also a great truth. There are not so many neutrinos coming from our sun as there ought to be; something has gone wrong, not with the sun but with our knowledge. There are radioastronomical instruments for listening to the leftover sounds of the creation of the universe; the astronomers are dumbstruck, they can hardly hear themselves think.

The social scientists have a long way to go to catch up, but they may be up to the most important scientific business of all, if and when they finally get down to the right questions. Our behavior toward each other is the strangest, most unpredictable, and almost entirely unaccountable of all the phenomena with which we are obliged to live. In all of nature there is nothing so threatening to humanity as humanity itself. We need, for this most worrying of puzzles, the brightest and youngest of our most agile minds, capable of dreaming up ideas not dreamed before, ready to carry the imagination to great depths and, I should hope, handy with big computers but skeptical about long questionnaires and big numbers.

Fundamental science did not become a national endeavor in this country until the time of World War II, when it was pointed out by some influential and sagacious advisers to the government that whatever we needed for the technology of warfare could be achieved only after the laying of a solid foundation of basic research. During the Eisenhower administration a formal mechanism was created in the White House for the explicit purpose of furnishing scientific advice to the President, the President's Science Advisory Committee (PSAC), chaired by a new administration officer, the Science Adviser. The National Institutes of Health, which had existed before the war as a relatively small set of laboratories for research on cancer and infectious disease, expanded rapidly in the postwar period to encompass all disciplines of biomedical science. The National Science Foundation was organized specifically for the sponsorship of basic science. Each of the federal departments and agencies developed its own research capacity, relevant to its mission; the programs of largest scale were those in defense, agriculture, space, and atomic energy.

Most of the country's basic research has been carried out by the universities, which have as a result become increasingly dependent on the federal government for their sustenance, even their existence, to a degree now causing alarm signals from the whole academic community. The ever-rising costs of doing modern science, especially the prices of today's sophisticated and complex instruments, combined with the federal efforts to reduce all expenditures, are placing the universities in deep trouble. Meanwhile, the philanthropic foundations, which were the principal source of funds for university research before the war, are no longer capable of more than a minor contribution to science.

Besides the government's own national laboratories and the academic institutions there is a third resource for the country's scientific enterprise—industry. Up to very recently, industrial research has been conducted in relative isolation, unconnected with the other two. There are signs that this is beginning to change, and the change should be a source of encouragement for the future. Some of the corporations responsible for high technology, especially those involved in energy, have formed solid linkages with a few research universities—MIT and Cal Tech, for example—and are investing substantial sums in long-range research in physics and chemistry. Several pharmaceutical companies have been investing in fundamental biomedical research in association with medical schools and private research institutions.

There needs to be much more of this kind of partnership. The nation's future may well depend on whether we can set up within the private sector a new system for collaborative research. Although there are some promising partnership ventures now in operation, they are few in number; within industry the tendency remains to concentrate on applied research and development, excluding any consideration of basic science. The academic community tends, for its part, to stay out of fields closely related to the development of new products. Each side maintains adversarial and largely bogus images of the other, money-makers on one side and impractical academics on the other. Meanwhile, our competitors in Europe and Japan have long since found effective ways to link industrial research to government and academic science, and they may be outclassing this country before long. In some fields, most conspicuously the devising and production of new scientific instruments, they have already moved to the front.

There are obvious difficulties in the behavior of the traditional worlds of research in the United States. Corporate research is obliged by its nature to concentrate on profitable products and to maintain a high degree of secrecy during the process; academic science, by its nature, must be carried out in the open and depends for its progress on the free exchange of new information almost at the moment of finding. But these are not impossible barriers to collaboration. Industry already has a life-or-death stake in what will emerge from basic research in the years ahead; there can be no more prudent investment for the corporate world, and the immediate benefit for any corporation in simply having the "first look" at a piece of basic science would be benefit enough in the long run. The university science community, for all the talk of ivory towers, hankers day and night for its work to turn out useful; a close working connection with industrial researchers might well lead to an earlier perception of potential applicability than is now the case.

The age of science did not really begin three hundred years ago. That was simply the time when it was realized that human curiosity about the world represented a deep wish, perhaps embedded somewhere in the chromosomes of human beings, to learn more about nature by experiment and the confirmation of experiment. The doing of science on a scale appropriate to the problems at hand was launched only in the twentieth century and has been moving into high gear only within the last fifty years. We have not lacked explanations at any time in our recorded history, but now we must live and think with the new habit of requiring reproducible observations and solid facts for the explanations. It is not as easy a time for us as it used to be: we are raised through childhood in skepticism and disbelief; we feel the need of proofs all around, even for matters as deep as the working of our own consciousness, where there is as yet no clear prospect of proof about anything. Uncertainty, disillusion, and despair are prices to be paid for living in an age of science. Illumination is the product sought, but it comes in small bits, only from time to time, not ever in broad, bright flashes of public comprehension, and there can be no promise that we will ever emerge from the great depths of the mystery of being.

Nevertheless, we have started to do science on a world scale, and to rely on it, and hope for it. Not just the scientists, everyone, and not for the hope of illumination, but for the sure predictable prospect of new technologies, which have always come along, like spray in the wake of science. We need better ways of predicting how a piece of new technology is likely to turn out, better measures available on an international level to shut off the ones that carry hazard to the life of the planet (including, but perhaps not always so much *first of all*, as is usually the only consideration, our own species' life). We will have to go more warily with technology in the future, for the demands will be increasing and the stakes will be very high. Instead of coping, or trying to cope, with the wants of four billion people, we will very soon be facing the needs, probably desperate, of double that number and, soon there-after, double again. The real challenge to human ingenuity, and to science, lies in the century to come.

I cannot guess at the things we will need to know from science to get through the time ahead, but I am willing to make one prediction about the method: we will not be able to call the shots in advance. We cannot say to ourselves, we need this or that sort of technology, therefore we should be doing this or that sort of science. It does not work that way. We will have to rely, as we have in the past, on science in general, and on basic, undifferentiated science at that, for the new insights that will open up the new opportunities for technological development. Science is useful, indispensable sometimes, but whenever it moves forward it does so by producing a surprise; you cannot specify the surprise you'd like. Technology should be watched closely, monitored, criticized, even voted in or out by the electorate, but science itself must be given its head if we want it to work.

Suggestions for Discussion

1. In the first paragraph, Thomas makes clear that scientific experimentation of the last three hundred years has had helpful as well as dangerous consequences. Why does he begin the essay this way?

2. What has been a popular negative response to science? What has caused this response? How do scientists view the record? Why is their response different from that of the general public?

3. How does Thomas use developments in DNA to illustrate the attitude of scientists toward science?

4. What are the positive consequences of scientific experimentation for Thomas? What positive use will come from advances in computer science?

5. In this brief essay, Thomas surveys advances and issues in a number of different sciences. How does he tie all of these together? How does he relate the social sciences to the "hard" sciences?

6. What bureaucratic structures has the government created to deal with scientific advances? What is the role of these bureaus in university research? How is industry a resource for scientific advancement? What argument does Thomas make for partnership among the three areas? What obstacles exist to prevent it? What are the incentives to achieve it?

7. What are the prices we pay for living in an age of science?

8. What distinctions does Thomas make between technology and science?

Suggestions for Writing

1. Choose one concrete example from the remarkable achievements in biology, physics, or astronomy mentioned in this essay and write a clear account of it. You will have to read additional material about DNA if you write about it, for example, but be certain that you give proper credit to your sources and paraphrase the material accurately.

2. Thomas asserts that the world of science is exciting, stimulating, and dangerous. Write an essay in which you explain this position. Use examples from sources other than this essay.

David S. Wilcove

What I Saw When I Went to the Forest

David S. Wilcove, who received a Ph.D. in biology from Princeton University in 1985, is a staff ecologist for the Wilderness Society and the author of numerous scientific publications and popular articles on the conservation of biological diversity. For a series published by the Wilderness Society called *On National Policies for the Forest of the Future*, he has contributed a volume, *Protecting Biological Diversity*. In this essay he narrates his firsthand experience of the dangers to the forest ecosystem created by the timber industry's practice of clearing too rapidly.

"The penalty of an ecological education," Aldo Leopold wrote, "is that one lives alone in a world of wounds." Wounds I was prepared to see when I went to the Pacific Northwest, but not the mutilated and hemorrhaging patient that is the old-growth forest. Now, half a year later when I look back on my trip, I find myself alternating between two very different sets of feelings: a sense of wonder and affection for the forest itself—for its complexity, its antiquity, and, of course, its beauty—and a sense of sadness and anger for what we are doing to it. I make no apologies for my shifting moods. Schizophrenia of this sort is common among ecologists.

There were two of us from The Wilderness Society—Chief Forester Barry Flamm and I—who together traveled from San Francisco to Seattle, visiting the old-growth forests and meeting the people who study them, defend them, manage them, and destroy them. What follows is a summary of my experiences—a blending, I hope, of ecological awe and environmentalist outrage, beginning with a small plane buzzing over the Willamette National Forest in south-central Oregon.

It looked for all the world as though some alien force had attacked the land with a giant cookie-cutter. As far as the eye could see, there were clearcuts, each one crisply excised from the surrounding forest. The most recent of them still showed signs of the fires used to dispose of the slash: charred earth and all too often a fringe of dead trees where the flames had escaped into the forest. In death, the needles of the burned trees had turned bright orange, creating a grotesque and incongruous burst of New England autumn color in a landscape that was otherwise green. A quick pass over some of the private forestlands fringing the Willamette confirmed what we already suspected: outside the public lands, the old growth was simply gone. In its stead were acre upon acre of young Douglas-fir trees. They were a young and exuberant lot, these saplings, but in aggregate about as exciting as a cornfield. As the little plane bobbed and weaved its way back to the airstrip, I found myself wishing it were thirty years earlier, when we had more old-growth and more time to protect it.

Spokesmen from the timber industry are fond of pointing out how much of the old-growth is already "locked up" in parks, wilderness areas, and research natural areas. Whether or not their numbers are accurate is almost irrelevant, because simple numbers cannot begin to convey the complexity and variety of the old-growth ecosystem or the subtle changes in species composition and stand structure that are caused by nuances of topography, elevation, exposure, and history. To lump a Sitka spruce forest in the Coast Range with a mid-elevation Douglas-fir forest in the Cascades is to ignore the senses and overrule the mind, for the two forests look, sound, and smell very differently. As near as I can tell, the easiest and safest generality to make about old-growth is that all of it seems to be disappearing rapidly.

Nor do acreage figures reflect the on-going fragmentation of the old-growth ecosystem. A generation of research has revealed that when natural landscapes are chopped into little pieces, ecological processes go awry and species go extinct. It can be an insidiously slow process, as the sensitive species wink out one after the other over a period of decades or even centuries. The fact that young spotted owls have had abysmal success in establishing themselves in new territories is indicative of the old-growth fragmentation that already has occurred. The spotted owl, of course, has attracted the lion's share of attention, and it may well be the first to go. And if the logging continues unabated, other species will follow.

Consider, for example, the Vaux's swift. It is not a bird one hears much about, and despite my fondness for it, I must admit that it isn't much to look at. The field guides accurately but heartlessly describe this small, brown, almost tailless bird as "a cigar with wings." Like all swifts, it is a creature of the air, invariably seen streaking across the sky, its long, stiff wings beating furiously as it runs down some hapless insect. Vaux's swifts are not particularly fussy about where they forage, and during my trip I often saw them hawking insects over open fields and small towns. But when it comes time to nest, they seek out large fire-hollowed snags. There they cement their saucer-shaped nests against the inner walls, using their own saliva as the glue. Snags of this sort occur in old-growth forests, but not in the young, intensively managed stands that are rapidly replacing the old-growth.

About two centuries ago, an identical problem faced the chimney swift, a close relative of the Vaux's swift, which inhabits eastern North America. As the settlers began felling the primeval forests of the East, some of the chimney swifts began nesting in dormant chimneys, an adaptive response that may have spared them a rather grim fate. Unfortunately, Vaux's swifts have not caught on to the trick as quickly as their eastern counterparts, and relatively few of them now nest in chimneys. It has become a race between natural selection, which is pushing the swifts away from the snags and into the chimneys, and the loggers, who are destroying the forests where the birds currently reside. There is a third possibility, however: our own species could voluntarily leave enough old growth for the swifts to continue living as they have for thousands of years.

Swifts and snags. It's easy to rhapsodize about swifts—their aeronautical prowess stirs our terrestrial imaginations—but by devoting so much attention to them we may be doing an injustice to the snags. To portray a snag as simply a condominium for swifts is to overlook its multi-faceted talents, such as the center of a termite civilization, a place where a long-eared bat can pass the time of day, or the feeding grounds for fungal filaments. Part of the elegance of the old-growth ecosystem lies in the fact that linkages between the living forest and the dead trees are so strong. Even the word "old growth" expresses this fact: strictly speaking, the term *ought* to be an oxymoron— "old" implying stasis or even decay, and "growth" implying youth, vigor, and change—but it isn't. Seeing the old-growth forests and thinking about these linkages brought to mind the issue of old-growth "management."

Most of the scientists I met, whether in the Forest Service or academia, were respectful of the complexity of the old-growth ecosystem. They were trying to find ways to juggle rotation times, cutting patterns and the like, not with any confidence that we can have our old-growth cake and eat it, too, but out of concern for what would assuredly happen to the forests without their input. Yet here and there in the forestry literature one occasionally encounters papers that purport to show how old-growth conditions can be recreated by intensively managing second-growth stands: the "you tell us what you want and we'll take our chainsaws into the woods and create it" mentality. I do not question the sincerity of the authors of these papers, but I find their self-confidence nothing short of astounding. Despite considerable training as an ecologist, I am not entirely confident of my ability to manage that quarter-acre collection of crab grass and dandelions that masquerades as my front lawn, much less an ancient, complex assemblage of plants and animals, individual trees of which were around when King John was forced to consider the Magna Carta.

Politically astute conservationists tend to avoid emphasizing the importance of the spotted owl in the old-growth matrix. The issue, they rightly point out, is not survival of an owl, but survival of an entire ecosystem, and until the public realizes this, the timber industry will have the upper hand. Yet I am nevertheless compelled to talk about the spotted owl. For a simple reason: I like owls. And I have always wanted to see a spotted owl, even before it bore the weight of the old-growth ecosystem upon its fluffly brown shoulders.

My own encounter with the spotted owl was, like most momentous events in birdwatching, a breathlessly sedate event. We hiked into a large and undisturbed section of old-growth forest within the Willamette National Forest and began hooting like a spotted owl. Within a few minutes, an honest-to-goodness spotted owl answered back. Unfortunately, it did not call long enough for us to get a bearing on its location, and all we could ascertain was that it was somewhere very close, perhaps even watching us.

We tried all manner of owl calls but could not get the bird to hoot back. Either it recognized a phony when it heard one or had no interest in defending its turf from an intruding owl. Finally, with nothing to lose we fanned out into the forest, walking quietly and scanning the trees. While scrambling over a log, I glanced ahead and noticed a Buddha-shaped object sitting in a small yew tree. A closer look through my binocular confirmed it: a spotted owl. In what I thought was a calm voice, but one which probably sounded delirious, I beckoned for the others to come quickly. I was afraid the wily creature would slip away before they had a chance to see it.

I needn't have worried. That bird had no intention of flying away. As we crept closer, snapping twigs underfoot, stumbling, and otherwise making all the noise that people make when they try to slip silently through the forest, the owl just yawned, stretched its wings, and dozed off. The sounds of our cameras, our whispered "oohs and aahs," our presence just a few feet away—none of this seemed to faze it in the least. This, I was told, is fairly typical of spotted owls. Why, we wondered, are they so fearless, even trusting, of the very species that seems hell-bent on driving them to extinction?

The answer came to me when a vole darted across a log, behind and out of view of the owl. Instantly, the owl swiveled its head and glared in the direction of the vole. Apparently the sound of cameras clicking and humans whispering meant nothing to the bird. But the sound of a rodent's feet scurrying across the forest floor—now *that* was a sound worth hearing. I realized then that spotted owls are neither fearless nor trusting of humans. They are simply oblivious to them. Their world revolves around what for countless generations have been the essentials for survival in the old-growth forest: expertise in the art of capturing voles and flying squirrels, fear of great horned owls, knowledge of the right hoots and whistles for attracting a mate. A fear of humans? My guess is that natural selection hasn't had time to get around to that particular lesson, not when there have been so many other pressing issues to resolve.

Had we been slower in our assault on old growth, logging the trees over the course of millennia rather than decades, the spotted owls, the Vaux's swifts, and all of the other inhabitants might have found a way to coexist with us. But it didn't happen that way because we turned out to be as competent at cutting down trees as spotted owls are at capturing voles. Perhaps, in a rather perverse way, it is a measure of our own success as a species that we have destroyed so much of the old growth in such a short span of time. If so, a better measure will surely be our willingness to save what little is left.

There is some irony in the fact that when I finally saw a spotted owl, it was perched in a Pacific yew tree. For years, foresters have shunned the small, slow-growing yew as a worthless "weed" tree. It isn't replanted on logged sites, it has no place in the managed forest. Only recently have we discovered that the bark of the Pacific yew contains a chemical that combats cancerous tumors, causing medical researchers to engage in a frenzied search for yew trees in the old-growth forests. I am not suggesting that we will derive fabulous pharmaceutical compounds from spotted owls, long-eared bats, Vaux's swifts, or big, old snags. But I am suggesting that each of them has important things to teach us, lessons we will never learn at the rate we're going.

Suggestions for Discussion

1. The author obviously believes that preservation of "old-growth" forests is a much more complicated matter than that of the protection of Vaux's swifts and spotted owls. Yet he devotes much of his essay to those two species. Why? What important argument does he make by stressing the need to save these birds?

2. Wilcove says that the very term "old growth" ought to be an oxymoron, and yet it is not. What is an oxymoron? What point does Wilcove make here about ecosystems?

3. Three of the essays on conservation are highly personal and familiar. Which are they? Why is this kind of essay effective in presenting an argument for the environmental movement?

Suggestions for Writing

1. What are some examples, other than those in this essay, of species that have been destroyed as people have, so to speak, tamed nature? Write an essay in which you argue for or against the inevitability of this extinction.

2. If you do not understand what Wilcove means by "ecosystems," do some research and then consider the importance to civilization of maintaining them. Write an essay in which you describe the dangers of such destruction. You may want to explore in your paper the famous example of the Amazonian rain forests that Jonathan Weiner discusses in this text in "Fire and Rain."

Jonathan Weiner

Fire and Rain

Jonathan David Weiner (b. 1953) was born in New York City and educated at Harvard University. He was senior editor of *The Sciences* from 1978 until 1984 and has remained a contributing editor and an author of a column "Field Notes" for that publication. "Field Notes" was named best column of 1985 by the National Association of Science Publications. His book *Planet Earth*, which received a special award in 1986 from the American Geological Institute, was followed by *The Next One Hundred Years* (1990), and *The Beak of the Finch* (1994). In this essay he warns of the widespread danger to the environment brought about by the destruction of the rain forests.

> The world is too much with us; late and soon,
> Getting and spending, we lay waste our powers:
> Little we see in Nature that is ours. . . .
> —**William Wordsworth**

By "the world," of course, Wordsworth meant the human sphere, which even in his day already seemed to surround, enclose, and completely absorb its citizens. By "Nature," he meant the rest of the planet.

Today the world is too much with us in ways that go beyond Wordsworth's meaning. At the North Pole, in the middle of the Pacific Ocean, and above the Antarctic icecap, the atmosphere is loaded with carbon, sulfur, nitrogen, phosphorus, chlorine. There are holes in the sky, and the sunlight that streams through is not as benign as it was in Wordsworth's day. The very climate threatens to change.

Most of the alterations we have made in nature's arrangements have occurred since Wordsworth wrote his lament in the early 1800s. From our point of view that may seem like a long time; from the point of view of other species, it is nearly instantaneous.

Sudden global change does more than offend romantic sensibilities: It leads, inevitably, to the extinction of species.

At the end of the last Ice Age, when the great ice sheets collapsed and melted, sea levels rose several hundred feet. Peninsulas around the world were drowned. Outlying hills were cut off from continents. Millions of animals and plants were marooned on brand-new islands.

Ecologists have made a study of these islands: Britain off the coast of Europe; Borneo and Java off Southeast Asia; Tasmania off Australia; Trinidad off South America; Fernando Po off the coast of Africa.

In the beginning each new island was like Noah's Ark. Its passenger list was a more or less complete inventory of the flora and fauna of its continent. Then the islands began to lose population—not just individuals but whole species. On the very smallest islands, those of less than 50 square kilometers, extinction rates ran so high that after 10,000 years virtually all population was gone.

Today the number of "islands" on this planet is increasing much faster than at the end of the Ice Age. The cause is not an elevation in sea level but rather the rising tide of human beings. As a rule, the longer a place has been inhabited, the more fragmented is the landscape; ours today looks like a checkerboard. And as the tide of human beings rises in the next century (demographers project that the human population will double within the next 100 years) and we push toward a controlling interest of 80 percent of the planet, the landscape can only get even more fragmented.

These new "islands" are not literally surrounded by water; they are islands of nature surrounded by people, created by human expansion into previously undeveloped wilderness. However, what is happening on the manmade islands is much like what happened on the islands that were formed at the end of the Ice Age. Whenever a bit of biosphere (i.e., the thin layer of life that coats the planet) is isolated, by rising tides or by any other catastrophe, natural or artificial, the results are the same.

In the 1960s, two mathematically minded ecologists, E. O. Wilson and Robert H. MacArthur, drew up formulas for predicting how many species can survive on a given island, based on its size and its distance from the mainland. Their theory applied to any island, real or metaphorical. The smaller the island and the farther it is from the mainland, they hypothesized, the greater the disparity between the rate of extinction and the rate of replacement. The eventual result would always be a decline in the number of species: what has come to be known as the island effect.

Partly as a result of Wilson and MacArthur's findings, ecologists realized that the fate of much of the biosphere in the next 100 years would depend upon the island effect, just as the fate of much of Earth's climate depends upon global warming, otherwise known as the greenhouse effect. But to expand their knowledge, they needed a test case: a giant, brand-new archipelago that could be watched from the moment of its isolation. Enter Thomas E. Lovejoy.

In 1965, while working on a Yale Ph.D. in biology, Lovejoy made his first trip to the Amazonian rain forest. He was overwhelmed by what he saw. Part of a green belt around the equator, the Amazon is in Earth's zone of strongest sunshine, where rates of evaporation and precipitation are greatest. Though the belt covers less than 10 percent of Earth's land area, it contains more than half its species of animals and plants. Within the city limits of Belém, on the edge of the rain forest near the mouth of the Amazon River, more than 425 different species of birds have been spotted. On the outskirts of Belém, in a single 11-acre patch of the Mocambo forest, a botanist has counted 295 species of trees. Lovejoy has called the world's rain forests "the greatest expression of life on the planet."

While completing his doctorate, Lovejoy also began a long association with the World Wildlife Fund, a tiny organization in those days, where he helped draft recommendations for nature preserves in the Amazon and all over the map. At the time, no one knew how large a nature park should be. Political as well as ecological concerns came into play: Make a park too big and no government would go for it; make it too small and precious few species would be preserved. But how small was too small? How much land does a wild cheetah really need to live on? Or an antelope? An Amazonian harpy eagle? A frog?

Just before Christmas 1976, Lovejoy was brainstorming with some fellow ecologists at the National Science Foundation in Washington, D.C. The subject was the island effect and how it could be studied. In his mind's eye, Lovejoy could see the Amazon: He remembered the dramatic scenes he'd witnessed of ranchers and homesteaders torching tens of thousands of acres of rain forest to make way for cattle pasture. The pioneer explosion in the rain forest was just beginning when Lovejoy was there, fueled by debt and hunger; throughout Latin America, in fact, squatters could claim rights to parcels of rain forest by cutting down trees ("improving the land"). The land could then be sold at a profit.

According to local law, a landowner in the rain forest could not clear his whole property: Half the forest had to be left standing. In practice, though, each time the land was sold, whatever rain forest was left could be cut in half again. Driving down the new dirt roads, Lovejoy had seen a sea of scrubby farmland in which bits of rain forest stood out here and there like tropical islands.

It now occurred to him that if the landowners could be persuaded to leave some of these islands standing—ideally, blocks of rain forest of different sizes—he would have a test case. Here was a giant archipelago of wilderness parks, he excitedly told his colleagues, that could be watched from the moment of isolation. A gifted diplomat, fluent in Portuguese, Lovejoy flew to Brazil and began negotiating with local officials.

Lovejoy's archipelago became the biggest planned experiment in the history of ecology. (Thanks to support from the World Wildlife Fund and other sources, he was able to hire a number of field assistants.) It is located just north of the Amazonian city of Manaus—"two hours and many thousands of potholes," as the project leaders say. Until recently this was still virgin forest, home of jaguars, pumas, tapirs, harpy eagles, and crested eagles. Today, flying overhead in a small plane, one can see thousands of acres where farmers have cut and burned away the forests. Here and there in the muddy fields are remnant patches of trees, and some of these patches are neat squares and rectangles. These are Lovejoy's islands, and they stand out so sharply that a visiting naturalist once observed, on approaching one by plane, "It looks like a piece of shag carpet tossed down on a dirt floor." Today there are ten islands in the ecologist's archipelago, ranging in size from 1 hectare to 100 hectares (a hectare is about two and a half acres). Lovejoy plans to have 24 islands eventually, including a giant of 10,000 hectares.

Projeto Lovejoy, as the experiment is known in Brazil's popular press, would have to be studied by hundreds of ecologists and volunteers for centuries before the full consequences of the island effect would appear. Nevertheless, as soon as the first of Lovejoy's islands was carved out in the early 1980s, there was a cascade of effects.

First, birds flocked in. Tropical ecologists can count birds by stringing invisibly fine nets—mist nets—across clearings in the forests before dawn. In the newly isolated forest, the rate at which the ecologists caught birds in the mist nets doubled. This is called a refugee effect. Displaced birds flocked to the island in the middle of the new field as if alighting upon an ark.

Six months later the population of refugees crashed—the ark was too small. Trees at the edge of the forest—unaccustomed to so much sunlight—began to crash, too. This is called an edge effect. One tree in the family Bombacaceae burst into flower six months out of season. Botanists had never seen that happen before.

Monkeys were in trouble, too. A band of golden-handed tamarins fled across the new fields and were seen no more. Saki monkeys normally range in troops across hundreds of hectares. Two of them were marooned together on the little island. They ate almost all the fruits and seeds of the trees in their reserve. Then the saki monkeys disappeared.

On the windward side of the island, the number of felled and broken trees was striking. Lovejoy attributes their destruction to the high winds that blew in from the open pasture—another edge effect. Each felled tree opened up more of the forest within to sunlight, which meant weeds from the pasture could creep farther into the forest. The edge crept inward.

Indeed the ten-hectare plot was really all edge. There was no core where the forest was untouched or unchanged—even in the very center of the reserve. Lovejoy says, "The number of standing dead trees jumped dramatically from nine in 1981 to 65 in 1982."

Volunteers who had explored and surveyed the area before it became an island began to find the place unfamiliar. The dawn chorus of the birds and the midnight chorus of the frogs had been silenced. Familiar butterflies were nowhere to be seen. Instead there were strange butterflies, some of them from the very roof of the forest, that fluttered near the ground as if the floor of the forest had begun to seem confusingly as bright as the top. The air was hot and dry, and each week there were fewer catches in the mist nets.

After only a year of isolation, the island had begun to resemble the nightmare fable that opens Rachel Carson's book *Silent Spring*. The groves had lost their voice, and life had fled from the trees. Here, though, there had been no spraying of poison, only the innocent clearing of a field. Lovejoy foresees slow, progressive losses for all his islands, large and small, though those of 100 hectares or 1,000 will not deteriorate as quickly as those of 1 or 10.

Events like those that created Lovejoy's islands are being repeated at a rate of about one acre per second in rain forests around the world, and despite an infinity of local variations on the theme, everywhere there will be the same pattern of attrition. The only fundamental difference is that here in the Amazon, the losses are being watched.

Outside the rain forests, where pioneer explosions have been going on longer, the islands are older, and in many of them, the last stages of ecological decay are now on display. Giant pandas, for instance, which once ranged across almost half of China, are now confined to a few small reserves in the wooded mountains of Sichuan province, on the eastern edge of the Tibetan plateau. In 1987 there were about 35 isolated populations in the wild, most of them consisting of fewer than 20 pandas each.

When islands are that small, the island effect is at its most extreme. An entire generation can turn out all male or all female, or the only breeding male in the group may die in a trap that a poacher sets for musk deer. With each group cut off from the rest, no roving bachelor is likely to come along and discover the languishing harem. The stranger never comes to dinner— and that is the end of the line.

The pronghorn antelope of Wyoming's Great Divide Basin escape the cold each winter by ranging south across the grasslands, as they have done since the depths of the last Ice Age. But cattlemen are putting up more and more barbed wire to fence in their cattle, thus cutting the antelopes' range and blocking their escape routes south. The barbed wire has helped turn the West into a set of enclosures that are, for the antelope, almost impermeable. In a single fierce winter in 1983 more than half the pronghorn antelopes died.

When we try to save species like the antelope we generally do so by setting aside more national parks—more islands. These parks are supposed to serve as arks, carrying the nation's wildlife through the next millennium and beyond. But it is now clear that very few arks on Earth are really large enough for the purpose. A recent study by the ecologist William D. Newmark found that in the United States, 14 western national parks are too small to save all the mammals that once lived there. The smallest reserve in Newmark's study, Bryce Canyon, 144 square kilometers, has already lost more than a third of its mammal species. Yosemite, at 2,083 square kilometers, had lost a quarter of its species even before the fires of the summer of '88.

If the giant parks of the West are too small, what about the parks of the East, or the vest-pocket parks in Europe? Creatures that depend upon those arks may not last through the next century, much less the next millennium. "We thought we could put a wall around nature and preserve it," says one ecologist. "But we were wrong."

As we keep forgetting—and as the planet keeps reminding us—no global change proceeds in isolation. If the greenhouse effect, caused by the buildup of carbon dioxide and other gases, combines with the island effect, the biosphere could be stressed far more powerfully than by either effect alone.

The excess of carbon dioxide—released into the atmosphere through the burning of fossil fuels and of rain forests—is already causing problems by itself, even without the accompanying greenhouse effect. The more this gas piles up in the air, the more it changes the terms of the struggle for existence in every patch of greenery on the planet. Carbon dioxide is like fertilizer for plants: Putting more of it in the air gives a competitive edge to those species that can utilize it in photosynthesis most efficiently. Many of those plants are opportunists: weeds.

The future of much of the world's flora and fauna, trapped on shrinking islands, requires particular plants to stay just as they are. The diet of the giant panda, for instance, consists almost entirely of bamboo. If carbon dioxide favors some other grass over bamboo, the pandas may starve. The fertilization effect will unsettle every fragment of woods, marshes, and tundra on Earth. For millions of plants and animals already living on the edge, the gas we are putting into the air may tip the balance.

The greenhouse effect would be a worse shock. A warming will redraw the boundaries of Earth's climate zones, shifting the tropics into what is now the temperate zone and the temperate zone toward the poles. Animals and plants that are adapted to cooler climates will have to move, forced to chase their shifting climate zones or die. (No air conditioners on Lovejoy's islands.)

As the world warms up, consider what happens to a population on the slope of a mountain. The peak is smaller than the base, so as the climate gets warmer and the species shifts upward, it is forced into a smaller and smaller space. Soon the population is cut off from those of neighboring peaks; where once it was joined to others at the base of the mountain, it now lives on an island. As the climate gets warmer and warmer the species is confined to a smaller and smaller island.

And if the temperature climbs even higher, where do the animals go from there?

Ecosystems, the homes of species, are made up of the climate of a place and of the interwoven lives of all of the species that live there. With rapid global warming, ecologists foresee the unraveling of whole ecosystems, a transformation of tundra, wetlands, boreal forests, and rain forests around the world.

Not only could the greenhouse effect hasten species on the path to extinction in the next 100 years. The loss of so many species and ecosystems may also help to change the climate, in a chain reaction.

There are a thousand links between life and air. The atmosphere and biosphere exchange carbon dioxide, as well as water vapor. In fact, rain forests make their own rain. These forests differ from most of the world's forests in having several distinct layers of canopy. The trees look like open umbrellas on stems of three or four different heights. These staggered layers of canopy break the fall of rain more than a single layer could do. Because of their vast surface area, they also spread moisture out in thin layers where it can evaporate quickly. If you dab a drop of rubbing alcohol on your palm and streak it across the skin, you can feel how much faster the fluid evaporates and cools when it is spread thin. With staggered canopies and shallow roots, the rain forest catches a rain, holds it, and spreads it out to dry. Evaporation takes place as if from a single immense green leaf many times larger than the great Amazon Basin itself.

From the air, one can see the result. Giant pillars of cloud seem to boil out of the tops of the trees and rise straight into the sky. Wherever the carpet of trees is thick these pillars rise, as if to link the forest and the sky. It almost looks as if the green canopy below is supporting, with those white pillars, the canopy of clouds overhead. The trees are rainmakers: "a neat trick," as Lovejoy observes, "and one people have lusted after for centuries."

Where forests have been thinned, there are fewer pillars and fewer clouds. The island of Marajó, at the mouth of the Amazon, is carpeted with trees on the western half but not on the eastern half. Thunderclouds seem to love the western half of Marajó, and it rains there every day. The eastern half often goes dry.

Everyone working in Lovejoy's project has commented on the hot, dry wind that blows across the clearings and through the new reserves. One never feels such a wind in the heart of a healthy rain forest. It is almost as if an organism larger than the rain forest itself has been disturbed. This curious impression leaves even Lovejoy, an articulate man, at a loss for words. He told one prospective visitor, "The whole—I don't know what you want to call it—physical functioning of air, temperature, and moisture in the cleared area is very different from the uncut forest. You'll feel it."

Because a farm does not give back its rainwater to the sky, the clouds overhead are thinner. That hurts the woods around the farm. The loss of rain can slowly eat away at the forests around each large clearing. Runoff also carves deep channels in the ground and carries sod away. Along the road from Belém to Brasília, large fields have been so overgrazed and eroded that they have been called "a ghost landscape."

Climatologists believe the clearings may raise temperatures in large areas of the tropics by as much as 3 to 5 degrees C.—a local warming that is larger than the tropics can expect from the greenhouse effect. That may drive the climate of the tropics beyond the conditions that gave rise to the forests in the first place. In the next hundred years large portions of the equatorial rain forest belt, the greenest wilderness in the world, could turn into some of the fiercest desert.

So the island effect extends far beyond the island: It alters the ecosystem's exchanges with the atmosphere and the hydrosphere (i.e., the waters of Earth), and through these restless spheres it alters conditions everywhere. "No man is an island," said John Donne. Not even an island is an island.

A spider spins a web of silken threads in the garden, and the biosphere spins a web of gases in the atmosphere. If the spider loses a few legs, they will grow back, and it can still spin its web, although the pattern may be somewhat altered. Something like that is happening in our atmosphere and hydrosphere today: The patterns that life on Earth weaves in the air, water, and soil are already changing slightly from year to year.

If the garden spider is disoriented by a drug or by various other means that have been devised over the years by experimental entomologists, then the spirals of the web it spins may be dramatically changed. That is what we fear could happen to our planet in the near future. With the sudden losses of so many ecosystems from the biosphere, our air, water, and soil will be significantly altered.

This is the ultimate replay to the philistine question "So what?" as we lose species after species. What if we do lose a snail darter, or an elephant, or a blue whale? What if we do lose the tropical rain forests? Most of the creatures in the rain forests are unnamed and unknown in any case, and they will vanish without a trace, like the dreams of deep sleep. And anyway, aren't most of them insects?

The answer is that the loss of a single species of spider alters the ability of the biosphere to weave the web of life. We are riding a Fate, an Atropos, that cuts the thread of life. How many threads can we cut before we cut the one thread upon which our own lives depend? We simply do not know.

Suggestions for Discussion

1. The essay has as an epigraph the opening lines of a sonnet by William Words-worth, the English Romantic poet. What use does Weiner make of the poem in his argument? Look up the entire sonnet, which is an attack on the Industrial Age at the beginning of the nineteenth century. On the basis of this sonnet, do you believe that Wordsworth would have agreed with Weiner's essay?

2. Why is Weiner interested in the "island effect"? Describe the role of Thomas E. Lovejoy in establishing "islands" as a method of saving species threatened by civilization. What does Weiner report to be the limits of this method?

3. Why are the Amazonian rain forests excellent examples of the destruction resulting from development? Summarize the stages of destruction described. What other examples does Weiner use? How do all of his examples fit together to make his argument?

4. What is the possible effect on humankind of the destruction of nature?

Suggestions for Writing

1. Numerous writers have discussed the Amazonian rain forests and the possible consequences of their devastation. Write a brief research paper on this topic in which you explore the causes of the destruction and suggestions for stopping it. Include Weiner as one of your sources and compare his treatment of the problem with other treatments.

2. Write a paper in which you explain how Weiner stimulates the reader's interest in his argument. How effective is his use of examples?

3. Weiner quotes John Donne's statement, "No man is an island" and continues "Not even an island is an island." Write an essay explaining what Weiner means.

Captain X

Mr. Spock

Captain X (b. 1922) is the pseudonym for the airline pilot Rodney Stich and the professional writer Reynolds Dodson. Together they wrote *Unfriendly Skies: Revelations of a Deregulated Airline Pilot* (1989). They have also written *The Real Unfriendly Skies: A Saga of Corruption* (1990), an updating of the original work from which this selection is taken. In it, the authors use a straightforward narrative to demonstrate the dangers of excessive abdication of government control.

It should have been routine.

We were bringing a 727 into Saginaw, Michigan.[1] The weather was clear, and we had already begun our descent. I could see the airport spread out below me in a little geometric spill among the snowbanks.

In one of those boardroom maneuvers that's become endemic in our industry, my company had recently merged with a smaller airline. This had given us some new and, to me, unfamiliar routes. I had never been to Saginaw. I had spent the past several years flying DC-9s and 10s along the southern tier, and although I knew about 200 U.S. airports like the palm of my hand, this particular field was not among them.

On coming aboard I had introduced myself to the crew members. My copilot and my flight engineer were both new to me. They were employees of the now-absorbed smaller airline. My flight engineer looked eager. Like all flight engineers, he undoubtedly hoped someday to move into the copilot's seat, and from there into the captain's seat where I was sitting. My copilot was a man of about my age. I was forty-two.

Saginaw was the second leg of our trip. The flight had originated in Miami, and, following the custom of our industry, I had turned the controls over to the copilot after the first leg. During our preflight checkout I had asked him how long he had been driving the Seven-Two.

"Eight years," he said as he busied himself with the hundreds of minute details that go into every preflight checklist.

Eight years, I said to myself. That's pretty good.

While I was qualified to fly the 727, I was not as comfortable on it as I might have been. My experience on it had been mostly of a training nature, and I was glad to have a man at my side who had been living with the plane on such an intimate basis.

"And you know Saginaw," I said.

"Been flying there since the day I joined the company," came the succinct and perhaps slightly smug reply.

Terrific, Superterrific.

Through Flight Control, we had learned that the airport was undergoing renovation. The longer of her two runways—about 6,800 feet—had been temporarily shortened. It was now about 5,500 feet, which was well within the requirements of a 727, but considerably short of the 7,000 or so feet that would be considered average.

Her second runway—Runway 18—was about 5,000 feet.

Now 5,000 feet on a 727 is cutting it pretty close. Technically the plane can land in shorter runway space, but unless you've been making your home in that cockpit for quite a while you really don't want to go around testing a plane's minimum landing requirements.

As we neared our destination, air traffic control was reporting a twenty-five-knot headwind on Runway 18. This was significant. A strong headwind would greatly reduce ground speed, slowing the plane to a velocity acceptable to the shorter runway space.

"How do you plan to take her in?" I asked. (As captain, I'm the copilot's chief and mentor. From gate to gate, no matter who is actually handling the controls, everything that happens is the captain's responsibility.)

---

[1] Not the true location. Where necessary, airports and locales have been changed to protect the author and his airline.

"Runway 18," he said. "I'll bring her in at a forty flap."

As you might imagine, a plane's flap setting is crucial to the landing procedure. The farther the flaps are down, the lower the nose is tilted. It's what we call the *deck angle*. The usual flap setting—the one I had been performing day in and day out along the southern tier—is thirty degrees. By choosing a forty-degree setting, my copilot was indicating that he was planning to alter our deck angle, augment the amount of "drag" (resistance of air as it flows across the wings), and take advantage of the headwind to lessen our velocity. These factors would enable us to land the plane at a relatively slow 120 knots and come to a stop well within the 5,000-foot limit.

"Good decision," I said.

As a passenger, you've probably applauded when the pilot brings the plane in on one of those smooth-as-glass, I-hardly-even-felt-us-touch-the-ground grease jobs. From where you sit, there's no greater testimony to your pilot's skill than that he didn't ruffle your in-flight reading matter. That's great. But what you don't know is that sometimes those ultra-smooth landings can kill you. If the weather is bad . . . if there's just a little too much ice out there on the tarmac . . . if the runway is too slick, or too short, or too sloped, or too *any*thing, sometimes the *right* decision is to bring that plane down, cut your forward momentum to a crawl, and *slam* the wheels onto the pavement. That way you'll get full braking power and diminish the risk of skidding or hydroplaning.

That's the *right* decision.

Which is not to say it's the greatest crowd-pleaser.

In this case, it took me about half a second to conclude that my copilot was making an absolutely 100 percent *right* decision, and once again I congratulated myself on having the good fortune to draw Mr. Spock as my first officer.

So there I sat, ignorant and blissful, my arms folded across my chest, my Coke and my peanuts at my side, 152 equally ignorant and blissful passengers in the cabin behind me, and none of us having the faintest idea we had about ninety-seven seconds to live.

One of the great thrills of flying is that you're constantly getting to experience what other men spend their entire lives clawing and scratching to achieve—namely, that awe-inspiring, ego-swelling phenomenon called "The View from the Fortieth Floor." I never tire of it. The landscape is constantly changing. As I crisscross the country, I marvel at what most other people get to see only a relatively few times in their lives. I wouldn't trade offices with Donald Trump on a bet.

But when you're coming in for that delicate operation called the landing, "The View from the Fortieth Floor" takes on a special significance. You're not sitting in an office with your feet up on the desk, you're sitting at the tip of a very fast and very powerful falling arrow. Your decisions are crucial. You're scanning your instrument panel. You're making numerous small adjustments in your ailerons and your elevators. You're watching to see that your wings are level, your airspeed's steady, your landing gear's down, your altitude's proper. And while you're doing all that, and while you're looking at your engine pressure and your compass headings and your rate of descent and your altitude gauges, you're also looking through your windshield and you're comparing what you're seeing on the ground with what you've seen a thousand times before in a thousand other similar landings. It's all very fast, and very instinctive. Only when the airport is new to you; when the terrain is just a little different from any you've ever seen before; when it's a plane you're not quite comfortable with, and it's coming in on a configuration that is almost never used except in the most unusual circumstances, sometimes then your instincts don't work right. You sit there and you stare and you realize that all your exhaustive training has not prepared you for the unique and somewhat confusing sensations you're actually experiencing. And when that happens, all you can do is marvel at what a weird and unsettling feeling this is, and you look for support in your copilot's competence.

As I sat there, I couldn't help thinking. Now isn't this strange? As many times as I've looked at runways through these windshields . . . as many hours as I've spent training on a Seven-Two and lifting her off and setting her down and going through God-knows-how-many exercises and emergency training procedures with her, isn't it strange how, when you come in at this steep angle toward a runway you've never seen before, you have the optical illusion you're about to crash?

I rolled a peanut over on my tongue.

The ground rose closer.

And isn't it strange, I thought, the way it looks like you may not even clear those trees down there, but even if you do clear those trees you're certainly going to hit those lights, and aren't you lucky that Mr. Spock here knows so much more than you do, and that the lump rising in your throat, which seems to be getting larger with every passing moment, is apparently not rising in his much more knowledgeable one.

In twenty years of service, I've listened to more than my share of dead men's chatter on voice recorders. I've sat through more than my share of postcrash conferences and listened to more than my share of ghostly conversations coming from those charred and battered "black boxes." And I know that the last word a pilot often utters before his plane disappears in a fiery ball of flame is *shit*. That may not be a very noble way to depart this planet, but that's the way we usually exit.

I can't swear that that particular Anglo-Saxonism was the one that escaped my lips at that moment, but if it wasn't, it wasn't for lack of thinking it.

Snapping forward, I grabbed the yoke with one hand and pushed the throttle forward with the other. We were a good hundred yards short of the runway, and we were doomed to crash.

Looking back on it now, I realize how silly it was. I realize how foolish I was to have placed so much confidence in a man I didn't know and whose only collateral was his self-assured arrogance. The group dynamics of cockpit crew members are pivotal to the success or failure of every flight, and it is just this kind of misunderstanding that can snuff out lives in a fraction of a second. But I didn't have the luxury of thinking about all that at that moment. There was the ground, here came the airplane, and all I could do was to act reflexively.

"*Power . . . full power!*" I cried.

I knew that my only chance, if I had a chance, was to bring the nose up, push the throttles to the limit, and hope like hell we would clear those approach lights. Straining forward against my shoulder harness, I slammed the throttles against the firewall.

The plane leaped forward.

I won't even venture to guess what the passengers must have thought at that moment. Even through the closed cockpit door I could hear the first of what would be many crashes as dirty food trays, coffeepots, and various pieces of overhead baggage shifted violently in their compartments. Within microseconds the airspeed indicator shot from 122 to 143 knots. The plane bolted, flared—then hit the pavement.

Later inspection would show that our main gear had cleared the end of the runway by less than thirty inches. A pilot is trained to land a plane within the first thousand feet of runway space. Landing it within the first thirty inches of runway space is cutting it just a little closer than the company that owns the airplane might wish.

But that wasn't the bad part. The bad part—the part that would bring my heart almost literally into my throat and make me wonder how my mother's little boy had ever come to be in this predicament—was that we were now hurtling down a dwarf-sized runway at a speed approximating a Grand Prix race car's!

As any pilot will tell you, when you have executed a landing as sloppy and screwed-up as this one, there is only one right thing to do. The right thing to do is keep the throttle shoved forward, lift the plane back off the ground, and execute what's called a "go-around." It's an inelegant and rather embarrassing maneuver, but it's the one the experts consider most prudent.

And the experts are right.

Unfortunately, that is not the procedure my reflexes chose to perform. The procedure my reflexes chose was to cut the throttle, reverse the engine thrust, raise the spoilers (those are the big noisy flaps on the tops of the wings), and apply the brakes. In other words, in the split-second's confusion caused by the poorly planned landing, my instincts overrode my training— and I decided to *stop the goddamn airplane!*

If you think the crashes in the cabin were bad before, you should have heard the outlandish noises coming from that quarter now. Everything that was not nailed down in the galley flew against the forward bulkhead. Along the aisle, the overhead compartments began springing open, *pop, pop, pop,* showering overcoats, garment bags, pillows, blankets, you name it, onto the hapless heads of the people below them. All the oxygen masks came down. These masks are held in place by barometric latches which release during pressure changes. The reactionary force of our landing had pulled the pins, and now there were a hundred-and-some-odd oxygen masks and hoses dangling before the bewildered and panic-stricken eyes of our whiplashed passengers.

Still the plane roared on.

I sat clench-jawed at the controls. I could see the end of the runway rising up before me. The plane was skipping and skidding along the pavement, its tires alternately grabbing and sliding as we heaved and rattled across the asphalt. My feet were pressed as hard as they would go against the brake pedals. In another few seconds the plane would nose-dive off the far end of the runway, slide along the ground on its belly, and end up in the same fiery inferno we had so narrowly averted at the runway's near end.

God have mercy on us all.

The fact that that didn't happen is, to me, still a bit of a miracle. Somehow the combined forces of brakes and spoilers and Lady Luck managed to slow our momentum, and the plane, after no small amount of protest, shuddered to a halt. We were sitting with our nose practically overhanging the end of the runway, but we were breathing.

The next few minutes are unclear. Somehow I managed to get the plane turned around and taxied toward the gate. Somehow I managed to get the switches off and the knobs turned and the levers pulled and the engines shut down. Somehow the ground crew managed to get the stairs rolled over to the passenger door, the cabin crew managed to get the passenger door open, and those poor scared passengers managed to crawl out of the Valley of Death and into the lap of sweet terra firma. (*"Thanks for flying with us, and we do hope you'll choose us again the next time you travel!"*)

The three of us in the cockpit sat there white-faced. For the next couple of minutes you could hear a pin drop. Finally—softly, and as offhandedly as possible—I suggested that the flight engineer might want to go out and get a cup of coffee.

"Roger!" said the flight engineer, and you've never seen a man exit a cockpit door as fast as that one did.

This left just me and Mr. Spock.

"I will try to put this as kindly and succinctly as I can," I said. "Just what the bloody fuck did you think you were doing back there? Just what the bloody fuck did you, in your eight distinguished years of flying Seven-Twos, mean by coming in on such an erroneous and obviously half-assed approach angle? Didn't you see we were about to crash? Didn't you in your infinite wisdom see that that was completely the wrong sight picture we were getting through the windshield, and that we were all about two seconds away from becoming crispy critters on this North Woods landscape?"

Mr. Spock squirmed uncomfortably.

I won't belabor this poor fellow's humiliation. Suffice it to say that it was as sincere as it was deserved. Suffice it also to say that when the dust had settled, not to mention my pulse rate, I learned that everything he had told me during our preflight checkout was true. He *had* been flying 727s for eight years. He *had* been coming into the Saginaw airport since the day he joined his company. As a *flight engineer!* This was only his third trip as a copilot! He had never actually *landed* a plane at Saginaw, and he had never made a forty-flap landing in his life!

In the years since, I've had a lot of time to think about that incident. I've awakened in the middle of the night, and I can still see the end of that runway racing toward me like some ghostly image from Christmas Future. And it never ceases to impress me that, had we crashed, the report issued by the National Transportation Safety Board would have attributed the carnage to "pilot error." About seven out of ten airline accidents in this country are labeled that way, and this, most assuredly, would have been one of them.

But as someone once wrote, "Most pilot errors are not really pilot errors so much as booby traps that the pilot has fallen into." Indeed, "pilot error" is itself an error. That pilots are human and make mistakes is self-evident; but there are reasons for those mistakes, and those are the factors which must be examined.

Let's take another look at that incident, and this time let's see it for what it really was:

Factor 1: Both my copilot and my flight engineer were new to me.

This in and of itself is not unusual. The airline I work for has more than 5,000 assorted pilots, copilots, and flight engineers. It is not unlikely that I am going to have many strangers share my flight deck as we sail about the world from this city to that.

What is worth noting is that, before deregulation, I could usually assume that my associates were competent. Since we worked for the same company, we had probably been hired with the same criteria in mind; we had gone through the same academic and practical exercises; and we were subject to the same corporate objectives and operations guidelines.

We were a *team*.

Since deregulation, there have been dozens of mergers involving hundreds of air routes and many thousands of disconsolate employees. This means that on a significant number of flights part of the crew will have been trained on one airline, part on another. Many of today's crew members come from small airlines who have neither the money nor the equipment to give them the sophisticated jet training they need. The result can be disastrous.

This was shown on a snowy afternoon in November 1987. That was the day a Continental DC-9 tipped a wing on takeoff from Denver's Stapleton Airport and flipped over, strewing bodies, glass, and twisted debris along a thousand feet of windswept runway. Twenty-eight of the eighty-two people on board were killed. Subsequent investigation showed that the captain had spent a mere thirty-three hours in the airplane's captain's seat. His first officer, who was at the controls at the time, had been hired a couple of months earlier from a small commuter airline in Texas. He had flown a DC-9 on only one previous scheduled flight, and he had never taken off in snow. This may not have been the most *immediate* cause of this accident (accidents are almost always the result of a series of errors, misjudgments, flukes, and coincidences), but the unfortunate pairing of these two men was undoubtedly a factor that helped to precipitate it.

In my case, the only information I had about my copilot was that he had been "flying" a 727 for a considerable length of time. It never occurred to me to question his definition of "flying." Nor did I doubt his meaning when he said that he had been landing planes in Saginaw since the day he joined the company. In retrospect, I can see how the misunderstanding arose. I can assure you that I have been much more careful in my questioning of copilots since that incident, but at the time that it happened it had just never occurred to me, and the fact that it didn't almost cost us all dearly.

Factor 2: I, as captain, didn't know the airport.

Before deregulation, when a crew took off in an airplane, there was at least a pretty good chance that the place they were going was familiar to one or more of the crew members. Because the industry was so controlled, air routes were fairly static. A pilot for, say, Piedmont knew the Southern and Mid-Atlantic areas like the back of his hand. He didn't have to wake up one morning and start worrying about thunderstorms in Dallas/Fort Worth or the Chinook winds that whip the Rockies.

Today it's different. Our schedules are so rushed, the economics of flying are so tight, the distances we travel are so great, that we often find ourselves caroming this way and that like so many billiard balls around a pool table. To take but one example: In the twelve-month period that included Texas Air's now famous merger binge (that's the period when Continental was merged with Eastern, Frontier, People Express, and New York Air), that one company alone added 177 new cities to its route structure. At the same time it shuffled some 61,000 employees, including approximately 8,000 pilots and copilots. You can imagine the chaos. While many of the pilots may have known many of the airports they now had to serve, it was not unusual for a pilot from one airline to be teamed with a copilot from another, and the two of them sent off to some hell-and-gone airport neither one of them had ever seen before.

That's a formula for disaster.

Pilots don't like to admit that this is a problem. Every pilot likes to think that, as a professional, he can handle any new circumstance as it arises. But I can tell you from personal experience: not knowing an airport, or not knowing a geographical or meteorological area through which you have to fly in order to reach that airport, is one more factor that can lead to misjudgment.

Factor 3: The copilot and I were about the same age.

In commercial aviation, flight crews advance in one way and one way only: seniority. When you are hired, your name goes on at the bottom of a list. From that moment on your career will consist of climbing that list one number at a time. You will climb it first as a flight engineer, then as a first officer, and finally as a captain. That's the way it has always been, and that's the way it will probably always be.

Unfortunately, the seniority track at one airline may be quite different from the seniority track at another. If your airline is financially unhealthy—if it is poorly managed, or if it is caught between the price-slashing big guys and the aggressive commuters—your chances for advancement are nil. I know many highly capable men—men who have just as much commercial flight time as I do, and probably a great deal more military flight time—who, even after fifteen or twenty years, are still flying as flight engineers or copilots. It's not their fault, it's just the luck of the draw. Those who in their youth were fortunate enough to link up with a well-managed company with growth potential have made out okay. Those who weren't—too bad.

Looking back on it, I'm convinced that this "unevenness" of seniority contributed to our near-disaster in Saginaw. I had been with my airline thirteen years. My airline was healthy, and I had long been a captain. My copilot had been with his airline twelve years, and he had barely made it past flight engineer. What could be more natural than his not wanting to admit—to me, of all people—that he had never actually landed in Saginaw.

It's been said that a pilot's ego is exceeded only by the size of his wristwatch. In this case, my copilot's ego (ably abetted by my own complacency) almost killed us.

Of course deregulation isn't the only thing that keeps things jumping in the airplane business nowadays. Flying one of today's new jets—an MD-80, say, or a 767—verges on something out of "Star Trek." Since my brush with fate in Michigan, I've flown 727s, 737s and 747s, and now I fly the near-state-of-the-art 767s almost exclusively. I'm one of a fairly select number of pilots who's qualified to do so. And my experiences on these planes—my run-ins with passengers, my relations with stewardesses, my tangles with weather and crazies and security problems—are probably enough to fill a book.

In fact, they *are* enough to fill a book.

The question is, Where to begin?

Well, there's an old saying in our industry: When an air traveler dies, it makes no difference whether he's going to heaven or hell. Either way (come on, you know this) . . . either way, he has to change in Atlanta.

Suggestions for Discussion

1. What is the tone of the narrator's account of his landing at the airport at Saginaw, Michigan? Show how it is suitable for his purpose.

2. Does the co-pilot's confession come as a surprise? What is its function in the narrative?

3. Discuss the factors listed by the author that led to the near-disaster of the landing.

4. What is the function of the final sentence in the essay?

Suggestions for Writing

1. Using this essay as a model, write a narrative in which you attempt to persuade the reader of your position on some social, economic, or political issue.

2. Following some of the leads in this essay, write a short research paper on the arguments for and against airline deregulation. Try to be as specific as Captain X.

Ursula K. Le Guin

Winged
The Creatures on My Mind

Ursula K. Le Guin (b. 1929) was born in Berkeley, California, and holds a B.A. from Radcliffe College and an M.A. from Columbia University. She has been a visiting lecturer and writer in residence at many universities in the United States and abroad. Her career as a writer of fiction, including science fiction, has been a distinguished one. Among her works are Planet of Exile (1967), The Left Hand of Darkness (1969), The Farthest Shore (1972), The Compass Rose (1982), and Always Coming Home (1985). She has also written numerous short stories, poems, criticism, and screenplays and has received numerous awards, including the National Book Award. This deeply personal essay shows by example how we can become more aware of and sensitive to other species that we tend to ignore.

I. The Beetle

When I stayed for a week in New Orleans, out near Tulane, I had an apartment with a balcony. It wasn't one of those cast-iron-lace showpieces of the French Quarter, but a deep, wood-railed balcony made for sitting outside in privacy, just the kind of place I like. But when I first stepped out on it, the first thing I saw was a huge beetle. It lay on its back directly under the light fixture. I thought it was dead, then saw its legs twitch and twitch again. No doubt it had been attracted by the light the night before, and had flown into it, and damaged itself mortally.

Big insects horrify me. As a child I feared moths and spiders, but adolescence cured me, as if those fears evaporated in the stew of hormones. But I never got enough hormones to make me easy with the large, hard-shelled insects: wood roaches, June bugs, mantises, cicadas. This beetle was a couple of inches long; its abdomen was ribbed, its legs long and jointed; it was dull reddish brown; it was dying. I felt a little sick seeing it lie there twitching, enough to keep me from sitting out on the balcony that first day.

Next morning, ashamed of my queasiness, I went out with the broom to sweep it away. But it was still twitching its legs and antennae, still dying. With the end of the broom handle I pushed it very gently a little farther toward the corner of the balcony, and then I sat to read and make notes in the wicker chair in the other corner, turned away from the beetle because its movements drew my eyes. My intense consciousness of it seemed to have something to do with my strangeness in that strange city, New Orleans, and my sense of being on the edge of the tropics—a hot, damp, swarming, fetid, luxuriant existence—as if my unease took the beetle as its visible sign. Why else did I think of it so much? I weighed maybe two thousand times what it weighed, and lived in a perceptual world utterly alien from its world. My feelings were quite out of proportion.

And if I had any courage or common sense, I kept telling myself, I'd step on the poor damned creature and put it out of its misery. We don't know what a beetle may or may not suffer, but it was, in the proper sense of the word, in agony, and the agony had gone on two nights and two days now. I put on my leather-soled loafers. But then I couldn't do it. It would crunch, ooze, squirt under my shoe. Could I hit it with the broom handle? No, I couldn't. I have had a cat with leukemia put down, and have stayed with a cat while he died; I think that if I were hungry, if I had reason to, I could kill for food, wring a chicken's neck, as my grandmothers did, with no more guilt and no less fellow feeling than they. My inability to kill this creature had nothing ethical about it, and no kindness in it. It was mere squeamishness. It was a little rotten place in me, like the soft brown spots in fruit; a sympathy that came not from respect but from loathing. It was a responsibility that would not act. It was guilt itself.

On the third morning the beetle was motionless, shrunken, dead. I got the broom again and swept it into the gutter of the balcony among dry leaves. And there it still is in the gutter of my mind, among dry leaves, a tiny dry husk, a ghost.

II. The Sparrow

In the humid New England summer the small cooling plant ran all day, making a deep, loud noise. Around the throbbing machinery was a frame of coarse wire net. I thought the bird was outside that wire net, then I hoped it was, then I wished it was. It was moving back and forth with the regularity of the trapped: the zoo animal that paces twelve feet east and twelve feet west and twelve feet east and twelve feet west, hour after hour; the heartbeat of the prisoner in the cell before the torture; the unending recurrence; the silent, steady panic. Back and forth, steadily fluttering between two wooden uprights just above a beam that supported the wire screen: a sparrow, ordinary, dusty, scrappy. I've seen sparrows fighting over territory till the feathers fly, and fucking cheerfully on telephone wires, and in winter gathering in trees in crowds like dirty little Christmas ornaments and talking all together like noisy children, chirp, charp, chirp, charp! But this sparrow was alone, and back and forth it went in terrible silence, trapped in wire and fear. What could I do? There was a door to the wire cage, but it was padlocked. I went on. I tell you I felt that bird beat its wings right here, here under my breastbone in the hollow of my heart. I said in my mind, Is it my fault? Did I build the cage? Just because I happened to see it, is it my sparrow? But my heart was low already, and I knew now that I would be down, down like a bird whose wings won't bear it up, a starving bird.

Then on the path I saw the man, one of the campus managers. The bird's fear gave me courage to speak. "I'm so sorry to bother you," I said. "I'm just visiting here at the librarians' conference—we met the other day in the office. I didn't know what to do, because there's a bird that got into the cooling plant there, inside the screen, and it can't get out." That was enough, too much, but I had to go on. "The noise of the machinery, I think the noise confuses it, and I didn't know what to do. I'm sorry." Why did I apologize? For what?

"Have a look," he said, not smiling, not frowning.

He turned and came with me. He saw the bird beating back and forth, back and forth in silence. He unlocked the padlock. He had the key.

The bird didn't see the door open behind it. It kept beating back and forth along the screen. I found a little stick on the path and threw it against the outside of the screen to frighten the bird into breaking its pattern. It went the wrong way, deeper into the cage, toward the machinery. I threw another stick, hard, and the bird veered and then turned and flew out. I watched the open door, I saw it fly.

The man and I closed the door. He locked it. "Be getting on," he said, not smiling, not frowning, and went on his way, a man with a lot on his mind, a hardworking man. But did he have no joy in it? That's what I think about now. Did he have the key, the power to set free, the will to do it, but no joy in doing it? It is his soul I think about now, if that is the word for it, the spirit, that sparrow.

III. The Gull

They were winged, all the creatures on my mind.

This one is hard to tell about. It was a seagull. Gulls on Klatsand Beach, on any North Pacific shore, are all alike in their two kinds: white adults with black wingtips and yellow bills; and yearlings, adult-sized but with delicately figured brown features. They soar and cry, swoop, glide, dive, squabble, and grab; they stand in their multitudes at evening in the sunset shallows of the creek mouth before they rise in silence to fly out to sea, where they will sleep the night afloat on waves far out beyond the breakers, like a fleet of small white ships with sails furled and no riding lights. Gulls eat anything, gulls clean the beach, gulls eat dead gulls. There are no individual gulls. They are magnificent flyers, big, clean, strong birds, rapacious, suspicious, fearless. Sometimes as they ride the wind I have seen them as part of the wind and the sea, exactly as the foam, the sand, the fog is part of it all, all one, and in such moments of vision I have truly seen the gulls.

But this was one gull, an individual, for it stood alone near the low-tide water's edge with a broken wing. I saw first that the left wing dragged, then saw the naked bone jutting like an ivory knife up from blood-rusted feathers. Something had attacked it, something that could half tear away a wing, maybe a shark when it dove to catch a fish. It stood there. As I came nearer, it saw me. It gave no sign. It did not sidle away, as gulls do when you walk toward them, and then fly if you keep coming on. I stopped. It stood, its flat red feet in the shallow water of a tidal lagoon above the breakers. The tide was on the turn, returning. It stood and waited for the sea.

The idea that worried me was that a dog might find it before the sea did. Dogs roam that long beach. A dog chases gulls, barking and rushing, excited; the gulls fly up in a rush of wings; the dog trots back, maybe a little hangdog, to its owner strolling far down the beach. But a gull that could not fly and the smell of blood would put a dog into a frenzy of barking, lunging, teasing, torturing. I imagined that. My imagination makes me human and makes me a fool; it gives me all the world and exiles me from it. The gull stood waiting for the dog, for the other gulls, for the tide, for what came, living its life completely until death. Its eye looked straight through me, seeing truly, seeing nothing but the sea, the sand, the wind.

Suggestions for Discussion

1. This essay has a subtitle, "The Creatures on My Mind." What do the creatures under reflection have in common? How do they determine the organization of the essay?

2. What is the underlying idea that binds these reflections together? What conclusions based on her experiences does the author suggest? What do these conclusions have in common?

3. How does the language of the reflections express the author's concerns? Is this a formal or an informal essay?

4. What is the connection between this essay and the others in its section? How do you respond to its very personal nature?

5. In what way are the author's conclusions unusual?

Suggestions for Writing

1. Many of us have had experiences with creatures in nature similar to those of the author. Write an essay in which you describe such an experience and in which you draw some conclusions based on it.

2. Keep a journal for one week in which you record your observations of birds or insects. You should try to examine the degree to which you either sympathize with or are repelled by them. Attempt to draw some conclusions about the world of nature from your own observations.

Colin Fletcher

A Bend in the Road

Colin Fletcher (b. 1922), born in Cardiff, Wales, studied at the West Buckland School in North Devon, England. He served in the Royal Marine Commandos, eventually becoming captain, from 1940 until 1947. He has been a manufacturer's representative, a farmer, and a road builder in Africa; he has worked in Canada for mining companies during the summer; he has worked as head janitor in a San Francisco hospital; and since 1958 he has been a writer, living in California. His books include *The Thousand-Mile Summer* (1964), *The Man Who Walked Through Time* (1968), *The Complete Walker III* (1984), and *The Secret Worlds of Colin Fletcher* (1989). He has also written *Learn of the Green World* (1991), which is an audiotape. This essay expresses an environmentalist's concern for the subtle way that development destroys the delicate balance between countryside and neighborhood.

When we contemplate such rents in the fabric as Los Angeles and the Love Canal, Beirut and Chernobyl, Ethiopia and the East Bronx, most of us tend to bleat about politicians or multi-nationals or drug cartels or other handy breeds of "them." Indictments of this kind are easy and exculpating and slightly titillating; but perhaps we should be looking closer to home.

A hundred yards from my house there is a bend in our little county road. The road is narrow and the bend is blind, and vehicles are apt to swing around it in wide, dangerous trajectories. If you are driving and if you have any sense, you slow down and sound your horn. If you are walking you hug the outside sweep of the bend, between the blacktop and the chain-link fence, close to the red fire hydrant; but if it is a good day, inside and outside your skin, you look beyond these tokens of "shruburbia" and discern curving harmonies.

The harmonies of the place were once far more resonant. At this bend, the road cuts through a notch between our valley's main southern slope and a hill-capped spur that geologic chance has thrust out from it. This notch or gap or saddle was once a room-sized patch of level ground, probably somewhat open, as such places tend to be. Grass grew, and a few small bushes, but the trees stood back. To the right, though, the slope was heavily wooded, and to the left a fringe of live oaks masked the outlier hill's steepsided dome. East and west, the saddle commanded vistas: down-valley to a glimpse of ocean; up-valley into a rich and rolling panorama of rising, interlocking ridges.

Once upon a time, this saddle held a peripherally pivotal place in valley life. Band-tailed pigeons and robins and other birds, journeying along the valley's flank from feeding place to feeding place, swept through in dense, swooshing flocks. Tule elk and black-tailed deer, traveling to and from their own feeding and sleeping and breeding places, also funnelled through. And predators passed by on their wider excursions: bobcats and foxes and coyotes and mountain lions and black and gizzly bears—but not, at that time, men.

668

The predators surely recognized the saddle as a natural place for an ambush; and after every successful strike the turkey vultures, or buzzards, that for hours had been in holding patterns above the dome of the outlier hill—floating on updrafts focused by its steep slopes—moved in to fulfill their role as garbage collectors.

For many, many years, this life continued at its slow, rhythmic pace. Animal populations waxed and waned. From time to time fire swept through the saddle; but afterward the vegetation resprouted and resumed its recurring program of succession.

When the first men appeared, nothing really changed. The men came only rarely to the saddle, passing by on their hunting and seed-gathering forays. They too knew a good ambush site when they saw one, and they duly lay in wait, flintheaded arrows ready, for the deer and elk, for the band-tailed pigeons and for any quail unwise enough to cross the open space. Or perhaps they set traps. But the men made just one more predator—and a rare and rather inefficient one, at that—so they disturbed no balances. And they altered the saddle, physically, not at all. It remained a beautiful, curving, harmonious place.

For many more years this state of affairs continued. The life-form cycles—of vegetation and birds and beasts, including humans—rolled on. Down decades and centuries, human hunting techniques improved only marginally, if at all, so men still disturbed no balances.

Then, little more than two centuries ago, a new, paler tribe of people came up from the south.

At first no newcomers visited this obscure saddle on the flanks of a long, outlying valley. They began, though, to kill off the local bears, both grizzly and black, and soon there were no bears visiting the saddle. The new tribe of men killed off the mountain lions, too, and before long the lions became rare, and most of the survivors lived deep in the forests. The newcomers established one of their red-roofed adobe missions at the mouth of the valley, and strove to change the habits of the darker and earlier people. Soon, these earlier humans rarely visited the saddle, either.

Then one day a party of pale newcomer land surveyors rode up into the saddle to mark a boundary of one of the vast estates into which they were dividing the whole countryside. They came to the saddle because the boundary happened to cut directly through it and then slant up a slope of the outlier hill. That first day, the men probably approached the saddle from the west, up a steep wooded gully, but certain local relics suggest that at some point they, the land surveyors, cut the first road to the saddle, angling it up at a gentler grade than the gully offered. Perhaps they just followed a deer trail. If it was not the surveyors who cut this road, then it was probably the men who in due course came to fence the boundary line. Anyway, a process had begun.

Within a few years, a different pale-faced tribe took over control of the land, and soon their homes began to dot the valley floor and flanks. Before long they cleared outlying fire roads to protect their houses from the summer brush fires. One of these dirt fire roads followed the line of the surveyors' road up to the saddle and pushed out beyond it. Because the hillside was steep, the upper side of the widened road now cut deep into it, above and below the saddle. The road therefore sliced more severely into the saddle's southern flank, sheering off almost half the root system of a live oak that grew there. For the first time, the curving harmony of the place suffered a serious wound.

Before long, someone built a cabin along the rough and ready road, half a mile beyond the saddle. Naturally, he improved his access road. In doing so he sliced off a little more from the saddle's flank, a little more from the live oak's root system. About this time—no more than fifty years ago—some local horseback riders cut a narrow bridle trail clear around the slope of the domed outlier hill. Soon, around on the plunging and friable far side of the hill, the trail crumbled away; but its useless, deep-cut beginning and ending remained, converging at the saddle as two stark and angular wounds in its once curving harmonies.

Down in the valley, the buildings grew more dense—and spread outward. Someone else built a house a little way down the fire road. A few more years, and the land around the saddle was subdivided. A dirt road was cut up the side of the outlier hill to the obvious building site at its summit—now leveled in readiness for a house. Down at the saddle, the road bisected the termini of the bridle trail, where the curves had once met in harmony. Soon, when a couple of people decided to build four or five houses along the old fire road and sell them, the county widened the road and blacktopped it. Saddle and live oak suffered further degradation.

Power poles now went in along the road. One pole stood on the lip of the saddle, so sited that to anyone standing there it rose stage center in the rich and rolling panorama of rising, interlocking ridges. The new houses needed a booster pump for their water supply, and the pump needed a meter, so two boxes appeared a few feet above the saddle, opposite the power pole. Access to the boxes was up a flight of wooden steps, set in a shallow cleft in the road embankment. Steps and gully were both reasonably discreet, but you could not pretend that they did anything to mend the tatters of the old harmonies.

This was the state of affairs when, thirteen years ago, I bought, from its second owner, the house nearest the saddle, just a hundred yards down the road.

At that time, the country around the saddle was, by shruburban standards, a quiet and reasonably harmonious place. Flocks of band-tailed pigeons— though probably smaller than when Indians lay waiting for them—still swooshed through the saddle. So, at certain seasons, did the robins. Spring and summer, quail families struttled querulously abroad. Deer sometimes glided through the oaks and skittered across the road. At night, raccoons roamed, and a pair of foxes often came to the water tub at the end of my veranda. Once or twice a year I would look out my picture window at the flank of the outlier hill and see a bobcat strolling across an open grassy patch just above three fire-charred fence posts that still survived from the original Spanish estate line.

In the years since I moved in, nothing dramatic has happened, really. Nothing at all, in fact, except natural events in the advance of what we label progress.

The county, for example, has applied normal civilized maintenance to the road. Periodically, it has resurfaced the blacktop. Because there was space to spare on one side of the saddle, the blackness tended to creep outward over what was once a room-sized grassy patch. The county also executed its annual spraying of roadside vegetation and tidy-up grading of ditches and embankments. Such deeds no doubt helped maintain the road—as much as they did anywhere else.

Meanwhile, five or six additional houses were built along our road. None stood within sight of the saddle, but because of them the saddle suffered a further series of improvements. Most of them were minor. Each was regarded by at least some of us locals as useful or even necessary.

All our homes face a severe fire hazard, and some years ago our excellent fire department installed a roadside hydrant on the level ground of the original saddle. At first it was painted bright yellow, then red.

About this time, a new house went in barely two hundred feet above the saddle—not for the owner to live in but for rental. Trees screen it, though, and the only obvious impact on the saddle comes when its renters are a rowdy bunch.

Soon afterward, a Midwesterner bought the subdivision that embraced the whole of the domed outlier hill, and although he was not yet ready to build he installed across the line of the saddle—which was the only place you could gain motorized access to "his" hill—an ugly galvanized chain link fence with an ugly galvanized gate. Somehow, the fence lay even more heavily on the saddle than the bulldozed road and bridle trail. It was possible, though, to hope that it lay less permanently.

Then the water company upgraded its booster pump and meter. It also tore down the flight of weathered wooden access steps, hacked its shallow cleft into a deep and angular trench, and installed a modern gray concrete stairway equipped with an equally soulless metal-pipe hand rail.

Soon, the electric company improved our supply—and the power pole that stood stage center in the panorama of rising, interlocking ridges became a kingpin in the upgraded local system. Seven lines now fed in and out of this pole, and its crown sprouted a wild assortment of gadgetry, including two extra cross arms festooned with massive double-dish porcelain insulators and a big gray metal transformer, unlovely as a garbage can. Sullen gray plastic or metal shields shrouded support stays and parts of the main pole. And so that no one, sober or otherwise, could possibly run into this repulsive, cobwebbed monstrosity—which even in Los Angeles would have stood out as a monument to ugliness—it bore at human eye level a pair of garish metal reflector strips that glittered by day and at night, in approaching headlights, glowed like evil rectangular eyes.

By this time, Friday-night teeny-boppers had bopped the gate in the new chain link fence and would drive up to the now-leveled summit of the hill and there—or, when it got crowded, down at the saddle, just inside the felled gate—they would, until the sheriffs arrived, bop their radios up to max and strew the place with beer cans and bottles and audio tapes and fragments of female underwear and condoms.

All these changes, you will note, had "utility" as an excuse. In somebody's eyes, anyway.

Then, a few years ago, the absentee Midwesterner sold "his" hill to a man with other homes on other continents, and this new man bulldozed the flat on the hill's summit flatter and bigger, and erected there a large and angular house, soon known locally as "the powerhouse," that probably had Frank

Lloyd Wright executing at least one turn in his grave—and then another turn when he saw the matching power gate that this man built down in the saddle, across his newly blacktopped access road. For the gate was also a power gate—one that could be opened and closed remotely, from the house—and this stark erection (stout sliding ironwork, painted off-white; two massive, ill-proportioned, off-white pillars; square box housing the machinery) stood dead center in what had once been a saddle. A friend of mine seeing it for the first time, said, "You know, it's difficult to imagine anyone putting up such a gate outside anything except a prison." Dead center on his pretentious gate, our new neighbor wired a cheap red plastic sign: "Beware of Dog." And once a week, on the day when all of us put out our offerings for the modern garbage disposers, he put out a galvanized garbage can so battered that its lid would not fit properly and the wind and passing animals often left a ring of refuse lying around it, there in the once beautiful, curving and harmonious saddle, beside the still-standing galvanized chain-link fence, midway between the red fire hydrant and the angular off-white gate complex, opposite the mutilated live oak roots and the water company's cement-and-metal stairway, in the lee of the grotesque, spider-webbed power pole.

A spin-off from the gate complex has been that local teeny-boppers, barred from the hill's summit, now favor the roadside space outside it as a small-scale substitute where they can—for short interludes, before one of us neighbors has time to summon the sheriff—at least max car radios and spread a little miscellaneous litter.

Yet I have to say that in spite of all the degradations our little enclave beyond the saddle remains, by modern standards, a quiet and relatively harmonious place. Band-tailed pigeons, and robins at their season, still swoosh through the saddle. Quail families still stroll. Buzzards still soar above the hill on its daily updrafts. Hawks, too. Raccoons still roam at night, I think, and deer still glide and skitter—though less freely since the powerhouse dweller extended his chain-link fence and girdled his garden with electrified wires. It is a long time, though, since the foxes visited my veranda. And I have not glimpsed a bobcat since the powerhouse went up. The saddest fact, it seems to me, is that the saddle, where most of our improvements seem to have focused—the saddle that was once the local jewel—has become our bleakest corner. What is even sadder, perhaps, is that few people seem to recognize quite what has happened—or even in some cases, to recognize that our bend in the road was once a saddle. For my part, I guess I had begun to resign myself—though by no means happily—to the slow toll exacted by "progress."

But one day last week as I walked along the road toward the bend I saw something lying on the blacktop, out in the middle of the road, midway between the water company's concrete stairway and the power pole. When I reached it, I saw that it was a white paper bag, and that something even whiter, and gooey, was oozing out of it. Carefully, I picked the bag up. It bore the insignia of a famous fast food dispensary. I pulled the mouth of the bag open, peered: several french fries; a plastic knife and fork; such unconsumed portions of a melting ice cream stick as had not already oozed out onto the blacktop; and four pennies.

I stood there for a moment, studying what I had found. In itself it was nothing, of course. Just a small sample of typical modern litter. But I stood for a long moment—dangerously, there in the middle of the blacktop, just beyond the bend around which vehicles are now apt to swing in wide trajectories; stood there in what had once been a beautiful saddle; stood there looking down at the unsavory little sample that had been jettisoned without thought; looking down in particular at the now-sticky pennies that someone could not be bothered to keep. Then I raised my eyes.

I found myself looking out over the red fire hydrant and the battered garbage can with its fringe of refuse, looking over and beyond the galvanized chain-link fence, looking through the gross and repulsive spider web of the power pole, with the off-white shape of the hideous gate complex tucked in at the left edge of my vision. And beyond the rich, rolling, ancient panorama of rising, interlocking ridges I saw—spread vividly out before my mind's unhappy eye—our modern panorama of Los Angeles and the Love Canal, Beirut and Chernobyl, Ethiopia and the East Bronx. Beyond them I perceived larger rents that we have torn in the fabric: polluted oceans, raped rainforests, the ozone rift. In that instant of looking I did not need mundane logical bridges to connect those vivid distant vistas with the tattered remnant rags of the saddle in which I stood, or with the paper bag still clutched in my hand and its attendant little pool of ice cream lying white and sticky on the blacktop at my feet. It was a short journey from one to the other, as the canker creeps.

Suggestions for Discussion

1. This essay begins and ends with what the author considers outrageous violations of the environment. What do these examples have in common? Are they all equally significant as disasters? Name other examples.

2. What is the emotional effect of the brief history of the valley and the hill above before it began to be transformed into a "neighborhood"?

3. The author is clearly conscious of and sensitive to the negative results of land development. How aware are you of similar events in your own neighborhood? If you live in a city, do you see examples of the ill effects of development?

4. How does the author organize his argument against development? What is the tone of this essay? How does the last episode of finding food in the road contribute to the tone?

Suggestions for Writing

1. Write an essay in which you describe the deterioration of a neighborhood or countryside with which you are familiar. Explain, if possible, the causes for deterioration. Are the causes often obscure or disguised?

2. Opponents of development cite the destruction of the environment as their primary concern. However, opponents of the environmental movement complain that environmentalists are insensitive to the loss of jobs that occurs when development is blocked. They also regard the environmental movement as white and middle-class. Write an essay in which you discuss these opposing views. Prepare for your essay by following newspaper and television debates on this issue.

Fiction

Aldous Huxley

Conditioning the Children

Aldous Huxley (1894–1963) was born in England and educated at Oxford. He is the author of many novels including *Point Counter Point* (1928) and the anti-utopian *Brave New World* (1932). He also wrote essays, short stories, poetry, and plays. After he moved to Southern California, he became increasingly interested in Hindu philosophy and mysticism. *The Doors of Perception* (1954) describes his experience with hallucinogenic drugs. This brief selection from *Brave New World* describes without comment painful experiments to condition the minds of newborn infants.

The D.H.C.[1] and his students stepped into the nearest lift and were carried up to the fifth floor.

INFANT NURSERIES. NEO-PAVLOVIAN CONDITIONING ROOMS, announced the notice board.

The Director opened a door. They were in a large bare room, very bright and sunny; for the whole of the southern wall was a single window. Half a dozen nurses, trousered and jacketed in the regulation white viscose-linen uniform, their hair aseptically hidden under white caps, were engaged in setting out bowls of roses in a long row across the floor. Big bowls, packed tight with blossom. Thousands of petals, ripeblown and silkily smooth, like the cheeks of innumerable little cherubs, but of cherubs, in that bright light, not exclusively pink and Aryan, but also luminously Chinese, also Mexican, also apoplectic with too much blowing of celestial trumpets, also pale as death, pale with the posthumous whiteness of marble.

The nurses stiffened to attention as the D.H.C. came in.

"Set out the books," he said curtly.

In silence the nurses obeyed his command. Between the rose bowls the books were duly set out—a row of nursery quartos opened invitingly each at some gaily coloured image of beast or fish or bird.

"Now bring in the children."

They hurried out of the room and returned in a minute or two, each pushing a kind of tall dumb-waiter laden, on all its four wire-netted shelves with eight-month-old babies, all exactly alike (a Bokanovsky Group, it was evident) and all (since their caste was Delta) dressed in khaki.

"Put them down on the floor."

The infants were unloaded.

"Now turn them so that they can see the flowers and books."

[1]Director of Hatcheries and Conditioning.

Turned, the babies at once fell silent, then began to crawl towards those clusters of sleek colors, those shapes so gay and brilliant on the white pages. As they approached, the sun came out of a momentary eclipse behind a cloud. The roses flamed up as though with a sudden passion from within; a new and profound significance seemed to suffuse the shining pages of the books. From the ranks of the crawling babies came little squeals of excitement, gurgles and twitterings of pleasure.

The Director rubbed his hands. "Excellent!" he said. "It might almost have been done on purpose."

The swiftest crawlers were already at their goal. Small hands reached out uncertainly, touched, grasped, unpetaling the transfigured roses, crumpling the illuminated pages of the books. The Director waited until all were happily busy. Then, "Watch carefully," he said. And, lifting his hand, he gave the signal.

The Head Nurse, who was standing by a switchboard at the other end of the room, pressed down a little lever.

There was a violent explosion. Shriller and ever shriller, a siren shrieked. Alarm bells maddeningly sounded.

The children started, screamed; their faces were distorted with terror.

"And now," the Director shouted (for the noise was deafening), "now we proceed to rub in the lesson with a mild electric shock."

He waved his hand again, and the Head Nurse pressed a second lever. The screaming of the babies suddenly changed its tone. There was something desperate, almost insane, about the sharp spasmodic yelps to which they now gave utterance. Their little bodies twitched and stiffened; their limbs moved jerkily as if to the tug of unseen wires.

"We can electrify that whole strip of floor," bawled the Director in explanation. "But that's enough," he signalled to the nurse.

The explosions ceased, the bells stopped ringing, the shriek of the siren died down from tone to tone into silence. The stiffly twitching bodies relaxed, and what had become the sob and yelp of infant maniacs broadened out once more into a normal howl of ordinary terror.

"Offer them the flowers and the books again."

The nurses obeyed; but at the approach of the roses, at the mere sight of those gaily-coloured images of pussy and cock-a-doodle-doo and baa-baa black sheep, the infants shrank away in horror; the volume of their howling suddenly increased.

"Observe," said the Director triumphantly, "observe."

Books and loud noises, flowers and electric shocks—already in the infant mind the couples were compromisingly linked; and after two hundred repetitions of the same or a similar lesson would be wedded indissolubly. What man has joined, nature is powerless to put asunder.

"They'll grow up with what the psychologists used to call an 'instinctive' hatred of books and flowers. Reflexes unalterably conditioned. They'll be safe from books and botany all their lives." The Director turned to his nurses. "Take them away again."

Still yelling, the khaki babies were loaded on to their dumb-waiters and wheeled out, leaving behind them the smell of sour milk and a most welcome silence.

Suggestions for Discussion

1. Summarize the Pavlovian experiment demonstrated on the children. Do the doctor and the student observers regard the experiment as cruel? Explain their attitude.

2. What details in the selection would you regard as contributing to the anti-utopian atmosphere? How does Huxley employ imagery in the details?

Suggestion for Writing

Write a story that describes a method of controlling human behavior. You may wish to place the events in a utopian, an anti-utopian, or a completely ordinary setting.

Bessie Head

The Wind and a Boy

Bessie Head (1937–1986), a prominent African writer, was born in Pieter-maritzburg and lived in Botswana from the mid-1960s. She wrote novels and tales, the latter based on the oral tradition. Her third novel, A Question of Power, demonstrated a connection between political integrity and personal morality. Among her other works are Maru (1971) and Serowe: Village of the Rain Wind (1981). Her works continue to be reprinted since her death. Her story, "The Wind and a Boy," from The Collector of Treasures (1977), reveals her skillful use of the oral tradition.

Like all the village boys, Friedman had a long wind blowing for him, but perhaps the enchanted wind that blew for him, filled the whole world with magic.

Until they became ordinary, dull grown men, who drank beer and made babies, the little village boys were a special set all on their own. They were kings whom no one ruled. They wandered where they willed from dawn to dusk and only condescended to come home at dusk because they were afraid of the horrible things in the dark that might pounce on them. Unlike the little girls who adored household chores and drawing water, it was only now and then that the boys showed themselves as useful attachments to any household. When the first hard rains of summer fell, small dark shapes, quite naked except for their loin-cloths, sped out of the village into the bush. They knew that the first downpour had drowned all the wild rabbits, moles, and porcupines in their burrows in the earth. As they crouched down near the entrances to the burrows, they would see a small drowned nose of an animal peeping out; they knew it had struggled to emerge from its burrow, flooded by the sudden rush of storm water and as they pulled out the animal, they would say, pityingly:

"Birds have more sense than rabbits, moles and porcupines. They build their homes in trees." But it was hunting made easy, for no matter how hard a boy and his dog ran, a wild rabbit ran ten times faster; a porcupine hurled his poisonous quills into the body; and a mole stayed where he thought it was safe—deep under the ground. So it was with inordinate pride that the boys carried home armfuls of dead animals for their families to feast on for many days. Apart from that, the boys lived very much as they pleased, with the wind and their own games.

Now and then, the activities of a single family could captivate the imagination and hearts of all the people of their surroundings; for years and years, the combination of the boy, Friedman and his grandmother, Sejosenye, made the people of Ga-Sefete-Molemo ward, smile, laugh, then cry.

They smiled at his first two phases. Friedman came home as a small bundle from the hospital, a bundle his grandmother nursed carefully near her bosom and crooned to day and night with extravagant care and tenderness.

"She is like that," people remarked, "because he may be the last child she will ever nurse. Sejosenye is old now and will die one of these days; the child is a gift to keep her heart warm."

Indeed, all Sejosenye's children were grown, married, and had left home. Of all her children, only her last-born daughter was unmarried and Friedman was the result of some casual mating she had indulged in, in a town a hundred miles away where she had a job as a typist. She wanted to return to her job almost immediately, so she handed the child over to her mother and that was that; she could afford to forget him as he had a real mother now. During all the time that Sejosenye haunted the hospital, awaiting her bundle, a friendly foreign doctor named Friedman took a fancy to her maternal, grandmotherly ways. He made a habit of walking out of his path to talk to her. She never forgot it and on receiving her bundle she called the baby, Friedman.

They smiled at his second phase, a small dark shadow who toddled silently and gravely beside a very tall grandmother; wherever the grandmother went, there went Friedman. Most women found this phase of the restless, troublesome toddler tedious; they dumped the toddler onto one of their younger girls and were off to weddings and visits on their own.

"Why can't you leave your handbag at home some times, granny?" they said.

"Oh, he's no trouble," Sejosenye would reply.

They began to laugh at his third phase. Almost overnight he turned into a tall, spindly-legged, graceful gazelle with large, grave eyes. There was an odd, musical lilt to his speech and when he teased, or was up to mischief, he moved his head on his long thin neck from side to side like a cobra. It was he who became the king of kings of all the boys in his area; he could turn his hand to anything and made the best wire cars with their wheels of shoe polish tins. All his movements were neat, compact, decisive, and for his age he was a boy who knew his own mind. They laughed at his knowingness and certainty on all things, for he was like the grandmother who had had a flaming youth all her own too. Sejosenye had scandalized the whole village in her days of good morals by leaving her own village ward to live with a married man in Ga-Sefete-Molemo ward. She had won him from his wife and married him and then lived down the scandal in the way only natural queens can.

Even in old age, she was still impressive. She sailed through the village, head in the air, with a quiet, almost expressionless face. She had developed large buttocks as time went by and they announced their presence firmly in rhythm with her walk.

Another of Sejosenye's certainties was that she was a woman who could plough, but it was like a special gift. Each season, in drought or hail or sun, she removed herself to her lands. She not only ploughed but nursed and brooded over her crops. She was there all the time till the corn ripened and the birds had to be chased off the land, till harvesting and threshing were done; so that even in drought years with their scanty rain, she came home with some crops. She was the envy of all the women of the surroundings.

"Sejosenye always eats fine things in her house," they said. "She ploughs and then sits down for many months and enjoys the fruits of her labour."

The women also envied her beautiful grandson. There was something special there, so that even when Friedman moved into his bad phase, they forgave him crimes other boys received a sound thrashing for. The small boys were terrible thieves who harassed people by stealing their food and money. It was all a part of the games they played but one which people did not like. Of them all, Friedman was the worst thief, so that his name was mentioned more and more in any thieving that had been uncovered.

"But Friedman showed us how to open the window with a knife and string," the sobbing, lashed boys would protest.

"Friedman isn't as bad as you," the parents would reply, irrationally. They were hypnotized by a beautiful creature. The boy Friedman, who had become a real nuisance by then, also walked around as though he were special. He couldn't possibly be a thief and he added an aloof, offended, disdainful expression to his pretty face. He wasn't just an ordinary sort of boy in Ga-Sefete-Molemo ward. He was . . .

It happened, quite accidentally, that his grandmother told him all those stories about the hunters, warriors, and emissaries of old. She was normally a quiet, absent-minded woman, given to dreaming by herself but she liked to sing the boy a little song now and then as they sat by the outdoor fire. A lot of them were church songs and rather sad; they more or less passed as her bed-time prayer at night—she was one of the old church-goers. Now and then she added a quaint little song to her repertoire and as the nighttime, fire-light flames flickered between them, she never failed to note that this particular song was always well received by the boy. A little light would awaken in his eyes and he would bend forward and listen attentively.

"Welcome, Robinson Crusoe, welcome," she would sing, in clear, sweet tones. "How could you stay, so long away, Robinson how could you do so?"

When she was very young, Sejosenye had attended the mission school of the village for about a year; made a slight acquaintance with the ABC and one, two, three, four, five, and the little song about Robinson Crusoe. But girls didn't need an education in those days when ploughing and marriage made up their whole world. Yet Robinson Crusoe lived on as a gay and out-of-context memory of her school-days. One evening the boy leaned forward and asked:

"Is that a special praise-poem song for Robinson Crusoe, grandmother?"

"Oh yes," she replied, smiling.

"It appears that the people liked Robinson Crusoe much," the boy observed. "Did he do great things for them?"

"Oh yes," she said, smiling.

"What great things did he do?" the boy asked, pointedly.

"They say he was a hunter who went by Gweta side and killed an elephant all by himself," she said, making up a story on the spot. "Oh! In those days, no man could kill an elephant by himself. All the regiments had to join together and each man had to thrust his sword into the side of the elephant before it died. Well, Robinson Crusoe was gone many days and people wondered about him: 'Perhaps he has been eaten by a lion,' they said. 'Robinson likes to be a solitary person and do foolish things. We won't ever go out into the bush by ourselves because we know it is dangerous.' Well, one day, Robinson suddenly appeared in their midst and people could see that he had a great thing on his mind. They all gathered around him. He said: 'I have killed an elephant for all the people.' The people were surprised: 'Robinson!' they said. 'It is impossible! How did you do it? The very thought of an elephant approaching the village makes us shiver!' And Robinson said: 'Ah, people, I saw a terrible sight! I was standing at the feet of the elephant. I was just a small ant. I could not see the world any more. Elephant was above me until his very head touched the sky and his ears spread out like great wings. He was angry but I only looked into one eye which was turning round and round in anger. What to do now? I thought it better to put that eye out. I raised my spear and threw it at the angry eye. People! It went right inside. Elephant said not a word and he fell to one side. Come I will show you what I have done.' Then the women cried in joy: 'Loo-loo-loo!' They ran to fetch their containers as some wanted the meat of the elephant; some wanted the fat. The men made their knives sharp. They would make shoes and many things from the skin and bones. There was something for all the people in the great work Robinson Crusoe did."

All this while, as he listened to the story, the boy's eyes had glowed softly. At the end of it, he drew in a long breath.

"Grandmother," he whispered, adroitly stepping into the role of Robinson Crusoe, the great hunter, "One day, I'm going to be like that. I'm going to be a hunter like Robinson Crusoe and bring meat to all the people." He paused for breath and then added tensely: "And what other great thing did Robinson Crusoe do?"

"Tsaa!" she said clicking her tongue in exhaustion. "Am I then going away that I must tell *all* the stories at once?"

Although his image of Robinson Crusoe, the great hunter, was never to grow beyond his everyday boyish activities of pushing wire cars, hunting in the fields for wild rabbits, climbing trees to pull down old bird's nests and yelling out in alarm to find that a small snake now occupied the abandoned abode, or racing against the wind with the spoils of his latest theft, the stories awakened a great tenderness in him. If Robinson Crusoe was not churning up the dust in deadly hand-to-hand combat with an enemy, he was crossing swollen rivers and wild jungles as the great messenger and ambassador of the chief—all his activities were touchingly in aid of or in defence of, the people. One day Friedman expressed this awakened compassion for life in a strange way. After a particularly violent storm, people found their huts invaded by many small mice and they were hard-pressed to rid themselves of these pests. Sejosenye ordered Friedman to kill the mice.

"But grandmother," he protested. "They have come to us for shelter. They lost all their homes in the storm. It's better that I put them in a box and carry them out into the fields again once the rains are over."

She had laughed in surprise at this and spread the story around among her women friends, who smiled tenderly then said to their own offspring: "Friedman isn't as bad as you."

Life and its responsibilities began to weigh down heavily on Friedman as he approached his fourteenth year. Less time was spent in boyish activities. He grew more and more devoted to his grandmother and concerned to assist her in every way. He wanted a bicycle so that he might run up and down to the shops for her, deliver messages, or do any other chore she might have in mind. His mother, who worked in a town far away, sent him the money to purchase the bicycle. The gift brought the story of his life abruptly to a close.

Towards the beginning of the rainy season, he accompanied his grandmother to her lands which were some twenty miles outside the village. They sowed seed together after the hired tractor had turned up the land but the boy's main chore was to keep the household pot filled with meat. Sometimes they ate birds Friedman had trapped, sometimes they ate fried tortoise-meat or wild rabbit; but there was always something as the bush abounded with animal life. Sejosenye only had to take a bag of mealie meal, packets of sugar, tea, and powdered milk as provisions for their stay at the lands; meat was never a problem. Mid-way through the ploughing season, she began to run out of sugar, tea, and milk.

"Friedman," she said that evening. "I shall wake you early tomorrow morning. You will have to take the bicycle into the village and purchase some more sugar, tea, and milk."

He was up at dawn with the birds, a solitary figure cycling on a pathway through the empty bush. By nine, he had reached the village and first made his way to Ga-Sefete-Molemo ward and the yard of a friend of his grandmother, who gave him a cup of tea and a plate of porridge. Then he put one foot on the bicycle and turned to smile at the woman with his beautiful gazelle eyes. His smile was to linger vividly before her for many days as a short while later, hard pounding feet came running into her yard to report that Friedman was dead.

He pushed the bicycle through the winding, sandy pathway of the village ward, reached the high embankment of the main road, peddled vigorously up it and out of the corner of his eye, saw a small green truck speeding towards him. In the devil-may-care fashion of all the small boys, he cycled right into its path, turned his head and smiled appealingly at the driver. The truck caught him on the front bumper, squashed the bicycle and dragged the boy along at a crazy speed for another hundred yards, dropped him and careered on another twenty yards before coming to a halt. The boy's pretty face was a smear all along the road and he only had a torso left.

People of Ga-Sefete-Molemo ward never forgot the last coherent words Sejosenye spoke to the police. A number of them climbed into the police truck and accompanied it to her lands. They saw her walk slowly and enquiringly towards the truck, they heard the matter-of-fact voice of the policeman

announce the death, then they heard Sejosenye say piteously: "Can't you return those words back?"

She turned away from them, either to collect her wits or the few possessions she had brought with her. Her feet and buttocks quivered anxiously as
she stumbled towards her hut. Then her feet tripped her up and she fell to
the ground like a stunned log.

The people of Ga-Sefete-Molemo ward buried the boy Friedman but none
of them would go near the hospital where Sejosenye lay. The stories brought
to them by way of the nurses were too terrible for words. They said the old
woman sang and laughed and talked to herself all the time. So they merely
asked each other: "Have you been to see Mma-Sejosenye?" "I'm afraid I cannot. It would kill my heart." Two weeks later, they buried her.

As was village habit, the incident was discussed thoroughly from all sides
till it was understood. In this timeless, sleepy village, the goats stood and
suckled their young ones on the main road or lay down and took their afternoon naps there. The motorists either stopped for them or gave way. But it
appeared that the driver of the truck had neither brakes on his car nor a
driving licence. He belonged to the new, rich civil-servant class whose salaries had become fantastically high since independence. They had to have cars
in keeping with their new status; they had to have any car, as long as it was a
car; they were in such a hurry about everything that they couldn't be bothered to take driving lessons. And thus progress, development, and a preoccupation with status and living-standards first announced themselves to the
village. It looked like being an ugly story with many decapitated bodies on
the main road.

Suggestions for Discussion

1. Why do the older people of the village have a special regard for the young boys?

2. How does the story of the boy Friedman and his grandmother Sejosenye serve to
   illustrate changing times in the village?

3. Describe the character of the grandmother in the story. How do her physical qualities and the manner in which she lives fit her character?

4. Is this a tragic story? Explain.

5. Relate the final paragraph to the rest of the story.

Suggestions for Writing

1. Write an essay in which you examine Sejosenye. Consider the following: How does
   her life serve to comment on the village? Why is it important for her to have a
   grandchild? What is the narrator's attitude toward her?

2. What elements of the story's style suggest that it arises out of an oral tradition? To
   clarify your remarks, compare and contrast the style of this story with that of another story in the text.

Poetry

Walt Whitman

When I Heard the Learn'd Astronomer

Walt Whitman (1819–1892), regarded by many as the greatest American poet, was born on Long Island, New York. He was a printer, a journalist, and a nurse during the Civil War. Strongly influenced by Ralph Waldo Emerson, he published *Leaves of Grass* in 1855 at his own expense. He added sections to new editions over the years. By the time of his death, he had become a major influence on younger poets who were moved by his experiments in free verse and by his transcendental ideas. In "When I Heard the Learn'd Astronomer," impatient with explanations of abstract science, he turns instead to silent contemplation of nature which, he implies, provides a profounder insight than do the "charts and diagrams" of science.

When I heard the learn'd astronomer,
When the proofs, the figures, were ranged in columns before me,
When I was shown the charts and diagrams, to add, divide, and measure
    them,
When I sitting heard the astronomer where he lectured with much applause
    in the lecture-room,
How soon unaccountable I became tired and sick,
Till rising and gliding out I wander'd off by myself,
In the mystical moist night-air, and from time to time,
Look'd up in perfect silence at the stars.

Suggestions for Discussion

1. Notice that this poem is contained in one sentence. How does Whitman organize the sentence to lead to the climax of the last line?

2. What is the poet's attitude toward the scientist? Why does he reject the scientific method of looking at nature? Why is his response "unaccountable"?

3. What is the significance of the phrase *perfect silence* in the last line?

Suggestion for Writing

Write an essay in which you explain not only the idea in the poem but how the idea is developed. Your essay should consider how a prose statement of the idea would differ.

Drama

Henrik Ibsen

An Enemy of the People

Henrik Ibsen (1828–1906), born in Norway, chose to live for over 20 years in Dresden, Rome, and Munich, which he found more congenial for his writing than the country of his birth. Ibsen wrote a number of significant plays, ranging from the poetic and romantic, such as *Peer Gynt* (1867); to plays with social themes, such as *A Doll's House* (1879) and *Ghosts* (1881); to psychological studies, such as *Hedda Gabler* (1890); and symbolic works, such as *When We Dead Awaken* (1899). However, all of his plays are rich and complex and have had a profound influence on the development of European and American drama in this century. He has also been greatly admired for his deeply intuitive creation of female characters, such as Hedda Gabler. *An Enemy of the People* (1882) raises the serious social issues of environmental pollution and the tendency of the majority to oppress the minority, but it also focuses on the many-sided character of Dr. Stockmann, who is both scientific and muddle-headed, a serious figure whom Ibsen described as a rather bumbling hero of a comedy.

Characters

DR. TOMAS STOCKMANN, *physician at the Baths*
MRS. KATRINE STOCKMANN, *his wife*
PETRA, *their daughter, a schoolteacher*
EJLIF & MORTEN, *their sons, aged thirteen and ten*
PETER STOCKMANN, *the doctor's elder brother; Mayor and Chief of Police; Chairman of the Board at the Baths*
MORTEN KIIL, *owner of a tannery; Mrs. Stockmann's foster-father*

HOVSTAD, *editor of* The People's Monitor
BILLING, *his colleague on the paper*
CAPTAIN HORSTER
ASLAKSEN, *a printer*

Citizens of various types and standing; some women and a number of schoolboys

The action takes place in a town on the South Coast of Norway.

Act I

SCENE: *Evening.* DOCTOR STOCKMANN'S *living room. It is decorated and furnished simply but neatly. In the side wall right are two doors, the upstage door leading to the hall and the one downstage to the doctor's study. In the opposite wall, facing the hall door, a door leading to the other rooms of the house. Against this wall, in the center of it, stands the stove: further down-*

683

*stage a sofa above which hangs a mirror, and in front of it an oval table:
on this table is a lighted lamp with a shade. In the back wall, an open door
leads to the dining room. The table is laid for supper and a lighted lamp
stands on it.*
     BILLING *is seated at the supper table; he has a napkin tucked under his
chin.* MRS. STOCKMANN *stands by the table and places a dish of cold roast
beef before him. The other seats round the table are empty; the table is in
disorder, as though a meal had recently been finished.*

MRS. STOCKMANN: I'm afraid you'll have to put up with a cold meal, Mr. Bill-
     ing; you were an hour late, you know.
BILLING (*Eating*): Never mind. It's delicious—absolutely delicious.
MRS. STOCKMANN: Stockmann is very strict about having his meals on time.
BILLING: It doesn't matter a bit. In fact I think food tastes even better when
     one's alone and undisturbed.
MRS. STOCKMANN: Well—as long as you enjoy it—(*Turns toward the hall
     door, listening*) That may be Mr. Hovstad—perhaps he's come to join you.
BILLING: Very likely.
     (THE MAYOR, PETER STOCKMANN, *enters. He wears an overcoat, and the gold-
     braided cap of his office. He carries a cane.*)
THE MAYOR: Good evening, Sister-in-law.
MRS. STOCKMANN: Well! Good evening. (*She comes forward into the living
     room*) So, it's you! How nice of you to look in.
THE MAYOR: I happened to be passing by, and so—(*With a glance toward the
     dining room*) Oh—you have company, I see.
MRS. STOCKMANN (*Slightly embarrassed*): No, no—not really. Mr. Billing just
     happened to drop in. Won't you join him for a bite to eat?
THE MAYOR: No, thank you—nothing for me! I never eat hot food at night—
     not with my digestion.
MRS. STOCKMANN: Oh, just for once! It surely couldn't hurt you.
THE MAYOR: I'm much obliged—but, no! I stick to my tea and bread and
     butter; it's much better for you—and it's more economical too.
MRS. STOCKMANN (*Smiling*): I hope you don't think Tomas and I are extrava-
     gant!
THE MAYOR: I know *you're* not, my dear; far be it from me to think that of
     you. (*Points to the doctor's study*) Is he home?
MRS. STOCKMANN: No. He went for a little walk after supper—with the boys.
THE MAYOR: Is that good for one's health, I wonder? (*Listens*) Here he comes
     now.
MRS. STOCKMANN: No, I don't think it can be he. (*A knock at the door*) Come
     in! (HOVSTAD *comes in from the hall*) Oh, it's Mr. Hovstad.
HOVSTAD: You must excuse me; I was held up at the printer's. Good evening,
     Mr. Mayor.
THE MAYOR (*Bowing rather stiffly*): Good evening. You're here on business, I
     presume?
HOVSTAD: Yes, partly. It's about an article for the paper.
THE MAYOR: I thought as much. I hear my brother has become quite a pro-
     lific contributor to *The People's Monitor*.
HOVSTAD: He's kind enough to write a piece for us now and then; whenever
     he has anything particular on his mind.

MRS. STOCKMANN (*To* HOVSTAD): But don't you want to—? (*She points toward the dining room.*)

THE MAYOR: It's natural, I suppose, that he should want to reach the kind of people who understand his point-of-view. Not that I have any personal objection to your paper, Mr. Hovstad—you may rest assured of that.

HOVSTAD: No—of course not.

THE MAYOR: We have a fine spirit of mutual tolerance here in our town, I'm glad to say; a truly co-operative spirit; it comes, of course, from the great common interest we all share—an interest that naturally concerns all right-thinking citizens.

HOVSTAD: The Baths, of course.

THE MAYOR: Precisely. Those splendid Mineral Baths of ours! You mark my words, Mr. Hovstad; the whole life of our community will center more and more around the Baths—there can be no doubt of that!

MRS. STOCKMANN: That's just what Tomas says.

THE MAYOR: The way the town has grown in these past two years is quite extraordinary. People are prosperous; housing-developments are springing up; the value of property is soaring; there's life and activity everywhere!

HOVSTAD: And far less unemployment too.

THE MAYOR: That's true, of course; and that's a great load off the upper classes; taxes for home-relief have already been reduced—and they will be reduced still further if we have a really prosperous summer; a good rush of visitors—plenty of invalids to give the Baths a reputation—

HOVSTAD: I hear there's a good chance of that.

THE MAYOR: Every day inquiries about living quarters—apartments and so forth—keep pouring in. Things look highly promising.

HOVSTAD: Then the doctor's article will be most timely.

THE MAYOR: So he's been writing again, has he?

HOVSTAD: This is something he wrote during the winter. It's an article about the Baths—strongly recommending them, and laying particular stress on the excellence of sanitary conditions here. But I didn't use it at the time—I held it over.

THE MAYOR: Why? Was he indiscreet, as usual?

HOVSTAD: No, nothing like that; I only thought it would be better to hold it over till the spring, when people start thinking about summer plans.

THE MAYOR: Very sensible; highly sensible, Mr. Hovstad.

MRS. STOCKMANN: Tomas never spares himself where the Baths are concerned.

THE MAYOR: As one of the staff that's no more than his duty.

HOVSTAD: And, after all, it was his idea in the first place.

THE MAYOR: His idea? Was it indeed? I know some people are of that opinion. But it seems to me I too had at least a modest share in the enterprise.

MRS. STOCKMANN: That's what Tomas always says.

HOVSTAD: Of course, Mr. Mayor, that's undeniable; you put it all on a practical basis—you made the whole thing possible; we all know that. I simply meant that the initial idea was Dr. Stockmann's.

THE MAYOR: My brother has had plenty of ideas in his time—unfortunately; but it takes a very different type of man to work them out. I should have thought the members of this household would be among the first to—

MRS. STOCKMANN: My dear Peter—

HOVSTAD: You surely don't—?

MRS. STOCKMANN: Do go in and have some supper, Mr. Hovstad; my husband is sure to be home directly.

HOVSTAD: Thank you; I think I will have just a bite. (*He goes into the dining room.*)

THE MAYOR (*Lowering his voice*): It's amazing! These people who come from peasant stock never seem to lose their want of tact.

MRS. STOCKMANN: Now, why should you be upset? You and Tomas are brothers—isn't it natural that you should share the honor?

THE MAYOR: One would think so, yes; but a share is not enough for some people, it seems.

MRS. STOCKMANN: What nonsense! You and Tomas get on so well together. (*Listening*) I think I hear him now. (*She goes and opens the hall door.*)

DR. STOCKMANN: (*Is heard laughing; he shouts in a loud voice, from the hall*): Here's another visitor for you, Katrine. Isn't this splendid, eh? Hang your coat up there on the peg, Captain Horster. But, I forgot—you don't wear an overcoat, do you? What do you think of this, Katrine? I met him on the street—I had a hard time persuading him; at first he wouldn't hear of coming up! (CAPTAIN HORSTER *enters and bows to* MRS. STOCKMANN) In with you boys! They're starving again, Katrine! Come along, Captain Horster; you must try a piece of our roast-beef—(*He forces* CAPTAIN HORSTER *into the dining room;* EJLIF *and* MORTEN *follow them.*)

MRS. STOCKMANN: But, Tomas, don't you see—!

DR. STOCKMANN (*Turns in the doorway*): Oh, it's you, Peter! (*Goes to him and holds out his hand*) Well, now this is really splendid!

THE MAYOR: I can only stay a minute—

DR. STOCKMANN: Nonsense! We'll have some hot toddy in a moment. You haven't forgotten the toddy, have you, Katrine?

MRS. STOCKMANN: Of course not! I've got the water boiling. (*She goes into the dining room.*)

THE MAYOR: Toddy, too—!

DR. STOCKMANN: Yes; let's sit down and be comfortable.

THE MAYOR: Thank you; I don't care for drinking parties.

DR. STOCKMANN: But this isn't a party!

THE MAYOR: It seems to me—(*He glances towards the dining room*) It's incredible the amount of food they can get through!

DR. STOCKMANN (*Rubs his hands*): Yes—it does one good to see young people eat! They're always hungry! That's the way it should be—they must keep up their strength. They've got things to stir up—they have to build the future!

THE MAYOR: May I ask what there is that requires "stirring up"—as you call it?

DR. STOCKMANN: You'll have to ask the young people about that—when the time comes. Of course we shan't live to see it. A couple of old fogies like you and me—

THE MAYOR: A fine way to talk, I must say!

DR. STOCKMANN: You mustn't mind my nonsense, Peter. I'm in such high spirits today. It makes me so happy to be a part of all this fertile, teeming life. What a wonderful age we live in! A whole new world is springing up around us!

THE MAYOR: Do you really think so?

DR. STOCKMANN: Of course you can't appreciate it as well as I do. You've spent your whole life surrounded by all this—you take it all for granted. But after being stuck away for years in that dreadful little hole up North— never seeing a soul—never exchanging a stimulating word with anyone—I feel as though I'd suddenly been transported into the heart of some great metropolis!

THE MAYOR: I should hardly call it a metropolis—

DR. STOCKMANN: Oh, I know it may seem small compared to lots of other places; but there's life here—there's a future—there are innumerable things to work and strive for; that's what's important, after all. (*Calls out*) Katrine! Did the postman bring anything for me?

MRS. STOCKMANN (*From the dining room*): No—he didn't come today.

DR. STOCKMANN: And to be getting a good salary, Peter! That's something you appreciate when you've lived on starvation-wages as long as we have—

THE MAYOR: Oh, come now—

DR. STOCKMANN: Things were often very hard for us up there, let me tell you; but now we can live like princes! Today, for instance, we had roast beef for dinner; and then we had it for supper too. Don't you want to taste it? At least let me show it to you—do come and see it!

THE MAYOR: Certainly not!

DR. STOCKMANN: Well—come over here then. Look! Isn't our new table-cover handsome?

THE MAYOR: Yes—I noticed it.

DR. STOCKMANN: And we have a lamp-shade too; Katrine has been saving up for them. It makes the room look much more cozy. Don't you think so? Stand over here—no, no; not over there—here! That's right! You see how it concentrates the light? I think it's quite magnificent! What do you think?

THE MAYOR: Of course, if one can afford such luxuries—

DR. STOCKMANN: Oh, we can afford them now. Katrine says I earn almost as much as we spend.

THE MAYOR: Almost—!

DR. STOCKMANN: Besides, a man of science should live in a certain amount of style. I'll bet you a mere county commissioner spends more money a year than I do.

THE MAYOR: Well—I should hope so! A high-ranking government official—!

DR. STOCKMANN: Take an ordinary business man, then. I'll bet you a man like that spends ever so much more—

THE MAYOR: Such things are purely relative—

DR. STOCKMANN: As a matter of fact I don't squander money, Peter. But I do so enjoy inviting people to my home—I can't resist it; I was an exile for so long, you see. I feel the need of company—buoyant, active people— liberal-minded people—like those young fellows enjoying their food in there. To me, that makes life worth while. I wish you'd make a point of getting to know Hovstad—

THE MAYOR: That reminds me—Hovstad was telling me just now he plans to publish another article of yours.

DR. STOCKMANN: Of mine?

THE MAYOR: Yes—about the Baths. An article you wrote last winter.

DR. STOCKMANN: Oh, that one! I'd rather that didn't appear just now.

THE MAYOR: Why not? This seems to me to be the ideal time for it.

DR. STOCKMANN: Yes—under ordinary circumstances— (*Paces across the room.*)

THE MAYOR (*Follows him with his eyes*): What is there so unusual about circumstances now?

DR. STOCKMANN (*Stands still*): I'm afraid I can't tell you about it just now, Peter—not this evening, at any rate. The circumstances may turn out to be in the highest degree unusual, you see. On the other hand it may all amount to nothing—just an illusion on my part.

THE MAYOR: You sound very mysterious. Are you keeping something from me? Is anything the matter? As chairman of the Bath Committee I demand the right to—!

DR. STOCKMANN: And I demand the right to—! Oh, don't let's fly off the handle, Peter.

THE MAYOR: I am not in the habit of "flying off the handle," as you express it. But I must emphatically insist that all matters concerning the Baths be handled in a business-like manner, and through the proper channels. I shall not tolerate devious or underhanded methods.

DR. STOCKMANN: When have I ever used devious or underhanded methods?

THE MAYOR: You have an incorrigible tendency to take things into your own hands; in a well-ordered community that is equally reprehensible. The individual must subordinate himself to Society as a whole; or, more precisely, to those authorities responsible for the well-being of that Society.

DR. STOCKMANN: That may be so; but I can't see how the devil it concerns me!

THE MAYOR: That is where you are wrong, my dear Tomas; I can't seem to get that into your head! But be careful; sooner or later you'll have to pay for it. Now I've warned you. Goodbye.

DR. STOCKMANN: You're out of your mind, I tell you! You're on the wrong track entirely—!

THE MAYOR: I am seldom on the wrong track. Moreover—I take strong exception to—! (*Bows in the direction of the dining room*) Goodbye, Katrine. Good-day, Gentlemen. (*He goes.*)

MRS. STOCKMANN (*Coming into the sitting room*): Has he gone?

DR. STOCKMANN: Yes—and in a towering rage too!

MRS. STOCKMANN: Tomas, dear! What did you do to him this time?

DR. STOCKMANN: Nothing at all! He can't very well expect me to give him an account of things—before they happen.

MRS. STOCKMANN: An account of what things?

DR. STOCKMANN: Never mind about that now, Katrine— It's very odd that the postman didn't come.

(HOVSTAD, BILLING *and* HORSTER *have risen from table and come into the sitting room*; EJLIF *and* MORTEN *follow presently.*)

BILLING (*Stretching himself*): What a meal! Strike me dead if I don't feel like a new man!

HOVSTAD: His Honor didn't seem in a very sunny mood this evening.

DR. STOCKMANN: It's his stomach; his digestion's bad, you know.

HOVSTAD: I think he found it hard to digest us! He has no great love for *The People's Monitor*, I gather.

MRS. STOCKMANN: I thought you seemed to get on very well.

HOVSTAD: Only a temporary truce, I fear me!

BILLING: A truce, yes. That's the word for it.

DR. STOCKMANN: We mustn't forget poor Peter is a lonely bachelor. He has no home to be happy in. Business—nothing but business! And then that damned tea he's always filling himself up with. Now then, boys! Draw your chairs up to the table! Katrine— what about that toddy!

MRS. STOCKMANN (*Going towards the dining room*): I'm just getting it.

DR. STOCKMANN: You sit here on the sofa with me, Captain Horster. We don't often have the chance of seeing you!— Go on, boys! Sit down! (*They sit down at the table.* MRS. STOCKMANN *brings in a tray with kettle, glasses, decanters, etc.*)

MRS. STOCKMANN: There you are! Now help yourselves. There's Arrak, rum, and this is cognac.

DR. STOCKMANN (*Taking a glass*): We're ready for it! (*While the toddy is being mixed*) Now—the cigars. Ejlif, you know where the box is. And Morten can get my pipe. (*The boys go into the room right*) I have a suspicion Ejlif sneaks a cigar now and then—but I pretend not to notice. (*Calls*) And my smoking-cap, Morten! Do you know where I left it, Katrine? Oh, he's found it. (*The boys bring in the various things*) Now, my friends, help yourselves! I stick to my pipe, you know; many's the long cold trip, up there in the North, that *this* has kept me company. (*They clink glasses*) Your health! It's a damn sight pleasanter to be sitting here in this warm comfortable room!

MRS. STOCKMANN (*Sits and starts to knit*): Are you sailing soon, Captain Horster?

HORSTER: I hope to be ready next week.

MRS. STOCKMANN: And you're going to America?

HORSTER: That's the intention.

BILLING: Then you won't be able to vote in the town election.

HORSTER: Oh, there's to be an election, is there?

BILLING: Didn't you know?

HORSTER: No—I don't bother about such things.

BILLING: You mean you have no interest in public affairs?

HORSTER: I don't know anything about them.

BILLING: Still—one ought at least to vote.

HORSTER: Even if you understand nothing about it?

BILLING: Not understand? How do you mean? Society is like a ship; it's up to every man to put his hand to the helm.

HORSTER: That may be all right on shore; but it would never do at sea.

HOVSTAD: Sailors rarely take an interest in public matters.

BILLING: Yes—it's amazing!

DR. STOCKMANN: Sailors are like birds of passage; North or South—every place is home to them! All the more reason for us to redouble our activities. Will there be anything of public interest in tomorrow's paper, Mr. Hovstad?

HOVSTAD: Nothing of local interest—no. But the day after tomorrow I thought I'd use your article.

DR. STOCKMANN: Oh, blast it, the article—of course! I'm afraid you'll have to hold it for a while.

HOVSTAD: Really? But we happen to have lots of space—and it seemed to me so timely.

DR. STOCKMANN: I dare say you're right—but you'll have to hold it all the same. I'll explain about it later—

(PETRA, *wearing a hat and cloak, enters from the hall; she carries a number of exercise books under her arm.*)

PETRA: Good evening.

DR. STOCKMANN: Oh, it's you Petra. Good evening.

(*General greetings.* PETRA *takes off her hat and cloak and puts them, with the exercise books, on a chair by the door.*)

PETRA: So while I slave away at school—you sit here enjoying yourselves!

DR. STOCKMANN: Now you must come and enjoy yourself too.

BILLING: May I mix you a little drink?

PETRA (*Goes to the table*): Thanks, I'll do it myself; you always make it too strong. Oh—by the way, Father, I have a letter for you. (*Goes to the chair where she left her things.*)

DR. STOCKMANN: A letter! From whom?

PETRA (*Looking in the pocket of her cloak*): I met the postman on my way out—

DR. STOCKMANN (*Rises and goes towards her*): You might have given it to me before!

PETRA: I really didn't have time to run upstairs again. Here it is.

DR. STOCKMANN (*Seizing the letter*): Let me see—let me see, child. (*He reads the address*) Yes! This is it!

MRS. STOCKMANN: Is it the one you've been expecting, Tomas?

DR. STOCKMANN: Yes. I must go in and read it at once. What about a light, Katrine? I suppose there's no lamp in my study again!

MRS. STOCKMANN: Oh, yes there is! It's already lighted on the desk.

DR. STOCKMANN: Good. Excuse me a moment— (*He goes into his study, right.*)

PETRA: What's all that about, Mother?

MRS. STOCKMANN: I don't know; these last few days he's done nothing but ask for the postman.

BILLING: Perhaps it's from one of his patients out of town—

PETRA: Poor father! He's getting to be frightfully busy. (*Mixes her toddy*) Ah! This will be most welcome!

HOVSTAD: Have you been teaching at night school again this evening?

PETRA (*Sipping her drink*): Two hours, yes.

BILLING: And four hours this morning at the girls' school—?

PETRA (*Sitting down at the table*): Five.

MRS. STOCKMANN: And you have some exercises to correct this evening as well, I see.

PETRA: Quite a lot.

HORSTER: You seem to keep busy too!

PETRA: Yes—but I like it. It's good to feel thoroughly exhausted!

BILLING: Do you enjoy that?

PETRA: It makes one sleep so well.

MORTEN: You must be a great sinner, Petra.

PETRA: A sinner?

MORTEN: Yes—or you wouldn't have to work so hard. Work is a punishment for our sins—that's what Mr. Rörlund always says.

EJLIF: How can you be such a fool! Believing all that nonsense!

MRS. STOCKMANN: Now, now—Ejlif!

BILLING (*Laughing*): That's a good one!

HOVSTAD: Shouldn't you like to work hard, Morten?

MORTEN: No, I shouldn't.

HOVSTAD: What do you want to do when you grow up?

MORTEN: I want to be a Viking.

EJLIF: You'd have to be a heathen, then.

MORTEN: Well—so I'd *be* a heathen!

BILLING: Good for you, Morten! That's the spirit!

MRS. STOCKMANN (*Makes a sign to him*): I'm sure you don't really mean that, Mr. Billing!

BILLING: Strike me dead if I don't! I'm a heathen and I'm proud of it. You'll see—we'll all be heathens before long.

MORTEN: Then we could do anything we liked, couldn't we?

BILLING: Well—I don't know about that, Morten—

MRS. STOCKMANN: You'd better run along, boys; you must have home-work to do.

EJLIF: Couldn't I stay a little bit longer—?

MRS. STOCKMANN: No—you couldn't. Now, run along—both of you.

(*The boys say goodnight and go into the room, left.*)

HOVSTAD: Do you think it's bad for them to hear that sort of talk?

MRS. STOCKMANN: I don't know; but I know I don't like it.

PETRA: Don't be so stuffy, Mother!

MRS. STOCKMANN: That's all very well—but I don't. Not in one's own home at any rate.

PETRA: All this hypocrisy! At home we're taught to hold our tongues; and at school we have to teach the children lies!

HORSTER: Teach them lies?

PETRA: Yes, of course— We have to teach all kinds of things we don't believe a word of!

BILLING: That's true enough.

PETRA: If I had enough money, I'd start a school myself—then I'd run things quite differently.

BILLING: Well—as far as the money goes—

HORSTER: If you're really serious about that, Miss Stockmann, I'd be glad to provide the necessary space; my father's old house is practically empty, and there's a huge dining-room on the ground floor that would—

PETRA: Oh, I don't suppose anything will come of it—but, thanks, all the same!

HOVSTAD: I've a feeling Miss Petra is more likely to take up journalism. And, that reminds me—have you had a chance to read that English story you promised to translate for us?

PETRA: No, not yet. But I'll get it done for you in time—don't worry.

(DR. STOCKMANN *comes in from his study with the letter open in his hand.*)

DR. STOCKMANN (*Flourishing the letter*): Well! Here's some news that will make the town sit up and take notice!

BILLING: News?

MRS. STOCKMANN: What sort of news, Tomas?

DR. STOCKMANN: A great discovery, Katrine!

HOVSTAD: Really?

MRS. STOCKMANN: A discovery of yours, you mean?

DR. STOCKMANN: Of mine—yes! (*Paces up and down*) And I defy them this time to call me a crack-pot, and laugh it off as nonsense. They won't dare! They simply won't dare!

PETRA: What is it, Father? Tell us!

DR. STOCKMANN: Just give me time, and I'll tell you all about it. I do wish Peter were here! It only goes to show how blind we are—just like a lot of moles!

HOVSTAD: What do you mean, Doctor?

DR. STOCKMANN: It's the general opinion that this town of ours is an exceedingly healthy place—isn't that true?

HOVSTAD: Of course.

DR. STOCKMANN: A quite exceptionally healthy place, as a matter of fact; a place to be highly recommended, not only to ordinary inhabitants, but to invalids as well—

MRS. STOCKMANN: My dear Tomas—

DR. STOCKMANN: And, as such, we have duly praised and recommended it; I myself have sung its praises innumerable times—not only in *The People's Monitor*, but in many pamphlets too—

HOVSTAD: Well—what then?

DR. STOCKMANN: And these Mineral Baths that have been called "the pulse of the town"—its "nerve center"—and the devil only knows what else besides—

BILLING: "The throbbing heart of our city" I remember I once called them—in a somewhat convivial mood—

DR. STOCKMANN: Yes—that too. Well—do you know what these Baths are? These precious, magnificent Baths that have been established at such great expense—can you guess what they really are?

HOVSTAD: No—what?

MRS. STOCKMANN: Tell us, Tomas!

DR. STOCKMANN: They're nothing but a pest hole!

PETRA: The Baths, Father?

MRS. STOCKMANN (*At the same time*): Our Baths!

HOVSTAD (*Simultaneously*): But, Doctor—!

BILLING: This is incredible!

DR. STOCKMANN: I tell you the whole institution is a whited-sepulcher, spreading poison; it's a menace to the Public Health! All that filth from the tanneries up at Milldale—and you know what a stench there is around there!—seeps into the feed-pipes of the pump-room; and, not only that, but this same poisonous offal seeps out onto the beach as well.

HOVSTAD: In the salt-water baths, you mean?

DR. STOCKMANN: Precisely.

HOVSTAD: How can you be sure of all this, Doctor?

DR. STOCKMANN: I've made the most painstaking investigations. I'd suspected something of the sort for quite some time, you see. I was struck by the curious amount of illness among the visitors at the Baths last year—there were several cases of typhoid and gastric fever—

MRS. STOCKMANN: Yes, I remember.

DR. STOCKMANN: At first we took it for granted that the visitors brought the infection with them; but later—this past winter—I began to think differently. I set to work to analyze the water, as best I could—

MRS. STOCKMANN: So that's what you've been working at!

DR. STOCKMANN: Yes—I've worked very hard at it, Katrine, but I didn't have the necessary equipment here; so I finally sent samples of the drinking-water and the sea-water by the beach to the laboratories at the university, and asked them to give me a full analysis.

HOVSTAD: And is that what you just received?

DR. STOCKMANN (*Showing the letter*): Yes—here it is! It proves beyond the shadow of a doubt the presence of decayed animal-matter in the water— millions of infusoria. The use of this water, both internally and externally, is in the highest degree dangerous to health.

MRS. STOCKMANN: What a blessing you found it out in time!

DR. STOCKMANN: It is indeed, Katrine!

HOVSTAD: What do you propose to do about it, Doctor?

DR. STOCKMANN: Set things straight, of course.

HOVSTAD: You think that can be done?

DR. STOCKMANN: It *must* be done. Otherwise the Baths are entirely useless— ruined! But there's no need for that to happen; I'm quite clear as to how we should proceed.

MRS. STOCKMANN: To think of your keeping all this secret, Tomas, dear!

DR. STOCKMANN: You wouldn't have had me rushing all over town gabbing about it before I was absolutely certain, would you? I'm not as mad as all that, you know!

PETRA: But, surely, to us—

DR. STOCKMANN: I couldn't say a word to a living soul! But tomorrow you can run and tell that badger of yours all about it—

MRS. STOCKMANN: Oh, Tomas!

DR. STOCKMANN: Well—your grandfather, then. That'll give the old man something to gape at! He thinks I'm cracked in the head—and a lot of other people think so too, I've noticed. But I'll show them! Yes—this time I'll show them! (*Walks up and down rubbing his hands*) What a commotion there'll be in the town, Katrine! Think of it; they'll have to re-lay all the waterpipes.

HOVSTAD (*Rising*): All the waterpipes—?

DR. STOCKMANN: Well—naturally. The intake must be moved much higher up; I always said it was down too low.

PETRA: You were right after all, Father.

DR. STOCKMANN: Yes—you remember, Petra? I sent in a protest before they even started on the work; but, of course, at that time, no one listened to me. Well—I'll let them have it now! I've prepared a report for the Board of Directors; it's been ready for a week—I was only waiting for this. (*Points to the letter*) I'll send it off at once. (*Goes into his study and returns with a manuscript*) Look! Four closely written pages! And I'll enclose this letter too. A paper, Katrine! Something to wrap this up in. Good. And now give this to—to—what the devil is that girl's name! To the maid—*you* know! Tell her to deliver it to the Mayor immediately!

(MRS. STOCKMANN *takes the package and goes out through the dining room.*)

PETRA: What do you think Uncle Peter will say, Father?

DR. STOCKMANN: What *can* he say? He can't fail to be pleased that such an important fact has come to light.

HOVSTAD: May we announce this in *The People's Monitor?*

DR. STOCKMANN: I'd be most grateful if you would.

HOVSTAD: It's important that the public should know of this without delay.

DR. STOCKMANN: It is indeed!

MRS. STOCKMANN (*Returning*): She's gone with it.

BILLING: Strike me dead if you're not hailed as the leading citizen of our community, Dr. Stockmann!

DR. STOCKMANN (*Walks up and down in high glee*): Oh, nonsense! I only did my duty. I simply was lucky enough to spot it—that's all. But still—

BILLING: Hovstad, don't you think the town should get up some sort of a demonstration in Dr. Stockmann's honor?

HOVSTAD: I shall certainly propose it.

BILLING: I'll talk it over with Aslaksen.

DR. STOCKMANN: No, no—my dear friends! You mustn't bother with such nonsense; I won't hear of it! And, I warn you, Katrine—if the Board of Directors should think of offering me a raise in salary—I shall refuse it. I simply won't accept!

MRS. STOCKMANN: You're quite right, Tomas, dear.

PETRA (*Raising her glass*): Your health, Father!

HOVSTAD *and* BILLING: Your good health, Doctor!

HORSTER (*Clinks glasses with him*): I hope this brings you joy.

DR. STOCKMANN: Thank you, thank you—my dear, dear friends! I can't tell you how happy I am—! It's a wonderful thing to feel you've deserved well of your own hometown, and of your fellow-citizens. Hurrah, Katrine!

(*He puts his arms round her and whirls her round the room.* MRS. STOCKMANN *screams and struggles to free herself. Laughter, applause and cheers for the doctor. The two boys poke their heads in the door to see what is going on.*) CURTAIN

Act II

SCENE: *The doctor's living room. The door to the dining room is closed. Morning.* MRS. STOCKMANN, *carrying a sealed letter in her hand, comes in from the dining room, goes to the door of the doctor's study and peeps in.*

MRS. STOCKMANN: Are you in there, Tomas?

DR. STOCKMANN (*From the study*): Yes, I just got back. (*Enters*) Do you want me?

MRS. STOCKMANN: Here's a letter from your brother. (*Hands it to him.*)

DR. STOCKMANN: Now—let's see. (*Opens the envelope and reads*) "The manuscript forwarded to me is returned herewith—" (*He reads on, mumbling to himself*) Hm.

MRS. STOCKMANN: Well? What does he say?

DR. STOCKMANN: Just that he'll be up to see me around noon.

MRS. STOCKMANN: You must be sure and be home, then.

DR. STOCKMANN: I can easily manage that; I've made all my morning calls.

MRS. STOCKMANN: I can't help wondering how he'll take it.

DR. STOCKMANN: He's sure to be annoyed that it was I, and not he, who discovered the whole business.

MRS. STOCKMANN: That's what I'm afraid of.

DR. STOCKMANN: He'll be glad at heart, of course. But still—; Peter's always so damnably resentful when anyone else does anything for the good of the town.

MRS. STOCKMANN: I know. I think it would be nice if you made a point of letting him share the honor; you might even imply that it was he who put you on the track—

DR. STOCKMANN: That's all right as far as I'm concerned. All I care about is getting the thing cleared up.

(*Old* MORTEN KIIL *sticks his head in at the hall door.*)

MORTEN KIIL (*Slyly*): Is—is all this true?

MRS. STOCKMANN (*Goes toward him*): Well! Here's Father.

DR. STOCKMANN: So it is! Good morning, Father-in-law!

MRS. STOCKMANN: Do come in.

MORTEN KIIL: If it's true, I will; otherwise I'll be off again.

DR. STOCKMANN: If what's true?

MORTEN KIIL: All this nonsense about the water-works. Well? Is it?

DR. STOCKMANN: Of course it's true. But how did *you* find out about it?

MORTEN KIIL: From Petra. She ran in to see me on her way to school—

DR. STOCKMANN: Oh, did she?

MORTEN KIIL: Yes, indeed; and she told me—at first I thought she must be joking! But that's not like Petra, come to think of it.

DR. STOCKMANN: Of course not! She'd never joke about a thing like that.

MORTEN KIIL: You never know; and I don't like to be made a fool of. So it really is true, is it?

DR. STOCKMANN: Unquestionably. Do sit down, Father. (*Forces him down on the sofa*) Well—what do you think? It's a lucky thing for the town, isn't it?

MORTEN KIIL (*With suppressed laughter*): A lucky thing for the town?

DR. STOCKMANN: Yes, that I made this discovery in time—

MORTEN KIIL (*As before*): Oh, of course! Of course!—I must say I never thought you'd try your monkey-tricks on your own brother!

DR. STOCKMANN: Monkey-tricks—!

MRS. STOCKMANN: Father, dear—!

MORTEN KIIL (*Rests his hands and chin on the top of his cane and blinks slyly at the doctor*): Let me see—what was it now? Oh! yes—the waterpipes are full of little animals—isn't that it?

DR. STOCKMANN: Infusoria, yes.

MORTEN KIIL: And Petra said there were a lot of them—whole swarms of them.

DR. STOCKMANN: Certainly; hundreds of thousands of them.

MORTEN KIIL: And yet no one can see them—isn't that the story?

DR. STOCKMANN: Of course no one can see them.

MORTEN KIIL (*With quiet chuckling laughter*): I'll be damned if this isn't the best thing you've hit on yet!

DR. STOCKMANN: What do you mean?

MORTEN KIIL: You'll never get the Mayor to believe this nonsense!

DR. STOCKMANN: We shall see.

MORTEN KIIL: You think he's as crazy as all that?

DR. STOCKMANN: I'm confident that the whole town will be as crazy as all that.

MORTEN KIIL: The whole town! Yes—I wouldn't put it past them. And it'll serve them right, too—teach them a lesson. We old-timers aren't good enough for them—oh, no! They think themselves so clever! They hounded me out of the Town Council—hounded me out like a dog, that's what they did! But they'll get paid back now! Just you go on playing your monkey-tricks with them, Stockmann—

DR. STOCKMANN: But, Father—listen—!

MORTEN KIIL (*Rising*): Give 'em all the monkey-tricks you can think of, say I! If you can put this over on the Mayor and his cronies—so help me, I'll give a hundred crowns to charity!

DR. STOCKMANN: Very handsome of you.

MORTEN KIIL: Mind you, I've little enough to spare! But just you put this over, and next Christmas I'll give fifty crowns to charity!

(HOVSTAD *enters from the hall.*)

HOVSTAD: Good morning! (*Pausing*) Oh, excuse me—

DR. STOCKMANN: No—come in; come in.

MORTEN KIIL (*Chuckling again*): Is he in on this?

HOVSTAD: What do you mean?

DR. STOCKMANN: Yes, of course he is.

MORTEN KIIL: I might have known it! He's to put it in his paper. Ah! You're a good one, Stockmann! Well—I'm off. I'll leave you two together.

DR. STOCKMANN: No, Father; don't go yet.

MORTEN KIIL: Yes—I'll be off. Just you think up all the monkey-tricks you can. You can be damn sure you won't lose by it!

(*He goes;* MRS. STOCKMANN *goes with him.*)

DR. STOCKMANN (*Laughing*): What do you think—? The old man doesn't believe a word about the water-works!

HOVSTAD: Oh, was that what you were talking about?

DR. STOCKMANN: Yes. I suppose you've come about that, too?

HOVSTAD: Yes, I have. Have you a few moments, Doctor?

DR. STOCKMANN: As many as you like.

HOVSTAD: Have you heard anything from the Mayor yet?

DR. STOCKMANN: No, not yet. But he's to be here presently.

HOVSTAD: Since I left here last night I've thought a great deal about this matter.

DR. STOCKMANN: You have?

HOVSTAD: Yes. As a doctor and a man of science you naturally think of this business of the water-works as a thing apart. I mean by that—you probably haven't stopped to realize how many other things it may involve.

DR. STOCKMANN: In what way—? Let's sit down, my dear fellow. No—here on the sofa. (HOVSTAD *sits down on the sofa and* STOCKMANN *in an armchair on the other side of the table*) So—you think—?

HOVSTAD: You said last night that the water was polluted by decayed matter in the soil.

DR. STOCKMANN: The trouble comes from that poisonous swamp by the tanneries at Milldale. I'm convinced of that.

HOVSTAD: Forgive me, Doctor—but I think the trouble comes from poison of quite another sort.

DR. STOCKMANN: What poison do you mean?

HOVSTAD: I mean the poison that is polluting and contaminating our whole community.

DR. STOCKMANN: What the devil do you mean by that?

HOVSTAD: Little by little the whole town has come under the control of a pack of bureaucrats.

DR. STOCKMANN: Oh, come now—they're not all bureaucrats.

HOVSTAD: Perhaps not—but those of them who are not bureaucrats are the friends and hangers-on of those who are. We are under the thumb of a small clique of powerful men; it's the old established families, the men of wealth and position, who rule the town.

DR. STOCKMANN: But, remember—they are also men of ability and insight.

HOVSTAD: I suppose it was their ability and insight that controlled the installation of the water-system?

DR. STOCKMANN: That was a colossal piece of stupidity, I grant you. But it will be corrected now.

HOVSTAD: Do you think that will be such a simple matter?

DR. STOCKMANN: Simple or not, it must be done.

HOVSTAD: Yes; especially if the press exerts its influence.

DR. STOCKMANN: That won't be necessary, I assure you; I'm certain that my brother—

HOVSTAD: Excuse me, Doctor, but I want you to know that I intend to publicize the matter.

DR. STOCKMANN: In the newspaper?

HOVSTAD: Yes. When I took over *The People's Monitor*, it was with the thought of breaking up this ring of obstinate old reactionaries who now have full control.

DR. STOCKMANN: With the result that you nearly wrecked the paper—you told me that yourself.

HOVSTAD: We were obliged to draw in our horns for a while—that's true enough; if these particular men had been put out of office at that time, the Bath scheme might have fallen through entirely. But now that danger's over; the Baths are an accomplished fact—and we can afford to do without these high and mighty gentlemen.

DR. STOCKMANN: Do without them, yes; but still, we have a lot to thank them for.

HOVSTAD: Oh, we shall make a point of acknowledging the debt! But a journalist of my liberal turn of mind cannot be expected to let an opportunity like this go by. This myth of official infallibility must be exploded. That kind of superstition must be rooted out.

DR. STOCKMANN: There I agree with you entirely, Mr. Hovstad; if it's a superstition, we must get rid of it!

HOVSTAD: I hesitate to attack the Mayor—since he's your brother; on the other hand, I'm sure you feel as I do, that truth comes first.

DR. STOCKMANN: Undoubtedly—of course. (*Vehemently*) But, all the same!

HOVSTAD: I don't want you to think ill of me. I'm no more egotistical—no more ambitious—than the majority of men.

DR. STOCKMANN: My dear fellow—! No one says you are.

HOVSTAD: I come of a very humble family, Dr. Stockmann; and my knowledge of the common people has been gained through personal experience. I know their needs—I understand their aims. It's because they wish to develop their own ability, knowledge and self-respect, that they claim the right to share in the responsibilities of government—

DR. STOCKMANN: That's very understandable—

HOVSTAD: Yes. And it seems to me a journalist would incur a heavy responsibility by failing to seize the slightest chance of furthering the emancipation of the down-trodden masses. Oh! I know the powers-that-be will call this anarchy. But, let them! I shall at least have done my duty.

DR. STOCKMANN: Quite so—quite so, dear Mr. Hovstad. Still—damn it all—you must remember—! (*A knock at the door*) Come in!

(ASLAKSEN, *the printer, appears at the hall door. He is shabbily but respectably dressed in a black suit with a slightly crumpled white necktie. He carries a silk hat and gloves.*)

ASLAKSEN (*Bowing*): Excuse me, Doctor, if I intrude—

DR. STOCKMANN (*Rising*): Well—well! It's Mr. Aslaksen!

ASLAKSEN: Yes, it's me, Doctor—

HOVSTAD (*Gets up*): Do you want me, Aslaksen?

ASLAKSEN: No; I didn't even know you were here. It's the doctor I—

DR. STOCKMANN: What can I do for you?

ASLAKSEN: Is it true, what Mr. Billing tells me, that you're planning to improve our water-system?

DR. STOCKMANN: For the Baths, yes.

ASLAKSEN: Just as I thought; then I'd like you to know, Doctor, that I shall support this plan with all my might.

HOVSTAD (*To the doctor*): You see!

DR. STOCKMANN: I'm most grateful to you, I'm sure; but—

ASLAKSEN: You never know—we small middle-class men might be very useful to you. We form what you might call a solid majority in the town; if we really make up our minds to it, that is. And it's always a good thing to have the support of the majority, Dr. Stockmann.

DR. STOCKMANN: That's unquestionably true; but I can't conceive that any special measures will be necessary in this case. The matter is so simple—so straightforward—

ASLAKSEN: It might be helpful all the same. I know the local authorities very well. Suggestions from people outside their immediate circle are not looked upon too favorably by the powers-that-be. So I thought it might be a good idea if we arranged a demonstration of some sort.

HOVSTAD: I quite agree.

DR. STOCKMANN: A demonstration? But what form would this demonstration take?

ASLAKSEN: Oh, it would be conducted with the utmost moderation, Doctor; I strive for moderation in all things; moderation is a citizen's prime virtue—at least in my opinion.

DR. STOCKMANN: Your moderation is well-known, dear Mr. Aslaksen.

ASLAKSEN: I think I may safely say it is. And to us small middle-class men, this business of the water-works is of very great importance. Our Baths bid fair to become a small gold mine, as it were. Many of us count on them to provide us with a means of livelihood—the home-owners especially; so we naturally wish to support the Baths in every possible way. Now, since I happen to be chairman of the Home-owners Association—

DR. STOCKMANN: Yes—?

ASLAKSEN: —and also an active worker in the Temperance Society—you know of course, Doctor, that I'm a temperance man—?

DR. STOCKMANN: That goes without saying—

ASLAKSEN: Then I need hardly tell you that I am in constant touch with a great number of my fellow-citizens. And since my reputation is that of a prudent, law-abiding man—as you yourself remarked—I have a certain influence in the town; a kind of modest authority—though I do say so myself.

DR. STOCKMANN: I'm well aware of that.

ASLAKSEN: So—should it be advisable—it would be a comparatively simple matter for me to get up some sort of a petition.

DR. STOCKMANN: A petition?

ASLAKSEN: Yes—a petition of thanks; of thanks to you, on behalf of the townspeople, for having taken up this all-important matter. It goes without saying that it must be worded with suitable moderation; it would never do to offend the authorities, or any of the men in power. But, if we keep this in mind, I see no reason for any possible objection.

HOVSTAD: Well—even if they did object—!

ASLAKSEN: No, no! There must be nothing in it to offend the powers-that-be, Mr. Hovstad. We can't afford to antagonize the men who control our destinies. I've seen plenty of that in my time—no good ever comes of it. But no one could object to a citizen expressing his opinion freely—provided it is couched in temperate terms.

DR. STOCKMANN: I am delighted, my dear Mr. Aslaksen, to know I can count on the support of my fellow-townsmen; I can't tell you how happy this makes me! And now—how about a glass of sherry?

ASLAKSEN: No—many thanks; I never indulge in spirits.

DR. STOCKMANN: Well—you surely won't refuse a glass of beer?

ASLAKSEN: Thank you—but I never touch anything so early in the day. Now I'll be on my way; I must talk to some of the home-owners, and set about preparing public opinion.

DR. STOCKMANN: It's extremely kind of you, Mr. Aslaksen; but I can't conceive that all this preparation should be necessary. The issue is clear—I can't see any room for disagreement.

ASLAKSEN: The authorities have a way of functioning very slowly, Dr. Stockmann. Oh, far be it from me to blame them—!

HOVSTAD: We'll give them a good stirring up in the paper tomorrow—

ASLAKSEN: But I beg you, Mr. Hovstad—no violence! If you wish to get results, you must use moderation. Take my advice; I speak from experience. Well—now I'll say goodbye. Remember, Doctor, we—of the middle-class—stand behind you to a man. The solid majority is on your side.

DR. STOCKMANN: I'm most grateful to you, Mr. Aslaksen. (*Holds out his hand*) Goodbye, goodbye!

ASLAKSEN: Are you coming to the office, Mr. Hovstad?

HOVSTAD: I'll be there presently. There are still a couple of things I'd like to discuss.

ASLAKSEN: Very well. (*He bows and goes out;* DR. STOCKMANN *shows him into the hall.*)

HOVSTAD (*As the doctor re-enters*): Well—now what do you say, Doctor? Don't you agree it's high time we put a stop to all this half-hearted, cowardly, shilly-shallying?

DR. STOCKMANN: Are you referring to Aslaksen?

HOVSTAD: Yes, I am. He's been infected by the poison too, you see—though he's not a bad sort, in his way. He's typical of most people around here; always wavering, always on the fence. They never dare take a definite stand—they're too full of doubts, and scruples, and caution.

DR. STOCKMANN: He seems like a thoroughly well-intentioned man.

HOVSTAD: Intentions may be all very well—but give me a man with some self-confidence, some self-assurance.

DR. STOCKMANN: Yes—I agree with you there.

HOVSTAD: I'm going to use this opportunity to inject a little back-bone into their good intentions. This servile worship of the "Powers-that-be" must be wiped out. The inexcusable bungling about the water-works must be fully exposed. Every single voter must be made aware of it.

DR. STOCKMANN: Very well; as long as you think it's for the good of the Community. But I must speak to my brother first.

HOVSTAD: Meanwhile—I'll be writing my editorial. And if the Mayor refuses to take action—

DR. STOCKMANN: That's inconceivable.

HOVSTAD: Perhaps not so inconceivable as you might think. But suppose he does—

DR. STOCKMANN: Then, my dear Mr. Hovstad—if that should happen—you may print my full report, word for word—just as it is.

HOVSTAD: Is that a promise?

DR. STOCKMANN (*Hands him the manuscript*): Look—here it is; take it with you. There's no harm in your reading it; you can return it to me later on.

HOVSTAD: Very good; I shall do so. Goodbye for now, dear Doctor.

DR. STOCKMANN: Goodbye. But, you'll see, this whole thing will be cleared up quite simply, Mr. Hovstad; I'm confident of that.

HOVSTAD: Well—we shall see (*He bows and goes out through the hall.*)

DR. STOCKMANN (*Goes to the dining room and looks in*): Katrine—! Oh! Are you back, Petra?

PETRA (*Enters the sitting room*): Yes; I just got back from school.

MRS. STOCKMANN (*Enters*): Hasn't he been here yet?

DR. STOCKMANN: Peter? No. But I had a long talk with Hovstad. He's quite excited about my discovery. He feels its implications are even more important than I thought. He's placed his newspaper at my disposal—in case I should require it.

MRS. STOCKMANN: But do you think you will?

DR. STOCKMANN: No! I'm sure I shan't. Still—it's very flattering to have the support of an enlightened, independent paper, such as his. I had a visit from the chairman of the Home-owners Association, too.

MRS. STOCKMANN: Really? What did he want?

DR. STOCKMANN: He, too, wanted to assure me of his support. They're all ready to stand by me, in case of need. Do you know what I have on my side, Katrine?

MRS. STOCKMANN: On your side? No—what?

DR. STOCKMANN: The solid majority.

MRS. STOCKMANN: And is that a good thing for you, Tomas, dear?

DR. STOCKMANN: A good thing! Well—I should hope so! (*He rubs his hands and paces up and down*) What a wonderful thing it is to feel in such close harmony with one's fellowmen!

PETRA: And to know one's doing good and valuable work!

DR. STOCKMANN: Especially when it's for your own home town, Petra.
MRS. STOCKMANN: There's the bell.
DR. STOCKMANN: That must be he. (*A knock at the door*) Come in!
THE MAYOR (*Enters from the hall*): Good morning.
DR. STOCKMANN: I'm glad to see you, Peter.
MRS. STOCKMANN: Good morning, Brother-in-law. And how are you today?
THE MAYOR: Thank you—only so-so. (*To the doctor*) Last night, after office-hours, I received a long dissertation from you on the subject of the Baths.
DR. STOCKMANN: Have you read it?
THE MAYOR: Yes—I have.
DR. STOCKMANN: Well—what do you think of it?
THE MAYOR (*With a side glance*): Hm—
MRS. STOCKMANN: Come along, Petra. (*She and* PETRA *go into the room left.*)
THE MAYOR: Why did you find it necessary to carry on these investigations behind my back?
DR. STOCKMANN: As long as I wasn't absolutely sure, I—
THE MAYOR: Then you think you're absolutely sure now?
DR. STOCKMANN: Didn't my report convince you of that?
THE MAYOR: Is it your intention to submit this report to the Board of Directors as an official document?
DR. STOCKMANN: Of course. Something must be done about it; and at once.
THE MAYOR: In your customary manner, you make use of some very strong expressions. You say among other things, that what we offer our visitors is nothing short of poison.
DR. STOCKMANN: But, Peter—what else can you call it? I tell you—whether you drink it or bathe in it—the water is poison! We can't do this to poor sick people who come here in good faith expecting to be cured!
THE MAYOR: You conclude your report by stating that a sewer must be built to carry off the alleged impurities at Milldale, and that the entire water-system must be redesigned and re-installed.
DR. STOCKMANN: Can you think of any other solution?
THE MAYOR: I found a pretext for calling on the town engineer this morning, and brought the matter up—in a joking way, of course—as something we should perhaps consider some time in the future.
DR. STOCKMANN: In the future!
THE MAYOR: He laughed at the extravagance of the suggestion—I naturally let him think it was my own idea. Have you taken the trouble to find out the cost of these proposed alterations? I gathered from the engineer it would amount to several hundred thousand crowns.
DR. STOCKMANN: As much as that?
THE MAYOR: Yes. But that's not the worst of it. The work would take at least two years.
DR. STOCKMANN: Two years? Two whole years?
THE MAYOR: At least. And what's to happen to the Baths in the meantime? Are we to close them? We'd have no alternative. You don't imagine people would go on coming here if it were rumored that the waters were injurious to the health?
DR. STOCKMANN: But, Peter—that's just what they are.
THE MAYOR: And that this should happen now—just when the Baths are beginning to gain a reputation. Other towns in this vicinity might qualify

equally well as health resorts. They'd bend every effort to divert this stream of visitors from us, to them; why shouldn't they? And we should be left stranded. All the money that has been invested in this costly undertaking would be wasted; most likely the whole scheme would have to be abandoned. The town would be completely ruined—thanks to you!

DR. STOCKMANN: Ruined—!

THE MAYOR: The only future the town has is through the Baths—the only future worth mentioning, that is! You know that as well as I do.

DR. STOCKMANN: Well? What do you think should be done?

THE MAYOR: I find myself unconvinced by your report. I cannot fully persuade myself that conditions are as critical as your statement represents.

DR. STOCKMANN: If anything they're worse! At least they will be, during the summer, when the hot weather sets in.

THE MAYOR: I repeat that in my opinion you greatly exaggerate the situation. I am certain that a competent physician would find adequate steps to take—would be able to counteract any harmful agents, should their presence be definitely established.

DR. STOCKMANN: I see. And then—?

THE MAYOR: The present water-system is an established fact and must, of course, be treated as such. At some future time the Directors might see their way clear—provided the cost was not too exorbitant—to inaugurate certain improvements.

DR. STOCKMANN: You don't imagine I could ever be party to such a swindle?

THE MAYOR: Swindle?

DR. STOCKMANN: Swindle, yes! It would be the worst kind of trickery—an out and out crime against Society!

THE MAYOR: I've already told you, I've not been able to persuade myself of the existence of any imminent danger.

DR. STOCKMANN: Yes, you have! You couldn't possibly have done otherwise. My report is so obviously clear and convincing. You understand the situation perfectly, Peter, but you simply refuse to face it. You were responsible for the placement of the Baths and the water-works—it was you who insisted on putting them where they are. It was a damnable mistake and now you refuse to admit it. Do you think I don't see through you?

THE MAYOR: And what if it were so? If I am concerned with protecting my reputation, it's only for the good of the town. I cannot possibly direct affairs in a manner conducive to the general welfare as I see it, unless my integrity and authority are unassailable. For this reason—among others—I consider it imperative that your report should not be brought to the notice of the Board of Directors. It must be withheld for the sake of the community. Later on I will bring the matter up for discussion and we will go to work quietly and see what can be done. Meanwhile not a word—not a breath—about this unfortunate business must be allowed to leak out.

DR. STOCKMANN: I'm afraid that can hardly be prevented, my dear Peter.

THE MAYOR: It must and shall be prevented.

DR. STOCKMANN: It's no use, I tell you; too many people know of it already.

THE MAYOR: Know of it! Whom? Surely not those fellows from *The People's Monitor*—?

DR. STOCKMANN: Yes—they know about it too. The free press will certainly see to it that you're made to do your duty.

THE MAYOR: You're an incredibly rash man, Tomas. Hasn't it occurred to you that all this might have serious consequences for you?

DR. STOCKMANN: Consequences—for me?

THE MAYOR: For you—and those dear to you, yes.

DR. STOCKMANN: What the devil do you mean by that?

THE MAYOR: As your brother, I've always been ready and willing to help you—I think I may say that?

DR. STOCKMANN: You have indeed—and I thank you for it.

THE MAYOR: I don't ask for thanks. In a way I was forced into it—for my own sake. By helping you to greater financial security I had hoped to keep you in check, to some extent.

DR. STOCKMANN: Do you mean to tell me you only did it for your own sake?

THE MAYOR: In a way, I said. It's extremely awkward for an official, when his closest relative is continuously compromising himself.

DR. STOCKMANN: You think I do that, do you?

THE MAYOR: Yes, you do—unfortunately; I daresay you're not even aware of it. You have a restless, violent, rebellious nature, and you can't resist going into print indiscriminately on any and all subjects. No sooner does a thought strike you than you dash off an article to the newspaper—or you write a whole pamphlet on the subject.

DR. STOCKMANN: Surely if one has new ideas, it's one's duty to share them with the public!

THE MAYOR: Believe me, the public has no need of new ideas; it's better off without them. The best way to serve the public is to give it what it's used to.

DR. STOCKMANN: That's a very bald statement!

THE MAYOR: For once I must be frank with you. I've tried to avoid it hitherto, because I know how irritable you are; but it's time I told you the truth, Tomas. You don't realize how you antagonize people by this intolerant attitude of yours. You criticize the authorities—you even criticize the Government; you do nothing but find fault. And then you complain of being slighted—of being persecuted. With your difficult nature, what can you expect?

DR. STOCKMANN: Oh—so I'm difficult too, am I?

THE MAYOR: Yes, Tomas; you are an extremely difficult man to get along with. I speak from experience. You seem to forget that you have me to thank for your present position as medical adviser to the Baths—

DR. STOCKMANN: I was entitled to that position—it belonged to me by right! It was I who first saw the possibility of creating a health resort here, and I was the only one at that time who believed in it. I fought for the idea single-handed for many years. I wrote about it—publicized it—

THE MAYOR: That is undeniable. But at that time the scheme was premature. Living as you did then, in that out-of-the-way corner of the world, you naturally couldn't be a judge of that. But later, when circumstances seemed more favorable, I—and the others—took the matter in hand—

DR. STOCKMANN: Yes. And a fine mess you made of it! You took my splendid plan and ruined it. And now the results of your cleverness and shrewdness are all too obvious.

THE MAYOR: Only one thing is obvious, in my opinion: you feel the need to be belligerent—to strike out at your superiors; that's an old habit of yours.

You refuse to submit to the slightest authority; you regard anyone above you as a personal enemy, and are prepared to use every conceivable weapon against him. I have now pointed out to you what is at stake for the town as a whole—and consequently for me personally. I warn you, Tomas, I shall be completely ruthless unless you accept certain conditions.

DR. STOCKMANN: What conditions?

THE MAYOR: Since you have seen fit to go round gossiping about a subject, which should, of course, have been treated with the utmost discretion as an official secret, it is too late to hush the matter up. There are bound to be all sorts of rumors, and malicious-minded people will of course elaborate them. It will therefore be necessary for you publicly to refute them.

DR. STOCKMANN: I? But how? I don't understand.

THE MAYOR: We shall expect you, on further investigation, to come to the conclusion that the situation is not nearly as pressing or as dangerous as you had at first imagined.

DR. STOCKMANN: Oh! You expect that of me, do you?

THE MAYOR: Furthermore we will expect you to make a public statement expressing your faith in the management's integrity and in their intention to take thorough and conscientious steps to remedy any possible defects.

DR. STOCKMANN: But that's out of the question, Peter. No amount of patching or tinkering can put this matter right; I tell you I *know!* It is my firm and unalterable conviction—

THE MAYOR: As a member of the staff you have no right to personal convictions.

DR. STOCKMANN (*With a start*): No right to—?

THE MAYOR: Not as a member of the staff—no! As a private individual—that's of course another matter. But as a subordinate in the employ of the Baths you have no right openly to express convictions opposed to those of your superiors.

DR. STOCKMANN: This is too much! Do you mean to tell me that as a doctor—a scientific man—I have no right to—!

THE MAYOR: But this is not purely a scientific matter; there are other questions involved—technical and economic questions.

DR. STOCKMANN: To hell with all that! I insist that I am free to speak my mind on any and all questions!

THE MAYOR: You are free to do anything you please—as long as it doesn't concern the Baths. But we forbid you to touch on that subject.

DR. STOCKMANN (*Shouts*): Forbid it—you! A bunch of—!

THE MAYOR: *I* forbid it. I personally—your superior in chief. And when I give an order I expect to be obeyed.

DR. STOCKMANN (*Controlling himself*): By God! If you weren't my brother, Peter—!

PETRA (*Flings open the door*): Don't put up with this, Father!

MRS. STOCKMANN (*Following her*): Petra! Petra!

THE MAYOR: So! We've been listening at doors, have we?

MRS. STOCKMANN: You talked so loud—we couldn't very well help hearing—

PETRA: That's not true. I was listening on purpose.

THE MAYOR: Well—I can't say I'm sorry—

Dr. Stockmann (*A step toward him*): You talked to me in terms of forbidding—of forcing me to obedience—

The Mayor: I had to; you gave me no choice.

Dr. Stockmann: So you expect me to recant in public.

The Mayor: We consider it imperative that you issue a statement along the
lines indicated.

Dr. Stockmann: And what if I refuse?

The Mayor: Then—in order to reassure the public—we shall have to issue a
statement ourselves.

Dr. Stockmann: Very well. I shall attack you in the newspapers; I shall use
every means to prove that I am right and that you are wrong. What do you
say to that?

The Mayor: In that case I shall not be able to prevent your dismissal.

Dr. Stockmann: What—!

Petra: Dismissal! Father!

Mrs. Stockmann: Dismissal!

The Mayor: I shall be obliged to advise the Board to give you your notice
and to see that you have no further connection with the Baths.

Dr. Stockmann: You would dare do that!

The Mayor: It is you who force me to it.

Petra: Uncle! This is a disgraceful way to treat a man like Father!

Mrs. Stockmann: Do be quiet, Petra!

The Mayor (*Looking at* petra): So! We already presume to have opinions, do
we? I suppose it's only natural. (*To* mrs. stockmann) Sister-in-law, you
seem to be the only sensible member of this household. I advise you to use
what influence you have on your husband; try and make him realize what
this will mean both for his family—

Dr. Stockmann: My family is my own concern!

The Mayor: I repeat—both for his family, and for the town he lives in.

Dr. Stockmann: I'm the one who has the good of the town at heart—you
know that perfectly well! This is my home town and I love it. That's why I
want to expose this dangerous situation that, sooner or later, must come to
light.

The Mayor: And in order to prove your love for it you insist on destroying
the town's one hope of prosperity?

Dr. Stockmann: But it's a *false* hope, man! Are you mad? Do you want the
town to grow rich by selling filth and poison? Must its prosperity be
founded on a lie?

The Mayor: That's worse than nonsense—it's downright libelous! Only an
enemy of Society could insinuate such things against his native town.

Dr. Stockmann (*Steps towards him*): You dare to—!

Mrs. Stockmann (*Throws herself between them*): Tomas!

Petra (*Seizes her father's arm*): Steady, Father!

The Mayor: I refuse to expose myself to violence. You've been warned. I
advise you to remember what you owe to yourself and to your family.
Goodbye. (*He goes.*)

Dr. Stockmann: They expect me to put up with that kind of treatment, do
they? And in my own house too! What do you say to that, Katrine?

Mrs. Stockmann: It's disgraceful, Tomas, I know—it's shameful—

PETRA: I wish I could have a talk with Uncle—!

DR. STOCKMANN: I suppose it's my own fault; I should have stood up to them long ago—held my own—defied them! An enemy of Society, am I? I'm damned if I'll put up with that!

MRS. STOCKMANN: Remember, Tomas—your brother has the power on his side—

DR. STOCKMANN: But I have the right on mine!

MRS. STOCKMANN: The right—yes, I daresay; but what good is right against might?

PETRA: Mother! How can you talk like that!

DR. STOCKMANN: Might, might! Don't talk nonsense, Katrine. In a free society to be *right* is what counts! I have the free press behind me, and the solid majority on my side—you heard what Aslaksen said. Isn't that might enough for you?

MRS. STOCKMANN: But, Tomas—you're surely not thinking of—?

DR. STOCKMANN: Of what?

MRS. STOCKMANN: Of going against your brother's wishes?

DR. STOCKMANN: What the devil do you expect me to do? What else *can* I do if I'm to stick up for what's honest and right?

PETRA: That's what I'd like to know!

MRS. STOCKMANN: But you know it won't be of any use! If they won't do it— they won't!

DR. STOCKMANN: Just give me time, Katrine. I'll succeed in the end— you'll see.

MRS. STOCKMANN: You'll succeed in getting dismissed—that's what it'll end with.

DR. STOCKMANN: In any case I shall have done my duty to Society—even though I am supposed to be its enemy!

MRS. STOCKMANN: But what about your family, Tomas? What about those dependent on you? Would you be doing your duty to us?

PETRA: Oh, do stop putting us first, Mother!

MRS. STOCKMANN: It's all very well for you to talk—you can manage alone, if need be. But what about the boys, Tomas? And yourself? And me?

DR. STOCKMANN: You must be stark, raving mad, Katrine! If I were such a coward as to kow-tow to Peter and his blasted crew—do you think I'd ever again have a moment's happiness?

MRS. STOCKMANN: I don't know about that; but God preserve us from the sort of happiness we'll have if you persist in defying them! We'll have nothing to live on; you'll be jobless, penniless—just as you were in the old days. We can't go through that again! Be sensible, Tomas; think of the consequences!

DR. STOCKMANN (*Struggling with himself and clenching his hands*): It's disgraceful that these damned bureaucrats should be able to do this to a free, honorable man! Don't you agree, Katrine?

MRS. STOCKMANN: They've treated you abominably—there's no doubt about that. But there's so much injustice in the world—one must just put up with it. Think of the boys, Tomas! Look at them! What's to become of them? You surely wouldn't have the heart to—

(EJLIF *and* MORTEN *have entered while she speaks; they carry their schoolbooks.*)

DR. STOCKMANN: The boys—! (*Firmly and decisively*) I don't care if the whole world crumbles, I refuse to be a slave to any man! (*He goes towards his study.*)

MRS. STOCKMANN (*Follows him*): Tomas! What are you going to do?

DR. STOCKMANN (*At the door*): When my boys grow up to be free men, I want to be able to look them in the face! (*He goes into his study.*)

MRS. STOCKMANN (*Bursting into tears*): God help us all!

PETRA: Father's wonderful, Mother! He'll never give in!   CURTAIN

Act III

SCENE: *The editorial office of* The People's Monitor. *The entrance door is in the background to the left; in the same wall to the right another door with glass panes, through which can be seen the composing-room. A door in the wall right. A large table stands in the middle of the room covered with papers, newspapers and books. Down left a window and by it a desk with a high stool. A couple of armchairs by the table; other chairs along the walls. The room is dingy and cheerless, the furniture old and the arm-chairs dirty and torn. In the composing-room some printers can be seen at work; further back a hand-press is in operation.*

HOVSTAD is seated at the desk writing. In a few moments BILLING enters from the door right, with the doctor's manuscript in his hand.

BILLING: Well, I must say—!

HOVSTAD (*Still writing*): Have you read it?

BILLING (*Laying the ms. on the desk*): I have indeed!

HOVSTAD: The doctor has courage, hasn't he? It's a strong statement!

BILLING: Strong! Strike me dead—it's positively crushing! Every word has the impact of a sledge-hammer.

HOVSTAD: It'll take more than one blow to knock those fellows out.

BILLING: That's true enough; but we'll keep on pounding at them and one of these days they'll come crashing down. As I sat there reading that article I could almost hear the revolution thundering in the distance.

HOVSTAD (*Turning round*): Careful! Don't let Aslaksen hear that.

BILLING: Aslaksen is a chicken-hearted milksop—he hasn't an ounce of manly feeling in him! But you'll insist on having your own way this time, won't you? You'll definitely use the doctor's statement?

HOVSTAD: If the Mayor doesn't give in—yes.

BILLING: It'd be a damn nuisance if he did!

HOVSTAD: Well—fortunately we're bound to gain by the situation in any case. If the Mayor doesn't agree to the doctor's proposition he'll have all the little people on his neck—the Home-owners Association, and all the rest of them. And if he does agree to it, all the rich people will be up in arms; all the people who've hitherto been his chief supporters—including of course those who have the biggest investment in the Baths—

BILLING: Yes; I suppose it would cost them a pretty penny to make the alter-ations—

HOVSTAD: There's no doubt of that! And once the reactionary party is split up, we can continue to expose the Mayor's total inefficiency, and convince the public that the Liberals must be brought to power, for the general good of the community.

BILLING: Strike me dead if that isn't the truth! I feel it—I feel it—the revolution is approaching!

(*A knock at the door.*)

HOVSTAD: Hush! (*Calls out*) Come in!

(DR. STOCKMANN *enters from the door upper left.*)

HOVSTAD (*Going to meet him*): Ah, here's the doctor now. Well?

DR. STOCKMANN: You may go ahead and print it, Mr. Hovstad.

HOVSTAD: So it's really come to that, has it?

BILLING: Hurrah!

DR. STOCKMANN: Yes—it's come to that; so print away, I say! They've asked for war, now let them have it.

BILLING: War to the death, I hope; war to the death!

DR. STOCKMANN: This first article is only the beginning; I have four or five others in mind—my head's bursting with ideas. Where's Aslaksen?

BILLING (*Calling into the printing room*): Oh, Aslaksen! Come here a minute, will you!

HOVSTAD: Four or five others, you say? On the same subject?

DR. STOCKMANN: Oh, by no means; they'll deal with quite different matters. They all stem from the water-works and the sewerage-system, of course—one thing leads to another. It's exactly like trying to patch up an old building.

BILLING: Strike me dead—that's the truth! You do a bit here and a bit there, but the whole thing's so rotten, you end by tearing it down!

ASLAKSEN (*Enters from the printing room*): Tearing down! Surely, Doctor, you're not thinking of tearing down the Baths!

HOVSTAD: No, of course not; you needn't be alarmed.

DR. STOCKMANN: We were talking about something quite different. Well—what do you think of my article, Mr. Hovstad?

HOVSTAD: I think it's an absolute masterpiece—

DR. STOCKMANN: Yes, isn't it—? I'm so glad you agree!

HOVSTAD: It's clear and to the point—anyone could follow it; there's no need to be a specialist. You'll have every intelligent man on your side.

ASLAKSEN: And the prudent ones as well, I hope.

BILLING: Prudent—and imprudent too! Pretty nearly the whole town in fact—

ASLAKSEN: In that case, I think we might safely venture to print it.

DR. STOCKMANN: Well—I should hope so!

HOVSTAD: It'll be in tomorrow morning.

DR. STOCKMANN: Splendid! There's no time to lose, you know. By the way, Mr. Aslaksen, there's one thing I'd like to ask you; you'll supervise the printing of the article yourself, won't you?

ASLAKSEN: Indeed I will.

DR. STOCKMANN: It's very precious, remember. We don't want any errors; every word is important. I'll drop in again presently—you might let me see a proof. I can't wait to have the thing in print—to get it launched.

BILLING: It'll be a bombshell!

DR. STOCKMANN: I want every enlightened citizen to read it and judge for himself. You've no idea what I've been through today. I've been exposed to every kind of pressure; my rights as an individual have been threatened—

BILLING: Your rights—!

DR. STOCKMANN: Yes! I was expected to crawl and humble myself. My deepest—my most sacred convictions were to be sacrificed for purely personal ends—

BILLING: Strike me dead! This is an outrage!

DR. STOCKMANN: But this time they've gone too far—and they shall be told so in no uncertain terms! I shall set up my headquarters here at *The People's Monitor*, and continue to attack them daily—

ASLAKSEN: But, just a minute—

BILLING: Hurrah! It's war—war!

DR. STOCKMANN: I'll run them into the ground; smash them to pieces—wipe them out! I'll show the public what they really are—that's what I'll do!

ASLAKSEN: But you will use moderation, my dear Doctor; attack—but prudently.

BILLING: No! Don't spare the dynamite!

DR. STOCKMANN: It's no longer merely a question of sewers and water-works, you see; it's a question of cleaning up the whole community—

BILLING: That's the way to talk!

DR. STOCKMANN: All those old fogies must be kicked out of office, no matter what position they may hold. I have such a clear perspective on everything today; I don't see all the details yet, but I'll soon work them out. What we need, my friends, is young and vital leaders—new captains at the outposts.

BILLING: Hear, hear!

DR. STOCKMANN: If we stand together, we're bound to win. This whole revolution will be launched quite smoothly—like a new ship gliding down the ways. Don't you believe that?

HOVSTAD: I believe we have every hope of putting the right people into power at last.

ASLAKSEN: And if we proceed with caution, I see no reason why we should run into any danger.

DR. STOCKMANN: Who the hell cares about danger! This is a matter of truth and conscience!

HOVSTAD: You deserve every support, Doctor.

ASLAKSEN: Dr. Stockmann is a true friend of the town; a friend of Society—that's what he is.

BILLING: Strike me dead! He's a friend of the People, Aslaksen!

ASLAKSEN: I'm sure the Home-owners Association will use that as a slogan.

DR. STOCKMANN: My dear friends—I can't thank you enough for all your loyalty; it does me good to hear you. My sainted brother called me something very different; but he'll be repaid—with interest! I'll be off now—I have to see a poor devil of a patient—but I'll be back. Take good care of my article, won't you, Mr. Aslaksen? And don't cut out any exclamation-marks! You can even add a few if you like! Well—goodbye for now; I'll be back shortly. Goodbye.

(*General goodbyes as they accompany him to the door; he goes.*)

HOVSTAD: He can be exceedingly useful to us.

ASLAKSEN: Yes, providing he sticks to this matter of the Baths; if he goes beyond that, it might be unwise to follow him.

HOVSTAD: Hm; it all depends on—

BILLING: You're always so damned frightened, Aslaksen.

ASLAKSEN: Frightened? Yes, when it comes to attacking the local authorities I am frightened, Mr. Billing. I've learned in a hard school, you see. National politics however are another matter; in such things you wouldn't find me frightened, I assure you—even if you were to pit me against the Government itself.

BILLING: I dare say not; that's where you're so inconsistent.

ASLAKSEN: Where the good of the town is concerned, I am very conscientious. There's no harm in attacking the Government—what does the Government care? Those men at the top are unassailable. But the local authorities are different—they can be dismissed; and should their power fall into the hands of inexperienced men, not only the Home-owners but the entire community would suffer.

HOVSTAD: If the People are never allowed self-government how can they ever gain experience? Haven't you thought of that?

ASLAKSEN: When one has vested interests, Mr. Hovstad, one must protect them. A man can't think of everything.

HOVSTAD: Vested interests! Then I hope I never have any!

BILLING: Hear, hear!

ASLAKSEN (*With a smile*): Hm. (*Points to the desk*) There was a time when Commissioner Stensgaard sat in that editor's chair, if you remember.

BILLING (*Spitting*): Pooh! That turncoat!

HOVSTAD: Well—I'm no weathercock, and never will be!

ASLAKSEN: A politician should never say "never" about anything, Mr. Hovstad. And as for you, Mr. Billing—I understand you've applied for the post of secretary to the Town Council; hadn't you better use a little caution?

BILLING: I—!

HOVSTAD: Billing—is this true?

BILLING: As a matter of fact, it is. I'm only doing it to spite the Bigwigs, mind you!

ASLAKSEN: Well—it's no business of mine. I may be accused of cowardice and inconsistency, but my political record is an open book. I've never changed in any way—except, possibly, to become more moderate. My heart is, and always has been, with the People; I must admit, however, that my common-sense inclines me towards the side of the authorities, to some extent; the local authorities, I mean. (*He goes into the printing office.*)

BILLING: Shouldn't we try and get rid of him, Hovstad?

HOVSTAD: Do you know of anybody else who'd be willing to pay our expenses?

BILLING: It's damnable to have no capital!

HOVSTAD (*Sits down at the desk*): Yes; we'd be all right if we had that!

BILLING: Why don't you talk to Dr. Stockmann?

HOVSTAD (*Looking through some papers*): What good would that do? He hasn't a penny.

BILLING: No—but he has connections; old Morten Kiil—"the badger" as they call him.

HOVSTAD (*Writing*): You really think he has money?

BILLING: Strike me dead—of course he has! And Stockmann's family is bound to get part of it. The old man's sure to provide for—for the children, at any rate.

HOVSTAD (*Half turning*): Are you counting on that?

BILLING: What do you mean—"counting?" You know I never count on anything.

HOVSTAD: You're wise. And you'd better not count on that job as secretary either; I assure you, you won't get it.

BILLING: Do you suppose I don't know that? That's the very reason I've applied for it. A slight of that sort fires the spirit of rebellion in one—gives one a fresh supply of vitriol, as it were; and that's a very necessary thing in a God-forsaken hole like this where nothing really stimulating ever seems to happen.

HOVSTAD (*Still writing*): Yes, yes; I know, I know.

BILLING: But—one of these days they'll hear from me, I promise you! —Well—I'd better go in and write that appeal to the Home-owners Association. (*He goes into the room on the right.*)

HOVSTAD (*At the desk: he bites the end of his penholder and says slowly*): Hm. —I see. —So that's it. (*A knock at the door*) Come in!
(PETRA *enters from the back, left.*)

HOVSTAD (*Rising*): Well! It's you, is it? What are you doing here?

PETRA: You must excuse me for—

HOVSTAD (*Pushes an armchair forward*): Do sit down.

PETRA: No thanks; I can only stay a minute.

HOVSTAD: Is it a message from your father—?

PETRA: No I've come on my own account. (*Takes a book out of her coat pocket*) I've brought back that English story.

HOVSTAD: Brought it back—why?

PETRA: Because I don't want to translate it after all.

HOVSTAD: But you gave me a definite promise—

PETRA: I know; but I hadn't read it then. You haven't read it, have you?

HOVSTAD: No—I don't read English; but—

PETRA: That's what I thought; so I felt I should advise you to look around for something else. (*Putting the book on the table*) This would never do for *The People's Monitor*.

HOVSTAD: Why not?

PETRA: Because it's against everything you stand for.

HOVSTAD: Well, as far as that goes—

PETRA: No—you don't see my point; this story claims that there's a supernatural power looking after all the so-called good people in the world, so that everything turns out well for them in the end—whereas all the so-called bad people get punished.

HOVSTAD: Splendid! Just what the public wants.

PETRA: Yes; but you surely wouldn't want to be the one to give them such nonsense. You don't believe a word of it yourself; you know perfectly well that's not the way things really happen.

HOVSTAD: You're right, of course; but, you see, a publisher can't always do as he pleases—he often has to cater to the public in minor matters. Politics, after all, are the main thing—to a newspaper at any rate; if I want to steer people towards a more liberal way of thinking, I can't afford to scare them off. If they come across a nice moral tale like that tucked away somewhere in the back pages of the paper they feel safer, and they're more willing to accept what we give them on the front page.

PETRA: But that's disgusting! I'm sure you'd never play a trick like that. You're not a hypocrite!

HOVSTAD (*Smiling*): I'm glad you think so well of me. As a matter of fact it's Billing's idea, not mine.

PETRA: Billing's!

HOVSTAD: Yes; at least he was talking along those lines only the other day. It was Billing who wanted to print the story; I don't know anything about it.

PETRA: Mr. Billing! But that seems impossible; he has such a modern point of view!

HOVSTAD: Well, you see—Billing is a man of many parts. He's now decided he wants to become secretary to the Town Council—or so I hear.

PETRA: I don't believe that for a moment, Mr. Hovstad. He could never lower himself to that!

HOVSTAD: You'd better ask him about it.

PETRA: I never would have thought such a thing of Mr. Billing.

HOVSTAD (*Looks at her intently*): No? Is it really such a surprise to you?

PETRA: Yes, indeed it is. And yet—perhaps it isn't really. I don't know what to think—

HOVSTAD: We newspaper men are worthless fellows, Miss Petra.

PETRA: Do you really mean that?

HOVSTAD: Yes; at least, I sometimes think so.

PETRA: That may be true as far as ordinary petty everyday matters are concerned. But now that you're involved in a great cause—

HOVSTAD: You mean this business about your father?

PETRA: Yes, of course. It must give you a proud feeling; a sense of being worth more than just ordinary people.

HOVSTAD: You're right; I do feel a bit like that today.

PETRA: I'm sure you must. What a wonderful career you've chosen! To be a pioneer; to promote the truth; to fight for bold ideas—new ways of thinking! The mere fact of coming to the defense of someone who's been wronged—

HOVSTAD: Especially when that someone is—I don't quite know how to put it—

PETRA: When he's so true and honorable, you mean?

HOVSTAD (*In a low voice*): Yes; and especially when he happens to be your father.

PETRA (*Suddenly taken aback*): You mean—? Oh, no!

HOVSTAD: Yes, Petra—Miss Petra.

PETRA: Is that your reason—? Is that what matters most to you? Then, it isn't the thing itself; the truth means nothing to you—and my father's generosity of soul means nothing either!

HOVSTAD: Yes, of course it does, but—

PETRA: Thank you, Mr. Hovstad. You've said more than enough. I shall never trust you again in anything.

HOVSTAD: Come now—you mustn't be too hard on me! Even if it is mainly for your sake—

PETRA: What makes me angry is that you haven't been honest with my father. You let him think you were concerned with the truth, with the good of the community, when all the time—! You've made fools of us both, Mr. Hovstad. You're not at all the sort of man you pretended to be. I shall never forgive you for it—never!

HOVSTAD: I wouldn't be too caustic, Miss Petra; this is not the time for that.

PETRA: Not the time? Why not?

HOVSTAD: Because your father can't very well get on without my help.

PETRA: I see. So you're that sort of a person too.

HOVSTAD: No, no—really I'm not! I didn't think what I was saying; you must believe me!

PETRA: I know what to believe, I assure you. Goodbye.

ASLAKSEN (*Enters hurriedly and mysteriously from the printing office*): Hell and damnation, Mr. Hovstad—! (*Sees* PETRA) Oh, I beg your pardon—

PETRA: There's the book. Get someone else to do it for you. (*Goes towards the main entrance.*)

HOVSTAD (*Following her*): But, Miss Petra—

PETRA: Goodbye. (*She goes.*)

ASLAKSEN: Mr. Hovstad, listen!

HOVSTAD: Well—what is it? What's the matter?

ASLAKSEN: It's the Mayor! He's out in the printing office.

HOVSTAD: The Mayor?

ASLAKSEN: Yes; he says he wants to talk to you. He came in the back way—didn't want to be seen, I suppose.

HOVSTAD: What does this mean, I wonder? Wait a minute—I'll go myself—(*He goes toward the printing office, opens the door, bows and invites* THE MAYOR *to come in.*)

HOVSTAD: Be on the look-out, Aslaksen, and see that no one—

ASLAKSEN: I understand— (*He goes into the printing office.*)

THE MAYOR: I don't suppose you expected to see me here, Mr. Hovstad.

HOVSTAD: No, I can't say I did.

THE MAYOR (*Looking round*): A nice place you have here; most comfortable.

HOVSTAD: Well—

THE MAYOR: You must forgive me for dropping in like this, and taking up your time.

HOVSTAD: I'm only too delighted, Mr. Mayor; always at your service. Let me take your things— (*Takes* THE MAYOR'S *hat and cane and puts them on a chair*) And now—won't you sit down?

THE MAYOR (*Sits by the table*): Thanks. (HOVSTAD *sits down at the table also*) I've been faced with—with a very troubling matter today, Mr. Hovstad.

HOVSTAD: Really? But, of course, you must have so many duties—

THE MAYOR: It concerns my brother, Mr. Hovstad.

HOVSTAD: Dr. Stockmann?

THE MAYOR: Yes. He's written a sort of memorandum to the directors of the Baths, alleging that there are certain defects in the establishment.

HOVSTAD: Really? Has he?

THE MAYOR: Hasn't he told you? I thought he said—

HOVSTAD: Now I come to think of it, I believe he did mention—

ASLAKSEN (*Enters from the printing office*): I'd better have that manuscript—

HOVSTAD (*With annoyance*): It's over on the desk.

ASLAKSEN: Ah, yes—here it is.

THE MAYOR: But surely— Isn't that—?

ASLAKSEN: It's Dr. Stockmann's article.

HOVSTAD: Oh—was that what you were referring to?

THE MAYOR: Precisely— What do you think of it?

HOVSTAD: I've only just glanced at it—and, of course, I'm not an expert—

THE MAYOR: And yet you intend to print it?

HOVSTAD: I can't very well refuse anything signed by—

ASLAKSEN: I've nothing to do with editing the paper, Mr. Mayor.

THE MAYOR: No, of course not.

ASLAKSEN: I just do the printing.

THE MAYOR: I understand.

ASLAKSEN: So—if you'll excuse me— (*Goes towards the press-room.*)

THE MAYOR: Just one moment, Mr. Aslaksen. With your permission, Mr. Hovstad—?

HOVSTAD: Of course.

THE MAYOR: Mr. Aslaksen—you seem to me to be a discreet and sensible man.

ASLAKSEN: It's very kind of you to say so—

THE MAYOR: And a man of widespread influence too.

ASLAKSEN: Only among the little people, Your Honor.

THE MAYOR: It's the small taxpayers who form the majority—here, as everywhere.

ASLAKSEN: That's true enough.

THE MAYOR: And I've no doubt you are familiar with the general trend of sentiment among them. Are you not?

ASLAKSEN: I think I may say I am, Your Honor.

THE MAYOR: Well—since there appears to be such a fine feeling of self-sacrifice among the poorer classes—

ASLAKSEN: How do you mean?

HOVSTAD: Self-sacrifice?

THE MAYOR: It indicates an admirable sense of public-spirit. I find it a little surprising, I admit; but then I don't know the public sentiment as well as you do.

ASLAKSEN: But, Your Honor—

THE MAYOR: And it will entail no small sacrifice to the town, I can assure you.

HOVSTAD: To the town?

ASLAKSEN: I don't understand; surely, this concerns the Baths—

THE MAYOR: At a rough preliminary estimate, the alterations Dr. Stockmann has in mind will cost in the neighborhood of two hundred thousand crowns.

ASLAKSEN: That's a lot of money; but—

THE MAYOR: A municipal loan will naturally be necessary.

HOVSTAD (*Rising*): You surely can't mean that the town—?

ASLAKSEN: You mean the townspeople would have to pay for it out of their own pockets?

THE MAYOR: My dear Mr. Aslaksen, where else should the money come from?

ASLAKSEN: I should think the owners of the Baths would be responsible.

THE MAYOR: The owners are not prepared to increase their investment at this time.

ASLAKSEN: Are you quite sure of that?

THE MAYOR: I have positive information to that effect. So if these alterations are to be made, the town itself will have to pay for them.

ASLAKSEN: But then, damn it all, Mr. Hovstad—excuse me, Your Honor—this puts the matter in quite a different light!

HOVSTAD: It does indeed.

THE MAYOR: The worst part of it is we shall be obliged to close down the Baths for a couple of years.

HOVSTAD: Close them? Completely close them?

ASLAKSEN: For two years!

THE MAYOR: Yes; it will take at least two years to do the work.

ASLAKSEN: But, damn it! We could never survive that, Your Honor; we home-owners depend on these visitors—what are we to live on in the meantime?

THE MAYOR: That is a difficult question to answer, Mr. Aslaksen. But what's to be done? Once people get this notion into their heads that the waters are tainted, that the whole place is a pest-hole—we can hardly expect them to come here.

ASLAKSEN: Then you think it's no more than a notion?

THE MAYOR: Try as I will, I can't persuade myself to think otherwise.

ASLAKSEN: Then it's downright inexcusable of Dr. Stockmann—I beg pardon, Your Honor, but—

THE MAYOR: Unfortunately you're quite right, Mr. Aslaksen; my brother has always been an exceedingly rash man.

ASLAKSEN: And yet you are prepared to back him up in this, Mr. Hovstad!

HOVSTAD: But, who would ever have thought that—!

THE MAYOR: I've drawn up a short statement on the matter, interpreting the facts from a more rational point of view; I've also indicated ways in which any small defects that might conceivably exist can be taken care of within the scope of the present financial budget.

HOVSTAD: Have you it with you?

THE MAYOR (*Feeling in his pocket*): Yes; I thought I'd better bring it in case you—

ASLAKSEN (*Quickly*): Damn it—there he is!

THE MAYOR: Who? My brother?

HOVSTAD: Where?

ASLAKSEN: Coming through the press-room.

THE MAYOR: This is unfortunate! I don't want to run into him here—yet there are several things I'd still like to talk to you about.

HOVSTAD (*Pointing to the door on the right*): Wait in there for a moment.

THE MAYOR: But—?

HOVSTAD: There's no one in there but Billing.

ASLAKSEN: Quick, Your Honor! Here he comes!

THE MAYOR: Very well; get rid of him as soon as you can, though. (*He goes out by the door right which* ASLAKSEN *opens, and closes after him.*)

HOVSTAD: Pretend to be busy, Aslaksen. (*He sits down and starts to write.* ASLAKSEN *goes through a pile of newspapers on a chair, right.*)

DR. STOCKMANN (*Enters from the composing-room*): Well—Here I am, back again. (*Puts down his hat and stick.*)

HOVSTAD (*Writing*): Already, Doctor? Get on with what we were just talking about, Aslaksen. We've no time to waste today.

DR. STOCKMANN (*To* ASLAKSEN): No proofs yet, I hear.

ASLAKSEN (*Without turning round*): You could hardly expect them yet, Doctor.

DR. STOCKMANN: No, of course not. It's just that I'm impatient—you can understand that; I can't wait to see the thing in print.

HOVSTAD: It'll be another hour at least; wouldn't you say so, Aslaksen?

ASLAKSEN: I'm afraid so, yes.

DR. STOCKMANN: Never mind; I'll come back. I don't mind coming back twice if need be. What's a little inconvenience compared to the welfare of the town—! (*Starts to go but stops and comes back*) By the way, there's something I must discuss with you.

HOVSTAD: I'm afraid, just now, you must excuse me, Doctor—

DR. STOCKMANN: It'll only take a moment. I was just thinking: when people read this article of mine tomorrow morning, and realize I devoted my whole winter to working for the good of the town—

HOVSTAD: But, after all, Doctor—

DR. STOCKMANN: Oh, I know what you're going to say—it was no more than my duty as a citizen—I know that as well as you do. But my fellow-townsmen—well, bless their hearts, they're so fond of me, you see—

ASLAKSEN: Yes—they've thought very highly of you up to now—

DR. STOCKMANN: I know; that's why I'm so afraid they might—what I mean is this: the people, especially the poorer classes, are bound to take this article of mine as a rousing call to action—as a summons to run things for themselves from now on—

HOVSTAD (*Rising*): As a matter of fact, Doctor, I think I ought to tell you—

DR. STOCKMANN: I knew it! I was sure they'd be up to something. But I won't hear of it, I tell you! So if they're planning anything like that—

HOVSTAD: Like what?

DR. STOCKMANN: Oh, I don't know—a parade, or a banquet, or a testimonial dinner of some sort—I count on you to put a stop to it. You, too, Mr. Aslaksen—remember now!

HOVSTAD: Excuse me, Doctor; I think you'd better know the truth once and for all—

(MRS. STOCKMANN *enters from the rear door, left*.)

MRS. STOCKMANN (*Seeing the doctor*): Just as I thought!

HOVSTAD (*Goes towards her*): You here too, Mrs. Stockmann?

DR. STOCKMANN: What the devil do you want here, Katrine?

MRS. STOCKMANN: You know very well what I want.

HOVSTAD: Won't you sit down? Or perhaps you'd rather—

MRS. STOCKMANN: Thanks—but please don't bother about me; and forgive my coming here to fetch my husband. I'm the mother of three children, let me tell you.

DR. STOCKMANN: Don't talk nonsense! As if we didn't all know that!

MRS. STOCKMANN: You don't seem to be giving much thought to it—otherwise you wouldn't be so anxious to ruin us all!

DR. STOCKMANN: You must be stark raving mad, Katrine! Just because he has a wife and children, can't a man stand up for the truth? Be a useful citizen? Serve the town he lives in?

MRS. STOCKMANN: If you'd only use a little moderation, Tomas!

ASLAKSEN: That's what I always say: everything in moderation!

MRS. STOCKMANN: It's very wrong of you, Mr. Hovstad, to lure my husband away from house and home; persuading him to get mixed up in all this—making a fool of him!

HOVSTAD: I don't make a fool of anyone—

DR. STOCKMANN: A fool! You think I let people make a fool of me!

MRS. STOCKMANN: Yes, Tomas—you do! Oh, I know you're the cleverest man in town, but you're easily fooled all the same. (*To* HOVSTAD) Don't you realize he'll lose his position if you print that article of his—

ASLAKSEN: What!

HOVSTAD: As a matter of fact, Dr. Stockmann—

DR. STOCKMANN (*Laughing*): They can't do a thing to me—they'd never dare! Don't forget, my dear, the solid majority is with me.

MRS. STOCKMANN: More's the pity. You'd be better off without it!

DR. STOCKMANN: Don't talk nonsense, Katrine; go home and tend to your house-work and leave Society to me. What is there to be afraid of! Can't you see how happy and confident I am? (*Rubs his hands and walks up and down*) The truth will conquer—I'm convinced of it. The people will band together in the cause of truth and freedom, and nothing can stop them—! (*Stops suddenly by a chair*) Why—what the devil's this doing here?

ASLAKSEN (*Realizing*): Oh, Lord.

HOVSTAD (*The same*): Hm—

DR. STOCKMANN (*He picks up* THE MAYOR'S *cap and holds it gingerly aloft*): The crown of authority, is it not?

MRS. STOCKMANN: It's the Mayor's cap!

DR. STOCKMANN: And the staff of office, too! But what the devil are they doing here?

HOVSTAD: You might as well know—

DR. STOCKMANN: Ah, I see! He came to try and win you over. Well—he chose the wrong customer for once! I suppose he caught sight of me in the office and— (*Bursts out laughing*) Did he turn tail, Mr. Aslaksen?

ASLAKSEN (*Hurriedly*): Yes, Doctor, he—he turned tail.

DR. STOCKMANN: Ran off and left his stick and— But, wait a minute—that's not a bit like Peter. What have you done with him? Oh, of course—he's hiding in there. Now you're going to see something, Katrine!

MRS. STOCKMANN: Please, Tomas—!

ASLAKSEN: Be careful, Doctor!

(DR. STOCKMANN *has put on* THE MAYOR'S *cap and seized his stick; he goes to the door, flings it open and makes a military salute.* THE MAYOR *enters, flushed with anger, followed by* BILLING.)

THE MAYOR: What is the meaning of these antics?

DR. STOCKMANN: Show some respect, Peter, if you please. (*Struts up and down*) I'm in authority now!

MRS. STOCKMANN (*Almost in tears*): Tomas—for heaven's sake!

THE MAYOR (*Following him*): Give me my cap and stick!

DR. STOCKMANN (*As before*): You may be chief of police, but I'm the Mayor—I'm king of the whole town!

THE MAYOR: Take off that cap, I tell you. Don't you realize it's a badge of office!

DR. STOCKMANN: Listen to him! We've roused the spirit of democracy—do you think a bit of gold braid can frighten me? Tomorrow the revolution starts, I'd have you know. You threatened to dismiss me, did you? Well now it's my turn to dismiss you—I'm going to kick you out of office! And if you don't think I can do it, you'll soon find out! The power is on my side— the power of an aroused public! Hovstad and Billing here will thunder away at you in the *Monitor*, and Aslaksen will lead the entire Home-own- ers Association into battle—!

ASLAKSEN: No, Doctor; I'll do nothing of the sort.

DR. STOCKMANN: Nonsense! Of course you will—

THE MAYOR: I see, so perhaps Mr. Hovstad will decide to join the rebels after all?

HOVSTAD: No, Your Honor.

ASLAKSEN: Mr. Hovstad's no fool; he's not likely to ruin both himself and the paper for the sake of a delusion.

DR. STOCKMANN (*Looks from one to the other*): What does this mean?

HOVSTAD: You've presented this whole matter in a false light, Doctor; that is why I cannot possibly give you my support.

BILLING: After what the Mayor so kindly explained to me just now—

DR. STOCKMANN: A false light, eh? Leave that part of it to me—you just print my article; I'll prove the truth of every word of it.

HOVSTAD: I shall not print it. I neither can, nor will, nor dare.

DR. STOCKMANN: Not *dare*? But that's absurd. You're the editor, aren't you? Don't you control your own paper?

ASLAKSEN: No—the subscribers do.

THE MAYOR: Fortunately—yes.

ASLAKSEN: Public opinion, majority interests, the Home-owners Association and other similar groups—they control the paper.

DR. STOCKMANN (*Calmly*): And they would all be against me, you think?

ASLAKSEN: Unquestionably. If your article were printed it would mean the ruin of the town.

DR. STOCKMANN: I see.

THE MAYOR: And now, my cap and stick!

(DR. STOCKMANN *takes off the cap and lays it on the table; he places the stick beside it.*)

THE MAYOR (*Picking them up*): Your term of office came to rather an abrupt end, didn't it?

DR. STOCKMANN: This is not the end, Peter—believe me. (*To* HOVSTAD) So you find it impossible to print my article in the *Monitor?*

HOVSTAD: Quite impossible; apart from anything else, consideration for your family would—

DR. STOCKMANN: Kindly leave my family to me, Mr. Hovstad.

THE MAYOR (*Takes a manuscript from his breast pocket*): This will put the necessary facts before the public. It is an official statement; I trust you to deal with it accordingly.

HOVSTAD (*Taking the manuscript*): Very good. We shall take care of it; it will appear without delay.

DR. STOCKMANN: But mine will be suppressed. Do you think you can sup- press the truth? You'll find it's not so easy! Mr. Aslaksen, please take my manuscript and print it as a pamphlet—at my own expense—I'll publish it myself. I want four hundred copies; no, five—better make it six.

ASLAKSEN: I can't possibly use my printing-press for such a purpose, Doc- tor—not if you were to pay me its weight in gold. I dare not offend public opinion. No one in town will print it, I assure you.

DR. STOCKMANN: Then give it back to me.

HOVSTAD (*Hands it to him*): Gladly.

DR. STOCKMANN (*Takes up his hat and stick*): But you won't be able to suppress it all the same! I'll call a public meeting—I'll read it to the people myself; my fellow-townsmen are going to hear the truth!

THE MAYOR: It won't be any good; not a single hall will be available to you.

ASLAKSEN: Not one—I'll vouch for that.

BILLING: That's true—strike me dead if it isn't!

MRS. STOCKMANN: But this is disgraceful, Tomas! Why are they suddenly all against you?

DR. STOCKMANN: I'll tell you why. It's because all the men in this town are a lot of old women—just like you! They think of nothing but themselves; they don't care a damn about the general good!

MRS. STOCKMANN: Then I'll show them here's at least one old woman who knows how to be a man. I'll stand by you, Tomas!

DR. STOCKMANN: Well said, Katrine! Nothing can stop me; if I can't rent a hall, I'll hire a drum and march through the town with it. I'll read my statement at the corner of every street, of every square—the people are going to know the truth!

THE MAYOR: You can't do that! Are you a raving lunatic?

DR. STOCKMANN: Yes, I am!

ASLAKSEN: No one will go with you, Doctor Stockmann.

BILLING: Strike me dead—I'm sure of that!

MRS. STOCKMANN: Don't give in now, Tomas. I'll ask the boys—they'll go with you.

DR. STOCKMANN: That's a splendid thought!

MRS. STOCKMANN: Morten would be delighted—and I'm certain Ejlif would go too.

DR. STOCKMANN: Yes—and then there's Petra! And you, Katrine!

MRS. STOCKMANN: Oh, no; it wouldn't do for me to go. But I tell you what I'll do—I'll watch you from the window.

DR. STOCKMANN (*Throws his arms round her*): Thanks! Well—the fight is on, gentlemen! We'll see if you and your chicanery can prevent an honest citizen from cleaning up the town he lives in! Come, Katrine!

(*He and* MRS. STOCKMANN *go out by the door upper left.*)

THE MAYOR (*Shakes his head thoughtfully*): He's managed to turn her head at last! Now she's as mad as he is.   CURTAIN

Act IV

SCENE: A *large old-fashioned room in* CAPTAIN HORSTER'S *house. Open double doors in the back wall lead to an anteroom. In the wall left are three windows; in the center of the opposite wall is a platform on which stands a small table with two candles, a carafe of water, a glass and a bell placed on it. Sconces between the windows provide the general lighting. Down left a small table with a candle, and a chair beside it. Down right a door and near it a couple of chairs.*

There is a large gathering of townspeople of various types. Among the crowd are seen a few women and schoolboys. People continue to stream in from the anteroom until the main room is quite full.

FIRST MAN (*as he bumps into another one*): You're here too, are you Lamstad?

SECOND MAN: I never miss a public meeting.

ANOTHER MAN: I see you've brought your whistle.

SECOND MAN: Of course; haven't you?

THIRD MAN: I should hope so! Skipper Evensen said he was going to bring his big horn!

SECOND MAN: That Evensen's a good one, he is!

(*Laughter in the group.*)

FOURTH MAN (*Joining them*): Tell me—what's going on here this evening?

SECOND MAN: Doctor Stockmann and the Mayor are holding a debate.

FOURTH MAN: But the Mayor's his brother, isn't he?

FIRST MAN: That makes no difference; Doctor Stockmann's not afraid of anyone.

THIRD MAN: But he's all wrong; it says so in the *Monitor*.

SECOND MAN: He must be wrong this time; no one would let him have a hall—not the Home-owners Association, nor the Citizens' Club either.

FIRST MAN: Even the Baths refused him.

SECOND MAN: That's not surprising.

A MAN (*In another group*): Whom do we support in this business?

ANOTHER MAN (*In the same group*): Just keep an eye on Aslaksen and do as he does.

BILLING (*With a portfolio under his arm pushes his way through the crowd*): Excuse me, gentlemen. May I get by please? I'm reporting for *The People's Monitor*. Thanks—thank you! (*He sits at the table left.*)

A WORKMAN: Who's he?

ANOTHER WORKMAN: Don't you know him? That's Billing—he writes for Aslaksen's paper.

(CAPTAIN HORSTER *ushers in* MRS. STOCKMANN *and* PETRA *through the door down right.* EJLIF *and* MORTEN *follow them.*)

CAPTAIN HORSTER: I thought this would be a good place for you to sit; it'll be easy for you to slip away if anything should happen.

MRS. STOCKMANN: Will there be any disturbance, do you think?

HORSTER: It's hard to say—with all these people. But don't be anxious—just sit here quietly.

MRS. STOCKMANN (*Sitting down*): It was so kind of you to let Stockmann have the room.

HORSTER: Since nobody else would, I thought I—

PETRA (*Who has also seated herself*): And it was brave of you too, Captain Horster.

HORSTER: I don't see anything specially brave about it.

(HOVSTAD *and* ASLAKSEN *enter at the same time, but separately, and make their way through the crowd.*)

ASLAKSEN (*Going up to* HORSTER): Isn't Doctor Stockmann here yet?

HORSTER: He's waiting in there.

(*A movement in the crowd by the door at the back of the room.*)

HOVSTAD (*To* BILLING): Here comes the Mayor! Look!

BILLING: Yes—strike me dead! So he's put in an appearance after all!

(MAYOR STOCKMANN *advances graciously through the crowd, bowing to right and left. He takes his stand near the wall on the left. A moment later*

DR. STOCKMANN *enters from the door down right. He wears a black frock coat and a white tie. There is scattered applause countered by subdued hissing. Then, silence.*)

DR. STOCKMANN (*In a low tone*): How do you feel, Katrine?

MRS. STOCKMANN: I'm all right, thank you, dear. (*Whispers to him*) Don't lose your temper, Tomas!

DR. STOCKMANN: Don't worry—I'll keep myself in hand. (*Looks at his watch, mounts the platform and bows*) It's a quarter past; I'm going to begin— (*Takes out his manuscript.*)

ASLAKSEN: Wait! We must elect a chairman first.

DR. STOCKMANN: That won't be necessary.

SEVERAL GENTLEMEN (*Shouting*): Yes! Yes!

THE MAYOR: By all means; of course we must have a chairman.

DR. STOCKMANN: But I've called this meeting to read a paper, Peter.

THE MAYOR: All the same—your paper is likely to cause discussion.

SEVERAL VOICES IN THE CROWD: A chairman! We want a chairman!

HOVSTAD: The general voice seems to be in favor of a chairman.

DR. STOCKMANN (*Controlling himself*): Oh, very well— Let the "general voice" have its way.

ASLAKSEN: Perhaps the Mayor will honor us?

THREE GENTLEMEN (*Clapping*): Bravo! Bravo!

THE MAYOR: Many thanks. But for various obvious reasons, I must decline. However, we are fortunate in having in our midst a man who, I am certain, will be acceptable to all. I refer, of course, to the chairman of the Home-owners Association—Mr. Aslaksen.

MANY VOICES: Yes! Yes! Long live Aslaksen! Hurrah for Aslaksen!

(DR. STOCKMANN *takes his manuscript and leaves the platform.*)

ASLAKSEN: Since my fellow-citizens are pleased to show me this signal mark of confidence—who am I to refuse?

(*Applause and cheers.* ASLAKSEN *ascends the platform.*)

BILLING (*Making notes*): Mr. Aslaksen elected by acclamation—

ASLAKSEN: And now—since I stand here as your chairman—allow me to say a few brief words to you. I am a quiet peace-loving man, gentlemen; a man in favor of discreet moderation, and of—and of—moderate discretion. All those who know me are aware of that.

SEVERAL VOICES: Yes, yes! To be sure, Aslaksen!

ASLAKSEN: I have learned in the great common school of life and of experience, that moderation is the citizen's prime virtue—a virtue from which he reaps the highest benefits—

THE MAYOR: Hear! Hear!

ASLAKSEN: —and that discretion and moderation are also the best servants of Society. Allow me therefore to suggest to our respected fellow-citizen who has seen fit to call this meeting, that he take note; let us hope he will bend every effort to keep within the bounds of moderation.

A MAN (*By the door*): I propose a toast to the Temperance Society! Hurrah!

A VOICE: Shame! Shame!

VOICES: Sh! Quiet!

ASLAKSEN: No interruptions if you please, gentlemen! —Does anyone wish to offer any observations?

THE MAYOR: Mr. Chairman!

ASLAKSEN: The Mayor has the floor!

THE MAYOR: Because of my close relationship to the present medical adviser to the Baths—a relationship of which most of you are undoubtedly aware—I should have preferred not to speak here this evening. But my position as Chairman of the Board, as well as my deep concern for the welfare of the town, force me to make this motion. I think I may venture to assume that not a single soul here present would condone the spreading of exaggerated and irresponsible statements concerning the sanitary conditions of our Baths and of our town.

MANY VOICES: No, no! Never! Certainly not! We protest!

THE MAYOR: I therefore move that this meeting pass the following resolution: Dr. Stockmann cannot be allowed to read his paper or to address this assembly on this particular subject.

DR. STOCKMANN (*Flaring up*): Cannot be allowed—! What do you mean?

MRS. STOCKMANN (*Coughing*): Hm, hm!

DR. STOCKMANN (*Controlling himself*): So, I'm not to be allowed; I see.

THE MAYOR: I have acquainted the Public with the relevant facts through my statement in *The People's Monitor*, so that all right-thinking citizens may have no difficulty in forming their own judgment. It will be clearly seen that the doctor's report on the situation—apart from being a direct vote of censure against the leading men in the community—simply means saddling the tax-payers with a totally unnecessary outlay of at least one hundred thousand crowns.

(*Cries of protest and scattered whistles.*)

ASLAKSEN (*Rings the bell*): Order, order, gentlemen! I beg to second the Mayor's motion. I share the opinion that there are other motives behind the doctor's agitation; he may talk about the Baths, but his real aim is nothing short of revolution—the complete overthrow of the parties now in power. No one doubts the doctor's integrity of purpose—there can be no two opinions about that. I too am in favor of self-government by the People, provided it doesn't result in too great a burden on the tax-payer; in this case that is precisely what would occur. For this reason—well, damn it—excuse me, gentlemen!—on this occasion I cannot possibly side with Dr. Stockmann. You can pay too high a price—even for gold. At all events, that's my opinion.

(*Loud applause from all sides.*)

HOVSTAD: I too should like to make my position clear in this matter. At first Dr. Stockmann's agitation met with considerable favor in many quarters and I did my best to give it my impartial support. It soon appeared however that we had been misled; that the facts had been presented in a false light—

DR. STOCKMANN: False—!

HOVSTAD: —an ambiguous light, if you prefer. The Mayor's report leaves no doubt on that score. I trust no one here questions my liberal principles; on the great political issues of the day, the views of *The People's Monitor* are well-known to you all. But I have learned from men of judgment and experience that when it comes to purely local matters, a newspaper should proceed with a certain amount of caution.

ASLAKSEN: I whole-heartedly endorse the speaker's views.

HOVSTAD: In the matter now under discussion public opinion is quite obviously against Dr. Stockmann. Now—what is a publisher's first and foremost duty, gentlemen? Is it not to work in harmony with his readers? Is he not obligated—by a tacit mandate, as it were—to serve indefatigably and tenaciously the interests of the majority? Or am I mistaken?

MANY VOICES: No, no! Hovstad is right!

HOVSTAD: It has not been easy, I assure you, to break with a man in whose home I have been a frequent guest of late. A man who up to this very day has enjoyed the unqualified goodwill of his fellow-citizens. A man whose only, or perhaps one should say whose chief fault, consists in following his heart rather than his head.

A FEW SCATTERED VOICES: That's true! Hurrah for Dr. Stockmann!

HOVSTAD: But my duty to Society has forced me, much against my will, to make this break. And there's another consideration that impels me to oppose him, and try, if I can, to stop him on the rash course on which he is embarked: consideration for his family, gentlemen—

DR. STOCKMANN: Stick to the sewers and water-works!

HOVSTAD: —consideration for his wife, and for his helpless children.

MORTEN: Does he mean us, Mother?

MRS. STOCKMANN: Hush!

ASLAKSEN: I shall now put the Mayor's resolution to a vote.

DR. STOCKMANN: That won't be necessary! I don't intend to speak about the filth and corruption of the Baths this evening. No! You're going to hear about something very different.

THE MAYOR (*Half to himself*): Now what's he up to?

A DRUNKEN MAN (*Near the main entrance*): I'm entitled to pay taxes—so I suppose I'm entitled to an opinion too. And it is my irrefutable and incomprehensible opinion that—

SEVERAL VOICES: Silence over there!

OTHERS: He's drunk! Throw him out!

(*The drunken man is put out.*)

DR. STOCKMANN: May I speak?

ASLAKSEN (*Ringing the bell*): Dr. Stockmann has the floor.

DR. STOCKMANN: I'd like to have seen anyone try—even a few days ago—to gag me as I've been gagged this evening. I should have fought like a lion for what I know to be my sacred rights. But that doesn't matter to me now. Now I have more important things to say.

(*The people crowd closer round him.* MORTEN KIIL *appears among the crowd.*)

DR. STOCKMANN (*Continuing*): I've done a lot of thinking these past days—turning things over in my mind, till my brain seemed all muddled and confused—

THE MAYOR (*Coughing*): Hm—!

DR. STOCKMANN: But gradually things straightened out, and I saw them in their true perspective. That's why I'm here this evening. I'm going to expose many things to you, my friends! The fact that our water-works are poisoned and that our health-resort is nothing but a pest-hole is comparatively unimportant compared to the discovery I'm about to reveal now.

MANY VOICES: No mention of the Baths! We won't listen! Leave them out of it!

DR. STOCKMANN: I've just told you—I'm going to speak about a great discovery I've made in these past days—and this is it: The very sources of our spiritual life are poisoned, and our whole community is founded on a pestilential lie!

A MURMUR OF AMAZED VOICES: What's he saying?

THE MAYOR: How dare he—!

ASLAKSEN (*His hand on the bell*): I call upon the speaker to moderate his language!

DR. STOCKMANN: No man could love his native town more than I've loved mine! I was very young when I left here, and distance, memory and homesickness combined to cast a kind of aura round the place and round its people. (*Scattered applause and expressions of approval*) I spent many years in the far North, in a God-forsaken hole of a place. I used to visit the few starving wretches scattered about in that rocky wilderness, and I often thought a horse-doctor would have served their purpose better than a man of science like myself.

(*Murmurs throughout the room.*)

BILLING (*Laying down his pen*): Strike me dead! I've never heard such—

HOVSTAD: An insult to honest country-folk!

DR. STOCKMANN: Just wait a minute! —All that time I don't think anyone could have accused me of forgetting my home town. I sat there brooding over an idea—like an eider-duck on her eggs—and what I finally hatched out was the plan for our Baths. (*Applause and protests*) And when at last fate was kind enough to make my return home possible—I felt as though my every wish had been fulfilled. I still had one wish, though; an ardent, unwavering, passionate desire to serve my home town and my fellow-citizens.

THE MAYOR (*Gazing into space*): A strange way to show it—!

DR. STOCKMANN: I was supremely happy—basking in joyous illusions. Then, yesterday morning—no, the preceding evening to be exact—I received a mental jolt; my eyes were suddenly wide open and the first thing I saw was the colossal stupidity of our reigning authorities—

(*Noise, cries and laughter.* MRS. STOCKMANN *coughs repeatedly.*)

THE MAYOR: Mr. Chairman!

ASLAKSEN (*Ringing his bell*): By virtue of my office—!

DR. STOCKMANN: Let the expression pass, Mr. Aslaksen—there's no need to be petty! I simply mean that the whole disgraceful situation at the Baths was suddenly revealed to me—a mess for which the so-called leading men of the town must take the blame. These leading men—I'm sick of them and all their works! They're like a lot of goats let loose in a young orchard—destroying everything; they stand in the way of free men and hamper them at every turn. For my part I'd like to see them exterminated together with all other predatory creatures—

(*Uproar in the room.*)

THE MAYOR: Mr. Chairman—can such things be allowed?

ASLAKSEN (*His hand on the bell*): Dr. Stockmann—!

DR. STOCKMANN: I can't conceive why it should have taken me so long to see through these gentlemen; every single day I've had a prime example before my very eyes—my brother Peter—empty of ideas and filled with prejudice—

(*Laughter, noise and catcalls.* MRS. STOCKMANN *coughs.* ASLAKSEN *violently rings his bell.*)

THE DRUNKEN MAN (*Who has returned*): Are you referring to me? My name's Pettersen all right—but I'll be damned if—

ANGRY VOICES: Throw him out! Throw that drunk out!
(*They throw him out again.*)
THE MAYOR: Who was that person?
A BYSTANDER: I don't know him, Your Honor.
ANOTHER MAN: He's not from around here.
A THIRD MAN: He must be that lumber-dealer from— (*The rest is inaudible.*)
ASLAKSEN: The man was unquestionably intoxicated. Proceed, Dr. Stockmann; but with moderation, if you please!
DR. STOCKMANN: Well, fellow-citizens, I shall say no more about our leading men. And if anyone imagines, after what I have just said, that I'm here to attack these gentlemen this evening, he is quite wrong I assure you. You see, I cherish the comfortable conviction that these reactionaries, these relics of another age, are busily engaged in cutting their own throats—they don't need a doctor to help them. And besides, they are not the worst menace to Society; it is not primarily due to them that our spiritual well-being is endangered, and that the very ground we stand on reeks with corruption. They are not the most dangerous enemies to truth and freedom!
CRIES FROM ALL SIDES: Who then? Who do you mean? Name them! Name them!
DR. STOCKMANN: Oh, I shall name them—never fear! You see, that is my great discovery; I made it yesterday. (*Raising his voice*) In our Society, the worst enemy to truth and freedom is the majority. Yes! The damnable, solid, liberal majority—that's the great menace! There's your answer! (*Great commotion in the room. Most of the audience are shouting, stamping and whistling. A few old gentlemen exchange covert glances and seem to be enjoying the situation.* MRS. STOCKMANN *gets up anxiously;* EJLIF *and* MORTEN *advance threateningly towards the schoolboys who are making catcalls.* ASLAKSEN *rings his bell and calls for order.* HOVSTAD *and* BILLING *both try to speak but are drowned out. At last quiet is restored.*)
ASLAKSEN: The speaker is requested to withdraw this outrageous statement.
DR. STOCKMANN: Never, Mr. Aslaksen—never! This same great majority robs me of my freedom, and wishes to prevent me from stating the truth!
HOVSTAD: The majority is always right.
BILLING: Yes—but, strike me dead—truth is right too!
DR. STOCKMANN: The majority is never right—never, I tell you! That's one of those social lies against which every free, intelligent man ought to rebel. What does the majority consist of—of wise men or of fools? I think we must all of us agree that from one end of the world to the other the proportion is overwhelmingly in favor of the fools. And are wise men to be ruled by fools? What could be more senseless! (*Uproar and yells*) You can shout me down if you like, but you can't deny it! The majority has the power, unfortunately—but right is on the side of people like me—of the few—of the individual. It's the minority that's always right! (*Renewed commotion.*)
HOVSTAD: Ha, ha! Dr. Stockmann has turned aristocrat!
DR. STOCKMANN: I've said I won't waste any words on that little rear-guard of puny, narrow-chested, self-important men—the stream of life has already left them far behind. I'm thinking of the few—those rare spirits among us who have had the vision to recognize the truth in new ideas, new ways of thought—and have made those ways their own. These men are in the van-

guard—so far ahead that the solid majority can't begin to reach them; and there they fight for new-born truths—too new and too daring to be accepted by that sacred majority of yours.

HOVSTAD: Now he's a revolutionist!

DR. STOCKMANN: Yes, by Heaven, I am, Mr. Hovstad! I intend to revolt against the lie that truth belongs exclusively to the majority. And what are these truths the majority worships? They're truths so old and worn— they're practically decrepit. And when a truth reaches that age you can hardly tell it from a lie! (*Laughter and jeers*) You can believe me or not as you like; but truths are not such tough old Methuselahs as most people imagine. A normal, ordinary truth is good for, say, seventeen or eighteen—at most twenty years; seldom more. And truths as venerable as that are nothing but skin and bones; yet it isn't until then that the great majority adopts them and prescribes them to Society as wholesome spiritual food. But there's not much nourishment in that kind of a diet, I assure you; as a doctor you can take my word for that. These tired old truths are as rancid and moldly as last year's bacon; they're the cause of all that moral scurvy that plagues Society.

ASLAKSEN: Our honored speaker appears to have strayed somewhat from his subject.

THE MAYOR: I heartily endorse the chairman's observation.

DR. STOCKMANN: You must be mad, Peter! I'm doing my best to stick to my subject; I'm saying that it's the masses—that damnable solid majority— that poison the sources of our spiritual life and corrupt the very ground we walk on.

HOVSTAD: I see; in other words you condemn the great majority of liberal-minded men for having sense enough to rely on truths that are fundamental and conclusive.

DR. STOCKMANN: My dear Mr. Hovstad, don't speak about fundamental truths! The truths endorsed by the great majority of men today were considered fundamental by the vanguard in our grandfather's time; they are no longer endorsed by the vanguard of today. There's only one fundamental truth, in my opinion—and that is that Society cannot live a healthy life based on truths that have become old and spineless.

HOVSTAD: Can't you be more explicit? Instead of this vague talk, give us some examples of these so-called spineless truths you say we base our lives on. (*Approval from several parts of the room.*)

DR. STOCKMANN: I could give you innumerable examples—but one will serve: the fundamental truth which, though basically a lie, you and your *People's Monitor* and its adherents swear by all the same—

HOVSTAD: —which is?

DR. STOCKMANN: A doctrine inherited from your grandparents, and that you thoughtlessly go on proclaiming far and wide; the doctrine that the common herd, the crowd, the masses, are the very flower of the people—in fact *are* the people—and that the uncouth man, the vulgar man, the ignorant and unevolved, have the same right to condemn and sanction, to govern and counsel, as the intellectually and spiritually distinguished few.

BILLING: Well—strike me dead! I've never—!

HOVSTAD (*Shouting at the same time*): Take note of this, citizens!

ANGRY VOICES: Aren't we the people? Are we to have no say?

A WORKMAN: A man who talks like that deserves to be kicked out!

OTHERS: Throw him out!

A MAN (*Shouting*): Now's the time to blow your horn, Evensen!

(*The deep notes of a horn are heard; whistles, catcalls and uproar.*)

DR. STOCKMANN (*As the noise subsides*): Be reasonable! Can't you endure the truth? I don't expect you all to agree with me—but I certainly thought Mr. Hovstad would calm down and back me up. Mr. Hovstad lays claim to being a free-thinker—

SEVERAL VOICES (*Subdued and astonished*): A free-thinker, did he say? What? Hovstad a free-thinker?

HOVSTAD: I dare you to prove it, Dr. Stockmann! Have I ever said so in black and white?

DR. STOCKMANN: No, damn it—you've never had the courage! Well, I don't want to get you into trouble; I'm the one who's the free-thinker, Mr. Hovstad. And now—let me prove to you all, scientifically, that *The People's Monitor* makes fools of you and leads you by the nose when it tells you that you, the masses, the crowd, are the flower of the people. That's just a journalistic lie! The masses are only the raw material from which a People can be made. (*Murmurs, laughter and general disturbance*) It's the same thing in all other forms of life. Fine animals are created by breeding and selection. Take an ordinary common hen, for instance—she's not much good for eating, and her eggs are not much better than a crow's eggs—or a raven's; she can't be compared with a really fine strain of poultry. But now take a Japanese or Spanish hen—a pheasant or a turkey—and you'll soon see the difference! Or in the case of dogs—so closely related to mankind; think first of a common ordinary cur—one of those filthy, ragged, plebian mongrels that haunt the gutters and dirty up the side-walks; and compare that mongrel with a pedigreed poodle, bred for generations from the finest stock, used to good food and accustomed to well-modulated voices and the sound of music. Don't you suppose the poodle's brain shows a marked superiority? Of course it does! A trainer can take a poodle pup like that and teach it the most fantastic tricks—things a common mongrel could never dream of learning!

(*Noise and laughter.*)

A MAN (*Shouting*): Are you comparing us with dogs?

ANOTHER: We're not animals, Doctor!

DR. STOCKMANN: Of course you are! We're all animals, my friend! What are we else? But there aren't many well-bred animals among us. There's a tremendous difference between poodle-men and mongrel-men. And it's so ridiculous—Mr. Hovstad agrees with me entirely as long as it's four-legged animals we're talking of—

HOVSTAD: An animal's an animal—and there's an end of it!

DR. STOCKMANN: Perhaps; but as soon as I apply the rule to two-legged animals, Mr. Hovstad rebels; he no longer has the courage of his convictions—he refuses to think things through to the end; so he turns the rule upside down and proclaims in the *Monitor* that the ordinary hen and the common cur are the prize specimens in the menagerie. And that's the way it'll always be, while we allow the cur in us to triumph, instead of working our way up to some sort of spiritual distinction.

HOVSTAD: I make no pretense of being distinguished in any way; I come from simple peasant stock and I'm proud of it. I'm proud to belong to those common people you're insulting!

SOME WORKMEN: Hurrah for Hovstad! Hurrah! Hurrah!

DR. STOCKMANN: The kind of common people I mean don't necessarily come from the lower classes; they're crawling and swarming all around us—you often find them in the very top ranks of Society. You've only to look at that smug, respectable Mayor of yours! He's about as low as any man that ever walked on two feet—

THE MAYOR: I must protest against these personal remarks!

DR. STOCKMANN: —and that has nothing to do with the fact that one of our ancestors was a disgusting old pirate from somewhere in Pomerania—

THE MAYOR: Pure invention! Utterly groundless!

DR. STOCKMANN: —no! It's because he thinks the thoughts of his superiors in office, and kow-tows to their opinions. And people who do that are common in spirit; that's why, in spite of his magnificence, my brother Peter is so fundamentally lacking in distinction, and is consequently so anti-liberal.

THE MAYOR: Mr. Chairman—!

HOVSTAD: So it seems you have to be a liberal to be distinguished! That's a new point of view if you like!

(*Laughter.*)

DR. STOCKMANN: Yes, that's part of my new discovery too. And there's something else: I've discovered that morality and liberalism are almost precisely the same thing. That's why I consider it downright inexcusable of *The People's Monitor* to go on proclaiming day in and day out that morality and liberalism are the sole monopoly of the mob and the masses; and that culture automatically generates vice and spiritual depravity—just as the filth from the Milldale Tanneries generates the poison that pollutes our waterworks. (*Noise and interruptions*) And yet this same *People's Monitor* prates about raising the masses to a higher level! Why, damn it—if the *Monitor*'s premise were really sound, raising them to a higher level would be equivalent to hurling them straight to perdition! Fortunately the theory that culture demoralizes is just another of those lies handed down from the past. No! Stupidity, poverty and ugliness are the true evils—they're demoralizing if you like! And to live in a house that is never aired, and where the floors are never swept—my wife, incidentally, claims that floors should be *scrubbed* every day, but that's a debatable point—that's demoralizing too! Lack of oxygen weakens the moral fiber. And there must be precious little oxygen in the houses around here, if the moral fiber of our citizens is so feeble that the great majority of them are anxious and willing to build the future of our town on a foundation of hypocrisy and lies!

ASLAKSEN: This is an insult to the entire community—we shall not tolerate it!

A GENTLEMAN: I move that the speaker be called to order!

EAGER VOICES: Yes, yes! He's right! Sit down! Sit down!

DR. STOCKMANN (*Flaring up*): Then I shall shout it from the house-tops! I'll write to all the newspapers! I'll let the whole country know of the situation here!

HOVSTAD: Dr. Stockmann is evidently bent on ruining the town.

DR. STOCKMANN: I love my native town so much that I'd rather see it ruined than prosper on a lie!

ASLAKSEN: There's a statement for you!

(*Noise and catcalls,* MRS. STOCKMANN *coughs in vain; the doctor no longer hears her.*)

HOVSTAD (*Shouting above the tumult*): You're an enemy to this whole community, or you couldn't talk so lightly of the ruin of the town!

DR. STOCKMANN (*With growing excitement*): A community based on lies and corruption deserves to be destroyed! Men who live on lies should be wiped out like a lot of vermin. This poison will spread throughout the country, and eventually the whole country will deserve to be destroyed; and, should it ever come to that, I'd say from the bottom of my heart: let it be destroyed, and let all its people perish!

A MAN (*In the crowd*): He's the People's enemy—that's what he is!

BILLING: Strike me dead! Did you hear that? The Voice of the People!

THE WHOLE CROWD (*Shouting*): Yes, yes, yes! He's an enemy of the People! He's a traitor to his country! He's against the People!

ASLAKSEN: As a citizen of this town, and as a human being, I am deeply shocked by what I have heard here tonight. I must regretfully concur with the sentiments expressed by so many of my fellow-citizens, and I move that those sentiments be formulated in the following resolution: "This meeting hereby declares the former medical adviser to the Baths, Dr. Tomas Stockmann, to be an enemy of the People."

(*Thunders of applause and cheers. A number of people crowd around* DR. STOCKMANN, *jeering and booing.* MRS. STOCKMANN *and* PETRA *have risen.* MORTEN *and* EJLIF *exchange blows with some of the schoolboys who have joined in the jeering. Some grownups separate them.*)

DR. STOCKMANN (*To the jeering crowd*): Fools! You fools! I tell you that—

ASLAKSEN (*Ringing his bell*): Doctor Stockmann is out of order! A formal vote must now be taken. However, out of consideration for personal feelings, it will be by secret ballot. Have you any sheets of blank paper, Mr. Billing?

BILLING: Yes—I have some here; both blue and white.

ASLAKSEN: Splendid. That will expedite matters. We'll just cut it into slips— There! (*To the meeting*) Blue stands for no, and white for yes. I shall collect the votes myself.

(THE MAYOR *leaves the room.* ASLAKSEN *and a couple of others circulate about the room with the pieces of paper in hats.*)

A GENTLEMAN (*To* HOVSTAD): What can be the matter with the doctor? I don't know what to make of it!

HOVSTAD: He's a dreadfully impetuous man, you know!

ANOTHER GENTLEMAN (*To* BILLING): You've been a guest there; tell me—does the fellow drink?

BILLING: Strike me dead—I don't know how to answer that. I know there's always plenty of hot toddy in the house!

A THIRD GENTLEMAN: He strikes me as unbalanced.

FIRST GENTLEMAN: Is there any insanity in the family, I wonder?

BILLING: I don't know—I shouldn't be surprised.

A FOURTH GENTLEMAN: It's pure malice, if you ask me. He's got a chip on his shoulder about something.

BILLING: I remember one day he mentioned wanting a raise in salary—but I know he didn't get it.

ALL THE GENTLEMEN (*Together*): Then that must be it, of course!

THE DRUNKEN MAN (*In the crowd*): Give me a blue one! And I want a white one, too!

SEVERAL PEOPLE: There's that drunk again! Throw him out!

MORTEN KIIL (*Comes up to* STOCKMANN): Well, Stockmann! Look where your monkey-tricks have led to!

DR. STOCKMANN: I've simply done my duty.

MORTEN KIIL: What was that you said about the Milldale Tanneries?

DR. STOCKMANN: You heard; I said they generated filth.

MORTEN KIIL: You mean mine too?

DR. STOCKMANN: Yours is among the worst.

MORTEN KIIL: And are you going to print that in the papers?

DR. STOCKMANN: I shall keep nothing back.

MORTEN KIIL: It'll cost you dear—I warn you! (*He goes out.*)

A FAT GENTLEMAN (*Goes up to* HORSTER *without bowing to the ladies*): I see you lend your house to enemies of the People, Captain.

HORSTER: I've a right to use my property as I see fit, sir.

THE GENTLEMAN: Very good. Then I shall follow your example.

HORSTER: What do you mean by that?

THE GENTLEMAN: You'll hear from me tomorrow. (*Turns away and goes out.*)

PETRA: Captain Horster—wasn't that the owner of your ship?

HORSTER: Mr. Vik, yes.

ASLAKSEN (*His hands full of slips of paper, mounts the platform and rings*): Allow me to announce the result of the vote, gentlemen. All the voters, with one exception—

A YOUNG GENTLEMAN: That must have been the drunk!

ASLAKSEN: With the exception of one intoxicated person this meeting unanimously declares Dr. Tomas Stockmann to be an enemy of the People. (*Cheers and applause*) Three cheers for our deeply loved and honorable community! (*Cheers*) And three cheers for our able and energetic Mayor who has so loyally set family prejudice aside! (*Cheers*) The meeting is adjourned. (*He steps down from the platform.*)

BILLING: Let's have three cheers for the chairman!

ALL: Three cheers for Aslaksen!

DR. STOCKMANN: Give me my hat and coat, Petra. Captain—have you room for any passengers on your trip to the New World?

HORSTER: There'll always be room for you and yours, Dr. Stockmann.

DR. STOCKMANN (*As* PETRA *helps him with his coat*): Thanks. Come, Katrine! Come, boys! (*He gives his wife his arm.*)

MRS. STOCKMANN (*In a low voice*): Let's go out the back way, Tomas, dear.

DR. STOCKMANN: No back ways for us, Katrine. (*Raises his voice*) You'll hear more from the enemy of the People before he finally shakes the dust off his feet! I'm not as forbearing as a certain person I could mention; I can't bring myself to say "I forgive you, for you know not what you do."

ASLAKSEN: That comparison is blasphemous, Doctor Stockmann!

BILLING: Strike me—! If that isn't too much for a decent man to stand!

A COARSE VOICE: And he actually threatens us, too!

ANGRY SHOUTS: Let's smash in his windows! Duck him in the fjord!

A MAN (*In the crowd*): Blow your horn, Evensen! Go on, man! Blow! (*Horn-blowing, whistles and catcalls; wild shouts.* DR. STOCKMANN *and his family go towards the door—*CAPTAIN HORSTER *clears the way for them.*)

ALL (*Yelling after them as they go out*): Enemy of the People! Enemy of the People! Enemy of the People!

BILLING: Strike me dead! I wouldn't want to drink toddy at the Stockmanns' house tonight!

(*The people throng towards the door; the shouting is taken up outside; from the street cries of "Enemy of the People! Enemy of the People!" are heard.*)   CURTAIN

Act V

SCENE: DR. STOCKMANN's *study. The walls are lined with bookshelves and glass cabinets containing various medicines. In the back wall is the door to the living room. Two windows in the wall right, with all the panes smashed in. In the center of the room is the doctor's desk covered with books and papers. The room is in disorder. It is morning.* DR. STOCKMANN *in a dressing-gown and slippers and with a skull-cap on his head is stooping down and raking under one of the cabinets with an umbrella; he succeeds in raking out a stone.*

DR. STOCKMANN (*Calling through the open door*): Here's another one, Katrine!

MRS. STOCKMANN (*From the living room*): You'll find a lot more, I expect.

DR. STOCKMANN (*Adds the stone to a pile on the table*): I'm going to keep these stones, Katrine; they're precious relics. I want Morten and Ejlif to have them constantly before their eyes—and I'll leave them as a heritage. (*Raking about under the book-case*) By the way, hasn't—what the devil *is* that girl's name—hasn't she been to the glazier yet?

MRS. STOCKMANN (*Coming in*): Yes; but he wasn't sure he could come today.

DR. STOCKMANN: I suppose he doesn't dare.

MRS. STOCKMANN: That's what Randina thinks; she thinks he's afraid of the neighbors. (*Talks to someone in the living room*) What is it, Randina? Oh, thanks. (*Goes out and returns immediately*) A letter for you, dear.

DR. STOCKMANN: Let's see. (*Opens the letter and reads*) Well—it's not surprising!

MRS. STOCKMANN: Who is it from?

DR. STOCKMANN: The landlord. He's giving us notice.

MRS. STOCKMANN: Not really! He's such a nice man, too—!

DR. STOCKMANN (*Glancing at the letter*): He daren't do otherwise, he says. He's very sorry; but he daren't do otherwise—public opinion—he has to earn his living—he's afraid of offending certain influential men—and so on.

MRS. STOCKMANN: That just shows you, Tomas.

DR. STOCKMANN: Oh, yes; it shows me right enough. They're all cowards in this town; no one dares do anything for fear of offending someone else. (*Flings the letter on the table*) Well—what do we care, Katrine; we're off to the New World—

MRS. STOCKMANN: You really think that's a wise decision, Tomas?

DR. STOCKMANN: You don't expect me to stay here, do you? After being spat on? After being branded as an enemy of the People and having my win-

dows smashed? And, look, Katrine! Somebody actually tore a hole in my
black trousers!

MRS. STOCKMANN: Oh, Tomas! And they're your best ones too!

DR. STOCKMANN: Yes! Well—you should never wear your best trousers when
you go out to fight for truth and freedom! But I don't care so much about
the trousers—you can always patch them up for me. What I can't stomach
is having that mob attack me as though they were my equals!

MRS. STOCKMANN: I know, Tomas; they've behaved abominably to you here.
But does that necessarily mean we have to leave the country altogether?

DR. STOCKMANN: It'd be just as bad in all the other towns; the mob is just as
insolent-minded there as here. Well—to Hell with it! Let the mongrels
yap; that's not the worst of it. The worst of it is that all over the country
men are nothing but abject slaves to the party-bosses. Not that the so-
called Free West is apt to be much better; I daresay enlightened public
opinion, the solid majority and all the rest of the trash is just as rampant
there—but at least it's on a bigger scale; they may kill a man, but they
don't put him to slow torture; they don't clamp a free soul into a strait
jacket. And, at a pinch, there's room to get away. (*Walks up and down*) If
only I knew of some primeval forest, some little South-Sea island that was
going cheap—

MRS. STOCKMANN: But—what about the boys, Tomas?

DR. STOCKMANN (*Comes to a standstill*): What an amazing woman you are,
Katrine! You wouldn't really want the boys to grow up in a society like
ours, would you? You must have seen last night that half the population of
this town is raving mad—and if the other half hasn't lost its wits, it's only
because they're such block-heads that they have no wits to lose!

MRS. STOCKMANN: Dear Tomas—you say such reckless things!

DR. STOCKMANN: Well—isn't it true? They turn every idea upside-down;
they make a hotch-potch out of right and wrong; they take lies for truth
and truth for lies. But the craziest thing of all is to see a lot of grownup
men calling themselves Liberals, parading about pretending to themselves
and others that they're friends of freedom! You must admit that's pretty
silly!

MRS. STOCKMANN: Yes; I suppose it is, but— (PETRA *enters from the living
room*) Home from school already, Petra?

PETRA: I've been dismissed.

MRS. STOCKMANN: Dismissed!

DR. STOCKMANN: You too!

PETRA: Mrs. Busk gave me my notice—so I thought I'd better leave at once.

DR. STOCKMANN: You were quite right!

MRS. STOCKMANN: Fancy Mrs. Busk doing a thing like that! How disgraceful
of her!

PETRA: It wasn't disgraceful of her, Mother. I could see how upset she was.
But she didn't dare do otherwise, she said. So—I'm dismissed.

DR. STOCKMANN (*Laughs and rubs his hands*): She didn't dare do otherwise—
just like the rest! This is delightful!

MRS. STOCKMANN: I suppose—after that dreadful scene last night—

PETRA: It wasn't only that. Father—listen to this!

DR. STOCKMANN: Well?

PETRA: Mrs. Busk showed me at least three letters she'd received this morning—

DR. STOCKMANN: Anonymous, of course?

PETRA: Yes.

DR. STOCKMANN: They never dare sign their names, Katrine!

PETRA: Two of them warned her that a certain gentleman—a frequent visitor at our house, so he said—had been talking at the club last night, and telling everyone that my views on certain subjects were decidedly advanced—

DR. STOCKMANN: I hope you didn't deny it!

PETRA: Of course not! Mrs. Busk has fairly advanced views too—that is, in private; but since I'd been publicly accused, she dared not keep me on.

MRS. STOCKMANN: A frequent visitor—just think of it! You see, Tomas—that's what comes of all your hospitality!

DR. STOCKMANN: We won't stay in this pig sty any longer. Get packed as soon as you can, Katrine. We'll leave this place at once—the sooner the better!

MRS. STOCKMANN: Be quiet a moment; I thought I heard someone in the hall. See who it is, Petra.

PETRA (*Opens the hall door*): Oh, it's you, Captain Horster! Do come in.

HORSTER (*From the hall*): Good morning. I thought I'd just come over and see how you were getting on.

DR. STOCKMANN (*Shaking his hand*): Thanks; that's very kind of you.

MRS. STOCKMANN: And thank you, Captain Horster, for helping us last night.

PETRA: How did you ever manage to get home?

HORSTER: It wasn't bad—I'm a pretty hefty man, you know. And, anyway—there was more noise than action!

DR. STOCKMANN: Isn't it amazing what cowards those people are? Come here—I want to show you something. Here are all the stones they threw in at us last night. Just look at them! There aren't more than two decent stones among the lot; most of them are pebbles—a lot of gravel! And yet they stood out there shouting and yelling that they were going to kill me! But as for really doing it—oh, no! Nothing as positive as that!

HORSTER: Well—for once—I should think you'd have been grateful, Doctor!

DR. STOCKMANN: Oh, I am—of course! But it's tragic all the same; I sometimes think—supposing a really serious struggle of national proportions were involved; you can be sure enlightened public opinion would instantly take to its heels and run away, and the great solid majority would scatter like a herd of frightened sheep; that's the depressing part of it—it makes me sick to think of. But, damn it—why should I care what they do! They've called me an enemy of the People, so I might as well *be* an enemy of the People!

MRS. STOCKMANN: You'll never be that, Tomas.

DR. STOCKMANN: I wouldn't be too sure, Katrine. One ugly word can act as an irritant sometimes—and that damned expression—! I can't get rid of it; it's dug its way into the pit of my stomach— I feel it gnawing away there like a bitter acid. All the magnesia tablets in the world won't make it stop!

PETRA: They're not worth taking seriously, Father.

HORSTER: Some day they'll change their minds, Doctor—you'll see.

MRS. STOCKMANN: Yes, Tomas; I'm sure of that.

DR. STOCKMANN: They may—when it's too late. Well—serve them right! Let them wallow in their filth and cry their hearts out with remorse at having driven a patriot into exile. When do you sail, Captain?

HORSTER: Hm—that's really what I wanted to talk to you about—

DR. STOCKMANN: Oh? Is anything the matter with the ship?

HORSTER: No, nothing; except—I shan't be with her.

PETRA: You surely haven't been dismissed?

HORSTER (*With a smile*): But I have, you see.

PETRA: You, too.

MRS. STOCKMANN: That just shows you, Tomas.

DR. STOCKMANN: And all for the sake of truth! If I'd thought anything like this could happen—!

HORSTER: You mustn't be upset. Some other company will take me on.

DR. STOCKMANN: And to think that a man like Vik—! A man of means—who can afford to be completely independent—! How disgusting!

HORSTER: He's not such a bad man, really. He told me himself he'd like to keep me on—only he didn't dare—

DR. STOCKMANN: He didn't dare! Of course not!

HORSTER: He said it wasn't always easy—when you're a member of a party—

DR. STOCKMANN: He hit the nail on the head that time! A party—! A sausage-machine—that's what a party's like! All the brains are ground up together and reduced to hash; and that's why the world is filled with a lot of brainless, empty-headed numskulls!

MRS. STOCKMANN: Tomas! Please!

PETRA (*To* HORSTER): If you hadn't seen us home, this mightn't have happened.

HORSTER: I don't regret it.

PETRA (*Holds out her hand to him*): Thank you!

HORSTER: But I wanted to tell you this: if you're really bent on going—there's another way it could be—

MRS. STOCKMANN: Hush! I thought I heard a knock.

PETRA: I believe it's Uncle.

DR. STOCKMANN: Aha! (*Calls*) Come in!

MRS. STOCKMANN: Now, Tomas—promise me, please—!

(THE MAYOR *enters from the hall.*)

THE MAYOR (*In the doorway*): Oh, you're busy. Then I'd better—

DR. STOCKMANN: No, no. Come in.

THE MAYOR: I wanted to speak to you alone.

MRS. STOCKMANN: We'll go into the living room.

HORSTER: I'll come back later, then.

DR. STOCKMANN: No, Captain Horster—don't go away. I'm anxious to hear more about—

HORSTER: Very well; I'll wait.

(*He follows* MRS. STOCKMANN *and* PETRA *into the living room.* THE MAYOR *says nothing, but glances at the windows.*)

DR. STOCKMANN: A bit draughty, isn't it? Better put on your hat.

THE MAYOR: Thanks—if I may. (*Does so*) I think I caught cold last night. I felt a sudden chill—

DR. STOCKMANN: Really? I thought it was a bit on the warm side!

THE MAYOR: I regret I was unable to prevent that most unfortunate business.

DR. STOCKMANN: Is there anything special you want to say to me?

THE MAYOR (*producing a large envelope*): The management of the Baths sends you this document.

DR. STOCKMANN: My dismissal, I suppose.

THE MAYOR: Yes—as of today. We regret this decision but, frankly, we didn't dare do otherwise. Out of respect for public opinion, you understand.

DR. STOCKMANN: Didn't dare do otherwise. I seem to have heard those words before, today.

THE MAYOR: I think you should face the fact that from now on you won't be able to count on any practice here.

DR. STOCKMANN: To hell with my practice! But why are you so sure of that?

THE MAYOR: The Home-owners Association is circulating a petition urging all respectable citizens to refrain from calling on your services. Of course everyone will sign it—they wouldn't dare do otherwise.

DR. STOCKMANN: I don't doubt that. What else?

THE MAYOR: If you take my advice, you'll leave town for a while.

DR. STOCKMANN: Yes; I've already given serious thought to that.

THE MAYOR: You're wise. Then—after six months or so—when you've had time to think things over, you might perhaps feel ready to write us a few words of apology, admitting your mistake—

DR. STOCKMANN: And then I might be re-instated, do you think?

THE MAYOR: You might; it's by no means impossible.

DR. STOCKMANN: But what about public opinion? Aren't you forgetting that?

THE MAYOR: Public opinion has a way of changing; and, quite frankly, it would be greatly to our advantage to have a signed statement from you to that effect.

DR. STOCKMANN: Yes—I dare say it would be most convenient! I've already told you how I feel about that kind of crookedness.

THE MAYOR: You were in a very different position then. At that time you imagined you had the whole town at your back—

DR. STOCKMANN: And now, it seems, I have the whole town *on* my back! (*Flaring up*) But I don't care if the devil himself were on my back, I'll never consent to—! Never, I tell you; never!

THE MAYOR: As a family man you have no right to take this stand, Tomas. You simply have no right!

DR. STOCKMANN: I have no right, have I? There's only one thing in this world a free man has no right to do; you don't know what that is, do you?

THE MAYOR: No, I don't.

DR. STOCKMANN: Of course not; then I'll tell you. A free man has no right to wallow in filth. A free man has no right to debase himself to the point of wanting to spit in his own face!

THE MAYOR: That might sound quite convincing if there were no other explanation for your pig-headedness; but of course we know there is—

DR. STOCKMANN: What do you mean?

THE MAYOR: You know quite well what I mean. However as your brother, and as a man of some experience, I advise you not to put too much faith in certain hopes and prospects that may prove disappointing.

DR. STOCKMANN: What on earth are you getting at?

THE MAYOR: Don't try to tell me you're unaware of the terms of old Morten Kiil's will!

DR. STOCKMANN: I only know he's left what little he has to a home for indigent workmen. It's no business of mine.

THE MAYOR: To begin with, "what little he has" amounts to a considerable sum. Morten Kiil is a very wealthy man.

DR. STOCKMANN: I had no idea of that—

THE MAYOR: No? Are you sure? Perhaps you had no idea either that a large part of his fortune is to be placed in a trust fund for your children; and that during your lifetime you and your wife are to enjoy the income from this trust. Did he never tell you that?

DR. STOCKMANN: He never breathed a word of it! In fact he does nothing but complain how poor he is, and grumble about taxes. Peter—are you quite sure of this?

THE MAYOR: Quite sure. My information is most reliable.

DR. STOCKMANN: But—good heavens! Then the children are provided for— and Katrine too! I must tell her this at once— (Calls) Katrine, Katrine!

THE MAYOR (Holding him back): No, wait! Don't tell her yet.

MRS. STOCKMANN (Opens the door): What is it, dear?

DR. STOCKMANN: It's nothing; never mind.

(MRS. STOCKMANN closes the door again.)

DR. STOCKMANN (Pacing up and down): To think of it—provided for! All of them provided for—and for life too. How wonderful to feel one is provided for!

THE MAYOR: But that's just what you're not, you see. Morten Kiil can change his will whenever he sees fit.

DR. STOCKMANN: Oh, but he won't, Peter! The old badger's much too pleased with me for unmasking you and your precious friends.

THE MAYOR (Starts and looks at him intently): I see! That puts things in quite a different light.

DR. STOCKMANN: What things?

THE MAYOR: So it was all a put-up job! Those violent attacks you made on the leading men of the town—all in the name of truth, of course—were actually nothing but—!

DR. STOCKMANN: But what?

THE MAYOR: —nothing but a kind of sop to that vindictive old miser Morten Kiil. That was his reward for leaving all that money to you in his will!

DR. STOCKMANN: Peter—upon my word you are the lowest of the low!

THE MAYOR: I shall have no further dealings with you; your dismissal is irrevocable. We are well armed against you now. (He goes out.)

DR. STOCKMANN: Of all the filthy—! (Calls) Katrine! Have this floor scrubbed at once! Tell the girl—what the devil's her—you know—the girl with the smutty nose—to bring her pail and scrub-brush!

MRS. STOCKMANN (In the doorway): Tomas, Tomas! Hush!

PETRA (Also in the doorway): Father; Grandfather's here. He wants to know if he can speak to you alone.

DR. STOCKMANN: Of course he can. (By the door) Come in, sir.

(MORTEN KIIL enters. STOCKMANN closes the door behind him.)

DR. STOCKMANN: Well, what is it? Won't you sit down?

MORTEN KIIL: No thanks. (He looks round) Well, Stockmann—things look very cozy here.

DR. STOCKMANN: Yes, don't they?

MORTEN KIIL: Very cozy indeed; a nice lot of fresh air too; plenty of that oxygen you talked so much about. Your moral fiber must be flourishing.

DR. STOCKMANN: It is.

MORTEN KIIL: Yes, to be sure. (*Tapping his breast pocket*) But do you know what I have here?

DR. STOCKMANN: Plenty of moral fiber too, I hope.

MORTEN KIIL: Something much better than that, I can assure you. (*Takes out a large wallet, opens it, and shows* STOCKMANN *a bundle of papers.*)

DR. STOCKMANN (*Looks at him in amazement*): Shares? Shares in the Baths?

MORTEN KIIL: They were easy enough to get today.

DR. STOCKMANN: Do you mean to say you've bought up—?

MORTEN KIIL: All I could lay my hands on!

DR. STOCKMANN: But, my dear sir—you know the present situation at the Baths—!

MORTEN KIIL: If you behave like a sensible man, you'll soon set that right again.

DR. STOCKMANN: You know I've tried to do everything I can—but these people are all lunatics!

MORTEN KIIL: You said last night that the worst filth came from my tannery. Now supposing that were true—it means that my father and my grandfather before me, and I myself for many years, have been poisoning the town—like three demons of destruction. You don't expect me to accept that accusation calmly, do you?

DR. STOCKMANN: I'm afraid you'll have to.

MORTEN KIIL: No thank you; my good name and reputation mean too much to me. People call me "the badger," so I'm told; and a badger's a kind of a pig, they tell me. But I intend to prove them wrong. While I live and after I die, my name shall be kept spotless.

DR. STOCKMANN: How are you going to manage that?

MORTEN KIIL: *You* are going to manage that for me, Stockmann. You are going to clear my name for me.

DR. STOCKMANN: I!

MORTEN KIIL: Do you know what money I used to buy these shares? No, of course you don't—but now I'm going to tell you. I used all the money Katrine, Petra and the boys were to inherit from me. For, in spite of everything, I have managed to save quite a bit, you see.

DR. STOCKMANN (*Flaring up*): Do you mean to say you used Katrine's money to do this!

MORTEN KIIL: Yes—I've invested every penny of it in the Baths. Now let's see how much of a madman you really are, Stockmann. Now if you keep on spreading this story that a lot of filthy animals seep into the water from my tannery, you'll just be flaying pieces of skin off Katrine, and off Petra too—to say nothing of the boys, of course. No decent father would dream of doing that—unless he were a madman.

DR. STOCKMANN (*Pacing up and down*): But I am a madman; I *am* a madman, don't you see?

MORTEN KIIL: Sacrifice your wife and children? You couldn't be as stark raving mad as that!

DR. STOCKMANN (*Stopping in front of him*): Why in God's name didn't you talk to me before buying all this rubbish?

MORTEN KIIL: What's done is done; it's too late now.

DR. STOCKMANN (*Walking about restlessly*): If only I weren't so absolutely certain—! But I'm absolutely positive I'm right.

MORTEN KIIL (*Weighing the wallet in his hand*): If you persist in this lunacy, these things won't be worth much, will they? (*Puts the wallet back in his pocket.*)

DR. STOCKMANN: Damn it! Surely there must be some scientific way of purifying the water—some sort of disinfectant—

MORTEN KIIL: To kill those animals, you mean?

DR. STOCKMANN: Yes—or at least to make them harmless.

MORTEN KIIL: You might try rat-poison.

DR. STOCKMANN: Oh! Don't talk nonsense! —And since everyone says it's merely an illusion on my part—why not let it be an illusion then! Let them have their way! Ignorant, damnable mongrels that they are! They've called me an enemy of the People—torn the clothes off my back—

MORTEN KIIL: And smashed in all your windows!

DR. STOCKMANN: And one has a duty toward one's family, after all. I must talk it over with Katrine. She's better at these things than I am.

MORTEN KIIL: A good idea; she'll give you sensible advice.

DR. STOCKMANN (*Turns on him angrily*): How could you behave in this fantastic manner? Gambling with Katrine's money; putting me through this agony—this torment! What kind of a devil are you!

MORTEN KIIL: If I'm a devil, perhaps I'd better go. But I want your decision—either yes or no—by two o'clock. If the answer's "no," I'll make these over to charity at once—this very day.

DR. STOCKMANN: And what will Katrine get?

MORTEN KIIL: Not a damn penny! (*The door to the hall opens;* HOVSTAD *and* ASLAKSEN *are seen outside*) I certainly never expected to meet them here!

DR. STOCKMANN (*Staring at them*): What does this mean? How dare you come to see me?

HOVSTAD: We have our reasons.

ASLAKSEN: We've something to discuss with you.

MORTEN KIIL (*In a whisper*): Yes or no—by two o'clock.

ASLAKSEN (*With a glance at* HOVSTAD): Aha!

(MORTEN KIIL *goes out.*)

DR. STOCKMANN: Well, what do you want? Be quick about it.

HOVSTAD: It's natural you should resent the attitude we were forced to take last night—

DR. STOCKMANN: So that's what you call an attitude, is it? A fine attitude! Behaving like a couple of cowards—a couple of old women—!

HOVSTAD: Call it what you like; but, you see, we have no alternative—

DR. STOCKMANN: You didn't dare do otherwise, I suppose!

HOVSTAD: If that's how you choose to put it.

ASLAKSEN: You should have given us some inkling, Dr. Stockmann. The slightest hint to Mr. Hovstad or to me—

DR. STOCKMANN: Hint? What about?

ASLAKSEN: About your real motive in this matter.

DR. STOCKMANN: I don't know what you mean.

ASLAKSEN (*Nods confidentially*): Of course you do, Dr. Stockmann.

HOVSTAD: Why make a mystery of it now?

DR. STOCKMANN (*Looks from one to the other*): What the devil's all this about—?

ASLAKSEN: You know your father-in-law's been all over town buying up shares in the Baths—isn't that so?

DR. STOCKMANN: Yes, he has—but what of that?

ASLAKSEN: It might have been wiser to choose somebody else to do it for you; the connection is a bit too obvious.

HOVSTAD: And wouldn't it have been more prudent if you hadn't mixed yourself up personally in this affair? The attack on the Baths should have been made by someone else. Why didn't you take me into your confidence, Dr. Stockmann?

DR. STOCKMANN (*Staring straight in front of him; a light seems to dawn on him, and he says as though thunderstruck*): This is incredible! Can such things be!

ASLAKSEN (*Smiling*): Well—obviously! But they should be handled with more delicacy, it seems to me.

HOVSTAD: And it was unwise to attempt it single-handed; it's always easier to avoid responsibility for a matter of this sort, if you have others working with you.

DR. STOCKMANN (*Calmly*): Come to the point, gentlemen. What is it you want?

ASLAKSEN: Perhaps Mr. Hovstad had better—

HOVSTAD: No; you explain it, Aslaksen.

ASLAKSEN: It's simply this: Now that we know how matters really stand, we feel safe in venturing to place *The People's Monitor* at your disposal.

DR. STOCKMANN: You feel safe, do you? What about public opinion? Aren't you afraid of raising a storm of protest?

HOVSTAD: We are prepared to weather it.

ASLAKSEN: And, before long, you can make a sudden change of tactics, Doctor. As soon as the charges made against the Baths have the desired effect—

DR. STOCKMANN: As soon as my father-in-law and I have bought up the shares at an attractive price, I suppose you mean—?

HOVSTAD: It's mainly for scientific reasons, I presume, that you wish to gain control of the establishment—?

DR. STOCKMANN: That goes without saying; and of course it was for scientific reasons too that I persuaded the old badger to become my partner in this plan. We'll patch up the pipes a bit, make a few little adjustments at the Beach—and it won't cost the town a penny. What do you think? That ought to do the trick!

HOVSTAD: I should think so—provided you have the *Monitor* to back you up.

ASLAKSEN: In a free community the Press is all-powerful, Doctor Stockmann.

DR. STOCKMANN: Unquestionably! And so is public opinion too. I suppose you'll answer for the Home-owners Association, Mr. Aslaksen?

ASLAKSEN: The Home-owners Association, and the Temperance Society too; you may depend on that.

DR. STOCKMANN: Now, tell me, gentlemen—I'm almost ashamed to mention such a thing—what is your price?

HOVSTAD: I beg you to believe, Doctor, that we'd be only too happy to give you our support for nothing. But, unfortunately, the status of *The People's*

Monitor is somewhat precarious; it's not as financially successful as it deserves to be. And it would seem a pity, just now when there's so much to be done in the field of general politics, to have to close our doors.

DR. STOCKMANN: I understand; I realize that would be very hard for a friend of the People, like yourself. (*Flaring up*) But *I*'m the People's enemy! An enemy of the People—have you forgotten that? (*Striding about the room*) Where's my stick? Where the devil is my stick?

HOVSTAD: What do you mean?

ASLAKSEN: You surely don't intend—?

DR. STOCKMANN (*Comes to a halt*): And what if I refuse to give you a penny of those shares? You must remember we rich people don't like parting with our money!

HOVSTAD: I advise *you* to remember that this business can be presented in a very ugly light.

DR. STOCKMANN: Yes; and you're just the man to do it! If I don't come to the rescue of your *Monitor*, I've no doubt you'll see to that. You'll hound me, won't you? You'll bait me—you'll slaughter me as a dog slaughters a hare!

HOVSTAD: That's the law of nature; every animal for himself, you know.

ASLAKSEN: We all have to take our food where we can find it.

DR. STOCKMANN: Then go out into the gutter, where you belong, and find it there! (*Striding about the room*) I'll show you who the strongest animal is here! (*Finds his umbrella and brandishes it at them*) Now—get out!

HOVSTAD: You wouldn't dare attack us—!

ASLAKSEN: Be careful with that umbrella—!

DR. STOCKMANN: Out of the window with you, Mr. Hovstad!

HOVSTAD (*By the hall door*): Have you gone raving mad?

DR. STOCKMANN: Out of the window, Mr. Aslaksen! Jump, I tell you—and be quick about it!

ASLAKSEN (*Running round the desk*): Moderation, Doctor Stockmann—moderation! I'm not a strong man, you know; I can't stand things like this— (*Screams*) Help! Help!

(MRS. STOCKMANN, HORSTER and PETRA *enter from the living room.*)

MRS. STOCKMANN: Good gracious, Tomas! What are you doing?

DR. STOCKMANN (*Brandishing the umbrella*): Go on—jump, I tell you! Into the gutter where you belong!

HOVSTAD: You're a witness to this, Captain Horster! An unprovoked assault—! (*Rushes out to the hall.*)

ASLAKSEN (*Bewildered*): I must look up the law on matters of this sort—! (*He escapes through the door to the living room.*)

MRS. STOCKMANN (*Clinging to the doctor*): Tomas—for heaven's sake control yourself!

DR. STOCKMANN (*Throws down the umbrella*): They both got away—damn them!

MRS. STOCKMANN: But what did they want, Tomas, dear?

DR. STOCKMANN: I'll tell you presently; I've other things to attend to now. (*Goes to his desk and writes something on a visiting-card*) Look, Katrine! I want you to see what I've written here.

MRS. STOCKMANN: Three large "No's"—what can that mean?

DR. STOCKMANN: I'll tell you that presently too. (*Giving* PETRA *the card*) Here, Petra; tell Smudgy-face to run over to the badger and give him this. And hurry! (PETRA *goes out with the card*) I never expected to have so many visits from the devil's emissaries as I've had today! But I know how to deal with them; I'll sharpen my pen against them till it becomes a goad; I'll dip it in gall and venom; I'll hurl my entire ink-pot at their brazen heads!

MRS. STOCKMANN: But, Tomas—aren't we going away?

(PETRA *returns*.)

DR. STOCKMANN: Well?

PETRA: She's gone with it.

DR. STOCKMANN: Splendid! —Did you say going away? No, I'll be damned if we are, Katrine—we're going to stay right here!

MRS. STOCKMANN: Here in the town?

DR. STOCKMANN: Here in the town. The battle-field is here, and here the battle must be fought, and here I shall win the victory! As soon as you've patched my trousers I'll be off and try to find a place for us to live. We can't get through the winter without a roof over our heads!

HORSTER: Will my roof do?

DR. STOCKMANN: You really mean it?

HORSTER: Of course. I've such a lot of room, and I'm hardly ever home myself.

MRS. STOCKMANN: Oh, Captain Horster—that is kind of you!

PETRA: Thanks!

DR. STOCKMANN (*Shaking his hand*): Thanks—and thanks again! That's a great load off my mind. Now I can set to work in earnest. Oh, there's such a lot to do, Katrine! And I'll have all my time to myself—that's just as well; for, I forgot to tell you—I've been dismissed—

MRS. STOCKMANN (*Sighing*): Yes—I expected that!

DR. STOCKMANN: —and now they want to take away my practice, too! Well— let them! There are always the poor people—those that can't afford to pay; they're really the ones that need me most, you see. But, by God, they're going to hear from me! I'll harangue them every single day—"in season and out of season," as somebody or other put it.

MRS. STOCKMANN: Haven't you done enough talking, Tomas, dear?

DR. STOCKMANN: Don't be absurd, Katrine! Do you think I'd allow public opinion, and the solid majority, and all the rest of it to drive me from the field? No, thank you! Besides, my aim is perfectly simple and straightforward. I just want to din into the heads of these poor misguided mongrels, that these so-called Liberals are freedom's bitterest enemies—that party programs do nothing but stifle living truths—that justice and morality are being turned upside-down by expediency and greed—until eventually life itself will scarcely be worth living! Surely I ought to be able to make the people see that, Captain Horster? Don't you think so?

HORSTER: Perhaps; I don't know much about such things myself.

DR. STOCKMANN: It's all quite simple—let me explain it to you! First, the party-bosses have got to be wiped out; they're just like wolves, you see— like ravening wolves! They batten on the small-fry. In order to keep themselves alive they devour literally hundreds of them every single year. Take Hovstad and Aslaksen, for instance—think of the small-fry they devour! Or if they don't devour them, they debase them and corrupt them till all they're good for is to become Home-owners or subscribers to *The People's Monitor!* (*Sits on the edge of the table*) Come here, Katrine! Just look at that radiant, gallant sunshine! And doesn't the air smell fresh and clear this morning?

MRS. STOCKMANN: If only we could live on air and sunshine, Tomas, dear!

DR. STOCKMANN: Oh, but we can—with a little help from you! You'll scrimp and save away and we shall manage splendidly. That's the least of my worries. One thing does worry me though; where am I to find a decent freedom-loving man to carry on the work after I'm gone?

PETRA: Don't start worrying about that, Father; you've still got lots of time ahead of you! —Why, look; here are the boys!

(EJLIF and MORTEN enter from the living room.)

MRS. STOCKMANN: What's happened? It's not a holiday today!

MORTEN: We got into a fight with some of the other boys—

EJLIF: No, we didn't! They got into a fight with us!

MORTEN: And Mr. Rörlund said we'd better stay home for a few days.

DR. STOCKMANN (Snapping his fingers and jumping down from the table): That gives me an idea! Yes, by heaven, that gives me an idea! You shan't set foot in that blasted school again!

THE BOYS: Not go to school!

MRS. STOCKMANN: But, Tomas—

DR. STOCKMANN: Never again, I say! I'll start teaching you myself; or, better still—you shan't be taught a blessed thing—

MORTEN: Hurrah!

DR. STOCKMANN: The only thing I'll teach you, is to become decent freedom-loving men. —You'll help me, Petra, won't you?

PETRA: I'd love to, Father.

DR. STOCKMANN: We'll have the school in the very room where they branded me an enemy of the People. But we'll have to have more pupils—I want a dozen boys at least.

MRS. STOCKMANN: You'll never get them to come, Tomas; not in this town.

DR. STOCKMANN: Wait and see. (To the boys) You must know a few street-urchins—some regular guttersnipes—?

MORTEN: Oh, yes, Father! I know lots of them!

DR. STOCKMANN: Then find a few good specimens and bring them to me. I'm going to experiment with a few mongrels for a change; there's plenty of good raw-material there.

MORTEN: What are we to do, Father, when we grow up to be decent freedom-loving men?

DR. STOCKMANN: Drive the wolves away to the Far West, my boys!

MRS. STOCKMANN: But suppose it's the wolves who drive you away, Tomas, dear?

DR. STOCKMANN: Drive me away! Are you stark raving mad, Katrine? I'm the strongest man in the town! Don't you know that?

MRS. STOCKMANN: The strongest—? You mean, now?

DR. STOCKMANN: Yes! I'll even go so far as to say that I'm one of the strongest men in the whole world!

MORTEN: Are you really, Father?

DR. STOCKMANN (Dropping his voice): Hush! You mustn't say a word about it yet; I've made a great discovery, you see.

MRS. STOCKMANN: Not another, Tomas, dear!

Dr. Stockmann: Another, yes—another! (*Gathers them round him and speaks in a confidential tone*) And I'll tell you what it is: the strongest man in the world is the man who stands alone.

Mrs. Stockmann (*Smiles and shakes her head*): Oh, Tomas, dear—!

Petra (*Grasps his hands and says with eyes full of faith*): Father!

CURTAIN

Suggestions for Discussion

1. What opposing political camps does Ibsen establish in the first act? As the play develops, how do these camps shift ground?

2. What arguments does Dr. Stockmann make against the power of the majority? How do these arguments dating from the nineteenth century relate to the reader over a hundred years later?

3. What is the modern reader (or modern audience) to make of Stockmann's attitude toward his wife? Is Stockmann a good family man? Explain.

4. Why does the town reject Dr. Stockmann's position on the environmental pollution in the city's Baths? Would a small town in the United States or Europe today respond similarly?

Suggestions for Writing

1. Write an essay that focuses on Dr. Stockmann as the hero of the play. What qualities make him heroic? How do you reconcile his strong character with his bumbling response to the town's opposition? Why is he called an "Enemy of the People"?

2. For a brief research paper, use newspaper files to compare and contrast a case history of present-day environmental pollution with the situation in the play. You may wish to focus on the causes of the incident and the public's responses to it.

3. The protection of the minority against majority rule is anticipated in the Constitution of the United States. Write an essay in which you relate those sections of the Constitution that would apply to the issue in the play or to one in our own time.

Freedom and
Human Dignity

"Liberty consists in being able to do anything which is not
harmful to another or to others. . . ."
> —**"The Declaration of the Rights of Man,"** Paris, August
> 27, 1789

I believe that man will not merely endure: he will prevail. He
is immortal, not because he alone among creatures has an
inexhaustible voice but because he has a soul, a spirit capable of compassion and sacrifice and endurance.
> —**William Faulkner,** "Nobel Prize Award Speech," 1949

Was he free? Was he happy? The question is absurd:
Had anything been wrong, we should certainly have heard.
> —**W. H. Auden,** "The Unknown Citizen"

Anti-Semitism does not fall within the category of ideas protected by the right of free opinion.
> —**Jean-Paul Sartre,** "The Passion of the Anti-Semite"

Tell me, then, whether you agree with and assent to my first
principle, that neither injury nor retaliation nor warding off
evil by evil is ever right.
> —**Plato,** "The Crito"

I think we can find a compassionate way to accompany one
another to the outer edges of life without mercy killing. If we
don't do that, then yeah, we're going to see the legalization of
euthanasia and it will be our own fault.
> —**Patrick Cooke,** "The Gentle Death"

At the heart of medicine is the principle of healing; in law it is that of justice; in theology, that of spiritual search; and in science and academic life, the quest for knowledge and truth.

    —**Robert Jay Lifton,** "The Genocidal Mentality"

. . . thanks to the miracle of speech, we know probably better than the other animals that we actually know very little, in other words we are conscious of the existence of mystery.

    —**Václav Havel,** "Words on Words"

It is essential for a moral decision about abortion to be made in an atmosphere of open, critical thinking.

    —**Mary Gordon,** "A Moral Choice"

We know through painful experience that freedom is never voluntarily given by the oppressor; it must be demanded by the oppressed. . . . For years now I have heard the word "Wait!" It rings in the ear of every Negro with a piercing familiarity. This "wait" has almost always meant "never."

    —**Martin Luther King, Jr.,** "Letter from Birmingham Jail"

Something was burning, the side of me that knew I was treated different, would always be treated different because I was born on a particular side of a fence, a fence that separated me from others, that separated me from a past, that separated me from the country of my genesis and glued me to the country I did not love because it demanded something of me I could not give.

    —**Benjamin Alire Sáenz,** Prologue to "Exiled: The Winds of Sunset Heights"

The history of mankind is a history of repeated injuries and usurpations on the part of man toward woman, having in direct object the establishment of an absolute tyranny over her.

    —**Seneca Falls Convention,** Declaration of Sentiments and Resolutions, 1848

Personal Reminiscences

W. E. B. Du Bois

On Being Crazy

William Edward Burghardt Du Bois (1868–1963) was born in Massachusetts. In the course of his life he became a major influence on American blacks. By 1903 he had written *The Souls of Black Folk*, which stated his major objections to the attitudes found in the writings of Booker T. Washington, the most influential black figure in the early twentieth century. In 1909 he helped found the National Association for the Advancement of Colored People. He edited *Crisis*, the magazine of the NAACP, and also founded the influential quarterly *Phylon* at Atlanta University. In this brief sketch (1907), Du Bois, in a series of conversations, touches ironically on the insanity of the relations between blacks and whites in the early days of the twentieth century. It might be instructive to consider just how different the relations between the races are today.

It was one o'clock and I was hungry. I walked into a restaurant, seated myself, and reached for the bill of fare. My table companion rose.

"Sir," said he, "do you wish to force your company on those who do not want you?"

No, said I, I wish to eat.

"Are you aware, sir, that this is social equality?"

Nothing of the sort, sir, it is hunger—and I ate.

The day's work done, I sought the theatre. As I sank into my seat, the lady shrank and squirmed.

I beg pardon, I said.

"Do you enjoy being where you are not wanted?" she asked coldly.

Oh no, I said.

"Well you are not wanted here."

I was surprised. I fear you are mistaken, I said, I certainly want the music, and I like to think the music wants me to listen to it.

"Usher," said the lady, "this is social equality."

"No, madame," said the usher, "it is the second movement of Beethoven's Fifth Symphony."

After the theatre, I sought the hotel where I had sent my baggage. The clerk scowled.

"What do you want?"

Rest, I said.

"This is a white hotel," he said.

I looked around. Such a color scheme requires a great deal of cleaning, I said, but I don't know that I object.

"We object," said he.

Then why, I began, but he interrupted.

"We don't keep niggers," he said, "we don't want social equality."

Neither do I, I replied gently, I want a bed.

I walked thoughtfully to the train. I'll take a sleeper through Texas. I'm a little bit dissatisfied with this town.

"Can't sell you one."

I only want to hire it, said I, for a couple of nights.

"Can't sell you a sleeper in Texas," he maintained. "They consider that social equality."

I consider it barbarism, I said, and I think I'll walk.

Walking, I met another wayfarer, who immediately walked to the other side of the road, where it was muddy. I asked his reason.

"Niggers is dirty," he said.

So is mud, said I. Moreover, I am not as dirty as you—yet.

"But you're a nigger, ain't you?" he asked.

My grandfather was so called.

"Well then!" he answered triumphantly.

Do you live in the South? I persisted, pleasantly.

"Sure," he growled, "and starve there."

I should think you and the Negroes should get together and vote out starvation.

"We don't let them vote."

We? Why not? I said in surprise.

"Niggers is too ignorant to vote."

But, I said, I am not so ignorant as you.

"But you're a nigger."

Yes, I'm certainly what you mean by that.

"Well then!" he returned, with that curiously inconsequential note of triumph. "Moreover," he said, "I don't want my sister to marry a nigger."

I had not seen his sister, so I merely murmured, let her say no.

"By God, you shan't marry her, even if she said yes."

But—but I don't want to marry her, I answered, a little perturbed at the personal turn.

"Why not!" he yelled, angrier than ever.

Because I'm already married and I rather like my wife.

"Is she a nigger?" he asked suspiciously.

Well, I said again, her grandmother was called that.

"Well then!" he shouted in that oddly illogical way.

I gave up.

Go on, I said, either you are crazy or I am.

"We both are," he said as he trotted along in the mud.

Suggestions for Discussion

1. Why has Du Bois chosen these specific scenes for his conversations with white people?

2. In what way is the final conversation different from those preceding it?

3. Discuss some of the examples of Du Bois's use of irony.

Suggestion for Writing

Write an essay in which you examine the areas of racism dealt with in this selection from today's perspective. What significant differences would you find? What similarities? In what way is "On Being Crazy" relevant for our time?

Richard Wright

The Ethics of Living Jim Crow

A major American black writer, Richard Wright (1908–1960) wrote stories, novels, an autobiography, and other books about America's racial problems. His best-known works are Native Son (1940), Black Boy (1945), and White Man, Listen (1957). The following autobiographical account of his education in race relations in a totally segregated South is from Uncle Tom's Children (1938).

I

My first lesson in how to live as a Negro came when I was quite small. We were living in Arkansas. Our house stood behind the railroad tracks. Its skimpy yard was paved with black cinders. Nothing green ever grew in that yard. The only touch of green we could see was far away, beyond the tracks, over where the white folks lived. But cinders were good enough for me and I never missed the green growing things. And anyhow cinders were fine weapons. You could always have a nice hot war with huge black cinders. All you had to do was crouch behind the brick pillars of a house with your hands full of gritty ammunition. And the first woolly black head you saw pop out from behind another row of pillars was your target. You tried your very best to knock it off. It was great fun.

I never fully realized the appalling disadvantages of a cinder environment till one day the gang to which I belonged found itself engaged in a war with the white boys who lived beyond the tracks. As usual we laid down our cinder barrage, thinking that this would wipe the white boys out. But they replied with a steady bombardment of broken bottles. We doubled our cinder barrage, but they hid behind trees, hedges, and the sloping embankments of their lawns. Having no such fortifications, we retreated to the brick pillars of our homes. During the retreat a broken milk bottle caught me behind the ear, opening a deep gash which bled profusely. The sight of blood pouring over my face completely demoralized our ranks. My fellow-combatants left me standing paralyzed in the center of the yard, and scurried for their homes. A kind neighbor saw me and rushed me to a doctor, who took three stitches in my neck.

I sat brooding on my front steps, nursing my wound and waiting for my mother to come from work. I felt that a grave injustice had been done me. It was all right to throw cinders. The greatest harm a cinder could do was leave a bruise. But broken bottles were dangerous; they left you cut, bleeding, and helpless.

When night fell, my mother came from the white folks' kitchen. I raced down the street to meet her. I could just feel in my bones that she would understand. I knew she would tell me exactly what to do next time. I grabbed

749

her hand and babbled out the whole story. She examined my wound, then slapped me.

"How come yuh didn't hide?" she asked me. "How come yuh awways fightin'?"

I was outraged, and bawled. Between sobs I told her that I didn't have any trees or hedges to hide behind. There wasn't a thing I could have used as a trench. And you couldn't throw very far when you were hiding behind the brick pillars of a house. She grabbed a barrel stave, dragged me home, stripped me naked, and beat me till I had a fever of one hundred and two. She would smack my rump with the stave, and, while the skin was still smarting, impart to me gems of Jim Crow wisdom. I was never to throw cinders any more. I was never to fight any more wars. I was never, never, under any conditions, to fight *white* folks again. And they were absolutely right in clouting me with the broken milk bottle. Didn't I know she was working hard every day in the hot kitchens of the white folks to make money to take care of me? When was I ever going to learn to be a good boy? She couldn't be bothered with my fights. She finished by telling me that I ought to be thankful to God as long as I lived that they didn't kill me.

All that night I was delirious and could not sleep. Each time I closed my eyes I saw monstrous white faces suspended from the ceiling, leering at me.

From that time on, the charm of my cinder yard was gone. The green trees, the trimmed hedges, the cropped lawns grew very meaningful, became a symbol. Even today when I think of white folks, the hard, sharp outlines of white houses surrounded by trees, lawns, and hedges are present somewhere in the background of my mind. Through the years they grew into an over-reaching symbol of fear.

It was a long time before I came in close contact with white folks again. We moved from Arkansas to Mississippi. Here we had the good fortune not to live behind the railroad tracks, or close to white neighborhoods. We lived in the very heart of the local Black belt. There were black churches and black preachers; there were black schools and black teachers; black groceries and black clerks. In fact, everything was so solidly black that for a long time I did not even think of white folks, save in remote and vague terms. But this could not last forever. As one grows older one eats more. One's clothing costs more. When I finished grammar school I had to go to work. My mother could no longer feed and clothe me on her cooking job.

There is but one place where a black boy who knows no trade can get a job, and that's where the houses and faces are white, where the trees, lawns, and hedges are green. My first job was with an optical company in Jackson, Mississippi. The morning I applied I stood straight and neat before the boss, answering all his questions with sharp yessirs and nosirs. I was very careful to pronounce my *sirs* distinctly, in order that he might know that I was polite, that I knew where I was, and that I knew he was a *white* man. I wanted that job badly.

He looked me over as though he were examining a prize poodle. He questioned me closely about my schooling, being particularly insistent about how much mathematics I had had. He seemed very pleased when I told him I had had two years of algebra.

"Boy, how would you like to try to learn something around here?" he asked me.

"I'd like it fine, sir," I said, happy. I had visions of "working my way up."
Even Negroes have those visions.

"All right," he said. "Come on."

I followed him to the small factory.

"Pease," he said to a white man of about thirty-five, "this is Richard. He's
going to work for us."

Pease looked at me and nodded.

I was then taken to a white boy of about seventeen.

"Morrie, this is Richard, who's going to work for us."

"Whut yuh sayin' there, boy!" Morrie boomed at me.

"Fine!" I answered,

The boss instructed these two to help me, teach me, give me jobs to do,
and let me learn what I could in my spare time.

My wages were five dollars a week.

I worked hard, trying to please. For the first month I got along O.K. Both
Pease and Morrie seemed to like me. But one thing was missing. And I kept
thinking about it. I was not learning anything and nobody was volunteering to
help me. Thinking they had forgotten that I was to learn something about the
mechanics of grinding lenses, I asked Morrie one day to tell me about the
work. He grew red.

"Whut yuh tryin' t' do, nigger, get smart?" he asked.

"Naw; I ain't tryin t' git smart," I said.

"Well, don't, if yuh know whut's good for yuh!"

I was puzzled. Maybe he just doesn't want to help me, I thought. I went
to Pease.

"Say, are yuh crazy, you black bastard?" Pease asked me, his gray eyes
growing hard.

I spoke out, reminding him that the boss had said I was to be given a
chance to learn something.

"Nigger, you think you're *white*, don't you?"

"Naw, sir!"

"Well, you're acting mighty like it!"

"But, Mr. Pease, the boss said . . ."

Pease shook his fist in my face.

"This is a *white* man's work around here, and you better watch yourself!"

From then on they changed toward me. They said good-morning no more.
When I was just a bit slow in performing some duty, I was called a lazy black
son-of-a-bitch.

Once I thought of reporting all this to the boss. But the mere idea of what
would happen to me if Pease and Morrie should learn that I had "snitched"
stopped me. And after all the boss was a white man, too. What was the use?

The climax came at noon one summer day. Pease called me to his workbench. To get to him I had to go between two narrow benches and stand
with my back against a wall.

"Yes, sir," I said.

"Richard, I want to ask you something," Pease began pleasantly, not looking up from his work.

"Yes, sir," I said again.

Morrie came over, blocking the narrow passage between the benches. He
folded his arms, staring at me solemnly.

I looked from one to the other, sensing that something was coming.

"Yes, sir," I said for the third time.

Pease looked up and spoke very slowly.

"Richard, *Mr.* Morrie here tells me you called me *Pease.*"

I stiffened. A void seemed to open up in me. I knew this was the show-down.

He meant that I had failed to call him Mr. Pease. I looked at Morrie. He was gripping a steel bar in his hands. I opened my mouth to speak, to protest, to assure Pease that I had never called him simply *Pease*, and that I had never had any intentions of doing so, when Morrie grabbed me by the collar, ramming my head against the wall.

"Now, be careful, nigger!" snarled Morrie, baring his teeth. "*I* heard yuh call 'im *Pease!*" 'N' if yuh say yuh didn't yuh're callin' me a *lie*, see?" He waved the steel bar threateningly.

If I had said: No, sir, Mr. Pease, I never called you *Pease*, I would have been automatically calling Morrie a liar. And if I had said: Yes, sir, Mr. Pease, I called you *Pease*, I would have been pleading guilty to having uttered the worst insult that a Negro can utter to a southern white man. I stood hesitating, trying to frame a neutral reply.

"Richard, I asked you a question!" said Pease. Anger was creeping into his voice.

"I don't remember calling you *Pease*, Mr. Pease," I said cautiously. "And if I did, I sure didn't mean . . ."

"You black son-of-a-bitch! You called me *Pease*, then!" he spat, slapping me till I bent sideways over a bench. Morrie was on top of me, demanding:

"Didn't yuh call 'im *Pease?* If yuh say yuh didn't, I'll rip yo' gut string loose with this bar, yuh black granny dodger! Yuh can't call a white man a liar 'n' git erway with it, you black son-of-a-bitch!"

I wilted. I begged them not to bother me. I knew what they wanted. They wanted me to leave.

"I'll leave," I promised. "I'll leave right *now.*"

They gave me a minute to get out of the factory. I was warned not to show up again, or tell the boss.

I went.

When I told the folks at home what had happened, they called me a fool. They told me that I must never again attempt to exceed my boundaries. When you are working for white folks, they said, you got to "stay in your place" if you want to keep working.

II

My Jim Crow education continued on my next job, which was portering in a clothing store. One morning, while polishing brass out front, the boss and his twenty-year-old son got out of their car and half dragged and half kicked a Negro woman into the store. A policeman standing at the corner looked on, twirling his night-stick. I watched out of the corner of my eye, never slackening the strokes of my chamois upon the brass. After a few minutes, I heard shrill screams coming from the rear of the store. Later the woman stumbled out, bleeding, crying, and holding her stomach. When she reached the end of the block, the policeman grabbed her and accused her of being drunk. Silently, I watched him throw her into a patrol wagon.

When I went to the rear of the store, the boss and his son were washing their hands at the sink. They were chuckling. The floor was bloody and strewn with wisps of hair and clothing. No doubt I must have appeared pretty shocked, for the boss slapped me reassuringly on the back.

"Boy, that's what we do to niggers when they don't want to pay their bills," he said, laughing.

His son looked at me and grinned.

"Here, hava cigarette," he said.

Not knowing what to do, I took it. He lit his and held the match for me. This was a gesture of kindness, indicating that even if they had beaten the poor old woman, they would not beat me if I knew enough to keep my mouth shut.

"Yes, sir," I said, and asked no questions.

After they had gone, I sat on the edge of a packing box and stared at the bloody floor till the cigarette went out.

That day at noon, while eating in a hamburger joint, I told my fellow Negro porters what had happened. No one seemed surprised. One fellow, after swallowing a huge bite, turned to me and asked:

"Huh! Is tha' all they did t' her?"

"Yeah. Wasn't tha' enough?" I asked.

"Shucks! Man, she's a lucky bitch!" he said, burying his lips deep into a juicy hamburger. "Hell, it's a wonder they didn't lay her when they got through."

III

I was learning fast, but not quite fast enough. One day, while I was delivering packages in the suburbs, my bicycle tire was punctured. I walked along the hot, dusty road, sweating and leading my bicycle by the handlebars.

A car slowed at my side.

"What's the matter, boy?" a white man called.

I told him my bicycle was broken and I was walking back to town.

"That's too bad," he said. "Hop on the running board."

He stopped the car. I clutched hard at my bicycle with one hand and clung to the side of the car with the other.

"All set?"

"Yes, sir," I answered. The car started.

It was full of young white men. They were drinking. I watched the flask pass from mouth to mouth.

"Wanna drink, boy?" one asked.

I laughed as the wind whipped my face. Instinctively obeying the freshly planted precepts of my mother, I said:

"Oh, no!"

The words were hardly out of my mouth before I felt something hard and cold smash me between the eyes. It was an empty whisky bottle. I saw stars, and fell backwards from the speeding car into the dust of the road, my feet becoming entangled in the steel spokes of my bicycle. The white men piled out and stood over me.

"Nigger, ain' yuh learned no better sense'n tha' yet?" asked the man who hit me. "Ain' yuh learned t' say *sir* t' a white man yet?"

Dazed, I pulled to my feet. My elbows and legs were bleeding. Fists doubled, the white man advanced, kicking my bicycle out of the way.

"Aw, leave the bastard alone. He's got enough," said one.

They stood looking at me. I rubbed my shins, trying to stop the flow of blood. No doubt they felt a sort of contemptuous pity, for one asked:

"Yuh wanna ride t' town now, nigger? Yuh reckon yuh know enough t' ride now?"

"I wanna walk," I said, simply.

Maybe it sounded funny. They laughed.

"Well, walk, yuh black son-of-a-bitch!"

When they left they comforted me with:

"Nigger, yuh sho better be damn glad it wuz us yuh talked t' tha' way. Yuh're a lucky bastard, 'cause if yuh'd said tha' t' somebody else, yuh might've been a dead nigger now."

IV

Negroes who had lived South know the dread of being caught alone upon the streets in white neighborhoods after the sun has set. In such a simple situation as this the plight of the Negro in America is graphically symbolized. While white strangers may be in these neighborhoods trying to get home, they can pass unmolested. But the color of a Negro's skin makes him easily recognizable, makes him suspect, converts him into a defenseless target.

Late one Saturday night I made some deliveries in a white neighborhood. I was pedaling my bicycle back to the store as fast as I could, when a police car, swerving toward me, jammed me into the curbing.

"Get down and put up your hands!" the policemen ordered.

I did. They climbed out of the car, guns drawn, faces set, and advanced slowly.

"Keep still!" they ordered.

I reached my hands higher. They searched my pockets and packages. They seemed dissatisfied when they could find nothing incriminating. Finally, one of them said:

"Boy, tell your boss not to send you out in white neighborhoods after sundown."

As usual, I said:

"Yes, sir."

V

My next job was a hall-boy in a hotel. Here my Jim Crow education broadened and deepened. When the bell-boys were busy, I was often called to assist them. As many of the rooms in the hotel were occupied by prostitutes, I was constantly called to carry them liquor and cigarettes. These women were nude most of the time. They did not bother about clothing, even for bell-boys. When you went into their rooms, you were supposed to take their nakedness for granted, as though it startled you no more than a blue vase or a red rug. Your presence awoke in them no sense of shame, for you were not regarded as human. If they were alone, you could steal sidelong glimpses at them. But if they were receiving men, not a flicker of your eyelids could show. I remember one incident vividly. A new woman, a huge, snowy-skinned blonde, took a room on my floor. I was sent to wait upon her. She was in bed with a thick-set man; both were nude and uncovered. She said she wanted some liquor and slid out of bed and waddled across the floor to get her money from a dresser drawer. I watched her.

"Nigger, what in hell you looking at?" the white man asked me, raising himself upon his elbows.

"Nothing," I answered, looking miles deep into the blank wall of the room.

"Keep your eyes where they belong, if you want to be healthy!" he said.

"Yes, sir."

VI

One of the bell-boys I knew in this hotel was keeping steady company with one of the Negro maids. Out of a clear sky the police descended upon his home and arrested him, accusing him of bastardy. The poor boy swore he had had no intimate relations with the girl. Nevertheless, they forced him to marry her. When the child arrived, it was found to be much lighter in complexion than either of the two supposedly legal parents. The white men around the hotel made a great joke of it. They spread the rumor that some white cow must have scared the poor girl while she was carrying the baby. If you were in their presence when this explanation was offered, you were supposed to laugh.

VII

One of the bell-boys was caught in bed with a white prostitute. He was castrated and run out of town. Immediately after this all the bell-boys and hall-boys were called together and warned. We were given to understand that the boy who had been castrated was a "mighty, mighty lucky bastard." We were impressed with the fact that next time the management of the hotel would not be responsible for the lives of "trouble-makin' niggers." We were silent.

VIII

One night, just as I was about to go home, I met one of the Negro maids. She lived in my direction, and we fell in to walk part of the way home together. As we passed the white night-watchman, he slapped the maid on her buttock. I turned around, amazed. The watchman looked at me with a long, hard, fixed-under stare. Suddenly he pulled his gun and asked:

"Nigger, don't yuh like it?"

I hesitated.

"I asked yuh don't yuh like it?" he asked again, stepping forward.

"Yes, sir," I mumbled.

"Talk like it, then!"

"Oh, yes, sir!" I said with as much heartiness as I could muster.

Outside, I walked ahead of the girl, ashamed to face her. She caught up with me and said:

"Don't be a fool! Yuh couldn't help it!"

This watchman boasted of having killed two Negroes in self-defense.

Yet, in spite of all this, the life of the hotel ran with an amazing smoothness. It would have been impossible for a stranger to detect anything. The maids, the hall-boys, and the bell-boys were all smiles. They had to be.

IX

I had learned my Jim Crow lessons so thoroughly that I kept the hotel job till I left Jackson for Memphis. It so happened that while in Memphis I applied for a job at a branch of the optical company. I was hired. And for some reason, as long as I worked there, they never brought my past against me.

Here my Jim Crow education assumed quite a different form. It was no longer brutally cruel, but subtly cruel. Here I learned to lie, to steal, to dissemble. I learned to play that dual role which every Negro must play if he wants to eat and live.

For example, it was almost impossible to get a book to read. It was assumed that after a Negro had imbibed what scanty schooling the state furnished he had no further need for books. I was always borrowing books from men on the job. One day I mustered enough courage to ask one of the men to let me get books from the library in his name. Surprisingly, he consented. I cannot help but think that he consented because he was a Roman Catholic and felt a vague sympathy for Negroes, being himself an object of hatred. Armed with a library card, I obtained books in the following manner: I would write a note to the librarian, saying: "Please let this nigger boy have the following books." I would then sign it with the white man's name.

When I went to the library, I would stand at the desk, hat in hand, looking as unbookish as possible. When I received the books desired I would take them home. If the books listed in the note happened to be out, I would sneak into the lobby and forge a new one. I never took any chances guessing with the white librarian about what the fictitious white man would want to read. No doubt if any of the white patrons had suspected that some of the volumes they enjoyed had been in the home of a Negro, they would not have tolerated it for an instant.

The factory force of the optical company in Memphis was much larger than that in Jackson, and more urbanized. At least they liked to talk, and would engage the Negro help in conversation whenever possible. By this means I found that many subjects were taboo from the white man's point of view. Among the topics they did not like to discuss with Negroes were the following: American white women; the Ku Klux Klan; France, and how Negro soldiers fared while there; French women; Jack Johnson; the entire northern part of the United States; the Civil War; Abraham Lincoln; U. S. Grant; General Sherman; Catholics; the Pope; Jews; the Republican Party; slavery; social equality; Communism; Socialism; the 13th and 14th Amendments to the Constitution; or any topic calling for positive knowledge or manly self-assertion on the part of the Negro. The most accepted topics were sex and religion.

There were many times when I had to exercise a great deal of ingenuity to keep out of trouble. It is a southern custom that all men must take off their hats when they enter an elevator. And especially did this apply to us blacks with rigid force. One day I stepped into an elevator with my arms full of packages. I was forced to ride with my hat on. Two white men stared at me coldly. Then one of them very kindly lifted my hat and placed it upon my armful of packages. Now the most accepted response for a Negro to make under such circumstances is to look at the white man out of the corner of his eye and grin. To have said: "Thank you!" would have made the white man *think* that you *thought* you were receiving from him a personal service. For such an act I have seen Negroes take a blow in the mouth. Finding the first alternative distasteful, and the second dangerous, I hit upon an acceptable course of action which fell safely between these two poles. I immediately—no sooner than my hat was lifted—pretended that my packages were about to spill, and appeared deeply distressed with keeping them in my arms. In this fashion I evaded having to acknowledge his service, and, in spite of adverse circumstances, salvaged a slender shred of personal pride.

How do Negroes feel about the way they have to live? How do they discuss it when alone among themselves? I think this question can be answered in a single sentence. A friend of mine who ran an elevator once told me:

"Lawd, man! Ef it wuzn't fer them polices 'n' them ol' lynch-mobs, there wouldn't be nothin' but uproar down here!"

Suggestions for Discussion

1. Analyze Wright's sketch in terms of (a) structure, (b) progression and unity in nine segments, (c) expository-narrative style, and/or (d) themes.

2. How does Wright's title contribute to the development of the major themes of the sketch? Why does he use *ethics* and *living?*

3. Discuss his use of personal experiences to illustrate his themes.

4. Discuss his use of violence in the sketch. Is it believable? Significant? Explain.

Suggestions for Writing

1. Analyze the motivation behind an incident of discrimination that you have observed or experienced.

2. Analyze the dramatic irony in the last line and its climactic effect as the final comment on the whole sketch.

Benjamin Alire Sáenz

Prologue to
Exiled: The Winds of Sunset Heights

Benjamin Alire Sáenz, born in Las Cruces in southern New Mexico, teaches at the University of Texas in El Paso. He holds an M.A. from the University of Louvain in Belgium and from the University of Texas at El Paso. He also has a Ph.D. from Stanford University where he was granted a Stegner Fellowship. He has published in numerous journals and magazines. His first book of poems, *Calendar of Dust*, won the Before Columbus Foundation American Book Award in 1992. He is the winner of the 1993 Lannan Poetry Fellowship. This prologue records the anger that a native-born Chicano, living near the border, feels over the frequent harassment by the border patrol.

That morning—when the day was new, when the sun slowly touched the sky, almost afraid to break it—that morning I looked out my window and stared at the Juárez Mountains. Mexican purples—burning. I had always thought of them as sacraments of belonging. That was the first time it happened. It had happened to others, but it had never happened to me. And when it happened, it started a fire, a fire that will burn for a long time.

As I walked to school, I remember thinking what a perfect place Sunset Heights was: turn of the century houses intact; remodeled houses painted pink and turquoise; old homes tastefully gentrified by the aspiring young; the rundown Sunset Grocery store decorated with the protest art of graffiti on one end and a plastic-signed "Circle K" on the other.

This was the edge of the piece of paper that was America, the border that bordered the University—its buildings, its libraries; the border that bordered the freeway—its cars coming and going, coming and going endlessly; the border that bordered downtown—its banks and businesses and bars; the border that bordered the border between two countries.

The unemployed poor from Juárez knocking on doors and asking for jobs—or money—or food. Small parks filled with people whose English did not exist. The upwardly mobile living next to families whose only concern was getting enough money to pay next month's rent. Some had lived here for generations, would continue living here into the next century; others would live here a few days. All this color, all this color, all this color beneath the shadow of the Juárez Mountains. Sunset Heights: a perfect place with a perfect name, and a perfect view of the river.

After class, I went by my office and drank a cup of coffee, sat and read, and did some writing. It was a quiet day on campus, nothing but me and my work—the kind of day the mind needs to catch up with itself, the kind of uneventful day so necessary for living. I started walking home at about three o'clock, after I had put my things together in my torn backpack. I made a mental note to sew the damn thing. *One day everything's gonna come tumbling out—better sew it.* I'd made that mental note before.

Walking down Prospect, I thought maybe I'd go for a jog. I hoped the spring would not bring too much wind this year. The wind, common desert rain; the wind blew too hard and harsh sometimes; the wind unsettled the desert—upset things, ruined the calmness of the spring. My mind wandered, searched the black asphalt littered with torn papers; the chained dogs in the yards who couldn't hurt me; the even bricks of all the houses I passed. I belonged here, yes. I belonged. Thoughts entered like children running through a park. This year, maybe the winds would not come.

I didn't notice the green car drive up and stop right next to me as I walked. The border patrol interrupted my daydreaming: "Where are you from?"

I didn't answer. I wasn't sure who the agent, a woman, was addressing. She repeated the question in Spanish, *"¿De dónde eres?"*

Without thinking, I almost answered her question—in Spanish. A reflex. I caught myself in midsentence and stuttered in a nonlanguage.

"¿Dónde naciste?" she asked again.

By then my mind had cleared, and quietly I said: "I'm a U.S. citizen."

"Were you born in the United States?"

She was browner than I was. I might have asked her the same question. I looked at her for awhile—searching for something I recognized.

"Yes," I answered.

"Where in the United States were you born?"

"In New Mexico."

"Where in New Mexico?"

"Las Cruces."

"What do you do?"

"I'm a student."

"And are you employed?"

"Sort of."

"Sort of?" She didn't like my answer. Her tone bordered on anger. I looked at her expression and decided it wasn't hurting anyone to answer her questions. It was all very innocent, just a game we were playing.

"I work at the University as a teaching assistant."

She didn't respond. She looked at me as if I were a blank. Her eyes were filling in the empty spaces as she looked at my face. I looked at her for a second and decided she was finished with me. I started walking away. "Are you sure you were born in Las Cruces?" she asked again.

I turned around and smiled, "Yes, I'm sure." She didn't smile back. She and the driver sat there for awhile and watched me as I continued walking. They drove past me slowly and then proceeded down the street.

I didn't much care for the color of their cars.

"Sons of bitches," I whispered, "pretty soon I'll have to carry a passport in my own neighborhood." I said it to be flippant; something in me rebelled against people dressed in uniforms. I wasn't angry—not then, not at first, not really angry. In less than ten minutes I was back in my apartment playing the scene again and again in my mind. It was like a video I played over and over—memorizing the images. Something was wrong. I was embarrassed, ashamed because I'd been so damned compliant like a piece of tin foil in the uniformed woman's hand. Just like a child in the principal's office, in trouble for speaking Spanish. "I should have told that witch exactly what I thought of her and her green car and her green uniform."

I lit a cigarette and told myself I was overreacting. "Breathe in—breathe out—breathe in—breathe out—no big deal—you live on a border. These things happen—just one of those things. Just a game . . ." I changed into my jogging clothes and went for a run. At the top of the hill on Sunbowl Drive, I stopped to stare at the Juárez Mountains. I felt the sweat run down my face. I kept running until I could no longer hear *Are you sure you were born in Las Cruces?* ringing in my ears.

School let out in early May. I spent the last two weeks of that month relaxing and working on some paintings. In June I got back to working on my stories. I had a working title, which I hated, but I hated it less than the actual stories I was writing. It would come to nothing; I knew it would come to nothing.

From my window I could see the freeway. It was then I realized that not a day went by when I didn't see someone running across the freeway or walking down the street looking out for someone. They were people who looked not so different from me—except that they lived their lives looking over their shoulders.

One Thursday, I saw the border patrol throw some men into their van— throw them—as if they were born to be thrown like baseballs, like rings in a carnival ringtoss, easy inanimate objects, dead bucks after a deer hunt. The illegals didn't even put up a fight. They were aliens, from somewhere else, somewhere foreign, and it did not matter that the "somewhere else" was as close as an eyelash to an eye. What mattered was that someone had once drawn a line, and once drawn, that line became indelible and hard and could not be crossed.

The men hung their heads so low that they almost scraped the littered asphalt. Whatever they felt, they did not show; whatever burned did not burn for an audience. I sat at my typewriter and tried to pretend I saw nothing. *What do you think happens when you peer out windows? Buy curtains.*

I didn't write the rest of the day. I kept seeing the border patrol woman against a blue sky turning green. I thought of rearranging my desk so I wouldn't be next to the window, but I thought of the mountains. No, I would keep my desk near the window, but I would look only at the mountains.

Two weeks later, I went for a walk. The stories weren't going well that day; my writing was getting worse instead of better; my characters were getting on my nerves—I didn't like them—no one else would like them either. They did not burn with anything. I hadn't showered, hadn't shaved, hadn't combed my hair. I threw some water on my face and walked out the door. It was summer; it was hot; it was afternoon, the time of day when everything felt as if it were on fire. The worst time of the day to take a walk. I wiped the sweat from my eyelids; it instantly reappeared. I wiped it off again, but the sweat came pouring out—a leak in the dam. Let it leak. I laughed. A hundred degrees in the middle of a desert afternoon. Laughter poured out of me as fast as my sweat. I turned the corner and headed back home. I saw the green van. It was parked right ahead of me.

A man about my height got out of the van and approached me. Another man, taller, followed him. "*¿Tienes tus papeles?*" he asked. His gringo accent was as thick as the sweat on my skin.

"I can speak English," I said. I started to add: *I can probably speak it better than you*, but I stopped myself. No need to be aggressive, no need to get any hotter.

"Do you live in this neighborhood?"

"Yes."

"Where?"

"Down the street."

"Where down the street?"

"Are you planning on making a social visit?"

He gave me a hard look—cold and blue—then looked at his partner. He didn't like me. I didn't care. I liked that he hated me. It made it easier.

I watched them drive away and felt as hot as the air, felt as hot as the heat that was burning away the blue in the sky.

There were other times when I felt watched. Sometimes, when I jogged, the green vans would slow down, eye me. I felt like prey, like a rabbit who smelled the hunter. I pretended not to notice them. I stopped pretending. I started noting their presence in our neighborhood more and more. I started growing suspicious of my own observations. Of course, they weren't everywhere. But they *were* everywhere. I had just been oblivious to their presence, had been oblivious because they had nothing to do with me; their presence had something to do with someone else. I was not a part of this. I wanted no part of it. The green cars and the green vans clashed with the purples of the Juárez Mountains. Nothing looked the same. I never talked about their presence to other people. Sometimes the topic of the *Migra* would come up in conversations. I felt the burning; I felt the anger, would control it. I casually referred to them as the Gestapo, the traces of rage carefully hidden from the expression on my face—and everyone would laugh. I hated them.

When school started in the fall, I was stopped again. Again I had been walking home from the University. I heard the familiar question: "Where are you from?"

"Leave me alone."

"Are you a citizen of the United States?"

"Yes."

"Can you prove it?"

"No. No, I can't."

He looked at my clothes: jeans, tennis shoes, and a casual California shirt. He noticed my backpack full of books.

"You a student?"

I nodded and stared at him.

"There isn't any need to be unfriendly—"

"I'd like you to leave me alone."

"Just doing my job," he laughed. I didn't smile back. *Terrorists. Nazis did their jobs. Death squads in El Salvador and Guatemala did their jobs, too.* An unfair analogy. An unfair analogy? Yes, unfair. I thought it; I felt it; it was no longer my job to excuse—someone else would have to do that, someone else. The Juárez Mountains did not seem purple that fall. They no longer burned with color.

In early January I went with Michael to Juárez. Michael was from New York, and he had come to work in a home for the homeless in South El Paso. We weren't in Juárez very long—just looking around and getting gas. Gas was cheap in Juárez. On the way back, the customs officer asked us to declare our citizenship. "U.S. citizen," I said. "U.S. citizen," Michael followed. The customs officer lowered his head and poked it in the car. "What are you bringing over?"

"Nothing."

He looked at me. "Where in the United States were you born?"

"In Las Cruces, New Mexico."

He looked at me a while longer. "Go ahead," he signaled.

I noticed that he didn't ask Michael where he was from. But Michael had blue eyes; Michael had white skin. Michael didn't have to tell the man in the uniform where he was from.

That winter, Sunset Heights seemed deserted to me. The streets were empty like the river. One morning, I was driving down Upson Street toward the University, the wind shaking the limbs of the bare trees. Nothing to shield them—unprotected by green leaves. The sun burned a dull yellow. In front of me, I noticed two border patrol officers chasing someone, though that someone was not visible. One of them put his hand out, signaling me to slow down as they ran across the street in front of my car. They were running with their billy clubs in hand. The wind blew at their backs as if to urge them on, as if to carry them.

In late January, Michael and I went to Juárez again. A friend of his was in town, and he wanted to see Juárez. We walked across the bridge, across the river, across the line into another country. It was easy. No one there to stop us. We walked the streets of Juárez, streets that had seen better years, that were tired now from the tired feet that walked them. Michael's friend wanted to know how it was that there were so many beggars. "Were there always so many? Has it always been this way?" I didn't know how it had always been. We sat in the Cathedral and in the old chapel next to it and watched people rubbing the feet of statues; when I touched a statue, it was warmer than my own hand. We walked to the marketplace and inhaled the smells. Grocery stores in the country we knew did not have such smells. On the way back we stopped in a small bar and had a beer. The beer was cold and cheap. Walking back over the bridge, we stopped at the top and looked out at the city of El Paso. "It actually looks pretty from here, doesn't it?" I said. Michael nodded. It did look pretty. We looked off to the side—down the river—and for a long time watched the people trying to get across. Michael's friend said it was like watching the *CBS Evening News*.

As we reached the customs building, we noticed that a border patrol van pulled up behind the building where the other green cars were parked. The officers jumped out of the van and threw a handcuffed man against one of the parked cars. It looked like they were going to beat him. Two more border patrol officers pulled up in a car and jumped out to join them. One of the officers noticed we were watching. They straightened the man out and walked him inside—like gentlemen. They would have beat him. They would have beat him. But we were watching.

My fingers wanted to reach through the wire fence, not to touch it, not to feel it, but to break it down, to melt it down with what I did not understand. The burning was not there to be understood. Something was burning, the side of me that knew I was treated different, would always be treated different because I was born on a particular side of a fence, a fence that separated me from others, that separated me from a past, that separated me from the country of my genesis and glued me to the country I did not love because it demanded something of me I could not give. Something was burning now, and if I could have grasped the source of that rage and held it in my fist, I would have melted that fence. Someone built that fence; someone could tear it down. Maybe I could tear it down; maybe I was the one. Maybe then I would no longer be separated.

The first day in February, I was walking to a downtown Chevron station to pick up my car. On the corner of Prospect and Upson, a green car was parked—just sitting there. A part of my landscape. I was walking on the opposite side of the street. For some reason, I knew they were going to stop me. My heart clenched like a fist; the muscles in my back knotted up. *Maybe they'll leave me alone. I should have taken a shower this morning. I should have worn a nicer sweater. I should have put on a pair of socks, worn a nicer pair of shoes. I should have cut my hair; I should have shaved . . .*

The driver rolled down his window. I saw him from the corner of my eye. He called me over to him—*whistled me over*—much like he'd call a dog. I kept walking. He whistled me over again. *Here, boy.* I stopped for a second. Only a second. I kept walking. The border patrol officer and a policeman rushed out of the car and ran toward me. I was sure they were going to tackle me, drag me to the ground, handcuff me. They stopped in front of me.

"Can I see your driver's license?" the policeman asked.

"Since when do you need a driver's license to walk down the street?" Our eyes met. "Did I do something against the law?"

The policeman was annoyed. He wanted me to be passive, to say: "Yes, sir." He wanted me to approve of his job.

"Don't you know what we do?"

"Yes, I know what you do."

"Don't give me a hard time. I don't want trouble. I just want to see some identification."

I looked at him—looked, and saw what would not go away: neither him, nor his car, nor his job, nor what I knew, nor what I felt. He stared back. He hated me as much as I hated him. He saw the bulge of my cigarettes under my sweater and crumpled them.

I backed away from his touch. "I smoke. It's not good for me, but it's not against the law. Not yet, anyway. Don't touch me. I don't like that. Read me my rights, throw me in the can, or leave me alone." I smiled.

"No one's charging you with anything."

My eyes followed them as they walked back to their car. Now it was war, and *I had won this battle.* Had I won this battle? Had I won?

This spring morning, I sit at my desk, wait for the coffee to brew, and look out my window. This day, like every day, I look out my window. Across the street, a border patrol van stops and an officer gets out. So close I could touch him. On the freeway—this side of the river—a man is running. I put on my glasses. I am afraid he will be run over by the cars. I cheer for him. *Be careful. Don't get run over.* So close to the other side he can touch it. The border patrol officer gets out his walkie-talkie and runs toward the man who has disappeared from my view. I go and get my cup of coffee. I take a drink—slowly, it mixes with yesterday's tastes in my mouth. The officer in the green uniform comes back into view. He has the man with him. He puts him in the van. I can't see the color in their eyes. I see only the green. They drive away. There is no trace that says they've been there. The mountains watch the scene and say nothing. The mountains, ablaze in the spring light, have been watching—and guarding—and keeping silent longer than I have been alive. They will continue their vigil long after I am dead.

The green vans. They are taking someone away. They are taking. Green vans. This is my home, I tell myself. But I am not sure if I want this to be my home anymore. The thought crosses my mind that maybe the *Migra* will stop me again. I will let them arrest me. I will let them warehouse me. I will let them push me in front of a judge who will look at me like he has looked at the millions before me. I will be sent back to Mexico. I will let them treat me like I am illegal. But the thoughts pass. I am not brave enough to let them do that to me.

Today, the spring winds blow outside my window. The reflections in the pane, graffiti burning questions into the glass: *Sure you were born . . . Identification . . . Do you live?* . . . The winds will unsettle the desert—cover Sunset Heights with green dust. The vans will stay in my mind forever. I cannot banish them. I cannot banish their questions: *Where are you from?* I no longer know.

This is a true story.

Suggestions for Discussion

1. Discuss the incidents in this memoir that describe and explain the author's anger over the actions of the border patrol. Are the patrol's actions consistently racist?

2. Why does the writer dislike the color of the border patrol officers' uniforms? The color of their cars and vans?

3. Describe Sáenz's feelings about the landscape of the border country in which he lives. How do these passages serve to portray the writer?

4. In the next to the last scene of the memoir, the writer describes a confrontation with a member of the border patrol. He wonders whether he has won this conflict. Has he? Explain your response.

Suggestions for Writing

1. Write a personal essay describing an incident, or a series of incidents, in which you confronted authority. Try to record how you behaved, what you felt, what your opponent felt, and so forth.

2. Most rational people despise the persistence of racism in this country. Write an essay describing a racist incident you observed or a racist conversation you overheard or participated in. Try to summarize the feelings generated by the incident or conversation and how you responded.

Rigoberta Menchú

Things Have Happened to Me
as in a Movie

Rigoberta Menchú (b. 1962), a Quiché Indian, was born in Guatemala. She taught herself Spanish when she was twenty. A founder of the Committee for the Peasants' Unity, she has widely traveled as an ambassador of the Indian people. She won the Casa de las Américas Prize of Cuba for her book, I, Rigoberta, and the Nobel Peace Prize in 1992. In this short memoir, resulting from an interview with César Chelala and translated by Regina M. Kreger, the writer recalls details from the Guatemalan suppression of the Indian people that are almost too painful to read.

I am Rigoberta Menchú; I am a native of the Quiché people of Guatemala. My life has been a long one. Things have happened to me as in a movie. My parents were killed in the repression. I have hardly any relatives living, or if I have, I don't know about them. It has been my lot to live what has been the lot of many, many Guatemalans.

We were a very poor family. All their lives my parents worked cutting cotton, cutting coffee. We lived about four months of the year on the high plain of Guatemala, where my father had a small piece of land; but that only supported us a short time, and then we had to go down to the plantations to get food.

During the whole time my mother was pregnant with me, she was on the plantation cutting coffee and cotton. I was paid twenty cents, many years ago, when I started to work in my town in Guatemala. There, the poor, the children, didn't have the opportunity for school; we did not have the opportunity to achieve any other life but working for food and to help our parents buy medicine for our little brothers and sisters. Two of my brothers died on the plantation cutting coffee. One of them got sick, couldn't be cured, and died. The other died when the landowner ordered the cotton sprayed while we were in the field. My brother was poisoned, there was no way to cure him and he died on the plantation, where we buried him.

We didn't know why those things happened. It's a miracle we were saved several times. When we got sick our mother looked for plants to cure us. The natives in Guatemala depended very much on nature. My mother cured us many times with the leaves of plants, with roots. That is how we managed to grow up. At ten years old, I started to work more in collaboration with my community, where my father, a local, native Mayan leader, was known by all the Indians of the region.

Little by little, my father got us involved in the concerns of the community. And so we grew up with that consciousness. My father was a catechist, and in Guatemala, a catechist is a leader of the community, and what he does especially is preach the Gospel. We, his children, began to evolve in the Catholic religion, and became catechists.

765

Little by little, we grew up—and really you can't say we started fighting only a short time ago, because it has been twenty-two years since my father fought over the land. The landowners wanted to take away our land, our little bit of land, and so my father fought for it. So he went to speak with the mayors, and with the judges in various parts of Guatemala. Afterwards, my father joined INTA, the land reform institution in Guatemala. For many years, my father was tricked because he did not speak Spanish. None of us spoke Spanish. So they made my father travel all over Guatemala to sign papers, letters, telegrams, which meant that not only he, but the whole community, had to sacrifice to pay the travel expenses. All this created an awareness in us from a very young age.

In the last years, my father was imprisoned many times, the first of those in 1954. My father landed in jail when he was accused of causing unrest among the population. When our father was in jail, the army kicked us out of our houses. They burned our clay pots. In our community we don't use iron or steel; we use clay pots, which we make ourselves with earth. But the army broke everything, and it was really hard for us to understand this situation.

Then my father was sentenced to eighteen years in prison, but he didn't serve them because we were able to work with lawyers to get him released. After a year and two months, my father got out of prison and returned home with more courage to go on fighting and much angrier because of what had happened. When that was over my mother had to go right to work as a maid in the city of Santa Cruz del Quiché, and all of us children had to go down to work on the plantations.

A short time later, my father was tortured by the landowners' bodyguards. Some armed men came to my house and took my father away. We got the community together and found my father lying in the road, far away, about two kilometers from home. My father was badly beaten and barely alive. The priests of the region had to come out to take my father to the hospital. He had been in the hospital for six months when we heard he was going to be taken out and killed. The landowners had been discussing it loudly, and the information came to us by way of their servants, who are also natives, and with whom we were very close. And so we had to find another place for my father, a private clinic the priests found for him so he would heal. But my father could no longer do hard work like he did before. A little later my father dedicated himself exclusively to working for the community, traveling, living off the land.

Several years passed, and again, in the year 1977, my father was sentenced to death. He landed in jail again. When we went to see him in the Pantán jail, the military told us they didn't want us to see my father, because he had committed many crimes. My mother went to Santa Cruz to find lawyers, and from them we learned that my father was going to be executed. When the time of the execution came, many union workers, students, peasants and some priests demonstrated for my father's freedom. My father was freed, but before he left he was threatened; he was told that he was going to be killed anyway for being a communist. From that moment on, my father had to carry out his activities in secret. He had to change the rhythm of his life. He lived hidden in several houses in Quiché, and then he went to the capital city. And so he became a leader of struggle for the peasants. It was then that my father said, "We must fight as Christians," and from there came the idea, along with other catechists, of forming Christian organizations which would participate in the process.

For us it was always a mystery how my father could carry out all those activities, which were very important, despite being illiterate. He never learned to read or write in his life. All his children were persecuted because of his activities, and our poverty really didn't help us defend ourselves, because we were in very sad circumstances.

All my father's activities had created a resentment in us because we couldn't have our parents' affection, because there were a lot of us children and a bigger worry was how to survive. On top of all this were the problems of the land, which upset my father very much. Many years before, rocks had fallen from the mountain and we had to go down from where we lived. When we went down and cultivated new land, the landowners appeared with documents and they told us the land was theirs before we came. But we knew very well the land had no owner before we got there.

They couldn't catch my father, but in the year 1979, they kidnapped one of my little brothers. He was sixteen. We didn't know who did it. We only knew that they were five armed men, with their faces covered. Since my father couldn't go out, we went with my mother and members of the community to make a complaint to the army, but they said they didn't know anything about what had happened to my brother. We went to City Hall, we went to all the jails in Guatemala, but we didn't find him. After many trips all over my mother was very upset. It had taken a lot for my brother to survive, and so for my mother it was very hard to accept his disappearance.

At that time the army published a bulletin saying there was going to be a guerrilla council. They said they had some guerrillas in their custody and that they were going to punish them in public. My mother said, "I hope to God my son shows up. I hope to God my son is there. I want to know what has happened to him." So we went to see what was happening. We walked for one day and almost the whole night to get to the other town. There were hundreds of soldiers who had almost the whole town surrounded, and who had gathered the people together to witness what they were going to do. There were natives of other areas as well as natives of that town. After a while an army truck arrived with twenty people who had been tortured in different ways. Among them we recognized my brother, who, along with the other prisoners, had been tortured for fifteen days. When my mother saw my little brother she almost gave herself away, but we had to calm her down, telling her that if she gave herself away she was going to die right there for being family of a guerrilla. We were crying, but almost all the rest of the people were crying also at the sight of the tortured people. They had pulled out my little brother's fingernails, they had cut off parts of his ears and other parts of his body, his lips, and he was covered with scars and swollen all over. Among the prisoners was a woman and they had cut off parts of her breasts and other parts of her body.

An army captain gave us a very long speech, almost three hours, in which he constantly threatened the people, saying that if we got involved with communism the same things were going to happen to us. Then he explained to us one by one the various types of torture they had applied to the prisoners. After three hours, the officer ordered the troops to strip the prisoners, and said: "Part of the punishment is still to come." He ordered the prisoners tied to some posts. The people didn't know what to do and my mother was overcome with despair in those few moments. And none of us knew how we could bear the situation. The officer ordered the prisoners covered with gasoline and they set fire to them, one by one.

Suggestions for Discussion

1. Menchú's account of the life-history of her Indian family is not meant to represent an unusual case. How does the writer make it seem representative?

2. What examples best reveal the punishing poverty of the Indians? How do they respond?

3. What roles do the mother and father play in this memoir? What qualities do they possess that make them seem heroic?

4. What is the relation of the title to the memoir?

Suggestions for Writing

1. Write a brief profile of Menchú's father. Summarize and evaluate his efforts to help the Indians of Guatemala. Was his life's effort a failure? Explain.

2. Compare and contrast the soldiers in Menchú's memoir with the border patrol guards in Sáenz's prologue. What accounts for the significant differences between the two groups? What about Menchú's memoir makes your reading of it so painful?

Vo Thi Tam

From Vietnam, 1979

Vo Thi Tam escaped from South Vietnam after the Communist victory. Like thousands of other refugees she endured the hardships recounted in this memoir, which first appeared in *American Mosaic* (edited by Joan Morison and Charlotte Fox Zabrisky, 1980). Vo Thi Tam's story reminds the reader that throughout the twentieth century hundreds of thousands of people from many lands have overcome terrible suffering and overwhelming odds in their search for freedom.

My husband was a former officer in the South Vietnamese air force. After the fall of that government in 1975, he and all the other officers were sent to a concentration camp for reeducation. When they let him out of the camp, they forced all of us to go to one of the "new economic zones," that are really just jungle. There was no organization, there was no housing, no utilities, no doctor, nothing. They gave us tools and a little food, and that was it. We just had to dig up the land and cultivate it. And the land was very bad.

It was impossible for us to live there, so we got together with some other families and bought a big fishing boat, about thirty-five feet long.

Altogether, there were thirty-seven of us that were to leave—seven men, eight women, and the rest children. I was five months pregnant.

After we bought the boat we had to hide it, and this is how: We just anchored it in a harbor in the Mekong Delta. It's very crowded there and very many people make their living aboard the boats by going fishing, you know. So we had to make ourselves like them. We took turns living and sleeping on the boat. We would maneuver the boat around the harbor, as if we were fishing or selling stuff, you know, so the Communist authorities could not suspect anything.

Besides the big boat, we had to buy a smaller boat in order to carry supplies to it. We had to buy gasoline and other stuff on the black market—everywhere there is a black market—and carry these supplies, little by little, on the little boat to the big boat. To do this we sold jewelry and radios and other things that we had left from the old days.

On the day we left we took the big boat out very early in the morning—all the women and children were in that boat and some of the men. My husband and the one other man remained in the small boat, and they were to rendezvous with us outside the harbor. Because if the harbor officials see too many people aboard, they might think there was something suspicious. I think they were suspicious anyway. As we went out, they stopped us and made us pay them ten taels of gold—that's a Vietnamese unit, a little heavier than an ounce. That was nearly all we had.

Anyway, the big boat passed through the harbor and went ahead to the rendezvous point where we were to meet my husband and the other man in the small boat. But there was no one there. We waited for two hours, but we did not see any sign of them. After a while we could see a Vietnamese navy boat approaching, and there was a discussion on board our boat and the end of it was the people on our boat decided to leave without my husband and the other man. [*Long pause.*]

When we reached the high seas, we discovered, unfortunately, that the water container was leaking and only a little bit of the water was left. So we had to ration the water from then on. We had brought some rice and other food that we could cook, but it was so wavy that we could not cook anything at all. So all we had was raw rice and a few lemons and very little water. After seven days we ran out of water, so all we had to drink was the sea water, plus lemon juice.

Everyone was very sick and, at one point, my mother and my little boy, four years old, were in agony, about to die. And the other people on the boat said that if they were agonizing like that, it would be better to throw them overboard so as to save them pain.

During this time we had seen several boats on the sea and had waved to them to help us, but they never stopped. But that morning, while we were discussing throwing my mother and son overboard, we could see another ship coming and we were very happy, thinking maybe it was people coming to save us. When the two boats were close together, the people came on board from there—it happened to be a Thai boat—and they said all of us had to go on the bigger boat. They made us all go there and then they began to search us—cutting off our blouses, our bras, looking everywhere. One woman, she had some rings she hid in her bra, and they undressed her and took out everything. My mother had a statue of our Lady, a very precious one, you know, that she had had all her life—she begged them just to leave the statue to her. But they didn't want to. They slapped her and grabbed the statue away.

Finally they pried up the planks of our boat, trying to see if there was any gold or jewelry hidden there. And when they had taken everything, they put us back on our boat and pushed us away.

They had taken all our maps and compasses, so we didn't even know which way to go. And because they had pried up the planks of our boat to look for jewelry, the water started getting in. We were very weak by then. But we had no pump, so we had to use empty cans to bail the water out, over and over again.

That same day we were boarded again by two other boats, and these, too, were pirates. They came aboard with hammers and knives and everything. But we could only beg them for mercy and try to explain by sign language that we'd been robbed before and we had nothing left. So those boats let us go and pointed the way to Malaysia for us.

That night at about 9:00 P.M. we arrived on the shore, and we were so happy finally to land somewhere that we knelt down on the beach and prayed, you know, to thank God.

While we were kneeling there, some people came out of the woods and began to throw rocks at us. They took a doctor who was with us and they beat him up and broke his glasses, so that from that time on he couldn't see anything at all. And they tied him up, his hands behind him like this [demonstrates], and they beat up the rest of the men, too. They searched us for anything precious that they could find, but there was nothing left except our few clothes and our documents. They took these and scattered them all over the beach.

Then five of the Malaysian men grabbed the doctor's wife, a young woman with three little children, and they took her back into the woods and raped her—all five of them. Later, they sent her back, completely naked, to the beach.

After this, the Malaysians forced us back into the boat and tried to push us out to sea. But the tide was out and the boat was so heavy with all of us on board that it just sank in the sand. So they left us for the night. . . .

In the morning, the Malaysian military police came to look over the area, and they dispersed the crowd and protected us from them. They let us pick up our clothes and our papers from the beach and took us in a big truck to some kind of a warehouse in a small town not far away. They gave us water, some bread, and some fish, and then they carried us out to Bidong Island. . . .

Perhaps in the beginning it was all right there, maybe for ten thousand people or so, but when we arrived there were already fifteen to seventeen thousand crowded onto thirty acres. There was no housing, no facilities, nothing. It was already full near the beach, so we had to go up the mountain and chop down trees to make room for ourselves and make some sort of a temporary shelter. There was an old well, but the water was very shallow. It was so scarce that all the refugees had to wait in a long line, day and night, to get our turn of the water. We would have a little can, like a small Coke can at the end of a long string, and fill that up. To fill about a gallon, it would take an hour, so we each had to just wait, taking our turn to get our Coke can of water. Sometimes one, two, or three in the morning we would get our water. I was pregnant, and my boys were only four and six, and my old mother with me was not well, but we all had to wait in line to get our water. That was just for cooking and drinking of course. We had to do our washing in the sea.

The Malaysian authorities did what they could, but they left most of the administration of the camp to the refugees themselves, and most of us were sick. There were, of course, no sanitary installations, and many people had diarrhea. It was very hard to stop sickness under those conditions. My little boys were sick and my mother could hardly walk. And since there was no man in our family, we had no one to chop the wood for our cooking, and it was very hard for us just to survive. When the monsoons came, the floor of our shelter was all mud. We had one blanket and a board to lie on, and that was all. The water would come down the mountain through our shelter, so we all got wet.

After four months in the camp it was time for my baby to be born. Fortunately, we had many doctors among us, because many of them had tried to escape from Vietnam, so we had medical care but no equipment. There was no bed there, no hospital, no nothing, just a wooden plank to lie down on and let the baby be born, that was all. Each mother had to supply a portion of boiling water for the doctor to use and bring it with her to the medical hut when it was time. It was a very difficult delivery. The baby came legs first. But, fortunately, there were no complications. After the delivery I had to get up and go back to my shelter to make room for the next woman.

When we left Vietnam we were hoping to come to the United States, because my sister and her husband were here already. They came in 1975 when the United States evacuated so many people. We had to wait in the camp a month and a half to be interviewed, and then very much longer for the papers to be processed. Altogether we were in the camp seven months.

All this time I didn't know what had happened to my husband, although I hoped that he had been able to escape some other way and was, perhaps, in another camp, and that when I came to the United States I would find him.

We flew out here by way of Tokyo and arrived the first week in July. It was like waking up after a bad nightmare. Like coming out of hell into paradise if only—. [*Breaks down, rushes from room.*]

Shortly after she arrived in this country, Vo Thi Tam learned that her husband had been captured on the day of their escape and was back in a "reeducation" camp in Vietnam.

Suggestions for Discussion

1. What impression of Vo Thi Tam develops as we read her narrative? Discuss the details that serve to create her self-portrait.

2. What conditions in Vietnam lead the family and the others in the group to attempt an escape? Discuss the horrors that the refugees are forced to face. How might you have acted under similar circumstances?

3. What is the effect on the reader of the interviewer's comments?

Suggestions for Writing

1. If you live in an area where Vietnamese or other refugees from oppression live, record and transcribe some interviews and discuss them in a brief research paper, with Vo Thi Tam's narrative serving as background. Think carefully of the questions you will need to ask to elicit meaningful responses. One of your questions might deal with the expectations of the immigrant on arriving in the United States and whether those expectations have been realized.

2. Choose a different group of immigrants escaping oppression or terror, such as the Armenians from Turkey or Iran, the Nicaraguans, or the Guatemalans. Do library research to enable you to compare their experience with that of the Vietnamese. Write a paper discussing the similarities and differences of the experiences of the two groups.

Essays

Thomas Jefferson

The Declaration of Independence

The Continental Congress assembled in Philadelphia in 1776 delegated to
Thomas Jefferson the task of writing a declaration of independence from
Great Britain, which the Congress amended and adopted on July 4. After the
Revolution, Jefferson (1743–1826) became Governor of Virginia and in 1801
the third President of the United States. He was the father of what is called
"Jeffersonian democracy," which exceeded the democracy then advocated
by either Washington or Jefferson's rival, Alexander Hamilton. After leaving
the presidency, he founded the University of Virginia as a place where truth
could assert itself in free competition with other ideas. In its theory as well
as in its style, the Declaration is a typical eighteenth-century view of man's
place in society, which included the right to overthrow a tyrannical ruler.

When in the course of human events, it becomes necessary for one people
to dissolve the political bands which have connected them with another, and
to assume among the powers of the earth, the separate and equal station to
which the Laws of Nature and of Nature's God entitle them, a decent respect
to the opinions of mankind requires that they should declare the causes
which impel them to the separation.

We hold these truths to be self-evident, that all men are created equal,
that they are endowed by their Creator with certain inalienable rights, that
among these are life, liberty, and the pursuit of happiness. That to secure
these rights, governments are instituted among men, deriving their just powers from the consent of the governed. That whenever any form of government becomes destructive of these ends, it is the right of the people to alter
or to abolish it, and to institute new government, laying its foundation on
such principles and organizing its powers in such form, as to them shall seem
most likely to effect their safety and happiness. Prudence, indeed, will dictate that governments long established should not be changed for light and
transient causes; and accordingly all experience hath shown, that mankind are
more disposed to suffer, while evils are sufferable, than to right themselves
by abolishing the forms to which they are accustomed. But when a long train
of abuses and usurpations, pursuing invariably the same object, evinces a design to reduce them under absolute despotism, it is their right, it is their
duty, to throw off such government, and to provide new guards for their
future security. Such has been the patient sufferance of these Colonies; and
such is now the necessity which constrains them to alter their former systems
of government. The history of the present King of Great Britain is a history of
repeated injuries and usurpations, all having in direct object the establishment of an absolute tyranny over these States. To prove this, let facts be
submitted to a candid world.

773

He has refused his assent to laws, the most wholesome and necessary for the public good.

He has forbidden his Governors to pass laws of immediate and pressing importance, unless suspended in their operation till his assent should be obtained; and when so suspended, he has utterly neglected to attend to them.

He has refused to pass other laws for the accommodation of large districts of people, unless those people would relinquish the right of representation in the legislature, a right inestimable to them and formidable to tyrants only.

He has called together legislative bodies at places unusual, uncomfortable, and distant from the depository of their public records, for the sole purpose of fatiguing them into compliance with his measures.

He has dissolved representative houses repeatedly, for opposing with manly firmness his invasions on the rights of the people.

He has refused for a long time, after such dissolutions, to cause others to be elected; whereby the legislative powers, incapable of annihilation, have returned to the people at large for their exercise; the State remaining in the meantime exposed to all the dangers of invasion from without and convulsions within.

He has endeavoured to prevent the population of these states; for that purpose obstructing the laws for naturalization of foreigners; refusing to pass others to encourage their migration hither, and raising the conditions of new appropriations of lands.

He has obstructed the administration of justice, by refusing his assent to laws for establishing judiciary powers.

He has made judges dependent on his will alone, for the tenure of their offices, and the amount and payment of their salaries.

He has erected a multitude of new offices, and sent hither swarms of officers to harass our people, and eat out their substance.

He has kept among us, in times of peace, standing armies without the consent of our legislatures.

He has affected to render the military independent of and superior to the civil power.

He has combined with others to subject us to a jurisdiction foreign of our constitution, and unacknowledged by our laws; giving his assent to their acts of pretended legislation:

For quartering large bodies of armed troops among us:

For protecting them, by a mock trial, from punishment for any murders which they should commit on the inhabitants of these States:

For cutting off our trade with all parts of the world:

For imposing taxes on us without our consent:

For depriving us in many cases of the benefits of trial by jury:

For transporting us beyond seas to be tried for pretended offences:

For abolishing the free system of English laws in a neighbouring Province, establishing therein an arbitrary government, and enlarging its boundaries so as to render it at once an example and fit instrument for introducing the same absolute rule into these Colonies:

For taking away our Charters, abolishing our most valuable laws, and altering fundamentally the forms of our governments:

For suspending our own legislatures, and declaring themselves invested with power to legislate for us in all cases whatsoever.

He has abdicated government here, by declaring us out of his protection and waging war against us.

He has plundered our seas, ravaged our coasts, burnt our towns, and destroyed the lives of our people.

He is at this time transporting large armies of foreign mercenaries to complete the works of death, desolation, and tyranny, already begun with circumstances of cruelty and perfidy scarcely paralleled in the most barbarous ages, and totally unworthy the head of a civilized nation.

He has constrained our fellow citizens taken captive on the high seas to bear arms against their country, to become the executioners of their friends and brethren, or to fall themselves by their hands.

He has excited domestic insurrections amongst us, and has endeavored to bring on the inhabitants of our frontiers, the merciless Indian savages, whose known rule of warfare, is an undistinguished destruction of all ages, sexes, and conditions.

In every stage of these oppressions we have petitioned for redress in the most humble terms: our repeated petitions have been answered only by repeated injury. A prince whose character is thus marked by every act which may define a tyrant is unfit to be the ruler of a free people.

Nor have we been wanting in attention to our British brethren. We have warned them from time to time of attempts by their legislature to extend an unwarrantable jurisdiction over us. We have reminded them of the circumstances of our emigration and settlement here. We have appealed to their native justice and magnanimity, and we have conjured them by the ties of our common kindred to disavow these usurpations, which would inevitably interrupt our connections and correspondence. They too have been deaf to the voice of justice and of consanguinity. We must, therefore, acquiesce in the necessity, which denounces our separation, and hold them, as we hold the rest of mankind, enemies in war, in peace friends.

We, therefore, the Representatives of the United States of America, in General Congress assembled, appealing to the Supreme Judge of the world for the rectitude of our intentions, do, in the name, and by authority of the good people of these Colonies, solemnly publish and declare, That these United Colonies are, and of right ought to be, Free and Independent States; that they are absolved from all allegiance to the British Crown, and that all political connection between them and the state of Great Britain, is and ought to be totally dissolved; and that as Free and Independent States, they have full power to levy war, conclude peace, contract alliances, establish commerce, and to do all other acts and things which Independent States may of right do. And for the support of this declaration, with a firm reliance on the protection of Divine Providence, we mutually pledge to each other our lives, our fortunes, and our sacred honor.

Suggestions for Discussion

1. What is the basis for Jefferson's belief that "all men are created equal"?

2. In the eighteenth century, the notion of the "divine right" of kings was still popular. How does Jefferson refute that notion?

3. Discuss the list of tyrannical actions which Jefferson attributes to the King of Great Britain. Account for the order in which he lists them.

4. This essay has been called a "model of clarity and precision." Explain your agreement with this statement. How does Jefferson balance strong feeling with logical argument?

Suggestion for Writing

Jefferson asserts that "all men are created equal," and yet he does not include black slaves as equals. In Jefferson's *Autobiography*, he wrote that a clause "reprobating the enslaving the inhabitants of Africa" was omitted in the final draft "in complaisance to South Carolina and Georgia." Was Jefferson merely opportunistic in agreeing to strike this clause? Write an essay in which you relate the ideas of the Declaration to the ideas in Lincoln's Gettysburg Address. Show how one set of ideas leads to the other.

The Declaration of the Rights of Man

Soon after the fall of the Bastille on July 14, 1789, a day celebrated in France as July 4th is celebrated in the United States, the National Assembly was asked to provide a declaration that would correspond to the American Declaration of Independence. The Assembly appointed a committee of five to draft the document. After several weeks of debate and compromise, the completed declaration was approved and proclaimed on August 27, 1789. An analysis of the Declaration shows that while a number of phrases resemble the American model, it derived more particularly from the English Bill of Rights of 1689. Ironically, the basis for democratic government embodied in this document was to be subverted by a leader of the new republic who would declare himself Emperor.

The representatives of the French people, gathered in the National Assembly, believing that ignorance, neglect, and disdain of the rights of men are the sole causes of public misfortunes and of the corruption of governments, have resolved to set forth, in solemn declaration, the natural, inalienable, and sacred rights of men, in order that this Declaration, held always before the members of the body social, will forever remind them of their rights and duties; that the acts of legislative and executive power, always identifiable with the ends and purposes of the whole body politic, may be more fully respected; that the complaints of citizens, founded henceforth on simple and incontrovertible principles, may be turned always to the maintaining of the Constitution and to the happiness of all.

The National assembly therefore recognizes and declares, in the presence and under the auspices of the Supreme Being, the following rights of Man and of citizen:

1. Men are born and will remain free and endowed with equal rights. Social distinctions can be based only upon usefulness to the common weal.

2. The end and purpose of all political groups is the preservation of the

natural and inalienable rights of Man. These rights are Liberty, the Possession of Property, Safety, and Resistance to Oppression.

3. The principle of all sovereignty will remain fundamentally in the State. No group and no individual can exercise authority which does not arise expressly from the State.

4. Liberty consists in being able to do anything which is not harmful to another or to others; therefore, the exercise of the natural rights of each individual has only such limits as will assure to other members of society the enjoyment of the same rights. These limits can be determined only by the Law.

5. The Law has the right to forbid only such actions as are harmful to society. Anything not forbidden by the Law can never be forbidden; and none can be forced to do what the Law does not prescribe.

6. The Law is the expression of the will of the people. All citizens have the right and the duty to concur in the formation of the Law, either in person or through their representatives. Whether it punishes or whether it protects, the Law must be the same for all. All citizens, being equal in the eyes of the Law, are to be admitted equally to all distinctions, ranks, and public employment, according to their capacities, and without any other discrimination than that established by their individual abilities and virtues.

7. No individual can be accused, arrested, or detained except in cases determined by the Law, and according to the forms which the Law has prescribed. Those who instigate, expedite, execute, or cause to be executed any arbitrary or extralegal prescriptions must be punished; but every citizen called or seized through the power of the Law must instantly obey. He will render himself culpable by resisting.

8. The Law should establish only those penalties which are absolutely and evidently necessary, and none can be punished except through the power of the Law, as already established and proclaimed for the public good and legally applied.

9. Every individual being presumed innocent until he has been proved guilty, if it is considered necessary to arrest him, the Law must repress with severity any force which is not required to secure his person.

10. None is to be persecuted for his opinions, even his religious beliefs, provided that his expression of them does not interfere with the order established by the Law.

11. Free communication of thought and opinion is one of the most precious rights of Man; therefore, every citizen can speak, write, or publish freely, except that he will be required to answer for the abuse of such freedom in cases determined by the Law.

12. The guarantee of the rights of Man and of the citizen makes necessary a Public Force and Administration; this Force and Administration has therefore been established for the good of all, and not for the particular benefit of those to whom it has been entrusted.

13. For the maintaining of this Public Force and Administration, and for the expense of administering it, a common tax is required; it must be distributed equally among the people, in accordance with their ability to pay.

14. All citizens have the right and duty to establish, by themselves or by their representatives, the requirements of a common tax, to consent to it

freely, to indicate its use, and to determine its quota, its assessment, its collection, and its duration.

15. Society has the right and duty to demand from every public servant an accounting of his administration.

16. No society in which the guarantee of rights is not assured nor the distinction of legal powers determined can be said to have a constitution.

17. The possession of property being an inviolable and sacred right, none can be deprived of it, unless public necessity, legally proved, clearly requires the deprivation, and then only on the necessary condition of a previously established just reparation.

Suggestions for Discussion

1. What is the major purpose of setting forth the principles enunciated in this declaration?

2. The declaration refers to a Supreme Being. Why did not the writers of the declaration refer simply to God?

3. How do the seventeen "rights of the Man and of the citizen" define the relationship between the individual person and the State?

4. How does the declaration define the function of the Law and of the State?

5. How does the declaration propose to guarantee freedom of speech?

6. Can you explain why the declaration says that the possession of property is an "inviolable and sacred right"? How does this statement basically differ from modern revolutionary thought?

7. On what principles is this declaration based?

Suggestions for Writing

1. Write an essay about the similarities to and differences from this declaration with the American Declaration of Independence and with the Bill of Rights of the American Constitution.

2. Examine the English Bill of Rights of 1689 and write an essay in which you explain the close relationship between the French and English declarations.

Seneca Falls Convention

Declaration of Sentiments and Resolutions, 1848

On July 19–20, 1848, between one and two hundred delegates (women and men) representing suffragist, abolitionist, and temperance groups met in Seneca Falls, New York, at a convention to discuss women's rights. The

Declaration of Sentiments and Resolutions was written by Elizabeth Cady Stanton and Lucretia Coffin Mott, assisted by the delegates present. The first major document that sought to define the issues and goals of the nineteenth-century women's movement, it was modeled after the Declaration of Independence in order to suggest the natural line of development from the American Revolution. Consequently, it stated women's demands for legal, political, economic, and social equality. The only resolution that created an objection was the one on women's suffrage, but after debate it too was included. Sixty-eight women and thirty-two men signed the declaration.

When, in the course of human events, it becomes necessary for one portion of the family of man to assume among the people of the earth a position different from that which they have hitherto occupied, but one to which the laws of nature and of nature's God entitle them, a decent respect to the opinions of mankind requires that they should declare the causes that impel them to such a course.

We hold these truths to be self-evident: that all men and women are created equal; that they are endowed by their Creator with certain inalienable rights; that among these are life, liberty, and the pursuit of happiness; that to secure these rights governments are instituted, deriving their just powers from the consent of the governed. Whenever any form of government becomes destructive of these ends, it is the right of those who suffer from it to refuse allegiance to it, and to insist upon the institution of a new government, laying its foundation on such principles, and organizing its powers in such form, as to them shall seem most likely to effect their safety and happiness. Prudence, indeed, will dictate that governments long established should not be changed for light and transient causes; and accordingly all experience hath shown that mankind are more disposed to suffer, while evils are sufferable, than to right themselves by abolishing the forms to which they were accustomed. But when a long train of abuses and usurpations, pursuing invariably the same object, evinces a design to reduce them under absolute despotism, it is their duty to throw off such government, and to provide new guards for their future security. Such has been the patient sufferance of the women under this government, and such is now the necessity which constrains them to demand the equal station to which they are entitled.

The history of mankind is a history of repeated injuries and usurpations on the part of man toward woman, having in direct object the establishment of an absolute tyranny over her. To prove this, let facts be submitted to a candid world.

He has never permitted her to exercise her inalienable right to the elective franchise.

He has compelled her to submit to laws, in the formation of which she had no voice.

He has withheld from her rights which are given to the most ignorant and degraded men—both natives and foreigners.

Having deprived her of this first right of a citizen, the elective franchise, thereby leaving her without representation in the halls of legislation, he has oppressed her on all sides.

He has made her, if married, in the eye of the law, civilly dead.

He has taken from her all right in property, even to the wages she earns.

He has made her, morally, an irresponsible being, as she can commit many crimes with impunity, provided they be done in the presence of her husband. In the covenant of marriage, she is compelled to promise obedience to her husband, he becoming to all intents and purposes, her master—the law giving him power to deprive her of her liberty, and to administer chastisement.

He has so framed the laws of divorce, as to what shall be the proper causes, and in case of separation, to whom the guardianship of the children shall be given, as to be wholly regardless of the happiness of women—the law, in all cases, going upon a false supposition of the supremacy of man, and giving all power into his hands.

After depriving her of all rights as a married woman, if single, and the owner of property, he has taxed her to support a government which recognizes her only when her property can be made profitable to it.

He has monopolized nearly all the profitable employments, and from those she is permitted to follow, she receives but a scanty remuneration. He closes against her all the avenues to wealth and distinction which he considers most honorable to himself. As a teacher of theology, medicine, or law, she is not known.

He has denied her the facilities for obtaining a thorough education, all colleges being closed against her.

He allows her in Church, as well as State, but a subordinate position, claiming Apostolic authority for her exclusion from the ministry, and, with some exceptions, from any public participation in the affairs of the Church.

He has created a false public sentiment by giving to the world a different code of morals for men and women, by which moral delinquencies which exclude women from society, are not only tolerated, but deemed of little account in man.

He has usurped the prerogative of Jehovah himself, claiming it as his right to assign for her a sphere of action, when that belongs to her conscience and to her God.

He has endeavored, in every way that he could, to destroy her confidence in her own powers, to lessen her self-respect, and to make her willing to lead a dependent and abject life.

Now, in view of this entire disfranchisement of one-half the people of this country, their social and religious degradation—in view of the unjust laws above mentioned, and because women do feel themselves aggrieved, oppressed, and fraudulently deprived of their most sacred rights, we insist that they have immediate admission to all the rights and privileges which belong to them as citizens of the United States.

In entering upon the great work before us, we anticipate no small amount of misconception, misrepresentation, and ridicule; but we shall use every instrumentality within our power to effect our object. We shall employ agents, circulate tracts, petition the State and National legislatures, and endeavor to enlist the pulpit and the press in our behalf. We hope this Convention will be followed by a series of Conventions embracing every part of the country.

Whereas, The great precept of nature is conceded to be, that "man shall pursue his own true and substantial happiness." Blackstone in his Commentaries remarks, that this law of Nature being coeval with mankind, and dictated by God himself, is of course superior in obligation to any other. It is binding over all the globe, in all countries and at all times; no human laws are of any validity if contrary to this, and such of them as are valid, derive all their force, and all their validity, and all their authority, mediately and immediately, from this original; therefore,

Resolved, That such laws as conflict, in any way, with the true and substantial happiness of woman, are contrary to the great precept of nature and of no validity, for this is "superior in obligation to any other."

Resolved, That all laws which prevent woman from occupying such a station in society as her conscience shall dictate, or which place her in a position inferior to that of man, are contrary to the great precept of nature, and therefore of no force or authority.

Resolved, That woman is man's equal—was intended to be so by the Creator, and the highest good of the race demands that she should be recognized as such.

Resolved, That the women of this country ought to be enlightened in regard to the laws under which they live, that they may no longer publish their degradation by declaring themselves satisfied with their present position, nor their ignorance, by asserting that they have all the rights they want.

Resolved, That inasmuch as man, while claiming for himself intellectual superiority, does accord to woman moral superiority, it is pre-eminently his duty to encourage her to speak and teach, as she has an opportunity, in all religious assemblies.

Resolved, That the same amount of virtue, delicacy, and refinement of behavior that is required of woman in the social state, should also be required of man, and the same transgressions should be visited with equal severity on both man and woman.

Resolved, That the objection of indelicacy and impropriety, which is so often brought against woman when she addresses a public audience, comes with a very ill-grace from those who encourage, by their attendance, her appearance on the stage, in the concert, or in feats of the circus.

Resolved, That woman has too long rested satisfied in the circumscribed limits which corrupt customs and a perverted application of the Scriptures have marked out for her, and that it is time she should move in the enlarged sphere which her great Creator has assigned her.

Resolved, That it is the duty of the women of this country to secure to themselves their sacred right to the elective franchise.

Resolved, That the equality of human rights results necessarily from the fact of the identity of the race in capabilities and responsibilities.

Resolved, therefore, That, being invested by the Creator with the same capabilities, and the same consciousness of responsibility for their exercise, it is demonstrably the right and duty of woman, equally with man, to promote every righteous cause by every righteous means; and especially in regard to the great subjects of morals and religion, it is self-evidently her right to participate with her brother in teaching them, both in private and in public, by writing and by speaking, by any instrumentalities proper to be used, and in any assemblies proper to be held; and this being a self-evident truth growing out of the divinely implanted principles of human nature, any custom or authority adverse to it, whether modern or wearing the hoary sanction of antiquity, is to be regarded as a self-evident falsehood, and at war with mankind.

Resolved, That the speedy success of our cause depends upon the zealous and untiring efforts of both men and women, for the overthrow of the monopoly of the pulpit, and for the securing to woman an equal participation with men in the various trades, professions, and commerce.

Suggestions for Discussion

1. Compare the Declaration of Independence with the Seneca Falls Declaration and discuss their parallel structure. Note particularly the basis, the "whereas" statement, for the resolution that follows.

2. Examine and discuss the preliminary list of grievances that lead to the need for the resolutions.

3. How might a contemporary declaration on the rights of women differ from this one? What other resolutions might appear at a similar convention today?

4. Why was there objection to women's suffrage?

5. The convention was attended by abolitionists and members of the temperance movement. How were these causes compatible with a convention on women's rights?

Suggestions for Writing

1. Write a paper comparing the Declaration of Independence with the Seneca Falls Declaration. What was missing from the first of these declarations?

2. Write a paper in which you discuss how a contemporary convention might stress different grievances. Be specific. Try to write some contemporary resolutions.

Abraham Lincoln

The Gettysburg Address

Abraham Lincoln (1809–1865), the sixteenth President of the United States, is generally regarded, along with Thomas Jefferson, as one of the greatest American prose stylists. On November 19, 1863, he traveled to Gettysburg in southern Pennsylvania to dedicate the cemetery for the soldiers killed there the previous July. The simple words he composed form the most famous speech ever delivered in America. A close reading reveals why it continues to live for Americans today.

Four score and seven years ago our fathers brought forth on this continent, a new nation, conceived in Liberty, and dedicated to the proposition that all men are created equal.

Now we are engaged in a great civil war, testing whether that nation, or any nation so conceived and so dedicated, can long endure. We are met on a great battlefield of that war. We have come to dedicate a portion of that field, as a final resting place for those who here gave their lives that that nation might live. It is altogether fitting and proper that we should do this.

But, in a larger sense, we can not dedicate—we can not consecrate—we can not hallow—this ground. The brave men, living and dead, who struggled here, have consecrated it, far above our poor power to add or detract. The world will little note nor long remember what we say here, but it can never forget what they did here. It is for us the living, rather, to be dedicated here to the unfinished work which they who fought here have thus far so nobly advanced. It is rather for us to be here dedicated to the great task remaining before us—that from these honored dead we take increased devotion to that cause for which they gave the last full measure of devotion—that we here highly resolve that these dead shall not have died in vain—that this nation, under God, shall have a new birth of freedom—and that government of the people, by the people, for the people, shall not perish from the earth.

Suggestions for Discussion

1. How is the proposition "that all men are created equal" related to the issues of the Civil War?

2. Why does Lincoln not simply begin his essay "Eighty-seven years ago"? What would he lose in tone if he had done so?

3. In paragraph three, Lincoln says "The world will little note, nor long remember what we say here." How do you account for the fact that he was wrong? Why did he make this statement? What function does it serve?

4. How does Lincoln use the verbs *dedicate, consecrate, hallow?* Could one easily change the order of these words?

5. How does Lincoln connect the first paragraph of his speech to the last?

6. What was the "unfinished work" of the soldiers who died at the Battle of Gettysburg?

Suggestion for Writing

Write an essay in which you relate the power of this speech to the simplicity of its language.

Niccolò Machiavelli

Of Cruelty and Clemency, and Whether It Is Better to Be Loved or Feared

Niccolò Machiavelli (1469–1527) was a Florentine statesman. His best-known work, The Prince, written in 1513, is an astute analysis of the contemporary political scene. The work was first translated into English in 1640.

This selection from *The Prince*, translated by Luigi Ricci and revised by E. R. P. Vincent, explains by examples from history why the prince must rely on the fear he creates rather than the love he might generate. Machiavelli explains also why the prince, though causing fear, must avoid incurring hatred.

Proceeding to the other qualities before named, I say that every prince must desire to be considered merciful and not cruel. He must, however, take care not to misuse this mercifulness. Cesare Borgia was considered cruel, but his cruelty had brought order to the Romagna, united it, and reduced it to peace and fealty. If this is considered well, it will be seen that he was really much more merciful than the Florentine people, who, to avoid the name of cruelty, allowed Pistoia to be destroyed. A prince, therefore, must not mind incurring the charge of cruelty for the purpose of keeping his subjects united and faithful; for, with a very few examples, he will be more merciful than those who, from excess of tenderness, allow disorders to arise, from whence spring bloodshed and rapine; for these as a rule injure the whole community, while the executions carried out by the prince injure only individuals. And of all princes, it is impossible for a new prince to escape the reputation of cruelty, new states being always full of dangers. Wherefore Virgil through the mouth of Dido says:

Res dura, et regni novitas me talia cogunt
Moliri, et late fines custode tueri.*

Nevertheless, he must be cautious in believing and acting, and must not be afraid of his own shadow, and must proceed in a temperate manner with prudence and humanity, so that too much confidence does not render him incautious, and too much diffidence does not render him intolerant.

From this arises the question whether it is better to be loved more than feared, or feared more than loved. The reply is, that one ought to be both feared and loved, but as it is difficult for the two to go together, it is much safer to be feared than loved, if one of the two has to be wanting. For it may be said of men in general that they are ungrateful, voluble dissemblers, anxious to avoid danger, and covetous of gain; as long as you benefit them, they are entirely yours; they offer you their blood, their goods, their life, and their children, as I have before said, when the necessity is remote; but when it approaches, they revolt. And the prince who has relied solely on their words, without making other preparations, is ruined; for the friendship which is gained by purchase and not through grandeur and nobility of spirit is bought but not secured, and at a pinch is not to be expended in your service. And men have less scruple in offending one who makes himself loved than one who makes himself feared; for love is held by a chain of obligation which, men being selfish, is broken whenever it serves their purpose; but fear is maintained by a dread of punishment which never fails.

Still, a prince should make himself feared in such a way that if he does not gain love, he at any rate avoids hatred; for fear and the absence of hatred may

*Our harsh situation and the newness of our kingdom compel me to contrive such measures and to guard our territory far and wide. (Dido offers this explanation to the newly landed Trojans of why her guards received them with hostile and suspicious measures.)

well go together, and will be always attained by one who abstains from inter-
fering with the property of his citizens and subjects or with their women.
And when he is obliged to take the life of anyone, let him do so when there is
proper justification and manifest reason for it; but above all he must abstain
from taking the property of others, for men forget more easily the death of
their father than the loss of their patrimony. Then also pretexts for seizing
property are never wanting, and one who begins to live by rapine will always
find some reason for taking the goods of others, whereas causes for taking life
are rarer and more fleeting.

But when the prince is with his army and has a large number of soldiers
under his control, then it is extremely necessary that he should not mind
being thought cruel; for without this reputation he could not keep an army
united or disposed to any duty. Among the noteworthy actions of Hannibal is
numbered this, that although he had an enormous army, composed of men of
all nations and fighting in foreign countries, there never arose any dissension
either among them or against the prince, either in good fortune or in bad.
This could not be due to anything but his inhuman cruelty, which together
with his infinite other virtues, made him always venerated and terrible in the
sight of his soldiers, and without it his other virtues would not have sufficed
to produce that effect. Thoughtless writers admire on the one hand his actions, and on the other blame the principal cause of them.

And that it is true that his other virtues would not have sufficed may be
seen from the case of Scipio (famous not only in regard to his own times, but
all times of which memory remains), whose armies rebelled against him in
Spain, which arose from nothing but his excessive kindness, which allowed
more licence to the soldiers than was consonant with military discipline. He
was reproached with this in the senate by Fabius Maximus, who called him a
corrupter of the Roman militia. Locri having been destroyed by one of Scipio's officers was not revenged by him, nor was the insolence of that officer
punished, simply by reason of his easy nature; so much so, that some one
wishing to excuse him in the senate, said that there were many men who
knew rather how not to err, than how to correct the errors of others. This
disposition would in time have tarnished the fame and glory of Scipio had he
persevered in it under the empire, but living under the rule of the senate
this harmful quality was not only concealed but became a glory to him.

I conclude, therefore, with regard to being feared and loved, that men love
at their own free will, but fear at the will of the prince, and that a wise prince
must rely on what is in his power and not on what is in the power of others,
and he must only contrive to avoid incurring hatred, as has been explained.

Suggestions for Discussion

1. How does Machiavelli show that Cesare Borgia, known for his cruelty, was more
   merciful than the people of Florence?

2. Explain the use of the quotation from Virgil.

3. Explain Machiavelli's argument that the prince cannot rely on the love of his subjects.

4. What attitudes does Machiavelli express when he says that "men forget more easily
   the death of their father than the loss of their patrimony"?

5. Compare and contrast the actions of Scipio and Hannibal. How does Machiavelli explain their actions to prove his point about the need of the prince to inspire fear?

Suggestion for Writing

Write an essay in which you comment on the ideas in this selection which may be brilliant but not admirable. What aspects of life does the author ignore? Why? Why does this selection not express the concern for freedom and human dignity that characterizes most of the selections in this section?

Martin Luther King, Jr.

Letter from Birmingham Jail

Martin Luther King, Jr. (1929–1968), more than twenty-five years after his death by assassination in Memphis, remains the most charismatic leader of the civil rights movement of the 1950s and 1960s. He led sit-ins and demonstrations throughout the South and was founder and president of the Southern Christian Leadership Conference, leader of the 1963 March on Washington, as well as pastor of a large Baptist congregation in Atlanta. King followed the principles of Gandhi and Thoreau in all of his public actions and writings. In 1964 he received the Nobel Peace Prize. His writings include *Strength to Love* (1963) and *Conscience for Change* (1967). The occasion for "Letter from Birmingham Jail" was provided by a public statement by eight Alabama clergymen calling on civil rights leaders to abandon the public demonstrations in Birmingham and press their claims for justice in the courts. The letter, revised and published in *Why We Can't Wait* (1964), is printed here in its original form. King began to write it on the margins of the newspaper in which the public statement by the eight Alabama clergymen appeared. That statement is also printed here.

Public Statement by Eight Alabama Clergymen

(April 12, 1963)

We the undersigned clergymen are among those who, in January, issued "An Appeal for Law and Order and Common Sense," in dealing with racial problems in Alabama. We expressed understanding that honest convictions in racial matters could properly be pursued in the courts, but urged that decisions of those courts should in the meantime be peacefully obeyed.

Since that time there had been some evidence of increased forbearance and a willingness to face facts. Responsible citizens have undertaken to work on various problems which cause racial friction and unrest. In Birmingham, recent public events have given indication that we all have opportunity for a new constructive and realistic approach to racial problems.

However, we are now confronted by a series of demonstrations by some of our Negro citizens, directed and led in part by outsiders. We recognize the natural impatience of people who feel that their hopes are slow in being realized. But we are convinced that these demonstrations are unwise and untimely.

We agree rather with certain local Negro leadership which has called for honest and open negotiation of racial issues in our area. And we believe this kind of facing of issues can best be accomplished by citizens of our own metropolitan area, white and Negro, meeting with their knowledge and experience of the local situation. All of us need to face that responsibility and find proper channels for its accomplishment.

Just as we formerly pointed out that "hatred and violence have no sanction in our religious and political traditions," we also point out that such actions as incite to hatred and violence, however technically peaceful those actions may be, have not contributed to the resolution of our local problems. We do not believe that these days of new hope are days when extreme measures are justified in Birmingham.

We commend the community as a whole, and the local news media and law enforcement officials in particular, on the calm manner in which these demonstrations have been handled. We urge the public to continue to show restraint should the demonstrations continue, and the law enforcement officials to remain calm and continue to protect our city from violence.

We further strongly urge our own Negro community to withdraw support from these demonstrations, and to unite locally in working peacefully for a better Birmingham. When rights are consistently denied, a cause should be pressed in the courts and in negotiations among local leaders, and not in the streets. We appeal to both our white and Negro citizenry to observe the principles of law and order and common sense.

Signed by:

C. C. J. CARPENTER, D.D., LL.D., Bishop of Alabama
JOSEPH A. DURICK, D.D., Auxiliary Bishop, Diocese of Mobile, Birmingham
Rabbi MILTON L. GRAFMAN, Temple Emanu-El, Birmingham, Alabama
Bishop PAUL HARDIN, Bishop of the Alabama-West Florida Conference of the Methodist Church
Bishop NOLAN B. HARMON, Bishop of the North Alabama Conference of the Methodist Church
GEORGE M. MURRAY, D.D., LL.D., Bishop Coadjutor, Episcopal Diocese of Alabama
EDWARD V. RAMAGE, Moderator, Synod of the Alabama Presbyterian Church in the United States
EARL STALLINGS, Pastor, First Baptist Church, Birmingham, Alabama

Letter from Birmingham Jail

MARTIN LUTHER KING, JR.
Birmingham City Jail
April 16, 1963

Bishop C. C. J. CARPENTER
Bishop JOSEPH A. DURICK
Rabbi MILTON L. GRAFMAN
Bishop PAUL HARDIN
Bishop NOLAN B. HARMON
The Rev. GEORGE M. MURRAY
The Rev. EDWARD V. RAMAGE
The Rev. EARL STALLINGS

My dear Fellow Clergymen,

While confined here in the Birmingham City Jail, I came across your recent statement calling our present activities "unwise and untimely." Seldom, if ever, do I pause to answer criticism of my work and ideas. If I sought to answer all of the criticisms that cross my desk, my secretaries would be engaged in little else in the course of the day and I would have no time for constructive work. But since I feel that you are men of genuine good will and your criticisms are sincerely set forth, I would like to answer your statement in what I hope will be patient and reasonable terms.

I think I should give the reason for my being in Birmingham, since you have been influenced by the argument of "outsiders coming in." I have the honor of serving as president of the Southern Christian Leadership Conference, an organization operating in every Southern state with headquarters in Atlanta, Georgia. We have some eighty-five affiliate organizations all across the South—one being the Alabama Christian Movement for Human Rights. Whenever necessary and possible we share staff, educational, and financial resources with our affiliates. Several months ago our local affiliate here in Birmingham invited us to be on call to engage in a nonviolent direct action program if such were deemed necessary. We readily consented and when the hour came we lived up to our promises. So I am here, along with several members of my staff, because we were invited here. I am here because I have basic organizational ties here. Beyond this, I am in Birmingham because injustice is here. Just as the eighth century prophets left their little villages and carried their "thus saith the Lord" far beyond the boundaries of their home town, and just as the Apostle Paul left his little village of Tarsus and carried the gospel of Jesus Christ to practically every hamlet and city of the Graeco-Roman world, I too am compelled to carry the gospel of freedom beyond my particular home town. Like Paul, I must constantly respond to the Macedonian call for aid.

Moreover, I am cognizant of the interrelatedness of all communities and states. I cannot sit idly by in Atlanta and not be concerned about what happens in Birmingham. Injustice anywhere is a threat to justice everywhere. We are caught in an inescapable network of mutuality tied in a single garment of destiny. Whatever affects one directly affects all indirectly. Never again can we afford to live with the narrow, provincial "outside agitator" idea. Anyone who lives inside the United States can never be considered an outsider anywhere in this country.

You deplore the demonstrations that are presently taking place in Birmingham. But I am sorry that your statement did not express a similar concern for the conditions that brought the demonstrations into being. I am sure that each of you would want to go beyond the superficial social analyst who looks merely at effects, and does not grapple with underlying causes. I would not hesitate to say that it is unfortunate that so-called demonstrations are taking place in Birmingham at this time, but I would say in more emphatic terms that it is even more unfortunate that the white power structure of this city left the Negro community with no other alternative.

In any nonviolent campaign there are four basic steps: (1) collection of the facts to determine whether injustices are alive; (2) negotiation; (3) self-purification; and (4) direct action. We have gone through all of these steps in Birmingham. There can be no gainsaying of the fact that racial injustice engulfs this community. Birmingham is probably the most thoroughly segregated city in the United States. Its ugly record of police brutality is known in every section of this country. Its unjust treatment of Negroes in the courts is a notorious reality. There have been more unsolved bombings of Negro homes and churches in Birmingham than any city in this nation. These are the hard, brutal, and unbelievable facts. On the basis of these conditions Negro leaders sought to negotiate with the city fathers. But the political leaders consistently refused to engage in good faith negotiation.

Then came the opportunity last September to talk with some of the leaders of the economic community. In these negotiating sessions certain promises were made by the merchants—such as the promise to remove the humiliating racial signs from the stores. On the basis of these promises Rev. Shuttlesworth and the leaders of the Alabama Christian Movement for Human Rights agreed to call a moratorium on any type of demonstrations. As the weeks and months unfolded we realized that we were the victims of a broken promise. The signs remained. As in so many experiences of the past we were confronted with blasted hopes, and the dark shadow of a deep disappointment settled upon us. So we had no alternative except that of preparing for direct action, whereby we would present our very bodies as a means of laying our case before the conscience of the local and national community. We were not unmindful of the difficulties involved. So we decided to go through a process of self-purification. We started having workshops on nonviolence and repeatedly asked ourselves the questions, "Are you able to accept blows without retaliating?" "Are you able to endure the ordeals of jail?"

We decided to set our direct action program around the Easter season, realizing that with the exception of Christmas, this was the largest shopping period of the year. Knowing that a strong economic withdrawal program would be the by-product of direct action, we felt that this was the best time to bring pressure on the merchants for the needed changes. Then it occurred to us that the March election was ahead, and so we speedily decided to postpone action until after election day. When we discovered that Mr. Connor was in the run-off, we decided again to postpone so that the demonstrations could not be used to cloud the issues. At this time we agreed to begin our nonviolent witness the day after the run-off.

This reveals that we did not move irresponsibly into direct action. We too wanted to see Mr. Connor defeated; so we went through postponement after postponement to aid in this community need. After this we felt that direct action could be delayed no longer.

You may well ask, "Why direct action? Why sit-ins, marches, etc.? Isn't negotiation a better path?" You are exactly right in your call for negotiation. Indeed, this is the purpose of direct action. Nonviolent direct action seeks to create such a crisis and establish such creative tension that a community that has constantly refused to negotiate is forced to confront the issue. It seeks so to dramatize the issue that it can no longer be ignored. I just referred to the creation of tension as a part of the work of the nonviolent resister. This may sound rather shocking. But I must confess that I am not afraid of the word tension. I have earnestly worked and preached against violent tension, but there is a type of constructive nonviolent tension that is necessary for growth. Just as Socrates felt that it was necessary to create a tension in the mind so that individuals could rise from the bondage of myths and half-truths to the unfettered realm of creative analysis and objective appraisal, we must see the need of having nonviolent gadflies to create the kind of tension in society that will help men rise from the dark depths of prejudice and racism to the majestic heights of understanding and brotherhood. So the purpose of the direct action is to create a situation so crisis-packed that it will inevitably open the door to negotiation. We, therefore, concur with you in your call for negotiation. Too long has our beloved Southland been bogged down in the tragic attempt to live in monologue rather than dialogue.

One of the basic points in your statement is that our acts are untimely. Some have asked, "Why didn't you give the new administration time to act?" The only answer that I can give to this inquiry is that the new administration must be prodded about as much as the outgoing one before it acts. We will be sadly mistaken if we feel that the election of Mr. Boutwell will bring the millennium to Birmingham. While Mr. Boutwell is much more articulate and gentle than Mr. Connor, they are both segregationists dedicated to the task of maintaining the status quo. The hope I see in Mr. Boutwell is that he will be reasonable enough to see the futility of massive resistance to desegregation. But he will not see this without pressure from the devotees of civil rights. My friends, I must say to you that we have not made a single gain in civil rights without determined legal and nonviolent pressure. History is the long and tragic story of the fact that privileged groups seldom give up their privileges voluntarily. Individuals may see the moral light and voluntarily give up their unjust posture; but as Reinhold Niebuhr has reminded us, groups are more immoral than individuals.

We know through painful experience that freedom is never voluntarily given by the oppressor; it must be demanded by the oppressed. Frankly I have never yet engaged in a direct action movement that was "well timed," according to the timetable of those who have not suffered unduly from the disease of segregation. For years now I have heard the word "Wait!" It rings in the ear of every Negro with a piercing familiarity. This "wait" has almost always meant "never." It has been a tranquilizing thalidomide, relieving the emotional stress for a moment, only to give birth to an ill-formed infant of frustration. We must come to see with the distinguished jurist of yesterday that "justice too long delayed is justice denied." We have waited for more than three hundred and forty years for our constitutional and God-given rights. The nations of Asia and Africa are moving with jet-like speed toward the goal of political independence, and we still creep at horse and buggy pace toward the gaining of a cup of coffee at a lunch counter.

I guess it is easy for those who have never felt the stinging darts of segregation to say wait. But when you have seen vicious mobs lynch your mothers and fathers at will and drown your sisters and brothers at whim; when you have seen hate filled policemen curse, kick, brutalize, and even kill your black brothers and sisters with impunity; when you see the vast majority of your twenty million Negro brothers smothering in an air-tight cage of poverty in the midst of an affluent society; when you suddenly find your tongue twisted and your speech stammering as you seek to explain to your six-year-old daughter why she can't go to the public amusement park that has just been advertised on television, and see tears welling up in her little eyes when she is told that Funtown is closed to colored children, and see the depressing clouds of inferiority begin to form in her little mental sky, and see her begin to distort her little personality by unconsciously developing a bitterness toward white people; when you have to concoct an answer for a five-year-old son asking in agonizing pathos: "Daddy, why do white people treat colored people so mean?"; when you take a cross country drive and find it necessary to sleep night after night in the uncomfortable corners of your automobile because no motel will accept you; when you are humiliated day in and day out by nagging signs reading "white" men and "colored"; when your first name becomes "nigger" and your middle name becomes "boy" (however old you are) and your last name becomes "John," and when your wife and mother are never given the respected title "Mrs."; when you are harried by day and haunted by night by the fact that you are a Negro, living constantly at tip-toe stance never quite knowing what to expect next, and plagued with inner fears and outer resentments; when you are forever fighting a degenerating sense of "nobodiness";—then you will understand why we find it difficult to wait. There comes a time when the cup of endurance runs over, and men are no longer willing to be plunged into an abyss of injustice where they experience the bleakness of corroding despair. I hope, sirs, you can understand our legitimate and unavoidable impatience.

You express a great deal of anxiety over our willingness to break laws. This is certainly a legitimate concern. Since we so diligently urge people to obey the Supreme Court's decision of 1954 outlawing segregation in the public schools, it is rather strange and paradoxical to find us consciously breaking laws. One may well ask, "How can you advocate breaking some laws and obeying others?" The answer is found in the fact that there are two types of laws. There are *just* laws and there are *unjust* laws. I would be the first to advocate obeying just laws. One has not only a legal but moral responsibility to obey just laws. Conversely, one has a moral responsibility to disobey unjust laws. I would agree with Saint Augustine that "An unjust law is no law at all."

Now what is the difference between the two? How does one determine when a law is just or unjust? A just law is a man-made code that squares with the moral law or the law of God. An unjust law is a code that is out of harmony with the moral law. To put it in the terms of Saint Thomas Aquinas, an unjust law is a human law that is not rooted in eternal and natural law. Any law that uplifts human personality is just. Any law that degrades human personality is unjust. All segregation statutes are unjust because segregation distorts the soul and damages the personality. It gives the segregator a false sense of superiority and the segregated a false sense of inferiority. To use the words of Martin Buber, the great Jewish philosopher, segregation substitutes an "I-it" relationship for the "I-thou" relationship, and ends up relegating persons to the status of things. So segregation is not only politically, economically, and sociologically unsound, but it is morally wrong and sinful. Paul Tillich has said that sin is separation. Isn't segregation an existential expression of man's tragic separation, an expression of his awful estrangement, his terrible sinfulness? So I can urge men to obey the 1954 decision of the Supreme Court because it is morally right, and I can urge them to disobey segregation ordinances because they are morally wrong.

Let us turn to a more concrete example of just and unjust laws. An unjust law is a code that a majority inflicts on a minority that is not binding on itself. This is *difference* made legal. On the other hand a just law is a code that a majority compels a minority to follow that it is willing to follow itself. This is *sameness* made legal.

Let me give another explanation. An unjust law is a code inflicted upon a minority which that minority had no part in enacting or creating because they did not have the unhampered right to vote. Who can say the legislature of

Alabama which set up the segregation laws was democratically elected? Throughout the state of Alabama all types of conniving methods are used to prevent Negroes from becoming registered voters and there are some counties without a single Negro registered to vote despite the fact that the Negro constitutes a majority of the population. Can any law set up in such a state be considered democratically structured?

These are just a few examples of unjust and just laws. There are some instances when a law is just on its face but unjust in its application. For instance, I was arrested Friday on a charge of parading without a permit. Now there is nothing wrong with an ordinance which requires a permit for a parade, but when the ordinance is used to preserve segregation and to deny citizens the First Amendment privilege of peaceful assembly and peaceful protest, then it becomes unjust.

I hope you can see the distinction I am trying to point out. In no sense do I advocate evading or defying the law as the rabid segregationist would do. This would lead to anarchy. One who breaks an unjust law must do it *openly, lovingly* (not hatefully as the white mothers did in New Orleans when they were seen on television screaming "nigger, nigger, nigger") and with a willingness to accept the penalty. I submit that an individual who breaks a law that conscience tells him is unjust, and willingly accepts the penalty by staying in jail to arouse the conscience of the community over its injustice, is in reality expressing the very highest respect for law.

Of course there is nothing new about this kind of civil disobedience. It was seen sublimely in the refusal of Shadrach, Meshach, and Abednego to obey the laws of Nebuchadnezzar because a higher moral law was involved. It was practiced superbly by the early Christians who were willing to face hungry lions and the excruciating pain of chopping blocks, before submitting to certain unjust laws of the Roman Empire. To a degree academic freedom is a reality today because Socrates practiced civil disobedience.

We can never forget that everything Hitler did in Germany was "legal" and everything the Hungarian freedom fighters did in Hungary was "illegal." It was "illegal" to aid and comfort a Jew in Hitler's Germany. But I am sure that, if I had lived in Germany during that time, I would have aided and comforted my Jewish brothers even though it was illegal. If I lived in a communist country today where certain principles dear to the Christian faith are suppressed, I believe I would openly advocate disobeying those antireligious laws.

I must make two honest confessions to you, my Christian and Jewish brothers. First I must confess that over the last few years I have been gravely disappointed with the white moderate. I have almost reached the regrettable conclusion that the Negroes' great stumbling block in the stride toward freedom is not the White Citizens' "Counciler" or the Ku Klux Klanner, but the white moderate who is more devoted to "order" than to justice; who prefers a negative peace which is the absence of tension to a positive peace which is the presence of justice; who constantly says "I agree with you in the goal you seek, but I can't agree with your methods of direct action"; who paternalistically feels that he can set the timetable for another man's freedom; who lives by the myth of time and who constantly advises the Negro to wait until a "more convenient season." Shallow understanding from people of good will is more frustrating than absolute misunderstanding from people of ill will. Lukewarm acceptance is much more bewildering than outright rejection.

I had hoped that the white moderate would understand that law and order exist for the purpose of establishing justice, and that when they fail to do this they become the dangerously structured dams that block the flow of social progress. I had hoped that the white moderate would understand that the present tension in the South is merely a necessary phase of the transition from an obnoxious negative peace, where the Negro passively accepted his unjust plight, to a substance-filled positive peace, where all men will respect the dignity and worth of human personality. Actually, we who engage in nonviolent direct action are not the creators of tension. We merely bring to the surface the hidden tension that is already alive. We bring it out in the open where it can be seen and dealt with. Like a boil that can never be cured as long as it is covered up but must be opened with all its pus-flowing ugliness to the natural medicines of air and light, injustice must likewise be exposed, with all of the tension its exposing creates, to the light of human conscience and the air of national opinion before it can be cured.

In your statement you asserted that our actions, even though peaceful, must be condemned because they precipitate violence. But can this assertion be logically made? Isn't this like condemning the robbed man because his possession of money precipitated the evil act of robbery? Isn't this like condemning Socrates because his unswerving commitment to truth and his philosophical delvings precipitated the misguided popular mind to make him drink the hemlock? Isn't this like condemning Jesus because His unique God consciousness and never-ceasing devotion to His will precipitated the evil act of crucifixion? We must come to see, as federal courts have consistently affirmed, that it is immoral to urge an individual to withdraw his efforts to gain his basic constitutional rights because the quest precipitates violence. Society must protect the robbed and punish the robber.

I had also hoped that the white moderate would reject the myth of time. I received a letter this morning from a white brother in Texas which said: "All Christians know that the colored people will receive equal rights eventually, but is it possible that you are in too great of a religious hurry? It has taken Christianity almost 2,000 years to accomplish what it has. The teachings of Christ take time to come to earth." All that is said here grows out of a tragic misconception of time. It is the strangely irrational notion that there is something in the very flow of time that will inevitably cure all ills. Actually time is neutral. It can be used either destructively or constructively. I am coming to feel that the people of ill will have used time much more effectively than the people of good will. We will have to repent in this generation not merely for the vitriolic words and actions of the bad people, but for the appalling silence of the good people. We must come to see that human progress never rolls in on wheels of inevitability. It comes through the tireless efforts and persistent work of men willing to be co-workers with God, and without this hard work time itself becomes an ally of the forces of social stagnation.

We must use time creatively, and forever realize that the time is always ripe to do right. Now is the time to make real the promise of democracy, and transform our pending national elegy into a creative psalm of brotherhood. Now is the time to lift our national policy from the quicksand of racial injustice to the solid rock of human dignity.

You spoke of our activity in Birmingham as extreme. At first I was rather disappointed that fellow clergymen would see my nonviolent efforts as those of the extremist. I started thinking about the fact that I stand in the middle of two opposing forces in the Negro community. One is a force of complacency made up of Negroes who, as a result of long years of oppression, have been so completely drained of self-respect and a sense of "somebodiness" that they have adjusted to segregation, and of a few Negroes in the middle class who, because of a degree of academic and economic security, and because at points they profit by segregation, have unconsciously become insensitive to the problems of the masses. The other force is one of bitterness and hatred and comes perilously close to advocating violence. It is expressed in the various black nationalist groups that are springing up over the nation, the largest and best known being Elijah Muhammad's Muslim movement. This movement is nourished by the contemporary frustration over the continued existence of racial discrimination. It is made up of people who have lost faith in America, who have absolutely repudiated Christianity, and who have concluded that the white man is an incurable "devil." I have tried to stand between these two forces saying that we need not follow the "do-nothingism" of the complacent or the hatred and despair of the black nationalist. There is the more excellent way of love and nonviolent protest. I'm grateful to God that, through the Negro church, the dimension of nonviolence entered our struggle. If this philosophy had not emerged I am convinced that by now many streets of the South would be flowing with floods of blood. And I am further convinced that if our white brothers dismiss us as "rabble rousers" and "outside agitators"—those of us who are working through the channels of nonviolent direct action—and refuse to support our nonviolent efforts, millions of Negroes, out of frustration and despair, will seek solace and security in black nationalist ideologies, a development that will lead inevitably to a frightening racial nightmare.

Oppressed people cannot remain oppressed forever. The urge for freedom will eventually come. This is what has happened to the American Negro. Something within has reminded him of his birthright of freedom; something without has reminded him that he can gain it. Consciously and unconsciously, he has been swept in by what the Germans call the *Zeitgeist*, and with his black brothers of Africa, and his brown and yellow brothers of Asia, South America, and the Caribbean, he is moving with a sense of cosmic urgency toward the promised land of racial justice. Recognizing this vital urge that has engulfed the Negro community, one should readily understand public demonstrations. The Negro has many pent-up resentments and latent frustrations. He has to get them out. So let him march sometime; let him have his prayer pilgrimages to the city hall; understand why he must have sit-ins and freedom rides. If his repressed emotions do not come out in these nonviolent ways, they will come out in ominous expressions of violence. This is not a threat; it is a fact of history. So I have not said to my people, "Get rid of your discontent." But I have tried to say that this normal and healthy discontent can be channeled through the creative outlet of nonviolent direct action. Now this approach is being dismissed as extremist. I must admit that I was initially disappointed in being so categorized.

But as I continued to think about the matter I gradually gained a bit of satisfaction from being considered an extremist. Was not Jesus an extremist in love? "Love your enemies, bless them that curse you, pray for them that despitefully use you." Was not Amos an extremist for justice—"Let justice roll down like waters and righteousness like a mighty stream." Was not Paul an extremist for the gospel of Jesus Christ—"I bear in my body the marks of the Lord Jesus." Was not Martin Luther an extremist—"Here I stand; I can do none other so help me God." Was not John Bunyan an extremist—"I will stay in jail to the end of my days before I make a butchery of my conscience." Was not Abraham Lincoln an extremist—"This nation cannot survive half slave and half free." Was not Thomas Jefferson an extremist—"We hold these truths to be self evident that all men are created equal." So the question is not whether we will be extremist but what kind of extremist will we be. Will we be extremists for hate or will we be extremists for love? Will we be extremists for the preservation of injustice—or will we be extremists for the cause of justice? In that dramatic scene on Calvary's hill three men were crucified. We must never forget that all three were crucified for the same crime—the crime of extremism. Two were extremists for immorality, and thus fell below their environment. The other, Jesus Christ, was an extremist for love, truth, and goodness, and thereby rose above His environment. So, after all, maybe the South, the nation, and the world are in dire need of creative extremists.

I had hoped that the white moderate would see this. Maybe I was too optimistic. Maybe I expected too much. I guess I should have realized that few members of a race that has oppressed another race can understand or appreciate the deep groans and passionate yearnings of those that have been oppressed, and still fewer have the vision to see that injustice must be rooted out by strong, persistent, and determined action. I am thankful, however, that some of our white brothers have grasped the meaning of this social revolution and committed themselves to it. They are still all too small in quantity, but they are big in quality. Some like Ralph McGill, Lillian Smith, Harry Golden, and James Dabbs have written about our struggle in eloquent, prophetic, and understanding terms. Others have marched with us down nameless streets of the South. They have languished in filthy, roach-infested jails, suffering the abuse and brutality of angry policemen who see them as "dirty nigger lovers." They, unlike so many of their moderate brothers and sisters, have recognized the urgency of the moment and sensed the need for powerful "action" antidotes to combat the disease of segregation.

Let me rush on to mention my other disappointment. I have been so greatly disappointed with the white Church and its leadership. Of course there are some notable exceptions. I am not unmindful of the fact that each of you has taken some significant stands on this issue. I commend you, Rev. Stallings, for your Christian stand on this past Sunday, in welcoming Negroes to your worship service on a nonsegregated basis. I commend the Catholic leaders of this state for integrating Springhill College several years ago.

But despite these notable exceptions I must honestly reiterate that I have been disappointed with the Church. I do not say that as one of those negative critics who can always find something wrong with the Church. I say it as a minister of the gospel, who loves the Church; who was nurtured in its bosom; who has been sustained by its spiritual blessings and who will remain true to it as long as the cord of life shall lengthen.

I had the strange feeling when I was suddenly catapulted into the leadership of the bus protest in Montgomery several years ago that we would have the support of the white Church. I felt that the white ministers, priests, and rabbis of the South would be some of our strongest allies. Instead, some have been outright opponents, refusing to understand the freedom movement and misrepresenting its leaders; all too many others have been more cautious than courageous and have remained silent behind the anesthetizing security of stained glass windows.

In spite of my shattered dreams of the past, I came to Birmingham with the hope that the white religious leadership of the community would see the justice of our cause and, with deep moral concern, serve as the channel through which our just grievances could get to the power structure. I had hoped that each of you would understand. But again I have been disappointed.

I have heard numerous religious leaders of the South call upon their worshippers to comply with a desegregation decision because it is the law, but I have longed to hear white ministers say follow this decree because integration is morally right and the Negro is your brother. In the midst of blatant injustices inflicted upon the Negro, I have watched white churches stand on the sideline and merely mouth pious irrelevancies and sanctimonious trivialities. In the midst of a mighty struggle to rid our nation of racial and economic injustice, I have heard so many ministers say, "Those are social issues with which the Gospel has no real concern," and I have watched so many churches commit themselves to a completely otherworldly religion which made a strange distinction between body and soul, the sacred and the secular.

So here we are moving toward the exit of the twentieth century with a
religious community largely adjusted to the status quo, standing as a tail light
behind other community agencies rather than a headlight leading men to
higher levels of justice.

I have travelled the length and breadth of Alabama, Mississippi, and all the
other Southern states. On sweltering summer days and crisp autumn mornings
I have looked at her beautiful churches with their spires pointing heavenward. I
have beheld the impressive outlay of her massive religious education
buildings. Over and over again I have found myself asking: "Who worships
here? Who is their God? Where were their voices when the lips of Governor
Barnett dripped with words of interposition and nullification? Where were they
when Governor Wallace gave the clarion call for defiance and hatred? Where
were their voices of support when tired, bruised, and weary Negro men and
women decided to rise from the dark dungeons of complacency to the bright
hills of creative protest?"

Yes, these questions are still in my mind. In deep disappointment, I have
wept over the laxity of the Church. But be assured that my tears have been
tears of love. There can be no deep disappointment where there is not deep
love. Yes, I love the Church; I love her sacred walls. How could I do otherwise?
I am in the rather unique position of being the son, the grandson, and the
great grandson of preachers. Yes, I see the Church as the body of Christ. But,
oh! How we have blemished and scarred that body through social neglect and
fear of being nonconformists.

There was a time when the Church was very powerful. It was during that
period when the early Christians rejoiced when they were deemed worthy to
suffer for what they believed. In those days the Church was not merely a
thermometer that recorded the ideas and principles of popular opinion; it was
a thermostat that transformed the mores of society. Wherever the early
Christians entered a town the power structure got disturbed and immediately
sought to convict them for being "disturbers of the peace" and "outside
agitators." But they went on with the conviction that they were a "colony of
heaven" and had to obey God rather than man. They were small in number but
big in commitment. They were too God-intoxicated to be "astronomically
intimidated." They brought an end to such ancient evils as infanticide and
gladiatorial contest.

Things are different now. The contemporary Church is so often a weak,
ineffectual voice with an uncertain sound. It is so often the archsupporter of
the status quo. Far from being disturbed by the presence of the Church, the
power structure of the average community is consoled by the Church's silent
and often vocal sanction of things as they are.

But the judgment of God is upon the Church as never before. If the Church
of today does not recapture the sacrificial spirit of the early Church, it will lose
its authentic ring, forfeit the loyalty of millions, and be dismissed as an
irrelevant social club with no meaning for the twentieth century. I am meeting
young people every day whose disappointment with the Church has risen to
outright disgust.

Maybe again I have been too optimistic. Is organized religion too
inextricably bound to the status quo to save our nation and the world? Maybe
I must turn my faith to the inner spiritual Church, the church within the
Church, as the true *ecclesia* and the hope of the world. But again I am thankful
to God that some noble souls from the ranks of organized religion have broken
loose from the paralyzing chains of conformity and joined us as active partners
in the struggle for freedom. They have left their secure congregations and
walked the streets of Albany, Georgia, with us. They have gone through the
highways of the South on torturous rides for freedom. Yes, they have gone to

jail with us. Some have been kicked out of their churches and lost the support of their bishops and fellow ministers. But they have gone with the faith that right defeated is stronger than evil triumphant. These men have been the leaven in the lump of the race. Their witness has been the spiritual salt that has preserved the true meaning of the Gospel in these troubled times. They have carved a tunnel of hope through the dark mountain of disappointment.

I hope the Church as a whole will meet the challenge of this decisive hour. But even if the Church does not come to the aid of justice, I have no despair about the future. I have no fear about the outcome of our struggle in Birmingham, even if our motives are presently misunderstood. We will reach the goal of freedom in Birmingham and all over the nation, because the goal of America is freedom. Abused and scorned though we may be, our destiny is tied up with the destiny of America. Before the pilgrims landed at Plymouth, we were here. Before the pen of Jefferson etched across the pages of history the majestic words of the Declaration of Independence, we were here. For more than two centuries our foreparents labored in this country without wages; they made cotton "king"; and they built the homes of their masters in the midst of brutal injustice and shameful humiliation—and yet out of a bottomless vitality they continued to thrive and develop. If the inexpressible cruelties of slavery could not stop us, the opposition we now face will surely fail. We will win our freedom because the sacred heritage of our nation and the eternal will of God are embodied in our echoing demands.

I must close now. But before closing I am impelled to mention one other point in your statement that troubled me profoundly. You warmly commended the Birmingham police force for keeping "order" and "preventing violence." I don't believe you would have so warmly commended the police force if you had seen its angry violent dogs literally biting six unarmed, nonviolent Negroes. I don't believe you would so quickly commend the policemen if you would observe their ugly and inhuman treatment of Negroes here in the city jail; if you would watch them push and curse old Negro women and young Negro girls; if you would see them slap and kick old Negro men and young Negro boys; if you will observe them, as they did on two occasions, refuse to give us food because we wanted to sing our grace together. I'm sorry that I can't join you in your praise for the police department.

It is true that they have been rather disciplined in their public handling of the demonstrators. In this sense they have been rather publicly "nonviolent." But for what purpose? To preserve the evil system of segregation. Over the last few years I have consistently preached that nonviolence demands that the means we use must be as pure as the ends we seek. So I have tried to make it clear that it is wrong to use immoral means to attain moral ends. But now I must affirm that it is just as wrong, or even more so, to use moral means to preserve immoral ends. Maybe Mr. Connor and his policemen have been rather publicly nonviolent, as Chief Pritchett was in Albany, Georgia, but they have used the moral means of nonviolence to maintain the immoral end of flagrant racial injustice. T. S. Eliot has said that there is no greater treason than to do the right deed for the wrong reason.

I wish you had commended the Negro sit-inners and demonstrators of Birmingham for their sublime courage, their willingness to suffer, and their amazing discipline in the midst of the most inhuman provocation. One day the South will recognize its real heroes. They will be the James Merediths, courageously and with a majestic sense of purpose, facing jeering and hostile mobs and the agonizing loneliness that characterizes the life of the pioneer. They will be old, oppressed, battered Negro women, symbolized in a seventy-two year old woman of Montgomery, Alabama, who rose up with a sense of dignity and with her people decided not to ride the segregated buses, and responded to one who inquired about her tiredness with ungrammatical profundity: "My feets is tired, but my soul is rested." They will be young high school and college students, young ministers of the gospel and a host of the elders, courageously and nonviolently sitting in at lunch counters and willingly going to jail for conscience sake. One day the South will know that when these disinherited children of God sat down at lunch counters they were in reality standing up for the best in the American dream and the most sacred values in our Judeo-Christian heritage, and thus carrying our whole nation back to great wells of democracy which were dug deep by the founding fathers in the formulation of the Constitution and the Declaration of Independence.

Never before have I written a letter this long (or should I say a book?). I'm afraid that it is much too long to take your precious time. I can assure you that it would have been much shorter if I had been writing from a comfortable desk, but what else is there to do when you are alone for days in the dull monotony of a narrow jail cell other than write long letters, think strange thoughts, and pray long prayers?

If I have said anything in this letter that is an overstatement of the truth and is indicative of an unreasonable impatience, I beg you to forgive me. If I have said anything in this letter that is an understatement of the truth and is indicative of my having a patience that makes me patient with anything less than brotherhood, I beg God to forgive me.

I hope this letter finds you strong in the faith. I also hope that circumstances will soon make it possible for me to meet each of you, not as an integrationist or a civil rights leader, but as a fellow clergyman and a Christian brother. Let us all hope that the dark clouds of racial prejudice will soon pass away and the deep fog of misunderstanding will be lifted from our fear-drenched communities and in some not too distant tomorrow the radiant stars of love and brotherhood will shine over our great nation with all of their scintillating beauty.

Yours for the cause of
Peace and Brotherhood
MARTIN LUTHER KING, JR.

Suggestions for Discussion

1. What is the rhetorical tone of King's letter? How does he achieve that tone? List and explain a half-dozen examples.

2. How does King deal with the eight clergymen's accusation that the demonstrators are "outsiders"?

3. In the letter King refers to a number of enemies of integration; for example, Eugene "Bull" Connor, Albert Bantwell, Ross R. Barnett, George C. Wallace, and Laurie Pritchett. Identify these people and explain their role in the fight against integration.

4. How does King answer the charge that his actions, though peaceful, are dangerous because they lead to violence?

5. What are King's objections to the white churches' response to the fight for integration? What are his objections to white moderates?

Suggestions for Writing

1. Write an essay in which you comment on King's statement: "I submit that an individual who breaks a law that conscience tells him is unjust, and willingly accepts

the penalty by staying in jail to arouse the conscience of the community over its injustice, is in reality expressing the very highest respect for the law."

2. Write a paper in which you explain King's use of the examples of Nazi Germany and Communist-controlled Hungary to defend his fight for civil rights.

3. Write a paper in which you agree or disagree with King's assessment of white moderates. Give explicit examples to support your position.

4. King calls his movement a viable alternative to black complacency, or acceptance of the status quo, and to the militant opposition of the black nationalists. Write a paper evaluating his assessment.

5. Write a paper in which you evaluate the civil rights movement of King's day in terms of the present. To what extent did his movement succeed? Fail?

William Faulkner

Nobel Prize Award Speech

William Faulkner (1897–1962) lived most of his life in Oxford, Mississippi. After a year at the university of his native state, he joined the Royal Canadian Air Force, eager to participate in World War I. His novels set in his imaginary Yoknapatawpha County include *The Sound and the Fury* (1929), *Light in August* (1932), *Absalom, Absalom!* (1936), and *The Hamlet* (1940). In his speech accepting the Nobel Prize for Literature in 1949, he states his belief in the significance and dignity of humankind and the need for the writer to reassert the universal truths of "love and honor and pity and pride and compassion and sacrifice."

I feel that this award was not made to me as a man but to my work—a life's work in the agony and sweat of the human spirit, not for glory and least of all for profit, but to create out of the materials of the human spirit something which did not exist before. So this award is only mine in trust. It will not be difficult to find a dedication for the money part of it commensurate with the purpose and significance of its origin. But I would like to do the same with the acclaim too, by using this moment as a pinnacle from which I might be listened to by the young men and women already dedicated to the same anguish and travail, among whom is already that one who will some day stand here where I am standing.

Our tragedy today is a general and universal physical fear so long sustained by now that we can even bear it. There are no longer problems of the spirit. There is only the question: When will I be blown up? Because of this, the young man or woman writing today has forgotten the problems of the human heart in conflict with itself which alone can make good writing because only that is worth writing about, worth the agony and the sweat.

He must learn them again. He must teach himself that the basest of all things is to be afraid; and, teaching himself that, forget it forever, leaving no room in his workshop for anything but the old verities and truths of the heart, the old universal truths lacking which any story is ephemeral and doomed—love and honor and pity and pride and compassion and sacrifice. Until he does so, he labors under a curse. He writes not of love but of lust, of defeats in which nobody loses anything of value, of victories without hope and, worst of all, without pity or compassion. His griefs grieve on no universal bones, leaving no scars. He writes not of the heart but of the glands.

Until he relearns these things, he will write as though he stood alone and watched the end of man. I decline to accept the end of man. It is easy enough to say that man is immortal simply because he will endure; that when the last ding-dong of doom has clanged and faded from the last worthless rock hanging tideless in the last red and dying evening, that even then there will still be one more sound: that of his puny inexhaustible voice, still talking. I refuse to accept this. I believe that man will not merely endure: he will prevail. He is immortal, not because he alone among creatures has an inexhaustible voice but because he has a soul, a spirit capable of compassion and sacrifice and endurance. The poet's, the writer's, duty is to write about these things. It is his privilege to help man endure by lifting his heart, by reminding him of the courage and honor and hope and pride and compassion and pity and sacrifice which have been the glory of his past. The poet's voice need not merely be the record of man, it can be one of the props, the pillars to help him endure and prevail.

Suggestions for Discussion

1. Do you agree with Faulkner's optimistic statement about man's ability to "endure and prevail"? Explain.

2. Do you think Faulkner's speech too brief for a major occasion such as the Nobel Prize Awards? Explain your answer.

3. Discuss whether or not man still lives in that state of general and universal physical fear to which Faulkner refers.

Suggestions for Writing

1. Summarize your own opinions about man's ability to survive the challenges of the next hundred years.

2. Prepare a formal speech in which you accept an international prize for literature or some other accomplishment.

Harriet Jacobs

The Women

Harriet Jacobs (1818–1896) describes the effects of Nat Turner's Rebellion in *Incidents in the Life of a Slave Girl* (1861). The following selection, from *Black Slave Narratives*, pinpoints with simple clarity the moral dilemmas that face a young female slave caught between her owner's desires and his wife's jealousy.

I would ten thousand times rather that my children should be the half-starved paupers of Ireland than to be the most pampered among the slaves of America. I would rather drudge out my life on a cotton plantation, till the grave opened to give me rest, than to live with an unprincipled master and a jealous mistress. The felon's home in a penitentiary is preferable. He may repent, and turn from the error of his ways, and so find peace, but it is not so with a favorite slave. She is not allowed to have any pride of character. It is deemed a crime in her to wish to be virtuous.

Mrs. Flint possessed the key to her husband's character before I was born. She might have used this knowledge to counsel and to screen the young and the innocent among her slaves; but for them she had no sympathy. They were the objects of her constant suspicion and malevolence. She watched her husband with unceasing vigilance; but he was well practiced in means to evade it. What he could not find opportunity to say in words he manifested in signs. He invented more than were ever thought of in a deaf and dumb asylum. I let them pass, as if I did not understand what he meant; and many were the curses and threats bestowed on me for my stupidity. One day he caught me teaching myself to write. He frowned, as if he was not well pleased; but I suppose he came to the conclusion that such an accomplishment might help to advance his favorite scheme. Before long, notes were often slipped into my hand. I would return them, saying, "I can't read them, sir." "Can't you?" he replied; "then I must read them to you." He always finished the reading by asking, "Do you understand?" Sometimes he would complain of the heat of the tea room, and order his supper to be placed on a small table in the piazza. He would seat himself there with a well-satisfied smile, and tell me to stand by and brush away the flies. He would eat very slowly, pausing between the mouthfuls. These intervals were employed in describing the happiness I was so foolishly throwing away, and in threatening me with the penalty that finally awaited my stubborn disobedience. He boasted much of the forbearance he had exercised toward me, and reminded me that there was a limit to his patience. When I succeeded in avoiding opportunities for him to talk to me at home, I was ordered to come to his office, to do some errand. When there, I was obliged to stand and listen to such language as he saw fit to address to me. Sometimes I so openly expressed my contempt for him that he would become violently enraged, and I wondered why he did not strike me. Circumstanced as he was, he probably thought it was better policy to be forebearing. But the state of things grew worse and worse daily. In desperation I told him that I must and would apply to my grandmother for protection. He threatened me with death, and worse than death, if I made my complaint to her. Strange to say, I did not despair. I was naturally of a buoyant disposition, and always I had a hope of somehow getting out of his clutches. Like many a poor, simple slave before me, I trusted that some threads of joy would yet be woven into my dark destiny.

I had entered my sixteenth year, and every day it became more apparent that my presence was intolerable to Mrs. Flint. Angry words frequently passed between her and her husband. He had never punished me himself, and he would not allow anybody else to punish me. In that respect, she was never satisfied; but, in her angry moods, no terms were too vile for her to bestow upon me. Yet I, whom she detested so bitterly, had far more pity for her than he had, whose duty it was to make her life happy. I never wronged her, or wished to wrong her; and one word of kindness from her would have brought me to her feet.

After repeated quarrels between the doctor and his wife, he announced his intention to take his youngest daughter, then four years old, to sleep in his apartment. It was necessary that a servant should sleep in the same room, to be on hand if the child stirred. I was selected for that office, and informed for what purpose that arrangement had been made. By managing to keep within sight of people, as much as possible, during the daytime, I had hitherto succeeded in eluding my master, though a razor was often held to my throat to force me to change this line of policy. At night I slept by the side of my great aunt, where I felt safe. He was too prudent to come into her room. She was an old woman, and had been in the family many years. Moreover, as a married man, and a professional man, he deemed it necessary to save appearances in some degree. But he resolved to remove the obstacle in the way of his scheme; and he thought he had planned it so that he should evade suspicion. He was well aware how much I prized my refuge by the side of my old aunt, and he determined to dispossess me of it. The first night the doctor had the little child in his room alone. The next morning, I was ordered to take my station as nurse the following night. A kind Providence interposed in my favor. During the day Mrs. Flint heard of this new arrangement, and a storm followed. I rejoiced to hear it rage.

After a while my mistress sent for me to come to her room. Her first question was, "Did you know you were to sleep in the doctor's room?"

"Yes, ma'am."

"Who told you?"

"My master."

"Will you answer truly all the questions I ask?"

"Yes, ma'am."

"Tell me, then, as you hope to be forgiven, are you innocent of what I have accused you?"

"I am."

She handed me a Bible, and said, "Lay your hand on your heart, kiss this holy book, and swear before God that you tell me the truth."

I took the oath she required, and I did it with a clear conscience.

"You have taken God's holy word to testify your innocence," said she. "If you have deceived me, beware! Now take this stool, sit down, look me directly in the face, and tell me all that has passed between your master and you."

I did as she ordered. As I went on with my account her color changed frequently, she wept, and sometimes groaned. She spoke in tones so sad, that I was touched by her grief. The tears came to my eyes; but I was soon convinced that her emotions arose from anger and wounded pride. She felt that her marriage vows were desecrated, her dignity insulted; but she had no compassion for the poor victim of her husband's perfidy. She pitied herself as a martyr; but she was incapable of feeling for the condition of shame and misery in which her unfortunate, helpless slave was placed.

Yet perhaps she had some touch of feeling for me; for when the conference was ended, she spoke kindly, and promised to protect me. I should have been much comforted by this assurance if I could have had confidence in it; but my experiences in slavery had filled me with distrust. She was not a very refined woman, and had not much control over her passions. I was an object of her jealousy, and, consequently, of her hatred; and I knew I could not expect kindness or confidence from her under the circumstances in which I was placed. I could not blame her. Slaveholders' wives feel as other women would under similar circumstances. The fire of her temper kindled from small sparks, and now the flame became so intense that the doctor was obliged to give up his intended arrangement.

I knew I had ignited the torch, and I expected to suffer for it afterward; but I felt too thankful to my mistress for the timely aid she rendered me to care much about that. She now took me to sleep in a room adjoining her own. There I was an object of her especial care, though not of her especial comfort, for she spent many a sleepless night to watch over me. Sometimes I woke up, and found her bending over me. At other times she whispered in my ear, as though it was her husband who was speaking to me, and listened to hear what I would answer. If she startled me, on such occasions, she would glide stealthily away; and the next morning she would tell me I had been talking in my sleep, and ask who I was talking to. At last I began to be fearful for my life. It had been often threatened; and you can imagine, better than I can describe, what an unpleasant sensation it must produce to wake up in the dead of night and find a jealous woman bending over you. Terrible as this experience was, I had fears that it would give place to one more terrible.

My mistress grew weary of her vigils; they did not prove satisfactory. She changed her tactics. She now tried the trick of accusing my master of crime, in my presence, and gave my name as the author of the accusation. To my utter astonishment, he replied, "I don't believe it; but if she did acknowledge it, you tortured her into exposing me." Tortured into exposing him! Truly, Satan had no difficulty in distinguishing the color of his soul! I understood his object in making this false representation. It was to show me that I gained nothing by seeking the protection of my mistress; that the power was still all in his own hands. I pitied Mrs. Flint. She was a second wife, many years the junior of her husband; and the hoary-headed miscreant was enough to try the patience of a wiser and better woman. She was completely foiled, and knew not how to proceed. She would gladly have had me flogged for my supposed false oath; but, as I have already stated, the doctor never allowed anyone to whip me. The old sinner was politic. The application of the lash might have led to remarks that would have exposed him in the eyes of his children and grandchildren. How often did I rejoice that I lived in a town where all the inhabitants knew each other! If I had been on a remote plantation, or lost among the multitude of a crowded city, I should not be a living woman at this day.

The secrets of slavery are concealed like those of the Inquisition. My master was, to my knowledge, the father of eleven slaves. But did the mothers dare to tell who was the father of their children? Did the other slaves dare to allude to it, except in whispers among themselves? No, indeed! They knew too well the terrible consequences.

My grandmother could not avoid seeing things which excited her suspicions. She was uneasy about me, and tried various ways to buy me; but the never-changing answer was always repeated: "Linda does not belong to *me*. She is my daughter's property, and I have no legal right to sell her." The conscientious man! He was too scrupulous to *sell* me; but he had no scruples whatever about committing a much greater wrong against the helpless young girl placed under his guardianship, as his daughter's property. Sometimes my persecutor would ask me whether I would like to be sold. I told him I would rather be sold to anybody than to lead such a life as I did. On such occasions he would assume the air of a very injured individual, and reproach me for my ingratitude. "Did I not take you into the house, and make you the companion of my own children?" he would say. "Have I ever treated you like a Negro? I have never allowed you to be punished, not even to please your mistress. And this is the recompense I get, you ungrateful girl!" I answered that he had reasons of his own for screening me from punishment, and that the course he pursued made my mistress hate me and persecute me. If I wept, he would say, "Poor child! Don't cry! don't cry! I will make peace for you with your mistress. Only let me arrange matters in my own way. Poor, foolish girl! you don't know what is for your own good. I would cherish you. I would make a lady of you. Now go, and think of all I have promised you."

I did think of it.

Reader, I draw no imaginary pictures of southern homes. I am telling you the plain truth. Yet when victims make their escape from this wild beast of Slavery, northerners consent to act the part of bloodhounds, and hunt the poor fugitive back into his den, "full of dead men's bones, and all uncleanness." Nay, more, they are not only willing, but proud, to give their daughters in marriage to slaveholders. The poor girls have romantic notions of a sunny clime, and of the flowering vines that all the year round shade a happy home. To what disappointments are they destined! The young wife soon learns that the husband in whose hands she has placed her happiness pays no regard to his marriage vows. Children of every shade of complexion play with her own fair babies, and too well she knows that they are born unto him of his own household. Jealousy and hatred enter the flowery home, and it is ravaged of its loveliness.

Southern women often marry a man knowing that he is the father of many little slaves. They do not trouble themselves about it. They regard such children as property, as marketable as the pigs on the plantation; and it is seldom that they do not make them aware of this by passing them into the slave-trader's hands as soon as possible, and thus getting them out of their sight. I am glad to say there are some honorable exceptions.

I have myself known two southern wives who exhorted their husbands to free those slaves toward whom they stood in a "parental relation"; and their request was granted. These husbands blushed before the superior nobleness of their wives' natures. Though they had only counseled them to do that which it was their duty to do, it commanded their respect, and rendered their conduct more exemplary. Concealment was at an end, and confidence took the place of distrust.

Though this bad institution deadens the moral sense, even in white women, to a fearful extent, it is not altogether extinct. I have heard southern ladies say of Mr. Such-a-one, "He not only thinks it no disgrace to be the father of those little niggers, but he is not ashamed to call himself their master. I declare, such things ought not to be tolerated in any decent society!"

Suggestions for Discussion

1. Discuss the effectiveness of the author's narrative method. Compare it with that used by Richard Wright.

2. How successfully does she communicate her desperation? How does she do so?

Suggestion for Writing

Write a newspaper editorial commenting on the events reported by Harriet Jacobs.

Chief Joseph

His Message of Surrender, 1876

Chief Joseph, one of the leaders of the Nez Percé tribes, fought against the destruction of his people in a manner that made him a hero (along with other chiefs, such as Tecumseh, Crazy Horse, and Sitting Bull) in the eyes of white settlers in Montana and Idaho. As part of an effort to drive the Plains Indians off their lands and onto reservations, the army commissioners decided that Joseph's Nez Percé should be moved to join others on the Lapwai Reservation in Montana. When Joseph resisted, a series of battles followed, and the Nez Percé attempted to cross the Bitterroot Mountains to Idaho. In the skirmishes that followed, most of the Nez Percé were killed. After four months of fighting and a journey of thirteen hundred miles, they were stopped in a battle a short distance from the Canadian border. Chief Joseph persuaded the approximately 120 remaining warriors to surrender and sent a message to the American officer in command. The following brief passage is an extract from a larger message and is taken from an article, "Chief Joseph, the Nez Percé," by C. E. S. Wood in the *Century Monthly Illustrated* magazine (May 1884).

Hear Me, My Warriors

Hear me, my warriors; my heart is sick and sad.
Our chiefs are killed,
The old men are all dead
It is cold, and we have no blankets;
The little children are freezing to death.
Hear me, my warriors; my heart is sick and sad.
From where the sun now stands I will fight no more forever!

Suggestions for Discussion

1. Although Chief Joseph's message is addressed to General Howard, it seems to have a larger audience. How do you imagine that wider audience reacted? The interpreter of the message is reported to have wept as he delivered it. The original message was not in the form of a poem.

2. Examine several history books that describe the destruction of the Plains Indians and give a full account of Chief Joseph's defeat. Organize a group discussion of the incident. Attempt to interpret the meaning of the episode in American history. How does this brief document relate to the theme of freedom and human dignity?

Suggestion for Writing

Find and read the lengthier message in an account of the Nez Percé. Then write a paper on the differences between it and the extract printed in this text.

Chief Seattle

Speech on the Signing of the Treaty of Port Elliott, 1855

Chief Seattle (1786–1866) of the Suquamish and Dewamish tribes was a significant figure among Native Americans of the Pacific Northwest. The city of Seattle was named in his honor. He was one of several chiefs in the Northwest who maintained peaceful relations with the continually encroaching white settlers. This speech, translated by a doctor named Henry Smith, acknowledges the defeat of the Native Americans and their willingness to live on a reservation in the state of Washington, provided that the American government agrees to treat them humanely and to respect the differences in their culture.

Yonder sky that has wept tears of compassion upon my people for centuries untold, and which to us appears changeless and eternal, may change. Today is fair. Tomorrow may be overcast with clouds. My words are like the stars that never change. Whatever Seattle says the great chief at Washington can rely upon with as much certainty as he can upon the return of the sun or the seasons. The White Chief says that Big Chief at Washington sends us greetings of friendship and goodwill. That is kind of him for we know he has little need of our friendship in return. His people are many. They are like the grass that covers vast prairies. My people are few. They resemble the scattering trees of a storm-swept plain. The great, and—I presume—good, White Chief sends us word that he wishes to buy our lands but is willing to allow us enough to live comfortably. This indeed appears just, even generous, for the Red Man no longer has rights that he need respect, and the offer may be wise also, as we are no longer in need of an extensive country. . . . I will not dwell on, nor mourn over, our untimely decay, nor reproach our paleface brothers with hastening it, as we too may have been somewhat to blame.

Youth is impulsive. When our young men grow angry at some real or imaginary wrong, and disfigure their faces with black paint, it denotes that their hearts are black, and then they are often cruel and relentless, and our old men and old women are unable to restrain them. Thus it has ever been. Thus it was when the white men first began to push our forefathers westward. But let us hope that the hostilities between us may never return. We would have everything to lose and nothing to gain. Revenge by young men is considered gain, even at the cost of their own lives, but old men who stay at home in times of war, and mothers who have sons to lose, know better.

Our good father at Washington—for I presume he is now our father as well as yours, since King George has moved his boundaries further north— our great good father, I say, sends us word that if we do as he desires he will protect us. His brave warriors will be to us a bristling wall of strength, and his wonderful ships of war will fill our harbors so that our ancient enemies far to the northward—the Hydas and Tsimpsians—will cease to frighten our women, children, and old men. Then in reality will he be our father and we his children. But can that ever be? Your God is not our God! Your God loves your people and hates mine. He folds his strong and protecting arms lovingly about the paleface and leads him by the hand as a father leads his infant son—but He has forsaken His red children—if they really are his. Our God, the Great Spirit, seems also to have forsaken us. Your God makes your people wax strong every day. Soon they will fill the land. Our people are ebbing away like a rapidly receding tide that will never return. The white man's God cannot love our people or He would protect them. They seem to be orphans who can look nowhere for help. How then can we be brothers? How can your God become our God and renew our prosperity and awaken in us dreams of returning greatness? If we have a common heavenly father He must be partial—for He came to his paleface children. We never saw Him. He gave you laws but He had no word for His red children whose teeming multitudes once filled this vast continent as stars fill the firmament. No; we are two distinct races with separate origins and separate destinies. There is little in common between us.

To us the ashes of our ancestors are sacred and their resting place is hallowed ground. You wander far from the graves of your ancestors and seemingly without regret. Your religion was written upon tables of stone by the iron finger of your God so that you could not forget. The Red Man could never comprehend nor remember it. Our religion is the traditions of our ancestors—the dreams of our old men, given them in solemn hours of night by the Great Spirit; and the visions of our sachems; and it is written in the hearts of our people.

Your dead cease to love you and the land of their nativity as soon as they pass the portals of the tomb and wander way beyond the stars. They are soon forgotten and never return. Our dead never forget the beautiful world that gave them being.

Day and night cannot dwell together. The Red Man has ever fled the approach of the White Man, as the morning mist flees before the morning sun. However, your proposition seems fair and I think that my people will accept it and will retire to the reservation you offer them. Then we will dwell apart in peace, for the words of the Great White Chief seem to be the words of nature speaking to my people out of dense darkness.

It matters little where we pass the remnant of our days. They will not be many. A few more moons; a few more winters—and not one of the descendants of the mighty hosts that once moved over this broad land or lived in happy homes, protected by the Great Spirit, will remain to mourn over the graves of a people once more powerful and hopeful than yours. But why should I mourn at the untimely fate of my people? Tribe follows tribe, and nation follows nation, like the waves of the sea. It is the order of nature, and regret is useless. Your time of decay may be distant, but it will surely come, for even the White Man whose God walked and talked with him as friend with friend, cannot be exempt from the common destiny. We may be brothers after all. We will see.

We will ponder your proposition, and when we decide we will let you know. But should we accept it, I here and now make this condition that we will not be denied the privilege without molestation of visiting at any time the tombs of our ancestors, friends and children. Every part of this soil is sacred in the estimation of my people. Every hillside, every valley, every plain and grove, has been hallowed by some sad or happy event in days long vanished. . . . The very dust upon which you now stand responds more lovingly to their footsteps than to yours, because it is rich with the blood of our ancestors and our bare feet are conscious of the sympathetic touch. . . . Even the little children who lived here and rejoiced here for a brief season will love these somber solitudes and at eventide they greet shadowy returning spirits. And when the last Red Man shall have perished, and the memory of my tribe shall have become a myth among the White Men, these shores will swarm with the invisible dead of my tribe, and when your children's children think themselves alone in the field, the store, the shop, upon the highway, or in the silence of the pathless woods, they will not be alone. . . . At night when the streets of your cities and villages are silent and you think them deserted, they will throng with the returning hosts that once filled and still love this beautiful land. The White Man will never be alone.

Let him be just and deal kindly with my people, for the dead are not powerless. Dead, did I say? There is no death, only a change of worlds.

Suggestions for Discussion

1. Discuss the figurative language that Chief Seattle uses in the speech. How are similes and metaphors used to characterize white settlers and Native Americans?

2. What is the tone of the speech? How does its tone fit Chief Seattle's purposes?

3. Experts have argued that this translation by Dr. Smith reflects a stereotypical picture of the Native American. What examples can you find in support of this claim? Why might this have occurred despite Dr. Smith's fluency in tribal languages?

4. Identify some ironic aspects of the speech. How might Americans of the mid-nineteenth century have responded to Chief Seattle's predictions?

Suggestions for Writing

1. Chief Seattle's speech refers to Native American enemies from whom he expects the government to protect his tribes. Write a short research paper in which you explain who those enemies were and the grounds for their enmity.

2. Write a paper comparing and contrasting the poetic nature of this speech with that of the Gettysburg Address. How do the two speeches reflect not only the differences between the two speakers and the occasions for their speeches, but cultural differences as well?

3. Chief Seattle converted to Christianity in the 1830s. Does this speech reflect his conversion? Write a paper in which you contrast the fact of his conversion with what he says about God in the speech.

E. M. Forster

Jew-Consciousness

Edward Morgan Forster (1879–1970) was a British novelist educated at King's College, Cambridge. He lived for a time in Italy, was a member of the Bloomsbury Group of writers and artists in London, and spent the major part of his life in Cambridge. His works include *Where Angels Fear to Tread* (1905), *A Room with a View* (1908), *Howards End* (1910), and *A Passage to India* (1924). In this selection (written in 1939) from *Two Cheers for Democracy* (1951) he tends to equate anti-Semitism with the nonsensical ideas that he says were prevalent in his public school days in the nineteenth century. His ironic stance was suitable for the English temperament of 1939. One wonders what he might have said had he known of the Holocaust that was soon to descend on European Jewry.

Long, long ago, while Queen Victoria reigned, I attended two preparatory schools. At the first of these, it was held to be a disgrace to have a sister. Any little boy who possessed one was liable to get teased. The word would go round: "Oh, you men, have you seen the Picktoes' sister?" The men would then reel about with sideway motions, uttering cries of "sucks" and pretending to faint with horror, while the Picktoes, who had hitherto held their own socially in spite of their name, found themselves banished into the wilderness, where they mourned. Major with Minor, in common shame. Naturally anyone who had a sister hid her as far as possible, and forbade her to sit with him at a Prizegiving or to speak to him except in passing and in a very formal manner. Public opinion was not bitter on the point, but it was quite definite. Sisters were disgraceful. I got through all right myself, because my conscience was clear, and though charges were brought against me from time to time they always fell through.

It was a very different story at my second school. Here, sisters were negligible, but it was a disgrace to have a mother. Crabbe's mother, Gob's mother, eeugh! No words were too strong, no sounds too shrill. And since mothers at that time of life are commoner than sisters, and also less biddable, the atmosphere of this school was less pleasant, and the sense of guilt stronger. Nearly every little boy had a mother in a cupboard, and dreadful revelations occurred. A boy would fall ill and a mother would swoop and drive him away in a cab. A parcel would arrive with "From Mummy for her darling" branded upon it. Many tried to divert suspicion by being aggressive and fastening female parents upon the weak. One or two, who were good at games and had a large popularity-surplus, took up a really heroic line, acknowledged their mother brazenly, and would even be seen walking with her across the playing-field, like King Carol with Madame Lupescu. We admired such boys and envied them, but durst not imitate them. The margin of safety was too narrow. The convention was established that a mother spelt disgrace, and no individual triumph could reverse this.

Those preparatory schools prepared me for life better than I realised, for having passed through two imbecile societies, a sister-conscious and a mother-conscious, I am now invited to enter a third. I am asked to consider whether the people I meet and talk about are or are not Jews, and to form no opinion on them until this fundamental point has been settled. What revolting tosh! Neither science nor religion nor common sense has one word to say in its favour. All the same, Jew-consciousness is in the air, and it remains to be seen how far it will succeed in poisoning it. I don't think we shall ever reintroduce ghettos in England; I wouldn't say for certain, since no one knows what wickedness may not develop in his country or in himself if circumstances change. I don't think we shall go savage. But I do think we shall go silly. Many people have gone so already. Today, the average man suspects the people he dislikes of being Jews, and is surprised when the people he likes are Jews. Having been a Gentile at my first preparatory school and a Jew at my second, I know what I am talking about. I know how the poison works, and I know too that if the average man is anyone in particular he is a preparatory school boy. On the surface, things do not look too bad. Labour and Liberalism behave with their expected decency and denounce persecution, and respectability generally follows suit. But beneath the surface things are not so good, and anyone who keeps his ears open in railway carriages or pubs or country lanes can hear a very different story. A nasty side of our nation's character has been scratched up—the sniggering side. People who would not ill-treat Jews themselves, or even be rude to them, enjoy tittering over their misfortunes; they giggle when pogroms are instituted by someone else and synagogues defiled vicariously. "Serve them right really, Jews." This makes unpleasant reading, but anyone who cares to move out of his own enlightened little corner will discover that it is true. The grand Nordic argument, "He's a bloody capitalist so he must be a Jew, and as he's a Jew he must be a Red," has already taken root in our filling-stations and farms. Men employ it more frequently than women, and young men more frequently than old ones. The best way of confuting it is to say sneeringly, "That's propaganda." When "That's propaganda" has been repeated several times, the sniggering stops, for no goose likes to think that he has been got at. There is another reply which is more intellectual but which requires more courage. It is to say, "Are you sure you're not a Jew yourself? Do you know who your eight great-grandparents were? Can you swear that all the eight are Aryan?" Cool reasonableness would be best of all, of course, but it does not work in the world of today any better than in my preparatory schools. The only effective check to silliness is silliness of a cleverer type.

Jew-mania was the one evil which no one foretold at the close of the last war. All sorts of troubles were discerned and discernible—nationalism, class-warfare, the split between the haves and the have-nots, the general lowering of cultural values. But no prophet, so far as I know, had foreseen this anti-Jew horror, whereas today no one can see the end of it. There had been warnings, of course, but they seemed no more ominous than a poem by Hilaire Belloc. Back in India, in 1921, a Colonel lent me the Protocols of the Elders of Zion, and it was such an obvious fake that I did not worry. I had forgotten my preparatory schools, and did not see that they were about to come into their own. To me, anti-Semitism is now the most shocking of all things. It is destroying much more than the Jews; it is assailing the human mind at its source, and inviting it to create false categories before exercising judgment. I am sure we shall win through. But it will take a long time. Perhaps a hundred years must pass before men can think back to the mentality of 1918, or can say with the Prophet Malachi, "Have we not all one father? Hath not one God created us?" For the moment, all that we can do is to dig in our heels, and prevent silliness from sliding into insanity.

Suggestions for Discussion

1. Discuss the pictures of life in preparatory schools with which Forster opens his essay. What do his comments on "sister-consciousness" and "mother-consciousness" have to do with the rest of the essay?

2. Define what he calls the "grand Nordic argument" against the Jews. What does he mean by "Jew-mania"?

3. In this chapter from *Two Cheers for Democracy* (copyrighted in 1951), Forster refers to "the mentality of 1918." Define that mentality and discuss whether or not it still exists.

Suggestion for Writing

Write an essay discussing how widespread and how serious, in your experience, anti-Semitism is today.

George Orwell

The Principles of Newspeak

George Orwell (1903–1950), pseudonym of Eric Arthur Blair, a British writer with socialist sympathies, wrote essays and novels based on his experiences as a British imperial policeman in Burma, as an impoverished writer in Paris and London, and as a volunteer in the republican army in the Spanish Civil War. He was for a few years the editor of the magazine of the British Labour Party. Although his essays and letters are considered masterpieces of prose style, he is probably best known for the satirical anticommunist fable *Animal Farm* (1945) and for the novel *1984* published in 1949. Orwell conceived a terrifying vision of a future where mechanized language and thought have become the tools of a totalitarian society. This essay, written as an appendix to *1984*, presents "Newspeak," the official language of Oceania, as the logical outcome and instrument of a repressive government. It also suggests the Newspeak has its basis in what Orwell considered our degradation of the English language.

Newspeak was the official language of Oceania and had been devised to meet the ideological needs of Ingsoc, or English Socialism. In the year 1984 there was not as yet anyone who used Newspeak as his sole means of communication, either in speech or writing. The leading articles in the *Times* were written in it, but this was a tour de force which could only be carried out by a specialist. It was expected that Newspeak would have finally superseded Oldspeak (or Standard English, as we should call it) by about the year 2050. Meanwhile it gained ground steadily, all Party members tending to use Newspeak words and grammatical constructions more and more in their everyday speech. The version in use in 1984, and embodied in the Ninth and Tenth Editions of the Newspeak dictionary, was a provisional one, and contained many superfluous words and archaic formations which were due to be suppressed later. It is with the final, perfected version, as embodied in the Eleventh Edition of the dictionary, that we are concerned here.

The purpose of Newspeak was not only to provide a medium of expression for the world-view and mental habits proper to the devotees of Ingsoc, but to make all other modes of thought impossible. It was intended that when Newspeak had been adopted once and for all and Oldspeak forgotten, a heretical thought—that is, a thought diverging from the principles of Ingsoc—should be literally unthinkable, at least so far as thought is dependent on words. Its vocabulary was so constructed as to give exact and often very subtle expression to every meaning that a Party member could properly wish to express, while excluding all other meanings and also the possibility of arriving at them by indirect methods. This was done partly by the invention of new words, but chiefly by eliminating undesirable words and by stripping such words as remained of unorthodox meanings, and so far as possible of all secondary meanings whatever. To give a single example. The word *free* still existed in

Newspeak, but it could only be used in such statements as "This dog is free from lice" or "This field is free from weeds." It could not be used in its old sense of "politically free" or "intellectually free," since political and intellectual freedom no longer existed even as concepts, and were therefore of necessity nameless. Quite apart from the suppression of definitely heretical works, reduction of vocabulary was regarded as an end in itself, and no word that could be dispensed with was allowed to survive. Newspeak was designed not to extend but to *diminish* the range of thought, and this purpose was indirectly assisted by cutting the choice of words down to a minimum.

Newspeak was founded on the English language as we now know it, though many Newspeak sentences, even when not containing newly created words, would be barely intelligible to an English-speaker of our own day. Newspeak words were divided into three distinct classes, known as the A vocabulary, the B vocabulary (also called compound words), and the C vocabulary. It will be simpler to discuss each class separately, but the grammatical peculiarities of the language can be dealt with in the section devoted to the A vocabulary, since the same rules held good for all three categories.

The A vocabulary. The A vocabulary consisted of the words needed for the business of everyday life—for such things as eating, drinking, working, putting on one's clothes, going up and down stairs, riding in vehicles, gardening, cooking, and the like. It was composed almost entirely of words that we already possess—words like *hit, run, dog, tree, sugar, house, field*—but in comparison with the present-day English vocabulary, their number was extremely small, while their meanings were far more rigidly defined. All ambiguities and shades of meaning had been purged out of them. So far as it could be achieved, a Newspeak word of this class was simply a staccato sound expressing *one* clearly understood concept. It would have been quite impossible to use the A vocabulary for literary purposes or for political or philosophical discussion. It was intended only to express simple, purposive thoughts, usually involving concrete objects or physical actions.

The grammar of Newspeak had two outstanding peculiarities. The first of these was an almost complete interchangeability between different parts of speech. Any word in the language (in principle this applied even to very abstract words such as *if* or *when*) could be used either as verb, noun, adjective, or adverb. Between the verb and the noun form, when they were of the same root, there was never any variation, this rule of itself involving the destruction of many archaic forms. The word *thought*, for example, did not exist in Newspeak. Its place was taken by *think*, which did duty for both noun and verb. No etymological principle was involved here; in some cases it was the original noun that was chosen for retention, in other cases the verb. Even where a noun and a verb of kindred meaning were not etymologically connected, one or other of them was frequently suppressed. There was, for example, no such word as *cut*, its meaning being sufficiently covered by the noun-verb *knife*. Adjectives were formed by adding the suffix *-ful* to the noun-verb, and adverbs by adding *-wise*. Thus, for example, *speedful* meant "rapid" and *speedwise* meant "quickly." Certain of our present-day adjectives, such as *good, strong, big, black, soft*, were retained, but their total number was very small. There was little need for them, since almost any adjectival meaning could be arrived at by adding *-ful* to a noun-verb. None of the now-existing adverbs was retained, except for a very few already ending in -*wise;* the -*wise* termination was invariable. The word *well,* for example, was replaced by *goodwise.*

In addition, any word—this again applied in principle to every word in the language—could be negatived by adding the affix *un-,* or could be strengthened by the affix *plus-,* or, for still greater emphasis, *doubleplus-.* Thus, for example, *uncold* meant "warm," while *pluscold* and *doublepluscold* meant, respectively, "very cold" and "superlatively cold." It was also possible, as in present-day English, to modify the meaning of almost any word by prepositional affixes such as *ante-, post-, up-, down-,* etc. By such methods it was found possible to bring about an enormous diminution of vocabulary. Given, for instance, the word *good,* there was no need for such a word as *bad,* since the required meaning was equally well—indeed, better—expressed by *ungood.* All that was necessary, in any case where two words formed a natural pair of opposites, was to decide which of them to suppress. *Dark,* for example, could be replaced by *unlight,* or *light* by *undark,* according to preference.

The second distinguishing mark of Newspeak grammar was its regularity. Subject to a few exceptions which are mentioned below, all inflections followed the same rules. Thus, in all verbs the preterite and the past participle were the same and ended in -*ed.* The preterite of *steal* was *stealed,* the preterite of *think* was *thinked,* and so on throughout the language, all such forms as *swam, gave, brought, spoke, taken,* etc., being abolished. All plurals were made by adding -*s* or -*es* as the case might be. The plurals of *man, ox, life* were *mans, oxes, lifes.* Comparison of adjectives was invariably made by adding -*er,* -*est* (*good, gooder, goodest*), irregular forms and the *more, most* formation being suppressed.

The only classes of words that were still allowed to inflect irregularly were the pronouns, the relatives, the demonstrative adjectives, and the auxiliary verbs. All of these followed their ancient usage, except that *whom* had been scrapped as unnecessary, and the *shall, should* tenses had been dropped, all their uses being covered by *will* and *would.* There were also certain irregularities in word-formation arising out of the need for rapid and easy speech. A word which was difficult to utter, or was liable to be incorrectly heard, was held to be ipso facto a bad word; occasionally therefore, for the sake of euphony, extra letters were inserted into a word or an archaic formation was retained. But this need made itself felt chiefly in connection with the B vocabulary. *Why* so great an importance was attached to ease of pronunciation will be made clear later in this essay.

The B vocabulary. The B vocabulary consisted of words which had been deliberately constructed for political purposes: words, that is to say, which not only had in every case a political implication, but were intended to impose a desirable mental attitude upon the person using them. Without a full understanding of the principles of Ingsoc it was difficult to use these words correctly. In some cases they could be translated into Oldspeak, or even into words taken from the A vocabulary, but this usually demanded a long paraphrase and always involved the loss of certain overtones. The B words were a sort of verbal shorthand, often packing whole ranges of ideas into a few syllables, and at the same time more accurate and forcible than ordinary language.

The B words were in all cases compound words.* They consisted of two or more words, or portions of words, welded together in an easily pronounceable form. The resulting amalgam was always a noun-verb, and inflected according to the ordinary rules. To take a single example: the word *goodthink*, meaning, very roughly, "orthodoxy," or, if one chose to regard it as a verb, "to think in an orthodox manner." This inflected as follows: noun-verb, *goodthink*; past tense and past participle, *goodthinked*; present participle, *goodthinking*; adjective, *goodthinkful*; adverb, *goodthinkwise*; verbal noun, *goodthinker*.

The B words were not constructed on any etymological plan. The words of which they were made up could be any parts of speech, and could be placed in any order and mutilated in any way which made them easy to pronounce while indicating their derivation. In the word *crimethink* (thoughtcrime), for instance, the *think* came second, whereas in *thinkpol* (Thought Police) it came first, and in the latter word police had lost its second syllable. Because of the greater difficulty in securing euphony, irregular formations were commoner in the B vocabulary than in the A vocabulary. For example, the adjectival forms of *Minitrue*, *Minipax*, and *Miniluv* were, respectively, *Minitruthful*, *Minipeaceful*, and *Minilovely*, simply because *-trueful*, *paxful*, and *loveful* were slightly awkward to pronounce. In principle, however, all B words could inflect, and all inflected in exactly the same way.

Some of the B words had highly subtilized meanings, barely intelligible to anyone who had not mastered the language as a whole. Consider, for example, such a typical sentence from a *Times* leading article as *Oldthinkers unbellyfeel Ingsoc*. The shortest rendering that one could make of this in Oldspeak would be: "Those whose ideas were formed before the Revolution cannot have a full emotional understanding of the principles of English Socialism." But this is not an adequate translation. To begin with, in order to grasp the full meaning of the Newspeak sentence quoted above, one would have to have a clear idea of what is meant by *Ingsoc*. And, in addition, only a person thoroughly grounded in Ingsoc could appreciate the full force of the word *bellyfeel*, which implied a blind, enthusiastic acceptance difficult to imagine today; or of the word *oldthink*, which was inextricably mixed up with the idea of wickedness and decadence. But the special function of certain Newspeak words, of which *oldthink* was one, was not so much to express meanings as to destroy them. These words, necessarily few in number, had had their meanings extended until they contained within themselves whole batteries of words which, as they were sufficiently covered by a single comprehensive term, could now be scrapped and forgotten. The greatest difficulty facing the compilers of the Newspeak dictionary was not to invent new words, but, having invented them, to make sure what they meant: to make sure, that is to say, what ranges of words they canceled by their existence.

As we have already seen in the case of the word *free*, words which had once borne a heretical meaning were sometimes retained for the sake of convenience, but only with the undesirable meanings purged out of them. Countless other words such as *honor, justice, morality, internationalism, democracy, science,* and *religion* had simply ceased to exist. A few blanket words covered them, and, in covering them, abolished them. All words

---

*Compound words, such as *speakwrite*, were of course to be found in the A vocabulary, but these were merely convenient abbreviations and had no special ideological color.

grouping themselves round the concepts of liberty and equality, for instance, were contained in the single word *crimethink*, while all words grouping themselves round the concepts of objectivity and rationalism were contained in the single word *oldthink*. Greater precision would have been dangerous. What was required in a Party member was an outlook similar to that of the ancient Hebrew who knew, without knowing much else, that all nations other than his own worshipped "false gods." He did not need to know that these gods were called Baal, Osiris, Moloch, Ashtaroth, and the like; probably the less he knew about them the better for his orthodoxy. He knew Jehovah and the commandments of Jehovah; he knew, therefore, that all gods with other names or other attributes were false gods. In somewhat the same way, the Party member knew what constituted right conduct, and in exceedingly vague, generalized terms he knew what kinds of departure from it were possible. His sexual life, for example, was entirely regulated by the two Newspeak words *sexcrime* (sexual immorality) and *goodsex* (chastity). *Sexcrime* covered all sexual misdeeds whatever. It covered fornication, adultery, homosexuality, and other perversions, and in addition, normal intercourse practiced for its own sake. There was no need to enumerate them separately, since they were all equally culpable, and, in principle, all punishable by death. In the C vocabulary, which consisted of scientific and technical words, it might be necessary to give specialized names to certain sexual aberrations, but the ordinary citizen had no need of them. He knew what was meant by *goodsex*—that is to say, normal intercourse between man and wife, for the sole purpose of begetting children, and without physical pleasure on the part of the woman; all else was *sexcrime*. In Newspeak it was seldom possible to follow a heretical thought further than the perception that it *was* heretical; beyond that point the necessary words were nonexistent.

No word in the B vocabulary was ideologically neutral. A great many were euphemisms. Such words, for instance, as *joycamp* (forced-labor camp) or *Minipax* (Ministry of Peace, i. e., Ministry of War) meant almost the exact opposite of what they appeared to mean. Some words, on the other hand, displayed a frank and contemptuous understanding of the real nature of Oceanic society. An example was *prolefeed*, meaning the rubbishy entertainment and spurious news which the Party handed out to the masses. Other words, again, were ambivalent, having the connotation "good" when applied to the Party and "bad" when applied to its enemies. But in addition there were great numbers of words which at first sight appeared to be mere abbreviations and which derived their ideological color not from their meaning but from their structure.

So far as it could be contrived, everything that had or might have political significance of any kind was fitted into the B vocabulary. The name of every organization, or body of people, or doctrine, or country, or institution, or public building, was invariably cut down into the familiar shape; that is, a single easily pronounced word with the smallest number of syllables that would preserve the original derivation. In the Ministry of Truth, for example, the Records Department, in which Winston Smith worked, was called *Recdep*, the Fiction Department was called *Ficdep*, the Teleprograms Department was called *Teledep*, and so on. This was not done solely with the object of saving time. Even in the early decades of the twentieth century, telescoped words and phrases had been one of the characteristic features of political language; and it had been noticed that the tendency to use abbreviations of this kind was most marked in totalitarian countries and totalitarian organizations. Examples were such words as *Nazi, Gestapo, Comintern, Inprecorr, Agitprop.* In the beginning the practice had been adopted as it were instinctively, but in Newspeak it was used with a conscious purpose. It was perceived that in thus abbreviating a name one narrowed and subtly altered its meaning, by cutting out most of the associations that would otherwise cling to it. The words *Communist International,* for instance, call up a composite picture of universal human brotherhood, red flags, barricades, Karl Marx, and the Paris Commune. The word Comintern, on the other hand, suggests merely a tightly knit organization and a well-defined body of doctrine. It refers to something almost as easily recognized, and as limited in purpose, as a chair or a table. *Comintern* is a word that can be uttered almost without taking thought, whereas *Communist International* is a phrase over which one is obliged to linger at least momentarily. In the same way, the associations called up by a word like *Minitrue* are fewer and more controllable than those called up by *Ministry of Truth.* This accounted not only for the habit of abbreviating whenever possible, but also for the almost exaggerated care that was taken to make every word easily pronounceable.

In Newspeak, euphony outweighed every consideration other than exactitude of meaning. Regularity of grammar was always sacrificed to it when it seemed necessary. And rightly so, since what was required, above all for political purposes, were short clipped words of unmistakable meaning which could be uttered rapidly and which roused the minimum of echoes in the speaker's mind. The words of the B vocabulary even gained in force from the fact that nearly all of them were very much alike. Almost invariably these words—*goodthink, Minipax, prolefeed, sexcrime, joycamp, Ingsoc, bellyfeel, thinkpol,* and countless others—were words of two or three syllables, with the stress distributed equally between the first syllable and the last. The use of them encouraged a gabbling style of speech, at once staccato and monotonous. And this was exactly what was aimed at. The intention was to make speech, and especially speech on any subject not ideologically neutral, as nearly as possible independent of consciousness. For that purpose of everyday life it was no doubt necessary, or sometimes necessary, to reflect before speaking, but a Party member called upon to make a political or ethical judgment should be able to spray forth the correct opinions as automatically as a machine gun spraying forth bullets. His training fitted him to do this, the language gave him an almost foolproof instrument, and the texture of the words, with their harsh sound and a certain willful ugliness which was in accord with the spirit of Ingsoc, assisted the process still further.

So did the fact of having very few words to choose from. Relative to our own, the Newspeak vocabulary was tiny, and new ways of reducing it were constantly being devised. Newspeak, indeed, differed from almost all other languages in that its vocabulary grew smaller instead of larger every year. Each reduction was a gain, since the smaller the area of choice, the smaller the temptation to take thought. Ultimately it was hoped to make articulate speech issue from the larynx without involving the higher brain centers at all. This aim was frankly admitted in the Newspeak word *duckspeak,* meaning "to quack like a duck." Like various other words in the B vocabulary, *duckspeak* was ambivalent in meaning. Provided that the opinions which were quacked out were orthodox ones, it implied nothing but praise, and when the *Times* referred to one of the orators of the Party as a *double-plusgood duckspeaker* it was paying a warm and valued compliment.

The C vocabulary. The C vocabulary was supplementary to the others and consisted entirely of scientific and technical terms. These resembled the scientific terms in use today, and were constructed from the same roots, but the usual care was taken to define them rigidly and strip them of undesirable meanings. They followed the same grammatical rules as the words in the other two vocabularies. Very few of the C words had any currency either in everyday speech or in political speech. Any scientific worker or technician could find all the words he needed in the list devoted to his own speciality, but he seldom had more than a smattering of the words occurring in the other lists. Only a very few words were common to all lists, and there was no vocabulary expressing the function of Science as a habit of mind, or a method of thought, irrespective of its particular branches. There was, indeed, no word for "Science," any meaning that it could possibly bear being already sufficiently covered by the word *Ingsoc.*

From the foregoing account it will be seen that in Newspeak the expression of unorthodox opinions, above a very low level, was well-nigh impossible. It was of course possible to utter heresies of a very crude kind, a species of blasphemy. It would have been possible, for example, to say *Big Brother is ungood.* But this statement, which to an orthodox ear merely conveyed a self-evident absurdity, could not have been sustained by reasoned argument, because the necessary words were not available. Ideas inimical to Ingsoc could only be entertained in a vague wordless form, and could only be named in very broad terms which lumped together and condemned whole groups of heresies without defining them in doing so. One could, in fact, only use Newspeak for unorthodox purposes by illegitimately translating some of the words back into Oldspeak. For example, *All mans are equal* was a possible Newspeak sentence, but only in the same sense in which *All men are red-haired* is a possible Oldspeak sentence. It did not contain a grammatical error, but it expressed a palpable untruth, i.e., that all men are of equal size, weight, or strength. The concept of political equality no longer existed, and the secondary meaning had accordingly been purged out of the word *equal.* In 1984, when Oldspeak was still the normal means of communication, the danger theoretically existed that in using Newspeak words one might remember their original meanings. In practice it was not difficult for any person well grounded in *doublethink* to avoid doing this, but within a couple of generations even the possibility of such a lapse would have vanished. A person growing up with Newspeak as his sole language would no more know that *equal* had once had the secondary meaning of "politically equal," or that *free* had once meant "intellectually free," than, for instance, a person who had never heard of chess would be aware of the secondary meanings attaching to *queen* and *rook.* There would be many crimes and errors which it would be beyond his power to commit, simply because they were nameless and therefore unimaginable. And it was to be foreseen that with the passage of time the distinguishing characteristics of Newspeak would become more and more pronounced—its words growing fewer and fewer, their meanings more and more rigid, and the chance of putting them to improper uses always diminishing.

When Oldspeak had been once and for all superseded, the last link with the past would have been severed. History had already been rewritten, but fragments of the literature of the past survived here and there, imperfectly censored, and so long as one retained one's knowledge of Oldspeak it was possible to read them. In the future such fragments, even if they chanced to survive, would be unintelligible and untranslatable. It was impossible to translate any passage of Oldspeak into Newspeak unless it either referred to some techincal process or some very simple everyday action, or was already orthodox (*goodthinkful* would be the Newspeak expression) in tendency. In practice this meant that no book written before approximately 1960 could be translated as a whole. Prerevolutionary literature could only be subjected to ideological translation—that is, alteration in sense as well as language. Take for example the well-known passage from the Declaration of Independence:

> We hold these truths to be self-evident, that all men are created equal, that they are endowed by their Creator with certain inalienable rights, that among these are life, liberty and the pursuit of happiness. That to secure these rights, Governments are instituted among men, deriving their powers from the consent of the governed. That whenever any form of Government becomes destructive of those ends, it is the right of the People to alter or abolish it, and to institute new Government . . .

It would have been quite impossible to render this into Newspeak while keeping to the sense of the original. The nearest one could come to doing so would be to swallow the whole passage up in the single word *crimethink*. A full translation could only be an ideological translation, whereby Jefferson's words would be changed into a panegyric on absolute government.

A good deal of the literature of the past was, indeed, already being transformed in this way. Considerations of prestige made it desirable to preserve the memory of certain historical figures, while at the same time bringing their achievements into line with the philosophy of Ingsoc. Various writers, such as Shakespeare, Milton, Swift, Byron, Dickens, and some others were therefore in process of translation; when the task had been completed, their original writings, with all else that survived of the literature of the past, would be destroyed. These translations were a slow and difficult business, and it was not expected that they would be finished before the first or second decade of the twenty-first century. There were also large quantities of merely utilitarian literature—indispensable technical manuals and the like—that had to be treated in the same way. It was chiefly in order to allow time for the preliminary work of translation that the final adoption of Newspeak had been fixed for so late a date as 2050.

Suggestions for Discussion

1. Explain Orwell's statement that Newspeak was designed to "diminish the range of thought." How does he demonstrate this statement by the use of the word *free?*

2. Summarize the uses of the A Vocabulary. Contrast it with present-day English and discuss the former's use of the parts of speech. Why are verbs usually suppressed? Why were most existing adverbs abolished? Why were all noun plurals formed by adding -s or -es?

3. Define the B Vocabulary. What were its uses? Discuss the examples given, particularly the sentence, "Oldthinkers unbellyfeel Ingsoc."

4. What difficulties faced the compilers of the Newspeak dictionary?

5. What are the precedents for Newspeak word combinations such as *Recdep* and *Ficdep?* What comment on current standard English does Orwell make here?

6. How does the word *duckspeak* symbolize the purpose of Newspeak?

7. What are the uses of the C Vocabulary? Why did the word *science* cease to exist?

8. Discuss the sentences, "Big Brother is ungood" and "All mans are equal" as examples of Newspeak.

9. What is the Newspeak equivalent of the opening passage of the Declaration of Independence? Discuss Orwell's reasons for inventing this translation. Relate the translation to the entire essay.

Suggestions for Writing

1. Examine your local newspaper for examples of words that resemble Newspeak and write an essay discussing the reasons for your choice.

2. Write an essay explaining how Newspeak is an instrument of power. Why is it a necessary ideal of Oceania? Discuss some words or sentences from contemporary political speeches or essays that come close to Newspeak.

Jean-Paul Sartre

The Passion of the Anti-Semite

Translated by George J. Becker

Jean-Paul Sartre (1905–1980), existentialist philosopher, novelist, and playwright, played a leading role in post-World War II French intellectual life. His writings portray human beings as alone, responsible for their own acts, given the frightening need to choose their actions in a world without religious meaning. His fiction includes Nausea, Intimacy, and The Age of Reason; his plays The Flies, No Exit, and The Respectful Prostitute; his philosophy Being and Nothingness. However, all of his works reveal his philosophic ideas. Sartre refused the Nobel Prize for Literature believing that the award exaggerated a writer's influence. In this selection from Anti-Semite and Jew (1948), he describes the irrational passion that governs the thoughts and behavior of the anti-Semite.

If a man attributes all or part of his own misfortunes and those of his country to the presence of Jewish elements in the community, if he proposes to remedy this state of affairs by depriving the Jews of certain of their rights, by keeping them out of certain economic and social activities, by expelling them from the country, by exterminating all of them, we say that he has anti-Semitic *opinions*.

This word *opinion* makes us stop and think. It is the word a hostess uses to bring to an end a discussion that threatens to become acrimonious. It suggests that all points of view are equal; it reassures us, for it gives an inoffensive appearance to ideas by reducing them to the level of tastes. All tastes are natural; all opinions are permitted. Tastes, colors, and opinions are not open to discussion. In the name of democratic institutions, in the name of freedom of opinion, the anti-Semite asserts the right to preach the anti-Jewish crusade everywhere.

At the same time, accustomed as we have been since the Revolution to look at every object in an analytic spirit, that is to say, as a composite whose elements can be separated, we look upon persons and characters as mosaics in which each stone coexists with the others without that coexistence affecting the nature of the whole. Thus anti-Semitic opinion appears to us to be a molecule that can enter into combination with other molecules of any origin whatsoever without undergoing any alteration. A man may be a good father and a good husband, a conscientious citizen, highly cultivated, philanthropic, *and* in addition an anti-Semite. He may like fishing and the pleasures of love, may be tolerant in matters of religion, full of generous notions on the condition of the natives in Central Africa, *and* in addition detest the Jews. If he does not like them, we say, it is because his experience has shown him that they are bad, because statistics have taught him that they are dangerous, because certain historical factors have influenced his judgment. Thus this opinion seems to be the result of external causes, and those who wish to study it are prone to neglect the personality of the anti-Semite in favor of a consideration of the percentage of Jews who were mobilized in 1914, the percentage of Jews who are bankers, industrialists, doctors, and lawyers, or an examination of the history of the Jews in France since early times. They succeed in revealing a strictly objective situation that determines an equally objective current of opinion, and this they call anti-Semitism, for which they can draw up charts and determine the variations from 1870 to 1944. In such wise anti-Semitism appears to be at once a subjective taste that enters into combination with other tastes to form a personality, and an impersonal and social phenomenon which can be expressed by figures and averages, one which is conditioned by economic, historical, and political constants.

I do not say that these two conceptions are necessarily contradictory. I do say that they are dangerous and false. I would admit, if necessary, that one may have an opinion on the government's policy in regard to the wine industry, that is, that one may decide, *for certain reasons*, either to approve or condemn the free importation of wine from Algeria: here we have a case of holding an opinion on the administration of things. But I refuse to characterize as opinion a doctrine that is aimed directly at particular persons and that seeks to suppress their rights or to exterminate them. The Jew whom the anti-Semite wishes to lay hands upon is not a schematic being defined solely by his function, as under administrative law; or by his status or his acts, as under the Code. He is a Jew, the son of Jews, recognizable by his physique, by the color of his hair, by his clothing perhaps, and, so they say, by his character. Anti-Semitism does not fall within the category of ideas protected by the right of free opinion.

Indeed, it is something quite other than an idea. It is first of all a *passion*. No doubt it can be set forth in the form of a theoretical proposition. The "moderate" anti-Semite is a courteous man who will tell you quietly: "Personally, I do not detest the Jews. I simply find it preferable, for various reasons, that they should play a lesser part in the activity of the nation." But a moment later, if you have gained his confidence, he will add with more abandon: "You see, there must be *something* about the Jews; they upset me physically."

This argument, which I have heard a hundred times, is worth examining. First of all, it derives from the logic of passion. For, really now, can we imagine anyone's saying seriously: "There must be something about tomatoes, for I have a horror of eating them"? In addition, it shows us that anti-Semitism in its most temperate and most evolved forms remains a syncretic whole which may be expressed by statements of reasonable tenor, but which can involve even bodily modifications. Some men are suddenly struck with impotence if they learn from the woman with whom they are making love that she is a Jewess. There is a disgust for the Jew, just as there is a disgust for the Chinese or the Negro among certain people. Thus it is not from the body that the sense of repulsion arises, since one may love a Jewess very well if one does not know what her race is; rather it is something that enters the body from the mind. It is an involvement of the mind, but one so deep-seated and complete that it extends to the physiological realm, as happens in cases of hysteria.

This involvement is not caused by experience. I have questioned a hundred people on the reasons for their anti-Semitism. Most of them have confined themselves to enumerating the defects with which tradition has endowed the Jews. "I detest them because they are selfish, intriguing, persistent, oily, tactless, etc."—"But, at any rate, you associate with some of them?"—"Not if I can help it!" A painter said to me: "I am hostile to the Jew because, with their critical habits, they encourage our servants to insubordination." Here are examples a little more precise. A young actor without talent insisted that the Jews had kept him from a successful career in the theatre by confining him to subordinate roles. A young woman said to me: "I have had the most horrible experiences with furriers; they robbed me, they burned the fur I entrusted to them. Well, they were all Jews." But why did she choose to hate Jews rather than furriers? Why Jews or furriers rather than such and such a Jew or such and such a furrier? Because she had in her a predisposition toward anti-Semitism.

A classmate of mine at the lycée told me that Jews "annoy" him because of the thousands of injustices that "Jew-ridden" social organizations commit in their favor. "A Jew passed his *agrégation** the year I was failed, and you can't make me believe that that fellow, whose father came from Cracow or Lemberg, understood a poem by Ronsard or an eclogue by Virgil better than I." But he admitted that he disdained the *agrégation* as a mere academic exercise, and that he didn't study for it. Thus, to explain his failure, he made use of two systems of interpretation, like those madmen who, when they are far gone in their madness, pretend to be the King of Hungary but, if questioned sharply, admit to being shoemakers. His thoughts moved on two planes with-

*Competitive state teachers' examination. [Translator's note]

out his being in the least embarrassed by it. As a matter of fact, he will in time manage to justify his past laziness on the grounds that it really would be too stupid to prepare for an examination in which Jews are passed in preference to good Frenchmen. Actually he ranked twenty-seventh on the official list. There were twenty-six ahead of him, twelve who passed and fourteen who failed. Suppose Jews had been excluded from the competition; would that have done him any good? And even if he had been at the top of the list of unsuccessful candidates, even if by eliminating one of the successful candidates he would have had a chance to pass, why should the Jew Weil have been eliminated rather than the Norman Mathieu or the Breton Arzell? To understand my classmate's indignation we must recognize that he had adopted in advance a certain idea of the Jew, of his nature and of his role in society. And to be able to decide that among twenty-six competitors who were more successful than himself, it was the Jew who robbed him of his place, he must a priori have given preference in the conduct of his life to reasoning based on passion. Far from experience producing his idea of the Jew, it was the latter which explained his experience. If the Jew did not exist, the anti-Semite would invent him.

That may be so, you will say, but leaving the question of experience to one side, must we not admit that anti-Semitism is explained by certain historical data? For after all it does not come out of the air. It would be easy for me to reply that the history of France tells us nothing about the Jews: they were oppressed right up to 1789; since then they have participated as best they could in the life of the nation, taking advantage, naturally, of freedom of competition to displace the weak, but no more and no less than other Frenchmen. They have committed no crimes against France, have engaged in no treason. And if people believe there is proof that the number of Jewish soldiers in 1914 was lower than it should have been, it is because someone had the curiosity to consult statistics. This is not one of those facts which have the power to strike the imagination by themselves; no soldier in the trenches was able on his own initiative to feel astonishment at not seeing any Jews in the narrow sector that constituted his universe. However, since the information that history gives on the role of Israel depends essentially on the conception one has of history, I think it would be better to borrow from a foreign country a manifest example of "Jewish treason" and to calculate the repercussions this "treason" may have had on contemporary anti-Semitism.

In the course of the bloody Polish revolts of the nineteenth century, the Warsaw Jews, whom the czars handled gently for reasons of policy, were very lukewarm toward the rebels. By not taking part in the insurrection they were able to maintain and improve their position in a country ruined by repression.

I don't know whether this is true or not. What is certain is that many Poles believe it, and this "historical fact" contributes not a little to their bitterness against the Jews. But if I examine the matter more closely, I discover a vicious circle: The czars, we are told, treated the Polish Jews well whereas they willingly ordered pogroms against those in Russia. These sharply different courses of action had the same cause. The Russian government considered the Jews in both Russia and Poland to be unassimiliable; according to the needs of their policy, they had them massacred at Moscow and Kiev because they were a danger to the Russian empire, but favored them at Warsaw as a means of stirring up discord among the Poles. The latter showed nothing but hate and scorn for the Jews of Poland, but the reason was the same: For them Israel could never become an integral part of the national collectivity. Treated as Jews by the czar and as Jews by the Poles, provided, quite in spite of themselves, with Jewish interests in the midst of a foreign community, is it any wonder that these members of a minority behaved in accordance with the representation made of them?

In short, the essential thing here is not an "historical fact" but the idea that the agents of history formed for themselves of the Jew. When the Poles of today harbor resentment against the Jews for their past conduct, they are incited to it by that same idea. If one is going to reproach little children for the sins of their grandfathers, one must first of all have a very primitive conception of what constitutes responsibility. Furthermore one must form his conception of the children on the basis of what the grandparents have been. One must believe that what their elders did the young are capable of doing. One must convince himself that Jewish character is inherited. Thus the Poles of 1940 treated the Israelites in the community as *Jews* because their ancestors in 1848 had done the same with their contemporaries. Perhaps this traditional representation would, under other circumstances, have disposed the Jews of today to act like those of 1848. It is therefore the *idea* of the Jew that one forms for himself which would seem to determine history, not the "historical fact" that produces the idea.

People speak to us also of "social facts," but if we look at this more closely we shall find the same vicious circle. There are too many Jewish lawyers, someone says. But is there any complaint that there are too many Norman lawyers? Even if all the Bretons were doctors would we say anything more than that "Brittany provides doctors for the whole of France"? Oh, someone will answer, it is not at all the same thing. No doubt, but that is precisely because we consider Normans as Normans and Jews as Jews. Thus wherever we turn it is the *idea of the Jew* which seems to be the essential thing.

It has become evident that no external factor can induce anti-Semitism in the anti-Semite. Anti-Semitism is a free and total choice of oneself, a comprehensive attitude that one adopts not only toward Jews but toward men in general, toward history and society; it is at one and the same time a passion and a conception of the world. No doubt in the case of a given anti-Semite certain characteristics will be more marked than in another. But they are always all present at the same time, and they influence each other. It is this syncretic totality which we must now attempt to describe.

I noted earlier that anti-Semitism is a passion. Everybody understands that emotions of hate or anger are involved. But ordinarily hate and anger have a *provocation:* I hate someone who has made me suffer, someone who contemns or insults me. We have just seen that anti-Semitic passion could not have such a character. It precedes the facts that are supposed to call it forth; it seeks them out to nourish itself upon them; it must even interpret them in a special way so that they may become truly offensive. Indeed, if you so much as mention a Jew to an anti-Semite, he will show all the signs of a lively irritation. If we recall that we must always *consent* to anger before it can manifest itself and that, as is indicated so accurately by the French idiom, we "put ourselves" into anger, we shall have to agree that the anti-Semite has *chosen* to live on the plane of passion. It is not unusual for people to elect to live a life of passion rather than one of reason. But ordinarily they love the *objects* of passion: women, glory, power, money. Since the anti-Semite has chosen hate, we are forced to conclude that it is the *state* of passion that he loves. Ordinarily this type of emotion is not very pleasant: a man who passionately desires a woman is impassioned because of the woman and in spite of his passion. We are wary of reasoning based on passion, seeking to support by all possible means opinions which love or jealousy or hate have dictated. We are wary of the aberrations of passion and of what is called monoideism. But that is just what the anti-Semite chooses right off.

How can one choose to reason falsely? It is because of a longing for impenetrability. The rational man groans as he gropes for the truth; he knows that his reasoning is no more than tentative, that other considerations may supervene to cast doubt on it. He never sees very clearly where he is going; he is "open"; he may even appear to be hesitant. But there are people who are attracted by the durability of a stone. They wish to be massive and impenetrable; they wish not to change. Where, indeed, would change take them? We have here a basic fear of oneself and of truth. What frightens them is not the content of truth, of which they have no conception, but the form itself of truth, that thing of indefinite approximation. It is as if their own existence were in continual suspension. But they wish to exist all at once and right away. They do not want any acquired opinions; they want them to be innate. Since they are afraid of reasoning, they wish to lead the kind of life wherein reasoning and research play only a subordinate role, wherein one seeks only what he has already found, wherein one becomes only what he already was. This is nothing but passion. Only a strong emotional bias can give a lightning-like certainty; it alone can hold reason in leash; it alone can remain impervious to experience and last for a whole lifetime.

The anti-Semite has chosen hate because hate is a faith; at the outset he has chosen to devaluate words and reasons. How entirely at ease he feels as a result. How futile and frivolous discussions about the rights of the Jews appear to him. He has placed himself on other ground from the beginning. If out of courtesy he consents for a moment to defend his point of view, he lends himself but does not give himself. He tries simply to project his intuitive certainty onto the plane of discourse. I mentioned awhile back some remarks by anti-Semites, all of them absurd: "I hate Jews because they make servants insubordinate, because a Jewish furrier robbed me, etc." Never believe that anti-Semites are completely unaware of the absurdity of their replies. They know that their remarks are frivolous, open to challenge. But they are amusing themselves, for it is their adversary who is obliged to use words responsibly, since he believes in words. The anti-Semites have the *right* to play. They even like to play with discourse for, by giving ridiculous reasons, they discredit the seriousness of their interlocutors. They delight in acting in bad faith, since they seek not to persuade by sound argument but to intimidate and disconcert. If you press them too closely, they will abruptly fall silent, loftily indicating by some phrase that the time for argument is past. It is not that they are afraid of being convinced. They fear only to appear ridiculous or to prejudice by their embarrassment their hope of winning over some third person to their side.

If then, as we have been able to observe, the anti-Semite is impervious to reason and to experience, it is not because his conviction is strong. Rather his conviction is strong because he has chosen first of all to be impervious.

He has chosen also to be terrifying. People are afraid of irritating him. No one knows to what lengths the aberrations of his passion will carry him—but he knows, for this passion is not provoked by something external. He has it well in hand; it is obedient to his will: now he lets go the reins and now he pulls back on them. He is not afraid of himself, but he sees in the eyes of others a disquieting image—his own—and he makes his words and gestures conform to it. Having this external model, he is under no necessity to look for his personality within himself. He has chosen to find his being entirely outside himself, never to look within, to be nothing save the fear he inspires in others. What he flees even more than Reason is his intimate awareness of himself. But someone will object: What if he is like that only with regard to the Jews? What if he otherwise conducts himself with good sense? I reply that that is impossible. There is the case of a fishmonger who, in 1942, annoyed by the competition of two Jewish fishmongers who were concealing their race, one fine day took pen in hand and denounced them. I have been assured that this fishmonger was in other respects a mild and jovial man, the best of sons. But I don't believe it. A man who finds it entirely natural to denounce other men cannot have our conception of humanity; he does not see even those whom he aids in the same light as we do. His generosity, his kindness are not like our kindness, our generosity. You cannot confine passion to one sphere.

The anti-Semite readily admits that the Jew is intelligent and hardworking; he will even confess himself inferior in these respects. This concession costs him nothing, for he has, as it were, put those qualities in parentheses. Or rather they derive their value from the one who possesses them: the more virtues the Jew has the more dangerous he will be. The anti-Semite has no illusions about what he is. He considers himself an average man, modestly average, basically mediocre. There is no example of an anti-Semite's claiming individual superiority over the Jews. But you must not think that he is ashamed of his mediocrity; he takes pleasure in it; I will even assert that he has chosen it. This man fears every kind of solitariness, that of the genius as much as that of the murderer; he is the man of the crowd. However small his stature, he takes every precaution to make it smaller, lest he stand out from the herd and find himself face to face with himself. He has made himself an anti-Semite because that is something one cannot be alone. The phrase, "I hate the Jews," is one that is uttered in chorus; in pronouncing it, one attaches himself to a tradition and to a community—the tradition and community of the mediocre.

We must remember that a man is not necessarily humble or even modest because he has consented to mediocrity. On the contrary, there is a passionate pride among the mediocre, and anti-Semitism is an attempt to give value to mediocrity as such, to create an elite of the ordinary. To the anti-Semite, intelligence is Jewish; he can thus disdain it in all tranquility, like all the other virtues which the Jew possesses. They are so many ersatz attributes that the Jew cultivates in place of that balanced mediocrity which he will never have. The true Frenchman, rooted in his province, in his country, borne along by a tradition twenty centuries old, benefiting from ancestral wisdom, guided by tried customs, does not *need* intelligence. His virtue depends upon the assimilation of the qualities which the work of a hundred generations has lent to the objects which surround him; it depends on property. It goes without saying that this is a matter of inherited property, not property one buys. The anti-Semite has a fundamental incomprehension of the various forms of modern property: money, securities, etc. These are abstractions, entities of reason related to the abstract intelligence of the Semite. A security belongs to no one because it can belong to everyone; moreover, it is a sign of wealth, not a concrete possession. The anti-Semite can conceive only of a type of primitive ownership of land based on a veritable magical rapport, in which the thing possessed and its possessor are united by a bond of mystical participation; he is the poet of real property. It transfigures the proprietor and endows him with a special and concrete sensibility. To be sure, this sensibility ignores eternal truths or universal values: the universal is Jewish, since it is an object of intelligence. What his subtle sense seizes upon is precisely that which the intelligence cannot perceive. To put it another way, the principle underlying anti-Semitism is that the concrete possession of a particular object gives as if by magic the meaning of that object. Maurras said the same thing when he declared a Jew to be forever incapable of understanding this line of Racine:

Dans l'Orient désert, quel devint mon ennui.

But the way is open to me, mediocre me, to understand what the most subtle, the most cultivated intelligence has been unable to grasp. Why? Because I possess Racine—Racine and my country and my soil. Perhaps the Jew speaks a purer French than I do, perhaps he knows syntax and grammar better, perhaps he is even a writer. No matter; he has spoken this language for only twenty years, and I for a thousand years. The correctness of his style is abstract, acquired; my faults of French are in conformity with the genius of the language. We recognize here the reasoning that Barrès used against the holders of scholarships. There is no occasion for surprise. Don't the Jews have all the scholarships? All that intelligence, all that money can acquire one leaves to them, but it is as empty as the wind. The only things that count are irrational values, and it is just these things which are denied the Jews forever. Thus the anti-Semite takes his stand from the start on the ground of irrationalism. He is opposed to the Jew, just as sentiment is to intelligence, the particular to the universal, the past to the present, the concrete to the abstract, the owner of real property to the possessor of negotiable securities.

Besides this, many anti-Semites—the majority, perhaps—belong to the lower middle class of the towns; they are functionaries, office workers, small businessmen, who possess nothing. It is in opposing themselves to the Jew that they suddenly become conscious of being proprietors: in representing the Jew as a robber, they put themselves in the enviable position of people who could be robbed. Since the Jew wishes to take France from them, it follows that France must belong to them. Thus they have chosen anti-Semitism as a means of establishing their status as possessors. The Jew has more money than they? So much the better: money is Jewish, and they can despise it as they despise intelligence. They own less than the gentleman-farmer of Périgord or the large-scale farmer of the Beauce? That doesn't matter. All they have to do is nourish a vengeful anger against the robbers of Israel and they feel at once in possession of the entire country. True Frenchmen, good Frenchmen are all equal, for each of them possesses for himself alone France whole and indivisible.

Thus I would call anti-Semitism a poor man's snobbery. And in fact it would appear that the rich for the most part exploit this passion for their own uses rather than abandon themselves to it—they have better things to do. It is propagated mainly among the middle classes, because they possess neither land nor house nor castle, having only some ready cash and a few securities in the bank. It was not by chance that the petty bourgeoisie of Germany was anti-Semitic in 1925. The principal concern of this "white-collar proletariat" was to distinguish itself from the real proletariat. Ruined by big industry, bamboozled by the Junkers, it was nonetheless to the Junkers and the great industrialists that its whole heart went out. It went in for anti-Semitism with the same enthusiasm that it went in for wearing bourgeois dress: *because* the workers were internationalists, because the Junkers possessed Germany and it wished to possess it also. Anti-Semitism is not merely the joy of hating; it brings positive pleasures too. By treating the Jew as an inferior and pernicious being, I affirm at the same time that I belong to the elite. This elite, in contrast to those of modern times which are based on merit or labor, closely resembles an aristocracy of birth. There is nothing I have to do to merit my superiority, and neither can I lose it. It is given once and for all. It is a *thing*.

We must not confuse this precedence the anti-Semite enjoys by virtue of his principles with individual merit. The anti-Semite is not too anxious to possess individual merit. Merit has to be sought, just like truth; it is discovered with difficulty; one must deserve it. Once acquired, it is perpetually in question: a false step, an error, and it flies away. Without respite, from the beginning of our lives to the end, we are responsible for what merit we enjoy. Now the anti-Semite flees responsibility as he flees his own consciousness, and choosing for his personality the permanence of rock, he chooses for his morality a scale of petrified values. Whatever he does, he knows that he will remain at the top of the ladder; whatever the Jew does, he will never get any higher than the first rung.

We begin to perceive the meaning of the anti-Semite's choice of himself. He chooses the irremediable out of fear of being free; he chooses mediocrity out of fear of being alone, and out of pride he makes of this irremediable mediocrity a rigid aristocracy. To this end he finds the existence of the Jew absolutely necessary. Otherwise to whom would he be superior? Indeed, it is vis-à-vis the Jew and the Jew alone that the anti-Semite realizes that he has rights. If by some miracle all the Jews were exterminated as he wishes, he would find himself nothing but a concierge or a shopkeeper in a strongly hierarchical society in which the quality of "true Frenchman" would be at a low valuation, because everyone would possess it. He would lose his sense of rights over the country because no one would any longer contest them, and that profound equality which brings him close to the nobleman and the man of wealth would disappear all of a sudden, for it is primarily negative. His frustrations, which he has attributed to the disloyal competition of the Jew, would have to be imputed to some other cause, lest he be forced to look within himself. He would run the risk of falling into bitterness, into a melancholy hatred of the privileged classes. Thus the anti-Semite is in the unhappy position of having a vital need for the very enemy he wishes to destroy.

The equalitarianism that the anti-Semite seeks with so much ardor has nothing in common with that equality inscribed in the creed of the democracies. The latter is to be realized in a society that is economically hierarchical, and is to remain compatible with a diversity of functions. But it is in protest *against* the hierarchy of functions that the anti-Semite asserts the equality of Aryans. He does not understand anything about the division of labor and doesn't care about it. From his point of view each citizen can claim the title of Frenchman, not because he co-operates, in his place or in his occupation, with others in the economic, social, and cultural life of the nation, but because he has, in the same way as everybody else, an imprescriptible and inborn right to the indivisible totality of the country. Thus the society that the anti-Semite conceives of is a society of juxtaposition, as one can very well imagine, since his ideal of property is that of real and basic property. Since, in point of fact, anti-Semites are numerous, each of them does his part in constituting a community based on mechanical solidarity in the heart of organized society.

The degree of integration of each anti-Semite with this society, as well as the degree of his equality, is fixed by what I shall call the temperature of the community. Proust has shown, for example, how anti-Semitism brought the duke closer to his coachman, how, thanks to their hatred of Dreyfus, bourgeois families forced the doors of the aristocracy. The equalitarian society that the anti-Semite believes in is like that of mobs or those instantaneous societies which come into being at a lynching or during a scandal. Equality in them is the product of the non-differentiation of functions. The social bond is anger; the collectivity has no other goal than to exercise over certain individuals a diffused repressive sanction. Collective impulsions and stereotypes are imposed on individuals all the more strongly because none of them is defended by any specialized function. Thus the person is drowned in the crowd, and the ways of thinking and reacting of the group are of a purely primitive type. Of course, such collectivities do not spring solely from anti-Semitism; an uprising, a crime, an injustice can cause them to break out suddenly. But those are ephemeral formations which soon vanish without leaving any trace.

Since anti-Semitism survives the great crises of Jew-hatred, the society which the anti-Semites form remains in a latent state during normal periods, with every anti-Semite celebrating its existence. Incapable of understanding modern social organization, he has a nostalgia for periods of crisis in which the primitive community will suddenly reappear and attain its temperature of fusion. He wants his personality to melt suddenly into the group and be carried away by the collective torrent. He has this atmosphere of the pogrom in mind when he asserts "the union of all Frenchmen." In this sense anti-Semitism is, in a democracy, a covert form of what is called the struggle of the citizen against authority. Question any one of those turbulent young men who placidly break the law and band together to beat up a Jew in a deserted street: He will tell you that he wants a strong authority to take from him the crushing responsibility of thinking for himself. Since the Republic is weak, he is led to break the law out of love of obedience. But is it really strong authority that he wishes? In reality he demands rigorous order for others, and for himself disorder without responsibility. He wishes to place himself above the law, at the same time escaping from the consciousness of his liberty and his isolation. He therefore makes use of a subterfuge: The Jews take part in elections; there are Jews in the government; therefore the legal power is vitiated at its base. As a matter of fact, it no longer exists, so it is legitimate to ignore its decrees. Consequently there is no disobedience—one cannot disobey what does not exist. Thus for the anti-Semite there is a *real* France with a government *real* but diffused and without special organs, and an abstract France, official, Jew-ridden, against which it is proper to rebel.

Naturally this permanent rebellion is the act of a group; the anti-Semite would under no circumstances dare to act or think on his own. And the group would be unable to conceive of itself as a minority party, for a minority party is obliged to devise a program and to determine on a line of political action, all of which implies initiative, responsibility, and liberty. Anti-Semitic associations do not wish to invent anything; they refuse to assume responsibility; they would be horrified at setting themselves up as a certain fraction of French opinion, for then they would have to draw up a program and seek legal means of action. They prefer to represent themselves as expressing in all purity, in all passivity, the sentiments of the *real* country in its indivisible state.

Any anti-Semite is therefore, in varying degree, the enemy of constituted authority. He wishes to be the disciplined member of an undisciplined group; he adores order, but a *social* order. We might say that he wishes to provoke political disorder in order to restore social order, the social order in his eyes being a society that, by virtue of juxtaposition, is egalitarian and primitive, one with a heightened temperature, one from which Jews are excluded. These principles enable him to enjoy a strange sort of independence, which I shall call an inverted liberty. Authentic liberty assumes responsibilities, and the liberty of the anti-Semite comes from the fact that he escapes all of his. Floating between an authoritarian society which has not yet come into existence and an official and tolerant society which he disavows, he can do anything he pleases without appearing to be an anarchist, which would horrify him. The profound seriousness of his aims—which no word, no statement, no act can express—permits him a certain frivolity. He is a hooligan, he beats people up, he purges, he robs; it is all in a good cause. If the government is strong, anti-Semitism withers, unless it be a part of the program of the government itself, in which case it changes its nature. Enemy of the Jews, the anti-Semite has need of them. Anti-democratic, he is a natural product of democracies and can only manifest himself within the framework of the Republic.

We begin to understand that anti-Semitism is more than a mere "opinion" about the Jews and that it involves the entire personality of the anti-Semite.

Suggestions for Discussion

1. Why does Sartre call anti-Semitism "a poor man's snobbery"? Do you agree? Explain your point of view.

2. Why does Sartre reject the notion that anti-Semitism is simply a matter of opinion based on observation? How does he argue that not all opinions are equal?

3. Explain Sartre's observation that if the Jew did not exist, the anti-Semite would have to invent him.

4. Compare Sartre's essay with Forster's "Jew-Consciousness." How do the arguments, examples, and tone of the two essays differ?

Suggestions for Writing

1. Write an essay of 500 words in which you apply Sartre's attitude toward the anti-Semite to racist feelings toward another minority.

2. Write a defense of Sartre's assertion that "Anti-Semitism does not fall within the category of ideas protected by the rights of free opinion."

Plato

The Crito

Translated by Benjamin Jowett,
revised by Peter White

Plato (428–348 B.C.), born of a noble family, lived in Athens during troubled political times. After the defeat of Athens in the Peloponnesian War, an autocratic and repressive government replaced the democracy, and it, in turn, was succeeded by a regime more demagogic than democratic. Under this government in 399 B.C., Socrates was prosecuted, tried, and condemned to death for subversive activities. In the Apology and the Crito (neither of them typical Platonic dialogues), Plato undertook the task of rehabilitating Socrates' reputation. Although the historian Xenophon has provided a somewhat different version of Socrates' trial, Plato's portrait of Socrates explains why he regarded him as the best of men. The Crito (and the Phaedo) presents Socrates in prison as he awaits execution. Crito, a wealthy Athenian, whose primary loyalty in this case is to his friend rather than to the state, urges Socrates to accept his help in escaping. In the course of the dialogue, Socrates leads Crito to agree that a respect for the law and a belief in personal integrity demand that Socrates accept his execution with dignity. Toward the end of the Crito, Plato personifies the laws of Athens to explain Socrates' decision to obey them.

Plato's Republic, written later than the Crito, and additional dialogues in which he uses Socrates to argue his own position on ethics, politics, and other philosophical issues, are Plato's versions of Socrates' conversations. He uses Socrates, however, as teacher of the Socratic method of discourse, which Plato employed in his dialogues, and so it is not surprising that soon after his fortieth year, Plato founded the Academy, the first institute for the purpose of educating suitable rulers for Athens, a school that became a model for many that followed.

SOCRATES: Why have you come at this hour, Crito? It must be quite early?
CRITO: Yes, certainly.
SOCRATES: What is the exact time?

CRITO: The dawn is breaking.

SOCRATES: I wonder that the keeper of the prison would let you in.

CRITO: He knows me, because I often come, Socrates; moreover, I have done him a kindness.

SOCRATES: And are you only just arrived?

CRITO: I came some time ago.

SOCRATES: Then why did you sit and say nothing instead of at once awakening me?

CRITO: That I could never have done, Socrates. I only wish I were not so sleepless and distressed myself. I have been looking at you, wondering how you can sleep so comfortably, and I didn't wake you on purpose, so that you could go on sleeping in perfect comfort. All through your life, I have often thought you were favored with a good disposition, but I have never been so impressed as in the present misfortune, seeing how easily and tranquilly you bear it.

SOCRATES: Why, Crito, when a man has reached my age he ought not to be repining at the approach of death.

CRITO: And yet other old men find themselves in similar misfortunes, and age does not prevent them from repining.

SOCRATES: That is true. But you have not told me why you come at this early hour.

CRITO: I come with a message which is painful—not, I expect, to you, but painful and oppressive for me and all your friends, and I think it weighs most heavily of all on me.

SOCRATES: What? Has the ship come from Delos, on the arrival of which I am to die?*

CRITO: No, the ship has not actually arrived, but she will probably be here today, as persons who have come from Sunium tell me that they left her there; and therefore tomorrow, Socrates, will be the last day of your life.

SOCRATES: Very well, Crito; if such is the will of the gods, I am willing; but my belief is that there will be a day's delay.

CRITO: Why do you think so?

SOCRATES: I will tell you. I am to die on the day after the arrival of the ship.

CRITO: Yes; that is what the authorities say.

SOCRATES: But I do not think that the ship will be here until tomorrow; this I infer from a vision which I had last night, or rather only just now, when you fortunately allowed me to sleep.

CRITO: And what was the nature of the vision?

SOCRATES: There appeared to me the likeness of a woman, fair and comely, clothed in bright raiment, who called to me and said: O Socrates,

"The third day hence to fertile Phthia shalt thou come."†

CRITO: What a singular dream, Socrates!

SOCRATES: There can be no doubt about the meaning, Crito, I think.

---

*Once every year Athens sent a state ship on a ceremonial pilgrimage to the island of Delos; no executions could be carried out between its departure and return.

†The apparition borrows the words in which Achilles contemplated a return from Troy to his home, *Iliad* 9.363.

CRITO: Yes; the meaning is only too clear. But, oh! my beloved Socrates, let me entreat you once more to take my advice and escape. For if you die, I shall not only lose a friend who can never be replaced, but there is another evil: people who do not know you and me will believe that I might have saved you if I had been willing to give money but that I did not care. Now, can there be a worse disgrace than this—that I should be thought to value money more than the life of a friend? For the many will not be persuaded that I wanted you to escape and that you refused.

SOCRATES: But why, my dear Crito, should we care about the opinion of the many? Good men, and they are the only persons who are worth considering, will think of these things truly as they occurred.

CRITO: But you see, Socrates, that the opinion of the many must be regarded, for what is now happening shows that they can do the greatest evil to anyone who has lost their good opinion.

SOCRATES: I only wish it were so, Crito, and that the many could do the greatest evil; for then they would also be able to do the greatest good—and what a fine thing this would be! But in reality they can do neither; for they cannot make a man either wise or foolish, and whatever result they produce is the result of chance.

CRITO: Well, I will not dispute with you; but please tell me, Socrates, whether you are not acting out of regard to me and your other friends: Are you not afraid that, if you escape from prison, we may get into trouble with the informers for having stolen you away and lose either the whole or a great part of our property—or that even a worse evil may happen to us? Now, if you fear on our account, be at ease; for in order to save you, we ought surely to run this or even a greater risk; be persuaded, then, and do as I say.

SOCRATES: Yes, Crito, that is one fear which you mention, but by no means the only one.

CRITO: Fear not—there are persons who are willing to get you out of prison at no great cost; and as for the informers, they are far from being exorbitant in their demands—a little money will satisfy them. My means, which are certainly ample, are at your service; and if, out of solicitude about me, you hesitate to use mine, there are non-Athenians here who will give you the use of theirs; and one of them, Simmias the Theban, has brought a large sum of money for this very purpose; and Cebes and many others are prepared to spend their money in helping you to escape. Therefore do not hesitate to save yourself because you are worried about this, and do not say, as you did in the court, that you will have difficulty in knowing what to do with yourself anywhere else. For men will love you in other places to which you may go, and not in Athens only; there are friends of mine in Thessaly, if you would like to go to them, who will value and protect you, and no Thessalian will give you any trouble. Nor can I think that you are at all justified, Socrates, in betraying your own life when you might be saved. You are only working to bring about what your enemies, who want to destroy you, would and did in fact work to accomplish. And further, I should say that you are deserting your own children; for you might bring them up and educate them, instead of which you go away and leave them, and they will have to take their chances; and if they do not meet with the usual fate of orphans, there will be small thanks to you. No man should bring children into the world who is unwilling to persevere to the end in their nurture and education. But you appear to be choosing the easier part, not the better and manlier, which would have been more becoming in one who has professed a life-long concern for virtue, like yourself. And indeed, I am ashamed not only of you but of us, who are your friends, when I reflect that the whole business will be attributed entirely to our want of courage. The trial need never have come on or might have been managed differently. And now it may seem that we have made a ridiculous bungle of this last chance, thanks to our lack of toughness and courage, since we failed to save you and you failed to save yourself, even though it was possible and practicable if we were good for anything at all. So, Socrates, you must not let this turn into a disgrace as well as a tragedy for yourself and us. Make up your mind then, or rather have your mind already made up; for the time of deliberation is over, and there is only one thing to be done, which must be done this very night, and, if we delay at all, it will be no longer practicable or possible; I beseech you therefore, Socrates, be persuaded by me, and do not be contrary.

SOCRATES: My dear Crito, your solicitude is invaluable if it is rightly directed, but otherwise, the more intense, the more difficult it is to deal with. And so we should consider whether I ought to follow this course or not. You know it has always been true that I paid no heed to any consideration I was aware of except that argument which, on reflection, seemed best to me. I cannot throw over the arguments I used to make in times past just because this situation has arisen: they look the same to me as before, and I respect and honor them as much as ever. You must therefore understand that if, on the present occasion, we cannot make better arguments, I will not yield to you—not even if the power of the people conjures up the bugaboos of imprisonment and death and confiscation, as though we could be scared like little children. What will be the fairest way of considering the question? Shall I return to your old argument about the opinions of men? We were saying that some of them are to be regarded, and others not. Now were we right in maintaining this before I was condemned? And has the argument which was once good now proved to be talk for the sake of talking—mere childish nonsense? That is what I want to consider with your help, Crito: whether, under my present circumstances, the argument will appear to be in any way different or not, and whether we shall subscribe to it or let it go. That argument, which, as I believe, is maintained by many persons of authority, was to the effect, as I was saying, that the opinions of some men are to be regarded, and of other men not to be regarded. Now you, Crito, are not going to die tomorrow—at least, there is no human probability of this—and therefore you are disinterested and not liable to be deceived by the circumstances in which you are placed. Tell me, then, whether I am right in saying that some opinions, and the opinions of some men only, are to be valued and that other opinions, and the opinions of other men, are not to be valued. I ask you whether I was right in maintaining this?

CRITO: Certainly.

SOCRATES: The good opinions are to be regarded, and not the bad?

CRITO: Yes.

SOCRATES: And the opinions of the wise are good, and the opinions of the unwise are bad?

CRITO: Certainly.

SOCRATES: Now what was the argument about this: does the serious athlete attend to the praise and blame and opinion of every man or of one man only—his physician or trainer, whoever he may be?

CRITO: Of one man only.

SOCRATES: And he ought to fear the censure and welcome the praise of that one only, and not of the many?

CRITO: Clearly so.

SOCRATES: And he ought to act and train and eat and drink in the way which seems good to his single master, who has understanding, rather than according to the opinion of all other men put together?

CRITO: True.

SOCRATES: And if he disobeys and disregards the opinion and approval of the one, and regards the opinion of the many who have no understanding, will he not suffer harm?

CRITO: Certainly he will.

SOCRATES: And what will the harm be: where will it be localized, and what part of the disobedient person will it affect?

CRITO: Clearly, it will affect the body; that is what is destroyed.

SOCRATES: Very good, and is not this true, Crito, of other things, which we need not separately enumerate? In questions of just and unjust, fair and foul, good and evil, which are the subjects of our present consultation, ought we to follow the opinion of the many, and to fear them, or the opinion of the one man who has understanding? Ought we not to fear and reverence him more than all the rest of the world, and, if we desert him, shall we not ruin and mutilate that principle in us which is improved by justice and deteriorated by injustice—there is such a principle?

CRITO: Certainly there is, Socrates.

SOCRATES: Take a parallel instance: if, ignoring the advice of those who have understanding, we destroy that which is improved by health and is deteriorated by disease, would life be worth having? and that which has been destroyed is—the body?

CRITO: Yes.

SOCRATES: Would life be worth living with an evil and corrupted body?

CRITO: Certainly not.

SOCRATES: And will life be worth living if that faculty which injustice damages and justice improves is ruined? Do we suppose that principle—whatever it may be in man which has to do with justice and injustice—to be inferior to the body?

CRITO: Certainly not.

SOCRATES: More honorable than the body?

CRITO: Far more.

SOCRATES: Then, my friend, we must not regard what the many say of us but what he, the one man who has understanding of just and unjust, will say and what the truth will say. And therefore you begin in error when you advise that we should regard the opinion of the many about just and unjust, good and evil, honorable and dishonorable. "Well," someone will say, "but the many can kill us."

CRITO: That is plain, and a person might well say so. You are right, Socrates.

SOCRATES: But dear Crito, the argument which we have gone over still seems as valid as before. And I should like to know whether I may say the same of another proposition—that not life, but a good life, is to be chiefly valued?

CRITO: Yes, that also remains unshaken.

SOCRATES: And a good life is equivalent to an honorable and just one—that holds also?

CRITO: Yes, it does.

SOCRATES: From these premises I proceed to argue the question whether I am justified in trying to escape without the consent of the Athenians; and if I am clearly right in escaping, then I will make the attempt, but, if not, I will abstain. The other considerations which you mention—of money and loss of character and the duty of educating one's children—are, I fear, only the doctrines of the multitude, who, if they could, would restore people to life as readily as they put them to death—and with as little reason. But since we have been forced this far by the logic of our argument, the only question which remains to be considered is whether we shall do right in giving money and thanks to those who will rescue me, and in taking a direct role in the rescue ourselves, or whether in fact we will be doing wrong. And if it appears that we will be doing wrong, then neither death nor any other calamity that follows from staying and doing nothing must be judged more important than that.

CRITO: I think that you are right, Socrates. How then shall we proceed?

SOCRATES: Let us consider the matter together, and you, either refute me if you can, and I will be convinced, or else cease, my dear friend, from repeating to me that I ought to escape against the wishes of the Athenians. It is most important to me that I act with your assent and not against your will. And now please consider whether my starting point is adequately stated, and also try to answer my questions as you think best.

CRITO: I will.

SOCRATES: Are we to say that we are never intentionally to do wrong, or that in one way we ought and in another we ought not to do wrong? Or is doing wrong always evil and dishonorable, as we often concluded in times past? Or have all those past conclusions been thrown overboard during the last few days? And have we, at our age, been earnestly discoursing with one another all our life long only to discover that we are no better than children? Or, in spite of the opinion of the many, and in spite of consequences, whether better or worse, shall we insist on the truth of what was then said, that injustice is always an evil and a dishonor to him who acts unjustly? Shall we say so or not?

CRITO: Yes.

SOCRATES: Then we must do no wrong?

CRITO: Certainly not.

SOCRATES: Nor, when injured, injure in return, as the many imagine; for we must injure no one at all?

CRITO: Clearly not.

SOCRATES: Again, Crito, may we do evil?

CRITO: Surely not, Socrates.

SOCRATES: And what of doing evil in return for evil, which is the morality of the many—is that just or not?

CRITO: Not just.

SOCRATES: For doing evil to another is the same as injuring him?

CRITO: Very true.

SOCRATES: Then we ought not to retaliate or render evil for evil to anyone, whatever evil we may have suffered from him. But I would have you consider, Crito, whether you really mean what you are saying. For this opinion has never been held, and never will be held, by any considerable number of persons; and those who are agreed and those who are not agreed upon this point have no common ground and can only despise one another when they see how widely they differ. Tell me, then, whether you agree with and assent to my first principle, that neither injury nor retaliation nor warding off evil by evil is ever right. And shall that be the premise of our argument? Or do you decline and dissent from this? For so I have ever thought, and continue to think; but, if you are of another opinion, let me hear what you have to say. If, however, you remain of the same mind as formerly, I will proceed to the next step.

CRITO: You may proceed, for I have not changed my mind.

SOCRATES: The next thing I have to say, or, rather, my next question, is this: Ought a man to do what he admits to be right, or ought he to betray the right?

CRITO: He ought to do what he thinks right.

SOCRATES: In light of that, tell me whether or not there is some victim—a particularly undeserving victim—who is hurt if I go away without persuading the city. And do we abide by what we agree was just or not?

CRITO: I cannot answer your question, Socrates, because I do not see what you are getting at.

SOCRATES: Then consider the matter in this way: imagine that I am about to run away (you may call the proceeding by any name which you like), and the laws and the government come and interrogate me: "Tell us, Socrates," they say; "what are you up to? are you not going by an act of yours to destroy us—the laws, and the whole state—as far as in you lies? Do you imagine that a state can subsist and not be overthrown in which the decisions of law have no power but are set aside and trampled upon by individuals?" What will be our answer, Crito, to questions like these? Anyone, and especially a rhetorician, would have a good deal to say against abrogation of the law that requires a sentence to be carried out. He will argue that this law should not be set aside. Or shall we retort, "Yes; but the state has injured us and given an unjust sentence." Suppose I say that?

CRITO: Very good, Socrates.

SOCRATES: "And was that our agreement with you?" the laws would answer; "or were you to abide by the sentence of the state?" And if I were to express my astonishment at their talking this way, they would probably add: "Take control of your astonishment and answer, Socrates—you are in the habit of asking and answering questions. Tell us: What complaint have you to make against us which justifies you in attempting to destroy us and the state? In the first place, did we not bring you into existence? Your father married your mother by our aid and brought you into the world. Say whether you have any objection to urge against those of us who regulate marriage." None, I should reply. "Or against those of us who after birth regulate the nurture and education of children, in which you also were trained? Were not the laws, which have the charge of education, right in commanding your father to train you in music and athletics?" Right, I should reply. "Well then, since you were brought into the world and nurtured and educated by us, can you deny in the first place that you are our child and slave, as your fathers were before you? And if this is true, do you really think you have the same rights as we do and that you are entitled to do to us whatever we do to you? Would you have any right to strike or revile or do any other evil to your father or your master, if you had one, because you had been struck or reviled by him or received some other evil at his hands?—you would not say this? And because we think it right to destroy you, do you think that you have any right to destroy us in return, and your country, as far as in you lies? Will you, O professor of true virtue, pretend that you are justified in this? Has a philosopher like you failed to discover that our country is more to be valued and higher and holier far more than mother or father or any ancestor, and more to be regarded in the eyes of the gods and of men of understanding? Also to be soothed and gently and reverently entreated when angry, even more than a father, and either to be persuaded or, if not persuaded, to be obeyed? And when we are punished by her, whether with imprisonment or beatings, the punishment is to be endured in silence; and if she leads us to wounds or death in battle, there we follow as is right; neither may anyone yield or retreat or leave his rank, but whether in battle, or in a court of law, or in any other place, he must do what his city and his country order him, or he must change their view of what is just; and if he may do no violence to his father or mother, much less may he do violence to his country." What answer shall we make to this, Crito? Do the laws speak truly, or do they not?

CRITO: I think that they do.

SOCRATES: Then the laws will say, "Consider, Socrates, if we are speaking truly that in your present attempt you are going to do us an injury. For, having brought you into the world, and nurtured and educated you, and given you and every other citizen a share in every good which we had to give, we further proclaim to any Athenian, by the liberty which we allow him, that if he does not like us when he has come of age and has seen the ways of the city and made our acquaintance, he may go where he pleases and take his goods with him. None of us laws will stand in the way if any of you who are dissatisfied with us and the city want to go to a colony or to move anywhere else. None of us forbids anyone to go where he likes, taking his property with him. But he who has experience of the manner in which we order justice and administer the state, and still remains, has entered into an implied contract that he will do as we command him. And he who disobeys us is, as we maintain, thrice wrong: first, because in disobeying us he is disobeying his parents; secondly, because we are the authors of his education; thirdly, because he has made an agreement with us that he will duly obey our commands, but he neither obeys them nor convinces us that our commands are unjust. We show flexibility. We do not brutally demand his compliance but offer him the choice of obeying or persuading us; yet he does neither.

"These are the sorts of accusations to which, as we were saying, you, Socrates, will be exposed if you accomplish your intentions; you, above all other Athenians." Suppose now I ask, why I rather than anybody else? They might reasonably take me to task because I above all other men have acknowledged the agreement. "There is clear proof," they will say, "Socrates, that we and the city were not displeasing to you. Of all Athenians you have been the most constant resident in the city, which, as you never leave it, you may be supposed to love. For you never went out of the city either to see the games, except once, when you went to the Isthmus, or to any other place unless when you were on military service; nor did you travel as other men do. Nor had you any curiosity to know other states or their laws: your affections did not go beyond us and our state; we were your special favorites, and you acquiesced in our government of you; and here in this city you had your children, which is a proof of your satisfaction. Moreover, you might in the course of the trial, if you had liked, have fixed the penalty at banishment, and then you could have done with the city's consent what you now attempt against its will. But you pretended that you preferred death to exile and that you were not unwilling to die. And now you do not blush at the thought of your old arguments and pay no respect to us, the laws, of whom you are the destroyer, and are doing what only a miserable slave would do, running away and turning your back on the compacts and agreements by which you agreed to act as a citizen. And, first of all, answer this very question: Are we right in saying that by your actions if not in words you agreed to our terms of citizenship? Is that true or not?" How shall we answer, Crito? Must we not assent?

CRITO: We cannot help it, Socrates.

SOCRATES: Then will they not say: "You, Socrates, are breaking the covenants and agreements which you made with us. You were not compelled to agree, or tricked, or forced to make up your mind in a moment, but had a period of seventy years during which you were free to depart if you were dissatisfied with us and the agreements did not seem fair. You did not pick Sparta or Crete, whose fine government you take every opportunity to praise, or any other state of the Greek or non-Greek world. You spent less time out of Athens than men who are crippled or blind or otherwise handicapped. That shows how much more than other Athenians you valued the city and us too, its laws (for who would value a city without laws?). And will you not now abide by your agreements? You will if you listen to us, Socrates, and you will not make yourself ridiculous by leaving the city.

"For just consider: if you transgress and err in this sort of way, what good will you do either to yourself or to your friends? That your friends will be driven into exile and deprived of citizenship or will lose their property is tolerably certain. And you yourself, if you go to one of the neighboring cities, like Thebes or Megara (both being well-ordered states, of course), will come as an enemy of their government, and all patriotic citizens will eye you suspiciously as a subverter of the laws, and you will confirm in the minds of the judges the justice of their own condemnation of you. For he who is a corrupter of the laws is more than likely to be a corrupter of the young and foolish portion of mankind. Will you then flee from well-ordered cities and law-abiding men? And will life be worth living if you do that? Or will you approach them and discourse unashamedly about—about what, Socrates? Will you discourse as you did here, about how virtue and justice and institutions and laws are the best things among men? Don't you think that such behavior coming from Socrates will seem disgusting? Surely one must think so. But if you go away from well-governed states to Crito's friends in Thessaly, where there is great disorder and license, they will be charmed to hear the tale of your escape from prison, set off with ludicrous particulars of the manner in which you were wrapped in a goatskin or some other disguise and metamorphosed in the usual manner of runaways. But will there be no one to comment that in your old age, when in all probability you had only a little time left to live, you were not ashamed to violate the most sacred laws from the greedy desire of a little more life? Perhaps not, if you keep them in good temper; but if they are out of temper, you will hear many degrading things. You will live as the flatterer and slave of all men, achieving what else but the chance to feast in Thessaly, as though you had gone abroad in order to get a meal? And where will the old arguments be, about justice and virtue? Say that you wish to live for the sake of your children—you want to bring them up and educate them—will you take them into Thessaly and deprive them of Athenian citizenship? Is this the benefit which you will confer upon them? Or are you under the impression that they will be better cared for and educated here if you are still alive, although absent from them; for your friends will take care of them? Do you fancy that, if you move to Thessaly, they will take care of them but that, if you move into the other world, they will not take care of them? No, if those who call themselves friends are good for anything, they will—to be sure, they will.

"Listen, then, Socrates, to us who have brought you up. Think not of life and children first and of justice afterwards but of justice first, so that you may defend your conduct to the rulers of the world below. For neither will you nor any that belong to you be happier or holier or juster in this life, or happier in another, if you do as Crito bids. Now you depart in innocence, a sufferer and not a doer of evil; a victim, not of the laws but of men. But if you escape, returning evil for evil and injury for injury, breaking the covenants and agreements which you have made with us and wronging those you ought least of all to wrong—that is to say, yourself, your friends, your country, and us—we shall be angry with you while you live, and our brethren, the laws in the world below, will receive you in no kindly spirit; for they will know that you have done your best to destroy us. Listen, then, to us and not to Crito."

This, dear Crito, is the voice I seem to hear murmuring in my ears, like the sound of the flute in the ears of the mystic; that voice, I say, is humming in my ears and prevents me from hearing any other. You must realize that you will be wasting your time if you speak against the convictions I hold at the moment. But if you think you will get anywhere, go ahead.

CRITO: No, Socrates, I have nothing to say.

SOCRATES: Then be resigned, Crito, and let us follow this course, since this is the way the god points out.

Suggestions for Discussion

1. What arguments does Crito use to urge Socrates to escape? To what extent do you agree with his position? How does Socrates counter his arguments?

2. Why does Socrates say that one should only consider the opinion of good people?

3. What qualities of character does Plato create for both Crito and Socrates? Which of the two men is more like most of us?

4. Explain Socrates' use of the analogy of the athlete and his trainer and the parallel question of whether life is worth living in a corrupted body.

5. How does Socrates distinguish between the value of "life" and "a good life"?

6. Socrates persuades Crito that a good man should never intentionally commit a wrong act. How does he relate this assertion to the issue of whether he should attempt to escape from prison?

7. Why does Socrates summon up the laws of Athens to discuss his strict obedience to them? What arguments do they offer?

8. Why does Socrates say that he must listen to the voice of the god? How does he connect the laws of the state to the god?

Suggestions for Writing

1. Socrates' arguments for obeying the laws of the state have not always found universal agreement. How do you relate these arguments to those of Antigone in Sophocles' play? In modern times, civil disobedience has moved men like Henry David Thoreau, Mahatma Gandhi, and Martin Luther King, Jr. A research paper of five pages could compare and contrast the writings of Thoreau, Gandhi, and King with this dialogue by Plato.

2. Have you ever broken the law or been tempted to do so? What reasons have restrained you or otherwise guided your behavior? Write a paper of 500 words in which you analyze your own motives as Socrates analyzes his.

Patrick Cooke

The Gentle Death

Patrick Cooke is a contributing editor to the magazine In Health (formerly Hippocrates). He examines here the complex and sensitive issue of euthanasia and explains why its practice in the Netherlands may not be a suitable guide for the United States.

Joop Michels was a young man the first time he witnessed killing in the name of mercy. It was 1944. The cities of central Holland, south beyond the forests of Utrecht, were in flames; there were corpses floating past on the River Waal. Thousands were dead and the German army was fleeing across the border to the Rhineland. In the windy countryside, the Dutch were eating tulip bulbs to stay alive.

"I was just twenty-one years old when the Americans came," says Michels, lighting an unfiltered cigarette on a dark afternoon at his home near Nijmegen. He is nearing 70 now; a few miles away, tall trees sway over the deserted military cemetery at Oosterbeek. "One day on the battlefield, not far from where we are sitting now, I saw an American soldier. His jaw was shot away but he was alive. There were no medical services at all, no medics or drugs of any kind. He was going to die. One of your officers walked past and shot him in the head. And I thought at the time: This is the right thing to do. Why should he suffer in this manner? These were simply hopeless circumstances."

For the last 25 years, Michels has been a nursing home doctor in the eastern province of Gelderland. At any given time, half of his patients are near death. In his working life he has seen more than 5,000 of them die. And many of those in his care have asked to be killed.

The gentle death, the Dutch call it, the mild death. Every year in the Netherlands, doctors perform euthanasia on anywhere from 2,000 to 6,000 people. Patients who are near death account for most cases, but recently people with chronic bronchitis, multiple sclerosis, and debilitating rheumatism have also been granted their wish to die. So open is the idea now—two-thirds of the Dutch favor the practice—that two years ago the Royal Dutch Pharmacists' Association published a doctor's guide to the most efficient and least painful drugs to use in carrying out mercy killing. Even the prime minister admitted he'd request it if matters came right down to the hopeless circumstance.

Officially, euthanasia is against the law in the Netherlands; the penalty is 12 years in prison. But while Dutch lawmakers feel the taking of a life should remain an answerable offense, doctors routinely satisfy prosecutors by pleading "conflict of duty." Their patient's justifiable wish to die, they say, outweighs any attempt to prolong life. If doctors follow certain guidelines—set by the court itself after a case came to trial in 1972—they will not be charged.

There are a number of criteria for euthanasia now, but the most important remain these: There must be an explicit and repeated request by the patient to be killed. The physical or mental pain must be severe and without hope of relief. The patient's decision must be of free will and enduring. All other options must be either exhausted or refused by the patient. The doctor must consult another physician and must record for the local prosecutor all events leading up to the final hour.

"Five years ago, every established medical organization in the world condemned the Netherlands for our stand on euthanasia—our Nazi policies, they called them," says Henk Rigter, the executive director of the Health Council of the Netherlands. "Today Britain, Canada, the United States, and others are talking seriously about whether the need exists for it in their own medical systems. No one wanted to talk to us before. Now articles appear, and afterward we receive phone calls asking how to get one-way tickets to the Netherlands."

As for why the Netherlands should become a proving ground for the rights of the dying, there are only guesses. You will hear vague talk about the tradition of tolerance and the consensus society. But, in fact, politics in the Netherlands are as divisive as ours. In a country half the size of Maine, with a population of roughly 16 million people, there are dozens of squabbling religious sects—some of them gloomy descendants of the same Calvinists who brought their discontent to America. The Dutch are not as liberal as the Swedes, or as fanatical as the Germans, or as *laissez-faire* as the French.

But they are patient, and open. Joop Michels's old battlefield is a wide lovely meadow now. The day I passed it there was an unbroken breeze sailing across a countryside so flat I could see church spires and windmills miles away beyond the wet empty fields. There were bicycle riders pedaling in the middle of nowhere, and on the highways, cops driving Porsches with the convertible tops down. In the villages at night no one ever seemed to shut the curtains. The Dutch, with their mechanical names—Vaandragger, Vanderboom, Spronk—sat in living rooms popping chocolates into their mouths and watching television.

Such openness encourages a kind of candor. The Dutch go about their lives with nothing to hide. And sometimes they choose to leave life the same way.

Report Submitted to the Public Prosecutor: In the first week of March 1987, my patient Mrs. A. Jansen-Verhaak,* born 3-4-1952, was diagnosed to have a malignant growth in the lower abdomen, which appeared to have spread from a malignant stomach tumor.

After consultation with my patient and her husband it was decided that she was to be treated with chemotherapy in the hospital. . . . These courses, however, did not have any effect. The tumor grew rapidly and the patient complained about severe pain, nausea, and vomiting.

On 1, 4, and 7 April 1987 I discussed at length with Mrs. Jansen and her husband, on their request, the possibility of termination of the patient's life should her suffering become unacceptable in the future. I declared myself prepared to terminate the patient's life in the cases of unacceptable suffering. For her this came as a great relief.

She was discharged from hospital on 11 May 1987 with morphine suppositories and strong anti-nausea medication. The patient was very drowsy as a result of the morphine and vomited several times a day. In spite of the morphine she still suffered a great deal of pain.

After consultation with the patient I asked Dr. Duikmans* to discuss with her her wish of active termination of her life. Dr. Duikmans agreed that curative treatment was not possible. The patient was well aware of her situation and the consequence of her decision. In his opinion the patient had come to her decision of her own free will.

Taxes are murder in the Netherlands, but there is virtually no poverty in the country, and anyone who wants insurance under the national health plan is entitled to the best care the western world can offer—from the beginning of life to the end. But even the Dutch cannot escape certain realities of modern medicine.

"Before 1940 most people died rather quickly of some infection and without much pain," says Heleen Dupuis as we walk along the narrow canals in the city of Leiden. She is a professor of bioethics at the local university, small, attractive, and a little melancholy. For four years she was president of the 35,000-member Netherlands Society for Voluntary Euthanasia. "Now, it takes people much longer to die. Some of our cases are AIDS victims," she says, "but mostly it is still cancer patients who are living longer. Medicine keeps changing the pattern of disease and the pattern of dying."

Physicians in the Netherlands feel assured that all patients have equal access to treatment for pain. But they also know that for a small percentage, there will be no drug strong enough to relieve suffering, and that from within

These names have been changed.

this shadowy margin will come the pleas to die. How often euthanasia is truly justified is a matter of some debate—Joop Michels would say the hopeless circumstance arises for only one in 10,000 patients. But most doctors concede that sometimes, euthanasia can be the final step in compassionate care.

Critics of euthanasia, particularly some physicians in the United States, argue that life in any form has meaning, that medicine's highest duty is to preserve life, despite pain and suffering. What lends medicine its heroic element is its insistence on remaining the "enemy of death."

But, Dupuis says, "I think in America you have such an enormous belief in medical science that you look upon it and say, 'Isn't it wonderful, it can do anything.' That's one reason why there is so much aggressive effort in the system. But that is absurd. It is horrible when doctors are afraid to stop treating, feeling it's their duty to go on and on. We in the Netherlands look at medical science and say, 'It is indeed wonderful, but it has its limits.' If you always vote for life, you never accept death, and of course we all must."

Euthanasia's supporters argue that it is well and good to preserve life, but that it is a basic human right for the one dying, and no one else, to decide when life no longer holds meaning. Choosing to die is the ultimate act of human self-determination. If free will doesn't count at these times, when does it count?

One physician who has honored his patients' freedom by helping them to die is Herbert Cohen, although he won't say how often. "That only encourages sensationalism—the number is enough to know what I am talking about." Cohen, who is Jewish, spent the war hiding from the Nazis in and around Amsterdam. Today he is a family doctor in the town of Capelle—"Only a bedroom community, it would bore you"—just east of Rotterdam.

"The act is a discreet, personal situation that does not impose itself on others," he says, looking out the window of a hotel bar at the drizzle and the evening commuters in The Hague. "There is more reason to make laws about abortion because the object cannot speak for itself. Euthanasia is forced on no one, so why does the world demand a moral consensus? It is totally personal. Whether or not even the family or clergyman agrees is completely irrelevant. I don't have to talk anyone into it. That is not my job as a doctor. Usually the family does agree, but even if they do not, that is their problem.

"There is another aspect which is very much overlooked. Offering euthanasia often prolongs life. Take AIDS patients. Quite a number of them will commit suicide early in the disease while they have the strength. The paradox is that they don't have to do that. They can stand it longer; with the euthanasia option they feel they will still have a card left to play when they are helpless and dependent. If you are so weak that you need a nurse to chase a fly from your forehead, it is marvelous to have the power to say, 'That is enough.'"

Mrs. Jansen continued to be in pain, the vomiting did not decrease and she was continuously drowsy. I suggested that she have a catheter inserted, through which morphine could be injected into the spinal cord. The catheterization took place 22 May 1987. The morphine was then injected once a day by the district nurse and once a day by myself.

The pain was adequately suppressed and the drowsiness disappeared, but the vomiting was still a major problem. Anti-nausea medication, sedation, and anti-acid medication had no effect.

In the 23 days between 11 May and 2 June 1987 the patient and I discussed euthanasia three times. Each time she expressed her wish to have euthanasia if the situation became unacceptable to her. Several times the patient and her husband expressed their relief that the possibility of an acceptable death existed.

On Friday afternoon, 2 June 1987, I was called to see Mrs. Jansen, who had been suffering from a pain in the chest all afternoon. . . . I told her that I could not do more than attempt to relieve the pain by administering morphine suppositories again. The patient was adamant in her refusal to be admitted to the hospital for insertion of a stomach tube and being drip fed, since she considered this a senseless prolongation of her life. The alternative of dehydration and reinstatement of sedating and pain-killing morphine medication was discussed and rejected.

At 19.00 hours I left the patient with the request to think about her wishes. At 21.00 hours I returned to administer the evening dose of morphine. The patient then expressed her wish for active termination of her life by means of an injection, preferably that same evening.

People told me that Delft was a "messy little town." It was, in fact, immaculate, astonishingly beautiful, and disconcertingly quiet. It is a merciful trait of the Dutch that they do not make a lot of unnecessary noise. Even teenagers who walked along the perfect 13th century red-bricked lanes—cowboy boots and Confederate belt buckles—talked in low tones and courteously stepped aside at the ping of a bicycle bell.

The loudest person in Delft seemed to be Pieter Admiraal, Reinier de Graaf hospital's senior anesthesiologist and arguably the person who has performed euthanasia more often than anyone else on earth. The day I called him to ask for an interview, he yelled into the telephone, "*Ja*, you *must* come to see me on Friday!" When I described myself for our first meeting as tall and blond—the unhelpful description of nearly everyone in the Netherlands—he shouted, "Never mind, ask anyone for Ah-mi-*RAWL!*" and hung up.

This was not intended as rudeness; it was simply Dutch directness, which can be startling. Admiraal had, in fact, a booming laugh and a surprisingly gentle way for a man so outwardly imposing. Even in baggy hospital scrubs he appeared to have only just tumbled out of a Rembrandt painting: stern and watchful, with a big belly. Four hundred years ago he might have been one of the grand burghers of Delft. Because he is larger than life and the Netherlands' most outspoken supporter of euthanasia, he has become both famous and infamous. So much is said of Admiraal that even he refers to himself, somewhat self-deprecatingly, in the third person.

"They say that Admiraal is a chilling individual," he howled after we shook hands. "They write about Admiraal the euthanasist and his poor victims!" We were sitting in his office adjacent to the hospital operating and recovery wards, a room out of a Chekhov play: heavy furniture, dark bookshelves, stuffed mallards and pheasants. "They do not say that I founded the Dutch Society for the Study of Pain to find better ways to help patients. When any patient asks to discuss euthanasia with me, my first thought is that we are not doing *enough* for him. We must work harder to make him change his mind!" Whenever Admiraal pounded the desktop with his fist, the steady foot traffic of nurses and orderlies in the next room stopped for a moment, then hurried away.

We talked throughout the afternoon as big clouds rolled off the North Sea and past the windows of Delft. Admiraal told me that in 28 years of working the operating rooms he had seen probably 4,000 people die. One of his most nettlesome critics, he said, was a dermatologist who'd experienced nothing of the sort. During those years he had come to know well the patients whom medicine could no longer rescue. The only thing left a doctor could give, he believed, was an open door to a threshold they now wished to pass.

I asked him how many times he had performed euthanasia. "Hundreds," he said, without hesitation. "But I do not keep a count. We have done it fifteen years now, so if I have done ten a year that is already one hundred and fifty."

I tried to imagine what the enemies of euthanasia saw when they looked at Admiraal: He was the doctor who turned his back on the preservation of life and instead pretended his mission was the relief of suffering. Until recently, granting someone the right to die was merely a sin of omission—like starving the comatose—but Admiraal's was a sin of commission, active killing. His frankness about it they took as coldbloodedness; only a murderer would talk this way. If The Great Admiraal cleared the path of ethical brambles, then physicians everywhere would emulate him.

It was easy to see why his critics exasperated him, but even his admirers caused him grief. "Let me show you something!" he hooted, and began pawing through a cabinet. "This is my file from people all around the world asking me for euthanasia." What he dropped on the table was as fat as a New York City phone book; the previous week's mail alone was an inch thick. "I get calls also at home in the night from AIDS patients in California. I say, I cannot *do* anything for you! I only hope that they find help somewhere rather than blowing their brains out with a pistol."

I asked him if he remembered his first mercy killing. "I do not recall," he said, but for the first time he stopped shouting. "Others I remember very well, however. There was a woman who had cancer of the tongue. She could not eat or swallow. She was suffocating. I came in and she wrote on a piece of paper, 'Please help me.'

"You realize that pain is not always the only reason they ask for euthanasia. It is loss of human dignity. That is what it is. It is a complex idea and I am not sure I can give you a definition . . . Can you imagine me lying there, incontinent, without even the strength to turn in bed? Fatigued in a way that is horrible but still unable to sleep? Perhaps there is no pain at all, just a continual hiccup, or thirst that won't go away. Can you imagine I would say that this is not a life? I do not want anyone to see me this way. I want to go away. I want to sleep forever."

Admiraal sat up on the edge of his chair and for a long moment stared down at his big white hospital clogs. "I remember a man, he was a taxi driver," he said. "His wife worked in a bar. They decided they wanted to have a baby and she became pregnant. But he began coughing a lot and it was discovered that he had cancer of the esophagus.

"He was in our hopsital until the end. We tried to keep him alive until the baby was born. And we did. But like many of these patients he was . . ." Admiraal stopped, looked up with a doomed expression, and began an indescribable rasping gurgle in his throat.

"It was on a Sunday that I stopped in to see him," he went on slowly. "This man said, 'How nice it is that you are here, I want to die now.' I wasn't prepared for this. His wife and baby were in the room. It so happened that he had said farewell to all of his family that morning. He had made a list of all his friends and given each one a little present.

"So I did it . . . It is very difficult to speak of the feelings you have at that moment." He turned away toward the window and closed his eyes. "I am always saying goodbye and I am kissing them when I do it. You may laugh at this but I say, 'I wish you a good journey . . . to an unknown land I have never seen before.'"

And then The Great Admiraal began to cry.

"*This* is what I am doing with my patients!" he continued. Tears rolled down his big cheeks, and he was yelling again. "Sometimes I cannot cry . . . I am so sorry for this . . . But these are my friends! I know them for *months*. I would blame myself if I did not do it. I say that you *must* blame the doctor who does not stop this suffering."

> I then asked Mrs. Jansen to fill in and sign the form given to her by Dr. Duikmans. The patient did this together with her husband. A friend of the patient, Mrs. Klein, was present and signed the declaration as a witness. Support from a priest or similar help was rejected. Her children of 14 and 15 were well informed and were, in my opinion, adequately taken care of and guided by their father and other relatives.
>
> After consultation with the patient and her husband it was decided that a possible termination of her life would take place the following afternoon. I strongly emphasized to the patient that she could retract her decision at any time.
>
> I then personally notified senior police officer K. van Droest of the Ypenburg police station at 22.30 hours of my intention to perform active euthanasia on one of my patients.

In the Santa Ynez Valley in Southern California, the temperature can easily reach 115 degrees in summer. Because the sky is dazzlingly blue, the mountains spectacular, and because the area looks like no place in particular, moviemakers have traveled the 130 miles here from Los Angeles to film what audiences will eventually believe to be Morocco, say, or Umbria in Italy.

The village of Solvang, a few miles off the Pacific Coast Highway on the valley's southern edge, was settled 75 years ago by Danish immigrants. There are Tudor buildings with high-pitched roofs on the main streets, artificial storks nesting on rooftops, and phony windmills squatting among the palm trees. Solvang is a movie-set town in a make-believe valley.

Teresa Takken lives just north of here and directs the non-denominational Pacific Institute for Bioethics in nearby Santa Barbara. Like the town itself, her life appears, from certain angles, beyond belief: She speaks 11 languages fluently, including Dutch—her uncle led the Netherlands railway strike against Hitler. She has a photographic and audiographic memory. She once had a lucrative recording career in opera—the money went to charity—and still plays any number of musical instruments. She has a doctorate in bioethics, and is working on a second in law. She is charming and pretty and shockingly earthy at times for a Roman Catholic nun of the Sisters for Christian Community. She is also only 36 years old.

Much of what the English-speaking world has read about euthanasia in the Netherlands was translated by Takken, who lived there while the Dutch moved toward its acceptance. Now, as legalization in America appears only a matter of time—California, Oregon, Washington, Florida, and Hawaii are considering some form of it—she has become a voice in the opposition. There aren't many with her, and they're starting from behind.

"Physicians tell me all the time that euthanasia already goes on," she says across a lunchtime helping of Solvang's fine Belgian waffles. "I've had doctors tell me they've done it with no reservations whatever. It happens right here in this area. One guy told me he's performed it a number of times on Alzheimer's patients. He said, 'You just overmedicate. Who's every going to find out?' He's almost flippant about it."

No one disputes that euthanasia secretly goes on in the United States. But there is only oblique evidence as to the extent. Last year, in a University of Colorado poll of roughly 2,000 state physicians, more than half said euthanasia would have been justified for some of their patients. Another third said they had actually given pain medication they knew would hasten a patient's death. The American Medical Association, too, discovered last year that 80 percent of the physicians who responded to its survey favored passive euthanasia—ending life support for the hopelessly ill if that's what the patients and their families wanted.

In January of 1988, the *Journal of the American Medical Association* printed its now notorious "Debbie Letter." In it, an anonymous physician claims to have carried out euthanasia on a 20-year-old woman suffering from ovarian cancer. The doctor wrote that the patient's somewhat vague request consisted of one sentence: "Let's get this over with." There followed a shower of indignant letters from the nation's anti-euthanasia physicians, but the subject had been broached. In a March issue of the *New England Journal of Medicine*, ten prominent doctors acknowledged that many of their colleagues were already giving patients the means with which to end their lives. "It is not immoral for a physician to assist in the rational suicide of a terminally ill person," they wrote. Active euthanasia, they cautiously added, is something we should be talking about.

All this naturally spooks those who see euthanasia as the erosion of respect for life. What will be the point, they ask, of looking for better ways to control pain once mercy killing becomes accepted? Why even look for cures for disease? Won't insurance companies eventually withhold payment when euthanasia is an option? They foresee hospices converted to gentle death clinics done up in soothing mauve and canned music.

"Let's face it," Takken says. "Euthanasia will become the quick fix in America. Let's just put people out of their misery. Let's get them off our backs. It's cheap, it's easy. Why not?"

Advocates of euthanasia ridicule such visions, but no one denies that there is historical precedent for mercy killing getting out of control. In the late 1930s, German doctors began killing psychiatric and medical patients for "compassionate" reasons. Steadily, other categories were added to cleanse society of its "useless eaters."

That the strong should come to dominate the weak on such a scale seems too horrible to be repeated. But no one is sure that euthanasia can be managed successfully, not even Admiraal. "I know a doctor who is very dedicated to euthanasia, and one of his fears is that if there are no young people to care for the elderly, in the next generation they will decide to kill a person simply because he is demented. And do you know the name of that famous doctor I am speaking of? It is Admiraal!"

Those who fret about this "slippery slope" say euthanasia should never be given a place in society. Certainly there are patients whose suffering will be difficult to watch, they say, but medicine's highest responsibility is to the common good, not to the individual. If you never draw the line, you needn't worry about what lies on the other side.

In my opinion this was a desperately critical situation and a case of unacceptable suffering. The patient's fear and expectation of not being able to die with dignity was justified.

The patient expressed her wish in total freedom and confirmed it after careful consideration. Her wish was based on a sustained desire. She had expressed this wish to her husband and to two general practitioners from 1 April 1987 onwards. In the following two months she never indicated that she was in doubt about her wish to have euthanasia in the case of an approaching unacceptable end.

On Friday evening, 2 June 1987, the patient was sound of mind and totally capable of exercising her own free will. Since the best possible terminal care had been given, there was no other possibility of making the suffering acceptable to her.

An American doctor once asked Herbert Cohen of Rotterdam about his standard fee for performing euthanasia. Cohen patiently told the man that he didn't charge anything.

Ask around in the Netherlands whether the idea of euthanasia seems transportable to America, and the Dutch will look up painfully with their pale blue eyes and try to formulate a reply that is not too offensive. The most they usually manage is, "Perhaps matters of profit in the States would make things . . . suspect."

The Dutch were naive, of course, if they believed euthanasia could be confined to their own society, where families are not financially ruined by sickness, where everyone is well-educated, and where the size and structure of the country allows for social experimentation. Perhaps no one in the Netherlands ever considered that other countries less suited to mercy killing would follow their lead.

"America does not have any business even talking about legalizing euthanasia," says Takken, as a hot wind blows through the doorway of a tiny mountain cabin she's using as a study. Nearby are the estates of Michael Jackson and Bo Derek. Ronald Reagan's Rancho del Cielo is just a few doors away, by valley standards. "We aren't ready socially, financially, or philosophically. Americans are morally schizophrenic—look at the diverse values we have. You can't compare the United States to the Netherlands. The Dutch don't go around bombing abortion clinics, thinking that's the way to solve problems. We do. It's a completely different setting."

Different, too, says Takken, is the oftentimes close relationship between doctor and patient in the Netherlands that makes euthanasia largely a matter between two people who have known one another for many years. The American health maintenance organization, on the other hand, isn't exactly the intimate setting in which one might imagine discussing the gentle death.

"The American health care system breeds more contempt for doctors than camaraderie," she says.

None of these arguments has fazed the Hemlock Society—an organization the Dutch, by and large, seem to want to distance themselves from—which has led the fight for legalized euthanasia in the United States. Hemlock was born ten years ago out of the helplessness felt by its founder, Derek Humphry, as his wife died painfully of cancer. Today the society has 32,000 members and publishes a newsletter with an odd mix of legislative updates and suicide instruction, such as how to kill yourself, or a loved one, with an ordinary plastic bag.

Last year Hemlock's legal wing, Americans Against Human Suffering, fought for passage of the California Humane and Dignified Death Act. The law would have allowed patients to request euthanasia if it was determined by two doctors that they would die within six months. Unlike in the Netherlands, mercy killing would also have been possible by proxy: a friend or relative with power of attorney could authorize it if the terminal patient became unable to.

The society had good reason to believe the measure would pass a popular vote. In 1988 a nationwide Roper poll found that more than half of its respondents favored legalization. Moreover, juries and grand juries have been almost uniformly sympathetic in cases of assisted suicide, when people have ended the lives of others in agony.

The initiative failed to collect the signatures needed to bring the issue to California voters—organizational difficulties, Humphry says—but plans are in the works to introduce it again in 1992.

"The things they were asking for in that bill were ridiculous," says Takken. "How can you ascertain beyond the shadow of a doubt if a person is going to die in six months? That's impossible.

"Look, ten years ago I *was* the dying patient. I went through hell with a freak medical condition no one could find a cause for. I lost all of my friends because nobody wants to see anyone down to ninety pounds and dying, which all the doctors agreed looked like a certainty. The pain, indignity, hopelessness, abandonment, isolation—it was all there. But I never once thought of asking for someone to kill me. And I *didn't* die."

Takken went head-to-head with Derek Humphry and made several speeches on her own during last year's California debate. She came away astonished at how little voters seemed to know about euthanasia. "There has been no education of the American people about just what the consequences might be if this were passed. How can they be expected to make an informed choice? You'd be shocked how many people of voting age think the word euthanasia, no lie, has something to do with young people in the Orient somewhere."

Takken worries most about the effect of legalization on the ever-increasing numbers of elderly. With health care costs beyond the reach of many Americans, the elderly may feel pressured to ask for mercy killing simply to spare their families the crushing financial burden of hanging on—making euthanasia less a personal choice than a social responsibility. And those families, knowing the realities, may not be terribly eager to argue the decision.

So who would fight for the patient? Nobody, Takken believes. Hospitals and nursing homes are struggling to contain costs. Medicare is on the skids. The elderly only use up what little resources exist, she says, and what better way to trim costs than offering the gentle death. In the 1930s, the rationale for mercy killing was racial purity; in the next century, perhaps, it will be budget considerations. A useless eater is still a useless eater.

"I know a nursing home administrator here who just loves the old-timers and is really dedicated to them," Takken says, walking out onto the cabin deck where there are bright flowers all around and golden pastures under an endless California sky. "But he's beginning to say, 'What's the use. Kill 'em.' Every day he fights a system that won't pay for their care. The place stinks, there's no money. The patients feel useless in a use-oriented society. But what's he going to do, put them out on the street? It only takes a little morphine, and he has a real hard time thinking, 'No, don't do it.'

"Euthanasia is the perfect Band-aid. But what we should be doing is taking a long hard look at the inequities in the system. Don't give me this crap about, well, the Dutch do it and things seem to work okay. I know how it works in the Netherlands; everyone has insurance and an equal chance. How many millions are there in America who can't possibly afford basic health care?

"Listen, I just lost a good friend to cancer. He was poor. The system sent this guy around and around and finally shoved him off in the corner because there was nobody to pay for his treatment. It happens so often in this state they call it being Medi-Caled. In the end he, literally, died in a shack outside of town. I was so pissed at that funeral . . . People go around shouting about how euthanasia is a human right. Well, why isn't proper care for a person like that a human right first?

"I think we can find a compassionate way to accompany one another to the outer edges of life without mercy killing. If we don't do that, then yeah, we're going to see the legalization of euthanasia and it will be our own fault. Maybe our *own* pain will be eased because we just won't have to deal with them any longer. But *someone* should look down on that person lying there and ask, 'What could we have done differently for you? Why do you want to leave us? Were you in pain? Were you lonely? Didn't we love you enough?'"

On Saturday morning, 3 June 1987, I visited Mrs. Jansen at 9.00 hours to administer morphine. The patient was a little drowsy due to the 20 mg. morphine suppositories that she had been using every three hours to relieve pain behind the sternum. She was nevertheless well capable of expressing her wishes and feelings. In the presence of her husband she confirmed her wish for termination of her life that afternoon.

I returned to the patient's house in the afternoon. In the presence of her husband, her friend, her sister, and her brother, I asked her once more whether she wished me to terminate her life. She confirmed this. Then, at approximately 14.15 I injected 1.0 g thiopental intravenously in her right forearm. The patient immediately lost consciousness. Then I injected 10 mg. alcuronium in her right forearm. After approximately 10 minutes, all heart activity had ceased.

Suggestions for Discussion

1. The essay alternates an analysis of euthanasia with an actual narrative told by a Dutch doctor who practices it. Why is this an effective organization for the essay?

2. What distinctions between Dutch and American society does Cooke report that might make a difference in the practice of euthanasia? Do you agree with the assertion that the United States is not a suitable place for euthanasia?

3. What are the political and social arguments for and against euthanasia?

4. Explain the title of the essay in connection with its subject.

5. Discuss Cooke's interview with the Dutch Dr. Admiraal. To what extent do you agree or disagree with Teresa Takken, a leader of the opposition to euthanasia in the United States?

Suggestions for Writing

1. Attempt to summarize your own position on euthanasia and write an essay in which you defend your position with clear arguments and facts.

2. How would you feel if someone you love wanted euthanasia? Write an essay in which you examine your own feelings and reach some conclusion based on them.

Robert Jay Lifton

The Genocidal Mentality

Robert Jay Lifton (b. 1926), born in New York City, graduated from Cornell University Medical School in 1948 and received many honorary doctorate degrees. He is director of the Center on Violence and Human Survival at John Jay College of the City University of New York, and has written books on psychiatric and social issues. He won the National Book Award and the Van Wyck Brooks Award for *Death in Life; Survivors of Hiroshima* in 1969. *The Nazi Doctors: Medical Killing and the Psychology of Genocide* (1986) received the National Jewish Book Award and the Los Angeles Times National Book Prize for History. In 1984 he won the Gandhi Peace Award and the Bertrand Russell Society Award. He explores the difficulties of the survival of the human race in *The Future of Immortality and Other Essays for a Nuclear Age*, with Eric Marcusen (1987), and in *The Genocidal Mentality: Nazi Holocaust and Nuclear Threat* (1990). He is a member of the American Academy of Arts and Sciences. On the occasion of his award of an honorary degree, Lifton, a scientist with humanitarian concerns, reminds his German audience of the genocide committed by Nazi doctors and explains the various ways they prepared themselves for their inhuman acts.

What I feel deeply in receiving this degree is the confirmation of an alliance with a special network of contemporary Germans. It is an alliance of shared ethical commitment—and yes, even of love. The commitment is toward confrontation of Nazi genocide on behalf of its victims—and for the sake of both the German future and the human future. That confrontation is

Reprinted by permission of *Tikkun* Magazine, a bimonthly Jewish critique of politics, culture, and society. Subscriptions are available for $25/yr (6 issues) from 5100 Leona St., Oakland, CA 94619 not easy for anyone, least of all for Germans and for Jews, and we do well to make it together.

There are certain vignettes from my research on Nazi doctors that I will not easily forget. One of them is from an interview with a Jewish dentist who had miraculously survived three years in Auschwitz. We spoke in the sitting room of his attractive house overlooking the beautiful Haifa harbor. He told me a great deal about the behavior of Nazi doctors and about his own experiences, all of which was as painful to him as it was important for my work. At the end of our talk he looked about, sighed deeply, and said, "This world is not this world!"

What I believe he meant was that, however comfortable one's immediate surroundings, having known Auschwitz one knows that menace lurks underneath. I had encountered similar tones in Hiroshima years earlier when interviewing people subjected to the first use of an atomic bomb on a human population. They too could be sitting with me in an apparently comfortable setting and yet convey that sense of never-absent menace. For they carried within them special memories that went beyond even the extensive killing and maiming that occurs in conventional bombing—memories of one plane, one bomb, one city.

In this kind of work one must struggle to combine mind and heart. Somewhere in the intellectual history of the West there developed the wrongheaded idea that mind and heart are antagonists, that scholarship must be divested of emotion, that spiritual journeys must avoid intellectual concerns. In my view, quite the opposite is true. Who has ever heard of an outstanding piece of scholarship that was not infused with moral passion? Or of a powerful spiritual quest that did not include intellectual clarity? In my developing scholarly work, therefore, I have put forward a model or paradigm in which I speak of advocacy and detachment: sufficient detachment to bring to bear one's intellectual discipline on the subject, and sufficient moral passion to motivate and humanize the work. From that standpoint all psychological work is both a scientific and a moral enterprise, one whose vocabulary may have to include a concept of evil.

I want to pause a bit here on the subject of evil, and to suggest three different views of it that have to be taken into account. The first is the classical religious view, the notion of evil as a strictly moral state that is only to be judged and never probed in terms of causation. A second view carries that notion further and approaches evil as a visitation from without, from a dark, more-than-natural source—Satan or the Devil—whose extreme manifestations cannot be understood in human terms. But there is a third view, closer to my own, which sees evil as a specifically human trait—we do not consider horses or cats to be evil—which can be influenced by psychological and historical forces. Evil, that is, can be illuminated by probing and grasping those forces. One is then investigating psychological and historical conditions conducive to evil, while retaining the term and thereby holding to ethical judgments. I choose this secular approach, but recognize that the theological views remain important because they convey a sense of the demonic dimensions that are possible in the perpetration of evil.

Rolf Hochhuth, the admirable Austrian writer, raised these issues in his brilliant 1963 play, *The Deputy*. The play was a powerful indictment of Pope

Pius XII for his failure to speak out against Nazi mass murder of Jews. The play's characters were actual historical figures depicted more or less realistically—except for one, a Mengele-like figure. Known only as "The Doctor," this character (according to Hochhuth) "has the stature of Absolute Evil" and so contrasts with "anything that has been learned about human beings" as to resemble "an uncanny visitant from another world." One must view him "as a figure of Satan in a Medieval morality play." During a talk I had with Hochhuth, he explained to me that he depicted his character in that way in order to suggest an extreme dimension of evil. I of course understood what he meant, but must also insist that Satan is a human creation, and that any perpetration of evil, no matter how spectacular, has something to do with the rest of us.

That principle was at issue in my embarking on a study of Nazi doctors. At the time a number of friends spoke to me of their uneasiness about my undertaking such painful work. They frequently used the phrase "strong stomach" for what they thought was needed—and hoped I had one. While they were expressing concern about a friend, some of them were also suggesting that extreme evil of that kind should not be touched, should be somehow walled off and kept absolutely separate from the rest of us. But the fact is that no such walling off is possible; that evil, however extreme, is part of human capability. And therein lies the justification—indeed the urgency—for this kind of work.

One friend, an Auschwitz survivor deeply concerned about the work, asked, in reference to the Nazi doctors doing what they did, "Were they beasts or human beings? And when I answered that they were human beings and that was the problem, his reply was an interesting one: "But it is *demonic* that they were *not* demonic." What he meant was that it would be easier for us, psychologically and morally, if Nazi doctors had the mark of Cain on their foreheads, or if they were clearly insane, or belonged to some category that separated them absolutely from the rest of us. But actually they were very ordinary men; there was nothing unusual about them. Prior to arriving at Auschwitz they would not have been identified as either particularly good or particularly bad, and none had murdered anyone. One is reminded of Hannah Arendt's famous thesis about the banality of evil, but the thesis requires some modification. The men were indeed banal, but the evil they perpetrated was not; nor did the men themselves, over time, remain banal.

For instance, I was able to interview at some length the daughter of a man who had been a prominent Nazi doctor at Auschwitz and killed himself upon being taken into custody soon after the war's end. A middle-aged housewife when I met her, she was by no means an unsympathetic figure to me—groping to understand how her father, a kindly and conscientious physician whom she had loved and thought a decent man, could have been associated with the terrible things she came to learn that he and others did in Auschwitz. Toward the end of our interview she asked a question that was as simple as it was difficult to answer: "Can a good man do bad things?" The only reply I could think of was, "Yes, but he is then no longer a good man." When involved in evil, one changes.

What can we learn from Nazi doctors? Let me mention three principles that have enormous importance for our present world.

The first has to do with the power of a genocidal ideology. In the Nazi case, that genocidal ideology included killing in the name of healing and a

pseudo-biological or "biomedical" worldview. Doctors were centrally involved in five terrible steps: coercive sterilization (of those considered to possess harmful genes); "euthanasia" (actually mass murder) of children designated as "life unworthy of life"; "euthanasia" or mass killing of adults (mostly
mental patients); the extension to concentration camps of "euthanasia" or direct medical killing; and finally, the construction of death camps in Poland by
transferring the killing centers of the "euthanasia" program from Germany,
including both equipment and personnel.

There were key individual doctors, Nazi true believers, who took the lead
in each of these steps. The Nazis combined terror with visionary idealism,
and one must recognize that visionary idealism if one is to understand the
power of the Nazi project for so many Germans. Indeed, it is impossible to
kill great masses of people without the claim of virtue, of higher purpose. But
most of the doctors I saw were by no means true believers; they embraced
ideological fragments rather than the full ideology. They were especially
drawn to the Nazi promise of individual and national revitalization, as were
Germans in general. That response could combine with added bits and pieces
of Nazi ideology, fervent nationalism, elements of anti-Semitism and authoritarianism, and corruptibility. An overall combination of that kind could be
enough.

One must be constantly aware of the danger of potentially genocidal ideologies, particularly when they project a principle of sickness and cure that
requires harming or destroying another group for the sake of the therapy of
one's own. Here there is a parallel to the ideology I call nuclearism—the
embrace of, and exaggerated dependency upon, weapons to the point of near
worship, a tendency that has long been rampant in the United States, the
Soviet Union, and other countries that possess nuclear weapons. Nuclearism
too is an ideology, embraced totally by some and in fragments by many more,
an ideology that could propel groups and nations toward genocide, or what is
now called omnicide—the destruction of everything.

A second major lesson from Nazi doctors has to do with the direct involvement of professionals, most of them ordinary professionals. I chose to study
Nazi doctors because I came to recognize, from trial documents, their special
importance for Nazi genocide; and also because I am a physician myself. But
in another sense, Nazi doctors simply reflected the behavior of German professionals at that time. One must not speak of deprofessionalization in Nazi
Germany, but rather of the professions becoming reconstituted so that medicine could become killing in the name of healing, law could become legitima-
tion of that killing, and theology its spiritual justification.

A perceptive reviewer of my book on Nazi doctors asked when I might
mount a study of what he called "nuclear doctors." I had in fact already embarked on precisely such a study. Whatever the enormous differences in the
two historical situations, one cannot help being impressed by parallels in the
role of professionals in nuclear-weapons projects, whether as physicists who
design the weapons or strategists (mostly drawn from social science or physical science) who project their use.

A Nazi doctor went far in conveying the amoral capacity of professionals
when he said to me, "Ethical . . . the word does not exist (in Auschwitz)."
He went on to explain that the killing process became "purely a technical
matter," with a focus always on what worked best. By means of that naked

pragmatism and technicism, Nazi doctors sought to retain a sense of themselves as scientists and physicians. They could also try to hold onto the medical identity by means of professional discussions with prisoner physicians (who, unlike Nazi doctors, did engage in actual therapeutic work) and by means of their notorious "research" experiments on their literally captive population.

I did not make medical ethics the central concern of my study, but have been pleased to find the issues it raised taken up widely at medical centers in the United States. There has been considerable recognition that the very extremity of Nazi medical behavior can help illuminate some of our own more nuanced moral questions. My main focus has been on the mass killing, where professionals' involvement was made possible by an amoral focus on technical issues. And most professions have been even more negligent than medicine in articulating and maintaining individual ethical principles.

A third lesson to be learned from Nazi doctors has to do with psychological states that make possible genocidal projects. Here I would emphasize what can be called a dissociative field, which can include patterns I have described as psychic numbing and as doubling. Dissociation is a mechanism by which a portion of the self separates from the rest of the self, as described in detail early in the twentieth century by the great French psychiatrist Pierre Janet, and as taken up by Freud under the concept of splitting. Psychic numbing is a form of dissociation and consists of diminished capacity or inclination to feel. I first observed psychic numbing in Hiroshima survivors (where it had a useful purpose as a psychological defense), but came to recognize it as taking on even more importance in perpetrators or potential perpetrators. With psychic numbing and other forms of dissociation, there can be a radical separation of knowledge from feeling—perhaps the most malignant overall psychological tendency of our era—whether occurring in Nazi doctors, nuclear-weapons professionals, or other educated participants in lethal projects.

Doubling consists of the formation of a part self that becomes functionally a whole self. A Nazi doctor could develop an "Auschwitz self," attuned to that environment, which enabled him not only to perform experiments but to supervise the entire killing process: from the selections at the ramp to the insertion of the gas to the determination that Jewish victims in the gas chamber were dead. Yet that same doctor could return to his home in Germany for a few days' leave and, by calling forth his prior, relatively more humane self, function as an ordinary husband and father.

The dissociative field, then, is likely to involve doubling within those closest to the center of killing projects, and psychic numbing in those at their periphery, so that in the case of the Nazis the numbing came to include much of the German population. There is a parallel dissociative field surrounding nuclear weapons: a form of doubling, in weapons scientists and strategists, less intense than that of Nazi doctors but highly significant nonetheless; and, in the general population, patterns of psychic numbing affecting groups that participate more indirectly in weapons projects. It is important to understand that the people involved in this dissociative field are in no way abnormal in a clinical psychiatric sense. Indeed, the mentally ill do relatively little harm to a society. It is the normal people who are dangerous, as they take on patterns of numbing and doubling that enable them to sever connections between knowledge and feeling in pursuing potentially genocidal projects. But whatever the psychological mechanisms, the people involved are responsible for what they do.

We may summarize what we have learned from Nazi doctors, then, as a malignant constellation that includes: a genocidal ideology, which provides the rationale and motor for mass killing; the participation of professionals, who are needed for the intellectual, technical, and organizational requirements of the genocidal project; and the dissociative field, characterized mainly by doubling and psychic numbing, that enables people at all levels to join in murderous behavior uncharacteristic of their previous individual lives.

In discussing actual genocide, I have been talking mostly about Germans. We cannot forget that the Nazis were a German phenomenon, and that it was Germans who killed six million Jews and about as many in other groups. These groups included Gypsies, Poles, Russians, and other Slavs, as well as fellow Germans. The German victims were, for the most part, mental patients and others considered to be "life unworthy of life"—homosexuals, Jehovah's Witnesses, and those designated as political and religious opponents. That is why contemporary Germans have a special responsibility that extends to universities like this one for confronting their own institutional behavior during the Nazi era.

Yet it must be understood that genocide is hardly a specific German trait. Just as any individual human being is capable of evil, so is any culture or state capable of genocide. We need only point to the all-too-frequent examples of genocide that have both preceded and followed the Nazi case. In that sense, Nazi genocide is part of human history, and there are partial parallels to it in other destructive events.

But saying that in no way justifies the recent revisionist trend among certain German historians, according to which Nazi genocide is nothing special, just another historical example of human cruelty—one mainly in response to Stalinism at that. Such a formulation embraces half-truths, distortions, and falsehoods in erasing the full dimensions of Nazi genocide and denying its unique features. We must clearly recognize the historical uniqueness of the attempt to round up every Jew from anywhere in the world for mass murder, and of the further impulse toward the mass murder of other peoples and the creation of what has been called a "genocidal universe." I would insist that we stress the special features of Nazi genocide while at the same time viewing it as part of history and seeking from it a grasp of those principles and patterns of behavior that can apply to other situations. From that perspective, what we learn from the Nazis can contribute greatly to combating potential genocide from any direction.

A genocidal mentality is not our only recourse. As human beings, as meaning-hungry creatures and inveterate symbolizers, we ourselves have created the meanings and symbolizations that take us along a genocidal path. We ourselves are equally capable of altering these meanings and symbolizations—of replacing a genocidal mentality with what I call a species mentality. All I have learned about Nazi doctors, about Hiroshima survivors, and about our present nuclear threat suggests the urgency of that alternative. And here there is a source of hope, however unlikely it may seem. These very genocidal possibilities—including our assaults on the earth's ecology—can prod the contemporary self toward a sense of shared fate. Each of us increasingly perceives that what is at issue is not Americans and Soviets, or West or East Germans, or Thais, Iranians, or Nigerians. What is at issue is the survival or demise of humankind. Each of us comes to feel, in significant degree, that his or her sense of self is bound up with every individual sense of self on the planet.

This more inclusive identity does not mean that one surrenders more immediate identifications; one cannot live on the species self alone. Speaking personally, I continue being an American, a Jew, a professor, a psychiatrist, a teacher, a writer, a husband, a father, an avid tennis player. But all of these aspects of myself—to the extent that I form a species self—are importantly subsumed by my sense of being a member of the human species. As that happens to any of us, we feel the pain, let us say, of a Jewish victim of anti-Semitism anywhere, but also of a Palestinian victim of Israeli harassment on the West Bank, of a South African Black treated cruelly simply because of being a Black, or of a Chinese student encountering official violence in his or her pursuit of democracy.

Many people throughout the world can already claim elements of such species consciousness, but it needs to be nurtured individually and collectively. Once more the professions are of great importance—this time in their potential for developing attitudes and behavior that enhance, rather than threaten, the human project. Here a simple image comes to mind: a scene from a film made during a visit by a group of American doctors to their counterparts in the Soviet Union, as part of the international physicians' antinuclear movement. The movement itself is species oriented, but that is not the point I wish to make. The scene took place in a Moscow hospital room in which an extremely sick man lay on his bed and two physicians examined him in turn. The first was the head of the American physicians' group, the second of the Soviet group, since both leaders happened to be cardiologists. As each doctor applied his stethoscope, it became quite clear that the two men had forgotten about being Americans or Russians, even about the nuclear weapons problem which brought them together. They were simply focused on applying their knowledge and experience, their commitment as healers, to maintaining the life of an extremely fragile fellow human being.

There is a species principle at the heart of every profession, even if covered over by struggles for power, money, and recognition within that profession. At the heart of medicine is the principle of healing; in law it is that of justice; in theology, that of spiritual search; and in science and academic life, the quest for knowledge and truth. During our better moments as professionals we live out these principles and are capable of extending our relationship to them. But nothing is automatic, either in the professions or in our culture in general. We can hardly expect a "greening of the species"—unless we work hard at cultivating our shared gardens.

I put forward the species self as not only a goal but an existing psychological construct. In that sense, without minimizing the forces in the world antagonistic to it, we can say that there are many levels of actual and potential support for the species self. There is its pragmatic importance in the face of our genocidal inclinations. It has significant *historical* roots. On recognizing its necessity, we rediscover figures who were ahead of their time in expressing species principles—Gandhi in India, Martin Luther King, Jr., in the

United States, or, for that matter, Jesus, the Buddha, or Abraham. In secular tradition, one may point to the universalism of Freud and Marx, whatever the sectarian directions of their disciples.

The species self also represents an important *evolutionary* step: the self, in a collective sense, evolves in a manner necessary to adaptation and to survival. It is also a *biological* truth. We are, all of us, members of the same species. When one group embarks upon violence toward another, it tends to engage in what Erik Erikson called pseudo-speciation, which means treating others as if they were members of a different species.

Finally, the species self is *psychologically and morally feasible*. Its existence is observable and expandable. We speak of ideas whose time has come: the species principle is one that has been thrust upon us. We confront Nazi atrocity and the genocidal mentality as a way of moving toward a species mentality. We look into the abyss in order to see beyond it.

For genocidal and victimizing mentalities remain active in various places in the world: in Russian anti-Semitism, Eastern European ethnic antagonisms, Chinese and South African repression, and the continuing American and Soviet nuclear stockpiling. And surely all Germans must understand that any plan for their country's reunification has to evoke fearful images of Nazi mass murder—in Jews especially, but not only in Jews. Approaching these matters with a species mentality would require that German arrangements include confronting the past and providing safeguards against destructive expressions of nationalism; and that governments and peoples everywhere reconsider their relationship to a still besieged, but increasingly self-aware, human species.

Yet this is a time for hope. As we observe events taking place right now in Europe and elsewhere, we have the sense that we are in what could be called a species moment. It is what the Greeks refer to as a *kairos* moment, one so crucial that it has a decisive effect on all that follows. It is a time when, as the American poet Louis Simpson puts it, "Strange dreams occur / For dreams are licensed as they never were."

I want to give the last word to a man who endured Nazi cruelty and emerged from it with considerable wisdom. He is a Jewish doctor who survived Auschwitz. He described to me how, at a certain point, he and a few other prisoner-doctors were overwhelmed with moribund patients, with suffering people clamoring for relief. They did what they could, dispensed the few aspirin they had, but made a point of offering a few words of reassurance and hope. He found, almost to his surprise, that the words had an effect, that what they had done "in that situation . . . really helped." He concluded that even under the most extreme conditions he was impressed with how much he could do by maintaining his determination to try to heal.

Suggestions for Discussion

1. This essay, based on a speech Lifton gave in accepting an honorary doctorate from the University of Munich, is in part shaped by its audience and the occasion. Discuss the rhetorical devices of the essay and point out how Lifton uses his own background and the history of his audience to create his argument.

2. Analyze Lifton's discussion of differing approaches to evil. While his own approach is secular, how does he manage to make it compatible with religious views?

3. How does the author use the play *The Deputy* by Hochhuth to advance his argument about genocide?

4. Lifton often refers to survivors of Auschwitz or others connected with the camp. What special tone do these references lend to the essay?

5. Although Lifton stresses the German history of genocide by focusing his talk on the Nazi destruction of millions, he suggests the potential for genocide in other cultures. What examples does he give? Can you think of others he does not mention?

6. One of the topics Lifton discusses is the use of euthanasia by Nazi doctors. Relate his discussion to the essay in this text, "The Gentle Death" by Patrick Cooke. Does the history of the Nazi use of euthanasia influence your own ideas on the subject? Explain.

7. Summarize the stages Lifton describes by which a doctor—or some other professional—becomes a willing participant in genocide. What is Lifton's answer to the question of whether a good man can commit evil acts?

8. Lifton suggests hope for humanity on the develoment of one's "species identity." Define this term and show how it might protect us from genocide or other destructive acts.

Suggestions for Writing

1. This essay provides a good basis for a research paper on a variety of topics. Choose one of Lifton's ideas that you would like to explore and do research on its currency in other writers. (For example, Lifton amplifies philosopher Hannah Arendt's discussions of the banality of evil.)

2. Write a research paper on the general potentiality for genocide in many societies. Use different examples.

3. Summarize Lifton's discussion of the psychological conditions that permit an otherwise ordinary person to commit genocidal acts. Do you agree with his position? State your opinion at the conclusion of your paper.

4. Read *The Deputy* and write a paper in which you state your agreement or disagreement with Lifton's statement about its main subject.

5. Lifton includes hostile acts against the environment as genocidal. Write an essay in which you discuss this point in specific detail.

Václav Havel

Words on Words

Václav Havel (b. 1936) was born in Prague, Czechoslovakia. He attended a technical college as well as Prague's Academy of Art. He is considered one of the most significant playwrights of Eastern and Central Europe despite the fact that, following the Soviet invasion of Czechoslovakia in 1968, his plays were banned and he became a frequent and well-known prisoner of conscience. His first play *The Garden Party* was published in England in 1969, and during the years in which his works were banned in his own country they were often performed in Western Europe and the United States. For many years he was an active leader of the dissident movement and participated in the peaceful Czech revolution of 1989. In 1990 he was chosen as the first president of the newly organized Czech government, a position considerably narrowed, by the subsequent division of Czechoslovakia into three separate countries, to president of the Czech Republic. In his acceptance speech for the German Booksellers Association's Peace Prize, he talks about the power of words, the authoritarian government's urge to censor and suppress writing, and the need for thoughtful people of good will to use language carefully and honestly.

The prize which it is my honor to receive today is called a peace prize and has been awarded to me by booksellers, in other words, people whose business is the dissemination of words. It is therefore appropriate, perhaps, that I should reflect here today on the mysterious link between words and peace, and in general on the mysterious power of words in human history.

In the beginning was the Word; so it states on the first page of one of the most important books known to us. What is meant in that book is that the Word of God is the source of all creation. But surely the same could be said, figuratively speaking, of every human action? And indeed, words can be said to be the very source of our being, and in fact the very substance of the cosmic life-form we call Man. Spirit, the human soul, or self-awareness, our ability to generalize and think in concepts, to perceive the world as the world (and not just as our locality), and lastly, our capacity for knowing that we will die—and living in spite of that knowledge: surely all these are mediated or actually created by words?

If the Word of God is the source of God's entire creation then that part of God's creation which is the human race exists as such only thanks to another of God's miracles—the miracle of human speech. And if this miracle is the key to the history of mankind, then it is also the key to the history of society. Indeed it might well be the former just because it is the latter. For the fact is that if they were not a means of communication between two or more human "I"s, then words would probably not exist at all.

All these things have been known to us—or people have at least suspected them—since time immemorial. There has never been a time when a sense of the importance of words was not present in human consciousness.

But that is not all: thanks to the miracle of speech, we know probably better than the other animals that we actually know very little, in other words we are conscious of the existence of mystery. Confronted by mystery—and at the same time aware of the virtually constitutive power of words for us—we have tried incessantly to address that which is concealed by mystery, and influence it with our words. As believers, we pray to God, as magicians we summon up or ward off spirits, using words to intervene in natural or human events. As subjects of modern civilization—whether believers or not—we use words to construct scientific theories and political ideologies with which to tackle or redirect the mysterious course of history— successfully or otherwise.

In other words, whether we are aware of it or not, and however we explain it, one thing would seem to be obvious: we have always believed in the power of words to change history—and rightly so, in a sense.

Why "rightly so"?

Is the human word truly powerful enough to change the world and influence history? And even if there were epochs when it did exert such a power, does it still do so today?

You live in a country with considerable freedom of speech. All citizens without exception can avail themselves of that freedom for whatever purpose, and no one is obliged to pay the least attention, let alone worry their heads over it. You might, therefore, easily get the impression that I overrate the importance of words quite simply because I live in a country where words can still land people in prison.

Yes, I do live in a country where the authority and radioactive effect of words are demonstrated every day by the sanctions which free speech attracts. Just recently, the entire world commemorated the bicentenary of the great French Revolution. Inevitably we recalled the famous Declaration of the Rights of Man and of Citizens, which states that every citizen has the right to own a printing press. During the same period, i.e., exactly two hundred years after that Declaration, my friend Frantisek Stárek was sent to prison for two-and-a-half years for producing the independent cultural journal *Vokno*—not on some private printing press but with a squeaky, antediluvian duplicator. Not long before, my friend Ivan Jirous was sentenced to sixteen months' imprisonment for berating, on a typewriter, something that is common knowledge: that our country has seen many judicial murders and that even now it is possible for a person unjustly convicted to die from ill-treatment in prison. My friend Petr Cibulka is in prison for distributing samizdat texts and recordings of nonconformist singers and bands.

Yes, all that is true. I do live in a country where a writers' congress or some speech at it is capable of shaking the system. Could you conceive of something of the kind in the Federal Republic of Germany? Yes, I live in a country which, twenty-one years ago, was shaken by a text from the pen of my friend Ludvik Vaculik. And as if to confirm my conclusions about the power of words, he entitled his statement: "Two Thousand Words." Among other things, that manifesto served as one of the pretexts for the invasion of our country one night by five foreign armies. And it is by no means fortuitous that as I write these words, the present regime in my country is being shaken by a single page of text entitled—again as if to illustrate what I am saying—"A few words." Yes, I really do inhabit a system in which words are capable of shaking the entire structure of government, where words can prove mightier than ten military divisions, where Solzhenitsyn's words of truth were regarded as something so dangerous that it was necessary to bundle their author into an airplane and transport him. Yet, in the part of the world I inhabit the word Solidarity was capable of shaking an entire power bloc.

All that is true. Reams have been written about it and my distinguished predecessor in this place, Lev Kopelev,* spoke about it also.

*Lev Kopelev received the Peace Prize of the German Booksellers Association in 1981.

But it is a slightly different matter that concerns me here. It is not my intention solely to speak about the incredible importance that unfettered words assume in totalitarian conditions. Nor do I wish to demonstrate the mysterious power of words by pointing exclusively to those countries where a few words can count for more than a whole train of dynamite somewhere else.

I want to talk in more general terms and consider the wider and more controversial aspects of my topic.

We live in a world in which it is possible for a citizen of Great Britain to find himself the target of a lethal arrow aimed—publicly and unashamedly—by a powerful individual in another country merely because he had written a particular book. That powerful man apparently did it in the name of millions of his fellow believers. And moreover, it is possible in this world that some portion of those millions—one hopes only a small portion—will identify with the death sentence pronounced.

What's going on? What does it mean? Is it no more than an icy blast of fanaticism, oddly finding a new lease on life in the era of the various Helsinki agreements, and oddly resuscitated by the rather crippling results of the rather crippling Europeanization of worlds which initially had no interest in the import of foreign civilization, and on account of that ambivalent commodity ended up saddled with astronomical debts they can never repay?

It certainly is all that.

But it is something else as well. It is a symbol.

It is a symbol of the mysteriously ambiguous power of words.

In truth, the power of words is neither unambiguous nor clear-cut. It is not merely the liberating power of Walesa's words or the alarm-raising power of Sakharov's. It is not just the power of Rushdie's—clearly misconstrued—book.

The point is that alongside Rushdie's words we have Khomeini's. Words that electrify society with their freedom and truthfulness are matched by words that mesmerize, deceive, inflame, madden, beguile, words that are harmful—lethal, even. The word as arrow.

I don't think I need to go to any lengths to explain to you of all people the diabolic power of certain words: you have fairly recent first-hand experience of what indescribable historical horrors can flow, in certain political and social constellations, from the hypnotically spellbinding, though totally demented, words of a single, average, petit bourgeois. Admittedly I fail to understand what it was that transfixed a large number of your fathers and mothers, but at the same time I realize that it must have been something extremely compelling as well as extremely insidious if it was capable of beguiling, albeit only briefly, even that great genius who lent such modern and penetrating meaning to the words: "Sein," "Da-Sein," and "Existenz."

The point I am trying to make is that words are a mysterious, ambiguous, ambivalent, and perfidious phenomenon. They are capable of being rays of light in a realm of darkness, as Belinsky once described Ostrovsky's Storm. They are equally capable of being lethal arrows. Worst of all, at times they can be the one and the other. And even both at once!

The words of Lenin—what were they? Liberating or, on the contrary, deceptive, dangerous, and ultimately enslaving? This is still a bone of contention among aficionados of the history of communism and the controversy is likely to go on raging for a good while yet. My own impression of these words is that they were invariably frenzied.

And what about Marx's words? Did they serve to illuminate an entire hidden plane of social mechanisms, or were they just the inconspicuous germ of all the subsequent appalling gulags? I don't know: most likely they are both at once.

And what about Freud's words? Did they disclose the secret cosmos of the human soul, or were they no more than the fountainhead of the illusion now benumbing half of America that it is possible to shed one's torments and guilt by having them interpreted away by some well-paid specialist?

But I'd go further and ask an even more provocative question: What was the true nature of Christ's words? Were they the beginning of an era of salvation and among the most powerful cultural impulses in the history of the world—or were they the spiritual source of the crusades, inquisitions, the cultural extermination of the Americas, and, later, the entire expansion of the white race that was fraught with so many contradictions and had so many tragic consequences, including the fact that most of the human world has been consigned to that wretched category known as the "Third World"? I still tend to think that His words belonged to the former category, but at the same time I cannot ignore the umpteen books that demonstrate that, even in its purest and earliest form, there was something unconsciously encoded in Christianity which, when combined with a thousand and one other circumstances, including the relative permanence of human nature, could in some way pave the way spiritually, even for the sort of horrors I mentioned.

Words can have histories too.

There was a time, for instance, when for whole generations of the downtroden and oppressed, the word socialism was a mesmerizing synonym for a just world, a time when, for the ideal expressed in that word, people were capable of sacrificing years and years of their lives, and their very lives even. I don't know about your country, but in mine, that particular word—"socialism"—was transformed long ago into just an ordinary truncheon used by certain cynical, parvenu bureaucrats to bludgeon their liberal-minded fellow citizens from morning until night, labeling them "enemies of socialism" and "antisocialist forces." It's a fact: in my country, for ages now, that word has been no more than an incantation that should be avoided if one does not wish to appear suspect. I was recently at an entirely spontaneous demonstration, not dissident-organized, protesting the sell-off of one of the most beautiful parts of Prague to some Australian millionaires. When one of the speakers there, loudly decrying the project, sought to bolster his appeal to the government by declaring that he was fighting for his home in the name of socialism, the crowd started to laugh. Not because they had anything against a just social order, but quite simply because they heard a word which has been incanted for years and years in every possible and impossible context by a regime that only knows how to manipulate and humiliate people.

What a weird fate can befall certain words! At one moment in history, courageous, liberal-minded peple can be thrown into prison because a particular word means something to them, and at another moment, people of the selfsame variety can be thrown into prison because that word has ceased to mean anything to them, because it has changed from a symbol of a better world into the mumbo jumbo of a doltish dictator.

No word—at least not in the rather metaphorical sense I am employing the word "word" here—comprises only the meaning assigned to it by an etymological dictionary. The meaning of every word also reflects the person who utters it, the situation in which it is uttered, and the reason for the utterance. The selfsame word can, at one moment, radiate great hopes, at another, it can emit lethal rays. The selfsame word can be true at one moment and false the next, at one moment illuminating, at another, deceptive. On one occasion it can open up glorious horizons, on another, it can lay down the tracks to an entire archipelago of concentration camps. The selfsame word can at one time be the cornerstone of peace, while at another, machine-gun fire resounds in its every syllable.

Gorbachev wants to save socialism through the market economy and free speech, while Li Peng protects socialism by massacring students, and Ceauşescu by bulldozing his people. What does the word actually mean on the lips of the one and the lips of the other two? What is this mysterious thing that is being rescued in such disparate ways?

I referred to the French Revolution and that splendid declaration that accompanied it. That declaration was signed by a gentleman who was later among the first to be executed in the name of that superbly humane text. And hundreds and possibly thousands followed him. *Liberté, Egalité, Fraternité*—what superb words! And how terrifying their meaning can be. Freedom: the shirt unbuttoned before execution. Equality: the constant speed of the guillotine's fall on different necks. Fraternity: some dubious paradise ruled by a Supreme Being!

The world now reechoes to the wonderfully promising word "perestroika." We all believe that it harbors hopes for Europe and the whole world.

I am bound to admit, though, that I sometimes shudder at the thought that this word might become just one more incantation, and in the end turn into yet another truncheon for someone to beat us with. It is not my own country I am thinking of: when our rulers utter that word it means about the same as the word "our monarch" when uttered by the Good Soldier Svejk. No, what I have in mind is the fact that even the intrepid man who now sits in the Kremlin occasionally, and possibly only from despair, accuses striking workers, rebellious nations or national minorities, or holders of rather too unusual minority opinions, of "jeopardizing perestroika." I can understand his feelings. It is terribly difficult to fulfill the enormous task he has undertaken. It all hangs by the finest of threads and almost anything could break that thread. Then we would all fall into the abyss. But even so I cannot help wondering whether all this "new thinking" does not contain some disturbing relics of the old. Does it not contain some echoes of former stereotyped thinking and the *ancien régime*'s verbal rituals? Isn't the word perestroika starting to resemble the word socialism, particularly on the odd occasion when it is discreetly hurled at the very people who, for so long, were unjustly lambasted with the word socialism?

Your country made an enormous contribution to modern European history. I refer to the first wave of détente: the celebrated "*Ostpolitik.*"

But even that word managed at times to be well and truly ambivalent. It signified, of course, the first glimmer of hope of a Europe without cold wars or iron curtains. At the same time—unhappily—there were also occasions when it signified the abandonment of freedom: the basic preconditon for all real peace. I still vividly recall how, at the beginning of the Seventies, a number of my West German colleagues and friends avoided me for fear that contact with me—someone out of favor with the government here—might needlessly provoke that government and thereby jeopardize the fragile foundations of nascent détente. Naturally I am not mentioning it on account of myself personally, let alone out of any sort of self-pity. After all, even in those days it was rather I who pitied them, since it was not I but they who were voluntarily renouncing their freedom. I mention it only in order to demonstrate yet again from another angle how easy it is for a well-intentioned cause to be transformed into the betrayal of its own good intentions—and yet again because of a word whose meaning does not seem to have been kept under adequate observation. Something like that can happen so easily that it almost takes you unawares: it happens inconspicuously, quietly, by stealth—and when at last you realize it, there is only one option left to you: belated astonishment.

However, that is precisely the fiendish way that words are capable of betraying us—unless we are constantly circumspect about their use. And frequently—alas—even a fairly minor and momentary lapse in this respect can have tragic and irreparable consequences, consequences for transcending the nonmaterial world of mere words and penetrating deep into a world that is all too material.

I'm finally getting around to that beautiful word "peace."

For forty years now I have read it on the front of every building and in every shop window in my country. For forty years, an allergy to that beautiful word has been engendered in me as in every one of my fellow citizens because I know what the word has meant here for the past forty years: ever mightier armies ostensibly to defend peace.

In spite of that lengthy process of systematically divesting the word "peace" of all meaning—worse than that, investing it instead with quite the opposite meaning to that given in the dictionary—a number of Don Quixotes in Charter 77 and several of their younger colleagues in the Independent Peace Association have managed to rehabilitate the word and restore its original meaning. Naturally, though, they had to pay a price for their "semantic perestroika"—i.e., standing the word "peace" back on its feet again: almost all the youngsters who fronted the Independent Peace Association were obliged to spend a few months inside for their pains. It was worth it, though. One important word has been rescued from total debasement. And it is not just a question of saving a word, as I have been trying to explain throughout my speech. Something far more important is saved.

The point is that all important events in the real world—whether admirable or monstrous—are always spearheaded in the realm of words.

As I've already stated, my intention here today is not to convey to you the experience of one who has learned that words still count for something when you can still go to prison for them. My intention was to share with you another lesson that we in this corner of the world have learned about the importance of words. I am convinced it is a lesson which has universal application: namely, that it always pays to be suspicious of words and to be wary of them, and that we can never be too careful in this respect.

There can be no doubt that distrust of words is less harmful than unwarranted trust in them.

Besides, to distrust words, and indict them for the horrors that might slumber unobtrusively within them—isn't this, after all, the true vocation of the intellectual? I recall that André Glucksmann, the dear colleague who preceded me here today, once spoke in Prague about the need for intellectuals to emulate Cassandra: to listen carefully to the words of the powerful, to be watchful of them, to forewarn of their danger, and to proclaim their dire implications or the evil they might invoke.

There is something that should not escape our attention and it concerns the fact that for centuries we—the Germans and the Czechs—had all sorts of problems with living together in Central Europe. I cannot speak for you, but I think I can rightly say that as far as we Czechs are concerned, the age-old animosities, prejudices and passions, constantly fuelled and fanned in numerous ways over the centuries, have evaporated in the course of recent decades. And it is by no means coincidental that this has happened at a time when we have been saddled with a totalitarian regime. Thanks to this regime we have developed a profound distrust of all generalizations, ideological platitudes, clichés, slogans, intellectual steroetypes, and insidious appeals to various levels of our emotions, from the baser to the loftier. As a result, we are now largely immune to all hypnotic enticements, even of the traditionally persuasive national or nationalistic variety. The stifling pall of hollow words that have smothered us for so long has cultivated in us such a deep mistrust of the world of deceptive words that we are now better equipped than ever before to see the human world as it really is: a complex community of thousands of millions of unique, individual human beings in whom hundreds of beautiful characteristics are matched by hundreds of faults and negative tendencies. They must never be lumped together into homogeneous masses beneath a welter of hollow clichés and sterile words and then en bloc—as "classes," "nations," or "political forces"—extolled or denounced, loved or hated, maligned or glorified.

This is just one small example of the good that can come from treating words with caution. I have chosen the example especially for the occasion, i.e., for the moment when a Czech has the honor to address an audience that is overwhelmingly German.

In the beginning of everything is the word.

It is a miracle to which we owe the fact that we are human.

But at the same time it is a pitfall and a test, a snare and a trial.

More so, perhaps, than it appears to you who have enormous freedom of speech, and might therefore assume that words are not so important.

They are.

They are important everywhere.

The selfsame word can be humble at one moment and arrogant the next. And a humble word can be transformed quite easily and imperceptibly into an arrogant one, whereas it is a very difficult and protracted process to transform an arrogant word into one that is humble. I tried to demonstrate this by referring to the fate of the word "peace" in my country.

As we approach the end of the second millennium, the world, and particularly Europe, finds itself at a peculiar crossroads. It is a long time since there were so many grounds for hoping that everything will turn out well. At the same time, there have never been so many reasons for us to fear that if everything went wrong the catastrophe would be final.

It is not hard to demonstrate that all the main threats confronting the world today, from atomic war and ecological disaster to social and civilizational catastrophe — by which I mean the widening gulf between rich and poor individuals and nations — have hidden within them just one root cause: the imperceptible transformation of what was originally a humble message into an arrogant one.

Arrogantly, Man started to believe that, as the pinnacle and lord of creation, he had a total understanding of nature and could do what he liked with it.

Arrogantly, he started to think that as the possessor of reason he was capable of understanding totally his own history and therefore of planning a life of happiness for all. This even gave him the right, in the name of an ostensibly better future for all — to which he had found the one and only key — to sweep from his path all those who did not fall for his plan.

Arrogantly he started to think that since he was capable of splitting the atom he was now so perfect that there was no longer any danger of nuclear arms rivalry, let alone nuclear war.

In all those cases he was fatally mistaken. That is bad. But in each case he is already beginning to realize his mistake. And that is good.

Having learned all those lessons, we should all fight together against arrogant words and keep a weather eye out for any insidious germs of arrogance in words that are seemingly humble.

Obviously this is not just a linguistic task. Responsibility for and toward words is a task which is intrinsically ethical.

As such, however, it is situated beyond the horizon of the visible world, in that realm wherein dwells the Word that was in the beginning and is not the word of Man.

I won't explain why this is so. It has been explained far better than I ever could by your great forebear Immanuel Kant.

Suggestions for Discussion

1. Two months after Havel's speech to the German Booksellers Association, he appeared before a crowd of hundreds of thousands of Czechs in Prague to announce the formation of a new government of which he became president. Do research on Havel's career so that you can be prepared to discuss the appropriateness of the award he was acknowledging in this speech and his later selection as president of Czechoslovakia.

2. Havel talks about both the religious and secular meaning of words. On which of these two levels does he place major emphasis? Why?

3. Relate Havel's remarks about the Declaration of the Rights of Man of the French Revolution (also in this text) and his own attitudes toward the power of the word as either an instrument of freedom or tyranny.

4. What is the relevance of Havel's reference to Salman Rushdie's novel *Satanic Verses* and its condemnation by Khomeini of Iran?

5. How does Havel politely remind his German audience of the negative power of words in their own recent history? Look up the controversy that has risen over the degree to which the German philosopher Heidegger was guilty of being pro-Nazi. What particular irony does Havel find in this issue?

6. Havel discusses the possible meanings of particular words such as "peace" and "socialism," and of the ambiguous meanings possible in the writings of men such as Lenin, Marx, and Freud. Summarize his arguments on this issue. Do you agree with him? Why?

7. Toward the end of his speech, Havel introduces a number of very short paragraphs. What is the rhetorical effect of doing this?

Suggestions for Writing

1. One of the main points of Havel's speech, that words are ambiguous and slippery and changing in their meaning, is one that most people would agree with. Choose some important abstract word (Havel talks about freedom, socialism, peace) and show by example how it can mean different things to different people.

2. Havel's career as a writer has been primarily as a playwright. Read several of his plays and write an essay relating the ideas in the plays to those in this speech.

3. Write an essay based on this speech in which you try to summarize Havel's ideas on politics, economics, or religion. How similar are his ideas to your own? Can you figure out the reasons for any differences that you find?

Mary Gordon

A Moral Choice

Mary Gordon (b. 1949) was born on Long Island, New York, and educated at Barnard College and the University of Syracuse, and has taught English at Dutchess County Community College and at Amherst College. She has published short stories, poems, and novels that have received critical and popular success, including *Final Payments* (1978); *The Company of Women* (1981); *Men and Angels* (1985); *The Other Side* (1989); a collection of stories, *Temporary Shelter* (1990); and a collection of three novellas, *The Rest of Life* (1993). A writer often identified as a Catholic, she frequently deals with theological themes. In this essay, she calls for clear definitions of the moral issues surrounding abortion and explains why she has taken a pro-choice position.

I am having lunch with six women. What is unusual is that four of them are in their seventies, two of them widowed, the other two living with husbands beside whom they've lived for decades. All of them have had children.

Had they been men, they would have published books and hung their paintings on the walls of important galleries. But they are women of a certain generation, and their lives were shaped around their families and personal relations. They are women you go to for help and support. We begin talking about the latest legislative act that makes abortion more difficult for poor women to obtain. An extraordinary thing happens. Each of them talks about the illegal abortions she had during her young womanhood. Not one of them was spared the experience. Any of them could have died on the table of whatever person (not a doctor in any case) she was forced to approach, in secrecy and in terror, to end a pregnancy that she felt would blight her life.

I mention this incident for two reasons: first as a reminder that all kinds of women have always had abortions; second because it is essential that we remember that an abortion is performed on a living woman who has a life in which a terminated pregnancy is only a small part. Morally speaking, the decision to have an abortion doesn't take place in a vacuum. It is connected to other choices that a woman makes in the course of an adult life.

Anti-choice propagandists paint pictures of women who choose to have abortions as types of moral callousness, selfishness, or irresponsibility. The woman choosing to abort is the dressed-for-success yuppie who gets rid of her baby so that she won't miss her Caribbean vacation or her chance for promotion. Or she is the feckless, promiscuous ghetto teenager who couldn't bring herself to just say no to sex. A third, purportedly kinder, gentler picture has recently begun to be drawn. The woman in the abortion clinic is there because she is misinformed about the nature of the world. She is having an abortion because society does not provide for mothers and their children, and she mistakenly thinks that another mouth to feed will be the ruin of her family, not understanding that the temporary truth of family unhappiness doesn't stack up beside the eternal verity that abortion is murder. Or she is the dupe of her husband or boyfriend, who talks her into having an abortion because a child will be a drag on his life-style. None of these pictures created by the anti-choice movement assumes that the decision to have an abortion is made responsibly, in the context of a morally lived life, by a free and responsible moral agent.

The Ontology of the Fetus

How would a woman who habitually makes choices in moral terms come to the decision to have an abortion? The moral discussion of abortion centers on the issue of whether or not abortion is an act of murder. At first glance it would seem that the answer should follow directly upon two questions: Is the fetus human? and Is it alive? It would be absurd to deny that a fetus is alive or that it is human. What would our other options be—to say that it is inanimate or belongs to another species? But we habitually use the terms "human" and "live" to refer to parts of our body—"human hair," for example, or "live red-blood cells"—and we are clear in our understanding that the nature of these objects does not rank equally with an entire personal existence. It then seems important to consider whether the fetus, this alive human thing, is a *person*, to whom the term "murder" could sensibly be applied. How would anyone come to a decision about something so impalpable as person-hood? Philosophers have struggled with the issue of personhood, but in language that is so abstract that it is unhelpful to ordinary people making decisions in the course of their lives. It might be more productive to begin thinking about the status of the fetus by examining the language and customs that surround it. This approach will encourage us to focus on the choosing, acting woman, rather than the act of abortion—as if the act were performed by abstract forces without bodies, histories, attachments.

This focus on the acting woman is useful because a pregnant woman has an identifiable, consistent ontology, and a fetus takes on different ontological identities over time. But common sense, experience, and linguistic usage point clearly to the fact that we habitually consider, for example, a seven-week-old fetus to be different from a seven-month-old one. We can tell this by the way we respond to the involuntary loss of one as against the other. We have different language for the experience of the involuntary expulsion of the fetus from the womb depending upon the point of gestation at which the experience occurs. If it occurs early in the pregnancy, we call it a miscarriage; if late, we call it a stillbirth.

We would have an extreme reaction to the reversal of those terms. If a woman referred to a miscarriage at seven weeks as a stillbirth, we would be alarmed. It would shock our sense of propriety; it would make us uneasy; we would find it disturbing, misplaced—as we do when a bag lady sits down in a restaurant and starts shouting, or an octogenarian arrives at our door in a sailor suit. In short, we would suspect that the speaker was mad. Similarly, if a doctor or a nurse referred to the loss of a seven-month-old fetus as a miscarriage, we would be shocked by that person's insensitivity: could she or he not understand that a fetus that age is not what it was months before?

Our ritual and religious practices underscore the fact that we make distinctions among fetuses. If a woman took the bloody matter—indistinguishable from a heavy period—of an early miscarriage and insisted upon putting it in a tiny coffin and marking its grave, we would have serious concerns about her mental health. By the same token, we would feel squeamish about flushing a seven-month-old fetus down the toilet—something we would quite normally do with an early miscarriage. There are no prayers for the matter of a miscarriage, nor do we feel there should be. Even a Catholic priest would not baptize the issue of an early miscarriage.

The difficulties stem, of course, from the odd situation of a fetus's ontology: a complicated, differentiated, and nuanced response is required when we are dealing with an entity that changes over time. Yet we are in the habit of making distinctions like this. At one point we know that a child is no longer a child but an adult. That this question is vexed and problematic is clear from our difficulty in determining who is a juvenile offender and who is an adult criminal and at what age sexual intercourse ceases to be known as statutory rape. So at what point, if any, do we on the pro-choice side say that the developing fetus is a person, with rights equal to its mother's?

The anti-choice people have one advantage over us; their monolithic position gives them unity on this question. For myself, I am made uneasy by third-trimester abortions, which take place when the fetus could live outside the mother's body, but I also know that these are extremely rare and often performed on very young girls who have had difficulty comprehending the realities of pregnancy. It seems to me that the question of late abortions should be decided case by case, and that fixation on this issue is a deflection from what is most important: keeping early abortions, which are in the majority by far, safe and legal. I am also politically realistic enough to suspect that bills restricting late abortions are not good-faith attempts to make distinctions about the nature of fetal life They are, rather, the cynical embodiments of the hope among anti-choice partisans that technology will be on their side and that medical science's ability to create situations in which younger fetuses are viable outside their mothers' bodies will increase dramatically in the next few years. Ironically, medical science will probably make the issue of abortion a minor one in the near future. The RU-486 pill, which can induce abortion early on, exists, and whether or not it is legally available (it is not on the market here, because of pressure from anti-choice groups), women will begin to obtain it. If abortion can occur through chemical rather than physical means, in the privacy of one's home, most people not directly involved will lose interest in it. As abortion is transformed from a public into a private issue, it will cease to be perceived as political; it will be called personal instead.

An Equivocal Good

But because abortion will always deal with what it is to create and sustain life, it will always be a moral issue. And whether we like it or not, our moral thinking about abortion is rooted in the shifting soil of perception. In an age in which much of our perception is manipulated by media that specialize in the sound bite and the photo op, the anti-choice partisans have a twofold advantage over us on the pro-choice side. The pro-choice moral position is more complex, and the experience we defend is physically repellent to contemplate. None of us in the pro-choice movement would suggest that abortion is not a regrettable occurrence. Anti-choice proponents can offer pastel photographs of babies in buntings, their eyes peaceful in the camera's gaze. In answer, we can't offer the material of an early abortion, bloody, amorphous in a paper cup, to prove that what has just been removed from the woman's body is not a child, not in the same category of being as the adorable bundle in an adoptive mother's arms. It is not a pleasure to look at the physical evidence of abortion, and most of us don't get the opportunity to do so.

The theologian Daniel Maguire, uncomfortable with the fact that most theological arguments about the nature of abortion are made by men who have never been anywhere near an actual abortion, decided to visit a clinic and observe abortions being performed. He didn't find the experience easy, but he knew that before he could in good conscience make a moral judgment on abortion, he needed to experience through his senses what an aborted fetus is like: he needed to look at and touch the controversial entity. He held in his hand the bloody fetal stuff; the eight-week-old fetus fit in the palm of his hand, and it certainly bore no resemblance to either of his two children when he had held them moments after their birth. He knew at that point what women who have experienced early abortions and miscarriages know:

that some event occurred, possibly even a dramatic one, but it was not the death of a child.

Because issues of pregnancy and birth are both physical and metaphorical, we must constantly step back and forth between ways of perceiving the world. When we speak of gestation, we are often talking in terms of potential, about events and objects to which we attach our hopes, fears, dreams, and ideals. A mother can speak to the fetus in her uterus and name it; she and her mate may decorate a nursery according to their vision of the good life; they may choose for an embryo a college, a profession, a dwelling. But those of us who are trying to think morally about pregnancy and birth must remember that these feelings are our own projections onto what is in reality an inappropriate object. However charmed we may be by an expectant father's buying a little football for something inside his wife's belly, we shouldn't make public policy based on such actions, nor should we force others to live their lives conforming to our fantasies.

As a society, we are making decisions that pit the complicated future of a complex adult against the fate of a mass of cells lacking cortical development. The moral pressure should be on distinguishing the true from the false, the real suffering of living persons from our individual and often idiosyncratic dreams and fears. We must make decisions on abortion based on an understanding of how people really do live. We must be able to say that poverty is worse than not being poor, that having dignified and meaningful work is better than working in conditions of degradation, that raising a child one loves and has desired is better than raising a child in resentment and rage, that it is better for a twelve-year-old not to endure the trauma of having a child when she is herself a child.

When we put these ideas against the ideas of "child" or "baby," we seem to be making a horrifying choice of life-style over life. But in fact we are telling the truth of what it means to bear a child, and what the experience of abortion really is. This is extremely difficult, for the object of the discussion is hidden, changing, potential. We make our decisions on the basis of approximate and inadequate language, often on the basis of fantasies and fears. It will always be crucial to try to separate genuine moral concern from phobia, punitiveness, superstition, anxiety, a desperate search for certainty in an uncertain world.

One of the certainties that is removed if we accept the consequences of the pro-choice position is the belief that the birth of a child is an unequivocal good. In real life we act knowing that the birth of a child is not always a good thing: people are sometimes depressed, angry, rejecting, at the birth of a child. But this is a difficult truth to tell; we don't like to say it, and one of the fears preyed on by anti-choice proponents is that if we cannot look at the birth of a child as an unequivocal good, then there is nothing to look toward. The desire for security of the imagination, for typological fixity, particularly in the area of "the good," is an understandable desire. It must seem to some anti-choice people that we on the pro-choice side are not only murdering innocent children but also murdering hope. Those of us who have experienced the birth of a desired child and felt the joy of that moment can be tempted into believing that it was the physical experience of the birth itself that was the joy. But it is crucial to remember that the birth of a child itself is a neutral occurrence emotionally: the charge it takes on is invested in it by the people experiencing or observing it.

The Fear of Sexual Autonomy

These uncertainties can lead to another set of fears, not only about abortion but about its implications. Many anti-choice people fear that to support abortion is to cast one's lot with the cold and technological rather than with the warm and natural, to head down the slippery slope toward a brave new world where handicapped children are left on mountains to starve and the old are put out in the snow. But if we look at the history of abortion, we don't see the embodiment of what the anti-choice proponents fear. On the contrary, excepting the grotesqe counterexample of the People's Republic of China (which practices forced abortion), there seems to be a real link between repressive anti-abortion stances and repressive governments. Abortion was banned in Fascist Italy and Nazi Germany; it is illegal in South Africa and in Chile. It is paid for by the governments of Denmark, England, and the Netherlands, which have national health and welfare systems that foster the health and well-being of mothers, children, the old, and the handicapped.

Advocates of outlawing abortion often refer to women seeking abortion as self-indulgent and materialistic. In fact these accusations mask a discomfort with female sexuality, sexual pleasure, and sexual autonomy. It is possible for a woman to have a sexual life unriddled by fear only if she can be confident that she need not pay for a failure of technology or judgment (and who among us has never once been swept away in the heat of a sexual moment?) by taking upon herself the crushing burden of unchosen motherhood.

It is no accident, therefore, that the increased appeal of measures to restrict maternal conduct during pregnancy—and a new focus on the physical autonomy of the pregnant woman—have come into public discourse at precisely the time when women are achieving unprecedented levels of economic and political autonomy. What has surprised me is that some of this new anti-autonomy talk comes to us from the left. An example of this new discourse is an article by Christopher Hitchens that appeared in *The Nation* last April, in which the author asserts his discomfort with abortion. Hitchens's tone is impeccably British: arch, light, we're men of the left.

> Anyone who has ever seen a sonogram or has spent even an hour with a textbook on embryology knows that the emotions are not the deciding factor. In order to terminate a pregnancy, you have to still a heartbeat, switch off a developing brain, and whatever the method, break some bones and rupture some organs. As to whether this involves pain on the "Silent Scream" scale, I have no idea. The "right to life" leadership, again, has cheapened everything it touches.

"It is a pity," Hitchens goes on to say, "that . . . the majority of feminists and their allies have stuck to the dead ground of 'Me Decade' possessive individualism, an ideology that has more in common than it admits with the prehistoric right, which it claims to oppose but has in fact encouraged." Hitchens proposes, as an alternative, a program of social reform that would make contraception free and support a national adoption service. In his opinion, it would seem, women have abortions for only two reasons: because they are selfish or because they are poor. If the state will take care of the economic problems and the bureaucratic messiness around adoption, it remains only for the possessive individuals to get their act together and walk with their babies into the communal utopia of the future. Hitchens would allow victims of rape or incest to have free abortions, on the grounds that since they didn't choose to have sex, the women should not be forced to have the babies. This would seem to put the issue of volition in a wrong and telling place. To Hitchens's mind, it would appear, if a woman chooses to have sex, she can't choose whether or not to have a baby. The implications of this are clear. If a woman is consciously and volitionally sexual, she should be prepared to take her medicine. And what medicine must the consciously sexual male take? Does Hitchens really believe, or want us to believe, that every male who has unintentionally impregnated a woman will be involved in the lifelong responsibility for the upbringing of the engendered child? Can he honestly say that he has observed this behavior—or, indeed, would want to see it observed—in the world in which he lives?

Real Choices

It is essential for a moral decision about abortion to be made in an atmosphere of open, critical thinking. We on the pro-choice side must accept that there are indeed anti-choice activists who take their position in good faith. I believe, however, that they are people for whom childbirth is an emotionally overladen topic, people who are susceptible to unclear thinking because of their unrealistic hopes and fears. It is important for us in the pro-choice movement to be open in discussing those areas involving abortion which are nebulous and unclear. But we must not forget that there are some things that we know to be undeniably true. There are some undeniable bad consequences of a woman's being forced to bear a child against her will. First is the trauma of going through a pregnancy and giving birth to a child who is not desired, a trauma more long-lasting than that experienced by some (only some) women who experience an early abortion. The grief of giving up a child at its birth—and at nine months it is a child whom one has felt move inside one's body—is underestimated both by anti-choice partisans and by those for whom access to adoptable children is important. This grief should not be forced on any woman—or, indeed, encouraged by public policy.

We must be realistic about the impact on society of millions of unwanted children in an overpopulated world. Most of the time, human beings have sex not because they want to make babies. Yet throughout history sex has resulted in unwanted pregnancies. And women have always aborted. One thing that is not hidden, mysterious, or debatable is that making abortion illegal will result in the deaths of women, as it has always done. Is our historical memory so short that none of us remember aunts, sisters, friends, or mothers who were killed or rendered sterile by septic abortions? Does no one in the anti-choice movement remember stories or actual experiences of midnight drives to filthy rooms from which aborted women were sent out, bleeding, to their fate? Can anyone genuinely say that it would be a moral good for us as a society to return to those conditions?

Thinking about abortion, then, forces us to take moral positions as adults who understand the complexities of the world and the realities of human suffering, to make decisions based on how people actually live and choose, and not on our fears, prejudices, and anxieties about sex and society, life and death.

Suggestions for Discussion

1. What is the function of the personal episode the author uses in the opening paragraph of the essay?

2. What reasons for abortion do anti-choice people ascribe to those who want abortions? What are the author's responses to those reasons?

3. How does the author deal with the issue of whether a fetus is live and human? Is her discussion of this issue valid or persuasive? Do you agree with the distinctions she makes between the terms "miscarriage" and "stillbirth"?

4. What does Gordon mean by the term "the ontology of the fetus"? How does this term become crucial to her argument in favor of choice?

5. For the author, what are the real moral choices surrounding a woman's decision to have an abortion? How complex does she believe the issue to be?

6. Gordon objects to the positions of the political left and right on this issue. Explain.

Suggestions for Writing

1. Write a paper in which you argue for or against Gordon's position on abortion. Summarize her argument and try to agree or disagree with it by reference to the points she makes.

2. Look at the last three paragraphs of Gordon's essay. Do you agree or disagree with her conclusions? Write an essay in which you state your position clearly and concretely.

Shelby Steele

On Being Black and Middle Class

Shelby Steele (b. 1946), born in Cedar Rapids, Iowa, has studied at Coe College and the University of Utah. He has contributed essays to many journals and has written *The Content of Our Character: A New Vision of Race in America* (1990). He is a professor of English at California State University, San Jose. The following essay, which originally appeared in the journal *Commentary*, examines the tensions and dilemmas facing a successful member of the black middle class who wants to retain his ethnic heritage.

Not long ago a friend of mine, black like myself, said to me that the term "black middle class" was actually a contradiction in terms. Race, he insisted, blurred class distinctions among blacks. If you were black, you were just black and that was that. When I argued, he let his eyes roll at my naiveté. Then he went on. For us, as black professionals, it was an exercise in self-flattery, a pathetic pretension, to give meaning to such a distinction. Worse, the very idea of class threatened the unity that was vital to the black community as a whole. After all, since when had white America taken note of anything but color when it came to blacks? He then reminded me of an old Malcolm X line that had been popular in the sixties. Question: What is a black man with a Ph.D.? Answer: A nigger.

For many years I had been on my friend's side of this argument. Much of my conscious thinking on the old conundrum of race and class was shaped during my high school and college years in the race-charged sixties, when the fact of my race took on an almost religious significance. Progressively, from the mid-sixties on, more and more aspects of my life found their explanation, their justification, and their motivation in race. My youthful concerns about career, romance, money, values, and even styles of dress became a subject to consultation with various oracular sources of racial wisdom. And these ranged from a figure as ennobling as Martin Luther King, Jr., to the underworld elegance of dress I found in jazz clubs on the South Side of Chicago. Everywhere there were signals, and in those days I considered myself so blessed with clarity and direction that I pitied my white classmates who found more embarrassment than guidance in the fact of *their* race. In 1968, inflated by my new power, I took a mischievous delight in calling them culturally disadvantaged.

But now, hearing my friend's comment was like hearing a priest from a church I'd grown disenchanted with. I understood him, but my faith was weak. What had sustained me in the sixties sounded monotonous and off the mark in the eighties. For me, race had lost much of its juju, its singular capacity to conjure meaning. And today, when I honestly look at my life and the lives of many other middle-class blacks I know, I can see that race never fully explained our situation in American society. Black though I may be, it is impossible for me to sit in my single-family house with two cars in the driveway and a swing set in the back yard and *not* see the role class has played in my life. And how can my friend, similarly raised and similarly situated, not see it?

Yet despite my certainty I felt a sharp tug of guilt as I tried to explain myself over my friend's skepticism. He is a man of many comedic facial expressions and, as I spoke, his brow lifted in extreme moral alarm as if I were uttering the unspeakable. His clear implication was that I was being elitist and possibly (dare he suggest?) anti-black—crimes for which there might well be no redemption. He pretended to fear for me. I chuckled along with him, but inwardly I did wonder at myself. Though I never doubted the validity of what I was saying, I felt guilty saying it. Why?

After he left (to retrieve his daughter from a dance lesson) I realized that the trap I felt myself in had a tiresome familiarity and, in a sort of slow-motion epiphany, I began to see its outline. It was like the suddenly sharp vision one has at the end of a burdensome marriage when all the long-repressed incompatibilities come undeniably to light.

What became clear to me is that people like myself, my friend, and middle-class blacks generally are caught in a very specific double bind that keeps two equally powerful elements of our identity at odds with each other. The middle-class values by which we were raised—the work ethic, the importance of education, the value of property ownership, of respectability, of "getting ahead," of stable family life, of initiative, of self-reliance, etc.—are, in themselves, raceless and even assimilationist. They urge us toward participation in the American mainstream, toward integration, toward a strong identification with the society—and toward the entire constellation of qualities that are implied in the word "individualism." These values are almost rules for how to prosper in a democratic, free-enterprise society that admires and rewards individual effort. They tell us to work hard for ourselves and our families and to seek our opportunities whenever they appear, inside or outside the confines of whatever ethnic group we may belong to.

But the particular pattern of racial identification that emerged in the sixties and that still prevails today urges middle-class blacks (and all blacks) in the opposite direction. This pattern asks us to see ourselves as an embattled minority, and it urges an adversarial stance toward the mainstream, an emphasis on ethnic consciousness over individualism. It is organized around an implied separatism.

The opposing thrust of these two parts of our identity results in the double bind of middle-class blacks. There is no forward movement on either plane that does not constitute backward movement on the other. This was the familiar trap I felt myself in while talking with my friend. As I spoke about class, his eyes reminded me that I was betraying race. Clearly, the two indispensable parts of my identity were a threat to each other.

Of course when you think about it, class and race are both similar in some ways and also naturally opposed. They are two forms of collective identity with boundaries that intersect. But whether they clash or peacefully coexist has much to do with how they are defined. Being both black and middle class becomes a double bind when class and race are defined in sharply antagonistic terms, so that one must be repressed to appease the other.

But what is the "substance" of these two identities, and how does each establish itself in an individual's overall identity? It seems to me that when we identify with any collective we are basically identifying with images that tell us what it means to be a member of that collective. Identity is not the same thing as the fact of membership in a collective; it is, rather, a form of self-definition, facilitated by images of what we wish our membership in the collective to mean. In this sense, the images we identify with may reflect the aspirations of the collective more than they reflect reality, and their content can vary with shifts in those aspirations.

But the process of identification is usually dialectical. It is just as necessary to say what we are *not* as it is to say what we are—so that finally identification comes about by embracing a polarity of positive and negative images. To identify as middle class, for example, I must have both positive and negative images of what being middle class entails; then I will know what I should and should not be doing in order to be middle class. The same goes for racial identity.

In the racially turbulent sixties the polarity of images that came to define racial identification was very antagonistic to the polarity that defined middle-class identification. One might say that the positive images of one lined up with the negative images of the other, so that to identify with both required either a contortionist's flexibility or a dangerous splitting of the self. The double bind of the black middle class was in place.

The black middle class has always defined its class identity by means of positive images gleaned from middle- and upper-class white society, and by means of negative images of lower-class blacks. This habit goes back to the institution of slavery itself, when "house" slaves both mimicked the whites they served and held themselves above the "field" slaves. But in the sixties the old bourgeois impulse to dissociate from the lower classes (the "we-they" distinction) backfired when racial identity suddenly called for the celebration of this same black lower class. One of the qualities of a double bind is that one feels it more than sees it, and I distinctly remember the tension and strange sense of dishonesty I felt in those days as I moved back and forth like a bigamist between the demands of class and race.

Though my father was born poor, he achieved middle-class standing through much hard work and sacrifice (one of his favorite words) and by identifying fully with solid middle-class values—mainly hard work, family life, property ownership, and education for his children (all four of whom have advanced degrees). In his mind these were not so much values as laws of nature. People who embodied them made up the positive images in his class polarity. The negative images came largely from the blacks he had left behind because they were "going nowhere."

No one in my family remembers how it happened, but as time went on, the negative images congealed into an imaginary character named Sam, who, from the extensive service we put him to, quickly grew to mythic proportions. In our family lore he was sometimes a trickster, sometimes a boob, but always possessed of a catalogue of sly faults that gave up graphic images of everything we should not be. On sacrifice: "Sam never thinks about tomorrow. He wants it now or he doesn't care about it." On work: "Sam doesn't favor it too much." On children: "Sam likes to have them but not to raise them." On money: "Sam drinks it up and pisses it out." On fidelity: "Sam has to have two or three women." On clothes: "Sam features loud clothes. He likes to see and be seen." And so on. Sam's persona amounted to a negative instruction manual in class identity.

I don't think that any of us believed Sam's faults were accurate representations of lower-class black life. He was an instrument of self-definition, not of sociological accuracy. It never occurred to us that he looked very much like the white racist stereotype of blacks, or that he might have been a manifestation of our own racial self-hatred. He simply gave us a counterpoint against which to express our aspirations. If self-hatred was a factor, it was not, for us, a matter of hating lower-class blacks but of hating what we did not want to be.

Still, hate or love aside, it is fundamentally true that my middle-class identity involved a dissociation from images of lower-class black life and a corresponding identification with values and patterns of responsibility that are common to the middle class everywhere. These values sent me a clear message: be both an individual and a responsible citizen; understand that the quality of your life will approximately reflect the quality of effort you put into it; know that individual responsibility is the basis of freedom and that the limitations imposed by fate (whether fair or unfair) are no excuse for passivity.

Whether I live up to these values or not, I know that my acceptance of them is the result of lifelong conditioning. I know also that I share this conditioning with middle-class people of all races and that I can no more easily be free of it than I can be free of my race. Whether all this got started because the black middle class modeled itself on the white middle class is no longer relevant. For the middle-class black, conditioned by these values from birth, the sense of meaning they provide is as immutable as the color of his skin.

I started the sixties in high school feeling that my class-conditioning was the surest way to overcome racial barriers. My racial identity was pretty much taken for granted. After all, it was obvious to the world that I was black. Yet I ended the sixties in graduate school a little embarrassed by my class background and with an almost desperate need to be "black." The tables had turned. I knew very clearly (though I struggled to repress it) that my aspirations and my sense of how to operate in the world came from my class background, yet "being black" required certain attitudes and stances that made me feel secretly a little duplicitous. The inner compatibility of class and race I had known in 1960 was gone.

For blacks, the decade between 1960 and 1969 saw racial identification undergo the same sort of transformation that national identity undergoes in times of war. It became more self-conscious, more narrowly focused, more prescribed, less tolerant of opposition. It spawned an implicit party line, which tended to disallow competing forms of identity. Race-as-identity was lifted from the relative slumber it knew in the fifties and pressed into service in a social and political war against oppression. It was redefined along sharp adversarial lines and directed toward the goal of mobilizing the great mass of black Americans in this warlike effort. It was imbued with a strong moral authority, useful for denouncing those who opposed it and for celebrating those who honored it as a positive achievement rather than as a mere birthright.

The form of racial identification that quickly evolved to meet this challenge presented blacks as a racial monolith, a singular people with a common experience of oppression. Differences within the race, no matter how ineradicable, had to be minimized. Class distinctions were one of the first such differences to be sacrificed, since they not only threatened racial unity but also seemed to stand in contradiction to the principle of equality which was the announced goal of the movement for racial progress. The discomfort I felt in 1969, the vague but relentless sense of duplicity, was the result of a historical necessity that put my race and class at odds, that was asking me to cast aside the distinction of my class and identify with a monolithic view of my race.

If the form of this racial identity was the monolith, its substance was victimization. The civil rights movement and the more radical splinter groups of the late sixties were all dedicated to ending racial victimization, and the form of black identity that emerged to facilitate this goal made blackness and victimization virtually synonymous. Since it was our victimization more than any other variable that identified and unified us, moreover, it followed logically that the purest black was the poor black. It was images of him that clustered around the positive pole of the race polarity; all other blacks were, in effect, required to identify with him in order to confirm their own blackness.

Certainly there were more dimensions to the black experience than victimization, but no other had the same capacity to fire the indignation needed for war. So, again out of historical necessity, victimization became the overriding focus of racial identity. But this only deepened the double bind for middle-class blacks like me. When it came to class we were accustomed to defining ourselves against lower-class blacks and identifying with at least the values of middle-class whites; when it came to race we were now being asked to identify with images of lower-class blacks and to see whites, middle class or otherwise, as victimizers. Negative lining up with positive, we were called upon to reject what we had previously embraced and to embrace what we had previously rejected. To put it still more personally, the Sam figure I had been raised to define myself against had now become the "real" black I was expected to identify with.

The fact that the poor black's new status was only passively earned by the condition of his victimization, not by assertive, positive action, made little difference. Status was status apart from the means by which it was achieved, and along with it came a certain power—the power to define the terms of access to that status, to say who was black and who was not. If a lower-class black said you were not really "black"—a sellout, an Uncle Tom—the judgment was all the more devastating because it carried the authority of his status. And this judgment soon enough came to be accepted by many whites as well.

In graduate school I was once told by a white professor, "Well, but . . . you're not really black. I mean, you're not disadvantaged." In his mind my lack of victim status disqualified me from the race itself. More recently I was complimented by a black student for speaking reasonably correct English, "proper" English as he put it. "But I don't know if I really want to talk like that," he went on. "Why not?" I asked. "Because then I wouldn't be black no more," he replied without a pause.

To overcome his marginal status, the middle-class black had to identify with a degree of victimization that was beyond his actual experience. In college (and well beyond) we used to play a game called "nap matching." It was a game of one-upmanship, in which we sat around outdoing each other with stories of racial victimization, symbolically measured by the naps of our hair. Most of us were middle class and so had few personal stories to relate, but if we could not match naps with our own biographies, we would move on to those legendary tales of victimization that came to us from the public domain.

The single story that sat atop the pinnacle of racial victimization for us was that of Emmett Till, the Northern black teenager who, on a visit to the South in 1955, was killed and grotesquely mutilated for supposedly looking at or whistling at (we were never sure which, though we argued the point endlessly) a white woman. Oh, how we probed his story, finding in his youth and Northern upbringing the quintessential embodiment of black innocence, brought down by a white evil so portentous and apocalyptic, so gnarled and hideous, that it left us with a feeling not far from awe. By telling his story and others like it, we came to *feel* the immutability of our victimization, its utter indigenousness, as a thing on this earth like dirt or sand or water.

Of course, these sessions were a ritual of group identification, a means by which we, as middle-class blacks, could be at one with our race. But why were we, who had only a moderate experience of victimization (and that offset by opportunities our parents never had), so intent on assimilating or appropriating an identity that in so many ways contradicted our own? Because, I think, the sense of innocence that is always entailed in feeling victimized filled us with a corresponding feeling of entitlement, or even license, that helped us endure our vulnerability on a largely white college campus.

In my junior year in college I rode to a debate tournament with three white students and our faculty coach, an elderly English professor. The experience of being the lone black in a group of whites was so familiar to me that I thought nothing of it as our trip began. But then halfway through the trip the professor casually turned to me and, in an isn't-the-world-funny sort of tone, said that he had just refused to rent an apartment in a house he owned to a "very nice" black couple because their color would "offend" the white couple who lived downstairs. His eyebrows lifted helplessly over his hawkish nose, suggesting that he too, like me, was a victim of America's racial farce. His look assumed a kind of comradeship: he and I were above this grimy business of race, though for expediency we had occasionally to concede the world its madness.

My vulnerability in this situation came not so much from the professor's blindness to his own racism as from his assumption that I would participate in it, that I would conspire with him against my own race so that he might remain comfortably blind. Why did he think I would be amenable to this? I can only guess that he assumed my middle-class identity was so complete and all-encompassing that I would see his action as nothing more than a trifling concession to the folkways of our land, that I would in fact applaud his decision not to disturb propriety. Blind to both his own racism and to me—one blindness serving the other—he could not recognize that he was asking me to betray my race in the name of my class.

His blindness made me feel vulnerable because it threatened to expose my own repressed ambivalence. His comment pressured me to choose between my class identification, which had contributed to my being a college student and a member of the debating team, and my desperate desire to be "black." I could have one but not both; I was double-bound.

Because double binds are repressed there is always an element of terror in them: the terror of bringing to the conscious mind the buried duplicity, self-deception, and pretense involved in serving two masters. This terror is the stuff of vulnerability, and since vulnerability is one of the least tolerable of all human feelings, we usually transform it into an emotion that seems to restore the control of which it has robbed us; most often, that emotion is anger. And so, before the professor had even finished his little story, I had become a furnace of rage. The year was 1967, and I had been primed by endless hours of nap-matching to feel, at least consciously, completely at one with the victim-focused black identity. This identity gave me the license, and the impunity, to unleash upon this professor one of those volcanic eruptions of racial indignation familiar to us from the novels of Richard Wright. Like Cross Damon in *Outsider*, who kills in perfectly righteous anger, I tried to annihilate the man. I punished him not according to the measure of his crime but according to the measure of my vulnerability, a measure set by the cumulative tension of years of repressed terror. Soon I saw that terror in *his* face, as he stared hollow-eyed at the road ahead. My white friends in the back seat, knowing no conflict between their own class and race, were astonished that someone they had taken to be so much like themselves could harbor a rage that for all the world looked murderous.

Though my rage was triggered by the professor's comment, it was deepened and sustained by a complex of need, conflict, and repression in myself of which I had been wholly unaware. Out of my racial vulnerability I had developed the strong need of an identity with which to defend myself. The only such identity available was that of me as victim, him as victimizer. Once in the grip of this paradigm, I began to do far more damage to myself than he had done.

Seeing myself as a victim meant that I clung all the harder to my racial identity, which, in turn, meant that I suppressed my class identity. This cut me off from all the resources my class values might have offered me. In those values, for instance, I might have found the means to a more dispassionate response, the response less of a victim attacked by a victimizer than of an individual offended by a foolish old man. As an individual I might have reported this professor to the college dean. Or I might have calmly tried to reveal his blindness to him, and possibly won a convert. (The flagrancy of his remark suggested a hidden guilt and even self-recognition on which I might have capitalized. Doesn't confession usually signal a willingness to face oneself?) Or I might have simply chuckled and then let my silence serve as an answer to his provocation. Would not my composure, in any form it might take, deflect into his own heart the arrow he'd shot at me?

Instead, my anger, itself the hair-trigger expression of a long-repressed double bind, not only cut me off from the best of my own resources, it also distorted the nature of my true racial problem. The righteousness of this anger and easy catharsis it brought buoyed the delusion of my victimization and left me as blind as the professor himself.

As a middle-class black I have often felt myself *contriving* to be "black." And I have noticed this same contrivance in others—a certain stretching away from the natural flow of one's life to align oneself with a victim-focused black identity. Our particular needs are out of sync with the form of identity available to meet those needs. Middle-class blacks need to identify racially; it is better to think of ourselves as black and victimized than not black at all; so we contrive (more unconsciously than consciously) to fit ourselves into an identity that denies our class and fails to address the true source of our vulnerability.

For me this once meant spending inordinate amounts of time at black faculty meetings, though these meetings had little to do with my real racial anxieties or my professional life. I was new to the university, one of two blacks in an English department of over seventy, and I felt a little isolated and vulnerable, though I did not admit it to myself. But at these meetings we discussed the problems of black faculty and students within a framework of victimization. The real vulnerability we felt was covered over by all the adversarial drama the victim/victimized polarity inspired, and hence went unseen and unassuaged. And this, I think, explains our rather chronic ineffectiveness as a group. Since victimization was not our primary problem—the university had long ago opened its doors to us—we had to contrive to make it so, and there is not much energy in contrivance. What I got at these meetings was ultimately an object lesson in how fruitless struggle can be when it is not grounded in actual need.

At our black faculty meetings, the old equation of blackness with victimization was ever present—to be black was to be a victim; therefore, not to be a victim was not to be black. As we contrived to meet the terms of this formula there was an inevitable distortion of both ourselves and the larger university. Through the prism of victimization the university seemed more impenetrable than it actually was, and we more limited in our powers. We fell prey to the victim's myopia, making the university an institution from which we could seek redress but which we could never fully join. And this mind-set often led us to look more for compensations for our supposed victimization than for opportunities we could pursue as individuals.

The discomfort and vulnerability felt by middle-class blacks in the sixties, it could be argued, was a worthwhile price to pay considering the progress achieved during that time of racial confrontation. But what may have been tolerable then is intolerable now. Though changes in American society have made it an anachronism, the monolithic form of racial identification that came out of the sixties is still very much with us. It may be more loosely held, and its power to punish heretics has probably diminished, but it continues to catch middle-class blacks in a double bind, thus impeding not only their own advancement but even, I would contend, that of blacks as a group.

The victim-focused black identity encourages the individual to feel that his advancement depends almost entirely on that of the group. Thus he loses sight not only of his own possibilities but of the inextricable connection between individual effort and individual advancement. This is a profound emcumbrance today, when there is more opportunity for blacks than ever before, for it reimposes limitations that can have the same oppressive effect as those the society has only recently begun to remove.

It was the emphasis on mass action in the sixties that made the victim-focused black identity a necessity. But in the eighties and beyond, when racial advancement will come only through a multitude of individual advancements, this form of identity inadvertently adds itself to the forces that hold us back. Hard work, education, individual initiative, stable family life, property ownership—these have always been the means by which ethnic groups have moved ahead in America. Regardless of past or present victimization, these "laws" of advancement apply absolutely to black Americans also. There is no getting around this. What we need is a form of racial identity that energizes the individual by putting him in touch with both his possibilities and his responsibilities.

It has always annoyed me to hear from the mouths of certain arbiters of blackness that middle-class blacks should "reach back" and pull up those blacks less fortunate than they—as though middle-class status were an unearned and essentially passive condition in which one needed a large measure of noblesse oblige to occupy one's time. My own image is of reaching back from a moving train to lift on board those who have no tickets. A noble enough sentiment—but might it not be wiser to show them the entire structure of principles, effort, and sacrifice that puts one in a position to buy a ticket any time one likes? This, I think, is something members of the black middle class can realistically offer to other blacks. Their example is not only a testament to possibility but also a lesson in method. But they cannot lead by example until they are released from a black identity that regards that example as suspect, that sees them as "marginally" black, indeed that holds *them* back by catching them in a double bind.

To move beyond the victim-focused black identity we must learn to make a difficult but crucial distinction: between actual victimization, which we must resist with every resource, and identification with the victim's status. Until we do this we will continue to wrestle more with ourselves than with the new opportunities which so many paid so dearly to win.

Suggestions for Discussion

1. How has the author's personal history brought him into conflict with the political movement to overcome racism?

2. Steele identifies and explains what it means to be a member of the middle class. Discuss his definition.

3. What is the negative consequence, for Steele, of seeing himself as a victim of racism?

4. Discuss the episode related by Steele of his anger with a white professor as they travel to a debating match.

Suggestions for Writing

1. Write an essay in which you evaluate Steele's statement of his dilemma both as student and professor. Do you sympathize with him? Do you agree or disagree with his position? Explain your position.

2. Take the part of a white or black student, and write a paper in which you discuss the "double bind" Steele describes. Try to examine carefully your own relation with a member of the opposite race.

3. Write a paper in which you evaluate Steele's solution to what he sees as the problem of being a member of the black middle class.

Fiction

William Faulkner

Dry September

William Faulkner (1897–1962) lived most of his life in Oxford, Mississippi. After a year at the university of his native state, he joined the Royal Canadian Air Force, eager to participate in World War I. His novels set in his imaginary Yoknapatawpha County include *The Sound and the Fury* (1929), *Light in August* (1932), *Absalom, Absalom!* (1936), and *The Hamlet* (1940). This story, taken from the section of Faulkner's *Collected Stories* (1950) called "The Village," offers an acute social and psychological analysis of life in a small Southern town after World War I. Notice how Faulkner focuses on the gentle barber, the hysterical spinster, and the brutal ex-soldier to provide social commentary.

I

Through the bloody September twilight, aftermath of sixty-two rainless days, it had gone like a fire in dry grass—the rumor, the story, whatever it was. Something about Miss Minnie Cooper and a Negro. Attacked, insulted, frightened: none of them, gathered in the barber shop on that Saturday evening where the ceiling fan stirred, without freshening it, the vitiated air, sending back upon them, in recurrent surges of stale pomade and lotion, their own stale breath and odors, knew exactly what had happened.

"Except it wasn't Will Mayes," a barber said. He was a man of middle age; a thin, sand-colored man with a mild face, who was shaving a client. "I know Will Mayes. He's a good nigger. And I know Minnie Cooper, too."

"What do you know about her?" a second barber said.

"Who is she?" the client said. "A young girl?"

"No," the barber said. "She's about forty, I reckon. She ain't married. That's why I dont believe—"

"Believe, hell!" a hulking youth in a sweat-stained silk shirt said. "Wont you take a white woman's word before a nigger's?"

"I dont believe Will Mayes did it," the barber said. "I know Will Mayes."

"Maybe you know who did it, then. Maybe you already got him out of town, you damn niggerlover."

"I dont believe anybody did anything. I dont believe anything happened. I leave it to you fellows if them ladies that get old without getting married dont have notions that a man cant—"

"Then you are a hell of a white man," the client said. He moved under the cloth. The youth had sprung to his feet.

"You dont?" he said. "Do you accuse a white woman of lying?"

The barber held the razor poised above the half-risen client. He did not look around.

886

"It's this durn weather," another said. "It's enough to make a man do anything. Even to her."

Nobody laughed. The barber said in his mild, stubborn tone: "I ain't accusing nobody of nothing. I just know and you fellows know how a woman that never—"

"You damn niggerlover!" the youth said.

"Shut up, Butch," another said. "We'll get the facts in plenty of time to act."

"Who is? Who's getting them?" the youth said. "Facts, hell! I—".

"You're a fine white man," the client said. "Aint you?" In his frothy beard he looked like a desert rat in the moving pictures. "You tell them, Jack," he said to the youth. "If there aint any white men in this town, you can count on me, even if I aint only a drummer and a stranger."

"That's right, boys," the barber said. "Find out the truth first. I know Will Mayes."

"Well, by God!" the youth shouted. "To think that a white man in this town—"

"Shut up, Butch," the second speaker said. "We got plenty of time."

The client sat up. He looked at the speaker. "Do you claim that anything excuses a nigger attacking a white woman? Do you mean to tell me you are a white man and you'll stand for it? You better go back North where you came from. The South dont want your kind here."

"North what?" the second said. "I was born and raised in this town."

"Well, by God!" the youth said. He looked about with a strained, baffled gaze, as if he was trying to remember what it was he wanted to say or to do. He drew his sleeve across his sweating face. "Damn if I'm going to let a white woman—"

"You tell them, Jack," the drummer said. "By God, if they—"

The screen door crashed open. A man stood in the floor, his feet apart and his heavy-set body poised easily. His white shirt was open at the throat; he wore a felt hat. His hot, bold glance swept the group. His name was McLendon. He had commanded troops at the front in France and had been decorated for valor.

"Well," he said, "are you going to sit there and let a black son rape a white woman on the streets of Jefferson?"

Butch sprang up again. The silk of his shirt clung flat to his heavy shoulders. At each armpit was a dark halfmoon. "That's what I been telling them! That's what I—"

"Did it really happen?" a third said. "This aint the first man scare she ever had, like Hawkshaw says. Wasn't there something about a man on the kitchen roof, watching her undress, about a year ago?"

"What?" the client said. "What's that?" The barber had been slowly forcing him back into the chair; he arrested himself reclining, his head lifted, the barber still pressing him down.

McLendon whirled on the third speaker. "Happen? What the hell difference does it make? Are you going to let the black sons get away with it until one really does it?"

"That's what I'm telling them!" Butch shouted. He cursed, long and steady, pointless.

"Here, here," a fourth said. "Not so loud. Dont talk so loud."

"Sure," McLendon said; "no talking necessary at all. I've done my talking. Who's with me?" He poised on the balls of his feet, roving his gaze.

The barber held the drummer's face down, the razor poised. "Find out the facts first, boys. I know Willy Mayes. It wasn't him. Let's get the sheriff and do this thing right."

McLendon whirled upon him his furious, rigid face. The barber did not look away. They looked like men of different races. The other barbers had ceased also above their prone clients. "You mean to tell me," McLendon said, "that you'd take a nigger's word before a white woman's? Why, you damn niggerloving—"

The third speaker rose and grasped McLendon's arm; he too had been a soldier. "Now, now. Let's figure this thing out. Who knows anything about what really happened?"

"Figure out hell!" McLendon jerked his arm free. "All that're with me get up from there. The ones that aint—" He roved his gaze, dragging his sleeve across his face.

Three men rose. The drummer in the chair sat up. "Here," he said, jerking at the cloth about his neck; "get this rag off me. I'm with him. I dont live here, but by God, if our mothers and wives and sisters—" He smeared the cloth over his face and flung it to the floor. McLendon stood in the floor and cursed the others. Another rose and moved toward him. The remainder sat uncomfortable, not looking at one another, then one by one they rose and joined him.

The barber picked the cloth from the floor. He began to fold it neatly. "Boys, dont do that. Will Mayes never done it. I know."

"Come on," McLendon said. He whirled. From his hip pocket protruded the butt of a heavy automatic pistol. They went out. The screen door crashed behind them reverberant in the dead air.

The barber wiped the razor carefully and swiftly, and put it away, and ran to the rear, and took his hat from the wall. "I'll be back as soon as I can," he said to the other barbers. "I cant let—" He went out, running. The two other barbers followed him to the door and caught it on the rebound, leaning out and looking up the street after him. The air was flat and dead. It had a metallic taste at the base of the tongue.

"What can he do?" the first said. The second one was saying "Jees Christ, Jees Christ" under his breath. "I'd just as lief be Will Mayes as Hawk, if he gets McLendon riled."

"Jees Christ, Jees Christ," the second whispered

"You reckon he really done it to her?" the first said.

II

She was thirty-eight or thirty-nine. She lived in a small frame house with her invalid mother and a thin, sallow, unflagging aunt, where each morning between ten and eleven she would appear on the porch in a lace-trimmed boudoir cap, to sit swinging in the porch swing until noon. After dinner she lay down for a while, until the afternoon began to cool. Then, in one of the three or four new voile dresses which she had each summer, she would go downtown to spend the afternoon in the stores with the other ladies, where they would handle the goods and haggle over the prices in cold, immediate voices, without any intention of buying.

She was of comfortable people—not the best in Jefferson, but good people enough—and she was still on the slender side of ordinary looking, with a bright, faintly haggard manner and dress. When she was young she had had a slender, nervous body and a sort of hard vivacity which had enabled her for a time to ride upon the crest of the town's social life as exemplified by the high school party and church social period of her contemporaries while still children enough to be unclassconscious.

She was the last to realize that she was losing ground; that those among whom she had been a little brighter and louder flame than any other were beginning to learn the pleasure of snobbery—male—and retaliation—female. That was when her face began to wear that bright, haggard look. She still carried it to parties on shadowy porticoes and summer lawns, like a mask or a flag, with that bafflement of furious repudiation of truth in her eyes. One evening at a party she heard a boy and two girls, all schoolmates, talking. She never accepted another invitation.

She watched the girls with whom she had grown up as they married and got homes and children, but no man ever called on her steadily until the children of the other girls had been calling her "aunty" for several years, the while their mothers told them in bright voices about how popular Aunt Minnie had been as a girl. Then the town began to see her driving on Sunday afternoons with the cashier in the bank. He was a widower of about forty—a high-colored man, smelling always faintly of the barber shop or of whisky. He owned the first automobile in town, a red runabout; Minnie had the first motoring bonnet and veil the town ever saw. Then the town began to say: "Poor Minnie." "But she is old enough to take care of herself," others said. That was when she began to ask her old schoolmates that their children call her "cousin" instead of "aunty."

It was twelve years now since she had been relegated into adultery by public opinion, and eight years since the cashier had gone to a Memphis bank, returning for one day each Christmas, which he spent at an annual bachelors' party at a hunting club on the river. From behind their curtains the neighbors would see the party pass, and during the over-the-way Christmas day visiting they would tell her about him, about how well he looked, and how they heard that he was prospering in the city, watching with bright, secret eyes her haggard, bright face. Usually by that hour there would be the scent of whisky on her breath. It was supplied her by a youth, a clerk at the soda fountain: "Sure; I buy it for the old gal. I reckon she's entitled to a little fun."

Her mother kept to her room altogether now; the gaunt aunt ran the house. Against that background Minnie's bright dresses, her idle and empty days, had a quality of furious unreality. She went out in the evenings only with women now, neighbors, to the moving pictures. Each afternoon she dressed in one of the new dresses and went downtown alone, where her young "cousins" were already strolling in the late afternoons with their delicate, silken heads and thin, awkward arms and conscious hips, clinging to one another or shrieking and giggling with paired boys in the soda fountain when she passed and went

on along the serried store fronts, in the doors of which the sitting and lounging men did not even follow her with their eyes any more.

III

The barber went swiftly up the street where the sparse lights, insect-
swirled, glared in rigid and violent suspension in the lifeless air. The day had
died in a pall of dust; above the darkened square, shrouded by the spent
dust, the sky was as clear as the inside of a brass bell. Below the east was a
rumor of the twice-waxed moon.

When he overtook them McLendon and three others were getting into a
car parked in an alley. McLendon stooped his thick head, peering out beneath the top. "Changed your mind, did you?" he said. "Damn good thing;
by God, tomorrow when this town hears about how you talked tonight—"

"Now, now," the other ex-soldier said. "Hawkshaw's all right. Come on,
Hawk; jump in."

"Will Mayes never done it, boys," the barber said. "If anybody done it.
Why, you all know well as I do there ain't any town where they got better
niggers than us. And you know how a lady will kind of think things about
men when there aint any reason to, and Miss Minnie anyway—"

"Sure, sure," the soldier said. "We're just going to talk to him a little;
that's all."

"Talk hell!" Butch said. "When we're through with the—"

"Shut up, for God's sake!" the soldier said. "Do you want everybody in
town—"

"Tell them, by God!" McLendon said. "Tell every one of the sons that'll
let a white woman—"

"Let's go; let's go: here's the other car." The second car slid squealing out
of a cloud of dust at the alley mouth. McLendon started his car and took the
lead. Dust lay like fog in the street. The street lights hung nimbused as in
water. They drove on out of town.

A rutted lane turned at right angles. Dust hung above it too, and above all
the land. The dark bulk of the ice plant, where the Negro Mayes was night
watchman, rose against the sky. "Better stop here, hadn't we?" the soldier
said. McLendon did not reply. He hurled the car up and slammed to a stop,
the headlights glaring on the blank wall.

"Listen here, boys," the barber said, "if he's here, dont that prove he
never done it? Dont it? If it was him, he would run. Dont you see he
would?" The second car came up and stopped. McLendon got down; Butch
sprang down beside him. "Listen, boys," the barber said.

"Cut the lights off!" McLendon said. The breathless dark rushed down.
There was no sound in it save their lungs as they sought air in the parched
dust in which for two months they had lived; then the diminishing crunch of
McLendon's and Butch's feet, and a moment later McLendon's voice:

"Will! . . . Will!"

Below the east the wan hemorrhage of the moon increased. It heaved
above the ridge, silvering the air, the dust, so that they seemed to breathe,
live, in a bowl of molten lead. There was no sound of nightbird nor insect, no

sound save their breathing and a faint ticking of contracting metal about the cars. Where their bodies touched one another they seemed to sweat dryly, for no more moisture came. "Christ!" a voice said; "let's get out of here."

But they didn't move until vague noises began to grow out of the darkness ahead; then they got out and waited tensely in the breathless dark. There was another sound: a blow, a hissing expulsion of breath and McLendon cursing in undertone. They stood a moment longer, then they ran forward. They ran in a stumbling clump, as though they were fleeing something. "Kill him, kill the son," a voice whispered. McLendon flung them back.

"Not here," he said. "Get him into the car." "Kill him, kill the black son!" the voice murmured. They dragged the Negro to the car. The barber had waited beside the car. He could feel himself sweating and he knew he was going to be sick at the stomach.

"What is it, captains?" the Negro said. "I aint done nothing. 'Fore God, Mr. John." Someone produced handcuffs. They worked busily about the Negro as though he were a post, quiet, intent, getting in one another's way. He submitted to the handcuffs, looking swiftly and constantly from dim face to dim face. "Who's here, captains?" he said, leaning to peer into the faces until they could feel his breath and smell his sweaty reek. He spoke a name or two. "What you all say I done, Mr. John?"

McLendon jerked the car door open. "Get in!" he said.

The Negro did not move. "What you all going to do with me, Mr. John? I aint done nothing. White folks, captains, I aint done nothing: I swear 'fore God." He called another name.

"Get in!" McLendon said. He struck the Negro. The others expelled their breath in a dry hissing and struck him with random blows and he whirled and cursed them, and swept his manacled hands across their faces and slashed the barber upon the mouth, and the barber struck him also. "Get him in there," McLendon said. They pushed at him. He ceased struggling and got in and sat quietly as the others took their places. He sat between the barber and the soldier, drawing his limbs in so as not to touch them, his eyes going swiftly and constantly from face to face. Butch clung to the running board. The car moved on. The barber nursed his mouth with his handkerchief.

"What's the matter, Hawk?" the soldier said.

"Nothing," the barber said. They regained the highroad and turned away from town. The second car dropped back out of the dust. They went on, gaining speed; the final fringe of houses dropped behind.

"Goddamn, he stinks!" the soldier said.

"We'll fix that," the drummer in front beside McLendon said. On the running board Butch cursed into the hot rush of air. The barber leaned suddenly forward and touched McLendon's arm.

"Let me out, John," he said.

"Jump out, niggerlover," McLendon said without turning his head. He drove swiftly. Behind them the sourceless lights of the second car glared in the dust. Presently McLendon turned into a narrow road. It was rutted with disuse. It led back to an abandoned brick kiln—a series of reddish mounds and weed- and vine-choked vats without bottom. It had been used for pasture once, until one day the owner missed one of his mules. Although he prodded carefully in the vats with a long pole, he could not even find the bottom of them.

"John," the barber said.

"Jump out, then," McLendon said, hurling the car along the ruts. Beside the barber the Negro spoke:

"Mr. Henry."

The barber sat forward. The narrow tunnel of the road rushed up and past. Their motion was like an extinct furnace blast: cooler, but utterly dead. The car bounded from rut to rut.

"Mr. Henry," the Negro said.

The barber began to tug furiously at the door. "Look out, there!" the soldier said, but the barber had already kicked the door open and swung onto the running board. The soldier leaned across the Negro and grasped at him, but he had already jumped. The car went on without checking speed.

The impetus hurled him crashing through dust-sheathed weeds, into the ditch. Dust puffed about him, and in a thin, vicious crackling of sapless stems he lay choking and retching until the second car passed and died away. Then he rose and limped on until he reached the highroad and turned toward town, brushing at his clothes with his hands. The moon was higher, riding high and clear of the dust at last, and after a while the town began to glare beneath the dust. He went on, limping. Presently he heard cars and the glow of them grew in the dust behind him and he left the road and crouched again in the weeds until they passed. McLendon's car came last now. There were four people in it and Butch was not on the running board.

They went on; the dust swallowed them; the glare and the sound died away. The dust of them hung for a while, but soon the eternal dust absorbed it again. The barber climbed back onto the road and limped on toward town.

IV

As she dressed for supper on that Saturday evening, her own flesh felt like fever. Her hands trembled among the hooks and eyes, and her eyes had a feverish look, and her hair swirled crisp and crackling under the comb. While she was still dressing the friends called for her and sat while she donned her sheerest underthings and stockings and a new voile dress. "Do you feel strong enough to go out?" they said, their eyes bright too, with a dark glitter. "When you have had time to get over the shock, you must tell us what happened. What he said and did; everything."

In the leafed darkness, as they walked toward the square, she began to breathe deeply, something like a swimmer preparing to dive, until she ceased trembling, the four of them walking slowly because of the terrible heat and out of solicitude for her. But as they neared the square she began to tremble again, walking with her head up, her hands clenched at her sides, their voices about her murmurous, also with that feverish, glittering quality of their eyes.

They entered the square, she in the center of the group, fragile in her fresh dress. She was trembling worse. She walked slower and slower, as children eat ice cream, her head up and her eyes bright in the haggard banner of her face, passing the hotel and the coatless drummers in chairs along the curb looking around at her: "That's the one: see? The one in pink in the middle." "Is that her? What did they do with the nigger? Did they—?" "Sure. He's all right." "All right, is he?" "Sure. He went on a little trip."

Then the drug store, where even the young men lounging in the doorway tipped their hats and followed with their eyes the motions of her hips and legs when she passed.

They went on, passing the lifted hats of the gentlemen, the suddenly ceased voices, deferent, protective. "Do you see?" the friends said. Their voices sounded like long, hovering sighs of hissing exultation. "There's not a Negro on the square. Not one."

They reached the picture show. It was like a miniature fairyland with its lighted lobby and colored lithographs of life caught in its terrible and beautiful mutations. Her lips began to tingle. In the dark, when the picture began, it would be all right; she could hold back the laughing so it would not waste away so fast and so soon. So she hurried on before the turning faces, the undertones of low astonishment, and they took their accustomed places where she could see the aisle against the silver glare and the young men and girls coming in two and two against it.

The lights flicked away; the screen glowed silver, and soon life began to unfold, beautiful and passionate and sad, while still the young men and girls entered, scented and sibilant in the half dark, their paired backs in silhouette delicate and sleek, their slim, quick bodies awkward, divinely young, while beyond them the silver dream accumulated, inevitably on and on. She began to laugh. In trying to suppress it, it made more noise than ever; heads began to turn. Still laughing, her friends raised her and led her out, and she stood at the curb, laughing on a high, sustained note, until the taxi came up and they helped her in.

They removed the pink voile and the sheer underthings and the stockings, and put her to bed, and cracked ice for her temples, and sent for the doctor. He was hard to locate, so they ministered to her with hushed ejaculations, renewing the ice and fanning her. While the ice was fresh and cold she stopped laughing and lay still for a time, moaning only a little. But soon the laughing welled again and her voice rose screaming.

"Shhhhhhhhhhh! Shhhhhhhhhhhhhh!" they said, freshening the icepack, smoothing her hair, examining it for gray; "poor girl!" Then to one another: "Do you suppose anything really happened?" their eyes darkly aglitter, secret and passionate. "Shhhhhhhhhh! Poor girl! Poor Minnie!"

V

It was midnight when McLendon drove up to his neat new house. It was trim and fresh as a birdcage and almost as small, with its clean, green-and-white paint. He locked the car and mounted the porch and entered. His wife rose from a chair beside the reading lamp. McLendon stopped in the floor and stared at her until she looked down.

"Look at that clock," he said, lifting his arm, pointing. She stood before him, her face lowered, a magazine in her hands. Her face was pale, strained, and weary-looking. "Haven't I told you about sitting up like this, waiting to see when I come in?"

"John," she said. She laid the magazine down. Poised on the balls of his feet, he glared at her with his hot eyes, his sweating face.

"Didn't I tell you?" He went toward her. She looked up then. He caught her shoulder. She stood passive, looking at him.

"Don't, John. I couldn't sleep . . . The heat; something. Please, John. You're hurting me."

"Didn't I tell you?" He released her and half struck, half flung her across the chair, and she lay there and watched him quietly as he left the room.

He went on through the house, ripping off his shirt, and on the dark, screened porch at the rear he stood and mopped his head and shoulders with the shirt and flung it away. He took the pistol from his hip and laid it on the table beside the bed, and sat on the bed and removed his shoes, and rose and slipped his trousers off. He was sweating again already, and he stooped and hunted furiously for the shirt. At last he found it and wiped his body again, and, with his body pressed against the dusty screen, he stood panting. There was no movement, no sound, not even an insect. The dark world seemed to lie stricken beneath the cold moon and the lidless stars.

Suggestions for Discussion

1. Faulkner tells this story of a lynching in five parts. Discuss the relation of the parts to each other.

2. What is the function of Hawkshaw? Why is it appropriate for the story to open in a barber shop? Explain the discussion between the barbers and the customers.

3. In what ways is John McLendon different from the other men? What explains his power over them?

4. Explain the significance of the scene in which Will Mayes hits Hawkshaw in the mouth.

5. How do you know that nothing has happened to Miss Minnie Cooper? What aspects of her character make clear that she has invented an affront?

6. Explain the title of the story. How does Faulkner use weather as a force in the story? What has weather to do with the lynching?

Suggestions for Writing

1. Write an essay in which you explain how this story is an eloquent attack on lynching. Does the author permit himself to comment on what has occurred?

2. Write an essay in which you explain how the characters in this story provide a comment on the relation between the races.

Ray Bradbury

Perhaps We Are Going Away

Ray Bradbury (b. 1920), who lives in Southern California, is among the most popular and prolific of science fiction writers. He is particularly well known for *The Martian Chronicles* (1950), *The Illustrated Man* (1951), and *Dandelion Wine*

(1957). In this brief and powerful story from *The Machineries of Joy* (1963), Bradbury imagines the sense of danger and of coming disaster which a young Indian boy feels as he gets his first glimpse of European soldiers in America.

It was a strange thing that could not be told. It touched along the hairs on his neck as he lay wakening. Eyes shut, he pressed his hands to the dirt.

Was the earth, shaking old fires under its crust, turning over in its sleep?

Were buffalo on the dust prairies, in the whistling grass, drumming the sod, moving this way like a dark weather?

No.

What? What, then?

He opened his eyes and was the boy Ho-Awi, of a tribe named for a bird, by the hills named for the shadows of owls, near the great ocean itself, on a day that was evil for no reason.

Ho-Awi stared at the tent flaps, which shivered like a great beast remembering winter.

Tell me, he thought, the terrible thing, where does it come from? Whom will it kill?

He lifted the flap and stepped out into his village.

He turned slowly, a boy with bones in his dark cheeks like the keels of small birds flying. His brown eyes saw god-filled, cloud-filled sky, his cupped ear heard thistles ticking the war drums, but still the greater mystery drew him to the edge of the village.

Here, legend said, the land went on like a tide to another sea. Between here and there was as much earth as there were stars across the night sky. Somewhere in all that land, storms of black buffalo harvested the grass. And here stood Ho-Awi, his stomach a fist, wondering, searching, waiting, afraid.

You too? said the shadow of a hawk.

Ho-Awi turned.

It was the shadow of his grandfather's hand that wrote on the wind.

No. The grandfather made the sign for silence. His tongue moved soft in a toothless mouth. His eyes were small creeks running behind the sunken flesh beds, the cracked sand washes of his face.

Now they stood on the edge of the day, drawn close by the unknown.

And Old Man did as the boy had done. His mummified ear turned, his nostril twitched. Old Man too ached for some answering growl from any direction that would tell them only a great timberfall of weather had dropped from a distant sky. But the wind gave no answer, spoke only to itself.

The Old Man made the sign which said they must go on the Great Hunt. This, said his hands like mouths, was a day for the rabbit young and the featherless old. Let no warrior come with them. The hare and the dying vulture must track together. For only the very young saw life ahead, and only the very old saw life behind; the others between were so busy with life they saw nothing.

The Old Man wheeled slowly in all directions.

Yes! He knew, he was certain, he was sure! To find this thing of darkness would take the innocence of the newborn and the innocence of the blind to see very clear.

Come! said the trembling fingers.

And snuffing rabbit and earthbound hawk shadowed out of the village into changing weather.

They searched the high hills to see if the stones lay atop each other, and they were so arranged. They scanned the prairies, but found only the winds which played there like tribal children all day. And found arrowheads from old wars.

No, the Old Man's hand drew on the sky, the men of this nation and that beyond smoke by the summer fires while the squaws cut wood. It is not arrows flying that we almost hear.

At last, when the sun sank into the nation of buffalo hunters, the Old Man looked up.

The birds, his hands cried suddenly, are flying south! Summer is over!

No, the boy's hands said, summer has just begun! I see no birds!

They are so high, said the Old Man's fingers, that only the blind can feel their passage. They shadow the heart more than the earth. I feel them pass south in my blood. Summer goes. We may go with it. Perhaps we are going away.

No! cried the boy aloud, suddenly afraid. Go where? Why? For what?

Who knows? said the Old Man, and perhaps we will not move. Still, even without moving, perhaps we are going away.

No! Go back! cried the boy, to the empty sky, the birds unseen, the un-shadowed air. Summer, stay!

No use, said the Old One's single hand, moving by itself. Not you or me or our people can stay this weather. It is a season changed, come to live on the land for all time.

But from where does it come?

This way, said the Old Man at last.

And in the dusk they looked down at the great waters of the east that went over the edge of the world, where no one had ever gone.

There. The Old Man's hand clenched and thrust out. There *it* is.

Far ahead, a single light burned on the shore.

With the moon rising, the Old Man and the rabbit boy padded on the sands, heard strange voices in the sea, smelled wild burnings from the now suddenly close fire.

They crawled on their bellies. They lay looking in at the light.

And the more he looked, the colder Ho-Awi became, and he knew that all the Old Man had said was true.

For drawn to this fire built of sticks and moss, which flickered brightly in the soft evening wind which was cooler now, at the heart of summer, were such creatures as he had never seen.

These were men with faces like white-hot coals, with some eyes in these faces as blue as sky. All these men had glossy hair on their cheeks and chins, which grew to a point. One man stood with raised lightning in his hand and a great moon of sharp stuff on his head like the face of a fish. The others had bright round tinkling crusts of material cleaved to their chests which gonged slightly when they moved. As Ho-Awi watched, some men lifted the gonging bright things from their heads, unskinned the eye-blinding crab shells, the turtle casings from their chests, their arms, their legs, and tossed these discarded sheaths to the sand. Doing this, the creatures laughed, while out in the bay stood a black shape on the waters, a great dark canoe with things like torn clouds hung on poles over it.

After a long while of holding their breath, the Old Man and the boy went away.

From a hill, they watched the fire that was no bigger than a star now. You could wink it out with an eyelash. If you closed your eyes, it was destroyed.

Still, it remained.

Is this, asked the boy, the great happening?

The Old One's face was that of a fallen eagle, filled with dreadful years and unwanted wisdom. The eyes were resplendently bright, as if they welled with a rise of cold clear water in which all could be seen, like a river that drank the sky and earth and knew it, accepted silently and would not deny the accumulation of dust, time, shape, sound and destiny.

The Old Man nodded, once.

This was the terrible weather. This was how summer would end. This made the birds wheel south, shadowless, through a grieving land.

The worn hands stopped moving. The time of questions was done.

Far away, the fire leaped. One of the creatures moved. The bright stuff on his tortoise-shell body flashed. It was like an arrow cutting a wound in the night.

Then the boy vanished in darkness, following the eagle and the hawk that lived in the stone body of his grandfather.

Below, the sea reared up and poured another great salt wave in billions of pieces which crashed and hissed like knives swarming along the continental shores.

Suggestions for Discussion

1. Explain the power of this account of the advent of Western man in America.

2. Discuss Bradbury's characterizations. Are they as important to the story as the events that occur or the descriptions of the setting? Explain.

3. This story is extremely brief. Would you want it any longer? Explain.

Suggestions for Writing

1. Describe the first encounter between the Indians and the Europeans.

2. Write an essay in which you try to warn the Indians to be wary of the Europeans. Be as convincing as possible.

Poetry

Wole Soyinka

Telephone Conversation

Wole Soyinka (b. 1934) was born in Ake, Nigeria, a member of the Yoruba tribe. He was educated at the Universities of Ibadan and Leeds, has received numerous honorary degrees, and has taught in the United States, England, and Africa. In 1986 he won the Nobel Prize for Literature, honoring his publications in fiction, nonfiction prose, poetry, drama, and opera. His many works include A Man Died: Prison Notes (1972); Myth, Literature and the African Novel (1976); a collection of poetry, Ogun Ahibimen (1976); another memoir, Ake: The Years of Childhood (1982); the play, Requiem for a Futurologist (1985); and Art, Dialogue and Outrage (1988). He was Goldwyn Smith Professor of African Studies and Theatre at Cornell from 1988 to 1992. At present he resides in Nigeria. "Telephone Conversation" details the painful and ludicrous niceties of racial discrimination.

The price seemed reasonable, location
Indifferent. The landlady swore she lived
Off premises. Nothing remained
But self-confession. "Madam," I warned,
"I hate a wasted journey—I am African."
Silence. Silenced transmission of
Pressurized good-breeding. Voice, when it came,
Lipstick coated, long gold-rolled
Cigarette-holder pipped. Caught I was, foully.
"HOW DARK?" . . . I had not misheard. . . . "ARE YOU LIGHT
OR VERY DARK?" Button B. Button A. Stench
Of rancid breath of public hide-and-speak.
Red booth. Red pillar-box. Red double-tiered
Omnibus squelching tar. It was real! Shamed
By ill-mannered silence, surrender
Pushed dumbfoundment to beg simplification.
Considerate she was, varying the emphasis—
"ARE YOU DARK? OR VERY LIGHT?" Revelation came.
"You mean—like plain or milk chocolate?"
Her assent was clinical, crushing in its light
Impersonality. Rapidly, wave-length adjusted,
I chose. "West African sepia"—and as afterthought,
"Down in my passport." Silence for spectroscopic
Flight of fancy, till truthfulness clanged her accent
Hard on the mouthpiece. "WHAT'S THAT?" conceding
"DON'T KNOW WHAT THAT IS." "Like brunette."
"THAT'S DARK, ISN'T IT?" "Not altogether.
Facially, I am brunette, but madam, you should see

The rest of me. Palm of my hand, soles of my feet
Are a peroxide blonde. Friction, caused—
Foolishly madam—by sitting down, has turned
My bottom raven black—One moment madam!"—sensing
Her receiver rearing on the thunderclap
About my ears—"Madam," I pleaded, "wouldn't you rather
See for yourself?"

Suggestions for Discussion

1. What tone does Soyinka give the poem? How is that tone revealed in the questions and answers of the telephone conversation?

2. Why does the prospective renter reveal that he is black? What does this tell us about the attitude of the landlady? The general relation of the two races?

3. Explain why the poet chooses to end the poem with a witty question.

Suggestions for Writing

1. Write a paper in which you relate the incident described in Soyinka's poem to a similar circumstance in the United States.

2. In a paper explain the decision by the prospective renter to remain polite instead of abruptly ending the telephone conversation. Which response is more effective? Why?

Wilfred Owen

Dulce et Decorum Est

Wilfred Owen (1893–1918) was born in Shropshire, England, and educated at Birkenhead Institute. Among the most celebrated of the English war poets, he was killed in action in World War I. Another war poet, Siegfried Sassoon, collected Owen's poems, which were first published in 1920. Other collections followed as did critical studies and memoirs. "Dulce et Decorum Est" (taken from Horace's statement, "It is sweet and fitting to die for one's country") opposes vivid and devastating images of the casualties of war with statements of sentimental patriotism. It shows war as the ultimate insult to human dignity.

Bent double, like old beggars under sacks,
Knock-kneed, coughing like hags, we cursed through sludge,
Till on the haunting flares we turned our backs,

And towards our distant rest began to trudge.
Men marched asleep. Many had lost their boots,
But limped on, blood-shod. All went lame, all blind;
Drunk with fatigue; deaf even to the hoots
Of gas-shells dropping softly behind.

Gas! Gas! Quick, boys!—An ecstasy of fumbling,
Fitting the clumsy helmets just in time,
But someone still was yelling out and stumbling
And flound'ring like a man in fire or lime.—
Dim through the misty panes and thick green light,
As under a green sea, I saw him drowning.
In all my dreams before my helpless sight
He plunges at me, guttering, choking, drowning.

If in some smothering dreams, you too could pace
Behind the wagon that we flung him in,
And watch the white eyes writhing in his face,
His hanging face, like a devil's sick of sin,
If you could hear, at every jolt, the blood
Come gargling from the froth-corrupted lungs
Bitter as the cud
Of vile, incurable sores on innocent tongues,—
My friend, you would not tell with such high zest
To children ardent for some desperate glory,
The old lie: *Dulce et decorum est
Pro patria mori.*

Suggestions for Discussion

1. In the first two stanzas, Owen presents two connected scenes of war. How are
   these two stanzas related to the final one?

2. Discuss the use of irony in the poem. Show why Owen uses the quotation from
   Horace.

3. Examine the series of images that Owen uses to describe war. Do they progress
   through the poem? Show why one cannot interchange the first two stanzas.

Suggestion for Writing

Owen's picture of the destruction of lives constitutes a poetic statement against war.
Does this poem lead you to a belief in pacifism? Are there "just" and "unjust" wars?
Try to sort out your attitudes and write an essay explaining under what conditions, if
any, you might be willing to fight for your country. Support your statements with
detailed arguments.

W. H. Auden

The Unknown Citizen

Wystan Hugh Auden (1907–1973), educated at Oxford University, was early recognized as a leader of the poets of his generation. His volumes of poetry include *The Orators* (1932), *The Double Man* (1941), and *The Age of Anxiety* (1947), which won a Pulitzer Prize in 1948. Born in England, he came to the United States at the outbreak of World War II. His autobiography, *Certain World: A Commonplace Book*, published in 1970, traces his return from leftist agnostic to the Church of England. In 1967 he was made a fellow of Christ Church, Oxford. In the following poem, published in 1940, Auden comments satirically on the behavior of a good citizen in a totalitarian state that resembles not only fascist Italy and Nazi Germany but democratic America and Britain as well.

(To JS/07/M/378 This Marble Monument Is Erected by the State)

He was found by the Bureau of Statistics to be
One against whom there was no official complaint,
And all the reports on his conduct agree
That, in the modern sense of an old-fashioned word, he was a saint,
For in everything he did he served the Greater Community.
Except for the War till the day he retired
He worked in a factory and never got fired,
But satisfied his employers, Fudge Motors Inc.
Yet he wasn't a scab or odd in his views,
For his Union reports that he paid his dues,
(Our report on his Union shows it was sound)
And our Social Psychology workers found
That he was popular with his mates and liked to drink.
The Press are convinced that he bought a paper every day
And that his reactions to advertisements were normal in every way.
Policies taken out in his name prove that he was fully insured,
And his Health-card shows he was once in a hospital but left it cured,
Both Producers Research and High-Grade Living declare
He was fully sensible to the advantages of the Installment Plan
And had everything necessary to the Modern Man,
A phonograph, a radio, a car and a frigidaire.
Our researchers into Public Opinion are content
That he held the proper opinions for the time of year;
When there was peace, he was for peace; when there was war, he went.
He was married and added five children to the population,
Which our Eugenist says was the right number for a parent of his generation,
And our teachers report that he never interfered with their education.
Was he free? Was he Happy? The question is absurd:
Had anything been wrong, we should certainly have heard.

Suggestions for Discussion

1. Discuss reasons for the state to bother erecting such a monument.
2. Analyze the strengths and weaknesses of the society described by Auden.
3. Discuss Auden's use of irony in the poem. Find specific examples.

Suggestions for Writing

1. Write a sketch describing and evaluating a typical day in the life of the unknown citizen.
2. Provide an alternative inscription for the monument.

Drama

Sophocles

Antigone

Translated by Dudley Fitts and Robert Fitzgerald

The Greek tragic playwright Sophocles (495?–406? B.C.) wrote a great number of plays, of which only seven have survived. He is best known for *Oedipus the King* whose name in our day, because of Sigmund Freud, has become synonymous with too close an attachment between mother and son. The play *Antigone* recounts the fate of the children of Oedipus and his wife-mother, particularly his older daughter Antigone, who gives her life choosing to obey the laws of the gods rather than those of men. This play counterpoises clearly the conflicting demands of government and religion or of government and individual conscience. A French translation and adaptation of the play by Jean Anouilh during the German occupation of France illustrated clearly to the French the relevance of *Antigone* to modern times. Beyond the pleasure and excitement of reading this fine translation by Dudley Fitts and Robert Fitzgerald, the student should keep in mind the significance of the play for his or her own life. The dilemmas that the characters face in *Antigone* are morally demanding whenever people choose to question the wisdom or legitimacy of the actions of the state.

Because of the curse that their father had laid upon them, ETEOCLES *and* POLYNEICES *quarreled about the royal power, and* POLYNEICES *was finally driven from Thebes. He took refuge in Argos and married the daughter of* KING ADRASTOS; *then, as one of seven captains whose commander was* ADRASTOS, *he marched upon Thebes to recover his throne. In the assault,* ETEOCLES *and* POLYNEICES *met at the Seventh Gate and killed each other in combat.* CREON *became king, and his first official act was to forbid, on pain of death, the burial of* POLYNEICES.

Dramatis Personæ

ANTIGONE	A SENTRY
ISMENE	HAIMON
EURYDICE	TEIRESIAS
CREON	CHORAG
A MESSENGER	CHORUS

SCENE: *Before the palace of* CREON, *King of Thebes. A central double door, and two lateral doors. A platform extends the length of the façade, and from this platform three steps lead down into the orchestra, or chorus-ground. Time: dawn of the day after the repulse of the Argive army from the assault on Thebes.*

Prologue

[ANTIGONE *and* ISMENE *enter from the central door of the Palace.*]

ANTIG: Ismenê, dear sister,
You would think that we had already suffered enough
For the curse on Oedipus:
I cannot imagine any grief
That you and I have not gone through. And now—
Have they told you the new decree of our King Creon?

ISMENE: I have heard nothing: I know
That two sisters lost two brothers, a double death
In a single hour; and I know that the Argive army
Fled in the night; but beyond this, nothing.

ANTIG: I thought so. And that is why I wanted you
To come out here with me. There is something we must do.

ISMENE: Why do you speak so strangely?

ANTIG: Listen, Ismenê:
Creon buried our brother Eteoclês
With military honours, gave him a soldier's funeral,
And it was right that he should; but Polyneicês,
Who fought as bravely and died as miserably,—
They say that Creon has sworn
No one shall bury him, no one mourn for him,
But his body must lie in the fields, a sweet treasure
For carrion birds to find as they search for food.
That is what they say, and our good Creon is coming here
To announce it publicly; and the penalty—
Stoning to death in the public square!
                               There it is,
And now you can prove what you are:
A true sister, or a traitor to your family.

ISMENE: Antigonê, you are mad! What could I possibly do?

ANTIG: You must decide whether you will help me or not.

ISMENE: I do not understand you. Help you in what?

ANTIG: Ismenê, I am going to bury him. Will you come?

ISMENE: Bury him! You have just said the new law forbids it.

ANTIG: He is my brother. And he is your brother, too.

ISMENE: But think of the danger! Think what Creon will do!

ANTIG: Creon is not strong enough to stand in my way.

ISMENE: Ah sister!
Oedipus died, everyone hating him
For what his own search brought to light, his eyes

Ripped out by his own hand; and Iocastê died,
His mother and wife at once: she twisted the cords
That strangled her life; and our two brothers died,
Each killed by the other's sword. And we are left:
But oh, Antigonê,
Think how much more terrible than these
Our own death would be if we should go against Creon
And do what he has forbidden! We are only women,
We cannot fight with men, Antigonê!
The law is strong, we must give in to the law
In this thing, and in worse. I beg the Dead
To forgive me, but I am helpless: I must yield
To those in authority. And I think it is dangerous business
To be always meddling.

ANTIG: If that is what you think,
I should not want you, even if you asked to come.
You have made your choice, you can be what you want to be.
But I will bury him; and if I must die,
I say that this crime is holy: I shall lie down
With him in death, and I shall be as dear
To him as he to me.
                                  It is the dead,
Not the living, who make the longest demands:
We die for ever . . .
                                  You may do as you like,
Since apparently the laws of the gods mean nothing to you.

ISMENE: They mean a great deal to me; but I have no strength
To break laws that were made for the public good.

ANTIG: That must be your excuse, I suppose. But as for me,
I will bury the brother I love.

ISMENE: Antigonê,
I am so afraid for you!

ANTIG: You need not be:
You have yourself to consider, after all.

ISMENE: But no one must hear of this, you must tell no one!
I will keep it a secret, I promise!

ANTIG: Oh tell it! Tell everyone!
Think how they'll hate you when it all comes out
If they learn that you knew about it all the time!

ISMENE: So fiery! You should be cold with fear.

ANTIG: Perhaps. But I am doing only what I must.

ISMENE: But can you do it? I say that you cannot.

ANTIG: Very well: when my strength gives out, I shall do no more.

ISMENE: Impossible things should not be tried at all.

ANTIG: Go away, Ismenê:
          I shall be hating you soon, and the dead will too,
          For your words are hateful. Leave me my foolish plan:
          I am not afraid of the danger; if it means death,
          It will not be the worst of deaths—death without honour.

ISMENE: Go then, if you feel that you must.
          You are unwise,
          But a loyal friend indeed to those who love you.
               [*Exit into the Palace.* ANTIGONE *goes off, L. Enters the* CHORUS.]

Parodos

CHORUS: Now the long blade of the sun, lying   [STROPHE 1]
          Level east to west, touches with glory
          Thebes of the Seven Gates. Open, unlidded
          Eye of golden day! O marching light
          Across the eddy and rush of Dircê's stream,*
          Striking the white shields of the enemy
          Thrown headlong backward from the blaze of morning!

CHORAG: Polyneicês their commander
          Roused them with windy phrases,
          He the wild eagle screaming
          Insults above our land,
          His wings their shields of snow,
          His crest their marshalled helms.

CHORUS: Against our seven gates in a yawning ring   [ANTISTROPHE 1]
          The famished spears came onward in the night;
          But before his jaws were sated with our blood,
          Or pinefire took the garland of our towers,
          He was thrown back; and as he turned, great Thebes—
          No tender victim for his noisy power—
          Rose like a dragon behind him, shouting war.

CHORAG: For God hates utterly
          The bray of bragging tongues;
          And when he beheld their smiling,
          Their swagger of golden helms,
          The frown of his thunder blasted
          Their first man from our walls.

Dircê's stream: Dirce was the wife of King Lycus, King of Thebes when Oedipus' father
Laios was a minor. Her sister-in-law, Antiope, who had loved Zeus and bore him twin sons, had
fled Thebes to avoid her husband's wrath. Lycus punished Antiopê but, after his death, Antiopê
and her sons had Dircê killed by having her dragged to death on the horns of a bull. The two
sons of Antiopê built the walls of Thebes with its seven gates, and one of them, Zethus, married
the nymph Thebê from whose name came the name of the city.

CHORUS: We heard his shout of triumph high in the air   [STROPHE 2]
Turn to a scream; far out in a flaming arc
He fell with his windy torch, and the earth struck him.
And others storming in fury no less than his
Found shock of death in the dusty joy of battle.

CHORAG: Seven captains at seven gates
Yielded their clanging arms to the god
That bends the battle-line and breaks it.
These two only, brothers in blood,
Face to face in matchless rage,
Mirroring each the other's death,
Clashed in long combat.

CHORUS: But now in the beautiful morning of victory   [ANTISTROPHE 2]
Let Thebes of the many chariots sing for joy!
With hearts for dancing we'll take leave of war:
Our temples shall be sweet with hymns of praise,
And the long night shall echo with our chorus.

Scene I

CHORAG: But now at last our new King is coming:
Creon of Thebes, Menoiceus' son.
In this auspicious dawn of his reign
What are the new complexities
That shifting Fate has woven for him?
What is his counsel? Why has he summoned
The old men to hear him?

[*Enter* CREON *from the Palace. He addresses the* CHORUS *from the top step.*]

CREON: Gentlemen: I have the honour to inform you that our Ship of State, which recent storms have threatened to destroy, has come safely to harbour at last, guided by the merciful wisdom of Heaven. I have summoned you here this morning because I know that I can depend upon you: your devotion to King Laïos was absolute; you never hesitated in your duty to our late ruler Oedipus; and when Oedipus died, your loyalty was transferred to his children. Unfortunately, as you know, his two sons, the princes Eteoclês and Polyneicês, have killed each other in battle; and I, as the next in blood, have succeeded to the full power of the throne.

I am aware, of course, that no Ruler can expect complete loyalty from his subjects until he has been tested in office. Nevertheless, I say to you at the very outset that I have nothing but contempt for the kind of Governor who is afraid, for whatever reason, to follow the course that he knows is best for the State; and as for the man who sets private friendship above the public welfare,—I have no use for him, either. I call God to witness that if I saw my country headed for ruin, I should not be afraid to speak out plainly; and I need hardly remind you that I would never have any dealings with an enemy of the people. No one values friendship more highly than I; but we must remember that friends made at the risk of wrecking our Ship are not real friends at all.

These are my principles, at any rate, and that is why I have made the following decision concerning the sons of Oedipus: Eteoclês, who died as a man should die, fighting for his country, is to be buried with full military honours, with all the ceremony that is usual when the greatest heroes die; but his brother Polyneicês, who broke his exile to come back with fire and sword against his native city and the shrines of his fathers' gods, whose one idea was to spill the blood of his blood and sell his own people into slavery—Polyneicês, I say, is to have no burial: no man is to touch him or say the least prayer for him; he shall lie on the plain, unburied; and the birds and the scavenging dogs can do with him whatever they like.

This is my command, and you can see the wisdom behind it. As long as I am King, no traitor is going to be honoured with the loyal man. But whoever shows by word and deed that he is on the side of the State,—he shall have my respect while he is living, and my reverence when he is dead.

CHORAG: If that is your will, Creon son of Menoiceus,
You have the right to enforce it: we are yours.

CREON: That is my will. Take care that you do your part.

CHORAG: We are old men: let the younger ones carry it out.

CREON: I do not mean that: the sentries have been appointed.

CHORAG: Then what is it that you would have us do?

CREON: You will give no support to whoever breaks this law.

CHORAG: Only a crazy man is in love with death!

CREON: And death it is; yet money talks, and the wisest
Have sometimes been known to count a few coins too many.

[*Enter* SENTRY.]

SENTRY: I'll not say that I'm out of breath from running, King, because every time I stopped to think about what I have to tell you, I felt like going back. And all the time a voice kept saying, 'You fool, don't you know you're walking straight into trouble?'; and then another voice: 'Yes, but if you let somebody else get the news to Creon first, it will be even worse than that for you!' But good sense won out, at least I hope it was good sense, and here I am with a story that makes no sense at all; but I'll tell it anyhow, because, as they say, what's going to happen's going to happen, and—

CREON: Come to the point. What have you to say?

SENTRY: I did not do it. I did not see who did it. You must not punish me
for what someone else has done.

CREON: A comprehensive defence! More effective, perhaps,
If I knew its purpose. Come: what is it?

SENTRY: A dreadful thing . . . I don't know how to put it—

CREON: Out with it!

SENTRY: Well, then;
The dead man—
                    Polyneicês—

[*Pause. The* SENTRY *is overcome, fumbles for words.* CREON *waits impassively.*]

                    out there—

                              someone,—

New dust on the slimy flesh!

                    [*Pause. No sign from* CREON.]

Someone has given it burial that way, and
Gone . . .

          [*Long pause.* CREON *finally speaks with deadly control:*]

CREON: And the man who dared do this?

SENTRY: I swear I
Do not know! You must believe me!
                              Listen:
The ground was dry, not a sign of digging, no,
Not a wheeltrack in the dust, no trace of anyone.
It was when they relieved us this morning: and one of them,
The corporal, pointed to it.
                              There it was,
The strangest—
          Look:
The body, just mounded over with light dust: you see?
Not buried really, but as if they'd covered it
Just enough for the ghost's peace. And no sign
Of dogs or any wild animal that had been there.

And then what a scene there was! Every man of us
Accusing the other: we all proved the other man did it,
We all had proof that we could not have done it.
We were ready to take hot iron in our hands,
Walk through fire, swear by all the gods,
It was not I!
I do not know who it was, but it was not I!

[CREON'*s rage has been mounting steadily, but the* SENTRY *is too intent upon
his story to notice it.*]

And then, when this came to nothing, someone said
A thing that silenced us and made us stare
Down at the ground: you had to be told the news,
And one of us had to do it! We threw the dice,
And the bad luck fell to me. So here I am,
No happier to be here than you are to have me:
Nobody likes the man who brings bad news.

CHORAG: I have been wondering, King: can it be that the gods have done
this?

CREON: [*Furiously.*] Stop!
Must you doddering wrecks
Go out of your heads entirely? 'The gods!'
Intolerable!
The gods favour this corpse? Why? How had he served them?
Tried to loot their temples, burn their images,
Yes, and the whole State, and its laws with it!
Is it your senile opinion that the gods love to honour bad men?
A pious thought!—
                   No, from the very beginning
There have been those who have whispered together,
Stiff-necked anarchists, putting their heads together,
Scheming against me in alleys. These are the men,
And they have bribed my own guard to do this thing.

[*Sententiously.*] Money!
There's nothing in the world so demoralising as money.
Down go your cities,
Homes gone, men gone, honest hearts corrupted,
Crookedness of all kinds, and all for money!

                   [*To* Sentry:]   But you—!
I swear by God and by the throne of God,
The man who has done this thing shall pay for it!
Find that man, bring him here to me, or your death
Will be the least of your problems: I'll string you up
Alive, and there will be certain ways to make you
Discover your employer before you die;
And the process may teach you a lesson you seem to have missed:
The dearest profit is sometimes all too dear.
That depends on the source. Do you understand me?
A fortune won is often misfortune.

SENTRY: King, may I speak?

CREON: Your very voice distresses me.

SENTRY: Are you sure that it is my voice, and not your conscience?

CREON: By God, he wants to analyse me now!

SENTRY: It is not what I say, but what has been done, that hurts you.

CREON: You talk too much.

SENTRY: Maybe; but I've done nothing.

CREON: Sold your soul for some silver: that's all you've done.

SENTRY: How dreadful it is when the right judge judges wrong!

CREON: Your figures of speech
May entertain you now; but unless you bring me the man,
You will get little profit from them in the end.

> [*Exit* CREON *into the Palace.*]

SENTRY: 'Bring me the man'—!
I'd like nothing better than bringing him the man!
But bring him or not, you have seen the last of me here.
At any rate, I am safe!   [*Exit* SENTRY.]

Ode I

CHORUS: Numberless are the world's wonders, but none   [STROPHE 1]
More wonderful than man; the stormgrey sea
Yields to his prows, the huge crests bear him high;
Earth, holy and inexhaustible, is graven
With shining furrows where his plows have gone
Year after year, the timeless labour of stallions.

[ANTISTROPHE 1]

The lightboned birds and beasts that cling to cover,
The lithe fish lighting their reaches of dim water,
All are taken, tamed in the net of his mind;
The lion on the hill, the wild horse windy-maned,
Resign to him; and his blunt yoke has broken
The sultry shoulders of the mountain bull.

Words also, and thought as rapid as air,   [STROPHE 2]
He fashions to his good use; statecraft is his,
And his the skill that deflects the arrows of snow,
The spears of winter rain: from every wind
He has made himself secure—from all but one:
In the late wind of death he cannot stand.

O clear intelligence, force beyond all measure!   [ANTISTROPHE 2]
O fate of man, working both good and evil!
When the laws are kept, how proudly his city stands!
When the laws are broken, what of his city then?
Never may the anarchic man find rest at my hearth,
Never be it said that my thoughts are his thoughts.

Scene II

[*Re-enter* SENTRY *leading* ANTIGONE.]

CHORAG: What does this mean? Surely this captive woman
Is the Princess, Antigonê. Why should she be taken?

SENTRY: Here is the one who did it! We caught her
In the very act of burying him.— Where is Creon?

CHORAG: Just coming from the house.

[*Enter* CREON, C.]

CREON: What has happened?
Why have you come back so soon?

SENTRY: [*Expansively.*] O King,
A man should never be too sure of anything:
I would have sworn
That you'd not see me here again: your anger
Frightened me so, and the things you threatened me with;
But how could I tell then
That I'd be able to solve the case so soon?

No dice-throwing this time: I was only too glad to come!

Here is this woman. She is the guilty one:
We found her trying to bury him.

Take her, then; question her; judge her as you will.
I am through with the whole thing now, and glad of it.

CREON: But this is Antigonê! Why have you brought her here?

SENTRY: She was burying him, I tell you!

CREON: [*Severely,*] Is this the truth?

SENTRY: I saw her with my own eyes. Can I say more?

CREON: The details: come, tell me quickly!

SENTRY: It was like this:
After those terrible threats of yours, King,
We went back and brushed the dust away from the body.
The flesh was soft by now, and stinking,
So we sat on a hill to windward and kept guard.
No napping this time! We kept each other awake.
But nothing happened until the white round sun
Whirled in the centre of the round sky over us:
Then, suddenly,
A storm of dust roared up from the earth, and the sky
Went out, the plain vanished with all its trees
In the stinging dark. We closed our eyes and endured it.
The whirlwind lasted a long time, but it passed;

And then we looked, and there was Antigonê!
I have seen
A mother bird come back to a stripped nest, heard
Her crying bitterly a broken note or two
For the young ones stolen. Just so, when this girl
Found the bare corpse, and all her love's work wasted,
She wept, and cried on heaven to damn the hands
That had done this thing
     And then she brought more dust
And sprinkled wine three times for her brother's ghost.

We ran and took her at once. She was not afraid,
Not even when we charged her with what she had done.
She denied nothing.
     And this was a comfort to me,
And some uneasiness: for it is a good thing
To escape from death, but it is no great pleasure
To bring death to a friend.
     Yet I always say
There is nothing so comfortable as your own safe skin!

CREON: [*Slowly, dangerously.*] And you, Antigonê,
You with your head hanging,—do you confess this thing?

ANTIG: I do. I deny nothing.

CREON: [*To* SENTRY:] You may go.

            [*Exit* SENTRY.]

[*To* ANTIGONE:]   Tell me, tell me briefly:
Had you heard my proclamation touching this matter?

ANTIG: It was public. Could I help hearing it?

CREON: And yet you dared defy the law.

ANTIG: I dared.
It was not God's proclamation. That final Justice
That rules the world below makes no such laws.

Your edict, King, was strong,
But all your strength is weakness itself against
The immortal unrecorded laws of God.
They are not merely now: they were, and shall be,
Operative for ever, beyond man utterly.

I knew I must die, even without your decree:
I am only mortal. And if I must die
Now, before it is my time to die,
Surely this is no hardship: can anyone
Living, as I live, with evil all about me,
Think Death less than a friend? This death of mine
Is of no importance; but if I had left my brother

Lying in death unburied, I should have suffered.
Now I do not.
                    You smile at me. Ah Creon,
Think me a fool, if you like; but it may well be
That a fool convicts me of folly.

CHORAG: Like father, like daughter: both headstrong, deaf to reason!
She has never learned to yield.

CREON: She has much to learn.
The inflexible heart breaks first, the toughest iron
Cracks first, and the wildest horses bend their necks
At the pull of the smallest curb.
                                    Pride? In a slave?
This girl is guilty of a double insolence,
Breaking the given laws and boasting of it.
Who is the man here,
She or I, if this crime goes unpunished?
Sister's child, or more than sister's child,
Or closer yet in blood—she and her sister
Win bitter death for this!

[To SERVANTS:]   Go, some of you,
Arrest Ismenê. I accuse her equally.
Bring her: you will find her sniffling in the house there.

Her mind's a traitor: crimes kept in the dark
Cry for light, and the guardian brain shudders;
But how much worse than this
Is brazen boasting of barefaced anarchy!

ANTIG: Creon, what more do you want than my death?

CREON: Nothing.
That gives me everything.

ANTIG: Then I beg you: kill me.
This talking is a great weariness: your words
Are distasteful to me, and I am sure that mine
Seem so to you. And yet they should not seem so:
I should have praise and honour for what I have done.
All these men here would praise me
Were their lips not frozen shut with fear of you.

[Bitterly.] Ah the good fortune of kings,
Licensed to say and do whatever they please!

CREON: You are alone here in that opinion.

ANTIG: No, they are with me. But they keep their tongues in leash.

CREON: Maybe. But you are guilty, and they are not.

ANTIG: There is no guilt in reverence for the dead.

CREON: But Eteoclês—was he not your brother too?

ANTIG: My brother too.

CREON: And you insult his memory?

ANTIG: [*Softly.*] The dead man would not say that I insult it.

CREON: He would: for you honour a traitor as much as him.

ANTIG: His own brother, traitor or not, and equal in blood.

CREON: He made war on his country. Eteoclês defended it.

ANTIG: Nevertheless, there are honours due all the dead.

CREON: But not the same for the wicked as for the just.

ANTIG: Ah Creon, Creon,
Which of us can say what the gods hold wicked?

CREON: An enemy is an enemy, even dead.

ANTIG: It is my nature to join in love, not hate.

[*Finally losing patience.*]

CREON: Go join them, then; if you must have your love,
Find it in hell!

CHORAG: But see, Ismenê comes:

[*Enter* ISMENE, *guarded.*]

Those tears are sisterly, the cloud
That shadows her eyes rains down gentle sorrow.

CREON: You too, Ismenê,
Snake in my ordered house, sucking my blood
Stealthily—and all the time I never knew
That these two sisters were aiming at my throne!

Ismenê,
Do you confess your share in this crime, or deny it?
Answer me.

ISMENE: Yes, if she will let me say so. I am guilty.

ANTIG: [*Coldly:*] No, Ismenê. You have no right to say so.
You would not help me, and I will not have you help me.

ISMENE: But now I know what you meant; and I am here
To join you, to take my share of punishment.

ANTIG: The dead man and the gods who rule the dead
Know whose act this was. Words are not friends.

ISMENE: Do you refuse me, Antigonê? I want to die with you:
I too have a duty that I must discharge to the dead.

ANTIG: You shall not lessen my death by sharing it.

ISMENE: What do I care for life when you are dead?

ANTIG: Ask Creon. You're always hanging on his opinions.

ISMENE: You are laughing at me. Why, Antigonê?

ANTIG: It's a joyless laughter, Ismenê.

ISMENE: But can I do nothing?

ANTIG: Yes. Save yourself. I shall not envy you.
          There are those who will praise you; I shall have honour, too.

ISMENE: But we are equally guilty!

ANTIG: No, more, Ismenê.
          You are alive, but I belong to Death.

CREON: [*To the* CHORUS:]   Gentlemen, I beg you to observe these girls:
          One has just now lost her mind; the other
          It seems, has never had a mind at all.

ISMENE: Grief teaches the steadiest minds to waver, King.

CREON: Yours certainly did, when you assumed guilt with the guilty!

ISMENE: But how could I go on living without her?

CREON: You are.
          She is already dead.

ISMENE: But your own son's bride!

CREON: There are places enough for him to push his plow.
          I want no wicked women for my sons!

ISMENE: O dearest Haimon, how your father wrongs you!

CREON: I've had enough of your childish talk of marriage!

CHORAG: Do you really intend to steal this girl from your son?

CREON: No; Death will do that for me.

CHORAG: Then she must die?

CREON: You dazzle me.
                    —But enough of this talk!

          [*To* GUARDS:] You, there, take them away and guard them well:
          For they are but women, and even brave men run
          When they see Death coming.
                              [*Exeunt* ISMENE, ANTIGONE, *and* GUARDS.]

Ode II

[STROPHE 1]

CHORUS: Fortunate is the man who has never tasted God's vengeance!
          Where once the anger of heaven has struck, that house is shaken
          For ever: damnation rises behind each child
          Like a wave cresting out of the black northeast,

When the long darkness under sea roars up
And bursts drumming death upon the windwhipped sand.

[ANTISTROPHE 1]

I have seen this gathering sorrow from time long past
Loom upon Oedipus' children: generation from generation
Takes the compulsive rage of the enemy god.
So lately this last flower of Oedipus' line
Drank the sunlight! but now a passionate word
And a handful of dust have closed up all its beauty.

What mortal arrogance   [STROPHE 2]
Transcends the wrath of Zeus?
Sleep cannot lull him, nor the effortless long months
Of the timeless gods: but he is young for ever,
And his house is the shining day of high Olympus.*
All that is and shall be,
And all the past, is his.
No pride on earth is free of the curse of heaven.

The straying dreams of men   [ANTISTROPHE 2]
May bring them ghosts of joy:
But as they drowse, the waking embers burn them;
Or they walk with fíxed éyes, as blind men walk.
But the ancient wisdom speaks for our own time:
*Fate works most for woe
With Folly's fairest show.*
Man's little pleasure is the spring of sorrow.

Scene III

CHORAG: But here is Haimon, King, the last of all your sons.
Is it grief for Antigonê that brings him here,
And bitterness at being robbed of his bride?

[*Enter* HAIMON.]

CREON: We shall soon see, and no need of diviners.
—Son,
You have heard my final judgment on that girl:
Have you come here hating me, or have you come
With deference and with love, whatever I do?

HAIMON: I am your son, father. You are my guide.
You make things clear for me, and I obey you.
No marriage means more to me than your continuing wisdom.

Olympus: the summit of this mountain was regarded in Greek myth as the residence of the gods.

CREON: Good. That is the way to behave: subordinate
Everything else, my son, to your father's will.
That is what a man prays for, that he may get
Sons attentive and dutiful in his house,
Each one hating his father's enemies,
Honouring his father's friends. But if his sons
Fail him, if they turn out unprofitably,
What has he fathered but trouble for himself
And amusement for the malicious?
                              So you are right
Not to lose your head over this woman.
Your pleasure with her would soon grow cold, Haimon,
And then you'd have a hellcat in bed and elsewhere.
Let her find her husband in Hell!
Of all the people in this city, only she
Has had contempt for my law and broken it.

Do you want me to show myself weak before the people?
Or to break my sworn word? No, and I will not.
The woman dies.

I suppose she'll plead 'family ties.' Well, let her.
If I permit my own family to rebel,
How shall I earn the world's obedience?
Show me the man who keeps his house in hand,
He's fit for public authority.
                              I'll have no dealings
With law-breakers, critics of the government:
Whoever is chosen to govern should be obeyed—
Must be obeyed, in all things, great and small,
Just and unjust! O Haimon,
The man who knows how to obey, and that man only,
Knows how to give commands when the time comes.
You can depend on him, no matter how fast
The spears come: he's a good soldier, he'll stick it out.

Anarchy, anarchy! Show me a greater evil!
This is why cities tumble and the great houses rain down,
This is what scatters armies!

No, no: good lives are made so by discipline.
We keep the laws then, and the lawmakers,
And no woman shall seduce us. If we must lose,
Let's lose to a man, at least! Is a woman stronger than we?

CHORAG: Unless time has rusted my wits,
What you say, King, is said with point and dignity.

HAIMON: [Boyishly earnest:] Father:
Reason is God's crowning gift to man, and you are right
To warn me against losing mine. I cannot say—
I hope that I shall never want to say!—that you

Have reasoned badly. Yet there are other men
Who can reason, too; and their opinions might be helpful.
You are not in a position to know everything
That people say or do, or what they feel:
Your temper terrifies them—everyone
Will tell you only what you like to hear.
But I, at any rate, can listen; and I have heard them
Muttering and whispering in the dark about this girl.
They say no woman has ever, so unreasonably,
Died so shameful a death for a generous act:
'She covered her brother's body. Is this indecent?
'She kept him from dogs and vultures. Is this a crime?
'Death?—She should have all the honour that we can give her!'

This is the way they talk out there in the city.

You must believe me:
Nothing is closer to me than your happiness.
What could be closer? Must not any son
Value his father's fortune as his father does his?
I beg you, do not be unchangeable:
Do not believe that you alone can be right.
The man who thinks that,
The man who maintains that only he has the power
To reason correctly, the gift to speak, the soul—
A man like that, when you know him, turns out empty.

It is not reason never to yield to reason!

In flood time you can see how some trees bend,
And because they bend, even their twigs are safe,
While stubborn trees are torn up, roots and all.
And the same thing happens in sailing:
Make your sheet fast, never slacken,—and over you go,
Head over heels and under: and there's your voyage.
Forget you are angry! Let yourself be moved!
I know I am young; but please let me say this:
The ideal condition
Would be, I admit, that men should be right by instinct;
But since we are all too likely to go astray,
The reasonable thing is to learn from those who can teach.

CHORAG: You will do well to listen to him, King,
If what he says is sensible. And you, Haimon,
Must listen to your father.—Both speak well.

CREON: You consider it right for a man of my years and experience
To go to school to a boy?

HAIMON: It is not right
If I am wrong. But if I am young, and right,
What does my age matter?

CREON: You think it right to stand up for an anarchist?

HAIMON: Not at all. I pay no respect to criminals.

CREON: Then she is not a criminal?

HAIMON: The City would deny it, to a man.

CREON: And the City proposes to teach me how to rule?

HAIMON: Ah. Who is it that's talking like a boy now?

CREON: My voice is the one voice giving orders in this City!

HAIMON: It is no City if it takes orders from one voice.

CREON: The State is the King!

HAIMON: Yes, if the State is a desert.

                                     [*Pause.*]

CREON: This boy, it seems, has sold out to a woman.

HAIMON: If you are a woman: my concern is only for you.

CREON: So? Your 'concern'! In a public brawl with your father!

HAIMON: How about you, in a public brawl with justice?

CREON: With justice, when all that I do is within my rights?

HAIMON: You have no right to trample on God's right.

CREON: [*Completely out of control:*] Fool, adolescent fool! Taken in by a woman!

HAIMON: You'll never see me taken in by anything vile.

CREON: Every word you say is for her!

HAIMON: [*Quietly, darkly:*] And for you.
And for me. And for the gods under the earth.

CREON: You'll never marry her while she lives.

HAIMON: Then she must die.—But her death will cause another.

CREON: Another?
Have you lost your senses? Is this an open threat?

HAIMON: There is no threat in speaking to emptiness.

CREON: I swear you'll regret this superior tone of yours!
You are the empty one!

HAIMON: If you were not my father,
I'd say you were perverse.

CREON: You girlstruck fool, don't play at words with me!

HAIMON: I am sorry. You prefer silence.

CREON: Now, by God—!
I swear, by all the gods in heaven above us,
You'll watch it, I swear you shall!

[*To the* SERVANTS.]   Bring her out!
Bring the woman out! Let her die before his eyes,
Here, this instant, with her bridegroom beside her!

HAIMON: Not here, no; she will not die here, King.
And you will never see my face again.
Go on raving as long as you've a friend to endure you.
[*Exit* HAIMON.]

CHORAG: Gone, gone.
Creon, a young man in a rage is dangerous!

CREON: Let him do, or dream to do, more than a man can.
He shall not save these girls from death.

CHORAG: These girls?
You have sentenced them both?

CREON: No, you are right.
I will not kill the one whose hands are clean.

CHORAG: But Antigonê?

CREON: [*Somberly:*] I will carry her far away
Out there in the wilderness, and lock her
Living in a vault of stone. She shall have food,
As the custom is, to absolve the State of her death.
And there let her pray to the gods of Hell:
They are her only gods:
Perhaps they will show her an escape from death,
Or she may learn,
                    though late,
That piety shown the dead is pity in vain.
[*Exit* CREON.]

Ode III

CHORUS: Love, unconquerable   [STROPHE]
Waster of rich men, keeper
Of warm lights and all-night vigil
In the soft face of a girl:
Sea-wanderer, forest-visitor!
Even the pure Immortals cannot escape you,
And mortal man, in his one day's dusk,
Trembles before your glory.

Surely you swerve upon ruin   [ANTISTROPHE]
The just man's consenting heart,
As here you have made bright anger
Strike between father and son—
And none has conquered but Love!

A girl's glánce wórking the will of heaven:
Pleasure to her alone who mocks us,
Merciless Aphroditê.*

Scene IV

[As ANTIGONE *enters guarded.*]

CHORAG: But I can no longer stand in awe of this,
Nor, seeing what I see, keep back my tears.
Here is Antigonê, passing to that chamber
Where all find sleep at last.

ANTIG: Look upon me, friends, and pity me   [STROPHE 1]
Turning back at the night's edge to say
Good-bye to the sun that shines for me no longer;
Now sleepy Death
Summons me down to Acheron,† that cold shore:
There is no bridesong there, nor any music.

CHORUS: Yet not unpraised, not without a kind of honour,
You walk at last into the underworld;
Untouched by sickness, broken by no sword.
What woman has ever found your way to death?

ANTIG: How often I have heard the story of Niobê,‡   [ANTISTROPHE 1]
Tantalos' wretched daughter, how the stone
Clung fast about her, ivy-close: and they say
The rain falls endlessly
And sifting soft snow; her tears are never done.
I feel the loneliness of her death in mine.

CHORUS: But she was born of heaven, and you
Are woman, woman-born. If her death is yours,
A mortal woman's, is this not for you
Glory in our world and in the world beyond?

ANTIG: You laugh at me. Ah, friends, friends,   [STROPHE 2]
Can you not wait until I am dead? O Thebes,
O men many-charioted, in love with Fortune,
Dear springs of Dircê, sacred Theban grove,

---

*Aphroditê: Aphrodite was the Greek goddess of love.
†Acheron: in Greek myth, one of the rivers of the lower world, the other being Styx. The land of the living is separated from Hades by these rivers and the dead were rowed across them by Charon.
‡Niobê: the daughter of Tantalos (who was punished in Hades by the gods by being deprived of food and drink just as he reached for it or by pushing a large stone up a hill only to have it roll back). Niobê had seven children. Because she boasted that their number made her superior to Leto, the mother of Apollo and Artemis, the two gods killed them with arrows. Niobê wept for her children until she turned into a column of stone from which her tears flowed.

Be witnesses for me, denied all pity,
Unjustly judged! and think a word of love
For her whose path turns
Under dark earth, where there are no more tears.

CHORUS: You have passed beyond human daring and come at last
Into a place of stone where Justice sits.
I cannot tell
What shape of your father's guilt appears in this.

ANTIG: You have touched it at last: that bridal bed   [ANTISTROPHE 2]
Unspeakable, horror of son and mother mingling:
Their crime, infection of all our family!
O Oedipus, father and brother!
Your marriage strikes from the grave to murder mine.
I have been a stranger here in my own land:
All my life
The blasphemy of my birth has followed me.

CHORUS: Reverence is a virtue, but strength
Lives in established law: that must prevail.
You have made your choice,
Your death is the doing of your conscious hand.

ANTIG: Then let me go, since all your words are bitter,   [EPODE]
And the very light of the sun is cold to me.
Lead me to my vigil, where I must have
Neither love nor lamentation; no song, but silence.

[CREON interrupts impatiently.]

CREON: If dirges and planned lamentations could put off death,
Men would be singing for ever.

[To the SERVANTS:] Take her, go!
You know your orders: take her to the vault
And leave her alone there. And if she lives or dies,
That's her affair, not ours: our hands are clean.

ANTIG: O tomb, vaulted bride-bed in eternal rock,
Soon I shall be with my own again
Where Persephonê* welcomes the thin ghosts underground:
And I shall see my father again, and you, mother,
And dearest Polyneicês— dearest indeed
To me, since it was my hand
That washed him clean and poured the ritual wine:
And my reward is death before my time!

---

*Persephonê: the daughter of Zeus and Demeter, who was kidnapped by Hades and brought to the underworld to be his queen. Demeter demanded her return, and Zeus agreed, but because she had eaten of the forbidden pomegranate there, she was forced to spend half of each year with Hades.

And yet, as men's hearts know, I have done no wrong,
I have not sinned before God. Or if I have,
I shall know the truth in death. But if the guilt
Lies upon Creon who judged me, then, I pray,
May his punishment equal my own.

CHORAG: O passionate heart,
Unyielding, tormented still by the same winds!

CREON: Her guards shall have good cause to regret their delaying.

ANTIG: Ah! That voice is like the voice of death!

CREON: I can give you no reason to think you are mistaken.

ANTIG: Thebes, and you my fathers' gods,
And rulers of Thebes, you see me now, the last
Unhappy daughter of a line of kings,
Your kings, led away to death. You will remember
What things I suffer, and at what men's hands,
Because I would not transgress the laws of heaven.

[*To the* GUARDS, *simply:*]   Come: let us wait no longer.
[*Exit* ANTIGONE, *L.*, *guarded.*]

Ode IV

CHORUS: All Danaê's beauty* was locked away   [STROPHE 1]
In a brazen cell where the sunlight could not come:
A small room, still as any grave, enclosed her.
Yet she was a princess too,
And Zeus in a rain of gold poured love upon her.
O child, child,
No power in wealth or war
Or tough sea-blackened ships
Can prevail against untiring Destiny!

And Dryas' son† also, that furious king,   [ANTISTROPHE 1]
Bore the god's prisoning anger for his pride:
Sealed up by Dionysos in deaf stone,
His madness died among echoes.
So at the last he learned what dreadful power

---

*Danaê's beauty: Danaê was the daughter of Acrisius, the king of Artos, who locked her in a tower because of the prophecy that he would be killed by her son. Zeus, however, visited her in a shower of gold. She bore Zeus a son, Perseus, who unintentionally killed his grandfather.

†Dryas' son: Lycurgus, the king of Thrace, opposed the worship of Dionysus, who imprisoned him and drove him mad.

His tongue had mocked:
For he had profaned the revels,
And fired the wrath of the nine
Implacable Sisters that love the sound of the flute.

And old men tell a half-remembered tale*   [STROPHE 2]
Of horror done where a dark ledge splits the sea
And a double surf beats on the grey shores:
How a king's new woman, sick
With hatred for the queen he had imprisoned,
Ripped out his two sons' eyes with her bloody hands
While grinning Arês watched the shuttle plunge
Four times: four blind wounds crying for revenge,

                                                            [ANTISTROPHE 2]
Crying, tears and blood mingled.— Piteously born,
Those sons whose mother was of heavenly birth!
Her father was the god of the North Wind
And she was cradled by gales,
She raced with young colts on the glittering hills
And walked untrammeled in the open light:
But in her marriage deathless Fate found means
To build a tomb like yours for all her joy.

Scene V

[Enter blind TEIRESIAS, *led by a boy. The opening speeches of* TEIRESIAS
should be in singsong contrast to the realistic lines of CREON.*]*

TEIRES: This is the way the blind man comes, Princes, Princes,
         Lock-step, two heads lit by the eyes of one.

CREON: What new thing have you to tell us, old Teiresias?

TEIRES: I have much to tell you: listen to the prophet, Creon.

CREON: I am not aware that I have ever failed to listen.

TEIRES: Then you have done wisely, King, and ruled well.

CREON: I admit my debt to you. But what have you to say?

TEIRES: This, Creon: you stand once more on the edge of fate.

CREON: What do you mean? Your words are a kind of dread.

TEIRES: Listen, Creon:
         I was sitting in my chair of augury, at the place
         Where the birds gather about me. They were all a-chatter,

---

*And old men tell a half-remembered tale . . . for all her joy: Strophe 2 refers to the story of
Phineus, king of Salmydessus, who had two children by his first wife, Cleopatra. His second
wife, Eidothea, put out the eyes of these two children. Antistrophe 2 refers to the sorrow of
Cleopatra, the daughter of the god Boreus, the North Wind. The tales of calamity and death in
Ode IV provide analogies of suffering for the fate of Antigone.

As is their habit, when suddenly I heard
A strange note in their jangling, a scream, a
Whirring fury; I knew that they were fighting,
Tearing each other, dying
In a whirlwind of wings clashing. And I was afraid.
I began the rites of burnt-offering at the altar,
But Hephaistos failed me: instead of bright flame,
There was only the sputtering slime of the fat thigh-flesh
Melting: the entrails dissolved in grey smoke,
The bare bone burst from the welter. And no blaze!

This was a sign from heaven. My boy described it,
Seeing for me as I see for others.

I tell you, Creon, you yourself have brought
This new calamity upon us. Our hearths and altars
Are stained with the corruption of dogs and carrion birds
That glut themselves on the corpse of Oedipus' son.
The gods are deaf when we pray to them, their fire
Recoils from our offering, their birds of omen
Have no cry of comfort, for they are gorged!
With the thick blood of the dead.
                              O my son,
These are no trifles! Think: all men make mistakes,
But a good man yields when he knows his course is wrong.
And repairs the evil. The only crime is pride.

Give in to the dead man, then: do not fight with a corpse—
What glory is it to kill a man who is dead?
Think, I beg you:
It is for your own good that I speak as I do.
You should be able to yield for your own good.

CREON: It seems that prophets have made me their especial province.
All my life long.
I have been a kind of butt for the dull arrows
Of doddering fortune-tellers!
                          No, Teiresias:
If your birds—if the great eagles of God himself
Should carry him stinking bit by bit to heaven,
I would not yield. I am not afraid of pollution:
No man can defile the gods.
                          Do what you will,
Go into business, make money, speculate
In India gold or that synthetic gold from Sardis,
Get rich otherwise than by my consent to bury him.
Teiresias, it is a sorry thing when a wise man
Sells his wisdom, lets out his words for hire!

TEIRES: Ah Creon! Is there no man left in the world—

CREON: To do what?—Come, let's have the aphorism!

TEIRES: No man who knows that wisdom outweighs any wealth?

CREON: As surely as bribes are baser than any baseness.

TEIRES: You are sick, Creon! You are deathly sick!

CREON: As you say: it is not my place to challenge a prophet.

TEIRES: Yet you have said my prophecy is for sale.

CREON: The generation of prophets has always loved gold.

TEIRES: The generation of kings has always loved brass.

CREON: You forget yourself! You are speaking to your King.

TEIRES: I know it. You are a king because of me.

CREON: You have a certain skill; but you have sold out.

TEIRES: King, you will drive me to words that—

CREON: Say them, say them!
          Only remember: I will not pay you for them.

TEIRES: No, you will find them too costly.

CREON: No doubt. Speak:
          Whatever you say, you will not change my will.

TEIRES: Then take this, and take it to heart!
          The time is not far off when you shall pay back
          Corpse for corpse, flesh of your own flesh.
          You have thrust the child of this world into living night,
          You have kept from the gods below the child that is theirs:
          The one in a grave before her death, the other,
          Dead, denied the grave. This is your crime:
          And the Furies and the dark gods of Hell
          Are swift with terrible punishment for you.

          Do you want to buy me now, Creon?

                                       Not many days,
          And your house will be full of men and women weeping,
          And curses will be hurled at you from far
          Cities grieving* for sons unburied, left to rot before the walls of
              Thebes.

          These are my arrows, Creon: they are all for you.

          [*To* BOY:]   But come, child: lead me home.
          Let him waste his fine anger upon younger men.
          Maybe he will learn at last
          To control a wiser tongue in a better head.   [*Exit* TEIRESIAS.]

CHORAG: The old man has gone, King, but his words
          Remain to plague us. I am old, too,
          But I can not remember that he was ever false.

CREON: That is true. . . . It troubles me.

Cities grieving: Creon had decreed that the corpses of Polyneices' allies also be left unburied.

Oh it is hard to give in! but it is worse
To risk everything for stubborn pride.

CHORAG: Creon: take my advice.

CREON: What shall I do?

CHORAG: Go quickly: free Antigonê from her vault
And build a tomb for the body of Polyneicês.

CREON: You would have me do this?

CHORAG: Creon, yes!
And it must be done at once: God moves
Swiftly to cancel the folly of stubborn men.

CREON: It is hard to deny the heart! But I
Will do it: I will not fight with destiny.

CHORAG: You must go yourself, you cannot leave it to others.

CREON: I will go.
          — Bring axes, servants:
Come with me to the tomb. I buried her, I
Will set her free.
               Oh quickly!
My mind misgives—
The laws of the gods are mighty, and a man must serve them
To the last day of his life!   [*Exit* CREON.]

Pæan

CHORAG: God of many names   [STROPHE 1]

CHORUS: O Iacchos*
                              son
of Cadmeian Sémelê
                    O born of the Thunder!
Guardian of the West
                    Regent
of Eleusis' plain
               O Prince of mænad Thebes
and the Dragon Field by rippling Ismenos:

CHORAG: God of many names   [ANTISTROPHE 1]
                    the flame of torches

Iacchos: Strophe 1, one of three deities (the others, Demeter and Persephone) at the Mysteries at Eleusis on the coast near Athens. These were rites revealed only to initiates and which celebrated life after death. The god Dionysus, son of Zeus and Sémelê, was also celebrated at these rites under the name of Iacchos. Dionysus was accompanied by possessed or intoxicated male and female Maenads, Satyrs, and Silenae. Cadmus, the father of Sémelê, was directed by the gods to the spot where he founded the citadel of the future city of Thebes. He was helped in this by the five surviving warriors, who sprang up from the dragon's teeth he had sown under Athenê's instructions. These five warriors were the ancestors of the noble families of Thebes.

CHORUS: flares on our hills
       the nymphs of Iacchos
  dance at the spring of Castalia:*

  from the vine-close mountain
          come ah come in ivy:
  Evohé evohé! sings through the streets of Thebes

CHORAG: God of many names   [STROPHE 2]

CHORUS: Iacchos of Thebes
  heavenly Child
       of Sémelê bride of the Thunderer!
  The shadow of plague is upon us:
          come
  with clement feet
       oh come from Parnasos†
  down the long slopes
  across the lamenting water

CHORAG: Iô Fire! Chorister of the throbbing stars!   [ANTISTROPHE 2]
  O purest among the voices of the night!
  Thou son of God, blaze for us!

CHORUS: Come with choric rapture of circling Mænads
  Who cry *Iô Iacche!*
      God of many names!

Exodos

[*Enter* MESSENGER.]

MESS: Men of the line of Cadmos, you who live
  Near Amphion's citadel:
        I cannot say
  Of any condition of human life 'This is fixed,
  This is clearly good, or bad.' Fate raises up,
  And Fate casts down the happy and unhappy alike:
  No man can foretell his Fate.
         Take the case of Creon:
  Creon was happy once, as I count happiness:
  Victorious in battle, sole governor of the land,
  Fortunate father of children nobly born.
  And now it has all gone from him! Who can say
  That a man is still alive when his life's joy fails?
  He is a walking dead man. Grant him rich,
  Let him live like a king in his great house:

---

spring of Castalia: the spring at Delphi, sacred to Apollo and the nine Muses.
†*Parnasos:* the mountain above Delphi, sacred to Apollo and Dionysus.

If his pleasure is gone, I would not give
So much as the shadow of smoke for all he owns.

CHORAG: Your words hint at sorrow: what is your news for us?

MESS: They are dead. The living are guilty of their death.

CHORAG: Who is guilty? Who is dead? Speak!

MESS: Haimon.
Haimon is dead; and the hand that killed him
Is his own hand.

CHORAG: His father's? or his own?

MESS: His own, driven mad by the murder his father had done.

CHORAG: Teiresias, Teiresias, how clearly you saw it all!

MESS: This is my news: you must draw what conclusions you can from it.

CHORAG: But look: Eurydicê, our Queen:
Has she overheard us?

                    [Enter EURYDICE from the Palace, C.]

EURYD: I have heard something, friends:
As I was unlocking the gate of Pallas' shrine,
For I needed her help today, I heard a voice
Telling of some new sorrow. And I fainted
There at the temple with all my maidens about me.
But speak again: whatever it is, I can bear it:
Grief and I are no strangers.

MESS: Dearest Lady,
I will tell you plainly all that I have seen.
I shall not try to comfort you: what is the use,
Since comfort could lie only in what is not true?
The truth is always best.

                    I went with Creon
To the outer plain where Polyneicês was lying,
No friend to pity him, his body shredded by dogs.
We made our prayers in that place to Hecatê*
And Pluto*, that they would be merciful. And we bathed
The corpse with holy water, and we brought
Fresh-broken branches to burn what was left of it,
And upon the urn we heaped up a towering barrow
Of the earth of his own land.

                    When we were done, we ran
To the vault where Antigonê lay on her couch of stone.
One of the servants had gone ahead,
And while he was yet far off he heard a voice

*Hecate and Pluto: gods of the underworld.

Grieving within the chamber, and he came back
And told Creon. And as the King went closer,
The air was full of wailing, the words lost,
And he begged us to make all haste.'Am I a prophet?'
He said, weeping, 'And must I walk this road,
'The saddest of all that I have gone before?
'My son's voice calls me on. Oh quickly, quickly!
'Look through the crevice there, and tell me
'If it is Haimon, or some deception of the gods!'

We obeyed; and in the cavern's farthest corner
We saw her lying:
She had made a noose of her fine linen veil
And hanged herself. Haimon lay beside her,
His arms about her waist, lamenting her,
His love lost under ground, crying out
That his father had stolen her away from him.

When Creon saw him the tears rushed to his eyes
And he called to him: 'What have you done, child? Speak to me.
'What are you thinking that makes your eyes so strange?
'O my son, my son, I come to you on my knees!'
But Haimon spat in his face. He said not a word,
Staring—
          And suddenly drew his sword
And lunged. Creon shrank back, the blade missed; and the boy,
Desperate against himself, drove it half its length
Into his own side, and fell. And as he died
He gathered Antigonê close in his arms again,
Choking, his blood bright red on her white cheek.
And now he lies dead with the dead, and she is his
At last, his bride in the houses of the dead.

[Exit EURYDICE into the Palace.]

CHORAG: She has left us without a word. What can this mean?

MESS: It troubles me, too; yet she knows what is best,
         Her grief is too great for public lamentation,
         And doubtless she has gone to her chamber to weep
         For her dead son, leading her maidens in his dirge.

CHORAG: It may be so: but I fear this deep silence.

[Pause.]

MESS: I will see what she is doing. I will go in.

[Exit MESSENGER into the Palace.]

[Enter CREON with attendants, bearing HAIMON's body.]

CHORAG: But here is the King himself: oh look at him,
         Bearing his own damnation in his arms.

CREON: Nothing you say can touch me any more.
         My own blind heart has brought me

From darkness to final darkness. Here you see
The father murdering, the murdered son—
And all my civic wisdom!
Haimon my son, so young, so young to die,
I was the fool, not you; and you died for me.

CHORAG: That is the truth; but you were late in learning it.

CREON: This truth is hard to bear. Surely a god
Has crushed me beneath the hugest weight of heaven,
And driven me headlong a barbaric way
To trample out the thing I held most dear.

The pains that men will take to come to pain!

[*Enter* MESSENGER *from the Palace.*]

MESS: The burden you carry in your hands is heavy,
But it is not all: you will find more in your house.

CREON: What burden worse than this shall I find there?

MESS: The Queen is dead.

CREON: O port of death, deaf world,
Is there no pity for me? And you, Angel of evil,
I was dead, and your words are death again.
Is it true, boy? Can it be true?
Is my wife dead? Has death bred death?

MESS: You can see for yourself.

[*The doors are opened, and the body of* EURYDICE *is disclosed within.*]

CREON: Oh pity!
All true, all true, and more than I can bear!
O my wife, my son!

MESS: She stood before the altar, and her heart
Welcomed the knife her own hand guided,
And a great cry burst from her lips for Megareus dead,
And for Haimon dead, her sons; and her last breath
Was a curse for their father, the murderer of her sons.
And she fell, and the dark flowed in through her closing eyes.

CREON: O God, I am sick with fear.
Are there no swords here? Has no one a blow for me?

MESS: Her curse is upon you for the deaths of both.

CREON: It is right that it should be. I alone am guilty.
I know it, and I say it. Lead me in,
Quickly, friends.
I have neither life nor substance. Lead me in.

CHORAG: You are right, if there can be right in so much wrong.
The briefest way is best in a world of sorrow.

CREON: Let it come,
Let death come quickly, and be kind to me.
I would not ever see the sun again.

CHORAG: All that will come when it will; but we, meanwhile,
Have much to do. Leave the future to itself.

CREON: All my heart was in that prayer!

CHORAG: Then do not pray any more: the sky is deaf.

CREON: Lead me away. I have been rash and foolish.
I have killed my son and my wife.
I look for comfort; my comfort lies here dead.
Whatever my hands have touched has come to nothing.
Fate has brought all my pride to a thought of dust.

[As CREON is being led into the house, the CHORAGOS advances and speaks directly to the audience.]

CHORAG: There is no happiness where there is no wisdom;
No wisdom but in submission to the gods.
Big words are always punished,
And proud men in old age learn to be wise.

Suggestions for Discussion

1. In the Prologue, Ismene states the argument for obeying authority. What is that argument? On what facts and feelings is it based?

2. What are Antigone's reasons for rejecting Creon's decree forbidding the burial of Polyneices? How do the characters of Ismene and Antigone correspond to the arguments they make for their differing actions?

3. What is the function of the Parados? How does it relate to the preceding Prologue? In what way are the speeches of the Choragos different from those of the Chorus?

4. In Scene I, Creon states the rationale for his decree. To what extent do you agree with his argument? What reason does the Choragos give for obeying Creon?

5. Once Creon has learned that someone has performed burial rites for Polyneices, he suggests reasons. What are these reasons? Why does he reject at once the suggestion that the gods have intervened? How does Sophocles treat the sentry in Scenes I and II?

6. What is the function of the Odes in the play?

7. In Scene II, we have the first confrontation between Creon and Antigone. Who makes the better argument and how?

8. What does Creon's treatment of Ismene in Scene II tell us about his character? Why is the nature of Creon's character an important aspect of the play?

9. Scene III shows Creon with his son. How does this scene add to Creon's anger at being disobeyed? What do we learn about the king's attitude toward women? Toward the difference between youth and age?

10. Discuss the difference between the speeches of the Choragos in the first and fourth scenes.

11. How does Antigone face death? Do we remain totally sympathetic toward her suffering?

12. Discuss the confrontation between Creon and Teiresias in Scene V. How are Teiresias' prophecies borne out?

13. What are the functions of the last two parts of the play, the Paean and the Exodos? How does the final speech of the Choragos at the end of the play summarize the tragedy that has occurred?

Suggestions for Writing

1. People have disagreed about who is the more important character, Creon or Antigone. Write a 500-word paper in which you state and explain your opinion on this issue.

2. Write a 500–750-word paper in which you discuss the laws of the state as opposed to either some higher authority or to individual conscience. Are you familiar with modern analogies of the conflict between two authorities? How would you behave in a situation in which you would have to choose as Antigone does? How would most people behave?

3. Write a 500-word paper in which you define tragic irony and elaborate on the definition by giving examples from *Antigone*.

The Examined Life: Education

I knew right there in prison that reading had changed forever the course of my life.

—**Malcolm X,** "A Homemade Education"

We survived. The depths had been icy and dark, but now a bright sun spoke to our souls. I was no longer simply a member of the proud graduating class of 1940; I was a proud member of the wonderful, beautiful Negro race.

—**Maya Angelou,** "Graduation"

Part of teaching is helping students learn how to tolerate ambiguity, consider possibilities, and ask questions that are unanswerable.

—**Bill Moyers,** "Interview with Sara Lawrence Lightfoot"

But more than therapy, that freewheeling, wide-ranging, exuberant talk functioned as an outlet for the tremendous creative energy they possessed.

—**Paule Marshall,** "From the Poets in the Kitchen"

The education of humanists cannot be regarded as complete, or even adequate, without exposure in some depth to where things stand in the various branches of science, and particularly, as I have said, in the areas of our ignorance.

—**Lewis Thomas,** "Humanities and Science"

Education doesn't end until life ends, because you never know when you're going to understand something you hadn't understood before.

—**Frank Conroy,** "Think About It"

More than any other time in history, mankind faces a cross-roads. One path leads to despair and utter hopelessness. The other, to total extinction. Let us pray we have the wisdom to choose correctly.

    —**Woody Allen,** "My Speech to the Graduates"

The challenge for the educational community is to figure out profiles of young people and then to help them find roles in which they can use their abilities in a productive way.

    —**Howard Gardner,** "Human Intelligence Isn't What We Think It Is"

If I intend for my life to matter to me, I had better read seriously, starting with newspapers and working up to philosophy and novels.

    —**Harold Brodkey,** "Reading, the Most Dangerous Game"

No doubt the best things that happen in universities *are* the things that happen in "the classroom."

    —**Gerald Graff,** "Off Course"

I was happy. I fell asleep at once. I had prayed for everybody: my talking family, cousins far away, passersby, and all the lonesome Christians. I expected to be heard. My voice was certainly the loudest.

    —**Grace Paley,** "The Loudest Voice"

Personal Reminiscences

Lincoln Steffens

I Go to College

Joseph Lincoln Steffens (1866–1936) was born in San Francisco and graduated from the University of California at Berkeley. After his return from three years of study in Europe, he became a well-known muckraker and journalist. As editor of *McClure's, American,* and *Everybody's* magazines, he exposed corruption in business and government. His collections of essays include *The Shame of the Cities* (1904) and *The Struggle for Self-Government* (1906). His *Autobiography* (1931) is a very personal account of the history not only of journalism in the United States but of the leftist movement as well. This selection from it recalls his carefree days as an undergraduate and the beginnings of his serious interest in learning, while it questions the connection between the search for knowledge and the baccalaureate degree.

Going to college is, to a boy, an adventure into a new world, and a very strange and complete world too. Part of his preparation for it is the stories he hears from those that have gone before; these feed his imagination, which cannot help trying to picture the college life. And the stories and the life are pretty much the same for any college. The University of California was a young, comparatively small institution when I was entered there in 1885 as a freshman. Berkeley, the beautiful, was not the developed villa community it is now; I used to shoot quail in the brush under the oaks along the edges of the college grounds. The quail and the brush are gone now, but the oaks are there and the same prospect down the hill over San Francisco Bay out through the Golden Gate between the low hills of the city and the high hills of Marin County. My class numbered about one hundred boys and girls, mostly boys, who came from all parts of the State and represented all sorts of people and occupations. There was, however, a significant uniformity of opinion and spirit among us, as there was, and still is, in other, older colleges. The American is molded to type early. And so are our college ways. We found already formed at Berkeley the typical undergraduate customs, rights, and privileged vices which we had to respect ourselves and defend against the faculty, regents, and the State government.

One evening, before I had matriculated, I was taken out by some upper classmen to teach the president a lesson. He had been the head of a private preparatory school and was trying to govern the private lives and the public morals of university "men" as he had those of his schoolboys. Fetching a long ladder, the upper classmen thrust it through a front window of Prexy's house and, to the chant of obscene songs, swung it back and forth, up and down, round and round, till everything breakable within sounded broken and the drunken indignation outside was satisfied or tired.

This turned out to be one of the last battles in the war for liberty against that president. He was allowed to resign soon thereafter and I noticed that

937

not only the students but many of the faculty and regents rejoiced in his downfall and turned with us to face and fight the new president when, after a lot of politics, he was appointed and presented. We learned somehow a good deal about the considerations that governed our college government. They were not only academic. The government of a university was—like the State government and horse-racing and so many other things—not what I had been led to expect. And a college education wasn't, either, nor the student mind.

Years later, when I was a magazine editor, I proposed a series of articles to raise and answer the question: Is there any intellectual life in our colleges? My idea sprang from my remembered disappointment at what I found at Berkeley and some experiences I was having at the time with the faculties and undergraduates of the other colleges in the east. Berkeley, in my day, was an Athens compared with New Haven, for example, when I came to know Yale undergraduates.

My expectations of college life were raised too high by Nixon's Saturday nights. I thought, and he assumed, that at Berkeley I would be breathing in an atmosphere of thought, discussion, and some scholarship; working, reading, and studying for the answers to questions which would be threshed out in debate and conversation. There was nothing of the sort. I was primed with questions. My English friends never could agree on the answers to any of the many and various questions they disputed. They did not care; they enjoyed their talks and did not expect to settle anything. I was more earnest. I was not content to leave things all up in the air. Some of those questions were very present and personal to me, as some of those Englishmen meant them to be. William Owen was trying to convert me to the anarchistic communism in which he believed with all his sincere and beautiful being. I was considering his arguments. Another earnest man, who presented the case for the Roman Catholic Church, sent old Father Burchard and other Jesuits after me. Every conversation at Mr. Nixon's pointed some question, academic or scientific, and pointed them so sharp that they drove me to college with an intense desire to know. And as for communism or the Catholic Church, I was so torn that I could not answer myself. The Jesuits dropped me and so did Owen, in disgust, when I said I was going to wait for my answer till I had heard what the professors had to say and had learned what my university had to teach me upon the questions underlying the questions Oxford and Cambridge and Rome quarreled over and could not agree on. Berkeley would know.

There were no moot questions in Berkeley. There was work to do, knowledge and training to get, but not to answer questions. I found myself engaged, as my classmates were, in choosing courses. The choice was limited and, within the limits, had to be determined by the degree we were candidates for. My questions were philosophical, but I could not take philosophy, which fascinated me, till I had gone through a lot of higher mathematics which did not interest me at all. If I had been allowed to take philosophy, and so discovered the need and the relation of mathematics, I would have got the philosophy and I might have got the mathematics which I miss now more than I do the Hegelian metaphysics taught at Berkeley. Or, if the professor who put me off had taken the pains to show me the bearing of mathematical thought on theoretical logic, I would have undertaken the preparation intelligently. But no one ever developed for me the relation of any of my required subjects to those that attracted me; no one brought out for me the relation of anything I was studying to anything else, except, of course, to that wretched degree. Knowledge was absolute, not relative, and it was stored in compartments, categorical and independent. The relation of knowledge to life, even to student life, was ignored, and as for questions, the professors asked them, not the students; and the students, not the teachers, answered them—in examinations.

The unknown is the province of the student; it is the field for his life's adventure, and it is a wide field full of beckonings. Curiosity about it would drive a boy as well as a child to work through the known to get at the unknown. But it was not assumed that we had any curiosity or the potential love of skill, scholarship, and achievement or research. And so far as I can remember now, the professors' attitude was right for most of the students who had no intellectual curiosity. They wanted to be told not only what they had to learn, but what they had to want to learn—for the purpose of passing. That came out in the considerations which decided the choice among optional courses. Students selected subjects or teachers for a balance of easy and hard, to fit into their time and yet "get through." I was the only rebel of my kind, I think. The nearest to me in sympathy were the fellows who knew what they wanted to be: engineers, chemists, professional men, or statesmen. They grunted at some of the work required of them, studies that seemed useless to their future careers. They did not understand me very well, nor I them, because I preferred those very subjects which they called useless, highbrow, cultural. I did not tell them so; I did not realize it myself definitely; but I think now that I had had as a boy an exhausting experience of *being* something great. I did not want now to be but rather to know things.

And what I wanted to know was buried deep under all this "college stuff" which was called "shop." It had nothing to do with what really interested us in common. Having chosen our work and begun to do it as a duty, we turned to the socially important question: which fraternity to join. The upper classmen tried to force our answers. They laid aside their superiority to "rush" those of us whose antecedents were known and creditable. It was all snobbish, secret, and exclusive. I joined a fraternity out of curiosity: What were the secrets and the mystic rites? I went blindfold through the silly initiation to find that there were no secrets and no mysteries, only pretensions and bunk, which so disgusted me that I would not live at the clubhouse, preferring for a year the open doors of a boarding-house. The next great university question was as to athletics. My ex-athletes from Oxford and Cambridge, with their lung and other troubles, warned me; but it was a mistake that saved me. I went with the other freshmen to the campus to be tried out for football, baseball, running, jumping, etc. Caught by the college and class spirit, I hoped to give promise of some excellence. Baseball was impossible for me; I had been riding horses when the other boys were preparing for college on the diamond. I had learned to run at the military academy and in the first freshman tests I did one hundred yards enough under eleven seconds to be turned over to an athletic upper classman for instruction. Pointing up to Grizzly Peak, a high hill back of the college, he said: "All you need is wind and muscle. Climb that mountain every day for a year; then come back and we'll see."

I did not climb Grizzly Peak every day, but I went up so often that I was soon able to run up and back without a halt. At the end of the year I ran around the cinder track so long that my student instructor wearied of watching me, but, of course, I could not do a hundred yards much under twelve seconds. Muscle and wind I had, but all my physical reactions were so slow that I was of no social use in college athletics. I was out of the crowd as I had been as a boy.

I shone only in the military department. The commandant, a U.S. Army officer, seeing that I had had previous training, told me off to drill the awkward squad of my class, and when I had made of them the best-drilled company in college, he gave me the next freshman class to drill. In the following years I was always drillmaster of the freshmen and finally commanded the whole cadet corps. Thus I led my class in the most unpopular and meaningless of undergraduate activities. I despised it myself, prizing it only for the chances it gave me to swank and, once a week, to lord it over my fellow students, who nicknamed me the "D. S."—damn stinker.

My nickname was won not only as a disciplinarian, however; I rarely punished any one; I never abused my command. I could persuade the freshmen to drill by arguing that, since it was compulsory, they could have more fun doing it well than badly; and that it was the one exercise in which they could beat and shame the upper classmen whose carelessness was as affected as their superiority. That is to say, I engaged their enthusiasm. All other student enthusiasms, athletics, class and college politics, fashions, and traditions I laughed at and damned. I was a spoilsport. I was mean, as a horse is mean, because I was unhappy myself. I could be enthusiastic in a conversation about something we were learning, if it wasn't too cut and dried; we had such talks now and then at the clubhouse in my later years. But generally speaking we were discussing the news or some prank of our own.

One night, for example, we sallied forth to steal some chickens from Dr. Bonte, the popular treasurer of the university. I crawled into the coop and selected the chickens, wrung their necks, and passed them out with comments to the other fellows who held the bag.

"Here," I said, "is the rooster, Dr. Bonte himself; he's tough, but good enough for the freshmen. Next is a nice fat hen, old Mrs. Bonte. This one's a pullet, Miss Bonte," and so on, naming each of the Bonte girls, till we were interrupted.

There was a sound from the house, the lights flashed in the windows, and—some one was coming. The other fellows ran, and I—when I tore myself out—I ran too. Which was all right enough. But when I caught up with the other thieves I learned that they had left the sack of chickens behind! Our Sunday dinner was spoiled, we thought, but no: the next day the whole fraternity was invited to dinner at Dr. Bonte's on Sunday. We accepted with some suspicion, we went in some embarrassment, but we were well received and soon put at our ease by Dr. Bonte, who explained that some thieves had been frightened while robbing his roost. "They were not students, I take it," he said. "Students are not so easily frightened; they might have run away, but students would have taken the bag of chickens with them. I think they were niggers or Chinamen."

So seated hospitably at table we watched with deep interest the great platter of roasted chickens borne in and set down before Dr. Bonte, who rose, whetted his carving-knife, and turning first to me, said: "Well, Steffens, what will you have, a piece of this old cock, Dr. Bonte? Or is he too tough for any but a freshman? Perhaps you would prefer the old hen, Mrs. Bonte, or, say, one of the Bonte girls."

I couldn't speak. No one could; and no one laughed, least of all Dr. Bonte, who stood there, his knife and fork in the air, looking at me, at the others, and back at me. He wanted an answer; I must make my choice, but I saw a gleam of malicious humor in his eye; so I recovered and I chose the prettiest of the girls, pointing to the tenderest of the pullets. Dr. Bonte laughed, gave me my choice, and we had a jolly, ample dinner.

We talked about that, we and the students generally and the faculty—we discussed that incident long enough and hard enough to have solved it, if it had been a metaphysical problem. We might have threshed out the psychology of thieves, or gamblers, but no. We liked to steal, but we didn't care to think about it, not as stealing. And some of us gambled. We had to get money for theaters, operas, and other expenses in the city. I had only my board, lodging, and clothes paid for by my father, and others had not even that. We played cards, therefore, among ourselves, poker and whist, so that a lucky few got each month about all the money all of the other hard-ups had, and so had all the fun. We played long, late, and hard, and for money, not sport. The strain was too great.

One night my roommate, sunk low in his chair, felt a light kick on one of his extended legs; a second later there were two kicks against his other leg. Keeping still and watching the hands shown down, he soon had the signal system of two men playing partners, the better hand staying in the game. We said nothing but, watching, saw that others cheated, too. We knew well an old professional gambler from the mining-camps who was then in San Francisco. We told him all about it.

"Sure," he said, "cheating will sneak into any game that's played long enough. That's why you boys oughtn't to gamble. But if you do, play the game that's played. Cards is like horse-racing. I never bet a cent except I know, and know how, the game is crooked."

Having advised against it, he took us around to the gambling-houses and the race course and showed us many of the tricks of his trade, how to spot and profit by them—if we must play. "Now you won't need never to be suckers," he said. "And ye needn't be crooks either," he added after a pause. But we had it in for our opponents. We learned several ways to cheat; we practiced them till we were cool and sure. After that our "luck" was phenomenal. We had money, more than we needed. In my last two years at the university I had a salary as military instructor at a preparatory school in the town, and my roommate, the adopted son of a rich goldminer, had a generous allowance. But we went on playing and cheating at cards for the excitement of it, we said, but really it was for the money. And afterward, when I was a student in Germany, I played on, fair but hard—and for money I did not need, till one night at the Café Bauer in Berlin, sitting in a poker game that had been running all night, an American who had long been playing in hard luck, lost a large amount, of which I carried away more than my share. The next day we read in the papers that when he got home he had shot himself. I have never gambled since—at cards.

I Become a Student

It is possible to get an education at a university. It has been done; not often, but the fact that a proportion, however small, of college students do get a start in interested, methodical study, proves my thesis, and the two personal experiences I have to offer illustrate it and show how to circumvent the faculty, the other students, and the whole college system of mind-fixing. My method might lose a boy his degree, but a degree is not worth so much as the capacity and the drive to learn, and the undergraduate desire for an empty baccalaureate is one of the holds the educational system has on students. Wise students some day will refuse to take degrees, as the best men (in England, for instance) give, but do not themselves accept, titles.

My method was hit on by accident and some instinct. I specialized. With several courses prescribed, I concentrated on the one or two that interested me most, and letting the others go, I worked intensively on my favorites. In my first two years, for example, I worked at English and political economy and read philosophy. At the beginning of my junior year I had several cinches in history. Now I liked history; I had neglected it partly because I rebelled at the way it was taught, as positive knowledge unrelated to politics, art, life, or anything else. The professors gave us chapters out of a few books to read, con, and be quizzed on. Blessed as I was with a "bad memory," I could not commit to it anything that I did not understand and intellectually need. The bare record of the story of man, with names, dates, and irrelative events, bored me. But I had discovered in my readings of literature, philosophy, and political economy that history had light to throw upon unhistorical questions. So I proposed in my junior and senior years to specialize in history, taking all the courses required and those also that I had flunked in. With this in mind I listened attentively to the first introductory talk of Professor William Cary Jones on American constitutional history. He was a dull lecturer, but I noticed that, after telling us what pages of what books we must be prepared in, he mumbled off some other references "for those that may care to dig deeper."

When the rest of the class rushed out into the sunshine, I went up to the professor and, to his surprise, asked for this memorandum. He gave it to me. Up in the library I ran through the required chapters in the two different books, and they differed on several points. Turning to the other authorities, I saw that they disagreed on the same facts and also on others. The librarian, appealed to, helped me search the book-shelves till the library closed, and then I called on Professor Jones for more references. He was astonished, invited me in, and began to approve my industry, which astonished me. I was not trying to be a good boy; I was better than that: I was a curious boy. He lent me a couple of his books, and I went off to my club to read them. They only deepened the mystery, clearing up the historical question, but leaving the answer to be dug for and written.

The historians did not know! History was not a science, but a field for research, a field for me, for any young man, to explore, to make discoveries in and write a scientific report about. I was fascinated. As I went on from chapter to chapter, day after day, finding frequently essential differences of opinion and of fact, I saw more and more work to do. In this course, Ameri-

can constitutional history, I hunted far enough to suspect that the Fathers of
the Republic who wrote our sacred Constitution of the United States not only
did not, but did not want to, establish a democratic government, and I
dreamed for a while—as I used as a child to play I was Napoleon or a trap-
per—I promised myself to write a true history of the making of the American
Constitution. I did not do it; that chapter has been done or well begun since
by two men: Smith of the University of Washington and Beard (then) of Columbia (afterward forced out, perhaps for this very work). I found other
events, men, and epochs waiting for students. In all my other courses, in
ancient, in European, and in modern history, the disagreeing authorities carried me back to the need of a fresh search for (or of) the original documents
or other clinching testimony. Of course I did well in my classes. The history
professors soon knew me as a student and seldom put a question to me except when the class had flunked it. Then Professor Jones would say, "Well,
Steffens, tell them about it."

Fine. But vanity wasn't my ruling passion then. What I had was a quickening sense that I was learning a method of studying history and that every
chapter of it, from the beginning of the world to the end, is crying out to be
rewritten. There was something for Youth to do; these superior old men had
not done anything, finally.

Years afterward I came out of the graft prosecution office in San Francisco
with Rudolph Spreckels, the banker and backer of the investigation. We were
to go somewhere, quick, in his car, and we couldn't. The chauffeur was trying to repair something wrong. Mr. Spreckels smiled; he looked closely at the
defective part, and to my silent, wondering inquiry he answered: "Always,
when I see something badly done or not done at all, I see an opportunity to
make a fortune. I never kick at bad work by my class: there's lots of it and we
suffer from it. But our failures and neglects are chances for the young fellows
coming along and looking for work."

Nothing is done. Everything in the world remains to be done or done
over. "The greatest picture is not yet painted, the greatest play isn't written
(not even by Shakespeare), the greatest poem is unsung. There isn't in all the
world a perfect railroad, nor a good government, nor a sound law." Physics,
mathematics, and especially the most advanced and exact of the sciences, are
being fundamentally revised. Chemistry is just becoming a science; psychology, economics, and sociology are awaiting a Darwin, whose work in turn is
awaiting an Einstein. If the rah-rah boys in our colleges could be told this,
they might not all be such specialists in football, petting parties, and unearned degrees. They are not told it, however; they are told to learn what is
known. This is nothing, philosophically speaking.

Somehow or other in my later years at Berkeley, two professors, Moses
and Howison, representing opposite schools of thought, got into a controversy, probably about their classes. They brought together in the house of
one of them a few of their picked students, with the evident intention of
letting us show in conversation how much or how little we had understood of
their respective teachings. I don't remember just what the subject was that
they threw into the ring, but we wrestled with it till the professors could
stand it no longer. Then they broke in, and while we sat silent and highly
entertained, they went at each other hard and fast and long. It was after
midnight when, the debate over, we went home. I asked the other fellows

what they had got out of it, and their answers showed that they had seen nothing but a fine, fair fight. When I laughed, they asked me what I, the D.S., had seen that was so much more profound.

I said that I had seen two highly trained, well-educated Masters of Arts and Doctors of Philosophy disagreeing upon every essential point of thought and knowledge. They had all there was of the sciences; and yet they could not find any knowledge upon which they could base an acceptable conclusion. They had no test of knowledge; they didn't know what is and what is not. And they have no test of right and wrong; they have no basis for even an ethics.

Well, and what of it? They asked me that, and that I did not answer. I was stunned by the discovery that it was philosophically true, in a most literal sense, that nothing is known; that it is precisely the foundation that is lacking for science; that all we call knowledge rested upon assumptions which the scientists did not all accept; and that, likewise, there is no scientific reason for saying, for example, that stealing is wrong. In brief: there was no scientific basis for an ethics. No wonder men said one thing and did another; no wonder they could settle nothing either in life or in the academies.

I could hardly believe this. Maybe these professors, whom I greatly respected, did not know it all. I read the books over again with a fresh eye, with a real interest, and I could see that, as in history, so in other branches of knowledge, everything was in the air. And I was glad of it. Rebel though I was, I had got the religion of scholarship and science; I was in awe of the authorities in the academic world. It was a release to feel my worship cool and pass. But I could not be sure. I must go elsewhere, see and hear other professors, men these California professors quoted and looked up to as their high priests. I decided to go as a student to Europe when I was through Berkeley, and I would start with the German universities.

My father listened to my plan, and he was disappointed. He had hoped I would succeed him in his business; it was for that that he was staying in it. When I said that, whatever I might do, I would never go into business, he said, rather sadly, that he would sell out his interest and retire. And he did soon after our talk. But he wanted me to stay home and, to keep me, offered to buy an interest in a certain San Francisco daily paper. He had evidently had this in mind for some time. I had always done some writing, verse at the poetical age of puberty, then a novel which my mother alone treasured. Journalism was the business for a boy who liked to write, he thought, and he said I had often spoken of a newspaper as my ambition. No doubt I had in the intervals between my campaigns as Napoleon. But no more. I was now going to be a scientist, a philosopher. He sighed; he thought it over, and with the approval of my mother, who was for every sort of education, he gave his consent.

Suggestions for Discussion

1. The first part of this reminiscence tells us about Steffens's carefree days as a student at Berkeley in the late nineteenth century. How does he describe student life? What was the main interest of most students at the university?

2. Why did Steffens fail to get ahead in athletics while achieving great success as a drillmaster? Why did military drill appeal to him?

3. What was Steffens's attitude toward money while he was a student? Why did he gamble? Explain how he learned to be a successful gambler. Explain why he gave up gambling.

4. Why was Steffens disappointed in his fraternity?

5. Explain the significance of the incident of the stealing of Dr. Bonte's chickens. Why is it included in this section?

6. What is the major difference between the first and second parts of the reminiscence?

7. How does Steffens get interested in the study of history? What determines his decision to continue his education in Germany?

8. Why were most of the students whom Steffens knew attending Berkeley? Does he respect their reasons? What does he think is the real reason for education?

9. How would you describe Steffens during his student days? Was he likeable? Explain your answer.

Suggestions for Writing

1. Using Steffens as a model, write an essay in which you attempt to summarize most of your classmates' reasons for going to college. Try to develop a questionnaire in which you sample opinion so that you have information to summarize. Write an opinion of the reasons you discover.

2. College life differs greatly from one institution to another. Write an essay in which you compare college life at your own college or university with that of another. You may wish to ask someone much older than yourself how his or her college life differed from yours. You may wish to contrast your own experiences with those of Steffens.

Malcolm X

A Homemade Education

Malcolm X (1925–1965), who became a Muslim while serving a prison sentence, was an early minister of the Nation of Islam's mosque in New York. Before his assassination, he was a spiritual leader, writer, lecturer, and political activist who worked for worldwide African-American unity and equality. The following selection is taken from his powerful *Autobiography of Malcolm X* (1965).

It was because of my letters that I happened to stumble upon starting to acquire some kind of a homemade education.

I became increasingly frustrated at not being able to express what I wanted to convey in letters that I wrote, especially those to Mr. Elijah Muhammad. In the street, I had been the most articulate hustler out there—I had commanded attention when I said something. But now, trying to write simple English, I not only wasn't articulate, I wasn't even functional. How would I sound writing in slang, the way I would *say* it, something such as, "Look, daddy, let me pull your coat about a cat, Elijah Muhammad—"

Many who today hear me somewhere in person, or on television, or those who read something I've said, will think I went to school far beyond the eighth grade. This impression is due entirely to my prison studies.

It had really begun back in the Charlestown Prison, when Bimbi first made me feel envy of his stock of knowledge. Bimbi had always taken charge of any conversations he was in, and I had tried to emulate him. But every book I picked up had few sentences which didn't contain anywhere from one to nearly all of the words that might as well have been in Chinese. When I just skipped those words, of course, I really ended up with little idea of what the book said. So I had come to the Norfolk Prison Colony still going through only book-reading motions. Pretty soon, I would have quit even these motions, unless I had received the motivation that I did.

I saw that the best thing I could do was get hold of a dictionary—to study, to learn some words. I was lucky enough to reason also that I should try to improve my penmanship. It was sad. I couldn't even write in a straight line. It was both ideas together that moved me to request a dictionary along with some tablets and pencils from the Norfolk Prison Colony school.

I spent two days just riffling uncertainly through the dictionary's pages. I'd never realized so many words existed! I didn't know *which* words I needed to learn. Finally, just to start some kind of action, I began copying.

In my slow, painstaking, ragged handwriting, I copied into my tablet everything printed on that first page, down to the punctuation marks.

I believe it took me a day. Then, aloud, I read back, to myself, everything I'd written on the tablet. Over and over, aloud, to myself, I read my own handwriting.

I woke up the next morning, thinking about those words—immensely proud to realize that not only had I written so much at one time, but I'd written words that I never knew were in the world. Moreover, with a little effort, I also could remember what many of these words meant. I reviewed the words whose meanings I didn't remember. Funny thing, from the dictionary first page right now, that "aardvark" springs to my mind. The dictionary had a picture of it, a long-tailed, long-eared, burrowing African mammal, which lives off termites caught by sticking out its tongue as an anteater does for ants.

I was so fascinated that I went on—I copied the dictionary's next page. And the same experience came when I studied that. With every succeeding page, I also learned of people and places and events from history. Actually the dictionary is like a miniature encyclopedia. Finally the dictionary's A section had filled a whole tablet—and I went on into the B's. That was the way I started copying what eventually became the entire dictionary. It went a lot faster after so much practice helped me to pick up handwriting speed. Between what I wrote in my tablet, and writing letters, during the rest of my time in prison I would guess I wrote a million words.

I suppose it was inevitable that as my word-base broadened, I could for the first time pick up a book and read and now begin to understand what the book was saying. Anyone who has read a great deal can imagine the new world that opened. Let me tell you something: from then until I left that prison, in every free moment I had, if I was not reading in the library, I was reading on my bunk. You couldn't have gotten me out of books with a wedge. Between Mr. Muhammad's teachings, my correspondence, my visitors—usually Ella and Reginald—and my reading of books, months passed without my even thinking about being imprisoned. In fact, up to then, I never had been so truly free in my life.

The Norfolk Prison Colony's library was in the school building. A variety of classes was taught there by instructors who came from such places as Harvard and Boston universities. The weekly debates between inmate teams were also held in the school building. You would be astonished to know how worked up convict debaters and audiences would get over subjects like "Should Babies Be Fed Milk?"

Available on the prison library's shelves were books on just about every general subject. Much of the big private collection that Parkhurst had willed to the prison was still in crates and boxes in the back of the library—thousands of old books. Some of them looked ancient: covers faded; old-time parchment-looking binding. Parkhurst, I've mentioned, seemed to have been principally interested in history and religion. He had the money and the special interest to have a lot of books that you wouldn't have in general circulation. Any college library would have been lucky to get that collection.

As you can imagine, especially in a prison where there was heavy emphasis on rehabilitation, an inmate was smiled upon if he demonstrated an unusually intense interest in books. There was a sizable number of well-read inmates, especially the popular debaters. Some were said by many to be practically walking encyclopedias. They were almost celebrities. No university would ask any student to devour literature as I did when this new world opened to me, of being able to read and *understand*.

I read more in my room than in the library itself. An inmate who was known to read a lot could check out more than the permitted maximum number of books. I preferred reading in the total isolation of my own room.

When I had progressed to really serious reading, every night at about ten P.M. I would be outraged with the "lights out." It always seemed to catch me right in the middle of something engrossing.

Fortunately, right outside my door was a corridor light that cast a glow into my room. The glow was enough to read by, once my eyes adjusted to it. So when "lights out" came, I would sit on the floor where I could continue reading in that glow.

At one-hour intervals the night guards paced past every room. Each time I heard the approaching footsteps, I jumped into bed and feigned sleep. And as soon as the guard passed, I got back out of bed onto the floor area of that light-glow, where I would read for another fifty-eight minutes—until the guard approached again. That went on until three or four every morning. Three or four hours of sleep a night was enough for me. Often in the years in the streets I had slept less than that.

The teachings of Mr. Muhammad stressed how history had been "whitened"—when white men had written history books, the black man simply had been left out. Mr. Muhammad couldn't have said anything that would have struck me much harder. I had never forgotten how when my class, me and all of those whites, had studied seventh-grade United States history back in Mason, the history of the Negro had been covered in one paragraph, and the teacher had gotten a big laugh with his joke, "Negroes' feet are so big that when they walk, they leave a hole in the ground."

This is one reason why Mr. Muhammad's teachings spread so swiftly all over the United States, among *all* Negroes, whether or not they became followers of Mr. Muhammad. The teachings ring true—to every Negro. You can hardly show me a black adult in America—or a white one, for that matter—who knows from the history books anything like the truth about the black man's role. In my own case, once I heard of the "glorious history of the black man," I took special pains to hunt in the library for books that would inform me on details about black history.

I can remember accurately the very first set of books that really impressed me. I have since bought that set of books and I have it at home for my children to read as they grow up. It's called *Wonders of the World*. It's full of pictures of archaeological finds, statues that depict, usually, non-European people.

I found books like Will Durant's *Story of Civilization*. I read H. G. Wells' *Outline of History*. *Souls of Black Folk* by W. E. B. Du Bois gave me a glimpse into the black people's history before they came to this country. Carter G. Woodson's *Negro History* opened my eyes about black empires before the black slave was brought to the United States, and the early Negro struggles for freedom.

J. A. Rogers' three volumes of *Sex and Race* told about race-mixing before Christ's time; about Aesop being a black man who told fables; about Egypt's Pharaohs; about the great Coptic Christian Empires; about Ethiopia, the earth's oldest continuous black civilization, as China is the oldest continuous civilization.

Mr. Muhammad's teaching about how the white man had been created led me to *Findings in Genetics* by Gregor Mendel. (The dictionary's G section was where I had learned what "genetics" meant.) I really studied this book by the Austrian monk. Reading it over and over, especially certain sections, helped me to understand that if you started with a black man, a white man could be produced; but starting with a white man, you never could produce a black man—because the white chromosome is recessive. And since no one disputes that there was but one Original Man, the conclusion is clear.

During the last year or so, in the *New York Times*, Arnold Toynbee used the word "bleached" in describing the white man. (His words were: "White [i.e., bleached] human beings of North European origin. . . .") Toynbee also referred to the European geographic area as only a peninsula of Asia. He said there is no such thing as Europe. And if you look at the globe, you will see for yourself that America is only an extension of Asia. (But at the same time Toynbee is among those who have helped to bleach history. He won't write that again. Every day now, the truth is coming to light.)

I never will forget how shocked I was when I began reading about slavery's total horror. It made such an impact upon me that it later became one of my favorite subjects when I became a minister of Mr. Muhammad's. The world's most monstrous crime, the sin and the blood on the white man's hands, are almost impossible to believe. Books like the one by Frederick Olmstead opened my eyes to the horrors suffered when the slave was landed in the United States. The European woman, Fannie Kimball, who had married a Southern white slaveowner, described how human beings were degraded. Of course I read *Uncle Tom's Cabin*. In fact, I believe that's the only novel I have ever read since I started serious reading.

Parkhurst's collection also contained some bound pamphlets of the Abolitionist Anti-Slavery Society of New England. I read descriptions of atrocities, saw those illustrations of black slave women tied up and flogged with whips; of black mothers watching their babies being dragged off, never to be seen by their mothers again; of dogs after slaves, and of the fugitive slave catchers, evil white men with whips and clubs and chains and guns. I read about the slave preacher Nat Turner, who put the fear of God into the white slavemaster. Nat Turner wasn't going around preaching pie-in-the-sky and "nonviolent" freedom for the black man. There in Virginia one night in 1831, Nat and seven other slaves started out at his master's home and through the night they went from one plantation "big house" to the next, killing, until by the next morning 57 white people were dead and Nat had about 70 slaves following him. White people, terrified for their lives, fled from their homes, locked themselves up in public buildings, hid in the woods, and some even left the state. A small army of soldiers took two months to catch and hang Nat Turner. Somewhere I have read where Nat Turner's example is said to have inspired John Brown to invade Virginia and attack Harper's Ferry nearly thirty years later, with thirteen white men and five Negroes.

I read Herodotus, "the father of History," or, rather, I read about him. And I read the histories of various nations, which opened my eyes gradually, then wider and wider, to how the whole world's white men had indeed acted like devils, pillaging and raping and bleeding and draining the whole world's non-white people. I remember, for instance, books such as Will Durant's *The Story of Oriental Civilization*, and Mahatma Gandhi's accounts of the struggle to drive the British out of India.

Book after book showed me how the white man had brought upon the world's black, brown, red, and yellow peoples every variety of the sufferings of exploitation. I saw how since the sixteenth century, the so-called "Christian trader" white man began to ply the seas in his lust for Asian and African empires, and plunder, and power. I read, I saw, how the white man never has gone among the non-white peoples bearing the Cross in the true manner and spirit of Christ's teachings—meek, humble, and Christlike.

I perceived, as I read, how the collective white man had been actually nothing but a piratical opportunist who used Faustian machinations to make his own Christianity his initial wedge in criminal conquests. First, always "religiously," he branded "heathen" and "pagan" labels upon ancient non-white cultures and civilizations. The stage thus set, he then turned upon his non-white victims his weapons of war.

I read how, entering India—half a *billion* deeply religious brown people—the British white man, by 1759, through promises, trickery and manipulations, controlled much of India through Great Britain's East India Company. The parasitical British administration kept tentacling out to half of the subcontinent. In 1857, some of the desperate people of India finally mutinied—and, excepting the African slave trade, nowhere has history recorded any more unnecessary bestial and ruthless human carnage than the British suppression of the non-white Indian people.

Over 115 million African blacks—close to the 1930s population of the United States—were murdered or enslaved during the slave trade. And I read how when the slave market was glutted, the cannibalistic white powers of Europe next carved up, as their colonies, the richest areas of the black continent. And Europe's chancelleries for the next century played a chess game of naked exploitation and power from Cape Horn to Cairo.

Ten guards and the warden couldn't have torn me out of those books. Not even Elijah Muhammad could have been more eloquent than those books were in providing indisputable proof that the collective white man had acted like a devil in virtually every contact he had with the world's collective non-white man. I listen today to the radio, and watch television, and read the headlines about the collective white man's fear and tension concerning China. When the white man professes ignorance about why the Chinese hate him so, my mind can't help flashing back to what I read, there in prison, about how the blood forebears of this same white man raped China at a time when China was trusting and helpless. Those original white "Christian traders" sent into China millions of pounds of opium. By 1839, so many of the Chinese were addicts that China's desperate government destroyed twenty thousand chests of opium. The first Opium War was promptly declared by the white man. Imagine! Declaring *war* upon someone who objects to being narcotized! The Chinese were severely beaten, with Chinese-invented gunpowder.

The Treaty of Nanking made China pay the British white man for the destroyed opium: forced open China's major ports to British trade; forced China to abandon Hong Kong; fixed China's import tariffs so low that cheap British articles soon flooded in, maiming China's industrial development.

After a second Opium War, the Tientsin Treaties legalized the ravaging opium trade, legalized a British-French-American control of China's customs. China tried delaying that Treaty's ratification; Peking was looted and burned.

"Kill the foreign white devils!" was the 1901 Chinese war cry in the Boxer Rebellion. Losing again, this time the Chinese were driven from Peking's choicest areas. The vicious, arrogant white man put up the famous signs, "Chinese and dogs not allowed."

Red China after World War II closed its doors to the Western white world. Massive Chinese agricultural, scientific, and industrial efforts are described in a book that *Life* magazine recently published. Some observers inside Red China have reported that the world never has known such a hate-white campaign as is now going on in this non-white country where, present birthrates continuing, in fifty more years Chinese will be half the earth's population. And it seems that some Chinese chickens will soon come home to roost, with China's recent successful nuclear tests.

Let us face reality. We can see in the United Nations a new world order being shaped, along color lines—an alliance among the non-white nations. America's U.N. Ambassador Adlai Stevenson complained not long ago that in the United Nations "a skin game" was being played. He was right. He. was facing reality. A "skin game" *is* being played. But Ambassador Stevenson sounded like Jesse James accusing the marshal of carrying a gun. Because who in the world's history ever has played a worse "skin game" than the white man?

Mr. Muhammad, to whom I was writing daily, had no idea of what a new world had opened up to me through my efforts to document his teachings in books.

When I discovered philosophy, I tried to touch all the landmarks of philosophical development. Gradually, I read most of the old philosophers, Occidental and Oriental. The Oriental philosophers were the ones I came to prefer; finally, my impression was that most Occidental philosophy had largely been borrowed from the Oriental thinkers. Socrates, for instance, traveled in Egypt. Some sources even say that Socrates was initiated into some of the Egyptian mysteries. Obviously Socrates got some of his wisdom among the East's wise men.

I have often reflected upon the new vistas that reading opened to me. I knew right there in prison that reading had changed forever the course of my life. As I see it today, the ability to read awoke inside me some long dormant craving to be mentally alive. I certainly wasn't seeking any degree, the way a college confers a status symbol upon its students. My homemade education gave me, with every additional book that I read, a little bit more sensitivity to the deafness, dumbness, and blindness that was afflicting the black race in America. Not long ago, an English writer telephoned me from London, asking questions. One was, "What's your alma mater?" I told him, "Books." You will never catch me with a free fifteen minutes in which I'm not studying something I feel might be able to help the black man.

Yesterday I spoke in London, and both ways on the plane across the Atlantic I was studying a document about how the United Nations proposes to insure the human rights of the oppressed minorities of the world. The American black man is the world's most shameful case of minority oppression. What makes the black man think of himself as only an internal United States issue is just a catch-phrase, two words, "civil rights." How is the black man going to get "civil rights" before first he wins his *human* rights? If the American black man will start thinking about his *human* rights, and then start thinking of himself as part of one of the world's great peoples, he will see he has a case for the United Nations.

I can't think of a better case! Four hundred years of black blood and sweat invested here in America, and the white man still has the black man begging for what every immigrant fresh off the ship can take for granted the minute he walks down the gangplank.

But I'm digressing. I told the Englishman that my alma mater was books, a good library. Every time I catch a plane, I have with me a book that I want to read—and that's a lot of books these days. If I weren't out here every day battling the white man, I could spend the rest of my life reading, just satisfying my curiosity—because you can hardly mention anything I'm not curious about. I don't think anybody ever got more out of going to prison than I did. In fact, prison enabled me to study far more intensively than I would have if my life had gone differently and I had attended some college. I imagine that one of the biggest troubles with colleges is there are too many distractions, too much panty-raiding, fraternities, and boola-boola and all of that. Where else but in a prison could I have attacked my ignorance by being able to study intensely sometimes as much as fifteen hours a day?

Suggestions for Discussion

1. Discuss the significance of the title "A Homemade Education."

2. Explain how Malcolm X used his dictionary to improve his education.

3. Discuss his observation that "the ability to read awoke inside me some long dormant craving to be mentally alive."

4. Comment on his assertion that his "alma mater was books."

5. What details help make clear his passion for learning?

Suggestions for Writing

1. Compare and contrast "A Homemade Education" with another section of Malcolm X's *Autobiography*.

2. Write about one or more books that have played an important role in shaping your thinking, attitudes, and behavior.

Maya Angelou

Graduation

Maya Angelou (b. 1928) was born in Stamps, Arkansas, to a childhood of poverty and pain. She has been a dancer and an actress, a coordinator of the Southern Christian Leadership Conference, a television writer and producer, and a poet. She is best known for her autobiographical works, I *Know Why the Caged Bird Sings* (1970), from which "Graduation" is taken, and *The Heart of a Woman* (1981). Her poem, "On the Pulse of Morning," delivered at the inauguration of President Bill Clinton, was published in 1992. In "Graduation" Angelou captures the pain of racial discrimination, but reaffirms the power of the black community to survive.

The children in Stamps trembled visibly with anticipation. Some adults were excited too, but to be certain the whole young population had come down with graduation epidemic. Large classes were graduating from both the grammar school and the high school. Even those who were years removed from their own day of glorious release were anxious to help with preparations as a kind of dry run. The junior students who were moving into the vacating classes' chairs were tradition-bound to show their talents for leadership and management. They strutted through the school and around the campus exerting pressure on the lower grades. Their authority was so new that occasionally if they pressed a little too hard it had to be overlooked. After all, next term was coming, and it never hurt a sixth-grader to have a play sister in the eighth grade, or a tenth-year student to be able to call a twelfth-grader Bubba. So all was endured in a spirit of shared understanding. But the graduating classes themselves were the nobility. Like travelers with exotic destinations on their minds, the graduates were remarkably forgetful. They came to school without their books, or tablets or even pencils. Volunteers fell over themselves to secure replacements for the missing equipment. When accepted, the willing workers might or might not be thanked, and it was of no importance to the pregraduation rites. Even teachers were respectful of the now quiet and aging seniors, and tended to speak to them, if not as equals, as beings only slightly lower than themselves. After tests were returned and grades given, the student body, which acted like an extended family, knew who did well, who excelled, and what piteous ones had failed.

Unlike the white high school, Lafayette County Training School distinguished itself by having neither lawn, nor hedges, nor tennis court, nor climbing ivy. Its two buildings (main classrooms, the grade school and home economics) were set on a dirt hill with no fence to limit either its boundaries or those of bordering farms. There was a large expanse to the left of the school which was used alternately as a baseball diamond or a basketball court. Rusty hoops on the swaying poles represented the permanent recreational equipment, although bats and balls could be borrowed from the P.E. teacher if the borrower was qualified and if the diamond wasn't occupied.

Over this rocky area relieved by a few shady tall persimmon trees the graduating class walked. The girls often held hands and no longer bothered to speak to the lower students. There was a sadness about them, as if this old world was not their home and they were bound for higher ground. The boys, on the other hand, had become more friendly, more outgoing. A decided change from the closed attitude they projected while studying for finals. Now they seemed not ready to give up the old school, the familiar paths and classrooms. Only a small percentage would be continuing on to college—one of the South's A & M (agricultural and mechanical) schools, which trained Negro youths to be carpenters, farmers, handymen, masons, maids, cooks and baby nurses. Their future rode heavily on their shoulders, and blinded them to the collective joy that had pervaded the lives of the boys and girls in the grammar school graduating class.

Parents who could afford it had ordered new shoes and ready-made clothes for themselves from Sears, Roebuck or Montgomery Ward. They also engaged the best seamstresses to make the floating graduating dresses and to cut down secondhand pants which would be pressed to a military slickness for the important event.

Oh, it was important, all right. Whitefolks would attend the ceremony, and two or three would speak of God and home, and the Southern way of life, and Mrs. Parsons, the principal's wife, would play the graduation march while the lower-grade graduates paraded down the aisles and took their seats below the platform. The high school seniors would wait in empty classrooms to make their dramatic entrance.

In the Store I was the person of the moment. The birthday girl. The center. Bailey had graduated the year before, although to do so he had had to forfeit all pleasures to make up for his time lost in Baton Rouge.

My class was wearing butter-yellow piqué dresses, and Momma launched out on mine. She smocked the yoke into tiny crisscrossing puckers, then shirred the rest of the bodice. Her dark fingers ducked in and out of the lemony cloth as she embroidered raised daisies around the hem. Before she considered herself finished she had added a crocheted cuff on the puff sleeves, and a pointy crocheted collar.

I was going to be lovely. A walking model of all the various styles of fine hand sewing and it didn't worry me that I was only twelve years old and merely graduating from the eighth grade. Besides, many teachers in Arkansas Negro schools had only that diploma and were licensed to impart wisdom.

The days had become longer and more noticeable. The faded beige of former times had been replaced with strong and sure colors. I began to see my classmates' clothes, their skin tones, and the dust that waved off pussy willows. Clouds that lazed across the sky were objects of great concern to me. Their shiftier shapes might have held a message that in my new happiness and with a little bit of time I'd soon decipher. During that period I looked at the arch of heaven so religiously my neck kept a steady ache. I had taken to smiling more often, and my jaws hurt from the unaccustomed activity. Between the two physical sore spots, I suppose I could have been uncomfortable, but that was not the case. As a member of the winning team (the graduating class of 1940) I had outdistanced unpleasant sensations by miles. I was headed for the freedom of open fields.

Youth and social approval allied themselves with me and we trammeled memories of slights and insults. The wind of our swift passage remodeled my features. Lost tears were pounded to mud and then to dust. Years of withdrawal were brushed aside and left behind, as hanging ropes of parasitic moss.

My work alone had awarded me a top place and I was going to be one of the first called in the graduating ceremonies. On the classroom blackboard, as well as on the bulletin board in the auditorium, there were blue stars and white stars and red stars. No absences, no tardinesses, and my academic work was among the best of the year. I could say the preamble to the Constitution even faster than Bailey. We timed ourselves often: "Wethepeople-oftheUnitedStatesinordertoformamoreperfectunion . . ." I had memorized the Presidents of the United States from Washington to Roosevelt in chronological as well as alphabetical order.

My hair pleased me too. Gradually the black mass had lengthened and thickened, so that it kept at last to its braided pattern, and I didn't have to yank my scalp off when I tried to comb it.

Louise and I had rehearsed the exercises until we tired out ourselves. Henry Reed was class valedictorian. He was a small, very black boy with hooded eyes, a long, broad nose and an oddly shaped head. I had admired him for years because each term he and I vied for the best grades in our class. Most often he bested me, but instead of being disappointed I was pleased that we shared top places between us. Like many Southern Black children, he lived with his grandmother, who was as strict as Momma and as kind as she knew how to be. He was courteous, respectful, and soft-spoken to elders, but on the playground he chose to play the roughest games. I admired him. Anyone, I reckoned, sufficiently afraid or sufficiently dull could be polite. But to be able to operate at a top level with both adults and children was admirable.

His valedictory speech was entitled "To Be or Not to Be." The rigid tenth-grade teacher had helped him write it. He'd been working on the dramatic stresses for months.

The weeks until graduation were filled with heady activities. A group of small children were to be presented in a play about buttercups and daisies and bunny rabbits. They could be heard throughout the building practicing their hops and their little songs that sounded like silver bells. The older girls (nongraduates, of course) were assigned the task of making refreshments for the night's festivities. A tangy scent of ginger, cinnamon, nutmeg and chocolate wafted around the home economics building as the budding cooks made samples for themselves and their teachers.

In every corner of the workshop, axes and saws split fresh timber as the woodshop boys made sets and stage scenery. Only the graduates were left out of the general bustle. We were free to sit in the library at the back of the building or look in quite detachedly, naturally, on the measures being taken for our event.

Even the minister preached on graduation the Sunday before. His subject was, "Let your light so shine that men will see your good works and praise your Father, Who is in Heaven." Although the sermon was purported to be addressed to us, he used the occasion to speak to backsliders, gamblers, and general ne'er-do-wells. But since he had called our names at the beginning of the service we were mollified.

Among Negroes the tradition was to give presents to children going only from one grade to another. How much more important this was when the person was graduating at the top of the class. Uncle Willie and Momma had sent away for a Mickey Mouse watch like Bailey's. Louise gave me four embroidered handkerchiefs. (I gave her three crocheted doilies.) Mrs. Sneed, the minister's wife, made me an underskirt to wear for graduation, and nearly every customer gave me a nickel or maybe even a dime with the instruction "Keep on moving to higher ground," or some such encouragement.

Amazingly the great day finally dawned and I was out of bed before I knew it. I threw open the back door to see it more clearly, but Momma said, "Sister, come away from that door and put your robe on."

I hoped the memory of that morning would never leave me. Sunlight was itself still young, and the day had none of the insistence maturity would bring it in a few hours. In my robe and barefoot in the backyard, under cover of going to see about my new beans, I gave myself up to the gentle warmth and thanked God that no matter what evil I had done in my life He had allowed me to live to see this day. Somewhere in my fatalism I had expected to die, accidentally, and never have the chance to walk up the stairs in the auditorium and gracefully receive my hard-earned diploma. Out of God's merciful bosom I had won reprieve.

Bailey came out in his robe and gave me a box wrapped in Christmas paper. He said he had saved his money for months to pay for it. It felt like a box of chocolates, but I knew Bailey wouldn't save money to buy candy when we had all we could want under our noses.

He was as proud of the gift as I. It was a soft-leatherbound copy of a collection of poems by Edgar Allan Poe, or, as Bailey and I called him, "Eap." I turned to "Annabel Lee" and we walked up and down the garden rows, the cool dirt between our toes, reciting the beautifully sad lines.

Momma made a Sunday breakfast although it was only Friday. After we finished the blessing, I opened my eyes to find the watch on my plate. It was a dream of a day. Everything went smoothly and to my credit. I didn't have to be reminded or scolded for anything. Near evening I was too jittery to attend to chores, so Bailey volunteered to do all before his bath.

Days before, we had made a sign for the Store, and as we turned out the lights Momma hung the cardboard over the doorknob. It read clearly: CLOSED. GRADUATION.

My dress fitted perfectly and everyone said that I looked like a sunbeam in it. On the hill, going toward the school, Bailey walked behind with Uncle Willie, who muttered, "Go on, Ju." He wanted him to walk ahead with us because it embarrassed him to have to walk so slowly. Bailey said he'd let the ladies walk together, and the men would bring up the rear. We all laughed, nicely.

Little children dashed by out of the dark like fireflies. Their crepe-paper dresses and butterfly wings were not made for running and we heard more than one rip, dryly, and the regretful "uh uh" that followed.

The school blazed without gaiety. The windows seemed cold and unfriendly from the lower hill. A sense of ill-fated timing crept over me, and if Momma hadn't reached for my hand I would have drifted back to Bailey and Uncle Willie, and possibly beyond. She made a few slow jokes about my feet getting cold, and tugged me along to the now-strange building.

Around the front steps, assurance came back. There were my fellow "greats," the graduating class. Hair brushed back, legs oiled, new dresses and pressed pleats, fresh pocket handkerchiefs and little handbags, all homesewn. Oh, we were up to snuff, all right. I joined my comrades and didn't even see my family go in to find seats in the crowded auditorium.

The school band struck up a march and all classes filed in as had been rehearsed. We stood in front of our seats, as assigned, and on a signal from the choir director, we sat. No sooner had this been accomplished than the band started to play the national anthem. We rose again and sang the song, after which we recited the pledge of allegiance. We remained standing for a brief minute before the choir director and the principal signaled to us, rather desperately I thought, to take our seats. The command was so unusual that our carefully rehearsed and smooth-running machine was thrown off. For a full minute we fumbled for our chairs and bumped into each other awkwardly. Habits change or solidify under pressure, so in our state of nervous tension we had been ready to follow our usual assembly pattern: the American national anthem, then the pledge of allegiance, then the song every Black person I knew called the Negro National Anthem. All done in the same key, with the same passion and most often standing on the same foot.

Finding my seat at last, I was overcome with a presentiment of worse things to come. Something unrehearsed, unplanned, was going to happen, and we were going to be made to look bad. I distinctly remember being explicit in the choice of pronoun. It was "we," the graduating class, the unit, that concerned me then.

The principal welcomed "parents and friends" and asked the Baptist minister to lead us in prayer. His invocation was brief and punchy, and for a second I thought we were getting back on the high road to right action. When the principal came back to the dais, however, his voice had changed. Sounds always affected me profoundly and the principal's voice was one of my favorites. During assembly it melted and lowed weakly into the audience. It had not been in my plan to listen to him, but my curiosity was piqued and I straightened up to give him my attention.

He was talking about Booker T. Washington, our "late great leader," who said we can be as close as the fingers on the hand, etc. . . . Then he said a few vague things about friendship and the friendship of kindly people to those less fortunate than themselves. With that his voice nearly faded, thin, away. Like a river diminishing to a stream and then to a trickle. But he cleared his throat and said, "Our speaker tonight, who is also our friend, came from Texarkana to deliver the commencement address, but due to the irregularity of the train schedule, he's going to, as they say, 'speak and run.'" He said that we understood and wanted the man to know that we were most grateful for the time he was able to give us and then something about how we were willing always to adjust to another's program, and without more ado— "I give you Mr. Edward Donleavy."

Not one but two white men came through the door offstage. The shorter one walked to the speaker's platform, and the tall one moved over to the center seat and sat down. But that was our principal's seat, and already occupied. The dislodged gentleman bounced around for a long breath or two before the Baptist minister gave him his chair, then with more dignity than the situation deserved, the minister walked off the stage.

Donleavy looked at the audience once (on reflection, I'm sure that he wanted only to reassure himself that we were really there), adjusted his glasses and began to read from a sheaf of papers.

He was glad "to be here and to see the work going on just as it was in the other schools."

At the first "Amen" from the audience I willed the offender to immediate death by choking on the word. But Amens and Yes, sir's began to fall around the room like rain through a ragged umbrella.

He told us of the wonderful changes we children in Stamps had in store. The Central School (naturally, the white school was Central) had already been granted improvements that would be in use in the fall. A well-known artist was coming from Little Rock to teach art to them. They were going to have the newest microscopes and chemistry equipment for their laboratory. Mr. Donleavy didn't leave us long in the dark over who made these improvements available to Central High. Nor were we to be ignored in the general betterment scheme he had in mind.

He said that he had pointed out to people at a very high level that one of the first-line football tacklers at Arkansas Agricultural and Mechanical College had graduated from good old Lafayette County Training School. Here fewer Amen's were heard. Those few that did break through lay dully in the air with the heaviness of habit.

He went on to praise us. He went on to say how he had bragged that "one of the best basketball players at Fisk sank his first ball right here at Lafayette County Training School."

The white kids were going to have a chance to become Galileos and Madame Curies and Edisons and Gauguins, and our boys (the girls weren't even in on it) would try to be Jesse Owenses and Joe Louises.

Owens and the Brown Bomber were great heroes in our world, but what school official in the white-goddom of Little Rock had the right to decide that those two men must be our only heroes? Who decided that for Henry Reed to become a scientist he had to work like George Washington Carver, as a bootblack, to buy a lousy microscope? Bailey was obviously always going to be too small to be an athlete, so which concrete angel glued to what country seat had decided that if my brother wanted to become a lawyer he had to first pay penance for his skin by picking cotton and hoeing corn and studying correspondence books at night for twenty years?

The man's dead words fell like bricks around the auditorium and too many settled in my belly. Constrained by hard-learned manners I couldn't look behind me, but to my left and right the proud graduating class of 1940 had dropped their heads. Every girl in my row had found something new to do with her handkerchief. Some folded the tiny squares into love knots, some into triangles, but most were wadding them, then pressing them flat on their yellow laps.

On the dais, the ancient tragedy was being replayed. Professor Parsons sat, a sculptor's reject, rigid. His large, heavy body seemed devoid of will or willingness, and his eyes said he was no longer with us. The other teachers examined the flag (which was draped stage right) or their notes, or the windows which opened on our now-famous playing diamond.

Graduation, the hush-hush magic time of frills and gifts and congratulations and diplomas, was finished for me before my name was called. The accomplishment was nothing. The meticulous maps, drawn in three colors of ink, learning and spelling decasyllabic words, memorizing the whole of *The Rape of Lucrece*—it was for nothing. Donleavy had exposed us.

We were maids and farmers, handymen and washerwomen, and anything higher that we aspired to was farcical and presumptuous.

Then I wished that Gabriel Prosser and Nat Turner had killed all whitefolks in their beds and that Abraham Lincoln had been assassinated before the signing of the Emancipation Proclamation, and that Harriet Tubman had been killed by that blow on her head and Christopher Columbus had drowned in the *Santa María*.

It was awful to be Negro and have no control over my life. It was brutal to be young and already trained to sit quietly and listen to charges brought against my color with no chance of defense. We should all be dead. I thought I should like to see us all dead, one on top of the other. A pyramid of flesh with the whitefolks on the bottom, as the broad base, then the Indians with their silly tomahawks and teepees and wigwams and treaties, the Negroes with their mops and recipes and cotton sacks and spirituals sticking out of their mouths. The Dutch children should all stumble in their wooden shoes and break their necks. The French should choke to death on the Louisiana Purchase (1803) while silkworms ate all the Chinese with their stupid pigtails. As a species, we were an abomination. All of us.

Donleavy was running for election, and assured our parents that if he won we could count on having the only colored paved playing field in that part of Arkansas. Also—he never looked up to acknowledge the grunts of acceptance—also, we were bound to get some new equipment for the home economics building and the workshop.

He finished, and since there was no need to give any more than the most perfunctory thank-you's, he nodded to the men on the stage, and the tall white man who was never introduced joined him at the door. They left with the attitude that now they were off to something really important. (The graduation ceremonies at Lafayette Country Training School had been a mere preliminary.)

The ugliness they left was palpable. An uninvited guest who wouldn't leave. The choir was summoned and sang a modern arrangement of "Onward, Christian Soldiers," with new words pertaining to graduates seeking their place in the world. But it didn't work. Elouise, the daughter of the Baptist minister, recited "Invictus," and I could have cried at the impertinence of "I am the master of my fate, I am the captain of my soul."

My name had lost its ring of familiarity and I had to be nudged to go and receive my diploma. All my preparations had fled. I neither marched up to the stage like a conquering Amazon, nor did I look in the audience for Bailey's nod of approval. Marguerite Johnson, I heard the name again, my honors were read, there were noises in the audience of appreciation, and I took my place on the stage as rehearsed.

I thought about colors I hated: ecru, puce, lavender, beige and black.

There was shuffling and rustling around me, then Henry Reed was giving his valedictory address, "To Be or Not to Be." Hadn't he heard the whitefolks? We couldn't *be*, so the question was a waste of time. Henry's voice came out clear and strong. I feared to look at him. Hadn't he got the message? There was no "nobler in the mind" for Negroes because the world didn't think we had minds, and they let us know it. "Outrageous fortune"? Now, that was a joke. When the ceremony was over I had to tell Henry Reed some things. That is, if I still cared. Not "rub," Henry, "erase." "Ah, there's the erase." Us.

Henry had been a good student in elocution. His voice rose on tides of promise and fell on waves of warnings. The English teacher had helped him to create a sermon winging through Hamlet's soliloquy. To be a man, a doer, a builder, a leader, or to be a tool, an unfunny joke, a crusher of funky toadstools. I marveled that Henry could go through with the speech as if we had a choice.

I had been listening and silently rebutting each sentence with my eyes closed; then there was a hush, which in an audience warns that something unplanned is happening. I looked up and saw Henry Reed, the conservative, the proper, the A student, turn his back to the audience and turn to us (the proud graduating class of 1940) and sing, nearly speaking,

> "Lift ev'ry voice and sing*
> Till earth and heaven ring
> Ring with the harmonies of Liberty . . ."

It was the poem written by James Weldon Johnson. It was the music composed by J. Rosamond Johnson. It was the Negro national anthem. Out of habit we were singing it.

Our mothers and fathers stood in the dark hall and joined the hymn of encouragement. A kindergarten teacher led the small children onto the stage and the buttercups and daisies and bunny rabbits marked time and tried to follow:

> "Stony the road we trod
> Bitter the chastening rod

*"Lift Ev'ry Voice and Sing"—words by James Weldon Johnson and music by J. Rosamond Johnson. Copyright by Edward B. Marks Music Corporation. Used by permission.

Felt in the days when hope, unborn, had died.
'Yet with a steady beat
Have not our weary feet
Come to the place for which our fathers sighed?"

Every child I knew had learned that song with his ABC's and along with "Jesus Loves Me This I Know." But I personally had never heard it before. Never heard the words, despite the thousands of times I had sung them. Never thought they had anything to do with me.

On the other hand, the words of Patrick Henry had made such an impression on me that I had been able to stretch myself tall and trembling and say, "I know not what course others may take, but as for me, give me liberty or give me death."

And now I heard, really for the first time:

"We have come over a way that with tears
has been watered,
We have come, treading our path through
the blood of the slaughtered."

While echoes of the song shivered in the air, Henry Reed bowed his head, said "Thank you," and returned to his place in the line. The tears that slipped down many faces were not wiped away in shame.

We were on top again. As always, again. We survived. The depths had been icy and dark, but now a bright sun spoke to our souls. I was no longer simply a member of the proud graduating class of 1940; I was a proud member of the wonderful, beautiful Negro race.

Oh, Black known and unknown poets, how often have your auctioned pains sustained us? Who will compute the lonely nights made less lonely by your songs, or the empty pots made less tragic by your tales?

If we were a people much given to revealing secrets, we might raise monuments and sacrifice to the memories of our poets, but slavery cured us of that weakness. It may be enough, however, to have it said that we survive in exact relationship to the dedication of our poets (include preachers, musicians and blues singers).

Suggestions for Discussion

1. Describe the feeling that comes over the students and teachers at school at the prospect of graduation.

2. How does Angelou describe the feelings in her own family? How is she treated by her brother? Her grandmother?

3. How does the black community become involved in the graduation? What special meaning does it have for them?

4. When do you begin to understand that something will go wrong? What details help you to understand? How do you know that the disappointment will come about from racial causes?

5. Summarize Donleavy's speech. How does Angelou make us feel its condescension and contempt?

6. How does the black community respond? What is the meaning of this response to Angelou? Explain.

Suggestions for Writing

1. Write an essay in which you contrast Angelou and Charles in John Cheever's story "Expelled." Your paper should include an explanation of why school has such different significance for the two of them.

2. Angelou describes a situation once common in segregated Southern schools that were separate but "unequal." Since the 1960s that situation has presumably changed. Write a research paper of 1,000 words in which you report your findings about schools in the South since desegregation. What new problems may have replaced those that Angelou describes?

Bill D. Moyers

Interview with Sara Lawrence Lightfoot

Bill D. Moyers (b. 1934) is one of the most distinguished television journalists in the world, the winner of a host of Emmy Awards, and author of such works as *The Secret Government* (1990) and *Healing and the Mind* (1993).

Sara Lawrence Lightfoot, professor of education at Harvard University, won the prestigious MacArthur Prize Award in 1984. Her books include *Worlds Apart: Relationships Between Families and School* (1978); *Balm in Gilead: Journey of a Healer* (1988); and *The Good High School*, the basis for the following discussion about good teachers and good schools with Bill Moyers.

MOYERS: You use an expression I like very much—the "playfulness of learning." You don't mean something frivolous or trivial, do you?

LIGHTFOOT: No, not at all. A lot of learning has lost its play and has become very concrete, very literal, very exacting. It moves towards an end or conclusion rather than turning ideas on their sides and considering them and laughing about them and being whimsical about them. Some of the best teachers are humorous teachers who see the playfulness of language and are quick and intuitive. Learning is at its best when it's deadly serious and very playful at the same time. When I say deadly serious, I mean that learning should be disciplined and that people should find ways of learning how to ask questions, how to think about evidence, and how to find the truths that are out there. That's a very serious pursuit. On the other hand, in every serious thought, there's a line of laughter. In my own teaching, I'm at my best when I have something that I feel passionate about and talk seriously about, but at the same time, that I can find a way of presenting the play in.

MOYERS: Shakespeare's plays pursue a very serious intent but with a lot of witty lines that reveal the relationship between the tragedy and comedy.

LIGHTFOOT: There is an art—or maybe just a craft—in that interplay of discipline and humor. There is a dynamic, a dialectic.

MOYERS: Do you find this kind of playful learning in schools today?

LIGHTFOOT: Not enough. You can go into a classroom that is an oasis and feel it almost immediately. And you don't hear it everyday in every classroom even when it goes on there. To have this sense of play, you have to be very confident as a thinker and confident in building relationships with students. In most schools today, teachers and students don't feel comfortable enough to be playful. When you're worried about discipline or preoccupied with completing a prescribed curriculum in a particular amount of time, you lose the sense of joy and possibility—the sense of play.

MOYERS: You've got a wonderful example in your book of a teacher who's teaching his class about the impact of Freud on the individual psyche.

LIGHTFOOT: This is a teacher at a very privileged preparatory school in New England working with seniors who have already been accepted to college, and so they are a very relaxed group. They are relatively sophisticated and well schooled. He's teaching them an elective course on Freud at eight o'clock in the morning. He's really trying to guide them through the major themes of Freudian theory, and they're fumbling through these ideas. A number of the students want more certainty, but the teacher really wants them to think, to explore, to weigh the ideas, to consider what might have happened. At one point, a girl comments with cynicism about how old-fashioned and primitive these ideas were. The teacher says, "You know, it takes a very, very long time for ideas to evolve and take shape. It's very hard to challenge authority and change one's view of the world if it's been in place for a long time." This teacher was seeking to give his students a sense of the adventure of learning.

MOYERS: And were they caught up in this?

LIGHTFOOT: Increasingly, as the class went on, they were. Initially, the students were impatient for the answer.

MOYERS: Not the search.

LIGHTFOOT: Exactly. In our schools, students are mostly trained to get to the answer quickly. Part of teaching is helping students learn how to tolerate ambiguity, consider possibilities, and ask questions that are unanswerable. Adolescents have been called "the truth tellers." I don't know that they always tell the truth, but they *do* listen for the truth. They can tell when adults are not authentic—so if you're asking them to take on adventure through a hard set of ideas, and you're not willing to go along, it's unlikely that they will be.

MOYERS: You describe in your book how at the end of one class, the teacher shouts out, "The struggle—I love it! I love it!" If, as you say, "high school is theater," he was having a good play. When did you first learn about the playfulness of education?

LIGHTFOOT: I'm sure I learned it at home and not in school. Our dinner table was always lively with conversation that was both serious and playful. There was never an asymmetry between the adults who had the serious conversation and the kids who watched and listened. All of us were part of the exchange. I learned very early that these two things could go together, so I found the tone of school to be quite monotonous for the most part. There was very little drama, very little play, and very little laughter.

MOYERS: Do you think that's common?

LIGHTFOOT: It's different for different families and subcultural groups. My own parents were very explicit about teaching what I now regard as a counter-curriculum at home. This included reading Frederick Douglass and W. E. B. Du Bois and some of the black poets from our own literary tradition. We also learned how to sing Negro spirituals in what my parents thought was the traditional classic way, which wasn't being taught at all in the schools I went to.

My parents also taught us an ideological counter-curriculum. They were leftists and pacifists. So there was always this contrary conversation going on at home and an attempt to reconcile what we were learning in school with what it was that my parents believed. We became very practiced in the art of negotiating which environment we were in and how to express ourselves in that environment.

MOYERS: So you could change gears from home to school. But what about the child that goes from a difficult home to a bad school? There's almost no hope for that child, is there?

LIGHTFOOT: It's very, very hard because in many families there is not a great conflict between what's taught in school and what's taught at home. The same sort of monotonous values get expressed in both places. It's problematic for a good education because children don't learn to be critical or to ask probing questions. They are just socialized to believe in a set of ideas or ideals that go unchallenged, either at school or at home. I consider myself very privileged to have experienced this dissonance. Most people don't.

The families of poor kids often have no idea what's happening in schools. They send their children off to a setting where they have no participation, no accountability, no voice. There's very little opportunity for them to become critics of that institution.

MOYERS: When did you know you wanted to be a teacher? Was it early?

LIGHTFOOT: No. There were several generations of teachers in my family, so as an adolescent, I wanted to do something different, more exciting. I imagined things like theater and the arts, something more risk-taking and more colorful. My parents had lots of friends in the arts, and I used them as models for what I might become. But I never imagined becoming a professor and doing research and teaching.

Some people regard teaching as a calling; they have wanted it for all of their lives. They may have had wonderful experiences in first grade or in kindergarten, and they say, "That's what I want to be." Then, for the rest of their lives, that's their purpose. Many of them are extraordinary. But teachers can emerge at any time. One of the hopeful signs across the country today is that people are leaving professions like engineering, business, law, and medicine, and becoming what they want to become—teachers. I think that's extraordinary. That's wonderful. Career change of all varieties is invigorating. In careers that are relational, like teaching, it's very important to be able to move out and in because teaching requires such energy and commitment and passion to do well.

MOYERS: I read an essay by your sister, Paula, who is a master teacher and a principal, in which she described the school as "a gathering of gifts." She said, "Everyone—the teacher, the administrator, the principal, the stu-

dent—brings gifts to that classroom, to that school." Do you see it as a
sharing of gifts?

LIGHTFOOT: At its very best. My sister, with her extraordinary talent and
commitment, tries very hard to make that kind of environment in her
school. She manages, most of the time, to do it. It requires extraordinary
courage, nurturance, attention, energy, commitment, empathy, a sense of
orchestration—all of that.

MOYERS: The child brings a gift to school and is not simply coming as an
empty vessel to receive.

LIGHTFOOT: That's right. The whole experience is negotiated. The child
brings himself or herself quite full of history and preoccupations and
dreams and hopes and concerns and fears. And the teacher comes with her
or his own set of those. That's negotiated every day throughout the year,
and it changes over time.

MOYERS: But so much of this individuality gets parked at the door.

LIGHTFOOT: Yes, much of the rich diversity will fade out as school goes on
throughout the year. This problem is much broader than school classrooms,
however. When we draw people together into a group or a community, we
think that's in opposition to individuality—

MOYERS: —that you can't become a member of the community without giving up your own individuality, your own gifts.

LIGHTFOOT: Social scientists often talk about forming the collective as being
opposed to individual initiative. But my sense is that it doesn't have to be
that way at all. There can be a difficult but harmonious coming together—
the building of a rich community *and* individual expression. As a matter of
fact, if we would let some of those individual gifts thrive, there would be
more possibility for a rich community life.

MOYERS: How do we encourage children to recognize what they have to give
in school?

LIGHTFOOT: They need to be praised for individual expression, for the ways in
which they are different from others and not always praised for the ways
that they are like others. Kids are proud of their gifts. If they do something
well when they're little, they announce it. They want praise for it. So it's
not so hard to figure out how to get them to feel good about their gifts. But
once we've told them that those gifts aren't appropriate or legitimate in the
school environment, then it's very hard to rekindle that later on, and
they'll stop bringing them there.

MOYERS: Many classrooms are overcrowded. It must be very hard for a
teacher to both deal with those thirty children as individuals and at the
same time meld them into a community.

LIGHTFOOT: Teachers at their best are wonderful with this process of trying to
get kids to recognize what's very special and different about themselves.
Good teachers also manage to teach kids about being empathetic and help
them recognize that group life in school is different from home life or from
"play" life outside. School life is group life, and part of what they're learning in school is how to live effectively in a group.

Good teachers come in all forms and express themselves very differently. Teachers don't always connect successfully with all thirty kids in a
classroom. But I think one thing all good teachers have in common is that

they regard themselves as thinkers, as existing in the world of ideas. This is true for a nursery teacher and a professor in the most distinguished university. The currency is ideas—but ideas as conveyed through relationships.

MOYERS: I think it was John Henry Newman who said, "We can get information from books, but real knowledge must come from those in whom it lives." The idea has to be incarnate.

LIGHTFOOT: Yes, you not only have to have the knowledge, but you also have to *want* to communicate it. You have to feel deeply about wanting those people to know it. In some sense you have to see yourself reflected in the eyes of those you teach—or at least see your destiny reflected in them.

MOYERS: Your destiny?

LIGHTFOOT: Your future after you're long gone. When teachers can't imagine themselves in their students, when there is no reflection back and forth, then there can be pernicious, discriminatory behavior on the part of the teacher, which is often expressed quite passively. This happens in a lot of schools where kids are very poor or predominantly minority or speak another language.

MOYERS: These are the kids who look around and see devastation and poverty. There are few opportunities and few rewards, so they don't think there's much ahead for them.

LIGHTFOOT: And the teachers don't see the kids' futures as a part of this civilization, or as counting in this world in a significant way.

MOYERS: As you talk, I think about what your book says about how a school takes on the personality of its internal community.

LIGHTFOOT: It's terribly important to recognize that there is a culture alive and throbbing in a school. It takes on the character and color and vitality of those who live inside, the students and teachers. When it doesn't have that kind of reflection of who's inside, then there's something askew.

MOYERS: What does this mean in terms of those schools that are located in the bleak wastelands of the inner city?

LIGHTFOOT: There are all kinds of suggestions for school reform that I absolutely agree with. We need to build schools smaller. We need to give teachers much more of a say in developing curriculum and in seeing themselves as major educational actors in the school and the community. We have to find ways of engaging parents or caretakers in the work of the school and building bridges between families and schools.

But I think what we're talking about here is even more subtle. Somehow we've got to find people to inhabit these schools—adults, teachers—people who see that this work is valuable and valued work and that these children are very much wrapped up in *the teacher's* own future.

MOYERS: The teacher sees her or his destiny in the student, and the student has to see his or her destiny in the teacher.

LIGHTFOOT: It's a very complicated and subtle dynamic, but you can hear it in the voices of teachers when they're talking about their students—you can hear whether they are in fact engaged with people whose lives and futures they care about.

MOYERS: Can you in good conscience urge some of your students to consider going into the inner city of Newark for Philadelphia or Detroit to teach?

LIGHTFOOT: Yes, I can. I think it's imperative that they do.

MOYERS: But how do you teach a teacher to go into a classroom and compensate for broken homes, for alcoholic parents, for a social structure that has collapsed?

LIGHTFOOT: It takes a lot of *chutzpah*. You have to believe that this is possible. I don't think there's any way you could be in this business and not have an optimistic spirit.

Teachers need a very broad outlook on what they're doing. Part of what I try to do with teachers is sketch out the landscape within which they're working. I talk about the origins of some of that deterioration they're experiencing within the school and the community so that they are better able to understand what it is that might motivate their students to tune into school more fully. My whole interest is in trying to get people to understand more comprehensively how to look at communities and school culture so that they can be more effective actors in it.

MOYERS: Do you find a lot of burnout in teachers today? Or is that a cliché?

LIGHTFOOT: It's not a cliché, but it's the wrong word for it. I would call it "boredom"—the need for renewal, change, inspiration, and rewards. When I say rewards, I don't mean only higher salaries, although that's terribly important. It's appreciation, respect, dignity, the recognition that this is a tremendously important role in society and that this is very precious work. The distortions of the negative cultural imagery that is now attached to teaching make it very hard to go in to school every day and work productively.

MOYERS: Do you think there really is a negative image of teaching?

LIGHTFOOT: Oh, absolutely.

MOYERS: But we see movies about teachers changing schools and "60 Minutes" reports on teachers who are dynamically engaging their children.

LIGHTFOOT: This is a new phenomenon—choosing people who are doing extraordinary work in schools and giving them visibility. But for the most part, teachers are demeaned. For example, given a chance, highly educated, high-status, privileged women who now have greater choice are unlikely to go into teaching. They are more likely to choose business, law, medicine, or any of those fields that used to be dominated solely by males.

MOYERS: There's that little saying: "Those who can, do; those who can't, teach."

LIGHTFOOT: There are lots of people who think that and who believe that teaching is a mediocre professional choice. That does a lot of damage to people who have to go in there and work at it every single day.

MOYERS: I cut out from the newspaper this morning a survey by the Carnegie Foundation for the Advancement of Teaching which says that most teachers feel excluded from the most critical decisions on school policy, that they feel like front-row spectators in a reform movement in which the signals are being called by governors, legislators, state education figures—everybody but the teacher on the ground.

LIGHTFOOT: That's a piece of the burnout. When teachers burn out, they aren't saying, "I've worked too hard." They're saying, "I haven't had the opportunity to participate fully in this enterprise." Some teachers are speaking about the politics of teacher's voice. They're saying, "We want more control over our lives in this school." Some of them are making an even more subtle point—they're talking about voice as knowledge. "We know things about this enterprise that researchers and policy makers can never know. We have engaged in this intimate experience, and we have things to tell you if you'd only learn how to ask, and if you'd only learn how to listen." Teachers are talking about their voice as knowledge and insight and control and power.

MOYERS: Why doesn't anybody listen?

LIGHTFOOT: School systems are highly bureaucratized, with people at the top far away from the action, making the decisions about what should go on, and people at the bottom engaged in the enterprise supposedly being the empty vessels through which those decisions get transmitted. When I speak to teachers and talk about this image of teachers as empty vessels, you can just hear moans of recognition and sadness in the room—because that's how they have felt. When you're not participating in making the decisions about what it is you do every day, you feel powerless. It is infantilizing—it makes people feel like children.

MOYERS: One of your brightest recent graduates told me yesterday that she was not going into the classroom because she just didn't feel the system gave her the professional autonomy that she wants. She wasn't talking about more money or more time off. She was talking about her professional voice.

LIGHTFOOT: One of the characteristics of the good schools I looked at was that teachers seemed to have more voice in these ways: in decision-making, in being regarded as having special knowledge, and in being given autonomy to express that knowledge. The good schools supported individual teachers in their personal, idiosyncratic expression. They allowed them, as one principal put it, to "disturb the inertia." I like teachers who disturb the inertia and schools that are colorful with diversity among the teachers. Inevitably, that also allows for color and diversity of expression among students.

MOYERS: A school with less fear, a place where the relationship between the characters grows, and where there's a dialogue between the audience and the teacher.

LIGHTFOOT: Right, although obviously, kids should not be perceived as the audience, but as participants in the drama that unfolds. I think that's terribly important.

MOYERS: You talk about good schools. But every time I mention the word "high school," I can see people's eyes reflecting back to me truancy, dropouts, illiteracy, racial conflict, violence, alcohol, and drug addiction. The image of schools today in the mind of the public is very negative.

LIGHTFOOT: Oh, indeed, I think it is, and some of that imagery is correct. There are too many schools that look like the schools you are describing. But there are many more good schools than we imagine and many more good teachers than we imagine. Part of what I want to do is to describe things that work and not merely things that don't work. I don't want to focus on the pathological or the fragile and weak, but really try to find examples of education at its best and begin to document that in all of its subtlety, complexity, and generosity. I want to convey that portrait so that others might feel inspired to do similar sorts of things. More importantly, others might see themselves in the stories I tell and be able to make up their own story of goodness.

MOYERS: Are there certain things that good schools have in common whether they're in the suburbs, the inner city, or are private academies or church schools?

LIGHTFOOT: Yes, although these may get expressed differently. Good schools have a sense of mission that kids and adults can all articulate. They have an identity. They have a character, a quality that's their own, that feels quite sturdy. They have a set of values. If you walk down the hall, kids will say, in their own language, "This is what this school is about. This is who we are." And adults will echo those same kinds of values. There is a kind of ideological stance that brings coherence to the school.

Also, in a good school, there has to be in the teaching and learning both seriousness and playfulness going on most of the time. Good schools tend to be a chemistry of extraordinary teachers, relatively good teachers, and mediocre teachers. In any professional group we can't expect that we will have goodness throughout. But there has to be this chemistry of wonderful people who are rewarded for being wonderful rather than denigrated for being wonderful, and of good people who continue to be good, and of relatively mediocre folks who are inspired or nudged or supported in becoming better.

Good schools are also disciplined places. I don't mean by that just behavioral discipline, but a place where people set goals and standards and hold each other accountable.

MOYERS: I was struck by the fact that all of the good schools you visited required a lot of the students and expected them to maintain a certain code of behavior. There was a strong respect for law and order and swift punishment for acts of violence.

LIGHTFOOT: That's right, but that requirement is experienced against a backdrop of love and respect. In other words, that respect doesn't come down hard as merely punitive. It's experienced as, "I expect a great deal of you. You are someone." That's a very different message than discipline, which refers to policing schools.

MOYERS: What about the role of the leader—the principal? Do all of these schools have a certain kind of leader?

LIGHTFOOT: The schools had very different leaders. But one quality all of the leaders shared was their focus on nurturance—supporting people and reaching for the best in those who work with them and developing strength rather than expecting blind allegiance and unquestioning loyalty from people. They are people who orchestrate relationships. As one of the principals said to me, "the metaphors are decidedly feminine." In all of these schools, it happened that the six principals were male—but all of them in various ways described the feminine sides of their natures when they talked about leadership in schools. They talked about listening, building a sense of community, sustaining relationships, and supporting people through failure.

MOYERS: Mothering.

LIGHTFOOT: Yes, in the best sense. Interestingly, a few of these principals had stereotypic jock masculine images. A couple of them had been successful coaches in big schools and talked proudly about their athletic heritage and success. But if you watched them in action, they were doing very nonstereotyped things.

MOYERS: Can you teach that to someone, or does that come with the genes?
LIGHTFOOT: It comes with experience, but you can find ways of providing the experience. That can start very young. It has to do with increasing the repertoire of possibilities for male and female children. If we think of leadership as taking the best of the stereotypic characteristics of male and female and deciding when and how to use them, then we recognize that we must offer boys and girls opportunities for developing in myriad ways that most of them haven't been offered before.
MOYERS: If the new President called you and said, "Professor Lightfoot, how should I address the school crisis?"—what would you tell him?
LIGHTFOOT: I would ask him to focus on teaching and learning, on the essence of the enterprise rather than on how to restructure the institution. Somehow the American public has to get back to the great richness and mystery of learning, the playfulness and seriousness of learning, and how that can be nurtured in schools by teachers in classrooms. I would ask him to focus on how to attract good people back into this profession, and how we can continue to support them once they have entered the profession.
MOYERS: There's a general lament in the country that the schools aren't meeting our great expectations of them, that they are not producing civilized and literate populations, that they're not mending inequalities, and that they're not encouraging innovation, creativity, and discovery. Do you share the general view that our schools are in crisis?
LIGHTFOOT: I agree with that lament to a certain extent. But I think we have expected far too much of schools. We have had very high aspirations for schools, asking them to solve all of our cultural, social, and economic crises. This is such an extraordinary set of agendas. Schools have never lived up to our hopes and dreams, even as far back as John Dewey and Horace Mann, who had great hopes for the way schools would reconstruct American society and make it more cohesive and healthy. So this is an old lament.

Part of what we have to do is to look at the broad ecology of education, at the other institutions that educate. We must develop a more realistic view of the roles that schools can play. It isn't only up to schools to undo racism and social privilege and poverty. It is very much a part of their responsibilities, but other institutions have to participate in that process as well.
MOYERS: Teachers can't be parents and preachers and doctors. A lot of teachers say they're expected to play every role.
LIGHTFOOT: In some sense schools have been our most visible and vulnerable institutions. They are the stage on which a lot of cultural crises get played out. We see in schools most vividly the inequities and the hypocrisy. It's right there in front of you, and it's enraging. We tend to blame the teachers, who are the primary adult actors there, or the system, if we don't want to blame individuals. But schools are connected to other institutions of learning and development. This is not a back-to-basics sermon. I'm not saying that schools should omit things like art, theater, or physical education. But we do have to more realistically appraise what it is that schools can do.
MOYERS: For what should schools be held accountable?

LIGHTFOOT: Anyone who graduates from high school should be literate and should be able to reason and think analytically. That's a very basic account- ability that we must hold schools to. I don't think we can hold schools accountable for all students feeling good about themselves, for example, or for making sure that kids don't smoke or don't get pregnant. Those respon- sibilities are broader in scope.

MOYERS: We blame the schools when schools are not the only teachers. Cul- ture teaches all the time. We learn from television, politics, sports, ath- letes, and business.

LIGHTFOOT: The learning is going on all the time. It's useful to think about the difference between schooling and education. Schooling is what happens inside the walls of the school, some of which is educational. Education hap- pens everywhere, and it happens from the moment a child is born—and some people say before—until a person dies. It's a far more complicated, overarching process than can ever be handled inside the walls of a school. Good teachers know the various ways in which children are educated out- side of the school and what their particular responsibilities are inside of the school.

MOYERS: What do we do about bad teachers?

LIGHTFOOT: I am really very disturbed about the processes of tenuring teach- ers. It takes a very short time for people to be tenured, and the standards tend to be so low that most people, if they are not absolutely pernicious, will get tenure. Once having gotten tenure, many people, particularly poor teachers, relax into getting worse. There is something very wrong with a system that allows that. We need a system to reevaluate teachers and to support them in doing a good job.

MOYERS: That would include a lot of peer judgments.

LIGHTFOOT: Yes. Teaching is a very autonomous experience—but the flip side of autonomy is that teachers experience loneliness and isolation. Teachers tend to miss other adult company, colleagueship, relationship, criticism, camaraderie, support, and intellectual stimulation. There must be time and space in school days for teachers to come together to support one another, to respond critically to one another, and to develop plans together.

MOYERS: Like motherhood, which is the most isolated work in the world.

LIGHTFOOT: Yes, there are very few opportunities for mothers to get together with other mothers and to ask, "Am I going crazy, or does this happen to all mothers of two-year-olds?" That's the real question all the time. Is this just me, or is this quite typical? Do lots of kids do this? Do lots of mothers experience this? The need for company in one's work, for criticism and support, for scrutiny, for someone to tell you you're not crazy, is there in all of us. It's very hard if you are living within the cellular environment of a classroom, and there are no rewards for collegial relationship or discourse.

MOYERS: Do you know what I thought you would have told the new Presi- dent? Something you have said before: "Tell the country that the way to better schools is to choose better teachers and treat them like chosen people."

LIGHTFOOT: Yes, I think that's right. We need to attract the best people into teaching and then to keep on telling them that they are chosen because they're so good—and to believe that, to be commenting on the reality.

MOYERS: Do you feel like a chosen person?

LIGHTFOOT: I feel privileged to be doing what I'm doing, and I do feel a call-ing in my work. I feel that my mission is broader than academic inquiry. I want to be part of the world. I want to be part of social change and social transformation. I'm constantly trying to find ways of communicating what I know to broader audiences, and trying to get more people engaged in the conversation that often stops at glib rhetoric about our schools. How can we get teachers involved in thinking about schools, in sharing their knowl-edge about schools, and in voicing it? Part of it is to write books with which they can identify, not the academic pieces that seem impenetrable and with which they feel no identity.

MOYERS: So it's possible to be within the academy and not be out of touch with the other world out there.

LIGHTFOOT: It's difficult because the rewards of the academy often go with thinking about esoteric abstractions that are difficult for most people in the outer world to penetrate. But there are those of us who see our role as quite different. I am very definitely a boundary sitter, someone who really thinks that knowledge has a great deal to do with how people live and how people think about their living. I want to be able to describe that with a clear enough voice so that people will be able to relate to it, and be identi-fied with it, perhaps even be inspired by it. Communicating what we know is not merely an intellectual, cerebral exercise. We must also try to move people, speak to their head *and* their heart, so that they might do some-thing about it. That's my hope.

Suggestions for Discussion

1. What does Lightfoot mean by the "playfulness of learning"?

2. Describe her education.

3. In what sense does every child bring "a gift to school"?

4. How does Lightfoot view the role of the teacher in today's school?

5. What common characteristics do good schools have?

Suggestions for Writing

1. Using your own experiences in education, describe a good teacher, a good class-room, and a good school.

2. What attractions and drawbacks do you see in teaching as a profession?

Paule Marshall

From the Poets in the Kitchen

Paule Marshall (b. 1929), whose family came from Barbados, is the author of Brown Girl (1981), The Chosen Place, the Timeless People (1984), and Daughters (1991). In this selection she writes about the importance of informal kitchen talk in acquiring language skills.

Some years ago, when I was teaching a graduate seminar in fiction at Columbia University, a well-known male novelist visited my class to speak on his development as a writer. In discussing his formative years, he didn't realize it but he seriously endangered his life by remarking that women writers are luckier than those of his sex because they usually spend so much time as children around their mothers and their mothers' friends in the kitchen.

What did he say that for? The women students immediately forgot about being in awe of him and began readying their attack for the question and answer period later on. Even I bristled. There again was that awful image of women locked away from the world in the kitchen with only each other to talk to, and their daughters locked in with them.

But my guest wasn't really being sexist or trying to be provocative or even spoiling for a fight. What he meant—when he got around to examining himself more fully—was that, given the way children are (or were) raised in our society, with little girls kept closer to home and their mothers, the woman writer stands a better chance of being exposed, while growing up, to the kind of talk that goes on among women, more often than not in the kitchen; and that this experience gives her an edge over her male counterpart by instilling in her an appreciation for ordinary speech.

It was clear that my guest lecturer attached great importance to this, which is understandable. Common speech and the plain, workaday words that make it up are, after all, the stock in trade of some of the best fiction writers. They are the principal means by which a character in a novel or story reveals himself and gives voice sometimes to profound feelings and complex ideas about himself and the world. Perhaps the proper measure of a writer's talent is his skill in rendering everyday speech—when it is appropriate to his story—as well as his ability to tap, to exploit, the beauty, poetry and wisdom it often contains.

"If you say what's on your mind in the language that comes to you from your parents and your street and friends you'll probably say something beautiful." Grace Paley tells this, she says, to her students at the beginning of every writing course.

It's all a matter of exposure and a training of the ear for the would-be writer in those early years of his or her apprenticeship. And, according to my guest lecturer, this training, the best of it, often takes place in as unglamorous a setting as the kitchen.

He didn't know it, but he was essentially describing my experience as a little girl. I grew up among poets. Now they didn't look like poets—whatever that breed is supposed to look like. Nothing about them suggested that poetry was their calling. They were just a group of ordinary housewives and mothers, my mother included, who dressed in a way (shapeless housedresses, dowdy felt hats and long, dark, solemn coats) that made it impossible for me to imagine they had ever been young.

Nor did they do what poets were supposed to do—spend their days in an attic room writing verses. They never put pen to paper except to write occasionally to their relatives in Barbados. "I take my pen in hand hoping these few lines will find you in health as they leave me fair for the time being," was the way their letters invariably began. Rather, their day was spent "scrubbing floor," as they described the work they did.

Several mornings a week these unknown bards would put an apron and a pair of old house shoes in a shopping bag and take the train or streetcar from our section of Brooklyn out to Flatbush. There, those who didn't have steady jobs would wait on certain designated corners for the white housewives in the neighborhood to come along and bargain with them over pay for a day's work cleaning their houses. This was the ritual even in the winter.

Later, armed with the few dollars they had earned, which in their vocabulary became "a few raw-mouth pennies," they made their way back to our neighborhood, where they would sometimes stop off to have a cup of tea or cocoa together before going home to cook dinner for their husbands and children.

The basement kitchen of the brownstone house where my family lived was the usual gathering place. Once inside the warm safety of its walls the women threw off the drab coats and hats, seated themselves at the large center table, drank their cups of tea or cocoa, and talked. While my sister and I sat at a smaller table over in a corner doing our homework, they talked—endlessly, passionately, poetically, and with impressive range. No subject was beyond them. True, they would indulge in the usual gossip: whose husband was running with whom, whose daughter looked slightly "in the way" (pregnant) under her bridal gown as she walked down the aisle. That sort of thing. But they also tackled the great issues of the time. They were always, for example, discussing the state of the economy. It was the mid and late 30's then, and the aftershock of the Depression, with its soup lines and suicides on Wall Street, was still being felt.

Some people, they declared, didn't know how to deal with adversity. They didn't know that you had to "tie up your belly" (hold in the pain, that is) when things got rough and go on with life. They took their image from the bellyband that is tied around the stomach of a newborn baby to keep the navel pressed in.

They talked politics. Roosevelt was their hero. He had come along and rescued the country with relief and jobs, and in gratitude they christened their sons Franklin and Delano and hoped they would live up to the names.

If F.D.R. was their hero, Marcus Garvey was their God. The name of the fiery, Jamaican-born black nationalist of the 20's was constantly invoked around the table. For he had been their leader when they first came to the United States from the West Indies shortly after World War I. They had contributed to his organization, the United Negro Improvement Association (UNIA), out of their meager salaries, bought shares in his ill-fated Black Star Shipping Line, and at the height of the movement they had marched as members of his "nurses' brigade" in their white uniforms up Seventh Avenue in Harlem during the great Garvey Day parades. Garvey: He lived on through the power of their memories.

And their talk was of war and rumors of wars. They raged against World War II when it broke out in Europe, blaming it on the politicians. "It's these politicians. They're the ones always starting up all this lot of war. But what they care? It's the poor people got to suffer and mothers with their sons." If it was *their* sons, they swore they would keep them out of the Army by giving them soap to eat each day to make their hearts sound defective. Hitler? He was for them "the devil incarnate."

Then there was home. They reminisced often and at length about home. The old country. Barbados—or Bimshire, as they affectionately called it. The little Caribbean island in the sun they loved but had to leave. "Poor—poor but sweet" was the way they remembered it.

And naturally they discussed their adopted home. America came in for both good and bad marks. They lashed out at it for the racism they encountered. They took to task some of the people they worked for, especially those who gave them only a hard-boiled egg and a few spoonfuls of cottage cheese for lunch. "As if anybody can scrub floor on an egg and some cheese that don't have no taste to it!"

Yet although they caught H in "this man country," as they called America, it was nonetheless a place where "you could at least see your way to make a dollar." That much they acknowledged. They might even one day accumulate enough dollars, with both them and their husbands working, to buy the brownstone houses which, like my family, they were only leasing at that period. This was their consuming ambition: to "buy house" and to see the children through.

There was no way for me to understand it at the time, but the talk that filled the kitchen those afternoons was highly functional. It served as therapy, the cheapest kind available to my mother and her friends. Not only did it help them recover from the long wait on the corner that morning and the bargaining over their labor, it restored them to a sense of themselves and reaffirmed their self-worth. Through language they were able to overcome the humiliations of the work-day.

But more than therapy, that freewheeling, wide-ranging, exuberant talk functioned as an outlet for the tremendous creative energy they possessed. They were women in whom the need for self-expression was strong, and since language was the only vehicle readily available to them they made of it an art form that—in keeping with the African tradition in which art and life are one—was an integral part of their lives.

And their talk was a refuge. They never really ceased being baffled and overwhelmed by America—its vastness, complexity and power. Its strange customs and laws. At a level beyond words they remained fearful and in awe. Their uneasiness and fear were even reflected in their attitude toward the children they had given birth to in this country. They referred to those like myself, the little Brooklyn-born Bajans (Barbadians), as "these New York children" and complained that they couldn't discipline us properly because of the laws here. "You can't beat these children as you would like, you know, because the authorities in this place will dash you in jail for them. After all, these is New York children." Not only were we different, American, we had, as they saw it, escaped their ultimate authority.

Confronted therefore by a world they could not encompass, which even limited their rights as parents, and at the same time finding themselves permanently separated from the world they had known, they took refuge in language. "Language is the only homeland," Czeslaw Milosz, the emigré Polish writer and Nobel Laureate, has said. This is what it became for the women at the kitchen table.

It served another purpose also, I suspect. My mother and her friends were after all the female counterpart of Ralph Ellison's invisible man. Indeed, you might say they suffered a triple invisibility, being black, female and foreigners. They really didn't count in American society except as a source of cheap labor. But given the kind of women they were, they couldn't tolerate the fact of their invisibility, their powerlessness. And they fought back, using the only weapon at their command: the spoken word.

Those late afternoon conversations on a wide range of topics were a way for them to feel they exercised some measure of control over their lives and the events that shaped them. "Soully-gal, talk yuh talk!" they were always exhorting each other. "In this man world you got to take yuh mouth and make a gun!" They were in control, if only verbally and if only for the two hours or so that they remained in our house.

For me, sitting over in the corner, being seen but not heard, which was the rule for children in those days, it wasn't only what the women talked about—the content—but the way they put things—their style. The insight, irony, wit and humor they brought to their stories and discussions and their poet's inventiveness and daring with language—which of course I could only sense but not define back then.

They had taken the standard English taught them in the primary schools of Barbados and transformed it into an idiom, an instrument that more adequately described them—changing around the syntax and imposing their own rhythm and accent so that the sentences were more pleasing to their ears. They added the few African sounds and words that had survived, such as the derisive suck-teeth sound and the word "yam," meaning to eat. And to make it more vivid, more in keeping with their expressive quality, they brought to bear a raft of metaphors, parables, Biblical quotations, sayings and the like:

"The sea ain't got no back door," they would say, meaning that it wasn't like a house where if there was a fire you could run out the back. Meaning that it was not to be trifled with. And meaning perhaps in a larger sense that man should treat all of nature with caution and respect.

"I has read hell by heart and called every generation blessed!" They sometimes went in for hyperbole.

A woman expecting a baby was never said to be pregnant. They never used that word. Rather, she was "in the way" or, better yet, "tumbling big." "Guess who I butt up on in the market the other day tumbling big again!"

And a woman with a reputation of being too free with her sexual favors was known in their book as a "thoroughfare"—the sense of men like a steady stream of cars moving up and down the road of her life. Or she might be dubbed "a free-bee," which was my favorite of the two. I liked the image it conjured up of a woman scandalous perhaps but independent, who flitted from one flower to another in a garden of male beauties, sampling their nectar, taking her pleasure at will, the roles reversed.

And nothing, no matter how beautiful, was ever described as simply beautiful. It was always "beautiful-ugly": the beautiful-ugly dress, the beautiful-ugly house, the beautiful-ugly car. Why the word "ugly," I used to wonder, when the thing they were referring to was beautiful, and they knew it. Why the antonym, the contradiction, the linking of opposites? It used to puzzle me greatly as a child.

There is the theory in linguistics which states that the idiom of a people, the way they use language, reflects not only the most fundamental views they hold of themselves and the world but their very conception of reality. Perhaps in using the term "beautiful-ugly" to describe nearly everything, my mother and her friends were expressing what they believed to be a fundamental dualism in life: the idea that a thing is at the same time its opposite, and that these opposites, these contradictions make up the whole. But theirs was not a Manichean brand of dualism that sees matter, flesh, the body, as inherently evil, because they constantly addressed each other as "soullygal"—soul: spirit; gal: the body, flesh, the visible self. And it was clear from their tone that they gave one as much weight and importance as the other. They had never heard of the mind/body split.

As for God, they summed up His essential attitude in a phrase. "God," they would say, "don' love ugly and He ain't stuck on pretty."

Using everyday speech, the simple commonplace words—but always with imagination and skill—they gave voice to the most complex ideas. Flannery O'Connor would have approved of how they made ordinary language work, as she put it, "double-time," stretching, shading, deepening its meaning. Like Joseph Conrad they were always trying to infuse new life in the "old old words worn thin . . . by . . . careless usage." And the goals of their oral art were the same as his: "to make you hear, to make you feel . . . to make you see." This was their guiding esthetic.

By the time I was 8 or 9, I graduated from the corner of the kitchen to the neighborhood library, and thus from the spoken to the written word. The Macon Street Branch of the Brooklyn Public Library was an imposing half block long edifice of heavy gray masonry, with glass-paneled doors at the front and two tall metal torches symbolizing the light that comes of learning flanking the wide steps outside.

The inside was just as impressive. More steps—of pale marble with gleaming brass railings at the center and sides—led up to the circulation desk, and a great pendulum clock gazed down from the balcony stacks that faced the entrance. Usually stationed at the top of the steps like the guards outside Buckingham Palace was the custodian, a stern-faced West Indian type who for years, until I was old enough to obtain an adult card, would immediately shoo me with one hand into the Children's Room and with the other threaten me into silence, a finger to his lips. You would have thought he was the chief librarian and not just someone whose job it was to keep the brass polished and the clock wound. I put him in a story called "Barbados" years later and had terrible things happen to him at the end.

I was sheltered from the storm of adolescence in the Macon Street library, reading voraciously, indiscriminately, everything from Jane Austen to Zane Grey, but with a special passion for the long, full-blown, richly detailed 18th- and 19th-century picaresque tales: *Tom Jones, Great Expectations, Vanity Fair.*

But although I loved nearly everything I read and would enter fully into the lives of the characters—indeed, would cease being myself and become them—I sensed a lack after a time. Something I couldn't quite define was missing. And then one day, browsing in the poetry section, I came across a book by someone called Paul Laurence Dunbar, and opening it I found the photograph of a wistful, sad-eyed poet who to my surprise was black. I turned to a poem at random. "Little brown-baby wif spa'klin' / eyes / Come to yo' pappy an' set on his knee." Although I had a little difficulty at first with the words in dialect, the poem spoke to me as nothing I had read before of the closeness, the special relationship I had had with my father, who by then had become an ardent believer in Father Divine and gone to live in Father's "kingdom" in Harlem. Reading it helped to ease somewhat the tight knot of sorrow and longing I carried around in my chest that refused to go away. I read another poem. "Lias! Lias! Bless de Lawd! / Don' you know de day's / erbroad? / Ef you don' get up, you scamp / Dey'll be trouble in dis camp." I laughed. It reminded me of the way my mother sometimes yelled at my sister and me to get out of bed in the mornings.

And another: "Seen my lady home las' night / Jump back, honey, jump back. / Hel' huh han' an' sque'z it tight . . ." About love between a black man and a black woman. I had never seen that written about before and it roused in me all kinds of delicious feelings and hopes.

And I began to search then for books and stories and poems about "The Race" (as it was put back then), about my people. While not abandoning Thackeray, Fielding, Dickens and the others, I started asking the reference librarian, who was white, for books by Negro writers, although I must admit I did so at first with a feeling of shame—the shame I and many others used to experience in those days whenever the word "Negro" or "colored" came up.

No grade school literature teacher of mine had ever mentioned Dunbar or James Weldon Johnson or Langston Hughes. I didn't know that Zora Neale Hurston existed and was busy writing and being published during those years. Nor was I made aware of people like Frederick Douglass and Harriet Tubman—their spirit and example—or the great 19th-century abolitionist and feminist Sojourner Truth. There wasn't even Negro History Week when I attended P.S. 35 on Decatur Street!

What I needed, what all the kids—West Indian and native black American alike—with whom I grew up needed, was an equivalent of the Jewish shul, someplace where we could go after school—the schools that were shortchanging us—and read works by those like ourselves and learn about our history.

It was around that time also that I began harboring the dangerous thought of someday trying to write myself. Perhaps a poem about an apple tree, although I had never seen one. Or the story of a girl who could magically transplant herself to wherever she wanted to be in the world—such as

Father Divine's kingdom in Harlem. Dunbar—his dark, eloquent face, his large volume of poems—permitted me to dream that I might someday write, and with something of the power with words my mother and her friends possessed.

When people at readings and writers' conferences ask me who my major influences were, they are sometimes a little disappointed when I don't immediately name the usual literary giants. True, I am indebted to those writers, white and black, whom I read during my formative years and still read for instruction and pleasure. But they were preceded in my life by another set of giants whom I always acknowledge before all others: the group of women around the table long ago. They taught me my first lesson in the narrative art. They trained my ear. They set a standard of excellence. This is why the best of my work must be attributed to them; it stands as testimony to the rich legacy of language and culture they so freely passed on to me in the word-shop of the kitchen.

Suggestions for Discussion

1. Explain how the education of the would-be writer could take "place in as unglamorous a setting as the kitchen."

2. Discuss kitchen talk as "therapy" or as an outlet for "tremendous creative energy."

3. Identify and discuss three or four examples of lively "talk" as presented by Marshall.

Suggestions for Writing

1. Record and analyze informal language use in a familiar setting.

2. Examine how your own language use has been shaped by "freewheeling, wide-ranging, exuberant talk."

Essays

Lewis Thomas

Humanities and Science

Lewis Thomas (1913–1993) was a physician whose medical career centered on the Sloan Kettering Cancer Care Center in New York, the city of his birth. He has written for medical journals at the same time that he has written popular essays to present science and the scientist's view of the world to the lay public. He won the National Book Award in 1974 for *The Lives of a Cell: Notes of a Biology Watcher.* Other collections include *More Notes of a Biology Watcher* (1979), *The Youngest Science: Notes of a Medicine-Watcher* (1983), *Late Night Thoughts on Listening to Mahler's Ninth* (1984), and *The Fragile Species* (1992). In the following essay, Dr. Thomas advocates open discussion of what science does not yet know or understand.

Lord Kelvin was one of the great British physicists of the late nineteenth century, an extraordinarily influential figure in his time, and in some ways a paradigm of conventional, established scientific leadership. He did a lot of good and useful things, but once or twice he, like Homer, nodded. The instances are worth recalling today, for we have nodders among our scientific eminences still, from time to time, needing to have their elbows shaken.

On one occasion, Kelvin made a speech on the overarching importance of numbers. He maintained that no observation of nature was worth paying serious attention to unless it could be stated in precisely quantitative terms. The numbers were the final and only test, not only of truth but about meaning as well. He said, "When you can measure what you are speaking about, and express it in numbers, you know something about it. But when you cannot— your knowledge is of a meagre and unsatisfactory kind."

But, as at least one subsequent event showed, Kelvin may have had things exactly the wrong way round. The task of converting observations into numbers is the hardest of all, the last task rather than the first thing to be done, and it can be done only when you have learned, beforehand, a great deal about the observations themselves. You can, to be sure, achieve a very deep understanding of nature by quantitative measurement, but you must know what you are talking about before you can begin applying the numbers for making predictions. In Kelvin's case, the problem at hand was the age of the earth and solar system. Using what was then known about the sources of energy and the loss of energy from the physics of that day, he calculated that neither the earth nor the sun were older than several hundred million years. This caused a considerable stir in biological and geological circles, especially among the evolutionists. Darwin himself was distressed by the numbers; the time was much too short for the theory of evolution. Kelvin's figures were described by Darwin as one of his "sorest troubles."

T. H. Huxley had long been aware of the risks involved in premature extrapolations from mathematical treatment of biological problems. He said, in an 1869 speech to the Geological Society concerning numbers, "This seems to be one of the many cases in which the admitted accuracy of mathematical processes is allowed to throw a wholly inadmissible appearance of authority over the results obtained by them. . . . As the grandest mill in the world will not extract wheat flour from peascods, so pages of formulas will not get a definite result out of loose data."

The trouble was that the world of physics had not moved fast enough to allow for Kelvin's assumptions. Nuclear fusion and fission had not yet been dreamed of, and the true age of the earth could not even be guessed from the data in hand. It was not yet the time for mathematics in this subject.

There have been other examples, since those days, of the folly of using numbers and calculations uncritically. Kelvin's own strong conviction that science could not be genuine science without measuring things was catching. People in other fields of endeavor, hankering to turn their disciplines into exact sciences, beset by what has since been called "physics envy," set about converting whatever they knew into numbers and thence into equations with predictive pretensions. We have it with us still, in economics, sociology, psychology, history, even, I fear, in English-literature criticism and linguistics, and it frequently works, when it works at all, with indifferent success. The risks of untoward social consequences in work of this kind are considerable. It is as important—and as hard—to learn *when* to use mathematics as *how* to use it, and this matter should remain high on the agenda of consideration for education in the social and behavioral sciences.

Of course, Kelvin's difficulty with the age of the earth was an exceptional, almost isolated instance of failure in quantitative measurement in the nineteenth-century physics. The instruments devised for approaching nature by way of physics became increasingly precise and powerful, carrying the field through electromagnetic theory, triumph after triumph, and setting the stage for the great revolution of twentieth-century physics. There is no doubt about it: measurement works when the instruments work, and when you have a fairly clear idea of what it is that is being measured, and when you know what to do with the numbers when they tumble out. The system for gaining information and comprehension about nature works so well, indeed, that it carries another hazard: the risk of convincing yourself that you know everything.

Kelvin himself fell into this trap toward the end of the century. (I don't mean to keep picking on Kelvin, who was a very great scientist; it is just that he happened to say a couple of things I find useful for this discussion.) He stated, in a summary of the achievements of nineteenth-century physics, that it was an almost completed science; virtually everything that needed knowing about the material universe had been learned; there were still a few anomalies and inconsistencies in electromagnetic theory, a few loose ends to be tied up, but this would be done within the next several years. Physics, in these terms, was not a field any longer likely to attract, as it previously had, the brightest and most imaginative young brains. The most interesting part of the work had already been done. Then, within the next decade, came radiation, Planck, the quantum, Einstein, Rutherford, Bohr, and all the rest—quantum mechanics—and the whole field turned over and became a brand-new sort of human endeavor, still now, in the view of many physicists, almost a full century later, a field only at its beginnings.

But even today, despite the amazements that are turning up in physics each year, despite the jumps taken from the smallest parts of nature—particle physics—to the largest of all—the cosmos itself—the impression of science that the public gains is rather like the impression left in the nineteenth-century public mind by Kelvin. Science, in this view, is first of all a matter of simply getting all the numbers together. The numbers are sitting out there in nature, waiting to be found, sorted and totted up. If only they had enough robots and enough computers, the scientists could go off to the beach and wait for their papers to be written for them. Second of all, what we know about nature today is pretty much the whole story: we are very nearly home and dry. From here on, it is largely a problem of tying up loose ends, tidying nature up, getting the files in order. The only real surprises for the future— and it is about those that the public is becoming more concerned and apprehensive—are the technological applications that the scientists may be cooking up from today's knowledge.

I suggest that the scientific community is to blame. If there are disagreements between the world of the humanities and the scientific enterprise as to the place and importance of science in a liberal-arts education, and the role of science in twentieth-century culture, I believe that the scientists are themselves responsible for a general misunderstanding of what they are really up to.

Over the past half century, we have been teaching the sciences as though they were the same academic collection of cut-and-dried subjects as always, and—here is what has really gone wrong—as though they would always be the same. The teaching of today's biology, for example, is pretty much the same kind of exercise as the teaching of Latin was when I was in high school long ago. First of all, the fundamentals, the underlying laws, the essential grammar, and then the reading of texts. Once mastered, that is that: Latin is Latin and forever after will be Latin. And biology is precisely biology, a vast array of hard facts to be learned as fundamentals, followed by a reading of the texts.

Moreover, we have been teaching science as though its facts were somehow superior to the facts in all other scholarly disciplines, more fundamental, more solid, less subject to subjectivism, immutable. English literature is not just one way of thinking, it is all sorts of ways. Poetry is a moving target. The facts that underlie art, architecture, and music are not really hard facts, and you can change them any way you like by arguing about them, but science is treated as an altogether different kind of learning: an unambiguous, unalterable, and endlessly useful display of data needing only to be packaged and installed somewhere in one's temporal lobe in order to achieve a full understanding of the natural world.

And it is, of course, not like this at all. In real life, every field of science that I can think of is incomplete, and most of them—whatever the record of accomplishment over the past two hundred years—are still in the earliest stage of their starting point. In the fields I know best, among the life sciences, it is required that the most expert and sophisticated minds be capable of changing those minds, often with a great lurch, every few years. In some branches of biology the mind-changing is occurring with accelerating velocities. The next week's issue of any scientific journal can turn a whole field upside down, shaking out any number of immutable ideas and installing new bodies of dogma, and this is happening all the time. It is an almost everday event in physics, in chemistry, in materials research, in neurobiology, in genetics, in immunology. The hard facts tend to soften overnight, melt away, and vanish under the pressure of new hard facts, and the interpretations of what appear to be the most solid aspects of nature are subject to change, now more than at any other time in history. The conclusions reached in science are always, when looked at closely, far more provisional and tentative than are most of the assumptions arrived at by our colleagues in the humanities.

The running battle now in progress between the sociobiologists and the antisociobiologists is a marvel for students to behold, close up. To observe, in open-mouthed astonishment, the polarized extremes, one group of highly intelligent, beautifully trained, knowledgeable, and imaginative scientists maintaining that all sorts of behavior, animal and human, are governed exclusively by genes, and another group of equally talented scientists saying precisely the opposite and asserting that all behavior is set and determined by the environment, or by culture, and both sides brawling in the pages of periodicals such as *The New York Review of Books*, is an educational experience that no college student should be allowed to miss. The essential lesson to be learned has nothing to do with the relative validity of the facts underlying the argument, it is the argument itself that is the education: we do not yet know enough to settle such questions.

It is true that at any given moment there is the appearance of satisfaction, even self-satisfaction, within every scientific discipline. On any Tuesday morning, if asked, a good working scientist will gladly tell you that the affairs of the field are nicely in order, that things are finally looking clear and making sense, and all is well. But come back again, on another Tuesday, and he may let you know that the roof has just fallen in on his life's work, that all the old ideas—last week's ideas in some cases—are no longer good ideas, that something strange has happened.

It is the very strangeness of nature that makes science engrossing. That ought to be at the center of science teaching. There are more than seven-times-seven types of ambiguity in science, awaiting analysis. The poetry of Wallace Stevens is crystal-clear alongside the genetic code.

I prefer to turn things around in order to make precisely the opposite case. Science, especially twentieth-century science, has provided us with a glimpse of something we never really knew before, the revelation of human ignorance. We have been used to the belief, down one century after another, that we more or less comprehend everything bar one or two mysteries like the mental processes of our gods. Every age, not just the eighteenth century, regarded itself as the Age of Reason, and we have never lacked for explanations of the world and its ways. Now, we are being brought up short, and this has been the work of science. We have a wilderness of mystery to make our way through in the centuries ahead, and we will need science for this but not science alone. Science will, in its own time, produce the data and some of the meaning in the data, but never the full meaning. For getting a full grasp, for perceiving real significance when significance is at hand, we shall need minds at work from all sorts of brains outside the fields of science, most of all the brains of poets, of course, but also those of artists, musicians, philosophers, historians, writers in general.

It is primarily because of this need that I would press for changes in the way science is taught. There is a need to teach the young people who will be doing the science themselves, but this will always be a small minority among us. There is a deeper need to teach science to those who will be needed for thinking about it, and this means pretty nearly everyone else, in hopes that a few of these people—a much smaller minority than the scientific community and probably a lot harder to find—will, in the thinking, be able to imagine new levels of meaning that are likely to be lost on the rest of us.

In addition, it is time to develop a new group of professional thinkers, perhaps a somewhat larger group than the working scientists, who can create a discipline of scientific criticism. We have had good luck so far in the emergence of a few people ranking as philosophers of science and historians and journalists of science, and I hope more of these will be coming along, but we have not yet seen a Ruskin or a Leavis or an Edmund Wilson. Science needs critics of this sort, but the public at large needs them more urgently.

I suggest that the introductory courses in science, at all levels from grade school through college, be radically revised. Leave the fundamentals, the so-called basics, aside for a while, and concentrate the attention of all students on the things that are *not* known. You cannot possibly teach quantum mechanics without mathematics, to be sure, but you can describe the strangeness of the world opened up by quantum theory. Let it be known, early on, that there are deep mysteries, and profound paradoxes, revealed in their distant outlines, by the quantum. Let it be known that these can be approached more closely, and puzzled over, once the language of mathematics has been sufficiently mastered.

Teach at the outset, before any of the fundamentals, the still imponderable puzzles of cosmology. Let it be known, as clearly as possible, by the youngest minds, that there are some things going on in the universe that lie beyond comprehension, and make it plain how little is known.

Do not teach that biology is a useful and perhaps profitable science; that can come later. Teach instead that there are structures squirming inside all our cells, providing all the energy for living, that are essentially foreign creatures, brought in for symbiotic living a billion or so years ago, the lineal descendants of bacteria. Teach that we do not have the ghost of an idea how they got there, where they came from, or how they evolved to their present structure and function. The details of oxidative phosphorylation and photosynthesis can come later.

Teach ecology early on. Let it be understood that the earth's life is a system of interliving, interdependent creatures, and that we do not understand at all how it works. The earth's environment, from the range of atmospheric gases to the chemical constituents of the sea, has been held in an almost unbelievably improbable state of regulated balance since life began, and the regulation of stability and balance is accomplished solely by the life itself, like the internal environment of an immense organism, and we do not know how *that* one works, even less what it means. Teach that.

Go easy, I suggest, on the promises sometimes freely offered by science. Technology relies and depends on science these days, more than ever before, but technology is nothing like the first justification for doing research, nor is it necessarily an essential product to be expected from science. Public decisions about what to have in the way of technology are totally different problems from decisions about science, and the two enterprises should not be tangled together. The central task of science is to arrive, stage by stage, at a clearer comprehension of nature, but this does not mean, as it is sometimes claimed to mean, a search for mastery over nature. Science may provide us, one day, with a better understanding of ourselves, but never, I hope, with a set of technologies for doing something or other to improve ourselves. I am made nervous by assertions that human consciousness will someday be unraveled by research, laid out for close scrutiny like the workings of a computer, and then, *and then!* I hope with some fervor that we can learn a lot more than we now know about the human mind, and I see no reason why this strange puzzle should remain forever and entirely beyond us. But I would be deeply disturbed by any prospect that we might use the new knowledge in order to begin doing something about it, to improve it, say. This is a different matter from searching for information to use against schizophrenia or dementia, where we are badly in need of technologies, indeed likely one day to be sunk without them. But the ordinary, everyday, more or less normal human mind is too marvelous an instrument ever to be tampered with by anyone, science or no science.

The education of humanists cannot be regarded as complete, or even adequate, without exposure in some depth to where things stand in the various branches of science, and particularly, as I have said, in the areas of our ignorance. This does not mean that I know how to go about doing it, nor am I unaware of the difficulties involved. Physics professors, most of them, look with revulsion on assignments to teach their subject to poets. Biologists, caught up by the enchantment of their new power, armed with flawless instruments to tell the nucleotide sequences of the entire human genome, nearly matching the physicists in the precision of their measurements of living processes, will resist the prospect of broad survey courses; each biology professor will demand that any student in his path must master every fine detail within that professor's research program. The liberal-arts faculties, for their part, will continue to view the scientists with suspicion and apprehension. "What do the scientists want?" asked a Cambridge professor in Francis Cornford's wonderful *Microcosmographia Academica.* "Everything that's going," was the quick answer. That was back in 1912, and universities haven't much changed.

The worst thing that has happened to science education is that the great fun has gone out of it. A very large number of good students look at it as slogging work to be got through on the way to medical school. Others look closely at the premedical students themselves, embattled and bleeding for grades and class standing, and are turned off. Very few see science as the high adventure it really is, the wildest of all explorations ever undertaken by human beings, the chance to catch close views of things never seen before, the shrewdest maneuver for discovering how the world works. Instead, they become baffled early on, and they are misled into thinking that bafflement is simply the result of not having learned all the facts. They are not told, as they should be told, that everyone else—from the professor in his endowed chair down to the platoons of postdoctoral students in the laboratory all night—is baffled as well. Every important scientific advance that has come in looking like an answer has turned, sooner or later—usually sooner—into a question. And the game is just beginning.

An appreciation of what is happening in science today, and of how great a distance lies ahead for exploring, ought to be one of the rewards of a liberal-arts education. It ought to be a good in itself, not something to be acquired on the way to a professional career but part of the cast of thought needed for getting into the kind of century that is now just down the road. Part of the intellectual equipment of an educated person, however his or her time is to be spent, ought to be a feel for the queernesses of nature, the inexplicable things.

And maybe, just maybe, a new set of courses dealing systematically with ignorance in science might take hold. The scientists might discover in it a new and subversive technique for catching the attention of students driven by curiosity, delighted and surprised to learn that science is exactly as Bush described it: an "endless frontier." The humanists, for their part, might take considerable satisfaction watching their scientific colleagues confess openly to not knowing everything about everything. And the poets, on whose shoulders the future rests, might, late nights, thinking things over, begin to see some meanings that elude the rest of us. It is worth a try.

Suggestions for Discussion

1. Summarize Thomas's complaints about "the impression of science that the public gains."

2. How would he have science taught?

3. What advantages might there be in "a new set of courses dealing systematically with ignorance in science"?

Suggestions for Writing

1. Discuss one or more unanswered questions that you have encountered in your study of science.

2. Tell about an experience in which you had to change your mind because of new information.

Frank Conroy

Think About It

Frank Conroy (b. 1936), a jazz pianist and critic, is director of the Writers Workshop at the University of Iowa. His books include an autobiography, *Stop-Time* (1967); *Midair* (1986); *Game Day* (1990); and *Body and Soul* (1993). In the following essay he uses autobiographical material to comment on the importance of continuity in education.

When I was sixteen I worked selling hot dogs at a stand in the Fourteenth Street subway station in New York City, one level above the trains and one below the street, where the crowds continually flowed back and forth. I worked with three Puerto Rican men who could not speak English. I had no Spanish, and although we understood each other well with regard to the tasks at hand, sensing and adjusting to each other's body movements in the extremely confined space in which we operated, I felt isolated with no one to talk to. On my break I came out from behind the counter and passed the time with two old black men who ran a shoeshine stand in a dark corner of the corridor. It was a poor location, half hidden by columns, and they didn't have much business. I would sit with my back against the wall while they stood or moved around their ancient elevated stand, talking to each other or to me, but always staring into the distance as they did so.

As the weeks went by I realized that they never looked at anything in their immediate vicinity — not at me or their stand or anybody who might come within ten or fifteen feet. They did not look at approaching customers once they were inside the perimeter. Save for the instant it took to discern the color of the shoes, they did not even look at what they were doing while they worked, but rubbed in polish, brushed, and buffed by feel while looking over their shoulders, into the distance, as if awaiting the arrival of an important person. Of course there wasn't all that much distance in the underground station, but their behavior was so focused and consistent they seemed somehow to transcend the physical. A powerful mood was created, and I came almost to believe that these men could see through walls, through girders, and around corners to whatever hyperspace it was where whoever it was they were waiting and watching for would finally emerge. Their scattered talk was hip, elliptical, and hinted at mysteries beyond my white boy's ken, but it was the staring off, the long, steady staring off, that had me hypnotized. I left for a better job, with handshakes from both of them, without understanding what I had seen.

Perhaps ten years later, after playing jazz with black musicians in various Harlem clubs, hanging out uptown with a few young artists and intellectuals, I began to learn from them something of the extraordinarily varied and complex riffs and rituals embraced by different people to help themselves get through life in the ghetto. Fantasy of all kinds — from playful to dangerous — was in the very air of Harlem. It was the spice of uptown life.

Only then did I understand the two shoeshine men. They were trapped in a demeaning situation in a dark corner in an underground corridor in a filthy subway system. Their continuous staring off was a kind of statement, a kind of dance. Our bodies are here, went the statement, but our souls are receiving nourishment from distant sources only we can see. They were powerful magic dancers, sorcerers almost, and thirty-five years later I can still feel the pressure of their spell.

The light bulb may appear over your head, is what I'm saying, but it may be a while before it actually goes on. Early in my attempts to learn jazz piano, I used to listen to recordings of a fine player named Red Garland, whose music I admired. I couldn't quite figure out what he was doing with his left hand, however; the chords eluded me. I went uptown to an obscure club where he was playing with his trio, caught him on his break, and simply asked him. "Sixths," he said cheerfully. And then he went away.

I didn't know what to make of it. The basic jazz chord is the seventh, which comes in various configurations, but it is what it is. I was a self-taught pianist, pretty shaky on theory and harmony, and when he said sixths I kept trying to fix the information into what I already knew, and it didn't fit. But it stuck in my mind—a tantalizing mystery.

A couple of years later, when I began playing with a bass player, I discovered more or less by accident that if the bass played the root and I played a sixth based on the fifth note of the scale, a very interesting chord involving both instruments emerged. Ordinarily, I suppose I would have skipped over the matter and not paid much attention, but I remembered Garland's remark and so I stopped and spent a week or two working out the voicings, and greatly strengthened my foundations as a player. I had remembered what I hadn't understood, you might say, until my life caught up with the information and the light bulb went on.

I remember another, more complicated example from my sophomore year at the small liberal-arts college outside Philadelphia. I seemed never to be able to get up in time for breakfast in the dining hall. I would get coffee and a doughnut in the Coop instead—a basement area with about a dozen small tables where students could get something to eat at odd hours. Several mornings in a row I noticed a strange man sitting by himself with a cup of coffee. He was in his sixties, perhaps, and sat straight in his chair with very little extraneous movement. I guessed he was some sort of distinguished visitor to the college who had decided to put in some time at a student hangout. But no one ever sat with him. One morning I approached his table and asked if I could join him.

"Certainly," he said. "Please do." He had perhaps the clearest eyes I had ever seen, like blue ice, and to be held in their steady gaze was not, at first, an entirely comfortable experience. His eyes gave nothing away about himself while at the same time creating in me the eerie impression that he was looking directly into my soul. He asked a few quick questions, as if to put me at my ease, and we fell into conversation. He was William O. Douglas from the Supreme Court, and when he saw how startled I was he said, "Call me Bill. Now tell me what you're studying and why you get up so late in the morning." Thus began a series of talks that stretched over many weeks. The fact that I was an ignorant sophomore with literary pretensions who knew nothing about the law didn't seem to bother him. We talked about everything from Shakespeare to the possibility of life on other planets. One day I mentioned that I was going to have dinner with Judge Learned Hand. I explained that Hand was my girlfriend's grandfather. Douglas nodded, but I could tell he was surprised at the coincidence of my knowing the chief judge of the most important court in the country save the Supreme Court itself. After fifty years on the bench Judge Hand had become a famous man, both in and out of legal circles—a living legend, to his own dismay. "Tell him hello and give him my best regards," Douglas said.

Learned Hand, in his eighties, was a short, barrel-chested man with a large, square head, huge, thick, bristling eyebrows, and soft brown eyes. He radiated energy and would sometimes bark out remarks or questions in the living room as if he were in court. His humor was sharp, but often leavened with a touch of self-mockery. When something caught his funny bone he would burst out with explosive laughter—the laughter of a man who enjoyed laughing. He had a large repertoire of dramatic expressions involving the use of his eyebrows—very useful, he told me conspiratorially, when looking down on things from behind the bench. (The court stenographer could not record the movement of his eyebrows.) When I told him I'd been talking to William O. Douglas, they first shot up in exaggerated surprise, and then lowered and moved forward in a glower.

"*Justice* William O. Douglas, young man," he admonished. "Justice Douglas, if you please." About the Supreme Court in general, Hand insisted on a tone of profound respect. Little did I know that in private correspondence he had referred to the Court as "The Blessed Saints, Cherubim and Seraphim," "The Jolly Boys," "The Nine Tin Jesuses," "The Nine Blameless Ethiopians," and my particular favorite, "The Nine Blessed Chalices of the Sacred Effluvium."

Hand was badly stooped and had a lot of pain in his lower back. Martinis helped, but his strict Yankee wife approved of only one before dinner. It was my job to make the second and somehow slip it to him. If the pain was particularly acute he would get out of his chair and lie flat on the rug, still talking, and finish his point without missing a beat. He flattered me by asking for my impression of Justice Douglas, instructed me to convey his warmest regards, and then began talking about the Dennis case, which he described as a particularly tricky and difficult case involving the prosecution of eleven leaders of the Communist party. He had just started in on the First Amendment and free speech when we were called in to dinner.

William O. Douglas loved the outdoors with a passion, and we fell into the habit of having coffee in the Coop and then strolling under the trees down toward the duck pond. About the Dennis case, he said something to this effect: "Eleven Communists arrested by the government. Up to no good, said the government; dangerous people, violent overthrow, etc. First Amendment, said the defense, freedom of speech, etc." Douglas stopped walking. "Clear and present danger."

"What?" I asked. He often talked in a telegraphic manner, and one was expected to keep up with him. It was sometimes like listening to a man thinking out loud.

"Clear and present danger," he said. "That was the issue. Did they constitute a clear and present danger? I don't think so. I think everybody took the language pretty far in Dennis." He began walking, striding along quickly. Again, one was expected to keep up with him. "The FBI was all over them. Phones tapped, constant surveillance. How could it be clear and present danger with the FBI watching every move they made? That's a ginkgo," he said suddenly, pointing at a tree. "A beauty. You don't see those every day. Ask Hand about clear and present danger."

I was in fact reluctant to do so. Douglas's argument seemed to me to be crushing—the last word, really—and I didn't want to embarrass Judge Hand. But back in the living room, on the second martini, the old man asked about Douglas. I sort of scratched my nose and recapitulated the conversation by the ginkgo tree.

"What?" Hand shouted. "Speak up, sir, for heaven's sake."

"He said the FBI was watching them all the time so there couldn't be a clear and present danger," I blurted out, blushing as I said it.

A terrible silence filled the room. Hand's eyebrows writhed on his face like two huge caterpillars. He leaned forward in the wing chair, his face settling, finally, into a grim expression. "I am astonished," he said softly, his eyes holding mine, "at Justice Douglas's newfound faith in the Federal Bureau of Investigation." His big, granite head moved even closer to mine, until I could smell the martini. "I had understood him to consider it a politically corrupt, incompetent organization, directed by a power-crazed lunatic." I realized I had been holding my breath throughout all of this, and as I relaxed, I saw the faintest trace of a smile cross Hand's face. Things are sometimes more complicated than they first appear, his smile seemed to say. The old man leaned back. "The proximity of the danger is something to think about. Ask him about that. See what he says."

I chewed the matter over as I returned to campus. Hand had pointed out some of Douglas's language about the FBI from other sources that seemed to bear out his point. I thought about the words "clear and present danger," and the fact that if you looked at them closely they might not be as simple as they had first appeared. What degree of danger? Did the word "present" allude to the proximity of the danger, or just the fact that the danger was there at all—that it wasn't an anticipated danger? Were there other hidden factors these great men were weighing of which I was unaware?

But Douglas was gone, back to Washington. (The writer in me is tempted to create a scene here—to invent one for dramatic purposes—but of course I can't do that.) My brief time as a messenger boy was over, and I felt a certain frustration, as if, with a few more exchanges, the matter of *Dennis* v. *United States* might have been resolved to my satisfaction. They'd left me high and dry. But, of course, it is precisely because the matter did not resolve that has caused me to think about it, off and on, all these years. "The Constitution," Hand used to say to me flatly, "is a piece of paper. The Bill of Rights is a piece of paper." It was many years before I understood what he meant. Documents alone do not keep democracy alive, nor maintain the state of law. There is no particular safety in them. Living men and women, generation after generation, must continually remake democracy and the law, and that involves an ongoing state of tension between the past and the present which will never completely resolve.

Education doesn't end until life ends, because you never know when you're going to understand something you hadn't understood before. For me, the magic dance of the shoeshine men was the kind of experience in which understanding came with a kind of click, a resolving kind of click. The same with the experience at the piano. What happened with Justice Douglas and Judge Hand was different, and makes the point that understanding does not always mean resolution. Indeed, in our intellectual lives, our creative lives, it is perhaps those problems that will never resolve that rightly claim the lion's share of our energies. The physical body exists in a constant state of tension as it maintains homeostasis, and so too does the active mind embrace the tension of never being certain, never being absolutely sure, never being done, as it engages the world. That is our special fate, our inexpressibly valuable condition.

Suggestions for Discussion

1. Discuss the four examples Conroy uses to comment on the continuity of education in life.

2. Which of Conroy's experiences interests you most? Explain why.

Suggestions for Writing

1. Use an example from your own experience to show that you may not understand until later what or how much you have learned from the experience.

2. Describe an encounter with a colorful, interesting person.

Margo Kaufman

Who's Educated? Who Knows?

Margo Kaufman, the New York journalist, explores what it means to be an educated person in the 1990s.

What is an educated person? Someone who watches public television voluntarily and cites *The Atlantic* magazine and *Harper's* instead of *People* and *Us?* Is it someone who breaks into Tennyson at odd moments or programs a computer in machine language?

Confucius believed that the educated person knows "the ordinances of Heaven," "the rules of propriety" and the "force of words." But some people envision a walking course catalogue. Dr. H. Keith H. Brodie, president of Duke University, suggested that the all-knowing should know "something of history and literature; of the rules and laws of the universe; of human laws, government and behavior, and something of art—how to understand and respect the play of imagination, and how to be enriched and kept whole by it."

Of course, while such a smartypants would do very well on a game show like "Jeopardy," he or she might be judged lacking by someone with different priorities—which is just about everyone, since in high-minded circles nobody agrees on what educated people should know.

This Is Serious!

There does seem to be consensus that this is no laughing matter; even the most amusing turn solemn if not downright ponderous when the subject is broached. Take Bertice Berry, a former university professor who is now a stand-up comic. "I'd have to include curriculums from a diverse group of people, whether they won the battle or not," Ms. Berry said. "Works of women, Native Americans, Hispanics and African-Americans. And they'd probably take precedence over the dead white men."

At least the well-schooled dead white men. "An educated person is often an idiot," said the comedian Jackie Mason. "Having a lot of information doesn't mean you know how to deal with the reality of making intelligent adjustments in terms of real life and society. An educated person should be the kind of person who understands how to deal with people, with his job and with his family." Not surprisingly, Mr. Mason says that by his standards he is "one of the most educated people who ever lived." But then, people often define education in self-flattering terms.

"It's someone who always wants to learn more," said the Pulitzer Prize-winning playwright Wendy Wasserstein. "Someone who questions. Someone who thinks he doesn't know anything yet." Does she consider herself educated? "I still need to learn more, too," Ms. Wasserstein said.

Marjorie David, a Los Angeles writer-producer who says she was overeducated at Harvard and Columbia, suggested this definition: "It's the ability to critically assess material. People who can't put information in a context respond to the most superficial things. When they watch TV and are told to buy soap they buy it. But an education teaches you to assess the soap pitch." And to be suspicious of any product described as "feminine" or "all natural" or pitched by an old coot who looks as if he stepped out of a Norman Rockwell painting.

John Callahan, the syndicated cartoonist whose latest collection is titled "Do What He Says! He's Crazy!!!" declared that an educated person "knows what a cat wants for dinner" and "can read George Bush's lips." Sha-ri Pendleton, better known as Blaze on the television program "American Gladiators," felt that the educated man or woman combines the "insight of Dr. David Viscott," a radio psychologist, "the intelligence of a Nobel Peace Prize winner and the drive of Michael Jackson."

Pendleton, whose speciality is playing a female Little John in a high altitude, high-technology version of his encounter with Robin Hood on the log, said she "aspires to possess all these qualities."

English and Calculus?

Back in academia, Steven B. Simple, president of the University of Southern California, said that for an American, "To be educated means proficiency in English and the second major language of our time, calculus." Mastery of English entails not just reading billboards and making oneself understood in supermarkets, but having a full understanding of the literature past and present and the ability to communicate, to serve people."

As for calculus, a subject that has led many a math phobic to a university without distribution requirements, "it has become the *lingua franca* of science and technology," said Mr. Simple, a professor of electrical engineering. Fortunately, it is still not a big icebreaker at parties.

Hanna H. Gray, president of the University of Chicago, offered what could be a recipe for the arts. The main ingredients are "the capacity for independent thought, a sense of relationship between different options, a sense of history, respect for evidence and a sense of how to define and approach important questions."

L. Jay Oliva, president of New York University, seasoned the soup with "strength of character, ethical behavior, understanding one's role in society as an active participant and feeling that helping other people is one of the most instructive and beneficial things you can do."

Lloyd Richards, professor emeritus at the Yale School of Drama, threw in "wit, wisdom, tolerance and the ability and willingness to share."

Experts ascribe the variety of definitions to the complexity of the subject. "There's no way either temporally or spatially of limiting what it means to be educated," said George Rupp, president of Rice University. "Knowledge is continually escalating, and spatially we don't have any easy limits to set around what we need to know."

Mr. Rupp pointed out that 1,000 years ago, a person who grew up in Christian Europe needed to understand the traditions of biblical and Greek culture to be considered educated. "Today we ask, 'Do we have to know about Buddhism, the history of Japan prior to Westernization and all the ranges of experience the Chinese have?' And there are exactly the same kinds of questions in social sciences and natural sciences."

Luckily for those of us who never heard of Gondwanaland, fractals or semiotics, Samuel Johnson postulated that knowledge is of two kinds—that which you know and that which you know how to find.

More than 2,000 years ago, Plato wrote that "The sum and substance of education is the right training, which effectively leads the soul of the child at play onto the love of the calling in which he will have to be perfect when he is a man."

By this definition, Steve Smith, director of the Ringling Bros. and Barnum & Bailey Clown College, is a sage. "You need the vision to know the world doesn't revolve around your ego," Mr. Smith said, "and in our case, juggling, magic, pantomime and how to ride a unicycle."

Suggestions for Discussion

1. Analyze three or four of the definitions of an educated person introduced by Kaufman.

2. Discuss the distinction between having knowledge and knowing how to use it.

Suggestions for Writing

1. What does it mean to you to be an educated person? Give examples.

2. To what extent has the concept of an educated person changed in your lifetime?

Woody Allen

My Speech to the Graduates

Woody Allen (b. 1935) is an American actor, filmmaker, and writer, best known for such outstanding films as *Annie Hall* (1977), *Interiors* (1978), *Manhattan* (1979), *Zelig* (1983), *Alice* (1990), and *Manhattan Murder Mystery* (1993). His humorous essays have appeared in *The New Yorker* and in the collections *Getting Even* (1971), *Without Feathers* (1975), *The Floating Lightbulb* (1981), and

Side Effects (1986). In the following parody of a commencement address, Allen faces a world of gloom and chaos with humorous platitudes and endless goodwill as he displays his mastery of the anticlimax and the *non sequitur.*

More than any other time in history, mankind faces a crossroads. One path leads to despair and utter hopelessness. The other, to total extinction. Let us pray we have the wisdom to choose correctly. I speak, by the way, not with any sense of futility but with a panicky conviction of the absolute meaninglessness of existence which could easily be misinterpreted as pessimism. It is not. It is merely a healthy concern for the predicament of modern man. (Modern man is here defined as any person born after Nietzsche's edict that "God is dead," but before the hit recording "I Wanna Hold Your Hand.") This "predicament" can be stated one of two ways, though certain linguistics philosophers prefer to reduce it to a mathematical equation where it can be easily solved and even carried around in the wallet.

Put in its simplest form, the problem is: How is it possible to find meaning in a finite world given my waist and shirt size? This is a very difficult question when we realize that science has failed us. True, it has conquered many diseases, broken the genetic code, and even placed human beings on the moon, and yet when a man of 80 is left in a room with two 18-year-old cocktail waitresses nothing happens. Because the real problems never change. After all, can the human soul be glimpsed through a microscope? Maybe—but you'd definitely need one of those very good ones with two eyepieces. We know that the most advanced computer in the world does not have a brain as sophisticated as that of an ant. True, we could say that of many of our relatives but we only have to put up with them at weddings or special occasions. Science is something we depend on all the time. If I develop a pain in the chest I must take an X-ray. But what if the radiation from the X-ray causes me deeper problems? Before I know it, I'm going in for surgery. Naturally, while they're giving me oxygen an intern decides to light up a cigarette. The next thing you know I'm rocketing over the World Trade Center in bed clothes. Is this science? True, science has taught us how to pasteurize cheese. And true, this can be fun in mixed company—but what of the H-bomb? Have you ever seen what happens when one of those things falls off a desk accidentally? And where is science when one ponders the eternal riddles? How did the cosmos originate? How long has it been around? Did matter begin with an explosion or by the word of God? And if by the latter, could He not have begun it just two weeks earlier to take advantage of some of the warmer weather? Exactly what do we mean when we say, man is mortal? Obviously it's not a compliment.

Religion too has unfortunately let us down. Miguel de Unamuno writes blithely of the "eternal persistence of consciousness," but this is no easy feat. Particularly when reading Thackeray. I often think how comforting life must have been for early man because he believed in a powerful, benevolent Creator who looked after all things. Imagine his disappointment when he saw his wife putting on weight. Contemporary man, of course, has no such peace of mind. He finds himself in the midst of a crisis of faith. He is what we fashionably call "alienated." He has seen the ravages of war, he has known natural catastrophes, he has been to singles bars. My good friend Jacques Monod spoke often of the randomness of the cosmos. He believed everything in existence occurred by pure chance with the possible exception of his breakfast, which he felt certain was made by his housekeeper. Naturally belief in a divine intelligence inspires tranquility. But this does not free us from our human responsibilities. Am I my brother's keeper? Yes. Interestingly, in my case I share that honor with the Prospect Park Zoo. Feeling godless then, what we have done is made technology God. And yet can technology really be the answer when a brand new Buick, driven by my close associate, Nat Persky, winds up in the window of Chicken Delight causing hundreds of customers to scatter? My toaster has never once worked properly in four years. I follow the instructions and push two slices of bread down in the slots and seconds later they rifle upward. Once they broke the nose of a woman I loved very dearly. Are we counting on nuts and bolts and electricity to solve our problems? Yes, the telephone is a good thing—and the refrigerator—and the air conditioner. But not every air conditioner. Not my sister Henny's, for instance. Hers makes a loud noise and still doesn't cool. When the man comes over to fix it, it gets worse. Either that or he tells her she needs a new one. When she complains, he says not to bother him. This man is truly alienated. Not only is he alienated but he can't stop smiling.

The trouble is, our leaders have not adequately prepared us for a mechanized society. Unfortunately our politicians are either incompetent or corrupt. Sometimes both on the same day. The Government is unresponsive to the needs of the little man. Under five-seven, it is impossible to get your Congressman on the phone. I am not denying that democracy is still the finest form of government. In a democracy at least, civil liberties are upheld. No citizen can be wantonly tortured, imprisoned, or made to sit through certain Broadway shows. And yet this is a far cry from what goes on in the Soviet Union. Under their form of totalitarianism, a person merely caught whistling is sentenced to 30 years in a labor camp. If, after 15 years, he still will not stop whistling they shoot him. Along with this brutal fascism we find its handmaiden, terrorism. At no other time in history has man been so afraid to cut his veal chop for fear that it will explode. Violence breeds more violence and it is predicted that by 1990 kidnapping will be the dominant mode of social interaction. Overpopulation will exacerbate problems to the breaking point. Figures tell us there are already more people on earth than we need to move even the heaviest piano. If we do not call a halt to breeding, by the year 2000 there will be no room to serve dinner unless one is willing to set the table on the heads of strangers. Then they must not move for an hour while we eat. Of course energy will be in short supply and each car owner will be allowed only enough gasoline to back up a few inches.

Instead of facing these challenges we turn instead to distractions like drugs and sex. We live in far too permissive a society. Never before has pornography been this rampant. And those films are lit so badly! We are a people who lack defined goals. We have never learned to love. We lack leaders and coherent programs. We have no spiritual center. We are adrift alone in the cosmos wreaking monstrous violence on one another out of frustration and pain. Fortunately, we have not lost our sense of proportion. Summing up, it is clear the future holds great opportunities. It also holds pitfalls. The trick will be to avoid the pitfalls, seize the opportunities, and get back home by six o'clock.

Suggestions for Discussion

1. Discuss Allen's use of exaggeration and understatement as sources of humor.
2. What real social problems does Allen address?
3. How does Allen's choice of allusion and vocabulary contribute to the effectiveness of his parody?

Suggestion for Writing

Write an essay in which, without diminishing Allen's skill as a comic writer, you consider why it is easy to parody a commencement address. Is it possible to compose an address that does not invite parody? What might be the content and tone of an effective address?

Howard Gardner

Human Intelligence Isn't What We Think It Is

Howard Gardner (b. 1943) is professor of education at Harvard University. His books include *Frames of Mind: The Theory of Multiple Intelligences* (1985), *To Open Minds* (1989), *The Unschooled Mind: How Children Think and How Schools Should Teach* (1991), and *Multiple Intelligences: The Theory in Practice* (1993). In the following essay he discusses the importance of recognizing and cultivating different kinds of intelligence.

"People Have Multiple Intelligences"

Intelligence is not an absolute such as height that can be measured simply, largely because people have multiple intelligences rather than one single intelligence.

In all, I have identified seven forms of intelligence. The two that are valued most highly in this society are linguistic and logical-mathematical intelligences. When people think of someone as smart, they are usually referring to those two, because individuals who possess linguistic and logical-mathematical abilities do well on tests that supposedly measure intelligence.

But there are five other kinds of intelligence that are every bit as important: Spatial, musical, bodily-kinesthetic and two forms of personal intelligence—interpersonal, knowing how to deal with others, and intrapersonal, knowledge of self. None of these ought to have a priority over others.

topic of a well-balanced personality

"Shifting Importance" of the Seven Varieties

The relative importance of these seven intelligences has shifted over time and varies from culture to culture. In a hunting society, for example, it is a lot more important to have extremely good control of your body and know your way around than to add or subtract quickly. In Japanese society, interpersonal intelligence—the ability to work well in groups and to arrive at joint decisions—is very important.

Historically, different systems of education have emphasized different blends of intelligence. In the old apprenticeship system, bodily, spatial and interpersonal abilities were valued. In old-fashioned religious schools, the focus was on linguistic and interpersonal abilities. The modern secular school emphasizes the linguistic and logical-mathematical, but in the school of the near future I think that linguistic will become much less crucial. For working with computers, logical-mathematical intelligence will be important for programing, and intrapersonal intelligence will be important for individual planning.

What I'm saying is that while both logical-mathematical and linguistic are important today, it won't always be that way. We need to be sensitive to the fact that blends of intelligences keep shifting so that in the future we don't get locked into a specific blend.

Secrets Unlocked by Biological Research

Research in biology has laid the foundation for the theory of multiple intelligences.

Studies show that when someone suffers damage to the nervous system through a stroke or tumor, all abilities do not break down equally. If you have an injury to areas of the left hemisphere of the brain, you will lose your language ability almost entirely, but that will not affect your musical, spatial or interpersonal skills to the same extent.

Conversely, you can have lesions in your right hemisphere that leave language capacity intact but that seriously compromise spatial, musical or interpersonal abilities. So we have a special capacity for language that is unconnected to our capacity for music or interpersonal skills, and vice versa.

I'm not suggesting that this analysis is the last word. I would like to think of it as the first word in a new way of looking at human abilities.

"America Wastes Potential!"

In America, we are wasting a lot of human potential by focusing on only linguistic and logical intelligence. If an individual doesn't happen to be good in these, he or she often gets thrown on society's scrap heap.

What happens is that a youngster takes an IQ test and doesn't do very well. He gets labeled as not very smart and the teacher treats him accordingly.

But there are many roles in society in which it is not important that a person have a high intelligence in language and logic so long as he or she can function at a basic level in these domains.

For example, somebody good at working with his hands and figuring out how machines function might find a responsible position in a science lab or working backstage in a theater. If kids with such abilities were encouraged— rather than discouraged because they can't figure out who wrote the *Iliad*— they could be extremely valuable to society.

IQ Tests "Have Destructive Social Effects"

I would like to get rid of intelligence and aptitude tests; they measure only two forms of intelligence and have destructive social effects. These tests have been successful because they serve as a good predictor of how people will do in school in the short run. But how much does doing well in school predict success outside of school? Very little.

Those of us who take a position against IQ tests have the burden of coming up with ways of assessing abilities that are not completely impractical. My notion is something between a report card and a test score.

I would assess intellectual propensities from an early age. I use the word *propensities* because I don't believe intelligences are fixed for many years. The earlier a strength is discovered, the more flexibility there is to develop it. Similarly, if a child has a low propensity, the earlier intervention begins, the easier it is to shore up the child. So early diagnosis is important.

Preschools Where "Children Can Do Exploring"

I would not assess abilities through traditional paper-and-pencil tests. Instead, we need learning environments—preschools—in which children can do a lot of exploring on their own or with help from adults.

All children play with blocks, for example, but what do they do with them? How complex are the structures they make? How well can they remember them? Can they revise them in various ways? All of these questions can be answered by adults observing and playing with the children.

The same environment could be equipped with musical materials, and, again, children could explore on their own and with adults. If we had such environments, with periodic monitoring we could develop very good profiles of a child's propensities. This would give parents and teachers a better way of thinking about children than one or two test scores. Instead of looking at a child and saying, "He's smart" or "He's dumb," people would talk in terms of a child's strengths and weaknesses. It is a much more realistic view.

But no theory is going to tell people what to do once a child's propensities are assessed. That decision would depend on the value of those around the child. Some people would say, "Let's go with the child's strengths for all they are worth." Others would say, "It's very important to be good in language, so even though this kid isn't good in it, we're going to work on it."

"The Challenge for Education"

As children mature, the assessments would continue in a different vein. By the age of 10 or 11, the monitoring would shift to "domains," where you might come up with analyses such as "this person has the talent to be a doctor."

While having a high intelligence in an area doesn't predict exactly what you are going to do, it predicts the direction you are likely to move in. If somebody has a very highly developed bodily intelligence, he or she could become an athlete, dancer or surgeon. If somebody has a highly developed spatial intelligence, he or she might be at home in architecture, engineering, sculpture or painting.

The challenge for the educational community is to figure out profiles of young people and then to help them find roles in which they can use their abilities in a productive way.

Recognizing the Diversity of Our Capabilities

The Suzuki method of teaching music, developed in Japan, shows what can be done to foster a specific intelligence when the effort is undertaken intensively at an early age and a lot of energy is put into it. This method creates an environment that is rich with music; mothers play with the youngsters for 2 hours a day from the time they reach age 2. Within a few years, all participants become decent musicians.

In theory, we could "Suzuki" everything. The more time and energy invested early in life on a particular intelligence, the more you can buoy it up. I am not advocating this approach, merely pointing out the possibilities. But before we can make these kinds of decisions, we have to take a first step— recognizing the diverse intelligences of which human beings are capable.

Suggestions for Discussion

1. Name the seven forms of intelligence identified by Gardner.

2. What suggestions does he make for replacing traditional intelligence and aptitude tests?

3. How might the development of intelligence be enhanced?

Suggestions for Writing

1. Write about your strongest intelligence. Give examples from your experience.

2. Rank your own intelligences from strongest to least strong.

Henry Louis Gates, Jr.

Talking Black

Henry Louis Gates, Jr. (b. 1950), is the W. E. B. Du Bois Professor of the Humanities at Harvard University. His seminal books include *Figures in Black* (1987), *The Signifying Monkey: A Theory of Afro-American Literary Criticism* (1988), *Loose Canons: Notes of the Culture Wars* (1992), and a memoir entitled *Colored People* (1994). In the following essay he explores the importance of "the language of black difference."

> For a language acts in diverse ways, upon the spirit of a people; even as the spirit of a people acts with a creative and spiritualizing force upon a language.
>
> **—Alexander Crummell, 1860**

> A new vision began gradually to replace the dream of political power—a powerful movement, the rise of another ideal to guide the unguided, another pillar of fire by night after a clouded day. It was the ideal of "book-learning"; the curiosity, born of compulsory ignorance, to know and test the power of the cabalistic letters of the white man, the longing to know.
>
> **—W. E. B. Du Bois, 1903**

> The knowledge which would teach the white world was Greek to his own flesh and blood . . . and he could not articulate the message of another people.
>
> **—W. E. B. Du Bois, 1903**

Alexander Crummell, a pioneering nineteenth-century Pan-Africanist, statesman, and missionary who spent the bulk of his creative years as an Anglican minister in Liberia, was also a pioneering intellectual and philosopher of language, founding the American Negro Academy in 1897 and serving as the intellectual godfather of W. E. B. Du Bois. For his first annual address as president of the academy, delivered on 28 December 1897, Crummell selected as his topic "The Attitude of the American Mind Toward the Negro Intellect." Given the occasion of the first annual meeting of the great intellectuals of the race, he could not have chosen a more timely or appropriate subject.

Crummell wished to attack, he said, "the denial of intellectuality in the Negro; the assertion that he was not a human being, that he did not belong to the human race." He argued that the desire "to becloud and stamp out the intellect of the Negro" led to the enactment of "laws and Statutes, closing the pages of every book printed to the eyes of Negroes; barring the doors of every school-room against them!" This, he concluded, "was the systematized method of the intellect of the South, to stamp out the brains of the Negro!"—a program that created an "almost Egyptian darkness [which] fell upon the mind of the race, throughout the whole land."

Crummell next shared with his audience a conversation between two Boston lawyers which he had overheard when he was "an errand boy in the Anti-slavery office in New York City" in 1833 or 1834:

> While at the Capitol they happened to dine in the company of the great John C. Calhoun, then senator from South Carolina. It was a period of great ferment upon the question of Slavery, States Rights, and Nullification; and consequently the Negro was the topic of conversation at the table. One of the utterances of Mr. Calhoun was to this effect—"That if he could find a Negro who knew the Greek syntax, he would then believe that the Negro was a human being and should be treated as a man."

"Just think of the crude asininity," Crummell concluded rather generously, "of even a great man!"

The salient sign of the black person's humanity—indeed, the only sign for Calhoun—would be the mastering of the very essence of Western civilization, of the very foundation of the complex fiction upon which white Western culture had been constructed. It is likely that "Greek syntax," for John C. Calhoun, was merely a hyperbolic figure of speech, a trope of virtual impossibility; he felt driven to the hyperbolic mode, perhaps, because of the long racist tradition in Western letters of demanding that black people *prove* their full humanity. We know this tradition all too well, dotted as it is with the names of great intellectual Western racialists, such as Francis Bacon, David Hume, Immanuel Kant, Thomas Jefferson, and G. W. F. Hegel. Whereas each of these figures demanded that blacks write poetry to prove their humanity, Calhoun—writing in a post-Phillis Wheatley era—took refuge in, yes, Greek syntax.

In typical African-American fashion, a brilliant black intellectual accepted Calhoun's bizarre challenge. The anecdote Crummell shared with his fellow black academicians turned out to be his shaping scene of instruction. For Crummell himself jumped on a boat, sailed to England, and matriculated at Queen's College, Cambridge, where he mastered (naturally enough) the intricacies of Greek syntax. Calhoun, we suspect, was not impressed.

Crummell never stopped believing that mastering the master's tongue was the sole path to civilization, intellectual freedom, and social equality for the black person. It was Western "culture," he insisted, that the black person "must claim as his rightful heritage, as a man—not stinted training, not a caste education, not," he concluded prophetically, "a Negro curriculum." As he argued so passionately in his speech of 1860, "The English Language in Liberia," the acquisition of the English language, along with Christianity, is the wonderful sign of God's providence encoded in the nightmare of African enslavement in the racist wilderness of the New World. English, for Crummell, was "the speech of Chaucer and Shakespeare, of Milton and Wordsworth, of Bacon and Burke, of Franklin and Webster," and its potential mastery was "this one item of compensation" that "the Almighty has bestowed upon us" in exchange for "the exile of our fathers from their African homes to

America." In the English language are embodied "the noblest theories of liberty" and "the grandest ideas of humanity." If black people master the master's tongue, these great and grand ideas will become African ideas, because "ideas conserve men, and keep alive the vitality of nations."

In dark contrast to the splendors of the English language, Crummell set the African vernacular languages, which, he wrote, have "definite marks of inferiority connected with them all, which place them at the widest distances from civilized languages." Any effort to render the master's discourse in our own black tongue is an egregious error, for we cannot translate sublime utterances "in[to] broken English—a miserable caricature of their noble tongue." We must abandon forever both indigenous African vernacular languages and the neo-African vernacular languages that our people have produced in the New World:

> All low, inferior, and barbarous tongues are, doubtless, but the lees and dregs of noble languages, which have gradually, as the soul of a nation has died out, sunk down to degradation and ruin. We must not suffer this decay on these shores, in this nation. We have been made, providentially, the deposit of a noble trust; and we should be proud to show our appreciation of it. Having come to the heritage of this language we must cherish its spirit, as well as retain its letter. We must cultivate it among ourselves; we must strive to infuse its spirit among our reclaimed and aspiring natives.

I cite the examples of John C. Calhoun and Alexander Crummell as metaphors for the relation between the critic of black writing and the larger institution of literature. Learning the master's tongue, for our generation of critics, has been an act of empowerment, whether that tongue be New Criticism, humanism, structuralism, Marxism, poststructuralism, feminism, new historicism, or any other -ism. But even as Afro-American literature and criticism becomes institutionalized, our pressing question now becomes this: in what tongue shall we choose to speak, and write, our own criticisms? What are we now to do with the enabling masks of empowerment that we have donned as we have practiced one mode of "white" criticism or another?

The Afro-American literary tradition is distinctive in that it evolved in response to allegations that its authors did not, and could not, create literature, a capacity that was considered the signal measure of a race's innate "humanity." The African living in Europe or in the New World seems to have felt compelled to create a literature not only to demonstrate that blacks did indeed possess the intellectual ability to create a written art, but also to indict the several social and economic institutions that delimited the "humanity" of all black people in Western cultures.

So insistent did these racist allegations prove to be, at least from the eighteenth to the early twentieth century, that it is fair to describe the subtext of the history of black letters in terms of the urge to refute them. Even as late as 1911, when J. E. Casely-Hayford published *Ethiopia Unbound* (the "first" African novel), he felt it necessary to address this matter in the first two paragraphs of his text. "At the dawn of the twentieth century," the novel opens, "men of light and leading both in Europe and in America had not yet made up their minds as to what place to assign to the spiritual aspirations of the black man." Few literary traditions have begun with such a complex and curious relation to criticism: allegations of an absence led directly to a presence, a literature often inextricably bound in a dialogue with its harshest critics.

Black literature and its criticism, then, have been put to uses that were not primarily aesthetic: rather, they have formed part of a larger discourse on the nature of the black, and his or her role in the order of things. Even so, a sense of integrity has arisen in the Afro-American tradition, though it has less to do with the formal organicism of the New Critics than with an intuitive notion of "ringing true," or Houston Baker's concept of "sounding." (One of the most frequently used critical judgments in the African-American tradition is "That shit don't sound right," or, as Alice Walker puts it in *The Color Purple,* "Look like to me only a fool would want to talk in a way that feel peculiar to your mind.") That is the sense I am calling on here, understanding how problematic even this can be. Doubleness, alienation, equivocality: since the turn of the century at least, these have been recurrent tropes for the black tradition.

To be sure, this matter of the language of criticism and the integrity of its subject has a long and rather tortured history in all black letters. It was David Hume, after all, who called Francis Williams, the Jamaican poet of Latin verse, "a parrot who merely speaks a few words plainly." Phillis Wheatley, too, has long suffered from the spurious attacks of black and white critics alike for being the *rara avis* of a school of so-called mockingbird poets, whose use of European and American literary conventions has been considered a corruption of a "purer" black expression, found in forms such as the blues, signifying, spirituals, and Afro-American dance. Can we, as critics, escape a "mockingbird" posture?

Only recently have some scholars attempted to convince critics of black literature that we can. Perhaps predictably, a number of these attempts share a concern with that which has been most repressed in the received tradition of Afro-American criticism: close readings of the texts themselves. And so we are learning to read a black text within a black formal cultural matrix. That means reading a literary culture that remains, for the most part, intransigently oral. If the black literary imagination has a privileged medium, it is what Douglass called the "live, calm, grave, clear, pointed, warm, sweet, melodious and powerful human voice." And the salient contribution of black literature may lie in its resolute vocality. But there is no black voice; only voices, diverse and mutable. Familiarly, there's the strut, confidence laced with bitters—

> I am a Waiter's Waiter. I know all the moves, all the pretty, fine moves that big book will never teach you . . . I built the railroad with my moves. (James Alan McPherson, "Solo Song")

Or the boisterous revelator:

> When he was on, Reverend Jones preached his gospel hour in a Texas church that held no more than 250 people, but the way he had the old sisters banging on them bass drums and slapping them tambourines, you'd think that God's Own Philharmonic was carrying on inside that old church where the loudspeaks blasted Jones's message to the thousands who stood outside. At the conclusion of Reverend Jones's sermon, the church didn't need no fire, because it was

being warmed by the spirit of the Lord. By the spirit of Jesus. (Ishmael Reed,
The Terrible Threes)

Yet how tonally remote they are from this cento of Baldwin, a preacher's son
for whom King Jamesian inversions were second nature:

In the case of the Negro the past was taken from him whether he would or no;
yet to forswear it was meaningless and availed him nothing, since his shameful
history was carried, quite literally, on his brow. Shameful; for he was heathen as
well as black and would never have discovered the healing blood of Christ had
not we braved the jungles to bring him these glad tidings. . . .

Where the Negro face appears, a tension is created, the tension of a silence
filled with things unutterable. ("Many Thousands Gone")

Baldwin wrote of "something ironic and violent and perpetually understated
in Negro speech," and in this he was describing his own careful, ungentle
cadences. Contrast, again, the homeliest intimacies of nuance that Morrison
will unexpectedly produce:

There is a loneliness that can be rocked. Arms crossed, knees drawn up; holding, holding on, this motion, unlike a ship's, smooths and contains the rockers.
It's an inside kind—wrapped tight like skin. *(Beloved)*

There's no hidden continuity or coherence among them. History makes them
like beads on a string: there's no necessary resemblance; but then again, no
possible separation.

And so we've had to learn to "read black" as a textual effect because the
existence of a black canon is a historically contingent phenomenon; it is not
inherent in the nature of "blackness," not vouchsafed by the metaphysics of
some racial essence. The black tradition exists only insofar as black artists
enact it. Only because black writers have read and responded to other black
writers with a sense of recognition and acknowledgment can we speak of a
black literary inheritance, with all the burdens and privileges that has entailed. Race is a text (an array of discursive practices), not an essence. It must
be *read* with painstaking care and suspicion, not imbibed.

The disjunction between the language of criticism and the language of its
subject helps defamiliarize the texts of the black tradition: ironically, it is necessary to create distance between reader and texts in order to go beyond
reflexive responses and achieve critical insight into and intimacy with their
formal workings. I have done this to respect the integrity of these texts, by
trying to avoid confusing my experiences as an Afro-American with the black
act of language that defines a text. This is the challenge of the critic of black
literature in the 1980s: not to shy away from white power—that is, a new
critical vocabulary—but to translate it into the black idiom, *renaming* principles of criticism where appropriate, but especially naming indigenous black
principles of criticism and applying them to our own texts. *Any* tool that enables the critic to explain the complex workings of the language of a text is
appropriate here. For it is language, the black language of black texts, that
expresses the distinctive quality of our literary tradition. Once it may have
seemed that the only critical implements black critics needed were the pom-
pom and the twirled baton; in fact, there is no deeper form of literary disre-
spect. We will not protect the integrity of our tradition by remaining afraid

of, or naive about, literary analysis; rather, we will inflict upon it the violation of reflexive, stereotypical reading—or nonreading. We are the keepers of the black literary tradition. No matter what approach we adopt, we have more in common with each other than we do with any other critic of any other litera- ture. We write for each other, and for our own contemporary writers. This relation is a critical trust.

It is also a *political* trust. How can the demonstration that our texts sustain ever closer and more sophisticated readings *not* be political at a time when all sorts of so-called canonical critics mediate their racism through calls for "pu- rity" of "the tradition," demands as implicitly racist as anything the Southern Agrarians said? How can the deconstruction of the forms of racism itself not be political? How can the use of literary analysis to explicate the racist social text in which we still find ourselves be anything *but* political? To be political, however, does not mean that I have to write at the level of a Marvel comic book. My task, as I see it, is to help guarantee that black and so-called Third World literature is taught to black and Third World and white students by black and Third World and white professors in heretofore white mainstream departments of literature, and to train students to think, to read, and to write clearly, to expose false uses of language, fraudulent claims, and muddled ar- guments, propaganda, and vicious lies—from all of which our people have suffered just as surely as we have from an economic order in which we were zeroes and a metaphysical order in which we were absences. These are the "values" which should be transmitted through the languages of cultural and literary study.

In the December 1986 issue of the *Voice Literary Supplement*, in an essay entitled "Cult-Nats Meet Freaky-Deke," Greg Tate argued cogently and compellingly that "black aestheticians need to develop a coherent criticism to communicate the complexities of our culture. There's no periodical on black cultural phenomena equivalent to *The Village Voice* or *Artforum*, no publica- tion that provides journalism on black visual art, philosophy, politics, eco- nomics, media, literature, linguistics, psychology, sexuality, spirituality, and pop culture. Though there are certainly black editors, journalists, and aca- demics capable of producing such a journal, the disintegration of the black cultural nationalist movement and the brain-drain of black intellectuals to white institutions have destroyed the vociferous public dialogue that used to exist between them." While I would argue that *Sage, Callaloo,* and *Black American Literature Forum* are indeed fulfilling that function for academic critics, I am afraid that the truth of Tate's claim is irresistible.

But his most important contribution to the future of black criticism is to be found in his most damning allegation. "What's unfortunate," he writes, "is that while black artists have opened up the entire 'text of blackness' for fun and games, not many black critics have produced writing as fecund, eclectic, and freaky-deke as the art, let alone the culture, itself. . . . For those who prefer exegesis with a polemical bent, just imagine how critics as fluent in black and Western culture as the postliberated artists could strike terror into that bastion of white supremacist thinking, the Western art [and literary] world[s]." To which I can only say, "Amen, Amen."

Tate's challenge is a serious one because neither ideology nor criticism nor blackness can exist as entities of themselves, outside their forms or their texts. This is the central theme of Ralph Ellison's *Invisible Man* and Ishmael Reed's *Mumbo Jumbo*, for example. But how can we write or read the text of "Blackness"? What language(s) do black people use to represent their critical or ideological positions? In what forms of language do we speak or write? Can we derive a valid, integral "black" text of criticism or ideology from borrowed or appropriated forms? Can a black woman's text emerge authentically as borrowed, or "liberated," or revised, from the patriarchal forms of the slave narratives, on the one hand, or from the white matriarchal forms of the sentimental novel, on the other, as Harriet Jacobs and Harriet Wilson attempted to do in *Incidents in the Life of a Slave Girl* (1861) and *Our Nig* (1859)? Where lies the liberation in revision, the ideological integrity of defining freedom in the modes and forms of difference charted so cogently by so many poststructural critics of black literature?

For it is in these spaces of difference that black literature has dwelled. And while it is crucial to read these patterns of difference closely, we should understand as well that the quest was lost, in an important sense, before it had even begun, simply because the terms of our own self-representation have been provided by the master. It is not enough for us to show that refutation, negation, and revision exist, and to define them as satisfactory gestures of ideological independence. Our next concern will be to address the black political signified, that is, the cultural vision and the black critical language that underpin the search through literature and art for a profound reordering and humanizing of everyday existence. We encourage our writers and critics to undertake the fullest and most ironic exploration of the manner and matter, the content and form, the structure and sensibility so familiar and poignant to us in our most sublime form of art, black music, where ideology and art are one, whether we listen to Bessie Smith or to postmodern and poststructural John Coltrane.

Just as we encourage our writers to meet this challenge, we as critics can turn to our own peculiarly black structures of thought and feeling to develop our own language of criticism. We do so by drawing on the black vernacular, the language we use to speak to each other when no white people are around. Unless we look to the vernacular to ground our modes of reading, we will surely sink in the mire of Nella Larsen's quicksand, remain alienated in the isolation of Harriet Jacobs' garret, or masked in the received stereotype of the Black Other helping Huck to return to the raft, singing "China Gate" with Nat King Cole under the Da Nang moon, or reflecting our balded heads in the shining flash of Mr. T's signifying gold chains.

We can redefine reading itself from within our own black cultures, refusing to grant the racist premise that criticism is something that white people do, so that we are doomed to imitate our white colleagues, like reverse black minstrel critics done up in whiteface. We should not succumb, as did Alexander Crummell, to the tragic lure of white power, the mistake of accepting the empowering language of white criticism as "universal" or as our own language, the mistake of confusing its enabling mask with our own black faces. Each of us has, in some literal or figurative manner, boarded a ship and sailed to a metaphorical Cambridge, seeking to master the master's tools. (I myself, being quite literal-minded, booked passage some fourteen years ago on the *QE2*.) Now we can at last don the empowering mask of blackness and talk *that* talk, the language of black difference. While it is true that we must, as Du Bois said so long ago, "know and test the power of the cabalistic letters of the white man," we must also know and test the dark secrets of a black discursive universe that awaits its disclosure through the black arts of interpretation. The future of our language and literature may prove black indeed.

Suggestions for Discussion

1. To what extent do Gates's historical and biographical allusions add weight and substance to his argument?

2. Discuss the writer's assertion that to "read black" is now a political trust. Cite examples.

3. Analyze Gates's discussion of the opinions of Alexander Crummell.

Suggestions for Writing

1. Discuss the significance of the three epigraphs that preface the essay. In what ways does each contribute to your understanding and appreciation of the essay?

2. Write a short analytical essay explaining what Gates means by his title, "Talking Black."

Harold Brodkey

Reading, the Most Dangerous Game

Harold Brodkey, educated at Harvard University, writes fiction and commentary for The New Yorker. His books include First Love and Other Sorrows (1988), Stories in an Almost Classical Mode (1989), and the novel The Runaway Soul (1991). In the following essay he explores the act of reading and advocates reading "seriously."

Reading is an intimate act, perhaps more intimate than any other human act. I say that because of the prolonged (or intense) exposure of one mind to another that is involved in it, and because it is the level of mind at which feelings and hopes are dealt in by consciousness and words.

Reading a good book is not much different from a love affair, from love, complete with shyness and odd assertions of power and of independence and with many sorts of incompleteness in the experience. One can marry the book: reread it, add it to one's life, live with it. Or it might be compared to pregnancy—serious reading even if you're reading trash: one is inside the experience and is about to be born; and one is carrying something, a sort of self inside oneself that one is about to give birth to, perhaps a monster. Of course, for men this is always verging on something else (part of which is a primitive rage with being masculine, a dismay felt toward women and the world, a reader's odd sense of women).

The act of reading as it really occurs is obscure: the decision to read a book in a real minute, how one selects the book, how one flirts with the choice, how one dawdles on the odd path of getting it read and then reread, the oddities of rereading, the extreme oddities of the procedures of continuing with or without interruptions to read, getting ready to read a middle chapter in its turn after going off for a while, then getting hold of the book physically, having it in one's hand, letting one's mind fill with thoughts in a sort of warm-up for the exercise of mind to come—one riffles through remembered scenes from this and other books, one diddles with half-memories of other pleasures and usefulnesses, one wonders if one can afford to read, one considers the limitations and possibilities of this book, one is humiliated in anticipation or superior or thrilled in anticipation, or nauseated in retrospect or as one reads. One has a sense of talk and of reviews and essays and of anticipation or dread and the will to be affected by the thing of reading, affected lightly or seriously. One settles one's body to some varying degree, and then one enters on the altered tempos of reading, the subjection to being played upon, one passes through phases, starting with reacting to or ignoring the cover of the book and the opening lines.

The piercing things, the stabbingly emotional stuff involved in reading, leads to envy, worse even than in sibling or neighborhood rivalry, and it leads to jealousy and possessiveness. If a book is not religious or trashy, the problem of salesmanship, always partly a con, arises in relation to it, to all the problems it presents. A good reader of Proust complains constantly as a man might complain of a wife or a woman of her husband. And Proust perhaps had such a marriage in mind with the reader. A good book, like pregnancy or a woman known to arouse love, or a man, is something you praise in the light of a general reluctance to risk the experience; and the quality of praise warns people against the book, warns them to take it seriously; you warn them about it, not wanting to be evangelical, a matchmaker or a malicious pimp for a troubled and troubling view of the world.

I can't imagine how a real text can be taught in a school. Even minor masterpieces, "Huckleberry Finn" or "The Catcher in the Rye," are too much for a classroom, too real an experience. No one *likes* a good book if they have actually read it. One is fanatically attached, restlessly attached, criminally attached, violently and criminally opposed, sickened, unable to bear it. In Europe, reading is known to be dangerous. Reading always leads to personal metamorphosis, sometimes irreversible, sometimes temporary, sometimes large-scale, sometimes less than that. A good book leads to alterations in one's sensibility and often becomes a premise in one's beliefs. One associates truth with texts, with impressive texts anyway; and when trashy books vanish from sight, it is because they lie too much and too badly and are not worth one's intimacy with them. Print has so much authority, however, that sometimes it is only at the beginning of an attempt at a second reading or at the end of it, and only then, if one is self-assured, that one can see whether a book was not really worth reading the first time; one tells by how alterable the truth in it seems in this more familiar light and how effective the book remains or, contrarily, how amazingly empty of meaning it now shows itself to be. It is a strange feeling to be a practiced enough reader and writer to see in some books that there is nothing there. It is eerie: why did the writer bother? What reward is there in being a fraud in one's language and in one's ideas? To believe they just didn't know is more unsettling than to doubt oneself or to claim to be superficial or prejudiced or to give up reading entirely, at least for a while.

Or, in our country, we deny what we see of this and even reverse it: fraud is presented as happiness; an empty book is said to be well constructed; a foolish argument is called innovative. This is a kind of bliss; but lying of that sort, when it is nearly universal, wrecks the possibility of our having a literary culture or even of our talking about books with each other with any real pleasure. It is like being phony yachtsmen who only know smooth water and who use their motors whenever they can. This guarantees an immense personal wretchedness, actually.

Of course, in Europe, cultural patterns exist which slow the rate of change in you as a reader (as well as supplying evidence to use in comprehending what happens and will happen to you if you change because of a book). Of course, such change is never entirely good or wise. In our country, we have nothing to hold us back from responding to any sort of idea. With us everything is for sale—everything is up for grabs, including ourselves—and we have very little tradition worth hanging onto except the antic.

The country is organized not by religion or political machinery but by what are seen as economic realities but which are fashions in making money and spending money. We are an army marching in the largest conceivable mass so entirely within cultural immediacy that it can be said this is new in the history in the world, emotionally new in that while this has been true of other cultures for brief periods in the past, it was never true as completely or for such a large part of the population or so continuously, with so few periods of stasis. We pretend to tradition but really, nothing prevents us changing.

And we do change. Divorce, born-again Christianity, the computer revolution, a return to the farm, a move to the city. In Boston, at college at Harvard, I first knew people who claimed to be cultivated to the degree they remained unchanged not only in spite of the reading they claimed to have done but with the help of it. They did not realize what an imbecile and provincial notion that was—it was simply untrue: you could see it, the untruth of it. A rule of thumb about culture is that personal or public yearning for a better time to come or one in the past and nostalgia of any sort are reliable signs of the counterfeit. The past is there to be studied in its reality, moment by moment, and the future can be discussed in its reality to come, which will be a reality moment by moment; but doing that means being honest just as doing it makes you too busy to yearn; and doing it shows you that nostalgia is a swindler's trick. A sense of the real is what is meant by good sense. And because of the nature of time and because of how relentlessly change occurs, good sense has to contain a good deal of the visionary as well as of ironic apology to cover the inevitable mistakes. And this is doubly so with us, in the United States. Reality here is special. And part of reality here or elsewhere is that novels, plays, essays, fact pieces, poems, through conversion or in the process of argument with them, change you or else—to use an idiom—you haven't listened.

If the reader is not at risk, he is not reading. And if the writer is not at risk, he is not writing. As a rule, a writer and a book or a poem are no good if the writer is essentially unchanged morally after having written it. If the work is really a holding operation, this will show in a closed or flat quality in the prose and in the scheme of the thing, a logiclessness, if you will pardon the neologism, in the writing. Writing always tends toward a kind of moral stance—this is because of the weight of logic and of truth in it—but judging the ways in which it is moral is hard for people who are not cultivated. Profoundly educated persons make the best judges.

The general risk in being a man or woman of cultivation is then very high, and this is so in any culture, and perhaps requires too much strength for even a small group to practice in ours. But should such a guerrilla group arise, it will have to say that cultivation and judgment issue from the mouths of books and can come from no other source. Over a period of centuries, ignorance has come, justifiably, to mean a state of booklessness. Movie-educated people are strained; they are decontextualized; they are cultivated in a lesser way. Television and contemporary music are haunted by the search for messiahs; the usual sign of mass inauthenticity is a false prophet (which usually means a war will shortly break out and be lost). The absence of good sense signals the decline of a people and of a civilization. Shrewdness without good sense is hell unleashed.

I would propose as a social cure that in fourth grade and in the first year at college, this society mandate that we undergo a year of reading with or without argument as the soul can bear, including argument with teachers and parents and local philosophers if there are any. Of course something like this happens anyway but we probably ought to institutionalize it in our faddish way.

After all, if you don't know what's in good books, how can your life not be utterly miserable all in all? Won't it fall apart with fearsome frequency? The best of what this species knows is in books. Without their help, how can you manage?

If I intend for my life to matter to me, I had better read seriously, starting with newspapers and working up to philosophy and novels. And a book in what it teaches, and in what it does in comforting and amusing us, in what it does in granting asylum to us for a while, had better be roughly equivalent to, or greater in worth than, an event involving other people in reality that teaches us or that grants us asylum for a while in some similar way, or there is no reason to bother with it. And I am careful toward books that offer refuge to my ego or my bad conscience. A writer who is opposed to notions of value and instruction is telling you he or she does not want to have to display loyalty or insight or sensitivity—to prose or to people: that would limit his or her maneuverability; and someone who does not believe that loyalty or insight or sensitivity or meaning has any meaning is hardly worth knowing in books or on the page although such people are unavoidable in an active life.

The procedures of real reading, if I may call it that, are not essentially shrewd, although certain writers, Twain and Proust for instance, often do play to the practice of shrewdness in their readers.

But the disappearance from the immediate world of one's attention, that infidelity to one's alertness toward outside attack, and then the gullibility required for a prolonged act of attention to something not directly inferior to one's own methods and experiences, something that emanates from someone else, that and the risk of conversion, the certainty that if the book is good, one will take on ideas and theories, a sense of style, a sense of things different from those one had before—if you think of those, you can see the elements of middle-class leisure and freedom, or upper-class insolence and power, or lower-class rebelliousness and hiddenness and disloyalty to one's surroundings, that are required for real reading.

And you can also see what the real nature of literature is—it is a matter of one's attention being removed from the real world and regarding nature and the world verbally: it is a messy mathematics in its way; it is a kind of science dealing in images and language, and it has to be right in the things it says; it has to be right about things.

I learned very early that when you were infatuated with someone, you read the same books the other person read or you read the books that had shaped the other person or you committed an infidelity and read for yourself and it was the beginning of trouble. I think reading and writing are the most dangerous human things because they operate on and from that part of the mind in which judgments of reality are made; and because of the authority language has from when we learn to speak and use its power as a family matter, as an immediate matter, and from when we learn to read and see its modern, middle-class power as a public matter establishing our rank in the world.

When a book is technically uninteresting, when such a book is not a kind of comically enraged protest against the pretensions of false technique and ludicrously misconceived subject matter, it is bound to be a phony. The democratic subversion of objects, of techniques, can never without real dishonesty stray far from its ostensible purpose, which is the democratic necessity of making our lives interesting to us. Folk art is, inevitably, a kind of baby talk in relation to high art—and this is shaming, but so is much in life, including one's odor giving one's secrets away (showing one's nervousness or one's lechery), but it is better to do that than live messageless and without nerves or desire. The moral extravagance of reading—its spiritual element and its class element—is bound to reflect both an absence of humility and a new kind of humility and both in odd ways. Two of our most conceited writers, Gertrude Stein and Ernest Hemingway, overtly wrote baby talk. Nowadays the young like financial reporting as a window on the world, and television and the interview. They are pursuing fact in the plethora of baby talk, and they are trying to exercise judgment in the middle of the overenthusiastic marketing of trash.

American colleges have taught our intellectuals to read politically in order to enter and stay in a group or on a track. One reads skimmingly then, and one keeps placing the authority for what one reads outside oneself. But actually people cannot read in a two-souled way, shrewdly, and with a capacity to feel and learn. Learning involves fear and sometimes awe and just plain factually is not shrewd—it is supershrewd if you like, it is a very grand speculation indeed; and graduate school stuff won't open out into awe and discovery or recognition or personal knowledge of events but only onto academic hustling. I mean when you stop theorizing and think about what is really there. Do I need to go on? One of the primary rules of language is that there must be a good reason for the listener to attend to a second sentence after the first one; to supply a good reason is called "being interesting." Not to attend to the second sentence is called "not listening." The reasons to listen are always selfish, but that does not mean they are only selfish.

It is hard to listen. It is also hard to write well and to think. These ought not to be unfamiliar statements. This ought not to be news.
See you in the bookstore soon.

Suggestions for Discussion

1. Discuss the significance of Brodkey's title.

2. Explain Brodkey's belief that the United States is organized by "fashions in making money and spending money."

3. Discuss the difficulties a reader encounters in Brodkey's lengthy, complex, and energetic sentences.

Suggestions for Writing

1. Analyze the reading that you do on a regular basis.

2. Discuss Brodkey's observation that "shrewdness without good sense is hell unleashed."

Gerald Graff

Off Course

Gerald Graff is the George M. Pullman Professor of English at the University of Chicago. His books include *Literature Against Itself* (1981), *Professing Literature* (1989), *Beyond the Culture Wars* (1992), *The Myth of Cultural Decline* (1992), and *The Struggle for the University* (1992). In the following essay he discusses "the best things that happen in universities."

An undergraduate tells of an art history course in which the instructor observed one day, "As we now know, the idea that knowledge can be objective is a positivist myth that has been exploded by postmodern thought." It so happens the student is concurrently enrolled in a political science course in which the instructor speaks confidently about the objectivity of his discipline as if it had not been "exploded" at all. What do you do? the student is asked. "What else can I do?" he says. "I trash objectivity in art history, and I presuppose it in political science."

A second undergraduate describes a history teacher who stresses the superiority of Western culture in developing the ideas of freedom, democracy, and free market capitalism that the rest of the world is now rushing to imitate. She also has a literature teacher who describes such claims of Western supremacy as an example of the hegemonic ideology by which the United States arrogates the right to police the world. Asked which course she prefers, she replies, "Well, I'm getting an A in both."

To some of us these days, the moral of these stories would be that students have become cynical relativists who care less about convictions than about grades and careers. In fact, if anything is surprising, it is that more students do not behave in this cynical fashion, for the established curriculum encourages it. The disjunction of the curriculum is a far more powerful source of relativism than any doctrine preached by the faculty.

One of the oddest things about the university is that it calls itself a community of scholars yet organizes its curriculum in a way that conceals the links of the community from those who are not already aware of them. The courses being given at any moment on a campus represent any number of rich potential conversations within and across the disciplines. But since students experience these conversations only as a series of monologues, the conversations become actual only for the minority who can reconstruct them on their own. No self-respecting educator would deliberately design a system guaranteed to keep students dependent on the whim of the individual instructor. Yet this is precisely the effect of a curriculum composed of courses that are not in dialogue with one another.

Among the factors that make academic culture more confusing today than in the past is not only that there is more controversy but that there is even controversy about what can legitimately be considered controversial. Traditionalists are often angry that there should even *be* a debate over the canon, while revisionists are often angry that there should even be a debate over "political correctness," or the relevance of ideology and politics to their subjects.

A recent feminist critic says she finds it "astonishing" that it still needs repeating at this late date that "the perspective assumed to be 'universal' which has dominated knowledge . . . has actually been male and culture-bound." Since the feminist argument, however, is that we still fail to see how culture-bound our thinking is, it is hard to see why this critic should be astonished that she still needs to make the point. Another political critic writes that "we are perhaps already weary of the avalanche of papers, books, and conferences entitled 'The Politics of X,' and we have recently begun to question that most hallowed of all political slogans on the left, 'everything is political.'" Yet the idea of politics that this critic and her audience are already "weary of" is one that most people have not yet encountered and might well find incomprehensible. The "advanced" academic and the layperson (or the traditional academic) are so far apart that what is already old news to one has not yet become intelligible to the other.

Imagine how this affects students who, at the moment they are negotiating the difficult transition from the lay culture to the academic culture, must also negotiate the unpredictable and unfathomable discrepancies between academic departments and factions. When there is no correlation of the different discourses to which students are exposed, it becomes especially difficult for them to infer which assumptions are safe and which are likely to be challenged. The problem is that knowledge of what is and is not considered potentially or legitimately controversial cannot be learned *a priori*; you cannot get it out of E. D. Hirsch's *Dictionary of Cultural Legacy*. Such knowledge comes only through interaction with a community, and that interaction is precisely what is prevented by a disconnected system of courses. Then, too, assumptions about what is and is not potentially controversial tend to change from one moment to the next and one sub-community to the next, and they are changing at a faster rate today than in the past.

Thomas S. Kuhn in *The Structure of Scientific Revolutions* describes moments of crisis or "paradigm shift" in the sciences, when "a law that cannot even be demonstrated to one group of scientists may . . . seem intuitively obvious to another." The fate of Kuhn's own book is an interesting case in point. Even as his sociological account of scientific paradigm change has been treated as virtual holy writ by many literary theorists (for a while it seemed almost obligatory to begin every book or essay with a respectful bow to Kuhn), his work has often been ignored or dismissed by scientists and philosophers of science, who accuse him of subverting the concept of objective truth in reducing scientific discovery to "mob psychology." As the controversy over Kuhn has revealed, both the literati and the scientists have remained largely walled up within their clashing assumptions about objectivity, the smugness of which might have been punctured had these parties been forced to argue with each other in their teaching. This mutual smugness has persisted in the sniper fire that continues to be exchanged over the issue of objectivity and the extent to which knowledge is independent of the social situation of the knower; revisionists sneer at the concept and traditionalists sneer at the very idea of questioning it.

The question neither group seems to ask is what it must be like to be a student caught in the crossfire between these conflicting views of objectivity, each one prone to present itself as "intuitively obvious" and uncontroversial. A rhetoric scholar, Gregory Columb, has studied the disorientation experienced by a bright high school graduate who, after doing well in a humanities course as a freshman at the University of Chicago, tried to apply her mastery to a social science course, only to come up with a grade of C. Imagine trying to write an academic paper when you sense that almost anything you say can be used against you and that the intellectual moves that got you an A in existentialist philosophy may get you a C minus and a dirty look in Skinnerian behaviorism.

Consider the fact that the passive voice that is so standard in sociology writing ("it will be contended in this paper . . . .") has been perennially rebuked in English courses. Or consider something so apparently trivial as the convention of using the present tense to describe actions in literature and philosophy and the past tense to describe them in history. Plato *says* things in literary and philosophical accounts while in historical accounts he *said* them. Experienced writers become so accustomed to such tense shifting that it seems a simple matter, but it reflects deep-rooted and potentially controversial differences between disciplines. Presumably, Plato speaks in the present in literary and philosophical contexts because ideas there are considered timeless; only when we move over to history does it start to matter that the writer is dead. We English teachers write "tense shift" in the margin when student writers betray uncertainty about this convention, but how do we expect them to "get" it when they pass from the very different time zones of history and philosophy/English with no engagement of the underlying issues?

One of the most frequent comments teachers make on student papers is "What's your evidence?" but nobody would ever finish a piece of writing if it were necessary to supply evidence for everything being said, so in order to write, one must acquire a sense of which statements have to be supported by evidence (or further argument) and which ones a writer can get away with because they are already taken for granted by the imagined audience. What happens, then, when a writer has no way of knowing whether an assumption that he or she got away with with audience A will also be conceded by audience B? It is no wonder that students protect themselves from the insecurity of such a situation by "psyching out" each course as it comes—and then forgetting about it as soon as possible after the final exam in order to clear their minds for the seemingly unrelated demands of the next set of courses.

It is not only ideas and reasoning processes but the recall of basic information as well that figure to be impaired by disjunctive curricular organization. To use the jargon of information theory, an information system that is experienced as an unrelated series of signals will be weak in the kind of redundancy that is needed for information to be retained. Faced with a curriculum overloaded with data and weak in redundancy, students may find it difficult to know which items of information they are supposed to remember. Then, too, a student may be exposed to the same information in several courses while failing to recognize it as "the same," since it is contextualized differently in each course. When students fail to identify a cultural literacy item on a test, the problem may be not that they don't know the information but that they don't know they know it; they may have learned it in a context whose relevance to the test questions they don't recognize. What is learned seems so specific to a particular course that it is difficult for students to see its application beyond.

The critic Kenneth Burke once compared the intellectual life of a culture to a parlor in which different guests are forever dropping in and out. As the standard curriculum represents the intellectual life, however, there is no parlor; the hosts congregate in separate rooms with their acolytes and keep their differences and agreements to themselves.

To venture a comparison, it is as if you were to try to learn the game of baseball by being shown a series of rooms in which you see each component of the game separately: pitchers going through their windups in one room; hitters swinging their bats in the next; then infielders, outfielders, umpires, fans, field announcers, ticket scalpers, broadcasters, hot dog vendors, and so on. You see them all in their different roles, but since you see them separately you get no clear idea of what the game actually looks like or why the players do what they do. No doubt you would come away with a very imperfect understanding of baseball under these conditions. Yet it does not seem farfetched to compare these circumstances with the ones students face when they are exposed to a series of disparate courses, subjects, and perspectives and expected not only to infer the rules of the academic intellectual game but to play it competently themselves.

It is tempting to blame these problems on bad teaching, seemingly rectifiable by encouraging instructors to be more sensitive to their students' predicament. Certainly more sensitivity on the part of teachers would help. But even the most sympathetic and sensitive teacher cannot be sure which of his or her views may be flatly contradicted by the next teacher encountered by his or her students. Then, too, though good teaching may have its inherently individualistic aspects, we all need others at times to counteract our biases and to make up for our gaps in knowledge. For this reason the problems I have been discussing cannot be effectively addressed at the level of individual teaching. They are curricular problems, and a curriculum is not simply the sum total of separate acts of teaching but a systematic organization of teaching. In fact, the habit of reducing all questions about education to questions about individual *teaching* discourages us from thinking systematically about the curriculum. Our very use of the term "the classroom" to stand for the entire educational process is a symptom of this constricted way of thinking, which I call the "course fetish," though it might also be called the "cult of the great teacher."

How well one can teach depends not just on individual virtuosity but on the possibilities and limits imposed by the structure in which one works. It may not hold for everyone, but I believe I am a better teacher when I am able to take my colleagues as reference points in my classroom. As long as teaching is viewed as an inherently solo performance, too much is made to depend on the teacher's personal resources, something which puts teachers under inordinate pressure and makes for burnout. Only a weak system would depend on perpetual feats of personal virtuosity to keep it functioning at its best.

This point has been made by a powerful critic of the course system, Joseph Tussman, a reformer who helped develop an experimental program at the University of California at Berkeley. In a book on the program published in 1969, Tussman pointed out that the course system had become so pervasive "that we have come to regard the conditions of course teaching as the conditions of teaching in general." He argued that the problem with the course system is that since "the courses are generally unrelated and competitive, . . . each professor knows that he has a valid claim to only a small fraction of the student's time and attention. The effect is that no teacher is in a position to be responsible for, or effectively concerned with, the student's total educational situation. The student presents himself to the teacher in fragments, and not even the advising system can put him back together again." These limiting conditions, noted Tussman, are ones "of which every sensitive teacher is bitterly aware. But there is nothing he can do about it. He can develop a coherent course, but a collection of coherent courses may be simply an incoherent collection."

As Tussman maintained, the only effective unit for educational planning is the *program*, not the course. We tend, however, to associate programs and systems with bureaucracy, mechanization, and institutionalization, terms lacking in the sentimental emotional resonance that we attach to the idea of "the classroom" presided over by the great teacher. The magical aura of "the classroom" lies in the illusion that it is not part of a system at all, that it is an island somehow exempt from the incursions of bureaucracy. We know that the truth is otherwise, that courses have to be scheduled, assigned to rooms, listed in the catalog, and assimilated to the grid of credit hours, requirements, and grades. The course, however, is experienced not as an extension of bureaucratic organization but as a force that transcends and redeems bureaucratic organization and makes it tolerable.

This explains why we frequently hear academics speak irreverently about the existence of *departments* but hardly ever about their courses, though the course is an expression of the same process of bureaucratic specialization and privatization that produced the department. The department is thought to epitomize the divisive, competitive, meanly professionalized aspects of academic life. Its existence is a reminder of the arbitrary fences with which each discipline selfishly guards its disciplinary turf, of factional rivalry and a narrowly self-serving and proprietary view of intellectual life. The faculty meeting, an expression of the departmental ethos, typifies this realm of petty strife from which the course is felt to be a saving escape. As Tussman put it, "the faculty meeting—college, departmental, or committee—is the abrasive ordeal from which one flees to the delicious, healing privacy of one's own course."

Whereas the department epitomizes the bureaucratic aspects of academic life, the course does not feel like a bureaucratic entity at all. Thus "the classroom" is believed to be what the university is really all about after we factor out the necessary evils of administration, departments, publish or perish, research, faculty meetings, and even the curriculum itself, which are seen as realms of conflict. This symbolic opposition in all its sentimentality is neatly exemplified in the recent popular film *The Dead Poets Society*, in which a brilliantly creative and eccentric teacher of literature is pitted against a puritanical, repressive, and life-denying prep school administration.

But the most familiar representation of the sentimental image of the course as a scene of conflict-free community is the one presented on untold numbers of college catalog covers: A small, intimate class is sprawled informally on the gently sloping campus greensward, shady trees overhead and ivy-covered buildings in the background. Ringed in a casual semicircle, the students gaze with rapt attention at a teacher who is reading aloud from a small book—a volume of poetry, we inevitably assume, probably Keats or Dickinson or Whitman. The classroom, in these images, is a garden occupying a redemptive space inside the bureaucratic and professional machine. It is a realm of unity and presence in a world otherwise given over to endless difference, conflict, competition, and factionalism.

The classroom resembles the primitive Protestant Church, freed from the ecclesiastical externals that only tend to intervene between the believer and the authentic experience of the sacred texts. The curriculum, by contrast, is identified with the bureaucratic machine and is represented in the catalog not in pastoral images but in mechanically numbered lists of departments, courses, and requirements, although the cold linearity of this organization in its own way obscures the conflicts between departments and courses.

To the extent that the curriculum is associated with alien bureaucracy, the course fetish carries with it a certain disbelief in the very need for a curriculum. Underlying the course fetish finally is a conviction (as I recently heard a prominent philosopher and educational theorist say) that there is nothing wrong with today's education that cannot be cured by getting good teachers together and simply turning them loose. And there is a certain truth to this view.

No doubt the best things that happen in universities *are* the things that happen in "the classroom." But the romance of "the classroom" blinds us to the steep educational prices we pay when classrooms are isolated from one another.

"The classroom" embodies a contradiction: In the process of creating one kind of community it thwarts the community that it could be constituting with other courses. It is not surprising that professors flock in increasing numbers to professional conferences and symposia, where they find the kind of collegial discussion that rarely occurs at home. No wonder they feel a lack of community at home when they spend so much of their time there isolated from one another in their courses.

To say this, to be sure, is to go against the widespread belief that professors now spend all too *little* of their time in their courses. This is sometimes indeed the case—though I think far less commonly than is thought. The more fundamental question we should be asking in most cases is not *how much* time teachers are spending in the classroom but *under what conditions.* Spending adequate time in the classroom is obviously crucial, but that time would be spent less wastefully if each classroom were not off limits to other classrooms, if classrooms formed a conversation instead of a set of ships passing in the night.

Suggestions for Discussion

1. Discuss Graff's observation that the "disjunction of the curriculum is a far more powerful source of relativism than any doctrine preached by the faculty."

2. Explain his key assertion that the "romance" of the classroom blinds us to the steep educational price we pay when classrooms are isolated from one another.

3. Discuss problems students have with traditional course and program arrangements. Cite examples from your own experience.

Suggestions for Writing

1. Examine how the courses you are currently taking are (or might be) related to one another in theory and practice.

2. Using specific examples from your experience, identify the classes and programs of study that have impressed you. Compare and contrast them with those that have not satisfied you.

Loren Eiseley

The Hidden Teacher

Loren Eiseley (1907–1977) was an anthropologist and academic administrator at the University of Pennsylvania. His publications include *Darwin's Century* (1958), which won the National Phi Beta Kappa Science Award, *The Mind as Nature* (1962), *The Unexpected Universe* (1969), *The Invisible Pyramid* (1970), and his autobiography, *All the Strange Hours: The Excavation of a Life* (1975). In the following essay, he emphasizes the importance of continuing exploration and discovery.

> Sometimes the best teacher teaches only once to a single child or a grownup past hope.
> —Anonymous

I

The putting of formidable riddles did not arise with today's philosophers. In fact, there is a sense in which the experimental method of science might be said merely to have widened the area of man's homelessness. Over two thousand years ago, a man named Job, crouching in the Judean desert, was moved to challenge what he felt to be the injustice of his God. The voice in the whirlwind, in turn, volleyed pitiless questions upon the supplicant— questions that have, in truth, precisely the ring of modern science. For the Lord asked of Job by whose wisdom the hawk soars, and who had fathered the rain, or entered the storehouses of the snow.

A youth standing by, one Elihu, also played a role in this drama, for he ventured diffidently to his protesting elder that it was not true that God failed to manifest Himself. He may speak in one way or another, though men do not perceive it. In consequence of this remark perhaps it would be well, whatever our individual beliefs, to consider what may be called the hidden teacher, lest we become too much concerned with the formalities of only one aspect of the education by which we learn.

We think we learn from teachers, and we sometimes do. But the teachers are not always to be found in school or in great laboratories. Sometimes what we learn depends upon our own powers of insight. Moreover, our teachers may be hidden, even the greatest teacher. And it was the young man Elihu who observed that if the old are not always wise, neither can the teacher's way be ordered by the young whom he would teach.

For example, I once received an unexpected lesson from a spider.

It happened far away on a rainy morning in the West. I had come up a long gulch looking for fossils, and there, just at eye level, lurked a huge yellow-and-black orb spider, whose web was moored to the tall spears of buffalo grass at the edge of the arroyo. It was her universe, and her senses did not extend beyond the lines and spokes of the great wheel she inhabited. Her extended claws could feel every vibration throughout that delicate structure. She knew the tug of wind, the fall of a raindrop, the flutter of a trapped moth's wing. Down one spoke of the web ran a stout ribbon of gossamer on which she could hurry out to investigate her prey.

Curious, I took a pencil from my pocket and touched a strand of the web. Immediately there was a response. The web, plucked by its menacing occupant, began to vibrate until it was a blur. Anything that had brushed claw or wing against that amazing snare would be thoroughly entrapped. As the vibrations slowed, I could see the owner fingering her guidelines for signs of struggle. A pencil point was an intrusion into this universe for which no precedent existed. Spider was circumscribed by spider ideas; its universe was spider universe. All outside was irrational, extraneous, at best raw material for spider. As I proceeded on my way along the gully, like a vast impossible shadow, I realized that in the world of spider I did not exist.

Moreover, I considered, as I tramped along, that to the phagocytes, the white blood cells, clambering even now with some kind of elementary intelligence amid the thin pipes and tubing of my body—creatures without whose ministrations I could not exist—the conscious "I" of which I was aware had no significance to these amoeboid beings. I was, instead, a kind of chemical web that brought meaningful messages to them, a natural environment seemingly immortal if they could have thought about it, since generations of them had lived and perished, and would continue to so live and die, in that odd fabric which contained my intelligence—a misty light that was beginning to seem floating and tenuous even to me.

I began to see that among the many universes in which the world of living creatures existed, some were large, some small, but that all, including man's, were in some way limited or finite. We were creatures of many different dimensions passing through each other's lives like ghosts through doors.

In the years since, my mind has many times returned to that far moment of my encounter with the orb spider. A message has arisen only now from the misty shreds of that webbed universe. What was it that had so troubled me about the incident? Was it that spidery indifference to the human triumph?

If so, that triumph was very real and could not be denied. I saw, had many times seen, both mentally and in the seams of exposed strata, the long backward stretch of time whose recovery is one of the great feats of modern science. I saw the drifting cells of the early seas from which all life, including our own, has arisen. The salt of those ancient seas is in our blood, its lime is in our bones. Every time we walk along a beach some ancient urge disturbs us so that we find ourselves shedding shoes and garments, or scavenging among seaweed and whitened timbers like the homesick refugees of a long war.

And war it has been indeed—the long war of life against its inhospitable environment, a war that has lasted for perhaps three billion years. It began with strange chemicals seething under a sky lacking in oxygen; it was waged through long ages until the first green plants learned to harness the light of the nearest star, our sun. The human brain, so frail, so perishable, so full of inexhaustible dreams and hungers, burns by the power of the leaf.

The hurrying blood cells charged with oxygen carry more of that element to the human brain than to any other part of the body. A few moments' loss of vital air and the phenomenon we know as consciousness goes down into the black night of inorganic things. The human body is a magical vessel, but its life is linked with an element it cannot produce. Only the green plant knows the secret of transforming the light that comes to us across the far reaches of space. There is no better illustration of the intricacy of man's relationship with other living things.

The student of fossil life would be forced to tell us that if we take the past into consideration the vast majority of earth's creatures—perhaps over 90 percent—have vanished. Forms that flourished for a far longer time than man has existed upon earth have become either extinct or so transformed that their descendants are scarcely recognizable. The specialized perish with the environment that created them, the tooth of the tiger fails at last, the lances of men strike down the last mammoth.

In three billion years of slow change and groping effort only one living creature has succeeded in escaping the trap of specialization that has led in time to so much death and wasted endeavor. It is man, but the word should be uttered softly, for his story is not yet done.

With the rise of the human brain, with the appearance of a creature whose upright body enabled two limbs to be freed for the exploration and manipulation of his environment, there had at last emerged a creature with a specialization—the brain—that, paradoxically, offered escape from specialization. Many animals driven into the nooks and crannies of nature have achieved momentary survival only at the cost of later extinction.

Was it this that troubled me and brought my mind back to a tiny universe among the grass blades, a spider's universe concerned with spider thought?

Perhaps.

The mind that once visualized animals on a cave wall is now engaged in a vast ramification of itself through time and space. Man has broken through the boundaries that control all other life. I saw, at last, the reason for my recollection of that great spider on the arroyo's rim, fingering its universe against the sky.

The spider was a symbol of man in miniature. The wheel of the web brought the analogy home clearly. Man, too, lies at the heart of a web, a web extending through the starry reaches of sidereal space, as well as backward into the dark realm of prehistory. His great eye upon Mount Palomar looks into a distance of millions of light-years, his radio ear hears the whisper of even more remote galaxies, he peers through the electron miscroscope upon the minute particles of his own being. It is a web no creature of earth has ever spun before. Like the orb spider, man lies at the heart of it, listening. Knowledge has given him the memory of earth's history beyond the time of his emergence. Like the spider's claw, a part of him touches a world he will never enter in the flesh. Even now, one can see him reaching forward into time with new machines, computing, analyzing, until elements of the shadowy future will also compose part of the invisible web he fingers.

Yet still my spider lingers in memory against the sunset sky. Spider thoughts in a spider universe—sensitive to raindrop and moth flutter, nothing beyond, nothing allowed for the unexpected, the inserted pencil from the world outside.

Is man at heart any different from the spider, I wonder: man thoughts, as limited as spider thoughts, contemplating now the nearest star with the threat of bringing with him the fungus rot from earth, wars, violence, the burden of a population he refuses to control, cherishing again his dream of the Adamic Eden he had pursued and lost in the green forests of America. Now it beckons again like a mirage from beyond the moon. Let man spin his web, I thought further; it is his nature. But I considered also the work of the phagocytes swarming in the rivers of my body, the unresting cells in their mortal universe. What is it we are a part of that we do not see, as the spider was not gifted to discern my face, or my little probe into her world?

We are too content with our sensory extensions, with the fulfillment of that Ice Age mind that began its journey amidst the cold of vast tundras and that pauses only briefly before its leap into space. It is no longer enough to see as a man sees—even to the ends of the universe. It is not enough to hold nuclear energy in one's hand like a spear, as a man would hold it, or to see the lightning, or times past, or time to come, as a man would see it. If we continue to do this, the great brain—the human brain—will be only a new version of the old trap, and nature is full of traps for the beast that cannot learn.

It is not sufficient any longer to listen at the end of a wire to the rustlings of galaxies; it is not enough even to examine the great coil of DNA in which is coded the very alphabet of life. These are our extended perceptions. But beyond lies the great darkness of the ultimate Dreamer, who dreamed the light and the galaxies. Before act was, or substance existed, imagination grew in the dark. Man partakes of that ultimate wonder and creativeness. As we turn from the galaxies to the swarming cells of our own being, which toil for something, some entity beyond their grasp, let us remember man, the self-fabricator who came across an ice age to look into the mirrors and the magic of science. Surely he did not come to see himself or his wild visage only. He came because he is at heart a listener and a searcher for some transcendent realm beyond himself. This he has worshiped by many names, even in the dismal caves of his beginning. Man, the self-fabricator, is so by reason of gifts he had no part in devising—and so he searches as the single living cell in the beginning must have sought the ghostly creature it was to serve.

II

The young man Elihu, Job's counselor and critic, spoke simply of the "Teacher," and it is of this teacher I speak when I refer to gifts man had no part in devising. Perhaps—though it is purely a matter of emotional reactions to words—it is easier for us today to speak of this teacher as "nature," that omnipresent all which contained both the spider and my invisible intrusion into her carefully planned universe. But nature does not simply represent reality. In the shapes of life, it prepares the future; it offers alternatives. Nature teaches, though what it teaches is often hidden and obscure, just as the voice from the spinning dust cloud belittled Job's thought but gave back no answers to its own formidable interrogation.

A few months ago I encountered an amazing little creature on a windy corner of my local shopping center. It seemed, at first glance, some long-limbed, feathery spider teetering rapidly down the edge of a store front. Then it swung into the air and, as hesitantly as a spider on a thread, blew away into the parking lot. It returned in a moment on a gust of wind and ran toward me once more on its spindly legs with amazing rapidity.

With great difficulty I discovered the creature was actually a filamentous seed, seeking a hiding place and scurrying about with the uncanny surety of a conscious animal. In fact, it *did* escape me before I could secure it. Its flexible limbs were stiffer than milkweed down, and, propelled by the wind, it ran rapidly and evasively over the pavement. It was like a gnome scampering somewhere with a hidden packet—for all that I could tell, a totally new one: one of the jumbled alphabets of life.

A new one? So stable seem the years and all green leaves, a botanist might smile at my imaginings. Yet bear with me a moment. I would like to tell a tale, a genuine tale of childhood. Moreover, I was just old enough to know the average of my kind and to marvel at what I saw. And what I saw was straight from the hidden Teacher, whatever be his name.

It is told in the Orient of the Hindu god Krishna that his mother, wiping his mouth when he was a child, inadvertently peered in and beheld the universe, though the sight was mercifully and immediately veiled from her. In a sense, this is what happened to me. One day there arrived at our school a newcomer, who entered the grade above me. After some days this lad, whose look of sleepy-eyed arrogance is still before me as I write, was led into my mathematics classroom by the principal. Our class was informed severely that we should learn to work harder.

With this preliminary exhortation, great rows of figures were chalked upon the blackboard, such difficult mathematical problems as could be devised by adults. The class watched in helpless wonder. When the preparations had been completed, the young pupil sauntered forward and, with a glance of infinite boredom that swept from us to his fawning teachers, wrote the answers, as instantaneously as a modern computer, in their proper place upon the board. Then he strolled out with a carelessly exaggerated yawn.

Like some heavy-browed child at the wood's edge, clutching the last stone hand ax, I was witnessing the birth of a new type of humanity—one so beyond its teachers that it was being used for mean purposes while the intangible web of the universe in all its shimmering mathematical perfection glistened untaught in the mind of a chance little boy. The boy, by then grown self-centered and contemptuous, was being dragged from room to room to encourage us, the paleanthropes, to duplicate what, in reality, our teachers could not duplicate. He was too precious an object to be released upon the playground among us, and with reason. In a few months his parents took him away.

Long after, looking back from maturity, I realized that I had been exposed on that occasion, not to human teaching, but to the Teacher, toying with some sixteen billion nerve cells interlocked in ways past understanding. Or, if we do not like the anthropomorphism implied in the word teacher, then nature, the old voice from the whirlwind fumbling for the light. At all events, I had been the fortunate witness to life's unbounded creativity—a creativity seemingly still as unbalanced and chance-filled as in that far era when a black-scaled creature had broken from an egg and the age of the giant reptiles, the creatures of the prime, had tentatively begun.

Because form cannot be long sustained in the living, we collapse inward with age. We die. Our bodies, which were the product of a kind of hidden teaching by an alphabet we are only beginning dimly to discern, are dismissed into their elements. What is carried onward, assuming we have descendants, is the little capsule of instructions such as I encountered hastening by me in the shape of a running seed. We have learned the first biological lesson: that in each generation life passes through the eye of a needle. It exists for a time molecularly and in no recognizable semblance to its adult condition. It *instructs* its way again into man or reptile. As the ages pass, so do variants of the code. Occasionally, a species vanishes on a wind as unreturning as that which took the pterodactyls.

Or the code changes by subtle degrees through the statistical altering of individuals; until I, as the fading Neanderthals must once have done, have looked with still-living eyes upon the creature whose genotype was quite possibly to replace me. The genetic alphabets, like genuine languages, ramify and evolve along unreturning pathways.

If nature's instructions are carried through the eye of a needle, through the molecular darkness of a minute world below the field of human vision and of time's decay, the same, it might be said, is true of those monumental structures known as civilizations. They are transmitted from one generation to another in invisible puffs of air known as words—words that can also be symbolically incised on clay. As the delicate printing on the mud at the water's edge retraces a visit of autumn birds long since departed, so the little scrabbled tablets in perished cities carry the seeds of human thought across the deserts of millennia. In this instance the teacher is the social brain, but it, too, must be compressed into minute hieroglyphs, and the minds that wrought the miracle efface themselves amidst the jostling torrent of messages, which, like the genetic code, are shuffled and reshuffled as they hurry through eternity. Like a mutation, an idea may be recorded in the wrong time, to lie latent like a recessive gene and spring once more to life in an auspicious era.

Occasionally, in the moments when an archaeologist lifts the slab over a tomb that houses a great secret, a few men gain a unique glimpse through that dark portal out of which all men living have emerged, and through which messages again must pass. Here the Mexican archaeologist Ruz Lhuillier speaks of his first penetration of the great tomb hidden beneath dripping stalactites at the pyramid of Palenque: "Out of the dark shadows, rose a fairytale vision, a weird ethereal spectacle from another world. It was like a magician's cave carved out of ice, with walls glittering and sparkling like snow crystals." After shining his torch over hieroglyphs and sculptured figures, the explorer remarked wonderingly: "We were the first people for more than a thousand years to look at it."

Or again, one may read the tale of an unknown pharaoh who had secretly arranged that a beloved woman of his household should be buried in the tomb of the god-king—an act of compassion carrying a personal message across the millennia in defiance of all precedent.

Up to this point we have been talking of the single hidden teacher, the taunting voice out of that old Biblical whirlwind which symbolizes nature. We have seen incredible organic remembrance passed through the needle's eye of a microcosmic world hidden completely beneath the observational powers of creatures preoccupied and ensorcelled by dissolution and decay. We have seen the human mind unconsciously seize upon the principles of that very code to pass its own societal memory forward into time. The individual, the momentary living cell of the society, vanishes, but the institutional structures stand, or if they change, do so in an invisible flux not too dissimilar from that persisting in the stream of genetic continuity.

Upon this world, life is still young, not truly old as stars are measured. Therefore it comes about that we minimize the role of the synapsid reptiles, our remote forerunners, and correspondingly exalt our own intellectual achievements. We refuse to consider that in the old eye of the hurricane we may be, and doubtless are, in aggregate, a slightly more diffuse and dangerous dragon of the primal morning that still enfolds us.

Note that I say "in aggregate." For it is just here, among men, that the role of messages, and, therefore, the role of the individual teacher—or, I should say now, the hidden teachers—began to be more plainly apparent and their instructions become more diverse. The dead pharaoh, though unintentionally, by a revealing act, had succeeded in conveying an impression of human tenderness that has outlasted the trappings of a vanished religion.

Like most modern educators I have listened to student demands to grade their teachers. I have heard the words repeated until they have become a slogan, that no man over thirty can teach the young of this generation. How would one grade a dead pharaoh, millennia gone, I wonder, one who did not intend to teach, but who, to a few perceptive minds, succeeded by the simple nobility of an act.

Many years ago, a student who was destined to become an internationally known anthropologist sat in a course in linguistics and heard his instructor, a man of no inconsiderable wisdom, describe some linguistic peculiarities of Hebrew words. At the time, the young student, at the urging of his family, was contemplating a career in theology. As the teacher warmed to his subject, the student, in the back row, ventured excitedly, "I believe I can understand that, sir. It is very similar to what exists in Mohegan."

The linguist paused and adjusted his glasses. "Young man," he said, "Mohegan is a dead language. Nothing has been recorded of it since the eighteenth century. Don't bluff."

"But sir," the young student countered hopefully, "It can't be dead so long as an old woman I know still speaks it. She is Pequot-Mohegan. I learned a bit of vocabulary from her and could speak with her myself. She took care of me when I was a child."

"Young man," said the austere, old-fashioned scholar, "be at my house for dinner at six this evening. You and I are going to look into this matter."

A few months later, under careful guidance, the young student published a paper upon Mohegan linguistics, the first of a long series of studies upon the forgotten languages and ethnology of the Indians of the northeastern forests. He had changed his vocation and turned to anthropology because of the attraction of a hidden teacher. But just who was the teacher? The young man himself, his instructor, or that solitary speaker of a dying tongue who had so yearned to hear her people's voice that she had softly babbled it to a child?

Later, this man was to become one of my professors. I absorbed much from him, though I hasten to make the reluctant confession that he was considerably beyond thirty. Most of what I learned was gathered over cups of coffee in a dingy campus restaurant. What we talked about were things some centuries older than either of us. Our common interest lay in snakes, scapulimancy, and other forgotten rites of benighted forest hunters.

I have always regarded this man as an extraordinary individual, in fact, a hidden teacher. But alas, it is all now so old-fashioned. We never protested the impracticality of his quaint subjects. We were all too ready to participate in them. He was an excellent canoeman, but he took me to places where I fully expected to drown before securing my degree. To this day, fragments of his unused wisdom remain stuffed in some back attic of my mind. Much of it I have never found the opportunity to employ, yet it has somehow colored my whole adult existence. I belong to that elderly professor in somewhat the same way that he, in turn, had become the wood child of a hidden forest mother.

There are, however, other teachers. For example, among the hunting peoples there were the animal counselors who appeared in prophetic dreams. Or, among the Greeks, the daemonic supernaturals who stood at the headboard while a man lay stark and listened—sometimes to dreadful things. "You are asleep," the messengers proclaimed over and over again, as though the man lay in a spell to hear his doom pronounced. "You, Achilles, you, son of Atreus. You are asleep, asleep," the hidden ones pronounced and vanished.

We of this modern time know other things of dreams, but we know also that they can be interior teachers and healers as well as the anticipators of disaster. It has been said that great art is the night thought of man. It may emerge without warning from the soundless depths of the unconscious, just as supernovas may blaze up suddenly in the farther reaches of void space. The critics, like astronomers, can afterward triangulate such worlds but not account for them.

A writer friend of mine with bitter memories of his youth, and estranged from his family, who, in the interim, had died, gave me this account of the matter in his middle years. He had been working, with an unusual degree of reluctance, upon a novel that contained certain autobiographical episodes. One night he dreamed; it was a very vivid and stunning dream in its detailed reality.

He found himself hurrying over creaking snow through the blackness of a winter night. He was ascending a familiar path through a long-vanished orchard. The path led to his childhood home. The house, as he drew near, appeared dark and uninhabited, but, impelled by the power of the dream, he stepped upon the porch and tried to peer through a dark window into his own old room.

"Suddenly," he told me, "I was drawn by a strange mixture of repulsion and desire to press my face against the glass. I knew intuitively they were all there waiting for me within, if I could but see them. My mother and my father. Those I had loved and those I hated. But the window was black to my gaze. I hesitated a moment and struck a match. For an instant in that freezing silence I saw my father's face glimmer wan and remote behind the glass. My mother's face was there, with the hard, distorted lines that marked her later years.

"A surge of fury overcame my cowardice. I cupped the match before me and stepped closer, closer toward that dreadful confrontation. As the match guttered down, my face was pressed almost to the glass. In some quick transformation, such as only a dream can effect, I saw that it was my own face into which I stared, just as it was reflected in the black glass. My father's haunted face was but my own. The hard lines upon my mother's aging countenance were slowly reshaping themselves upon my living face. The light burned out. I awoke sweating from the terrible psychological tension of that nightmare. I was in a far port in a distant land. It was dawn. I could hear the waves breaking on the reef."

"And how do you interpret the dream?" I asked, concealing a sympathetic shudder and sinking deeper into my chair.

"It taught me something," he said slowly, and with equal slowness a kind of beautiful transfiguration passed over his features. All the tired lines I had known so well seemed faintly to be subsiding.

"Did you ever dream it again?" I asked out of a comparable experience of my own.

"No, never," he said, and hesitated. "You see, I had learned it was just I, but more, much more, I had learned that I was they. It makes a difference. And at the last, late—much too late—it was all right. I understood. My line was dying, but I understood. I hope they understood, too." His voice trailed into silence.

"It is a thing to learn," I said. "You were seeking something and it came." He nodded, wordless. "Out of a tomb," he added after a silent moment, "my kind of tomb—the mind."

On the dark street, walking homeward, I considered my friend's experience. Man, I concluded, may have come to the end of that wild being who had mastered the fire and the lightning. He can create the web but not hold it together, not save himself except by transcending his own image. For at last, before the ultimate mystery, it is himself he shapes. Perhaps it is for this that the listening web lies open: that by knowledge we may grow beyond our past, our follies, and ever closer to what the Dreamer in the dark intended before the dust arose and walked. In the pages of an old book it has been written that we are in the hands of a Teacher, nor does it yet appear what man shall be.

Suggestions for Discussion

1. Discuss the rhetorical importance of the fourth paragraph, which introduces the "lesson from a spider."

2. In what sense is the "spider a symbol of man in miniature"?

3. Explain Eiseley's belief that man is "at heart a listener and a searcher."

Suggestions for Writing

1. Use your observations of the conduct of another creature to make generalizations about human behavior.

2. Speculate on Eiseley's notion that we are "a part of that we do not see."

Amoja Three Rivers

Cultural Etiquette: A Guide

Amoja Three Rivers is a cofounder of the Accessible African Herstory Project. In the following essay originally published in Ms. magazine in 1991, she discusses the serious task of dispelling racial myths and stereotypes through language.

Cultural Etiquette is intended for people of all "races," nationalities, and creeds, not necessarily just "white" people, because no one living in Western society is exempt from the influences of racism, racial stereotypes, race and cultural prejudices, and anti-Semitism. I include anti-Semitism in the discussion of racism because it is simply another manifestation of cultural and racial bigotry.

All people are people. It is ethnocentric to use a generic term such as "people" to refer only to white people and then racially label everyone else. This creates and reinforces the assumption that whites are the norm, the real people, and that all others are aberrations.

"Exotic," when applied to human beings, is ethnocentric and racist.

While it is true that most citizens of the U.S.A. are white, at least four fifths of the world's population consists of people of color. Therefore, it is statistically incorrect as well as ethnocentric to refer to us as minorities. The term "minority" is used to reinforce the idea of people of color as "other."

A cult is a particular system of religious worship. If the religious practices of the Yorubas constitute a cult, then so do those of the Methodists, Catholics, Episcopalians, and so forth.

A large radio/tape player is a boom-box, or a stereo or a box or a large metallic ham sandwich with speakers. It is not a "ghetto blaster."

Everybody can blush. Everybody can bruise. Everybody can tan and get sunburned. Everybody.

Judaism is no more patriarchal than any other patriarchal religion.

Koreans are not taking over. Neither are Jews. Neither are the Japanese. Neither are the West Indians. These are myths put out and maintained by the ones who really have.

All hair is "good" hair. Dreadlocks, locks, dreads, natty dreads, et cetera, is an ancient traditional way that African people sometimes wear their hair. It is not braided, it is "locked." Locking is the natural tendency of African hair to knit and bond to itself. It locks by itself, we don't have to do anything to it to make it lock. It is permanent; once locked, it cannot come undone. It gets washed just as regularly as anyone else's hair. No, you may not touch it, don't ask.

One of the most effective and insidious aspects of racism is cultural genocide. Not only have African Americans been cut off from our African tribal roots, but because of generations of whites pitting African against Indian, and Indian against African, we have been cut off from our Native American roots as well. Consequently, most African Native Americans no longer have tribal affiliations, or know for certain what people they are from.

Columbus didn't discover diddly-squat.

Slavery is not a condition unique to African people. In fact, the word "slave" comes from the Slav people of Eastern Europe. Because so many Slavs were enslaved by other people (including Africans), their very name came to be synonymous with the condition.

Native Americans were also enslaved by Europeans. Because it is almost impossible to successfully enslave large numbers of people in their own land, most enslaved Native Americans from the continental U.S. were shipped to Bermuda, and the West Indies, where many intermarried with the Africans.

People do not have a hard time because of their race or cultural background. No one is attacked, abused, oppressed, pogromed, or enslaved because of their race, creed, or cultural background. People are attacked, abused, oppressed, pogromed, or enslaved because of racism and anti-Semitism. There is a subtle but important difference in the focus here. The first implies some inherent fault or shortcoming within the oppressed person or group. The second redirects the responsibility back to the real source of the problem.

Asians are not "mysterious," "fatalistic," or "inscrutable."

Native Americans are not stoic, mystical, or vanishing.

Latin people are no more hot-tempered, hot-blooded, or emotional than anyone else. We do not have flashing eyes, teeth, or daggers. We are lovers pretty much like other people. Very few of us deal with any kind of drugs.

Middle Easterners are not fanatics, terrorists, or all oil-rich.

Jewish people are not particularly rich, clannish, or expert in money matters.

Not all African Americans are poor, athletic, or ghetto-dwellers.

Most Asians in the U.S. are not scientists, mathematicians, geniuses, or wealthy.

Southerners are no less intelligent than anybody else.

It is not a compliment to tell someone: "I don't think of you as Jewish/ Black/Asian/Latina/Middle Eastern/Native American." Or "I think of you as white."

Do not use a Jewish person or person of color to hear your confession of past racist transgressions. If you have offended a particular person, then apologize directly to that person.

Also don't assume that Jews and people of color necessarily want to hear about how prejudiced your Uncle Fred is, no matter how terrible you think he is.

If you are white and/or gentile, do not assume that the next Jewish person or person of color you see will feel like discussing this guide with you. Sometimes we get tired of teaching this subject.

If you are white, don't brag to a person of color about your overseas trip to our homeland. Especially when we cannot afford such a trip. Similarly, don't assume that we are overjoyed to see the expensive artifacts you bought.

Words like "gestapo," "concentration camp" and "Hitler" are only appropriate when used in reference to the Holocaust.

"Full-blood," "half-breed," "quarter-blood." Any inference that a person's "race" depends on blood is racist. Natives are singled out for this form of bigotry and are denied rights on that basis.

"Scalping": a custom also practiced by the French, the Dutch, and the English.

Do you have friends or acquaintances who are terrific except they're really racist? If you quietly accept that part of them, you are giving their racism tacit approval.

As an exercise, pretend you are from another planet and you want an example of a typical human being for your photo album. Having never heard of racism, you'd probably pick someone who represents the majority of the people on the planet—an Asian person.

How many is too many? We have heard well-meaning liberals say things like "This event is too white. We need more people of color." Well, how many do you need? Fifty? A hundred? Just what is your standard for personal racial comfort?

People of color and Jewish people have been so all their lives. Further, if we have been raised in a place where white gentiles predominate, then we have been subjected to racism/anti-Semitism all our lives. We are therefore experts on our own lives and conditions. If you do not understand or believe or agree with what someone is saying about their own oppression, do not automatically assume that they are wrong or paranoid or oversensitive.

It is not "racism in reverse" or "segregation" for Jews or people of color to come together in affinity groups for mutual support. Sometimes we need some time and space apart from the dominant group just to relax and be ourselves. If people coming together for group support makes you feel excluded, perhaps there's something missing in your own life or cultural connections.

The various cultures of people of color often seem very attractive to white people. (Yes, we are wonderful, we can't deny it.) But white people should not make a playground out of other people's cultures. We are not quaint. We are not exotic. We are not cool.

Don't forget that every white person alive today is also descended from tribal peoples. If you are white, don't neglect your own ancient traditions. They are as valid as anybody else's, and the ways of your own ancestors need to be honored and remembered.

"Race" is an arbitrary and meaningless concept. Races among humans don't exist. If there ever was any such thing as race, there has been so much constant crisscrossing of genes for the last 500,000 years that it would have lost all meaning anyway. There are no real divisions between us, only a continuum of variations that constantly change, as we come together and separate according to the movement of human populations.

Anyone who functions in what is referred to as the "civilized" world is a carrier of the disease of racism.

Does reading this guide make you uncomfortable? Angry? Confused? Are you taking it personally? Well, not to fret. Racism has created a big horrible mess, and racial healing can sometimes be painful. Just remember that Jews and people of color do not want or need anybody's guilt. We just want people to accept responsibility when it is appropriate, and actively work for change.

Suggestions for Discussion

1. Which of the writer's pithy observations strike you as particularly apt and on target? Which seem hyperbolic or unfair? Explain your choices.

2. Discuss how people might "accept responsibility" and "actively work for change." What might you do, as an individual? Give three or four specific examples.

3. Why might reading this guide make one uncomfortable?

Suggestions for Writing

1. Describe one or more examples of sexual, racial, or other stereotyping that you have experienced or observed.

2. Make your own list of ten or more words that might offend certain people.

Fiction

John Cheever

Expelled

John Cheever (1912–1982) was born in Massachusetts where he was expelled from a prep school, and thereby propelled into a literary career. He devoted himself primarily to writing novels and stories, and was published often in *The New Yorker*. He won the Pulitzer Prize in 1979 for the collection *The Stories of John Cheever*. His best-known novels of suburban life are *The Wapshot Chronicle* (1957) and *The Wapshot Scandal* (1964). The prep school in the story "Expelled," which Cheever wrote at seventeen, exists to prepare the sons of the middle class for admission into acceptable Eastern colleges with little concern for aesthetic, moral, or intellectual values.

It didn't come all at once. It took a very long time. First I had a skirmish with the English department and then all the other departments. Pretty soon something had to be done. The first signs were cordialities on the part of the headmaster. He was never nice to anybody unless he was a football star, or hadn't paid his tuition, or was going to be expelled. That's how I knew.

He called me down to his office with the carved chairs arranged in a semi-circle and the brocade curtains resting against the vacant windows. All about him were pictures of people who had got scholarships at Harvard. He asked me to sit down.

"Well, Charles," he said, "some of the teachers say you aren't getting very good marks."

"Yes," I said, "that's true." I didn't care about the marks.

"But Charles," he said, "you know the scholastic standard of this school is very high and we have to drop people when their work becomes unsatisfactory." I told him I knew that also. Then he said a lot of things about the traditions, and the elms, and the magnificent military heritage from our West Point founder.

It was very nice outside of his room. He had his window pushed open halfway and one could see the lawns pulling down to the road behind the trees and the bushes. The gravy-colored curtains were too heavy to move about in the wind, but some papers shifted around on his desk. In a little while I got up and walked out. He turned and started to work again. I went back to my next class.

The next day was very brilliant and the peach branches were full against the dry sky. I could hear people talking and a phonograph playing. The sounds came through the peach blossoms and crossed the room. I lay in bed and thought about a great many things. My dreams had been thick. I remembered two converging hills, some dry apple trees, and a broken blue egg cup. That is all I could remember.

I put on knickers and a soft sweater and headed toward school. My hands shook on the wheel. I was like that all over.

Through the cloudy trees I could see the protrusion of the new tower. It was going to be a beautiful new tower and it was going to cost a great deal of money. Some thought of buying new books for the library instead of putting up a tower, but no one would see the books. People would be able to see the tower five miles off when the leaves were off the trees. It would be done by fall.

When I went into the building the headmaster's secretary was standing in the corridor. She was a nice sort of person with brown funnels of hair furrowed about a round head. She smiled. I guess she must have known.

The Colonel

Every morning we went up into the black chapel. The brisk headmaster was there. Sometimes he had a member of the faculty with him. Sometimes it was a stranger.

He introduced the stranger, whose speech was always the same. In the spring life is like a baseball game. In the fall it is like football. That is what the speaker always said.

The hall is damp and ugly with skylights that rattle in the rain. The seats are hard and you have to hold a hymnbook in your lap. The hymnbook often slips off and that is embarrassing.

On Memorial Day they have the best speaker. They have a mayor or a Governor. Sometimes they have a Governor's second. There is very little preference.

The Governor will tell us what a magnificent country we have. He will tell us to beware of the Red menace. He will want to tell us that the goddam foreigners should have gone home a hell of a long time ago. That they should have stayed in their own goddam countries if they didn't like ours. He will not dare say this though.

If they have a mayor the speech will be longer. He will tell us that our country is beautiful and young and strong. That the War is over, but that if there is another war we must fight. He will tell us that war is a masculine trait that has brought present civilization to its fine condition. Then he will leave us and help stout women place lilacs on graves. He will tell them the same thing.

One Memorial Day they could not get a Governor or a mayor. There was a colonel in the same village who had been to war and who had a chest thick with medals. They asked him to speak. Of course he said he would like to speak.

He was a thin colonel with a soft nose that rested quietly on his face. He was nervous and pushed his wedding ring about his thin finger. When he was introduced he looked at the audience sitting in the uncomfortable chairs. There was silence and the dropping of hymnbooks like the water spouts in the aftermath of a heavy rain.

He spoke softly and quickly. He spoke of war and what he had seen. Then he had to stop. He stopped and looked at the boys. They were staring at their boots. He thought of the empty rooms in the other buildings. He thought of the rectangles of empty desks. He thought of the curtains on the stage and the four Windsor chairs behind him. Then he started to speak again.

He spoke as quickly as he could. He said war was bad. He said that there would never be another war. That he himself should stop it if he could. He swore. He looked at the young faces. They were all very clean. The boys' knees were crossed and their soft pants hung loosely. He thought of the empty desks and began to whimper.

The people sat very still. Some of them felt tight as though they wanted to giggle. Everybody looked serious as the clock struck. It was time for another class.

People began to talk about the colonel after lunch. They looked behind them. They were afraid he might hear them.

It took the school several weeks to get over all this. Nobody said anything, but the colonel was never asked again. If they could not get a Governor or a mayor they could get someone besides a colonel. They made sure of that.

Margaret Courtwright

Margaret Courtwright was very nice. She was slightly bald and pulled her pressed hair down across her forehead. People said that she was the best English teacher in this part of the country, and when boys came back from Harvard they thanked her for the preparation she had given them. She did not like Edgar Guest, but she did like Carl Sandburg. She couldn't seem to understand the similarity. When I told her people laughed at Galsworthy she said that people used to laugh at Wordsworth. She did not believe people were still laughing at Wordsworth. That was what made her so nice.

She came from the West a long time ago. She taught school for so long that people ceased to consider her age. After having seen twenty-seven performances of "Hamlet" and after having taught it for sixteen years, she became a sort of immortal. Her interpretation was the one accepted on college-board papers. That helped everyone a great deal. No one had to get a new interpretation.

When she asked me for tea I sat in a walnut armchair with grapes carved on the head and traced and retraced the arms on the tea caddy. One time I read her one of my plays. She thought it was wonderful. She thought it was wonderful because she did not understand it and because it took two hours to read. When I had finished, she said, "You know that thing just took right hold of me. Really it just swept me right along. I think it's fine that you like to write. I once had a Japanese pupil who liked to write. He was an awfully nice chap until one summer he went down to Provincetown. When he came back he was saying that he could express a complete abstraction. Fancy . . . a complete abstraction. Well, I wouldn't hear of it and told him how absurd it all was and tried to start him off with Galsworthy again, but I guess he had gone just too far. In a little while he left for New York and then Paris. It was really too bad. One summer in Provincetown just ruined him. His marks fell down . . . he cut classes to go to symphony. . . ." She went into the kitchen and got a tray of tarts.

The pastries were flaky and covered with a white coating that made them shine in the dead sunlight. I watched the red filling burst the thin shells and stain the triangles of bright damask. The tarts were good. I ate most of them.

She was afraid I would go the way of her Japanese pupil. She doubted anyone who disagreed with Heine on Shakespeare and Croce on expression.

One day she called me into her antiseptic office and spoke to me of reading Joyce. "You know, Charles," she said, "this sex reality can be quite as absurd as a hypercritical regard for such subjects. You know that, don't you? Of course, you do." Then she went out of the room. She had straight ankles and wore a gold band peppered with diamond chips on her ring finger. She seemed incapable of carrying the weight of the folds in her clothing. Her skirt was askew, either too long in front or hitching up on the side. Always one thing or the other.

When I left school she did not like it. She was afraid I might go too near Provincetown. She wished me good luck and moved the blotter back and forth on her desk. Then she returned to teaching "Hamlet."

Late in February Laura Driscoll got fired for telling her history pupils that Sacco and Vanzetti were innocent. In her farewell appearance the headmaster told everyone how sorry he was that she was going and made it all quite convincing. Then Laura stood up, told the headmaster that he was a damned liar, and waving her fan-spread fingers called the school a hell of a dump where everyone got into a rut.

Miss Courtwright sat closely in her chair and knew it was true. She didn't mind much. Professor Rogers with his anti-feminization movement bothered her a little, too. But she knew that she had been teaching school for a long time now and no movement was going to put her out of a job overnight— what with all the boys she had smuggled into Harvard and sixteen years of "Hamlet."

Laura Driscoll

History classes are always dead. This follows quite logically, for history is a dead subject. It has not the death of dead fruit or dead textiles or dead light. It has a different death. There is not the timeless quality of death about it. It is dead like scenery in the opera. It is on cracked canvas and the paint has faded and peeled and the lights are too bright. It is dead like old water in a zinc bathtub.

"We are going to study ancient history this year," the teacher will tell the pupils. "Yes, ancient history will be our field.

"Now of course, this class is not a class of children any longer. I expect the discipline to be the discipline of well-bred young people. We shall not have to waste any time on the scolding of younger children. No. We shall just be able to spend all our time on ancient history.

"Now about questions. I shall answer questions if they are important. If I do not think them important I shall not answer them, for the year is short, and we must cover a lot of ground in a short time. That is, if we all cooperate and behave and not ask too many questions we shall cover the subject and have enough time at the end of the year for review.

"You may be interested in the fact that a large percentage of this class was certified last year. I should like to have a larger number this year. Just think, boys: wouldn't it be fine if a very large number—a number larger than last year—was certified? Wouldn't that be fine? Well, there's no reason why we can't do it if we all cooperate and behave and don't ask too many questions.

"You must remember that I have twelve people to worry about and that you have only one. If each person will take care of his own work and pass in his notebook on time it will save me a lot of trouble. Time and trouble mean whether you get into college or not, and I want you all to get into college.

"If you will take care of your own little duties, doing what is assigned to you and doing it well, we shall all get along fine. You are a brilliant-looking group of young people, and I want to have you all certified. I want to get you into college with as little trouble as possible.

"Now about the books. . . ."

I do not know how long history classes have been like this. One time or another I suppose history was alive. That was before it died its horrible fly-dappled unquivering death.

Everyone seems to know that history is dead. No one is alarmed. The pupils and the teachers love dead history. They do not like it when it is alive. When Laura Driscoll dragged history into the classroom, squirming and smelling of something bitter, they fired Laura and strangled the history. It was too tumultuous. Too turbulent.

In history one's intellect is used for mechanical speculation on a probable century or background. One's memory is applied to a list of dead dates and names. When one begins to apply one's intellect to the mental scope of the period, to the emotional development of its inhabitants, one becomes dangerous. Laura Driscoll was terribly dangerous. That's why Laura was never a good history teacher.

She was not the first history teacher I had ever had. She is not the last I will have. But she is the only teacher I have ever had who could feel history with an emotional vibrance—or, if the person was too oblique, with a poetic understanding. She was five feet four inches tall, brown-haired, and bent-legged from horseback riding. All the boys thought Laura Driscoll was a swell teacher.

She was the only history teacher I have ever seen who was often ecstatical. She would stand by the boards and shout out her discoveries on the Egyptian cultures. She made the gargoylic churnings of Chartres in a heavy rain present an applicable meaning. She taught history as an interminable flood of events viewed through the distortion of our own immediacy. She taught history in the broad-handed rhythms of Hauptmann's drama, in the static melancholy of Egypt moving before its own shadow down the long sand, in the fluted symmetry of the Doric culture. She taught history as a hypothesis from which we could extract the evaluation of our own lives.

She was the only teacher who realized that, coming from the West, she had little business to be teaching these children of New England.

"I do not know what your reaction to the sea is," she would say. "For I have come from a land where there is no sea. My elements are the fields, the sun, the plastic cadence of the clouds and the cloudlessness. You have been brought up by the sea. You have been coached in the cadence of the breakers and the strength of the wind.

"My emotional viewpoints will differ from yours. Do not let me impose my perceptions upon you."

However, the college-board people didn't care about Chartres as long as you knew the date. They didn't care whether history was looked at from the mountains or the sea. Laura spent too much time on such trivia and all of her pupils didn't get into Harvard. In fact, very few of her pupils got into Harvard, and this didn't speak well for her.

While the other members of the faculty chattered over Hepplewhite legs and Duncan Phyfe embellishments, Laura was before five-handed Siva or the sexless compassion glorious in its faded polychrome. Laura didn't think much of America. Laura made this obvious and the faculty heard about it. The faculty all thought America was beautiful. They didn't like people to disagree.

However, the consummation did not occur until late in February. It was cold and clear and the snow was deep. Outside the windows there was the enormous roaring of broken ice. It was late in February that Laura Driscoll said Sacco and Vanzetti were undeserving of their treatment.

This got everyone all up in the air. Even the headmaster was disconcerted.

The faculty met.

The parents wrote letters.

Laura Driscoll was fired.

"Miss Driscoll," said the headmaster during her last chapel at the school, "has found it necessary to return to the West. In the few months that we have had her with us, she has been a staunch friend of the academy, a woman whom we all admire and love and who, we are sure, loves and admires the academy and its elms as we do. We are all sorry Miss Driscoll is leaving us. . . ."

Then Laura got up, called him a damned liar, swore down the length of the platform and walked out of the building.

No one ever saw Laura Driscoll again. By the way everyone talked, no one wanted to. That was all late in February. By March the school was quiet again. The new history teacher taught dates. Everyone carefully forgot about Laura Driscoll.

"She was a nice girl," said the headmaster, "but she really wasn't made for teaching history. . . . No, she really wasn't a born history teacher."

Five Months Later

The spring of five months ago was the most beautiful spring I have ever lived in. The year before I had not known all about the trees and the heavy peach blossoms and the tea-colored brooks that shook down over the brown rocks. Five months ago it was spring and I was in school.

In school the white limbs beyond the study hall shook out a greenness, and the tennis courts became white and scalding. The air was empty and hard, and the vacant wind dragged shadows over the road. I knew all this only from the classrooms.

I knew about the trees from the window frames. I knew the rain only from the sounds on the roof. I was tired of seeing spring with walls and awnings to intercept the sweet sun and the hard fruit. I wanted to go outdoors and see the spring. I wanted to feel and taste the air and be among the shadows. That is perhaps why I left school.

In the spring I was glad to leave school. Everything outside was elegant and savage and fleshy. Everything inside was slow and cool and vacant. It seemed a shame to stay inside.

But in a little while the spring went. I was left outside and there was no spring. I did not want to go in again. I would not have gone in again for anything. I was sorry, but I was not sorry over the fact that I had gone out. I was sorry that the outside and the inside could not have been open to one another. I was sorry that there were roofs on the classrooms and trousers on the legs of the instructors to insulate their contacts. I was not sorry that I had left school. I was sorry that I left for the reasons that I did.

If I had left because I had to go to work or because I was sick it would not have been so bad. Leaving because you are angry and frustrated is different. It is not a good thing to do. It is bad for everyone.

Of course it was not the fault of the school. The headmaster and faculty were doing what they were supposed to do. It was just a preparatory school trying to please the colleges. A school that was doing everything the colleges asked it to do.

It was not the fault of the school at all. It was the fault of the system—the noneducational system, the college-preparatory system. That was what made the school so useless.

As a college-preparatory school it was a fine school. In five years they could make raw material look like college material. They could clothe it and breed it and make it say the right things when the colleges asked it to talk. That was its duty.

They weren't prepared to educate anybody. They were members of a college-preparatory system. No one around there wanted to be educated. No sir.

They presented the subjects the colleges required. They had math, English, history, languages, and music. They once had had an art department but it had been dropped. "We have enough to do," said the headmaster, "just to get all these people into college without trying to teach them art. Yes sir, we have quite enough to do as it is."

Of course there were literary appreciation and art appreciation and musical appreciation, but they didn't count for much. If you are young, there is very little in Thackeray that is parallel to your own world. Van Dyke's "Abbé Scaglia" and the fretwork of Mozart quartets are not for the focus of your ears and eyes. All the literature and art that holds a similarity to your life is forgotten. Some of it is even forbidden.

Our country is the best country in the world. We are swimming in prosperity and our President is the best president in the world. We have larger apples and better cotton and faster and more beautiful machines. This makes us the greatest country in the world. Unemployment is a myth. Dissatisfaction is a fable. In preparatory school America is beautiful. It is the gem of the ocean and it is too bad. It is bad because people believe it all. Because they become indifferent. Because they marry and reproduce and vote and they know nothing. Because the tempered newspaper keeps its eyes ceilingwards and does not see the dirty floor. Because all they know is the tempered newspaper.

But I will not say any more. I do not stand in a place where I can talk.

And now it is August. The orchards are stinking ripe. The tea-colored brooks run beneath the rocks. There is sediment on the stone and no wind in the willows. Everyone is preparing to go back to school. I have no school to go back to.

I am not sorry. I am not at all glad.

It is strange to be so very young and to have no place to report to at nine o'clock. That is what education has always been. It has been laced curtseys and perfumed punctualities.

But now it is nothing. It is symmetric with my life. I am lost in it. That is why I am not standing in a place where I can talk.

The school windows are being washed. The floors are thick with fresh oil.

Soon it will be time for the snow and the symphonies. It will be time for Brahms and the great dry winds.

Suggestions for Discussion

1. Why is Charles expelled from his school? How does he respond to his expulsion?

2. Explain the form the story takes as a series of short portraits. How do these portraits serve to express Charles's view of the school?

3. Compare Margaret Courtwright with Laura Driscoll. Which was the better teacher? Why?

4. How did the Colonel embarrass the school on Memorial Day? What is Charles's reaction to him? What does his reaction reveal about Charles?

5. Explain the function of the last section of the story.

Suggestion for Writing

What do you believe to be the primary purpose of education? Is it different from that described in the story? What do you expect from an education? Write an essay in which you explain your ideas.

==========

Grace Paley

The Loudest Voice

Grace Paley (b. 1922) grew up in New York City and studied at Hunter College. Her works include *The Little Disturbances of Man* (1959), *Later the Same Day* (1985), and *New and Collected Poems* (1992). "The Loudest Voice" is a humorous look at the Christmas holidays in an ethnically diverse New York public school.

There is a certain place where dumb-waiters boom, doors slam, dishes crash; every window is a mother's mouth bidding the street shut up, go skate somewhere else, come home. My voice is the loudest.

There, my own mother is still as full of breathing as me and the grocer stands up to speak to her. "Mrs. Abramowitz," he says, "people should not be afraid of their children."

"Ah, Mr. Bialik," my mother replies, "if you say to her or her father 'Ssh,' they say, 'In the grave it will be quiet.' "

"From Coney Island to the cemetery," says my papa. "It's the same subway; it's the same fare."

I am right next to the pickle barrel. My pinky is making tiny whirlpools in the brine. I stop a moment to announce: "Campbell's Tomato Soup. Campbell's Vegetable Beef Soup. Campbell's S-c-otch Broth . . ."

"Be quiet," the grocer says, "the labels are coming off."

"Please, Shirley, be a little quiet," my mother begs me.

In that place the whole street groans: Be quiet! Be quiet! but steals from the happy chorus of my inside self not a tittle or a jot.

There, too, but just around the corner, is a red brick building that has been old for many years. Every morning the children stand before it in double lines which must be straight. They are not insulted. They are waiting anyway.

I am usually among them. I am, in fact, the first, since I begin with "A."

One cold morning the monitor tapped me on the shoulder. "Go to Room 409, Shirley Abramowitz," he said. I did as I was told. I went in a hurry up a down staircase to Room 409, which contained sixth-graders. I had to wait at the desk without wiggling until Mr. Hilton, their teacher, had time to speak.

After five minutes he said, "Shirley?"

"What?" I whispered.

He said, "My! My! Shirley Abramowitz! They told me you had a particularly loud, clear voice and read with lots of expression. Could that be true?"

"Oh yes," I whispered.

"In that case, don't be silly; I might very well be your teacher someday. Speak up, speak up."

"Yes," I shouted.

"More like it," he said. "Now, Shirley, can you put a ribbon in your hair or a bobby pin? It's too messy."

"Yes!" I bawled.

"Now, now, calm down." He turned to the class. "Children, not a sound. Open at page 39. Read till 52. When you finish, start again." He looked me over once more. "Now, Shirley, you know, I suppose, that Christmas is coming. We are preparing a beautiful play. Most of the parts have been given out. But I still need a child with a strong voice, lots of stamina. Do you know what stamina is? You do? Smart kid. You know, I heard you read 'The Lord is my shepherd' in Assembly yesterday. I was very impressed. Wonderful delivery. Mrs. Jordan, your teacher, speaks highly of you. Now listen to me, Shirley Abramowitz, if you want to take the part and be in the play, repeat after me, 'I swear to work harder than I ever did before.' "

I looked to heaven and said at once, "Oh, I swear." I kissed my pinky and looked at God.

"That is an actor's life, my dear," he explained. "Like a soldier's, never tardy or disobedient to his general, the director. Everything," he said, "absolutely everything will depend on you."

That afternoon, all over the building, children scraped and scrubbed the turkeys and the sheaves of corn off the schoolroom windows. Good-bye Thanksgiving. The next morning a monitor brought red paper and green paper from the office. We made new shapes and hung them on the walls and glued them to the doors.

The teachers became happier and happier. Their heads were ringing like the bells of childhood. My best friend Evie was prone to evil, but she did not get a single demerit for whispering. We learned "Holy Night" without an error. "How wonderful!" said Miss Glacé, the student teacher. "To think that some of you don't even speak the language!" We learned "Deck the Halls" and "Hark! The Herald Angels." . . . They weren't ashamed and we weren't embarrassed.

Oh, but when my mother heard about it all, she said to my father: "Misha, you don't know what's going on there. Cramer is the head of the Tickets Committee."

"Who?" asked my father. "Cramer? Oh yes, an active woman."

"Active? Active has to have a reason. Listen," she said sadly, "I'm surprised to see my neighbors making tra-la-la for Christmas."

My father couldn't think of what to say to that. Then he decided: "You're in America! Clara, you wanted to come here. In Palestine the Arabs would be eating you alive. Europe you had pogroms. Argentina is full of Indians. Here you got Christmas. . . . Some joke, ha?"

"Very funny, Misha. What is becoming of you? If we came to a new country a long time ago to run away from tyrants, and instead we fall into a creeping pogrom, that our children learn a lot of lies, so what's the joke? Ach, Misha, your idealism is going away."

"So is your sense of humor."

"That I never had, but idealism you had a lot of."

"I'm the same Misha Abramovitch, I didn't change an iota. Ask anyone."

"Only ask me," says my mama, may she rest in peace. "I got the answer."

Meanwhile the neighbors had to think of what to say too.

Marty's father said: "You know, he has a very important part, my boy."

"Mine also," said Mr. Sauerfeld.

"Not my boy!" said Mrs. Klieg. "I said to him no. The answer is no. When I say no! I mean no!"

The rabbi's wife said, "It's disgusting!" But no one listened to her. Under the narrow sky of God's great wisdom she wore a strawberry-blond wig.

Every day was noisy and full of experience. I was Right-hand Man. Mr. Hilton said: "How could I get along without you, Shirley?"

He said: "Your mother and father ought to get down on their knees every night and thank God for giving them a child like you."

He also said: "You're absolutely a pleasure to work with, my dear, dear child."

Sometimes he said: "For God's sakes, what did I do with the script? Shirley! Shirley! Find it."

Then I answered quietly: "Here it is, Mr. Hilton."

Once in a while, when he was very tired, he would cry out: "Shirley, I'm just tired of screaming at those kids. Will you tell Ira Pushkov not to come in till Lester points to that star the second time?"

Then I roared: "Ira Pushkov, what's the matter with you? Dope! Mr. Hilton told you five times already, don't come in till Lester points to that star the second time."

"Ach, Clara," my father asked, "what does she do there till six o'clock she can't even put the plates on the table?"

"Christmas," said my mother coldly.

"Ho! Ho!" my father said. "Christmas. What's the harm? After all, history teaches everyone. We learn from reading this is a holiday from pagan times also, candles, lights, even Chanukah. So we learn it's not altogether Christian. So if they think it's a private holiday, they're only ignorant, not patriotic. What belongs to history, belongs to all men. You want to go back to the Middle Ages? Is it better to shave your head with a secondhand razor? Does it hurt Shirley to learn to speak up? It does not. So maybe someday she won't live between the kitchen and the shop. She's not a fool."

I thank you, Papa, for your kindness. It is true about me to this day. I am foolish but I am not a fool.

That night my father kissed me and said with great interest in my career, "Shirley, tomorrow's your big day. Congrats."

"Save it," my mother said. Then she shut all the windows in order to prevent tonsillitis.

In the morning it snowed. On the street corner a tree had been decorated for us by a kind city administration. In order to miss its chilly shadow our neighbors walked three blocks east to buy a loaf of bread. The butcher pulled down black window shades to keep the colored lights from shining on his chickens. Oh, not me. On the way to school, with both my hands I tossed it a kiss of tolerance. Poor thing, it was a stranger in Egypt.

I walked straight into the auditorium past the staring children. "Go ahead, Shirley!" said the monitors. Four boys, big for their age, had already started work as propmen and stagehands.

Mr. Hilton was very nervous. He was not even happy. Whatever he started to say ended in a sideward look of sadness. He sat slumped in the middle of the first row and asked me to help Miss Glacé. I did this, although she thought my voice too resonant and said, "Show-off!"

Parents began to arrive long before we were ready. They wanted to make a good impression. From among the yards of drapes I peeked out at the audience. I saw my embarrassed mother.

Ira, Lester, and Meyer were pasted to their beards by Miss Glacé. She almost forgot to thread the star on its wire, but I reminded her. I coughed a few times to clear my throat. Miss Glacé looked around and saw that everyone was in costume and on line waiting to play his part. She whispered, "All right . . ." Then:

Jackie Sauerfeld, the prettiest boy in first grade, parted the curtains with his skinny elbow and in a high voice sang out:

> "Parents dear
> We are here
> To make a Christmas play in time.
> It we give
> In narrative
> And illustrate with pantomime."

He disappeared.

My voice burst immediately from the wings to the great shock of Ira, Lester, and Meyer, who were waiting for it but were surprised all the same. "I remember, I remember, the house where I was born . . ."

Miss Glacé yanked the curtain open and there it was, the house—an old hayloft, where Celia Kornbluh lay in the straw with Cindy Lou, her favorite doll. Ira, Lester, and Meyer moved slowly from the wings toward her, sometimes pointing to a moving star and sometimes ahead to Cindy Lou.

It was a long story and it was a sad story. I carefully pronounced all the words about my lonesome childhood, while little Eddie Braunstein wandered upstage and down with his shepherd's stick, looking for sheep. I brought up lonesomeness again, and not being understood at all except by some women everybody hated. Eddie was too small for that and Marty Groff took his place, wearing his father's prayer shawl. I announced twelve friends, and half the boys in the fourth grade gathered round Marty, who stood on an orange crate while my voice harangued. Sorrowful and loud, I declaimed about love and God and Man, but because of the terrible deceit of Abie Stock we came suddenly to a famous moment. Marty, whose remembering tongue I was, waited at the foot of the cross. He stared desperately at the audience. I groaned, "My God, my God why hast thou forsaken me?" The soldiers who were sheiks grabbed poor Marty to pin him up to die, but he wrenched free, turned again to the audience, and spread his arms aloft to show despair and the end. I murmured at the top of my voice, "The rest is silence, but as everyone in this room, in this city—in this world—now knows, I shall have life eternal."

That night Mrs. Kornbluh visited our kitchen for a glass of tea.

"How's the virgin?" asked my father with a look of concern.

"For a man with a daughter, you got a fresh mouth, Abramovitch."

"Here," said my father kindly, "have some lemon, it'll sweeten your disposition."

They debated a little in Yiddish, then fell in a puddle of Russian and Polish. What I understood next was my father, who said, "Still and all, it was certainly a beautiful affair, you have to admit, introducing us to the beliefs of a different culture."

"Well, yes," said Mrs. Kornbluh. "The only thing . . . you know Charlie Turner—that cute boy in Celia's class—a couple others? They got very small parts or no part at all. In very bad taste, it seemed to me. After all, it's their religion."

"Ach," explained my mother, "what could Mr. Hilton do? They got very small voices; after all, why should they holler? The English language they know from the beginning by heart. They're blond like angels. You think it's so important they should get in the play? Christmas . . . the whole piece of goods . . . they own it."

I listened and listened until I couldn't listen any more. Too sleepy, I climbed out of bed and kneeled. I made a little church of my hands and said, "Hear, O Israel . . ." Then I called out in Yiddish, "Please, good night, good night. Ssh." My father said, "Ssh yourself," and slammed the kitchen door.

I was happy. I fell asleep at once. I had prayed for everybody: my talking family, cousins far away, passersby, and all the lonesome Christians. I expected to be heard. My voice was certainly the loudest.

Suggestions for Discussion

1. Explain the significance of the title of the story.

2. Discuss Shirley's opportunity, her predicament, and the resolution of the story.

3. Discuss Paley's humorous, yet respectful interweaving of Jewish tradition and sensibility with the public school celebration of the Christmas season.

Suggestions for Writing

1. Write about several examples of Paley's humor.

2. Describe a situation in which you or someone you know encountered pressure to perform in public.

Poetry

Langston Hughes

Theme for English B

Langston Hughes (1902–1962), a prominent black poet, was born in Missouri and educated at Lincoln University in Pennsylvania. Often using dialect and jazz rhythms, his work expresses the concerns and feelings of American blacks. His collections of poetry include *The Weary Blues* (1926) and *Shakespeare in Harlem* (1940); his novels include *Not Without Laughter* (1930) and *The Best of Simple* (1950). In "Theme for English B" he clearly expresses the chasm between the races that exists even in the college classroom.

The instructor said,

> *Go home and write*
> *a page tonight.*
> *And let that page come out of you—*
> *Then, it will be true.*

I wonder if it's that simple?
I am twenty-two, colored, born in Winston-Salem.
I went to school there, then Durham, then here
to this college on the hill above Harlem.
I am the only colored student in my class.
The steps from the hill lead down into Harlem,
through a park, then I cross St. Nicholas,
Eighth Avenue, Seventh, and I come to the Y,
the Harlem Branch Y, where I take the elevator
up to my room, sit down, and write this page:

It's not easy to know what is true for you or me
at twenty-two, my age. But I guess I'm what
I feel and see and hear, Harlem, I hear you:
hear you, hear me—we two—you, me, talk on this page.
(I hear New York, too.) Me—who?

Well, I like to eat, sleep, drink, and be in love.
I like to work, read, learn, and understand life.
I like a pipe for a Christmas present,
or records—Bessie, bop, or Bach.
I guess being colored doesn't make me *not* like
the same things others folks like who are other races.
So will my page be colored that I write?

Being me, it will not be white.
But it will be
a part of you, instructor.
You are white—
yet a part of me, as I am a part of you.

That's American.
Sometimes perhaps you don't want to be a part of me.
Nor do I often want to be a part of you.
But we are, that's true!
As I learn from you,
I guess you learn from me—
Although you're older—and white—
and somewhat more free.

This is my page for English B.

Suggestions for Discussion

1. With what details does Hughes convey a strong sense of identity?
2. How does he reveal his feelings about composition, learning, Harlem, his racial background, and his instructor?

Suggestion for Writing

Write an essay in which you attempt to convey some of your feelings about your own background, your likes and dislikes. Try to focus on details as Hughes has done in his poem.

Lawrence Raab

The Shakespeare Lesson

Lawrence Raab (b. 1949) is professor of English at Williams College. His collections of poetry include *Other Children* (1987) and *What We Don't Know About Each Other* (1993). "The Shakespeare Lesson," a poem dedicated to his colleague at Williams, John Reichert, explores a classroom discussion of the play *Antony and Cleopatra.*

For John Reichert

None of the students liked Cleopatra.
    She was selfish, they said, and Antony
was a wimp—because he wouldn't decide
    how he felt, because he ran away,
and couldn't even kill himself.

They were so impatient
    with the languors of Egypt, the perfume
and the barges, those fond little games
    he felt so close to.
Is there anyone you admire? he asked,

himself half in love with Cleopatra.
Caesar, one student answered,
because Caesar knew what he wanted.
The sun caught in the smudged-up
panes of glass; he fiddled with the lectern.

Could he tell them Caesar
was the wrong answer?
Antony, after all, had betrayed the man
his soldiers needed him to be.
And Cleopatra was foolish, unpredictable . . .

Could he ask them not to feel
so certain about what they felt?
He said it was complicated.
Why does it have to be complicated?
someone asked. Is that always good?

And shouldn't they have talked,
figured out what they meant
to each other? Why does everybody
always have to die?
Let's look at the last scene, he said,

and saw a stage crowded with bodies,
saw her body displayed among the others.
How does it make you feel?
he asked, although he did not know anymore
what he wanted them to say.

Suggestions for Discussion

1. What problems does the professor have teaching Shakespeare's play?

2. Discuss Raab's resolution of the tension and anxiety in the class.

Suggestions for Writing

1. Describe a class of your own in which students and teacher did not seem to communicate effectively. Analyze the problems and tell how professor and students handled the situation.

2. Describe a class in which you, the other students, and the professor worked together with unusual effectiveness.

Theodore Roethke

Elegy for Jane: My Student,
Thrown by a Horse

Theodore Roethke (1908–1963) was born in Michigan and educated at the University of Michigan and Harvard. His poetry celebrated human relationships, the land, and all growing things with wit, an inventive verse form, and, at times, an almost surrealist language. He taught poetry writing for many years at the University of Washington in Seattle, and won the Pulitzer Prize for *The Waking* (1953). His other collections include *The Lost Son and Other Poems* (1949) and *The Far Field* (1964). Essays and lectures are collected in *The Poet and His Craft* (1965). "Elegy for Jane" is a tender poem expressing grief at the death of one of his students. Like many other modern poems on death, it achieves its force through wit and understatement.

I remember the neckcurls, limp and damp as tendrils;
And her quick look, a sidelong pickerel smile;
And how, once startled into talk, the light syllables leaped for her,
And she balanced in the delight of her thought,
A wren, happy, tail into the wind,
Her song trembling the twigs and small branches.
The shade sang with her;
The leaves, their whispers turned to kissing;
And the mold sang in the bleached valleys under the rose.

Oh, when she was sad, she cast herself down into such a pure depth,
Even a father could not find her:
Scraping her cheek against straw;
Stirring the clearest water.

My sparrow, you are not here,
Waiting like a fern, making a spiny shadow.
The sides of wet stones cannot console me,
Nor the moss, wound with the last light.

If only I could nudge you from this sleep,
My maimed darling, my skittery pigeon.
Over this damp grave I speak the words of my love:
I, with no rights in this matter,
Neither father nor lover.

Suggestions for Discussion

1. What is the relation of the first two stanzas to the rest of the poem?

2. How does the poet remember his dead student? What is the effect of the details he recalls?

3. Why does he call his dead student "my maimed darling" or "my skittery pigeon"? How would you describe this language?

4. Discuss the feelings that the poem expresses. How do you relate these feelings to the poet's language?

5. Explain the last two lines of the poem.

Suggestion for Writing

This poem expresses the feelings of a teacher for a dead student. Does this expression of feeling come as a surprise to you? Write an essay in which you discuss, from your experience, the kinds of relationships that exist between teachers and students. Relate your comments to the feelings expressed in this poem.

Marianne Moore

The Student

Marianne Moore (1887–1972) was born in Missouri, was graduated from Bryn Mawr College, taught at an Indian school, worked in the New York Public Library, and edited *The Dial* (1925–1929). Her early poems were published in 1921, her *Collected Poems* in 1951. She also wrote *Predilections* (1955), a volume of critical essays, a poetic translation of La Fontaine's *Fables* (1954), and a collection of poetry, *Tell Me, Tell Me* (1967). The following poem, taken from *What Are Years?* (1941, 1969), analyzes and praises the student.

"In America," began
the lecturer, "everyone must have a
degree. The French do not think that
all can have it, they don't say everyone
    must go to college." We
do incline to feel
    that although it may be unnecessary

to know fifteen languages,
one degree is not too much. With us, a
school—like the singing tree of which
the leaves were mouths singing in concert—is
    both a tree of knowledge
and of liberty,—
    seen in the unanimity of college
mottoes, *lux et veritas*,
Christo et ecclesiae, sapiet

felici. It may be that we
have not knowledge, just opinions, that we
    are undergraduates,
not students; we know
    we have been told with smiles, by expatriates

of whom we had asked "When will
your experiment be finished?" "Science
is never finished." Secluded
from domestic strife, Jack Bookworm led a
    college life, says Goldsmith;
and here also as
    in France or Oxford, study is beset with

dangers,—with bookworms, mildews,
and complaisancies. But someone in New
England has known enough to say
the student is patience personified,
    is a variety
of hero, "patient
    of neglect and of reproach,"—who can "hold by

himself." You can't beat hens to
make them lay. Wolf's wool is the best of wool,
but it cannot be sheared because
the wolf will not comply. With knowledge as
    with the wolf's surliness,
the student studies
    voluntarily refusing to be less

than individual. He
"gives his opinion and then rests on it";
he renders service when there is
no reward, and is too reclusive for
    some things to seem to touch
him, not because he
    has no feeling but because he has so much.

Suggestions for Discussion

1. What significance do you find in quotations from Einstein, lines 23–24, and Emerson, lines 34–35?

2. Finally, what values does Moore find in the student?

Suggestion for Writing

Define the life of the student in your college.

Richard Wilbur

A Finished Man

The distinguished American poet Richard Wilbur served as Poet Laureate of
the United States in 1987. Winner of the National Book Award, he has also
won the Pulitzer Prize for Poetry in 1957 and 1989. In addition to his translations of Molière's plays, Wilbur has published such collections of his own
poetry as *The Poems of Richard Wilbur* (1987) and *New and Collected Poems* (1988).

Of the four louts who threw him off the dock,
Three are now dead, and so more faintly mock
The way he choked and splashed and was afraid.
His memory of the fourth begins to fade.

It was himself whom he could not forgive;
Yet it has been a comfort to outlive
That woman, stunned by his appalling gaffe,
Who with a napkin half suppressed her laugh,

Or that gray colleague, surely gone by now,
Who, turning toward the window, raised his brow,
Embarrassed to have caught him in a lie.
All witness darkens, eye by dimming eye.

Thus he can walk today with heart at ease
Through the old quad, escorted by trustees,
To dedicate the monumental gym
A grateful college means to name for him.

Seated, he feels the warm sun sculpt his cheek
As the young president gets up to speak.
If the dead die, if he can but forget,
If money talks, he may be perfect yet.

Suggestions for Discussion

1. What thoughts run through the mind of the distinguished alumnus?

2. What values does he represent? Are they all attractive?

Suggestion for Writing

Describe a college ceremony you have attended. Speculate on the motives of various
participants, including yourself.

The Examined Life: Personal Values

If we put a high value on decency, if we put a high value on excellence and on family, if we love the people we share our lives with—our wives and husbands, our children—and if we don't shortchange them for a few bucks, if we can love the work we do and learn the skill of it, if we can give full measure to the people who pay us for our work, if we try not to lie, try not to cheat, try to do good just by doing well whatever we do . . . then we will have made a revolution.

Alan Alda, "You Have to Know What Your Values Are!"

Trexler felt invigorated. Suddenly his sickness seemed health, his dizziness stability. A small tree, rising between him and the light, stood there saturated with the evening, each gilt-edged leaf perfectly drunk with excellence and delicacy. Trexler's spine registered an ever so slight tremor as it picked up this natural disturbance in the lovely scene. "I want the second tree from the corner, just as it stands," he said, answering an imaginary question from an imaginary physician. And he felt a slow pride in realizing that what he wanted none could bestow, and that what he had none could take away. He felt content to be sick, unembarrassed at being afraid; and in the jungle of his fear he glimpsed (as he had so often glimpsed them before) the flashy tail feathers of the bird courage.

—E. B. White, "The Second Tree from the Corner"

I who am blind can give one hint to those who see—one admonition to those who would make full use of the gift of sight: Use your eyes as if tomorrow you would be stricken blind. And the same method can be applied to the other senses. Hear the music of voices, the song of a bird, the mighty strains of an orchestra, as if you would be stricken deaf tomorrow. Touch each object you want to touch as if tomorrow your tactile sense would fail. Smell the perfume of flowers, taste with relish each morsel, as if tomorrow you could never smell and taste again. Make the most of every sense; glory in all the facts of pleasure and beauty which the world reveals to you through the several means of contact which Nature provides. But of all the senses, I am sure that sight must be the most delightful.

Helen Keller, "Three Days to See"

The secret of seeing, then, is the pearl of great price. If I thought he could teach me to find it and keep it forever I would stagger barefoot across a hundred deserts after any lunatic at all. But although the pearl may be found, it may not be sought. The literature of illumination reveals this above all: although it comes to those who wait for it, it is always, even to the most practiced and adept, a gift and a total surprise.

Annie Dillard, "Sight into Insight"

I went to the woods because I wished to live deliberately, to front only the essential facts of life, and see if I could not learn what it had to teach, and not, when I came to die, discover that I had not lived. I did not wish to live what was not life, living is so dear; nor did I wish to practice resignation, unless it was quite necessary. I wanted to live deep and suck out all the marrow of life, to live so sturdily and Spartan-like as to put to rout all that was not life, to cut a broad swath and shave close, to drive life into a corner, and reduce it to its lowest terms, and, if it proved to be mean, why then to get the whole and genuine meanness of it, and publish its meanness to the world; or if it were sublime, to know it by experience, and be able to give a true account of it in my next excursion.

Henry David Thoreau, "Why I Went to the Woods"

Personal Reminiscences

Annie Dillard

Sight into Insight

Annie Dillard (b. 1945), a contributing editor to Harper's, won a Pulitzer Prize in 1974 for Pilgrim at Tinker Creek. More recent books include Living by Fiction and Teaching a Stone to Talk: Expeditions and Encounters, both published in 1982, and An American Childhood (1987). There are people of dull vision who don't really see and those like the writer for whom the effort truly to see is "a discipline requiring a lifetime of dedicated struggle."

When I was six or seven years old, growing up Pittsburgh, I used to take a precious penny of my own and hide it for someone else to find. It was a curious compulsion; sadly, I've never been seized by it since. For some reason I always "hid" the penny along the same stretch of sidewalk up the street. I'd cradle it at the roots of a maple, say, or in a hole left by a chipped-off piece of sidewalk. Then I'd take a piece of chalk and, starting at either end of the block, draw huge arrows leading up to the penny from both directions. After I learned to write I labeled the arrows "SURPRISE AHEAD" or "MONEY THIS WAY." I was greatly excited, during all this arrow-drawing, at the thought of the first lucky passerby who would receive in this way, regardless of merit, a free gift from the universe. But I never lurked about. I'd go straight home and not give the matter another thought, until, some months later, I would be gripped by the impulse to hide another penny.

There are lots of things to see, unwrapped gifts and free surprises. The world is fairly studded and strewn with pennies cast broadside from a generous hand. But—and this is the point—who gets excited by a mere penny? If you follow one arrow, if you crouch motionless on a bank to watch a tremulous ripple thrill on the water, and are rewarded by the sight of a muskrat kit paddling from its den, will you count that sight a chip of copper only, and go your rueful way? It is a very dire poverty indeed for a man to be so malnourished and fatigued that he won't stoop to pick up a penny. But if you cultivate a healthy poverty and simplicity, so that finding a penny will make your day, then, since the world is in fact planted in pennies, you have with your poverty bought a lifetime of days. What you see is what you get.

Unfortunately, nature is very much a now-you-see-it, now-you-don't affair. A fish flashes, then dissolves in the water before my eyes like so much salt. Deer apparently ascend bodily into heaven; the brightest oriole fades into leaves. These disappearances stun me into stillness and concentration; they say of nature that it conceals with a grand nonchalance, and they say of vision that it is a deliberate gift, the revelation of a dancer who for my eyes only flings away her seven veils.

For nature does reveal as well as conceal: now-you-don't-see-it, now-you-do. For a week this September migrating red-winged blackbirds were feeding heavily down by Tinker Creek at the back of the house. One day I went out to investigate the racket; I walked up to a tree, an Osage orange, and a hundred birds flew away. They simply materialized out of the tree. I saw a tree, then a whisk of color, then a tree again. I walked closer and another hundred blackbirds took flight. Not a branch, not a twig budged: the birds were apparently weightless as well as invisible. Or, it was as if the leaves of the Osage orange had been freed from a spell in the form of red-winged blackbirds; they flew from the tree, caught my eye in the sky, and vanished. When I looked again at the tree, the leaves had reassembled as if nothing had happened. Finally I walked directly to the trunk of the tree and a final hundred, the real diehards, appeared, spread, and vanished. How could so many hide in the tree without my seeing them? The Osage orange, unruffled, looked just as it had looked from the house, when three hundred red-winged blackbirds cried from its crown. I looked upstream where they flew, and they were gone. Searching, I couldn't spot one. I wandered upstream to force them to play their hand, but they'd crossed the creek and scattered. One show to a customer. These appearances catch at my throat: they are the free gifts, the bright coppers at the roots of trees.

It's all a matter of keeping my eyes open. Nature is like one of those line drawings that are puzzles for children: Can you find hidden in the tree a duck, a house, a boy, a bucket, a giraffe, and a boot? Specialists can find the most incredibly hidden things. A book I read when I was young recommended an easy way to find caterpillars: you simply find some fresh caterpillar droppings, look up, and there's your caterpillar. More recently an author advised me to set my mind at ease about those piles of cut stems on the ground in grassy fields. Field mice make them; they cut the grass down by degrees to reach the seeds at the head. It seems that when the grass is tightly packed, as in a field of ripe grain, the blade won't topple at a single cut through the stem; instead, the cut stem simply drops vertically, held in the crush of grain. The mouse severs the bottom again and again, the stem keeps dropping an inch at a time, and finally the head is low enough for the mouse to reach the seeds. Meanwhile the mouse is positively littering the field with its little piles of cut stems into which, presumably, the author is constantly stumbling.

If I can't see this minutiae, I still try to keep my eyes open. I'm always on the lookout for ant lion traps in sandy soil, monarch pupae near milkweed, skipper larvae in locust leaves. These things are utterly common, and I've not seen one. I bang on hollow trees near water, but so far no flying squirrels have appeared. In flat country I watch every sunset in hopes of seeing the green ray. The green ray is a seldom-seen streak of light that rises from the sun like a spurting fountain at the moment of sunset; it throbs into the sky for two seconds and disappears. One more reason to keep my eyes open. A photography professor at the University of Florida just happened to see a bird die in midflight; it jerked, died, dropped, and smashed on the ground.

I squint at the wind because I read Stewart Edward White: "I have always maintained that if you looked closely enough you could *see* the wind—the dim, hardly-made-out, fine débris fleeing high in the air." White was an excellent observer, and devoted an entire chapter of *The Mountains* to the subject of seeing deer: "As soon as you can forget the naturally obvious and construct an artificial obvious, then you too will see deer."

But the artificial obvious is hard to see. My eyes account for less than 1 percent of the weight of my head; I'm bony and dense; I see what I expect. I just don't know what the lover knows; I can't see the artificial obvious that those in the know construct. The herpetologist asks the native, "Are there snakes in that ravine?" "No, sir." And the herpetologist comes home with, yessir, three bags full. Are there butterflies on that mountain? Are the bluets in bloom? Are there arrowheads here, or fossil ferns in the shale?

Peeping through my keyhole I see within the range of only about 30 percent of the light that comes from the sun; the rest is infrared and some little ultraviolet, perfectly apparent to many animals, but invisible to me. A nightmare network of ganglia, charged and firing without my knowledge, cuts and splices what I do see, editing it for my brain. Donald E. Carr points out that the sense impressions of one-celled animals are *not* edited for the brain: "This is philosophically interesting in a rather mournful way, since it means that only the simplest animals perceive the universe as it is."

A fog that won't burn away drifts and flows across my field of vision. When you see fog move against a backdrop of deep pines, you don't see the fog itself, but streaks of clearness floating across the air in dark shreds. So I see only tatters of clearness through a pervading obscurity. I can't distinguish the fog from the overcast sky; I can't be sure if the light is direct or reflected. Everywhere darkness and the presence of the unseen appalls. We estimate now that only one atom dances alone in every cubic meter of intergalactic space. I blink and squint. What planet or power yanks Halley's Comet out of orbit? We haven't seen it yet; it's a question of distance, density, and the pallor of reflected light. We rock, cradled in the swaddling band of darkness. Even the simple darkness of night whispers suggestions to the mind. This summer, in August, I stayed at the creek too late.

Strangers to Darkness

Where Tinker Creek flows under the sycamore log bridge to the tear-shaped island, it is slow and shallow, fringed thinly in cattail marsh. At this spot an astonishing bloom of life supports vast breeding populations of insects, fish, reptiles, birds, and mammals. On windless summer evenings I stalk along the creek bank or straddle the sycamore log in absolute stillness, watching for muskrats. The night I stayed too late I was hunched on the lawn staring spellbound at spreading, reflected stains of lilac on the water. A cloud in the sky suddenly lighted as if turned on by a switch; its reflection just as suddenly materialized on the water upstream, flat and floating, so that I couldn't see the creek bottom, or life in the water under the cloud. Downstream, away from the cloud on the water, water turtles smooth as beans were gliding down with the current in a series of easy, weightless push-offs, as men bound on the moon. I didn't know whether to trace the progress of one turtle I was sure of, risking sticking my face in one of the bridge's spider webs made invisible by the gathering dark, or take a chance on seeing the carp, or scan the mudbank in hope of seeing a muskrat, or follow the last of the swallows who caught at my heart and trailed it after them like streamers as they appeared from directly below, under the log, flying upstream with their tails forked, so fast.

But shadows spread and deepened and stayed. After thousands of years we're still strangers to darkness, fearful aliens in an enemy camp with our arms crossed over our chests. I stirred. A land turtle on the bank, startled, hissed the air from its lungs and withdrew to its shell. An uneasy pink here, an unfathomable blue there, gave great suggestion of lurking beings. Things were going on. I couldn't see whether that rustle I heard was a distant rattle-snake, slit-eyed, or a nearby sparrow kicking in the dry flood debris slung at the foot of a willow. Tremendous action roiled the water everywhere I looked, big action, inexplicable. A tremor welled up beside a gaping muskrat burrow in the bank and I caught my breath, but no muskrat appeared. The ripples continued to fan upstream with a steady, powerful thrust. Night was knitting an eyeless mask over my face, and I still sat transfixed. A distant airplane, a delta wing out of a nightmare, made a gliding shadow on the creek's bottom that looked like a stingray cruising upstream. At once a black fin slit the pink cloud on the water, shearing it in two. The two halves merged together and seemed to dissolve before my eyes. Darkness pooled in the cleft of the creek and rose, as water collects in a well. Untamed, dream-ing lights flickered over the sky. I saw hints of hulking underwater shadows, two pale splashes out of the water, and round ripples rolling close together from a blackened center.

At last I stared upstream where only the deepest violet remained of the cloud, a cloud so high its underbelly still glowed, its feeble color reflected from a hidden sky lighted in turn by a sun halfway to China. And out of that violet, a sudden enormous black body arched over the water. Head and tail, if there was a head and tail, were both submerged in cloud. I saw only one ebony fling, a headlong dive to darkness; then the waters closed, and the lights went out.

I walked home in a shivering daze, up hill and down. Later I lay open-mouthed in bed, my arms flung wide at my sides to steady the whirling dark-ness. At this latitude I'm spinning 836 miles an hour round the earth's axis; I feel my sweeping fall as a breakneck arch like the dive of dolphins, and the hollow rushing of wind raises the hairs on my neck and the side of my face. In orbit around the sun I'm moving 64,800 miles an hour. The solar system as a whole, like a merry-go-round unhinged, spins, bobs, and blinks at the speed of 43,200 miles an hour along a course set east of Hercules. Someone has piped, and we are dancing a tarantella until the sweat pours. I open my eyes and I see dark, muscled forms curl out of water, with flapping gills and flattened eyes. I close my eyes and I see stars, deep stars giving way to deeper stars, deeper stars bowing to deepest stars at the crown of an infinite cone.

"Still," wrote Van Gogh in a letter, "a great deal of light falls on every-thing." If we were blinded by darkness, we are also blinded by light. Some-times here in Virginia at sunset low clouds on the southern or northern hori-zon are completely invisible in the lighted sky. I only know one is there because I can see its reflection in still water. The first time I discovered this mystery I looked from cloud to no-cloud in bewilderment, checking my bear-ings over and over, thinking maybe the ark of the covenant was just passing by south of Dead Man Mountain. Only much later did I learn the explana-tion: polarized light from the sky is very much weakened by reflection, but the light in clouds isn't polarized. So invisible clouds pass among visible clouds, till all slide over the mountains; so a greater light extinguishes a lesser as though it didn't exist.

In the great meteor shower of August, the Perseid, I wail all day for the shooting stars I miss. They're out there showering down, committing hara-kiri in a flame of fatal attraction, and hissing perhaps at last into the ocean. But at dawn what looks like a blue dome clamps down over me like a lid on a pot. The stars and planets could smash and I'd never know. Only a piece of ashen moon occasionally climbs up or down the inside of the dome, and our local star without surcease explodes on our heads. We have really only that one light, one source for all power, and yet we must turn away from it by universal decree. Nobody here on the planet seems aware of this strange, powerful taboo, that we all walk about carefully averting our faces, this way and that, lest our eyes be blasted forever.

Darkness appalls and light dazzles; the scrap of visible light that doesn't hurt my eyes hurts my brain. What I see sets me swaying. Size and distance and the sudden swelling of meanings confuse me, bowl me over. I straddle the sycamore log bridge over Tinker Creek in the summer. I look at the lighted creek bottom: snail tracks tunnel the mud in quavering curves. A crayfish jerks, but by the time I absorb what has happened, he's gone in a billowing smoke screen of silt. I look at the water: minnows and shiners. If I'm thinking minnows, a carp will fill my brain till I scream. I look at the water's surface: skaters, bubbles, and leaves sliding down. Suddenly, my own face, reflected, startles me witless. Those snails have been tracking my face! Finally, with a shuddering wrench of the will, I see clouds, cirrus clouds. I'm dizzy, I fall in.

This looking business is risky. Once I stood on a humped rock on nearby Purgatory Mountain, watching through binoculars the great autumn hawk migration below, until I discovered that I was in danger of joining the hawks on a vertical migration of my own. I was used to binoculars, but not, apparently, to balancing on humped rocks while looking through them. I reeled. Everything advanced and receded by turns; the world was full of unexplained foreshortenings and depths. A distant huge object, a hawk the size of an elephant, turned out to be the browned bough of a nearby loblolly pine. I followed a sharp-skinned hawk against a featureless sky, rotating my head unawares as it flew, and when I lowered the glass a glimpse of my own looming shoulder sent me staggering. What prevents the men on Palomar from falling, voiceless and blinded, from their tiny, vaulted chairs?

I reel in confusion; I don't understand what I see. With the naked eye I can see two million light-years to the Andromeda galaxy. Often I slop some creek water in a jar, and when I get home I dump it in a white china bowl. After the silt settles I return and see tracings of minute snails on the bottom, a planarian or two winding round the rim of water, roundworms shimmying frantically, and finally, when my eyes have adjusted to these dimensions, amoebae. At first the amoebae look like *muscae volitantes*, those curled moving spots you seem to see in your eyes when you stare at a distant wall. Then I see the amoebae as drops of water congealed, bluish, translucent, like chips of sky in the bowl. At length I choose one individual and give myself over to its idea of an evening. I see it dribble a grainy foot before it on its wet, unfathomable way. Do its unedited sense impressions include the fierce focus of my eyes? Shall I take it outside and show it Andromeda, and blow its little endoplasm? I stir the water with a finger, in case it's running out of oxygen. Maybe I should get a tropical aquarium with motorized bubblers and lights, and keep this one for a pet. Yes, it would tell its fissioned descendants, the universe is two feet by five, and if you listen closely you can hear the buzzing music of the spheres.

Oh, it's mysterious, lamplit evenings here in the galaxy, one after the other. It's one of those nights when I wander from window to window, looking for a sign. But I can't see. Terror and a beauty insoluble are a riband of blue woven into the fringes of garments of things both great and small. No culture explains, no bivouac offers real haven or rest. But it could be that we are not seeing something. Galileo thought comets were an optical illusion. This is fertile ground: since we are certain that they're not, we can look at what our scientists have been saying with fresh hope. What if there are *really* gleaming, castellated cities hung upside-down over the desert sand? What limpid lakes and cool date palms have our caravans always passed untried? Until, one by one, by the blindest of leaps, we light on the road to these places, we must stumble in darkness and hunger. I turn from the window. I'm blind as a bat, sensing only from every direction the echo of my own thin cries.

Learning to See

I chanced on a wonderful book called *Space and Sight,* by Marius Von Senden. When Western surgeons discovered how to perform safe cataract operations, they ranged across Europe and America operating on dozens of men and women of all ages who had been blinded by cataracts since birth. Von Senden collected accounts of such cases; the histories are fascinating. Many doctors had tested their patients' sense perceptions and ideas of space both before and after the operations. The vast majority of patients, of both sexes and all ages, had, in Von Senden's opinion, no idea of space whatsoever. Form, distance, and size were so many meaningless syllables. A patient "had no idea of depth, confusing it with roundness." Before the operation a doctor would give a blind patient a cube and a sphere; the patient would tongue it or feel it with his hands, and name it correctly. After the operation the doctor would show the same objects to the patient without letting him touch them; now he had no clue whatsoever to what he was seeing. One patient called lemonade "square" because it pricked on his tongue as a square shape pricked on the touch of his hands. Of another postoperative patient the doctor writes, "I have found in her no notion of size, for example, not even within the narrow limits which she might have encompassed with the aid of touch. Thus when I asked her to show me how big her mother was, she did not stretch out her hands, but set her two index fingers a few inches apart."

For the newly sighted, vision is pure sensation unencumbered by meaning. When a newly sighted girl saw photographs and paintings, she asked, "'Why do they put those dark marks all over them?' 'Those aren't dark marks,' her mother explained, 'those are shadows. That is one of the ways the eye knows that things have shape. If it were not for shadows, many things would look flat.' 'Well, that's how things do look,' Joan answered. 'Everything looks flat with dark patches.'"

In general the newly sighted see the world as a dazzle of "color-patches." They are pleased by the sensation of color, and learn quickly to name the colors, but the rest of seeing is tormentingly difficult. Soon after his operation, a patient "generally bumps into one of these color-patches and observes them to be substantial, since they resist him as tactual objects do. In walking about it also strikes him—or can if he pays attention—that he is continually passing in between the colors he sees, that he can go past a visual object, that a part of it then steadily disappears from view; and that in spite of this, however he twists and turns—whether entering the room from the door, for example, or returning back to it—he always has a visual space in front of him. Thus he gradually comes to realize that there is also space behind him, which he does not see."

The mental effort involved in these reasonings proves overwhelming for many patients. It oppresses them to realize, if they ever do at all, the tremendous size of the world, which they had previously conceived of as something touchingly manageable. It oppresses them to realize that they have been visible to people all along, perhaps unattractively so, without their knowledge or consent. A disheartening number of them refuse to use their new vision, continuing to go over objects with their tongues, and lapsing into apathy and despair.

On the other hand, many newly sighted people speak well of the world, and teach us how dull our own vision is. To one patient, a human hand, unrecognized, is "something bright and then holes." Shown a bunch of grapes, a boy calls out, "It is dark, blue and shiny. . . . It isn't smooth, it has bumps and hollows." A little girl visits a garden. "She is greatly astonished, and can scarcely be persuaded to answer, stands speechless in front of the tree, which she only names on taking hold of it, and then as 'the tree with the lights in it.'" Another patient, a twenty-two-year-old girl, was dazzled by the world's brightness and kept her eyes shut for two weeks. When at the end of that time she opened her eyes again, she did not recognize any objects, but "the more she now directed her gaze upon everything about her, the more it could be seen how an expression of gratification and astonishment overspread her features; she repeatedly exclaimed: 'Oh God! How beautiful!'"

I saw color-patches for weeks after I read this wonderful book. It was summer; the peaches were ripe in the valley orchards. When I woke in the morning, color-patches wrapped round my eyes, intricately, leaving not one unfilled spot. All day long I walked among shifting color-patches that parted before me like the Red Sea and closed again in silence, transfigured, wherever I looked back. Some patches swelled and loomed, while others vanished utterly, and dark marks flitted at random over the whole dazzling sweep. But I couldn't sustain the illusion of flatness. I've been around for too long. Form is condemned to an eternal danse macabre with meaning: I couldn't unpeach the peaches. Nor can I remember ever having seen without understanding; the color-patches of infancy are lost. My brain then must have been smooth as any balloon. I'm told I reached for the moon; many babies do. But the color-patches of infancy swelled as meaning filled them; they arrayed themselves in solemn ranks down distance which unrolled and stretched before me like a plain. The moon rocketed away. I live now in a world of shadows that shape and distance color, a world where space makes a kind of terrible sense. What Gnosticism is this, and what physics? The fluttering patch I saw in my nursery window—silver and green and shape-shifting blue—is gone; a row of Lombardy poplars takes its place, mute, across the distant lawn. That humming oblong creature pale as light that stole along the walls of my room at night, stretching exhilaratingly around the corners, is gone, too, gone the night I ate of the bittersweet fruit, put two and two together, and puckered forever my brain. Martin Buber tells this tale: "Rabbi Mendel once boasted to his teacher Rabbi Elimelekh that evenings he saw the angel who rolls away the light before the darkness, and mornings the angel who rolls away the darkness before the light. 'Yes,' said Rabbi Elimelekh, 'in my youth I saw that too. Later on you don't see these things anymore.'"

Why didn't someone hand these newly sighted people paints and brushes from the start, when they still didn't know what anything was? Then maybe we all could see color-patches too, the world unraveled from reason, Eden before Adam gave names. The scales would drop from my eyes; I'd see trees like men walking; I'd run down the road against all orders, hallooing and leaping.

Silver Flashes

Seeing is of course very much a matter of verbalization. Unless I call my attention to what passes before my eyes, I simply won't see it. If Tinker Mountain erupted, I'd be likely to notice. But if I want to notice the lesser cataclysms of valley life, I have to maintain in my head a running description of the present. It's not that I'm observant; it's just that I talk too much. Otherwise, especially in a strange place, I'll never know what's happening. Like a blind man at the ball game, I need a radio.

When I see this way I analyze and pry. I hurl over logs and roll away stones; I study the bank a square foot at a time, probing and tilting my head. Some days when a mist covers the mountains, when the muskrats won't show and the microscope's mirror shatters, I want to climb up the blank blue dome as a man would storm the inside of a circus tent, wildly, dangling, and with a steel knife claw a rent in the top, peep, and, if I must, fall.

But there is another kind of seeing that involves a letting go. When I see this way I sway transfixed and emptied. The difference between the two ways of seeing is the difference between walking with and without a camera. When I walk with a camera I walk from shot to shot, reading the light on a calibrated meter. When I walk without a camera, my own shutter opens, and the moment's light prints on my own silver gut. When I see this second way I am above all an unscrupulous observer.

It was sunny one evening last summer at Tinker Creek; the sun was low in the sky, upstream. I was sitting on the sycamore log bridge with the sunset at my back, watching the shiners the size of minnows who were feeding over the muddy sand in skittery schools. Again and again, one fish, then another, turned for a split second across the current and flash! the sun shot out from its silver side. I couldn't watch for it. It was always just happening somewhere else, and it drew my vision just as it disappeared: flash! like a sudden dazzle of the thinnest blade, a sparking over a dun and olive ground at chance intervals from every direction. Then I noticed white specks, some sort of pale petals, small, floating from under my feet on the creek's surface, very slow and steady. So I blurred my eyes and gazed toward the brim of my hat and saw a new world. I saw the pale white circles roll up, roll up, like the world's turning, mute and perfect, and I saw the linear flashes, gleaming silver, like stars being born at random down a rolling scroll of time. Something broke and something opened. I filled up like a new wineskin. I breathed an air like light; I saw a light like water. I was the lip of a fountain the creek filled forever; I was ether, the leaf in the zephyr; I was flesh-flake, feather, bone. When I see this way I see truly. As Thoreau says, I return to my senses. I am the man who watches the baseball game in silence in an empty stadium. I see the game purely; I'm abstracted and dazed. When it's all over and the white-suited players lope off the green field to their shadowed dugouts, I leap to my feet, I cheer and cheer.

But I can't go out and try to see this way. I'll fail, I'll go mad. All I can do is try to gag the commentator, to hush the noise of useless interior babble that keeps me from seeing just as surely as a newspaper dangled before my eyes. The effort is really a discipline requiring a lifetime of dedicated struggle; it marks the literature of saints and monks of every order east and west, under every rule and no rule, discalced and shod. The world's spiritual geniuses seem to discover universally that the mind's muddy river, this ceaseless flow of trivia and trash, cannot be dammed, and that trying to dam it is a waste of effect that might lead to madness. Instead you must allow the muddy river to flow unheeded in the dim channels of consciousness; you raise your sights; you look along it, mildly, acknowledging its presence without interest and gazing beyond it into the realm of the real where subjects and objects act and rest purely, without utterance. "Launch into the deep," says Jacques Ellul, "and you shall see."

The secret of seeing, then, is the pearl of great price. If I thought he could teach me to find it and keep it forever I would stagger barefoot across a hundred deserts after any lunatic at all. But although the pearl may be found, it may not be sought. The literature of illumination reveals this above all: although it comes to those who wait for it, it is always, even to the most practiced and adept, a gift and a total surprise. I return from one walk knowing where the killdeer nests in the field by the creek and the hour the laurel blooms. I return from the same walk a day later scarcely knowing my own name. Litanies hum in my ears; my tongue flaps in my mouth, *Alimonon*, alleluia! I cannot cause light; the most I can do is try to put myself in the path of its beam. It is possible, in deep space, to sail on solar wind. Light, be it particle or wave, has force: you rig a giant sail and go. The secret of seeing is to sail on solar wind. Hone and spread your spirit till you yourself are a sail, whetted, translucent, broadside to the merest puff.

When her doctor took her bandages off and led her into the garden, the girl who was no longer blind saw "the tree with the lights in it." It was for this tree I searched through the peach orchards of summer, in the forests of fall and down winter and spring for years. Then one day I was walking along Tinker Creek thinking of nothing at all and I saw the tree with the lights in it. I saw the backyard cedar where the mourning doves roost charged and transfigured, each cell buzzing with flame. I stood on the grass with the lights in it, grass that was wholly fire, utterly focused and utterly dreamed. It was less like seeing than like being for the first time seen, knocked breathless by a powerful glance. The flood of fire abated, but I'm still spending the power.

Gradually the lights went out in the cedar, the colors died, the cells un-flamed and disappeared. I was still ringing. I had been my whole life a bell, and never knew it until at that moment I was lifted and struck. I have since only very rarely seen the tree with the lights in it. The vision comes and goes, mostly goes, but I live for it, for the moment when the mountains open and a new light roars in spate through the crack, and the mountains slam.

Suggestions for Discussion

1. What is the central point of this essay?

2. How does the author's story about hiding pennies as a child relate to the thesis of the piece?

3. Discuss the tone of Dillard's description of observations of nature. How honest do you feel her reactions to nature are? Compare her reaction to nature with those of other naturalists you have read.

Suggestions for Writing

1. Recall a scene, either natural or social, to which you reacted strongly. Write about it.

2. Write a piece in which you analyze your attitude toward the natural world.

3. With wax crayons, magic markers, or water colors, attempt to represent a sight common to you as "patches of color." Then write a paper in which you describe the difficulties or pleasures you found in your attempt.

===

Richard Selzer

A Question of Mercy

Richard Selzer (b. 1928) is a physician, an associate professor of surgery at the Yale Medical School, and a writer. He was educated at Union College, Albany Medical College, and Yale. Holder of four honorary degrees, he has written a number of books, ranging from those dealing with his life as a surgeon, such as Mortal Lessons: Notes on the Art of Surgery (1976) and Confession of a Knife (1979), to fiction, Imagine a Woman and Other Tales (1990), to his widely acclaimed autobiographical works, Down from Troy (1992) and Raising the Dead (1994). In this selection he vividly depicts the ethical anguish he experiences when his personal and professional, moral and medical sensibilities come into conflict.

Almost two years ago, I received a phone call from a poet I knew slightly. Would I, he wondered, be willing to intervene on behalf of a friend of his who was dying of AIDS?

"Intervene?"

"His suffering is worthy of Job. He wants to commit suicide while he still has the strength to do it."

"Do you know what you're asking?"

"I know, I know."

"No," I told him. "I'm trained to preserve life, not end it. It's not in me to do a thing like that."

"Are you saying that a doctor should prolong a misfortune as long as possible?"

"There is society," I replied. "There is the law. I'm not a barbarian."

"You are precisely that," he said. "A barbarian."

His accusation reminded me of an incident in the life of Ambroise Paré, the father of surgery, who in the 16th century accompanied the armies of France on their campaigns. Once, on entering a newly captured city, Paré looked for a barn in which to keep his horse while he treated the wounded. Inside he found four dead soldiers and three more still alive, their faces contorted with pain, their clothes still smoldering where the gunpowder had burned them.

As Paré gazed at the wounded with pity, an old soldier came up and asked whether there was any way to cure them. Paré shook his head whereupon the old soldier went up to the men and, Paré recounted in his memoirs, cut their throats "gently, efficiently and without ill will." Horrified at what he thought a great cruelty, Paré cried out to the executioner that he was a villain.

"No," said the man. "I pray God that if ever I come to be in that condition someone will do the same for me." Was this an act of villainy, or mercy?

The question still resists answering. Last year, a Michigan court heard the case of a doctor who supplied a woman with his "suicide machine"—a simple apparatus that allows a patient to self-administer a lethal dose of drugs intravenously. Since then, it seems that each day brings reports of deaths assisted by doctors. A best-selling book, *Final Exit*, written by the director of the Hemlock Society, now instructs us in painless ways to commit suicide should the dreadful occasion arise. Even the most ideologically opposed must now hear the outcry of a populace for whom the dignity and mercy of a quick pharmacological death may be preferable to a protracted, messy and painful end.

"But why are you calling *me?*" I asked my friend.

"I've read your books. It occurred to me that you might just be the right one."

I let the poet know that I had retired from medicine five years before, that I was no longer a doctor.

"Once a doctor, always a doctor," he replied.

What I did not tell him was that each year I have continued to renew the license that allows me to prescribe narcotics. You never know. . . . Someday I might have need of them to relieve pain or to kill myself easily should the occasion arise. If for myself, then why not for another?

"I'll think about it," I said. He gave me the address and phone number.

"I implore you," said the poet.

The conversation shifted to the abominable gymnastics of writing, a little gossip. We hung up.

Don't! I told myself.

Diary: January 14, 1990

My friend's friend lives with a companion on the seventh floor of an apartment building about a 10-minute walk from my house. The doorman on duty is a former patient of mine. He greets me warmly, lifts his shirt to show me his gallbladder incision, how well it has healed.

"You can hardly see it," he says. That is the sort of thing that happens when I leave my study and re-enter the world. The doorman buzzes me in.

At precisely 4 P.M., as arranged, I knock on the apartment door. It is opened by L., a handsome, perhaps too handsome, man in his late 30's. We recognize each other as presences on the Yale campus. He is an ordained minister. He tells me that he has made use of my writings in his sermons. In the living room, R. is sitting on an invalid's cushion on the sofa. A short, delicate man, also in his 30's, R. is a doctor specializing in public health— women's problems, birth control, family planning, AIDS. He is surprisingly unwasted, although pale as a blank sheet of paper. He gives me a brilliant smile around even white teeth. The eyes do not participate in the smile. L. and R. have been lovers for six years.

R.'s hair is close-cropped, black; there is a neat lawn of beard. He makes a gesture as if to stand, but I stop him. His handshake is warm and dry and strong. There is a plate of chocolate chip cookies on a table. L. pours tea. L.'s speech is clipped, slightly mannered. R. has a Hispanic accent; he is Colombian.

For a few minutes we step warily around the reason I have come. Then, all at once, we are engaged. I ask R. about his symptoms. He tells me of his profound fatigue, the depression, the intractable diarrhea, his ulcerated hemorrhoids. He has Kaposi's sarcoma. Only yesterday a new lesion appeared in the left naso-orbital region, the area between the nose and eye. He points to it. Through his beard I see another large black tumor. His mouth is dry, encrusted from the dehydration that comes with chronic diarrhea. Now and then he clutches his abdomen, grimaces. There is the odor of stool.

"I want to die," he announces calmly.

"Is it so bad?"

"Yes, it is."

"But how can I be sure? On Tuesday, you want to die; by Thursday, perhaps you will have changed your mind."

He nods to L., who helps him to stand. The three of us go into their bedroom, where R., lying on his side, offers his lesions as evidence. I see that his anus is a great circular ulceration, raw and oozing blood. His buttocks are smeared with pus and liquid stool. With tenderness, L. bathes and dresses him in a fresh diaper. Even though I have been summoned here, I feel very much the intruder upon their privacy. And I am convinced.

We return to the living room. L. and R. sit side by side on the sofa, holding hands. A lethal dose of barbiturates is being mailed by a doctor friend in Colombia. R. wants to be certain that it will not fail, that someone will be on hand to administer a final, fatal dose if he should turn out to be physically too weak to take the required number of pills. He also wants L. to be with him, holding him. He asks that L. not cry. He couldn't bear that, he says. L. says that of course he will cry, that he must be allowed to. L. is afraid, too, that it might not work, that he will be discovered as an accomplice.

"I am the sole beneficiary of the will," he explains. L. does not want to be alone when the time comes. He has never seen anyone die before. (A minister? Has he never attended a deathbed?) "It has just worked out that way," he says, as though reading my mind. Still, I am shocked at such a state of virginity.

We have a discussion. It is about death as best friend, not enemy. How sensible were the pagans, for whom death was a return to the spirit world that resides in nature. One member of the tribe vanishes forever, but the tribe itself lives on. It is a far cry from the Christian concept of death and resurrection.

R. passes a hand across his eyes as if to brush away a veil. His vision is failing; soon he will be blind. He coughs, shifts on the pillow, swallows a pain pill. He tells me that he has taken all of the various experimental medicines without relief of the diarrhea. His entire day is spent medicating himself and dealing with the incontinence. Despite chemotherapy, the tumors are growing rapidly. His palate is covered with them. He opens his mouth for me to see. Above all, he wants to retain his dignity, to keep control of his life, which he equates with choosing the time and method of suicide. Soon he will be unable to do it.

"But death," I say. "It's so final."

"I want it," he says again, on his face a look of longing. He wants me to promise that I will obtain the additional narcotics that would insure death, if needed. I offer only to return in a few days to talk. R. urges me to think of myself as an instrument that he himself will use for his rescue. An instrument? But I am a man.

The tone turns conspiratorial. Our voices drop. We admonish each other to be secretive, tell no one. There are those who would leap to punish. I suggest that R. arrange for a codicil to his will requesting that there be no autopsy.

January 16

Four in the afternoon. R. answers the door. He has lost ground. His eyes are sunken, his gait tottering. He is in great pain, which he makes no effort to conceal. As arranged, he is alone. L. is to return in an hour. The barbiturates have arrived from Colombia. He shows me the bottles of tablets in the bottom drawer of the dresser. A quick calculation tells me that he has well over the lethal dose. The diarrhea has been unrelenting. The Kaposi's sarcoma is fulminating, with new lesions every day.

"I have always counted so much on my looks," he says shyly and without the least immodesty. "And now I have become something that no one would want to touch." Without a pause, he asks, "What if I vomit the pills?" I tell him to take them at a regular pace, each with only a sip of water so as not to fill up too quickly. If necessary, would I inject more medication? "I have good veins," he says, and rolls up a sleeve. I see that he does. There are several needle puncture marks at the antecubital fossa—the front of the elbow—where blood has been drawn. One more would not be noticed.

"When?" I ask him. No later than one month from today. Do I want to choose a date? R. rises with difficulty, gets a calendar from the kitchen. We bend over it.

"Are you free on February 10?" he asks. "It's a Saturday."

"I'm free."

February 10! There is a date!

I ask R. about his life. He was born and raised in Medellin, one of four sisters and three brothers. His mother had no formal education, but she is "very wise." It is clear that he loves her. No, she knows nothing; neither that he is gay nor that he is ill. He has written a letter to be sent after his death, telling her that he loves her, thanking her for all that she has done. In the family, only an older brother knows that he is gay, and to him it is a disgrace. He has forbidden R. to tell the others. His sisters live near his mother in Medellin. There are 12 grandchildren. She will not be alone. (He smiles at this.)

Had he always known he was gay? He discovered his attraction to men at age 8, but of course it was impossible to express it. Colombia is intolerant of homosexuality. At 17, he went to Bogotá to study medicine. For six years he lived in an apartment with four other students. There was close camaraderie but no sexual expression. It was a "quiet" student's life. After one year of internship in a hospital, he decided against clinical medicine.

It was while working toward a degree in public health at Yale that he met L. The year was 1983. After completing his studies, he was separated from L. for two years, working in another city, although he returned to visit L. frequently. There followed a three-year period when they lived together in New Haven. Shortly after they met, R. began to feel ill, thought he had an infection. He suspected it was AIDS. He told L. at once and they agreed to discontinue sex. Aside from mutual caressing, there has been no sexual contact between them since.

"It was not sex that brought us together," he says. "It was love." I lower my gaze, I who have always hesitated before expressing love.

L. returns. It is the first day of the semester at Yale. A day of meeting with students, advising, counseling. He is impeccably dressed. He is accompanied by a woman, someone I know slightly. He notices my surprise.

"This is M.," he announces. "She's all right." He places his arm about her waist, explaining that they have been close friends and confidantes for many years. "She is the sister I have always wanted." L. bends to kiss R. on the cheek.

"*Chiquito!* You are wearing your new shirt," says L. I am alarmed by the presence of M. It is clear that she knows everything. We sit around the table drinking tea.

"Tell me about death," says L.

"What do you mean?"

"The details. You're a doctor, you should know. What about the death rattle?"

"It has been called that." I explain about not being able to clear secretions from the lungs.

"What sort of equipment will we need?"

"Nothing. You already have the diapers."

"R. has to die in diapers?" I explain about the relaxation of the bowel and urinary sphincters, that it would be best.

"I shouldn't have asked." L. seems increasingly nervous. "I'm terrified of the police," he says. "I always have been. Should I see a lawyer? What if I'm caught and put in prison?" He begins to weep openly. "And I'm losing R. That is a fact, and there is not a thing I can do about it!" When he continues to cry without covering his face, R. reaches out to a hand to console him.

"Look," I say. "You're not ready for this and, to tell the truth, I'm not sure I am either."

"Oh please!" R.'s voice is a high-pitched whine of distress. "It is only a matter of a few minutes of misery. I would be dying anyway after that."

L. pulls himself together, nods to show that he understands. I begin to feel that my presence is putting pressure on him; it makes R.'s death real, imminent. I tell him that I am ready to withdraw. How easy that would be. A way out.

"You are the answer to R.'s prayers," he says. "To him you are an angel." But to L. I am the angel of death. "Of course, I agree to whatever R. wants to do," he says. It is R. who turns practical.

"If it is too hard for you, L., I won't mind if you are not here with me." And to me: "L. simply cannot lie. If questioned by the police, he would have to tell the truth." I see that the lying will be up to me. All the while, M. has remained silent.

We go through the "script"—L.'s word. In the bedroom, R. will begin taking the pills. I will help him. L. and M. will wait in the living room.

L.: "Will we be in the apartment all the time until he dies?"

M. (speaking for the first time): "Not necessary. We can go out somewhere and return to find him dead."

L.: "Where would we go?"

M.: "Anywhere. For a walk; to the movies."

L.: "How long will it take?"

Me: "Perhaps all day."

L.: "What if the doctors notify the police? R. has made no secret of his intentions at the clinic. They have even withheld pain medication because he is 'high risk.' "

Me (to R.): "Next time you go to the clinic, ask for a prescription for 50 Levo-Dromoran tablets. It's a narcotic. Maybe they'll give you that many. Maybe not."

L.: "I simply can't believe they would turn us in, but there's no way to be sure, is there?"

More and more we are like criminals, or a cell of revolutionaries. L.'s fear and guilt are infectious. But then there is R. I stand up to leave, assuring them that I will come again on Sunday at 4 in the afternoon. M. says that she will be there, too. L. hopes he has not shaken my resolve. He apologizes for his weakness.

"We'll talk further," I say. R. takes my hand. "You have become my friend. In such a short time. One of the best friends of my life."

January 17

In the mail there is a note from L. in his small, neat handwriting. He thanks me. Enclosed is a copy of a lecture he had given in 1984 in which he cited an incident from one of my books, about a doctor who, entreated by a suffering patient who wants to die, stays his hand out of mercy. It is strangely prophetic and appropriate to the circumstances.

My nights are ridden with visions: I am in the bedroom with R. We are sitting side by side on the bed. He is wearing only a large blue disposable diaper. The bottles of pills are on the night stand along with a pitcher of water and a glass. R. pours a handful of the tiny tablets into his palm, then with a shy smile begins to swallow them one at a time. Because of the dryness of his mouth and the fungal infection of his throat, it is painful. And slow.

"You're drinking too much water," I say. "You'll fill up too quickly."

"I will try," he says. What seems like hours go by. From the living room comes the sound of Mozart's Clarinet Quintet. R. labors on, panting, coughing. When he has finished one bottle, I open another. His head and arms begin to wobble. I help him to lie down.

"Quickly," I tell him. "We don't have much time left." I hold the glass for him, guide it to his lips. He coughs, spits out the pills.

"Hold me," he says. I bend above him, cradle his head in my arm.

"Let yourself go," I say. He does, and minutes later he is asleep. I free myself and count the pills that are left, calculate the milligrams. Not enough. It is too far below the lethal dose. I take a vial of morphine and a syringe from my pocket, a rubber tourniquet. I draw up 10 cc. of the fluid and inject it into a vein in R.'s arm. The respirations slow down at once. I palpate his pulse. It wavers, falters, stops. There is a long last sigh from the pillow.

All at once, a key turns in the door to the hallway. The door is flung open. Two men in fedoras and raincoats enter the bedroom. They are followed by the doorman whose gallbladder I had removed.

"You are under arrest," one of them announces.

"What is the charge?" I ask, clinging to a pretense of innocence. "For the murder of R. C." I am startled by the mention of his last name. Had I known it? I am led away.

January 21

M., L., R. and I.: R.'s smile of welcome plays havoc with my heart. It is easy to see why L. fell in love with him. I offer an alternative: R. could simply stop eating and drinking. It would not take too many days. Neither L. nor R. can accept this. L. cannot watch R. die of thirst. There is a new black tumor on R.'s upper lip. He has visited the clinic and obtained 30 Levo-Dromoran tablets. Suddenly, I feel I must test him again.

Me: "I don't think you're ready. February 10 is too soon."

R. (covering his face with his hands, moaning): "Why do you say that?"

Me: "Because you haven't done it already. Because you've chosen a method that is not certain. Because you're worrying about L."

L.: "I feel that I'm an obstruction."

Me: "No, but you're unreliable. You cannot tell the lies that may be necessary."

L.: "I'm sorry, I'm sorry."

Me: "Don't apologize for virtue. It doesn't make sense."

R.: "There is one thing. I prefer to do it at night, after dark. It would be easier for me." That, if nothing else, is comprehensible. Youth bids farewell to the moon more readily than to the sun.

We rehearse the revised plan. L., M. and R. will dine together, "love each other," say goodbye. L. and M. will take the train to New York for the night. At 6 P.M. R. will begin to take the pills. At 8:30 I will let myself into the apartment. The doorman may or may not question me, but I will have a key. I will stay only long enough to be sure that R. is dead. If he is not, I will use the morphine; if he is, I will not notify anyone. At noon the next day, L. and M. will return to discover the body and call the clinic. It is most likely that a doctor will come to pronounce death. Of course, he will ask questions, perhaps notice something, demand an autopsy. In that case, L. will show him the codicil to the will. M. asks whether the codicil is binding. At the end of the session we are all visibly exhausted.

February 3

Our final visit. R. is worried that because of the diarrhea he will not absorb the barbiturate. He has seen undigested potassium tablets in his stool. I tell him not to worry; I will make sure. His gratitude is infinitely touching, infinitely sad. We count the pills. There are 110 of them, totaling 11 grams. The lethal dose is 4.5. He also has the remaining Levo-Dromoran tablets. I have already obtained the vial of morphine and the syringe. R. is bent, tormented, but smiles when I hug him goodbye.

"I'll see you on Saturday," I tell him.

"But I won't see you," he replies with a shy smile. On the elevator, I utter aloud a prayer that I will not have to use the morphine.

February 7

Lunch at a restaurant with L. and M.

"It's no good," M. says to me. "You're going to get caught."

"What makes you think so?"

"Why would a doctor with a practice of one patient be present at his death, especially when the patient is known to be thinking about suicide?" She has contacted the Hemlock Society and talked with a sympathetic lawyer. She was told that there is no way to prevent an autopsy. By Connecticut law, the newly dead must be held for 48 hours before cremation, R.'s preference. The coroner will see the body. Because of R.'s youth and the suspicion of suicide, the coroner will order an autopsy. Any injected substance would be discovered. The time of death can be estimated with some accuracy. I would have been seen entering the building around that time. The police would ask questions. Interviewed separately, L., M. and I would give conflicting answers. I would be named. There would be the publicity, the press. It would be vicious. "No, you're fired, and that's that." I long to give in to the wave of relief that sweeps over me. But there is R.

"What about R. and my promise?"

"We just won't tell him that you're not coming."

"The coward's way," I say.

"That's what we are, aren't we?"

February 11

A phone call from L.: R. is "very much alive." He is at the hospital, in the intensive-care unit. They have put him on a respirator, washed out his stomach. He is being fed intravenously.

"I had to call the ambulance, didn't I?" he asks. "What else could I do? He was alive."

February 15

The intensive-care unit is like a concrete blockhouse. The sound of 20 respirators, each inhaling and exhaling at its own pace, makes a steady wet noise like the cascade from a fountain. But within minutes of one's arrival, it becomes interwoven with the larger fabric of sound—the clatter and thump, the quick footfalls, the calling out, the moaning. Absolute silence would be louder.

From the doorway I observe the poverty of R.'s body, the way he shivers like a wet dog. The draining away of his flesh and blood is palpable. The skin of his hands is as chaste and dry, as beautiful as old paper. I picture him as a small bird perched on an arrow that has been shot and is flying somewhere.

"R.!" I call out. He opens his eyes and looks up, on his face a look that I can only interpret as reproach or disappointment. He knows that I was not there. L. the Honest has told him.

"Do you want to be treated for the pneumonia?" I ask. He cannot speak for the tube in his trachea, but he nods. "Do you want to live?" R. nods again. "Do you still want to die?" R. shakes his head no.

Twelve days later, R. died in the hospital. Three days after that, I met L. on the street. We were shy, embarrassed, like two people who share a shameful secret.

"We must get together soon," said L.

"By all means. We should talk." We never did.

Suggestions for Discussion

1. R. wants above all "to retain his dignity, to keep control of his life, which he equates with choosing the time and method of suicide." Is it an act of mercy or villainy to assist in the suicide? Explain your position.

2. To L. Selzer is an angel of death. To R. he is an angel. What do you think?

3. In the end, the people whom R. had counted upon to assist in his death betray him. And yet, at the end, he says he does not want to die. Were they right in what they did? Explain.

Suggestions for Writing

1. Are there times when one might be justified in taking life? In taking one's own life? Describe a situation, if any, in which this might be the case.
2. Selzer is a physician. This poses a special set of problems for him. What are they?
3. Identify what you think constitutes human dignity. How can society protect these definitions or aspects of dignity? Should society be expected to do so? Explain.

Nancy Mairs

On Being a Cripple

Nancy Mairs (b. 1943) was born in California and received an M.F.A. degree from Wheaton College and a Ph.D. from the University of Arizona. Her professional career has been spent as editor, professor, and writer. She writes in a variety of genres, including essays, poetry, autobiography, and fiction. Her books include In All the Rooms of the House (1984), for which she received the Poetry Award from the Western States Arts Foundation; Plaintext (1986); Remembering the Bone House (1989); Carnal Acts (1990); Ordinary Time (1993); and Voice Lessons (1994). In the following selection she shares the experience of dealing with a chronic, crippling disease in the midst of the demanding richness of personal, family, and professional life.

> To escape is nothing. Not to escape is nothing.
> —**Louise Bogan**

The other day I was thinking of writing an essay on being a cripple. I was thinking hard in one of the stalls of the women's room in my office building, as I was shoving my shirt into my jeans and tugging up my zipper. Preoccupied, I flushed, picked up my book bag, took my cane down from the hook, and unlatched the door. So many movements unbalanced me, and as I pulled the door open I fell over backward, landing fully clothed on the toilet seat with my legs splayed in front me: the old beetle-on-its-back routine. Saturday afternoon, the building deserted, I was free to laugh aloud as I wriggled back to my feet, my voice bouncing off the yellowish tiles from all directions. Had anyone been there with me, I'd have been still and faint and hot with chagrin. I decided that it was high time to write the essay.

First, the matter of semantics. I am a cripple. I choose this word to name me. I choose from among several possibilities, the most common of which are "handicapped" and "disabled." I made the choice a number of years ago, without thinking, unaware of my motives for doing so. Even now, I'm not sure what those motives are, but I recognize that they are complex and not entirely flattering. People—crippled or not—wince at the word "cripple," as they do not at "handicapped" or "disabled." Perhaps I want them to wince. I want them to see me as a tough customer, one to whom the fates/gods/viruses have not been kind, but who can face the brutal truth of her existence squarely. As a cripple, I swagger.

But, to be fair to myself, a certain amount of honesty underlies my choice. "Cripple" seems to me a clean word, straightforward and precise. It has an honorable history, having made its first appearance in the Lindisfarne Gospel in the tenth century. As a lover of words, I like the accuracy with which it describes my condition: I have lost the full use of my limbs. "Disabled," by contrast, suggests an incapacity, physical or mental. And I certainly don't like "handicapped," which implies that I have deliberately been put at a disadvantage, by whom I can't imagine (my God is not a Handicapper General), in order to equalize chances in the great race of life. These words seem to me to be moving away from my condition, to be widening the gap between word and reality. Most remote is the recently coined euphemism "differently abled," which partakes of the same semantic hopefulness that transformed countries from "undeveloped" to "underdeveloped," then to "less developed," and finally to "developing" nations. People have continued to starve in those countries during the shift. Some realities do not obey the dictates of language.

Mine is one of them. Whatever you call me, I remain crippled. But I don't care what you call me, so long as it isn't "differently abled," which strikes me as pure verbal garbage designed, by its ability to describe anyone, to describe no one. I subscribe to George Orwell's thesis that "the slovenliness of our language makes it easier for us to have foolish thoughts." And I refuse to participate in the degeneration of the language to the extent that I deny that I have lost anything in the course of this calamitous disease; I refuse to pretend that the only differences between you and me are the various ordinary ones that distinguish any one person from another. But call me "disabled" or "handicapped" if you like. I have long since grown accustomed to them; and if they are vague, at least they hint at the truth. Moreover, I use them myself. Society is no readier to accept crippledness than to accept death, war, sex, sweat, or wrinkles. I would never refer to another person as a cripple. It is the word I use to name only myself.

I haven't always been crippled, a fact for which I am soundly grateful. To be whole of limb is, I know from experience, infinitely more pleasant and useful than to be crippled; and if that knowledge leaves me open to bitterness at my loss, the physical soundness I once enjoyed (though I did not enjoy it half enough) is well worth the occasional stab of regret. Though never any good at sports, I was a normally active child and young adult. I climbed trees, played hopscotch, jumped rope, skated, swam, rode my bicycle, sailed. I despised team sports, spending some of the wretchedest afternoons of my life sweaty and humiliated, behind a field-hockey stick and under a basketball hoop. I tramped alone for miles along the bridle paths that webbed the woods behind the house I grew up in. I swayed through countless dim hours in the arms of one man or another under the scattered shot of light from mirrored balls, and gyrated through countless more as Tab Hunter and Johnny Mathis gave way to the Rolling Stones, Creedence Clearwater Revival, Cream. I walked down the aisle. I pushed baby carriages, changed tires in the rain, marched for peace.

When I was twenty-eight I started to trip and drop things. What at first seemed my natural clumsiness soon became too pronounced to shrug off. I consulted a neurologist, who told me that I had a brain tumor. A battery of tests, increasingly disagreeable, revealed no tumor. About a year and a half later I developed a blurred spot in one eye. I had, at last, the episodes "disseminated in space and time" requisite for a diagnosis: multiple sclerosis. I have never been sorry for the doctor's initial misdiagnosis, however. For almost a week, until the negative results of the tests were in, I thought that I was going to die right away. Every day for the past nearly ten years, then, has been a kind of gift. I accept all gifts.

Multiple sclerosis is a chronic degenerative disease of the central nervous system, in which the myelin that sheathes the nerves is somehow eaten away and scar tissue forms in its place, interrupting the nerves' signals. During its course, which is unpredictable and uncontrollable, one may lose vision, hearing, speech, the ability to walk, control of bladder and/or bowels, strength in any or all extremities, sensitivity to touch, vibration, and/or pain, potency, coordination of movements—the list of possibilities is lengthy and yes, horrifying. One may also lose one's sense of humor. That's the easiest to lose and the hardest to survive without.

In the past ten years, I have sustained some of these losses. Characteristic of MS are sudden attacks, called exacerbations, followed by remissions, and these I have not had. Instead, my disease has been slowly progressive. My left leg is now so weak that I walk with the aid of a brace and a cane; and for distances I use an Amigo, a variation on the electric wheelchair that looks rather like an electrified kiddie car. I no longer have much use of my left hand. Now my right side is weakening as well. I still have the blurred spot in my right eye. Overall, though, I've been lucky so far. My world has, of necessity, been circumscribed by my losses, but the terrain left me has been ample enough for me to continue many of the activities that absorb me: writing, teaching, raising children and cats and plants and snakes, reading, speaking publicly about MS and depression, even playing bridge with people patient and honorable enough to let me scatter cards every which way without sneaking a peek.

Lest I begin to sound like Pollyanna, however, let me say that I don't like having MS. I hate it. My life holds realities—harsh ones, some of them— that no right-minded human being ought to accept without grumbling. One of them is fatigue. I know of no one with MS who does not complain of bone-weariness; in a disease that presents an astonishing variety of symptoms, fatigue seems to be a common factor. I wake up in the morning feeling the way most people do at the end of a bad day, and I take it from there. As a result, I spend a lot of time *in extremis* and, impatient with limitation, I tend to ignore my fatigue until my body breaks down in some way and forces rest. Then I miss picnics, dinner parties, poetry readings, the brief visits of old friends from out of town. The offspring of a puritanical tradition of exceptional venerability, I cannot view these lapses without shame. My life often seems a series of small failures to do as I ought.

I lead, on the whole, an ordinary life, probably rather like the one I would have led had I not had MS. I am lucky that my predilections were already solitary, sedentary, and bookish—unlike the world-famous French cellist I have read about, or the young woman I talked with one long afternoon who wanted only to be a jockey. I had just begun graduate school when I found out something was wrong with me, and I have remained, interminably, a graduate student. Perhaps I would not have if I'd thought I had the stamina to return to a full-time job as a technical editor; but I've enjoyed my studies.

In addition to studying, I teach writing courses. I also teach medical students how to give neurological examinations. I pick up freelance editing jobs here and there. I have raised a foster son and sent him into the world, where he has made me two grandbabies, and I am still escorting my daughter and son through adolescence. I go to Mass every Saturday. I am a superb, if messy, cook. I am also an enthusiastic laundress, capable of sorting a hamper full of clothes into five subtly differentiated piles, but a terrible housekeeper. I can do italic writing and, in an emergency, bathe an oil-soaked cat. I play a fiendish game of Scrabble. When I have the time and the money, I like to sit on my front steps with my husband, drinking Amaretto and smoking a cigar, as we imagine our counterparts in Leningrad and make sure that the sun gets down once more behind the sharp childish scrawl of the Tucson Mountains.

This lively plenty has its bleak complement, of course, in all the things I can no longer do. I will never run again, except in dreams, and one day I may have to write that I will never walk again. I like to go camping, but I can't follow George and the children along the trails that wander out of a campsite through the desert or into the mountains. In fact, even on the level I've learned never to check the weather or try to hold a coherent conversation: I need all my attention for my wayward feet. Of late, I have begun to catch myself wondering how people can propel themselves without canes. With only one usable hand, I have to select my clothing with care not so much for style as for ease of ingress and egress, and even so, dressing can be laborious. I can no longer do fine stitchery, pick up babies, play the piano, braid my hair. I am immobilized by acute attacks of depression, which may or may not be physiologically related to MS but are certainly its logical concomitant.

These two elements, the plenty and the privation, are never pure, nor are the delight and wretchedness that accompany them. Almost every pickle that I get into as a result of my weakness and clumsiness—and I get into plenty—is funny as well as maddening and sometimes painful. I recall one May afternoon when a friend and I were going out for a drink after finishing up at school. As we were climbing into opposite sides of my car, chatting, I tripped and fell, flat and hard, onto the asphalt parking lot, my abrupt departure interrupting him in mid-sentence. "Where'd you go?" he called as he came around the back of the car to find me hauling myself up by the door frame. "Are you all right?" Yes, I told him, I was fine, just a bit rattly, and we drove off to find a shady patio and some beer. When I got home an hour or so later, my daughter greeted me with "What have you done to yourself?" I looked down. One elbow of my white turtleneck with the green froggies, one knee of my white trousers, one white kneesock were blood-soaked. We peeled off the clothes and inspected the damage, which was nasty enough but not alarming. That part wasn't funny: The abrasions took a long time to heal, and one got a little infected. Even so, when I think of my friend talking earnestly, suddenly, to the hot thin air while I dropped from his view as though through a trap door, I find the image as silly as something from a Marx Brothers movie.

I may find it easier than other cripples to amuse myself because I live propped by the acceptance and the assistance and, sometimes, the amusement of those around me. Grocery clerks tear my checks out of my check-book for me, and sales clerks find chairs to put into dressing rooms when I want to try on clothes. The people I work with make sure I teach at times when I am least likely to be fatigued, in places I can get to, with the materi-als I need. My students, with one anonymous exception (in an end-of-the-semester evaluation) have been unperturbed by my disability. Some even like it. One was immensely cheered by the information that I paint my own fingernails; she decided, she told me, that if I could go to such trouble over fine details, she could keep on writing essays. I suppose I became some sort of bright-fingered muse. She wrote good essays, too.

The most important struts in the framework of my existence, of course, are my husband and children. Dismayingly few marriages survive the MS test, and why should they? Most twenty-two- and nineteen-year-olds, like George and me, can vow in clear conscience, after a childhood of chickenpox and summer colds, to keep one another in sickness and in health so long as they both shall live. Not many are equipped for catastrophe: the dismay, the de-pression, the extra work, the boredom that a degenerative disease can insinu-ate into a relationship. And our society, with its emphasis on fun and its asso-ciation of fun with physical performance, offers little encouragement for a whole spouse to stay with a crippled partner. Children experience similar stresses when faced with a crippled parent, and they are more helpless, since parents and children can't usually get divorced. They hate, of course, to be different from their peers, and the child whose mother is tacking down the aisle of a school auditorium packed with proud parents like a Cape Cod din-ghy in a stiff breeze jolly well stands out in a crowd. Deprived of legal di-vorce, the child can at least deny the mother's disability, even her existence, forgetting to tell her about recitals and PTA meetings, refusing to accompany her to stores or church or the movies, never inviting friends to the house. Many do.

But I've been limping along for ten years now, and so far George and the children are still at my left elbow, holding tight. Anne and Matthew vacuum floors and dust furniture and haul trash and rake up dog droppings and but-ton my cuffs and bake lasagne and Toll House cookies with just enough grum-bling so I know that they don't have brain fever. And far from hiding me, they're forever dragging me by racks of fancy clothes or through teeming school corridors, or welcoming gaggles of friends while I'm wandering through the house in Anne's filmy pink babydoll pajamas. George generally calls before he brings someone home, but he does just as many dumb thank-less chores as the children. And they all yell at me, laugh at some of my jokes, write me funny letters when we're apart—in short, treat me as an ordinary human being for whom they have some use. I think they like me. Unless they're faking. . . .

Faking. There's the rub. Tugging at the fringes of my consciousness always is the terror that people are kind to me only because I'm a cripple. My mother almost shattered me once, with that instinct mothers have—blind, I think, in this case, but unerring nonetheless—for striking blows along the fault-lines of their children's hearts, by telling me, in an attack on my selfish-ness, "We all have to make allowances for you, of course, because of the way you are." From the distance of a couple of years, I have to admit that I haven't any idea just what she meant, and I'm not sure that she knew either. She was awfully angry. But at the time, as the words thudded home, I felt my worst fear, suddenly realized. I could bear being called selfish: I am. But I couldn't bear the corroboration that those around me were doing in fact what I'd always suspected them of doing, professing fondness while silently putting up with me because of the way I am. A cripple. I've been a little cracked ever since.

Along with this fear that people are secretly accepting shoddy goods comes a relentless pressure to please — to prove myself worth the burdens I impose, I guess, or to build a substantial account of goodwill against which I may write drafts in times of need. Part of the pressure arises from social expectations. In our society, anyone who deviates from the norm had better find some way to compensate. Like fat people, who are expected to be jolly, cripples must bear their lot meekly and cheerfully. A grumpy cripple isn't playing by the rules. And much of the pressure is self-generated. Early on I vowed that, if I had to have MS, by God I was going to do it well. This is a class act, ladies and gentlemen. No tears, no recriminations, no faint-heartedness.

One way and another, then, I wind up feeling like Tiny Tim, peering over the edge of the table at the Christmas goose, waving my crutch, piping down God's blessing on us all. Only sometimes I don't want to play Tiny Tim. I'd rather be Caliban, a most scurvy monster. Fortunately, at home no one much cares whether I'm a good cripple or a bad cripple as long as I make vichyssoise with fair regularity. One evening several years ago, Anne was reading at the dining-room table while I cooked dinner. As I opened a can of tomatoes, the can slipped in my left hand and juice spattered me and the counter with bloody spots. Fatigued and infuriated, I bellowed, "I'm so sick of being crippled!" Anne glanced at me over the top of her book. "There now," she said, "do you feel better?" "Yes," I said, "yes, I do." She went back to her reading. I felt better. That's about all the attention my scurviness ever gets.

Because I hate being crippled, I sometimes hate myself for being a cripple. Over the years I have come to expect — even accept — attacks of violent self-loathing. Luckily, in general our society no longer connects deformity and disease directly with evil (though a charismatic once told me that I have MS because a devil is in me) and so I'm allowed to move largely at will, even among small children. But I'm not sure that this revision of attitude has been particularly helpful. Physical imperfection, even freed of moral disapprobation, still defies and violates the ideal, especially for women, whose confinement in their bodies as objects of desire is far from over. Each age, of course, has its ideal, and I doubt that ours is any better or worse than any other. Today's ideal woman, who lives on the glossy pages of dozens of magazines, seems to be between the ages of eighteen and twenty-five; her hair has body, her teeth flash white, her breath smells minty, her underarms are dry; she has a career but is still a fabulous cook, especially of meals that take less than twenty minutes to prepare; she does not ordinarily appear to have a husband or children; she is trim and deeply tanned; she jogs, swims, plays tennis, rides a bicycle, sails, but does not bowl; she travels widely, even to out-of-the-way places like Finland and Samoa, always in the company of the ideal man, who possesses a nearly identical set of characteristics. There are a few exceptions. Though usually white and often blonde, she may be black, Hispanic, Asian, or Native American, so long as she is unusually sleek. She may be old, provided she is selling a laxative or is Lauren Bacall. If she is selling a detergent, she may be married and have a flock of strikingly messy children. But she is never a cripple.

Like many women I know, I have always had an uneasy relationship with my body. I was not a popular child, largely, I think now, because I was peculiar: intelligent, intense, moody, shy, given to unexpected actions and inexplicable notions and emotions. But as I entered adolescence, I believed myself unpopular because I was homely: my breasts too flat, my mouth too wide, my hips too narrow, my clothing never quite right in fit or style. I was not, in fact, particularly ugly, old photographs inform me, though I was well off the ideal; but I carried this sense of self-alienation with me into adulthood, where it regenerated in response to the depredations of MS. Even with my brace I walk with a limp so pronounced that, seeing myself on the videotape of a television program on the disabled, I couldn't believe that anything but an inchworm could make progress humping along like that. My shoulders droop and my pelvis thrusts forward as I try to balance myself upright, throwing my frame into a bony S. As a result of contractures, one shoulder is higher than the other and I carry one arm bent in front of me, the fingers curled into a claw. My left arm and leg have wasted into pipe-stems, and I try always to keep them covered. When I think about how my body must look to others, especially to men, to whom I have been trained to display myself, I feel ludicrous, even loathsome.

At my age, however, I don't spend much time thinking about my appearance. The burning egocentricity of adolescence, which assures one that all the world is looking all the time, has passed, thank God, and I'm generally too caught up in what I'm doing to step back, as I used to, and watch myself as though upon a stage. I'm also too old to believe in the accuracy of self-image. I know that I'm not a hideous crone, that in fact, when I'm rested, well dressed, and well made up, I look fine. The self-loathing I feel is neither physically nor intellectually substantial. What I hate is not me but a disease.

I am not a disease.

And a disease is not—at least not singlehandedly—going to determine who I am, though at first it seemed to be going to. Adjusting to a chronic incurable illness, I have moved through a process similar to that outlined by Elizabeth Kübler-Ross in *On Death and Dying*. The major difference—and it is far more significant than most people recognize—is that I can't be sure of the outcome, as the terminally ill cancer patient can. Research studies indicate that, with proper medical care, I may achieve a "normal" life span. And in our society, with its vision of death as the ultimate evil, worse even than decrepitude, the response to such news is, "Oh well, at least you're not going to *die*." Are there worse things than dying? I think that there may be.

I think of two women I know, both with MS, both enough older than I to have served as models. One took to her bed several years ago and has been there ever since. Although she can sit in a high-backed wheelchair, because she is incontinent she refuses to go out at all, even though incontinence pants, which are readily available at any pharmacy, could protect her from embarrassment. Instead, she stays at home and insists that her husband, a small quiet man, a retired civil servant, stay there with her except for a quick weekly foray to the supermarket. The other woman, whose illness was diagnosed when she was eighteen, a nursing student engaged to a young doctor, finished her training, married her doctor, accompanied him to Germany when he was in the service, bore three sons and a daughter, now grown and gone. When she can, she travels with her husband; she plays bridge, embroiders, swims regularly; she works, like me, as a symptomatic-patient instructor of medical students in neurology. Guess which woman I hope to be.

At the beginning, I thought about having MS almost incessantly. And because of the unpredictable course of the disease, my thoughts were always terrified. Each night I'd get into bed wondering whether I'd get out again the next morning, whether I'd be able to see, to speak, to hold a pen between my fingers. Knowing that the day might come when I'd be physically incapable of killing myself, I thought perhaps I ought to do so right away, while I still had the strength. Gradually I came to understand that the Nancy who might one day lie inert under a bedsheet, arms and legs paralyzed, unable to feed or bathe herself, unable to reach out for a gun, a bottle of pills, was not the Nancy I was at present, and that I could not presume to make decisions for that future Nancy, who might well not want in the least to die. Now the only provision I've made for the future Nancy is that when the time comes— and it is likely to come in the form of pneumonia, friend to the weak and the old—I am not to be treated with machines and medications. If she is unable to communicate by then, I hope she will be satisfied with these terms.

Thinking all the time about having MS grew tiresome and intrusive, especially in the large and tragic mode in which I was accustomed to considering my plight. Months and even years went by without catastrophe (at least without one related to MS), and really I was awfully busy, what with George and children and snakes and students and poems, and I hadn't the time, let alone the inclination, to devote myself to being a disease. Too, the richer my life became, the funnier it seemed, as though there were some connection between largesse and laughter, and so my tragic stance began to waver until, even with the aid of a brace and cane, I couldn't hold it for very long at a time.

After several years I was satisfied with my adjustment. I had suffered my grief and fury and terror, I thought, but now I was at ease with my lot. Then one summer day I set out with George and the children across the desert for a vacation in California. Part way to Yuma I became aware that my right leg felt funny. "I think I've had an exacerbation," I told George. "What shall we do?" he asked. "I think we'd better get the hell to California," I said, "because I don't know whether I'll ever make it again." So we went on to San Diego and then to Orange, and up the Pacific Coast Highway to Santa Cruz, across to Yosemite, down to Sequoia and Joshua Tree, and so back over the desert to home. It was a fine two-week trip, filled with friends and fair weather, and I wouldn't have missed it for the world, though I did in fact make it back to California two years later. Nor would there have been any point in missing it, since in MS, once the symptoms have appeared, the neurological damage has been done, and there's no way to predict or prevent that damage.

The incident spoiled my self-satisfaction, however. It renewed my grief and fury and terror, and I learned that one never finishes adjusting to MS. I don't know now why I thought one would. One does not, after all, finish adjusting to life, and MS is simply a fact of my life—not my favorite fact, of course—but as ordinary as my nose and my tropical fish and my yellow

Mazda station wagon. It may at any time get worse, but no amount of worry or anticipation can prepare me for a new loss. My life is a lesson in losses. I learn one at a time.

And I had best be patient in the learning, since I'll have to do it like it or not. As any rock fan knows, you can't always get what you want. Particularly when you have MS. You can't, for example, get cured. In recent years researchers and the organizations that fund research have started to pay MS some attention even though it isn't fatal; perhaps they have begun to see that life is something other than a quantitative phenomenon, that one may be very much alive for a very long time in a life that isn't worth living. The researchers have made some progress toward understanding the mechanism of the disease: It may well be an autoimmune reaction triggered by a slow-acting virus. But they are nowhere near its prevention, control, or cure. And most of us want to be cured. Some, unable to accept incurability, grasp at one treatment after another, no matter how bizarre: megavitamin therapy, gluten-free diet, injections of cobra venom, hypothermal suits, lymphocytopharesis, hyperbaric chambers. Many treatments are probably harmless enough, but none are curative.

The absence of a cure often makes MS patients bitter toward their doctors. Doctors are, after all, the priests of modern society, the new shamans, whose business is to heal, and many an MS patient roves from one to another, searching for the "good" doctor who will make him well. Doctors too think of themselves as healers, and for this reason many have trouble dealing with MS patients, whose disease in its intransigence defeats their aims and mocks their skills. Too few doctors, it is true, treat their patients as whole human beings, but the reverse is also true. I have always tried to be gentle with my doctors, who often have more at stake in terms of ego than I do. I may be frustrated, maddened, depressed by the incurability of my disease, but I am not diminished by it, and they are. When I push myself up from my seat in the waiting room and stumble toward them, I incarnate the limitation of their powers. The least I can do is refuse to press on their tenderest spots.

This gentleness is part of the reason that I'm not sorry to be a cripple. I didn't have it before. Perhaps I'd have developed it anyway—how could I know such a thing?—and I wish I had more of it, but I'm glad of what I have. It has opened and enriched my life enormously, this sense that my frailty and need must be mirrored in others, that in searching for and shaping a stable core in a life wrenched by change and loss, change and loss, I must recognize the same process, under individual conditions, in the lives around me. I do not deprecate such knowledge, however I've come by it.

All the same, if a cure were found, would I take it? In a minute. I may be a cripple, but I'm only occasionally a loony and never a saint. Anyway, in my brand of theology God doesn't give bonus points for a limp. I'd take a cure; I just don't need one. A friend who also has MS startled me once by asking, "Do you ever say to yourself, 'Why me, Lord?'" "No, Michael, I don't," I told him, "because whenever I try, the only response I can think of is 'Why not?'" If I could make a cosmic deal, who would I put in my place? What in my life would I give up in exchange for sound limbs and a thrilling rush of energy? No one. Nothing. I might as well do the job myself. Now that I'm getting the hang of it.

Suggestions for Discussion

1. Why does Mairs prefer the word "cripple" to "handicapped" or "disabled" to describe her condition?

2. How does she characterize the plenty, the privation of her life?

3. What does she mean by "I'd take a cure; I just don't need one"?

Suggestions for Writing

1. Mairs asserts that her multiple sclerosis is only one part of her multifaceted self: "What I hate is not me but a disease. I am not a disease." Write about how people tend instead to identify with things that have happened to them or with aspects of themselves. Use an example from your own experience to support this idea.

2. "My life is a lesson in losses. I learn one at a time." What does this convey about Mairs's attitude toward life? How would you handle a life-long "crisis"?

3. Examine the role of humor as a survival tool. Use examples from the essay and your own experience to explore the topic.

Essays

Alan Alda

You Have to Know What Your Values Are!

Alan Alda, a professional actor and writer, has played the role of Captain Benjamin Franklin Pierce of M*A*S*H* fame. He has written several of the M*A*S*H* scripts and other TV shows and movies. In this excerpt from his 1979 commencement address to Drew University, he points to the contradictions in the American culture and urges his audience to articulate their values and bring meaning to their lives.

Someday it's very possible that you will look up from your work and wonder what the point of it all is. You'll wonder how much you are getting accomplished and how much it all means.

The sentence "What's the purpose of all this?" is written in large letters over the mid-life-crisis butcher shop. You can't miss it as you lug the carcass of your worldly success through the door to have it dressed and trimmed and placed in little plastic packages for people to admire. *"What's the purpose of all this?"* You may be asking yourself that question now or next year or in twenty years. When you do, consider this: Your life will have meaning when you can give meaning to it—and only then. No one else is going to give meaning to your life. There isn't a job or a title or a degree that has meaning in itself. The world can always go stumbling on without you no matter how high your office. There isn't a liquor that will give meaning to your life or a drug, or any type of sexual congress either.

I would like to suggest to you, just in case you haven't done it lately, that it's a good idea to find out what your values in life really are, and then to figure out how you are going to live by them. It seems to me that knowing what you care about and then devoting yourself to it is just about the only way you can have a sense of purpose in life, and it's probably the only way you can go through the minefield of existence and get out in one piece.

It can be a startling experience when you try to rank your values. Just ask yourself for a second what you feel is the most important thing in the world to you. Your family, your work, your money, your country, getting to heaven, sex, dope, alcohol? When you get the answer to that, ask yourself how much time you actually spend on your number-one value and how much time you spend on what you thought was number five, or number ten. What *in fact* is the thing you value most? This may not be so easy to decide, because we live in a time that seems to be split about its values, it seems almost schizophrenic. For instance, if you should pick up a magazine that specializes in psychology and social issues, you might see an article titled something like "White Collar Crime: It's More Widespread Than You Think," and then turn to the back of the magazine and find an ad that reads, "We'll Write Your Doctoral Thesis for Twenty-Five Dollars." (You see how our values are eroding? A doctoral thesis ought to go for at least a C-note!) Now, who is writing these institutionalized crib notes? Scholars? I'd love to send away for an article on the ethics of scholarship and see what they send back. The question is, Where are their values? *What* do they value?

Unfortunately, the people we look to for leadership seem to be providing it by negative example. All across the country, commencement speakers say to graduating classes, "We look to you for tomorrow's leaders." That's because *today's* leaders are all in jail. I don't mean to be too hard on politicians. Politics is a very useful, very old profession—in some ways it is the oldest profession. I may have become somewhat disillusioned about politicians in the past couple of years because of a few I've met while campaigning for the Equal Rights Amendment. I've crossed the paths of some very strange legislators.

One assemblyman in a Midwestern state where I campaigned told a woman who was lobbying for the Equal Rights Amendment that he would give her his vote, he would vote yes for the Equal Rights Amendment, if she showed up in his hotel room that night. Can you imagine a more inappropriate offer? That's like saying you will vote yes for emancipation in exchange for a couple of good slaves.

I was in the Washington office of a United States senator one day when he was trying to get a legislator back in his home state to vote yes on the amendment, and the guy he was talking to was absolutely opposed to it in principle. He just didn't believe in it. However, he would change his vote, he said, if the senator would pay his way to Washington and arrange for his son's high school band to march in the inaugural parade. Now, the question is, Where were these men's values? What did they hold as important? Anything? All that these men seemed to care about was sex, money and power.

There are people influencing our lives who seem to be operating according to no principle whatsoever. And you find them in every field, in every business, in our country. When you sell a product that you know will fall apart in a few months, when you sell the sizzle and you know there's no steak, when you take the money and run, when you write an article or a political speech or a television show that excites and titillates but doesn't lead to understanding and insight, when you are all style and no substance, you might as well be tossing poison into the reservoir we all drink from.

Think about that. Suppose somebody came up to you and offered you $50 to throw a little poison into the reservoir. He says, "Look, it's just a little poison, how much harm can it do?" What would you take to throw just a little poison into the reservoir? Would you take $50? Would you take $100? How about $10,000? Would you take $500,000 a year, with stock options and a Christmas bonus? The problem is that everyone who's throwing in a little bit of poison combines with everyone else who is doing it, and together we are tampering dangerously with our moral ecology.

No matter what our work is, we all have to face that choice—in my field no less than in others. There may not be a more important field for the dissemination of values in our country than the entire communications industry—most strikingly, television. Networks are very sensitive to that fact, and they employ dozens of censors to prevent all of us from using language on television that an eight year old might have to explain to his parents. But the point that censors miss, I think, is that it is not so much what we *say* that teaches as what we *don't* say. Even programs that attempt to make a moral point don't always make the point that they intended to, because when we sense we are being sold something, we automatically defend ourselves against it. I think it may be the unspoken assumptions that mold an audience.

Look at the way, for instance, that violence is treated on television. It is not only the quantity that offends. There probably is no more violence on television than there is in a Shakespearean tragedy. But on television you find *unfelt* violence and in Shakespeare you tend to find *felt* violence. In Shakespeare the characters react with a human response: They fear, they hurt, they mourn. Most of the time on television, violence is dealt with by sweeping it under the rug as fast as possible and by having people go on about their business as if nothing had happened. (If I can't have less violence, I want at least a better grade of violence.) One of the unspoken assumptions is that violence can be tolerated as long as you ignore it and have no reaction to it. But that seems to me to be dangerously close to psychopathic behavior. I wonder if there is any connection between the long acceptance by our people of the Vietnam war and the thousands and thousands of deaths that we have seen on television over the years that were never mourned, never even paused for except to sell shampoo for sixty seconds.

Maybe our greatest problem is that we have two separate sets of value systems that we use—the one we talk about and the one we live by. We seem to place a very high value on fairness and on human concerns. And yet we still have widespread discrimination based on race, sex and religion. You still don't find Jews, blacks or other minorities in any significant numbers in decision-making positions in the banking industry, for instance. You think that's an accident? I think somebody put a value on that. And you don't find women in any significant numbers in decision-making capacities in *any* industry. Why? Because we place a higher value on appeasing the fragile male ego than we do on fairness and decency? Maybe what we need is a declaration of interdependence.

Maybe we simply need to know what we care about.

If we put a high value on decency, if we put a high value on excellence and on family, if we love the people we share our lives with—our wives and our husbands, our children—and if we don't shortchange them for a few bucks, if we can love the work we do and learn the skill of it, the art of it, if we can give full measure to the people who pay us for our work, if we try not to lie, try not to cheat, try to do good just by doing well whatever we do . . . then we will have made a revolution.

Suggestions for Discussion

1. What does Alda mean when he says that "your life will have meaning when you can give meaning to it"? How do his subsequent remarks illuminate the statement?

2. What do Alda's reflections on the leaders of our country, and on politics, business, and the media tell you about his values?

3. What does Alda mean by our "moral ecology"?

4. What are Alda's views of television violence?

5. What contradictions does Alda see in contemporary society?

6. How would you sum up Alda's personal values?

7. How are the tone and substance of Alda's remarks affected by the fact that it is a commencement speech?

Suggestions for Writing

1. How would you place your values in hierarchical order? How will they serve to give meaning to your life?

2. Discuss the values of your parents or peers and evaluate them.

3. What do Alda's values have in common with those of other writers in this section?

Ronald Dworkin

Life Is Sacred: That's the Easy Part

Ronald Dworkin (b. 1931), a native of Massachusetts, was educated at Harvard and Oxford Universities. A legal authority, he taught for some years at Oxford, and since 1975 has been at New York University. He holds honorary degrees from three universities, and is a fellow of the British Academy as well as the American Academy of Arts and Letters. His books include *Taking Rights Seriously* (1977), *A Matter of Principle* (1985), *Law's Empire* (1986), and *Life's Dominion* (1993). In this article he articulates a common ground on which he believes proponents of intensely held opposing positions on abortion and euthanasia can meet to listen to one another.

The fierce argument about abortion and euthanasia now raging in America is this century's Civil War. When Dr. David Gunn was shot and killed in front of a Florida abortion clinic last March, any hope that the abortion battle had finally become less savage died with him. The argument over euthanasia has been less violent but equally intense. When Nancy Cruzan was finally allowed to die in a Missouri hospital in 1991, after seven years in a persistent vegetative state, people called her parents murderers and her nurses wept over what was being done to her.

These terrible controversies have been far more polarized and bitter than they need and should have been, however, because most Americans have misunderstood what the arguments are *about*. According to the usual explanation, the abortion struggle is about whether a fetus, from the moment of conception, is already a person—already a creature whose interests other people must respect and whose rights government must protect. If that is the correct way to understand the debate, then of course accommodation is impossible; people who think that abortion violates a fetus's right to life can no more compromise than decent people can compromise over genocide.

But in fact, in spite of the scalding rhetoric, almost none of those who believe abortion may be objectionable on moral grounds actually believe that an early fetus is a person with rights and interests of its own. The vast majority of them think abortion morally permissible when necessary to save the mother's life, and only somewhat fewer that it is permissible in cases of rape and incest. Many of them also think that even when abortion is morally wrong, it is none of the law's business to prohibit it. None of this is compatible with thinking that a fetus has interests of its own. Doctors are not permitted to kill one innocent person to save the life of another one; a fetus should not be punished for a sexual crime of which it is wholly innocent, and it is certainly part of government's business to protect the rights and interests of persons too weak to protect themselves.

So conservative opinion cannot consistently be based on the idea that a fetus has interests of its own from the moment of conception. Neither can liberal and moderate opinion be based simply on rejecting that idea. Most liberals insist that abortion is always a morally grave decision, not to be taken for frivolous or capricious reasons, and this positive moral position must be based on more than the negative claim that a fetus has no interests or rights.

I suggest a different explanation of the controversy: We disagree about abortion not because some of us think, and others deny, that an immature fetus is already a person with interests of its own but, paradoxically, because of an ideal we share. We almost all accept, as the inarticulate assumption behind much of our experience and conviction, that human life in all its forms is *sacred*—that it has intrinsic and objective value quite apart from any value it might have to the person whose life it is. For some of us, this is a matter of religious faith; for others, of secular but deep philosophical belief. But though we agree that life is sacred, we disagree about the source and character of that sacred value and therefore about which decisions respect and which dishonor it. I can best explain what the idea that life has intrinsic and objective value means by turning to the other agonizing controversy I mentioned, at the far edge of life.

Should a doctor prescribe enough pills to allow a patient with leukemia to kill herself, as Dr. Timothy Quill of Rochester did in 1991? Should he ever try to kill a patient in agony and pleading to die by injecting her with potassium chloride, as Dr. Nigel Cox did in Britain last year? Many people concede that in such terrible circumstances death would actually be in the patient's best interests, but nevertheless insist that killing her or letting her die would be wrong because human life has an independent, sacred value and should be preserved for that reason.

There is nothing odd or unusual about the idea that it is wrong to destroy some creatures or things, not because they themselves have interests that would be violated but because of the intrinsic value they embody. We take that view, for example, of great paintings and also of distinct animal species, like the Siberian tiger that we work to save from extinction. Paintings and species do not have interests: if it nevertheless seems terrible to destroy them, because of their intrinsic value, it can also seem terrible to destroy a human life, which most people think even more precious, though that human life has not yet developed into a creature with interests either. So people can passionately oppose abortion for that reason even though they do not believe that a collection of growing cells just implanted in a womb already has interests of its own.

Once we identify that different basis for thinking abortion wrong, we see that it actually unites as well as divides our society, because almost everyone—conservatives, moderates and liberals on the issue of abortion—accepts both that the life of a human fetus embodies an intrinsic value and that a frivolous abortion is contemptuous of that important value. Americans disagree about when abortion is morally permissible, not because many of them reject the idea that human life is sacred but because they disagree about how best to respect that value when continuing a pregnancy would itself frustrate or damage human life in some other grave way: when a child would be born seriously deformed, for example, or when childbirth would frustrate a teenage mother's chances to make something of her own life, or when the economic burden of another child would mean more privation for other children already living in poverty.

In such cases, respect for the inherent value of a human life pulls in two directions, and some resolution of the tragic conflict is necessary. How each of us resolves it will depend on our deeper, essentially religious or philosophical convictions about which of the different sources of life's sacred value is most important. People who think that biological life—the gift of God or nature—is the transcendently important source of that sacred value will think that the death of any human creature, even one whose life in earnest has not yet begun, is always the worst possible insult to the sanctity of life. Those who think that frustrating people's struggle to make something of their own lives, once those lives are under way, is sometimes an even greater affront to the value of life than an early abortion might resolve the conflict in the other direction.

That view of how and why we disagree about abortion also explains why so many people think that even when early abortion is morally wrong, government has no business forbidding it. There is no contradiction in insisting that abortion sometimes dishonors a sacred value and that government must nevertheless allow women to decide for themselves when it does. On the contrary, that very distinction is at the heart of one of the most important liberties modern democracies have established, a liberty America leads the world in protecting—freedom of conscience and religion. Once we see the abortion argument in this light, we see that it is an essentially *religious* argument— not about who has rights and how government should protect these, but a very different, more abstract and spiritual argument about the meaning and character and value of human life itself. Government does have a responsibility to help people understand the gravity of these decisions about life and death, but it has no right to dictate which decision they must finally make.

The same is true of euthanasia. Of course, any legal regime that permits doctors to help patients die must be scrupulously careful to protect the patient's real, reflective wishes and to avoid patients or relatives making an unwitting choice for death when there is a genuine chance of medical recovery. But government can do people great harm by not allowing them to die when that is their settled wish and in their best interests, as they themselves have judged or would judge their interests when competent to do so.

In both cases, the crucial question is not whether to respect the sanctity of life, but which decision best respects it. People who dread being kept alive, permanently unconscious or sedated beyond sense, intubated and groomed and tended as vegetables, think this condition degrades rather than respects what has been intrinsically valuable in their own living. Others disagree: They believe, about euthanasia as about abortion, that mere biological life is so inherently precious that nothing can justify deliberately ending it. The disagreement, once again, is an essentially religious or spiritual one, and a decent government, committed to personal integrity and freedom, has no business imposing a decision. Dictating how people should see the meaning of their own lives and deaths is a crippling, humiliating form of tyranny.

If we change our collective view of these two great controversies, if we realize that we are arguing not about whether abortion and euthansia are murder but about how best to honor a humane ideal we all share, then we can cure the bitterness in our national soul. Freedom of choice can be accepted by all sides with no sense of moral compromise, just as all religious groups and sects can accept, with no sense of compromise, freedom for other versions of spiritual truth, even those they think gravely mistaken. We might even hope for something more: a healing sense, after all the decades of hate, that what unites us is more important than our differences. It is inevitable that free people who really do believe that human life is sacred will disagree about how to live and die in the light of that conviction, because free people will insist on making that profound and self-defining decision for themselves.

Suggestions for Discussion

1. Discuss Dworkin's argument that the abortion debate is essentially a religious one.

2. The author believes that we share a humane ideal and that what divides us is how we would choose to enact that ideal. Explain why you agree or disagree.

3. Dworkin sets the resolution to the bitter debates over abortion and euthanasia within a framework of religious tolerance. Do you support this? Why or why not?

4. "[T] the crucial question is not whether to respect the sanctity of life, but which decision best respects it." Explain your reasons for agreeing or disagreeing with this statement.

Suggestions for Writing

1. Sometimes we find ourselves in situations in which there is nothing we can do, no way we can act, that does not call some principle we hold into question. Create a dialogue that depicts this.

2. Debate: "*Resolved;* The role of the government is to help us understand our decisions, not to make them for us."

Erich Fromm

Our Way of Life Makes Us Miserable

Erich Fromm (1900–1980) immigrated to the United States from Germany in 1934 and became an American citizen in 1940. He established his reputation as a psychoanalyst, social critic, and writer. His major books include *Escape from Freedom, The Sane Society, Life Without Illusions,* and *The Art of Loving.*

Fromm attributes the violence and misery in contemporary society to our confusion of means and ends, and suggests that if we recognize the alternatives to our present way of life we may yet achieve a humanist society.

Most Americans believe that our society of consumption-happy, fun-loving, jet-traveling people creates the greatest happiness for the greatest number. Contrary to this view, I believe that our present way of life leads to increasing anxiety, helplessness and, eventually, to the disintegration of our culture. I refuse to identify fun with pleasure, excitement with joy, business with happiness, or the faceless, buck-passing "organization man" with an independent individual.

From this critical view our rates of alcoholism, suicide and divorce, as well as juvenile delinquency, gang rule, acts of violence and indifference to life, are characteristic symptoms of our "pathology of normalcy." It may be argued that all these pathological phenomena exist because we have not yet reached our aim, that of an affluent society. It is true, we are still far from being an affluent society. But the material progress made in the last decades allows us to hope that our system might eventually produce a materially affluent society. Yet will we be happier then? The example of Sweden, one of the most prosperous, democratic and peaceful European countries, is not very encouraging: Sweden, as is often pointed out, in spite of all its material security has among the highest alcoholism and suicide rates in Europe, while a much poorer country like Ireland ranks among the lowest in these respects. Could it be that our dream that material welfare per se leads to happiness is just a pipe dream? . . .

Certainly the humanist thinkers of the eighteenth and nineteenth centuries, who are our ideological ancestors, thought that the goal of life was the full unfolding of a person's potentialities; what mattered to them was the person who *is* much, not the one who *has* much or *uses* much. For them economic production was a means to the unfolding of man, not an end. It seems that today the means have become ends, that not only "God is dead," as Nietzsche said in the nineteenth century, but also man is dead; that what is alive are the organizations, the machines; and that man has become their slave rather than being their master.

Each society creates its own type of personality by its way of bringing up children in the family, by its system of education, by its effective values (that is, those values that are rewarded rather than only preached). Every society creates the type of "social character" which is needed for its proper functioning. It forms men who *want* to do what they *have* to do. What kind of men does our large-scale, bureaucratized industrialism need?

It needs men who cooperate smoothly in large groups, who want to consume more and more, and whose tastes are standardized and can be easily influenced and anticipated. It needs men who feel free and independent, yet who are willing to be commanded, to do what is expected, to fit into the social machine without friction; men who can be guided without force, led without leaders, prompted without an aim except the aim to be on the move, to function, to go ahead.

Modern industrialism has succeeded in producing this kind of man. He is the "alienated" man. He is alienated in the sense that his actions and his own forces have become estranged from him; they stand above him and against him, and rule him rather than being ruled by him. His life forces have been transformed into things and institutions, and these things and institutions have become idols. They are something apart from him, which he worships and to which he submits. Alienated man bows down before the works of his own hands. He experiences himself not as the active bearer of his own forces and riches but as an impoverished "thing," dependent on other things outside of himself. He is the prisoner of the very economic and political circumstances which he has created.

Since our economic organization is based on continuous and ever-increasing consumption (think of the threat to our economy if people did not buy a new car until their old one was really obsolete), contemporary industrial man is encouraged to be consumption-crazy. Without any real enjoyment, he "takes in" drink, food, cigarettes, sights, lectures, books, movies, television, any new kind of gadget. The world has become one great maternal breast, and man has become the eternal suckling, forever expectant, forever disappointed.

Sex, in fact, has become one of the main objects of consumption. Our newsstands are full of "girlie" magazines; the percentages of girls having premarital sexual relations and of unwed mothers are on a steep incline. It can be argued that all this represents a welcome emancipation from Victorian morality, that it is a wholesome affirmation of independence, that it reflects the Freudian principle that repression may produce neurosis. But while all these arguments are true to some extent, they omit the main point. Neither independence nor Freudian principle is the main cause of our present-day sexual freedom. Our sexual mores are part and parcel of our *cult of consumption,* whose main principle was so succinctly expressed by Aldous Huxley in *Brave New World:* "Never put off till tomorrow the fun you can have today." Nature has provided men and women with the capacity for sexual excitement; but excitement in consumption, whether it is of sex or any other commodity, is not the same as aliveness and richness of experience.

In general, our society is becoming one of giant enterprises directed by a bureaucracy in which man becomes a small, well-oiled cog in the machinery. The oiling is done with higher wages, fringe benefits, well-ventilated factories and piped music, and by psychologists and "human-relations" experts; yet all this oiling does not alter the fact that man has become powerless, that he does not wholeheartedly participate in his work and that he is bored with it. In fact, the blue- and the white-collar workers have become economic puppets who dance to the tune of automated machines and bureaucratic management.

The worker and employee are anxious, not only because they might find themselves out of a job (and with installment payments due); they are anxious also because they are unable to acquire any real satisfaction or interest in life. They live and die without ever having confronted the fundamental realities of human existence as emotionally and intellectually productive, authentic and independent human beings.

Those higher up on the social ladder are no less anxious. Their lives are no less empty than those of their subordinates. They are even more insecure in some respects. They are in a highly competitive race. To be promoted or to fall behind is not only a matter of salary but even more a matter of self-esteem. When they apply for their first job, they are tested for intelligence as well as for the right mixture of submissiveness and independence. From that moment on they are tested again and again—by the psychologists, for whom testing is a big business, and by their superiors, who judge their behavior, sociability, capacity to get along, etc., their own and that of their wives. This constant need to *prove* that one is as good as or better than one's fellow-competitor creates constant anxiety and stress, the very causes of unhappiness and psychosomatic illness. *—again we go outside of ourselves to find satisfaction*

The "organization man" may be well fed, well amused and well oiled, yet he lacks a sense of identity because none of his feelings or his thoughts originates within himself; none is authentic. He has no convictions, either in politics, religion, philosophy or in love. He is attracted by the "latest model" in thought, art and style, and lives under the illusion that the thoughts and feelings which he has acquired by listening to the media of mass communication are his own.

He has a nostalgic longing for a life of individualism, initiative and justice, a longing that he satisfies by looking at Westerns. But these values have disappeared from real life in the world of giant corporations, giant state and military bureaucracies and giant labor unions. He, the individual, feels so small before these giants that he sees only one way to escape the sense of utter insignificance: He identifies himself with the giants and idolizes them as the true representatives of his own human powers, those of which he has dispossessed himself. His effort to escape his anxiety takes other forms as well. His pleasure in a well-filled freezer may be one unconscious way of reassuring himself. His passion for consumption—from television to sex—is still another symptom, a mechanism which psychiatrists often find in anxious patients who go on an eating or buying spree to evade their problems.

The man whose life is centered around producing, selling and consuming commodities transforms himself into a commodity. He becomes increasingly attracted to that which is man-made and mechanical, rather than to that which is natural and organic. Many men today are more interested in sports cars than in women; or they experience women as a car which one can cause to race by pushing the right button. Altogether they expect happiness is a matter of finding the right button, not the result of a productive, rich life, a life which requires making an effort and taking risks. In their search for the button, some go to the psychoanalyst, some go to church and some read "self-help" books. But while it is impossible to find the button for happiness, the majority are satisfied with pushing the buttons of cameras, radios, television sets, and watching science fiction becoming reality.

One of the strangest aspects of this mechanical approach to life is the widespread lack of concern about the danger of total destruction by nuclear weapons; a possibility people are consciously aware of. The explanation, I believe, is that they are more proud of than frightened by the gadgets of mass destruction. Also, they are so frightened of the possibility of their personal failure and humiliation that their anxiety about personal matters prevents them from feeling anxiety about the possibility that everybody and everything may be destroyed. Perhaps total destruction is even more attractive than total insecurity and never-ending personal anxiety.

Am I suggesting that modern man is doomed and that we should return to the preindustrial mode of production or to nineteenth-century "free enterprise" capitalism? Certainly not. Problems are never solved by returning to a stage which one has already outgrown. I suggest transforming our social system from a bureaucratically managed industrialism in which maximal production and consumption are ends in themselves (in the Soviet Union as well as in the capitalist countries) into a humanist industrialism in which man and the full development of his potentialities—those of love and of reason—are the aims of all social arrangements. Production and consumption should serve only as means to this end, and should be prevented from ruling man.

To attain this goal we need to create a Renaissance of Enlightenment and of Humanism. It must be an Enlightenment, however, more radically realistic and critical than that of the seventeenth and eighteenth centuries. It must be a Humanism that aims at the full development of the total man, not the gadget man, not the consumer man, not the organization man. The aim of a humanist society is the man who loves life, who has faith in life, who is productive and independent. Such a transformation is possible if we recognize that our present way of life makes us sterile and eventually destroys the vitality necessary for survival.

Whether such transformation is likely is another matter. But we will not be able to succeed unless we see the alternatives clearly and realize that the choice is still ours. Dissatisfaction with our way of life is the first step toward changing it. As to these changes, one thing is certain: They must take place in all spheres simultaneously—in the economic, the social, the political and the spiritual. Change in only one sphere will lead into blind alleys, as did the purely political French Revolution and the purely economic Russian Revolution. Man is a product of circumstances—but the circumstances are also his product. He has a unique capacity that differentiates him from all other living beings: the capacity to be aware of himself and of his circumstances, and hence to plan and to act according to his awareness.

Suggestions for Discussion

1. What are the aspects of our culture which Fromm believes may lead to its disintegration?

2. How does he account for the pathological phenomena in the society?

3. What evidence does he provide that affluence does not produce happiness?

4. How do we confuse means and ends?

5. What are the characteristics of the alienated person?

6. How does Fromm's use of imagery contribute to his thesis?

7. How does the author relate our sexual mores to our cult of consumption?

8. What are the principal sources of anxiety of both workers and their employers?

9. How does the author relate a life centered around producing, selling, and consuming commodities to a loss of self?

10. What is Fromm's hope for the individual and for society?

Suggestions for Writing

1. Although Fromm uses the masculine pronoun throughout his essay, to what degree does his description of the alienated person apply to women?

2. Challenge or support Fromm's thesis with reference to your experience or the observations you have made about men and women of your acquaintance.

3. Fromm refuses "to identify fun with pleasure, excitement with joy." Do you believe they are irreconcilable? Distinguish between each of these opposites.

Rollo May

The Man Who Was Put in a Cage

Rollo May (b. 1909) is a practicing psychotherapist in New York. He is a member of the William Alanson White Institute of Psychiatry, Psychoanalysis, and Psychology. In addition he has written *Man's Search for Himself* (1953), *Power and Innocence* (1972), *The Courage to Create* (1975), *Freedom and Destiny* (1981), *The Discovery of Being: Writings in Existential Psychology* (1983), *Love and Will* (1986), and *The Ageless Spirit* (1992), among many others. In this parable from *Psychology and the Human Dilemma* (1966), the psychologist is impelled to act on the man's impassioned cry in the dream: When any man's freedom is taken away, the freedom of everyone is also taken away.

> What a piece of work is man! how noble in reason! how infinite in faculty! in form and moving how express and admirable! . . . The paragon of animals!
> —Shakespeare, *Hamlet*

We have quite a few discrete pieces of information these days about what happens to a person when he is deprived of this or that element of freedom. We have our studies of sensory deprivation and of how a person reacts when put in different kinds of authoritarian atmosphere, and so on. But recently I have been wondering what pattern would emerge if we put these various pieces of knowledge together. In short, what would happen to a living, whole person if his total freedom—or as nearly total as we can imagine—were taken away? In the course of these reflections, a parable took form in my mind.

The story begins with a king who, while standing in reverie at the window of his palace one evening, happened to notice a man in the town square below. He was apparently an average man, walking home at night, who had taken the same route five nights a week for many years. The king followed this man in his imagination—pictured him arriving home, perfunctorily kissing his wife, eating his late meal, inquiring whether everything was all right with the children, reading the paper, going to bed, perhaps engaging in the sex relation with his wife or perhaps not, sleeping, and getting up and going off to work again the next day.

And a sudden curiosity seized the king, which for a moment banished his fatigue: "I wonder what would happen if a man were kept in a cage, like the animals at the zoo?" His curiosity was perhaps in some ways not unlike that of the first surgeons who wondered what it would be like to perform a lobotomy on the human brain.

So the next day the king called in a psychologist, told him of his idea, and invited him to observe the experiment. When the psychologist demurred saying, "It's an unthinkable thing to keep a man in a cage," the monarch replied that many rulers had in effect, if not literally, done so, from the time of the Romans through Genghis Khan down to Hitler and the totalitarian leaders; so why not find out scientifically what would happen? Furthermore, added the king, he had made up his mind to do it whether the psychologist took part or not; he had already gotten the Greater Social Research Foundation to give a large sum of money for the experiment, and why let that money go to waste? By this time the psychologist also was feeling within himself a great curiosity about what would happen if a man were kept in a cage.

And so the next day the king caused a cage to be brought from the zoo—a large cage that had been occupied by a lion when it was new, then later by a tiger; just recently it had been the home of a hyena who died the previous week. The cage was put in an inner private court in the palace grounds, and the average man whom the king had seen from the window was brought and placed therein. The psychologist, with his Rorschach and Wechsler-Bellevue tests in his brief case to administer at some appropriate moment, sat down outside the cage.

At first the man was simply bewildered, and he kept saying to the psychologist, "I have to catch the tram, I have to get to work, look what time it is, I'll be late for work!" but later on in the afternoon the man began soberly to realize what was up, and then he protested vehemently, "The king can't do this to me! It is unjust! It's against the law." His voice was strong, and his eyes full of anger. The psychologist liked the man for his anger, and he became vaguely aware that this was a mood he had encountered often in people he worked with in his clinic. "Yes," he realized, "this anger is the attitude of people who—like the healthy adolescents of any era—want to fight what's wrong, who protest directly against it. When people come to the clinic in this mood, it is good—they can be helped."

During the rest of the week the man continued his vehement protests. When the king walked by the cage, as he did every day, the man made his protests directly to the monarch.

But the king answered, "Look here, you are getting plenty of food, you have a good bed, and you don't have to work. We take good care of you; so why are you objecting?"

After some days had passed, the man's protests lessened and then ceased. He was silent in his cage, generally refusing to talk. But the psychologist could see hatred glowing in his eyes. When he did exchange a few words, they were short, definite words uttered in the strong, vibrant, but calm voice of the person who hates and knows whom he hates.

Whenever the king walked into the courtyard, there was a deep fire in the man's eyes. The psychologist thought, "This must be the way people act when they are first conquered." He remembered that he had also seen that expression of the eyes and heard that tone of voice in many patients at his clinic: the adolescent who had been unjustly accused at home or in school and could do nothing about it; the college student who was required by public and campus opinion to be a star on the gridiron, but was required by his professors to pass courses he could not prepare for if he were to be successful in football—and who was then expelled from college for the cheating that resulted. And the psychologist, looking at the active hatred in the man's eyes, thought, "It is still good; a person who has this fight in him can be helped."

Every day the king, as he walked through the courtyard, kept reminding the man in the cage that he was given food and shelter and taken good care of, so why did he not like it? And the psychologist noticed that, whereas at first the man had been entirely impervious to the king's statements, it now seemed more and more that he was pausing for a moment after the king's speech—for a second the hatred was postponed from returning to his eyes—as though he were asking himself if what the king said were possibly true.

And after a few weeks more, the man began to discuss with the psychologist how it was a useful thing that a man is given food and shelter; and how man had to live by his fate in any case, and the part of wisdom was to accept fate. He soon was developing an extensive theory about security and the acceptance of fate, which sounded to the psychologist very much like the philosophical theories that Rosenberg and others worked out for the fascists in Germany. He was very voluble during this period, talking at length, although the talk was mostly a monologue. The psychologist noticed that his voice was flat and hollow as he talked, like the voice of people in TV previews who make an effort to look you in the eye and try hard to sound sincere as they tell you that you should see the program they are advertising, or the announcers on the radio who are paid to persuade you that you should like high-brow music.

And the psychologist also noticed that now the corners of the man's mouth always turned down, as though he were in some gigantic pout. Then the psychologist suddenly remembered: this was like the middle-aged, middle-class people who came to his clinic, the respectable bourgeois people who went to church and lived morally but were always full of resentment, as though everything they did was conceived, born, and nursed in resentment. It reminded the psychologist of Nietzsche's saying that the middle class was consumed with resentment. He then for the first time began to be seriously worried about the man in the cage, for he knew that once resentment gets a firm start and becomes well rationalized and structuralized, it may become like cancer. When the person no longer knows whom he hates, he is much harder to help.

During this period the Greater Social Research Foundation had a board of trustees meeting, and they decided that since they were expending a fund to keep a man supported in a cage, it would look better if representatives of the Foundation at least visited the experiment. So a group of people, consisting of two professors and a few graduate students, came in one day to look at the man in the cage. One of the professors then proceeded to lecture to the group about the relation of the autonomic nervous system and the secretions of the ductless glands to human existence in a cage. But it occurred to the other professor that the verbal communications of the victim himself might just possibly be interesting, so he asked the man how he felt about living in a cage. The man was friendly toward the professors and students and explained to them that he had chosen this way of life, that there were great values in security and in being taken care of, that they would of course see how sensible this course was, and so on.

"How strange!" thought the psychologist, "and how pathetic; why is it he struggles so hard to get them to approve his way of life?"

In the succeeding days when the king walked through the courtyard, the man fawned upon him from behind the bars in his cage and thanked him for the food and shelter. But when the king was not in the yard and the man was not aware that the psychologist was present, his expression was quite different—sullen and morose. When his food was handed to him through the bars by the keeper, the man would often drop the dishes or dump over the water and then would be embarrassed because of his stupidity and clumsiness. His conversation became increasingly one-tracked; and instead of the involved philosophical theories about the value of being taken care of, he had gotten down to simple sentences such as "It is fate," which he would say over and over again, or he would just mumble to himself, "It is." The psychologist was surprised to find that the man should now be so clumsy as to drop his food, or so stupid as to talk in those barren sentences, for he knew from his tests that the man had originally been of good average intelligence. Then it dawned upon the psychologist that this was the kind of behavior he had observed in some anthropological studies among the Negroes in the South— people who had been forced to kiss the hand that fed and enslaved them, who could no longer either hate or rebel. The man in the cage took more and more to simply sitting all day long in the sun as it came through the bars, his only movement being to shift his position from time to time from morning through the afternoon.

It was hard to say just when the last phase set in. But the psychologist became aware that the man's face now seemed to have no particular expression; his smile was no longer fawning, but simply empty and meaningless, like the grimace a baby makes when there is gas on its stomach. The man ate his food and exchanged a few sentences with the psychologist from time to time; but his eyes were distant and vague, and though he looked at the psychologist, it seemed that he never really *saw* him.

And now the man, in his desultory conversations, never used the word "I" *any more.* He had accepted the cage. He had no anger, no hate, no rationalizations. But he was now insane.

The night the psychologist realized this, he sat in his apartment trying to write a concluding report. But it was very difficult for him to summon up words, for he felt within himself a great emptiness. He kept trying to reassure himself with the words, "They say that nothing is ever lost, that matter is merely changed to energy and back again." But he could not help feeling that something *had* been lost, that something had gone out of the universe in this experiment.

He finally went to bed with his report unfinished. But he could not sleep; there was a gnawing within him which, in less rational and scientific ages, would have been called a conscience. Why didn't I tell the king that this is the one experiment that no man can do—or at least why didn't I shout that I would have nothing to do with the whole bloody business? Of course, the king would have dismissed me, the foundations would never have granted me any more money, and at the clinic they would have said that I was not a real scientist. But maybe one could farm in the mountains and make a living, and maybe one could paint or write something that would make future men happier and more free. . . .

But he realized that these musings were, at least at the moment, unrealistic, and he tried to pull himself back to reality. All he could get, however, was this feeling of emptiness within himself, and the words, "Something has been taken out of the universe, and there is left only a void."

Finally he dropped off to sleep. Some time later, in the small hours of the morning, he was awakened by a startling dream. A crowd of people had gathered, in the dream, in front of the cage in the courtyard, and the man in the cage—no longer inert and vacuous—was shouting through the bars of the cage in impassioned oratory. "It is not only I whose freedom is taken away!" he was crying. "When the king puts me or any man in a cage, the freedom of each of you is taken away also. The king must go!" The people began to chant, "The king must go!" and they seized and broke out the iron bars of the cage, and wielded them for weapons as they charged the palace.

The psychologist awoke, filled by the dream with a great feeling of hope and joy—an experience of hope and joy probably not unlike that experienced by the free men of England when they forced King John to sign the Magna Charta. But not for nothing had the psychologist had an orthodox analysis in the course of his training, and as he lay surrounded by this aura of happiness, a voice spoke within him: "Aha, you had this dream to make yourself feel better; it's just a wish fulfillment."

"The hell it is!" said the psychologist as he climbed out of bed. "Maybe some dreams are to be acted on."

Suggestions for Discussion

1. What possible implicit judgment of the average man is evident in the king's imaginative recreation of his life? What is the significance of the king's selection of an average man for his experiment?

2. Formulate a plausible explanation of the fact that the anger and subsequent hate manifested by the man in the cage signified that he could be helped.

3. Define the various phases of the victim's response to his imprisonment and account for each of them. Include an analysis of the changes in his conversations with the several observers. How did the analogies cited contribute to your understanding of his metamorphosis?

4. Account for the reactions of the psychologist after his realization that the man was no longer sane, especially his feeling of emptiness within himself, the sense that "there is left only a void." Account for his final postdream resolution.

Suggestions for Writing

1. What does the form of the parable contribute to May's thesis? Write a paragraph elaborating on May's thesis. What is lost when you state it directly?

2. Using a vital subject like freedom of choice or love or the dignity of man, write a parable of your own in which you place it in fresh perspective.

3. Read a work that depicts a human as prisoner and victim. Write an analysis of the effects of incarceration on the human spirit, paying special attention to what qualities and activities of the mind distinguish one person from another under such adverse circumstances.

4. Relate the opening lines from *Hamlet* to the parable. Or develop an essay on the most difficult or the most crucial choices you have ever made, or are currently contemplating, and the factors you regard as central in arriving at a resolution.

5. May attributes the man's capitulation largely to the fact of his security. Defend or criticize this thesis. What if the victim were not an average man but a bright member of a youth commune, a poet, or a mystic? Rewrite the parable using one of the latter or any other victim as your protagonist.

Carol Tavris

Uncivil Rights—
The Cultural Rules of Anger

Carol Tavris (b. 1944) is a social psychologist with a doctorate from the University of Michigan. She teaches at the Human Relations Center of the New School for Social Research, and is senior editor of *Psychology Today*. She has written several books on anger, including *Anger: The Misunderstood Emotion* (1982) and *Controlling Anger* (1989). Her most recent book is *The Mismeasure of Woman* (1992). In the selection that follows she attempts to look at anger not as a personal response to a situation, but as part of a complex pattern of social control.

> The full potential of human fury cannot be reached until a friend of both parties tactfully intervenes.
> —G. K. Chesterton

The young wife leaves her house one afternoon to draw water from the local well. She saunters down the main street, chatting amiably with her neighbors, as her husband watches from their porch. On her return from the well, a stranger stops her and asks for a cup of water. She obliges, and in fact invites the man home for dinner. He accepts. The husband, wife, and guest spend a pleasant evening together, and eventually the husband puts the lamp out and retires to bed. The wife also retires to bed—with the guest. In the morning, the husband leaves early to bring back some breakfast for the household. Upon his return, he find his wife again making love with the visitor.

At what point in this sequence of events will the husband become angry or jealous? Is his anger inevitable? The answer, observes psychologist Ralph Hupka, depends on the tribe and culture he belongs to:

A Pawnee Indian husband, a century ago, would, in fury, bewitch any man who dared to request a cup of water from his wife.

An Ammassalik Eskimo husband who wants to be a proper host invites his guest to have sex with his wife; he signals his invitation by putting out the lamp. (The guest might feel angry if this invitation were not extended.) An Ammassalik husband would be angry, however, if he found his wife having sex with a man in circumstances other than the lamp game, such as that morning encore, or without a mutual agreement to exchange mates.

A middle-class husband belonging to most modern American tribes would tend to get angry with any guest who, however courteously, tried to seduce his wife, and with the wife who, however hospitably, slept with their guest.

A husband who belonged to the polyandrous Toda tribe of southern India at the turn of the century would find the whole sequence of events perfectly normal; nothing to raise a fuss about. The Todas practiced *mokhtoditi*, a custom that allowed both spouses to take lovers. If a man wanted to make love to a married woman, he first got her permission and then the permission of her husband or husbands; a yearly fee was negotiated; and then the wife was free to visit her new lover and the lover free to visit the wife at her home. But a Toda husband and wife would undoubtedly be angry with any man who tried to establish an affair by sneaking around the husband's back (and not paying the proper fee).

People everywhere get angry, but they get angry in the service of their culture's rules. Sometimes those rules are explicit ("Thou shalt not covet thy neighbor's wife"); more often they are implicit, disguised in the countless daily actions performed because "That's the way we do things around here." These unstated rules are often not apparent until someone breaks them, and anger is the sign that someone has broken them. It announces that someone is not behaving as (you think) she or he *ought*. This "assertion of an ought" is, according to psychologist Joseph de Rivera, the one common and essential feature of anger in all its incarnations. "Whenever we are angry," he writes, "we somehow believe that we can influence the object of our anger. We assume that the other is responsible for his actions and ought to behave differently."

This "ought" quality suggests that a major role of anger is its policing function. Anger, with its power of forcefulness and its threat of retaliation, helps to regulate our everyday social relations: in family disputes, neighborly quarrels, business disagreements, wherever the official law is too cumbersome, inappropriate, or unavailable (which is most of the time). Psychologist James Averill observes that for most of Western history, it has been up to individuals to see to it that their rights were respected and justice seen to; in the absence of a formal judiciary, anger operates as a personal one.

Perhaps the best way to understand the policing power of anger is to step outside of our own complex environment, and observe the way anger works in small societies. Small societies are highly revealing, whether they are families, tribes, high-school marching bands, or the U.S. Congress. Members of such groups understand very well the importance of the rules that govern anger, because everyone has to get along with each other in the morning. Anger is society's servant, and you can see this in the day-to-day life of small tribes. They may seem exotic, but they are, close up, a mirror on ourselves.

The Judicial Emotion

N!uhka, age seventeen, was furious. Her father had reminded her that she was getting on in years and that it was high time for her to marry. N!uhka, who was rebellious and vain, was uninterested in the eligible young men her father suggested, and at last, in the heat of argument, she cursed him aloud. He was shocked. *She* was shocked. So were all the neighbors and relations who had overheard her.

Now N!uhka was angry and also ashamed of her disrespectful outburst. She grabbed her blanket and stormed out of the camp to a lone tree some seventy yards away. There she sat, all day, covered in the blanket. This was not a trivial penance, since the temperature that day was 105 degrees Fahrenheit in the shade (without a blanket), but by the time she returned to camp her anger and embarrassment had subsided.

The !Kung hunter-gatherers of the Kalahari Desert are called "the harmless people" because of their renowned lack of aggression. This does not mean that they are free from the petty plagues of human life, such as jealousies, resentments, suspicions, and sulks. Teenagers disagree with their parents' wishes, relatives squabble about who owes what to whom, and husbands and wives bicker about marital matters. The difference is that the !Kung know that they must manage these emotions and dampen them down to tolerable levels, and that if they don't their very survival is endangered.

The !Kung are nomadic, foraging constantly for food, and their only insurance against hard times is each other. No individual can lay in a supply of frozen pizzas and beer in the event of famine and drought, and no individual could long survive on his or her own. Sharing is therefore the dominant value and obsession of their society. As one of their principal ethnographers, Elizabeth Marshall Thomas, observed: "It has never happened that a Bushman [today they are called !Kung or !Kung-san] failed to share objects, food, or water with the other members of his band, for without very rigid cooperation Bushmen could not survive the famines and droughts that the Kalahari offers them." Under such conditions, any antisocial or angry outburst threatens the whole group; so it is to the !Kung interest to avoid direct physical confrontation or violence, and to be suspicious of individuals who cannot control their behavior or their tempers. "Their hold on life," says Thomas, "is too tenuous to permit quarreling among themselves."

The same structure of camp life that increases the chances of group solidarity and survival—lack of privacy, each hut close to the other huts, extended family nearby—also means that every flare-up and dispute is immediately available for public discussion and resolution. Such lack of privacy would be cause enough for anger in the West, where "It's none of your business" is an accepted refrain. Among the !Kung, everything is everyone's business. "Once a person attacks his victim he is like a fly that attacks an insect already caught in a spider's web," writes anthropologist Patricia Draper. "Immediately both are caught. If the combatants forget the sticky web in the heat of their anger, the onlookers do not. Real anger frightens and sickens the !Kung, for it is so destructive of their web of relationships." Anyone who becomes angry will have the assistance ("interference" to the West) of the entire tribe, if need be. Perhaps this is why, in nearly a year and a half of fieldwork, one anthropologist saw only four examples of overt discord and heard of only a few others. Another recorded only three serious disputes: one over possession of an animal that had been killed, another about a marital disagreement, and a third in which a mother raged at a curer who failed to attend her sick child.

Although the !Kung are not aggressive, they are expert at bickering and complaint. "The outsider wonders how the !Kung can stand to live with each other," says Patricia Draper. "In the early months of my own fieldwork I despaired of ever getting away from continual harassment." Some psychoanalytically inclined observers take this as evidence of the !Kung's "displaced" aggressive instinct, which, if not released physically (they say), takes this verbal outlet. But a closer look at the content of the bickering reveals two things about it: It has a distinct social purpose, and although it may seem to outsiders like a sign of anger it is really a ritual game, devoid of anger's heat.

After several months, Draper discovered that the key to !Kung bickering was its emphasis on dunning for food. What idle conversation about the weather and the economy is to Europeans, she noticed, reminders about food obligations were to the !Kung. In time she learned the "properly melodramatic disclaimers" that allowed her to join the game:

> You expect *me*, one lonely European, a stranger in this territory, living away from my own kin, without even one spear or arrow or even a digging stick, and with no knowledge of the bush . . . you expect *me* to give *you* something to eat? You are a person whose hut is crammed full of good things to eat. Berries, billtong, sweet roots, stand shoulder high in your hut and you come to me saying you are hungry!

The !Kung visitor would be delighted with such a spirited reply (as would the inevitable onlookers), and once this exchange was completed, Draper and the !Kung could go on to talk about other things. But food-dunning jokes and complaints are important because they remind everyone of the responsibility to recirculate food and property. The have-nots press for their share; the haves are reminded that their fortune is only temporary.

I have found Draper's observations useful in understanding my own particular tribe, Eastern European Jews whose forebears came from the shtetls of Russia and Poland, and for whom ritual dunning has been a long tradition. Indeed, the rich curse repertoire of Yiddish makes the four-letter-word grunts of English a pale and gutless thing. As Barbara Myerhoff recorded in *Number Our Days:*

> *Jake:* In those days, everybody gave curses. You couldn't live without it. A woman there was on our street who could curse like Heifetz plays the violin. The things she would fix up for her enemies! "May your teeth get mad and eat your head off." "May you inherit a hotel with one hundred rooms and be found dead in every one." "May you have ten sons and all your daughters-in-law hate you." "May all your teeth fall out but one, and that one has a cavity." "May your chickens lay eggs in your neighbor's house." "May the gypsies camp on your stomach and their bears do the *kazotskhi* in your liver."
> *Basha:* This last one you are getting from Sholom Aleichem.
> *Jake:* And where do you think Sholom Aleichem learned it?

Today these curses are a fading talent (I think they require the original Yiddish), just as the ritual dunning is a mere shadow of its former self: "You don't call me any more"; "Write your Aunt Hannah a thank-you letter *today*"; "Do your fingers have leprosy that you can't pick up your socks?" But the curses and the dunning have their origin in survival needs as great as those for food in the African bush. The repeated bickering reminded shtetl Jews of their social obligations to the family and the culture, emphasizing the importance of staying in line and paying attention to the traditions that kept the precarious group together. A visitor to such cultures is likely, as Patricia Draper was among the !Kung, to feel under attack, at least until he or she learns the rules and can play the game.

A Brief Madness

A culture's values and needs determine not only our everyday angers but even when we may be allowed to "go crazy" with rage. "Anger," wrote Horace some two thousand years ago, "is a brief madness," succinctly noting the affinity between "mad" and "angry." The match is psychological as well as linguistic, because in many cultures (including our own) an enraged individual and an insane one are both regarded as being out of control, unable to take responsibility for their actions. Yet other cultures, such as the Eskimo, distinguish the two conditions: A person who is legitimately insane cannot be expected to control himself, but one who is merely angry can and must control himself. What distinguishes us from the Eskimo, aside from the weather? What role does the *belief* in the similarity between rage and madness play?

One evening, apparently out of the blue, a young Malay man armed himself with traditional weapons, the parang and the kris, and embarked on a killing spree. By the time his rampage was over, several hours later, he had accosted customers in three local coffeehouses and murdered five innocent men. His friends were surprised that the young man had "run amok"; he seemed so polite and well mannered.

In San Francisco in 1979, a civil servant named Dan White resigned his seat on the city's Board of Supervisors. Shortly thereafter he changed his mind, but he was too late: Mayor George Moscone had decided to give the job to someone else. White took his snubnosed revolver, climbed in through the window of City Hall (so the metal detectors wouldn't reveal his gun), and pumped nine bullets into Moscone and supervisor Harvey Milk, who had been one of White's outspoken opponents (and who was a homosexual whom White disliked). In what the press played up as the "Twinkie defense," White's lawyers argued that his excessive consumption of junk food had caused his "diminished mental capacity," leaving him unable to premeditate anything, much less murder. The jury agreed. White was convicted of voluntary manslaughter and given a maximum sentence of seven years and eight months in jail. (Twenty months after his release, he committed suicide.)

The Gururumba tribesman was behaving strangely. He had suddenly taken to looting his neighbors' huts, stealing food and objects, and one afternoon his kinsmen found him hiding behind a tree, shooting arrows at passersby. He was clearly suffering a mental aberration, the tribe agreed, which they diagnosed as "being a wild pig."

In New York in 1980, Jean Harris shot and killed Herman Tarnower, her lover of fourteen years, in what the prosecution called a "jealous rage" and the defense a "tragic accident." Tarnower was found with four bullets in his body; Harris said she was trying to kill herself, not him. The jury did not believe her. She was convicted of intentional murder and given a minimum sentence of fifteen years in prison.

Running amok, being a wild pig, and temporary insanity are, within their respective tribes, legitimate signs of "a brief madness." These rages are, however, regarded as something other than psychosis, true mental illness, or other sorts of "long" madnesses, and they are often treated differently. Certainly some individuals who suffer organic abnormalities or psychoses that produce rage attacks can properly be diagnosed as insane; they do not, for one thing, revert to normalcy after a violent episode. And there are other individuals, such as the disturbed loners who have tried to assassinate or succeeded in assassinating our presidents and heroes, whose aggressive acts have little to do with anger and more to do with fantasies of power and fame. But most cases of "temporary insanity" caused apparently by rage, those heralded cases that capture the public eye, can be explained better in terms of their social causes than their organic ones, junk food to the contrary notwithstanding.

Start with "running amok," a phenomenon that originally referred to violent, often homicidal attacks among the indigenous peoples of the Malay Archipelago. Most people assume that the acts committed while a person is in such a state are unconscious, random, and without purpose. The *pengamok* (those who run amok) themselves think so, and so do their neighbors and relatives. But a closer look suggests otherwise. The frequency of this supposedly impulsive, uncontrollable act declined precipitately when the cultural response to it shifted from supportive tolerance to vicious punishment (at one point in Malay history, the *pengamok* were drawn and quartered).

Further, the objects of amok attacks are not random victims: Almost all of them are known to the amok and have been continuing sources of provocation. In one study that compared true *pengamok* to a control group of psychotics, the victims of the *pengamok* proved to be "rational" choices: a wife suspected of infidelity, a quarrelsome neighbor, an oppressive religion teacher. The Malay who killed the five customers of coffeehouses had carefully assured that his victims were Chinese: As his record showed, he had harbored anger at the Chinese who had killed some Malays several years before. The so-called psychotic symptoms of the *pengamok* vanish within a month or two of the episode, which is hardly the case for true psychotics.

Traditionally, the Malay are expected to be courteous and self-effacing, never to reprimand each other, and never to strive for success at the expense of another. Other cultures that have invaded the Malay Archipelago, such as the Chinese, have had rather more aggressive values, and therefore interpreted Malay behavior as signs of weakness and inferiority—which they promptly exploited. "Running amok," whether on an individual level or at a group level of rebellion, is a brilliant solution for Malay conflict: It allows the Malay to remain true to his cultural values while attacking the sources of his oppression and rage.

"Being a wild pig" is to the Gururumba what "running amok" is to the Malay. The Malay think that amok results from witchcraft or possession by evil spirits; the Gururumba think it comes from being bitten by a ghost. But wild pigs, like the *pengamok*, are not randomly distributed throughout the society. The only people who seem to get bitten, for example, are men between the ages of twenty-five and thirty-five, which is an especially stressful decade for the Gururumba male. He must abandon his youthful irresponsibility, take a wife, and assume a sudden burden of social obligations to the group. Success or failure at meeting these obligations will reflect not only on him, but on his clan.

Anthropologist P. L. Newman thinks that "being a wild pig" is a way of calling attention to the difficulties of shouldering these obligations. The victim of ghost bite, by his wild behavior, thereby announces to the tightly knit group that he wants to do something that his kinsmen might otherwise prohibit: change wives, move somewhere else, give up a particular responsibility. In the same way that a vociferous display of anger in our own culture finally convinces the recipient that the angry person *means* it, wild-pigdom convinces the Gururumba that the victim really is having a hard time and that something must be done. (Some Gururumba, consciously or not, put themselves in places where they are likely to be bitten by a ghost—a remote part of the forest or a gravesite.)

The Gururumba react with tolerance to a man who is being a wild pig. They are sympathetic to him, because they believe he is not responsible for his actions; they expect the seizure to run its course in a few days, like the flu. While the man is in this state they gently direct his "craziness": They leave food and little things for him to steal, and they don't let him hurt anyone seriously. The victim retreats to the forest for a few days on his own—not unlike our paid vacations—and if he returns still in a "wild" state, the tribesmen set up a ritual to cure him. They "capture" him and treat him as if he *were* a pig that had gone wild: They hold him over a smoking fire and rub him all over with pig fat. (This, the anthropologists assure us, is not as bad as it sounds.) A prominent person kills a real pig in the victim's name, and the victim is given a feast of pig meat and roots. Most important, however, are the reassessment and usually reduction of his obligations that occur after this ritual. That component of the procedure seems most likely to prevent remissions.

The Malay and Gururumba examples suggest that acceptable varieties of "temporary insanity" occur in cultures in which two equally powerful value systems conflict. In Western culture, a powerful taboo exists against intentional acts of violence, especially murder; yet the culture often counteracts that taboo with as great a passion for revenge, retribution, and defense of moral values. In America, when "an eye for an eye" meets "turn the other cheek"; when "thou shalt not kill" meets "thou shalt not commit adultery," temporary insanity is a temporary solution. This is a legal loophole in a Gordian knot: the law allows individuals to become angry enough to kill, but only if they kill in the service of society's dominant values, and only if they kill without premeditation or self-control—"in the heat of passion."

This is one reason, I think, that Dan White got off with such a light sentence for murdering two men and Jean Harris got a severe sentence for killing one. White and Harris both had had time, before their actions, to think about what they were doing. Both packed up their little guns at home and sought their victims. Both believed that they had been cruelly and unfairly treated by their victims. But Dan White's lawyers played on his "diminished mental capacity" to the hilt, bringing in plenty of psychiatrists to testify to his unstable mental condition. "The killing was done out of passion," the foreman of the jury later said, "given the stress he was under." Jean Harris's defense emphasized the "tragic accident" explanation, and called on no psychiatrists to exonerate her behavior or describe the stress she was under. The only person to describe her mental state was Harris herself, and that was her undoing; for the anger she expressed, even there on the witness stand, was cold and deliberate. She gave no evidence of having been enraged at Tarnower; angry with the "other woman," yes, but with the lover who left her, no. Had she done so, had she used the enormous sympathy usually extended to scorned lovers, had she argued that she had committed a crime of passion, I believe the outcome would have been different. But she did not. She took responsibility for her emotions. And so the jury had to find her guilty of her actions.

Although people frequently deplore the association between anger and violence in the United States, our customs and our laws (to say nothing of the easy availability of handguns) encourage the link. Why do we resist the idea that we can control our emotions, that feeling angry need not inevitably cause us to behave violently? Seneca the Stoic had a good idea of the answer. We refuse to follow his philosophy of self-restraint, he suggested, "Because we are in love with our vices; we uphold them and prefer to make excuses for them rather than shake them off." And why do we make excuses for them? *Because they excuse us.*

In a timely update of Seneca's observation, James Averill notices that we do not abdicate responsibility for all of our emotions, just the negative ones. No one apologizes for being swept away by a tidal wave of kindness and donating five thousand dollars to a worthy cause. A bystander who intervenes to prevent an assault or mugging is unlikely to apologize for acting courageously. We want credit for our noble emotions and tolerance for our negative ones; and losing one's temper, "misplacing" it in a fleeting hour of insanity, is the apology that begs such tolerance. While anger serves our private uses, it also makes our social excuses.

Manners, Emotions, and the American Way

The class was basic English for foreign students, and an Arab student, during a spoken exercise, was describing a tradition of his home country. Something he said embarrassed a Japanese student in the front row, who reacted the proper Japanese way: He smiled. The Arab saw the smile and demanded to know what was so funny about Arab customs. The Japanese, who was now publicly humiliated as well as embarrassed, could reply only with a smile and, to his misfortune, he giggled to mask his shame. The Arab, who now likewise felt shamed, furiously hit the Japanese student before the teacher could intervene. Shame and anger had erupted in a flash, as each student dutifully obeyed the rules of his culture. Neither could imagine, of course, that his rules might not be universal.

Because a major function of anger is to maintain the social order, through its moralizing implications of how people "should" behave, it is predictable that when two social orders collide they would generate angry sparks. It is easiest to see this when the colliding cultures are foreign to each other, but we have plenty of such collisions within our society as well. For some groups in America, anger is an effective way to get your way; for others it is the last resort. (Some groups have to learn assertiveness training to deal with others.) You may find your attitudes about anger, and the rules you learned to govern it, in conflict with those of different groups. Often it is this conflict about anger rules, not the rules per se, that can stir up trouble.

Each of us is tied to a group—a minitribe, if you will—by virtue of our sex, status, race, and ethnicity, and with countless unconscious reactions we reveal those ties as surely as Eliza Doolittle did when she opened her mouth. Anthropologist Edward T. Hall speaks of the "deep biases and built-in blinders" that every culture confers on its members. You can observe them at work every time you hear someone grumble, "I'll never understand women," or, "Why can't he just say what he feels?" or, "The (Japanese) (Mexicans) (Irish) (etc.) are utterly inscrutable."

Hall, who lives in New Mexico, has long observed the clash that occurs between groups when deeply felt rules about the "correct" management of anger are broken. The Spanish are sensitive to the slightest suggestion of criticism, Hall explains. "Confrontations are therefore to be avoided at all costs." The resulting misunderstandings between Spanish- and Anglo-Americans, he says, would be amusing if they weren't so often tragic.

When Anglo-Americans are angry, they tend to proceed in stages from small steps to larger ones. First, they hint around ("Mort, are you sure that fence is on *your* side of the property line?"). Then they talk to neighbors and friends of Mort. If they get no results, they may talk directly, and calmly, to Mort ("Mort, can we discuss our fence problem?"). Next they will express anger directly to Mort ("Dammit, that fence is on my property"). Eventually, if they are angry enough, they will take the matter to the courts. And as a last resort, they may resort to violence—and burn the fence down.

These steps, from smallest to largest, seem natural, logical, and inevitable. Actually, they are not only not natural, they are not even very common, worldwide. In many societies, such as in Latin cultures and in the Middle East, the first step is . . . to do nothing. Think about it. Brood. This brooding may go on for weeks, months, or even years (some cultures have long memories). The second step is . . . to burn the fence down. Now that matters are back to square one, participants are ready for direct discussions, negotiations, lawyers, and intermediaries. But notice, says Hall, that the act of force, which is the last step to Anglos, signaling the failure of negotiation, is the start of the conversation to Hispanics.

A culture's rules of anger are not arbitrary; they evolve along with its history and structure. The Japanese practice of emotional restraint, for example, dates back many centuries, when all aspects of demeanor were carefully regulated: facial expressions, breathing, manner of sitting and standing, style of walking. Not only were all emotions—anger, grief, pain, even great happiness—to be suppressed in the presence of one's superiors, but also regulations specified that a person submit to any order with a pleasant smile and a properly happy tone of voice. At the time of the Samurai knights, these rules had considerable survival value, because a Samurai could legally execute any-one who he thought was not respectful enough. (You may notice the similar-ity to American blacks and to women, who likewise had to be careful to con-trol anger in the presence of the white man.)

Even today in Japan, an individual who feels very angry is likely to show it by excessive politeness and a neutral expression instead of by furious words and signs. A Japanese who shows anger the Western way is admitting that he has lost control, and therefore lost face; he is thus at the extreme end of a negotiation or debate. In other cultures, though, showing anger may simply mark the *beginning* of an exchange, perhaps to show that the negotiator is serious; a man may lose face if he does *not* show anger when it is appropriate and "manly" for him to do so.

Psychotherapy, of course, takes place within a culture and is deeply em-bedded in cultural rules. Arthur Kleinman, himself both an anthropologist and psychiatrist, tells of a psychiatrist in south-central China who was treat-ing a patient who had become depressed and anxious ever since her demand-ing mother-in-law had moved in. "She is your family member. It is your re-sponsibility to care for an old mother-in-law," the Chinese psychiatrist said. "You must contain your anger. You know the old adage: 'Be deaf and dumb! Swallow the seeds of the bitter melon! Don't speak out!'"

I am not recommending that Americans learn to "swallow the seeds of the bitter melon"; in our society, most of us would choke on them. Cultural prac-tices cannot be imported from society to society like so many bits of cheese, because they are part of a larger pattern of rules and relationships. Indeed, that is the reason we cannot avoid the anger we feel when someone breaks the rules that we have learned are the only civilized rules to follow. But we might emulate the Arapesh, who criticize the provocateur; or the Eskimo, who settle in for a good round of verbal dueling; or Mbuti, who have a good laugh, understanding as they do the healing power of humor. We might also retrieve the old-fashioned standard of manners, which is, as small tribes teach us, an organized system of anger management. The con-ventions of the U.S. Senate, for example—the ornate language, the rules of debate—regulate anger over disagreements into acceptable channels. A sen-ator does not call his or her opposition a stupid blithering moron, for in-stance. He says, "My distinguished colleague from the great state of Blitzhorn, an otherwise fine and noble individual, is, in this rare moment, erring in judgment." The elaborate language that seems so comically decep-tive to the rest of us is what keeps political conversation going without blood-shed and mayhem.

Good manners melt resentment because they maintain respect between the two disagreeing parties. Indeed, one of the basic principles of parliamen-tary law is courtesy, "respect for the rights of individuals and for the assem-bly itself." You don't have to join Congress to feel the effect of this principle at work. Someone steps on your toe, you feel angry, the person apologizes, your anger vanishes. Your toe may still hurt, but your dignity is intact. (A friend tells me he loudly shushed a talkative man sitting behind him at the movies, and immediately felt bad that he had expressed himself so angrily. After the show, the man touched him on the shoulder. "You were quite right to tell me to keep quiet," he said, "I was rude." "I could have kissed him," said my friend.)

Without rules for controlling anger, it can slip into emotional anarchy, lasting far longer than its original purposes require. Observe how friends and family react to someone undergoing a bitter divorce: They extend sympathy and a willing ear to the enraged spouse for a while, but eventually they expect the person to "shape up" and "get on with it." What these friends and relatives are doing is imposing unofficial rules of anger management. The victim may grouse and mutter about the loss of sympathy, but actually the friends and relatives are doing what any decent tribe would do: keeping anger in bounds after it has done its job and making sure the victim stays in the social circle. Well-meaning friends and therapists who encourage a vengeful spouse to ventilate rage for years are doing neither the spouse nor the tribe a service.

People in all cultures, even the pacifistic !Kung and the Utku, do occasionally feel irritable and angry. But they do not *value* anger. They strive for a state of mind that philosopher Robert Solomon calls "equanimity under trying circumstances," the worldview of small societies that live in dangerous environments. "The Utku," says Solomon, "much more than any of us, are used to extreme hardship and discomfort. Their philosophy, therefore, is that such things must be tolerated, not flailed against. Captain Ahab and Sisyphus would have no role in their literature."

In this country, the philosophy of emotional expression regards self-restraint as hypocrisy. The cultures of the Far East do not have this conflict; a person is expected to control and subdue the emotions because it is the relationship, not the individual, that comes first. Here, where the reverse is true, some people express their emotions even at the expense of the relationship, and manners seem to be as rare as egrets. This analogy is not arbitrary, for the same ideology that gave us emotional ventilation is responsible for the scarcity of egrets: the imperial "I."

Consider the gentle, forgiving environment of Tahiti, where people learn that they have limited control over nature and over other people. They learn that if they try to change nature, she will swiftly destroy them, but if they relax and accept the bounty of nature—and the nature of people—they will be taken care of. Anthropologist Robert Levy calls this resulting world view among the Tahitians "passive optimism."

Such a philosophy would not have lasted long among the ancient Hebrews, whose God gave them "dominion over the fish of the sea, and over the fowl of the air, and over the cattle, and over all the earth, and over every creeping thing that creepeth upon the earth" (Genesis 1:26). And a good thing He did, too, because in the harsh deserts of the Middle East, adherents of a laissez-faire Tahitian religion would have met a swift demise. The Judeo-Christian philosophy, however, produces "active pessimists": people who assume that nature and other people are to be conquered, indeed must be conquered, and that individual striving is essential to survival. But a universe defined as the Tahitians see it is intrinsically less infuriating than a universe in which almost everything is possible if the individual tries hard enough. The individualism of American life, to our glory and despair, creates anger and encourages its release; for when everything is possible, limitations are irksome. When the desires of the self come first, the needs of others are annoying. When we think we deserve it all, reaping only a portion can enrage.

Suggestions for Discussion

1. According to Tavris, because anger emerges from a sense of how a culture expects people to behave, its major function is to maintain the social order. Explain why you agree or disagree.

2. The author describes manners as an organized system of anger management. What does this suggest about our culture, in which many people feel that manners are a thing of the past?

3. Tavris talks about societies characterized by passive optimism or active pessimism. How are these cultures different? Why have they chosen different ways to adapt?

Suggestions for Writing

1. America is made up of many subcultures. In the subculture in which you live, what is a permissible cause for anger? Is it acceptable in your culture to get angry at all? Do people get angry often? Explain.

2. What do you think is the function of manners? Describe an instance in which you were treated in a fashion that you found "unmannerly"? What were the consequences?

Helen Keller

Three Days to See

Helen Keller (1880–1968) was deaf and blind from the age of nineteen months. Through her teacher, Annie Sullivan, she learned to communicate by using sign language and later through voice lessons. She graduated from Radcliffe College with honors and wrote a critically acclaimed autobiography, *Story of My Life* (1902). Other books are *Optimism* (1903), *The World I Live In* (1908), and *Out of the Dark* (1913). In this essay Keller movingly describes the delights she would experience were she to be given *Three Days to See.*

All of us have read thrilling stories in which the hero had only a limited and specified time to live. Sometimes it was as long as a year; sometimes as short as twenty-four hours. But always we were interested in discovering just how the doomed man chose to spend his last days or his last hours. I speak, of course, of free men who have a choice, not condemned criminals whose sphere of activities is strictly delimited.

Such stories set us thinking, wondering what we should do under similar circumstances. What events, what experiences, what associations should we crowd into those last hours as mortal beings? What happiness should we find in reviewing the past, what regrets?

Sometimes I have thought it would be an excellent rule to live each day as if we should die tomorrow. Such an attitude would emphasize sharply the values of life. We should live each day with a gentleness, a vigor, and a keenness of appreciation which are often lost when time stretches before us in the constant panorama of more days and months and years to come. There are those, of course, who would adopt the epicurean motto of "Eat, drink, and be merry," but most people would be chastened by the certainty of impending death.

In stories, the doomed hero is usually saved at the last minute by some stroke of fortune, but almost always his sense of values is changed. He becomes more appreciative of the meaning of life and its permanent spiritual values. It has often been noted that those who live, or have lived, in the shadow of death bring a mellow sweetness to everything they do.

Most of us, however, take life for granted. We know that one day we must die, but usually we picture that day as far in the future. When we are in buoyant health, death is all but unimaginable. We seldom think of it. The days stretch out in an endless vista. So we go about our petty tasks, hardly aware of our listless attitude toward life.

The same lethargy, I am afraid, characterizes the use of all our faculties and senses. Only the deaf appreciate hearing, only the blind realize the manifold blessings that lie in sight. Particularly does this observation apply to those who have lost sight and hearing in adult life. But those who have never suffered impairment of sight or hearing seldom make the fullest use of these blessed faculties. Their eyes and ears take in all sights and sounds hazily, without concentration and with little appreciation. It is the same old story of not being grateful for what we have until we lose it, of not being conscious of health until we are ill.

I have often thought it would be a blessing if each human being were stricken blind and deaf for a few days at some time during his early adult life. Darkness would make him more appreciative of sight; silence would teach him the joys of sound.

Now and then I have tested my seeing friends to discover what they see. Recently I was visited by a very good friend who had just returned from a long walk in the woods, and I asked her what she had observed. "Nothing in particular," she replied. I might have been incredulous had I not been accustomed to such responses, for long ago I became convinced that the seeing see little.

How was it possible, I asked myself, to walk for an hour through the woods and see nothing worthy of note? I who cannot see find hundreds of things to interest me through mere touch. I feel the delicate symmetry of a leaf. I pass my hands lovingly about the smooth skin of a silver birch, or the rough shaggy bark of a pine. In spring I touch the branches of trees hopefully in search of a bud, the first sign of awakening Nature after her winter's sleep. I feel the delightful, velvety texture of a flower, and discover its remarkable convolutions; and something of the miracle of Nature is revealed to me. Occasionally, if I am fortunate, I place my hand gently on a small tree and feel the happy quiver of a bird in full song. I am delighted to have the cool waters of a brook rush through my open fingers. To me a lush carpet of pine needles or spongy grass is more welcome than the most luxurious Persian rug. To me the pageant of seasons is a thrilling and unending drama, the action of which streams through my finger tips.

At times my heart cries out with longing to see all these things. If I can get so much pleasure from mere touch, how much more beauty must be revealed by sight. Yet, those who have eyes apparently see little. The panorama of color and action which fills the world is taken for granted. It is human, perhaps, to appreciate little that which we have and to long for that which we have not, but it is a great pity that in the world of light the gift of sight is used only as a mere convenience rather than as a means of adding fullness to life.

If I were the president of a university I should establish a compulsory course in "How to Use Your Eyes." The professor would try to show his pupils how they could add joy to their lives by really seeing what passes unnoticed before them. He would try to awake their dormant and sluggish faculties.

Perhaps I can best illustrate by imagining what I should most like to see if I were given the use of my eyes, say, for just three days. And while I am imagining, suppose you, too, set your mind to work on the problem of how you would use your own eyes if you had only three more days to see. If with the oncoming darkness of the third night you knew that the sun would never rise for you again, how would you spend those three precious intervening days? What would you most want to let your gaze rest upon?

I, naturally, should want most to see the things which have become dear to me through my years of darkness. You, too, would want to let your eyes rest long on the things that have become dear to you so that you could take the memory of them with you into the night that loomed before you.

If by some miracle I were granted three seeing days, to be followed by a relapse into darkness, I should divide the period into three parts.

On the first day, I should want to see the people whose kindness and gentleness and companionship have made my life worth living. First I should like to gaze long upon the face of my dear teacher, Mrs. Anne Sullivan Macy, who came to me when I was a child and opened the outer world to me. I should want not merely to see the outline of her face, so that I could cherish it in my memory, but to study that face and find in it the living evidence of the sympathetic tenderness and patience with which she accomplished the difficult task of my education. I should like to see in her eyes that strength of character which has enabled her to stand firm in the face of difficulties, and that compassion for all humanity which she has revealed to me so often.

I do not know what it is to see into the heart of a friend through that "window of the soul," the eye. I can only "see" through my finger tips the outline of a face. I can detect laughter, sorrow, and many other obvious emotions. I know my friends from the feel of their faces. But I cannot really picture their personalities by touch. I know their personalities, of course, through other means, through the thoughts they express to me, through whatever of their actions are revealed to me. But I am denied that deeper understanding of them which I am sure would come through sight of them, through watching their reactions to various expressed thoughts and circumstances, through noting the immediate and fleeting reactions of their eyes and countenance.

Friends who are near to me I know well, because through the months and years they reveal themselves to me in all their phases; but of casual friends I have only an incomplete impression, an impression gained from a handclasp, from spoken words which I take from their lips with my finger tips, or which they tap into the palm of my hand.

How much easier, how much more satisfying it is for you who can see to grasp quickly the essential qualities of another person by watching the subtleties of expression, the quiver of a muscle, the flutter of a hand. But does it ever occur to you to use your sight to see into the inner nature of a friend or acquaintance? Do not most of you seeing people grasp casually the outward features of a face and let it go at that?

For instance, can you describe accurately the faces of five good friends? Some of you can, but many cannot. As an experiment, I have questioned husbands of long standing about the color of their wives' eyes, and often they express embarrassed confusion and admit that they do not know. And, incidentally, it is a chronic complaint of wives that their husbands do not notice new dresses, new hats, and changes in household arrangements.

The eyes of seeing persons soon become accustomed to the routine of their surroundings, and they actually see only the startling and spectacular. But even in viewing the most spectacular sights the eyes are lazy. Court records reveal every day how inaccurately "eyewitnesses" see. A given event will be "seen" in several different ways by as many witnesses. Some see more than others, but few see everything that is within the range of their vision.

Oh, the things that I should see if I had the power of sight for just three days!

The first day would be a busy one. I should call to me all my dear friends and look long into their faces, imprinting upon my mind the outward evidences of the beauty that is within them. I should let my eyes rest, too, on the face of a baby, so that I could catch a vision of the eager, innocent beauty which precedes the individual's consciousness of the conflicts which life develops.

And I should like to look into the loyal, trusting eyes of my dogs—the grave, canny little Scottie, Darkie, and the stalwart, understanding Great Dane, Helga, whose warm, tender, and playful friendships are so comforting to me.

On that busy first day I should also view the small simple things of my home. I want to see the warm colors in the rugs under my feet, the pictures on the walls, the intimate trifles that transform a house into home. My eyes would rest respectfully on the books in raised type which I have read, but they would be more eagerly interested in the printed books which seeing people can read, for during the long night of my life the books I have read and those which have been read to me have built themselves into a great shining lighthouse, revealing to me the deepest channels of human life and the human spirit.

In the afternoon of that first seeing day, I should take a long walk in the woods and intoxicate my eyes on the beauties of the world of Nature, trying desperately to absorb in a few hours the vast splendor which is constantly unfolding itself to those who can see. On the way home from my woodland jaunt my path would lie near a farm so that I might see the patient horses plowing in the field (perhaps I should see only a tractor!) and the serene content of men living close to the soil. And I should pray for the glory of a colorful sunset.

When dusk had fallen, I should experience the double delight of being able to see by artificial light, which the genius of man has created to extend the power of his sight when Nature decrees darkness.

In the night of that first day of sight, I should not be able to sleep, so full would be my mind of the memories of the day.

The next day—the second day of sight—I should arise with the dawn and see the thrilling miracle by which night is transformed into day. I should behold with awe the magnificent panorama of light with which the sun awakens the sleeping earth.

This day I should devote to a hasty glimpse of the world, past and present. I should want to see the pageant of man's progress, the kaleidoscope of the ages. How can so much be compressed into one day? Through the museums, of course. Often I have visited the New York Museum of Natural History to touch with my hands many of the objects there exhibited, but I have longed to see with my eyes the condensed history of the earth and its inhabitants displayed there—animals and the races of men pictured in their native environment; gigantic carcasses of dinosaurs and mastodons which roamed the earth long before man appeared, with his tiny stature and powerful brain, to conquer the animal kingdom; realistic presentations of the processes of evolution in animals, in man, and in the implements which man has used to fashion for himself a secure home on this planet; and a thousand and one other aspects of natural history.

I wonder how many readers of this article have viewed this panorama of the face of living things as pictured in that inspiring museum. Many, of course, have not had the opportunity, but I am sure that many who *have* had the opportunity have not made use of it. There, indeed, is a place to use your eyes. You who see can spend many fruitful days there, but I, with my imaginary three days of sight, could only take a hasty glimpse, and pass on.

My next stop would be the Metropolitan Museum of Art, for just as the Museum of Natural History reveals the material aspects of the world, so does the Metropolitan show the myriad facets of the human spirit. Throughout the history of humanity the urge to artistic expression has been almost as powerful as the urge for food, shelter, and procreation. And here, in the vast chambers of the Metropolitan Museum, is unfolded before me the spirit of Egypt, Greece, and Rome, as expressed in their art. I know well through my hands the sculptured gods and goddesses of the ancient Nile-land. I have felt copies of Parthenon friezes, and I have sensed the rhythmic beauty of charging Athenian warriors. Apollos and Venuses and the Winged Victory of Samothrace are friends of my finger tips. The gnarled, bearded features of Homer are dear to me, for he, too, knew blindness.

My hands have lingered upon the living marble of Roman sculpture as well as that of later generations. I have passed my hands over a plaster cast of Michelangelo's inspiring and heroic Moses; I have sensed the power of Rodin; I have been awed by the devoted spirit of Gothic wood carving. These arts which can be touched have meaning for me, but even they were meant to be seen rather than felt, and I can only guess at the beauty which remains hidden from me. I can admire the simple lines of a Greek vase, but its figured decorations are lost to me.

So on this, my second day of sight, I should try to probe into the soul of man through his art. The things I knew through touch I should now see. More splendid still, the whole magnificent world of painting would be opened to me, from the Italian Primitives, with their serene religious devotion, to the Moderns, with their feverish visions. I should look deep into the canvases of Raphael, Leonardo da Vinci, Titian, Rembrandt. I should want to feast my eyes upon the warm colors of Veronese, study the mysteries of El Greco, catch a new vision of Nature from Corot. Oh, there is so much rich meaning and beauty in the art of the ages for you who have eyes to see!

Upon my short visit to this temple of art I should not be able to review a fraction of that great world of art which is open to you. I should be able to get only a superficial impression. Artists tell me that for a deep and true appreciation of art one must educate the eye. One must learn through experience to weigh the merits of line, of composition, of form and color. If I had eyes, how happily would I embark upon so fascinating a study! Yet I am told that, to many of you who have eyes to see, the world of art is a dark night, unexplored and unilluminated.

It would be with extreme reluctance that I should leave the Metropolitan Museum, which contains the key to beauty—a beauty so neglected. Seeing persons, however, do not need a Metropolitan to find this key to beauty. The same key lies waiting in smaller museums, and in books on the shelves of even small libraries. But naturally, in my limited time of imaginary sight, I should choose the place where the key unlocks the greatest treasures in the shortest time.

The evening of my second day of sight I should spend at a theater or at the movies. Even now I often attend theatrical performances of all sorts, but the action of the play must be spelled into my hand by a companion. But how I should like to see with my own eyes the fascinating figure of Hamlet, or the gusty Falstaff amid colorful Elizabethan trappings! How I should like to follow each movement of the graceful Hamlet, each strut of the hearty Falstaff! And since I could see only one play, I should be confronted by a many-horned dilemma, for there are scores of plays I should want to see. You who have eyes can see any you like. How many of you, I wonder, when you gaze at a play, a movie, or any spectacle, realize and give thanks for the miracle of sight which enables you to enjoy its color, grace, and movement?

I cannot enjoy the beauty of rhythmic movement except in a sphere restricted to the touch of my hands. I can envision only dimly the grace of a Pavlova, although I know something of the delight of rhythm, for often I can sense the beat of music as it vibrates through the floor. I can well imagine that cadenced motion must be one of the most pleasing sights in the world. I have been able to gather something of this by tracing with my fingers the lines in sculptured marble; if this static grace can be so lovely, how much more acute must be the thrill of seeing grace in motion.

One of my dearest memories is of the time when Joseph Jefferson allowed me to touch his face and hands as he went through some of the gestures and speeches of his beloved Rip Van Winkle. I was able to catch thus a meager glimpse of the world of drama, and I shall never forget the delight of that moment. But, oh, how much I must miss, and how much pleasure you seeing ones can derive from watching and hearing the interplay of speech and movement in the unfolding of a dramatic performance! If I could see only one play, I should know how to picture in my mind the action of a hundred plays which I have read or had transferred to me through the medium of the manual alphabet.

So, through the evening of my second imaginary day of sight, the great figures of dramatic literature would crowd sleep from my eyes.

The following morning, I should again greet the dawn, anxious to discover new delights, for I am sure that, for those who have eyes which really see, the dawn of each day must be a perpetually new revelation of beauty.

This, according to the terms of my imagined miracle, is to be my third and last day of sight. I shall have no time to waste in regrets or longings; there is too much to see. The first day I devoted to my friends, animate and inanimate. The second revealed to me the history of man and Nature. Today I shall spend in the workaday world of the present, amid the haunts of men going about the business of life. And where can one find so many activities and conditions of men as in New York? So the city becomes my destination.

I start from my home in the quiet little suburb of Forest Hills, Long Island. Here, surrounded by green lawns, trees, and flowers, are neat little houses, happy with the voices and movements of wives and children, havens of peaceful rest for men who toil in the city. I drive across the lacy structure of steel which spans the East River, and I get a new and startling vision of the power and ingenuity of the mind of man. Busy boats chug and scurry about the river—racy speed boats, stolid, snorting tugs. If I had long days of sight ahead, I should spend many of them watching the delightful activity upon the river.

I look ahead, and before me rise the fantastic towers of New York, a city that seems to have stepped from the pages of a fairy story. What an awe-inspiring sight, these glittering spires, these vast banks of stone and steel— structures such as the gods might build for themselves! This animated picture is a part of the lives of millions of people every day. How many, I wonder, give it so much as a second glance? Very few, I fear. Their eyes are blind to this magnificent sight because it is so familiar to them.

I hurry to the top of one of those gigantic structures, the Empire State Building, for there, a short time ago, I "saw" the city below through the eyes of my secretary. I am anxious to compare my fancy with reality. I am sure I should not be disappointed in the panorama spread out before me, for to me it would be a vision of another world.

Now I begin my rounds of the city. First, I stand at a busy corner, merely looking at people, trying by sight of them to understand something of their lives. I see smiles, and I am happy. I see serious determination, and I am proud. I see suffering, and I am compassionate.

I stroll down Fifth Avenue. I throw my eyes out of focus so that I see no particular object but only a seething kaleidoscope of color. I am certain that the colors of women's dresses moving in a throng must be a gorgeous spectacle of which I should never tire. But perhaps if I had sight I should be like most other women—too interested in styles and the cut of individual dresses to give much attention to the splendor of color in the mass. And I am convinced, too, that I should become an inveterate window shopper, for it must be a delight to the eye to view the myriad articles of beauty on display.

From Fifth Avenue, I make a tour of the city—to Park Avenue, to the slums, to factories, to parks where children play. I take a stay-at-home trip abroad by visiting the foreign quarters. Always my eyes are open wide to all the sights of both happiness and misery so that I may probe deep and add to my understanding of how people work and live. My heart is full of the images of people and things. My eye passes lightly over no single trifle; it strives to touch and hold closely each thing its gaze rests upon. Some sights are pleasant, filling the heart with happiness; but some are miserably pathetic. To these latter I do not shut my eyes, for they, too, are part of life. To close the eye on them is to close the heart and mind.

My third day of sight is drawing to an end. Perhaps there are many serious pursuits to which I should devote the few remaining hours, but I am afraid that on the evening of that last day I should again run away to the theater, to a hilariously funny play, so that I might appreciate the overtones of comedy in the human spirit.

At midnight my temporary respite from blindness would cease, and permanent night would close in on me again. Naturally in those three short days I should not have seen all I wanted to see. Only when darkness had again descended upon me should I realize how much I had left unseen. But my mind would be so crowded with glorious memories that I should have little time for regrets. Thereafter the touch of every object would bring a glowing memory of how that object looked.

Perhaps this short outline of how I should spend three days of sight does not agree with the program you would set for yourself if you knew that you were about to be sticken blind. I am, however, sure that if you actually faced that fate your eyes would open to things you had never seen before, storing up memories for the long night ahead. You would use your eyes as never before. Everything you saw would become dear to you. Your eyes would touch and embrace every object that came within your range of vision. Then, at last, you would really see, and a new world of beauty would open itself before you.

I who am blind can give one hint to those who see—one admonition to those who would make full use of the gift of sight: Use your eyes as if tomorrow you would be stricken blind. And the same method can be applied to the other senses. Hear the music of voices, the song of a bird, the mighty strains of an orchestra, as if you would be stricken deaf tomorrow. Touch each object you want to touch as if tomorrow your tactile sense would fail. Smell the perfume of flowers, taste with relish each morsel, as if tomorrow you could never smell and taste again. Make the most of every sense; glory in the facts of pleasure and beauty which the world reveals to you through the several means of contact which Nature provides. But of all the senses, I am sure that sight must be the most delightful.

Suggestions for Discussion

1. With what details does Keller suggest the manifold things she observes, feels, and touches after an hour's walk through the woods?

2. What were Keller's criteria for her choices for the first day of seeing? What does she feel she loses in her understanding of her friends because of her lack of sight?

3. What desires and curiosities would be satisfied on Keller's second day?

4. What aspects of the theater does Keller miss in not being able to see?

5. What are Keller's goals in her visit to New York City?

6. What is significant about her plan for the evening of the last day?

7. How would you sum up Keller's values as reflected in her priorities for the three days of seeing?

8. Compare what Keller would expect to see in nature with what Annie Dillard sees. What do the two writers have in common?

Suggestions for Writing

1. How would you live each day (or a particular day) if you were to die tomorrow?

2. Write an essay discussing some of the things you take for granted.

3. If you were creating a compulsory course on "How to Use Your Eyes," what assignments would you make?

4. Should you have only three more days to see, how would you spend them?

Jonathan Kozol

Distancing the Homeless

Jonathan Kozol (b. 1936) was educated at Harvard and at Oxford University, where he was a Rhodes Scholar. He has devoted most of his professional life to the field of basic education, and was for some years the director of the National Literacy Coalition. He has taught at a number of universities and has lectured at over four hundred. Among other honors, he has received the National Book Award (1968) and fellowships from the Field, Ford, Rockefeller, and Guggenheim Foundations. He is considered one of the nation's most serious and provocative social thinkers. Of his many books the most recent include *Rachel and Her Children* (1988), *Savage Inequalities* (1991), and *The Issue Is Race* (1992). In the following selection he analyzes the causes of homelessness and society's inability to face them.

It is commonly believed by many journalists and politicians that the homeless of America are, in large part, former patients of large mental hospitals who were deinstitutionalized in the 1970s—the consequence, it is sometimes said, of misguided liberal opinion, which favored the treatment of such persons in community-based centers. It is argued that this policy, and the subsequent failure of society to build such centers or to provide them in sufficient number, is the primary cause of homelessness in the United States.

Those who work among the homeless do not find that explanation satisfactory. While conceding that a certain number of the homeless are, or have been, mentally unwell, they believe that, in the case of most unsheltered people, the primary reason is economic rather than clinical. The cause of homelessness, they say with disarming logic, is the lack of homes and of income with which to rent or acquire them.

They point to the loss of traditional jobs in industry (two million every year since 1980) and to the fact that half of those who are laid off end up in work that pays a poverty-level wage. They point to the parallel growth of poverty in families with children, noting that children, who represent one-quarter of our population, make up 40 percent of the poor: since 1968, the number of children in poverty has grown by three million, while welfare benefits to families with children have declined by 35 percent.

And they note, too, that these developments have coincided with a time in which the shortage of low-income housing has intensified as the gentrification of our major cities has accelerated. Half a million units of low-income housing have been lost each year to condominium conversion as well as to arson, demolition, or abandonment. Between 1978 and 1980, median rents climbed 30 percent for people in the lowest income sector, driving many of these families into the streets. After 1980, rents rose at even faster rates. In Boston, between 1982 and 1984, over 80 percent of the housing units renting below three hundred dollars disappeared, while the number of units renting above six hundred dollars nearly tripled.

Hard numbers, in this instance, would appear to be of greater help than psychiatric labels in telling us why so many people become homeless. Eight million American families now pay half or more of their income for rent or a mortgage. Six million more, unable to pay rent at all, live doubled up with others. At the same time, federal support for low-income housing dropped from $30 billion (1980) to $9 billion (1986). Under Presidents Ford and Carter, five hundred thousand subsidized private housing units were constructed. By President Reagan's second term, the number had dropped to twenty-five thousand. "We're getting out of the housing business, period," said a deputy assistant secretary of the Department of Housing and Urban Development in 1985.

One year later, the *Washington Post* reported that the number of homeless families in Washington, D.C., had grown by 500 percent over the previous twelve months. In New York City, the waiting list for public housing now contains two hundred thousand names. The waiting is eighteen years.

Why, in the face of these statistics, are we impelled to find a psychiatric explanation for the growth of homelessness in the United States?

A misconception, once it is implanted in the popular imagination, is not easy to uproot, particularly when it serves a useful social role. The notion that the homeless are largely psychotics who belong in institutions, rather than victims of displacement at the hands of enterprising realtors, spares us from the need to offer realistic solutions to the fact of deep and widening extremes of wealth and poverty in the United States. It also enables us to tell ourselves that the despair of homeless people bears no intimate connection to the privileged existence we enjoy—when, for example, we rent or purchase one of those restored townhouses that once provided shelter for people now huddled in the street.

But there may be another reason to assign labels to the destitute. Terming economic victims "psychotic" or "disordered" helps to place them at a distance. It says that they aren't quite like us—and, more important, that we could not be like them. The plight of homeless families is a nightmare. It may not seem natural to try to banish human beings from our midst, but it *is* natural to try to banish nightmares from our minds.

So the rituals of clinical contamination proceed uninterrupted by the economic facts described above. Research that addresses homelessness as an *injustice* rather than as a medical *misfortune* does not win the funding of foundations. And the research which *is* funded, defining the narrowed borders of permissible debate, diverts our attention from the antecedent to the secondary cause of homelessness. Thus it is that perfectly ordinary women whom I know in New York City—people whose depression or anxiety is a realistic consequence of months and even years in crowded shelters or the streets—are interrogated by invasive research scholars in an effort to decode their poverty, to find clinical categories for their despair and terror, to identify the secret failing that lies hidden in their psyche.

Many pregnant women without homes are denied prenatal care because they constantly travel from one shelter to another. Many are anemic. Many are denied essential dietary supplements by recent federal cuts. As a consequence, some of their children do not live to see their second year of life. Do these mothers sometimes show signs of stress? Do they appear disorganized, depressed, disordered? Frequently. They are immobilized by pain, traumatized by fear. So it is no surprise that when researchers enter the scene to ask them how they "feel," the resulting reports tell us that the homeless are emotionally unwell. The reports do not tell us we have *made* these people ill. They do not tell us that illness is a natural response to intolerable conditions. Nor do they tell us of the strength and the resilience that so many of these people still retain despite the miseries they must endure. They set these men and women apart in capsules labeled "personality disorder" or "psychotic," where they no longer threaten our complacence.

I visited Haiti not many years ago, when the Duvalier family was still in power. If an American scholar were to have made a psychological study of the homeless families living in the streets of Port-au-Prince—sleeping amidst rotten garbage, bathing in open sewers—and if he were to return to the United States to tell us that the reasons for their destitution were "behavioral problems" or "a lack of mental health," we would be properly suspicious. Knowledgeable Haitians would not merely be suspicious. They would be enraged. Even to initiate such research when economic and political explanations present themselves so starkly would appear grotesque. It is no less so in the United States.

One of the more influential studies of this nature was carried out in 1985 by Ellen Bassuk, a psychiatrist at Harvard University. Drawing upon interviews with eight homeless parents, Dr. Bassuk contends, according to the *Boston Globe*, that "90 percent [of these people] have problems other than housing and poverty that are so acute they would be unable to live successfully on their own." She also precludes the possibility that illness, where it does exist, may be provoked by destitution. "Our data," she writes, "suggest that mental illness tends to precede homelessness." She concedes that living in the streets can make a homeless person's mental illness worse; but she insists upon the fact of prior illness.

The executive director of the Massachusetts Commission on Children and Youth believes that Dr. Bassuk's estimate is far too high. The staff of Massachusetts Human Services Secretary Phillip Johnston believes the appropriate number is closer to 10 percent.

In defending her research, Bassuk challenges such critics by claiming that they do not have data to refute her. This may be true. Advocates for the homeless do not receive funds to defend the sanity of the people they represent. In placing the burden of proof upon them, Dr. Bassuk has created an extraordinary dialectic: How does one prove that people aren't unwell? What homeless mother would consent to enter a procedure that might "prove" her mental health? What overburdened shelter operator would divert scarce funds to such an exercise? It is an unnatural, offensive, and dehumanizing challenge.

Dr. Bassuk's work, however, isn't the issue I want to raise here; the issue is the use or misuse of that work by critics of the poor. For example, in a widely syndicated essay published in 1986, the newspaper columnist Charles Krauthammer argued that the homeless are essentially a deranged segment of the population and that we must find the "political will" to isolate them from society. We must do this, he said, "whether they like it or not." Arguing even against the marginal benefits of homeless shelters, Krauthammer wrote: "There is a better alternative, however, though no one dares speak its name." Krauthammer dares: that better alternative, he said, is "asylum."

One of Mr. Krauthammer's colleagues at the *Washington Post*, the columnist George Will, perceives the homeless as a threat to public cleanliness and argues that they ought to be consigned to places where we need not see them. "It is," he says, "simply a matter of public hygiene" to put them out of sight. Another journalist, Charles Murray, writing from the vantage point of a social Darwinist, recommends the restoration of the almshouses of the 1800s. "Granted Dickensian horror stories about almshouses," he begins, there were nonetheless "good almshouses"; he proposes "a good correctional 'halfway house'" as a proper shelter for mother and child with no means of self-support.

In the face of such declarations, the voices of those who work with and know the poor are harder to hear.

Manhattan Borough President David Dinkins made the following observation on the basis of a study commissioned in 1986: "No facts support the belief that addiction or behavioral problems occur with more frequency in the homeless family population than in a similar socioeconomic population. Homeless families are not demographically different from other public assistance families when they enter the shelter system. . . . Family homelessness is typically a housing and income problem: the unavailability of affordable housing and the inadequacy of public assistance income."

In a "hypothetical world," write James Wright and Julie Lam of the University of Massachusetts, "where there were no alcoholics, no drug addicts, no mentally ill, no deinstitutionalization, . . . indeed, no personal social pathologies at all, there would still be a formidable homelessness problem, simply because at this stage in American history, there is not enough low-income housing" to accommodate the poor.

New York State's respected commissioner of social services, Cesar Perales, makes the point in fewer words: "Homelessness is less and less a result of personal failure, and more and more is caused by larger forces. There is no longer affordable housing in New York City for people of poor and modest means."

Even the words of medical practitioners who care for homeless people have been curiously ignored. A study published by the Massachusetts Medical Society, for instance, has noted that the most frequent illnesses among a sample of the homeless population, after alcohol and drug use, are trauma (31 percent), upper respiratory disorders (28 percent), limb disorders (19 percent), mental illness (16 percent), skin diseases (15 percent), hypertension (14 percent), and neurological illnesses (12 percent). (Excluded from this tabulation are lead poisoning, malnutrition, acute diarrhea, and other illnesses especially common among homeless infants and small children.) Why, we may ask, of all these calamities, does mental illness command so much political and press attention? The answer may be that the label of mental illness places the destitute outside the sphere of ordinary life. It personalizes an anguish that is public in its genesis; it individualizes a misery that is both general in cause and general in application.

The rate of tuberculosis among the homeless is believed to be ten times that of the general population. Asthma, I have learned in countless interviews, is one of the most common causes of discomfort in the shelters. Compulsive smoking, exacerbated by the crowding and the tension, is more common in the shelters than in any place that I have visited except prison. Infected and untreated sores, scabies, diarrhea, poorly set limbs, protruding elbows, awkwardly distorted wrists, bleeding gums, impacted teeth, and other untreated dental problems are so common among children in the shelters that one rapidly forgets their presence. Hunger and emaciation are everywhere. Children as well as adults can bring to mind the photographs of people found in camps for refugees of war in 1945. But these miseries bear no stigma, and mental illness does. It conveys a stigma in the Soviet Union. It conveys a stigma in the United States. In both nations the label is used, whether as a matter of deliberate policy or not, to isolate and treat as special cases those who, by deed or word or by sheer presence, represent a threat to national complacence. The two situations are obviously not identical, but they are enough alike to give Americans reason for concern.

Last summer, some twenty-eight thousand homeless people were afforded shelter by the city of New York. Of this number, twelve thousand were children and six thousand were parents living together in families. The average child was six years old, the average parent twenty-seven. A typical homeless family included a mother with two or three children, but in about one-fifth of these families two parents were present. Roughly ten thousand single persons, then, made up the remainder of the population of the city's shelters.

These proportions vary somewhat from one area of the nation to another. In all areas, however, families are the fastest-growing sector of the homeless population, and in the Northeast they are by far the largest sector already. In Massachusetts, three-fourths of the homeless now are families with children;

in certain parts of Massachusetts—Attleboro and Northampton, for example—the proportion reaches 90 percent. Two-thirds of the homeless children studied recently in Boston were less than five years old.

Of an estimated two to three million homeless people nationwide, about 500,000 are dependent children, according to Robert Hayes, counsel to the National Coalition for the Homeless. Including their parents, at least 750,000 homeless people in America are family members.

What is to be made, then, of the supposition that the homeless are primarily the former residents of mental hospitals, persons who were carelessly released during the 1970s? Many of them are, to be sure. Among the older men and women in the streets and shelters, as many as one-third (some believe as many as one-half) may be chronically disturbed, and a number of these people were deinstitutionalized during the 1970s. But in a city like New York, where nearly half the homeless are small children with an average age of six, to operate on the basis of such a supposition makes no sense. Their parents, with an average age of twenty-seven, are not likely to have been hospitalized in the 1970s, either.

Nor is it easy to assume, as was once the case, that single men—those who come closer to fitting the stereotype of the homeless vagrant, the drifting alcoholic of an earlier age—are the former residents of mental hospitals. The age of homeless men has dropped in recent years; many of them are only twenty-one to twenty-eight years old. Fifty percent of homeless men in New York City shelters in 1984 were there for the first time. Most had previously had homes and jobs. Many had never before needed public aid.

A frequently cited set of figures tells us that in 1955, the average daily census of nonfederal psychiatric institutions was 677,000, and that by 1984, the number had dropped to 151,000. Subtract the second number from the first, conventional logic tells us, and we have an explanation for the homelessness of half a million people. A closer look at the same number offers us a different lesson.

The sharpest decline in the average daily census of these institutions occurred prior to 1978, and the largest part of that decline, in fact, appeared at least a decade earlier. From 677,000 in 1955, the census dropped to 378,000 in 1972. The 1974 census was 307,000. In 1976 it was 230,000; in 1977 it was 211,000; and in 1978 it was 190,000. In no year since 1978 has the average daily census dropped by more than 9,000 persons, and in the six-year period from 1978 to 1984, the total decline was 39,000 persons. Compared with a decline of 300,000 from 1955 to 1972, and of nearly 200,000 more from 1972 to 1978, the number is small. But the years since 1980 are the period in which the present homeless crisis surfaced. Only since 1983 have homeless individuals overflowed the shelters.

If the large numbers of the homeless lived in hospitals before they reappeared in subway stations and in public shelters, we need to ask where they were and what they had been doing from 1972 to 1980. Were they living under bridges? Were they waiting out the decade in the basements of deserted buildings?

No. The bulk of those who had been psychiatric patients and were released from hospitals during the 1960s and early 1970s had been living in the meantime in low-income housing, many in skid-row hotels or boarding houses. Such housing—commonly known as SRO (single-room occupancy) units—was drastically diminished by the gentrification of our cities that began in 1970. Almost 50 percent of SRO housing was replaced by luxury apartments or by office buildings between 1970 and 1980, and the remaining units have been disappearing at even faster rates. As recently as 1986, after New York City had issued a prohibition against conversion of such housing, a well-known developer hired a demolition team to destroy a building in Times Square that had previously been home to indigent people. The demolition took place in the middle of the night. In order to avoid imprisonment, the developer was allowed to make a philanthropic gift to homeless people as a token of atonement. This incident, bizarre as it appears, reminds us that the profit motive for displacement of the poor is very great in every major city. It also indicates a more realistic explanation for the growth of homelessness during the 1980s.

Even for those persons who are ill and were deinstitutionalized during the decades before 1980, the precipitating cause of homelessness in 1987 is not illness but loss of housing. SRO housing, unattractive as it may have been, offered low-cost sanctuaries for the homeless, providing a degree of safety and mutual support for those who lived within them. They were a demeaning version of the community health centers that society had promised; they were the de facto "halfway houses" of the 1970s. For these people too, then—at most half of the homeless single persons in America—the cause of homelessness is lack of housing.

A writer in the *New York Times* describes a homeless woman standing on a traffic island in Manhattan. "She was evicted from her small room in the hotel just across the street," and she is determined to get revenge. Until she does, "nothing will move her from that spot. . . . Her argumentativeness and her angry fixation on revenge, along with the apparent absence of hallucinations, mark her as a paranoid." Most physicians, I imagine, would be more reserved in passing judgment with so little evidence, but this author makes his diagnosis without hesitation. "The paranoids of the street," he says, "are among the most difficult to help."

Perhaps so. But does it depend on who is offering the help? Is anyone offering to help this woman get back her home? Is it crazy to seek vengeance for being thrown into the street? The absence of anger, some psychiatrists believe, might indicate much greater illness.

The same observer sees additional symptoms of pathology ("negative symptoms," he calls them) in the fact that many homeless persons demonstrate a "gross deterioration in their personal hygiene" and grooming, leading to "indifference" and "apathy." Having just identified one woman as unhealthy because she is so far from being "indifferent" as to seek revenge, he now sees apathy as evidence of illness; so consistency is not what we are looking for in this account. But how much less indifferent might the homeless be if those who decide their fate were less indifferent themselves? How might their grooming and hygiene be improved if they were permitted access to a public toilet?

In New York City, as in many cities, homeless people are denied the right to wash in public bathrooms, to store their few belongings in a public locker, or, in certain cases, to make use of public toilets altogether. Shaving, cleaning of clothes, and other forms of hygiene are prohibited in the men's room of

Grand Central Station. The terminal's three hundred lockers, used in former times by homeless people to secure their goods, were removed in 1986 as "a threat to public safety," according to a study made by the New York City Council. At one-thirty every morning, homeless people are ejected from the station. Many once attempted to take refuge on the ramp that leads to Forty-second Street because it was protected from the street by wooden doors and thus provided some degree of warmth. But the station management responded to this challenge in two ways. The ramp was mopped with a strong mixture of ammonia to produce a noxious smell, and when the people sleeping there brought cardboard boxes and newspapers to protect them from the fumes, the entrance doors were chained wide open. Temperatures dropped some nights to ten degrees. Having driven these people to the streets, city officials subsequently determined that their willingness to risk exposure to cold weather could be taken as further evidence of mental illness.

At Pennsylvania Station in New York, homeless women are denied the use of toilets. Amtrak police come by and herd them off each hour on the hour. In June 1985, Amtrak officials issued this directive to police: "It is the policy of Amtrak to not allow the homeless and undesirables to remain. . . . Officers are encouraged to eject all undesirables. . . . Now is the time to train and educate them that their presence will not be tolerated as cold weather sets in." In an internal memo, according to CBS, an Amtrak official asked flatly: "Can't we get rid of this trash?"

I have spent many nights in conversation with the women who are huddled in the corridors and near the doorway of the public toilets in Penn Station. Many are young. Most are cogent. Few are dressed in the familiar rags suggested by the term *bag ladies*. Unable to bathe or use the toilets in the station, almost all are in conditions of intolerable physical distress. The sight of clusters of police officers, mostly male, guarding a toilet from use by homeless women speaks volumes about the public conscience of New York.

Where do these women defecate? How do they bathe? What will we do when, in her physical distress, a woman finally disrobes in public and begins to urinate right on the floor? "Gross deterioration," someone will call it, evidence of mental illness. In the course of an impromptu survey in the streets last September, Mayor Koch observed a homeless woman who had soiled her own clothes. Not only was the woman crazy, said the mayor, but those who differed with him on his diagnosis must be crazy, too. "I am the number one social worker in this town—with sanity," said he.

It may be that this woman was psychotic, but the mayor's comment says a great deal more about his sense of revulsion and the moral climate of a decade in which words like these may be applauded than about her mental state.

A young man who had lost his job, then his family, then his home, all in the summer of 1986, spoke with me for several hours in Grand Central Station on the weekend following Thanksgiving. "A year ago," he said, "I never thought that somebody like me would end up in a shelter. Nothing you've ever undergone prepares you. You walk into the place [a shelter on the Bowery]—the smell of sweat and urine hits you like a wall. Unwashed bodies and the look of absolute despair on many, many faces there would make you think you were in Dante's Hell. . . . What you fear is that you will be here forever. You do not know if it is ever going to end. You think to yourself: it is a dream and I will awake. Sometimes I think: it's an experiment. They are watching you to find out how much you can take. . . . I was a pretty stable man. Now I tremble when I meet somebody in the ordinary world. I'm trembling right now. . . . For me, the loss of work and loss of wife had left me rocking. Then the welfare regulations hit me. I began to feel that I would be reduced to trash. . . . Half the people that I know are suffering from chest infections and sleep deprivation. The lack of sleep leaves you debilitated, shaky. You exaggerate your fears. If a psychiatrist came along he'd say that I was crazy. But I was an ordinary man. There was nothing wrong with me. I lost my kids. I lost my home. Now would you say that I was crazy if I told you I was feeling sad?"

"If the plight of homeless adults is the shame of America," writes Fred Hechinger in the *New York Times,* "the lives of homeless children are the nation's crime."

In November 1984, a fact already known to advocates for the homeless was given brief attention by the press. Homeless families, the *New York Times* reported, "mostly mothers and young children, have been sleeping on chairs, counters, and floors of the city's emergency welfare offices." Reacting to such reports, the mayor declared: "The woman is sitting on a chair or on a floor. It is not because we didn't offer her a bed. We provide a shelter for every single person who knocks on our door." On the same day, however, the city reported that in the previous eleven weeks it had been unable to give shelter to 153 families, and in the subsequent year, 1985, the city later reported that about two thousand children slept in welfare offices because of lack of shelter space.

Some eight hundred homeless infants in New York City, reported the National Coalition for the Homeless, "routinely go without sufficient food, cribs, health care, and diapers." The lives of these children "are put at risk," while "high-risk pregnant women" are repeatedly forced to sleep in unsafe "barracks shelters" or welfare offices called Emergency Assistance Units (EAUs). "Coalition monitors, making sporadic random checks, found eight women in their *ninth* month of pregnancy sleeping in EAUs. . . . Two women denied shelter began having labor contractions at the EAU." In one instance, the Legal Aid Society was forced to go to court after a woman lost her child by miscarriage while lying on the floor of a communal bathroom in a shelter which the courts had already declared unfit to house pregnant women.

The coalition also reported numerous cases in which homeless mothers were obliged to choose between purchasing food or diapers for their infants. Federal guidelines issued in 1986 deepened the nutrition crisis faced by mothers in the welfare shelters by counting the high rent paid to the owners of the buildings as a part of family income, rendering their residents ineligible for food stamps. Families I interviewed who had received as much as $150 in food stamps monthly in June 1986 were cut back to $33 before Christmas.

"Now you're hearing all kinds of horror stories," said President Reagan, "about the people that are going to be thrown out in the snow to hunger and [to] die of cold and so forth. . . . We haven't cut a single budget." But in the four years leading up to 1985, according to the *New Republic*, Aid to Families with Dependent Children had been cut by $4.8 billion, child nutrition programs by $5.2 billion, food stamps by $6.8 billion. The federal government's authority to help low-income families with housing assistance was cut from $30 billion to $11 billion in Reagan's first term. In his fiscal 1986 budget, the president proposed to cut that by an additional 95 percent.

"If even one American child is forced to go to bed hungry at night," the president said on another occasion, "that is a national tragedy. We are too generous a people to allow this." But in the years since the president spoke these words, thousands of poor children in New York alone have gone to bed too sick to sleep and far too weak to rise the next morning to attend a public school. Thousands more have been unable to attend school at all because their homeless status compels them to move repeatedly from one temporary shelter to another. Even in the affluent suburbs outside New York City, hundreds of homeless children are obliged to ride as far as sixty miles twice a day in order to obtain an education in the public schools to which they were originally assigned before their families were displaced. Many of these children get to school too late to eat their breakfast; others are denied lunch at school because of federal cuts in feeding programs.

Many homeless children die—and others suffer brain damage—as a direct consequence of federal cutbacks in prenatal programs, maternal nutrition, and other feeding programs. The parents of one such child shared with me the story of the year in which their child was delivered, lived, and died. The child, weighing just over four pounds at birth, grew deaf and blind soon after, and for these reasons had to stay in the hospital for several months. When he was released on Christmas Eve of 1984, his mother and father had no home. He lived with his parents in the shelters, subways, streets, and welfare offices of New York City for four winter months, and was readmitted to the hospital in time to die in May 1985.

When we met and spoke the following year, the father told me that his wife had contemplated and even attempted suicide after the child's death, while he had entertained the thought of blowing up the welfare offices of New York City. I would tell him that to do so would be illegal and unwise. I would never tell him it was crazy.

"No one will be turned away," says the mayor of New York City, as hundreds of young mothers with their infants are turned from the doors of shelters season after season. That may sound to some like denial of reality. "Now you're hearing all these stories," says the president of the United States as he denies that anyone is cold or hungry or unhoused. On another occasion he says that the unsheltered "are homeless, you might say, by choice." That sounds every bit as self-deceiving.

The woman standing on the traffic island screaming for revenge until her room has been restored to her sounds relatively healthy by comparison. If three million homeless people did the same, and all at the same time, we might finally be forced to listen.

1988

Suggestions for Discussion

1. What according to Kozol is the primary cause of homelessness?
2. Does the writer view homelessness as a "clinical misfortune," as the end product of social forces, or as the result of personal failure?
3. Why is mental illness a popular explanation for homelessness, according to the author?
4. What arguments does Kozol use to disprove the theory that mental illness is the primary source of homelessness?

Suggestions for Writing

1. For the homeless child, what do you imagine would be the most painful aspects of having no home? Have you ever experienced this? How did you deal with it?
2. Homelessness is a growing problem. How might it be curtailed or eliminated altogether?

May Sarton

The Rewards of Living a Solitary Life

May Sarton (b. 1912) is the author of sixteen volumes of poetry, twenty-two novels—including *Faithful Are the Wounds* (1955), *Mrs. Stevens Hears the Mermaids Singing* (1965), and *Kinds of Love* (1970)—and a number of books of nonfiction. The author finds that a strong sense of self allows her to find happiness in a solitary life.

The other day an acquaintance of mine, a gregarious and charming man, told me he had found himself unexpectedly alone in New York for an hour or two between appointments. He went to the Whitney and spent the "empty" time looking at things in solitary bliss. For him it proved to be a shock nearly as great as falling in love to discover that he could enjoy himself so much alone.

What had he been afraid of, I asked myself? That, suddenly alone, he would discover that he bored himself, or that there was, quite simply, no self there to meet? But having taken the plunge, he is now on the brink of adventure; he is about to be launched into his own inner space, space as immense, unexplored, and sometimes frightening as outer space to the astronaut. His every perception will come to him with a new freshness and, for a time, seem startingly original. For anyone who can see things for himself with a naked eye becomes, for a moment or two, something of a genius. With another human being present vision becomes double vision, inevitably. We are busy wondering, what does my companion see or think of this, and what do I think of it? The original impact gets lost, or diffused.

"Music I heard with you was more than music." Exactly. And therefore music *itself* can only be heard alone. Solitude is the salt of personhood. It brings out the authentic flavor of every experience.

"Alone one is never lonely: the spirit adventures, walking/In a quiet garden, in a cool house, abiding single there."

Loneliness is most acutely felt with other people, for with others, even with a lover sometimes, we suffer from our differences of taste, temperament, mood. Human intercourse often demands that we soften the edge of perception, or withdraw at the very instant of personal truth for fear of hurting, or of being inappropriately present, which is to say naked, in a social situation. Alone we can afford to be wholly whatever we are, and to feel whatever we feel absolutely. That is a great luxury!

For me the most interesting thing about a solitary life, and mine has been that for the last twenty years, is that it becomes increasingly rewarding. When I can wake up and watch the sun rise over the ocean, as I do most days, and know that I have an entire day ahead, uninterrupted, in which to write a few pages, take a walk with my dog, lie down in the afternoon for a long think (why does one think better in a horizontal position?), read and listen to music, I am flooded with happiness.

I am lonely only when I am overtired, when I have worked too long without a break, when for the time being I feel empty and need filling up. And I am lonely sometimes when I come back home after a lecture trip, when I have seen a lot of people and talked a lot, and am full to the brim with experience that needs to be sorted out.

Then for a little while the house feels huge and empty, and I wonder where my self is hiding. It has be recaptured slowly by watering the plants, perhaps, and looking again at each one as though it were a person, by feeding the two cats, by cooking a meal.

It takes a while, as I watch the surf blowing up in fountains at the end of the field, but the moment comes when the world falls away, and the self emerges again from the deep unconscious, bringing back all I have recently experienced to be explored and slowly understood, when I can converse again with my hidden powers, and so grow, and so be renewed, till death do us part.

Suggestions for Discussion

1. In asking herself what her friend had been afraid of when he finally found himself alone at a museum, Sarton speculates as to whether he was afraid he would be bored or whether there was no self to meet. How does the presence or absence of a self relate to her thesis?

2. Why does vision become double vision in the presence of another human being?

3. How does the author distinguish between loneliness and solitude? Why does she feel that loneliness is felt most acutely with other people?

4. What details does Sarton offer to explain her happiness in leading a solitary life? What role does the self play in her satisfaction?

Suggestions for Writing

1. Are you persuaded by Sarton of the joys of the solitary life?

2. Defend or challenge her position that loneliness is most acutely felt in the presence of other people.

Henry David Thoreau

Why I Went to the Woods

Henry David Thoreau (1817–1862) was a philosopher and poet-naturalist whose independent spirit led him to the famous experiment recorded in *Walden, or Life in the Woods* (1854). Thoreau's passion for freedom and his lifetime resistance to conformity in thought and manners are forcefully present in his famous essay, "On the Duty of Civil Disobedience." Thoreau states that he went to the woods in order to encounter only the essential facts of life and avoid all that is petty, trivial, and unnecessary.

I went to the woods because I wished to live deliberately, to front only the essential facts of life, and see if I could not learn what it had to teach, and not, when I came to die, discover that I had not lived. I did not wish to live what was not life, living is so dear; nor did I wish to practice resignation, unless it was quite necessary. I wanted to live deep and suck out all the marrow of life, to live so sturdily and Spartan-like as to put to rout all that was not life, to cut a broad swath and shave close, to drive life into a corner, and reduce it to its lowest terms, and, if it proved to be mean, why then to get the whole and genuine meanness of it, and publish its meanness to the world; or if it were sublime, to know it by experience, and be able to give a true account of it in my next excursion. For most men, it appears to me, are in a strange uncertainty about it, whether it is of the devil or of God, and have *somewhat hastily* concluded that it is the chief end of man here to "glorify God and enjoy him forever."

Still we live meanly, like ants; though the fable tells us that we were long ago changed into men; like pygmies we fight with cranes; it is error upon error, and clout upon clout, and our best virtue has for its occasion a superfluous and evitable wretchedness. Our life is frittered away by detail. An honest man has hardly need to count more than his ten fingers, or in extreme cases he may add his ten toes, and lump the rest. Simplicity, simplicity, simplicity! I say, let your affairs be as two or three, and not a hundred or a thousand; instead of a million count half a dozen, and keep your accounts on your thumb-nail. In the midst of this chopping sea of civilized life, such are the clouds and storms and quicksands and thousand-and-one items to be allowed for, that a man has to live, if he would not founder and go to the bottom and not make his port at all, by dead reckoning, and he must be a great calculator indeed who succeeds. Simplify, simplify. Instead of three meals a day, if it be necessary eat but one; instead of a hundred dishes, five; and reduce other things in proportion. Our life is like a German Confederacy, made of up petty states, with its boundary forever fluctuating, so that even a German cannot tell you how it is bounded at any moment. The nation itself, with all its so-called internal improvements, which, by the way are all external and superficial, is just such an unwieldy and overgrown establishment, cluttered with furniture and tripped up by its own traps, ruined by luxury and heedless expense, by want of calculation and a worthy aim, as the million households in the lands; and the only cure for it, as for them, is in a rigid economy, a stern and more than Spartan simplicity of life and elevation of purpose. It lives too fast. Men think that it is essential that the *Nation* have commerce, and export ice, and talk through a telegraph, and ride thirty miles an hour, without a doubt, whether *they* do or not; but whether we should live like baboons or like men, is a little uncertain. If we do not get our sleepers, and forge rails, and devote days and nights to the work, but go to tinkering upon our *lives* to improve *them*, who will build railroads? And if railroads are not built, how shall we get to heaven in season? But if we stay at home and mind our business, who will want railroads? We do not ride on the railroad; it rides upon us. Did you ever think what those sleepers are that underlie the railroad? Each one is a man, an Irishman, or a Yankee man. The rails are laid on them, and they are covered with sand, and the cars run smoothly over them. They are sound sleepers, I assure you. And every few years a new lot is laid down and run over; so that, if some have the pleasure of riding on a rail, others have the misfortune to be ridden upon. And when they run over a man that is walking in his sleep, a supernumerary sleeper in the wrong position, and wake him up, they suddenly stop the cars, and make a hue and cry about it, as if this were an exception. I am glad to know that it takes a gang of men for every five miles to keep the sleepers down and level in their beds as it is, for this is a sign that they may sometimes get up again.

Why should we live with such hurry and waste of life? We are determined to be starved before we are hungry. Men say that a stitch in time saves nine, and so they take a thousand stitches to-day to save nine tomorrow. As for *work*, we haven't any of any consequence. We have the Saint Vitus' dance, and cannot possibly keep our heads still. If I should only give a few pulls at the parish bell-rope, as for a fire, that is, without setting the bell, there is hardly a man on his farm in the outskirts of Concord, notwithstanding that press of engagements which was his excuse so many times this morning, nor a boy, nor a woman, I might almost say, but would foresake all and follow that sound, not mainly to save property from the flames, but, if we will confess the truth, much more to see it burn, since burn it must, and we, be it known, did not set it on fire—or to see it put out, and have a hand in it, if that is done as handsomely; yes, even if it were the parish church itself. Hardly a man takes a half-hour's nap after dinner, but when he wakes he holds up his head and asks, "What's the news?" as if the rest of mankind had stood his sentinels. Some give directions to be waked every half-hour, doubtless for no other purpose; and then, to pay for it, they tell what they have dreamed. After a night's sleep the news is as indispensable as the breakfast. "Pray tell me anything new that has happened to a man anywhere on this globe"—and he reads it over his coffee and rolls, that a man has had his eyes gouged out this morning on the Wachito River; never dreaming the while that he lives in the dark unfathomed mammoth cave of this world, and has but the rudiment of an eye himself.

For my part, I could easily do without the post-office. I think that there are very few important communications made through it. To speak critically, I never received more than one or two letters in my life—I wrote this some years ago—that were worth the postage. The penny-post is, commonly, an institution through which you seriously offer a man that penny for his thoughts which is so often safely offered in jest. And I am sure that I never read any memorable news in a newspaper. If we read of one man robbed, or murdered, or killed by accident, or one house burned, or one vessel wrecked, or one steamboat blown up, or one cow run over on the Western Railroad, or one mad dog killed, or one lot of grasshoppers in the winter—we never need read of another. One is enough. If you are acquainted with the principle, what do you care for a myriad instances and applications? To a philosopher all *news*, as it is called, is gossip, and they who edit and read it are old women over their tea. Yet not a few are greedy after this gossip. There was such a rush, as I hear, the other day at one of the offices to learn the foreign news by the last arrival, that several large squares of plate glass belonging to the establishment were broken by the pressure—news which I seriously think a ready wit might write a twelvemonth, or twelve years, beforehand with sufficient accuracy. As for Spain, for instance, if you know how to throw in Don Carlos and the Infanta, and Don Pedro and Seville and Granada, from time to time in the right proportions—they may have changed the names a little since I saw the papers—and serve up a bull-fight when other entertainments fail, it will be true to the letter, and give us as good an idea of the exact state or ruin of things in Spain as the most succinct and lucid reports under this head in the newspapers; and as for England, almost the last significant scrap of news from that quarter was the revolution of 1649; and if you have learned the history of her crops for an average year, you never need attend to that thing again, unless your speculations are of a merely pecuniary character. If one may judge who rarely looks into the newspapers, nothing new does ever happen in foreign parts, a French revolution not excepted.

What news! how much more important to know what that is which was never old! "Kieou-he-yu (great dignitary of the state of Wei) sent a man to Khoung-tseu to know his news. Khoung-tseu caused the messenger to be seated near him, and questioned him in these terms: What is your master doing? The messenger answered with respect: My master desires to diminish the number of his faults, but he cannot come to the end of them. The messenger being gone, the philosopher remarked: What a worthy messenger! What a worthy messenger!" The preacher, instead of vexing the ears of drowsy farmers on their day of rest at the end of the week—for Sunday is the fit conclusion of an ill-spent week, and not the fresh and brave beginning of a new one—with this one other draggle-tail of a sermon, should shout with thundering voice, "Pause! Avast! Why so seeming fast, but deadly slow?"

Shams and delusions are esteemed for soundless truths, while reality is fabulous. If men would steadily observe realities only, and not allow themselves to be deluded, life, to compare it with such things as we know, would be like a fairy tale and the Arabian Nights' Entertainments. If we respected only what is inevitable and has a right to be, music and poetry would resound along the streets. When we are unhurried and wise, we perceive that only great and worthy things have any permanent and absolute existence, that petty fears and petty pleasures are but the shadow of the reality. This is always exhilarating and sublime. By closing the eyes and slumbering, and consenting to be deceived by shows, men establish and confirm their daily life of routine and habit everywhere, which still is built on purely illusory foundations. Children, who play life, discern its true law and relations more clearly than men, who fail to live it worthily, but who think that they are wiser by experience, that is, by failure. I have read in a Hindoo book, that "there was a king's son, who, being expelled in infancy from his native city, was brought up by a forester, and, growing up to maturity in that state, imagined himself to belong to the barbarous race with which he lived. One of his father's ministers having discovered him, revealed to him what he was, and the misconception of his character was removed, and he knew himself to be a prince. So soul," continues the Hindoo philosopher, "from the circumstances in which it is placed, mistakes its own character, until the truth is revealed to it by some holy teacher and then it knows itself to be *Brahme*." I perceive that we inhabitants of New England live this mean life that we do because our vision does not penetrate the surface of things. We think that that *is* which *appears* to be. If a man should walk through this town and see only the reality, where, think you, would the "Milldam" go to? If he should give us an account of the realities he beheld there, we should not recognize the place in his description. Look at the meetinghouse, or a courthouse, or a jail, or a shop, or a dwelling-house, and say what that thing really is before a true gaze, and they would all go to pieces in your account of them. Men esteem truth remote, in the outskirts of the system, behind the farthest star, before Adam and after the last man. In eternity there is indeed something true and sublime. But all these times and places and occasions are now and here. God himself culminates in the present moment, and will never be more divine in the lapse of all the ages. And we are enabled to apprehend at all what is sublime and noble only by the perpetual instilling and drenching of the reality that surrounds us. The universe constantly and obediently answers to our conceptions; whether we travel fast or slow, the track is laid for us. Let us spend our lives in conceiving then. The poet or the artist never yet had so fair and noble a design but some of his posterity at least could accomplish it.

Let us spend one day as deliberately as Nature, and not be thrown off the track by every nutshell and mosquito's wing that falls on the rails. Let us rise early and fast, or breakfast, gently and without perturbation; let company come and let company go, let the bells ring and the children cry—determined to make a day of it. Why should we knock under and go with the stream? Let us not be upset and overwhelmed in that terrible rapid and whirlpool called a dinner, situated in the meridian shallows. Weather this danger and you are safe, for the rest of the way is downhill. With unrelaxed nerves, with morning vigor, sail by it, looking another way, tied to the mast like Ulysses. If the engine whistles, let it whistle till it is hoarse for its pains. If the bell rings, why should we run? We will consider what kind of music they are like. Let us settle ourselves and work and wedge our feet downward through the mud and slush of opinion, and prejudice, and tradition, and delusion, and appearance, that alluvion which covers the globe, through Paris and London, through New York and Boston and Concord, through Church and State, through poetry and philosophy and religion, till we come to a hard bottom and rocks in place, which we can call *reality*, and say, This is, and no mistake; and then begin, having a *point d'appui*, below freshet and frost and fire, a place where you might found a wall or a state, or set a lamppost safely, or perhaps a gauge, not a Nilometer, but a Realometer, that future ages might know how deep a freshet of shams and appearances had gathered from time to time. If you stand right fronting and face to face to a fact, you will see the sun glimmer on both its surfaces, as if it were a cimeter, and feel its sweet edge dividing you through the heart and marrow, and so you will happily conclude your mortal career. Be it life or death, we crave only reality. If we are really dying, let us hear the rattle in our throats and feel cold in the extremities; if we are alive, let us go about our business.

Time is but the stream I go afishing in. I drink at it; but while I drink I see the sandy bottom and detect how shallow it is. Its thin current slides away but eternity remains. I would drink deeper; fish in the sky, whose bottom is pebbly with stars. I cannot count one. I know not the first letter of the alphabet. I have always been regretting that I was not as wise as the day I was born. The intellect is a cleaver; it discerns and rifts its way into the secret of things. I do not wish to be any more busy with my hands than is necessary. My head is hands and feet. I feel all my best faculties concentrated in it. My instinct tells me that my head is an organ for burrowing, as some creatures use their snout and fore paws, and with it I would mine and burrow my way through these hills. I think that the richest vein is somewhere hereabouts; so by the divining-rod and thin rising vapors, I judge; and here I will begin to mine.

Suggestions for Discussion

1. Why did Thoreau go to the woods?

2. With what details does Thoreau support his statement that "we live meanly like ants"?

3. Interpret Thoreau's rhetorical question in the context of his philosophy: "If you are acquainted with the principle, what do you care for a myriad instances and applications"?

4. With what details does Thoreau illustrate his impatience with man's proclivity for being deluded?

5. How do Thoreau's rhetorical questions, metaphors, and allusions contribute to substance and tone?

6. What aspects of American life does Thoreau repudiate and why?

7. What does he affirm? Paraphrase his last two paragraphs.

Suggestions for Writing

1. Discuss what you have learned from your observations of nature.

2. Discuss: "Our life is frittered away by detail."

3. Comment on: "Shams and delusions are esteemed for soundless truths, while reality is fabulous."

4. What would Thoreau's impressions be of our current preoccupations?

Jamaica Kincaid

A Small Place

Jamaica Kincaid (b. 1949), born and raised in St. John's, Antigua, has been a staff writer for the New Yorker since 1976. Winner of the 1983 Zabel Award from the American Academy of Arts and Letters for At the Bottom of the River, she has written a series of books on island life, particularly as experienced by a child. These include A Small Place (1988), from which the following selection is taken; Annie John (1985); Annie, Gwen, Lilly, Pam, and Tulip (1989); and Lucy (1990). Here we see her bitterness at the contrast between what she knows about life on Antigua and what she considers to be the fantasy world of the tourists who visit it.

If you go to Antigua as a tourist, this is what you will see. If you come by aeroplane, you will land at the V. C. Bird International Airport. Vere Cornwall (V. C.) Bird is the Prime Minister of Antigua. You may be the sort of tourist who would wonder why a Prime Minister would want an airport named after him—why not a school, why not a hospital, why not some great public monument? You are a tourist and you have not yet seen a school in Antigua, you have not yet seen the hospital in Antigua, you have not yet seen a public monument in Antigua. As your plane descends to land, you might say, What a beautiful island Antigua is—more beautiful than any of the other islands you have seen, and they were very beautiful, in their way, but they were much too green, much too lush with vegetation, which indicated to you, the tourist, that they got quite a bit of rainfall, and rain is the very thing that you, just now, do not want, for you are thinking of the hard and cold and dark and long days you spent working in North America (or, worse, Europe), earning some money so that you could stay in this place (Antigua) where the sun always shines and where the climate is deliciously hot and dry for the four to ten days you are going to be staying there; and since you are on your holiday, since you are a tourist, the thought of what it might be like for someone who had to live day in, day out in a place that suffers constantly from drought, and so has to watch carefully every drop of fresh water used (while at the same time surrounded by a sea and an ocean—the Caribbean Sea on one side, the Atlantic Ocean on the other), must never cross your mind.

You disembark from your plane. You go through customs. Since you are a tourist, a North American or European—to be frank, white—and not an Antiguan black returning to Antigua from Europe or North America with cardboard boxes of much needed cheap clothes and food for relatives, you move through customs swiftly, you move through customs with ease. Your bags are not searched. You emerge from customs into the hot, clean air: immediately you feel cleansed, immediately you feel blessed (which is to say special); you feel free. You see a man, a taxi driver; you ask him to take you to your destination; he quotes you a price. You immediately think that the price is in the local currency, for you are a tourist and you are familiar with these things

1133

(rates of exchange) and you feel even more free, for things seem so cheap, but then your driver ends by saying, "In U.S. currency." You may say, "Hmmmm, do you have a formal sheet that lists official prices and destinations?" Your driver obeys the law and shows you the sheet, and he apologises for the incredible mistake he has made in quoting you a price off the top of his head which is so vastly different (favouring him) from the one listed. You are driven to your hotel by this taxi driver in his taxi, a brand-new Japanese-made vehicle. The road on which you are travelling is a very bad road, very much in need of repair. You are feeling wonderful, so you say, "Oh, what a marvellous change these bad roads are from the splendid highways I am used to in North America." (Or, worse, Europe.) Your driver is reckless; he is a dangerous man who drives in the middle of the road when he thinks no other cars are coming in the opposite direction, passes other cars on blind curves that run uphill, drives at sixty miles an hour on narrow, curving roads when the road sign, a rusting, beat-up thing left over from colonial days, says 40 mph. This might frighten you (you are on your holiday; you are a tourist); this might excite you (you are on your holiday; you are a tourist), though if you are from New York and take taxis you are used to this style of driving: most of the taxi drivers in New York are from places in the world like this. You are looking out the window (because you want to get your money's worth); you notice that all the cars you see are brand-new, or almost brand-new, and that they are all Japanese-made. There are no American cars in Antigua—no new ones, at any rate; none that were manufactured in the last ten years. You continue to look at the cars and you say to yourself, Why, they look brand-new, but they have an awful sound, like an old car—a very old, dilapidated car. How to account for that? Well, possibly it's because they use leaded gasoline in these brand-new cars whose engines were built to use non-leaded gasoline, but you mustn't ask the person driving the car if this is so, because he or she has never heard of unleaded gasoline. You look closely at the car; you see that it's a model of a Japanese car that you might hesitate to buy; it's a model that's very expensive; it's a model that's quite impractical for a person who has to work as hard as you do and who watches every penny you earn so that you can afford this holiday you are on. How do they afford such a car? And do they live in a luxurious house to match such a car? Well, no. You will be surprised, then, to see that most likely the person driving this brand-new car filled with the wrong gas lives in a house that, in comparison, is far beneath the status of the car; and if you were to ask why you would be told that the banks are encouraged by the government to make loans available for cars, but loans for houses not so easily available; and if you ask again why, you will be told that the two main car dealerships in Antigua are owned in part or outright by ministers in government. Oh, but you are on holiday and the sight of these brand-new cars driven by people who may or may not have really passed their driving test (there was once a scandal about driving licences for sale) would not really stir up these thoughts in you. You pass a building sitting in a sea of dust and you think, It's some latrines for people just passing by, but when you look again you see the building has written on it PIGOTT'S SCHOOL. You pass the hospital, the Holberton Hospital, and how wrong you are not to think about this, for though you are a tourist on your holiday, what if your heart should miss a few beats? What if a blood vessel in your neck should break? What if one of those people driving those brand-new cars filled with the wrong gas fails to pass safely while going uphill on a curve and you are in the car going in the opposite direction? Will you be comforted to know that the hospital is staffed with doctors that no actual Antiguan trusts; that Antiguans always say about the doctors, "I don't want them near me"; that Antiguans refer to them not as doctors but as "the three men" (there are three of them); that when the Minister of Health himself doesn't feel well he takes the first plane to New York to see a real doctor; that if any one of the ministers in government needs medical care he flies to New York to get it?

It's a good thing that you brought your own books with you, for you couldn't just go to the library and borrow some. Antigua used to have a splendid library, but in The Earthquake (everyone talks about it that way— The Earthquake; we Antiguans, for I am one, have a great sense of things, and the more meaningful the thing, the more meaningless we make it) the library building was damaged. This was in 1974, and soon after that a sign was placed on the front of the building saying, THIS BUILDING WAS DAMAGED IN THE EARTHQUAKE OF 1974. REPAIRS ARE PENDING, The sign hangs there, and hangs there more than a decade later, with its unfulfilled promise of repair, and you might see this as a sort of quaintness on the part of these islanders, these people descended from slaves—what a strange, unusual perception of time they have. REPAIRS ARE PENDING, and here it is many years later, but perhaps in a world that is twelve miles long and nine miles wide (the size of Antigua) twelve years and twelve minutes and twelve days are all the same. The library is one of those splendid old buildings from colonial times, and the sign telling of the repairs is a splendid old sign from colonial times. Not very long after The Earthquake Antigua got its independence from Britain, making Antigua a state in its own right, and Antiguans are so proud of this that each year, to mark the day, they go to church and thank God, a British God, for this. But you should not think of the confusion that must lie in all that and you must not think of the damaged library. You have brought your own books with you, and among them is one of those new books about economic history, one of those books explaining how the West (meaning Europe and North America after its conquest and settlement by Europeans) got rich: the West got rich not from the free (free—in this case meaning got-for-nothing) and then undervalued labour, for generations, of the people like me you see walking around you in Antigua but from the ingenuity of small shopkeepers in Sheffield and Yorkshire and Lancashire, or wherever; and what a great part the invention of the wristwatch played in it, for there was nothing noble-minded men could not do when they discovered they could slap time on their wrists just like that (isn't that the last straw; for not only did we have to suffer the unspeakableness of slavery, but the satisfaction to be had from "We made you bastards rich" is taken away, too), and so you needn't let that slightly funny feeling you have from time to time about exploitation, oppression, domination develop into full-fledged unease, discomfort; you could ruin your holiday. They are not responsible for what you have; you owe them nothing; in fact, you did them a big favour, and you can provide one hundred examples. For here you are now, passing by Government House. And here you are now, passing by the Prime Minister's Office and the Parliament Building, and overlooking these, with a splendid view of St. John's Harbour, the American Embassy. If it were not for you, they would not have Government House, and Prime Minister's Office, and Parliament Building and embassy of powerful country. Now you are passing a mansion, an extraordinary house painted the colour of old cow dung, with more aerials and antennas attached to it than you will see even at the American Embassy. The people who live in this house are a merchant family who came to Antigua from the Middle East less than twenty years ago. When this family first came to Antigua, they sold dry goods door to door from suitcases they carried on their backs. Now they own a lot of Antigua; they regularly lend money to the government, they build enormous (for Antigua), ugly (for Antigua), concrete buildings in Antigua's capital, St. John's, which the government then rents for huge sums of money; a member of their family is the Antiguan Ambassador to Syria; Antiguans hate them. Not far from this mansion is another mansion, the home of a drug smuggler. Everybody knows he's a drug smuggler, and if just as you were driving by he stepped out of his door your driver might point him out to you as the notorious person that he is, for this drug smuggler is so rich people say he buys cars in tens—ten of this one, ten of that one—and that he bought a house (another mansion) near Five Islands, contents included, with cash he carried in a suitcase: three hundred and fifty thousand American dollars, and, to the surprise of the seller of the house, lots of American dollars were left over. Overlooking the drug smuggler's mansion is yet another mansion, and leading up to it is the best paved road in all of Antigua—even better than the road that was paved for the Queen's visit in 1985 (when the Queen came, all the roads that she would travel on were paved anew, so that the Queen might have been left with the impression that riding in a car in Antigua was a pleasant experience). In this mansion lives a woman sophisticated people in Antigua call Evita. She is a notorious woman. She's young and beautiful and the girlfriend of somebody very high up in the government. Evita is notorious because her relationship with this high government official has made her the owner of boutiques and property and given her a say in cabinet meetings, and all sorts of other privileges such a relationship would bring a beautiful young woman.

Oh, but by now you are tired of all this looking, and you want to reach your destination—your hotel, your room. You long to refresh yourself; you long to eat some nice lobster, some nice local food. You take a bath, you brush your teeth. You get dressed again; as you get dressed, you look out the window. That water—have you ever seen anything like it? Far out, to the horizon, the colour of the water is navy-blue; nearer, the water is the colour of the North American sky. From there to the shore, the water is pale, silvery, clear, so clear that you can see its pinkish-white sand bottom. Oh, what beauty! Oh, what beauty! You have never seen anything like this. You are so excited. You breathe shallow. You breathe deep. You see a beautiful boy skimming the water, godlike, on a Windsurfer. You see an incredibly unattractive, fat, pastrylike-fleshed woman enjoying a walk on the beautiful sand, with a man, an incredibly unattractive, fat, pastrylike-fleshed man; you see the pleasure they're taking in their surroundings. Still standing, looking out the window, you see yourself lying on the beach, enjoying the amazing sun (a sun so powerful and yet so beautiful, the way it is always overhead as if on permanent guard, ready to stamp out any cloud that dares to darken and so empty rain on you and ruin your holiday; a sun that is your personal friend).

You see yourself taking a walk on that beach, you see yourself meeting new people (only they are new in a very limited way, for they are people just like you). You see yourself eating some delicious, locally grown food. You see yourself, you see yourself . . . You must not wonder what exactly happened to the contents of your lavatory when you flushed it. You must not wonder where your bathwater went when you pulled out the stopper. You must not wonder what happened when you brushed your teeth. Oh, it might all end up in the water you are thinking of taking a swim in; the contents of your lavatory might, just might, graze gently against your ankle as you wade care-free in the water, for you see, in Antigua, there is no proper sewage-disposal system. But the Caribbean Sea is very big and the Atlantic Ocean is even bigger; it would amaze even you to know the number of black slaves this ocean has swallowed up. When you sit down to eat your delicious meal, it's better that you don't know that most of what you are eating came off a plane from Miami. And before it got on a plane in Miami, who knows where it came from? A good guess is that it came from a place like Antigua first, where it was grown dirt-cheap, went to Miami, and came back. There is a world of something in this, but I can't go into it right now.

The thing you have always suspected about yourself the minute you be-come a tourist is true: A tourist is an ugly human being. You are not an ugly person all the time; you are not an ugly person ordinarily; you are not an ugly person day to day. From day to day, you are a nice person. From day to day, all the people who are supposed to love you on the whole do. From day to day, as you walk down a busy street in the large and modern and prosperous city in which you work and live, dismayed, puzzled (a cliché, but only a cliché can explain you) at how alone you feel in this crowd, how awful it is to go unnoticed, how awful it is to go unloved, even as you are surrounded by more people than you could possibly get to know in a lifetime that lasted for millennia, and then out of the corner of your eye you see someone looking at you and absolute pleasure is written all over that person's face, and then you realise that you are not as revolting a presence as you think you are (for that look just told you so). And so, ordinarily, you are a nice person, an attractive person, a person capable of drawing to yourself the affection of other people (people just like you), a person at home in your own skin (sort of; I mean, in a way; I mean, your dismay and puzzlement are natural to you, because people like you just seem to be like that, and so many of the things people like you find admirable about yourselves—the things you think about, the things you think really define you—seem rooted in these feelings): a person at home in your own house (and all its nice house things), with its nice back yard (and its nice back-yard things), at home on your street, your church, in community activities, your job, at home with your family, your relatives, your friends— you are a whole person. But one day, when you are sitting somewhere, alone in that crowd, and that awful feeling of displacedness comes over you, and really, as an ordinary person you are not well equipped to look too far inward and set yourself aright, because being ordinary is already so taxing, and being ordinary takes all you have out of you, and though the words "I must get away" do not actually pass across your lips, you make a leap from being that nice blob just sitting like a boob in your amniotic sac of the modern experience to being a person visiting heaps of death and ruin and feeling alive and inspired at the sight of it; to being a person lying on some faraway beach, your stilled body stinking and glistening in the sand, looking like something first forgotten, then remembered, then not important enough to go back for; to being a person marvelling at the harmony (ordinarily, what you would say is the backwardness) and the union these other people (and they are other people) have with nature. And you look at the things they can do with a piece of ordinary cloth, the things they fashion out of cheap, vulgarly colored (to you) twine, the way they squat down over a hole they have made in the ground, the hole itself is something to marvel at, and since you are being an ugly person this ugly but joyful thought will swell inside you: their ancestors were not clever in the way yours were and not ruthless in the way yours were, for then would it not be you who would be in harmony with nature and backwards in that charming way? An ugly thing, that is what you are when you become a tourist, an ugly, empty thing, a stupid thing, a piece of rubbish pausing here and there to gaze at this and taste that, and it will never occur to you that the people who inhabit the place in which you have just paused cannot stand you, that behind their closed doors they laugh at your strangeness (you do not look the way they look); the physical sight of you does not please them; you have bad manners (it is their custom to eat their food with their hands; you try eating their way, you look silly; you try eating the way you always eat, you look silly); they do not like the way you speak (you have an accent); they collapse helpless from laughter, mimicking the way they imagine you must look as you carry out some everyday bodily function. They do not like you. *They do not like me!* That thought never actually occurs to you. Still, you feel a little uneasy. Still, you feel a little foolish. Still, you feel a little out of place. But the banality of your own life is very real to you; it drove you to this extreme, spending your days and your nights in the company of people who despise you, people you do not like really, people you would not want to have as your actual neighbour. And so you must devote yourself to puzzling out how much of what you are told is really, really true (Is ground-up bottle glass in peanut sauce really a delicacy around here, or will it do just what you think ground-up bottle glass will do? Is this rare, multicoloured, snout-mouthed fish really an aphrodisiac, or will it cause you to fall asleep permanently?). Oh, the hard work all of this is, and is it any wonder, then, that on your return home you feel the need of a long rest, so that you can recover from your life as a tourist?

That the native does not like the tourist is not hard to explain. For every native of every place is a potential tourist, and every tourist is a native of somewhere. Every native everywhere lives a life of overwhelming and crushing banality and boredom and desperation and depression, and every deed, good and bad, is an attempt to forget this. Every native would like to find a way out, every native would like a rest, every native would like a tour. But some natives—most natives in the world—cannot go anywhere. They are too poor. They are too poor to go anywhere. They are too poor to escape the reality of their lives; and they are too poor to live properly in the place where they live, which is the very place you, the tourist, want to go—so when the natives see you, the tourist, they envy you, they envy your ability to leave your own banality and boredom, they envy your ability to turn their own banality and boredom into a source of pleasure for yourself.

Suggestions for Discussion

1. Kincaid describes the visitor to Antigua as "An ugly thing, that is what you are when you become a tourist, an ugly, empty thing, a stupid thing, a piece of rubbish pausing here and there to gaze at this and taste that. . . ." What is the reason for her rage?

2. The author argues that people become tourists because their lives are filled with banality and boredom. Discuss why you agree or disagree.

3. There are many Antiguas: what the tourist sees; what the native sees; what we interpret; what they live; what we experience. What is the "real" Antigua? Is Antigua a puzzle to be solved? Explain.

Suggestions for Writing

1. Several people present at the same "event" might each experience it differently. Antigua is an "event" of this kind. Describe your hometown, or something that happened in it, from a series of perspectives.

2. What *is* the case and what may *seem* to be the case are often very different. From your own experience, describe a scene (such as a meal at home or an encounter with a stranger) in which this was the case.

Jean Bethke Elshtain

Battered Reason

Jean Bethke Elshtain (b. 1941) is a professor of political science at the University of Massachusetts where she has spent most of her career. Born in Canada, she was educated at Colorado State and the University of Colorado, and received her Ph.D. from Brandeis. The recipient of Woodrow Wilson and MacDowell Fellowships, she has concentrated on reframing the discipline of political science to include the realities of the experiences of women. Her recent books include *Women and War* (1987), *Power Trips and Other Journeys* (1990), *Women, Militarism, and War* (1990), and *But Was It Just?* (1992). Here we find her examining the internal fallacies entailed in asserting women's rights from a position of victimhood.

Feminism in the West has always been of at least two minds about the nature of male and female identity. Egalitarian feminists hold that there is a single, generic human being. People may, of course, differ in temperament, abilities, and power, but such differences must be assessed by a universal standard. What is excellent in a man, they argue, is excellent in a woman and vice versa. A nefarious deed is nefarious no matter who commits it. The problem for women historically is that men were the paradigmatic exemplars of humanity. Most feminists insisted that women too shared in the excellences wrongly deemed "masculine"; hence women could not fairly be denied access to education, property, the vote, and other civic rights.

This egalitarian or "assimilationist" feminism was always challenged by an argument from women who subscribed to a feminism of "difference." Why accept a single human standard—and a male one at that? Is it not only possible but even desirable that there are many human virtues, and that women may more likely serve as exemplars of some just as men stand for others? Perhaps valor is, in some sense, masculine even as compassion is, in some sense, feminine. The problem for women is that the qualities most linked to women have been devalued overall, that male virtues were rewarded (with medals and high office and official institutional power) while female virtues (succor, temperance, durability) were ranked low in the overall scheme of things. As one feminist puts it: "Men have had more pomp in their circumstances."

The most disquieting developments at the moment come from the "difference" end of the continuum. For, taken to an extreme, difference begins to blot out equality and to lay claim to privilege, or at least to open season on all the cumbersome rules and regulations aimed at achieving fair play. Fairness itself comes to seem a paltry thing in contrast to empowerment, as can be seen increasingly in academic feminist discourse. At one conference I attended, several women vehemently insisted that it would be best to jettison the notion of "equality" altogether. We want "nothing of equality," one participant exclaimed. We want nothing of this "male standard." What she aimed to put in the place of political fights about equality was a "celebration of the female will to power." This seemed a tad murky at best and not a little disquieting, considering how the will to power has worked itself out, politically, in the past. But the specter that is haunting feminism, the specter of difference constructed as a principle designed to trump all other principles, pops up everywhere these days.

One area where the argument from difference has made major inroads is feminist jurisprudence. One finds many, often quite interesting, discussions about whether the "female voice" might not differ—as defendant, witness, and victim—from the male voice and the like. But the debate has escaped the hothouse of the law classroom and academic journals and made its way into the courtroom, often in bizarre and troubling forms that reflect one side of the "will to power" coin. As Nietzsche himself observed, the flip side of an urge to dominate is an urge to submit and then to construe victimization as a claim to privilege.

In the social world of the radical feminist, women are routinely portrayed as debased, victimized, deformed, and mutilated. By construing herself as a victim, the woman, in this scheme of things, seeks to attain power through depictions of her victimization. The presumption is that the victim speaks in a voice more reliable than that of any other. (And in this world, remember, there are only two kinds of people—victims and oppressors.) The voice of the victim gains not only privilege but hegemony—provided she remains a victim, incapable, helpless, demeaned. This can be part and parcel of an explicit power play. Or it may serve as one feature of a strategy of exculpation—evasion of responsibility for a situation or outcome. A discussion in a recent book on race and rights by Patricia Williams, *The Alchemy of Race and Rights*, plays the victim card to achieve both ends simultaneously. Acknowledging that the Tawana Brawley accusations were part of a hoax, Williams goes on to say that doesn't really matter. For Brawley was a victim of "some unspeakable crime" even "if she did it to herself." She was the victim of a "meta-rape," and this secures both her victim status and the power plays of those who cynically manipulated the situation.

Suppose one shifts the terrain to an instance in which a woman is cast as both victim and victimizer. How does the difference argument—which seeks to preserve her victim status while simultaneously denying that she could, as well, abuse or "oppress" others—play out? Take a recent, dreadful case in Nashville, Tennessee. The facts are not in dispute. Summoned to an apartment by a man named Michael Bordis whose infant son had "stopped breathing," Metro Police confronted a horrific scene. They found a 13-week-old baby boy in the early stages of decomposition. The room occupied by the baby and his half-brother smelled so strongly of feces and urine that it "literally turned your stomach," according to the Metro Police detective who happened first on the scene. The infant's filthy 4-year-old half-brother was himself hungry and underweight. It appeared that he fed himself from the refrigerator and had been left alone with the starving infant.

Police arrested Bordis and his wife, Claudette. While in custody and awaiting trial, Claudette Bordis wrote her husband love letters exalting his sexual prowess in graphic terms and describing her favorite sexual activities with him.

Claudette Bordis went to trial first. According to her defense attorneys, the 23-year-old was the *real victim*. They mounted a defense based on the "battered woman syndrome," an exculpatory strategy not available in principle to a male defendant. She could "not be held accountable" for the neglect and death of her child because she was in thrall to her abusive, domineering husband. Although the husband was away at work all day, she claimed to be so bedeviled that it didn't occur to her to care for her child. She never intended to do wrong. To hold her responsible for her deeds was either a "male deal or a prosecution deal or a society deal, but some people just don't get it," the defense attorney insisted.

The defense called a psychologist to the stand who testified that Bordis was "stressed out." This explained the fact that she neglected to feed her son. It also accounted for why she agreed to "dress like a prostitute" and accompany her husband to bars where they picked up men for three-way sexual encounters. Finally, the psychologist testified that the "battered woman syndrome" propelled Bordis to exchange sexually explicit letters with seven male prisoners in other states following her incarceration. The psychologist claimed: "I think our society has conditioned women to accept that they're to serve the men." On this the defense rested. Note that her lawyer did not use the insanity defense; rather, the argument was that Bordis had been robotized by living with a lout. As a victim, her human responsibilities collapsed and she became mere putty in his hands—and this diminished entity could scarcely be held accountable for victimizing another.

The prosecutors weren't having any of it. Tacitly they offered a distinction between extenuating circumstances and exculpatory conditions. They agreed that Bordis was a disturbed woman and had been long before she married her creepy husband. But this didn't inhibit her ability to distinguish right from wrong. They insisted that she was just as accountable as her husband, perhaps even more so, for the knowing torment of her slowly starving child. She had the baby throughout the day and chose not to feed him. The Metro Public Defender's claim that the jurors had a duty to find Bordis "not guilty" because she was a victim of battered woman syndrome amounted to a "trumped-up defense" that itself constituted "an insult to women in the community who are battered." The prosecutor told the jury that Bordis could have put her infant in the hands of others to care for. She could have called her family—her mother had, at one point, cared for the woman's older child. She had choices and she chose, on some level, to destroy her child.

The jury, accepting the prosecutor's argument, found Bordis guilty of first-degree murder. Her husband goes on trial for the same offense soon. The jury decision prompted a letter to the *Tennessean*, one of Nashville's two daily newspapers, from Bordis's mother decrying the verdict and proclaiming, in language more and more familiar in contemporary cultural, legal, and political argument, that Bordis herself was the "victim." She was a "victim" of abuse and now a "victim of society's unwillingness to educate themselves." In fact, the grandmother continued, "I am a victim. I lost a grandson." As a victim she had suffered and her daughter had suffered and, for this reason, the daughter should be let off the hook as she was not responsible for what she did.

What are we to make of all this, and how does it connect to the heated debate over difference? In my own work over the years I have attempted to steer a course between a harsh rejection of difference and a strong plea that men and women seem to inhabit incommensurable moral, cognitive, ethical, and political universes. The stern rejection of any possibility of difference seems mistaken in its desire to forge one generic human standard and its refusal to countenance all distinctions that cannot be traced to some alterable arrangement in social structures; the second seems crazy in its refusal to see how much all creatures we call "human" share and in its repudiation of any possibility of reciprocity and commonality between men and women. Most feminist discourse operates somewhere in this middle range, although the antinomies—denial of difference altogether or making of difference an absolute—pop up more and more these days.

The Bordis case demonstrates how pernicious a difference argument can become when taken to exculpatory extremes. Women are not responsible human agents. They are once again found wanting in what Aristotle called a "deliberative" faculty. The Nashville jury refused to go this route. But other juries have bought a variety of exculpatory strategies, including the so-called PMS (pre-menstrual stress) defense, which has been used to clear women of charges including driving to endanger, assault, child abuse, even murder. In this matter women cannot indefinitely have it both ways. It is terrible to be abused. But for a 23-year-old woman with a range of options still open to her, despite her entanglement in a wretched relationship, to starve an infant to death is more terrible yet. Moral responsibility doesn't come to us in neat packages, one tied with a blue ribbon, the other in pink. Those who demand full civic standing must be prepared for its responsibilities and its burdens.

Suggestions for Discussion

1. How does Elshtain characterize the "egalitarian" versus the "difference" feminist positions?

2. What does she see as the conceptual pitfall in the argument from "difference"?

3. What have been the legal ramifications of the "woman as victim" position?

Suggestions for Writing

1. "Over the years I have attempted to steer a course between a harsh rejection of difference and a strong plea that men and women seem to inhabit incommensurable moral, cognitive, ethical, and political universes." Evaluate this statement in terms of your own experience.

2. How do you think men and women are alike? Different? The author describes how some interpretations of gender similarities and differences have come to have legal ramifications. What might be the educational ramifications of these interpretations? Explain.

Fiction

Anton Chekhov

The Bet

Translated by Constance Garnett

Anton Chekhov (1860–1904), Russian short-story writer and playwright, practiced medicine briefly before devoting himself to literature. Among his plays are *The Sea Gull* (1896), *Uncle Vanya* (1900), *The Three Sisters* (1901), and *The Cherry Orchard* (1904). His stories, translated by Constance Garnett, were published as *The Tales of Chekhov* (1916–1923). The drama of the lawyer's solitary existence constitutes the central action of the story; it culminates in his walking out of the lodge a few hours before fulfilling the conditions of the bet; and it reaches its highest point of intensity, and its resolution, in the letter that passionately expresses his nihilism and supreme contempt for his fellow men.

I

It was a dark autumn night. The old banker was pacing from corner to corner of his study, recalling to his mind the party he gave in the autumn fifteen years before. There were many clever people at the party and much interesting conversation. They talked among other things of capital punishment. The guests, among them not a few scholars and journalists, for the most part disapproved of capital punishment. They found it obsolete as a means of punishment, unfitted to a Christian State and immoral. Some of them thought that capital punishment should be replaced universally by life imprisonment.

"I don't agree with you," said the host. "I myself have experienced neither capital punishment nor life imprisonment, but if one may judge *a priori*, then in my opinion capital punishment is more moral and more humane than imprisonment. Execution kills instantly, life imprisonment kills by degrees. Who is the more humane executioner, one who kills you in a few seconds or one who draws the life out of you incessantly, for years?"

"They're both equally immoral," remarked one of the guests, "because their purpose is the same, to take away life. The State is not God. It has no right to take away that which it cannot give back, if it should so desire."

Among the company was a lawyer, a young man of about twenty-five. On being asked his opinion, he said:

"Capital punishment and life imprisonment are equally immoral; but if I were offered the choice between them, I would certainly choose the second. It's better to live somehow than not to live at all."

There ensued a lively discussion. The banker who was then younger and more nervous suddenly lost his temper, banged his fist on the table, and turning to the young lawyer, cried out:

"It's a lie. I bet you two millions you wouldn't stick in a cell even for five years."

"If you mean it seriously," replied the lawyer, "then I bet I'll stay not five but fifteen."

"Fifteen! Done!" cried the banker. "Gentlemen, I stake two millions."

"Agreed. You stake two millions, I my freedom," said the lawyer.

So this wild, ridiculous bet came to pass. The banker, who at that time had too many millions to count, spoiled and capricious, was beside himself with rapture. During supper he said to the lawyer jokingly:

"Come to your senses, young man, before it's too late. Two millions are nothing to me, but you stand to lose three or four of the best years of your life. I say three or four, because you'll never stick it out any longer. Don't forget either, you unhappy man, that voluntary is much heavier than enforced imprisonment. The idea that you have the right to free yourself at any moment will poison the whole of your life in the cell. I pity you."

And now the banker, pacing from corner to corner, recalled all this and asked himself:

"Why did I make this bet? What's the good? The lawyer loses fifteen years of his life and I throw away two millions. Will it convince people that capital punishment is worse or better than imprisonment for life? No, no! all stuff and rubbish. On my part, it was the caprice of a well-fed man; on the lawyer's, pure greed of gold."

He recollected further what happened after the evening party. It was decided that the lawyer must undergo his imprisonment under the strictest observation, in a garden wing of the banker's house. It was agreed that during the period he would be deprived of the right to cross the threshold, to see living people, to hear human voices, and to receive letters and newspapers. He was permitted to have a musical instrument, to read books, to write letters, to drink wine, and smoke tobacco. By the agreement he could communicate, but only in silence, with the outside world through a little window specially constructed for this purpose. Everything necessary, books, music, wine, he could receive in any quantity by sending a note through the window. The agreement provided for all the minutest details, which made the confinement strictly solitary, and it obliged the lawyer to remain exactly fifteen years from twelve o'clock of November 14th, 1870 to twelve o'clock of November 14th, 1885. The least attempt on his part to violate the conditions, to escape if only for two minutes before the time freed the banker from the obligation to pay him the two millions.

During the first year of imprisonment, the lawyer, as far as it was possible to judge from his short notes, suffered terribly from loneliness and boredom. From his wing day and night came the sound of the piano. He rejected wine and tobacco. "Wine," he wrote, "excites desires, and desires are the chief foes of a prisoner; besides, nothing is more boring than to drink good wine alone, and tobacco spoils the air in his room." During the first year the lawyer was sent books of a light character; novels with a complicated love interest, stories of crime and fantasy, comedies, and so on.

In the second year the piano was heard no longer and the lawyer asked only for classics. In the fifth year, music was heard again, and the prisoner asked for wine. Those who watched him said that during the whole of that year he was only eating, drinking, and lying on his bed. He yawned often and talked angrily to himself. Books he did not read. Sometimes at nights he would sit down to write. He would write for a long time and tear it all up in the morning. More than once he was heard to weep.

In the second half of the sixth year, the prisoner began zealously to study languages, philosophy, and history. He fell on these subjects so hungrily that the banker hardly had time to get books enough for him. In the space of four years about six hundred volumes were brought at his request. It was while that passion lasted that the banker received the following letter from the prisoner: "My dear gaoler, I am writing these lines in six languages. Show them to experts. Let them read them. If they do not find one single mistake, I beg you to give orders to have a gun fired off in the garden. By the noise I shall know that my efforts have not been in vain. The geniuses of all ages and countries speak in different languages; but in them all burns the same flame. Oh, if you knew my heavenly happiness now that I can understand them!" The prisoner's desire was fulfilled. Two shots were fired in the garden by the banker's order.

Later on, after the tenth year, the lawyer sat immovable before his table and read only the New Testament. The banker found it strange that a man who in four years had mastered six hundred erudite volumes, should have spent nearly a year in reading one book, easy to understand and by no means thick. The New Testament was then replaced by the history of religions and theology.

During the last two years of his confinement the prisoner read an extraordinary amount, quite haphazard. Now he would apply himself to the natural sciences, then he would read Byron or Shakespeare. Notes used to come from him in which he asked to be sent at the same time a book on chemistry, a text-book of medicine, a novel, and some treatise on philosophy or theology. He read as though he were swimming in the sea among broken pieces of wreckage, and in his desire to save his life was eagerly grasping one piece after another.

II

The banker recalled all this, and thought:

"To-morrow at twelve o'clock he receives his freedom. Under the agreement, I shall have to pay him two millions. If I pay, it's all over with me. I am ruined for ever. . . ."

Fifteen years before he had too many millions to count, but now he was afraid to ask himself which he had more of, money or debts. Gambling on the Stock-Exchange, risky speculation, and the recklessness of which he could not rid himself even in old age, had gradually brought his business to decay; and the fearless, self-confident, proud man of business had become an ordinary banker, trembling at every rise and fall in the market.

"That cursed bet," murmured the old man clutching his head in despair. . . . "Why didn't the man die? He's only forty years old. He will take away my last farthing, marry, enjoy life, gamble on the Exchange, and I will look on like an envious beggar and hear the same words from him every day:

'I'm obliged to you for the happiness of my life. Let me help you.' No, it's too much! The only escape from bankruptcy and disgrace—is that the man should die."

The clock had just struck three. The banker was listening. In the house every one was asleep, and one could hear only the frozen trees whining outside the windows. Trying to make no sound, he took out of his safe the key of the door which had not been opened for fifteen years, put on his overcoat, and went out of the house. The garden was dark and cold. It was raining. A damp, penetrating wind howled in the garden and gave the trees no rest. Though he strained his eyes, the banker could see neither the ground, nor the white statues, nor the garden wing, nor the trees. Approaching the garden wing, he called the watchman twice. There was no answer. Evidently the watchman had taken shelter from the bad weather and was now asleep somewhere in the kitchen or the greenhouse.

"If I have the courage to fulfill my intention," thought the old man, "the suspicion will fall on the watchman first of all."

In the darkness he groped for the steps and the door and entered the hall of the garden-wing, then poked his way into a narrow passage and struck a match. Not a soul was there. Some one's bed, with no bedclothes on it, stood there, and an iron stove loomed dark in the corner. The seals on the door that led into the prisoner's room were unbroken.

When the match went out, the old man, trembling from agitation, peeped into the little window.

In the prisoner's room a candle was burning dimly. The prisoner himself sat by the table. Only his back, the hair on his head and his hands were visible. Open books were strewn about on the table, the two chairs, and on the carpet near the table.

Five minutes passed and the prisoner never once stirred. Fifteen years' confinement had taught him to sit motionless. The banker tapped on the window with his finger, but the prisoner made no movement in reply. Then the banker cautiously tore the seals from the door and put the key into the lock. The rusty lock gave a hoarse groan and the door creaked. The banker expected instantly to hear a cry of surprise and the sound of steps. Three minutes passed and it was as quiet inside as it had been before. He made up his mind to enter.

Before the table sat a man, unlike an ordinary human being. It was a skeleton, with tight-drawn skin, with long curly hair like a woman's, and a shaggy beard. The colour of his face was yellow, of an earthy shade; the cheeks were sunken, the back long and narrow, and the hand upon which he leaned his hairy head was so lean and skinny that it was painful to look upon. His hair was already silvering with grey, and no one who glanced at the senile emaciation of the face would have believed that he was only forty years old. On the table, before his bended head, lay a sheet of paper on which something was written in a tiny hand.

"Poor devil," thought the banker, "he's asleep and probably seeing millions in his dreams. I have only to take and throw this half-dead thing on the bed, smother him a moment with the pillow, and the most careful examination will find no trace of unnatural death. But, first, let us read what he has written here."

The banker took the sheet from the table and read:

"Tomorrow at twelve o'clock midnight, I shall obtain my freedom and the right to mix with people. But before I leave this room and see the sun I think it necessary to say a few words to you. On my own clear conscience and before God who sees me I declare to you that I despise freedom, life, health, and all that your books call the blessings of the world.

"For fifteen years I have diligently studied earthly life. True, I saw neither the earth nor the people, but in your books I drank fragrant wine, sang songs, hunted deer and wild boar in the forests, loved women. . . . And beautiful women, like clouds ethereal, created by the magic of your poets' genius, visited me by night, and whispered to me wonderful tales, which made my head drunken. In your books I climbed the summits of Elbruz and Mont Blanc and saw from there how the sun rose in the morning, and in the evening suffused the sky, the ocean and the mountain ridges with a purple gold. I saw from there how above me lightnings glimmered cleaving the clouds; I saw green forests, fields, rivers, lakes, cities; I heard sirens singing, and the playing of the pipes of Pan; I touched the wings of beautiful devils who came flying to me to speak of God. . . . In your books I cast myself into bottomless abysses, worked miracles, burned cities to the ground, preached new religions, conquered whole countries. . . .

"Your books gave me wisdom. All that unwearying human thought created in the centuries is compressed to a little lump in my skull. I know that I am cleverer than you all.

"And I despise your books, despise all worldly blessings and wisdom. Everything is void, frail, visionary and delusive as a mirage. Though you be proud and wise and beautiful, yet will death wipe you from the face of the earth like the mice underground; and your posterity, your history, and the immorality of your men of genius will be as frozen slag, burnt down together with the terrestrial globe.

"You are mad, and gone the wrong way. You take falsehood for truth and ugliness for beauty. You would marvel if suddenly apple and orange trees should bear frogs and lizards instead of fruit, and if roses should begin to breathe the odour of a sweating horse. So do I marvel at you, who have bartered heaven for earth. I do not want to understand you.

"That I may show you in deed my contempt for that by which you live, I waive the two millions of which I once dreamed as of paradise, and which I now despise. That I may deprive myself of my right to them, I shall come out from here five minutes before the stipulated term, and thus shall violate the agreement."

When he had read, the banker put the sheet on the table, kissed the head of the strange man, and began to weep. He went out of the wing. Never at any other time, not even after his terrible losses on the Exchange, had he felt such contempt for himself as now. Coming home, he lay down on his bed, but agitation and tears kept him a long time from sleeping. . . .

The next morning the poor watchman came running to him and told him that they had seen the man who lived in the wing climb through the window into the garden. He had gone to the gate and disappeared. The banker instantly went with his servants to the wing and established the escape of his prisoner. To avoid unnecessary rumours he took the paper with the renunciation from the table and, on his return, locked it in his safe.

Suggestions for Discussion

1. If you agree that "The Bet" is primarily the lawyer's story, why is our view of the lawyer filtered through the reminiscences and observations of the banker? Why are we permitted to see the lawyer directly only twice? What artistic purposes are served by the use of hearsay and notes and letters, and by the sparseness and flatness of the account of the lawyer's years of confinement?

2. Trace the changes in the lawyer's activities as they mark the development and resolution of the action. What are the implications as to his ultimate fate?

3. How do the shifts in time contribute to suspense and tone?

4. Find examples of irony and paradox.

5. How do you reconcile the lawyer's nihilism with his lyrical assertion that he has known the beauty of earth and love, has seen nature in her glory and tempestuousness, and has achieved wisdom—"all that the unresting thought of man has created"? What evidence can you find that Chekhov's vision of life extends beyond negation of all values?

Suggestions for Writing

1. Chekhov has said, "When you depict sad or unlucky people and want to touch the reader's heart, try to be colder—it gives their grief, as it were, a background against which it stands out in greater relief. . . . You must be unconcerned when you write pathetic stories, . . . the more objective, the stronger will be the effect." Write an evaluation of Chekhov's theories in relation to the characters of the banker and the lawyer, the tone of the story, and its denouement.

2. Write a position paper on the lawyer's (banker's) "examined life."

3. Write your own preferred conclusion to "The Bet"; or describe the lawyer's next fifteen years; or recount a conversation in which the banker tells his story the next morning.

Walter Van Tilburg Clark

The Portable Phonograph

Walter Van Tilburg Clark (1909–1972) was an American short-story writer and novelist, many of whose works reflect his intense awareness of nature and of the relation between man and nature. His novels include *The Ox-Bow Incident* (1942), *The City of Trembling Leaves* (1945), and *The Track of the Cat* (1949). His collected stories have been published under the title *The Watchful Gods and Other Stories* (1950). In "The Portable Phonograph," survivors of war find momentary relief from their grim and threatened existence in the words of *The Tempest* and the music of Debussy.

The red sunset with narrow, black cloud strips like threads across it, lay on the curved horizon of the prairie. The air was still and cold, and in it settled the mute darkness and greater cold of night. High in the air there was wind, for through the veil of the dusk the clouds could be seen gliding rapidly south and changing shapes. A queer sensation of torment, of two-sided, unpredictable nature, arose from the stillness of the earth air beneath the violence of the upper air. Out of the sunset, through the dead, matted grass and isolated weed stalks of the prairie, crept the narrow and deeply rutted remains of a road. In the road, in places, there were crusts of shallow, brittle ice. There were little islands of an old oiled pavement in the road too, but most of it was mud, now frozen rigid. The frozen mud still bore the toothed impress of great tanks, and a wanderer on the neighboring undulations might have stumbled, in this light, into large, partially filled-in and weed-grown cavities, their banks channeled and beginning to spread into badlands. These pits were such as might have been made by falling meteors, but they were not. They were the scars of gigantic bombs, their rawness already made a little natural by rain, seed, and time. Along the road, there were rakish remnants of fence. There was also, just visible, one portion of tangled and multiple barbed wire still erect, behind which was a shelving ditch with small caves, now very quiet and empty, at intervals in its back wall. Otherwise there was no structure or remnant of a structure visible over the dome of the darkling earth, but only, in sheltered hollows, the darker shadows of young trees trying again.

Under the withering arch of the high wind a V of wild geese fled south. The rush of their pinions sounded briefly, and the faint, plaintive notes of their expeditionary talk. Then they left a still greater vacancy. There was the smell and expectation of snow, as there is likely to be when the wild geese fly south. From the remote distance, towards the red sky, came faintly the protracted howl and quick yap-yap of a prairie wolf.

North of the road, perhaps a hundred yards, lay the parallel and deeply intrenched course of a small creek, lined with leafless alders and willows. The creek was already silent under ice. Into the bank above it was dug a sort of cell, with a single opening, like the mouth of a mine tunnel. Within the cell there was a little red of fire, which showed dully through the opening, like a reflection or a deception of the imagination. The light came from the chary burning of four blocks of poorly aged peat, which gave off a petty warmth and much acrid smoke. But the precious remnants of wood, old fence posts and timbers from the long-deserted dugouts, had to be saved for the real cold, for the time when a man's breath blew white, the moisture in his nostrils stiffened at once when he stepped out, and the expansive blizzards paraded for days over the vast open, swirling and settling and thickening, till the dawn of the cleared day when the sky was thin blue-green and the terrible cold, in which a man could not live for three hours unwarmed, lay over the uniformly drifted swell of the plain.

Around the smoldering peat, four men were seated cross-legged. Behind them, traversed by their shadows, was the earth bench, with two old and dirty army blankets, where the owner of the cell slept. In a niche in the opposite wall were a few tin utensils which caught the glint of the coals. The host was rewrapping in a piece of daubed burlap four fine, leather-bound books. He worked slowly and very carefully, and at last tied the bundle securely with a piece of grass-woven cord. The other three looked intently upon the process, as if a great significance lay in it. As the host tied the cord, he spoke. He was an old man, his long, matted beard and hair gray to nearly white. The shadows made his brows and cheekbones appear gnarled, his eyes and cheeks deeply sunken. His big hands, rough with frost and swollen by rheumatism, were awkward but gentle at their task. He was like a prehistoric priest performing a fateful ceremonial rite. Also his voice had in it a suitable quality of deep, reverent despair, yet perhaps at the moment, a sharpness of selfish satisfaction.

"When I perceived what was happening," he said, "I told myself, 'It is the end. I cannot take much; I will take these.'"

"Perhaps I was impractical," he continued. "But for myself, I do not regret, and what do we know of those who will come after us? We are the doddering remnant of a race of mechanical fools. I have saved what I love; the soul of what was good in us is here; perhaps the new ones will make a strong enough beginning not to fall behind when they become clever."

He rose with slow pain and placed the wrapped volumes in the niche with his utensils. The others watched him with the same ritualistic gaze.

"Shakespeare, the Bible, *Moby Dick, the Divine Comedy,*" one of them said softly. "You might have done worse, much worse."

"You will have a little soul left until you die," said another harshly. "That is more than is true of us. My brain becomes thick, like my hands." He held the big, battered hands, with their black nails, in the glow to be seen.

"I want paper to write on," he said. "And there is none."

The fourth man said nothing. He sat in the shadow farthest from the fire, and sometimes his body jerked in its rags from the cold. Although he was still young, he was sick and coughed often. Writing implied a greater future than he now felt able to consider.

The old man seated himself laboriously, and reached out, groaning at the movement, to put another block of peat on the fire. With bowed heads and averted eyes, his three guests acknowledged his magnanimity.

"We thank you, Doctor Jenkins, for the reading," said the man who had named the books.

They seemed then to be waiting for something. Doctor Jenkins understood, but was loath to comply. In an ordinary moment he would have said nothing. But the words of *The Tempest,* which he had been reading, and the religious attention of the three made this an unusual occasion.

"You wish to hear the phonograph," he said grudgingly.

The two middle-aged men stared into the fire, unable to formulate and expose the enormity of their desire.

The young man, however, said anxiously, between suppressed coughs, "Oh, please," like an excited child.

The old man rose again in his difficult way, and went to the back of the cell. He returned and placed tenderly upon the packed floor, where the firelight might fall upon it, an old portable phonograph in a black case. He smoothed the top with his hand, and then opened it. The lovely green-felt-covered disk became visible.

"I have been using thorns as needles," he said. "But tonight, because we have a musician among us"—he bent his head to the young man, almost invisible in the shadow—"I will use a steel needle. There are only three left."

The two middle-aged men stared at him in speechless adoration. The one with the big hands, who wanted to write, moved his lips, but the whisper was not audible.

"Oh, don't!" cried the young man, as if he were hurt. "The thorns will do beautifully."

"No," the old man said. "I have become accustomed to the thorns, but they are not really good. For you, my young friend, we will have good music tonight."

"After all," he added generously, and beginning to wind the phonograph, which creaked, "they can't last forever."

"No, nor we," the man who needed to write said harshly. "The needle, by all means."

"Oh, thanks," said the young man. "Thanks," he said again in a low, excited voice, and then stifled his coughing with a bowed head.

"The records, though," said the old man when he had finished winding, "are a different matter. Already they are very worn. I do not play them more than once a week. One, once a week, that is what I allow myself."

"More than a week I cannot stand it; not to hear them," he apologized.

"No, how could you?" cried the young man. "And with them here like this."

"A man can stand anything," said the man who wanted to write, in his harsh, antagonistic voice.

"Please, the music," said the young man.

"Only the one," said the old man. "In the long run, we will remember more that way."

He had a dozen records with luxuriant gold and red seals. Even in that light the others could see that the threads of the records were becoming worn. Slowly he read out the titles and the tremendous, dead names of the composers and the artists and the orchestras. The three worked upon the names in their minds, carefully. It was difficult to select from such a wealth what they would at once most like to remember. Finally, the man who wanted to write named Gershwin's "New York."

"Oh, no," cried the sick young man, and then could say nothing more because he had to cough. The others understood him, and the harsh man withdrew his selection and waited for the musician to choose.

The musician begged Doctor Jenkins to read the titles again, very slowly, so that he could remember the sounds. While they were read, he lay back against the wall, his eyes closed, his thin, horny hand pulling at his light beard, and listened to the voices and the orchestras and the single instruments in his mind.

When the reading was done he spoke despairingly. "I have forgotten," he complained; "I cannot hear them clearly."

"There are things missing," he explained.

"I know," said Doctor Jenkins. "I thought that I knew all of Shelley by heart. I should have brought Shelley."

"That's more soul than we can use," said the harsh man. "*Moby Dick* is better."

"By God, we can understand that," he emphasized.

The Doctor nodded.

"Still," said the man who had admired the books, "we need the absolute if we are to keep a grasp on anything."

"Anything but these sticks and peat clods and rabbit snares," he said bitterly.

"Shelley desired an ultimate absolute," said the harsh man. "It's too much," he said. "It's no good; no earthly good."

The musician selected a Debussy nocturne. The others considered and approved. They rose to their knees to watch the Doctor prepare for the playing, so that they appeared to be actually in an attitude of worship. The peat glow showed the thinness of their bearded faces, and the deep lines in them, and revealed the condition of their garments. The other two continued to kneel as the old man carefully lowered the needle onto the spinning disk, but the musician suddenly drew back against the wall again, with his knees up, and buried his face in his hands.

At the first notes of the piano the listeners were startled. They stared at each other. Even the musician lifted his head in amazement, but then quickly bowed it again, strainingly, as if he were suffering from a pain he might not be able to endure. They were all listening deeply, without movement. The wet, blue-green notes tinkled forth from the old machine, and were individual, delectable presences in the cell. The individual, delectable presences swept into a sudden tide of unbearably beautiful dissonance, and then continued fully the swelling and ebbing of that tide, the dissonant inpourings, and the resolutions, and the diminishments, and the little, quiet wavelets of interlude lapping between. Every sound was piercing and singularly sweet. In all the men except the musician, there occurred rapid sequences of tragically heightened recollection. He heard nothing but what was there. At the final, whispering disappearance, but moving quietly so that the others would not hear him and look at him, he let his head fall back in agony, as if it were drawn there by the hair, and clenched the fingers of one hand over his teeth. He sat that way while the others were silent, and until they began to breathe again normally. His drawn-up legs were trembling violently.

Quickly Doctor Jenkins lifted the needle off, to save it and not to spoil the recollection with scraping. When he had stopped the whirling of the sacred disk, he courteously left the phonograph open and by the fire, in sight.

The others, however, understood. The musician rose last, but then abruptly, and went quickly out at the door without saying anything. The others stopped at the door and gave their thanks in low voices. The Doctor nodded magnificently.

"Come again," he invited, "in a week. We will have the 'New York.'"

When the two had gone together, out towards the rimed road, he stood in the entrance, peering and listening. At first, there was only the resonant boom of the wind overhead, and then far over the dome of the dead, dark plain, the wolf cry lamenting. In the rifts of clouds the Doctor saw four stars flying. It impressed the Doctor that one of them had just been obscured by the beginning of a flying cloud at the very moment he heard what he had been listening for, a sound of suppressed coughing. It was not nearby, however. He believed that down against the pale alders he could see the moving shadow.

With nervous hands he lowered the piece of canvas which served as his door, and pegged it at the bottom. Then quickly and quietly, looking at the piece of canvas frequently, he slipped the records into the case, snapped the lid shut, and carried the phonograph to his couch. There, pausing often to stare at the canvas and listen, he dug earth from the wall and disclosed a piece of board. Behind this there was a deep hole in the wall, into which he put the phonograph. After a moment's consideration, he went over and reached down for his bundle of books and inserted it also. Then, guardedly, he once more sealed up the hole with the board and the earth. He also changed his blankets, and the grass-stuffed sack which served as a pillow, so that he could lie facing the entrance. After carefully placing two more blocks of peat upon the fire, he stood for a long time watching the stretched canvas, but it seemed to billow naturally with the first gusts of a lowering wind. At last he prayed, and got in under his blankets, and closed his smoke-smarting eyes. On the inside of the bed, next the wall, he could feel with his hand the comfortable piece of lead pipe.

Suggestions for Discussion

1. What does the setting contribute to the tone of the story? What details prepare you for what follows? Describe the situation in which the four men find themselves.

2. The description of each man is restrained and sparse. With what details do you learn of the inner life and character of each? Of what they have in common? Of their differences?

3. Account for the old man's choice of books. Why would he take *The Tempest?* Explain the "harsh" man's allusion to Shelley with reference to the man's situation.

4. How does repetition contribute to tone and characterization?

5. How does the last sentence illuminate the action?

Suggestions for Writing

1. Compare Chekhov's "The Bet" and "The Portable Phonograph" as they portray their authors' respective structures of the world.

2. Place yourself in the host's position. What books or records would you have selected? Why?

E. B. White

The Second Tree from the Corner

E. B. White (1899–1985), perhaps America's best personal essayist, was a contributor of a monthly department to *Harper's* magazine (1938–1943) and a contributing editor of *The New Yorker* magazine since 1926. His lightly satirical essays show great depth of feeling. They have been published under the titles *One Man's Meat* (1942), *The Second Tree from the Corner* (1947), and *The Points of My Compass* (1962). Among his other books are *Stuart Little* (1945),

The Wild Flag (1946), *Charlotte's Web* (1952), and his revision, with additions, of William Strunk's *The Elements of Style* (1959, 1972, 1979). The second tree from the corner is a metaphor for what all men wanted, and Trexler was glad that "what he wanted, and what, in general, all men wanted . . . was both inexpressible and unattainable, and that it wasn't a wing."

"Ever had any bizarre thoughts?" asked the doctor.

Mr. Trexler failed to catch the word. "What kind?" he said.

"Bizarre," repeated the doctor, his voice steady. He watched his patient for any slight change of expression, any wince. It seemed to Trexler that the doctor was not only watching him closely but was creeping slowly toward him, like a lizard toward a bug. Trexler shoved his chair back an inch and gathered himself for a reply. He was about to say "Yes" when he realized that if he said yes the next question would be unanswerable. Bizarre thoughts, bizarre thoughts? Ever have any bizarre thoughts? What kind of thoughts *except* bizarre had he had since the age of two?

Trexler felt the time passing, the necessity for an answer. These psychiatrists were busy men, overloaded, not to be kept waiting. The next patient was probably already perched out there in the waiting room, lonely, worried, shifting around on the sofa, his mind stuffed with bizarre thoughts and amorphous fears. Poor bastard, thought Trexler. Out there all alone in that misshapen antechamber, staring at the filing cabinet and wondering whether to tell the doctor about that day on the Madison Avenue bus.

Let's see, bizarre thoughts. Trexler dodged back along the dreadful corridor of the years to see what he could find. He felt the doctor's eyes upon him and knew that time was running out. Don't be so conscientious, he said to himself. If a bizarre thought is indicated here, just reach into the bag and pick anything at all. A man as well supplied with bizarre thoughts as you are should have no difficulty producing one for the record. Trexler darted into the bag, hung for a moment before one of his thoughts, as a hummingbird pauses in the delphinium. No, he said, not that one. He darted to another (the one about the rhesus monkey), paused, considered. No, he said, not that.

Trexler knew he must hurry. He had already used up pretty nearly four seconds since the question had been put. But it was an impossible situation—just one more lousy, impossible situation such as he was always getting himself into. When, he asked himself, are you going to quit maneuvering yourself into a pocket? He made one more effort. This time he stopped at the asylum, only the bars were lucite—fluted, retractable. Not here, he said. Not this one.

He looked straight at the doctor. "No," he said quietly. "I never have any bizarre thoughts."

The doctor sucked in on his pipe, blew a plume of smoke toward the rows of medical books. Trexler's gaze followed the smoke. He managed to make out one of the titles, "The Genito-Urinary System." A bright wave of fear swept cleanly over him, and he winced under the first pain of kidney stones. He remembered when he was a child, the first time he ever entered a doctor's office, sneaking a look at the titles of the books—and the flush of fear, the shirt wet under the arms, the book on t.b., the sudden knowledge that

he was in the advanced stages of consumption, the quick vision of the hemorrhage. Trexler sighed wearily. Forty years, he thought, and I still get thrown
by the title of a medical book. Forty years and I still can't stay on life's little
bucky horse. No wonder I'm sitting here in this dreary joint at the end of this
woebegone afternoon, lying about my bizarre thoughts to a doctor who looks,
come to think of it, rather tired.

The session dragged on. After about twenty minutes, the doctor rose and
knocked his pipe out. Trexler got up, knocked the ashes out of his brain, and
waited. The doctor smiled warmly and stuck out his hand. "There's nothing
the matter with you—you're just scared. Want to know how I know you're
scared?"

"How?" asked Trexler.

"Look at the chair you've been sitting in! See how it has moved back away
from the desk? You kept inching away from me while I asked you questions.
That means you're scared."

"Does it?" said Trexler, faking a grin. "Yeah, I suppose it does."

They finished shaking hands. Trexler turned and walked out uncertainly
along the passage, then into the waiting room and out past the next patient, a
ruddy pin-striped man who was seated on the sofa twirling his hat nervously
and staring straight ahead at the files. Poor, frightened guy, thought Trexler,
he's probably read in the *Times* that one American male out of every two is
going to die of heart disease by twelve o'clock next Thursday. It says that in
the paper almost every morning. And he's also probably thinking about that
day on the Madison Avenue bus.

A week later, Trexler was back in the patient's chair. And for several
weeks thereafter he continued to visit the doctor, always toward the end of
the afternoon, when the vapors hung thick above the pool of the mind and
darkened the whole region of the East Seventies. He felt no better as time
went on, and he found it impossible to work. He discovered that the visits
were becoming routine and that although the routine was one to which he
certainly did not look forward, at least he could accept it with cool resignation, as once, years ago, he had accepted a long spell with a dentist who had
settled down to a steady fooling with a couple of dead teeth. The visits, moreover, were now assuming a pattern recognizable to the patient.

Each session would begin with a résumé of symptoms—the dizziness in
the streets, the constricting pain in the back of the neck, the apprehensions,
the tightness of the scalp, the inability to concentrate, the despondency and
the melancholy times, the feeling of pressure and tension, the anger at not
being able to work, the anxiety over work not done, the gas on the stomach.
Dullest set of neurotic symptoms in the world, Trexler would think, as he
obediently trudged back over them for the doctor's benefit. And then, having
listened attentively to the recital, the doctor would spring his question:
"Have you ever found anything that gives you relief?" And Trexler would
answer, "Yes. A drink." And the doctor would nod his head knowingly.

As he became familiar with the pattern Trexler found that he increasingly
tended to identify himself with the doctor, transferring himself into the doctor's seat—probably (he thought) some rather slick form of escapism. At any
rate, it was nothing new for Trexler to identify himself with other people.
Whenever he got into a cab, he instantly became the driver, saw everything
from the hackman's angle (and the reaching over with the right hand, the

nudging of the flag, the pushing it down, all the way down along the side of the meter), saw everything—traffic, fare, everything—through the eyes of Anthony Rocco, or Isidore Freedman, or Matthew Scott. In a barbershop, Trexler was the barber, his fingers curled around the comb, his hand on the tonic. Perfectly natural, then, that Trexler should soon be occupying the doctor's chair, asking the questions, waiting for the answers. He got quite interested in the doctor, in this way. He liked him, and he found him a not too difficult patient.

It was on the fifth visit, about halfway through, that the doctor turned to Trexler and said, suddenly, "What do you want?" He gave the word "want" special emphasis.

"I d'know," replied Trexler uneasily. "I guess nobody knows the answer to that one."

"Sure they do," replied the doctor.

"Do you know what you want?" asked Trexler narrowly.

"Certainly," said the doctor. Trexler noticed that at this point the doctor's chair slid slightly backward, away from him. Trexler stifled a small, internal smile. Scared as a rabbit, he said to himself. Look at him scoot!

"What *do* you want?" continued Trexler, pressing his advantage, pressing it hard.

The doctor glided back another inch away from his inquisitor. "I want a wing on the small house I own in Westport. I want more money, and more leisure to do the things I want to do."

Trexler was just about to say, "And what are those things you want to do, Doctor?" when he caught himself. Better not go too far, he mused. Better not lose possession of the ball. And besides, he thought, what the hell goes on here, anyway—me paying fifteen bucks a throw for these séances and then doing the work myself, asking the questions, weighing the answers. So he wants a new wing! There's a fine piece of theatrical gauze for you! A new wing.

Trexler settled down again and resumed the role of patient for the rest of the visit. It ended on a kindly, friendly note. The doctor reassured him that his fears were the cause of his sickness, and that his fears were unsubstantial. They shook hands, smiling.

Trexler walked dizzily through the empty waiting room and the doctor followed along to let him out. It was late; the secretary had shut up shop and gone home. Another day over the dam. "Goodbye," said Trexler. He stepped into the street, turned west toward Madison, and thought of the doctor all alone there, after hours, in that desolate hole—a man who worked longer hours than his secretary. Poor, scared, overworked bastard, thought Trexler. And that new wing!

It was an evening of clearing weather, the Park showing green and desirable in the distance, the last daylight applying a high lacquer to the brick and brownstone walls and giving the street scene a luminous and intoxicating splendor. Trexler meditated, as he walked, on what he wanted. "What do you want?" he heard again. Trexler knew what he wanted, and what, in general, all men wanted; and he was glad, in a way, that it was both inexpressible and unattainable, and that it wasn't a wing. He was satisfied to remember that it was deep, formless, enduring, and impossible of fulfillment, and that it made men sick, and that when you sauntered along Third Avenue and looked through the doorways into the dim saloon, you could sometimes pick out from the unregenerate ranks the ones who had not forgotten, gazing steadily into the bottoms of the glasses on the long chance that they could get another little peek at it. Trexler found himself renewed by the remembrance that what he wanted was at once great and microscopic, and that although it borrowed from the nature of large deeds and of youthful love and of old songs and early intimations, it was not any one of these things, and that it had not been isolated or pinned down, and that a man who attempted to define it in the privacy of a doctor's office would fall flat on his face.

Trexler felt invigorated. Suddenly his sickness seemed health, his dizziness stability. A small tree, rising between him and the light, stood there saturated with the evening, each gilt-edged leaf perfectly drunk with excellence and delicacy. Trexler's spine registered an ever so slight tremor as it picked up this natural disturbance in the lovely scene. "I want the second tree from the corner, just as it stands," he said, answering an imaginary question from an imaginary physician. And he felt a slow pride in realizing that what he wanted none could bestow, and that what he had none could take away. He felt content to be sick, unembarrassed at being afraid; and in the jungle of his fear he glimpsed (as he had so often glimpsed them before) the flashy tail feathers of the bird courage.

Then he thought once again of the doctor, and of his being left there all alone, tired, frightened. (The poor, scared guy, thought Trexler.) Trexler began humming "Moonshine Lullaby," his spirit reacting instantly to the hypodermic of Merman's healthy voice. He crossed Madison, boarded a downtown bus, and rode all the way to Fifty-second Street before he had a thought that could rightly have been called bizarre.

Suggestions for Discussion

1. Each paragraph describes Mr. Trexler's sessions in the psychiatrist's office or his subsequent reflections about them. How does each sequence contribute to the resolution of the narrative? Describe the changes in Trexler's behavior and attitudes toward the psychiatrist. State in your own words what Trexler wanted. What is he satirizing? What values is he affirming?

2. Discuss the appropriateness and effectiveness of the following images in relation to purpose and tone: "Trexler darted into the bag, hung for a moment before one of his thoughts, as a hummingbird pauses in the delphinium"; "he stopped at the asylum, only the bars were lucite—fluted, retractable"; "life's little bucky horse"; "the vapors hung thick above the pool of the mind"; "So he wants a new wing! There's a fine piece of theatrical gauze for you!"; "the flashy tail feathers of the bird courage"; "the hypodermic of Merman's healthy voice." In your analysis, generalize on the kinds of language represented by these quotations. What other contexts might you expect to contain such words as *hummingbird, bucky horse, theatrical gauze, tail feathers, hypodermic?* Why are the bars made of lucite and fluted and retractable? What is the effect on the reader of comparing Merman's voice to a hypodermic?

3. How does the use of specific details contribute to the illusion of reality? What sensory images do you find most vivid?

4. Characterize the humor. How does the diction, particularly the use of metaphor, contribute to the purpose and tone? Cite specific illustrations. How does the con-

trast between Trexler's unvoiced free associations and his actual statements in the psychiatrist's office contribute to the ironic tone?

5. From what point of view is the story written? What relationship does the narrator establish with the reader?

Suggestions for Writing

1. Write a narrative presenting your view of some aspect of our culture. Your feelings and attitudes should become apparent to the reader by implication rather than by explicit statement.

2. Write your own answer to the question "What do you want?" in the manner of the next to the last two paragraphs.

3. Recreate an imaginary session with one of your parents, your psychiatrist, your boss, your teacher, or your Congressman in which your feelings and attitudes are implicitly expressed.

Poetry

Matthew Arnold

Dover Beach

Matthew Arnold (1822–1888), son of the famous Headmaster of Rugby, Thomas Arnold, was first a poet but later abandoned poetry to become a lecturer, a critic of life and literature, and an inspector of schools. His *Collected Poems* appeared in 1869, *Essays in Criticism* in 1865 and 1888, *Culture and Anarchy* in 1869, *Friendship's Garland* in 1879, and *Mixed Essays* in 1879. In "Dover Beach," the speaker at a moment of emotional crisis, speaking to one he loves, raises the question of whether humans can find any peace or joy or release from pain in a world of conflict.

The sea is calm tonight.
The tide is full, the moon lies fair
Upon the straits; on the French coast the light
Gleams and is gone; the cliffs of England stand,
Glimmering and vast, out in the tranquil bay.
Come to the window, sweet is the night-air!
Only, from the long line of spray
Where the sea meets the moon-blanched land,
Listen! you hear the grating roar
Of pebbles which the waves draw back, and fling,
At their return, up the high strand,
Begin, and cease, and then again begin,
With tremulous cadence slow, and bring
The eternal note of sadness in.

Sophocles long ago
Heard it on the Aegean, and it brought
Into his mind the turbid ebb and flow
Of human misery; we
Find also in the sound a thought,
Hearing it by this distant northern sea.
The Sea of Faith
Was once, too, at the full, and round earth's shore
Lay like the folds of a bright girdle furled.
But now I only hear
Its melancholy, long, withdrawing roar,
Retreating, to the breath
Of the night-wind, down the vast edges drear
And naked shingles of the world.

Ah, love, let us be true
To one another! for the world, which seems
To lie before us like a land of dreams,

So various, so beautiful, so new,
Hath really neither joy, nor love, nor light,
Nor certitude, nor peace, nor help for pain;
And we are here as on a darkling plain
Swept with confused alarms of struggle and flight,
Where ignorant armies clash by night.

Suggestions for Discussion

1. How does the sea symbolize modern life?

2. What is the speaker seeking and what values does he affirm?

Mark Levine

About Face
(A Poem Called "Dover Beach")

Mark Levine, born in Toronto, was educated at Brown University and the University of Iowa, where he received his M.F.A. At present he teaches at the University of Montana. In addition to Debt (1993), from which "About Face" is taken, he has written Capital, and he was included in Best Poems of 1991. This poem uses the frame of Matthew Arnold's Victorian poem, "Dover Beach," to make a powerful commentary about the violence of our contemporary world.

It's dead out here. The sea is calm tonight.
Just me, the sand, the sand-like
things, wriggling like wet pockets.
I cover my eyes with some fingers; I have fingers
to spare. I open my mouth and hear the medicine
splashing on my tongue. The cliffs of England stand.

Behind enemy lines? Yes. Toujours. The Sea of Faith
was once, too, at the full. The barricades are stacked
like empty chairs after tonight's performance.
Is tonight's performance over?
I'm dragging bodies along as decoys, a dozen
well-dressed bodies, greasy, glazed with red sauce. Tonight's menu:
Peking duck. My stench is making me hungry.
Commander, may I have a body too?

Is someone quaking in my boots? To fear? Perchance, to flee.
Out here "advance" looks a lot like "retreat."
My wheels kick up sand as they spin.
Listen! you hear the grating.
My gears are caught. No use hurrying.
Time's nearly up. And I have
thoughts to collect, faces to grow.

My instructions read: "Come as you
were, leave as you are." Only, from the long
line of spray—
Commander, can you hear me?
I'm waiting for my answer.

Come to the window. Sweet is the night air.
My guests are here, clamoring to be let in.
I am here, clamoring to be let in.
In. Where is that? Come to the window.
Knocking twice, I greet myself at the door and am surprised.

Oh naked shingles of the world. My enemy's skin is bad
from eating boiled soap and scrubbing with potatoes.
My enemy's parts are detachable.
He is having a reaction to his medicine:
pain-free, confused. Am I

my enemy's enemy? My enemy's keeper? My
enemy? Ah, love, let us be true.
We're all a bit tired
to be killing so much, but we continue.
The tickets were bought through the mail long ago so why not.
No time to save face.

Action. Action.
A cardboard bomber flies by with its flaming nets.
We are here as on a darkling plain.
Make me an offer. I'm going fast.
The theater is so crowded no one can be sure
if the fire is in their hair
or in their wigs.

Suggestions for Discussion

1. Why does Levine choose to set what he has to say within the frame of Matthew Arnold's "Dover Beach"?

2. ". . . Am I / my enemy's enemy? My enemy's keeper? My / enemy? . . ." Who or what is the enemy in the poem?

3. There is a sense in Levine's poem that the despair that undergirds Arnold's poem has evolved in our time into the enactment of a death and destruction that overflows everything. If this is the case, what has brought it about?

4. The author uses theatrical metaphors throughout his poem. Why? What do they help us to understand?

Suggestions for Writing

1. A poet works not by explication, but by exemplification. Create ten images, or verbal pictures, that show to your reader something you want to convey. Try not to use modifiers. Nouns and verbs are most powerful by themselves.

2. War is a common subject of poetry. So is love. Find two other poems, on either of these topics, that say different things about the subject.

Marianne Moore

The Mind Is an Enchanting Thing

Marianne Moore (1887–1972) was born in Missouri, was graduated from Bryn Mawr College, taught at an Indian school, worked in the New York Public Library, and edited *The Dial* (1925–1929). Her early poems were published in 1921, her *Collected Poems* in 1951. She is also the author of *Predilections* (1955), a volume of critical essays, a poetic translation of La Fontaine's *Fables* (1954), and a collection of poetry, *Tell Me, Tell Me* (1967). The symbols of enchantment are drawn from nature, science, and art.

is an enchanted thing
  like the glaze on a
katydid-wing
    subdivided by sun
    till the nettings are legion.
Like Gieseking playing Scarlatti;

like the apteryx-awl
  as a beak, or the
kiwi's rain-shawl
    of haired feathers, the mind
    feeling its way as though blind,
walks along with its eyes on the ground.

It has memory's ear
  that can hear without
having to hear.
    Like the gyroscope's fall,
    truly unequivocal
because trued by regnant certainty,

it is a power of
  strong enchantment. It
is like the dove-
    neck animated by
    sun; it is memory's eye;
it's conscientious inconsistency.

It tears off the veil; tears
    the temptation, the
mist the heart wears,
        from its eyes,—if the heart
        has a face; it takes apart
dejection. It's fire in the dove-neck's

iridescence; in the
    inconsistencies
of Scarlatti.
        Unconfusion submits
        its confusion to proof; it's
not a Herod's oath that cannot change.

Suggestions for Discussion

1. The symbols of the poem derive from nature, art, and science. Identify them.

2. How do the similes contribute to the theme of enchantment? What paradoxes do you find, and how do they underscore the central theme?

Theodore Roethke

The Waking

Theodore Roethke (1908–1963), American poet, taught during the last years of his life at the University of Washington. The Waking: Poems, 1933–1953 was the winner of the Pulitzer Prize for Poetry in 1953. He received the Bollingen Award for Poetry in 1958. A collected volume, Words for the Wind, appeared in 1958, and The Far Field was published posthumously in 1964. Among the many modes of learning, the poet learns "by going where I have to go."

I wake to sleep, and take my waking slow.
I feel my fate in what I cannot fear.
I learn by going where I have to go.

We think by feeling. What is there to know?
I hear my being dance from ear to ear.
I wake to sleep, and take my waking slow.

Of those so close beside me, which are you?
God bless the Ground! I shall walk softly there,
And learn by going where I have to go.

Light takes the Tree; but who can tell us how?
The lowly worm climbs up a winding stair;
I wake to sleep, and take my waking slow.

Great Nature has another thing to do
To you and me; so take the lively air,
And, lovely, learn by going where to go.

This shaking keeps me steady. I should know.
What falls away is always. And is near.
I wake to sleep, and take my waking slow.
I learn by going where I have to go.

Suggestions for Discussion

1. Relate the title to the substance of the poem.

2. What are the modes of learning? Cite specific passages.

3. How does the use of paradox contribute to tone and substance? Comment on the rhythm, rhyme scheme, repetition of refrain, imagery, and diction.

Suggestion for Writing

Examine your own processes of learning and comment on their relative effectiveness. Relate the mode of learning to the nature of what is to be learned.

Jorge Luís Borges

The Web

Translated from the Spanish by Alastair Reid

Jorge Luís Borges (1899–1986), Argentinian poet, short-story writer, essayist, critic, and university professor, was regarded until his death in 1986 as the greatest living man of letters writing in Spanish. Best known for his esoteric short fiction, Borges received little recognition in America until the publication in 1968 of English translations of *Ficciónes, Labyrinths,* and *The Aleph.* In this poem, which appeared shortly after Borges's death, he reviews a number of the key experiences of his life, anticipates his death, and wonders when it will occur, a death he faces with "impatient hope."

Which of my cities
am I doomed to die in?
Geneva,
where revelation reached me
from Virgil and Tacitus

(certainly not from Calvin)?
Montevideo,
where Luis Melián Lafinur,
blind and heavy with years,
died among the archives
of that impartial
history of Uruguay
he never wrote?
Nara,
where in a Japanese inn
I slept on the floor
and dreamed the terrible
image of the Buddha
I had touched without seeing
but saw in my dream?
Buenos Aires,
where I verge on being a foreigner?
Austin, Texas,
where my mother and I
in the autumn of '61
discovered America?
What language
am I doomed to die in?
The Spanish my ancestors used
to call for the charge, or to play *truco*?
The English of the Bible
my grandmother read from
at the edges of the desert?
What time will it happen?
In the dove-colored twilight
when color drains away,
or in the twilight of the crow
when night abstracts and simplifies
all visible things?
Or at an inconsequential moment—
two in the afternoon?
These questions are
digressions that stem not from fear
but from impatient hope.
They form part of the fateful web
of cause and effect
that no man can foresee,
nor any god.

Suggestions for Discussion

1. Relate Borges's speculations to the title "The Web."

2. Recall the earlier piece, *Borges and Myself*. What relationship, if any, do you perceive between the two pieces?

3. What is the nature of Borges's memories?

4. What personal values are expressed?

Suggestions for Writing

1. Drawing upon your observation and experience, discuss the "fateful web of cause and effect."

2. Relate a series of key experiences that has played a role in shaping your attitudes.

Glossary

Abstraction, levels of Distinguished in two ways: in the range between the general and the specific and in the range between the abstract and the concrete.

A general word refers to a class, genus, or group; a specific word refers to a member of that group. *Ship* is a general word, but *ketch, schooner, liner,* and *tugboat* are specific. It must be remembered, however, that the terms *general* and *specific* are relative, not absolute. *Ketch,* for example, is more specific than *ship.* But *ketch,* on the other hand, is more general than *Tahiti ketch,* for a Tahiti ketch is a kind of ketch.

The distinction between the abstract and the concrete also is relative. Ideas, qualities, and characteristics which do not exist by themselves may be called abstract; physical things such as *house, shoes,* and *horse* are concrete. Notice, however, that concrete words not only can range further into the specific (*bungalow, moccasin,* and *stallion*), but they also can range back toward the general (*domicile, clothing,* and *cattle*). In making these distinctions between the abstract and the concrete and between the general and the specific, there is no implication that good writing should be specific and concrete and that poor writing is general and abstract. Certainly most good writing is concrete and specific, but it is also general and abstract, constantly moving from the general to the specific and from the abstract to the concrete.

Allusion Reference to a familiar person, place, or thing, whether real or imaginary: Woodrow Wilson or Zeus, Siam or Atlantis, kangaroo or phoenix. The allusion is an economical way to evoke an atmosphere, a historical era, or an emotion.

Analogy In exposition, usually a comparison of some length in which the unknown is explained in terms of the known, the unfamiliar in terms of the familiar, the remote in terms of the immediate.

In argument, an analogy consists of a series of likenesses between two or more dissimilar things, demonstrating that they are either similar or identical in other respects also. The use of analogy in argument is open to criticism, for two things alike in many respects are not necessarily alike in all (for example, lampblack and diamonds are both pure carbon; they differ only in their crystal structure). Although analogy never *proves* anything, its dramatic quality, its assistance in establishing tone, its vividness make it one of the most valuable techniques of the writer.

Analysis A method of exposition by logical division, applicable to anything that can be divided into component parts: an object, such as an automobile or a watch; an institution, such as a college; or a process, such as mining coal or writing a poem. Parts or processes may be described technically and factually or impressionistically and selectively. In the latter method the parts are organized in relation to a single governing idea so that the mutually supporting function of each of the components in the total structure becomes clear to the reader. Parts may be explained in terms of their characteristic function. Analysis may also be concerned with the connection of events; given this condition or series of conditions, what effects will follow?

Argument Often contains the following parts: the *proposition,* that is, an assertion that leads to the issue; the *issue,* that is, the precise phase of the proposition

1169

which the writer is attempting to prove and the question on which the whole argument rests; the *evidence*, the facts and opinions which the author offers as testimony. One may order the evidence deductively by proceeding from certain premises to a *conclusion;* or *inductively* by generalizing from a number of instances and drawing a *conclusion.* Informal arguments frequently make greater use of the methods of exposition than they do of formal logic. See Deduction, Induction, Logic, and Analogy.

The attempt to distinguish between argument and persuasion is sometimes made by reference to means (Argument makes appeals to reason: persuasion, to emotions); sometimes to ends (Argument causes someone to change his mind; persuasion moves him to action). These distinctions, however, are more academic than functional, for in practice argument and persuasion are not discrete entities. Yet the proof in argument rests largely upon the objectivity of evidence; the proof in persuasion, upon the heightened use of language.

Assumption   That part of an argument that is unstated because it is either taken for granted by the reader and writer or undetected by them. When the reader consciously disagrees with an assumption, the writer has misjudged his audience by assuming what the reader refuses to concede.

Attitude   Toward subject, see Tone. Toward audience, see Audience.

Audience   For the writer, his expected readers. When the audience is a general, unknown one, and the subject matter is closely related to the writer's opinions, preferences, attitudes, and tastes, then the writer's relationship to his audience is in a very real sense his relationship to himself. The writer who distrusts the intelligence of his audience or who adapts his material to what he assumes are the tastes and interests of his readers compromises his integrity.

On the other hand, if the audience is generally known (a college class, for example), and the subject matter is factual information, then the beginning writer may well consider the education, interests, and tastes of her audience. Unless she keeps a definite audience in mind, the beginner is apt to shift levels of usage, use inappropriate diction, and lose the reader by appealing to none of his interests.

"It is now necessary to warn the writer that his concern for the reader must be pure; he must sympathize with the reader's plight (most readers are in trouble about half the time) but never seek to know his wants. The whole duty of a writer is to please and satisfy himself, and the true writer always plays to an audience of one. Let him start sniffing the air, or glancing at the Trend Machine, and he is as good as dead although he may make a nice living." Strunk and White, *The Elements of Style* (Macmillan).

Cause and Effect   A seemingly simple method of development in which either the cause of a particular effect or the effects of a particular cause are investigated. However, because of the philosophical difficulties surrounding causality, the writer should be cautious in ascribing causes. For the explanation of most processes, it is probably safer to proceed in a sequential order, using transitional words to indicate the order of the process.

Classification   The division of a whole into the classes that compose it; or the placement of a subject into the whole of which it is a part. See Definition and Analysis.

Coherence   Literally, a sticking together, therefore, the joining or linking of one point to another. It is the writer's obligation to make clear to the reader the relationship of sentence to sentence and paragraph to paragraph. Sometimes coherence is simply a matter of putting the parts in a sequence that is meaningful and relevant—logical sequence, chronological order, order of importance. Other times it is helpful to underscore the relationship. An elementary but highly useful method of underscoring relationships is the use of transitional words: *but, how-*

ever, yet inform the reader that what is to follow contrasts with what went before; *furthermore, moreover, in addition to* continue or expand what went before.

Another elementary way of achieving coherence is the enumeration of ideas—*first, second, third*—so as to remind the reader of the development. A more subtle transition can be gained by repeating at the beginning of a paragraph a key word or idea from the end of the preceding paragraph. Such a transition reminds the reader of what has gone before and simultaneously prepares her for what is to come.

Comparison and Contrast   The presentation of a subject by indicating similarities between two or more things (comparison); by indicating differences (contrast). The basic elements in a comparative process, then, are (1) the terms of the comparison, or the various objects compared, and (2) the points of likeness or difference between the objects compared. Often comparison and contrast are used in definition and other methods of exposition.

Concreteness   See Abstraction, Levels of.

Connotation   All that the word suggests or implies in addition to its literal meaning. However, this definition is arbitrary and, from the standpoint of the writer, artificial, because the meaning of a word includes *all* that it suggests and implies.

Contrast   See Comparison.

Coordination   Elements of like importance in like grammatical construction. Less important elements should be placed in grammatically subordinate positions. See Parallelism and Subordination.

Deductive Reasoning   In logic, the application of a generalization to a particular; by analogy, in rhetoric, that development which moves from the general to the specific.

Definition   In logic, the placing of the word to be defined in a general class and then showing how it differs from other members of the class; in rhetoric, the meaningful extension (usually enriched by the use of detail, concrete illustration, anecdote, metaphor) of a logical definition in order to answer fully, clearly, and often implicitly the question, "What is——?"

Denotation   The literal meaning of a word. See Connotation.

Description   That form of discourse whose primary purpose is to present factual information about an object or experience (objective description); or to report the impression or evaluation of an object or experience (subjective description). Most description combines the two purposes. *It was a frightening night.* (An evaluation with which others might disagree.) *The wind blew the shingles off the north side of the house and drove the rain under the door.* (Two facts about which there can be little disagreement.)

Diction   Style as determined by choice of words. Good diction is characterized by accuracy and appropriateness to subject matter; weak diction, by the use of inappropriate, vague, or trite words. The relationship between the kinds of words a writer selects and his subject matter in large part determines tone. The deliberate use of inappropriate diction is a frequent device of satire.

Discourse, forms of   Traditionally, exposition, argument, description, and narration. See entries under each. These four kinds of traditional discourse are rarely found in a pure form. Argument and exposition may be interfused in the most complex fashion. Exposition often employs narration and description for purposes of illustration. It is important to remember, however, that in an effective piece of writing the use of more than one form of discourse is never accidental. It always serves the author's central purpose.

Emphasis   The arrangement of the elements of a composition so that the important meanings occur in structurally important parts of the composition. Repetition, order of increasing importance, exclamation points, rhetorical questions, and figures of speech are all devices to achieve emphasis.

Evidence   That part of argument or persuasion that involves proof. It usually takes the form of facts, particulars deduced from general principles, or opinions of authorities.

Exposition   That form of discourse which explains or informs. Most papers required of college students are expository. The *methods* of exposition presented in this text are identification, definition, classification, illustration, comparison and contrast, and analysis. See separate entries in glossary.

Figure of Speech   A form of expression in which the meanings of words are extended beyond the literal. The common figures of speech are metaphor, simile, analogy.

Generalization   A broad conception or principle derived from particulars. Often, simply a broad statement. See Abstraction.

Grammar   A systematic description of a language.

Identification   A process preliminary to definition of a subject. For the writer it is that vastly important period preliminary to writing when, wrestling with inchoate glimmerings, she begins to select and shape her materials. As a method of exposition, it brings the subject into focus by describing it.

Illustration   A particular member of a class used to explain or dramatize a class, a type, a thing, a person, a method, an idea, or a condition. The idea explained may be either stated or implied. For purposes of illustration, the individual member of a class must be a fair representation of the distinctive qualities of the class. The use of illustrations, examples, and specific instances adds to the concreteness and vividness of writing. See Narration.

Image   A word or statement which makes an appeal to the senses. Thus, there are visual images, auditory images, *etc.* As the most direct experience of the world is through the senses, writing which makes use of sense impressions (images) can be unusually effective.

Inductive Reasoning   In logic, the formulation of a generalization after the observation of an adequate number of particular instances; by analogy, in rhetoric, that development which moves from the particular to the general.

Intention   For the particular purpose or function of a single piece of writing, see Purpose. Intention determines the four forms of discourse. See Exposition, Argument, Description, Narration. These intentions may be explicitly or implicitly set forth by the writer.

Irony   At its simplest, involves a discrepancy between literal and intended meaning; at its most complex, it involves an utterance more meaningful (and usually meaningful in a different way) to the listener than to the speaker. For example, Oedipus's remarks about discovering the murderer of the king are understood by the audience in a way Oedipus himself cannot understand them. The inability to grasp the full implications of his own remark is frequently feigned by the satirist.

Issue   The limitation of a general proposition to the precise point on which the argument rests. Defeating the issue defeats the argument. Typically the main proposition of an argument will raise at least one issue for discussion and controversy.

Limitation of Subject   Restriction of the subject to one that can be adequately developed with reference to audience and purpose.

Metaphor   An implied comparison between two things that are seemingly different; a compressed analogy. Effectively used, metaphors increase clarity, interest, vividness, and concreteness.

Narration   A form of discourse the purpose of which is to tell a story. If a story is significant in itself, the particulars appealing to the imagination, it is *narration*. If a story illustrates a point in exposition or argument, it may be called *illustrative narration*. If a story outlines a process step by step, the particulars appealing to the understanding, it is designated as *expository narration*.

Organization, methods of   Vary with the form of discourse. Exposition uses in part, in whole, or in combination identification, definition, classification, illustration, comparison and contrast, and analysis. Argument and persuasion often use the method of organization of inductive or deductive reasoning, or analogy. Description is often organized either around a dominant impression or by means of a spatial arrangement. Narration, to give two examples, may be organized chronologically or in terms of point of view.

Paradox   An assertion or sentiment seemingly self-contradictory, or opposed to common sense, which may yet be true.

Paragraph   A division of writing that serves to discuss one topic or one aspect of a topic. The central thought is either implied or expressed in a topic sentence. Paragraphs have such a great variety of organization and function that it is almost impossible to generalize about them.

Parallelism   Elements of similar rhetorical importance in similar grammatical patterns. See Coordination.

Parody   Mimicking the language and style of another.

Perspective   The vantage point chosen by the writer to achieve his purpose, his strategy. It is reflected in his close scrutiny of, or distance from, his subject; his objective representation or subjective interpretation of it. See Diction, Purpose, Tone.

Persuasion   See Argument.

Point of View   In description, the position from which the observer looks at the object described; in narration, the person who sees the action, who tells the story; in exposition, the grammatical person of the composition. First person or the more impersonal third person is commonly used.

Proposition   See Argument.

Purpose   What the writer wants to accomplish with a particular piece of writing.

Rhetoric   The art of using language effectively.

Rhetorical Question   A question asked in order to induce thought and to provide emphasis rather than to evoke an answer.

Rhythm   In poetry and prose, patterned emphasis. Good prose is less regular in its rhythm than poetry.

Satire   The attempt to effect reform by exposing an object to laughter. Satire makes frequent recourse to irony, wit, ridicule, parody. It is usually classified under such categories as the following: social satire, personal satire, literary satire.

Style   "The essence of a sound style is that it cannot be reduced to rules—that it is a living and breathing thing, with something of the demoniacal in it—that it fits its proprietor tightly and yet ever so loosely, as his skin fits him. It is, in fact, quite as securely an integral part of him as that skin is . . . In brief, a style is always the outward and visible symbol of a man, and it cannot be anything else." H. L. Mencken, *On Style*, used with permission of Alfred A. Knopf, Inc.

"Young writers often suppose that style is a garnish for the meat of prose, a sauce by which a dull dish is made palatable. Style has no such separate entity; it is nondetachable, unfilterable. The beginner should approach style warily, realizing that it is himself he is approaching, no other; and he should begin by turning resolutely away from all devices that are popularly believed to indicate style—all mannerisms, tricks, adornments. The approach to style is by way of plainness, simplicity, orderliness, sincerity." E. B. White from *The Elements of Style* (Macmillan).

Subordination   Less important rhetorical elements in gramatically subordinate positions. See Parallelism and Coordination.

Syllogism   In formal logic, a deductive argument in three steps: a major premise, a minor premise, a conclusion. The major premise states a quality of a class (All men are mortal); the minor premise states that X is a member of the class (Socrates is a man); the conclusion states that the quality of a class is also a quality of a member of the class (Socrates is mortal). In rhetoric, the full syllogism is rarely used; instead, one of the premises is usually omitted. "You can rely on her; she is independent" is an abbreviated syllogism. Major premise: Independent people are reliable; minor premise: She is independent; conclusion: She is reliable. Constructing the full syllogism frequently reveals flaws in reasoning, such as the above, which has an error in the major premise.

Symbol   A concrete image which suggests a meaning beyond itself.

Tone   The manner in which the writer communicates his attitude toward the materials he is presenting. Diction is the most obvious means of establishing tone. See Diction.

Topic Sentence   The thesis that the paragraph as a whole develops. Some paragraphs do not have topic sentences, but the thesis is implied.

Transition   The linking together of sentences, paragraphs, and larger parts of the composition to achieve coherence. See Coherence.

Unity   The relevance of selected material to the central theme of an essay. See Coherence.

Index